Asian and Pacific Islander Americans in Congress
1900–2017

PREPARED UNDER THE DIRECTION OF

The Committee on House Administration of the United States House of Representatives

Gregg Harper, Chairman

Robert A. Brady, Ranking Minority Member

BY THE

Office of the Historian and Office of the Clerk United States House of Representatives

U.S. GOVERNMENT PUBLISHING OFFICE, WASHINGTON, DC, 2017

107th Congress
H. Con. Res. 130
House Document 108-226
U.S. Government Publishing Office
Washington, DC: 2017

Library of Congress Cataloging-in-Publication Data

Title: Asian and Pacific Islander Americans in Congress, 1900–2017.
Description: Washington, DC: U.S. Government Publishing Office, 2017. | "Prepared under the direction of the Committee on House Administration of the U.S. House of Representatives (Gregg Harper, Chairman; Robert A. Brady, Ranking Minority Member) by the Office of the Historian and the Office of the Clerk, U.S. House of Representatives." | "107th Congress, H. Con. Res. 130, House Document 108-226." | "Fourth book in the Minorities in Congress series."--Publisher. | Includes bibliographical references and index.
Identifiers: LCCN 2017056091 | ISBN 9780160943560 (case bound) | ISBN 9780160940408 (paper bound) | ISBN 9780160943683 (epub) | ISBN 9780160943720 (MOBI)
Subjects: LCSH: Asian American legislators--History. | Pacific Islander American legislators--History. | Asian American legislators--Registers. | Pacific Islander American legislators--Registers. | Asian Americans--Politics and government. | Pacific Islander Americans--Politics and government. | United States. Congress--History. | United States. Congress--Registers.
Classification: LCC E184.A75 A855 2017 | DDC 328.73/0922 [B] --dc23 LC

LC record available at https://lccn.loc.gov/2017056091

For sale by the Superintendent of Documents, U.S. Government Publishing Office
Internet: bookstore.gpo.gov Phone: toll free (866) 512-1800; DC area (202) 512-1800
Fax: (202) 512-2104 Mail: Stop IDCC, Washington, DC 20402-0001

ON THE COVER

Dalip Singh (Judge) Saund of California, who served in the U.S. House of Representatives from 1957 to 1963, was the first Asian Pacific American to serve in Congress as a full voting Member. For half a century before him, other Asian Pacific Americans from Hawaii and the Philippines had served as Delegates and Resident Commissioners. Saund, who everyone simply called "Judge," was a tireless champion of his southern California district and the farmers who called it home. But his unique backstory—born in India, naturalized U.S. citizen, successful businessman, county judge—also catapulted him to the international stage.

Dalip Singh Saund, Jon R. Friedman, 2007, Collection of the U.S. House of Representatives

House Concurrent Resolution No. 130

ONE HUNDRED SEVENTH CONGRESS, FIRST SESSION

SUBMITTED BY THE HONORABLE ROBERT A. UNDERWOOD

Resolved by the House of Representatives (the Senate concurring),

SECTION 1. ASIAN AND PACIFIC ISLANDER AMERICANS IN CONGRESS. (a) IN GENERAL.—The book entitled "Asian and Pacific Islander Americans in Congress", prepared by the Library of Congress under the direction of the Joint Committee on Printing, shall be printed as a House document. (b) SPECIFICATIONS.—The House document described in subsection (a) shall include illustrations and shall be in the style, form, manner, and binding as directed by the Joint Committee on Printing.

SEC. 2. NUMBER OF COPIES. In addition to the usual number of copies, there shall be printed the lesser of—(1) 30,700 copies of the document described in subsection (a) of section 1, of which—(A) 25,000 shall be for the use of the Committee on House Administration of the House of Representatives; and (B) 5,700 shall be for the use of the Committee on Rules and Administration of the Senate; or (2) such number of copies of the document described in subsection (a) of section 1 as does not exceed a total production and printing cost of $220,000, which copies shall be for the use of the Committee on House Administration of the House of Representatives and the Committee on Rules and Administration of the Senate in the same proportions as described in paragraph (1).

Agreed to November 9, 2001

COMPILED AND EDITED UNDER THE DIRECTION
OF THE

COMMITTEE ON HOUSE ADMINISTRATION OF THE UNITED STATES HOUSE OF REPRESENTATIVES

GREGG HARPER, Chairman
ROBERT A. BRADY, Ranking Minority Member

GREGG HARPER of Mississippi
RODNEY DAVIS of Illinois
BARBARA COMSTOCK of Virginia
MARK WALKER of North Carolina
ADRIAN SMITH of Nebraska
BARRY LOUDERMILK of Georgia

ROBERT A. BRADY of Pennsylvania
ZOE LOFGREN of California
JAMIE RASKIN of Maryland

KAREN L. HAAS, Clerk of the United States House of Representatives
MATTHEW A. WASNIEWSKI, Historian of the United States House of Representatives

Editor: Albin J. Kowalewski
Lead writers: Kenneth Kato, Joshua Litten
Co-writers: Jacqueline Burns, V. Grace Ethier, Erin Marie-Lloyd Hromada,
Michael Murphy, Laura Turner O'Hara, Terrance Rucker

Contents

Alphabetical List of Asian American and Pacific Islander Members of Congress, 1900–2017*

Daniel K. Akaka (1977–2013)

Steve Austria (2009–2013)

Ami Bera (2013–Present)

Ben Garrido Blaz (1985–1993)

Anh (Joseph) Cao (2009–2011)

Judy Chu (2009–Present)

Hansen Clarke (2011–2013)

Jaime C. de Veyra (1917–1923)

Francisco A. Delgado (1934–1936)

Charles Djou (2010–2011)

Tammy Duckworth (2013–Present)

Manuel Earnshaw (1912–1917)

Joaquin M. Elizalde (1938–1944)

Eni F. H. Faleomavaega (1989–2015)

Hiram L. Fong (1959–1977)

Isauro Gabaldon (1920–1928)

Tulsi Gabbard (2013–Present)

Pedro Guevara (1923–1935)

Colleen Hanabusa (2011–2015; 2016–Present)

Kamala Harris (2017–Present)

Samuel Ichiye (Sam) Hayakawa (1977–1983)

Mazie K. Hirono (2007–Present)

Mike Honda (2001–2017)

Victor S. (Kaleoaloha) Houston (1927–1933)

Daniel K. Inouye (1959–2012)

William P. Jarrett (1923–1927)

Pramila Jayapal (2017–Present)

Bobby Jindal (2005–2008)

Jonah Kuhio Kalanianaole (1903–1922)

Ro Khanna (2017–Present)

Jay C. Kim (1993–1999)

Samuel Wilder King (1935–1943)

S. Raja Krishnamoorthi (2017–Present)

Benito Legarda (1907–1912)

Ted Lieu (2015–Present)

Doris Matsui (2005–Present)

Robert T. Matsui (1979–2005)

Spark M. Matsunaga (1963–1990)

Grace Meng (2013–Present)

Norman Y. Mineta (1975–1995)

Patsy Takemoto Mink (1965–1977; 1990–2002)

Stephanie Murphy (2017–Present)

Pablo Ocampo (1907–1909)

Camilo Osias (1929–1935)

Quintin Paredes (1935–1938)

Manuel L. Quezon (1909–1916)

Aumua Amata Coleman Radewagen (2015–Present)

Carlos Peña Romulo (1944–1946)

Gregorio Kilili Camacho Sablan (2009–Present)

Patricia Saiki (1987–1991)

Dalip Singh (Judge) Saund (1957–1963)

Robert C. (Bobby) Scott (1993–Present)

Fofó I. F. Sunia (1981–1988)

Mark Takai (2015–2016)

Mark Takano (2013–Present)

Robert A. Underwood (1993–2003)

Robert W. Wilcox (1900–1903)

Antonio Borja Won Pat (1973–1985)

David Wu (1999–2011)

Teodoro R. Yangco (1917–1920)

* The closing date for this volume was July 1, 2017.

CERTIFICATE OF ELECTION

TERRITORY OF HAWAII

Executive Chamber

I, Sanford B. Dole, Governor of the Territory of Hawaii, do hereby certify that Robert W. Wilcox, was on the sixth day of November, nineteen hundred, duly elected a Delegate for the unexpired term of the Fifty-sixth Congress.

Given under my hand and the great seal of the Territory of Hawaii, at the Capitol in Honolulu, this thirtieth day of November, A.D. 1900.

Sanford B. Dole

By the Governor.

Henry E. Cooper

Secretary of the Territory.

Asian and Pacific Islander Americans in Congress
1900–2017

★ INTRODUCTION ★

On December 15, 1900, two weeks into the second session of the 56th Congress (1899–1901) of the United States, one of the early Hispanic Members of Congress, Delegate Pedro Perea of New Mexico, escorted a tall man with a handlebar moustache into the well of the U.S. House of Representatives. Facing the marble rostrum, Robert W. Wilcox, the son of a New England sea captain and a Native-Hawaiian mother, took the oath of office as the first Delegate from the Territory of Hawaii. Wilcox, along with his wife, two children, and an aide, had just arrived that morning in Washington, DC, after a long transcontinental train trip. Quickly surrounded by well-wishers, the first Asian Pacific American (APA) Member of Congress and, in fact, the first individual to represent a constituency outside the continental United States, set to work.[1]

During the course of the next century, another 59 individuals of Asian or Pacific Islander ancestry followed Delegate Wilcox into the U.S. Congress.[2] Their saga spans vast distances, stretching from Manila in the faraway Philippine archipelago to Capitol Hill in Washington, DC. Rooted in U.S. expansion into the Pacific Ocean, the story of APAs in Congress also was influenced by successive waves of immigrants and refugees who arrived on American shores. What follows is the story of how APAs moved from almost complete exclusion and marginalization to a rising influence at the center of American government.

This certificate of election from 1900 formalizes Robert W. Wilcox's election to Congress as a Delegate from the Territory of Hawaii. Wilcox was the first Asian Pacific American Member of Congress.

Image courtesy of the National Archives and Records Administration

This 1919 map of the United States includes insets for the territories of Samoa, Hawaii, Guam, the Philippine Islands, Puerto Rico, and the Virgin Islands.

Image courtesy of the Library of Congress

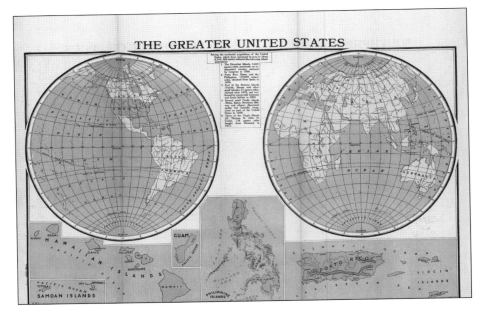

In some respects, the story of Asian Pacific Americans in Congress is similar to those portrayed in the earlier volumes in this series: *Women in Congress, 1917–2006; Black Americans in Congress, 1870–2008;* and *Hispanic Americans in Congress, 1822–2012.* Like these other groups who were previously unrepresented or excluded, some APA Members eventually came to see themselves as "surrogate representatives" legislating for APA constituencies nationwide and far beyond the borders of their states, territories, or individual House districts, though this was far from a universal sentiment. And, as their numbers increased, their careers progressed in stages very similar to these other legislators, from pioneers to apprentices, to power brokers with their own issues caucus.[3] Additionally, like the experiences of women, African-American, and Latino Members on Capitol Hill, the story of APAs in Congress overwhelmingly has been written in the U.S. House: of the 60 APAs who have served in Congress, just eight were Senators, five of whom first served in the House.[4]

From the start, foreign affairs, overseas expansion, colonial rule, and immigration policy exercised decisive influence upon Asian Pacific American experiences in Congress. The brief and lopsided American victory in the war with Spain in 1898 had long-lasting consequences, ultimately bringing the Philippines, Guam, and Samoa under the aegis of the United States. In the case of the Philippines, American troops had to first conquer Philippine liberation forces fighting the United States for independence in the bloody Philippine-American War from 1899 through 1902. A strong impulse to secure trade routes and overseas markets led the United States to annex Hawaii in 1898 as well. Each of these faraway territories eventually sent APA representatives to Congress. Since the mid-19th century, the twists and turns of U.S. immigration policy also have channeled the ebbs and flows of the APA storyline, from early efforts to secure cheap immigrant labor in the American West to many decades of exclusionary policies driven by xenophobia, to post–World War II reforms that lifted old barriers and spurred rapid APA population growth in the United States.

In 1908 the first Resident Commissioners from the Philippines met with Secretary of War William H. Taft. Seated, from left to right: Pablo Ocampo, Taft, and Benito Legarda. Standing behind Ocampo and Legarda are their respective secretaries, and behind Taft is Clarence Edwards, Chief of the Bureau of Insular Affairs.

Collection of the U.S. House of Representatives

In some aspects, the APA experience most closely parallels that of Hispanic Americans in Congress. The majority of the earliest Hispanic Members hailed from lands acquired by war: the New Mexico Territory and what would become California after the Mexican-American War (1846–1848) and Puerto Rico after the Spanish-American War of 1898, which is now also called the War of 1898. These individuals served as "statutory representatives," that is, Delegates or Resident Commissioners who possessed circumscribed legislative powers prescribed by federal statute, rather than by the Constitution. A majority of Hispanic Members who served through 1945 were statutory representatives.[5]

For the most part, the Constitution did not provide for such representation over the long term, leaving Congress to establish and manage these offices, whose powers were often strictly limited. Thus, like many of the Hispanic Americans who served with them, APA members employed legislative strategies different from those of most Representatives and Senators. Quite often these statutory representatives functioned more like envoys, ministers without portfolio, or public relations agents rather than lawmakers. Consequently, they often served as intercessors between their territorial governments and key congressional committees and select federal executive departments.

From Hawaiian Delegate Wilcox to the last Philippine Resident Commissioner, Carlos Peña Romulo, all 18 APA Members of Congress whose service fell within the five decades between the Spanish-American War and the end of World War II were statutory representatives. Most of these individuals represented far-flung locales that Congress and a long line of Presidents never contemplated incorporating fully into the Union. While in the period after 1990 far more APA Representatives and Senators have been elected than statutory representatives, 40 percent of all APA Members who have ever served on Capitol Hill (24 of 60) have been either Delegates or Resident Commissioners.

More so than the previous groups studied in this series, Asian Pacific Americans in Congress are unique because of their cultural diversity and many different national origins. This is, without a doubt, one of their defining features. Individuals whose roots extend to nearly a dozen Asian nations and Pacific Islands have served in Congress: Indian, Chinese, Filipino, Guamanian, Japanese, Korean, Native Hawaiian, Samoan, Thai, Vietnamese, and other South Asians. They have represented more than a dozen different states and territories stretching from New York to the Philippines.

Since Asian Pacific Americans became the fastest-growing group in the United States, that trend may only accelerate. When the landmark Hart–Celler immigration bill passed Congress and was signed into law by President Lyndon B. Johnson in 1965, Asian Pacific Americans accounted for less than 1 percent of the U.S. population. By 2010 their numbers had grown to roughly 18 million (about 6 percent of the U.S. population) based largely on family reunification and employer sponsorships. Key to America's changing demographics, Asians also recently overtook Hispanics as the largest percentage of legal immigrants arriving in the United States.[6] Additionally, the 2010 Census revealed that the Native-Hawaiian and other Pacific Islander populations had grown to approximately 1.2 million people.[7] By June 2016, as Asians continued to account for the largest number of immigrants, their mainland U.S. population

Carlos Peña Romulo presents a sword and flag taken from a Japanese officer in battle to House Speaker Sam Rayburn of Texas and Majority Leader John McCormack of Massachusetts in 1941. Two years later, Romulo became the final Resident Commissioner from the Philippines.

Image courtesy of the Library of Congress

surpassed 20 million, and the Pacific Islander population had grown to 1.5 million people.[8]

In 2010 the U.S. Census Bureau issued a list of the detailed groups covered by the terms "Asian" and "Native Hawaiian and Other Pacific Islanders." More than 40 subgroups were listed. Historians and social scientists who study Asian-Pacific American history and issues often observe that the term APA is, in reality, a catch-all, encompassing a wide range of peoples, cultures, and heritages that have very few shared distinguishing characteristics.[9] As this volume will elaborate, that lack of shared identity and cohesion is evident in the legislative interests of this manifold group. [**Table 1**]

TERMINOLOGY

We derived the roster of Members included in this publication from the official list of Asian and Pacific Islander Members of Congress compiled by the Congressional Research Service (CRS) of the Library of Congress.[10] In addition, in the course of our research, we discovered that three Hawaiian Delegates not covered in previous CRS reports also had Native-Hawaiian ancestry: William P. Jarrett, Victor S. (Kaleoaloha) Houston, and Samuel Wilder King. We added these men to the volume.[11]

Following the example of CRS, we use "the designation 'Asian Pacific American' … to identify a person having origins in East Asia, Southeast Asia,

Chamorro:

Indigenous inhabitants of the Mariana Islands and Guam who migrated from Southeast Asia almost 3,000 years ago. The term also denotes a distinct Austronesian language.

Table 1: U.S. Census Bureau's Detailed Groups of Asians, Native Hawaiians, and Other Pacific Islanders

Based on responses to the 2010 Census questionnaire.

Group	Subgroups	
Asian	Asian Indian	Korean
	Bangladeshi	Laotian
	Bhutanese	Malaysian
	Burmese	Maldivian
	Cambodian	Mongolian
	Chinese (except Taiwanese)	Nepalese
	Taiwanese	Okinawan
	Filipino	Pakistani
	Hmong	Singaporean
	Indonesian	Sri Lankan
	Iwo Jiman	Thai
	Japanese	Vietnamese
Polynesian	Native Hawaiian	Tongan
	Samoan	Tokelauan
	Tahitian	Other Polynesian
Micronesian	Guamanian or Chamorro	Pohnpeian
	Mariana Islander	Chuukese
	Saipanese	Yapese
	Palauan	Marshallese
	Carolinian	I-Kiribati
	Kosraean	Other Micronesian
Melanesian	Fijian	Ni-Vanuatu
	Papua New Guinean	Other Melanesian
	Solomon Islander	

Sources: *The Native Hawaiian and Other Pacific Islander Population: 2010*, C2010BR-12, prepared by Lindsay Hixon, Bradford B. Hepler, and Myoung Ouk Kim, U.S. Census Bureau (Washington, DC, issued May 2012); *The Asian Population: 2010*, C2010BR-11, prepared by Elizabeth M. Hoeffel, Sonya Rastogi, Myoung Ouk Kim, and Hasan Shahid, U.S. Census Bureau (Washington, DC, issued March 2012). Additionally, a large number of respondents checked the "Other Asian" or "Other Pacific Islander" on the Census questionnaire or wrote in a generic term such as "Asian," "Asiatic," or "Pacific Islander."

or the Indian subcontinent including, for example, Cambodia, China, India, Japan, Korea, Malaysia, Pakistan, the Philippine Islands, Thailand, Vietnam, and the original peoples of Hawaii, Guam, Samoa, or other Pacific Islands." The term, as CRS points out, is also incorporated into the formal name of the issues caucus, the Congressional Asian Pacific American Caucus (CAPAC), "founded in May 1994, and refers to those who have self-identified themselves as such." This volume uses the "Asian Pacific American" designation and its abbreviation, "APA," as an umbrella term to cover this wide range of ethnic and national identities.[12]

Where appropriate throughout the book, we reference individuals by their particular ethnic origins, for instance, "Japanese American" or "Chinese American" or "Native Hawaiian." We also use broader terms, "Asian American" or "Pacific Islander American," that encompass a subset of particular ethnicities. For instance, an individual of Vietnamese ancestry may be referenced as an "Asian American" while an individual from Guam may be designated as a "Pacific Islander American."

A note regarding the use of the word *internment* as it applied to Japanese Americans during World War II: the moral calculus behind internment and the actual language used to describe the policy have changed over time. Like many previous federal actions that were once considered acceptable, internment is now rightfully determined to have violated personal liberties and basic human rights. What was once deemed a wartime necessity is today considered one of the darkest chapters in American history.

Arguably, most people familiar with the systematic removal and relocation of nearly 120,000 Japanese Americans and Japanese immigrants know it under the umbrella term *internment*. The federal panel created in 1980 to study the event, for instance, was called the Commission on Wartime Relocation and Internment of Civilians. College-level textbooks written by noted historians like Alan Brinkley and David M. Kennedy, Lizabeth Cohen, and Thomas A. Bailey have used the terms *internment* and *internment camps*. And according to the historian Wendy Ng, "*internment* and *relocation* were the terms used by the government to describe the overall removal and detainment program." Moreover, Ng wrote in 2002, "Among former internees, the term *internment camp* or simply *camp* is still widely used and has become a standard part of the Japanese American vocabulary."[13]

Over the last few decades, historians have used other terms to describe the experiences of Japanese Americans during World War II. Noted scholars like Roger Daniels and Erika Lee have described the policy as *incarceration*, and Daniels and others, including Kennedy, Cohen, and Bailey, have labeled the guarded barracks where the internees lived as *concentration camps*. The most direct explanation for this wording comes from Daniels in his 1993 study, *Prisoners Without Trials: Japanese Americans in World War II*. "Although the later mass incarcerations are referred to as 'internments,' that is not really the appropriate term," Daniels wrote. "In law, internment can only apply to aliens. During World War II, in the United States, internment was individual and presumably based on something the individuals had done; the mass incarceration that took place was based simply on ethnic origin and geography." Rogers reiterated this point in a 2006 article in the *Journal of American Ethnic History*.[14]

At the Capitol in 1926, Hawaiian Delegate William P. Jarrett, left, smiles as he stands with Francis Kau, a 14-year-old marble champion from Hawaii, and Curran Swint, of Scripps-Howard newspapers.

Collection of the U.S. House of Representatives

After the bombing of Pearl Harbor in 1941, authorities removed Japanese Americans from their homes and businesses and placed them in internment camps. Before the evacuation, the Japanese-American owner of the Wanto Co. grocery store in Oakland, California, posted this sign reading, "I am an American."

Image courtesy of the National Archives and Records Administration

A group of Japanese Americans arrive at Heart Mountain Relocation Center in Park County, Wyoming, in 1942.

Image courtesy of the National Archives and Records Administration

The detailed and instructive summary of the debate over the use of *internment, incarceration*, and *concentration camps* in Wendy Ng's book *Japanese American Internment During World War II: A History and Reference Guide* underscores just how challenging it is for historians "to choose terminology that can be understood by everyone and that carries an accurate meaning and intention." Ng opted for *internment* in her own book because the commission used it and because she endeavored "to use the terminology that is best understood by the greatest number of people, while understanding their limitations."[15]

As such, this book uses *internment* to describe the federal government's policy to detain Japanese Americans and Japanese immigrants in camps often hundreds of miles from their homes. But this book also, at times, uses *incarceration* to describe the reality of the situation.

EMPIRE AND EXCLUSION, 1898–1941

The earliest persons of Asian and Pacific ancestries in Congress emerged from three distinct, but parallel, storylines: one set in America's colonial government in the Philippines, another in annexed Hawaii, and a third on the U.S. West Coast into which Chinese, Japanese, and Filipino immigrants flowed to meet the demand for labor during the late 19th century before being abruptly barred. In combination, these various historical strands not only shaped the first half-century of APA experiences in Congress, but, indeed, many of the contours of later eras, including the persistence of exclusionary immigration and citizenship policies as well as thorny issues arising from territorial representation.

All 18 APA individuals who served in Congress between the aftermath of the War of 1898 and the end of World War II shared a common status: each was a statutory representative with limited legislative powers. A total of 13 Resident Commissioners from the Philippines served in the House between 1907 and 1946 while five Native Hawaiians served in the chamber, including the first APA in Congress, Delegate Wilcox.[16] His successor, Prince Jonah Kuhio Kalanianaole, who was in the Hawaiian royal line of succession until the monarchy was overthrown in 1893, served nearly 19 years in the House. For many decades, he was the longest-serving APA in Congress, until Daniel K. Inouye, also from

Jonah Kuhio Kalanianaole was a Hawaiian prince when the monarchy was overthrown in 1893. He later became a Delegate and represented Hawaii in the U.S. Congress from 1903 until his death in 1922.

Image courtesy of the Library of Congress

Hawaii, eclipsed his mark in 1978. While some previous Members of Congress claimed to trace their distant lineage to kings and queens, Kuhio is the only individual ever to move directly from the ranks of royalty to service in the U.S. Congress.[17]

The Philippines

The Philippines is the only American territory with representation in Congress to ever achieve its independence, and its transition from colonial status to freedom is intertwined with the history of the archipelago's Resident Commissioners to Congress.

Located about 8,600 miles from Capitol Hill, the Philippines became part of the United States' insular orbit following back-to-back wars for independence, first against the Spanish (with aid from the United States), and then against the United States, which claimed sovereignty over the islands following the Treaty of Paris, with major combat operations lasting from 1899 to 1902. Over the next few years, Republican presidential administrations in Washington worked with key Filipino officials to erect a territorial government and establish new terms for trade and commerce.

In the half-century before World War II, those two policies—insular status and trade—dominated the transpacific relationship between the Philippines and the United States. Both issues forced Congress to confront nettlesome questions about the territorial status of the Philippines, in particular, and America's role in world affairs, in general: Was the Philippines a domestic entity entitled to U.S. military protection and annual appropriations? Was it foreign? Was it something else entirely? Democrats and Republicans rarely seemed to agree. For the first few decades of the 20th century, Republicans generally advocated retaining the islands. Democrats, meanwhile, tended to support more isolationist policies that would culminate in Philippine independence, freeing Congress from having to administer and protect a territory a half a world away.

Governor General of the Philippines Dwight Davis meets with members of the Special Philippine Mission in 1929 about tariffs. From left to right, front row: speaker of the Philippine house Manuel Roxas, Governor General Dwight Davis, Secretary of War James W. Good, president of the Philippine senate Sergio Osmeña. From left to right, back row: Resident Commissioner Pedro Guevara, Rafael Alunan, and Resident Commissioner Camilo Osias.

Image courtesy of the Library of Congress

In this 1902 political cartoon, Massachusetts Senator George Frisbie Hoar telegraphs a message of support from the Capitol to those fighting against U.S. expansion in the Philippines. At the time, Congress confronted questions about the territorial status of the distant archipelago.

Image courtesy of the Library of Congress

"WIRELESS TELEGRAPHY."

Francis Burton Harrison, governor general of the Philippines, left, and Manuel L. Quezon speak to a crowd in 1918. Quezon served as a Resident Commissioner from the Philippines from 1909 to 1916. He later served as president of the territorial senate and president of the Commonwealth of the Philippines.

Collection of the U.S. House of Representatives

This 1909 cartoon depicts Hawaiian Delegate Jonah Kuhio Kalanianaole, left, and Territorial Governor Walter Francis Frear as trains crashing in a head-on collision over Hawaiian politics.

Image courtesy of the Library of Congress

Almost to a man, the Philippines' 13 Resident Commissioners—the islands' representatives in Washington who initially served in pairs—lobbied for beneficial tariff rates and more territorial autonomy. For decades—well before Congress ever became involved in the Philippines—independence had been the ultimate goal for the islands' leaders, and for the vast majority of the people there, Philippine nationalism was the going intellectual currency. Gradually, behind the efforts of Resident Commissioners like Manuel L. Quezon, Jaime C. de Veyra, and Pedro Guevara, they chipped away at American authority in the Philippines. But timing was everything: win independence too quickly and the Philippines might flounder; pursue it too slowly and the Philippines might never get out from under America's shadow. Finally, in 1934 Congress and the territorial legislature approved the Philippine Independence Act (the Tydings–McDuffie Act), authorizing the creation of a new Philippine constitution.

But before the split became official, World War II cruelly intervened. Japan invaded the Philippines, and, at the behest of American officials, the commonwealth government went into exile in the United States. After U.S. troops seized control of Manila in 1944, Congress considered a new trade deal and rehabilitation package to help the islands rebuild after being devastated during the conflict. The Philippines became an independent country in 1946.

To this date, the nearly 40-year succession of Philippine Resident Commissioners accounts for the second largest group of APAs in Congress, behind only the 16 individuals who represented Hawaii from annexation to the present.

Hawaii

The APA Hawaiian Delegates contended with a set of issues familiar to the Philippine Resident Commissioners: protecting the rights of the native population, promoting economic growth, and educating colleagues and the American public about the unique cultural, social, and economic facets of the islands, all while navigating Capitol Hill without the right to vote. But, unlike the Philippines, which was never seriously considered for incorporation into the Union, Hawaii's strategic location in the Pacific made it a candidate for statehood.

As early as the 1820s, American Protestant missionaries traveled to the islands. But over the decades, fervor for spreading the gospel was supplanted by sugar production and development of the islands as a key port for merchant ships and, eventually, the U.S. Navy.

By the 1880s, the booming sugar businesses run by the American descendants of the missionaries dominated the islands' economy and began to usurp power from the Native Hawaiians. These *haole* businessmen eventually toppled the Hawaiian monarchy and established a fledgling republic positioned to be annexed by the United States. The war with Spain provided the momentum to do just that, and Congress passed an annexation bill signed into law by President William McKinley in July 1898. Two years later, Congress passed the Hawaiian Organic Act, which provided for a presidentially appointed territorial governor, an elected bicameral island legislature, and a popularly elected Delegate to the U.S. Congress.

Five of the first seven Hawaiian Delegates to Congress had Native-Hawaiian ancestry, and they represented the islands for virtually the entire period from 1900 to 1943, excepting just three years in that span.[18] Prince Kuhio set the bar for most who followed him. He acted as a one-man publicity bureau for the islands, educating official Washington and leading large annual congressional delegations to Hawaii. He emphasized Hawaii's strategic importance, eventually convincing the Navy brass and Congress to spend millions in federal appropriations to build up Pearl Harbor and other military installations around the islands. Kuhio also sought to improve the lot of Native Hawaiians who had suffered in the transition from the monarchy to U.S. rule, most notably with his Hawaiian Homes Commission Act. Kuhio and other Hawaiian Delegates also addressed issues such as protecting the sugar and tobacco industry from tariffs, advocating for Native-Hawaiian interests, and working with interests on the islands that were initially ambivalent about statehood.

Immigration

Finally, U.S. immigration policy fundamentally shaped APA experiences in this era. The history of the early laws that regulated Asian migration to the mainland United States and excluded those already here help to explain why only Pacific Islanders in Congress dominate this era's story, despite the fact that significant Chinese and Japanese communities had existed in the United States since the mid-19th century.

Beginning in the 1850s, young Chinese men streamed into the western United States in search of gold and later were recruited for constructing railroads, growing crops, or starting businesses. For a while, this flow of immigrant workers satiated a strong demand for cheap labor on the still sparsely populated frontier.

Driven by concerns that Asian immigrants would increase competition for jobs and never assimilate, nativist westerners demanded that state and federal governments limit Chinese immigration to the United States. By the 1870s, responding to agitation in states like California, Congress passed measures to do just that, culminating in the Chinese Exclusion Act of 1882 that prohibited the immigration of Chinese laborers, the first such law of its kind in U.S. history.

Workers load Hawaiian sugarcane onto carts around 1917.

Image courtesy of the Library of Congress

Haole:

A Hawaiian term that means "foreigner," but is mainly used to identify Caucasians.

Dalip Singh Saund, whose nickname "Judge" is used on this campaign ribbon, represented California in the U.S. House of Representatives from 1957 to 1963. Born in Amritsar, India, he became the first Asian Pacific American Member of Congress with full voting rights in the U.S. House.

Collection of the U.S. House of Representatives, Gift of Dr. Eric Saund

By the early 20th century, as Japan competed with the United States as a Pacific power, Japanese immigration became a flashpoint. When protests in San Francisco resulted in support to segregate schools and ban further immigration, a full-blown diplomatic crisis ensued. In 1913 California, followed by Oregon and Washington, passed sweeping alien land laws that barred foreign-born Asians from owning real estate.

The anti-immigrant undertow ran even stronger in 1917 when Congress approved the Asiatic Barred Zone Act, effectively blocking immigration from an entire section of the globe and excluding Asian Indians and most people from South Asia, East Asia, and Polynesia (the law at first exempted Filipinos because of their legal status as U.S. nationals). By the early 1920s, amid a wave of reinvigorated nativism, the United States adopted a quota system that restricted total immigration by capping the number of individuals eligible to immigrate from particular countries, especially in Europe and Africa. In 1924, with passage of the Johnson–Reed Immigration Act (also known as the National Origins Act), Congress completely cut off all Japanese immigration.

These laws restricting Asian immigration and prohibiting Asian immigrants from becoming naturalized citizens explain the absence of APA Members of Congress with full voting rights for nearly a century after they first began coming to the United States. Representative Dalip Singh (Judge) Saund of California, an immigrant from India, was the first to serve in the House in 1957. But Hiram L. Fong and Daniel K. Inouye, who both entered Congress in 1959 when Hawaii became a state, were the first Members of Congress of Chinese and Japanese ancestry, respectively. The first Japanese American and Chinese American from the mainland were not elected to Congress until California's Norman Y. Mineta in 1975 and David Wu of Oregon in 1999, respectively.

FROM EXCLUSION TO INCLUSION, 1941–1992

Japan's surprise attack on Pearl Harbor on December 7, 1941, and the congressional declaration of war the following day reverberated for decades.

The attack on Pearl Harbor was a tragic day for all Americans, but for Japanese Americans, years of exclusionary policies reached a climax in February 1942 when the Franklin D. Roosevelt administration broadly interpreted its wartime powers and mandated the internment—or what many historians call a mass incarceration—of Japanese-American men, women, and children. Long unwelcome in their adopted country, Japanese Americans were now considered by the federal government to be potential supporters of the Japanese military and a threat to the nation itself. Roughly 120,000 Americans of Japanese ancestry, largely from along the West Coast, were rounded up and sent to remote detention camps in the country's interior where they remained for much of the war.

Internment inflicted searing personal injustices—forced relocation, the loss of livelihoods, homes, and possessions, a complete lack of due process—not to mention deep psychological scars. It was not until decades after the war that Congress formally acknowledged that the treatment of Japanese Americans had been reprehensible and worthy of redress. Coming to grips with what happened

during the war forced the nation to confront long-simmering tensions that had kept many APAs from fully participating in American society.

"Dec. 7 was the worst date in history for Americans of Japanese ancestry," Daniel Inouye once observed. "And yet—maybe this is a horrible thing to say—Dec. 7 was one of the greatest breaks we ever had. The hatred erupted and gave us a chance to counteract it."[19]

Inouye served his country as a member of the now-legendary all-Japanese-American 442nd Regimental Combat Team, the most highly decorated unit in the war that the U.S. House and Senate later recognized with a Congressional Gold Medal. Inouye was separately awarded a Medal of Honor for his heroism. Though his dream of becoming a surgeon was dashed when he lost an arm in combat, he entered Hawaiian politics, became that state's first U.S. Representative, and served nearly a half-century in the U.S. Senate. He now stands as one of Congress's legislative titans.

Inouye was one of 14 APAs first elected to Congress in this time period, which spanned roughly from the United States' entry into World War II until the end of the Cold War. Seven of the 14 Members covered in this essay were Japanese Americans, a testament to the fact that this ethnic group remained the largest single subset of APAs until the 1970s. Inouye, along with other Japanese-American Members of Congress, including Californians Norman Mineta and Robert T. Matsui, both former internees, spearheaded one of the APA community's major legislative accomplishments of the era: redress for the internment of Japanese Americans.

With Philippine independence in 1946 and Hawaii entering the Union in 1959, the APA storyline shifted away from statutory representation to one in which most of these individuals served as full-fledged voting Members. This was a slow process, however. After the last Philippine Resident Commissioner,

Daniel K. Inouye observed that the bombing of Pearl Harbor was the worst day for Americans of Japanese ancestry but that the U.S. entry into the war also offered the opportunity to work against anti-Japanese sentiment. Inouye served in the U.S. Army's 442nd Regimental Combat Team and then as a U.S. Representative and Senator from Hawaii.

From left to right, Representatives Elijah Cummings of Maryland, Xavier Becerra of California, and Robert T. Matsui of California hold a press conference on civil rights in 1997.

Image courtesy of the Library of Congress

California Representative Dalip Singh (Judge) Saund joins other Members of Congress for a "congressional coffee hour" with President John F. Kennedy at the White House in 1961. From left to right: Representative Saund, Harold C. Ostertag of New York, James A. Haley of Florida, President Kennedy, Frank W. Boykin of Alabama, Harold T. Johnson of California, and John W. Byrnes of Wisconsin.

Image courtesy of the John F. Kennedy Presidential Library and Museum/National Archives and Records Administration

Carlos Romulo, departed Congress in 1946, a decade elapsed before a Punjabi Indian immigrant named Dalip Saund from Southern California became the next APA to serve in Congress and the first to represent a mainland state.

Most of these 14 APAs represented Hawaii and California. These included Patsy Takemoto Mink, the first woman of color to serve in Congress beginning in 1965, and Mineta, who served as president of the "Watergate Baby" freshman class a decade later and remains the only APA to chair a standing committee in the House. Others won assignments to influential committees for the first time; among them was Robert T. Matsui, who was the first APA to serve on three key panels: Judiciary, Interstate and Foreign Commerce, and Ways and Means.

America's combat with Japan in the Pacific Theater during World War II not only changed life for mainland Asian Americans, it reshaped America's relations with its current and former territories in the Pacific. An independent Philippines became a close ally during the Cold War, and Guam and American Samoa, because of their strategic importance, were further enveloped by the American embrace. Later in this period, they also received representation in Congress as their first Delegates, Antonio Borja Won Pat and Fofó I. F. Sunia, respectively, were sworn into the House.

The wartime loyalty and bravery of the Japanese-American community, the World War II alliance with China, and later the imperatives of Cold War policies in Asia collectively softened deeply ingrained negative perceptions about Asian Pacific Americans and gradually eroded long-standing immigration barriers. At first, these movements were symbolic, such as the wartime repeal of prior Chinese exclusion legislation, the extension of naturalization privileges, and the creation of a modest immigration quota from that country (a little more than 100 people annually).

When the global Cold War struggle between the United States and communist powers began in the late 1940s, Congress passed a series of bills allowing Asian refugees to enter the country. As Japan became a vital Cold War ally and Americans' perceptions about that country improved, the McCarran–Walter Act of 1952 extended naturalization privileges to Japanese immigrants

(*issei*). Later, American military interventions in Asian civil wars, most notably in Korea and Vietnam, opened the door for thousands of refugees from those nations to enter the United States.

The signal piece of immigration legislation in this era was the Hart–Celler Act of 1965, which replaced the existing national quotas that were racially based. Crafted during a burst of Great Society legislation, Hart–Celler not only overturned the last vestige of racial discrimination in immigration policy, it had the unexpected consequence of sharply increasing the flow of immigrants from Asia by putting into place two key components: family reunification and skilled workers' preferences.

A GROWING DIVERSITY, 1993 TO PRESENT

More Asian Pacific Americans have served in Congress during the past two decades than in any comparable period. In fact, roughly 47 percent of all the APAs who have ever served in Congress arrived on Capitol Hill after 1992. The 18 APA Members who served in the House and Senate at the opening of the 115th Congress (2017–2019) constituted a larger APA cohort than in any prior Congress. Several factors have contributed to this trend.

Within the last decade, Asian Pacific Americans have become the fastest-growing legal immigrant group in America, surpassing persons of Hispanic origins.[20] In large measure, this population growth is a legacy of the Hart–Celler Act. More recently, the demand for highly trained technical and medical workers has outstripped the United States' ability to fill those jobs with its own citizens, prompting Congress to expand the annual limits on H-1B visas aimed at bringing such workers into the country. Overwhelmingly, these have been filled by Asian immigrant workers.

Another major source of Asian immigration into the United States in the latter half of the 20th century was that of the refugees from countries torn by civil strife, military conflicts, and other unrest. U.S. withdrawal from and the subsequent collapse of South Vietnam in 1975 led to successive, multi-decadal waves of Vietnamese refugees. One of these refugees was Anh (Joseph) Cao, who more than three decades after fleeing Saigon as a child, became the first Vietnamese American elected to Congress. Other groups arrived via a similar path, including Cambodians, the Lao, and the Hmong people from Southeast Asia.

These various streams of immigrants and refugees have led to an expanding diversity of APA ethnicities on Capitol Hill: Jay C. Kim became the first Korean American elected to Congress, Hansen Clarke had Bangladeshi roots, and Charles Djou claimed both Chinese and Thai ancestry. Along with ethnic diversity, APAs also experienced a geographic diversification that reflected shifts in the general APA population. Whereas Hawaii and California as well as the Philippines had long been home to most APA Members of Congress from the previous eras, APAs in this era represented constituencies in New York City, New Orleans, Detroit, suburban Chicago, Virginia, Ohio, and Washington State.

Moreover, the number of APAs in Congress increased because of expanding representation for the United States' Pacific territories. In the fall of 2008, the Northern Mariana Islands elected its first Delegate to Congress, Gregorio Kilili Camacho Sablan, who joined post-war Delegates representing Guam and American Samoa.

Issei:

A Japanese term that identifies the generation of emigrants who left Japan to settle in the United States.

President Lyndon B. Johnson signs the Hart–Celler Act into law in 1965 at a special ceremony at the Statue of Liberty. The law has enabled Asian and Pacific Islander Americans to become the fastest-growing legal immigrant group in the United States.

Photograph by Yoichi Okamoto; image courtesy of the Lyndon B. Johnson Presidential Library/National Archives and Records Administration

In 1975, at the end of the Vietnam War, the U.S. government welcomed displaced children from South Vietnam during "Operation Babylift." President Gerald R. Ford cradles an infant refugee at the San Francisco International Airport.

Image courtesy of the Gerald R. Ford Presidential Library/National Archives and Records Administration

While investigating the Iran-Contra Affair, Senator Daniel K. Inouye of Hawaii (back row, center) maintained a nonconfrontational tone with witnesses, including principal witness Lieutenant Colonel Oliver North.

Image courtesy of the U.S. Senate Historical Office

A campaign button promotes the re-election of Representative Spark M. Matsunaga. During his youth, Matsunaga was teasingly nicknamed "Spark" and "Sparky" by his friends. After World War II, the future Representative and Senator from Hawaii legally changed his first name to "Spark."

Collection of the U.S. House of Representatives, Gift of Trent LeDoux

As more APAs served in Congress, they responded to the same impulse to organize and pool resources that had previously led women, African Americans, and Hispanic Americans to create their own separate issues caucuses. In 1994 APA Members, led by Patsy Mink and Norman Mineta, formed the Congressional Asian Pacific American Caucus in an effort to inject issues of common APA interest into the legislative agenda—among them immigration, civil liberties, and increased political participation. The caucus also sought to raise awareness about the contributions of APA Members within the institutions of the House and Senate. "We have to write our own history," admitted Mineta, who served as the group's first chairman.[21]

Better organization and growing numbers suggested an upward trajectory to this story and, by the end of the period, new trends and patterns emerged. As one generation passed from the scene, a new one took shape. When Congress convened for the opening of the 113th Congress (2013–2015) in January 2013, the name Daniel Inouye was not on the roll of Members in either the House or Senate for the first time since 1959. Inouye had passed away in December 2012, and only weeks later, his Hawaiian colleague Daniel Akaka, a congressional veteran of 35 years, retired. When the new Congress was sworn in, the most senior APA Member had only little more than a decade of House experience. But five new APAs had been elected to the House, and Hawaii's Mazie K. Hirono, who had served several terms in the House, made history when she took the oath of office, succeeding Akaka and becoming the first APA woman Senator.

HISTORIOGRAPHY AND STRUCTURE OF THIS VOLUME

The 107th Congress (2001–2003) ordered the production of new editions of *Women in Congress*, *Black Americans in Congress*, and *Hispanic Americans in Congress*. At the same time, Congress also mandated the preparation of a new publication, *Asian and Pacific Islander Americans in Congress*.[22] In the spring of 2001, Delegate Robert A. Underwood of Guam submitted House Concurrent Resolution 130. The resolution, which passed on October 9, 2001, and was agreed to by the Senate on November 9, 2001, authorized the Library of Congress to publish *Asian and Pacific Islander Americans in Congress*. The Library of Congress later transferred the project to the Office of the Clerk of the U.S. House of Representatives. The Office of the Historian ultimately became responsible for researching and writing the volume.

As with the latest editions of the books on women, African Americans, and Hispanic Americans in Congress, this volume features profiles of former Members, contextual essays that introduce the profiles chronologically and group them into generations, brief entries on current Members, and appendices. Each former Member profile consists of a section on the Member's precongressional career, followed, where possible, by a detailed analysis of the subject's first campaign for congressional office; subsequent re-election efforts; information about committee assignments, leadership, and major legislative initiatives; and a brief summary of the Member's post-congressional career. Photographs of each Member are included.

Bibliographic information is provided at the end of each profile, and, where applicable, the location of a Member's manuscript collection is included at the end of their individual profiles. Manuscript information has been drawn from House and Senate records used to compile and maintain the online *Biographical Directory of the United States Congress* at http://bioguide.congress.gov. The editors have referenced Members' major manuscript collections and other repositories with significant holdings, e.g., the transcript of an oral history or extended correspondence. This information is intended to be a resource for the general reader and a starting point for the scholarly researcher.

Additionally, contextual essays describing three successive generations of Members analyze social, political, and institutional developments affecting their participation in Congress. Appendices include tables on APA Members' committee assignments, leadership positions, and familial connections in Congress.

RESEARCHING THE HISTORY OF
ASIAN PACIFIC AMERICANS

The content of this publication reflects the growth and dynamism of the field of Asian-American studies since its emergence in the 1960s. Growing out of the social movements in the 1960s and 1970s that emphasized researching "history from below" and giving voice to previously neglected topics and groups, early works in the field focused on the experiences of Americans of Asian Indian, Chinese, Filipino, Japanese, and Korean descents.[23] Scholars have also used a transnational focus by analyzing the experiences of Asian immigrants in their home countries and comparing them to their experiences in the United States.[24]

The story of APAs is multifaceted, and we relied on the following general texts to help ground our discussions, particularly in the contextual essays: Sucheng Chan, *Asian Americans: An Interpretive History* (New York: Twayne

California Representative Judy Chu became chair of the Congressional Asian Pacific American Caucus in 2011.

Image courtesy of the U.S. House of Representatives Photography Office

This 1960 campaign handbill not only touts California Representative Dalip Singh (Judge) Saund's qualifications but also includes book reviews for his autobiography, *Congressman from India.*

Collection of the U.S. House of Representatives, Gift of Dr. Eric Saund

In the 1970s, the Philippine government issued a series of stamps honoring notable citizens, including former Resident Commissioner Teodoro R. Yangco.

Collection of the U.S. House of Representatives

"Troubles Which May Follow an Imperial Policy," Charles Nelan's 1898 cartoon, draws on racial anxiety about the effects of U.S. expansion. The print shows the House Chamber rostrum pierced by spears, as Speaker Thomas Brackett Reed fearfully eyes a man labeled "The Representative from the Philippines."

Image courtesy of the New York Public Library

Publishers, 1991); Roger Daniels, *Asian America: Chinese and Japanese in the United States since 1850* (Seattle: University of Washington Press, 1988); Erika Lee, *The Making of Asian America: A History* (New York: Simon and Schuster, 2015); Ronald Takaki, *Strangers from a Different Shore: A History of Asian Americans*, revised and updated edition (Boston, MA: Little, Brown, 1998); and Janelle Wong, S. Karthick Ramakrishnan, Taeku Lee, and Jane Junn, *Asian American Political Participation: Emerging Constituents and Their Political Identities* (New York: Russell Sage Foundation, 2011). We also benefitted from two useful reference works: David K. Yoo and Eiichiro Azuma, eds., *The Oxford Handbook of Asian American History* (New York: Oxford University Press, 2016), which includes excellent essays that summarize recent trends and developments in Asian-American studies; and Hyung-Chan Kim, *Dictionary of Asian American History* (Westport, CT: Greenwood Press, 1986), which provides useful descriptions of people, places, and events within Asian Pacific American history. Several documentary texts also proved valuable: Franklin S. Odo, *The Columbia Documentary History of the Asian American Experience* (New York: Columbia University Press, 2002); Hyung-Chan Kim, *Asian Americans and Congress: A Documentary History* (Westport, CT: Greenwood Press, 1996), which offers a detailed analysis of Congress's role in U.S. immigration policy and its effects on APAs; and Hyung-Chan Kim, *Asian Americans and the Supreme Court: A Documentary History* (Westport, CT: Greenwood Press, 1992), an edited collection of Supreme Court cases that defined U.S. immigration policies toward Asian Americans with useful explanatory essays.

The growth and management of the United States' overseas empire in the late 19th and early 20th centuries composes a major portion of this story. Two monographs in particular were critical to understanding U.S.-Philippine relations and the insular political context into which Filipino Resident Commissioners fit. Peter W. Stanley, *A Nation in the Making: The Philippines and the United States, 1899–1921* (Cambridge, MA: Harvard University Press, 1974) offers an overview of the Philippines' early history as an American territory often from the perspective of both U.S. and Filipino officials working in Manila. Stanley describes the asymmetrical relationship between the Philippines (which he describes as severely underdeveloped) and the United States (which he called an "ambivalent" superpower) as being "developmental and consensual."[25] Michael Cullinane, *Ilustrado Politics: Filipino Elite Responses to American Rule, 1898–1908* (Quezon City, PI: Ateneo de Manila University Press, 2003) examines in depth how the wealthiest and most-educated members of Philippine society—a handful of whom eventually served as Resident Commissioners in the U.S. Congress—helped to create and guide what Cullinane calls "the Filipino-American collaborative empire."[26] Similarly, Bonifacio S. Salamanca, *The Filipino Reaction to American Rule, 1901–1913* (Hamden, CT: Shoe String Press, 1968) offers a useful study of how then governor general and later President William H. Taft altered Philippine institutions and worked with Filipino elites to reinforce U.S. colonial rule over the islands. Frank H. Golay, *Face of Empire: United States-Philippine Relations, 1898–1946* (Quezon City, PI: Ateneo de Manila University Press, 1997) offers a detailed overview of the evolution of U.S. colonial policy in the Philippines from 1898 to 1946 using a large number of congressional sources. Unlike the collaborative and consensual framework suggested by Cullinane and Stanley, Golay's account emphasizes the United States' more heavy-handed, unilateral approach.

Other useful general accounts include H. W. Brands, *Bound to Empire: The United States and the Philippines* (New York: Oxford University Press, 1992); and Stanley Karnow, *In Our Image: America's Empire in the Philippines* (New York: Random House, 1989). Bernardita R. Churchill, *Philippine Independence Missions to the United States, 1919–1934* (Manila, PI: National Historical Institute, 1983) details the succession of independence missions to Washington that Filipino politicians organized to secure greater autonomy for their nation. Theodore Friend, *Between Two Empires: The Ordeal of the Philippines, 1929–1946* (New Haven, CT: Yale University Press, 1965) studies a transitional period between the Philippines' colonial status and the path to becoming an independent nation-state. Paul A. Kramer, *The Blood of Government: Race, Empire, the United States, and the Philippines* (Chapel Hill: University of North Carolina Press, 2006) describes how changing racial perceptions between Americans and Filipinos affected their interactions from the War of 1898 to Philippine independence in 1946. Tariff policy was a major preoccupation of Philippine Resident Commissioners, and Pedro E. Abelarde, *American Tariff Policy towards The Philippines* (New York: King's Crown Press, 1947), while dated, provides a comprehensive guide to Congress's main policy focus with the Philippines. Abelarde highlights the tension between American business interests and the Filipino people as well as the long-term consequences of America's transpacific trade policy.

We found the following general histories of the Hawaiian Islands to be helpful: Ralph S. Kuykendall and A. Grove Day, *Hawaii: A History—From Polynesian Kingdom to American State*, rev. ed. (Englewood Cliffs, NJ: Prentice-Hall, 1961); Gavan Daws, *Shoal of Time: A History of the Hawaiian Islands* (Honolulu: University of Hawaii Press, 1968); and H. Brett Melendy, *Hawaii: America's Sugar Territory, 1898–1959* (Lewiston, NY: Edwin Mellen Press, 1999). Several books helped us to understand Hawaii's long transition from territory to state: John S. Whitehead, *Completing the Union: Alaska, Hawai'i, and the Battle for Statehood* (Albuquerque: University of New Mexico Press, 2004); Roger Bell, *Last Among Equals: Hawaiian Statehood and American Politics* (Honolulu: University of Hawaii Press, 1984); and Tom Coffman, *The Island Edge of America: A Political History of Hawai'i* (Honolulu: University of Hawai'i Press, 2003).

For information on the United States' relations with other Pacific Island territories, including Guam, American Samoa, and Micronesia, we relied on Charles S. Campbell, *The Transformation of American Foreign Relations, 1865–1900* (New York: Harper and Row, 1975); Robert F. Rogers, *Destiny's Landfall: A History of Guam*, rev. ed. (Honolulu: University of Hawai'i Press, 2011); and Arnold H. Leibowitz, *Defining Status: A Comprehensive Analysis of United States Territorial Relations* (Dordrecht, Netherlands: Martinus Nijhoff, 1989).

Immigration and the policies the United States has used to regulate it during the last 150 years are central components of Asian Pacific Americans' experiences. We benefitted greatly from two major works on the topic: Mae M. Ngai, *Impossible Subjects: Illegal Aliens and the Making of Modern America*

This 1915 photograph shows 11 political leaders from Hawaii: from left to right, front row: Charles F. Chillingworth, Wade Warren Thayer, Lucius E. Pinkham, Delegate Jonah Kuhio Kalanianaole, Henry L. Holstein; from left to right, back row: J. H. Coney, William H. Rice, Norman Watkins, George H. Huddy, James L. Coke, and P. J. Goodness.

Collection of the U.S. House of Representatives

From left to right: Representative Spark M. Matsunaga, Senator Daniel K. Inouye, President Lyndon B. Johnson, and Senator Hiram L. Fong exit Air Force One on a visit to the Members' home state of Hawaii in 1966.

Photograph by Yoichi Okamoto; image courtesy of the Lyndon B. Johnson Presidential Library/National Archives and Records Administration

This 1942 Department of Justice notice, written in Italian, German, and Japanese, advised immigrants of these "enemy nationalities" to obtain a certificate of identification, which they were required to carry with them at all times. The identification program was intended as a wartime protection against suspected enemies living in the United States.

UNITED STATES DEPARTMENT OF JUSTICE

★

NOTICE TO ALIENS OF ENEMY NATIONALITIES

★ The United States Government requires all aliens of German, Italian, or Japanese nationality to apply at post offices nearest to their place of residence for a Certificate of Identification. Applications must be filed between the period February 9 through February 28, 1942. *Go to your postmaster today for printed directions.*

EARL G. HARRISON,
Special Assistant to the Attorney General.

FRANCIS BIDDLE,
Attorney General.

AVVISO

Il Governo degli Stati Uniti ordina a tutti gli stranieri di nazionalità Tedesca, Italiana e Giapponese di fare richiesta all' Ufficio Postale più prossimo al loro luogo di residenza per ottenere un Certificato d'Identità. Le richieste devono essere fatte entro il periodo che decorre tra il 9 Febbraio e il 28 Febbraio, 1942.
Andate oggi dal vostro Capo d'Ufficio Postale (Postmaster) per ricevere le istruzioni scritte.

BEKANNTMACHUNG

Die Regierung der Vereinigten Staaten von Amerika fordert alle Auslaender deutscher, italienischer und japanischer Staatsangehoerigkeit auf, sich auf das ihrem Wohnorte naheliegende Postamt zu begeben, um einen Personalausweis zu beantragen. Das Gesuch muss zwischen dem 9. und 28. Februar 1942 eingereicht werden.
Gehen Sie noch heute zu Ihrem Postmeister und verschaffen Sie sich die gedruckten Vorschriften.

敵國外人注意

日獨伊諸國ノ國籍ヲ有スル在留外人ハ二月九日ヨリ二十八日ニテ身分證明書ヲ申込ムベシ。近イ郵便局デ國分證明書ヲ申込ム可シ。合ニ早速郵便局ヘ行キテ説明書ヲ願ヒ願ヒマス。

(Princeton, NJ: Princeton University Press, 2004), a groundbreaking study that describes how the "illegal alien" became a pivotal issue in U.S. immigration policy in the early 20th century; and Roger Daniels, *Coming to America: A History of Immigration and Ethnicity in American Life* (New York: Harper Perennial, 1990), which is a standard survey text on U.S. immigration. For descriptions of the Asian-American experience particularly, see Roger Daniels, *Asian America: Chinese and Japanese in the United States since 1850* (Seattle: University of Washington Press, 1988); Bill Ong Hing, *Making and Remaking Asian America Through Immigration Policy, 1850–1990* (Stanford, CA: Stanford University Press, 1993); David M. Reimers, *Still the Golden Door: The Third World Comes to America* (New York: Columbia University Press, 1992); Stephan Thernstrom et al., *Harvard Encyclopedia of American Ethnic Groups* (Cambridge, MA: Belknap Press, 1980); Mary C. Waters and Reed Ueda, eds., *The New Americans: A Guide to Immigration since 1965* (Cambridge, MA: Harvard University Press, 2007); and Yuji Ichioka, *The Issei: The World of the First Generation Japanese Immigrants, 1885–1924* (New York: Free Press, 1988).

The story of Japanese-American internment during World War II and the long effort to right that historic injustice, culminating in redress in the 1980s, is perhaps the defining, unifying thread in the story of APAs in Congress. We relied on the authoritative work of Roger Daniels, including *Prisoners Without Trial: Japanese Americans in World War II* (New York: Hill and Wang, 1999) and *The Japanese American Cases: The Rule of Law in Time of War* (Lawrence: University Press of Kansas, 2013); Mitchell T. Maki et al., *Achieving the Impossible Dream: How Japanese Americans Obtained Redress* (Urbana: University of Illinois Press, 1999); and Leslie T. Hatamiya, *Righting a Wrong: Japanese Americans and the Passage of the Civil Liberties Act of 1988* (Stanford, CA: Stanford University Press, 1993).

Though the field of Asian Pacific studies has flourished in recent decades, it is still marked by significant historical gaps, including the underrepresentation of APAs in Congress in the secondary literature. A few individuals, such as Hawaiian Delegates Robert W. Wilcox and Prince Jonah Kuhio Kalanianaole and Philippine Resident Commissioner Carlos Peña Romulo, are the subject of published biographies, though emphases on the congressional phases of their careers vary. Others, such as Philippine Resident Commissioners Manuel L. Quezon and Camilo Osias, California Representative Dalip Singh (Judge) Saund, and Senator Daniel K. Inouye, wrote autobiographies. The daughter of Resident Commissioner Quintin Paredes wrote a memoir of her father's career. Unpublished academic theses explore the career of a handful of Members, such as Hawaii's Hiram L. Fong and Teodoro R. Yangco of the Philippines, but remain inaccessible to a general readership. No trade or scholarly biographies exist of other prominent legislative figures, such as Spark M. Matsunaga, Patsy Takemoto Mink, or Norman Y. Mineta. One aim of these profiles is to generate interest in future studies of such key Members as well as lesser-known, but equally significant, individuals, such as Jaime C. de Veyra of the Philippines, Hawaii's Samuel Wilder King, and Guamanian Delegate Antonio Borja Won Pat.[27]

Hawaiian Delegate Samuel Wilder King, left, and White House official Marvin McIntyre examine leis in 1936.

Image courtesy of the Library of Congress

METHODOLOGY AND USEFUL RESEARCH STRATEGIES

As with previous editions in this series of books on women and minorities in Congress, we consulted several standard sources that were indispensable starting points during the compilation of this book. Inquiries into Members' congressional careers should begin with the *Biographical Directory of the United States Congress* at http://bioguide.congress.gov. Maintained by the Office of the Historian of the U.S. House of Representatives and the Senate Historical Office, this publication contains basic biographical information about Members, pertinent bibliographic references, and information about manuscript collections. Previous editions of the *Congressional Directory* also provided important biographical information, particularly for the Philippine Resident Commissioners and Territorial Delegates from Hawaii. These U.S. Government Publishing Office (GPO) publications— produced once per Congress in recent Congresses, but often once per session in earlier Congresses—date back to the early 19th century. From the 104th Congress (1995–1997) onward, the series is available at http://www.gpo.gov/fdsys/.

In the early phase of our research, we also consulted standard secondary references such as the *American National Biography*, *Dictionary of American Biography*, and *Current Biography*. We used various editions of the *Almanac of American Politics* (Washington, DC: National Journal Inc.) and *Politics in America* (Washington, DC: Congressional Quarterly Press) as a starting point to research Members who served after 1971. We also consulted various editions of the United States Census and U.S. passport applications for biographical information about Members by using Ancestry Library at ancestrylibrary.com. All of these citations appear in the notes.

We obtained much of the information in this book from primary sources, particularly published official congressional records and scholarly compilations of congressional statistics. The following is a summary of the sources we consulted for information related to congressional elections, committee assignments, legislation, votes, floor debates, news accounts, and images:

Norman Y. Mineta, taking an oath early in his political career in San Jose, California, served 20 years in Congress.

Image courtesy of Japanese American Museum of San Jose

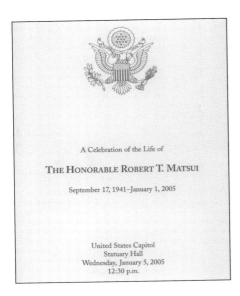

A Celebration of the Life of

THE HONORABLE ROBERT T. MATSUI

September 17, 1941–January 1, 2005

United States Capitol
Statuary Hall
Wednesday, January 5, 2005
12:30 p.m.

Representative Robert T. Matsui of California served in Congress from 1979 until his death on January 1, 2005. This program is from his memorial service, which took place in the Capitol's National Statuary Hall.

Collection of the U.S. House of Representatives

- For congressional election results for the biennial elections from 1920 onward, we consulted "Election Statistics," compiled by the Office of the Clerk, U.S. House of Representatives, and published by GPO and available in PDF format at http://history.house.gov/Institution/Election-Statistics/Election-Statistics/. Philippine Resident Commissioner elections are not included in "Election Statistics"; Hawaiian elections appear only in the 1926 edition before being consistently included in the series beginning in 1940. Michael J. Dubin, *United States Congressional Elections, 1788–1997* (Jefferson, NC: McFarland and Company, Publishing, Inc., 1998) contains results for both general and special elections, and it covers the period prior to the publication of the Clerk's "Election Statistics." It does not, however, include statistics for territorial elections. For election results for the Philippine Resident Commissioners, we relied primarily on the various journals of pre–World War II Philippine legislatures and newspapers. We also reviewed election certificates that were part of the records of the U.S. House of Representatives (RG 233) at the National Archives' Center for Legislative Archives. A useful source on state and national elections in Hawaii from 1900 through 1976 is Robert C. Schmitt, *Historical Statistics of Hawaii* (Honolulu: University Press of Hawaii, 1977), also available in PDF format online at http://files.hawaii.gov/dbedt/economic/data_reports/Historical-Statistics-of-Hawaii.pdf.

- For information on district boundaries and reapportionment, we relied on Kenneth C. Martis, *The Historical Atlas of Political Parties in the United States Congress, 1789–1989* (New York: Macmillan Publishing Company, 1989) and the three-volume work by Stanley B. Parsons et al., *United States Congressional Districts* (New York: Greenwood Press, 1986). Various editions of the *Congressional Directory* also proved useful.

- For committee assignments and information about jurisdiction, we used three indispensable scholarly compilations: David T. Canon, Garrison Nelson, and Charles Stewart III, *Committees in the U.S. Congress, 1789–1946*, 4 vols. (Washington, DC: Congressional Quarterly Press, 2002); Garrison Nelson, *Committees in the U.S. Congress, 1947–1992*, 2 vols. (Washington, DC: Congressional Quarterly Press, 1994); and Garrison Nelson and Charles Stewart III, *Committees in the U.S. Congress, 1993–2010* (Washington, DC: Congressional Quarterly Press, 2010). Committee rosters and information also are published in the *Congressional Directory*. However, this single source often does not track committee composition changes that occur mid-Congress.

- For legislation, floor debates, roll call votes, bills, resolutions, and public laws as far back as the 1980s, we searched the Library of Congress's legislative database at http://congress.gov. A particularly useful print resource that discusses historical acts of Congress is Steven W. Stathis's *Landmark Legislation, 1774–2012: Major U.S. Acts and Treaties*, 2nd ed. (Washington, DC: Congressional Quarterly Press, 2014). Floor debates about legislation are in the *Congressional Record* (1873 to the present), copies of which can be obtained at a local federal depository library. To find the nearest location, search http://www.fdlp.gov/about-the-fdlp/federal-depository-libraries. The

Record is available online dating back to the 104th Congress at the Library of Congress's website: https://www.congress.gov/congressional-record. We also consulted the official proceedings in the *House Journal* and the *Senate Journal*. For House roll call votes back to the second session of the 101st Congress (1989–1991), please visit http://clerk.house.gov/legislative/legvotes.aspx. For Senate roll call votes back to the first session of the 101st Congress, check the U.S. Senate website at http://www.senate.gov/. As with the *Congressional Record*, printed editions of the *Congressional Directory*, the *House Journal*, or the *Senate Journal* can be found at the nearest federal depository library. For presidential statements and addresses, we used John T. Woolley and Gerhard Peters, eds., *American Presidency Project*, at http://www.presidency.ucsb.edu/.

Using online databases, we reviewed key newspapers for the historical periods covered in this book, including the *Baltimore Sun, Christian Science Monitor, Chicago Daily Tribune, Indianapolis Star, Los Angeles Times, New York Times, Wall Street Journal*, and *Washington Post*. We also consulted Hawaiian newspapers such as the *Hawaiian Gazette, Hawaiian Star, Honolulu Advertiser*, and *Honolulu Star-Bulletin* via microfilm and the Library of Congress's "Chronicling America" database at http://chroniclingamerica.loc.gov. Finally, using the Library's Periodicals and Newspapers Reading Room, we reviewed microfilm editions of Philippine newspapers, including the *Cablenews-American* (Manila, PI); *Philippines Free Press* (Manila, PI); *Manila Times*; and *Philippines Herald*. News accounts and feature stories, particularly for Members who served before 1945, provided missing information. All newspaper articles are cited in the notes.

For readers interested in acquiring reproductions of the photographs in this book, we have provided information for images from public, private, and commercial repositories. Transmission or reproduction of protected items beyond that allowed by fair use requires the written permission of the copyright owners. Requesters must make their own assessments of rights in light of their intended use. The U.S. House of Representatives is not responsible for violation of copyright by users of the images nor does it assume responsibility for any claims resulting from the failure of users to secure reproduction rights. The following institutions provided photographs and/or assistance with locating images related to the history of Asian and Pacific Islander Americans in Congress: the U.S. House of Representatives Office of Photography; the U.S. Senate Historical Office; the Library of Congress Prints and Photographs Division; the Library of Congress Serial and Government Publications Division; the National Archives and Records Administration; the William J. Clinton Presidential Library; the Jimmy Carter Presidential Library; the Ronald Reagan Presidential Library; the John F. Kennedy Presidential Library; the Gerald R. Ford Presidential Library; the Filipinas Heritage Library; the Hawaii State Archives; the Densho Digital Repository; the University of Hawaii at Manoa Library; the Barack Obama Presidential Library; the Lyndon B. Johnson Presidential Library; the Franklin D. Roosevelt Presidential Library; the Daniel K. Inouye Institute; the Japanese American National Museum; and the United States Mint. The images of current Members were provided by their offices, which are the points of contact for those seeking official images.

From left to right: Senator Daniel K. Inouye of Hawaii, Representative Norman Y. Mineta of California, and Senator Spark M. Matsunaga of Hawaii watch as President Jimmy Carter signs the Commission on Wartime Relocation and Internment of Civilians Act into law in 1980. The three lawmakers played an instrumental role in the legislation.

Image courtesy of the Jimmy Carter Library/National Archives and Records Administration

Delegate Ben Garrido Blaz used the Chamorro slogan "Biba Guam," which translates to "Long Live Guam," on this campaign button.

Collection of the U.S. House of Representatives

The 442nd Regimental Combat Team, made up of Japanese Americans, salutes the U.S. flag during a review in June 1943.

Image courtesy of the Library of Congress

The coat of arms for the 100th Infantry Battalion, formed primarily of Japanese Americans from Hawaii, incorporates Hawaiian emblems into its heraldry. The *mahiole*, or feather helmet, was a symbol of early chiefs, and the taro plant, on the upper right, played an important role in the Hawaiian creation story. The motto, "Remember Pearl Harbor," memorializes the patriotism of the battalion even as Japanese-American citizens faced racism and internment.

Image courtesy of the National Archives and Records Administration

ACKNOWLEDGEMENTS

The writing team wishes to extend a special thanks to the area experts in Asian-American studies, U.S.-Philippines relations, immigration, and Congress who commented on all or portions of the manuscript. The following individuals graciously shared their time and insights: Professor Michael Cullinane, Associate Director of the Center for Southeast Asian Studies, University of Wisconsin-Madison; Roger Daniels, Charles Phelps Taft Professor of History Emeritus at the University of Cincinnati; Timothy S. Elliott, former Deputy Associate Solicitor for the Department of the Interior; Lorraine Tong of the Congressional Research Service; and Phil Wolgin, PhD, Managing Director for Immigration Policy at the Center for American Progress. Their suggestions and comments have greatly improved this volume, and any errors in the manuscript are the responsibility of the authors alone. We also thank our colleagues in the Senate Historical Office for reviewing the sections of the manuscript related to the APA Senators: Historian Betty Koed, Associate Historian Kate Scott, and Assistant Historian Dan Holt. For additional guidance on researching the Philippine Resident Commissioners, we thank Victoria Hill, the assistant chief (retired) of the Asian Division, Library of Congress. In addition, the staff of the Library of Congress's Newspaper and Periodical Reading Room and the reference staff of the Congressional Research Service provided valuable assistance.

We thank the supportive and collegial staff of the Office of the Clerk of the House of Representatives. As with earlier volumes in this series, Clerk Karen L. Haas and her staff provided instrumental support. The Office of Communications in the Office of the Clerk provided editorial support and designed and managed production of the print and digital versions of this publication. For their collaboration and enthusiasm, we especially thank Catherine Cooke, Communications Chief; January Layman-Wood, Deputy Communications Chief; Eric Christensen, Senior Content Developer; Ashlee

Laubon, Senior Graphic Designer; Christine Gennetti, Senior Multimedia Developer; Phoebe Doan, Design and Multimedia Producer; Whitney Wyszynski, Content and Multimedia Producer; Lindsay Williams, Content and Multimedia Producer; Y. Michelle Haynes, Administrative Assistant; and Charlene Wiltsie, Editor. As usual, the courteous and professional staffs at the libraries of the U.S. House of Representatives and the U.S. Senate provided timely research assistance.

We thank our colleagues in the Office of Art & Archives (OAA) in the Office of the Clerk for their help. OAA Chief and House Curator Farar Elliott and her staff helped with captions and credits related to artifacts from the House Collection. House Archivist and OAA Deputy Chief Robin Reeder and Archivists Heather Bourk and Alison Trulock provided information about manuscript collections and facilitated research visits to the National Archives. Photo Archivist Michelle Strizever acquired copies of rare images for this publication. Office Manager Selena Haskins performed all the administrative tasks necessary to keep the writers on track.

Finally, many semesters' worth of enthusiastic and talented college and graduate interns in the Historian's Office played a laborious but vital part finding primary source documents at the National Archives, as well as many microfilmed newspaper articles at the Library of Congress. We thank Caitlyn Borghi, Rebecca Czochor, Erica Fuller, Raymond Hyser III, Sean Krauss, Ayla Mangold, Aldo Ponterosso, Nick Shumate, Rosemary Townsend, Zack Wood, Doug Yang, and Samuel Winter.

Editors: Albin J. Kowalewski, Matthew Wasniewski

Lead writers: Kenneth Kato, Joshua Litten

Co-writers: Jacqueline Burns, V. Grace Ethier, Erin Marie-Lloyd Hromada, Michael Murphy, Laura Turner O'Hara, Terrance Rucker

NOTES

1   "Seat for an Hawaiian," 16 December 1900, *Washington Post*: 13. Federico Degetau, the first Puerto Rican Resident Commissioner, had visited the Capitol a day before Wilcox but would not be sworn in until the opening of the following Congress in March 1901. Moreover, he initially had none of the floor privileges afforded Wilcox and other Delegates.

2   As of July 1, 2017, the closing date of this publication.

3   For a useful essay on surrogate representation within a larger discussion about "descriptive" versus "substantive" representation, see Michele L. Swers and Stella M. Rouse, "Descriptive Representation: Understanding the Impact of Identity on Substantive Representation of Group Interests," in *The Oxford Handbook of the American Congress*, ed. Eric Schickler and Frances E. Lee (New York: Oxford University Press, 2011): 241–271. See also, Office of the Historian, U.S. House of Representatives, *Women in Congress, 1917–2006* (Washington, DC: Government Printing Office, 2007): 1–7, and Office of the Historian, U.S. House of Representatives, *Black Americans in Congress, 1870–2007* (Washington, DC: Government Printing Office, 2008): 1–7.

4   The proportions for the other three groups are similarly weighted toward House service. As of July 1, 2017, 325 women have served in Congress—287 in the House and 50 in the Senate (12 have served in both chambers); 153 African Americans have served in Congress—144

Representatives and 10 Senators (one has served in both chambers); and 116 Hispanics have served in Congress—110 in the House and nine in the Senate (three have served in both chambers).

5 Office of the Historian, U.S. House of Representatives, *Hispanic Americans in Congress, 1822–2012* (Washington, DC: Government Printing Office, 2013): 22–65. See for example, Abraham Holtzman, "Empire and Representation: The U.S. Congress," *Legislative Studies Quarterly* 11, no. 2 (May 1986): 249–273. Twenty-six of the first Hispanic Members of Congress, from the very first, Joseph Marion Hernández of Florida in 1822, through World War II, were statutory representatives.

6 Pew Research Center, "The Rise of Asian Americans" (4 April 2013): 1–2, http://www.pewsocialtrends.org/2012/06/19/the-rise-of-asian-americans/ (accessed 11 July 2016).

7 *The Native Hawaiian and Other Pacific Islander Population: 2010*, C2010BR-12, prepared by Lindsay Hixon, Bradford B. Hepler, and Myoung Ouk Kim, U.S. Census Bureau (Washington, DC, issued May 2012): 1–4.

8 Jesse J. Holland, "Census: Asians Remain Fastest Growing Racial Group in US," 23 June 2016, Associated Press, http://apnews.com/2dc421061f124a19a9b86fade21b097d/census-asians-remain-fastest-growing-racial-group-us (accessed 1 July 2016).

9 See for example, Erika Lee, *The Making of Asian America: A History* (New York: Simon and Schuster, 2015): 3; Janelle Wong, S. Karthick Ramakrishnan, Taeku Lee, and Jane Junn, *Asian American Political Participation: Emerging Constituents and Their Political Identities* (New York: Russell Sage Foundation, 2011): 9–12; Gary Y. Okihiro, *The Columbia Guide to Asian American History* (New York: Columbia University Press, 2001): xiv–xv. Policy consequences from overgeneralizing the APA community are discussed in Chieh-Hsin Lin, "Why Pacific Islanders are Dropping Out of School," 17 August 2011, *International Examiner* (Seattle, WA): 8; Suzanne Gamboa, "Asian Groups, White House Seek Better Race Data," 22 June 2013, *Northwest Asian Weekly* (Seattle, WA): 4, 16; Sucheng Chan, *Asian Americans: An Interpretive History* (New York: Twayne Publishers, 1991): 170.

10 Lorraine H. Tong, "Asian Pacific Americans in the United States Congress," Report 97-398, 7 May 2013, Congressional Research Service.

11 Riley Kawika (Office of Hawaiian Affairs) to Donald Kennon (U.S. Capitol Historical Society), 21 March 2013, Memorandum on Native Hawaiian Delegates, in the files of the Office of the Historian, U.S. House of Representatives.

12 Although the title of this book is *Asian and Pacific Islander Americans in Congress*, we have followed the lead of CRS and used the term Asian Pacific Americans throughout the text to describe the Members featured here. See Tong, "Asian Pacific Americans in the United States Congress": 1n1. As promulgated by the U.S. Office of Management and Budget, the official terms to be used in designating these Americans for federal reporting purposes are "Asians" and "Native Hawaiians and other Pacific Islanders." U.S. Office of Management and Budget, "Revisions to the Standards for the Classification of Federal Data on Race and Ethnicity," *Federal Register* 62, no. 210 (30 October 1997): 58782–58790. See also, *The Native Hawaiian and Other Pacific Islander Population: 2010*.

13 On textbooks, see Alan Brinkley, *American History: A Survey*, 10th ed. (New York: McGraw-Hill College, 1999): 946; David M. Kennedy, Lizabeth Cohen, and Thomas A. Bailey, *The American Pageant: A History of the Republic*, 13th ed. (Boston: Houghton Mifflin Company, 2006): 822–823. For the Ng quotations, see Wendy Ng, *Japanese American Internment During World War II: A History and Reference Guide* (Westport, CT: Greenwood, 2002): xiii–xiv.

14 For the Daniels quotation, see Roger Daniels, *Prisoners Without Trial: Japanese Americans in World War II* (New York: Hill and Wang, 1993): 27. See also Lee, *The Making of Asian America*; Roger Daniels, "Incarceration of Japanese Americans: A Sixty-year Perspective," *The History Teacher* 35, no. 3 (May 2002): 297–310; Roger Daniels, "Immigration Policy in a Time of War: The United States, 1939–1945," *Journal of American Ethnic History* 25, no. 2/3 (Spring, 2006): 107–116; Karen L. Miksch and David Ghere, "Teaching Japanese-American Incarceration," *The History Teacher* 37, no. 2 (Feb., 2004): 211–227. Wendy Ng also uses the term incarceration to describe the federal policy of removal. See Wendy Ng, "Exile and Incarceration: Japanese Americans in World War II," in *Asian America: History and Culture, An Encyclopedia*, ed. Huping Ling and Allan Austin (New York: Sharpe Reference, 2010): 400–404.

15 Ng, *Japanese American Internment During World War II*: xiv.

16 For purposes of continuity, Resident Commissioner Carlos Romulo's profile is included with his one dozen predecessors who fit chronologically in this essay. Romulo was the last Philippine Resident

Commissioner, appointed to a brief two-year term beginning in 1944 and ending with Philippine independence in 1946.

7   See, for example, "Blue Blood: American Descendants of Royalty," 20 February 1887, *San Francisco Chronicle*: 8.

8   Henry Alexander Baldwin briefly succeeded Kuhio after his death in late 1922. Lincoln Loy McCandless served a single term in between Victor Houston and Samuel Wilder King. See Office of the Historian, U.S. House of Representatives, "Henry Alexander Baldwin," http://history.house. gov/People/Detail/8888; Office of the Historian, U.S. House of Representatives, "Lincoln Loy McCandless," http://history.house.gov/People/Detail/17702.

9   Caryl Rivers, "A Career of Many Lifetimes," 15 January 1967, *Boston Globe*: A32.

10 See Pew Research Center, "The Rise of Asian Americans."

11 David S. Broder and Kenneth Cooper, "Politics: Asian Pacific Caucus," 22 May 1994, *Washington Post*: A10.

12 H. Con. Res. 130, 107th Cong. (2001).

13 David K. Yoo and Eiichiro Azuma, "Introduction," in *The Oxford Handbook of Asian American History* (New York: Oxford University Press, 2016): 1–6. Some of the seminal works of this field include Elmer Clarence Sandmeyer, *The Anti-Chinese Movement in California* (1939; repr., Urbana: University of Illinois Press, 1973); Roger Daniels, *The Politics of Prejudice: The Anti-Japanese Movement in California and the Struggle for Japanese Inclusion* (Berkeley: University of California Press, 1962); and Alexander Saxton, *The Indispensable Enemy: Labor and the Anti-Chinese Movement in California* (Berkeley: University of California Press, 1971).

14 Keith L. Camacho, "Filipinos, Pacific Islanders, and the American Empire," in *The Oxford Handbook of Asian American History*, ed. David K. Yoo and Eiichiro Azuma (New York: Oxford University Press, 2016): 13–29, quotation on p. 14. Camacho reviewed works that cover "labor and migration" of Filipinos and Pacific Islanders between their homelands and the United States; the military value and use of the islands throughout the 20th century; and the effects of U.S. colonial rule on the islands and their respective cultures.

15 Peter W. Stanley, *A Nation in the Making: The Philippines and the United States, 1899–1921* (Cambridge, MA: Harvard University Press, 1974): vi.

16 Michael Cullinane, *Ilustrado Politics: Filipino Elite Responses to American Rule, 1898–1908* (Quezon City, PI: Ateneo de Manila University Press, 2003): 1.

17 For a fuller explanation about Asian-American studies and politics, see Gordon H. Chang, "Asian Americans, Politics, and History," in *The Oxford Handbook of Asian American History*, ed. David K. Yoo and Eiichiro Azuma (New York: Oxford University Press, 2016): 331–344.

Asian and Pacific Islander Americans by Congress
56th–115th Congresses (1900–2017)*

Legend:
DELEGATES
REPRESENTATIVES
SENATORS
RESIDENT COMMISSIONERS
REPRESENTATIVE AND SENATOR⁺

NUMBER OF MEMBERS

CONGRESS

56th (1899–1901)
59th (1905–1907)
62nd (1911–1913)
65th (1917–1919)
68th (1923–1925)
71st (1929–1931)
74th (1935–1937)
77th (1941–1943)
80th (1947–1949)
83rd (1953–1955)
86th (1959–1961)
89th (1965–1967)
92nd (1971–1973)
95th (1977–1979)
98th (1983–1985)
101st (1989–1991)
104th (1995–1997)
107th (2001–2003)
110th (2007–2009)
113th (2013–2015)
115th (2017–2019)

Sources: Appendix A: Asian and Pacific Islander American Representatives, Senators, Delegates, and Resident Commissioners by Congress, 1900–2017, Office of the Historian, U.S. House of Representatives; U.S. Senate Historical Office.

*56th Congress (1899–1901) as of November 6, 1900; 115th Congress (2017–2019) as of July 1, 2017.

⁺Daniel K. Akaka served as both a Representative and Senator in the 101st Congress (1989–1991) from the state of Hawaii.

Asian and Pacific Islander American Members as a Percentage of Congress

56th–115th Congresses (1900–2017)*

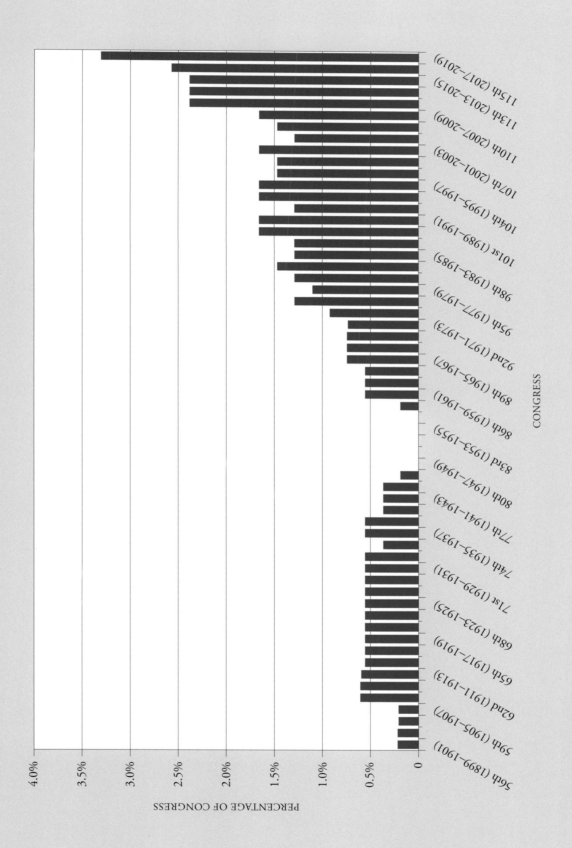

Sources: Appendix A: Asian Pacific Islander American Representatives, Senators, Delegates, and Resident Commissioners by Congress, 1900–2017; Office of the Historian, U.S. House of Representatives; U.S. Senate Historical Office.

*56th Congress (1899–1901) as of November 6, 1900; 115th Congress (2017–2019) as of July 1, 2017.

Asian and Pacific Islander American Members by Office
56th–115th Congresses (1900–2017)*

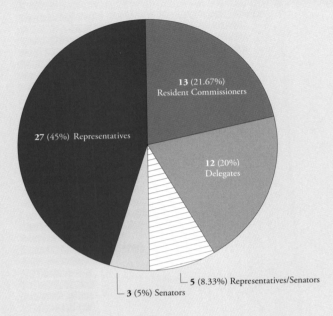

27 (45%) Representatives

13 (21.67%)
Resident Commissioners

12 (20%)
Delegates

5 (8.33%) Representatives/Senators

3 (5%) Senators

Length of Service of Asian and Pacific Islander American Members of Congress
56th–115th Congresses (1900–2017)*

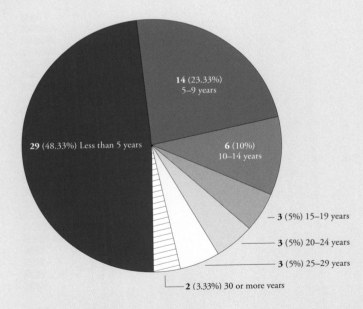

29 (48.33%) Less than 5 years

14 (23.33%)
5–9 years

6 (10%)
10–14 years

3 (5%) 15–19 years

3 (5%) 20–24 years

3 (5%) 25–29 years

2 (3.33%) 30 or more years

Sources: Appendix A: Asian and Pacific Islander American Representatives, Senators, Delegates, and Resident Commissioners by Congress, 1900–2017; Office of the Historian, U.S. House of Representatives; U.S. Senate Historical Office; *Biographical Directory of the United States Congress*, 1774–Present, http://bioguide.congress.gov.

*56th Congress (1899–1901) as of November 6, 1900; 115th Congress (2017–2019) as of July 1, 2017.

"WE HAVE TO WRITE
OUR OWN HISTORY."

Norman Y. Mineta
Washington Post, May 22, 1994

★ PART ONE ★

*Former Asian and Pacific Islander
American Members*

Exclusion and Empire

1898–1941

Around midnight, May 1, 1898, nine U.S. warships slipped past the strangely quiet guns on Corregidor Island, past the old Spanish fort guarding the entrance to Manila Bay, and sailed silently toward the Philippines' capital city. After about five hours, the U.S. Navy's Asiatic Squadron dipped down close to Sangley Point, just to the southwest of Manila, where a dozen Spanish ships rested at anchor. As dawn broke, the Luneta battery onshore began firing at the intruders.

Manuel L. Quezon, a 19-year-old law student in Manila, woke to the cannon fire and ran to the beach as Spanish forces lobbed volley after volley at the American squadron. Then, at 5:40 a.m., U.S. Commodore George Dewey gave the command to open fire. The American warships sailed in an elliptical pattern, each one emptying a broadside into the Spanish fleet before circling back around. Two hours later, Dewey broke off contact and sailed out into the bay. Quezon remembered hearing cheers of "Viva España!" until the Spanish ships began sinking into the shallow waters off Cavite. By 12:30 that afternoon, the Spanish forces had surrendered.[1]

What Quezon saw from the beaches of Manila Bay was the dawn of America's overseas empire. In a sudden energetic burst, the country defeated Spain in the War of 1898 (traditionally called the Spanish-American War) and took control of territory in the Caribbean while, in the Pacific, the United States annexed the Philippines and negotiated to obtain Hawaii.[2]

This 1898 Clifford K. Berryman cartoon from the *Washington Post* depicts tensions that arose between the United States and European imperialists in Asia after the American victory over Spain in 1898. Jealous of the newfound U.S. influence in Asia and the Pacific, and seeking to retain control of the Philippines and other Pacific islands, Kaiser Wilhelm II of Germany struggles to hold shut the door to the "East" as Uncle Sam's oversized leg squeezes through the opening.

Image courtesy of the National Archives and Records Administration

This 1898 Kurz & Allison lithograph depicts the Battle of Manila Bay on May 1, 1898, which marked the dawn of America's overseas empire.

Image courtesy of the Library of Congress

What became a relatively straightforward conflict—U.S. diplomat John Hay, speaking for many at the time, famously boasted that it was a "splendid little war"—gave way to enormously complicated ramifications.[3] Since 1789 American policymakers had encouraged the country's often violent westward expansion—displacing many American Indian nations as eastern settlers established new towns, territories, and, eventually, states on the push toward the Pacific coast. Beginning in 1898, Congress, for the first time in American history, became responsible for overseeing territories that existed beyond the shores of North America. Millions of new people were suddenly swept up into America's global footprint. Their very presence challenged long-held assumptions about citizenship and race and forced Congress to confront what it meant to be American.[4] Would the islands become states, and would their inhabitants become citizens? Was there room in the national narrative for Filipinos, Native Hawaiians, and other Pacific Islanders?

Congress, of course, had been wrestling with those questions since the mid-19th century, when immigrants from China and Japan began coming to America to work the gold mines, build the railroads, and tend the farms along the Pacific coast. Since 1868, with the ratification of the Fourteenth Amendment, the Constitution had guaranteed citizenship rights to people born on U.S. soil, regardless of whether they were white and lived in Massachusetts or whether they had once been enslaved in Mississippi. Since 1870 both white and black immigrants qualified for naturalization.

But as the number of Asian immigrants rose out west, Congress developed laws targeting them specifically. Over the course of 70 years, federal legislators and the courts worked to bar immigrants from China and Japan from coming to America while prohibiting those already stateside from becoming naturalized citizens. These exclusion acts were compounded by state laws that prevented Asian immigrants from owning land or participating in the political process in any way. This simple fact, more than anything, explains why there is not a single Asian or Pacific Islander American elected as a voting Representative or Senator before 1956.

Although this essay begins in the 1850s, the bulk of it covers the years between the War of 1898 and World War II. We have split it into two sections. The first section covers nearly a century of U.S. immigration law and explains how Congress and the western states, especially, envisioned and erected a policy of exclusion that systematically prevented people of Asian descent from integrating into American society. The second part investigates the history of America's global reach in the Pacific: the debates for and against acquiring new territory, Congress's approach to designing the territorial governments in the Philippines and Hawaii, territorial representation on Capitol Hill, the commercial relationship between mainland America and its overseas possessions, and the decades-long debates about independence and statehood.

Although the Philippine and Hawaiian "questions" entered the national conversation around the same time, the island territories had remarkably different experiences, culminating in starkly different results. In 1946 the Philippines, which from the start saw itself as a separate nation entirely, became the only territory in American history with representation in Congress to gain its independence. Meanwhile, by the 1940s, Hawaii was clearing a path to statehood. Because of this vast split, their stories are told separately. Although the end date for this chapter is 1941, we have extended the section on the Philippines an extra five years to 1946. From a narrative standpoint, this allows us to cover the entire scope of the Philippines as an American territory, from its acquisition all the way up to its independence.

In 1900 Hawaiian Delegate Robert W. Wilcox, whose mother was Polynesian, became the first Asian Pacific American (APA) Member of Congress. Less than 10 years later, Benito Legarda and Pablo Ocampo were sworn in as the first Resident Commissioners from the Philippines. Over the next five decades, 5 more APA Members served on Capitol Hill as either a Delegate from Hawaii (five total) or as a Resident Commissioner from the Philippines (13 total). For the 18 APA Members of Congress featured in this section, racism, exclusion, and imperialism were not abstract concepts. They were the products of everyday life, frequently dictating their personal legislative agendas and determining the very nature of their constituents' relationship with the federal government.

The two Resident Commissioners from the Philippine Islands, Isauro Gabaldon (pictured fourth from left) and Pedro Guevara (tenth from left), gather with a group of Filipino independence lobbyists and activists in Washington, DC, in 1923.

Image courtesy of the Filipinas Heritage Library

Asian immigrants played a key role in the development of the western United States. A photographer documented this team of Chinese men in Deadwood, Dakota Territory, in 1888.

Image courtesy of the Library of Congress

The title of this section, "Exclusion and Empire," is meant to underscore the two major forces at work in the United States' policy toward the Pacific prior to World War II: the process of expanding America's global presence while simultaneously restricting who could belong. In large measure, the two themes informed each other. By the time Congress assumed control over territory in the Pacific, it had decades of experience excluding people of Asian descent—especially the Chinese—from the American story. Over the next 40 years, as Congress supervised territorial governments in the Philippines and Hawaii, lawmakers continued to revise the requirements for citizenship.

FIRST ARRIVALS, FIRST REACTIONS

In the half-century between the California Gold Rush and the War of 1898, young men primarily from China and Japan flocked to the western states to fill an untold number of jobs brought about by America's push across the continent. The West was sparsely populated, and demand for labor was high. The influx of Asian workers, however, created a volatile mix of hostility and resentment among the region's white population that reverberated across the next few generations. On Capitol Hill, such anxieties were routinely codified into law. Even though America was home to thousands of Asian immigrants, they were almost completely prohibited from participating in the political process and were frequently ostracized from American society.

Beginning in 1849, Chinese immigrants came to California for the same reason everyone else did: to get rich mining gold. But when the federal government began a spirited race to build the western leg of the transcontinental railroad, American companies hired Chinese laborers by the thousands.[5] Chinese merchants followed, setting up shops that catered to the immigrants. Many became labor brokers themselves.[6] In 1868 the United States and China negotiated the Treaty of Trade, Consuls, and Emigration, known as the Burlingame Treaty, which established a reciprocal relationship for the movement of people and goods between the two countries.[7]

This 1869 cartoon from *Frank Leslie's Illustrated Newspaper* depicts the completion of the transcontinental railroad that connected the nation's coasts. Thousands of Chinese laborers laid track for the railroad, and Chinese merchants followed the construction. The predominantly white frontier population reacted by adopting anti-Chinese sentiments.

Image courtesy of the Library of Congress

Chinese Exclusion

The influx of Chinese into California during the 1850s and 1860s did not sit well with the white frontier population. The two groups were vastly different, and what white Californians did not understand they began to fear. It was not long before an anti-Chinese movement took root. In response, the California legislature produced an astonishing crop of laws hostile to the Chinese that raised taxes, discouraged immigration, restricted educational opportunities, and limited due process.[8]

When the transcontinental railroad was completed in 1869, thousands of Chinese laborers were suddenly left unemployed. Many returned to the West Coast, where anti-Chinese violence and labor unrest soon flared up. In late October 1871, for instance, "the largest mass lynching in U.S. history," as described by historian Erika Lee, took place in Los Angeles when a mob of 500 killed 17 Chinese in response to the shooting of a police officer.[9]

Over the next decade, Congress clamped down on Chinese immigration, recommending changes to both the Burlingame Treaty and existing immigration laws.[10] Presidential administrations went along with the effort by negotiating a new treaty ratified in 1881 that empowered Congress to "regulate, limit, or suspend" the flow of Chinese laborers into America.[11]

That year Congress doubled down on its anti-Chinese position and passed a bill that closed Chinese labor immigration for 20 years and excluded Chinese immigrants from becoming naturalized citizens. Business interests pushed back and President Chester A. Arthur vetoed the measure, but he hinted that a shorter suspension would work. Within months, a new bill had been approved that closed Chinese immigration for 10 years.[12]

The Chinese Exclusion Act of 1882 imposed the first restrictions on immigration in U.S. history. Like clockwork, Congress extended its provisions, including the citizenship prohibition, every 10 years. With the backing of the Supreme Court, subsequent renewals and amendments expanded the original act.[13] By 1892 Congress had streamlined deportation procedures and required Chinese immigrants to carry a certificate of residence. Six years later, Congress banned Chinese laborers living in Hawaii from entering the mainland. The ban against Chinese immigrants became permanent in 1904.[14]

Japanese Immigration and Exclusion

During the 19th century, Japan modernized its economy and, in the process, became a rising world power. Following Chinese exclusion, significant numbers of Japanese came to the United States to attend America's schools and work as diplomats and entrepreneurs. Unlike China, which had a weak central state and thus did not closely monitor its citizens living abroad, Japan's government, with its strong administrative structure, played an active role recruiting and vetting immigrants. In an effort to make sure Japanese immigrants avoided the kind of discrimination that befell the Chinese, Japanese envoys regularly checked on living conditions in the States.[15]

At the time, the Japanese presence on the mainland remained small and never approached the number of Chinese living on the West Coast, although their numbers in Hawaii before annexation were substantial.[16] The vigilance

President Chester A. Arthur signed the Chinese Exclusion Act in 1882, which placed the first restrictions on immigration in U.S. history. The law specifically targeted Chinese immigration.

Image courtesy of the Library of Congress

As mayor of San Francisco from 1897 to 1902, James D. Phelan publicly espoused anti-Chinese and anti-Japanese views. Phelan later served as a U.S. Senator from California from 1915 to 1921.

In the early 1900s, President Theodore Roosevelt grappled with the segregation of Japanese children in San Francisco schools and nativist attacks on Japanese businesses. He reluctantly decided to restrict Japanese immigration.

PANORAMIC SAN FRANCISCO, FROM CALIFORNIA STREET HILL
1877

of the Japanese government, which included formal inquiries and high-level diplomacy, helped solve problems before they worsened. America's expanding territorial footprint in the Pacific also contributed to the relationship: Washington sought to maintain good relations with Japan rather than risk its interests in the Philippines.[17]

Combined, those factors help explain the early lack of widespread anti-Japanese agitation beyond a few local hot spots like San Francisco, where several violent incidents occurred in the 1890s. By 1900, however, Japanese immigration had been swept up into larger anti-Asian movements.[18] "Chinese and Japanese … are not the stuff of which American citizens can be made," proclaimed San Francisco Mayor and future U.S. Senator James D. Phelan, ignoring the reality that the Constitution conferred citizenship to the children of Asian immigrants born in America. Although the Japanese government responded by halting passports for laborers, immigrants continued to travel freely from America's territories to the mainland.[19]

As more and more Japanese immigrants arrived to work on the West Coast, anti-Japanese agitation took hold especially in California, where the state government routinely petitioned Congress for wholesale Japanese exclusion.[20] Despite a short period of goodwill after Japan gave San Francisco a substantial donation to recover from a massive earthquake, anti-Japanese policies soon re-emerged.[21] In the fall of 1906, the San Francisco board of education announced that all Japanese children would attend segregated schools.[22] Japan's government criticized the measure, and in just a short while the United States had been whipped into a full-blown war scare before the city finally rescinded the segregation order. Only a few months later tempers flared again when mobs of California nativists attacked Japanese businesses during a San Francisco streetcar strike.[23] War threatened again, but President Theodore Roosevelt defused the situation before it escalated.[24]

Roosevelt was ever the optimist, but it all led him to a distressing thought: "I have been reluctantly forced to the conclusion that it is indispensable for the Japanese to be kept from coming in any numbers as settlers to the United States."[25]

Alien Land Laws and Citizenship

During the first two decades of the 20th century, the state of California enhanced its already stringent anti-Asian policies and explored ways to restrict the property rights of Japanese immigrants, further excluding them from American society.[26]

The process culminated in 1913, when the state government passed an act prohibiting "aliens ineligible to citizenship"—almost universally people of Asian descent—from owning land in California. As U.S. nationals, Filipinos were eligible for entry in the United States, but still ineligible for naturalization. Other states, particularly Oregon and Washington, passed their own laws based on California's formula.[27]

As a result, many *issei*—first-generation Japanese immigrants—registered property in the name of their native-born children. Others had to lease or own land using a corporation held in trust for their children. But California closed even these loopholes in 1920.[28]

The federal courts, moreover, sided with the states. In November 1923, the U.S. Supreme Court upheld both California's and Washington's alien land laws as well as a handful of other restrictions. Over the next two decades, California strengthened its property laws, even going so far as to seize land and assets from Japanese Americans incarcerated during World War II.[29]

But by the late 1940s, public opinion on the issue had started to shift, and the federal courts began reversing their earlier decisions. On April 17, 1952, in *Sei Fujii v. California*, the California supreme court declared the land laws unconstitutional. California voters finally erased the policy in a public referendum in November 1956. Washington State removed the country's last alien land law in 1966.[30]

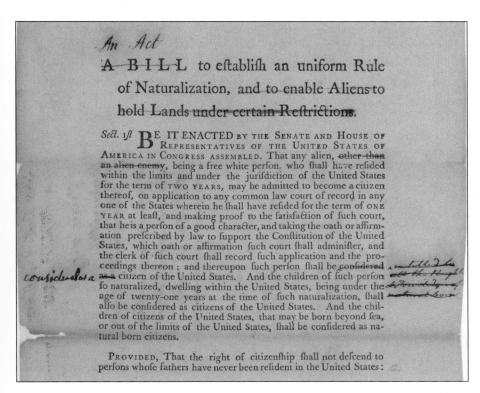

In March 1790, Congress debated America's first immigration law. The bill allowed a "free white person" to petition for U.S. citizenship after two years of residency. Congress quickly approved the bill, and the Naturalization Act of 1790 became law on March 26, 1790.

Image courtesy of the National Archives and Records Administration

At the root of the issue were the country's qualifications for citizenship, and for much of U.S. history, the courts severely circumscribed who was eligible to become a naturalized citizen. For 80 years (1790–1870) only "free white persons" qualified. In 1870 Congress added "persons of African descent."[31] For Asian immigrants, in the second half of the 19th century there was no standard national practice. At the time, local judges determined who was eligible for naturalization on a case-by-case basis. As immigrant numbers increased early in the 20th century, national eligibility requirements became a major issue. In a handful of cases that made it to the U.S. Supreme Court, Asian-American leaders decided to test whether Japanese immigrants could be classified as "white" for purposes of naturalization.[32]

In the early 1920s, the Supreme Court decided two significant cases that demonstrated the historical malleability of ideas about race. In *Ozawa v. United States*, the court validated the category of "aliens ineligible to citizenship" by arguing that, "The federal and state courts, in an almost unbroken line, have held that the words 'white person' [in the 1870 Naturalization Act] were meant to indicate only a person of what is popularly known as the Caucasian race."[33] This 1922 decision meant that Takao Ozawa could not classify as white and was disqualified from naturalized citizenship.[34] A year later, in *United States v. Bhagat Singh Thind*, an immigrant from the Punjab in India—who had served in the U.S. Army during World War I—claimed the right to become a naturalized American citizen. The Justices, however, unanimously agreed that Thind's ethnicity fell beyond the bounds of what "the common man" understood to classify as white. In doing so, the court upheld the ban against Thind, in particular, and Asian Indians, generally.[35]

Toward Total Exclusion

At a policy level, citizenship remained perhaps the most powerful tool at Congress's disposal and, during the 1910s, the national legislature completely overhauled the country's immigration laws. For the first time, the federal government prohibited people from whole areas of the globe—not just individual countries—from coming to America. During World War I, fears of espionage and sabotage encouraged the United States to clamp down on visas, giving Congress time to consider bigger and broader reform. With the Immigration Act of 1924, the effort to codify total bans culminated in a restrictive national origins quota system built on the legal invention of "aliens ineligible for citizenship" popular in various state laws.

As anti-Asian feelings grew more pronounced, immigrants from India— many of whom began arriving in the United States in the 1890s—became one of the first groups affected by the new laws. At the time, federal immigration restrictions fell into two categories: generalized groups (for example, paupers and anarchists) and individual nationalities (for example, Japanese and Chinese). But, by 1911, Asian Indians had become a category all their own. As a new target for exclusionists, the government classified them as "Hindu" no matter their religion or ethnicity.[36]

Congress went even further and passed the Immigration Act of 1917, creating an "Asiatic Barred Zone" that excluded Chinese, Asian Indians, Burmese, Thai,

President Woodrow Wilson vetoed the Immigration Act of 1917 because of its inclusion of literacy tests for immigrants. Congress overrode his veto to codify Asian exclusion.

Image courtesy of the Library of Congress

and Malays and extended to parts of Russia, the Arabian peninsula, Afghanistan, Polynesia, and all East Indian islands—about 500 million people in total. The Woodrow Wilson administration omitted Japan because its immigrants already faced a number of prohibitions. The law also exempted the Philippines since its residents, as members of an American territory, were U.S. nationals and legally eligible to move to the States.[37]

The eruption of World War I also had a pronounced effect on the number of people coming to the States. Immigration rates dropped during the war, encouraging Congress to build on the Asiatic Barred Zone and consider ways to close America's borders completely. But reform attempts struggled to get off the ground, and in 1920 Congress abandoned its crusade for an outright ban. Instead, it settled on a legislative formula creating a national origins quota system.[38]

After the White House changed hands in 1921, the Republican Congress, working with the new Republican presidential administration of Warren G. Harding, redoubled its efforts to overhaul America's immigration policy. Within a month of being introduced, the national origins quota system became law on May 19, 1921.[39] The quota law set total annual immigration at 355,000, or 3 percent of the foreign-born population during the last Census in 1910. Federal officials used the same calculus to determine the number of immigrants allowed on a nation-by-nation basis.[40]

Immigration hard-liners who had long opposed Asian immigration began worrying that America would experience a surge of refugees from hard-hit southern and eastern Europe after the war. In 1923 President Calvin Coolidge called for new legislation in order to limit immigration completely, and Congress quickly obliged. In the House, the Immigration and Naturalization Committee, led by Albert Johnson of Washington, who had long opposed Japanese immigration, began working on ways to tighten the quota system, pushing the baseline numbers back from the 1910 Census to the 1890 Census, which were lower and would therefore be more restrictive.[41]

On March 17, 1924, after a stalled first effort, Chairman Johnson introduced H.R. 7995, the committee's comprehensive immigration reform bill. The legislation filled in policy gaps, but, more importantly, devised a quota system organized by nationality that limited future immigration to a small fraction of the foreign-born population in 1890. Moreover, to effectively bar immigration from Japan, the legislation adopted the legal definition of "aliens ineligible to citizenship" popular in the Pacific states.[42]

The problem, however, was that Japan had become a global power whose naval strength trailed only the United States and Britain. State Department officials feared that, if the bill became law, whatever cooperation existed between America and Japan in their work to maintain political stability in the Pacific basin would end.[43] Nevertheless, the bill cruised through the House, passing 323 to 71. When the White House and the Japanese ambassador tried to pressure the Senate into removing the clause, the plan backfired. The Senate overwhelmingly approved the immediate exclusion clause. President Coolidge signed the immigration bill into law on May 26, 1924.[44]

As enacted, the Johnson–Reed Act limited annual immigration to the United States to 165,000, but placed few restrictions on people from the Western

Representative Albert Johnson of Washington chaired the House Immigration and Naturalization Committee from the 66th Congress to the 71st Congress (1919–1931), working to limit Japanese immigration to the United States.

Collection of the U.S. House of Representatives

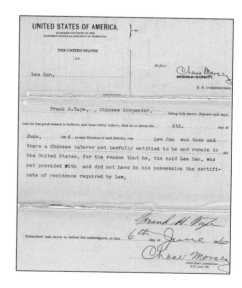

District courts around the country maintained case files for individuals excluded under Section 3 of the Chinese Exclusion Act. This 1906 case record for Lee San indicates that he lived and worked in the United States without the legally required certificate of residency and ordered him to be deported.

Image courtesy of the National Archives and Records Administration

Public Law 68-139, approved during the 68th Congress (1923–1925) and known as the Immigration Act of 1924, established a national origins quota system. It limited the number of immigrants allowed to enter the United States and barred immigration from most of Asia.

Image courtesy of the National Archives and Records Administration

---

Sixty-eighth Congress of the United States of America;

At the First Session,

Begun and held at the City of Washington on Monday, the third day of December, one thousand nine hundred and twenty-three.

AN ACT

To limit the immigration of aliens into the United States, and for other purposes.

Be it enacted by the Senate and House of Representatives of the United States of America in Congress assembled, That this Act may be cited as the " Immigration Act of 1924."

IMMIGRATION VISAS.

SEC. 2. (a) A consular officer upon the application of any immigrant (as defined in section 3) may (under the conditions hereinafter prescribed and subject to the limitations prescribed in this Act or regulations made thereunder as to the number of

---

Hemisphere. For the remaining transatlantic migrants, their admission quota was set at 2 percent of the total number of foreign-born nationals living in the United States in 1890. The new law closed America's borders to all Japanese men, women, and children. Combined with the earlier Chinese exclusion acts and the Asiatic Barred Zone, Congress's new Japanese exclusion clause had effectively stopped transpacific immigration to all but Filipinos.[45]

The impact of the law was arguably greatest in Japan, where many resented the section that singled them out as "an inferior race."[46] Somewhat optimistically, the Japanese government expected the immigration restriction to relax over time as the commercial interests between Japan and the United States strengthened. Nevertheless, Japan began viewing the United States, instead of the Soviet Union, as its primary military and naval adversary.[47] That shift would have devastating consequences for America's two major Pacific territories—the Philippines and Hawaii—during World War II.

But even the Philippines and Hawaii, which the United States assumed control over at the turn of the century, were not immune to some level of exclusion during the 40 years preceding the war. Beginning in 1898, the experience of the United States in the Philippines and Hawaii legalized the convergence of exclusionary practices at home and abroad as ideas about race and empire conflicted with American traditions of democracy and self-government.

1898: BIRTH OF AN OVERSEAS EMPIRE

In a way, America's empire in the Pacific began with an explosion roughly 100 miles or so off the coast of Florida in the quiet waters of Havana Harbor.

On February 15, 1898, the USS *Maine*, a battleship moored just outside Cuba's capital, erupted in flames and sank, killing hundreds of crew on board.

The ship had been sent there to monitor the growing conflict between Cuban revolutionaries and the Spanish regime that had maintained control of the island for centuries. It is not entirely clear how or why the ship exploded, but almost immediately war hawks in the United States blamed Spain. Tension grew until Congress declared war on April 25, 1898.[48]

Although the United States fought in two major theaters—the Philippines and the Caribbean—the war was over quickly. After the U.S. Navy dispatched the Spanish squadron in Manila, U.S. servicemen took all of about four months to capture Cuba. When it was all said and done, the William McKinley administration went on what George C. Herring, a leading historian of U.S. foreign policy, has called an "island land grab." By the time the ink dried on the Treaty of Paris ending the war, the United States had staked claim to Cuba, Puerto Rico, the Philippines, Samoa, and a handful of other Pacific islands and had used the conflict to begin the process of annexing Hawaii.[49]

The war and America's resulting overseas expansion came at the end of an anxious decade. The 1890s had unleashed an avalanche of social strife at home, including the collapse of the U.S. economy, the supposed closing of the American frontier, unemployment, labor unrest, and the entrenchment of Jim Crow laws limiting the rights of African Americans. The disorder at home led many to look abroad. "Since Jefferson's time," the historian Herring wrote, "Americans had sought to deal with pressing internal difficulties through expansion, and in the 1890s they increasingly looked outward for solutions to domestic problems."[50]

But by the turn of the century, looking outward only seemed to bring up more questions than answers. Many Americans wondered if expansion was a good idea, whether the United States should enter the 20th century as an imperial power. Mostly, the debate split the population into those for expansion and those against it.

Those in favor envisioned the United States as an emerging global power in which American ships crisscrossed the Pacific to trade with untapped markets. Geography bestowed the Philippines and Hawaii with immense value to U.S. industries looking to trade with Asia. Expansionists like Senator Albert

Senator Albert Beveridge of Indiana argued for an expanded U.S. role in the Pacific, suggesting that the Philippines and Hawaii could play an important part in U.S. commercial and military interests.

Image courtesy of the Library of Congress

Shown here entering the harbor of Havana, Cuba, on January 25, 1898, the USS *Maine* exploded three weeks later, on February 15. Despite the lack of definitive proof that Spain was responsible for destroying the ship, Congress responded to cries for action by declaring war on Spain two months later.

Image courtesy of the Naval History and Heritage Command

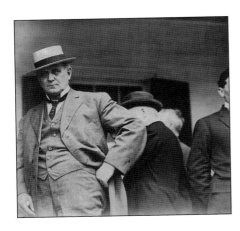

When the United States annexed Hawaii, Congress considered the racial demographics of the islands. Representative James Beauchamp (Champ) Clark of Missouri denounced the idea of eventual Hawaiian statehood, arguing that Congress would be unable to incorporate such a large foreign population into the country.

Collection of the U.S. House of Representatives

Beveridge of Indiana argued that the islands would be invaluable as way stations for American exporters and the U.S. military, lending credence to his theory that the Pacific would dominate "the commerce of the future."[51] Anti-imperialists, on the other hand, believed expansion endangered the future of the republic by antagonizing world powers and overextending America's resources.[52]

Almost immediately Congress confronted a host of moral and legal conundrums about the nation's new island possessions: Did the Constitution even allow the United States to reach beyond the boundaries of North America to govern new territory? What did it mean for a former colony to possess colonies of its own? Would these territories be eligible for statehood, or did Congress have the authority to prevent them from joining the Union?

Regardless of where fin de siècle Americans came down on expansion, they faced unavoidable questions about what would happen to the inhabitants of these new territories: Were they eligible for American citizenship? Could they move freely between the islands and the mainland United States? Would they have representation in Congress? From the start, America's racial politics featured prominently in debates about the Philippines and Hawaii. Popular ways of thinking, driven by trends like social Darwinism, shaped congressional discussions on citizenship, democracy, and the movement of goods and people across borders.[53]

When Congress approved the annexation of Hawaii in July 1898, for instance, a substantial part of the debate focused on the racial characteristics of the inhabitants of the islands.[54] As we have seen, the United States had for decades followed a policy of exclusion that prevented people of Asian descent from integrating into American society. But after years of transpacific immigration, Hawaii had substantial Japanese and Chinese populations. The question became whether the U.S. government could reconcile this with the strict exclusionary policies of its immigration law.

Some in Congress saw this as a problem the United States could easily overcome.[55] But others, like future Speaker James Beauchamp (Champ) Clark of Missouri, saw Hawaii's large Asian population as a direct threat to the republic. Clark deplored the idea that Hawaii might one day become a state—that Japanese and Chinese immigrants might one day become U.S. citizens—and he encouraged Congress to develop a solution "without polluting and weakening our system of government by taking to our bosom a horde of Asiatic savages."[56]

For Clark and Members of Congress who shared his beliefs, expansionism gambled with the future of the nation by overestimating the capacity of American society to assimilate new, nonwhite immigrants.[57] Imperial ambitions in the Pacific, Clark predicted, would lead the United States to acquire one new territory after another, reshaping the legislative branch along the way. He described what he considered to be a nightmarish future in which the House had to a hire an "interpreter to the Speaker" in order to translate the "discordant voices" during debate. Underwriting his argument with pseudoscientific theories about race popular at the time, he warned against a "polyglot House" populated by Members from Cuba, Fiji, Hong Kong, Korea, and "the Cannibal Islands," the last of which, he told the Speaker, would "gaze upon you with watering mouth and gleaming teeth."[58]

For others, like Senator Beveridge, future President William H. Taft, and British author Rudyard Kipling, who put these anxieties to verse in his 1899 poem "The White Man's Burden: The United States and the Philippine Islands," race was not a reason to avoid the Philippines. It was the very reason America needed to expand; it was the justification for American superiority. Beveridge dismissed Filipinos as "children utterly incapable of self-government." As the head of a U.S. mission to the islands, Taft called them America's "little brown brothers."[59] Beveridge understood the U.S. role in the Philippines as a "divine mission" to establish a "system where chaos reigns." American expansion was bigger than party politics, he said, bigger than popular opinion or constitutional authority. "It is elemental. It is racial."[60]

Taft likewise doubted the capacity of the Philippine people for self-government, a theory he based largely on the color of their skin, once predicting they would "need the training of fifty or a hundred years before they shall even realize what Anglo-Saxon liberty is." The Filipinos were "born politicians," Taft wrote to Secretary of War Elihu Root, "as ambitious as Satan and as jealous as possible of each others' [sic] preferment."[61]

Ultimately, the construction of an American empire contained an inseparable and volatile mix of race and nationhood. Americans for and against expansion used common racial theories and popular stereotypes to support their arguments. For some, the United States stood as a civilizing force in the Pacific territories. For others who saw no way of integrating America's new territories into the Union, race became the chief reason to dial back the country's overseas ambitions.[62] In the first half of the 20th century, America's dealings in the Philippines and Hawaii showcased the convergence of race and empire.

THE PHILIPPINES, 1898–1946

The relative ease with which the United States dispatched the Spanish squadron in Manila Bay was only the beginning of what would become a nearly 50-year American presence in the Philippines. It was one thing to capture the islands, but another thing entirely to set up a working administration. The Philippines encompasses about 7,100 islands and sits nearly 8,600 miles away from Washington, DC. By the late 1890s, it had an estimated population of 8 million.[63] Dewey's victory had come so fast that few in the McKinley administration appeared to have given much thought to what came next.[64]

President McKinley's strategy going into the conflict was to take as much of the Philippines as possible and then, during peace negotiations, to only "keep what we want."[65] From an administrative standpoint, McKinley envisioned the Philippines as an American protectorate or an American colony. Like many people on the mainland, he believed Filipinos were incapable of self-government and did not want another foreign power to take over the islands.[66]

The decision to keep the Philippines during the Treaty of Paris that the Senate approved in February 1899 set off an intense and emotional debate across the country and on Capitol Hill. Expansionists in Congress saw the decision to retain the islands as a continuation of America's "manifest destiny" to spread its reach beyond the West Coast and into the Pacific. Anti-imperialists, on the other hand, believed that America, which itself had once been an overseas colony, had no right to take the islands as the spoils of war.[67]

This circa 1899 image, "Uncle Sam's Burden (with apologies to Mr. Kipling)," shows a U.S. soldier carrying three children (representing the Philippines, Puerto Rico, and Cuba) in a backpack made from the U.S. flag. The scene was inspired by Rudyard Kipling's 1899 poem "The White Man's Burden: The United States and the Philippine Islands."

Image courtesy of the Library of Congress

On May 1, 1898, Commodore George Dewey led the U.S. Navy's Asiatic Squadron to a decisive victory against the Spanish fleet in Manila Bay. The following year, he was commissioned Admiral of the Navy.

Image courtesy of the Library of Congress

This Kurz & Allison lithograph depicts the December 10, 1898, signing of the Treaty of Paris, which set the terms that ended the Spanish-American War. Commissioners from the United States included Senator Cushman K. Davis of Minnesota, Secretary of State William R. Day, Senator William P. Frye of Maine, Senator George Gray of Delaware, and Ambassador Whitelaw Reid.

Image courtesy of the Library of Congress

THE SPANISH-AMERICAN TREATY OF PEACE, PARIS DEC. 10TH 1898.

By the time the United States took control of the Manila government in 1899, the Philippines had been in a state of war for the better part of three years. In 1896, when the Spanish regime refused long-standing Filipino requests to reform the islands' colonial government, the Philippines erupted into rebellion. Two years into that conflict the islands suddenly became a crucial theater in the War of 1898, as Spain's empire receded and America's expanded. Finally, in 1899, on the heels of the Treaty of Paris, as America's occupying force attempted to install a new colonial regime in the Philippines, Filipinos fought back in a second war for independence, beginning what would become a three-year conflict over the right to self-government in the Philippines.[68]

The United States began planning to administer the archipelago in January 1899 when President McKinley established the Philippine commission to gather information about the islands' "various populations," their "legislative needs," and to identify how best to maintain "order, peace and the public welfare."[69]

The Philippine-American War erupted less than a month later. The conflict pitted pro-independence Filipinos, who believed Spain's regime had simply been swapped for an American one, against the U.S. military that was based largely out of Manila. In response, the United States placed the Philippines under martial law until the fighting wound down in 1902.[70]

The multi-year conflict, which Filipinos saw as a continued fight for sovereignty but which Americans considered to be more of an insurrection, was bloody and devastating. What started as a more conventional struggle quickly gave way to a fierce guerrilla fight. According to one State Department estimate, 20,000 Filipino revolutionaries and 4,200 American troops died in combat while upward of 200,000 Filipino civilians starved to death, died of disease, or were killed in combat. Another estimate puts the total fatalities at nearly 300,000 Filipinos and 6,000 Americans. Reports of torture and other

President William McKinley established the first Philippine commission in 1899. Four of the members of the commission, shown here from left to right, were Jacob Schurman, Admiral George Dewey, Charles Denby, and Dean Worcester.

Image courtesy of the Library of Congress

atrocities, especially late in the conflict, underscored the brutality of the war.[71]

By 1902, even as the Theodore Roosevelt administration declared victory in the archipelago, the conflict had left an indelible mark on the identity of the Philippines. If the idea of the Philippines as a sovereign nation had simmered just out of reach during the late 19th century, the collective experience fighting the Spanish and then the Americans inspired the islands to embrace a sense of nationhood, to celebrate their commonalities and shared beliefs, and to eventually adopt an identity that made them Filipinos first and foremost. "Though there was no Filipino nation in the conflict," observed one recent history, "the Filipino nation could not have existed without the war."[72]

Despite the ruthless conflict and the widespread support in the Philippines for independence, McKinley's commission, headed by Cornell University president Jacob Schurman, went forward with its investigation and published its final report in four volumes in January 1900. It called on the United States to end martial law and revealed that Filipinos wanted their government to defend religious freedom, protect basic human rights, and guarantee home rule. But Schurman set the tone for future U.S. policy, concluding in no uncertain terms that the Filipinos would be unable to govern themselves in the short term. "No one," the report said, "can foresee when the diverse peoples of the Philippine Islands may be molded together into a nationality capable of exercising all the functions of independent self-government."[73]

Shortly after receiving Schurman's report, McKinley appointed a second Philippine commission, headed by federal judge William H. Taft, to begin designing a civil government based on America's model.[74]

During his research, Taft concluded, and overstated, that "the great majority of Filipinos" did not object to U.S. colonial rule in a general sense; they simply reserved their main "hostility" for America's "Military Government."[75] Nevertheless, his commission report, issued in August 1900, was a scathing indictment of the population at large. Filipino people were described as being "ignorant, superstitious, and credulous in remarkable degree." Taft laid out a plan to introduce government institutions, establish a civil service, and enact currency and tax programs. It also called for public works, capital investment, and educational reform. On the heels of its report, the commission assumed all legislative powers in the Philippines on September 1, 1900.[76]

With Taft's report in hand, the McKinley administration pushed Congress to follow its recommendations and approve a civil government for the islands. Taft envisioned an insular architecture that included "a Governor General and a legislative body, consisting of the Commission and possibly one or two reliable Filipinos to act as a provisional legislature for eighteen months or two years" until a larger government could be installed. In March 1901, Congress passed and McKinley signed a measure introduced by Senator John C. Spooner of Wisconsin that largely put Taft's recommendations into law.[77]

The transfer of power from the military to the temporary insular government in 1901 also marked the beginning of Filipino involvement in the Manila administration. Taft's dim view of the Filipino people carried over to nearly every class on the islands, from rich to poor, but there were a handful of *ilustrados*—the wealthiest and most-educated members of the Filipino elite—

While serving as the third president of Cornell University, Jacob Schurman chaired the first Philippine commission in 1899. He later served as the United States' top diplomat to Greece, Montenegro, China, and Germany.

Image courtesy of the Library of Congress

William H. Taft was a federal judge when President William McKinley chose him to lead the second Philippine commission in 1900. Taft later was appointed War Secretary, elected as the 27th President in 1908, and appointed Chief Justice of the Supreme Court in 1921.

Image courtesy of the Library of Congress

This stereoview shows Filipino children, each holding a flag, as they gather for a Fourth of July celebration in Manila in 1900.

Image courtesy of the Library of Congress

who accepted positions in the new government. It was these men that first gave shape to what the historian Michael Cullinane has called "the Filipino-American collaborative empire." "It was an empire," Cullinane wrote, "that from the outset mediated—though not without frequent strain—between the objectives and expediencies of the American colonial rulers and those of the incumbent political power holders among the Filipino educated elites."[78]

Among the "possibly one or two reliable Filipinos" Taft hoped to include on the commission was Benito Legarda, a wealthy businessman who six years later became one of the first two Resident Commissioners to represent the Philippines in Congress.[79]

Legarda's early involvement helps demonstrate the shifting foundation of this new "collaborative empire" in which "some Filipinos and Americans," Cullinane observed, "reached an accommodation and eventual collaboration" that satisfied both the *ilustrados'* ambitions and the United States' commercial blueprint for the Philippines.[80]

Legarda was one of the first to adopt and help shape this mutual understanding.[81] He had made a fortune in the tobacco and alcohol businesses under Spanish rule, and when the Philippines went to war with the Crown, he briefly advised the Philippines' revolutionary leader Emilio Aguinaldo. Legarda was by no means a revolutionary, but he did serve, again briefly, as the vice president of the Philippine congress in the town of Malolos.

But he was also an entrepreneur, and open warfare first with Spain and then with the United States made it difficult to run a business. When American officials set up the occupation government in Manila, Legarda, who maintained a home in the capital city, began working with the Taft commission to develop the Philippines' new civil government.

Taft hoped men like Legarda would be his gateway to every corner of the Philippines, and he worked to win over *ilustrados* sympathetic to America's goals in the Philippines. He believed that courting men of such stature would help end the Philippine-American War and convince the rest of the population to cast their lot with the United States. This "policy of attraction," the historian Peter Stanley observed, "transcended the interests of any particular group of ilustrados ... it was a pursuit of the loyalty of the Filipino people by the only means available."[82]

17543. Our young Filipinos in holiday attire at the Fourth of July celebration, Manila, P. I.

3514 The Stars and Stripes floating over the Walls of Old Manila, P. I.
COPYRIGHT 1901 BY H. C. WHITE CO.

This stereoview from around 1901 shows the U.S. flag raised over the walls of Manila, the capital of the Philippines.

Image courtesy of the Library of Congress

As it became increasingly apparent that the Philippine-American War was all but over, more and more *ilustrados* in Manila began to cooperate with Taft's provisional government. By the end of 1900, enough Filipino elites had recognized U.S. authority that many joined together to form the Partido Federal (Federal Party). That Taft virtually quashed the creation of any rival political parties only added to the Federalistas' influence, especially in areas where their party maintained an iron grip on the patronage system.[83]

Per the earlier Spooner bill, Taft became civil governor of the Philippines on July 4, 1901, and appointed Legarda and two other Filipinos to the commission in September. With its expanded roster, the commission looked to overhaul and Americanize virtually every segment of Filipino life, everything from the separation of church and state to education, currency, trade, and the islands' infrastructure. Perhaps most importantly, the commission shouldered the responsibility of designing the Philippines' governing structure going forward.[84]

The commission's plan, which Congress approved mostly intact, concentrated much of the Philippines' legislative and executive powers within the commission itself. Headed by a governor general, the commission would be evenly divided between four Americans and four Filipinos.[85] The resulting legislation—the Philippine Organic Act of 1902—made the Philippines into an American protectorate as an "unorganized" territory. It created a popularly elected assembly to govern alongside the commission pending the results of a territory-wide census. The legislation also provided the Philippines with two Resident Commissioners, one elected by the commission, the other elected by the assembly, each selection subject to the approval of the other chamber.[86]

The decision to give the Philippines two representatives in Washington is unique in American history, as all other overseas U.S. territories have been assigned either one Delegate or one Resident Commissioner. The justification for two appears to have come from Taft's desire to maintain U.S. authority in the Philippines while providing the territory with a measure of autonomy.

Because the commission was the United States' administrative arm in the Philippines, Taft believed the popularly elected assembly should also have a direct line to federal lawmakers. "The Filipinos … desire an opportunity to reach Congress, not through the executive in the islands, not through the

Helen Herron Taft wears a dramatic, Philippine-style gown in this studio photograph taken in Manila during the 1900–1903 governorship of her husband, William H. Taft.

Image courtesy of the Library of Congress

Benito Legarda, left, and Pablo Ocampo, the first two Resident Commissioners from the Philippines, pose together around 1908.

Image courtesy of the Library of Congress

Commission in the islands," he told the House Insular Affairs Committee in February 1902. "They desire a representation here." By keeping the Philippine commission an appointed body, Taft hoped "to retain American guidance and control and initiative." But since the Philippine assembly would be the people's voice on the islands, he told the committee, "a popular assembly with delegates to Washington gives to the Filipinos all the practice in self-government and a popular government that it is possible to give."[87]

Five months later, on July 4, 1902, President Theodore Roosevelt issued a full amnesty proclamation that pardoned anyone who fought against the United States in the Philippine-American War. In addition to signaling the end of the conflict, the general clemency sparked a shift in the islands' civic makeup: pro-independence sentiment that had once sparked a revolution became the bedrock of new political parties in peacetime.[88]

Philippine nationalists initially splintered into different factions, their main disagreement stemming from conflicting views on the urgency of independence. While some advocated for immediate, unequivocal independence, others sought a more prolonged process to allow the new government to find its footing. In 1907, on the eve of the opening of the Philippine assembly, the two main blocs pushing for immediate independence merged to form the Partido Nacionalista (Nationalist Party). By that point, the nationalist movement was so strong that even Federalistas, who had once advocated for annexation, rebranded themselves as the Partido Nacional Progresista (National Progressive Party) and began calling for gradual independence.[89]

Following the territorial census, American officials gave the go-ahead for an election to open the Philippine assembly. With a number of restrictions in place, only a fraction of the population qualified to vote, and within that fraction there seemed to be no consensus on the timeline for independence. Consequently, no party captured the majority. Nacionalistas took the most seats, followed by the Independientes, the Progresistas, the Immediatistas, and a handful of "other minor" parties, according to one history of the Philippine legislature. It was not until the legislature convened, however, that Filipino leaders assembled behind the Partido Nacionalista.[90]

Resident Commissioners

With the opening of the new territorial government, the Philippine legislature sent its first two Resident Commissioners—Benito Legarda and Pablo Ocampo—to Capitol Hill during the winter of 1907–1908. From then until 1946, when the Philippines became independent, the territory sent a total of 13 Resident Commissioners to Congress.

Like Legarda and Ocampo, most of the earliest Resident Commissioners were *ilustrados*, members of the Philippines' upper class. On the whole, the 13 came from traditionally wealthy and urban families. They attended the best schools both in Manila and occasionally abroad, and, alongside being fluent in Spanish and their own native languages, often spoke English fluently or well enough to get by. Ocampo was an exception and brought a translator with him to Congress.[91]

Every Resident Commissioner came from the main island of Luzon except Jaime C. de Veyra, who was from Leyte and who made a name for himself n Cebu, the territory's second largest city. Otherwise, even if the Resident Commissioners grew up in one of the rural provinces outside Manila, they used the capital city as their primary launching pad for their political careers.

A number of Resident Commissioners took part in the conflicts that ravaged the islands during the turn of the century, fighting against the Spanish, the Americans, or both. After fighting against Spain, Ocampo, for example, joined the forces trying to repel America's occupation army and served as the chief intelligence officer for Philippine general Emilio Aguinaldo. Afterward, U.S. officials arrested Ocampo and exiled him to the island of Guam. Just a few years later, in 1907, Ocampo was elected to Congress.

Before they entered politics, Resident Commissioners frequently started out in business, journalism, law, or some combination thereof. Five had been successful businessmen, five had law backgrounds, and four worked in journalism, including two who edited pro-independence newspapers and another who won the Pulitzer Prize on the eve of World War II.

Like Congressmen during any era, Resident Commissioners often started their political careers at the local level and served in their home provinces before making the jump to higher positions in Manila. Three Resident Commissioners were provincial governors, and others held more minor positions. Some, however, started closer to the top. Camilo Osias was the first Filipino superintendent of the islands' schools, and Joaquin M. Elizalde was an economic adviser to the Philippine president.

Before their tenures in Washington, five Resident Commissioners served in the lower chamber of the territorial legislature, either in the Philippine assembly or, later, the Philippine house of representatives. Legarda and de Veyra sat on the Philippine commission as two of its only Filipino members. Three others served in the Philippine senate, which replaced the commission in 1916.[92]

Revolutionary leader and general Emilio Aguinaldo fought for the Philippines' independence, first from Spain and then from the United States. Aguinaldo was captured in 1901 and consented to declare his allegiance to the United States.

Image courtesy of the Library of Congress

The Philippine legislature poses for a group photo sometime before 1924.

Image courtesy of the Library of Congress

GOVERNMENT OF THE PHILIPPINE ISLANDS.
PHILIPPINE COMMISSION.
MANILA.

November 23, 1907.

I, Wm. H. DONOVAN, Secretary of the Philippine Commission, do hereby certify that the Journal of the Philippine Commission of Friday, the twenty-second day of November, nineteen hundred and seven, shows that at twelve o'clock Meridian of said date Don Benito Legarda and Don Pablo Ocampo were elected by the Philippine Commission to the positions of Resident Commissioners to the United States, in accordance with the provisions of section eight of the Act of Congress of July first, nineteen hundred and two, by the following vote:

Yeas: Commissioners Worcester, Tavera, Luzuriaga, Forbes, Shuster and the President.

Nays: None.

(S E A L)   (Sgd) WM. H. DONOVAN,
                         Secretary, Philippine Commission.

This paperwork from the new Philippine government certifies the 1907 election of Benito Legarda and Pablo Ocampo as the first Resident Commissioners from the Philippine Islands. To balance the interests of both the Philippine commission and the assembly, the legislative bodies elected candidates who would be quickly ratified by the opposite chamber.

Image courtesy of the National Archives and Records Administration

Statutory Representation

U.S. territories have had a level of nonvoting representation in the national legislature since 1787, when the Northwest Ordinance created a Delegate for the region above the Ohio River. Following the adoption of the Constitution, the early federal Congresses continued the practice as the nation expanded westward. Because their positions were created by an act of Congress rather than delineated in the Constitution, Delegates and Resident Commissioners are considered statutory representatives and their rights and prerogatives as Members depend on a host of different variables, including House Rules and the whims of the majority.[93]

Resident Commissioners from the Philippines initially served two-year terms. But during a particularly nettlesome re-election contest in 1910, when the assembly and the commission refused to agree to one another's candidates, Congress was forced to intervene, lengthening the incumbents' terms to four years in order to give the insular legislature time to resolve its differences without causing a break in representation. Their terms were shortened to three years in 1916.[94] The next major change to the office occurred in 1934 when the Philippines became a commonwealth. As part of the deal giving the Philippines its eventual independence, the islands agreed to send a single Resident Commissioner per term rather than a pair.

Experience in Washington

For interested observers in Manila during the early 1900s, the new Resident Commissioners were a matter of speculation. "Just what the powers and prerogatives of the delegates will be upon their arrival in Washington is a matter of conjecture," the *Washington Post* reported from the territory's capital city. "The general impression is that their status will be the same as that of Territorial delegates to Congress, which would entitle them to a seat in the House of Representatives without a vote. But the law designates them as 'resident commissioners,' which may mean anything or nothing."[95]

In practice, there was little difference between Delegates and Resident Commissioners; Congress gave both offices little legislative agency. Because the House denied the Filipinos a vote and prohibited them from serving on committees, they functioned more like lobbyists and cultural ambassadors than legislators. They were given a salary, access to the House Floor, office space, and, eventually, franking privileges, but they had to wield power in different ways: pigeonholing Members, testifying before committees, and leaning on the Bureau of Insular Affairs. Certain Resident Commissioners, like Manuel Quezon, excelled at such behind-the-scenes lawmaking, meeting with Presidents and delicately maneuvering past Congress's parliamentary hurdles.

The Resident Commissioners were not so much the representatives of the Filipino people as they were the mouthpieces of the territorial government controlled by the Nacionalistas, and, in theory, they were supposed to follow the marching orders sent by party leaders.[96]

As part of the first set of Resident Commissioners from the Philippines, Legarda grasped the subtleties of his office early on. "We do not expect to have much weight when political questions are being discussed," he said in 1907,

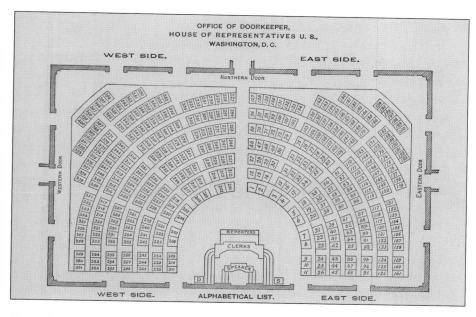

This diagram depicts the House Chamber seating chart for the 62nd Congress (1911–1913). Philippine Resident Commissioners Benito Legarda and Manuel L. Quezon were assigned to seats in the last two rows on the west side.

Collection of the U.S. House of Representatives

"but when economic matters pertaining to the Philippine Islands arise in either house of congress we expect to fully inform the homeland legislators."[97]

With a handful of exceptions, informing Members of Congress was often all they could do. Testifying before committees was perhaps the most common tool in the Resident Commissioners' legislative toolbox, and some, especially Quezon, developed alliances with influential chairmen.[98] Many took the opportunity to address the House during debate. For the years that we have records, Resident Commissioners were assigned seats in the back of the chamber with the minority party often in close proximity to one another, but not necessarily next to one another. In 1910, for instance, Legarda and Quezon sat at desks in the second-to-last row on the Democratic side of the chamber. But the next year, at the start of the 62nd Congress (1911–1913), after Democrats captured the majority during the fall elections, Legarda and Quezon were assigned to desks in the last two rows on the Republican side.[99]

Although the historical record is thin, some evidence suggests that the earliest Resident Commissioners interacted with other statutory representatives. "Four men wandered into the house of representatives today, took seats in the rear of the chamber and began [an] animated conversation," reported the *Detroit Free Press* in February 1908. "Their language was strange and the group attracted a good deal of attention. 'Who are they?' said a stranger in the gallery. 'Two are resident commissioners from the Philippines, one is the resident commissioner from Porto Rico, while the fourth one … is the delegate from Hawaii,' said a house [employee]."[100]

During Quezon's career in Congress specifically, Resident Commissioners who served in pairs developed something of a unique arrangement. One of them—often the one more well versed in the issues and able to navigate the ever-changing congressional landscape—handled the legislative lift. The other Resident Commissioner, as described by the historian Peter Stanley, was usually "rich, personally dignified as a representative of the Filipino people, and politically impotent."[101]

A steamboat transports William H. Taft, then Secretary of War, up the Pasig River in the Philippines in 1905.

Image courtesy of the Library of Congress

This 1905 political cartoon, "Back from Bololand," depicts William H. Taft with a group of Congressmen, Senators, and others in a train station. The terminals are labeled "Philippine Free Trade" and "Stand-Pat"—a reference to the debate in Washington about whether to levy steep tariffs on Philippine trade goods. Taft chides the others, "Now, boys, after all my talking, don't go and take the wrong train."

Image courtesy of the Library of Congress

Philippine Trade, 1898–1934

By the time America assumed possession of the Philippines, the territory's economy had grown at a decent clip.[102] But the gradual shift from subsistence farming to exporting on a global scale had left its mark. A number of the Philippines' chief products—sugar, tobacco, cordage, and coconut oil—had taken a considerable amount of farmland out of food production. For American officials, especially Governor Taft, the poor state of the islands' infrastructure, combined with pockets of poverty, necessitated a complete overhaul of the Philippine economy.[103] But Taft's vision conflicted with that of a skeptical Congress, and a series of events conspired to place the Philippines and its Resident Commissioners front and center in one of the most heated issues on Capitol Hill: the tariff.

After the Supreme Court declared income taxes unconstitutional in 1895, Congress continued to rely on tariffs—fees placed on imported goods—to raise money for the federal treasury. U.S. officials believed that low tariffs would generate trade, but invite competition from abroad. Higher tariffs, on the other hand, would restrict overseas commerce, but "protect" American industries from foreign competitors.[104]

By the fall of 1908, Taft, who had left the Philippines to head the War Department, won the U.S. presidency. As the Republican candidate, he had run, in part, on a promise to break with traditional GOP doctrine and lower America's tariffs. Not wanting to waste time, the new President called Congress into special session to deal expressly with the issue.[105]

Coincidentally, Taft's reforms dovetailed with the expiration of clauses in the Treaty of Paris that had prevented the United States from establishing new tariff rates on trade with the Philippines. As part of Spain's surrender, America agreed to favorable terms that gave the Spanish ready access to markets in the Philippines for the next decade. Spanish goods were essentially treated the same as U.S. goods. But when those 10 years were up, Congress was free to overhaul how America did business with its farthest territory. For Taft, that meant tightly binding the Philippines to the U.S. economy by making calculated investments in the islands and using trade to form a measure of economic dependence on the United States. It was dollar diplomacy in its purest form, the historian H. W. Brands once observed.[106]

With such high stakes, the territorial government leaned heavily on its new Resident Commissioners. This ensured that the first piece of legislation they dealt with would be one of the cornerstone bills governing the transpacific relationship.[107]

The tariff bill reported by the Ways and Means Committee, what became known as the Payne–Aldrich Tariff Act, provided American businesses with virtually unlimited access to the Philippine market while simultaneously installing quotas on Philippine imports to the United States. The effect would be to open the flow of U.S. goods going to the Philippines while severely restricting Philippine goods headed to the United States. Since the Philippines generated a large portion of its revenue from fees on imported goods and since the archipelago did a robust trade with the States, the proposal to remove tariffs on American products threatened to both unravel the territory's fiscal policy and prevent the Philippines from diversifying its economy.[108]

On paper, Congress had clear authority to dictate the rates of the Philippines' tariffs, but, in practice, the process was monumentally awkward. The territory may have been part of America's geopolitical orbit, but for many people on either side of the Pacific, the Philippines seemed like a separate nation entirely. Congress, for its part, had never been able to decide whether the archipelago was an international or domestic trading partner. House Republicans danced around its liminal status, but Democrats, as they said in a 1905 committee report, wanted Congress to decide whether the Philippines was "altogether American or altogether foreign."[109]

No one associated with the territorial government was happy about the terms of Payne–Aldrich, and Legarda and Ocampo protested the measure on the House Floor.[110] As Washington scrambled to bring the Philippines back onboard, Taft and the Bureau of Insular Affairs developed a revision that Sereno Payne of New York, chairman of the Ways and Means Committee, introduced as H.R. 9135 that promised to help the Philippines make up lost revenue once the new tariffs went into place.[111] Although Ocampo and Legarda disagreed about the new bill, the House passed the standalone Philippine tariff on May 24, 1909, and the Senate cleared it in July.[112] On August 2, the conference report for the Philippine trade bill was quickly approved, and a deeply satisfied Taft signed it into law three days later.[113]

Although the language of the 1909 Philippine Tariff Act remained the basis of the islands' economy over the next few years, Congress occasionally adjusted the terms of America's trade relationship with the Philippines. And ever so gradually Congress began treating the Philippines more and more like a foreign trading partner. In 1913, for instance, Congress passed the Underwood–Simmons Act, removing quotas placed on Philippine imports to the United States and more or less installing a policy of free trade. Three years later, as part of the Jones Act, Congress gave the Philippine legislature more control over the territory's commerce with other countries, empowering it to set "customs duties on all foreign goods entering the Islands," according to Pedro Abelarde, an historian of the tariff. Congress, however, retained oversight of the Philippines' trade with the United States.[114]

Sereno Payne of New York was chairman of the House Ways and Means Committee from 1899 to 1911, and introduced a revision to the Payne–Aldrich Tariff Act.

Sereno Payne, Cecilia Beaux, 1912, Collection of the U.S. House of Representatives

Sugar refineries in the Philippines processed the territory's sugarcane and prepared it for export. Sugar was one of the Philippines' major agricultural products.

Image courtesy of the Library of Congress

This 1906 political cartoon, "Upholding the Honor of the American Flag," shows a large figure personifying America's agricultural industry blasting Philippine commerce with a gun labeled "Dingley Tariff."

Image courtesy of the Library of Congress

This stereoview shows an American flag flying over the entrance to the Manila headquarters of Major General Arthur MacArthur Jr. during the Philippine-American War.

Image courtesy of the Library of Congress

The terms of the Jones Act remained on the books until 1934, when Congress passed the Jones–Costigan Act, giving the Agriculture Secretary the right to set quotas on goods coming into America. A while later, as part of the Tydings–McDuffie Act that granted the Philippines its independence, Congress cleared the way for the Philippines to assume the role of a completely unaffiliated trading partner.[115]

"For decades," Abelarde observed in 1947, a year after the Philippines became independent, "the Filipinos had been repeatedly advised with paternal solicitude to be more material-minded and devote more serious attention to their country's economic development."[116] As it turned out, that development often came in the form of one-dimensional commerce. By the late 1920s, goods from America made up 60 percent of the Philippines' total imports, and as late as 1934, the United States was the destination for 83 percent of the Philippines' exports and accounted for 75 percent of the Philippines' total trade.[117]

A large part of that commerce depended on the Philippines' agricultural sector and its two biggest crops, sugar and tobacco. But over the years, U.S. sugar and tobacco industries maintained powerful allies on Capitol Hill, meaning that, "in dealing with the Insular tariff," Abelarde concluded, "Congress acted, in the main, in the interest of American producers."[118]

Toward Independence, 1907–1934

If the tariff debates underscored the tenuous nature of the Philippines' economic relationship with official Washington, they also revealed the rather muddled nature of the Philippines' political status, especially early on: Was the Philippines foreign, American, or something else entirely? What became clear after tariff reform, however, was that the Philippines' economic future was in nearly every respect intimately bound to its insular status. The issues were two sides of the same coin.

With the new tariffs in place after 1909, Congress's dealings with the Philippines switched gears, and with the new Resident Commissioner, Manuel Quezon, taking the lead, debate began focusing more and more on the islands' long-term political future. Beginning with the 62nd Congress, Quezon received help from a new House majority after Democrats took back the chamber for the first time in 15 years.

Unlike the GOP, which saw huge economic possibilities in the Philippines but believed the territory needed to be carefully tutored in self-government, the Democratic Party had been on the record since 1900 as being firmly against acquiring the Philippines. According to the historian H. W. Brands, Democrats believed that retaining the Philippines as a territory "contradicted American ideals and prevented the natural development of Filipino society." Now in power, Democrats had a chance to link up with Filipino nationalists in an uneasy partnership to give the Philippines greater autonomy, if not full independence.[119]

Working alongside William A. Jones of Virginia, the new chairman of the House Committee on Insular Affairs, Quezon readied an independence bill he hoped to show voters back home in time for the upcoming territorial elections. The Resident Commissioner knew that as much as Democrats wanted to divest America of the Philippines they would not rush the separation; so, he designed legislation (H.R. 22143) that provided for independence after a period of eight years and committed the U.S. military to 20 years of protection to discourage predatory foreign powers.[120]

Quezon's bill, which came to be known as the Jones bill, made it out of Jones's committee, but quickly hit a snag in the form of Woodrow Wilson, then the Democratic nominee for President, who advised party leaders to sit on the matter.[121]

As Wilson quietly came around on the issue after winning the presidency, Quezon reworked his proposal into something more gradual. The crux of his new plan would swap the U.S.-backed Philippine commission for a popularly elected territorial senate, giving the Philippine people more control over their government but likely delaying independence until at least the 1930s.[122]

Over the winter of 1913–1914, Quezon teamed up with Frank McIntyre, chief of the Bureau of Insular Affairs, to put his new ideas into bill form. McIntyre briefed Wilson on the matter, and Quezon met with the President in January. The Resident Commissioner came away with the understanding that, although Wilson sympathized with the Philippines, the White House would not support immediate independence nor would it hamstring the administration by fixing a date for independence.[123] Taking this into account, Quezon and McIntyre's new bill creating the Philippine senate (H.R. 606) included a preamble that set no timetable for independence. Instead, it included a vague promise that independence would only be possible once the Philippines established a "stable" government.[124]

During House debate on the bill in the fall of 1914, the Resident Commissioner framed the struggle in the Philippines much like America's own past: "Remember how your forefathers felt when they were as we are now struggling for freedom," Quezon asked.[125] The bill passed, but died in the Senate when a small group of Senators threatened to filibuster the preamble's "stable" government clause.[126]

Despite the setback, Quezon had laid a solid foundation after years of work on the issue, and when the 64th Congress (1915–1917) opened, the Philippine government bill was the first piece of legislation offered in the House on the first day of the new Congress (H.R. 1). Within two weeks, Quezon testified before the Senate Committee on the Philippines and pointed out that his support for

William A. Jones, a Representative from Virginia, chaired the Committee on Insular Affairs from 1911 to 1918 and worked with Resident Commissioner Manuel L. Quezon on the issue of independence for the Philippines.

Collection of the U.S. House of Representatives

As chief of the Bureau of Insular Affairs from 1912 to 1929, Major General Frank McIntyre served as intermediary between Resident Commissioner Manuel L. Quezon of the Philippines and President Woodrow Wilson.

Image courtesy of the Library of Congress

Manuel L. Quezon, Resident Commissioner from the Philippine Islands, attends the 1912 Democratic National Convention in Baltimore.

Image courtesy of the Library of Congress

the bill was a huge political gamble. "As a practical man who takes what he can get that is good," he said, "I am 'standing pat' on this bill now." The Senate committee reported it favorably and urged Congress to act swiftly.[127]

The stable government clause, however, remained problematic. In 1916, an election year, Democrats, including Wilson, started to walk back their support for gradual independence. Eventually, Senator James Clarke of Arkansas offered an amendment to give the Philippines its independence in four years or less. The Senate cleared the amendment by one vote in early February.[128]

Quezon was stuck. The Clarke amendment would free the Philippines almost immediately, but such a truncated timeline could bring large-scale economic and social unrest. By supporting it, Quezon risked the Philippines' future. But if he opposed the amendment and the bill died, all his work would be for nothing. In the end, Quezon supported it, and Chairman Jones reluctantly brought the Clarke amendment to the House Floor. In a marathon session on May 1, 1916, Quezon and Jones urged House Democrats to vote for the new version.[129]

Despite the earlier pressure from party leadership, a number of Democrats broke ranks and stood with Republicans to vote down the Clarke amendment. Seeing an opportunity, Jones submitted his earlier draft containing the "stable" government clause, and the House quickly adopted it.[130] After a summer of uncertainty and delay in which Quezon urged the President to support the vague preamble, the Senate abandoned the Clarke amendment and cleared the Jones bill in mid-August. With Quezon looking on, Wilson signed it into law on August 29, 1916.[131]

Although the Jones Act was a major turning point, Quezon's successors in the House continued to deal with the same issues of trade and insular status. Independence remained a driving force in Manila, but in Washington, Philippine Resident Commissioners had to navigate between Republican and Democratic administrations that came down on different sides of the independence debate. Often the Resident Commissioners had to fight to protect the gains in autonomy the islands had won over the years.

In the waning days of the Wilson administration, for instance, Resident Commissioner Jaime de Veyra and other pro-independence activists worked to speed up the independence process before Republican President-elect Warren G. Harding took office. As former chairman of the Senate Committee on the Philippines, Harding, like many Republicans, believed the United States should retain the islands indefinitely.[132]

In December 1920, Wilson appeared ready to move on Philippine independence and told Congress that the territory had "succeeded in maintaining a stable government" and was therefore eligible for its freedom.[133] But it was too little, too late, and Congress mostly ignored the outgoing President.[134]

After taking office the next year, Harding met with the Philippine Resident Commissioners Isauro Gabaldon and de Veyra but refused to commit one way or the other on independence. Like Taft and McKinley before him, Harding sent a fact-finding mission to assess the "fitness" of the Philippines for self-rule. Led by General Leonard Wood and former Governor General W. Cameron Forbes, both opponents of independence, Harding assured the Resident Commissioners that he would make no policy decision until the commission submitted its report.[135]

The Wood–Forbes Mission visited the islands during the summer of 1921 and spoke with insular government officials, American expatriates, everyday Filipinos, and a host of other "foreigners." They visited all but one of the 49 provinces of the islands and held meetings in nearly 450 cities and towns.[136]

In its report, the mission not only opposed Philippine independence, it asked Congress to strengthen America's presence in Manila by expanding the powers of the governor general.[137] Gabaldon and de Veyra publicly protested the report, with Gabaldon calling it little more than "a clever, but unworthy attempt to change the issue from that of stable government to a multitude of other conditions not required by Congress."[138]

Nevertheless, President Harding endorsed the report and nominated General Wood to reassert the powers of the governor general over the islands. Confirmed in October 1921, Wood maintained cordial relations with Filipinos, but he soon ran afoul of insular politicians while navigating the shoals of a pitched political battle between Manuel Quezon, president of the Philippine senate, and Philippine assembly speaker Sergio Osmeña. To many in the capital city of Manila, Harding's decision to appoint Wood seemed to violate the intent of the Jones Act that gave the territorial legislature more control over the Philippines' daily affairs. As Wood tried to consolidate power, the division between Philippine and American officials only widened.[139]

The struggle for power in Manila—what came to be called the Cabinet Crisis—nearly put independence on the legislative agenda in the 68th Congress (1923–1925). After a Philippine independence mission met with a number of administration officials and Members of Congress to protest Wood's reforms, six bills taking steps toward independence were submitted between December 1923 and March 1924.[140] But the proposals struggled to gain traction. Lawmakers, backed by a negative propaganda campaign designed to curb Philippine autonomy and led largely by U.S. business interests, remained committed to maintaining American control over the islands.[141]

Philippine Resident Commissioner Pedro Guevara, left, visits the White House in 1923 with his secretary, J. E. Espinas.

Collection of the U.S. House of Representatives

To Provide for Independence

The symbiotic link between trade and status that so often characterized Congress's policy toward the Philippines entered a new phase by the early 1930s. As the U.S. economy plummeted amid the Great Depression and as Japan widened its global reach by invading Manchuria, Congress considered ways to free the Philippines perhaps less out of genuine interest for the islands and more because many considered the territory to be a financial and national security liability.[142] Moreover, Democrats, who traditionally opposed the retention of the Philippines, had once again captured the majority in the House to start the 72nd Congress (1931–1933), giving the independence movement something of a leg up. Whatever policy Congress designed, however, would depend on the support of the insular government in Manila.

As a coalition of U.S. industries and interest groups pushed to limit both Philippine trade and Philippine immigration in order to protect struggling markets at home, Congress responded by drafting a measure that granted the Philippines its independence after a relatively brief transition period. Named after its authors in the House and Senate—Butler Hare of South Carolina, chairman of the House Insular Affairs Committee, and Senators Harry Hawes of Missouri and Bronson Cutting of New Mexico—the Hare–Hawes–Cutting bill cleared the way for a new Philippine constitution, but kept immigration quotas low and tariffs high following the installment of independence.[143]

During the House debate on the bill, Resident Commissioner Pedro Guevara reminded everyone of the high stakes involved. The Philippine Organic Act of 1902 and the 1916 Jones Act were only temporary vehicles for the Philippines, he said. But granting outright independence would redeem America's promise for freedom. With Guevara watching, the House approved the bill in a landslide vote, 306 to 47. Although the Senate sat on the bill until after the fall elections, it passed on December 17, 1932. A conference committee swiftly changed the transition period to 10 years, and by the end of the month, both the House and Senate had cleared the new version.[144] In early 1933, the outgoing President, Republican Herbert Hoover, vetoed the bill, but the House and Senate quickly overrode him.[145]

Although the bill had become law, the insular legislature had to approve it before the graduated independence schedule began. Almost immediately a struggle for power on the islands derailed it. For much of 1933, the governing Partido Nacionalista had fractured into those for and those against the independence bill. Those in favor of the bill included power brokers like Resident Commissioner Camilo Osias, who had helped design the Hare–Hawes–Cutting Act, and Sergio Osmeña, who had lobbied for it. Those against it were led by former Resident Commissioner Manuel Quezon, perhaps the most powerful official in Manila. Quezon had once supported the bill, but quickly backtracked when he realized credit for independence might go to Osmeña instead of himself. At that point, he became a fierce critic of the Hare–Hawes–Cutting bill. Ultimately, Quezon prevailed and solidified his position in the Philippines when the insular government rejected the measure.[146]

Not to be outdone, Quezon traveled to Washington to negotiate a second and nearly identical independence bill during the 73rd Congress (1933–1935).

He initially received a chilly reception from the new Franklin D. Roosevelt (FDR) administration.[147] Nevertheless, FDR wanted to resolve the Philippine issue as quickly as possible. The President believed the United States was bound by the Jones Act to uphold the law's "stable" government provision, and in March 1934, he asked Congress to revisit Philippine independence.[148]

After a few days of intense debate, both houses of Congress approved the new version built largely on the framework of Hare–Hawes–Cutting, including the 10-year transition period to independence. President Roosevelt signed it into law on March 24, 1934. Dubbed the Tydings–McDuffie Act after Senator Millard Tydings of Maryland and Representative John McDuffie of Alabama, the Philippine legislature approved the law in May 1934. The Philippines then held a referendum on the new constitution and an island-wide plebiscite on independence. Philippine voters approved the package by huge margins.[149]

Under Tydings–McDuffie, the Philippines became a commonwealth, making the islands far more autonomous, but still subject to Congress's authority over the next decade as it prepared for independence. The law replaced the governor general with an American high commissioner, and it changed how the Philippines was represented on the Hill. Since 1907 the insular legislature had elected two Resident Commissioners, but the new law provided for only one and empowered the new Philippine president to appoint that person directly. Unsurprisingly, Quezon was elected the Philippines' first president a year later. Tydings–McDuffie also set graduated tariff rates on Philippine goods so that, by the time the islands became independent, they would have to pay the rates in full.[150]

But exactly when those full tariffs would go into effect remained unclear. Early in 1937, Quezon and FDR created the Joint Preparatory Committee (JPC) on Philippine Affairs, composed of Philippine and U.S. economists, to identify and begin addressing troublesome issues that would inevitably accompany independence. Among its many findings, the JPC recommended phasing in full tariff rates over 15 years, giving the Philippine economy five extra years to grow after independence.[151]

In order to avoid the potential pitfalls in the Tydings–McDuffie Act, FDR sent the JPC report to the Hill and asked Congress to frame legislation around the committee's recommendations. But the Senate and especially Tydings, who took it as a personal affront, greeted the report with disdain.[152] Only after FDR personally lobbied members of the House and Senate did the overseeing committees produce a bill that lengthened the trade window to match the JPC's recommendations. FDR signed the bill into law on August 7, 1939.[153]

Despite the changes, not everyone was happy with the final product. For his part, Quezon was not convinced the new law went far enough to solve the problems that would accompany the "economic readjustment" inherent in Philippine independence.[154]

Economics, of course, was not the only looming concern as independence approached. Philippine citizenship, for one, remained a confusing legal mess. In 1940, when Congress updated federal naturalization provisions, citizenship was limited to whites and African Americans. But legislators inserted a special provision allowing "native-born Filipinos having the honorable service in the United States Army, Navy, Marine Corps, or Coast Guard" to become

Alabama Representative John McDuffie, pictured here, and Maryland Senator Millard Tydings authored legislation during the 73rd Congress (1933–1935) that brought about Philippine independence after a 10-year transition period.

Collection of the U.S. House of Representatives

Philippine High Commissioner Francis B. Sayre, Philippine Vice President Sergio Osmeña, and Resident Commissioner Joaquin M. Elizalde (standing, left to right), watch as President Franklin D. Roosevelt signs a 1939 bill that adjusted duties on Philippine goods.

Image courtesy of the Library of Congress

Resident Commissioner Joaquin M. Elizalde and Philippine Vice President Sergio Osmeña meet with businessman John W. Hausserman (right) in Washington, DC, in 1938.

Image courtesy of the Library of Congress

naturalized citizens.[155] With independence, however, the rest of the civilian population would cease being U.S. nationals and would become "aliens ineligible to citizenship."[156]

The War in the Philippines

Despite its design to help the Philippines transition from colony to independence, the era of the Philippine commonwealth (1934–1944) turned out to be one of the more tumultuous periods in the history of the islands. With the onset of World War II, the Philippines suddenly became one of the most contested regions of the Pacific theater.

For years, American officials had worried that Japan would encroach on the Philippines once America began pulling out, and in December 1941, in a coordinated bombing campaign that targeted Manila and a host of other cities across the Pacific, Japan unleashed the full power of its military. Much of the Philippines' infrastructure built under the territorial government—new roads, hospitals, ports, and airfields—were lost as the archipelago was captured by Japan and then recaptured by the United States within a three-year period. Along the way, hundreds of thousands died and the commonwealth government was forced to flee to the United States until Allied forces retook Manila.

The first bombs fell on the Philippines on December 8, 1941, just hours after the attack on Pearl Harbor across the International Dateline. Dense fog had delayed the departure of the Japanese air force, but once the skies cleared, planes attacked for five straight days.[157]

Japan's decision to attack the Philippines was part of a larger strategy to seize oil reserves in the Dutch East Indies. To do so, however, Japan needed to eliminate the U.S. forces based in the Philippines. Under General Douglas MacArthur, the military had integrated nearly 100,000 Filipino troops and 30,000 American servicemen into the U.S. Army Forces in the Far East (USAFFE) that included dozens of bombers, more than 100 fighter planes, and a full complement of warships in the U.S. Navy's Asiatic Squadron.[158]

Japan's relentless bombing campaign, however, quickly overwhelmed the Philippines. The U.S. Navy withdrew, enabling Japanese forces to land on separate sides of Luzon. As Japanese troops marched toward Manila, U.S. and Filipino forces evacuated to the Bataan Peninsula while MacArthur removed his staff and the commonwealth government to the harbor fortress on Corregidor Island.[159]

President Quezon scrambled to keep the Philippines out of the conflict and pushed FDR to work out a deal with Japan that, among other things, would grant the islands immediate independence, establish guaranteed neutrality, demilitarize the archipelago, and enact new trade agreements with Japan and the United States. Roosevelt flatly denied Quezon's request.[160]

By the spring of 1942, after MacArthur and the commonwealth government were ordered to leave the Philippines for Australia, Japan broke the defensive lines on the island of Bataan, starving out the remaining USAFFE forces before leading them on the Bataan Death March in which thousands of American and Filipino troops died on the way to prison camps or during their incarceration. Following the final Japanese assault on the island fortress of Corregidor, the last organized resistance in the Philippines surrendered.[161]

General Douglas MacArthur presents a Distinguished Service Cross to Lieutenant Jack Dale of the U.S. Army Air Corps in Manila, Philippines, on December 22, 1941.

Image courtesy of the Library of Congress

At the urging of the Americans, Quezon's government-in-exile moved from Australia to the United States. With no need for an official go-between, FDR agreed to suspend the office of the high commissioner, in theory, strengthening Quezon's hand. But with no country to govern, the government-in-exile primarily handled ceremonial events.[162]

Hoping to negotiate with Japan directly, Quezon, whose health was deteriorating, pushed Congress to advance the date for independence. There was a widespread belief in the Philippines, which Quezon shared, that Japan's successful invasion stemmed directly from America's failure to fortify the territory's defenses. Complicating that sentiment was Japan's tactic to appeal to Filipinos on racial grounds: "Like it or not, you are Filipinos and belong to the Oriental race," read propaganda leaflets. "No matter how hard you try, you cannot become white people."[163]

Whatever inroads Japan may have made with the general population were swept aside in the wake of its brutal occupation. Even as the Japanese military erected a puppet government in Manila—granting the Philippines its "independence" while requiring the new administration to declare war on the United States—occupation forces imprisoned, tortured, and killed residents who objected or got in their way.[164]

By the summer of 1944, however, the war in the Pacific theater had swung in favor of the Allied forces. FDR gave General MacArthur the go-ahead to invade the Philippines, and on October 20, 1944, two months after Quezon died, U.S. forces landed on Leyte and met little resistance.[165] After defeating the Japanese navy in the Battle of Leyte Gulf, American GIs worked to secure the capital city. In a last stand in early 1945, Japanese forces hunkered down during the Battle of Manila in which an estimated 1,000 U.S. soldiers, 16,000 Japanese soldiers, and 100,000 Filipino noncombatants died. The heavy combat destroyed much of the city, leaving thousands homeless before the Japanese military finally surrendered.[166]

American troops surrender to Japanese
forces at Corregidor Island in the
Philippines on May 6, 1942.

Image courtesy of the National Archives
and Records Administration

Post-war Recovery and Independence

The liberation of the Philippines ended nearly three years of hardship that had robbed the territory of much-needed time and resources for the transition to independence. With independence scheduled to take effect in less than 18 months and the clock ticking, the commonwealth now faced a massive reconstruction program.

In Congress, the economic development of the islands became a hot-button issue after the war. More than ever, leaders in Manila argued, the Philippines needed a preferential trade deal with the United States to last well after independence.

Even before MacArthur recaptured Manila, Congress was thinking about how to rebuild the islands. In June 1944, it created the Philippine-American Rehabilitation Commission to study the financial ramifications of the war and identify areas where the commonwealth's economy would need the most help.[167] Almost a year later, President Harry S. Truman, after meeting with the new commonwealth president, Sergio Osmeña, asked Senator Tydings to lead an investigation into the recovery needs of the Philippines.[168]

Tydings eventually developed a Philippine rehabilitation package (S. 1488) that set aside hundreds of millions of dollars—total damage was estimated at $800 million in 1944—and developed a tariff schedule that would grow over time. The Senate eventually removed the tariff provisions after the House Ways and Means Committee asserted its constitutional prerogative to originate all revenue measures.[169] "Factories, homes, government and commercial buildings, roads, bridges, docks, harbors, and the like are in need of complete reconstruction or widespread repairs," Tydings's committee wrote in its report. The full Senate approved it in early December.[170]

In the House, however, the rehabilitation and trade packages took on different shapes entirely. If the Senate offered ways to diversify the islands' economy, the House worked to tightly link the Philippines to U.S. markets, submitting a plan to enact 20 years of free trade and giving American industries virtually unfettered access to the Philippines. Along with the new trade bill, the House made more than 140 changes to Tydings's bill, including one designed by the new high commissioner, Paul V. McNutt, that withheld the rehabilitation funding until the Philippines agreed to the new trade terms.[171]

McNutt's proposal, which had the support of the Insular Affairs Committee chairman, Democrat Jasper Bell of Missouri, promised to reverse more than 40 years of U.S. policy in the Philippines. In some of the earliest legislation governing the territory, Congress protected the islands from exploitative overseas interests by requiring a 60-percent Filipino ownership stake in utility companies working in industries like oil, timber, and coal. McNutt's amendment, on the other hand, promised to loosen those regulations and give American investors access to the Philippines' natural resources.[172]

By mid-April 1946, both bills and their controversial provisions had been sent to the White House. President Truman signed the Philippine Trade Act and the Philippine Rehabilitation Act, but he criticized Congress's decision to make the rehabilitation funds subject to the new trade agreement, especially since it required an amendment to the Philippine constitution.[173] After the fact, Minnesota Representative Harold Knutson of the Insular Affairs Committee

Ninth Philippine Legislature
FIRST SESSION

RESOLUTION OF BOTH HOUSES IN JOINT SESSION

RESOLUTION OF THE SENATE AND HOUSE OF REPRESENTATIVES OF THE PHILIPPINES IN JOINT SESSION ASSEMBLED, APPROVING AN INDEPENDENCE MEMORIAL

WHEREAS the Honorable Patrick Jay Hurley, Secretary of War of the United States of America, is now in the Philippine Islands investigating conditions; Now, therefore, be it

Resolved by the Senate and House of Representatives of the Philippines in Joint Session assembled, and by the authority of the same:

That the following Independence Memorial be, and the same hereby is, approved, to wit:

Independence Memorial

We, the members of the Philippine Legislature in joint session assembled, for ourselves and in behalf of the Filipino people, do hereby reiterate our petition for the immediate and complete political separation of the Philippine Islands from the United States.

Our desire for liberty was repeatedly manifested, in the course of our history, throughout our many struggles for political emancipation, culminating in the establishment of the Philippine Republic. We lost our independence because of the superior force of America; we expect to regain it because of her plighted word. We acquiesced in American rule only when we were assured that she came not as a conqueror but as a liberator. In all good faith we relied on her promise made through her highest executive officials and confirmed by the Congress of the United States when it declared that the independence of the Philippine Islands shall be granted upon the establishment of a stable government. This condition having been fulfilled, the Filipino people rightfully expect that their independence will be recognized without any further delay.

Practical considerations also justify this urgent desire for immediate separation. The present movement to exclude Filipinos from the United States is giving rise to friction and misunderstanding. The manner in which the campaign is being conducted cannot but arouse among the Filipino people a feeling that it is impelled by other than purely economic motives. Even at the present time it is not safe for Filipinos in some parts of the United States to engage in lawful occupation. So long as we remain under the American flag, justice demands that we shall be allowed freely to live, work, and travel in any American territory.

The dual responsibility in our government—the one assumed by the Governor-General and the other by Filipino officials—has been the source of serious conflicts in the past and is ever fraught with difficulties. Such an unsatisfactory situation must end. A backward step is unthinkable. The only solution is independence.

Our present trade relations with the United States are uncertain and unstable. Regulated exclusively by the American Congress, America's interests rather than our own are the dominant consideration. There is an increasing demand by American producers to maintain the American market solely for their benefit. Powerful American interests are now conducting a persistent campaign against the free entry of Philippine products. No one knows how long the American market will remain open to us. Doubts and misgivings have seized upon the minds of Philippine producers and investors, thus checking our development. We believe that enduring economic progress can only be achieved under an independent Philippines, free to dictate its own policies.

These facts prove the wisdom of the declared purpose of the United States to grant us independence. They also serve to strengthen our belief that political separation is the only solution to our problem. We see no other alternative. The happiness and prosperity of the Philippines and the economic interests of America are not to be found in the present artificial union which hampers our national development and injures economic progress, but in political separation, wherein each may live the life suited to its distinct individuality and its national interests. The independence of America from the Philippines would seem to be as imperative as the independence of the Philippines from America.

Therefore, with all due respect, with a deep feeling of gratitude to America, and with full consciousness of the burdens and responsibilities of an independent life, we hereby submit that the time has come for the redemption of America's solemn promise to declare and recognize the independence of the Philippine Islands.

RESOLVED, FURTHER, That the Presiding Officers of the Legislature appoint a Committee among its members, which shall deliver the aforesaid memorial to the Honorable, the Secretary of War, with the request that the same be transmitted to the President and the Congress of the United States.

This resolution, adopted by the Philippine legislature on September 24, 1931, called for the "immediate and complete political separation of the Philippine Islands from the United States." The Philippines gained independence in 1946, becoming the only territory in American history with representation in Congress to gain its independence.

Image courtesy of the National Archives and Records Administration

made a surprising confession by admitting that the committee "did not realize, because of the haste and urgency of the situation, that we were coercing the Philippines into signing a trade agreement and making other fundamental adjustments in their laws."[174]

The government in Manila was left with two less-than-ideal options: approve the trade deal and sacrifice economic sovereignty in exchange for reconstruction funding or oppose the trade bill and lose the rehabilitation package, but maintain a measure of economic self-determination. With the clock ticking down to independence, the legislature approved the trade pact in the closing hours of the commonwealth and, in the process, granted Americans the right to purchase and own property as majority shareholders. Ultimately, the rebuilding needs of the islands won out. As one Philippine legislator said, "I vote yes because we are flat broke, hungry, homeless, and destitute."[175]

The Philippines became independent on July 4, 1946. President Truman marked the occasion by releasing a statement pledging the support of the United States should the Philippines ever need it. "I am confident, however, that the

Minnesota Congressman Harold Knutson served in the House of Representatives from 1917 to 1949. In addition to chairing the Committee on Insular Affairs, Knutson also led the Committee on Indian Affairs, the Committee on Ways and Means, and the Joint Committee on Internal Revenue Taxation.

Collection of the U.S. House of Representatives

Filipino people will meet the challenge of independence with courage and determination," he said.[176] Just down Massachusetts Avenue, State Department officials were on hand as the Philippine flag was raised over its new embassy.[177]

In Manila, a similar scene unfolded. At around 10:00 a.m., a massive crowd watched as the American flag came down and the Philippine flag went up over the capital city. "Simultaneously, sirens wailed out in Manila and church bells rang all over the Philippines," observed H. Ford Wilkins, the *New York Times* reporter covering the event. The Associated Press reported that "cries of 'Kalayan' [*sic*] (freedom) rang from barrio to barrio, from island to island ... as Filipinos celebrated their newly gained independence."[178] But Wilkins sensed something other than euphoria in the Philippines that day. "Filipinos generally observed Independence Day more as a solemn occasion than one for spontaneous rejoicing at having attained a goal they had sought during the forty-eight years of American sovereignty," he wrote.[179]

For the first half of the 20th century, the Philippines had been the far edge of the United States' overseas empire, the physical limit of America's frontier. Throughout this period, the United States tried to keep the people of the Philippines at arm's length while controlling the political and economic affairs of the islands. But in the opinion of the Philippine president Manuel Roxas, July 4, 1946, signaled the opening of a whole new era. "We mark here today a forward thrust of the frontiers of freedom," he said from the park at Luneta, a massive green space adjacent to Manila Bay. It was virtually the same spot where Spain opened fire on Dewey's warships in 1898 that began the Philippines' nearly 50-year history as an American colony. In 1962 the Philippines changed the date of its independence to June 12, 1898, marking the day when General Emilio Aguinaldo declared the Philippines independent of Spain.[180]

HAWAII

As was the case in the Philippines, the APA experience in Hawaii developed as a direct consequence of America's imperial ambitions. American colonists and missionaries gradually usurped power from the Polynesian people native to the Hawaiian Islands who suddenly found their way of life divorced from the economic strength of the country. The new economy in Hawaii centered on the cultivation and refinement of sugar, run by white, non-native businessmen. Native Hawaiians began referring to these Caucasian colonials as *haoles*, loosely meaning "foreigner" in the Hawaiian language. The plantations, in turn, attracted immigrants from the other side of the Pacific, principally Japanese and Chinese contract laborers. What followed was a fight for power and security among four groups under the shadow of the United States: monarchs, Native Hawaiians, the sugar companies, and immigrants.

The Hawaiian Islands had long been a convenient port of call for American whalers, seal hunters, and traders to China. Since the 1820s, the American Board of Commissioners for Foreign Missions had sent Protestant missionaries from New England, many of whom eventually settled permanently in Hawaii. The missionaries' successes led the board to proclaim the islands Christianized and to turn over control of the missions to the locals. American settlers soon turned their energies from missionary work to profiteering and invested heavily

In 1897 the satirical magazine *Puck* printed this political cartoon depicting "another shotgun wedding, with neither party willing" between Uncle Sam and a female personification of Hawaii. President William McKinley officiates the wedding while Senator John Tyler Morgan of Alabama, who supported American expansion, stands watch.

Image courtesy of the Library of Congress

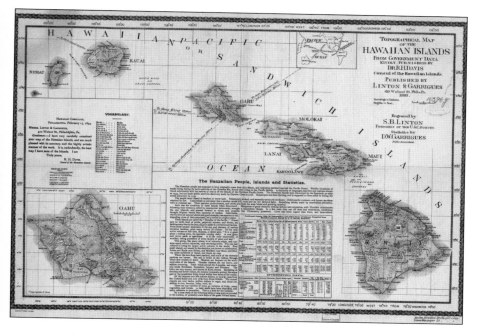

in sugar cultivation. Hawaiian monarchs provided favorable land grants. By 1870 these American descendants had become the "Big Five" sugar companies: Ladd & Company, H. Hackfeld & Company, C. Brewer & Company, Castle & Cooke, and Alexander & Baldwin.[181]

The United States began exercising direct influence over the Hawaiian monarchy with the Reciprocity Treaty of 1875. In exchange for exclusive use of Pearl Harbor near Honolulu, Hawaiian sugar would enter U.S. markets under favorable tariff rates. Sugar was suddenly the islands' premier crop, and revenue more than tripled, from $1.3 million in 1876 to $4.3 million in 1880.[182] This economic explosion granted the Big Five enormous leverage, leverage that they parlayed into a political revolution in 1887.

Bayonet Constitution

On June 30, 1887, an organization of *haole* lawyers and sugar planters, accompanied by an armed militia and led by attorneys Sanford B. Dole and Lorrin Thurston, forced King Kalakaua to sign a new constitution radically restructuring the Hawaiian government. The so-called "Bayonet Constitution" sharply restricted the powers of the monarchy and limited suffrage to property owners, which had the effect of disenfranchising most Native Hawaiians. New political parties emerged in the revolution's wake. Businessmen, missionaries, and planters rallied to the Reform Party while Native Hawaiians who met the voting requirements organized the National Reform Party in opposition.[183]

The assertion of *haole* influence changed the career trajectory of a young military student, Robert W. Wilcox. The government recalled Wilcox, a Native Hawaiian, from an exchange program in Italy, and he returned to Honolulu without a promised prestigious military appointment. In frustration, Wilcox turned to the more radical elements of the National Reform Party. Party conspirators plotted to force King Kalakaua's abdication in favor of his sister, Liliuokalani, who Native Hawaiians believed would show a firmer hand against

Hawaiian mills process sugar from cultivated cane. Sugar became the islands' most profitable crop by 1880.

Foreign lawyers and sugar planters forced King Kalakaua of Hawaii to sign a new constitution in 1887, which drastically restricted the power of his government.

Constructed in the late 19th century, Iolani Palace was briefly the residence of the Hawaiian royal family. After the monarchy was overthrown, the palace functioned as governmental headquarters until 1969.

Image courtesy of the Library of Congress

Robert W. Wilcox, a Native Hawaiian, attempted to force King Kalakaua to abdicate in 1888 so that the King's sister, Liliuokalani, could rule instead. Wilcox was captured, but found not guilty of conspiracy. He became Hawaii's first Delegate to Congress in 1900.

Image courtesy of the Hawaii State Archives

the *haole* government. Following a brief self-imposed exile in San Francisco in 1888 in fear of reprisal, Wilcox and his coconspirators moved forward with their plan on July 30, 1889. Relying on his military training, he marched roughly 150 men on Iolani Palace only to find the palace closed and the King spirited away. After hours of being holed up in a nearby bungalow under bombardment from the Royal Guard, Wilcox and his followers surrendered. First charged with treason, they were tried for conspiracy. A Native-Hawaiian jury found the defendants not guilty.[184]

That fall protectionist Republicans gained control of the U.S. Congress. Hawaiians viewed this development nervously, since the sugar trade with the United States funded three-fourths of the kingdom's imports and almost all of its exports.[185] Their fears proved to be well founded in 1890, when Congress passed the McKinley Tariff, named after its author, House Ways and Means Chairman William McKinley of Ohio. It eliminated all duties on raw sugar, effectively dismantling the special trade status Hawaii had enjoyed since 1875. Hawaiian diplomats raised objections to no avail. *Haole* officials began discussing the possibility of becoming either an American protectorate or being fully annexed by the United States. Both alternatives provoked opposition from Native Hawaiians.[186]

Rise of the Republic

The turmoil only increased when King Kalakaua died in January 1891. Queen Liliuokalani took the throne in the throes of an economic depression, determined to restore the power of the monarchy and Native Hawaiians. She surrounded herself with fellow royals, including 19-year-old Prince Jonah Kuhio Kalanianaole, a ward of King Kalakaua incorporated into the royal line. Known primarily as Kuhio, the young prince took on greater responsibilities when he became one of the queen's unofficial advisers after her husband died barely seven months into her reign.

Queen Liliuokalani's first opportunity to consolidate power and reverse the Bayonet Constitution arrived in the 1892 elections. However, Native Hawaiians split between the queen's National Reform Party and the more radical Liberal Party, which counted Wilcox among its members, while the planters' Reform Party held a plurality of seats. Liliuokalani desperately sought to appoint and maintain a new government, but the three parties refused to establish a stable partnership. No one party held a majority, leaving the situation, in U.S. Minister John Stevens's word, "feverish."[187]

During this time, anxious planters secretly formed the "Annexation Club" and contacted Stevens to gauge America's interest in taking on Hawaii as a territory. The club then sent Lorrin Thurston to Washington under the guise of arranging Hawaii's exhibit at the Chicago World's Fair. He met with Secretary of State James G. Blaine and the chairmen of the House and Senate Foreign Affairs Committees to assess U.S. reactions to a potential rebellion against Liliuokalani. Blaine assured Thurston the United States would welcome any Hawaiian annexation request. The *haole* planters were not alone in their dissatisfaction, however. Wilcox and other Native Hawaiians from the Liberal Party formed the Equal Rights League, also seeking annexation, abolition of the monarchy, and the democratic empowerment of the Native-Hawaiian people.[188]

Liliuokalani gave the annexationists the excuse they needed when she ended the 1892 legislative session by attempting to install a new constitution more favorable to Native Hawaiians. The Annexation Club reacted first and swiftly proclaimed itself a "Committee of Safety." The committee reached out to Minister Stevens and secured a promise of American military aid. With the support of American troops landing in Honolulu, the committee launched its revolution on January 15, 1893. Sanford Dole, who had since ascended to the Hawaiian supreme court and the queen's privy council, was offered and accepted the presidency of the provisional government. Liliuokalani's ministers met to discuss the crisis with the resident diplomats who advised them to avoid using force against the rebels. When two of the ministers met with Stevens, he refused to provide any assistance to the government. Working as a clerk at the government building, Prince Kuhio dutifully followed Dole's orders to send the letters out announcing the end of his own family's reign. Liliuokalani, Hawaii's final monarch, surrendered peacefully just after sunset.[189]

In one of the provisional government's first actions, Dole petitioned Stevens for American protection in the event of an uprising of Asian laborers and migrants who represented a sizable portion of the islands' population. U.S. flags flew over public buildings for weeks after the American minister assented to the request. The provisional government declared martial law to maintain order and appointed a delegation, including Lorrin Thurston, to negotiate a treaty of annexation in Washington, DC. The envoys arrived in early February 1893. Negotiations progressed quickly after Hawaiians assured State Department officials that they held no interest in statehood, which would enfranchise the Native-Hawaiian population and potentially interfere with the recruitment of migrant laborers from Japan and China. The treaty was signed on February 14, 1893, and quickly went to the Senate Foreign Relations Committee for consideration.[190]

Queen Liliuokalani was Hawaii's last monarch. She ascended to the throne in 1891 but surrendered her sovereignty two years later. Hawaii was formally annexed to the United States in 1898.

Image courtesy of the Library of Congress

Sanford B. Dole, who advocated the overthrow of the Hawaiian monarchy and urged the United States to annex the islands, became the first territorial governor of Hawaii in 1900.

Image courtesy of the Hawaii State Archives

William Richards Castle, Charles L. Carter, Joseph Marsden, William Chauncey Wilder, and Lorrin A. Thurston (clockwise from top) formed a commission in 1893 to negotiate the U.S. annexation of Hawaii.

Image courtesy of the Hawaii State Archives

Grover Cleveland's second inauguration as President, on March 4, 1893, marked the start of a slowdown of the U.S. annexation of Hawaii.

Image courtesy of the Library of Congress

All hope of immediate annexation evaporated once President Grover Cleveland took office two weeks later. A Democrat wary of angering his base in the Jim Crow South, Cleveland repudiated the protectorate status Stevens had arranged, halted progress on the annexation treaty in the Senate, and arranged for House Foreign Affairs Committee Chairman James Blount of Georgia to investigate conditions in Hawaii before moving forward. Blount blasted Stevens's involvement in the rebellion and predicted the Hawaiian republic would not last long. "The undoubted sentiment of the people is for the Queen," he wrote, "against the Provisional Government and against annexation."[191]

Cleveland's administration promptly replaced Stevens as the U.S. minister to Hawaii with Albert S. Willis. Willis apologized for the "reprehensible conduct of the American minister and the unauthorized presence on land of a military force of the United States" and urged Liliuokalani to accept amnesty for the members of the committee of safety. The queen, believing the United States had finally come to its senses and would back her return to power, initially insisted "such persons should be beheaded and their property confiscated to the government" before Willis managed to talk her down.[192] Willis then met with Dole, who flatly stated the provisional government would only give way to the queen if compelled by force. Dole further insisted erroneously that, by signing the February treaty, the United States had formally recognized Dole's administration as the legitimate government of the islands.[193]

With annexation stalled, the provisional government proceeded to draft a constitution. On July 4, 1894, the government declared itself the new Hawaiian republic, but discriminatory policies belied its true nature. Foremost among these was the full disenfranchisement of Native-Hawaiian and Asian laborers. The constitution of 1894 set up a tiered set of qualifications for voters who would elect the new Hawaiian bicameral legislature. Hawaiian house elections required voters to be males at least 20 years old, to speak English or Hawaiian, pay taxes, and hold at least one year's residency. Hawaiian senate voters had

the same requirements, but residency was increased to at least three years and a net property worth of at least $3,000 or an income of $600 was required. The constitution also excluded royalists from the voting rolls, leaving just 2,700 people able to vote in elections. Wilcox briefly worked with the provisional government, but quickly realized the *haole* bureaucracy held no position for him and returned to the role of agitator.[194]

In the last days of 1894, Wilcox joined Kuhio and other royalists to plot a counterrevolution that would restore Liliuokalani to the Hawaiian throne. With the deposed monarch's blessing, the conspirators smuggled arms into Honolulu and launched their revolt in the dusk hours of January 6, 1895. The republic had been informed of their plan, however, and Dole once more declared martial law on the islands. The royalist plot was scuttled within 36 hours after only scattered resistance. By January 10, the rebels had been caught and jailed, including Wilcox and Prince Kuhio.[195] Sentences ranged from a year of hard labor for the prince to death for Wilcox. Dole eventually commuted Wilcox's sentence to hard labor and offered a full pardon in 1898.[196]

Annexation and Transition

Despite this unrest, the Hawaiian republic continued to lobby for annexation in the hopes of boosting their flagging sugar trade. A path to annexation opened following the presidential election of Ohio Governor William McKinley in 1896. The Republican Party platform specifically called for U.S. control over the Hawaiian Islands. On June 16, 1897, McKinley sent a new treaty to the Senate for approval, but intense protests from the Japanese government shone a spotlight on the heavy presence of Asian contract laborers working Hawaii's sugar plantations. Progress on the treaty stalled, and the Senate adjourned on July 24 without acting on it. It became apparent that American fear over the ballooning population of Asian laborers on the islands would prove to be the greatest hurdle to Hawaiian annexation.[197]

Asian immigration to the Hawaiian Islands began in 1852 when the first ship from South China arrived in Honolulu Harbor laden with contract laborers for the sugar plantations. Among the early immigrants from China were relatives of future Senators Daniel K. Akaka and Hiram L. Fong, whose father, Sau Howe Fong, was recruited by a family member working for one of the Big Five sugar companies. The elder Fong's experience reflected the experiences of many Chinese immigrants in Hawaii. After finishing his contract in 1877, he found work at a fertilizer plant. Initially hired for five years, Chinese immigrants often settled their families in the islands once their contracts ended.[198]

By the 1880s, the sugar companies began importing Japanese laborers to balance against the growing Chinese population. The families of future Senators Daniel K. Inouye and Spark M. Matsunaga immigrated during this time, initially working the rich sugar fields of Maui. The Japanese government actively encouraged these first-generation Japanese emigrants, or *issei*, to agree to three-year contracts their government had negotiated with Hawaiian officials and sugar growers. Contrary to the United States and unlike the recruitment of Chinese laborers, Hawaii encouraged Japanese women to emigrate under the belief that family life would cool unrest. While this accomplished the

Prince Jonah Kuhio Kalanianaole served as the Hawaiian Delegate to the U.S. Congress from 1903 to 1922. President Theodore Roosevelt refused to pronounce his last name and instead referred to the Delegate by his middle name, Kuhio.

Image courtesy of the Library of Congress

Queen Liliuokalani took the throne in
1891 determined to restore the power
of the monarchy and Native Hawaiians.
This memorial, signed by Queen
Liliuokalani on December 19, 1898,
was her last attempt to return control
of her homeland to Native Hawaiians.

A crowd gathers outside Iolani Palace in
Honolulu on August 12, 1898, as legislation
annexing Hawaii to the United States went
into effect.

plantations' desired goals of maintaining stability among the labor force, it led
Japanese immigrants to follow the examples of their Chinese predecessors and
raise families on the island rather than return to Japan, as both governments had
envisioned. New minority communities sprang up as a result and created tight-
knit blocs of individual ethnic Asian minorities. Because of the importation of
cheap Japanese labor, Hawaiian plantations increased production while Japanese
emigration companies thrived and reinvigorated the Japanese economy. Roughly
30,000 Japanese contract laborers had poured into Hawaii by 1894.[199]

Dole's government attempted to address the influx of Japanese laborers
in 1897 when they turned back three ships with more than 1,000 Japanese
immigrants aboard. The Japanese government responded by sending its warship
Naniwa to Honolulu Harbor, causing the McKinley administration to dispatch
the U.S. Navy to Hawaii as well, while U.S. Secretary of State John Sherman
mediated the Japanese immigration issue. The increasingly martial Japanese
government viewed Hawaiian annexation as an attempt to avoid renegotiating
the highly profitable contract labor agreement between the two nations.
Japanese diplomats protested to the United States, but Secretary Sherman more
or less lied to Japanese diplomats that no annexation was contemplated. "It is
the white race against the yellow," one Honolulu newspaper opined. "Nothing
but annexation can save the islands."[200]

To that end, the Hawaiian legislature unanimously approved the annexation
treaty on September 6, 1897. Later that month, a joint congressional delegation
favoring annexation visited Honolulu. Hawaiian royalists presented evidence
before the delegation that many Native Hawaiians opposed annexation, which
gave the members pause.[201] Following another push by President McKinley
in his annual message on December 6, Secretary Sherman succeeded in his
efforts to remove the Japanese government's protest to the treaty and provided
assurances that Japan would suffer no discrimination from an annexed Hawaii.
The Senate launched into debate, and then progress came to a sudden halt
when the USS *Maine* exploded in Havana Harbor on February 15, 1898,
precipitating military conflict between America and Spain.

When the War of 1898 began in late April that year, events moved quickly and brought the Hawaiian Islands to the nation's attention with a new urgency. The destruction of the Spanish fleet in Manila Bay in early May made the Pacific Ocean an important component of the war. Hawaii suddenly became a key way station for the U.S. military as it provided supplies for U.S. troops to capture Manila and to hold the Philippines. The annexation of Hawaii had been revived mere months after its sudden demise.[202]

Representative Francis Newlands of Nevada introduced H. Res. 259 to annex Hawaii on May 4, 1898, and the House debated the resolution a month later, from June 11 to June 14. Champ Clark of Missouri opposed annexation because, in his view, Native Hawaiians could not become Americans. He dismissed them as "a lot of non-descript Asiatico-Polynesian ignoramuses." And he ended his speech with a warning about a future he wanted to avoid: "How can we endure our shame when a Chinese Senator from Hawaii, with his pigtail hanging down his back, with his pagan joss in his hand, shall rise from his curule chair and in pigeon [sic] English proceed to chop logic with George Frisbie Hoar or Henry Cabot Lodge? O tempora! O mores!"[203]

While Champ Clark's racial prejudices were widely shared, Hawaii's key position in the Pacific carried the day. "We owe the most solemn duty to reciprocate this friendly spirit," said Representative John Mitchell of New York, "and see that no possible harm shall come to them by reason of it."[204] When the House debated and voted on Newlands's resolution on June 15, 1898, it was approved, 290 to 91. Once Congress had decided to annex Hawaii by joint resolution rather than by treaty, Senate passage was certain. The Senate, having considered similar legislation several times over, wasted little time deliberating and approved the resolution, 42 to 21, on July 6. The President signed H. Res. 259 into law the next day.[205]

The Newlands Resolution authorized an interim government co-managed by the U.S. Army and Hawaiian republic leaders until Congress could set up a more permanent territorial government. Likewise, a commission was set up to recommend to Congress the legislation necessary to govern the islands. It included two Senators and the chairman of the House Foreign Affairs Committee. Hawaiian president Sanford Dole and Hawaiian supreme court justice Walter Frear, both *haoles*, rounded out the commission. Dole quickly set about persuading Congress to adopt discriminatory portions of the Hawaiian republic's constitution for the territory. For example, property qualifications were specified for legislators and senate voters, Asian citizens of the republic would not become U.S. citizens, and the territorial governor would appoint territorial judges. But Congress balked, and no territorial bill passed either chamber before the 55th Congress (1897–1899) concluded in early March 1899.[206]

Congressional indifference in the 56th Congress (1899–1901) allowed Wisconsin Senator John C. Spooner to strip out the property qualifications and insert an independent judiciary in the commission's bill.[207] President McKinley signed the resultant Hawaiian Organic Act into law on April 30, 1900. Like former territorial legislation, the Organic Act set aside the territorial governor, secretary, and judges as presidential appointments subject to Senate confirmation. McKinley obligingly nominated Sanford Dole as Hawaii's

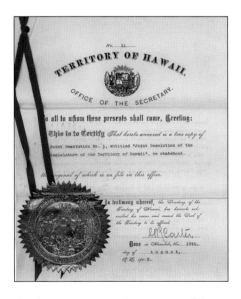

On August 15, 1903, the secretary of the Territory of Hawaii signed this resolution of the territorial legislature asking Congress to pass an act allowing Hawaii to hold a state constitutional convention and be admitted as a state to the Union. Hawaii was annexed by the United States only five years earlier, in July 1898.

Image courtesy of the National Archives and Records Administration

Following the enactment of the Hawaiian Organic Act on April 30, 1900, which created the Territory of Hawaii, President William McKinley nominated Sanford B. Dole to be territorial governor on May 4, 1900.

Image courtesy of the National Archives and Records Administration

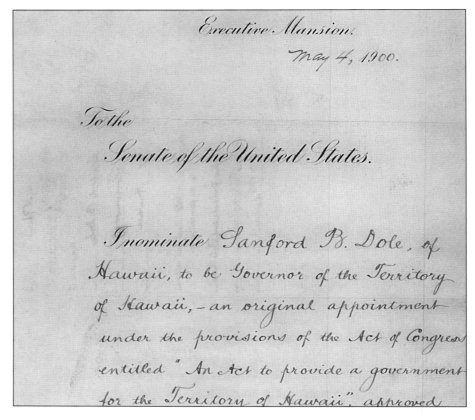

Executive Mansion.
May 4, 1900.

To the
Senate of the United States.

I nominate Sanford B. Dole, of Hawaii, to be Governor of the Territory of Hawaii, — an original appointment under the provisions of the Act of Congress entitled "An Act to provide a government for the Territory of Hawaii", approved

first territorial governor. The bill also created an elected bicameral legislature and provided for the election of a Territorial Delegate to the U.S. House of Representatives.[208] Though appointed officials retained considerable power over local politics, these changes ultimately restored Native Hawaiians as a majority of the electorate.

An extension of U.S. citizenship to all Hawaiian citizens notably excluded Asian laborers, who accounted for nearly 60 percent of the islands' population. At the time, U.S. law excluded Asian immigrants from becoming naturalized citizens, meaning that only those children born to Asian immigrants after annexation would gain citizenship. The act further required island-born Asians to produce a Hawaiian birth certificate before traveling to the U.S. mainland, but immigration officials implemented this section of the act by further requiring a creditable witness who had "seen the claimant at various times during his life."[209]

Meanwhile, Native Hawaiians asserted their renewed political power. The Organic Act went into effect in June 1900 and provided just enough time to hold the election for the first Territorial Delegate. While *haoles* adopted the political parties of their new nation, Native Hawaiians merged two patriotic leagues into the Hawaiian Independent Party (HIP) and demanded "Hawai'i for the Hawaiians" and "Equal Rights for the People." Robert Wilcox headed the HIP ticket. Wilcox distanced himself from the anti-*haole* tactics of the HIP's radical wing, and the party changed its name to Home Rule. When Democrats nominated Kuhio's older brother, David Kawananakoa, rumors swirled that Wilcox might withdraw his candidacy to avoid splitting the Native-Hawaiian vote. Unnerved, Wilcox hardened his rhetoric and lashed out at the *haoles* who had oppressed Native Hawaiians. He vowed to work toward the removal of Dole as territorial governor and staged rallies to highlight *haole* imperialism.[210] Wilcox's demagoguery bore fruit, and on November 6, 1900, he captured a narrow plurality of the votes to become Hawaii's first Delegate to Congress.

Creating a Legal Identity

Of the 10 Hawaiian Delegates to the U.S. Congress who served between 1900 and 1959, half were Native Hawaiian: Robert Wilcox, Jonah Kuhio Kalanianaole, William P. Jarrett, Victor S. (Kaleoaloha) Houston, and Samuel Wilder King. Together, these Delegates represented the islands in Congress for more than two-thirds of the period between annexation and statehood. These Native Hawaiians represented three different parties but wrestled with similar insular concerns. Arriving in Washington, most struggled to adjust to life on the mainland, and all faced congressional colleagues who knew little about the Hawaiian Islands. Granted floor privileges and the ability to introduce legislation, Hawaiian Delegates were nevertheless left without a vote and had to rely on personal relationships and lobbying efforts to cajole Congress into providing aid for the territory.

Robert Wilcox made a rough start of Hawaii's early congressional efforts when he failed to stir much sympathy in Washington, DC. During his tenure as a member of the Home Rule Party, he was unable to caucus with either Republicans or Democrats. He wound up on the Private Land Claims and Coinage, Weights, and Measures Committees; neither were plum assignments. Additionally, his anti-*haole* campaign and unsteady English hindered his effectiveness.[211]

When Prince Kuhio returned from an extended wedding honeymoon in 1901, he threw himself into Home Rule politics. However, the prince never felt entirely comfortable with the party's anti-*haole* rhetoric or Wilcox's tightfisted control. After a disastrous party convention resulted in a walkout of half of the Home Rule delegates, Kuhio entertained Republican outreach. Former Nebraska Senator John M. Thurston nudged Kuhio to the Republican Party with a line at the state convention: "You might as well send a frog to chipper at the doors of the Court of St. James for what you want as to send to Washington a Delegate who is not one of or in harmony with either of the two great political parties."[212] Kuhio's compromise with Republican business interests proved to be successful; he defeated Wilcox in the 1902 election and became Hawaii's second Delegate. Wilcox's Home Rule Party did not long survive his troubled House career, and Native Hawaiians quickly split between Republicans and Democrats.

In many ways, Kuhio set the tone for Hawaiian Delegates. He sought to correct congressional misconceptions about the islands through both formal and informal means. Like Wilcox, the prince made few floor speeches and did most of his work in committees, frequently testifying at length. Unlike Wilcox, Kuhio maintained far more confidence among his peers after years spent as an equal in foreign courts. Kuhio's successors continued this trend and acted more often as ambassadors than empowered legislators.

Kuhio quickly learned the depth of Members' ignorance regarding the islands while attempting to secure funding to repair lighthouses in the territory.

Hawaiian Delegate Samuel Wilder King, seated left, and Secretary of the Interior Harold Ickes receive leis in Washington, DC, in 1936.

Image courtesy of the Library of Congress

Illinois Representative James R. Mann and his wife wear leis during a 1915 congressional trip to Hawaii. The caption notes that they were "learning Hawaiian customs."

Collection of the U.S. House of Representatives

Hawaiian Delegate Victor S. (Kaleoaloha) Houston (right), and his wife, Pinao Brickwood Houston, present a lei—handmade by Mrs. Houston—to Speaker Nicholas Longworth (center) in 1929.

Collection of the U.S. House of Representatives

Bounced back and forth between the territorial lighthouse board, the Navy Department, the Appropriations Committee, and Speaker Joe Cannon, Kuhio discovered belatedly that some officials incorrectly believed that Hawaii was ineligible for federal funds.[213]

After the prince's eye-opening experience with the lighthouse board in late 1903, Kuhio took a new approach to educating his colleagues about Hawaii. He embraced his home's reputation as an exotic paradise among the Capitol Hill elite and sought to use that curiosity to his advantage. Kuhio and his wife purchased property near Pershing Square in the District of Columbia and transformed it into a social hotspot. Officials gambled, drank, and enjoyed dinner parties while Kuhio pontificated on the splendor and importance of the islands.[214]

The prince extended his educational campaign to sponsored tours of the islands beginning in 1907. These semiannual excursions often attracted funding from Hawaiian businesses and the territorial legislature itself. Members brought their families and enjoyed the full hospitality of the islands. These tours generally led to increased attention to Hawaiian needs back in Washington, DC. "I do not hesitate to say that I believe that the American congress will do a great deal for you this next session," Representative William Wilson of Illinois wrote to Kuhio after the 1915 tour. "I think you will find that the trip was of great benefit to you in that respect, as it was to us in every way."[215]

Kuhio's successors faced similar misapprehensions about Hawaii's status under the Organic Act. In the 71st Congress (1929–1931), Victor Houston struggled to extend provisions for federal highways that the Bureau of Public Roads had withheld for eight years because the territory had not been explicitly mentioned in the law.[216] William Jarrett wrestled with the strictures of the Organic Act throughout his tenure. He repeatedly testified before committees that, under the act, the territorial legislature required congressional approval to fund even basic governmental services like housing assistance and park management.[217] Samuel Wilder King continued to malign the act's obstruction in 1940 when Congress failed to approve reapportionment on the islands, leaving the territorial legislature under the control of Oahu's more cosmopolitan delegates.[218] Houston and King benefited from military contacts gained during their service in the U.S. Navy, and King in particular leaned on them to open wider avenues for lobbying in DC.[219]

Delegates continued to do much of their work in committees. The five Native-Hawaiian Delegates served on 13 standing committees, and all but Wilcox shared four in common: Agriculture, Military Affairs, Post Office and Post Roads, and Territories. These assignments represented the primary areas of concern for Hawaii. Jarrett, Houston, and King also served on the Committee on Public Lands, which gained much greater importance after Kuhio's signature piece of legislation, the Hawaiian Homes Commission Act, creating a homesteading program for Native Hawaiians on 200,000 acres of the former royal holdings. Delegates relied on these committee assignments to protect Hawaiian sugar, increase funding for military installations, improve infrastructure, and defend the rights of Hawaii's territorial government.

Legislative Interests

Early Hawaiian Delegates like Wilcox and Kuhio faced much greater political pressure on the islands. Both traveled to and from the mainland frequently in order to shore up support in a still uncertain political environment. Their greatest concerns were filling in the gaps the Organic Act had left behind. Wilcox clarified the terms of territorial senators and sought to transfer to the federal government the administrative responsibility for a community on the island of Molokai where people living with leprosy had been quarantined, a decision that likely cost him his seat after a visiting Congressman implied the United States would seek to relocate the residents upon taking control. In contrast, Kuhio drew federal attention to what had inspired annexation in the first place: the strategic position of the islands in the Pacific. He brought jobs and federal money to Hawaii to expand U.S. military resources. As a Republican, the prince also prioritized the economic concerns of his party's wealthy *haole* elites, most notably shipping concerns and protection of the sugar industry. Hawaii had been incorporated with the clear eventual goal of statehood, but Hawaiian businesses led by the Big Five and political elites were far more concerned with solidifying the status quo in the territory's early years.[220]

Where Kuhio began to diverge from his Republican bosses was in the "rehabilitation" of the Native-Hawaiian people. After years of *haole* control over nearly all facets of life during the republic, the economic strength of Native Hawaiians had waned considerably.[221] A homesteading program had been in the minds of Hawaiians since before the Organic Act. Wilcox had championed a similar program that aimed to benefit all Hawaiians, though that bill ultimately went nowhere. When Kuhio introduced the Hawaiian Rehabilitation Bill in April 1920, he presented it in testimony as "the first opportunity given to a poor man." Kuhio's version of homesteading was intended as a solution to what he saw as his people's decline.[222]

Kuhio intended to use the former Hawaiian Crown lands for this new homesteading program quickly renamed the Hawaiian Homes Commission Act. The Crown lands had long been a preoccupation of Kuhio. Until her death in 1917, Queen Liliuokalani pressured Kuhio to help her reacquire the lands ceded first to the republic and then to the American government. The prince dutifully made requests, but Congress and the territorial legislature held the lands under leases until 1920 and continually denied the claims. The Hawaiian Homes Commission Act took advantage of the leases' expirations to set aside 200,000 acres for 99-year leases to homesteaders who qualified as at least half Native Hawaiian. The bill, as passed, had many flaws. Successful lobbying by the Big Five ensured that the best lands were retained for sugar plantations, and the arbitrary nature of the Native-Hawaiian requirement meant that new generations often had trouble holding on to their family's land.[223]

King Sugar

The power of the sugar industry loomed large over the territory's politics. The mere threat of tariff reform effectively ended the career of Hawaii's first Democratic Delegate, William Jarrett. By that time, Republicans had controlled the House of Representatives since 1919 with no sign of waning. Mainland

interests itched to strengthen tariffs, a hallmark of the Republican platform, in order to protect American crops and products. As a Democrat, Jarrett did not devote much effort to maintaining the Big Five's unique place in the American economy. Well liked, but politically inexperienced, Jarrett found himself a victim of this blind spot in 1926 when Republicans ran Victor Houston, another political newcomer, against him. Only a Republican, the party insisted, could properly preserve the islands' economic interests in the face of certain tariff legislation.[224]

Republicans spent a great deal of time attending to the concerns of the sugar industry, particularly the constant labor shortages. By 1900 the Japanese population on the islands was roughly 60,000; 40,000 more arrived in the seven years after annexation. A significant number of these immigrants were women, which led to more permanent *issei* settlement in Hawaii. Planters faced with the abolition of the contract labor system after annexation encouraged family emigration to keep laborers living and working on the plantations. This new system culminated in the Gentlemen's Agreement in 1907 between the United States and Japan, in which Japan restricted emigration to the United States, but retained a loophole for the immediate relatives of immigrants already living there. The loophole resulted in more female and family migration and crystalized the permanent settlement of Japanese laborers in Hawaii.[225]

Native Hawaiians like Kuhio openly derided the Japanese population as "un-Americanizing the territory." Some of this unease developed due to Japan's rapid militarization and its tendency to engage in gunboat diplomacy. With the United States seemingly uninterested in building a Pacific defense on the foundation provided in the wake of the Spanish-American War, Hawaiians worried about Japan and the numerous emigrants the nation sent to the islands. Native Hawaiians and *haoles* alike feared the Asian majority likely to arise when the second generation of laborers, entitled to citizenship by birth after annexation, at last gained the vote. Kuhio responded to these fears by combating U.S. objections to importing Chinese immigrants whom the prince viewed much more favorably. The Hawaiian Homes Commission Act also prevented Japanese people from working on federal construction projects. The efforts of Hawaiian politicians paralleled what was occurring on the mainland, which led to complete Japanese exclusion in the Immigration Act of 1924.[226]

The immigration debate hardly ended there. Faced with a prohibition on Japanese immigration, Hawaiian planters once more had to seek other sources for their labor needs, which they found in another American possession: the Philippines. But not even this American territory was immune to the widespread concerns over Asian immigration, and in 1930 Delegate Victor Houston was forced to testify before the House Committee on Immigration and Naturalization to retain a loophole for Hawaii against any immigration restrictions on Filipinos. It was not Houston who won the loophole, however, but the powerful sugar lobby that had co-opted Kuhio's homesteading legislation. In his defense of that loophole, Houston offered rousing testimony about the multicultural society on the islands, calling them "a real melting-pot" that "is working and may possibly serve as an example to the rest of the world."[227]

Indeed, despite simmering racial tension on the islands, Hawaii's racial conflicts were typically rather muted in comparison to conditions on the mainland. Asian labor was vital to the territory's key industry, and many Japanese and Chinese immigrants actively invited and encouraged assimilation to American cultural norms. Many converted to Christianity, and second generations moved on from the sugar plantations to more industrial and professional careers. The Pan-Pacific Union (formerly Hands Around the Pacific) arose to represent Asian laborers and address racial concerns on the islands.[228] These concerns took on a new and dangerous form beginning in 1931 in response to an explosive legal case that threatened not only racial violence, but the territory's very sovereignty.

The Massie Affair and the Jones–Costigan Act

On the night of September 21, 1931, a white woman named Thalia Massie, the wife of U.S. Navy Lieutenant Thomas Massie, was attacked after leaving a party alone. Badly beaten—her jaw had been broken—she told police that a gang of "local boys" had forced her into their car, driven to a field, and there had beaten and raped her. Honolulu police charged five young men—two Japanese, two Native Hawaiians, and one Chinese Hawaiian—after Thalia Massie identified four of the men as her attackers. A sensationalized trial followed in which stories headlined on the mainland constantly shifted and evidence remained sparse. The jury, largely made up of Native Hawaiians and Asian Americans, was unable to come to a verdict. A mistrial was declared in early December.[229]

The trial's outcome infuriated *haoles* and military families on the islands. The lurid accusations of the trial put Hawaii under a microscope. One of the suspects was abducted and beaten by sailors days after the trial ended. Events escalated further when Honolulu police stopped a car carrying Lieutenant Massie, his mother-in-law, and two sailors on January 8, 1932. They had abducted and murdered one of the suspects and were on their way to toss

In 1931 a revenge killing known as the Massie affair increased racial tensions and shocked Hawaiians and U.S. Naval officers stationed at Pearl Harbor, shown here in an aerial view.

Image courtesy of the Naval History and Heritage Command

the body into the sea. Famed attorney Clarence Darrow defended Lieutenant Massie and his coconspirators at trial, but the court adjudged all four guilty of manslaughter and sentenced them to 10 years of hard labor. Fearing an uproar from the mainland, Delegate Houston urged territorial Governor Lawrence Judd to pardon the perpetrators. Judd obliged and commuted their sentences to a single hour spent in his office, at the conclusion of which the defendants fled Hawaii and the case ended. Houston's involvement cost him the following election when Democratic opponent Lincoln McCandless portrayed his action as meddling and "an act of treachery to the Hawaiian race."[230]

The combined series of events prompted a violent storm of emotion and denunciation from Hawaiians, the mainland press, the Navy, and—most ominously—the U.S. Congress. Many on Capitol Hill now pictured Hawaii through this racialized lens, concerned that the territorial government remained helpless to protect white inhabitants. More than one Representative responded by proposing territorial reorganization, and a Senate resolution (S. Res. 134) requested a Justice Department investigation of the islands' law enforcement efforts. In the resultant hearing, the Justice Department suggested an end to the residence requirement for appointed officials in Hawaii. No immediate change was forthcoming, but the issue did not go away.[231]

Upon entering office in 1933, President Franklin D. Roosevelt requested the residence requirement be lifted for the territorial governor, and Representative John Rankin of Mississippi, who opposed statehood for Hawaii, immediately introduced a bill (H.R. 5767) to that effect. Hawaiians panicked when the Rankin bill passed the House in early June. Governor Judd appointed a three-member Home Rule Commission to lobby against the bill in Washington. Notable among them was former naval officer Samuel Wilder King. Rankin's bill was narrowly defeated in the Senate after a protracted filibuster. The callous,

John Rankin, a Representative from Mississippi, introduced legislation in 1933 opposing Hawaiian statehood.

John Elliott Rankin, Margaret Brisbine, 1939, Collection of the U.S. House of Representatives

offhand manner in which Hawaiian politics were treated convinced King that the territory must seek statehood, and he pursued the Delegate seat in 1934 with that idea as his platform.[232]

The final major obstacle to a unified Hawaiian approach to statehood—the Big Five sugar companies—was removed after passage of the Jones–Costigan Act (H.R. 8861) of 1934. In the depths of the Great Depression and under immense pressure from mainland agricultural lobbies, Congress greatly reduced sugar quotas for Hawaii relative to the states. The issue became compounded when the Agriculture Department used outdated figures to set Hawaii's quota lower than it would have otherwise been. The new quota had an almost immediate effect. Sugar production in the islands dropped by 8 to 10 percent and farmers abandoned thousands of acres of fields. Perhaps more worrisome for the future of the territory, the Jones–Costigan Act set a troubling precedent by classifying Hawaii as a "foreign" market for the purpose of future reductions.[233] The Big Five's lobbying arm, the Hawaiian Sugar Planters' Association (HSPA), alleged unconstitutionality and unsuccessfully challenged the legislation in court. The Big Five had long relied on this lobbying network and often bypassed the elected Delegate whenever he proved to be inconvenient. After Jones–Costigan, the HSPA met and agreed that only statehood could guarantee equal economic privileges.[234]

Hawaiian Statehood: Gradually, Then Suddenly

Though the Organic Act had originally been intended to place Hawaii on a path to eventual statehood, few people in positions of power actively sought to speed that process along in the early days of the territory. For the most part, Hawaiians remained content for more than 30 years to work within the political structure provided. Territorial Governor Sanford Dole paid lip service to statehood in his 1900 inaugural address. The territorial legislature passed resolutions between 1903 and 1917 requesting permission from Congress to hold a constitutional convention, but these proposals had neither the backing of the powerful sugar

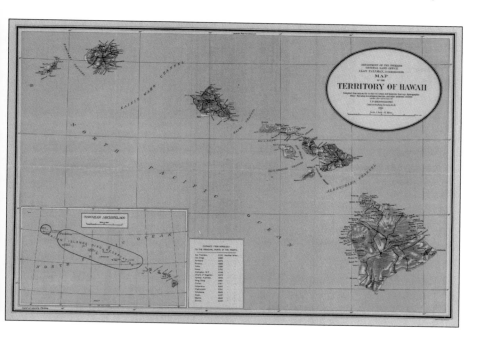

This 1915 map of the Territory of Hawaii includes a key listing the distances from Honolulu to other major ports in the Pacific. Trade, particularly of sugar, was a key factor in the annexation of the islands in 1898.

Image courtesy of the National Archives and Records Administration

This campaign button promotes the re-election of Samuel Wilder King as Hawaii's Delegate to the U.S. Congress. King ran on a pro-statehood platform in 1934 and continued lobbying for statehood throughout his four terms in the House of Representatives.

Collection of the U.S. House of Representatives

industry nor the enthusiasm of a majority of the voting population. While both of the territory's political parties included statehood in their platforms, neither party advocated for it immediately.[235]

Delegate Kuhio promised to offer legislation for statehood as early as 1910 but did not put forward the first statehood proposal until 1919. It received no support from the HSPA and quietly died in the Committee on Territories. In 1927, when asked about statehood, Sanford Dole's longtime ally, *Honolulu Advertiser* publisher Lorrin Thurston, responded, "Hawaii needs statehood as much as a cat needs two tails." Victor Houston appeared to genuinely support statehood when he proposed it in 1931, but his bill drowned amid the deluge of bad press surrounding the Massie affair. When Houston offered his bill on December 9, 1931, three days after the mistrial in the Massie case, Congress had practically ruled out statehood.[236]

Only after the twin crises of the Massie affair and the Jones–Costigan Act did the territory galvanize behind the statehood movement. Fresh from his lobbying efforts against the Rankin bill, Samuel Wilder King successfully campaigned for Delegate on a platform of achieving statehood for the islands. Later, as Delegate, he openly discussed his wish to one day become the state of Hawaii's first governor. King included a petition for statehood among his first bills in 1935. This bill differed from previous efforts by having the full monetary and lobbying support of the HSPA. Congress took note, and that autumn a subcommittee from the Committee on Territories held public hearings across the islands. Representatives of the Big Five readily admitted before the committee that their change of heart rested upon economic concerns. Much of the testimony compared Hawaii favorably in terms relative to states already in the Union, citing the territory's economy, size, population, and tax contribution. President Roosevelt, who had visited the territory in 1934, announced his opposition to statehood just as the hearings got under way. The committee ultimately agreed to forego further action.[237]

King immediately reintroduced his statehood bill in the 75th Congress (1937–1939). In addition, he worked with Senator Tydings to form a high-profile Joint Committee on Hawaii to more comprehensively study the territory's fitness for statehood.[238] The territorial legislature appropriated $20,000 for Hawaii's Equal Rights Commission (a statehood group created by the territorial legislature in 1935) to prepare for the hearings. Though supporters of statehood again rushed to plead their case before the joint committee, opponents voiced their own concerns. Native-Hawaiian dissenters were particularly worried that statehood would only allow further centralization of power under the Big Five. Most arguments against Hawaiian statehood, however, pointed to the large Asian population on the islands that opponents insisted could never be "truly thoroughly, fundamentally, and unequivocally American," especially given their suspect loyalties, insular communities, and tendencies to vote in a bloc.[239]

The joint committee did not offer statehood proponents their desired result. Representative Rankin, now the leading opponent of Hawaiian statehood, led the minority's report in recommending that statehood be postponed indefinitely in light of the islands' Japanese population and the increasing military aggression

Speaker William Bankhead of Alabama calls the House to order during a session of the 75th Congress (1937–1939), when Delegate Samuel Wilder King introduced his second Hawaii statehood bill.

Collection of the U.S. House of Representatives

of Japan on display in the outbreak of the Sino-Japanese War. The official report agreed that some postponement was necessary and cited "the present disturbed condition of international affairs" in Asia as a major reason that caution was necessary.[240]

Additionally, the Joint Committee on Hawaii determined that Congress could not act further on statehood until "the sentiment of the people" could be established.[241] King pressed the territorial legislature for a plebiscite on statehood, which it authorized in 1939 for the following November. The legislature then placed the Equal Rights Commission, in coordination with the HSPA, in charge of the statehood campaign. Taking Congress's fears over Japan into consideration, the commission changed its campaign from immediate statehood to eventual statehood. The question "Do you favor statehood for Hawaii?" was vaguely worded and allowed for equivocation, much to King's dismay. A Japanese diplomat sowed further unrest by characterizing Hawaiian Japanese as "all determined to undergo great sacrifices for Japan during the present uneasy condition." Just before the plebiscite King denounced as un-American any opposition due to prejudice against Japanese Americans.[242]

The plebiscite passed with 67 percent of voters favoring statehood, far from the resounding 80 percent King and other statehood proponents had hoped for and predicted. Furthermore, the vague wording and shifting campaign of the Equal Rights Commission meant that little could be done with the result.[243] King did what he could to address concerns of Japanese citizenship: passing a bill to naturalize all women born prior to Hawaiian annexation.

The next step toward statehood came into focus following a handful of nationwide surveys conducted during this period. *Fortune* magazine found in 1939 that "fewer people in the U.S. were willing to go to war to defend the Hawaiian Islands … than Canada," and a 1941 Gallup poll reported 48 percent of Americans favored statehood for Hawaii. For statehood advocates, these results suggested that the American people needed to become better educated on Hawaiian issues.[244]

Japan's surprise attack on Pearl Harbor on the morning of December 7, 1941, put all concerns of statehood on hold. The islands fell under martial law. King ceased agitating for statehood and instead spent much of his time traveling back and forth between Hawaii and Washington, DC. He defended the rights of Japanese Americans in the territory and urged restraint for the military government.[245] In Hawaii, many Asian Americans put politics on hold to enlist in the war effort and combat anti-Asian sentiment. Future Senator Hiram Fong, a Chinese American who had won election to the territorial legislature in 1938, forfeited his candidacy for re-election in early 1942 to serve in the U.S. Army Air Force as a judge advocate.[246] Delegate King likewise abandoned his plans to campaign for a fifth term and rejoined the U.S. Naval Reserve as a lieutenant commander. "I cannot remain in civil life when the training I received as a naval officer may better serve our country's present needs in active service," King declared in a radio address to the island.[247]

Following the conclusion of World War II, King returned to his advocacy of statehood. He served as president of the constitutional convention in 1950, and in 1953 he secured President Dwight D. Eisenhower's appointment to the territorial governorship. Hawaii had changed considerably after World War II, however, and King found himself a Republican governor dealing with a highly contentious Democratic territorial legislature. The Democratic revolution of 1954 swept into politics the generation of *nisei* (the American-born children of Japanese immigrants) like Daniel Inouye and Spark Matsunaga, veterans fresh from GI Bill–funded educations and eager to exert their political influence. In fact, Japanese Americans controlled half the seats in the legislature.[248] King's struggles with the legislature ended with his resignation in 1957. He died two years later, barely five months before Hawaii finally attained statehood in August 1959.

CONCLUSION

March 20, 1918, was one of those typical early-spring days in the nation's capital, partly cloudy and cool in the morning, but warm enough that the temperature eventually hit a pleasant 71 degrees. Just before the House opened at noon that day, more than 260 Members gathered on the East Front of the Capitol for a unique panoramic photo. Some sat, and some stood. Some held lit cigars. Nearly everyone squinted into the late-morning light. Seated in the middle of the group was Jeannette Rankin of Montana, the first woman elected to Congress, one chair over from Speaker Champ Clark.[249]

It had been 20 years since Clark ridiculed the idea of American expansion in the Pacific, his garish descriptions of cannibals serving in Congress, and the need for translators eliciting laughter and applause from his colleagues.[250] America was at war with Spain then, in 1898. In 1918 America was fighting in Europe in what was being called the Great War, a world conflict that itself brought up a host of new immigration and citizenship issues.

Nisei:

A Japanese term that identifies the generation of Japanese Americans who were born in the United States from their issei *immigrant parents.*

Off to the side of the photo stood three men, seemingly by themselves: Filipino Resident Commissioners Teodoro R. Yangco and Jaime de Veyra and, in between them, Puerto Rican Resident Commissioner Félix Córdova Dávila. A few feet away, mixed in with some of the other Members, Hawaiian Delegate Jonah Kuhio Kalanianaole stood slightly forward with his left hand on his hip, arm bent at the elbow, as if he was losing patience and was in a rush to get back to work.

By 1918 Hawaii and the Philippines had been American territories for two decades. The country's decision to expand into the Pacific a generation earlier was, in a sense, a continuation of what it had done throughout the 19th century: American society spreading westward across the continent, displacing indigenous peoples in order to access new land and resources. There were, of course, major differences. Antebellum and Gilded Age Americans had considered it their "manifest destiny" to link the Atlantic and Pacific Oceans under one nation. But as the 1800s gave way to a new century, many wondered, especially in Congress, whether it was "manifest" that America should plant its flag in far-flung locations overseas. America had once been a colony itself. What would it mean if it now had colonies of its own?

As the country wrestled with that question, Americans based arguments both for and against expansion in the racially charged language and pseudoscientific theories of the day that placed people of Asian descent, including Filipinos and Native Hawaiians, below white people of European origin on the racial hierarchy. But even after the United States gained possession of the Philippines and Hawaii, Congress confronted a litany of new issues, setting up island administrations that tried, often awkwardly, to balance the interests of American industries doing business in the Pacific with the hopes and ambitions of the people who actually lived there. Hawaii had been annexed with the eventual goal of statehood. The Philippines, however, had fought Spain for its independence and continued to fight for it after the United States, despite protests at home, staked claim to the archipelago. Three years of bloodshed during the Philippine-American War may have led to an American military victory, but it also sparked the formation of a popular national identity in the Philippines. And it was that identity which underwrote the peaceful independence efforts of the islands' leaders over the next four decades while the islands were under America's sphere of influence.

To help the territories make their cases on Capitol Hill, Congress gave Resident Commissioners to the Philippines and it gave Delegates to Hawaii. Limited in their legislative tools, statutory representatives had to be resourceful as they fought on behalf of the interests of their home islands. For the Philippines, that meant beneficial trade terms and independence, which it gained in 1946. For Hawaii, that meant shoring up the Organic Act and dealing with the demands of the powerful sugar conglomerates.

Top and middle: Resident Commissioners Teodoro R. Yangco (129) and Jaime C. de Veyra (131) of the Philippines and Delegate Jonah Kuhio Kalanianaole (162) of Hawaii stand at the periphery of a 65th Congress panoramic photograph (bottom) from 1918 that features Montana's Jeannette Rankin, the first woman in Congress (front row, fourth from the left).

Image courtesy of the Library of Congress

The 13 Filipino Resident Commissioners and five Hawaiian Delegates in this section—18 statutory representatives who served without a vote—made up the extent of APA representation on the Hill from 1898 through World War II. Remarkably, not a single Representative or Senator of Asian descent served during this period. Simply put, federal law prevented them from taking part in the political process. Since the last quarter of the 19th century, the federal government had adopted a policy of exclusion, keeping Asian immigrants primarily from China and Japan from taking the oath as American citizens. From outright bans to immigration quotas, federal lawmakers limited who could participate in American society even as the country acquired new territory and governed millions of new people.

Although the Philippines' story in Congress ended with its independence in 1946, Hawaii's story continued into statehood in 1959. If APA Members once stood on the periphery as they did in that early-spring photo from 1918, soon they would be front and center as some of the most powerful elected officials on Capitol Hill, legislators like Daniel Inouye and Patsy Takemoto Mink of Hawaii and Norman Y. Mineta of California. Once again the legacy of war propelled that change, forcing a major recalculation of policies at home, including an overhaul of who could qualify for citizenship. As barriers began to fall around midcentury, an immigrant farmer from the Punjab region of northern India who had settled in Southern California staked his claim as the first APA Member to serve in Congress with the same constitutional standing as anyone else.

NOTES

1   On the Battle of Manila Bay, see Michael Blow, *A Ship to Remember: The* Maine *and the Spanish-American War* (New York: William Morrow, 1992): 224–234. For Quezon's account, see Manuel Luis Quezon, *The Good Fight* (New York: Appleton-Century, 1946): 34–35. See also Stanley Karnow, *In Our Image: America's Empire in the Philippines* (New York: Random House, 1989): 103–105.

2   The War of 1898 is traditionally called the Spanish-American War, but recent scholarship has begun using the War of 1898 in order to include Cuban and Filipino combatants in the narrative. See George C. Herring, *From Colony to Superpower: U.S. Foreign Relations since 1776* (New York: Oxford University Press, 2008): 309.

3   For the Hay quote, see Herring, *From Colony to Superpower:* 316.

4   Ernest R. May, *Imperial Democracy: The Emergence of America as a Great Power* (New York: Harper Torchbooks, 1961); Robert L. Beisner, *From the Old Diplomacy to the New, 1865–1900*, 2nd ed. (Wheeling, WV: Harlan Davidson, 1986); and Warren Zimmermann, *First Great Triumph: How Five Americans Made Their Country a World Power* (New York: Farrar, Straus and Giroux, 2002).

5   Ronald Takaki, *A Different Mirror: A History of Multicultural America* (New York: Little, Brown and Company, 1993): 196; Erika Lee, *The Making of Asian America: A History* (New York: Simon and Schuster, 2015): 65, 72.

6   Ronald Takaki, *Strangers from a Different Shore: A History of Asian Americans*, rev. ed. (Boston, MA: Back Bay Books, 1998): 35–36.

7   Daniel J. Tichenor, *Dividing Lines: The Politics of Immigration Control in America* (Princeton, NJ: Princeton University Press, 2002): 93; Treaty of Trade, Consuls, and Emigration, U.S.-China, 16 Stat. 739 (1868).

8   Elmer Clarence Sandmeyer, *Anti-Chinese Movement in California* (1939; repr., Urbana: University of Illinois Press, 1991): 25–39; David Haward Bain, *Empire Express: Building the First Transcontinental Railroad* (New York: Penguin Books, 1999): 206.

Bain, *Empire Express*: 640, 671; Lee, *The Making of Asian America*: 93.

Charles S. Campbell, *Transformation of American Foreign Relations, 1865–1900* (New York: Harper and Row, 1975): 114; Lawrence H. Chamberlain, *President, Congress and Legislation* (1946; repr., New York: AMS Press, 1967): 353; Robert A. Divine, *American Immigration Policy, 1924–1952* (New Haven, CT: Yale University Press, 1957): 19–20.

Justus D. Doenecke, *The Presidencies of James A. Garfield and Chester A. Arthur* (Lawrence: University Press of Kansas, 1981): 82; Campbell, *Transformation of American Foreign Relations*: 116n30; Roger Daniels, *Asian America: Chinese and Japanese in the United States since 1850* (Seattle: University of Washington Press, 1988): 55; 22 Stat. 826 (1880).

Andrew Gyory, *Closing the Gate: Race, Politics, and the Chinese Exclusion Act* (Chapel Hill: University of North Carolina Press, 1998): 222–223; Sandmeyer, *Anti-Chinese Movement in California*: 92; Chamberlain, *President, Congress and Legislation*: 354; Campbell, *Transformation of American Foreign Relations*: 116n33, 117; Stephen W. Stathis, *Landmark Legislation, 1774–2002: Major U.S. Acts and Treaties* (Washington, DC: CQ Press, 2003): 122; Chinese Exclusion Act, 22 Stat. 58 (1882).

For legal examples, see Fong Yue Ting v. United States, 149 U.S. 698 (1893) and Chae Chan Ping v. United States, 130 U.S. 581 (1889). In the United States v. Wong Kim Ark, 169 U.S. 649 (1898), the Supreme Court upheld the Fourteenth Amendment in which a child born in the United States became an American citizen even if his or her parents were Chinese aliens. Melvin I. Urofsky and Paul Finkelman, *March of Liberty: A Constitutional History of the United States*, vol. 1, 2nd ed. (New York: Oxford University Press, 2002): 487–488; Daniels, *Asian America*: 58; Morton Keller, *Affairs of State: Public Life in Late Nineteenth Century America* (Cambridge, MA: Harvard University Press, 1977): 444; Lee, *The Making of Asian America*: 84–85.

Stathis, *Landmark Legislation*: 137; Sandmeyer, *Anti-Chinese Movement in California*: 106–108; Daniels, *Asian America*: 112.

Sucheng Chan, *Asian Americans: An Interpretive History* (New York: Twayne Publishers, 1991): 11; Takaki, *Strangers from a Different Shore*: 46; Daniels, *Asian America*: 104–105, 109.

The 1890 U.S. Census, for example, listed just 1,147 Japanese living in California. See Daniels, *Asian America*: 112.

Lewis L. Gould, *The Presidency of William McKinley* (Lawrence: University Press of Kansas, 1980): 133, 146, 203–204; Lewis L. Gould, *The Presidency of Theodore Roosevelt*, 2nd ed. (Lawrence: University Press of Kansas, 2011): 12–13.

Daniels, *Asian America*: 109–110, 112.

Ibid., 112; Raymond A. Esthus, *Theodore Roosevelt and Japan* (Seattle: University of Washington Press, 1966): 129.

Roger Daniels, *Politics of Prejudice: The Anti-Japanese Movement in California and the Struggle for Japanese Exclusion* (Berkeley: University of California Press, 1962): 8, 22, 113; Takaki, *Strangers from a Different Shore*: 200–201.

Charles E. Neu, *An Uncertain Friendship: Theodore Roosevelt and Japan, 1906–1909* (Cambridge, MA: Harvard University Press, 1967): 23, 130; Daniels, *Politics of Prejudice*: 32–33.

Roger Daniels, *Coming to America: A History of Immigration and Ethnicity in American Life* (New York: Harper Perennial, 1990): 256–257; Takaki, *Strangers from a Different Shore*: 201.

Neu, *Uncertain Friendship*: 62, 66–67, 79; Takaki, *Strangers from a Different Shore*: 201–203.

Gould, *Presidency of Theodore Roosevelt*: 252; Neu, *Uncertain Friendship*: 79–80; Daniels, *Politics of Prejudice*: 95; Chamberlain, *President, Congress and Legislation*: 369.

Esthus, *Theodore Roosevelt and Japan*: 295.

Takaki, *Strangers from a Different Shore*: 203; Esthus, *Theodore Roosevelt and Japan*: 287–291.

Lee, *The Making of Asian America*: 132; Takaki, *Strangers from a Different Shore*: 206–207.

Takaki, *Strangers from a Different Shore*: 205. The individual cases are: Terrace v. Thompson, 263 U.S. 197 (1923); Porterfield v. Webb, 263 U.S. 225 (1923); Webb v. O'Brien, 263 U.S. 313 (1923); and Frick v. Webb, 263 U.S. 326 (1923). See Chan, *Asian Americans*: 47.

Chan, *Asian Americans*: 95–96; Daniels, *Asian America*: 298–299; David M. Reimers,

Still the Golden Door: The Third World Comes to America, 2nd ed. (New York: Columbia University Press, 1992): 18–19.

30 Takaki, *Strangers from a Different Shore*: 412–413; Mitchell T. Maki, Harry H. L. Kitano, and S. Megan Berthold, *Achieving the Impossible Dream: How Japanese Americans Obtained Redress* (Chicago: University of Illinois Press, 1999): 55, 249n11.

31 Senator Lyman Trumbull of Illinois tried to extend naturalization privileges to Chinese immigrants, but it was voted down. Daniels, *Asian America*: 43, 43n31.

32 Yuji Ichioka, *The Issei: The World of the First Generation Japanese Immigrants, 1885–1924* (New York: Free Press, 1988): 216; Chan, *Asian Americans*: 47, 92–93.

33 Ozawa v. United States, 260 U.S. 178 (1922): 197.

34 Ichioka, *The Issei*: 221; Ozawa v. United States, 260 U.S. 178 (1922): 198; Daniels, *Politics of Prejudice*: 98.

35 United States v. Bhagat Singh Thind, 261 U.S. 204 (1923): 214–215; Takaki, *Strangers from a Different Shore*: 299; Chan, *Asian Americans*: 94.

36 Chan, *Asian Americans*: 55; Michael E. Parrish, *Anxious Decades: America in Prosperity and Depression, 1920–1941* (New York: W. W. Norton, 1994): 110; Bill Ong Hing, *Making and Remaking Asian America through Immigration Policy, 1850–1990* (Stanford, CA: Stanford University Press, 1993): 32.

37 Lee, *The Making of Asian America*: 171; Stathis, *Landmark Legislation*: 174; Daniels, *Asian America*: 149–150; Hing, *Making and Remaking Asian America*: 70.

38 John Higham, *Strangers in the Land: Patterns of American Nativism, 1860–1925*, 2nd ed. (New Brunswick, NJ: Rutgers University Press, 1988): 302, 304–307, 309–311; Chamberlain, *President, Congress and Legislation*: 367–369; Tichenor, *Dividing Lines*: 142–143; Daniels, *Coming to America*: 280; *Presidential Vetoes, 1789–1976* (Washington, DC: U.S. Government Printing Office, 1978): 216.

39 Daniels, *Politics of Prejudice*: 95; Chamberlain, *President, Congress and Legislation*: 369; Stathis, *Landmark Legislation*: 183; Public Law 67-5, 42 Stat. 5 (1921).

40 Parrish, *Anxious Decades*: 112; Lee, *The Making of Asian America*: 134.

41 Chamberlain, *President, Congress and Legislation*: 369; Higham, *Strangers in the Land*: 319; Parrish, *Anxious Decades*: 112.

42 Chamberlain, *President, Congress and Legislation*: 370–371; Higham, *Strangers in the Land*: 310–321; Parrish, *Anxious Decades*: 112; Daniels, *Coming to America*: 282–283.

43 Akira Iriye, *After Imperialism: The Search for a New Order in the Far East, 1921–1931* (1965; repr., Chicago, IL: Imprint Publications, 1990): 35.

44 Parrish, *Anxious Decades*: 112; Chamberlain, *President, Congress and Legislation*: 371–373; Immigration Act of 1924, Public Law 68-139, 43 Stat. 153 (1924).

45 Lee, *The Making of Asian America*: 135; Yuka Fujioka, "The Thought War: Public Diplomacy by Japan's Immigrants in the United States," in *Tumultuous Decade: Empire, Society, and Diplomacy in 1930s Japan*, ed. Masato Kimura and Tosh Minohara (Toronto, CN: University of Toronto Press, 2013): 164.

46 Takaki, *Strangers from a Different Shore*: 210.

47 Akira Iriye, *Across the Pacific: An Inner History of American-East Asian Relations* (New York: Harcourt, Brace and World, 1967): 115, 152–153.

48 Herring, *From Colony to Superpower*: 214–321; Jennifer K. Elsea and Matthew C. Weed, "Declarations of War and Authorizations for the Use of Military Force: Historical Background and Legal Implications," Report RL31133, 18 April 2014, Congressional Research Service: 4. On the USS *Maine's* assignment in the Caribbean, see Gould, *The Presidency of William McKinley*: 70–72.

49 Herring, *From Colony to Superpower*: 319.

50 Ibid., 299–309, quotation on p. 304.

51 *Congressional Record*, Senate, 56th Cong., 1st sess. (9 January 1900): 704.

52 For a take on the ideology behind anti-imperialism, see Robert L. Beisner, *Twelve Against*

Empire: The Anti-Imperialists, 1898–1900 (New York: McGraw Hill Book Company, 1968).

For a comprehensive look at the intersection of race, immigration, and empire, see Matthew Frye Jacobson, *Barbarian Virtues: The United States Encounters Foreign Peoples at Home and Abroad, 1876–1917* (New York: Hill and Wang, 2000).

Jacobson, *Barbarian Virtues*: 234.

Congressional Record, House, 55th Cong., 2nd sess. (11 June 1898): 5787.

Ibid., 5789.

Ibid., 5790.

Ibid., 5792. For a similar Clark quote, see "House Scene Recalls Champ Clark's Vision," 28 February 1908, *Detroit Free Press*: 2.

Congressional Record, Senate, 56th Cong., 1st sess. (9 January 1900): 705, 708; Peter W. Stanley, *A Nation in the Making: The Philippines and the United States, 1899–1921* (Cambridge, MA: Harvard University Press, 1974): 164.

Congressional Record, Senate, 56th Cong., 1st sess. (9 January 1900): 711.

Karnow, *In Our Image*: 173–174.

Jacobson, *Barbarian Virtues*: 261.

Report of the Philippine Commission to the President, vol. 1, 56th Cong., 1st sess., S. Doc. 138 (1900): 15; *The World Almanac and Book of Facts, 2015* (New York: World Almanac Books, 2014): 824.

Karnow, *In Our Image*: 102–105, 110–115.

H. Wayne Morgan, *William McKinley and His America*, rev. ed. (Kent, OH: Kent State University Press, 2003): 305.

H. W. Brands, *Bound to Empire: The United States and the Philippines* (New York: Oxford University Press, 1992): 24–25; Gould, *The Presidency of William McKinley*: 140.

For general discussions of American imperialism, see Ernest R. May, *American Imperialism: A Speculative Essay* (1968, repr., Chicago, IL: Imprint Publications, 1991) and Beisner, *Twelve Against Empire*. See also David Healy, *U.S. Expansionism: The Imperialist Urge in the 1890s* (Madison: University of Wisconsin Press, 1970); Robert L. Beisner, *From the Old Diplomacy to the New, 1865–1900* (New York: Crowell, 1975): 139–140; Gould, *Presidency of William McKinley*: 146, 150.

Stanley, *A Nation in the Making*: 47–51. On the war between the Philippines and the U.S., see Brian McAllister Linn, *The Philippine War, 1899–1902* (Lawrence: University Press of Kansas, 2000).

Brands, *Bound to Empire*: 51.

Stanley, *A Nation in the Making*: 55; Brands, *Bound to Empire*: 50, 51, 53, 60.

"The Philippine-American War, 1899–1902," Office of the Historian, U.S. Department of State, accessed 6 July 2016, https://history.state.gov/milestones/1899-1913/war; Michael Cullinane, *Ilustrado Politics: Filipino Elite Responses to American Rule, 1898–1908* (Quezon City, PI: Ateneo de Manila University Press, 2003): 52. For an interpretation of the Philippine-American War as a race war, see Paul A. Kramer, *The Blood of Government: Race, Empire, the United States, & the Philippines* (Chapel Hill: The University of North Carolina Press, 2006): 87–158. On torture, see Richard E. Welch Jr., "American Atrocities in the Philippines: The Indictment and the Response," *Pacific Historical Review* 43, no. 2 (May 1974): 233–253.

David J. Silbey, *A War of Frontier and Empire: The Philippine-American War, 1899–1902* (New York: Hill and Wang, 2007): xi–xvi, 207–218, quotation on p. xiv–xv.

Report of the Philippine Commission to the President, vol. 1: 113. See also Gould, *Presidency of William McKinley*: 185; Stanley, *A Nation in the Making*: 59; Brands, *Bound to Empire*: 54.

Julius W. Pratt, *America's Colonial Experiment: How the United States Gained, Governed, and in Part Gave Away a Colonial Empire* (New York: Prentice-Hall, 1950): 196–197; Stanley, *A Nation in the Making*: 61. Dean Worcester, a member of the first commission, agreed to serve on the second. Bernard Moses of the University of California, Henry Ide who served as U.S. magistrate in Samoa, and Luke Wright who had been attorney general for Tennessee filled out the commission's membership. See Stanley, *A Nation in the Making*: 62–63; Karnow, *In Our Image*: 168–169; Gould, *Presidency of William McKinley*: 186.

75 Frank Hindman Golay, *Face of Empire: United States-Philippine Relations, 1898–1946* (Madison, WI: Center for Southeast Asian Studies, 1998): 67.

76 Stanley, *A Nation in the Making*: 63–64. Through an oversight in the commission's instructions, Taft would not become governor general until July 4, 1901, when the military government was finally disbanded. See Karnow, *In Our Image*: 173; Lewis E. Gleeck Jr., *The American Governors-General and High Commissioners in the Philippines: Proconsuls, Nation-Builders, and Politicians* (Quezon City, PI: New Day Publishers, 1986): 22.

77 Stanley, *A Nation in the Making*: 76–77. There were a handful of changes to Taft's plan, including the decision to limit the commission's ability to approve long-term economic policies. See *Congressional Record*, Senate, 56th Cong., 2nd sess. (8 February 1901): 2117; Gould, *Presidency of William McKinley*: 235; Stathis, *Landmark Legislation*: 149; Golay, *Face of Empire*: 73–74; Stanley, *A Nation in the Making*: 88; William McKinley, "Message to Congress," 25 January 1901, in *American Presidency Project*, ed. John T. Woolley and Gerhard Peters, http://www.presidency.ucsb.edu/ws/?pid=668 (accessed 17 May 2016).

78 Cullinane, *Ilustrado Politics*: 1–2. See also Stanley, *A Nation in the Making*: 67.

79 Stanley, *A Nation in the Making*: 69, 72.

80 Cullinane, *Ilustrado Politics*: 52.

81 Ibid., 54.

82 Stanley, *A Nation in the Making*: 67. For more on this policy, see Kramer, *The Blood of Government*: 171–177.

83 For more on the creation of the Partido Federal and their growing influence, see Cullinane, *Ilustrado Politics*: 58, 66–72; Stanley, *A Nation in the Making*: 72–73; Golay, *Face of Empire*: 76.

84 Stanley, *A Nation in the Making*: 79, 82–99; Golay, *Face of Empire*: 76. For an in-depth look at the Philippine commission as a legislative body, see Celestina P. Boncan, "The Philippine Commission, 1900–1916," in *Philippine Legislature: 100 Years*, ed. Cesar P. Pobre (Quezon City, PI: Philippine Historical Association with New Day Publishers, 2000): 27–62.

85 Stanley, *A Nation in the Making*: 77.

86 Philippine Organic Act, Public Law 57-235, 32 Stat. 691 (1902); Brands, *Bound to Empire*: 99; Golay, *Face of Empire*: 85–87; Kramer, *The Blood of Government*: 162–166.

87 Hearings before the House Committee on Insular Affairs, *Statement of Conditions in the Philippines, by Hon. William H. Taft*, 57th Cong., 1st sess. (26 February 1902): 43–44.

88 Stanley, *A Nation in the Making*: 116.

89 According to the historian Peter W. Stanley, although the two major parties, the Nacionalistas and the Progresistas, disagreed on the timing of independence, they agreed on many other issues, including the need for more local autonomy, a greater Filipino presence in the government, tax reform, and new investments in agriculture and education. See Stanley, *A Nation in the Making*: 128–129. See also Celestina P. Boncan, "The Philippine Assembly, 1907–1916," in *Philippine Legislature: 100 Years*, ed. Cesar P. Pobre (Quezon City, PI: Philippine Historical Association with New Day Publishers, 2000): 65–66.

90 Boncan, "The Philippine Assembly, 1907–1916": 67.

91 For more on the *ilustrados*, see Cullinane, *Ilustrado Politics*.

92 After serving as Resident Commissioner, Manuel L. Quezon won election as the Philippine senate's first president.

93 Abraham Holtzman, "Empire and Representation: The U.S. Congress," *Legislative Studies Quarterly* 11, no. 2 (May 1986): 249–273. A statistically small but numerically consequential group, statutory representatives have constituted more than 1 percent of all House Members. From 1789 to 2016, 176 individuals have represented territories or insular possessions in the House (144 Delegates and 32 Resident Commissioners from Puerto Rico and the Philippines). See Office of the Historian, U.S. House of Representatives, "Total Members of the House & State Representation," http://history.house.gov/Institution/Seniority/Total-

Members/Total-Members/. For the development of the office of Delegate from a procedural perspective, see Chapter 43 of *Hinds' Precedents of the House of Representatives*, vol. 2 (Washington, DC: Government Printing Office, 1907): 861–868.

94 Stanley, *Nation in the Making*: 168–169; Philippine Assembly, *Election of Resident Commissioners to the United States*, Second Legislature, First Session, 1911, Document 250—A.38 (Manila, PI: Bureau of Printing, 1911), https://archive.org/details/aqw4348.0001.001. umich.edu (accessed 10 February 2016); *Congressional Record*, House, 61st Cong., 3rd sess. (6 February 1911): 2022–2024; Public Law 61-376, 36 Stat. 910 (1911). Congress applied a legal resolution to the Resident Commissioner dispute via Article IV, Section 3, §2, which gives Congress complete legislative authority over any U.S. territory.

95 Thomas F. Millard, "The Men Who Have Come to Washington to Represent the Filipinos," 2 February 1908, *Washington Post*: SM4.

96 *Congressional Record*, House, 61st Cong., 1st sess. (3 April 1909): 929–930; Stanley, *A Nation in the Making*: 151.

97 "'We Will Do Our Duty,' Says Legarda" 20 December 1907, *Manila Times*: 9.

98 Stanley, *A Nation in the Making*: 170.

99 *Congressional Directory*, 61st Cong., 2nd sess., 2nd ed. (Washington, DC: Government Printing Office, 1910): 240–241; *Congressional Directory*, 62nd Cong., 1st sess. (Washington, DC: Government Printing Office, 1911): 220–221.

100 "House Scene Recalls Champ Clark's Vision."

101 Stanley, *A Nation in the Making*: 182.

102 Ibid., 30, 33.

103 The governor's three-point plan to rejuvenate the territory's business sector called for new roads and commercial hubs, a large infusion of U.S. funding into the agricultural and natural resources industries, and targeted tariffs to generate trade. See Karnow, *In Our Image*: 209–210.

104 Kermit L. Hall, "The Courts, 1790–1920," in *The Cambridge History of Law in America*, vol. 2, *The Long Nineteenth Century (1790–1920)*, ed. Michael Grossberg and Christopher Tomlins (New York: Cambridge University Press, 2008): 131; Lewis L. Gould, *William Howard Taft Presidency* (Lawrence: University Press of Kansas, 2009): 51–57.

105 Paolo E. Coletta, *The Presidency of William Howard Taft* (Lawrence: University Press of Kansas, 1973): 56.

106 Taft said as much in a 1903 speech in Manila. See Golay, *Face of Empire*: 96; Brands, *Bound to Empire*: 98.

107 *Journal of the Philippine Commission*, inaugural session, vol. 1 (Manila, PI: Manila Bureau of Printing, 1908): 361–362, www.hathitrust.org (accessed 18 February 2016).

108 Stanley, *A Nation in the Making*: 148; Chamberlain, *President, Congress and Legislation*: 103; *Congressional Record*, House, 61st Cong., 1st sess. (3 April 1909): 929–930.

109 House Committee on Ways and Means, *Duties on Philippine Products Imported into the United States*, 59th Cong., 1st sess., H. Rept. 20 (1905): 1, 3. See also, Thomas F. Millard, "Philippines Not a 'Problem' Nor a 'Burden,'" 23 February 1908, *New York Times Magazine*: 2; Thomas F. Millard, "Our Interests and Our Duty in the Philippine Islands," 23 February 1908, *Washington Post Magazine*: 4; Thomas F. Millard, "Congress Holds the Key," 23 February 1908, *Chicago Daily Tribune*: A1.

110 "A Filipino Heard," 3 April 1909, *New York Tribune*: 2; "Test Vote Monday," 3 April 1909, *Washington Post*: 1; "House Debate Goes On," 4 April 1909, *New York Times*: 2; *Congressional Record*, House, 61st Cong., 1st sess. (3 April 1909): 929–930.

111 William H. Taft, "Special Message," 14 April 1909, in *American Presidency Project*, ed. John T. Woolley and Gerhard Peters, http://www.presidency.ucsb.edu/ws/?pid=68503 (accessed 18 May 2016); *Congressional Record*, House, 61st Cong., 1st sess. (15 April 1909): 1365; "New Philippine Tariff," 16 April 1909, *New York Tribune*: 2; *Congressional Record*, House, 61st Cong., 1st sess. (13 May 1909): 1998; Hearing before the House Committee on Ways and Means, *Philippine Tariff Bill*, 61st Cong., 1st sess. (20 April 1909): 17, 32.

112 *Congressional Record*, House, 61st Cong., 1st sess. (24 May 1909): 2338; "Philippine Tariff in Senate," 26 May 1909, *Wall Street Journal*: 6; "Philippine Tariff Bill Favored," 2 July 1909, *New York Tribune*: 3; *Congressional Record*, Senate, 61st Cong., 1st sess. (9 July 1909): 4337; "Passed Philippine Bill," 10 July 1909, *Baltimore Sun*: 2; "Island Bills Passed," 10 July 1909, *Washington Post*: 4; "Senate Fixes Insular Tariff," 10 July 1909, *Chicago Daily Tribune*: 1.

113 "House Completes the Philippine Tariff Bill," 3 August 1909, *San Francisco Chronicle*: 2; "Pass Philippine Bill," 3 August 1909, *Washington Post*: 1; Public Law 61-5, 36 Stat. 11 (1909).

114 Pedro E. Abelarde, *American Tariff Policy towards The Philippines* (New York: King's Crown Press, 1947): 114–124, 127, 202.

115 Ibid., 128; Jones–Costigan Act, Public Law 73-213, 48 Stat. 670 (1934); Appendix I: Constitutional Amendments, Treaties, Executive Orders, and Major Acts of Congress Referenced in the Text.

116 Abelarde, *American Tariff Policy towards the Philippines*: 131.

117 Brands, *Bound to Empire*: 98; Abelarde, *American Tariff Policy towards the Philippines*: 135.

118 Abelarde, *American Tariff Policy towards the Philippines*: 201–202.

119 Pratt, *America's Colonial Experiment*: 203; Stanley, *A Nation in the Making*: 172; Brands, *Bound to Empire*: vi.

120 A separate resolution introduced by Jones required the world powers to agree to stay out of Philippine affairs while the Manila government found its footing. Stanley, *A Nation in the Making*: 172–173; "Committee Head Steals Cline's Glory as Future Emancipator of Filipinos," 31 March 1912, *Indianapolis Star*: B11; "To Free Filipinos Eight Years Hence," 21 March 1912, *New York Times*: 1; "Filipino Bill In," 22 March 1912, *New York Times*: 3; "Nations May Pledge Filipinos Freedom," 26 March 1912, *New York Times*: 8.

121 Stanley, *A Nation in the Making*: 179, 212–213.

122 Ibid., 180, 212–213.

123 The briefing memo was included in a letter from the Secretary of War to the President. Lindley Miller Garrison to Woodrow Wilson, 19 January 1914, in *The Papers of Woodrow Wilson*, vol. 29, ed. Arthur Link (Princeton, NJ: Princeton University Press, 1979): 147–152. See also Stanley, *A Nation in the Making*: 213–214, quotation on p. 213. The President also met with Chairman Jones to discuss the situation in February that year. See, "Wilson Takes Up Philippines," 12 February 1914, *Baltimore Sun*: 2.

124 Stanley, *A Nation in the Making*: 213–215; Garrison to Wilson, 19 January 1914, in *The Papers of Woodrow Wilson*, vol. 29: 149; "'Watchful Waiting,' His Policy," 12 February 1914, *Washington Post*: 3; "Philippine Bill Offers Independence," 4 June 1914, *Christian Science Monitor*: 7; "Early Independence of Philippines Urged," 21 August 1914, *Indianapolis Star*: 16; "Step to Free Islands," 21 August 1914, *Washington Post*: 3.

125 *Congressional Record*, House, 63rd Cong., 2nd sess. (1 October 1914): 16019. For additional context on the debate, see "To Give Filipinos Self-Government," 4 June 1914, *New York Times*: 5; "Philippines Must Wait For Freedom," 5 June 1914, *New York Tribune*: 4; "A New Philippines Plan," 5 June 1914, *New York Times*: 10; Stanley, *A Nation in the Making*: 215, 220; "To Free Filipinos," 4 June 1914, *Los Angeles Times*: I1; "New Wilson Bill To Free Filipinos," 4 June 1914, *New York Tribune*: 1; *Congressional Record*, House, 63rd Cong., 2nd sess. (26 September 1914): 15800–15812.

126 Stanley, *A Nation in the Making*: 219.

127 Senate Committee on the Philippines, *Future Political Status of the People of the Philippine Islands*, 64th Cong., 1st sess., S. Rept. 18 (1915): 1, 3; Hearings before the Senate Committee on the Philippines, S. *381: Government of the Philippines*, 64th Cong., 1st sess. (1915): 71.

128 Stanley, *A Nation in the Making*: 221; House Committee on Insular Affairs, *Political Status of the Philippine Islands*, 64th Cong., 1st sess., H. Rept. 499 (1916): 1.

129 Stanley, *A Nation in the Making*: 223–224; "Will Keep Philippines," 2 May 1916, *Washington Post*: 1; *Congressional Record*, House, 64th Cong., 1st sess. (1 May 1916): 7144–7214; "No Independence for Philippines," 2 May 1916, *Atlanta Constitution*: 2.

130 "Will Keep Philippines"; "No Independence for Philippines."

131 "Senators Yield on Philippines," 9 May 1916, *New York Tribune*: 6; "Senate Hedges on Philippines," 17 August 1916, *New York Tribune*: 2; "See Filipinos Free by 1921," 26 August 1916, *New York Tribune*: 4; Public Law 64-240, 39 Stat. 545 (1916).

132 Stanley, *A Nation in the Making*: 251–258. See, for example, Randolph C. Downes, *The Rise of Warren Gamaliel Harding, 1865–1920* (Columbus: Ohio State University Press, 1970): 235–238.

133 Woodrow Wilson, "Eighth Annual Message," 7 December 1920, in *American Presidency Project*, ed. John T. Woolley and Gerhard Peters, http://www.presidency.ucsb.edu/ws/index.php?pid=29561 (accessed 15 January 2016). See also Jaime C. de Veyra, "The Philippine Problem: The Truth about the Philippines," 5 March 1921, *The Independent*: 12–14.

134 Bernardita Reyes Churchill, *Philippine Independence Missions to the United States, 1919–1934* (Manila, PI: National Historical Institute, 1983): 27.

135 "Policy in Philippines Waits on Wood's Report," 15 March 1921, *New York Tribune*: 4; "Harding Sees Filipinos," 15 March 1921, *New York Times*: 10. For more on Wood, see Jack C. Lane, "Leonard Wood," *American National Biography*, vol. 23 (New York: Oxford University Press, 1999): 767–768.

136 *Condition in the Philippine Islands*: *Report of the Special Mission to the Philippine Islands to the Secretary of War*, 67th Cong., 2nd sess., H. Doc. 325 (1922): 10–12.

137 *Condition in the Philippine Islands*: 45–46. Leonard Wood was especially critical of the territorial government, condemning it for a "lack of competent supervision and inspection." See David F. Schmitz, *Henry L. Stimson: The First Wise Man* (Wilmington, DE: SR Books, 2001): 63.

138 *Congressional Record*, House, 67th Cong., 2nd sess. (20 January 1922): 1483–1487, quotation on p. 1484; "Commissioner Attacks Report on Philippines," 21 January 1922, *Washington Post*: 10; "Criticize Philippine Report," 2 December 1921, *Washington Post*: 6.

139 Brands, *Bound to Empire*: 133.

140 Churchill, *Philippine Independence Missions to the United States*: 70–80, 87. The bills are: H.R. 2817, 68th Cong. (1923); H.R. 3924, 68th Cong. (1923); H.J. Res. 127, 68th Cong. (1924); H.J. Res 131, 68th Cong. (1924); S. 912, 68th Cong. (1923); and S. Res. 35, 68th Cong. (1923).

141 Coordinated largely by the American Chamber Commerce of the Philippines, the press campaign called on Congress to pass legislation that would ensure the United States retained the islands. From November 1924 to January 1925, the *Washington Post* published a series by Katherine Mayo called "Isles of Fear." Her crude stereotypes depicted Filipinos as lazy, irresponsible, and intellectually incapable of managing a modern nation-state. Retentionists, including the *Post* editorial board, praised Mayo's work. Resident Commissioners Guevara and Gabaldon, on the other hand, lambasted Mayo in a response published in the *Post*. During a speech in New York City, Guevara said Mayo's work was nothing more than a self-interested "campaign of misrepresentation." See Churchill, *Philippine Independence Missions to the United States*: 122–124; "'Isles of Fear' to Present Truth About Philippines," 28 November 1924, *Washington Post*: 10. The articles were compiled into a single volume, Katherine Mayo, *The Isles of Fear: The Truth About the Philippines* (New York: Harcourt, Brace, and Company: 1925). For biographical information about Mayo, see "Katherine Mayo, Writer, Is Dead," 10 October 1940, *New York Times*: 25. For the *Post's* supportive editorials, see "Conditions in the Philippines," 7 December 1924, *Washington Post*: EF1; "Vetoing Seditious Propaganda," 11 December 1924, *Washington Post*: 6; "The Philippines As They Are," 24 January 1925, *Washington Post*: 6. Gabaldon also described the connection between Mayo and the American Chamber of Commerce of the Philippines in his final remarks to the House. See *Congressional Record*, House, 70th Cong., 1st sess. (3 March 1928): 4016; *Congressional Record*, House, 68th Cong., 2nd sess. (3 March 1925): 5348–5350. Gabaldon's remarks about the Mayo articles are in *Congressional Record*, House, 68th Cong., 2nd sess. (3 January 1925): 1167–1173.

142 Karnow, *In Our Image*: 252–253.

143 Theodore Friend, *Between Two Empires: The Ordeal of the Philippines, 1929–1946* (New Haven, CT: Yale University Press, 1965): 90; "House Votes to Free Philippines in 1940; Stimson Is Opposed," 5 April 1932, *New York Times*: 1; *Congressional Record*, House, 72nd Cong., 1st sess. (4 April 1932): 7401–7412.

144 *Congressional Record*, House, 72nd Cong., 1st sess. (4 April 1932): 7410; Friend, *Between Two Empires*: 96. For House debate, see *Congressional Record*, House, 72nd Cong., 2nd sess. (29 December 1932): 1075–1095.

145 For the remarks by the Resident Commissioners on the veto override, see *Congressional Record*, House, 72nd Cong., 2nd sess. (13 January 1933): 1764, 1769. See also Friend, *Between Two Empires*: 106–108; "Hail Defeat of Veto: Filipino Commissioners Call Independence Grant Unprecedented," 18 January 1933, *New York Times*: 2; Philippine Independence Act, Public Law 72-311, 47 Stat. 761 (1933).

146 Friend, *Between Two Empires*: 129–132; Karnow, *In Our Image*: 254.

147 "Filipinos in Dispute on Independence," 26 December 1933, *New York Times*: 5; "Filipino Leaders to Ignore Osias," 27 December 1933, *New York Times*: 8.

148 President Roosevelt's special message was reprinted in *Congressional Record*, House, 73rd Cong., 2nd sess. (2 March 1934): 3580–3581.

149 Philippine Independence Act, Public Law 73-127, 48 Stat. 456 (1934); *Congressional Record*, House, 73rd Cong., 2nd sess. (19 March 1934): 4225, 4831, 4842; *Congressional Record*, Senate, 73rd Cong., 2nd sess. (20 March 1934): 4921, 5164; Public Law 73-127, 48 Stat. 456 (1934); Golay, *Face of Empire*: 320–327, 343.

150 Erwin D. Canham, "New Philippines Delegate Finds Problems Facing Him," 13 February 1936, *Christian Science Monitor*: 1. On the High Commissioner, see Vincente Albano Pacis, "Americans Leaving Islands to the Natives," 27 October 1934, *Washington Post*: 9; Robert Aura Smith, "Path of Basic Law Eased by Filipinos," 24 June 1934, *New York Times*: E8.

151 Brands, *Bound to Empire*: 170; Golay, *Face of Empire*: 360, 362–364; Friend, *Between Two Empires*: 157–158.

152 *Congressional Record*, House, 76th Cong., 1st sess. (26 January 1939): 859; *Congressional Record*, Senate, 76th Cong., 1st sess. (26 January 1939): 810; Golay, *Face of Empire*: 377; Friend, *Between Two Empires*: 158.

153 Public Law 76-30, 53 Stat. 1226 (1939); Golay, *Face of Empire*: 378–379; *Congressional Record*, House, 76th Cong., 1st sess. (10 July 1939): 8798; Friend, *Between Two Empires*: 159.

154 Friend, *Between Two Empires*: 159.

155 See Nationality Act of 1940, Public Law 76-853, 54 Stat. 1137 (1940). *Congressional Record*, House, 76th Cong., 3rd sess. (3 June 1940): 7433; *Congressional Record*, House, 76th Cong., 3rd sess. (11 September 1940): 11952; Veta R. Schlimgen, "Neither Citizens nor Aliens: Filipino 'American Nationals' in the U.S. Empire, 1900–1946" (PhD diss., University of Oregon, 2010): 450.

156 Schlimgen, "Neither Citizens nor Aliens": 450.

157 Louis Morton, *The Fall of the Philippines* (Washington, DC: Center of Military History, 1953): 77–84; Karnow, *In Our Image*: 288–290; Brands, *Bound to Empire*: 190.

158 Brands, *Bound to Empire*: 185; Michael A. Barnhart, *Japan Prepares for Total War: The Search for Economic Security, 1919–1941* (Ithaca, NY: Cornell University Press, 1987); Golay, *Face of Empire*: 404–405; Brands, *Bound to Empire*: 186, 188.

159 Golay, *Face of Empire*: 407; Brands, *Bound to Empire*: 190, 195; Karnow, *In Our Image*: 291–292, 295; Morton, *The Fall of the Philippines*: 90–92, 138–144.

160 Brands, *Bound to Empire*: 193–194, 195.

161 Karnow, *In Our Image*: 297–305; Brands, *Bound to Empire*: 197; Golay, *Face of Empire*: 417–418.

162 Golay, *Face of Empire*: 421, 424–428; Brands, *Bound to Empire*: 212–214.

163 Brands, *Bound to Empire*: 199, 201.

164 Golay, *Face of Empire*: 422, 438; Friend, *Between Two Empires*: 213–214; Brands, *Bound to Empire*: 198, 201–202; Karnow, *In Our Image*: 307.

165 Karnow, *In Our Image*: 312–313; Brands, *Bound to Empire*: 206; David M. Kennedy, *Freedom from Fear: The American People in Depression and War, 1929–1945* (New York: Oxford University Press, 1999): 821.

166 Brands, *Bound to Empire*: 209–210; Karnow, *In Our Image*: 313–314, 320–322.

Party Divisions in the House of Representatives
56th–84th Congresses (1899–1957)*

DEMOCRATS · **REPUBLICANS** · **OTHER**

NUMBER OF MEMBERS

340 320 300 280 260 240 220 200 180 160 140 120 100 80 60 40 20 0

56th (1899–1901)
57th (1901–1903)
58th (1903–1905)
59th (1905–1907)
60th (1907–1909)
61st (1909–1911)
62nd (1911–1913)
63rd (1913–1915)
64th (1915–1917)
65th (1917–1919)
66th (1919–1921)
67th (1921–1923)
68th (1923–1925)
69th (1925–1927)
70th (1927–1929)
71st (1929–1931)
72nd (1931–1933)
73rd (1933–1935)
74th (1935–1937)
75th (1937–1939)
76th (1939–1941)
77th (1941–1943)
78th (1943–1945)
79th (1945–1947)
80th (1947–1949)
81st (1949–1951)
82nd (1951–1953)
83rd (1953–1955)
84th (1955–1957)

Source: Office of the Historian, U.S. House of Representatives, "Party Divisions," http://history.house.gov.

*Party division totals are based on Election Day results.

Asian and Pacific Islander American Members by Office

First Elected 1900–1955

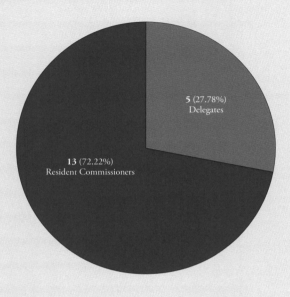

Asian and Pacific Islander American Members by State and Territory

First Elected 1900–1955

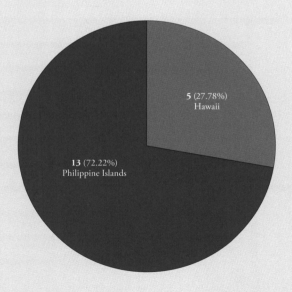

Sources: Appendix A: Asian and Pacific Islander American Representatives, Senators, Delegates, and Resident Commissioners by Congress, 1900–2017; Office of the Historian, U.S. House of Representatives; U.S. Senate Historical Office.

Congressional Service

For Asian and Pacific Islander Americans in Congress First Elected 1900–1955

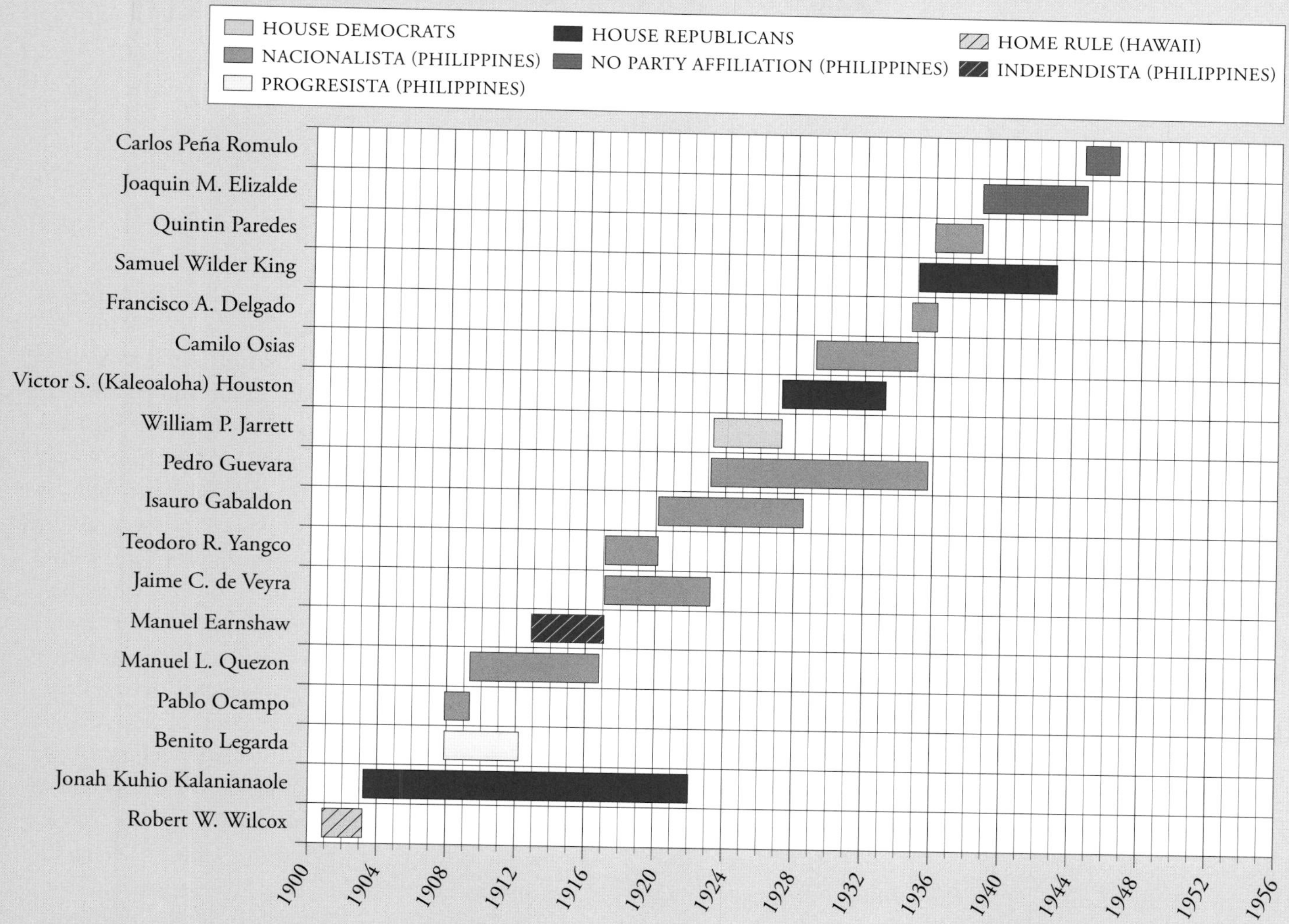

HOUSE DEMOCRATS
NACIONALISTA (PHILIPPINES)
PROGRESISTA (PHILIPPINES)
HOUSE REPUBLICANS
NO PARTY AFFILIATION (PHILIPPINES)
HOME RULE (HAWAII)
INDEPENDISTA (PHILIPPINES)
Carlos Peña Romulo
Joaquin M. Elizalde
Quintin Paredes
Samuel Wilder King
Francisco A. Delgado
Camilo Osias
Victor S. (Kaleoaloha) Houston
William P. Jarrett
Pedro Guevara
Isauro Gabaldon
Teodoro R. Yangco
Jaime C. de Veyra
Manuel Earnshaw
Manuel L. Quezon
Pablo Ocampo
Benito Legarda
Jonah Kuhio Kalanianaole
Robert W. Wilcox
1900
1904
1908
1912
1916
1920
1924
1928
1932
1936
1940
1944
1948
1952
1956

Robert W. Wilcox
1855–1903

DELEGATE 1900–1903
HOME RULE FROM HAWAII

An insurrectionist who fought to restore the Hawaiian monarchy, and who was sentenced to death for treason, Robert W. Wilcox eventually organized a potent home-rule movement, won election as the new territory's first Delegate, and became the first Asian Pacific American elected to Congress. A symbolic figure who embodied the complexities of managing the United States' growing empire in the Pacific, Wilcox exercised limited influence on Capitol Hill. His focus on territorial politics, devotion to Native-Hawaiian concerns, and strong preference for Hawaiian independence were all hallmarks of his brief U.S. House career.

Robert William Wilcox was born in Kahalu, Honuaula, on the island of Maui, in the Kingdom of Hawaii, on February 15, 1855. His parents were William S. Wilcox, an American sea captain, and Kalua Makoleokalani, said to be a direct descendant of Lonomakaihonua, brother to King Kaulahea of Maui. His mother died when Wilcox was 10 years old, about the time his father became a rancher at Makawao, Maui. He attended the Haleakala Boarding School in Makawao before attending school in Wailuku, Maui. He taught school in Honuaula.[1]

Wilcox was elected to represent Maui in the Hawaiian legislature in 1880. In 1881 a legislature-sponsored program, Education of Hawaiian Youths Abroad, selected Wilcox as one of its beneficiaries and allowed him to continue his education. He was assigned to the Royal Military School in Turin, Italy, for military training, graduating in 1885 as a sublieutenant of artillery. Wilcox then attended the Royal Application School for Engineer and Artillery Officers, also in Turin. While attending these military institutes, Wilcox married Gina Sobrero of the House of Colonna di Stigliano. Unrest in Hawaii in 1887, the bloodless Bayonet Revolution in which *haoles*—white, often wealthy landholders—usurped power from the

monarchy, led the government to recall its Education of Hawaiian Youths Abroad students.[2]

Upon his return to Hawaii, Wilcox found that, under the new status quo, no elected position and no army existed for him to serve in, and this experience fueled his anger and prejudice against the islands' white elites. With the monarchy's authority severely limited and Wilcox's former mentors out of power, there was no direct route to power for the ambitious politician. Wilcox and his wife moved to San Francisco, California, where he was a surveyor, and his wife grudgingly taught French and Italian. The couple had a daughter, Victoria, but the marriage was an increasingly unhappy one. Wilcox returned to Hawaii alone in 1889, and his wife returned to Italy with their child shortly thereafter, requesting an annulment of their marriage. Tragically, Victoria died en route to Italy.[3] In 1896 Wilcox married Princess Teresa Owana Kaohelelani, a distant descendant of Keona, the father of Kamehameha the Great. The couple had five children, Teresa Owana Kaohelelani, Robert, Virginia, Gideon, and Elizabeth; the latter two died as infants.[4]

Upon arriving in Honolulu in April 1889, Wilcox set himself up as a civil engineer and surveyor for hire. In mid-May, he hosted a meeting that resulted in the founding of the Kamehameha Rifle Association, an organization determined to undertake a hostile overturn of the Hawaiian government. Soon after, Wilcox founded the Liberal Patriotic Association, designed as the political arm of the revolt. The rebels plotted either to force King Kalakaua to sign a new constitution restoring monarchical power or to supplant him with his sister Liliuokalani with the same end in mind. Plans developed swiftly, and in the predawn hours of July 30 Wilcox led nearly 150 men to the palace as a display of force. The Royal Guard locked themselves in the palace and refused Wilcox an audience with the king, who

had fled to safety. Wilcox stubbornly refused to abandon his plan and stationed his men in a bungalow on the grounds until bombardment from government soldiers forced their surrender in the late afternoon.[5]

Members of the reform government decried the destructive activities of "two or three men, on whom this Government has spent some twenty thousand dollars to give them a foreign military education—for what?"[6] Wilcox was charged with treason, but the law dictated that he be judged by a jury of his peers of Native or part Hawaiians. Knowing no Hawaiian jury would convict him, the reform cabinet met with Wilcox's attorney to suggest he plead guilty to conspiracy and serve one year in prison, but Wilcox, embittered at his failed revolt and news of his infant daughter's recent death, refused that concession. Reluctantly, the government dropped the treason charge and tried Wilcox only for conspiracy. After two juries heard the case, Wilcox was found innocent and released, and became a native hero.

A few months out of jail, Wilcox embraced his newfound status and recognition. Along with political leader John E. Bush, Wilcox helped two of the opposition groups on the islands unite to form a new political party, the National Reform Party, a more moderate opposition party calling for democratic reforms and a return of some administrative duties to the monarchy. In 1890 Wilcox won election to represent Honolulu in the Hawaiian legislature. He won re-election in 1892.[7]

Wilcox and others who had grown impatient with the new queen, Liliuokalani, formed an alliance informally called the Equal Rights League, which favored annexation and the abolition of the monarchy coupled with empowerment of Native Hawaiians in politics. Their unstated goal was the removal of *haole* politicians from places of power in the government.[8] For participation in that scheme, Wilcox and other group leaders were briefly jailed.

But Wilcox changed his tack again. In the revolution of 1893, pro-annexationist forces overthrew Queen Liliuokalani. Wilcox worked for a short time with the new provisional government under Sanford B. Dole but eventually broke with it when he did not receive a

political appointment. Two years later, Wilcox joined a counterrevolution when it became apparent to him that the majority of Native Hawaiians supported the restoration of the monarchy under Liliuokalani. He joined the plot late as its commander in January 1895, but the effort was repulsed. Wilcox and the conspirators were rounded up, court-martialed, and sentenced to death.[9] President Dole offered a conditional pardon in 1896, commuting the sentence to several decades of hard labor and a hefty fine; in 1898 Dole granted a full pardon.[10]

Shortly after the United States annexed Hawaii, the Hawaiian Organic Act went into effect in mid-June 1900, ensuring time enough to hold elections in the fall for the territorial senate (15 members), the territorial house of representatives (30 members), and the Territorial Delegate to Congress. Its greatest immediate effect was the re-expanded suffrage to the Native Hawaiian population, most of which had been disenfranchised under the republic.[11] In preparation for the elections, the native patriotic leagues, Hui Aloha ʻĀina and the Hui Kalai ʻĀina, rallied behind the slogans of "Hawaiʻi for the Hawaiians" and "Equal Rights for the People" and merged into the Hawaiian Independent Party (HIP). At the same time, the *haole* population divided itself between the two mainland political parties, Republicans and Democrats.[12]

As the Organic Act went into effect, HIP nominated its slate of candidates, all Native Hawaiians, for the territorial offices. Wilcox headed the ticket as the nominee for Territorial Delegate and began campaigning on Oahu. Because the two major local newspapers, the *Pacific Commercial Advertiser* and the *Hawaiian Gazette*, criticized the convention establishing HIP as anti-white and radical, Wilcox distanced himself from those candidates who conducted anti-*haole* campaigns.[13] The other two parties chose not to nominate their candidates until the end of summer. The Republicans chose "the cowboy from Waimea," Sam Parker, as their nominee for Territorial Delegate. Parker, who served with Theodore Roosevelt in Cuba during his Rough Rider days, ran a well-funded campaign that promised to use Parker's pull with the new President to the territory's advantage.[14] The

Democrats hoped to capitalize on the newly enfranchised Native Hawaiian vote by nominating in October Prince David Kawananakoa.[15]

When rumors circulated that Wilcox intended to withdraw his candidacy in favor of the prince, one of the founders of HIP, George Markham, switched to the Republican Party, charging Wilcox had been bribed by the Democrats.[16] In response to these machinations, Wilcox's rhetoric became harsher. He promised that, as Delegate, he would work to have Sanford Dole removed as territorial governor. On the day before the election, Wilcox spoke at a rally by the ruins of the Kaumakapili Church. "This is the work of these stinking *haoles*," he said, pointing to the rubble. He predicted, "Tomorrow Wilcox will be a Napoleon and these other parties will be the Russians and Austrians who failed in their attempt to overwhelm him." Honolulu merchants plastered their newspapers with ads warning their employees against voting for Wilcox and his party.[17] On Election Day, November 6, Wilcox won both a term in the remaining months of the 56th Congress (1899–1901) and a full term in the 57th Congress (1901–1903), though the final results were not announced for two days. Wilcox won his seat in the 56th Congress with 4,083 votes to Parker's 3,856; Kawananakoa finished third with 1,650. Results for the full term in the 57th Congress were virtually identical: Wilcox with 4,108, Parker with 3,845, and Kawananakoa with 1,656.[18]

In mid-November 1900, HIP changed its name to the Independent Home Rule Party, though it was commonly known as the Home Rule Party (HRP) or, simply, Home Rulers. As a result, both Hui Aloha 'Āina and Hui Kalai 'Āina were permanently dissolved just before Wilcox set out for Washington, DC. "We are like little calves feeding from the mother cow," said party leader J. W. Kaulia at a farewell rally for Wilcox, "and America is the mother cow, and her milk constitutes all the benefits that are coming to us from her. We must let Americans know what we want, and she will let us have it."[19] On December 15, Wilcox was sworn in as the first Territorial Delegate from Hawaii at the start of the second session of the 56th Congress.[20]

Shortly after Wilcox's election, the *Hawaiian Star* reported on plans to contest his seating in the House. George D. Gear, leader of a Republican faction in Hawaii, organized a campaign founded on charges that the election proclamation was invalid and that Wilcox was unfit because he was a bigamist, alleging that Wilcox's 1895 divorce was not made final. By the time Wilcox was sworn in, Gear had mustered additional materials against him. He produced an 1899 Wilcox letter offering his services to Filipino rebel leader Emilio Aguinaldo and a letter from Celso C. Moreno, King Kalakaua's prime minister, denouncing Wilcox. The *Hawaiian Advertiser* criticized Gear's efforts to have Wilcox unseated.[21] The effort to challenge Wilcox's election received an initial hearing by the House in early February 1901 before being referred to the Committee on Elections. The Committee reported back to the House on the next-to-last day of the 56th Congress, dismissing the charges against Wilcox and letting his election stand.[22]

Wilcox participated in the House as best he could, but as with other Territorial Delegates, he was hampered by the lack of a vote. Wilcox's problems were amplified, too, by belonging to a political party that lacked any affiliation with either of the two national political parties. As some critics had predicted, this deprived him of the chance to participate in either of the party caucuses and develop working relationships.[23] "Thus, Wilcox remained throughout his Washington career a loner with little influence upon his congressional colleagues," noted his biographer. Several other factors were at play, too, including his dark complexion and prevailing discrimination toward people of color in that era. Most decisive, perhaps, was his halting English, which compromised his ability to effectively communicate on behalf of his constituency. As his biographer also conjectured, this likely made it "simply too difficult and embarrassing to buttonhole colleagues to try and secure their support."[24]

However, Wilcox did enjoy more privileges than other statutory representatives. Unlike the Resident Commissioners from the Philippines and Puerto Rico, he had immediate floor privileges and was entitled to address the House as a Member. But his grasp of spoken English, which in some transcripts was broken, may well have dissuaded him from speaking on the floor. The *Congressional Record* contains no speeches by him, not even inserted into the "Extensions of Remarks," and lists only one instance in which he participated in floor debate. Language barriers aside, he enjoyed the advantage of being able to serve on House committees. He arrived too late in the 56th Congress to be assigned to any panel. But at the opening of the 57th Congress in December 1901, he was assigned to the Private Land Claims Committee and the Committee on Coinage, Weights, and Measures.[25] These were middling assignments at best in terms of their influence and desirability, but they were relevant to several issues that mattered to him.

Unlike Resident Commissioners, Wilcox could introduce legislation. His major policy goal was to establish a homestead policy for Hawaii. This offered the chance for the *haole* estates to be redistributed to small Native Hawaiian farmers, a move that he and other Native Hawaiians saw as fundamentally egalitarian. Lands once under control of the Hawaiian monarchy, which had been seized by the provisional government and the oligarchs and now largely fell under federal oversight, might at least be returned to the people. Wilcox introduced H.R. 13906 on January 29, 1901, to achieve this goal. The bill called for the public land laws of the United States to be extended to the territory of Hawaii. It also empowered the Secretary of the Interior "to make rules and regulations for the entry of lands to be used for homestead purposes"; no land grant would exceed 100 acres.[26] The bill was referred to the Committee on Territories, where it died when the session concluded about a month later.[27]

Still Wilcox did not relinquish the goal of redistributing both federal land and plantation acreage to promote small-scale homesteading. At the opening of the 57th Congress, he introduced another measure, H.R. 3090, to provide for the classification of public lands ceded to the United States into four categories: urban/residential; land then under cultivation; land capable of being cultivated but unused

or uninhabited; and unusable lands, including reefs and small outlying islands. Of greatest interest were those in the second and third categories, with Wilcox pushing for timely surveys and distributions to homesteaders.[28] That bill also was dispatched to the Territories Committee, where it eventually died. When Wilcox testified before a congressional commission visiting Honolulu in the summer of 1902, he offered a laundry list of initiatives, although this bill was not on that list. He concluded by telling the commissioners, "My great idea is to get this land system so all the people—native, white, and every American citizen of this country [Hawaii]—can have land, and not as it is now, in the hands of a few men."[29]

Wilcox found himself drawn into considering legislation associated with converting Hawaii from an independent republic to a U.S. territory. For example, other Members turned to Wilcox as they considered the process of converting Hawaiian currency to that of the United States. "Our country being annexed to the United States," he told his colleagues, "we might as well have the same kind of dollars as the United States, rather than different dollars."[30] Wilcox may have been ambivalent because he saw the issue of retiring Hawaiian silver currency as affecting primarily financiers in Honolulu rather than his core constituents. This legislation, which had already passed the Senate, was amended by the House. But the Congress ended before any further action could be taken. At the opening of the 57th Congress in December 1901, Wilcox introduced H.R. 4343, a bill that retired Hawaiian coin currency.[31] A similar version of this legislation passed at the very end of that same Congress, though Wilcox, ill and a lame duck by that point, had ceased to advocate for it. The measure set out terms that placed each Hawaiian silver piece at face value on par with U.S. coins even though the Hawaiian coins were not minted at a silver weight ratio equal to U.S. coins. The federal government absorbed the cost difference.[32]

Wilcox also supported an effort to transfer over to the federal government administrative control of a community on the island of Molokai where people with leprosy had been quarantined, arguing that the local board of health administered it poorly and had lost the trust of Native Hawaiians. Just weeks after the opening of the 57th Congress, he introduced H.R. 6561, a bill to convert the colony into a federal reservation controlled by the Secretary of the Treasury. It was referred to the Committee on Territories. By transferring control, Wilcox believed the deplorable living conditions of the current colony would be improved. "They will build a hospital there, and the United States is a big Government, not like the one-horse concern here," he noted in the summer of 1902 while testifying before a congressional commission that was visiting Honolulu, "and they will see that the poor leper is well taken care of. This is my belief. I know all the natives are scared of that place, scared of these people, scared of the board of health."[33] He also supported bringing people suffering from leprosy from the United States—he estimated as many as 300—for resettlement at the new facility. Republican opponents latched onto this proposal to stir a backlash against Wilcox, arguing that Hawaiians of all stripes did not want the islands to become a "dumping ground" for Americans with leprosy. Though the commission backed the proposal, Congress never acted on it. Still the political consequences were serious. Wilcox had underestimated Hawaiians' fears of the disease despite their long history with it and, according to his biographer, "unquestionably made" his biggest political misstep as Delegate as Republicans would use the issue against him in the 1902 election.[34]

In spite of the distance between Washington, DC, and Hawaii, Wilcox continued to exert his influence over the territorial legislature's actions. "One blast upon the Wilcox bugle is worth a thousand men," proclaimed the *Hawaiian Advertiser*.[35] The truth of this characterization was demonstrated when the Wilcoxes returned to the islands from Washington in April 1901. Wilcox quickly began meeting with Home Rule Party territorial legislators to catch up on all that had taken place while he was gone, facilitating agreements and mending political fences. Among his first steps was to lobby the party to change its name to the Home Rule Republican Party to allow him the chance to caucus with the majority Republican Conference at the next session.[36]

Thereafter, Wilcox instructed legislators in his party and the Independents to end their obstruction of Territorial Governor Sanford Dole's nominations because their efforts at blocking all business had begun to have an adverse impact in Washington on Hawaii's capacity for self-government. By the time Wilcox prepared to return to Washington, his leadership over the ruling opposition had spread throughout the territorial legislature.[37]

In fact, the only Wilcox bill that was enacted into law was a measure that set the terms of some of the Hawaiian territorial senators, the lengths of which varied according to their share of the popular vote. The HRP controlled a majority of the 15 seats, but Republicans were floating a proposal to divide the longer four-year terms evenly between themselves and the Home Rulers. Initially, Wilcox responded by introducing a bill that would have provided four-year terms to all 15 Senators until the 1904 election, essentially ensuring Home Rule control for several more years. That bill was quickly shunted aside by the Territories Committee. But a month later Wilcox introduced H.R. 13076, a more politically feasible bill, which set the terms of seven of the Senators (four Home Rule, three Republican) at two years, based on their having received the lowest popular vote totals. Wilcox's biographer described this as a victory for the Delegate, in part, because, of the four Home Rulers, three had proven disappointing to Wilcox in the territorial legislature's inaugural term.[38] The bill passed the House on April 26, 1902, and shortly afterward passed the Senate. President Roosevelt signed it into law on May 19, 1902.[39]

In early 1902, Wilcox's health kept him from his congressional duties and largely confined him to home for several months. He suffered from severe stomach ulcers. His recurring health issues, coupled with the coming elections, shifted his attention away from Washington, where he had never fully been engaged, to back home, where his true interests were.

As 1902 opened, the first rumors about the upcoming election for Territorial Delegate appeared. Hawaiian newspapers reported a possible effort to merge the Home Rule Party with the Democrats, replacing Wilcox

with Democrat John Wise.[40] In early spring, Territorial Governor Sanford Dole predicted to California reporters that the Republican Party would do quite well in the fall since Wilcox had fulfilled none of his campaign promises, especially that of getting Dole removed as governor.[41] The *Evening Bulletin* ran a story on Wilcox's record as Territorial Delegate in June, just before the HRP convention would be held. "The impression Wilcox has created in national circles has cast no credit upon the people he was elected to represent," the paper reported. Wilcox "has aided those who have sought to represent Hawaiian Americans as unable to govern themselves."[42]

Wilcox opened the HRP convention on July 8 with a rousing speech calling upon all Hawaiians to accept annexation as a fact and embracing the Hawaiian Organic Act for bringing suffrage back to Native Hawaiians. He defended his record in Washington, blaming "missionaries" in Congress with thwarting his efforts. Wilcox also proposed that the party replace "Republican" in its name with "Democratic" in an effort to allow him to affiliate himself with the national party.[43] As the convention began its work, it was evident that Wilcox had laid the groundwork carefully, blocking a floor amendment demanding expanded federal spending on Hawaii. Wilcox had also managed to keep one of the most popular members of the Hawaiian royal family, Prince Jonah Kuhio Kalanianaole, participating in the party despite his growing unease with the party's direction and tactics. Kuhio had been appointed chairman of a reorganization committee that drafted proposals to make the party more effective, but when Kuhio's report was presented, Wilcox and his followers tabled it, preventing any further consideration of its proposals. This action enraged Kuhio, who led a walkout, taking 40 of the 100 delegates with him. Wilcox immediately took the floor denouncing the walkout, but urged tolerance towards Kuhio and his followers.[44] Nevertheless, the damage was done. The *Hawaiian Star* reported that Wilcox's political prospects were fading "not in the glory of the brilliant colors of the west, but sinking into a bank of clouds upon which can be read the gloomy word 'Failure.'"[45]

Rumors flew that Wilcox had lost the favor of the former queen, and both mainland parties hastened to recruit Kuhio as their candidate, with Republicans succeeding. Kuhio's nomination quickly gained support. The Portuguese community of workers as well as the *Evening Bulletin* and the *Pacific Commercial Advertiser* endorsed Kuhio.[46] Governor Dole reversed his opposition to Native Hawaiians having the vote and quickly cracked down on government corruption, minimizing criticism against him.[47] The single most important campaign issue, which Republicans eagerly seized upon, was Wilcox's plan to introduce federal control of the quarantined leprosy settlement on the island of Molokai, reported the *Washington Post*.[48] On Election Day, November 4, Wilcox lost to Kuhio, 4,696 to 6,636.[49] The pattern of voting made clear that Wilcox had lost the *haole* vote and a substantial bloc of Native Hawaiians shocked at his proposal to hand over Molokai to the federal government.[50]

But the damage was not confined to Wilcox's personal political fortunes: the HRP also lost seats and control of the house of representatives and senate. Many in Hawaii believed that HRP had been broken. One historian suggests it was a "watershed" moment in Hawaiian politics, marking the ascendancy of the Republican Party and the declining influence of native politicians.[51]

In 1903 Home Rulers implored Wilcox to run as their candidate for sheriff of Oahu. Against the strenuous objections of his wife and the advice of his doctors, he accepted. His declining health, combined with the grueling schedule of a campaign, contributed to his further deterioration just weeks before the election. With his wife and young children at his side, Wilcox died at his home at the foot of the Punchbowl volcanic crater in Honolulu from a massive hemorrhage caused by what news accounts called "consumption," likely tuberculosis, on October 23, 1903.[52] His career, opined the *San Francisco Chronicle*, was a "romantic and adventurous one."

Though government officials refused to give Wilcox a state funeral, throngs of mourners paid their respects to the late leader at the family estate, which led to the decision to postpone his funeral until after the elections. On November

8, after a funeral mass at the Catholic cathedral in Honolulu, Wilcox's casket was placed on a hearse and drawn through the streets by 200 Native Hawaiians to his grave site, where a crowd witnessed his interment.[53] The *Pacific Commercial Advertiser* eulogized Wilcox as a faithful voice for the people. "It may be justly said that no other Hawaiian, not of Royal blood, has ever exerted such a powerful influence on Hawaii as Robert W. Wilcox," the editors judged. "We may condemn the nature of that influence as we please; but the fact remains that it made history and gave Wilcox rank as a tribune of his people, a man stronger in the elements of leadership than all but one of his native kings."[54]

FOR FURTHER READING

Andrade, Ernest, Jr. *Unconquerable Rebel: Robert W. Wilcox and Hawaiian Politics* (Niwot: University Press of Colorado, 1996).

MANUSCRIPT COLLECTIONS

Cornell University Libraries, Division of Rare and Manuscript Collections (Ithaca, NY). *Papers*: In the Constance Goddard DuBois papers, 1897–1909, 1 cubic foot. The collection contains one folder about Robert Wilcox and the Hawaiian Rebellion.

Huntington Library, Manuscripts Department (San Marino, CA). *Papers*: In the Nathaniel Bright Emerson Papers, circa 1766–1944. Authors include R. W. Wilcox.

University of Hawaiʻi at Manoa, Hamilton Library (Honolulu, HI). *Papers*: 3 volumes. Materials contain articles from 19th-century American newspapers about the 1893 overthrow of the Hawaiian monarchy. Topics represented include R. W. Wilcox.

NOTES

1 "Robert W. Wilcox," *Biographical Directory of the United States Congress, 1774–Present*, http://bioguide.congress.gov/scripts/biodisplay.pl?index=W000459; and A. P. Taylor (Librarian of the Archives of Hawaii), "Biographical Sketch of Robert William Wilcox," Box 174, *Biographical Directory of the United States Congress* Research Collection, Office of the Historian, U.S. House of Representatives.

2 Ibid.

3 Sobrero arranged for an annulment that was granted by Pope Leo XIII and the Civil Court of Italy in 1895. See Taylor, "Biographical Sketch of Robert William Wilcox"; Ernest Andrade Jr., *Unconquerable Rebel: Robert W. Wilcox and Hawaiian Politics* (Niwot: University Press of Colorado, 1996): 65.

4 Taylor, "Biographical Sketch of Robert William Wilcox."

5 Andrade, *Unconquerable Rebel*: 58–60.

6 Editorial, 31 July 1889, *Pacific Commercial Advertiser*: 2.

7 "Robert W. Wilcox Dead," 27 October 1903, *Hawaiian Gazette*: 3.

8 Merze Tate, *The United States and the Hawaiian Kingdom* (New Haven, CT: Yale University Press, 1965): 114–115; Helena G. Allen, *Sanford Ballard Dole: Hawaii's Only President, 1844–1926* (Glendale, AZ: Arthur H. Clark Company, 1988): 182; Andrade, *Unconquerable Rebel*: 107.

9 Andrade, *Unconquerable Rebel*: 125–139.

10 Taylor, "Biographical Sketch of Robert William Wilcox."

11 Andrade, *Unconquerable Rebel*: 191; Stephen W. Stathis, *Landmark Legislation, 1774–2002: Major U.S. Acts and Treaties* (Washington, DC: CQ Press, 2003): 149.

12 Tom Coffman, *The Island Edge of America: A Political History of Hawaiʻi* (Honolulu: University of Hawaiʻi Press, 2003): 9; Ethel M. Damon, *Sanford Ballard Dole and His Hawaii* (Palo Alto, CA: Pacific Books, 1957): 340; Andrade, *Unconquerable Rebel*: 194. The Hawaiian Organic Act went into effect as 31 Stat. 141 (1900).

13 Andrade, *Unconquerable Rebel*: 194.

14 Allen, *Sanford Ballard Dole*: 239; Andrade, *Unconquerable Rebel*: 191–192.

15 Allen, *Sanford Ballard Dole*: 238–239; Andrade, *Unconquerable Rebel*: 195.

16 Andrade, *Unconquerable Rebel*: 195, 196.

17 Ibid., 196.

18 Ibid., 198; Taylor, "Biographical Sketch of Robert William Wilcox"; Robert C. Schmitt, *Historical Statistics of Hawaii* (Honolulu: The University Press of Hawaii, 1977): 603.

19 Andrade, *Unconquerable Rebel*: 200, 218.

20 Ibid., 219.

21 Ibid.

22 House Committee on Elections, No. 1, *Charges against Robert W. Wilcox*, 56th Cong., 2nd sess., H. Rept. 3001 (1 March 1901): 1–4. See also Chester H. Rowell, *A Historical and Legal Digest of all the Contested Election Cases in the House of Representatives from the First to the Fifty-Sixth Congress, 1789–1901* (Washington, DC: Government Printing Office, 1901): 601–603; Andrade, *Unconquerable Rebel*: 220.

23 "A Brilliant Speech," 24 October 1900, *The Independent*: 3.

24 Andrade, *Unconquerable Rebel*: 230–232.

25 David T. Cannon et al., *Committees in the U.S. Congress, 1789–1946*, vol. 3 (Washington, DC: CQ Press, 2002): 1128.

26 A Bill To Extend the General Land Laws of the United States to the Territory of Hawaii, with Rules and Regulations for Homestead

Entries by the Secretary of the Interior, H.R. 13906, 56th Cong., 2nd sess. (29 January 1901).

27 H.R. 6561, 57th Cong., 1st sess. (1901); Andrade, *Unconquerable Rebel*: 220.

28 A Bill To Provide Special Land Laws for the Territory of Hawaii, H.R. 3090, 57th Cong., 1st sess. (6 December 1901).

29 Testimony before the Senate Committee on Pacific Islands and Porto Rico, *Hawaiian Investigation*, Part 2, 57th Cong., 2nd sess. (1902): 526.

30 *Congressional Record*, House, 56th Cong., 2nd sess. (4 February 1901): 1915.

31 A Bill Relating to the Retirement of Hawaiian Coinage and Currency, H.R. 4343, 57th Cong., 1st sess. (10 December 1901); Andrade, *Unconquerable Rebel*: 223.

32 Andrade, *Unconquerable Rebel*: 224–225.

33 *Hawaiian Investigation*, Part 2: 525–526.

34 Andrade, *Unconquerable Rebel*: 226.

35 Ibid., 201–202.

36 Ibid., 204.

37 Ibid., 202.

38 Ibid., 223.

39 H.R. 13706, 57th Cong., 1st sess. (27 March 1902); Public Law 57-118, 32 Stat. 200 (1902).

40 Andrade, *Unconquerable Rebel*: 236.

41 Damon, *Sanford Ballard Dole and His Hawaii*: 343.

42 Andrade, *Unconquerable Rebel*: 228.

43 Ibid., 238.

44 Ibid., 239–240.

45 No title, 18 July 1902, *Hawaiian Star*: 4.

46 Andrade, *Unconquerable Rebel*: 243.

47 Ibid., 244–245.

48 "Prince in the House: Kalanianaole Defeats Delegate Wilcox in Hawaii," 13 November 1902, *Washington Post*: 3.

49 *Congressional Directory*, 58th Cong., 1st sess. (Washington, DC: Government Printing Office, 1903): 133; "Prince in the House: Kalanianaole Defeats Delegate Wilcox in Hawaii." For election results, see Schmitt, *Historical Statistics of Hawaii*: 603.

50 "Prince in the House: Kalanianaole Defeats Delegate Wilcox in Hawaii."

51 Andrade, *Unconquerable Rebel*: 246–247; "Prince in the House: Kalanianaole Defeats Delegate Wilcox in Hawaii."

52 "Robert Wilcox Died Last Night," 24 October 1903, *Hawaiian Star*: 1; "Robert W. Wilcox Dead."

53 "Hawaiians Mourn for Their Delegate," 25 October 1903, *San Francisco Chronicle*: 18.

54 "Robert W. Wilcox," 25 October 1903, *Pacific Commercial Advertiser*: 4.

"It may be justly said that no other Hawaiian, not of Royal blood, has ever exerted such a powerful influence on Hawaii as Robert W. Wilcox."

Pacific Commercial Advertiser,
October 25, 1903

Jonah Kuhio Kalanianaole
1871–1922

DELEGATE 1903–1922
REPUBLICAN FROM HAWAII

From royal prince to revolutionary to Hawaiian Delegate, Jonah Kuhio Kalanianaole traveled a unique route to the United States Congress. Known primarily as "Kuhio" or by his childhood nickname "Prince Cupid," he remains the only Member of Congress born into royalty. As a royal, Kuhio consistently attracted support from Native Hawaiians who were nostalgic for the fallen kingdom and from *haoles* who respected his symbolic status. In the nation's capital and on elaborate tours to the islands, however, the prince relied on his charm and personal diplomacy rather than his royal status to ensure advantages for Hawaiians. As the second Delegate from Hawaii, Kuhio won federal funds for infrastructure improvements, arranged the expansion of the Pearl Harbor naval base, and paid homage to his Hawaiian heritage through the Hawaiian Homes Commission Act, his final, most controversial, and, arguably, most important accomplishment.

Jonah Kuhio Kalanianaole Piikoi was born on March 26, 1871, in the village of Kukuiula in the Koloa District of the island of Kauai. Kuhio was the youngest of three sons of High Chief David Kahalepouli Piikoi and Princess Victoria Kinoiki Kekaulike, both members of the fast-disappearing Hawaiian royal caste.[1] Princess Victoria's sister, Kapiolani Napelakapuokakae, married into the royal line of Hawaii in 1863 when she wed King David Kalakaua. The couple remained childless so the king anointed his wife's family as his eventual heirs. In 1880 Kuhio's father, David Piikoi, died and King Kalakaua appointed Kuhio's mother governor of the island of Hawaii. The king issued a royal proclamation making Kuhio and his two brothers princes in 1883 and made them wards following their mother's death a year later. He then incorporated Princess Kekaulike's line into the Kalakaua dynasty through the so-called Bayonet Constitution of 1887.[2]

King Kalakaua provided the best education available for his sister-in-law's sons. As a child, Kuhio and his brothers lived in Honolulu, and it was at St. Alban's School where classmates first started calling him "Prince Cupid." Later Kuhio attended Oahu College, today known as Punahou School, in Honolulu, where he earned a reputation as an outdoor sportsman.[3] Kuhio then joined his brothers at St. Matthew's Military Academy in San Mateo, California, but their education was interrupted when the sudden death of Kuhio's brother, Edward, forced their return home. In 1888 King Kalakaua sent Kuhio to Japan with the hope of setting up a marriage with the Japanese royal family. Kuhio spent nearly a year as the guest of the Japanese government, learning the art of diplomacy, but he made no effort to secure a marriage.[4] Upon returning home, Kuhio briefly took up a position in the Ministry of Interior and Customs.

Continuing to groom Kuhio and his brother, David, to be potential heirs, Kalakaua sent them to study business in Gloucestershire, England, at the Royal Agricultural College. The pair toured Europe, greeted as equals in royal courts across the continent.[5] The brothers returned from England in early 1891; King Kalakaua died in January while visiting San Francisco. His sister, Liliuokalani, succeeded to the throne and set Princess Kaiulani, daughter of Kalakaua's youngest sister, Miriam Likelike, as her heir apparent, cementing Kawananakoa and Kuhio, respectively, as presumptive heirs behind the princess.

Liliuokalani took the throne in the midst of an economic depression and unrest among disenfranchised Native Hawaiians. Following her husband's passing, Kuhio became a close confidante and adviser to the queen.[6] At this time, he and his brother dropped their father's surname, Piikoi, leaving Kalanianaole and Kawananakoa as their surnames for official business, in order to stand out from one another as they gained increased political prominence.[7]

On January 16, 1893, Queen Liliuokalani attempted to install a new constitution, undoing what she saw as the deleterious effects of the Bayonet Constitution and restoring power to the monarchy. This shocked the wealthy business class, led by Sanford B. Dole, a *haole* who had muscled his way onto the Hawaiian supreme court and then Liliuokalani's privy council. Dole and his friends among the immigrant elite then formed the Committee of Safety. Three days later they marched an organized volunteer militia in to occupy the government building with the aim of appealing for annexation by the United States. Dole remembered that Kuhio, working as one of the clerks there, quickly acquiesced to the takeover and began sending letters informing foreign diplomats of the change in government. "I must say the young prince worked with a vim," Dole recalled, "although the overthrow of the monarchy meant the end of royal honors."[8]

After it became clear that President Grover Cleveland's administration would not annex the islands, a provisional government reorganized as the Republic of Hawaii on July 4, 1894. Its constitution emulated parts of the U.S. Constitution, though it also prohibited many Native Hawaiians and citizens of Asian descent from voting, frustrating Kuhio. In the last weeks of 1894, Kuhio plotted a coup alongside his friend John Wise and agitator Robert W. Wilcox. However, Kuhio and Wise encountered roadblocks in their attempt to join Wilcox at the government building at the center of the insurrection. They eventually gave up and returned home in the early hours of January 7, 1895. President Dole declared martial law, and the pair was arrested the next day and held without charge. On February 11, they were at last charged with neglect in reporting treason.[9] A military tribunal found Kuhio guilty and sentenced him to one year in prison and a fine of $1,000. Government officials offered him clemency if he revealed the names of his coconspirators, but Kuhio refused.

While serving his sentence, Kuhio received regular visits from Chiefess Elizabeth Kahanu Kaleiwohi-Kaauwai. Kuhio was released months ahead of schedule, in September 1895, and he married Kahanu soon after.[10] Faced with uncertainty about the future of the Hawaiian government on the eve of annexation and coping with the sudden deaths of his beloved cousin, Princess Kaiulani, and Queen Kapiolani, Kuhio left Hawaii with his new wife for a belated and prolonged honeymoon in late 1899. Part of his travels took him to South Africa at the height of the Second Boer War, where he was a guest of the British Army. The couple did not return until September 1901.[11]

In his absence, his former ally Wilcox defeated Kuhio's brother David to become the first Hawaiian Delegate in the U.S. Congress on the strength of Native Hawaiians who had been re-enfranchised under the Hawaiian Organic Act of 1900. Kuhio joined Wilcox's Home Rule Party, which became the dominant political party on a platform of restoring the rights and power of Native Hawaiians, but Kuhio grew disenchanted with the Home Rule Party after witnessing some of its racially charged politics firsthand. The party often derided *haoles* and conducted legislative business in the Hawaiian language rather than English in defiance of the Organic Act.[12]

In July 1902, the party tapped Kuhio to lead a reorganization committee. Kuhio's proposals prioritized attracting younger moderates, but Wilcox preferred the status quo, seeking to retain his ally David Kalauokalani as party president. When Wilcox loyalists tabled Kuhio's plan indefinitely at the convention, he resigned his party affiliation and led a walkout of nearly half the delegates. He demanded Kalauokalani's ouster in exchange for bringing his faction back under the party tent, but that was a nonstarter for Wilcox. On July 14, Kuhio and his followers formed the Independent Party, or Hui Kokoa, and newspapers rumored that Queen Liliuokalani had given her tacit support.[13] He also lured his old friend John Wise away from the Democrats. Hui Kokoa's platform read as a rebuke of Home Rulers' racial politics.

Meanwhile, business interests frustrated with the Home Rule Party turned to the Republican Party.[14] Republicans initially rejoiced at Home Rulers' fragmentation but soon worried that Kuhio's status as a royal could draw a decisive number of votes. Over the course of August, Kuhio considered merging his party with either one of the major parties from the mainland. Kuhio leaned toward Democrats, but Democrats remained skittish and afraid of insulting Wilcox and the remaining Home Rulers. Native Hawaiians viewed Republicans as the party of *haoles* and the reviled territorial governor Sanford B. Dole. But a speech at the opening of the territory's Republican convention cemented Kuhio's choice to run as a Republican. Former Nebraska Senator John M. Thurston declared, "You might as well send a frog to chipper at the doors of the Court of St. James for what you want as send to Washington a Delegate who is not one of or in harmony with either of the two great political parties." After Kuhio met with key Republican operatives, Republicans readily incorporated elements of his platform into their own. This included many former Home Rule positions: the creation of county and municipal government, a legislative settlement for Queen Liliuokalani, and the revision of the tax system.[15] Kuhio joined the convention as a nominee for Delegate, announcing, "I am a Republican from the top of my head to the bottom of my feet." Republicans nominated him by acclamation.[16]

The Home Rule-leaning newspaper *Independent* excoriated Kuhio as a race traitor, tying him to Dole and other *haoles*, whom it portrayed as oppressors. Wilcox called him "that very inconsequential little mouse."[17] Many more Hawaiian institutions lined up behind Kuhio's candidacy, however. The Portuguese Political Club even renamed itself the Portuguese Republican Club as a show of support for the prince.[18]

Democrats, led by Kuhio's brother David, even allied with the Home Rule Party to counterbalance Kuhio's popularity. The brothers bore no ill will toward one another, and in either outcome a member of the royal family would end up leading the party in power. Home Rulers emphasized "Hawai'i for the Hawaiians" and campaigned for Wilcox's re-election, while Republicans attacked the incumbent as an ineffective demagogue. Republicans zeroed in on Wilcox's proposal to cede control of the community of people on Molokai suffering from leprosy to the federal government. When it became clear that, under federal control, inhabitants of the settlement would be strictly separated by gender, among

other changes, residents reacted strongly, and Wilcox faltered.[19] Kuhio's campaign developed around embracing Americanism, saying at stump speeches, "Monarchy had accomplished a useful means, and democracy arises to carry on the work."[20] Ultimately, Republicans swept both the legislature and the delegacy. Kuhio won a large percentage of the white vote and attracted considerable Native Hawaiian support as well, tallying 6,636 votes to Wilcox's 4,696.[21] Kuhio's victory fatally weakened the Home Rule Party. For a few elections, they split votes with Democrats, who eventually absorbed the remaining Home Rulers.

Kuhio arrived in Washington, DC, with much exuberance, though the reality of his isolated position rapidly set in. When President Theodore Roosevelt greeted Kuhio in 1903, he balked at the name Kalanianaole. "I shall not call him Prince Cupid, and I cannot pronounce his last name. I never would be able to remember it, anyhow," the President complained. "Can't we cut it off somewhere and make it simpler?" From then on, most Washingtonians simply referred to him as "Kuhio" or "Prince Cupid," after his childhood nickname.[22] Racial prejudice was apparent in the House of Representatives' barbershop, when the proprietor curtly informed him, using a racial epithet, that he would not cut the Hawaiian's hair. Not one to suffer fools, Kuhio grabbed the barber by the collar and hauled him out of the shop.[23] On January 4, 1904, Kuhio gained some unwanted notoriety when he was arrested for disorderly conduct after scuffling outside a DC bar. He refused to pay a fine or to alert friends to his predicament and stayed overnight in jail, incorrectly claiming that, as a Member of Congress, he was exempt from arrest. The next morning the court notified friends, who bailed him out.[24]

He enjoyed better luck in his first lottery for a desk in the House Chamber, drawing ahead of powerful Appropriations Chairman James Hemenway of Indiana. When Hemenway asked to swap desks, Kuhio complied. He was only too happy to extend the small favor and win the indebtedness of a well-placed ally. Kuhio bragged to a friend, "This damn little Delegate had a seat that some of the fellows would give anything to get."[25]

After settling into his position, Kuhio wrestled with mainland ignorance of Hawaii. He was appointed to the traditional seats on the Territories Committee and the Post Office and Post Roads Committee, but often found himself testifying before the Merchant Marine and Fisheries or Naval Affairs panels instead.[26] He struggled to pass bills approving a franchise grant to expand the installation of electric lights in Hawaii. Afterward in the 59th Congress (1905–1907), he concentrated on getting money to build, repair, and maintain lighthouses on the islands and encouraging greater trade (H.R. 10512, H.R. 21927).[27] No one seemed to know whether funding existed for the project, so Kuhio shuffled back and forth between the Navy Department's Lighthouse Board, Speaker Joe Cannon, and a clerk of the Appropriations Committee before discovering the funds had been suspended under the belief that Hawaii was an insular possession, like Puerto Rico or the Philippines.[28]

Over and over the prince became aware that neither congressional colleagues nor federal bureaucrats knew much about Hawaii. So he dedicated himself to educating American administrators about the islands. Much of this process happened off the House Floor, and Kuhio reveled in these extracurricular venues.[29] Much of his time was spent in committee rooms hosting card games, playing golf, and attending various functions to expand his social circle and influence. Sometime after 1904, the prince set up a luxurious getaway for guests near Pershing Square, dubbing it the Bird's Nest. Furnished with a bar, poker tables, pool tables, and his African hunting trophies, it became a getaway for officials where Kuhio would hold forth on Hawaii's beauty, fertility, and strategic position in the Pacific. When Princess Kahanu made the trip to the capital, the couple hosted dinner parties for Members featuring the guest of honor from the islands.[30] Kuhio even arranged for an exhibit on Hawaii in the Alaska–Yukon–Pacific Exposition of 1909 in Seattle, Washington.[31]

However, starting in May 1907, Kuhio's preferred method was to host colleagues on extended tours of Hawaii.[32] The territorial legislature even chipped in for the three-week tour of Hawaii that spring. These excursions became more popular over time. The 1915 entourage included 27 Representatives, 10 Senators, congressional family members, staff, and a gaggle of press. Hawaiians sailed out to greet the congressional visitors before they reached land, presenting leis and playing Hawaiian music from an accompanying tugboat.[33] The firsthand experience often helped grease the skids for legislative action afterward. "I have a few things to take up with the prince about the merchant marine and transportation facilities that come within the jurisdiction of my committee," wrote Representative William Wilson of Illinois after one tour, "and I intend to help rectify those unreasonable sailing conditions when we get together."[34]

Kuhio's attempts to focus federal attention on the Hawaiian Islands also included more traditional efforts at legislative lobbying. In 1903 he wrote letters to every Member of Congress on the necessity to dredge and improve the Honolulu Harbor. When contacts at the War Department turned him aside the following year, Kuhio went directly to President Roosevelt himself, prevailing upon him to lean on the chairmen of the Rivers and Harbors and Appropriations Committees as well as the irascible Speaker Cannon. Kuhio even took to the House Floor on occasion, as he did in 1905, to implore the House not to ignore Hawaiian problems. "Do not make it possible for my people to reproach me because that in this great national family injustice is done to its youngest and weakest child," he said. "Do not leave it possible for any Hawaiian to say that, either politically or economically, he was better off under the old monarchy than he may be to-day under the American flag."[35]

More often than not, Congress applauded Kuhio's pluck but rewarded it with little substantive legislation. But his constant pressure prodded executive agencies into making some of the improvements requested of their own accord. By the end of 1906, the Department of Commerce and Labor had started construction of a lighthouse at Makapuu Point. Kuhio won appropriations for improvements across several omnibus bills, but did not manage to pass a full harbor improvement bill until 1916, when he pushed through Congress an overhaul to the Board of Harbor Commissioners.[36]

Faced with repeated stonewalling in committees, particularly on the issue of harbor improvements, Kuhio changed his tactics. In a period of increasing tensions between the United States and Japan, his new idea was to tie the federal government tighter to Hawaiian infrastructure through renewed focus on military and naval bases on the islands. He took his case before the House Naval Affairs Committee in 1908. "Gentlemen of the committee, this Government has for ten years neglected the safeguard of preparing a naval base in the mid-Pacific," Kuhio declared. It amounted to an "inexcusable neglect" not of a special Hawaiian interest, but of a national security necessity.[37] Kuhio's persistent lobbying on the issue over the course of a decade paid dividends after he led a 1919 tour for Navy Secretary Josephus Daniels and the navy board to visit Pearl Harbor. Daniels agreed with Kuhio's assessment, and Congress responded to the secretary's report with an appropriation of $27 million for recommended improvements and expansions.[38]

Kuhio spent much of his time protecting Hawaii from federal policy changes that conflicted with its interests. In 1917 he testified against the passage of a bill introduced by Missouri Democrat Joshua Alexander, which would have sharply regulated wireless radio usage and traffic within the United States. Laden with communications from Hawaiian businessmen, Kuhio argued that radio was essential to the growth and development of the islands and that new federal regulations would hurt Hawaiian economic expansion and the ability of its people to assimilate into American culture.[39] The committee accordingly scuttled the bill.

After World War I, Kuhio pressured Congress to continue the suspension of coastwise laws that forbade foreign ships from serving as passenger steamers between Honolulu and San Francisco without the payment of a hefty fine per passenger. Members on the House Merchant Marine and Fisheries Committee, however, were eager to roll back the wartime suspensions. But with American ships still pressed into service as military transports, Hawaiians relied primarily on foreign ships to travel to and from the mainland. Kuhio reasoned that an exemption for Hawaii would keep travel open until more American

ships were returned to service. The committee ignored Kuhio's plea.[40]

Prohibition dominated much of the political discussion during Kuhio's tenure in Congress, as the temperance issue was used as a wedge to critique Hawaiians' fitness for self-rule. The Hawaiian legislature passed a liquor licensing law in 1907 in the hope of slowing liquor traffic in the territory. In 1910 John G. Woolley of the Anti-Saloon League of America testified before Congress that the legislature's licensing law had failed. Portraying the average Hawaiian as a drunkard and local politicians as being in the pockets of liquor lobbyists, Woolley pushed Congress to dismantle territorial home rule. Kuhio took pains to point out the hypocrisy and cherry-picking in Woolley's testimony. "There are many good people in Hawaii who believe in prohibition but who do not believe that Congress should enact it," Kuhio countered. He defended the right of Hawaiian self-government and relied on the history and virtue of the Hawaiian constitution.[41] Only a couple weeks later Kuhio testified in favor of a congressionally approved referendum (H.J. Res. 155, S.J. Res. 80) on the prohibition of liquor sales in the territories, which gave control back to the Hawaiian people, but the referendum failed.[42]

Pressure in favor of prohibition grew, and, in 1917, when Oahu was declared a military zone, serving alcohol on the island was banned. Kuhio viewed the restriction as unfair, since the manufacture and sale of alcohol were still permitted. A year later Kuhio introduced his own bill to prohibit the traffic and manufacture of alcohol during the war (H.R. 9960, S. 3935). However, Kuhio continued to guard Hawaiians' right to self-government. "We are fully capable of settling all our domestic problems," he declared, "and the waiver of this right in the instance, I trust will not be made a precedent for future inroads by the Federal Government on the inherent right of the people of the islands to home rule." The bill passed the House a few months later by a vote of 238 to 30, following considerable lobbying from Kuhio.[43]

As a Republican, Kuhio spent most of his time protecting the islands' economy, but his position as a member of the fast-receding royalty stoked a deep sense of personal responsibility to his kin and Native Hawaiians generally. His brother, Prince David Kawananakoa, died in San Francisco in 1908.[44] This left Kuhio and Queen Liliuokalani as the last of the royal line. The queen seemed intent on regaining a measure of her authority and often pressured Kuhio to reacquire crown lands lost during annexation. Kuhio dutifully pressed what he knew to be a futile point. Congress repeatedly denied the land claim, but, at Kuhio's behest, eventually granted Liliuokalani a monthly payment. Still Kuhio's relationship with the queen remained turbulent until her death on November 11, 1917.[45]

Among his many legislative interests, Kuhio most forcefully advocated for Native Hawaiians, whom, he contended, had suffered terribly from the introduction of European disease and the changes in their culture. To that end, Kuhio encouraged the adoption of the English language and American cultural norms and styles to better integrate into the new Hawaii.[46] This motivation, combined with Kuhio's own hopes of becoming the first Native Hawaiian territorial governor, led to a feud with the sitting territorial governor, Walter Frear, a fellow Republican.

Kuhio and Frear had met and worked together on land use bills both in the territorial legislature and before the U.S. Congress. When Frear declined to release certain plots in the southern Kau District of Hawaii for purchase by Native Hawaiians in late 1909, the partnership broke down. Kuhio accused Frear of mismanaging public lands and kowtowing to plantation owners. "The sugar plantations can get anything they want from Frear, but the people do not get any chance," the Delegate railed. "Gov. Frear lied to the people and he lied to me and made me lie to the people in my promises."[47]

Kuhio's attacks grew more strident over Frear's tenure. Complaints that plantation owners were discouraging homesteaders by turning off their water supply or closing routes to market continued to pour in, and the prince vowed to put the issue before the President himself. If that failed, Kuhio pledged to ask Congress to set up a commission to investigate Frear's administration. President William H. Taft's Interior Secretary Walter Fisher requested

a written list of offenses before traveling to Honolulu. His investigation shifted from a focus on Frear's administration to a broader appraisal of the islands' public utilities and homesteading programs. Fisher recommended the creation of a public utilities commission to monitor these services separate from the territorial governor's administration. When many of the allegations against Frear's office proved to be unfounded, Kuhio withdrew his charges and backed Fisher's recommendations. The rivalry between the Delegate and governor cost both men in 1912: Kuhio battled opponent Lincoln McCandless for 54 percent of the vote in his toughest campaign to date and saw his hopes for the governor's office dashed while Frear failed to secure reappointment.[48]

Kuhio believed one of the simplest ways to ensure civil rights for his people was the admission of Hawaii to the Union. He struggled, however, against ambivalence among the more potent political groups on the islands, such as the sugar industry. "Hawaii will make the next bid for Statehood, and the request will come soon," he predicted in 1910, but momentum stalled. Although rumors spread that Kuhio planned to ask for statehood at the very next session of Congress, that request did not come for nine more years.[49] The Hawaiian legislature passed resolutions in favor of statehood in 1911, 1913, 1915, and 1917, but these efforts were largely perfunctory and lacked the full backing of the parties or funding for commissions organized to lobby for statehood in Washington. Each time Kuhio cautioned patience to statehood's proponents, sensing a lack of enthusiasm for the idea in both the halls of Congress and among the powerful agricultural oligarchs of the islands.[50] Kuhio finally brought the first statehood proposal (H.R. 12210) before Congress in 1919. The bill generated little fanfare in Washington and died before being debated in committee, leaving Kuhio to seek other means to protect his people. The *Honolulu Star-Bulletin*, Hawaii's premier paper, stated in 1920 that "Hawaii is not yet ready for statehood."[51]

Frustrated with the machinations of *haole* Republicans both in Hawaii and in their DC lobbying offices, Kuhio began to push more brazenly for accommodations for his own people, the Native Hawaiians.[52] This advocacy for homesteaders eventually culminated in his trademark accomplishment: the Hawaiian Homes Commission Act in 1921, a bill that Kuhio championed while bucking *haole* elites within his own party. Between the rapid *haole* acquisition of former native land and the domination of the labor market by Chinese and Japanese immigrants, the situation had become dire, Kuhio argued. "If conditions remain as they are today," he insisted, "it will only be a matter of a short space of time when this race of people, my people, renowned for their physique, their courage, their sense of justice, their straight-forwardness, and their hospitality, will be a matter of history." Kuhio joined the popular movement among Native Hawaiians for homesteading as a possible solution for the preservation or "rehabilitation," as it was termed, of the Hawaiian people. He pointed to the successful rehabilitation of the Maori people in New Zealand by the British government under a homesteading program. Circumstances aligned to push his own proposal in early 1920 as leases on significant portions of government land (the former "Crown lands" the queen had been eager to reacquire) were due to expire.[53]

In April 1920, the prince introduced what he initially termed the Hawaiian Rehabilitation Bill (H.R. 13500), which set up a comprehensive homesteading program and returned Hawaiians to farming the land. "The legislation proposed seeks to place the Hawaiian back on the soil, so that the valuable and sturdy traits of that race, peculiarly adapted to the islands, shall be preserved to posterity," Kuhio explained.[54] Later that year, testifying before the Senate Committee on Territories, he claimed, "This is the first opportunity given to a poor man," and he accused opponents of the bill of protecting the wealthy who were eager to retain their leases.[55] Senator Harry Stewart New of Indiana submitted a companion bill (S. 1881) the following session which quickly moved through Congress. S. 1881 passed the Senate and House by voice vote on June 27 and 30, 1921, respectively, and was signed into law by President Warren G. Harding.

The Hawaiian Homes Commission Act amended the Organic Act to set aside roughly 200,000 acres across

the Hawaiian Islands for 99-year leases to claimants at least 21 years old with 50 percent or more Hawaiian blood. However, the persistent lobbying of the islands' sugar industry managed to retain the best lands for their sugar plantations while relegating homesteaders to less fertile and more remote acreage. Kuhio supported the exemption for sugar producers as a necessity for both passage of the bill and the maintenance of the Hawaiian economy. He bristled at accusations that he had sold out Native Hawaiians, insisting that he had negotiated the best deal possible. While Kuhio conceded that the program "does have a second class choice of lands," he touted the provisions which made funds available for farming equipment and home construction. Ultimately, many homesteaders found themselves beholden to larger agricultural firms once again for even such basic needs as roads and irrigation.[56]

Tellingly, the bill also prohibited Japanese laborers from obtaining work on federal construction projects. The provision reflected Kuhio's tendency to protect Native Hawaiians, whom he frequently defended as prime examples of American values, at the expense of other ethnic groups. As the Native Hawaiian population dropped, he frequently warned, for instance, of competition from the growing pool of Japanese immigrant laborers. He feared the growing ethnic Japanese population would dominate island politics and have the effect of "un-Americanizing the territory."[57]

Kuhio's antipathy for Japanese immigrants seemed based less on competition for jobs than it was on racial prejudice, given that he touted economic advantages of bringing in cheap Chinese labor to relieve a severe labor shortage on the islands' sugar plantations. To bypass federal Chinese exclusion laws, Kuhio introduced H. Res. 93 in 1917 to authorize the immigration of 30,000 Chinese laborers to work rice fields and construct government buildings in Hawaii. Though proponents cited a long history of Chinese agricultural laborers on the islands, the bill received little consideration.[58]

The labor shortage continued, however, and garnered significant attention in 1921 after a strike by Japanese workers. Yet again Kuhio requested that Congress reverse its aversion to Chinese immigration and import Chinese laborers for a span of five years rather than allow further Japanese immigration. Texas Democrat John C. Box argued that Kuhio's proposal did not represent a "permanent" solution to Hawaii's problems. Kuhio countered that any permanent solution involving the importation of "European" labor would inevitably lead to inexcusable delays. For Hawaii's Chinese population Kuhio had nothing but praise. He attempted to distinguish Chinese immigrants from Japanese immigrants by insisting Chinese Hawaiians had a greater tendency to adopt American norms. "We have Chinese citizens there of whom we are proud," he said. "They make fine citizens."[59] Neither the House nor the Senate took up the proposal for a vote, and the legislation languished until after Kuhio's death a year later.

Kuhio encountered little serious competition for two decades. His election in 1904 was contested by King Kalakaua's former chamberlain, Democrat Curtis P. Iaukea, but the House rejected Iaukea's challenge.[60] Kuhio's campaign strategy was genial and quintessentially Hawaiian. He wrote his own campaign song based on the popular melody of "Aloha No Au I Ko Maka" and handed out white silk handkerchiefs with his initials and picture.[61] Kuhio's perennial opponent was Lincoln McCandless, who abandoned the Republican Party for the Democrats in 1908. Kuhio ignored attempts to replace him within his own party after his 1912 confrontation with Governor Frear, using an endorsement from Illinois Representative James Mann, the Republican leader, who credited Kuhio with $10.5 million in appropriations for Hawaii across his then decade of service.[62]

Kuhio faced unusually heavy opposition in his final campaign. Pressure built within the Republican Party to replace him. Party leaders, still largely *haoles*, had grown increasingly concerned with Kuhio's fervent support of the Hawaiian Rehabilitation Bill benefiting Native Hawaiians. Spurious charges circulated that Kuhio blocked a territorial women's suffrage bill, a policy Kuhio actually supported and that his wife had spoken in favor of in the territorial legislature. Kuhio's old friend and political manager

John Wise exposed the false whispering campaign, and Kuhio's prospects received an unexpected boost when the Nineteenth Amendment was ratified in August 1920, a mere month before the election.[63] Kuhio defeated McCandless one last time, winning 61 percent of the vote.

During the 1920 election, Kuhio was adamant that he would retire after his term expired in the 67th Congress (1921–1923). He once again eyed appointment as territorial governor, but lost out to Wallace R. Farrington, who had gathered endorsements from all previous living governors, including Kuhio's old nemesis Frear.[64] Exhaustive campaigning and the rigors of constant long-distance travel between Hawaii and Washington finally caught up with the prince. He fell ill in the fall of 1921 and ignored his doctors' prescriptions for bedrest. Kuhio died of a heart attack in Honolulu on January 7, 1922. He was accorded a state funeral in Hawaii with full military honors.[65]

FOR FURTHER READING

Kamae, Lori. *The Empty Throne: A Biography of Hawaii's Prince Cupid* (Honolulu: Topgallant Publishing, 1980).

Schlup, Leonard. "Prince Cupid: Jonah Kuhio Kalanianaole and the Quest for Hawaiian Progressivism," *International Review of History and Political Science* 19 (1982): 54–58.

MANUSCRIPT COLLECTION

Hawaii State Archives (Honolulu, HI). *Papers*: 1903–1922, 4.3 cubic feet. The papers of Jonah Kalanianaole document his 19 years as Hawaii's Delegate to Congress. The papers mainly consist of bill files and correspondence. The bill files concern his campaign for Hawaiian Home Lands legislation and federal public works legislation for Hawaii. The correspondence reflects an unusually close consultation between Delegate Kalanianaole and the governor on legislation of interest to Hawaii. A finding aid is available at the repository.

Photographs: circa 1875–1920, 1 folder. Photographs of Jonah Kalanianaole as a child, young man, and during his political career as Hawaii's Delegate to the U.S. Congress. Photos record his activities as a sportsman, as a student with his brothers in San Mateo, California, and as a member of the Order of Kamehameha. Several photographs of commemorations honoring him are also included.

NOTES

1 Barbara Bennett Peterson, "Kuhio," *American National Biography* 12 (New York: Oxford University Press, 1999): 943.

2 "Prince Cupid at Home," 24 May 1903, *Washington Post*: E10.

3 Peterson, "Kuhio": 943.

4 Lori Kamae, *The Empty Throne: A Biography of Hawaii's Prince Cupid* (Honolulu: Topgallant Publishing, 1980): 67–68.

5 Davianna Pomaika'I McGregor, "Prince Kuhio: An Introduction to His Life," in *Biography Hawaii: Five Lives—A Series of Public Remembrances*, University of Hawaii, http://hawaii.edu/biograph/pdf/kuhioguide.pdf (accessed 7 March 2013).

6 Kamae, *The Empty Throne*: 70–73.

7 Peterson, "Kuhio": 943.

8 Helena G. Allen, *Sanford Ballard Dole: Hawaii's Only President, 1844–1926* (Glendale, AZ: Arthur H. Clark Company, 1988): 190.

9 Kamae, *The Empty Throne*: 80–87.

10 Ibid., 91–96; "Thurston Is Recalled," 9 June 1895, *New York Times*: 5.

11 Kamae, *The Empty Throne*: 99.

12 Ibid., 106–107; Stephen W. Stathis, *Landmark Legislation, 1774–2002: Major U.S. Acts and Treaties* (Washington, DC: CQ Press, 2003): 149. The Hawaiian Organic Act went into effect as 31 Stat. 141 (1900).

13 Ernest Andrade Jr., *Unconquerable Rebel: Robert W. Wilcox and Hawaiian Politics* (Niwot: University Press of Colorado, 1996): 239–240.

14 Kamae, *The Empty Throne*: 107.

15 Andrade, *Unconquerable Rebel*: 242–243.

16 Kamae, *The Empty Throne*: 108.

17 "Wilcox and Cupid," 2 September 1902, *The Independent*: 2; "Review of the Press," 9 September 1902, *The Independent*: 1.

18 Andrade, *Unconquerable Rebel*: 243.

19 "Prince in the House," 13 November 1902, *Washington Post*: 3.

20 Kamae, *The Empty Throne*: 109.

21 "Prince in the House"; Robert C. Schmitt, *Historical Statistics of Hawaii* (Honolulu: University of Hawaii, 1977): 603.

22 "Prince Cupid's New Name," 29 November 1903, *Boston Daily Globe*: 31.

23 Kamae, *The Empty Throne*: 112.

24 "Jonah in the Jug," 6 January 1904, *Los Angeles Times*: 3; "'Prince Cupid' Arrested," 6 January 1904, *New York Times*: 9.

25 Kamae, *The Empty Throne*: 113.

26 For a full listing of Kuhio's committee assignments, see David T. Canon et al., *Committees in the U.S. Congress, 1789–1946*, vol. 3 (Washington, DC: CQ Press, 2002): 570.

27 Peterson, "Kuhio": 944.

28 Kamae, *The Empty Throne*: 113–115.

29 Ibid., 110–111.

30 Ibid., 112, 122; Peterson, "Kuhio": 944.

31 Hearing before the House Committee on Industrial Arts and Expositions, *Alaska-Yukon Exposition*, 60th Cong., 2nd sess. (27 January 1908): 44–45.

32 Kamae, *The Empty Throne*: 128.

33 Roderick Matheson, *Congressional Visit to Hawaii: 1915* (Honolulu: Advertiser Press, 1915): 14.

34 Kamae, *The Empty Throne*: 158.

35 *Congressional Record*, Appendix, 59th Cong., 1st sess. (23 February 1905): 75.

36 Kamae, *The Empty Throne*: 127–129.

37 Hearings before the House Committee on Naval Affairs, *Pearl Harbor Dry Dock*, 60th Cong., 2nd sess. (29 January 1908): 495–496.

38 Kamae, *The Empty Throne*: 176; Peterson, "Kuhio": 944.

39 Hearings before the House Committee on the Merchant Marine and Fisheries, *Radio Communications*, 64th Cong., 2nd sess. (11–26 January 1917): 383–384.

40 Hearings before the House Committee on the Merchant Marine and Fisheries, *Extending Relief to the Territory of Hawaii by Providing Additional Shipping Facilities Between the Territory of Hawaii and the Mainland*, 66th Cong., 1st sess. (14 July 1919): 3–7.

41 Statements before the Senate Committee on Pacific Islands and Porto Rico, *Liquor Traffic in Hawaii*, 61st Cong., 2nd sess. (11 February 1910): 18–20.

42 36 Stat. 878 (1910); Hearings before the House Committee on the Territories, *Special Prohibition Election in the Territory of Hawaii*, 61st Cong., 2nd sess. (25 February 1910): 6–9; Kamae, *The Empty Throne*: 141–142.

43 Kamae, *The Empty Throne*: 171–172.

44 Ibid., 132–133; "Hawaiian Prince Dead," 3 June 1908, *Washington Post*: 4.

45 Kamae, *The Empty Throne*: 129–130, 162, 173–75.

46 Ibid., 111.

47 "Fight Over Hawaiian Lands," 27 December 1909, *New York Times*: 4; "The Party Split—And After," 13 December 1909, *Hawaiian Star*: 4; "Island Press On Politics," 28 December 1909, *Hawaiian Gazette*: 3.

48 Kamae, *The Empty Throne*: 143–144; "Hawaiian Delegate to Fight Governor of Pacific Isles," 31 May 1911, *Los Angeles Times*: 13; "Knox and Fisher Land," 12 October 1912, *Washington Post*: 6.

49 "Hawaii Would Enter Union," 9 July 1910, *New York Times*: 1; "Views of Visitors in Washington," 1 August 1910, *Washington Post*: 6.

50 It is unclear for whose benefit the territorial legislature offered these proposals, given the lack of funding or serious push each resolution ultimately provided. Kuhio seemed to recognize, alongside much of the press at the time, the futility of pushing a proper statehood campaign in Congress without more potent backing from Hawaiian authorities. See Kamae, *The Empty Throne*: 178.

51 Roger Bell, *Last Among Equals*: *Hawaiian Statehood and American Politics* (Honolulu: University of Hawaii Press, 1984): 44–46; John S. Whitehead, *Completing the Union*: *Alaska, Hawaii, and the Battle for Statehood* (Albuquerque: University of New Mexico Press, 2004): 30.

52 Gavan Daws, *Shoal of Time*: *A History of the Hawaiian Islands* (Honolulu: University of Hawaii Press, 1968): 295–296.

53 Daws, *Shoal of Time*: 296–297; Hearings before the House Committee on Immigration and Naturalization, *Labor Problems in Hawaii*, 67th Cong., 1st sess. (7 July 1921): 450.

54 Kamae, *The Empty Throne*: 187.

55 Hearings before the Senate Committee on Territories, *Hawaiian Homes Commission Act, 1920*, 66th Cong., 3rd sess. (14 December 1920): 128–130.

56 Kamae, *The Empty Throne*: 197; Daws, *Shoal of Time*: 297–299; Peterson, "Kuhio": 944; "Hawaiian Rehabilitation Bill is Passed; Anti-Beer Measure Favored," 1 July 1921, *Sacramento Union*: 2.

57 Peterson, "Kuhio": 944; *Labor Problems in Hawaii*: 448.

58 Hearings before the House Committee on Immigration and Naturalization, *Relative to Chinese Immigration into Hawaii*, 65th Cong., 2nd sess. (17 January 1918): 1–3, 48–49.

59 Kuhio's efforts alongside those of businessman Walter Dillingham ultimately led to pressure for Japanese exclusion in the Immigration Act of 1924. See Tom Coffman, *The Island Edge of America* (Honolulu: University of Hawaii Press, 2003): 32; *Labor Problems in Hawaii*: 451–453.

60 The House rejected Iaukea's claim that an early mistake in dispensing the ballots necessarily voided the election and also noted that voting proportions did not fall significantly outside the broader numbers. See "Contest from Hawaii," 13 December 1904, *Washington Post*: 1; House Committee on Elections No. 3, *Iaukea v. Kalanianaole*, 59th Cong., 1st sess., H. Rept. 2651, (26 March 1906): 1–6.

61 Kamae, *The Empty Throne*: 138–139.

62 Ibid., 156.

63 Ibid., 178–180.

64 Coffman, *The Island Edge of America*: 13.

65 Kamae, *The Empty Throne*: 185, 200; Peterson, "Kuhio": 944.

"DO NOT LEAVE IT POSSIBLE
FOR ANY HAWAIIAN TO SAY
THAT, EITHER POLITICALLY
OR ECONOMICALLY, HE WAS
BETTER OFF UNDER THE OLD
MONARCHY THAN HE MAY
BE TO-DAY UNDER THE
AMERICAN FLAG."

Jonah Kuhio Kalanianaole
Congressional Record, February 23, 1905

Benito Legarda
1853–1915

RESIDENT COMMISSIONER 1907–1912
PROGRESISTA FROM THE PHILIPPINES

A prominent entrepreneur before entering Congress, Benito Legarda served as one of the first Resident Commissioners from the Philippines. Elected to the U.S. House of Representatives in 1907, Legarda used his vast business experience to influence tariff legislation in an effort to reshape the Philippines' economy. He was close friends with President William H. Taft—the two first met when Taft served as civil governor of the Philippines at the turn of the century—and Legarda worked closely with officials from the Bureau of Insular Affairs on a host of trade issues. While many Filipinos called for independence, Legarda took a more measured approach and believed the island government should first establish consistent sources of revenue before it sought independence. "He was a man of the highest repute," Democratic Senator William Stone of Missouri said about Legarda, "clear-headed, intelligent, patriotic, representative, and worthy in every way of the greatest confidence."[1]

Benito Legarda was born on September 27, 1853, in Binondo, Manila Province, Philippines, to Benito Legarda Sr., a Spaniard, and Cirila Tuason. Legarda attended the Ateneo de Manila University and matriculated to the University of Santo Tomas, also in Manila, where he graduated with a law degree in 1874. His family, according to one account, had been "distinguished for decades in the business and political life of the Spanish regime," and Legarda was himself an adept businessman, founding the Germinal cigar factory and making a fortune in the tobacco and alcohol industries. Legarda married twice, the second time to Teresa de la Paz, and together they had three children.[2]

In the midst of his lucrative business career, which made him one of the wealthiest men in the Philippines, Legarda won election to the municipal council of Manila and served as lieutenant mayor of the Quiapo District in 1891.[3]

Legarda belonged to a class of well-educated Filipinos commonly called the *ilustrados* (the enlightened ones), men who had often grown wealthy and successful under Spanish rule but who had also challenged the Spanish colonial structure from within. Their status as cultural elites may have given the *ilustrados* more conservative tendencies, but their history as internal reformers enabled men like Legarda to identify with the movement for political control that took shape in the 1890s. "They emphatically desired reform," wrote Peter W. Stanley in his history of Philippine independence, "particularly guaranteed civil liberties, decentralization of government, separation of church and state, and recognition of their position as leaders in Filipino life."[4]

As a result, when the Philippines went to war with Spain in 1896, Legarda backed the independence forces and served as an adviser to General Emilio Aguinaldo. Legarda was by no means a revolutionary, but he represented the Jolo Province in the revolutionary Malolos congress—named after the town about 30 miles north of Manila where the rebel government gathered—and nominally served as its vice president. Legarda only attended session twice, however, later telling American authorities, "I did not like it, and I did not swear to support the constitution." He also served as director of the new government's treasury department.[5]

With the American occupation of the islands in February 1898, Legarda drifted away from the objectives of his more radical counterparts in the revolutionary congress. War was bad for business, and he had a lot to lose if he backed the wrong side. Legarda resigned from the Malolos congress, and returned to Manila where he found allies in United States General and military governor of the Philippines Elwell S. Otis and William H. Taft, the islands' civil governor and future President of the United States.

By siding with the Americans, Legarda risked becoming a target of the nationalist guerrilla fighters, but he nevertheless remained in Manila, where he kept a large, "palatially furnished home."[6] Legarda ended up testifying before a panel of American investigators studying how best to install a new government. Called the first Philippines commission, the panel heard statements on a range of topics, including the archipelago's economic potential. Legarda, who touted his credentials as a captain of industry, complained to the commission that the Philippines lacked a stable currency and protections against foreign competition. "There is no security in business," he said.[7]

Legarda quickly became a key figure in newly formed Partido Federal (Federal Party), which controlled patronage and worked closely with the Americans to create a new civil government. After Taft assumed the office of civil governor, he appointed Legarda to the second Philippine commission on September 1, 1901. Taft formed a close personal and professional friendship with Legarda and once described him as "a public-spirited citizen of high character" in a letter to President Theodore Roosevelt.[8]

Since its creation at the turn of the century, the Philippine commission, which Legarda likened to the American Senate, functioned as an advisory board with legislative powers for the new Manila government. It was staffed by both U.S. officials and Filipino Federalistas sympathetic to America's goals in the Pacific. Within a short while, Legarda had won the reputation as one of "the prestigious figures at the center of the party," working to strengthen the relationship between the Philippines and the United States.[9] In fact, according to one historian of U.S.–Philippine relations, Legarda was one of a handful of *ilustrados* who questioned the Philippines' ability for "self-government" and "even advocated the indefinite continuation of American rule."[10] Legarda served on the commission for six years.

In 1904, when U.S. officials unveiled sweeping changes to the Philippines' tax system, Legarda flexed his own political muscle and fought the proposal. At one point, as the debate dragged on, he and one of his Filipino colleagues even threatened to resign from the commission in protest.[11]

Perhaps unsurprisingly, the debate over taxes in the Philippines revealed a rift in relations with America. Legarda challenged the notion that Filipinos would simply accept the recommendations from their American counterparts on the commission. At the time, both his party, which had changed its name to the Progresistas, and everyday Filipinos were thinking broadly about their home's political future. Although Legarda and many other business and cultural leaders remained wary of independence, it was not long before a younger generation of Filipinos built a nationalist movement. By the time Philippine voters elected their first assembly under U.S. control in 1907, independence had become a potent force.[12]

With the formation of the new Philippine government, Legarda suddenly found himself with a new job. As part of the new arrangement, the legislation authorized the Philippines to send two Resident Commissioners to Washington to represent it before Congress. In an attempt to balance the interests of both the Philippine commission, which had a notable American influence, and the assembly, which had a large nationalist contingent, the two legislative bodies agreed to elect a candidate of their own choosing who would then be quickly ratified by the opposite chamber.[13] The commission, as many expected, chose Legarda on November 22, 1907; the assembly selected Pablo Ocampo, who had played a prominent part in the rebellion.[14] Both seemed well regarded. "The presence of these commissioners should prove of value to the members of the House," wrote the *Washington Post*, "as it brings there men who are well posted on Philippine matters and who can, presumably, speak with authority on affairs in the archipelago."[15]

Legarda and Ocampo, both of whom were reportedly reluctant to accept the job, were somewhat different selections for the office of Resident Commissioner, and their appointments underscored the tension between the Philippine commission and the assembly. Whereas Legarda had risen to power by working with American officials, Ocampo made his name by routinely speaking out against foreign influence.[16]

The commission and the assembly wanted Legarda and Ocampo to leave for the United States as soon as possible in order to join the upcoming debate over U.S. tariffs on Philippine goods. Travel from Manila to the United States in the early 1900s required long boat rides, including a stop in Hong Kong in order to catch a steamer to San Francisco. Legarda became seasick easily, and the trip across the Pacific on a smaller vessel made him nervous.[17] By the time they left in late December, some Filipino businessmen feared that the Resident Commissioners would arrive in Washington too late to help craft tariff legislation, but Taft had reassured Legarda there would be plenty of time to address his concerns.[18]

Legarda was something of a media darling when he landed in America. Newspapers across the country covered his arrival, many of which applauded his long association with U.S. rule in the Philippines, a point Legarda was happy to reaffirm when he docked in San Francisco.[19] "The people are indefinitely better off under present conditions than they would be under other political management," he said.[20] Still, he quickly reminded American readers that U.S. occupation came at a steep price for the islands.[21]

Filipino political leaders saw the treaty to end the War of 1898 as a bad deal for their economy, and the government gave Legarda a long list of issues to address on the Hill, including the right for the Philippines to open independent trade agreements with countries that already consumed its goods, to open new trade partnerships without American oversight, to repeal tariffs that restricted a host of Philippine goods in the American market, and to repeal a trade bill giving U.S. ships sole discretion to move people and goods to and from the Philippines.[22] "Our particular object," Legarda said shortly before arriving in Washington, "will be to show Congress the great need of lowering the duty upon Philippine sugar and tobacco."[23]

For Legarda, political independence for the Philippines was a worthy, but long-term, goal—a discussion for another time. His main ambition was to industrialize and diversify the islands' economy so that, when independence arrived, the nation could stand on its own.[24] "We do not expect to have much weight when political questions are being discussed," he said in 1907, shortly after his election, "but when economic matters pertaining to the Philippine

Islands arise in either house of congress we expect to fully inform the homeland legislators."[25] This was also a personal concern for Legarda, who admitted that he wanted independence, but just was not sure how to get it. "That's the question," he said. "I do not want to stand the risk of possible civil war or anarchy, for I have property to lose."[26]

Like any lawmaker, Legarda's chances for success rested on his ability to influence the legislative process, which, in 1908, seemed tenuous. At least one Manila-based *Washington Post* correspondent wondered openly what kind of "powers and prerogatives" Legarda and Ocampo would have in the House. "The law designates them as 'resident commissioners,' which may mean anything or nothing," he wrote, speculating that the two would be marginalized so Congress could avoid defining the "status of the islands."[27] Well aware of the limitations placed on him as Resident Commissioner, Legarda offered an honest assessment a few days before he took office: "As we are the first delegates to represent our people officially in the United States," he said, "much more is expected of us than we will possibly accomplish."[28]

Legarda took his seat in Congress in early February 1908.[29] House leaders assigned him and Ocampo to desks on the Democratic side of the chamber, and while the new Resident Commissioners had access to both the House and Senate floors, had office space in the new House Office Building (now the Cannon building), and could participate in debate, they lacked the ability to vote and were prohibited from sitting on committees.[30]

Despite his limitations, Legarda focused on trade issues and tariff rates, guided by his desire to have the Philippines accorded the same treatment as America's other territories, Hawaii and Puerto Rico.[31] Legarda noted that the Treaty of Paris had severely circumscribed the Philippines' sugar and tobacco markets, two of its biggest exports. Without protected access to U.S. consumers, the archipelago's entire agricultural sector would suffer. A close partnership, he said, would ensure that "our political interests could never be severed."[32]

Legarda also had an ace up his sleeve. He planned to lean on his old friend, William H. Taft, who had since risen to the job of Secretary of War, even telling an Ohio newspaper that the Philippines would "depend on Governor Taft" to protect its interests in Washington.[33] Luckily for Legarda, the Insular Bureau, which oversaw America's colonial possessions, fell under Taft's War Department. When it came to tackling the Philippines' tariff concerns, Legarda quickly began working alongside the Insular Bureau's chief, Clarence Edwards. Barely a month into his term, Legarda appeared publicly with Edwards at a banquet in Ohio, speaking about the Philippines' economy and the need to remove U.S. import duties on Philippine goods.[34]

Legarda had additional support among the press. The *New York Tribune*, writing shortly after Legarda's speech, argued that, since Hawaii and Puerto Rico both had preferable trade deals with the United States, the Philippines should, too. "This is an unfair discrimination," it observed, noting that trade in sugar and tobacco from the Philippines might be tripled if duties were lowered. "Logic and good faith call for their reduction."[35]

Crafting tariff legislation, however, meant dealing with many moving parts, not the least of which was the Philippines' tenuous position in America's economic orbit. In effect, the archipelago was two things at once: a significant part of America's insular roster and a unique political entity that many on both sides of the Pacific saw as a separate country entirely. Nevertheless, the United States was in the driver's seat. "Practically speaking," a U.S. journalist wrote, "Congress holds the prosperity of these islands in the hollow of its hand."[36]

Congress, however, could not agree on how best to categorize the islands. For a decade it had gone back and forth, unable to decide if the Philippines was a domestic or international trading partner. Republicans built trade policy around the Philippines' ambiguous status. Meanwhile, Democrats called its insular position "anomalous and preposterous" and wanted Congress to decide whether the Philippines was "altogether American or altogether foreign."[37]

Because the Philippines collected much of its revenue from fees on imported goods from the United States, trade dictated much of the islands' annual budget. By the early 1900s, the Philippines depended on America to such an extent that, if free trade went into effect and tariffs were removed, one journalist estimated, the islands would lose three-quarters of its customs revenue, one of the main sources of money for the Philippines' treasury.[38]

During Legarda's first few months in the House, the trade relationship between the United States and the Philippines became something of a prelude to a much larger debate about America's export-import business.[39] But in the spring of 1908, the Philippine tariff moved briefly to the fore when the Ways and Means Committee considered H.R. 21449, amending sections of the Tariff Revision Law of 1905 that dealt specifically with goods imported to the islands.[40] Prior to the committee markup, Legarda and the Insular Bureau designed amendments to adjust a handful of rates, including those on imported buttons (to protect Manila's mother-of-pearl fisheries), and to eliminate entry fees for agricultural machinery and shipbuilding tools.[41]

At ten o'clock in the morning on May 5, 1908, the Ways and Means Committee began hearings on H.R. 21449. Three witnesses sat across from the committee: Legarda; the Insular Bureau chief, Clarence Edwards; and Edwards's assistant, Major Frank McIntyre. McIntyre had written the bulk of the amendments and did most of the talking. Legarda contributed every now and then, but for the most part, he sat quietly while the committee questioned the Insular Bureau officials.[42] The committee agreed with the proposed amendments and favorably reported the bill.[43]

After word reached the Philippines, businesses back home clamored to know the details. Despite Legarda's reserved role during the hearing, the island press made him the leading voice on the bill. Some headlines even listed him as coauthor: "Enthusiastic on Tariff"; "Legarda-Payne Tariff Bill Up"; "Contents of Legarda Bill"; "How Legarda Has Amended the Payne Bill"; "El bill Legarda-Payne."[44]

When the measure went to the floor on May 27, the resulting debate distilled the larger tariff question. Democrats criticized it and the GOP majority for ignoring the immediate trade concerns at home and for applying

different standards to the Philippines. "It is an emergency hodgepodge tariff bill—a sort of cross between the good and the bad—a miserable compromise," grumbled Democrat William Sulzer of New York.[45] Ways and Means Chairman Sereno Payne of New York, ever paternalistic, countered that he believed the bill would teach the Philippines a lesson in economics. Legarda, for his part, did not speak up during debate. The bill passed that day and went to the Senate, where it was referred to the Committee on the Philippines, but it never came up for a vote.[46]

About a year later, in the 61st Congress (1909–1911), the Ways and Means Committee took up the issue again, only this time in the form of two separate bills. Despite the earlier struggle for reform, a lot had changed over the preceding months. Legarda's old friend, Governor Taft, had won election as President and was calling for an overhaul of U.S. tariffs. It promised to be a huge undertaking. At the time, the United States had no income tax, meaning the federal Treasury generated vast sums of revenue from fees placed on imported goods.[47]

Payne introduced an omnibus tariff bill in mid-March, and at the end of the month, Legarda's former colleagues on the Philippine commission came out publicly in support of much of it, including the provision to open free trade with the Philippines. They asked that the United States help the islands adjust over the next three years.[48]

At around the same time, the commission sent Legarda and Ocampo "very specific instructions" on the tariffs affecting the Philippines in the Payne bill. Like the tariff legislation the year before, the new Payne measure dealt with a number of contingencies both in the United States and in the Pacific. For the last 10 years, the Philippines had assumed that the United States would open free trade, removing tariffs and costing the islands vast sums of revenue. To prepare for such a sudden loss of funding, the insular government levied direct taxes on its citizens. Even though the taxes went into effect, free trade never did, leaving the Philippines with a surplus. To put that money back into circulation, the insular government funded infrastructure projects to help industrialize the economy. With taxes fueling construction, tariffs helped run the

government. To suddenly remove the tariffs on goods imported to the Philippines would devastate the islands' budget and threaten its public works initiatives.[49]

On April 3, 1909, Legarda used the debate over what would become the Payne–Aldrich bill to make his first address on the House Floor. Ocampo had spoken the day before, protesting adamantly against the inequitable free trade proposal.[50] Legarda, as was his style, took a far more moderate approach. A major sticking point for the insular legislature and, thus, the Resident Commissioners was how the Payne bill treated Philippine sugar and tobacco imported to the mainland. If maintaining fees on goods imported to the Philippines promised to help the insular treasury, removing tariffs from Philippine goods imported to the mainland would have far-reaching benefits for Filipino farmers. Legarda told the House that his government had grown frustrated by Congress's inability to agree on how to regulate the entry of raw material from Manila. He faulted the Senate for the recent "nonaction" on the tariff and laid additional blame on U.S. sugar and tobacco industries. As they had in the past, Big Sugar and Big Tobacco saw Philippine producers as a threat to their market share at home and vigorously sought to maintain the fees on Philippine imports. Legarda, however, pointed out that production in the Philippines had slowed in recent years and that, even if Filipino farmers increased production, they "could never catch up with America's increased consumption."[51]

Legarda concluded his lengthy remarks by turning back to the situation at home. Free exports to the United States were one thing, but allowing the Philippines to continue to tax U.S. goods or at least finding some balance was vital to the islands' financial health. Legarda had no problem with U.S.-based businesses enjoying "a proper measure of protection," he said. But businesses in the Philippines which had operated under almost exactly the same conditions needed similar protection.[52]

"The Filipino people believe that, coming before this Congress with a just cause, they will receive the same measure of equity as that which the American people, through their Representatives in this Congress, have always in the past conceded under similar circumstances," Legarda said. The House erupted in applause after he finished.[53] After the bill passed the House, President Taft convinced the Senate Committee on Finance to raise the quota on imported Philippine sugar. The Associated Press called it a "signal victory," but Taft and the War Department feared it was not enough.[54]

The War Department, like Legarda, worried that free trade would disrupt key industries on the islands and cause a devastating loss of revenue. In response, on April 15, 1909, Taft called for a separate tariff bill entirely for the Philippines. Drafted by a team of "tariff experts" who had consulted with businesses in Manila, the new bill, Taft told Congress, "revises the present Philippine tariff, simplifies it and makes it to [sic] conform as nearly as possible to the regulations of the customs laws of the United States."[55] Taft intended the measure to spur revenue in the Philippines, maximizing customs fees to fund the government while protecting the islands' burgeoning industrial sector.[56] Chairman Payne agreed to the request.[57]

Five days later the Ways and Means Committee sat to hear testimony on the stand-alone Philippine bill. After hearing from its authors in the Insular Bureau who said the bill was designed "to create real competition," the committee turned to Legarda, who agreed that the bill would cover some of the projected deficit in the Philippines once free trade took effect.[58] A tense moment followed when the committee pushed Legarda on whether the bill included "fair and equitable" rates for the Philippines. At that point, Edwards of the Insular Bureau stepped in to remind the committee that "Commissioner Legarda is about as actively interested in every trade and pursuit and everything else in the Philippine Islands as anybody I know."[59] Using his experience in the tobacco industry, Legarda quickly broke down tariff problems in the Philippines before the three-hour hearing adjourned.[60]

The Ways and Means Committee favorably reported the Philippine tariff measure (H.R. 9135) on May 10, 1909, complete with a few amendments.[61] Despite appearing to have the support of both parties, the tariff divided the Philippines' own Resident Commissioners. Whereas Legarda

appeared to want to help shape the terms of the tariff bill, Ocampo opposed the idea of free trade outright. Not only did he not testify before the Ways and Means Committee, Ocampo also lent his support to Filipinos living on the mainland who petitioned Congress to kill the legislation.[62]

Throughout the tariff debate, the issue of Philippine independence percolated just below the surface. Ocampo and the Philippine assembly saw the tariff as an inherently political issue which would dictate the Philippines' relationship with Capitol Hill for the foreseeable future.[63] If Legarda seemed reluctant to address the politics of the tariff outright, however, it is likely because he and the Philippine commission realized they would be wasting their breath. Congress and Chairman Payne himself were not likely to budge on the issue.[64]

When the Philippine tariff bill went to the floor for the first time on May 13, there was a long discussion, a few partisan swipes, but only token opposition. In general, the criticisms dealt less with the bill's specifics and more with America's colonial policy.[65] On the bill itself, Democrats called it "experimental" and weak.[66] Over the next two weeks, the House failed to achieve a quorum, delaying final passage.[67] Finally, on May 24, the House approved the amendments to H.R. 9135.[68] Despite his earlier testimony before the Ways and Means Committee, Legarda appears not to have participated in the debate on the House Floor. After a number of revisions in the Senate which sat on the measure until Payne's larger tariff bill became law, the new rates effecting U.S.–Philippine trade cleared Congress on August 2.[69]

Taft signed the Philippine tariff bill into law on August 5, 1909, immediately after signing the larger Payne–Aldrich Tariff Act. For Taft, the changes to tariff rates governing trade with the Philippines were 10 years in the making. "It gratifies me exceedingly by my signature to give it the effect of law," he said. "I am sure it will greatly increase the trade between the two countries and it will do much to build up the Philippines to a healthful prosperity."[70] According to one journalist, Taft flashed "a broad smile of satisfaction" when he signed the new measures into law.[71]

Taken together, the separate tariff bill and the Payne–Aldrich bill overhauled trade between the Philippines and the United States. It required a number of deals with sugar, rice, and tobacco producers, but with the stand-alone Philippine bill, Congress and Insular Bureau officials had attempted to provide the islands' government with a means to raise revenue. With Payne–Aldrich, on the other hand, Congress worked to implement free trade between the archipelago and the mainland.[72]

In mid-May 1909, just as the House was working its way through the Philippine tariff bill, the Philippine commission unanimously elected Legarda to another term as Resident Commissioner. Ocampo, however, lost re-election to Manuel L. Quezon in the assembly.[73] Ambitious and powerful, Quezon had served as governor in the provinces before winning election as floor leader in the Philippine assembly. After presenting their credentials to Taft in late December 1909, Legarda and Quezon began efforts to reform the Philippines' tax code, to expand American citizenship on the islands, and to change the date on which service dates began in the Philippine assembly.[74]

If Legarda had taken the lead on legislation when he served alongside Ocampo, he seemed to pass along that responsibility to Quezon, now that the tariff issue was over. In early January 1911, when the two sat before the House Committee on Insular Affairs to discuss the four-year election cycle planned for the Philippines, for instance, Legarda deferred to Quezon's testimony, telling the chairman directly, "I have nothing to add to what Mr. Quezon said."[75] When the committee heard testimony on the islands' civil government that same day, Legarda again said little.[76]

Much of Legarda's activity from 1910 to 1912 took place away from Capitol Hill. He addressed crowds in a number of eastern cities, but his trip to Paris, France, was perhaps his most important. For a number of years, the Philippine government struggled to provide loans to farmers who needed help. In 1907 Congress passed a bill creating an agricultural bank in the Philippines, but few investors were willing to contribute seed money. Free trade, as required by the Payne–Aldrich law, may have

helped bolster the Philippines' economy, but loans in the archipelago still carried exorbitant interest rates.[77] In July 1911, however, Wall Street was surprised when the *New York Times* reported that French financiers had offered $10 million to help fund the languishing agricultural bank in the Philippines. That the deal had even been mentioned was thanks in large part to Legarda's business acumen. One American banker told the *Times* that, because the Philippines had a virtual monopoly over essential oils used to create perfume popular in Paris, Legarda was looking to corner the market in France. In order to meet supply in Europe, however, Philippine farmers needed capital to improve their operations, which is where an active agricultural bank would make the difference.[78]

In November 1910, the Philippine commission named Legarda to another term in the House, but the assembly shocked everyone by refusing to confirm his nomination. Over the next three months into early 1911, the commission and the assembly tried to work out a compromise. In the meantime, however, Congress passed H.R. 32004, which created four-year terms for the Philippines' Resident Commissioners and extended Legarda's existing tenure until he or his successor was elected. Importantly, the bill also provided funds for the Resident Commissioners to hire staff and gave them franking privileges.[79]

Legarda had few friends in the assembly during the nomination fight back home, and, according to one unnamed delegate, the lower house was willing to "accept almost any other man but Mr. Legarda."[80] On November 21, 1912, the logjam broke and the commission agreed to appoint Manuel Earnshaw in place of Legarda.[81] For his part, Legarda was done with politics anyway, confiding to friends that he planned to retire when his old friend, Taft, left the White House after losing re-election himself that fall.[82]

Following his congressional service, Legarda spent the rest of his life away from the Philippines, working alongside Europe's moneyed interests to bolster the islands' agricultural bank, which he called "my life work." On August 27, 1915, while in the town of Évian-les-Bains along Lake Geneva in western France, Legarda died suddenly. "It was as a brilliant scholar, charming gentleman and a financier of rare genius that Benito Legarda was known in many parts of the world," the *Manila Times* eulogized. "It was Benito Legarda's efforts which are said to have done more than any other thing to bring about peace between Americans and Filipinos in the days of the Empire and it was due in good part to his efforts that the American government was established here on such a firm foundation."[83] Legarda's remains were buried in his native Manila.

NOTES

1 *Congressional Record*, Senate, 61st Cong., 1st sess. (14 June 1909): 3208.

2 Quotation and family history from "Benito Legarda Called By Death in Paris," 30 August 1915, *Manila Times*: 1; "El Hon. Benito Legarda, Fallecido en París," 30 August 1915, *La Democracia* (Manila, PI): 1; Carlos Quirino, ed., *Who's Who in Philippine History* (Manila, PI: Tahanan Books, 1995): 124–125; Benito Legarda Passport Application, No. 578, *U.S. Passport Applications, Puerto Rico and Philippines, 1913–1925*, vol. 2, Box 4233, National Archives and Records Administration, Washington, DC, www.ancestrylibrary.com (accessed 24 February 2016).

3 G. H. Blakeslee, "The Gentlemen from Manila," 18 January 1908, *Harper's Weekly*: 14; Celestina P. Boncan, "The Philippine Commission, 1900–1916," in *Philippine Legislature: 100 Years*, ed. Cesar P. Pobre (Quezon City, PI: Philippines Historical Association, 2000): 41.

4 Frank H. Golay, *Face of Empire: United States–Philippine Relations, 1898–1946* (Manila, PI: Ateneo de Manila University Press, 1997): 32; Peter W. Stanley, *A Nation in the Making: The Philippines and the United States, 1899–1921* (Cambridge, MA: Harvard University Press, 1974): 44, quotation on p. 52. For a general discussion on the *ilustrados*, see Michael Cullinane, *Ilustrado Politics: Filipino Elites Respond to American Rule, 1898–1908* (Manila, PI: Ateneo de Manila University Press, 2003): 26–35.

5 *Report of the Philippine Commission*, vol. 2, *Testimony and Exhibits*, 56th Cong., 1st sess., S. Doc. 138: 387–388.

6 Thomas F. Millard, "The Men Who Have Come to Washington to Represent the Filipinos," 2 February 1908, *Washington Post Magazine*: 4; Stanley, *A Nation in the Making*: 64–65, 67; Cullinane, *Ilustrado Politics*: 29, 54, 57–58, 62; Boncan, "The Philippine Commission, 1900–1916": 44; "Philippine Delegates to Congress Arrive," 19 January 1908, *San Francisco Chronicle*: 17.

7 Blakeslee, "The Gentlemen from Manila"; *Report of the Philippine Commission, Vol. 2, Testimony and Exhibits*: 176–182. See also Stanley, *A Nation in the Making*: 93.

8 Stanley, *A Nation in the Making*: 72–73, 79; Boncan, "The Philippine Commission, 1900–1916": 40–41; Cullinane, *Ilustrado Politics*: 69–70; "Dual Role in the Philippines," 5 July 1901, *New York Times*: 1. For Taft's remarks on Legarda, see "Special Report of the Secretary of War," 23 January 1908, *Annual Report of the War Department, 1907*, vol. IX, 60th Cong., 1st sess., H. Doc. 2 (1908): 277.

9 Stanley, *A Nation in the Making*: 116; Cullinane, *Ilustrado Politics*: 66; "Free Trade for the Philippines," 20 January 1908, *San Francisco Chronicle*: 4. For more information on the Philippine Commission and its individual installments, see Boncan, "The Philippine Commission, 1900–1916": 27–62.

10 Golay, *Face of Empire*: 103.

11 Stanley, *A Nation in the Making*: 119–123, quotation on p. 123. See also Cullinane, *Ilustrado Politics*: 105–106; Golay, *Face of Empire*: 114–115.

12 Stanley, *A Nation in the Making*: 124, 127–128, 132–133. On the development of opposition parties and the fall of the Federal Party in the Philippines, see Cullinane, *Ilustrado Politics*: 73–143. For the rise of the Nationalist Party, see Cullinane, *Ilustrado Politics*: chapter 10. And for the new Progressive party, see Cullinane, *Ilustrado Politics*: 294–304.

13 Golay, *Face of Empire*: 139; "Two Filipino Delegates," 23 November 1907, *Washington Post*: 3; Millard, "The Men Who Have Come to Washington to Represent the Filipinos."

14 "Legarda One of The Delegates," 7 November 1907, *Manila Times*: 1; "Legarda is Chosen to Go to Washington," 16 November 1907, *Philippines Free Press*: 1.

15 "Our Cosmopolitan Congress," 26 November 1907, *Washington Post*: 6.

16 "Filipino Delegates on Way," 22 December 1907, *Washington Post*: 12. Quotation from "Free Trade for the Philippines." See also Millard, "The Men Who Have Come to Washington to Represent the Filipinos."

17 *Journal of the Philippine Commission, Inaugural Session*, vol. 1 (Manila Bureau of Printing, 1908): 115, 120, 358–370, www.hathitrust.org (accessed 18 February 2016).

18 "Delayed Departure," 26 November 1907, *Manila Times*: 1; "Resident Delegates," 13 December 1907, *Manila Times*: 1.

19 "Philippine Delegates to Congress Arrive," 19 January 1908, *San Francisco Chronicle*: 17; "Filipino Delegates Here," 28 January 1908, *Baltimore Sun*: 2; Millard, "The Men Who Have Come To Washington To Represent the Filipinos."

20 "Free Trade for the Philippines."

21 "Legarda's Straight Talk," 28 February 1908, *Cablenews-American* (Manila, PI): 2.

22 "Legarda's Straight Talk"; "Commissioners Leave Tonight," 20 December 1907, *Manila Times*: 1. The trade bill was Public Law 58-114, 33 Stat. 181 (1904).

23 Blakeslee, "The Gentlemen from Manila."

24 Millard, "The Men Who Have Come To Washington To Represent the Filipinos"; "Legarda Offends Some Assemblymen," 28 February 1908, *Cablenews-American* (Manila, PI): 3; "Filipino Makes A Practical Plea for Independence," 17 March 1912, *St. Louis Post Dispatch*: 10.

25 "'We Will Do Our Duty,' Says Legarda," 20 December 1907, *Manila Times*: 9.

26 Blakeslee, "The Gentlemen from Manila."

27 Millard, "The Men Who Have Come To Washington To Represent the Filipinos."

28 "People Met in Hotel Lobbies," 28 January 1908, *Washington Post*: 6.

29 "Needs Interpreter in Congress," 6 February 1908, *New York Tribune*: 7.

30 *Congressional Record*, House, 60th Cong., 1st sess. (4 February 1908): 1540; "Commissioners From Philippines to Sixtieth Congress," 13 February 1908, *Los Angeles Times*: 12; "They Get Rights There," 14 March 1908, *Cablenews-American* (Manila, PI): 6.

31 "Filipinos Urge Trade," 14 March 1908, *Washington Post*: 3.

32 "Free Trade for the Philippines."

33 Gus J. Karger, "Capitol Comment," 17 February 1908, *Times-Star* (Cincinnati, OH): 4; "A Great Big Man," 30 April 1908, *Manila Times*: 3.

34 "Filipinos Urge Trade."

35 "Trade With The Dependencies," 16 March 1908, *New York Tribune*: 6.

36 Thomas F. Millard, "Philippines Not a 'Problem' Nor a 'Burden,'" 23 February 1908, *New York Times Magazine*: 2; Thomas F. Millard, "Our Interests and Our Duty in the Philippine Islands," 23 February 1908, *Washington Post Magazine*: 4; Thomas F. Millard, "Congress Holds the Key," 23 February 1908, *Chicago Daily Tribune*: A1.

37 House Committee on Ways and Means, *Duties on Philippine Products Imported into the United States*, 59th Cong., 1st sess., H. Rept. 20 (20 December 1905): 1, 3.

38 Pedro E. Abelarde, *American Tariff Policy toward The Philippines, 1898–1946* (New York: King's Crown Press, 1947): 41–43; Millard, "Philippines Not a 'Problem' Nor a 'Burden.'"

39 "To Gather Revision Facts," 1 May 1908, *New York Times*: 2.

40 "Enthusiastic on Tariff," 5 May 1908, *Cablenews-American* (Manila, PI): 1; "Island Help Planned," 1 May 1908, *Indianapolis Star*: 2; "To Gather Revision Facts," 1 May 1908, *New York Times*: 2; "Legarda-Payne Tariff Bill Up," 7 May 1908, *Cablenews-American* (Manila, PI): 1.

41 "Legarda-Payne Tariff Bill Up"; "Contents of Legarda Bill," 9 May 1908, *Manila Times*: 1; "How Legarda Has Amended the Payne Bill," 9 May 1908, *Cablenews-American* (Manila, PI): 6. For more

42 Hearings before the House Committee on Ways and Means, *H.R. 21449: Philippine Island Tariff*, 60th Cong., 1st sess. (5 May 1908): 225–232.

43 House Committee on Ways and Means, *Philippine Tariff Laws*, 60th Cong., 1st sess., H. Rept. 1607 (4 May 1908).

44 "Enthusiastic on Tariff"; "Legarda-Payne Tariff Bill Up"; "Contents of Legarda Bill"; "How Legarda Has Amended the Payne Bill"; "El bill Legarda-Payne," 12 May 1908, *La Democracia* (Manila, PI): 1.

45 *Congressional Record*, House, 60th Cong., 1st sess. (27 May 1908): 7094.

46 Ibid., 7097; "Payne-Legarda Tariff Bill Passes The House," 29 May 1908, *Manila Times*: 1; "Railroad Gets Extension," 28 May 1908, *Washington Post*: 4.

47 Lewis L. Gould, *The William Howard Taft Presidency* (Lawrence: University Press of Kansas, 2009): 11.

48 "For the Payne Bill," 1 April 1909, *Boston Daily Globe*: 9; "House to Hasten Tariff Revision," 1 April 1909, *Chicago Daily Tribune*: 2; "Tariff in the Philippines," 1 April 1909, *Los Angeles Times*: 11.

49 *Congressional Record*, House, 61st Cong., 1st sess. (3 April 1909): 929–930.

50 "A Filipino Heard," 3 April 1909, *New York Tribune*: 2; "Test Vote Monday," 3 April 1909, *Washington Post*: 1; "House Debate Goes On," 4 April 1909, *New York Times*: 2.

51 *Congressional Record*, House, 61st Cong., 1st sess. (3 April 1909): 929–930.

52 Ibid., 930. See also "House on Monday to Ballot on Hide and Lumber Tariff," 3 April 1909, *Christian Science Monitor*: 1.

53 *Congressional Record*, House, 61st Cong., 1st sess. (3 April 1909): 931.

54 "President Wins Point for Philippine Sugar," 10 April 1909, *Los Angeles Times*: I12; Hearings before the House Committee on Ways and Means, *Philippine Tariff Bill*, 61st Cong., 1st sess. (20 April 1909): 44.

55 Quotation from "Message by Taft Demands Bill for Philippine Trade," 15 April 1909, *Christian Science Monitor*: 1. See also "Tariff Revision for Philippines," 16 April 1909, *Atlanta Constitution*: 2; "Taft Submits Bill for Insular Tariff," 16 April 1909, *New York Times*: 3; "Tariff Message from Taft Today," 15 April 1909, *New York Times*: 3; "Free Trade in Philippines," 15 April 1909, *Baltimore Sun*: 2.

56 "New Tariff for the Philippines," 16 April 1909, *San Francisco Chronicle*: 3; "Trade With the Philippines," 17 April 1909, *New York Times*: 8; "Low Rates for Philippines," 21 April 1909, *New York Times*: 1; "Beveridge to Lead New Subcommittee," 27 April 1909, *Indianapolis Star*: 1; House Committee on Ways and Means, *Philippine Tariff*, 61st Cong., 1st sess., H. Rept. 7 (10 May 1909): 1.

information on H.R. 21449, see Abelarde, *American Tariff Policy toward The Philippines*: 92–95.

57 "New Philippine Tariff," 16 April 1909, *New York Tribune*: 2.

58 *Congressional Record*, House, 61st Cong., 1st sess. (13 May 1909): 1998; *Philippine Tariff Bill*: 17, 32, 47.

59 *Philippine Tariff Bill*: 47.

60 Ibid., 46–49.

61 *Philippine Tariff*: 2; "Tariff Shadow Over Congress," 10 May 1909, *Atlanta Constitution*: 2; "Duties for Filipinos," 12 May 1909, *Washington Post*: 5; "New Philippine Bill," 11 May 1909, *Baltimore Sun*: 2; "Philippine Bill Reported to House," 11 May 1909, *Wall Street Journal*: 3.

62 "Filipinos Want Freedom," 13 May 1909, *Baltimore Sun*: 2; "Duties for Filipinos," 12 May 1909, *Washington Post*: 5.

63 "The Future of the Philippines," 3 April 1909, *Christian Science Monitor*: 14; "Ocampo for Protest," 13 May 1909, *Washington Post*: 4.

64 *Congressional Record*, House, 61st Cong., 1st sess. (13 May 1909): 2000.

65 "Philippine Bill Up," 14 May 1909, *New York Tribune*: 2; *Congressional Record*, House, 61st Cong., 1st sess. (13 May 1909): 1997–2012.

66 *Congressional Record*, House, 61st Cong., 1st sess. (13 May 1909): 2002, 2005.

67 *Congressional Record*, House, 61st Cong., 1st sess. (17 May 1909): 2126; *Congressional Record*, House, 61st Cong., 1st sess. (20 May 1909): 2237.

68 *Congressional Record*, House, 61st Cong., 1st sess. (24 May 1909): 2238.

69 "House Completes the Philippine Tariff Bill," 3 August 1909, *San Francisco Chronicle*: 2; "Pass Philippine Bill," 3 August 1909, *Washington Post*: 1.

70 "Party Pledges Fulfilled Says Taft, of Tariff Bill," 6 August 1909, *Detroit Free Press*: 1.

71 "Taft Signs Tariff Bill," 6 August 1909, *Detroit Free Press*: 1. See also "Tariff Bill Now a Law," 6 August 1909, *Baltimore Sun*: 1.

72 Abelarde, *American Tariff Policy toward The Philippines*: 100–109.

73 "Legarda and Quezon Chosen," 15 May 1909, *Manila Times*: 1.

74 "Filipinos Envoys Here," 29 December 1909, *Washington Post*: 4; Stanley, *A Nation in the Making*: 181–182.

75 Hearings before the House Committee on Insular Affairs, *H.R. 32004*, 61st Cong., 3rd sess. (26 January 1911): 6.

76 Hearings before the House Committee on Insular Affairs, *Administration of Civil Government in Philippine Islands*, Part 2, 61st Cong., 3rd sess. (26 January 1911).

77 "French to Finance Big Philippine Bank," 20 July 1911, *New York Times*: 4.

78 "French Bank in Philippines," 21 July 1911, *New York Times*: 11.

79 *Congressional Record*, House, 61st Cong., 3rd sess. (6 February 1911): 2022–2024; Public Law 61-376, 36 Stat. 910 (1911). For more information, see Philippine Legislature, *Election of Resident Commissioners to the United States*, 2nd legislature, 1st sess., Document No. 250—A. 38 (Manila: Bureau of Printing, 1911), https://archive.org/details/aqw4348.0001.001.umich.edu (accessed 10 February 2016).

80 "Tavera Vice Legarda Is Rumor," 8 November 1912, *Manila Times Weekly Edition*: 8.

81 "The Week and the Outlook," 22 November 1912, *Manila Times Weekly Edition*: 1; Stanley, *A Nation in the Making*: 168–169.

82 "Benito Legarda Called By Death in Paris."

83 Ibid.

"THE FILIPINO PEOPLE BELIEVE
THAT, COMING BEFORE THIS
CONGRESS WITH A JUST CAUSE,
THEY WILL RECEIVE THE
SAME MEASURE OF EQUITY AS
THAT WHICH THE AMERICAN
PEOPLE, THROUGH THEIR
REPRESENTATIVES IN THIS
CONGRESS, HAVE ALWAYS IN
THE PAST CONCEDED UNDER
SIMILAR CIRCUMSTANCES."

Benito Legarda
Congressional Record, April 3, 1909

Pablo Ocampo
1853–1925

RESIDENT COMMISSIONER 1907–1909
NACIONALISTA FROM THE PHILIPPINES

Pablo Ocampo served in the House as Resident Commissioner only briefly, but he was a powerful force on behalf of Philippine nationhood. From his early days as a leader in the revolutionary government to his election to the U.S. House of Representatives, Ocampo helped shape the terms of the Philippines' relationship with America. On Capitol Hill, he fought to protect the archipelago's economy from what he considered an unbalanced trade deal and worked to further the concerns of the Philippine assembly. He was, according to Sereno Payne of New York, the chairman of the House Ways and Means Committee, "a gentleman of education, a lawyer, and a man of ability."[1] Ocampo was not fluent in English, but during his time as Resident Commissioner, he spoke compellingly for his home islands.

Pablo Ocampo was born on January 25, 1853, to an established Manila family.[2] He attended Colegio de San Juan de Letran before graduating from the University of Santo Tomas in Manila in 1882. After studying law, Ocampo passed the bar and began practicing in Manila, starting what would become a very diverse career. From 1883 to 1884, he served as the prosecuting attorney in Manila's Tondo District along Manila Bay. And then, under the Spanish regime, he served as secretary of the royal court from 1885 to 1887 and as relator of the supreme court from 1887 to 1888. From 1888 to 1890, he was an adviser to the Economic Association of the Philippines.[3]

When the war broke out between the Philippines and Spain, Ocampo severed his ties with the empire and joined the revolution. The Spanish arrested him and threw him in jail in 1896, but Ocampo remained committed to the cause and became a close adviser to Emilio Aguinaldo, the general leading the insurrection. In 1898, as the United States beefed up its presence in the South Pacific, Ocampo was elected to the Philippines' revolutionary congress at Malolos, a town approximately 30 miles north of Manila.[4]

Ocampo's relationship with the U.S. occupying forces was rocky from the start. In 1899 the United States arrested him for his work with the revolution. Although he was eventually released, Ocampo stayed on America's radar.[5] During his time in Manila, Ocampo became the editor of *La Patria*, a newspaper openly critical of American occupation.[6] According to a *Los Angeles Times* correspondent in the Philippines, Ocampo was also reported to have been the mastermind behind the insurrection's intelligence operation, sending agents throughout Manila, Hong Kong, and other points in the Pacific. "His office was really the distributing point of all aid for the insurrectionists," the reporter said, "and he solicited contributions to keep up the battle."[7]

The reach of Ocampo's newspaper, alongside his history with Philippine nationalists, made United States authorities in the Philippines extremely nervous, so much so that, in the first part of 1901, American military officials deported him to the island of Guam, 1,500 miles to the east, where his political views on Philippine independence would be safely contained. But Ocampo's repeated imprisonments, first by the Spanish and then by the Americans, in addition to his work with the revolutionary government, may have only heightened his standing. Writing in the widely read *Harper's Weekly* a few years later, George H. Blakeslee, a leading American authority in the field of international relations, took stock of Ocampo's repeated sacrifices and concluded that the Manila lawyer was "a Filipino patriot."[8]

After spending two years exiled in Guam, Ocampo returned home. Despite concerns about his future in the Philippines, the former rebel leader took the loyalty oath to the United States and kept a comparatively low profile, focusing on his law practice.[9] His politics also seemed more

moderate. While Ocampo was gone, U.S. civil authorities, led by governor and future U.S. President William H. Taft, began exerting greater control over the Philippines. They worked closely with the Philippine Partido Federal (Federal Party), which saw U.S. occupation as a stabilizing force. It was a necessary evil that Ocampo hoped was a prelude to Philippine nationhood, a goal he now believed could be negotiated peacefully.[10]

Not long after he returned home, Ocampo fell in with a newly formed group of Filipino elites called the Comité de Intereses Filipinos (Committee of Filipino Interests), which opposed America's imperial government. Although the new group included a number of former revolutionaries, the committee's ambitions were rather moderate. "It functioned mainly as a coalition of oppositionists promoting the welfare of the indigenous population," wrote Michael Cullinane, a historian of Philippine politics. The committee was something of a political incubator, helping leaders of the opposition form an agenda. "The primary accomplishment of the Comité," Cullinane observed, "was that it provided an organization that brought together many of the men who eventually emerged as the leaders of the Partido Nacionalista in 1907."[11]

The Partido Nacionalista (Nationalist Party) was first conceived in 1906, the result of efforts to unite the many different opposition leaders in Manila. For much of the preceding decade, politics in the Philippines was unbalanced: there was the pro-American Partido Federal and then there was everyone else, a loose affiliation of factions opposed to American rule. These opposition groups all sought Philippine independence, but subscribed to different levels of urgency—everything from immediate independence to much more gradual freedom.

Ocampo, along with a number of his politically moderate colleagues from the committee, gravitated to a burgeoning party called Comité de la Unión Nacional (Committee of the National Union). Although its members did not push for immediate independence, they did seem to want it sooner rather than later. Eventually, in the spring of 1907, Manila's nationalist elements, led by the Comité de la Unión Nacional, fused together to form

the Partido Nacionalista, offering a stark contrast to the Federalistas' agenda (the Partido Federal changed its name to Partido Nacional Progresista [National Progressive Party] in 1907).[12]

The effort to unite the nationalist camps was still lurching forward when the campaign for the new Philippine assembly began. As part of the Philippine Organic Act of 1902, Congress created a bicameral legislature for the Philippines in which the commission functioned much like the U.S. Senate while the assembly would be popularly elected and fill a role similar to the U.S. House of Representatives.[13] It had taken five years, but by the summer of 1907, the Philippines was preparing to cast its first ballots for a popularly elected governing body when Ocampo entered the race.

The philosophical differences which made it so difficult to unify independence supporters in the first place remained a problem. During the nominating phase, numerous pro-independence groups ran candidates for seats in the assembly often from the same district. Late in the spring, Ocampo announced his candidacy for Manila's 2nd district, releasing a platform in June that the *Manila Times*, a newspaper sympathetic to American occupation, called "very safe, sane, and conservative."[14] Ocampo had become something of a realist over the years, and when he was approached about running for the assembly by calling for immediate independence, he flatly refused. American authorities would never grant it, and Ocampo did not want to waste time belaboring what he felt "constituted a deception of the people." It made more political sense to him to work alongside American authorities and prepare gradually for a lasting freedom. Because Ocampo refused to support immediate independence, the Nacionalista ticket fractured and cost him a seat in the assembly.[15]

Nevertheless, Ocampo suddenly found himself on the inside track for a historic appointment to Congress. The same Philippine Organic Act of 1902 that created the assembly also empowered the islands' legislature to elect two Resident Commissioners to the U.S. House of Representatives: the assembly and commission would each select one candidate who then had to be confirmed by the other chamber. In the fall of 1907, Ocampo's name was submitted to the assembly, and on November 22, 1907, he was elected with 42 votes, more than double his closest competitor. The commission elected Benito Legarda, one of the Philippines' wealthiest businessmen and a close ally of United States Secretary of War William H. Taft.[16]

Ocampo had a lot in his favor: even if he had mellowed a bit, he was committed to the cause of Philippine nationhood; he ran a successful law practice; and he was well regarded among the islands' ruling class. With Legarda, the commission had selected a member of the pro-American Progressive Party. But, with Ocampo, the assembly selected someone who it hoped could more ably represent the interests of its nationalist majority.[17] As Blakeslee, the American foreign policy scholar, pointed out at the time, Ocampo was also a native Filipino. "The majority of the Assembly were anxious to have their delegate a true representative of their race," Blakeslee observed. "This fact alone was enough to cause the defeat of other strong candidates who were in part of Spanish origin."[18]

Ocampo's politics and his long career in the public eye also seemed to make him the most viable compromise candidate. His service in the revolutionary government may have made him a radical, but by the time the assembly sent him to Washington, Ocampo had the reputation as a conservative leader among the Nacionalistas.[19]

The day after his election, an editorial in the *Manila Times* gave Ocampo a lukewarm endorsement, and mainland press accounts did so as well, describing the commission's decision to confirm his nomination as "a good omen." Ocampo, the *New York Times* surmised, was now the public face of the islands' nationalist movement. "The career of Delegate Ocampo will be watched with interest," the editors wrote.[20]

Secretary of War Taft might not have completely agreed with Ocampo's politics, but the future commander in chief also held him in high regard, telling then President Theodore Roosevelt that the new Resident Commissioner was "a prominent and able member of the bar of the Islands and a man of high character."[21]

The 60th Congress (1907–1909) was set to open on December 2, 1907, only 10 days after Ocampo's election, severely condensing the new Resident Commissioner's travel schedule. During the early 20th century, the trip from Manila to Washington, DC, took about a month and required travelers to set sail from Manila to Hong Kong in order to catch a steamer to San Francisco. So there was little hope Ocampo and Legarda would make it for the opening of the session. Congress, however, had a busy legislative agenda to start the 60th Congress, and the Bureau of Insular Affairs had told the Philippine commission that, in early January, the House would consider a major overhaul of the Dingley Tariff Act governing trade between the United States and the Philippines.[22]

Many people on the islands, especially in the Philippine legislature, were anxious for the Resident Commissioners to make it to Capitol Hill in time to participate in the tariff debate, but the quick turnaround from election to departure created a mess. After a series of schedule changes, Legarda and Ocampo agreed to leave Manila by December 21 in order to catch an America-bound ship sailing from southern China on Christmas Eve.[23] "At all events," one leading member of the Philippine legislature said, "it is important that they be in Washington at the time the bill is brought up in the House, so that it may have stout defenders in persons who are cognizant of all the facts in the case."[24]

Adjusting tariff rates was complicated, detailed work that contained a number of competing interests in both the private and public sectors on either side of the Pacific. Neither Ocampo nor Legarda could claim to be tariff experts. So the legislature agreed to compile "all the necessary data" they would need to help shape the section of the legislation covering Philippine sugar and tobacco, the islands' two major commodities.[25]

Ocampo and Legarda arrived in San Francisco on January 18, 1908, and almost immediately tried to sway public opinion to their side, telling the Associated Press that if Congress followed through on its plan to overhaul tariff rates prices back home would skyrocket.[26]

The Resident Commissioners made it to Washington two weeks later and took their seats in the House in early February 1908. On February 4, the House approved a measure giving them access to the House Floor and the right to participate in debate. They received suites in the new House Office Building (now the Cannon building), but were prohibited from voting or serving on committees.[27] A few days later, the House did the "proper and handsome thing," according to the *New York Tribune*, and voted to raise their salaries to match the rest of their House colleagues.[28]

Because they were the Philippines' only voices on Capitol Hill, Legarda and Ocampo had to steer legislation in both chambers. Building working relationships with both Members and Senators was crucial to whatever success they were going to have. In mid-February, for instance, Legarda and Ocampo, whom the *Baltimore Sun* incorrectly referred to as "Bonito Legarda" and "Tablo Ocampo de Leon," were formally introduced to the members of the Senate Committee on the Philippines.[29]

For Ocampo, establishing those relationships was likely going to be harder than normal. Unlike Legarda, Ocampo was not fluent in English and relied on his personal secretary, Antonio G. Escamilla, to translate for him. Escamilla and Ocampo likely knew one another from their time with the revolutionary government when they both served under General Aguinaldo.[30] Not long after Ocampo took his seat in the House, it was reported that he planned on asking Speaker Joe Cannon of Illinois if Escamilla could join him on the House Floor during debate, but it is not clear if this meeting ever occurred. Ocampo also hoped to have Legarda translate for him.[31]

Ocampo kept a relatively low profile during his first term in the House, but something as simple as his presence on the floor, especially when he sat and spoke with the Resident Commissioner from Puerto Rico and the Delegate from Hawaii, generated interest in the galleries above.[32] In an official capacity, however, Ocampo mostly stayed behind the scenes. Evidence in the *Congressional Record* suggests that Ocampo pigeonholed Members in the chamber to discuss living conditions back home and other issues affecting the Philippines.[33]

In late February 1908, Ocampo and Legarda accompanied Secretary Taft during his testimony before the House Insular Affairs Committee and nodded along in support as Taft asked the committee to raise the number of seats on the Philippine commission from eight to nine.[34] When the commission bill went to the floor two months later, Ocampo did not participate in debate, but Members pointed out that both he and Legarda favored the expansion.[35] Ultimately, the bill (H.R. 17516) passed the House and became law a few months later.

During his first term in the House, Ocampo juggled two often interrelated responsibilities, one as the Philippines' official representative before the federal legislature and another as a booster for his homeland. At least twice in his first year he traveled outside Washington to address crowds and participate in conferences. In mid-March, Ocampo, Legarda, and officials from the Bureau of Insular Affairs went to Cincinnati, Ohio—Taft's hometown—to attend an annual dinner hosted by the Cincinnati Commercial Club. Ocampo, speaking through a translator, touted the Philippines' natural resources and delivered remarks meant to entice American businesses to the Pacific.[36] Later in the year, in October, Ocampo traveled to Lake Mohonk, New York, for a conference titled simply "The Philippines," where he told the crowd that Filipinos across the island chain shared in "the vivid desire of being free and independent."[37]

A stable and lasting independence, however, required a healthy economy. Ever since the war, the Philippines had worked to build an infrastructure and a robust commercial sector. In large measure, however, the future of the islands' economy would be dictated by its trade relationship with the United States, and that trade relationship fell squarely within Congress's purview.

At the time, the United States had no income tax, which meant the government generated much of its revenue from fees placed on goods imported to America. Trade with the Philippines became problematic, however, because of its territorial status. On the one hand, the Philippines, as an American territory, could be seen as a domestic trading partner. On the other hand, many people on either side of the Pacific saw the Philippines as a separate country entirely. The question on everyone's mind was whether that unique status made the Philippines a foreign commercial entity.[38]

Before tackling tariff rates in 1909, Ocampo went before the House Insular Affairs Committee to address a completely separate concern the Philippine legislature had regarding the qualifications needed to serve in the islands' assembly. Manila wanted Congress to amend the Organic Act of 1902 so that the requirements to serve at the local level matched those for service in the insular government. The changes the Philippines wanted were modest but would have made service in the assembly slightly more difficult, raising the age limit from 25 to 26, tightening district residency regulations, and instituting a literacy test in "English or Spanish or any of the local dialects." The hearing lasted only a few minutes, and with his secretary Antonio Escamilla translating, Ocampo answered a series of questions on the electoral process back home.[39] The Insular Affairs Committee supported the bill, which came straight from the Philippine legislature, but with only two weeks left in the session, the full House appears to have taken a pass.[40] It would be another two years before Congress took a close look at the Philippines' civil government, and, at that point, Ocampo had already left the House.[41]

When the 61st Congress (1909–1911) opened on March 4, 1909, tariff reforms dominated everything. It was a monumental legislative task, and the Ways and Means Committee and its chairman, Sereno Payne, had spent much of the last term gathering research. The newly elected President Taft also threw the weight of his administration behind the reform effort. By 1909, however, the United States faced a budget shortfall of nearly $100 million, which put a substantial amount of pressure on Congress to set sustainable rates in order to cover the country's operating costs. As part of the debate, Congress was forced to consider options for the major industries in the Philippines: sugar and tobacco.[42]

Free trade with the Philippines had long been an ambition on Capitol Hill, but implementing it had proven difficult. Among other issues, U.S. sugar and tobacco interests had waged campaign after campaign to protect their market share and keep Philippine products out of the country while simultaneously insisting on direct and unfettered access to consumers in the Philippines.[43]

From the Philippines' perspective, free trade threatened economic collapse. Like Washington, the government in Manila filled its treasury with money derived in large measure from fees on imports. Recognizing Congress's ambition for free trade, however, the islands' legislature instituted a direct tax on its people in an effort to compensate for what would amount to a huge loss of annual revenue if and when free trade went into effect. Despite the foresight of the Philippines' legislature, by 1909, free trade had yet to begin, leaving the government in Manila with two sources of income: tariffs and taxes. Using tariffs to fund the government, the Philippines started a series of ambitious infrastructure projects to pump its tax revenue back into the economy. To suddenly implement free trade would risk that progress.[44]

By the spring of 1909, the House's solution to the Philippine tariff issue seemed woefully one sided. H.R. 1438, the tariff bill which would eventually become the Payne–Aldrich law, created what one member of the press called "a novel free trade system." The proposal gave American businesses unlimited access to the Philippines, but used quotas to restrict the entry of Philippine goods into America. It was free only in the sense that America could export its merchandise to the Philippines with no charge. There was no vice versa.[45]

On April 2, 1909, as the House was midway through its consideration of the tariff bill, Ocampo became the first Filipino to formally participate in debate. Speaking in halting English, he forcefully criticized the bill's treatment of his native Philippines. "The lack of absolute reciprocity in that provision of the bill," he said, "makes it inequitable, inasmuch as the Philippine Islands, considered a poor and small country, are under the protection of the United States, a gigantic Nation and a herald of wealth." As designed, the new U.S.–Philippine trade relationship would cost the Pacific territory vast sums every year. Compounding the problem, America's easy access to

Filipino consumers would deter international competition. "Once foreign goods are driven from the Philippine markets," Ocampo continued, "the importer of American products would control the situation, and, following the usual practice in trade as seen in the past and in the present, he will despotically dictate the prices to the detriment of the consuming public who shall be enslaved even in their most pressing needs."[46]

But the stakes involved in the tariff bill were not all financial, and Ocampo pivoted to another topic: the Philippines' future independence. In an ideal world, independence would allow the Philippines to impose tariffs on U.S. goods down the road if it wanted. But in Ocampo's assessment of H.R. 1438, he saw the Philippines struggling with its hoped-for freedom. He predicted that if the bill became law, the relaxed trade terms would embolden U.S. companies to move to the Philippines. Once American companies took root in the Philippines, Ocampo expected them to use their influence to halt the movement to give the territory its independence. He was not alone in this fear. Both the assembly and the Philippine commission, where Americans wielded considerable power, opposed free trade between the United States and the Philippines.[47]

Ocampo concluded his address by challenging the House to vote down the free trade provision in Payne–Aldrich, proving to the world that it was not merely trying to exploit the Philippines. Only after the Philippines won its independence would free trade "be more advantageous to both countries," he said before closing with one last ultimatum. If Congress really wanted to open free trade with the Pacific, it should first vote to free the islands. "In this way the American people will sanctify the noble work of liberating the Philippines as it liberated Cuba and other countries." Ocampo's remarks earned him a round of applause.[48]

A few weeks later he doubled down. "This free-trade proposition is a case of life and death with us," he told the press. "The ambition of the Filipinos to live an independent life is one which is undeniable and persistent, and any measure tending to oppose it would only stir the people of the islands and operate to prevent the development of a better feeling between Americans and Filipinos." Reaching back

two centuries, Ocampo contrasted America's past against Congress's reluctance. "Surely in the land of Washington, Jefferson, and Adams it can be permitted us to express the wish that we may be allowed to govern ourselves. It ought to be understood that in the centuries of protest against the rule of Spain we were not merely trying to throw off one foreign yoke to go under another."[49]

Despite Ocampo's strong words, Congress approved the unique tariff schedule that gave U.S. businesses virtually unlimited access to Philippine markets. Payne–Aldrich became law on August 5, 1909. But in an effort to help soften the blow to the islands' economy, President Taft, the Insular Bureau, and Resident Commissioner Legarda crafted a separate bill (H.R. 9135) adjusting certain rates to generate revenue for the Philippines.[50] It, too, became law in early August, but it is unclear what role Ocampo had in its passage. In fact, by the time the House voted on the revenue bill's final passage, Ocampo was already a lame-duck Resident Commissioner.[51]

A few months earlier, in mid-May, Manuel L. Quezon, a leader in the Philippine assembly and a member of the Partido Nacionalista, was elected to replace Ocampo in Washington.[52] Cabling Ocampo the day of Quezon's confirmation, Sergio Osmeña, the assembly's speaker, expressed his regret at having to break the bad news. He wished Ocampo a safe trip home and thanked him for his "brilliant work" on Capitol Hill.[53] There were conflicting reports about whether Ocampo was shocked and disappointed by his loss, but, regardless, the *Manila Times* reported that political forces beyond his control dictated the outcome. A likely theory had it that the Progresistas, confident they could flip Quezon's seat in the assembly if he was in Washington, threw him their votes just to get him out of Manila.[54] Ocampo, accompanied by his secretary Antonio Escamilla, left DC for San Francisco on August 11, 1909. He planned to set sail home for the final time as Resident Commissioner six days later.[55]

After returning to Manila, Ocampo won election to the second Philippine legislature and served in the assembly starting in October 1910, continuing his push for Philippine nationhood. He died of pneumonia on February 5, 1925.[56]

NOTES

1   *Congressional Record*, House, 60th Cong., 1st sess. (2 May 1908): 5609.

2   G. H. Blakeslee, "The Gentlemen from Manila," 18 January 1908, *Harper's Weekly*: 14.

3   "Pablo Ocampo," *Biographical Directory of the United States Congress, 1774–Present*, http://bioguide.congress.gov/scripts/biodisplay.pl?index=O000020.

4   Blakeslee, "The Gentlemen from Manila"; Thomas F. Millard, "The First Filipino Delegates to Washington," 2 February 1908, *New York Times Magazine*: 9; Frank H. Golay, *Face of Empire: United States-Philippine Relations, 1898–1946* (Madison: University of Wisconsin-Madison Center for Southeast Asian Studies, 1998): 32.

5   "Civil Rule for the Philippines," 21 August 1900, *New York Times*: 6.

6   Blakeslee, "The Gentlemen from Manila"; Millard, "The First Filipino Delegates to Washington."

7   "Filipino Rebels Who Will Go Free," 1 July 1902, *Los Angeles Times*: 4.

8   "Bribery Used on Insurgents," 8 March 1901, *Atlanta Constitution*: 3; *Special Report of William H. Taft, Secretary of War, to the President on the Philippines*, 60th Cong., 1st sess., S. Doc. 200 (1908): 46; Blakeslee, "The Gentlemen from Manila." For more on Blakeslee as a scholar and foreign policy specialist, see http://www.clarku.edu/research/archives/blakeslee/scope.cfm (accessed 23 February 2016), and "George Blakeslee, Educator, U.S. Aide," 6 May 1954, *New York Times*: 33.

9   "Filipino Rebels Who Will Go Free"; "Two Filipinos To Congress," 23 November 1907, *Chicago Daily Tribune*: 5.

10 Millard, "The First Filipino Delegates to Washington."

11 Michael Cullinane, *Ilustrado Politics: Filipino Elite Responses to American Rule, 1898–1908* (Manila, PI: Ateneo de Manila University Press, 2003): 128–129.

12 Cullinane, *Ilustrado Politics*: 286–294; Peter W. Stanley, *A Nation in the Making: The Philippines and the United States, 1899–1921* (Cambridge, MA: Harvard University Press, 1974): 128.

13 Julius W. Pratt, *America's Colonial Experiment: How the United States Gained, Governed, and in Part Gave away a Colonial Empire* (New York: Prentice-Hall, 1950): 199. The Philippine Organic Act of 1902 went into effect as Public Law 57-235, 32 Stat. 691 (1902).

14 As quoted in Cullinane, *Ilustrado Politics*: 306.

15 "The Official Count of the Vote Total In Manila," 31 July 1907, *Manila Times*: 1; Millard, "The First Filipino Delegates to Washington."

16 "Legarda and Ocampo Are Chosen," 22 November 1907, *Manila Times*: 1; *Journal of the Philippine Commission, Inaugural Session*, vol. 1 (Manila Bureau of Printing, 1908): 94, https://www.hathitrust.org (accessed 18 February 2016).

17 Millard, "The First Filipino Delegates to Washington."

18 Blakeslee, "The Gentlemen from Manila."

19 "Filipino Rebels Who Will Go Free"; Blakeslee, "The Gentlemen from Manila."

20 "The Selection of Ocampo," 23 November 1907, *Manila Times*: 4; "A Radical Filipino Delegate," 24 November 1907, *New York Times*: 8.

21 *Special Report of William H. Taft, Secretary of War, to the President on the Philippines*: 46.

22 *Journal of the Philippine Commission, Inaugural Session*, vol. 1: 115, 120, 362–363.

23 Ibid., 115, 120, 358–361, 369–370.

24 Ibid., 362.

25 Ibid., 361.

26 "Filipinos Fear Japan's Plans," 20 January 1908, *Los Angeles Times*: 12.

27 *Congressional Record*, House, 60th Cong., 1st sess. (4 February 1908): 1540; "Commissioners from Philippines to Sixtieth Congress," 13 February 1908, *Los Angeles Times*: 12.

28 No title, 8 February 1908, *New York Tribune*: 6.

29 "Briefs from Washington," 18 February 1908, *Baltimore Sun*: 2.

30 "People Met in Hotel Lobbies," 28 January 1908, *Washington Post*: 6; David R. Francis, *The Universal Exposition of 1904* (Louisiana Purchase Exposition Company, 1913): 566, http://books.google.com (accessed 19 February 2016); John T. Sidel, *Capital, Coercion, and Crime: Bossism in the Philippines* (Stanford, CA: Stanford University Press, 1999): 58; Murat Halstead, *The Story of the Philippines and Our New Possessions, Including the Ladrones, Hawaii, Cuba and Porto Rico* (Chicago, IL: Our Possessions Publishing Company, 1898): 61, https://archive.org/ (accessed 19 February 2016); "All Eyes on New York," 16 August 1908, *New York Tribune*: 1; "Wright Helped Out by Taft," 16 August 1908, *Chicago Daily Tribune*: 7.

31 "Needs Interpreter in Congress," 6 February 1908, *New York Tribune*: 7.

32 "House Scene Recalls Champ Clark's Vision," 28 February 1908, *Detroit Free Press*: 2; "Legislative Briefs," 28 February 1908, *Washington Post*: 4.

33 *Congressional Record*, House, 60th Cong., 1st sess. (1 April 1908): 4245.

34 Hearings before the House Committee on Insular Affairs, *Increase Membership of Philippine Commission*, 60th Cong., 1st sess. (20 February 1908): 4.

35 *Congressional Record*, House, 60th Cong., 1st sess. (2 May 1908): 5607–5609.

36 "Filipinos Urge Trade," 14 March 1908, *Washington Post*: 3; "Speaking Against Tariff," 17 March 1908, *Cablenews-American* (Manila, PI): 1; "Delegates Banquetted," 17 March 1908, *Manila Times*: 1.

37 "Philippines Under Debate," 23 October 1908, *Los Angeles Times*: 12.

38 Thomas F. Millard, "Philippines Not a 'Problem' Nor a 'Burden,'" 23 February 1908, *New York Times Magazine*: 2; Thomas F. Millard, "Our Interests and Our Duty in the Philippine Islands," 23 February

1908, *Washington Post Magazine*: 4; Thomas F. Millard, "Congress Holds the Key," 23 February 1908, *Chicago Daily Tribune*: A1.

39 Hearings before the House Committee on Insular Affairs, *Qualifications for Electors in the Philippine Legislature*, 60th Cong., 2nd sess. (17 February 1909): 1–2.

40 House Committee on Insular Affairs, *Qualifications for Electors in the Philippine Islands*, 60th Cong., 2nd sess., H. Rept. 2184 (15 February 1909).

41 Hearings before the House Committee on Insular Affairs, *H.R. 32004*, 61st Cong., 3rd sess. (26 January 1911); Hearings before the House Committee on Insular Affairs, *S. 7400, Administration of Civil Government in Philippine Islands*, Part 2, 61st Cong., 3rd sess. (26 January 1911).

42 Lewis L. Gould, *The William Howard Taft Presidency* (Lawrence: University Press of Kansas, 2009): 51–57.

43 Pedro E. Abelarde, *American Tariff Policy toward The Philippines, 1898–1946* (New York: King's Crown Press, 1947): 76–77.

44 *Congressional Record*, House, 61st Cong., 1st sess. (2 April 1909): 818; *Congressional Record*, House, 61st Cong., 1st sess. (3 April 1909): 929–930.

45 "Congress Hears Filipino Attack Tariff," 2 April 1909, *Christian Science Monitor*: 1.

46 *Congressional Record*, House, 61st Cong., 1st sess. (2 April 1909): 818. For research purposes, the *Congressional Record* is inconsistent in how it identifies Ocampo. At one point he's referred to as "Mr. de Leon" and at others as "Mr. Ocampo."

47 *Congressional Record*, House, 61st Cong., 1st sess. (2 April 1909): 819.

48 Ibid.

49 *Congressional Record*, Senate, 61st Cong., 1st sess. (21 May 1909): 2240.

50 Abelarde, *American Tariff Policy toward The Philippines*: 100.

51 *Congressional Record*, House, 61st Cong., 1st sess. (24 May 1909): 2238.

52 The election was lopsided: Quezon received 61 votes, Ocampo received four, and two other candidates received one vote each. "Legarda and Quezon Chosen," 15 May 1909, *Manila Times*: 1.

53 "Ocampo Not Puzzled," 20 May 1909, *Washington Post*: 12.

54 Ibid.; "Ocampo Much Disappointed," 22 May 1909, *Manila Times*: 1; *Journal of the Philippine Commission, Second Session of the First Philippine Legislature*, vol. 3 (Manila Bureau of Printing, 1908): 502–504, www.hathitrust.org (accessed 22 February 2016).

55 No title, 12 August 1909, *Washington Post*: 7.

56 "Ocampo Funeral Set for Saturday," 6 February 1925, *Manila Times*: 1; "Pablo Ocampo Dead," 7 February 1925, *New York Times*: 15.

"The ambition of the
Filipinos to live an
independent life is one
which is undeniable and
persistent, and any measure
tending to oppose it would
only stir the people of the
islands and operate to
prevent the development
of a better feeling between
Americans and Filipinos."

Pablo Ocampo
Congressional Record, May 21, 1909

Manuel L. Quezon
1878–1944

RESIDENT COMMISSIONER 1909–1916
NACIONALISTA FROM THE PHILIPPINES

During a career that spanned the length of America's colonial rule in the Philippines, Manuel L. Quezon held an unrivaled grasp upon territorial politics that culminated with his service as the commonwealth's first president. Although he once fought against the United States during its invasion of the islands in the early 1900s, Quezon quickly catapulted himself into a Resident Commissioner seat by the sheer force of his personality and natural political savvy. Young and brilliant, Quezon, according to a political rival, possessed "an ability and persistence rare and creditable to any representative in any parliament in the world."[1] Quezon was wary of immediate independence, but in the U.S. House of Representatives, he worked tirelessly to secure his nation a greater level of autonomy. He met privately with the President and powerful committee chairmen alike, gauging the issues and crafting legislative solutions, which culminated in perhaps his savviest political victory, the Jones Act of 1916. "Considering the time I have been here, the character of the subject, and the influences I had to fight, I feel inclined to say that I am almost surprised that I have secured so much," he said.[2] Long after he left Washington as a Resident Commissioner, he continued to shape the office by choosing and sometimes discarding his successors.

Manuel Luis Quezon was born on August 19, 1878, in Baler, a town on the island of Luzon in Tayabas Province, Philippines, to Lucio, a veteran of the Spanish Army and a small-business owner, and Maria Molina Quezon.[3] The family lived in the remote "mountainous, typhoon-plagued" swath of the province that hugged much of the eastern coastline of Luzon. Quezon's parents eventually became schoolteachers, which allowed the family to live comfortably in Baler. Manuel, the eldest of three sons, and his brothers, Pedro and Teodorico, were taught at home by a local parish priest. In 1888 Quezon left Baler to attend

Colegio de San Juan de Letran in Manila, graduating in 1894. Shortly after, he matriculated to the University of Santo Tomas, also in Manila, to study law.[4]

About a year later, however, Quezon left school and returned home during the Philippines' revolution against Spain. He resumed his studies in 1897, but when hostilities began between the United States and the Philippines in February 1899, Quezon joined General Emilio Aguinaldo's forces. Commissioned as a second lieutenant, he saw little action, but rose to captain and served on Aguinaldo's staff. After surrendering to U.S. forces in 1901, Quezon spent six hard months in prison, where he contracted malaria and tuberculosis. He suffered from complications of the diseases for the rest of his life.[5]

On his release, Quezon resumed his legal studies at Santo Tomas and earned a bachelor of laws degree in 1903 before returning to his home province. Only in his mid-20s, intelligent, and a natural "master of political intrigue," Quezon caught the attention of American administrators, particularly Harry H. Bandholtz, the director of the local constabulary, and district judge Paul Linebarger. The two Americans soon adopted Quezon as a protégé.[6]

As a result, Quezon routinely walked a fine line, balancing the colonial agenda of his powerful American associates, the interests of Philippine nationalists, and his own career ambitions. According to a recent study by Alfred W. McCoy, a leading historian of the Philippines, Quezon—in an arrangement that seemed equal parts quid pro quo and extortion—worked as an informant for American security officials who kept a detailed list of accusations against Quezon—ranging from corruption to murder—that they could use to destroy Quezon if he ever ceased being "a loyal constabulary asset," McCoy wrote. Quezon reportedly had damaging information on his American connections as well, but he continued to spy for

them, passing along information about Philippine radicals in exchange for political support and for help ascending the ranks of the insular government.[7]

Quezon's political career began in 1903, when Linebarger named him the provincial attorney, or fiscal, of Mindoro, an island province near Tayabas.[8] Quezon was quickly promoted to serve as fiscal of his home province, where he famously prosecuted Francis J. Berry, who owned the *Cablenews-American*, one of the largest daily newspapers in the Philippines, on charges of illegal land transactions. He won the case, but had to defend himself against charges of corruption by Berry's allies. Once the dust settled, Quezon resigned and returned to private practice.[9]

In 1906 Quezon ran for governor of Tayabas Province, campaigning not only on his reputation as a lawyer, but on his connections with Bandholtz and other American officials. Belying his inexperience—he had been in politics less than two years—Quezon deftly maneuvered past two other candidates and overcame shifting alliances to win his seat.[10]

As a local politician, Quezon had not yet aligned with any national political party. In fact, at the time, American administrators regulated much of the Philippines' civil activity and very little formal political organization existed outside Manila.[11] Following a trip to the capital for a convention of provincial governors in late 1906, Quezon, in the hopes of laying the groundwork for a shot at national office, joined the Partido Independista Immediatista, which pushed for immediate Philippine independence.[12] In 1907 the opportunity came. He resigned from the governorship and ran for the Tayabas seat in the Philippines' first national assembly, which would function much like the U.S. House and was created by a delayed provision in the Organic Act of 1902. On July 30, 1907, he won election decisively.[13]

With the opening of the Philippine legislature, political parties and new coalitions "sprang up like mushrooms," according to one historian of the era, catapulting Quezon into the national spotlight.[14] His party, the Partido Independista Immediatista, was absorbed by the Partido Nacionalista (Nationalist Party), creating a majority in the territorial legislature. After throwing his support

for speaker behind Sergio Osmeña, a powerful young assemblyman with a broad base of power, Quezon was rewarded with prestigious appointments as majority floor leader and chairman of the appropriations committee. From their first term in the assembly until Quezon's death, Osmeña and Quezon went back and forth in one of the Philippines' foremost political rivalries, vying for control over both the party and their country.[15]

After serving just one term in the Philippine assembly, Quezon looked nearly 9,000 miles away for his next political challenge. In 1907 the Philippines began sending two Resident Commissioners to the U.S. Congress to lobby on behalf of the territory's interests. The assembly and the commission selected one candidate each, which the opposite chamber then had to ratify. It is not entirely clear why Quezon wanted the position in Washington—one biographer has conjectured that Quezon wanted to be the hero who brought independence to the Philippines— but in 1909 he sought the Resident Commissioner seat occupied by Nacionalista Pablo Ocampo. Regardless of his motivations, Congress and the President controlled the fate of the islands, and the Resident Commissioners, despite not being able to vote in the House, were best positioned to influence the territory's political future on Capitol Hill.[16]

"I have every reason to believe that I shall succeed in my ambition, or I certainly should not permit my name to go before the Assembly," Quezon told the *Manila Times* when asked about his candidacy.[17] Though initial reports indicated that Ocampo was surprised by the challenge, the incumbent later published telegrams to and from Osmeña indicating his desire to retire.[18] Quezon won handily with 61 of the 71 available votes, Ocampo received four votes— ostensibly "complimentary" gestures out of respect for his service—and a third candidate received none.[19]

Quezon arrived in Washington, DC, in December 1909 wearing a thick fur overcoat to protect him from the early winter chill and took up residence at the Champlain Apartment House, a new building at the corner of 14th and K Streets in Northwest.[20] Quezon received House Floor and debate privileges but was not permitted to serve on any committees.

Already fluent in Spanish, Tagalog, and the local dialects in Tayabas, Quezon recalled the "most serious obstacle to the performance of my duties in Washington was my very limited knowledge of the English language." He hired a tutor, but soon began teaching himself using a Spanish–English dictionary to read books, magazines, and newspapers.[21] His American friends gave him the nickname Casey, an anglicization of Quezon.[22]

Quezon's first term in Congress was relatively quiet legislatively. Publicly, he toed the party line on immediate independence, but, privately, he believed his territory should wait for independence for at least a generation.[23] Quezon's primary goal as Resident Commissioner was to win the hearts and minds of the American people—and, consequently, Congress—to support greater political autonomy in the Philippines.[24] Accordingly, he acted more like a publicist than a lawmaker. "My opinion is that we don't so much need to have delegates here as to have a press," he confessed to a friend back home, "and money which has to be spent for delegates ought to be spent on publication."[25]

Calling the Capitol "at once the best university and the nicest playhouse in the world," Quezon wandered the corridors of the new House Office Building (now the Cannon building) strategically bantering with Members and journalists.[26] He was a bachelor and naturally gregarious, and he frequently mingled with Congressmen and administration officials at dinner parties and long lunches. Compared to the Philippines' older, more staid Resident Commissioner, Progresista Benito Legarda, Quezon displayed a flashier style. The two disagreed on certain policies, but they got along "tolerably well," according to Quezon's biographer.[27]

Quezon's maiden speech in the House on May 14, 1910, reflected his goal to win over popular opinion.[28] He thanked the United States for its investment in the Philippines and appealed to America's revolutionary past, observing that most people would rather "emancipate" the islands than "subjugate" them.[29] He carefully emphasized that his constituents would not be satisfied with anything short of independence. "Fillipinos [sic] are not, as yet, a happy people," Quezon said, hinting at his gradual strategy to win greater autonomy while playing up his nationalist bona fides.[30]

In the fall of 1910, the policy differences between Legarda and Quezon and, consequently, between the Philippine commission and the assembly threw their re-election into chaos. Because Legarda opposed immediate independence, the assembly refused to certify his nomination. In retaliation, the commission rejected Quezon's candidacy.[31] For months, the Philippine legislature tried and failed to settle the dispute.[32] Finally, in February 1911, the House stepped in and passed a bill extending Quezon and Legarda's terms until October 1912, giving the insular legislature time to resolve its differences while maintaining representation on the Hill. The bill also lengthened the general term of service for Filipino Resident Commissioners to four years and raised their office budgets to match those of the rest of Congress.[33]

It was not until the fall of 1912 that the assembly and the commission reached a deal. In November Quezon recommended Manuel Earnshaw, a conservative industrialist with little political experience, as a replacement for Legarda, who wanted to retire from politics anyway. With the commission on board, Quezon was re-elected to another term. As a result of his carefully crafted compromise, Quezon enjoyed a smooth re-election to the 63rd and 64th Congresses (1913–1917).[34]

Throughout the first decade of the 20th century, American corporations looking to open outposts in the Philippines had been stifled by a law preventing them from buying land in large enough quantities to open commercial farms. But when the insular government bought a huge tract that had once belonged to the Catholic Church and was then unable to sell it directly to Filipino farmers, the American Sugar Refining Corporation, which had a stranglehold on sugar refining in the States, quickly snapped up the vacant property. Democrats cried foul, criticizing the William H. Taft administration for approving the sale, and began considering ways to clamp down on deals with U.S. monopolies.[35]

In Washington Quezon called out Democrats for timing their criticism to coincide with the upcoming presidential election, but he joined the chorus opposing the sale of additional friar lands.[36] In mid-May 1912,

Quezon delivered two long, impassioned speeches on the House Floor, filling the *Congressional Record*. He argued in favor of a bill that would place the friar lands under the same size restrictions put on the sale of other public lands. Speaking on behalf of the Philippine assembly, Quezon told the House that Filipinos would rather pay to keep the land than to sell it off to "individuals for exploitation." Quezon did not oppose American investment outright, but he wanted to protect the islands from corporations that could hurt native businesses.[37] It was also a troubling sign, leading Quezon to suspect that American officials would not fulfill the promise of independence.[38] The House never acted on the Philippines' land bill and the land itself remained under Manila's control, but the fact that U.S. monopolies got wrapped up in the debate tarnished Taft's re-election bid that fall.[39]

Quezon's ambition for greater autonomy in the Philippines won him no friends in the Taft administration, which had long sought to tighten the relationship between the territory and the mainland. At one point, Clarence Edwards, the chief of the Insular Bureau, warned Quezon that he was "stirring up too much trouble" and threatened "to get rid of him," according to one account of their meeting. Despite his own reservations about independence, Quezon replied that he was simply doing the people's work and would continue to fight. President Taft reportedly "lost his temper completely" when he heard what the Resident Commissioner had said.[40]

Quezon, however, was not as worried about the Taft administration as he was about the party faithful in Manila. Hoping to shore up his standing back home before the upcoming election, he anxiously looked for a way to put an independence bill on the floor of the House. Early in his push, Quezon reportedly formed a close partnership with Democrat Cyrus Cline of Indiana. Cline had studied the situation in the Philippines and believed he could make independence a reality. Their relationship was so strong, the *Indianapolis Star* reported in March 1912, "that he and Quezon became almost like long-lost brothers. Quezon was so frequently in Mr. Cline's committee room that he began to take on the mannerisms of a native-born

Indianan, although his language was a little out of joint with the Hoosier dialect."[41]

Along with Cline, Quezon cultivated other more powerful allies in the House, including Democrat William A. Jones of Virginia, who chaired the Insular Affairs Committee. Jones was a consistent supporter of Philippine independence, but he was ill and worked slowly and methodically to build consensus on the issue within his committee.[42]

Looking for a way to hasten the independence process in order to give his party a campaign issue, Quezon put together his own proposal (H.R. 22143) that he knew Jones could get behind. The bill, which Jones put his name on after party leaders gave it the go-ahead, set an independence date eight years later and provided for the creation of a Philippine senate. The islands would remain under America's military umbrella for the next two decades while a separate resolution would force other foreign powers to stay clear of Manila while the new government settled in.[43]

"As a representative of the Filipino people in this country, I have given my hearty approval and co-operation to both the bill and the resolution," Quezon said in a letter to the *New York Tribune*. By creating an eight-year buffer in which the United States would still exercise a measure of control, he believed the bill would "[give] the people of the Philippines an opportunity to practice self-government before finally assuming all the responsibilities of a wholly independent nation."[44]

Despite support in Jones's committee, Quezon's independence measure hit a snag when the Democratic nominee for president, Woodrow Wilson, advised the chairman to sit on the bill. Wilson, who bluntly told Quezon he did not think leaders in Manila would ever be able to unite the Philippines' diverse population, worried that independence would distract U.S. voters from other issues.[45]

Over the summer of 1912, however, Wilson walked back his opposition, giving Quezon the opening he needed. Quezon told the Insular Bureau's new chief, Frank McIntyre, that full independence could wait if Congress would agree to subtler changes. The Philippine commission had become so unpopular, Quezon said, that simply creating a territorial senate would buy the federal government time to deal with the question of independence.[46]

As tariff issues ate up much of the legislative calendar in 1913, Quezon counseled patience back home. He worked the angles in Washington to influence territorial appointments and lobbied for changes to the Philippine commission.[47] In August Quezon won a substantial victory when he convinced President Wilson to appoint Democrat Francis Burton Harrison of New York, a supporter of independence and a powerful member of the House Ways and Means Committee, as the Philippines' new governor general.[48]

Quezon thought highly of Harrison, and Harrison returned the sentiment, later calling the Resident Commissioner "one of the greatest safety-valves" Manila had in Washington. "These delegates have no vote," Harrison later wrote about his friend, "but they are given a voice in the House, and the voice of Mr. Quezon was worth many votes.... His brilliant speeches made an impression upon Congress, and every American Representative who heard him felt sympathy for this young man so ably pleading for the independence of his race."[49]

Quezon and Harrison disagreed on one key issue, however: the urgency of independence. Harrison wanted to hand over the archipelago's government to the Filipinos as quickly as possible, according to one historian of the era, but Quezon, like other party leaders in Manila, knew the islands would stumble if America pulled its resources too quickly. With Sergio Osmeña's help, Quezon sidestepped Harrison, drafting a new independence bill with the cooperation of the Wilson administration in Washington.[50]

Quezon's new proposal postponed independence for almost a generation and gave the President a say in the Philippines' affairs, but it also transferred much of the daily management of the islands to the Filipino people. In other words, it was a huge risk, less about independence than it was about "increasing home rule," the historian Peter W. Stanley observed. In one conversation after another, Quezon leaned on McIntyre at the Insular Bureau for support, knowing full well that Harrison would fight back.[51]

Quezon sought similar assurances from the President, and after meeting with Wilson in early 1914, the Resident Commissioner believed he had at least the conditional support of the White House. Wilson was not comfortable setting a date for independence and was more or less content to step back and wait to see how things played out, according to the *Washington Post*. That was fine with Quezon, who, along with Osmeña and other leaders, proceeded to amend the draft bill to include two long-standing Democratic requests: first, that independence would be possible only after the Philippines established a "stable" government in Manila, and, second, that the bill set no timetable for independence.[52]

When Quezon gave the new bill to Chairman Jones, he ran into some familiar problems. Jones continued to drag his feet, and House Democrats pivoted to other issues as the 1914 elections neared.[53] Quezon stepped up his lobbying, speaking with the Insular Bureau, business leaders, and the White House before winning enough support that summer.[54] Although the Insular Affairs Committee opted not to hold public hearings on the bill, Jones said he was in regular contact with Quezon during the markup. Earnshaw, meanwhile, went home to the Philippines to rally support for the bill.[55]

Under Quezon's guidance, the House cleared the rule governing debate after two hours of discussion. Republicans moved to table the legislation, but Quezon fought them point by point, arguing that the looming threat of a world war made Philippine autonomy more important than ever. Moreover, he said, by creating a Philippine senate, the United States would simply be "rearranging" the existing government, not creating something new.[56]

When the bill came up for general debate two days later, Republicans ripped into the Insular Affairs Committee for marking it up behind closed doors. Chairman Jones had earlier called it "an emergency measure," but Republicans cautioned Quezon about trusting the motives of the committee.[57]

Quezon responded forcefully. "I am not a Democrat nor a Republican, nor even a Progressive," he said. "The Filipinos take no sides in your partisan differences." He reminded the House that the measure had wide support in the Philippines, and he implored his colleagues to keep election-year politicking out of the debate.[58]

Quezon gave a full-throated defense of the bill on the floor a few days later, telling the House that the self-government provisions would allow the Philippines to prepare for independence.[59] He also used America's own revolutionary history to highlight the sentiment in the Philippines, asking his colleagues to imagine what it felt like to fight for political freedom.[60] Democrats rallied to his words, and one Texan even went so far as to say that any other debate on the Jones bill would be an "anticlimax."[61]

Quezon dutifully monitored the bill during amendments: countering mischaracterizations, opposing certain suggestions, and defending others.[62] After the bill passed the House and went to the Senate, he faced a whole new task. The core of the bill bolstering home rule in the Philippines made it through unchanged, but a handful of legislators threatened to kill the measure unless the Senate reworked the independence clause in the preamble. Quezon hustled to iron out a deal, but the 63rd Congress closed without a solution.[63]

The 64th Congress picked up Quezon's bill right away, naming it H.R. 1, the first piece of legislation introduced in the House on the first day of the new session. Senate leaders placed it on the legislative calendar a day later (S. 381).[64]

For Quezon, however, the bill remained a huge political gamble. He told the Senate Committee on the Philippines that it was not ideal, but the measure was about as good as he thought he could win.[65] After approving the markup, the Senate committee pressed Congress to quickly pass this second version of the Jones bill.[66]

Things came to a screeching halt in January 1916, however, when Democratic Senator James Clarke of Arkansas offered an amendment replacing the preamble's "stable" government requirement with a provision requiring the United States to pull out of the Philippines completely within four years. Looking to distance themselves from earlier GOP policies toward the Philippines, Senate Democrats, with the support of President Wilson, approved the change in a close vote in early February.[67]

Clarke's amendment completely changed the course of debate for Quezon, who now had a monumental decision to make. If he backed the amendment, Stanley observed, the Philippines would likely become independent quicker than originally planned. But that threatened to bring a host of troublesome issues with it, including widespread financial problems that could derail the future of the Philippines.[68] If Quezon opposed the amendment, however, the bill could fail altogether, erasing years of work.[69]

Quezon ended up supporting the Clarke amendment, and when the bill went back to the House, Chairman Jones begrudgingly brought the Senate version to the floor on May 1, 1916. Debate that day lasted nearly 13 hours.[70]

When Quezon addressed the chamber, he did his best to convey the gravity of the situation: Congress, he said bluntly, had the power to determine the Philippines' future. Quezon admitted that much of the bill had become "defective," but that he was willing to compromise on the Clarke amendment rather than risk the best chance the Philippines had to become independent. If the alternative was the status quo, "I am for the Clarke amendment body and soul," he said.[71]

Despite Quezon's impassioned remarks, enough Democrats teamed up with Republicans to vote down Clarke's "poison pill." Jones offered a few changes in keeping with the Clarke amendment, but when those failed as well, the chairman submitted his own Philippine bill, which more or less mirrored the one the House passed at the end of the 63rd Congress and which contained the "stable" government provision. Jones's version quickly passed the House.[72]

Assuming that this version of the bill would again die in the Senate, Quezon was crushed. "This ends my work in Congress," he told the Associated Press after the vote. "I am not coming back. What is the use? The action of the House tonight makes the fight for independence harder. I notice not a single Republican voted for the Clarke amendment. They had it all figured out in advance."

Surprisingly enough, the bill did not die in conference with the Senate.[73] Not long after the Jones bill cleared the House there were whispers that the Senate would acquiesce and abandon the Clarke amendment as well. On May 8, Quezon visited the White House and implored President Wilson to back the revived legislation rather than risk having to start all over.[74] Nearly four months later, the Senate finally cleared the House bill, a version of which Quezon had helped write years earlier.[75] With Quezon in attendance, the President signed it into law on August 29, 1916.[76]

Following the success of the second Jones bill, Quezon resigned as Resident Commissioner on October 15, 1916.[77] Friends in Washington threw him a farewell banquet at the Willard Hotel, and his arrival in Manila—during a typhoon, no less—was akin to a national holiday. Bunting-wrapped boats and flotillas greeted his ship in the choppy downpour, beginning two days of public speeches and celebratory banquets.[78]

Back in the Philippines, Quezon was elected to the new territorial senate, where he was named president of the chamber.[79] In 1918 Quezon married his cousin, Aurora Aragon. The couple had four children, Maria Aurora, Maria Zeneida, Manuel Luis Jr., and Luisa Corazon Paz. Luisa died in infancy.[80]

Quezon also kept one foot in Washington. He continued to lobby for Filipino independence, traveling to the capital on several "independence missions" between 1919 and 1934.[81] Following the passage of the Tydings–McDuffie Act in 1934, which created the Commonwealth of the Philippines, Quezon won election as the first president of the Philippines in 1935. Throughout his post-congressional tenure, Quezon held near-dictatorial sway over the Partido Nacionalista, either personally selecting or approving each of the next nine Philippine Resident Commissioners. He leveraged the Resident Commissioner position as a means to solidify his support in Manila, enabling him to virtually exile political opponents. On the other hand, if an ally broke ranks with him on the Hill, Quezon was quick to name a replacement.[82]

As president in the 1930s, Quezon worked to strengthen his authority at home and tried to brace the nation for war as Japan began encroaching on the islands.[83] Despite an attempt to bolster his archipelago's defenses and under pressure from U.S. officials, Quezon and his family fled his home country and set up a government in exile after Japanese forces invaded in early 1942. He lived in Saranac Lake in Upstate New York as his health started to fail. Quezon died on August 1, 1944, succumbing to the long-term effects of his battle with tuberculosis.

After a funeral mass at St. Matthew's Cathedral in Washington attended by high-ranking American military officials, Quezon's body was placed in a mausoleum at Arlington National Cemetery until it could be repatriated to the Philippines.[84] American forces began an invasion of the Philippines in October 1944 and captured Manila in February 1945. Quezon's family, living in Los Angeles since his death, departed for the Philippines with his body on June 28, 1946.[85] He was reinterred on August 1, 1946, in Cementerio del Norte in Manila. In his honor, an outlying suburb of Manila was named Quezon City and became the site of the national capital of the Philippines.[86]

FOR FURTHER READING

Gwekoh, Sol H. *Manuel L. Quezon*: *His Life and Career*; *A Philippine President Biography* (Manila, PI: University Publishing Company, 1948).

McCoy, Alfred W. "Quezon's Commonwealth: The Emergence of Philippine Authoritarianism." In *Philippine Colonial Democracy*, edited by Ruby R. Paredes (Quezon City, PI: Ateneo de Manila University Press, 1988): 114–160.

Quezon, Manuel L. *The Good Fight* (New York: AMS Press, 1974, reprint of 1946 edition).

Quirino, Carlos. *Quezon*: *Paladin of Philippine Freedom*, with an introduction by Alejandro R. Roces (Manila, PI: Filipiniana Book Guild, 1971).

MANUSCRIPT COLLECTION

University of Michigan, Bentley Historical Library (Ann Arbor, MI). *Microfilm*: 1909–1944, 54 microfilm reels. The papers of Manuel Luis Quezon contain correspondence, speeches, articles, and other papers related to all phases of his career in the Philippines and as Resident Commissioner in the U.S. House of Representatives.

NOTES

1   *Congressional Record*, House, 64th Cong., 1st sess. (1 May 1916): 7158; *Congressional Record*, House, 65th Cong., 2nd sess. (18 August 1916): 12839.

2 *Congressional Record*, House, 65th Cong., 2nd sess. (18 August 1916): 12839.

3 There is some conflicting information surrounding Quezon's family history. The noted historian Alfred W. McCoy cites a U.S. military intelligence report claiming that Quezon's biological father was a "Padre" who had an affair with Quezon's mother which resulted in her getting pregnant with Manuel. Before he was born, Quezon's mother was forced to get married "thus assuring that [Quezon] would be born in wedlock." See Alfred W. McCoy, *Policing America's Empire*: *The United States, the Philippines, and the Rise of the Surveillance State* (Madison: The University of Wisconsin Press, 2009): 110.

4 Roger Soiset, "Quezon, Manuel Luis," *American National Biography* 18 (New York: Oxford University Press, 1999): 28–29; Michael Cullinane, "The Politics of Collaboration in Tayabas Province: The Early Political Career of Manuel Luis Quezon, 1903–1906," in *Reappraising an Empire*: *New Perspectives on Philippine-American History*, ed. Peter W. Stanley (Cambridge, MA: Harvard University Press, 1984): 64–69; Peter W. Stanley, "Quezon, Manuel Luis, (Aug. 19, 1878–Aug. 1, 1944)," *Dictionary of American Biography*, Supplement Three, 1941–1945 (New York: Charles Scribner's Sons, 1974): 613–615; Carlos Quirino, *Quezon*: *Paladin of Philippine Freedom* (Manila, PI: The Community Publishers, Inc., 1971): 18–23, 41, 48–52, 58.

5 Manuel Luis Quezon, *The Good Fight* (New York: D. Appleton-Century Company, 1946): 88.

6 The relationship between Quezon and American officials in the early 1910s is discussed in detail in Cullinane, "The Politics of Collaboration in Tayabas." The quotation is from Cullinane, "The Politics of Collaboration in Tayabas": 77.

7 According to McCoy, even after Quezon became Resident Commissioner, he continued to spy on Philippine radicals for America's colonial administrators. McCoy, *Policing America's Empire*: 96–97, 109–111, 187–188, quotation on p. 111.

8 Quirino, *Quezon*: *Paladin of Philippine Freedom*: 66; Quezon, *The Good Fight*, 92.

9 Quirino, *Quezon*: *Paladin of Philippine Freedom*: 63–71; Cullinane, "The Politics of Collaboration in Tayabas Province": 73–74; Frank L. Jenista, "Problems of the Colonial Civil Service: An Illustration from the Career of Manuel L. Quezon," *Southeast Asia*: *An International Quarterly* 3, no. 3 (1974): 809–829.

10 At the time, the provincial governors were not directly elected. Instead, they were elected by town councilors, who themselves had been popularly elected under restrictive suffrage laws. Quezon's complicated campaign for governor is discussed in detail in Cullinane, "The Politics of Collaboration in Tayabas Province": 79–81.

11 An exception was the Partido Federal—formed in December 1900, primarily among Manila elites uniting on a platform of peaceful American sovereignty and eventual Philippine statehood. As a formal political party, however, its reach never extended far outside the capital. See Michael Cullinane, *Ilustrado Politics*: *Filipino Elite Responses to American Rule, 1898–1908* (Manila, PI: Ateneo de Manila University Press, 1989): 63–64, 97–98.

12 Cullinane, *Ilustrado Politics*: 251, 256, 274.

13 Quirino, *Quezon*: *Paladin of Philippine Freedom*: 78.

14 Ibid.

15 Though specific timelines vary, several scholars discuss the development of the Partido Nacionalista and Partido Nacional Progresista in 1906 and 1907. See Peter W. Stanley, *A Nation in the Making*: *The Philippines and the United States, 1899–1921* (Cambridge, MA: Harvard University Press, 1974): 127–129; Cullinane, *Ilustrado Politics*: 286–315; Quirino, *Quezon*: *Paladin of Philippine Freedom*: 77–81.

16 Quirino, *Quezon*: *Paladin of Philippine Freedom*: 85.

17 "Quezon for Ocampo's Seat," 11 May 1909, *Manila Times*: 1.

18 "Ocampo Much Disappointed," 22 May 1909, *Manila Times*: 1; "Ocampo Not Puzzled," 20 May 1909, *Washington Post*: 12.

19 "Legarda and Quezon Chosen," 15 May 1909, *Manila Times*: 1; "Quezon for Ocampo's Seat"; *Congressional Directory*, 64th Cong., 1st sess. (Washington, DC: Government Printing Office, 1913): 125.

20 Quirino, *Quezon*: *Paladin of Philippine Freedom*: 89; Frank H. Golay, *Face of Empire*: *United States–Philippine Relations, 1898–1946* (Manila, PI: Ateneo de Manila University Press, 1998): 165–166.

21 Quezon, *The Good Fight*: 114–115; Felix F. Gabriel, "Manuel L. Quezon As Resident Commissioner, 1909–1916," *Philippine Historical Bulletin* (September 1962): 254.

22 Stanley Karnow, *In Our Image*: *America's Empire in the Philippines* (New York: Random House, 1990): 241.

23 Michael Paul Onorato argues that Quezon opposed complete independence, preferring a permanent political link to the United States. See Michael Paul Onorato, "Quezon and Independence: A Reexamination," *Philippine Studies* 37, no. 2 (1989): 221–239. See also Lindley Miller Garrison to Woodrow Wilson, 19 January 1914, in *The Papers of Woodrow Wilson*, vol. 29, ed. Arthur Link (Princeton, NJ: Princeton University Press, 1979): 147–152.

24 Gabriel, "Manuel L. Quezon As Resident Commissioner, 1909–1916": 254.

25 Quoted in Stanley, *A Nation in the Making*: 170.

26 Quezon, *Good Fight*: 114.

27 Quirino, *Quezon*: *Paladin of Philippine Freedom*: 93–94.

28 Gabriel, "Manuel L. Quezon As Resident Commissioner, 1909–1916": 254.

29 *Congressional Record*, House, 61st Cong., 2nd sess. (10 May 1910): 6312.

30 Ibid., 6310.

31 Stanley, *A Nation in the Making*: 168–169.

32 Philippine Assembly, *Election of Resident Commissioners to the United States*, 2nd Legislature, 1st sess., 1911, Document No. 250—A. 38 (Manila, PI: Bureau of Printing, 1911), https://archive.org/details/aqw4348.0001.001.umich.edu (accessed 10 February 2016).

33 *Congressional Record*, House, 61st Cong., 3rd sess. (6 February 1911): 2022–2024; Public Law 61-376, 36 Stat. 910 (1911).

34 Manuel L. Quezon Certificate of Election (endorsed 22 November 1912), Committee on Elections (HR63-AJ1), 63rd Congress, Records of the U.S. House of Representatives, Record Group 233, National Archives and Records Administration, Washington, DC; Philippines National Assembly, *Diario de Sesiones de la Asamblea Filipina*, Tomo VIII (Manila, PI: Bureau of Printing, 1913): 160–161; Stanley, *A Nation in the Making*: 181–182.

35 Stanley, *A Nation in the Making*: 157–163. For a more contemporary history of the friar lands, see Charles H. Cunningham, "Origin of the Friar Lands Question in the Philippines," *American Political Science Review* 10, no. 3 (August 1916): 465–480. For newspaper coverage of the friar land sales in newspapers, see, for example, "Protest Sale of Friar Lands in Philippines," 1 January 1912, *Christian Science Monitor*: 9; "Committee Asks Friars' Lands Be Sold Off in Lots," 11 January 1912, *Christian Science Monitor*: 1; "May 'Gobble' Friar Lands," 9 May 2012, *Washington Post*: 4; "Would Protect Friar Lands," 9 May 2012, *Baltimore Sun*: 11.

36 McCoy, *Policing America's Empire*: 255–256.

37 *Congressional Record*, House, 62nd Cong., 2nd sess. (1 May 1912): 5698–5703.

38 *Congressional Record*, House, 62nd Cong., 2nd sess. (15 May 1912): 6503–6510.

39 McCoy, *Policing America's Empire*: 256; Quirino, *Quezon: Paladin of Philippine Freedom*: 96–97.

40 Francis Burton Harrison, *The Corner-Stone of Philippine Independence: A Narrative of Seven Years* (New York: The Century Co., 1922): 47.

41 Stanley, *A Nation in the Making*: 172; "Committee Head Steals Cline's Glory as Future Emancipator of Filipinos," 31 March 1912, *Indianapolis Star*: B11.

42 Stanley, *A Nation in the Making*: 172–173; "Committee Head Steals Cline's Glory as Future Emancipator of Filipinos." On Jones's illness, see *Congressional Record*, Appendix, 63rd Cong., 2nd sess. (28 September 1914): 1291.

43 Stanley, *A Nation in the Making*: 173; "To Free Filipinos Eight Years Hence," 21 March 1912, *New York Times*: 1; "Filipino Bill In," 22 March 1912, *New York Times*: 3; "Nations May Pledge Filipinos Freedom," 26 March 1912, *New York Times*: 8.

44 Stanley, *A Nation in the Making*: 174; "Quezon for Independence," 1 April 1912, *New York Tribune*: 7.

45 Stanley, *A Nation in the Making*: 179.

46 Ibid., 180.

47 Ibid., 190.

48 Ibid., 198–201; Harrison, *The Corner-Stone of Philippine Independence*: 3–4; "Not A Good Philippine Counsellor," 29 August 1913, *New York Tribune*: 6.

49 Harrison, *The Corner-Stone of Philippine Independence*: 46–47. See also "Choice of Harrison Forced on Garrison," 22 August 1913, *New York Tribune*: 4; "Burton Harrison Confirmed," 22 August 1913, *Baltimore Sun*: 2; Stanley, *A Nation in the Making*: 198–200.

50 Stanley, *A Nation in the Making*: 212–213.

51 Garrison to Wilson, 19 January 1914, in *The Papers of Woodrow Wilson*, vol. 29: 147–152. See also Stanley, *A Nation in the Making*: 213–214, quotation on p. 213. The President also met with Chairman Jones to discuss the situation in February that year. See "Wilson Takes Up Philippines," 12 February 1914, *Baltimore Sun*: 2.

52 Stanley, *A Nation in the Making*: 213–215; Garrison to Wilson, 19 January 1914, in *The Papers of Woodrow Wilson*, vol. 29: 149; "'Watchful Waiting,' His Policy," 12 February 1914, *Washington Post*: 3; "Philippine Bill Offers Independence," 4 June 1914, *Christian Science Monitor*: 7; "Early Independence of Philippines Urged," 21 August 1914, *Indianapolis Star*: 16; "Step to Free Islands," 21 August 1914, *Washington Post*: 3.

53 "To Give Filipinos Self-Government," 4 June 1914, *New York Times*: 5; "Philippines Must Wait For Freedom," 5 June 1914, *New York Tribune*: 4; "A New Philippines Plan," 5 June 1914, *New York Times*: 10.

54 Stanley, *A Nation in the Making*: 215, 220; "To Free Filipinos," 4 June 1914, *Los Angeles Times*: I1; "New Wilson Bill To Free Filipinos," 4 June 1914, *New York Tribune*: 1.

55 *Congressional Record*, House, 63rd Cong., 2nd sess. (28 September 1914): 15843; *Congressional Record*, House, 63rd Cong., 2nd sess. (2 October 1914): 16079.

56 *Congressional Record*, House, 63rd Cong., 2nd sess. (26 September 1914): 15800–15812, quotation on p. 15806.

57 *Congressional Record*, House, 63rd Cong., 2nd sess. (28 September 1914): 15838, 15845.

58 *Congressional Record*, Appendix, 63rd Cong., 2nd sess. (28 September 1914): 1290–1291; *Congressional Record*, House, 63rd Cong., 2nd sess. (1 October 1914): 16022.

59 *Congressional Record*, House, 63rd Cong., 2nd sess. (1 October 1914): 16015–16016.

60 Ibid., 16019.

61 Ibid., 16031.

62 *Congressional Record*, House, 63rd Cong., 2nd sess. (3 October 1914): 16137–16138; *Congressional Record*, House, 63rd Cong., 2nd sess.

(6 October 1914): 16217, 16234; *Congressional Record*, House, 63rd Cong., 2nd sess. (9 October 1914): 16383.

63 Stanley, *A Nation in the Making*: 219.

64 Senate Committee on the Philippines, *Future Political Status of the People of the Philippine Islands*, 64th Cong., 1st sess., S. Rept. 18 (17 December 1915): 1.

65 Hearings before the Senate Committee on the Philippines, *S. 381: Government of the Philippines*, 64th Cong., 1st sess. (17 December 1915): 71.

66 *Future Political Status of the People of the Philippine Islands*: 3.

67 Stanley, *A Nation in the Making*: 221; House Committee on Insular Affairs, *Political Status of the Philippine Islands*, 64th Cong., 1st sess., H. Rept. 499 (6 April 1916): 1.

68 Stanley, *A Nation in the Making*: 223.

69 Ibid., 224.

70 "Will Keep Philippines," 2 May 1916, *Washington Post*: 1; *Congressional Record*, House, 64th Cong., 1st sess. (1 May 1916): 7144–7214; "No Independence for Philippines," 2 May 1916, *Atlanta Constitution*: 2.

71 *Congressional Record*, Appendix, 64th Cong., 1st sess. (1 May 1916): 2225.

72 "Will Keep Philippines"; "No Independence for Philippines."

73 "Clarke Amendment Defeated in House," 2 May 1916, *Los Angeles Times*: I1; "No Independence for Philippines."

74 "Senators Yield on Philippines," 9 May 1916, *New York Tribune*: 6.

75 "Senate Hedges on Philippines," 17 August 1916, *New York Tribune*: 2.

76 "See Filipinos Free by 1921," 26 August 1916, *New York Tribune*: 4.

77 *Congressional Record*, House, 64th Cong., 2nd sess. (2 January 1917): 748.

78 Quirino, *Quezon: Paladin of Philippine Freedom*: 114–118.

79 Ibid., 114.

80 Ibid., 127, 152, 192.

81 See Bernadita Reyes Churchill, *The Philippine Independence Missions to the United States, 1919–1934* (Manila, PI: National Historical Institute, 1983).

82 Eugenio S. De Garcia, "The Man Quintin Paredes," 5 September 1934, *Philippines Herald Mid-Week Magazine*: 3; "Osias Will Return to D.C. Tomorrow," 22 December 1933, *Washington Post*: 12; "Filipinos Reappoint Guevara, Drop Osias," 21 August 1934, *Christian Science Monitor*: 5.

83 For more on Quezon's time and his power as president, see Alfred W. McCoy, "Quezon's Commonwealth: The Emergence of Philippine Authoritarianism," in *Philippine Colonial Democracy*, ed. Ruby R. Paredes (Quezon City, PI: Ateneo de Manila University Press, 1988): 114–160; Theodore Friend, *Between Two Empires:*

The Ordeal of the Philippines, 1929–1946 (New Haven, CT: Yale University Press, 1965): 151–195.

84 "Quezon Rites Tomorrow," 3 August 1944, *New York Times*: 19; "High Dignitaries of State to Attend Quezon Rites Today," 4 August 1944, *Washington Post*: 9; "Arlington Burial, Tribute to Quezon," 5 August 1944, *New York Times*: 11; "Quezon to Rest at Arlington Until Philippines Are Freed," 5 August 1944, *Washington Post*: 2.

85 "Family of Late Filipino Chief in Southland," 4 November 1944, *Los Angeles Times*: 3; "Quezon's Body Starts for Manila Tuesday," 29 June 1946, *New York Times*: 19.

86 "New Capitol in Manila," 30 December 1946, *New York Times*: 3.

"I am not a Democrat nor a Republican, nor even a Progressive. The Filipinos take no sides in your partisan differences."

Manuel L. Quezon
Congressional Record, October 1, 1914

Manuel Earnshaw
1862–1936

RESIDENT COMMISSIONER 1912–1917
INDEPENDENT FROM PHILIPPINES

As a marine engineer and shipbuilder, Manuel Earnshaw never intended to dip his toes into political waters. Even when he did represent the Philippines in the U.S. Congress for two terms, he left nary a ripple.

But Earnshaw's selection as Resident Commissioner, engineered by the kingmaker of Filipino politics Manuel L. Quezon, ended an ugly impasse between the islands' commission and assembly and—not coincidentally—also cleared Quezon's path to single-handedly negotiate the first step toward Philippine independence: the Jones Act of 1916. Earnshaw readily admitted his lack of policy chops, noting that, when discussions turned to politics, he sought the refuge of "the billiard room or some other part of the club, for politics is not, nor has it ever been my game."[1] Still, he dutifully followed Quezon's lead and seemed content to serve as a symbol of the Philippines' thriving economy—an accompaniment to the political arguments advanced by Quezon of Filipinos' readiness for autonomy. Like all good businessmen, he longed for the stability and order that certainty brought. "The main thing, the essential thing in the whole matter is this: That something definite be given [to] us," Earnshaw told the *New York Times*. "We want something specific in the way of time, not 'when we are fit for self-government,' or 'when it shall seem best' in the eyes of somebody. We want the year, month and day—and until that date is set there will be unrest and disquiet in the Philippines."[2]

Manuel Earnshaw was born in Cavite City, Cavite Province, Philippines, on November 19, 1862. The oldest son of a British engineer, Daniel Earnshaw, and Gavina Noguera, a Filipina, Manuel grew up in the Manila area with his brothers, Tomas and Daniel. Earnshaw graduated from Ateneo de Manila University, a prominent secondary school. Cavite City sits on a peninsula jutting into Manila Bay just south of the city of Manila. Drawn to the sea, he learned the business of shipbuilding as an apprentice in his father's engineering business. He joined the Spanish Navy and earned a marine engineering degree from the Manila Nautical School.

Earnshaw worked for his father's business, D. Earnshaw & Company, as a marine engineer beginning in 1885. His career advanced rapidly when the Wilks & Boyle Company hired him in 1888. Four years later, he rose to partner in the company, and his name was emblazoned on the new masthead, Boyle & Earnshaw. In 1901 Earnshaw acquired full control of the company, later renamed Earnshaw Slipways & Engineering Company, and formed a new partnership that included his brothers. By 1912 Earnshaw's company had grown into the islands' largest shipbuilding plant—capable of repairing or building boats up to 460 feet in length at its docks and facility that spread across more than seven acres.[3] On February 4, 1888, Earnshaw married Maria Villar Ubalda; the couple had no children.[4]

While Earnshaw never seemed drawn to politics, politics eventually prevailed upon him when he was tapped as a compromise candidate to represent the Philippines on the Hill. By 1910 the process for choosing Resident Commissioners had broken down. Past practice had been to have the unelected Philippine commission choose one nominee—usually an *ilustrado* or prominent businessman—while the assembly chose its own candidate who had a progressive view toward independence. But to ratify those selections, each body had to approve both candidates. Benito Legarda became the sticking point in this internal schism. Legarda, who had served as Resident Commissioner since 1907, never had been very palatable to the assembly. But his public opposition to independence as Resident Commissioner rankled the popularly elected body, sinking his stock even further.[5]

Assembly speaker Sergio Osmeña manufactured a crisis when he pressed to have both nominees for Resident Commissioner be individuals who had wide popular backing, including meeting the approval of the assembly, which refused to support Legarda's renomination. By 1911 the conference between both bodies deadlocked and failed to reach a compromise. The U.S. Congress eventually had to step in with a temporary fix by extending the terms of both Legarda and his fellow Resident Commissioner, Manuel Quezon.[6]

Quezon resolved the crisis in 1912 by working with Governor General W. Cameron Forbes to secure consent from the William H. Taft administration that Legarda would be replaced with another prominent businessman. He then convinced Earnshaw to be that man. Earnshaw's background as a Filipino captain of industry pleased the conservative commission, which approved him. The Philippine assembly, at Quezon's prodding, eventually stood down, rubber-stamping Earnshaw's nomination to the 63rd Congress (1913–1915) in a 55 to 10 vote on November 21, 1912. It ended an embarrassing moment for the territorial government that undercut the case for Filipino self-rule.[7]

The day after the legislature formally approved both Quezon and Earnshaw, the *Manila Times* observed that the latter's selection as Resident Commissioner would "commend itself to all sections of the community. He is a business man, a native of the Philippines of high standing, ability, and integrity … and may be depended on for that wise union of conservatism and progress which the times demand." A week later, the paper reiterated the point by noting that Earnshaw's selection was a refreshing change. "It will be said at once that he is without political experience or knowledge," the editors conceded, "but to most spectators of the great political game here and elsewhere it is a positive relief to see a high office filled by one who is not a politician and cares little or nothing for the ways and methods of politicians."[8]

Quezon's motives were not purely altruistic. For one thing, the Earnshaw compromise cleared the path to his own re-election, now as the senior Resident Commissioner.

"Beyond this, moreover, it established a pattern, to which Quezon remained attached for as long as he held office as resident commissioner," observed historian Peter W. Stanley, "of yoking him with a colleague who was rich, personally dignified as a representative of the Filipino people, and politically impotent." Legarda and Earnshaw each filled the bill of being from the merchant-industrialist class, but the former, in addition to being senior in service to Quezon, enjoyed a warm friendship with President Taft and pursued an independent course, particularly on tariff issues. Earnshaw, on the other hand, was no political creature, and his position on independence more closely aligned with Quezon's. "The last thing Quezon wanted was a rival either in Filipino electoral politics or American legislative politics," Stanley writes. "Earnshaw knew nothing about American politics. He did as Quezon advised him."[9] He enjoyed traveling, however, and Washington seemed to him an agreeable excursion.[10]

Whatever the expectations for Earnshaw's service, it is clear that he left almost no legislative fingerprint during nearly four years in Washington. During Earnshaw's two terms of service in the 63rd and 64th Congresses (1913–1917), the *Congressional Record* barely mentioned his name, other than to note his attendance at various sessions of the House. After taking his seat on April 7, 1913, the Opening Day of the 63rd Congress, Earnshaw never gave a floor speech, introduced a single bill or resolution, or even inserted extensions of remarks or supplementary materials into the official debates, nor did he follow the example of other Resident Commissioners, who often gave copious testimony before congressional committees considering legislation that might affect the Philippines. He also spoke sparingly to the press. Earnshaw did have one thing in common with other Filipino colleagues, past and future; his powers were circumscribed by the fact that he could not vote on final legislation or even hold a committee assignment.

This silence seemed to be the way that he—and Quezon—wanted it. "I know nothing of politics," Earnshaw confided shortly after his election, and that clearly commended him, in Quezon's eyes. He admitted never having read the draft text of the proposed Jones

Act or even studied the particulars of the Payne–Aldrich Tariff of 1909. "When offered the post of Resident Commissioner," Earnshaw told the *Manila Weekly Times*, "I asked Manuel Quezon and other political leaders whether I should be obliged to have anything to do with occupying the post.... They all replied, 'Not unless you wish to do so' and on that condition I accepted the appointment." When reporters pressed him about his position on immediate independence for the Philippines, Earnshaw demurred, citing his inexperience: "I am at sea on all the principal things I should know about."[11] Indeed, he lived up to his end of the bargain, deferring to Quezon as the authority on all policy issues, including the question of Philippine autonomy.[12]

That pattern of deference was set from the beginning of this political marriage between the wealthy industrialist and the rising politico. When their ship landed in San Francisco in late December 1912, the *San Francisco Chronicle* reported that the delegation would press the new (and seemingly sympathetic) Woodrow Wilson administration for passage of an independence bill. But Quezon did all the talking, noting that "sentiment throughout the islands is extremely intense for home rule. The people believe that they are now able to govern themselves." Quezon also pointed to the islands' strong economy, which was "never in a more prosperous state." Earnshaw, a millionaire from the Philippines' industrialist class, seemed little more than a showcase for that claim, the very embodiment of the islands' economic vitality.[13] The new Resident Commissioner, the *Chronicle* noted, "travels in magnificence, having a retinue of servants with him."[14]

While Quezon took a highly public profile promoting the passage of the Jones bill as it percolated in the House during several sessions, Earnshaw lent the effort only an occasional public endorsement. He likely lobbied businesses with stakes in the Filipino economy as well. Otherwise, he appears exclusively to have been a silent partner who may well have helped to fund the lobbying effort with his own personal fortune by entertaining key committee members and government officials, but who was a mum wingman to the senior Resident Commissioner.[15]

Four months after the Jones Act became law, the *Manila Times* reported that Earnshaw had tendered his resignation and retired from the House in mid-January 1917, citing health issues and the pressing needs of his vast business enterprise.[16] His belief that his work was accomplished also seemed apparent in an address he made marking the 20th anniversary of the martyred patriot Jose Rizal weeks earlier. "The United States of America, which has always taken the lead in the advocacy of national liberty," he told a crowd at Washington's Ebbitt restaurant, "has begun to accede to the aspirations of our people by the congressional enactment last August of our new organic law, called the 'Jones law,' which gives us an ample autonomy and a clear, unmistakable promise of our independence."[17]

Earnshaw's and Quezon's terms were set to expire anyway in early March of that year to comply with the new provisions of the Jones Act. "I am more than happy to have had the opportunity to live in Washington and represent the Philippine Islands there," Earnshaw told the *Manila Times* on his return trip home, "but it is my intention to settle down … and devote myself to my private affairs and my business." During a stop in Japan on the journey back to Manila, he and Quezon briefed their successors, Jaime C. de Veyra and Teodoro R. Yangco, who were en route to Washington.[18]

Upon his return to the Philippines, Earnshaw resumed his business affairs until he retired in 1921. Earnshaw committed suicide with a revolver in his family's Manila mausoleum on February 13, 1936. His suicide note indicated that age, declining health, and financial reverses were to blame.[19]

Quezon, who remained on close terms with Earnshaw, recalled his colleague as a "wonderful man in every respect and a sincere patriot." He generously added in retrospect, "The part he took in getting through Congress the Jones act has given him a place in the history of the Philippines." Earnshaw's last wish was that his body not be removed from the family crypt but simply be buried there. He is interred in Manila's Cementerio del Norte, where six other Resident Commissioners also are buried.[20]

NOTES

1   "Earnshaw, Who Succeeds Legarda Talks on Independence Question," 29 November 1912, *Manila Weekly Times*: 43.

2   "Philippine Freedom Advocated by New Resident Commissioner," 30 March 1913, *New York Times*: SM6.

3   "Growth of Earnshaw Company," 18 October 1912, *Manila Times Weekly*: n.p.

4   *Congressional Directory*, 64th Cong., 1st sess. (Washington, DC: Government Printing Office, 1915): 125; "Manuel Earnshaw," *Biographical Directory of the United States Congress, 1774–Present*, http://bioguide.congress.gov/scripts/biodisplay.pl?index=E000015; "Growth of Earnshaw Company"; "Philippine Freedom Advocated by New Resident Commissioner"; "Reverses Drive Earnshaw to Suicide," 14 February 1936, *Manila Tribune*: 4; U.S. Passport Applications, Hawaii, Puerto Rico, and Philippines, 1907–1925, box 4251, vol 8., National Archives and Records Administration (hereinafter NARA), Washington, DC, http://search.ancestrylibrary.com (accessed 25 February 2015).

5   Peter W. Stanley, *A Nation in the Making: The Philippines and the United States, 1899–1921* (Cambridge, MA: Harvard University Press, 1974): 168–169.

6   Stanley, *A Nation in the Making*: 168–169.

7   Philippines Legislative Assembly, *Diario de Sesiones de la Asamblea Filipina*, Tomo VIII (Manila, PI: Bureau of Printing, 1913): 161; Manuel Earnshaw Certificate of Election (endorsed 22 November 1912), Committee on Elections (HR63A-J1), 63rd Cong., Records of the U.S. House of Representatives, Record Group 233, NARA; Stanley, *A Nation in the Making*: 181–182.

8   "The Week and the Outlook," 22 November 1912, *Manila Times Weekly Edition*: 1; "The Point of View—Topics of the Week: Delegate Manuel Earnshaw," 29 November 1912, *Manila Weekly Times*: 2.

9   Stanley, *A Nation in the Making*: 181–182.

10   "'One of the Finest Capitals'—Philippine Commissioner So States," 1 September 1913, *Washington Post*: CW6.

11   "Earnshaw, Who Succeeds Legarda Talks on Independence Question."

12   Stanley, *A Nation in the Making*: 181–182.

13   "Filipinos Want Home Rule; Will Urge Passage of Bill," 28 December 1912, *San Francisco Chronicle*: 18.

14   "Philippine Delegate Is Here; In Favor of Independence," 11 March 1913, *San Francisco Chronicle*: 1.

15   "Philippine Freedom Advocated by New Resident Commissioner"; "To Urge Island Independence: Philippine Delegate Arrives," 31 December 1913, *San Francisco Chronicle*: 18; "Reads Filipinos' Future," 31 December 1916, *Washington Post*: 4.

16   "Earnshaw Resigns Commissionership," 11 January 1917, *Cablenews-American* (Manila, PI): 1.

17   "Reads Filipinos' Future."

18   "Earnshaw Resigns Commissionership"; "Earnshaw for Private Life," 27 June 1917, *Manila Times*: 1.

19   "Noted Filipino Ends Life," 14 February 1936, *New York Times*: 9; "Reverses Drive Earnshaw to Suicide."

20   "Manuel Earnshaw Commits Suicide in Mausoleum," 22 February 1936, *Philippines Free Press*: 35; "Manuel Earnshaw," *Biographical Directory of the United States Congress, 1774–Present*, http://bioguide.congress.gov/scripts/biodisplay.pl?index=E000015; "Manila North Cemetery," http://www.manila.gov.ph/manilanorthcem.htm (accessed 13 April 2011).

"HE IS A BUSINESS MAN,
A NATIVE OF THE PHILIPPINES
OF HIGH STANDING, ABILITY,
AND INTEGRITY ... AND MAY
BE DEPENDED ON FOR THAT
WISE UNION OF CONSERVATISM
AND PROGRESS WHICH THE
TIMES DEMAND."

Manila Times, November 22, 1912

Jaime C. de Veyra
1873–1963

RESIDENT COMMISSIONER 1917–1923
NACIONALISTA FROM THE PHILIPPINES

As a journalist turned politician, Jaime de Veyra was the voice of the Philippines in Washington following enactment of the landmark Jones Act of 1916. As Manuel L. Quezon's successor in Congress, de Veyra spent six years as Resident Commissioner navigating the shifting U.S. political landscape, speaking on behalf of the Philippine legislature, and lobbying for an independent Philippines. "No benefits, however great, and no altruism, however splendid, can compensate any people for the lack of that national independence," de Veyra noted in a House Floor speech late in his career. "Without freedom wealth is nothing, culture is meaningless, existence itself is only the procession of idle images on a purposeless screen."[1]

Jaime Carlos de Veyra was born in Tanauan, which is on the northeast coast of Leyte Province in the Philippines, on November 4, 1873, to Felix de Veyra, the director of a private school, and Ildefonsa Diaz. Born into a middle-class family on an island 600 miles southeast of Manila, de Veyra received an education in the local schools. He left Tanauan at age 15 to attend the Colegio de San Juan de Letran in Manila. After he graduated with a bachelor of arts in 1893, de Veyra remained in Manila for two more years to study at the University of Santo Tomas, studying alongside future national leaders Sergio Osmeña and Manuel Quezon. The Philippine Revolution of 1896 interrupted de Veyra's studies, prompting him to return home and join the fight against the Spanish, eventually serving as secretary to provincial rebel commander General Ambrosio Mojica. On June 28, 1907, he married Sofia Reyes, a notable social worker who became one of the most prominent women on the islands. The couple had four children, Jesus María, Manuel, Lourdes Josefina, and Maria Rosario. In 1961, when de Veyra was in his late 80s, he received an honorary PhD in humane letters from Ateneo Municipal de Manila.[2]

After the war, de Veyra worked as a newspaper editor, starting *El Nuevo Día* (*The New Day*) with his former college classmate, Sergio Osmeña, on the neighboring island of Cebu. Together they dug into local political issues that arose during the transition from Spanish rule to American occupation. The publication was critical of the new U.S. administration, and cautious American bureaucrats viewed de Veyra "as anti-American with pro-Republic sympathies." Many worried that the paper might be too radical, but Osmeña's deft skills as a diplomat kept it from being censored or shut down.

El Nuevo Día ended up being a short-lived experiment. Osmeña quickly won election as governor of the province, leaving de Veyra to manage the paper by himself. But de Veyra was also gradually drawn into Cebu City politics, winning election as municipal councillor in 1901. When *El Nuevo Día* folded in November 1902, de Veyra jumped to another newspaper, *La Nueva Era* (*The New Era*) and oversaw its Tagalog section. He also managed a private school in Leyte. In 1904, after narrowly losing the race for governor of his home province of Leyte, de Veyra returned to Manila to join the staff of *El Renacimiento* (*The Renaissance*), a newspaper run by a former colleague from *El Nuevo Día*, Rafael Palma. Like their old publication, *El Renacimiento* criticized the U.S. colonial government.[3]

In 1906 de Veyra left journalism for good. That year he again ran for governor of Leyte against Peter Borseth, one of the few remaining Americans in a popularly elected office. According to one scholar, de Veyra was part of an emerging generation of politicians who commanded local bases of power outside Manila, their influence enhanced by U.S. officials who wanted native allies to help maintain control of the Philippines. Running as a Nacionalista, de Veyra was seen by Manila authorities as an unpalatable "radical." Officials in Leyte, on the other hand, celebrated

when he won the governorship. An American supporter cabled the news to Manila: "God lives. Leyte saved. Borseth overwhelmingly defeated."[4]

De Veyra served as provincial governor for little more than a year before running for a seat from Leyte in the newly created first Philippine assembly. Elected in July 1907, he served for two terms (1907–1912) alongside familiar faces. Osmeña, now a representative of Cebu Province, was speaker of the assembly, and his other college contemporary, Manuel Quezon, represented Tayabas and served as majority floor leader.

When *Outlook* magazine profiled the assembly shortly after it first convened, it noted that de Veyra had shed his reputation as a "revolutionary firebrand" in favor "of more moderate measures." De Veyra, according to *Outlook*, understood the assembly to be something of a "political training-school" where Filipino politicians could prove to the world that they were capable of handling the responsibilities of self-government.[5] During his time in the legislature, de Veyra earned the nickname "Protector of Children," steering government subsidies toward pasteurizing the islands' milk supply and authoring a law making women eligible to be schoolteachers.

After Quezon went to Washington as Resident Commissioner in 1909, he and de Veyra stayed in close contact.[6] That political connection advanced de Veyra's career at various turns, and in 1913 he was nominated to serve on the Philippine commission. Four other Filipinos were also selected so that, when the commission convened later that year, Native Filipinos held the majority for the first time. De Veyra eventually became the commission's executive secretary.[7]

Under the Jones Act of 1916, a formal, popularly elected senate replaced the Philippine commission, and in Washington neither Quezon nor Manuel Earnshaw stood for re-election as Resident Commissioner. De Veyra and Teodoro R. Yangco were nominated to take their places, and, as the nominee of the new senate, de Veyra sailed through the process. Facing only minor opposition, both men were elected to three-year terms by a joint session of the Philippine legislature on January 10, 1917.[8]

De Veyra's political skill, one Manila newspaper noted, made him "ably prepared" to direct the Philippines' agenda on Capitol Hill in the years following the Jones Act.[9] According to the *Christian Science Monitor*, he and Yangco shared the workload. In effect, de Veyra would represent the Filipino people while Yangco would work to protect the Philippines' commercial interests.[10] While Yangco did not stand for re-election in 1920, de Veyra was re-elected by the Philippine legislature on February 7, 1920. His second term commenced midway through the 66th Congress (1919–1921).[11]

Throughout his career on the Hill, de Veyra had the expert help of his wife, Sofia, who began her career as an educator and in her own right had become a leading proponent of Filipino women's issues. In 1907 she founded the first training school for nurses on the islands and later organized women's clubs throughout the archipelago that she then consolidated into the National Federation of Women's Clubs. The *Philippines Free Press* once observed that she was "the most envied woman of the Philippines" and a role model for many young women who aspired to careers in public service.[12]

When the Nineteenth Amendment granting U.S. women the right to vote went into effect, Sofia de Veyra spoke frequently on the East Coast lecture circuit, stressing the gains of Filipino women. Because of the matriarchal culture on the islands, they enjoyed progressive property rights and professional opportunities unavailable to women in the United States, Mrs. de Veyra noted. She voiced the strong desire among Filipinos for "progressive legislation" particularly in women's health care, child health, and day care. She confidently predicted that Filipino women would soon gain access to the ballot and was an unceasing advocate for the right of the Filipino people for self-rule.[13] "I want the Americans to know the truth about that distant country," Sofia said, "which is not infrequently misrepresented and misunderstood."[14]

During his entire six-year stint in Washington, House Rules barred Jaime de Veyra from serving on committees or voting. He spoke sparingly in debates, perhaps a half dozen times in all. He did not deliver his first floor speech until the closing weeks of the 65th Congress (1917–1919), when he eulogized William A. Jones, chairman of the Insular Affairs Committee and namesake of the Jones Act of 1916, calling him "the American most dear to our hearts."[15]

De Veyra was far less a legislator than he was a salesman, constantly publicizing the Nacionalista platform and calling for independence at the earliest possible moment.[16] Like Quezon, he was a pragmatist who leveraged a variety of opportunities to promote Philippine sovereignty. He often spoke to the press and privately lobbied Members of Congress and administration officials. He and Yangco frequently gave public lectures around the country, but principally in major East Coast cities, to publicize Philippine autonomy.[17] The pair also helped form a Philippine American Chamber of Commerce to encourage trade and rally support for independence. De Veyra was often found testifying before House and Senate committees on economic matters, including the adjustment of the Philippines' debt load, tax revisions for U.S. citizens living on the islands, and salary changes for U.S. colonial officials.[18]

When de Veyra went to Washington, Democrats controlled both the House and the presidency and were generally more focused on domestic reforms and mobilizing for World War I than the status of the Philippines. In 1916, the year before he arrived, Democrats agreed to support the Jones Act, gradually eliminating U.S. control over the Philippines, but when Republicans took over in 1919, Congress changed its approach.[19] When the GOP issued calls to strengthen U.S. authority in the Pacific, the Philippines' territorial legislature responded by more or less putting de Veyra in charge of an independence mission to Washington.[20]

De Veyra met the independence mission when it disembarked in San Francisco in February 1919, and over the next two months, the delegation traveled the country, publicizing Philippine independence. After meeting with Secretary of War Newton Baker, the delegation brought their cause to a number of cities, pushing for a final resolution on the Philippines' political status. Shortly after the mission's visit, the Philippines opened an official press bureau in Washington and put its two Resident

Commissioners in charge of placing key issues before the general public.[21] Two months later, de Veyra published a memorial calling for immediate independence in the *Congressional Record*, and in 1920 he led a Filipino delegation to the Democratic and Republican National Conventions to lobby for immediate autonomy.[22]

With Republican nominee Warren G. Harding's decisive victory in the 1920 presidential election, de Veyra and other pro-independence activists realized they would need to move quickly to secure as much as they could from the outgoing Wilson administration. A former chairman of the Senate Committee on the Philippines, President Harding, like many Republicans, believed the United States should hold the islands indefinitely.[23]

By November 1920, Horace M. Towner of Iowa, chairman of the House Insular Affairs Committee, publicly declared he would not consider immediate independence, forcing de Veyra and his newly elected colleague, Isauro Gabaldon, to shift their attention to the White House. Wilson had earlier told Congress that the Philippines had "succeeded in maintaining a stable government … and have thus fulfilled the condition" in the Jones Act as a prerequisite for independence.[24] In the fall, in order to move one step closer to sovereignty, the two Resident Commissioners persuaded Wilson's secretary to ask the President to support a bill certifying that the Philippines successfully fulfilled that requirement, but it was too little, too late. No Member in either chamber acted on Wilson's request.[25]

De Veyra backed one last, desperate measure in the waning days of the Wilson administration to speed an independence provision through Congress. Edward King of Illinois submitted H.R. 14481, a bill to enable the Philippine government, by means of a presidential proclamation, to form a constitutional convention within one year of its enactment. Once the Filipino people drafted and approved a constitution, the President could, at his sole discretion, declare the Philippines free and independent. In supporting the King bill, de Veyra cast aside concerns that the removal of U.S. military protection might embolden Japanese designs on the islands. "We are willing to take a chance and we are confident we shall be able to … defend ourselves from any possible aggression."[26] The bill went to the House Committee on Insular Affairs, but never resurfaced.

Early in the next Congress, de Veyra and Gabaldon met with President Harding to discuss the status of the Philippines in his new administration. The President refused to render an immediate decision about independence, but told the Resident Commissioners he would review the results of a fact-finding mission led by General Leonard Wood and former Governor General W. Cameron Forbes, who were sent to assess the Philippines' "fitness" for independence. Even before Wood and Forbes departed for the islands there were doubts their report would have much effect. "Nothing in connection with the investigation indicates that the movement to turn the islands loose from this country will be encouraged as a result of the inquiry," the *New York Tribune* reported.[27]

The Wood–Forbes Commission visited the islands from May to August 1921 and spoke with territorial government officials, Filipinos, American residents, and "foreigners of every walk of life." The commissioners spent a week in Manila, visited all but one of the 49 provinces of the islands, and held meetings in nearly 450 cities and towns.[28] In its final recommendation, the commission not only cautioned against independence "until the people have had time to absorb and thoroughly master the powers already in their hands," it actually recommended strengthening the powers of the governor general while weakening the territorial legislature.[29] President Harding endorsed the findings and nominated General Wood to reassert U.S. authority as the islands' new governor general.

In Washington, de Veyra and Gabaldon protested the commission's report in a joint statement. They took particular umbrage at the suggestion of curtailing the hard-won rights of the Philippine legislature: "To a subject people like us, the power of the Philippine senate to confirm or not to confirm appointments … is a bulwark against possible tyranny on the part of the governor general … therefore we can not surrender it." De Veyra also submitted a letter of protest and supporting documentation to President Harding, challenging the reported results in the *Congressional Record*.[30]

The Wood–Forbes Commission inspired a second Philippine independence mission to the United States in June 1922. As with the original mission three years earlier, de Veyra helped to coordinate its activities. Unlike the 1919 group, this one had a singular political goal: challenging the Wood–Forbes report to protect the promise of autonomy embodied in the Jones Act. Senator Quezon and Philippine house speaker Osmeña, the insular legislature's highest-ranking officers, led the delegation.

The House received the independence mission on June 21, 1922, shortly after their arrival in the United States. Peering down from the public gallery, they listened as Insular Affairs Committee Chairman Horace Towner complimented Manila's leaders as "educated men," "able orators," and "keen debaters," and he noted paternalistically that Congress was "proud to claim them as our legislative children. We have given them, and they have gladly received and assimilated, our form [of government] and most of our procedure." After being recognized on the floor, the mission delegates went to meet with Speaker Frederick Gillett of Massachusetts and other Members of the House.[31]

Nine days later, de Veyra submitted a "statement of conditions" demonstrating the viability of the Philippine government. The 23-page entry in the *Congressional Record* accompanied the official memorial that the delegation submitted to President Harding and Congress. Publicizing the message via the Philippine press bureau, de Veyra argued that the time was ripe for independence. Not only had the Philippines kept their end of the bargain by maintaining a "stable government" per the Jones Act, but each of the island's main political parties favored independence.[32]

In 1922 de Veyra opted not to stand for renomination as Resident Commissioner. In retrospect, the reasoning behind his decision is not all that clear. One could perhaps infer that de Veyra understood that, with the transition from Wilson to Harding, the case for immediate independence had been temporarily shelved. It is also plausible that, after more than 15 years in elected office, he was ready to return to private life. While he subsequently held appointed positions, de Veyra never again sought elected office and seemed content to focus on academic pursuits.

Three weeks before his term expired at the end of the 67th Congress (1921–1923), in early March 1923, de Veyra submitted a request from the Philippine legislature calling for a constitutional convention. The "holding of a constitutional convention," he said, was the "next logical step to be taken in the direction of … complete and absolute independence." He insisted that the desire for independence was requested "in no spirit of ingratitude, in no forgetfulness of the obligation of the Filipino people to the United States." Touting the United States' own history and noting that many U.S. citizens were sympathetic to Philippine autonomy, de Veyra asked how much longer Filipinos must wait. Citing the Jones Act, de Veyra noted that the stable government provision was the only requirement Congress asked of the Philippines prior to independence. Since the Philippines had met that obligation, de Veyra said, Congress's opposition to independence was meant only to benefit "small circles and private interests that derive profit from the present conditions."[33]

Upon the election of his successor Pedro Guevara, de Veyra returned to the Philippines, where he became a respected academic, widely recognized as "the peerless literary critic in Filipino-Spanish literature." He published broadly in periodicals and academic journals and also authored several well-received books. He served as the head of the Spanish language department at the University of the Philippines for nine years and was the assistant director of the National Library of the Philippines. At the urging of President Manuel Quezon, he headed the Institute of National Language from 1936 to 1944.[34] De Veyra also was a member of the Real Academia Española de la Lengua and the Philippine Historical Committee. He died in Manila on March 7, 1963.[35]

FOR FURTHER READING

De Veyra, Jaime C. *Efemérides Filipinas* (Manila, PI: Impr. y Libreria de I. R. Morales, 1914).

_____. *El Último Adiós de Rizal, Estudio Critico-Expositivo* (Manila, PI: Bureau of Printing, 1946).

_____. *Tandaya*; O, *Kandaya, Algunos Ensayos Historico-Literarios* (Manila, PI: 1948).

_____. *La Hispanidad en Filipinas* (Madrid, Spain: Publicaciones del Círculo Filipino, 1961).

MANUSCRIPT COLLECTIONS

The New York Public Library (New York, NY). George F. Parker Papers: 1919–1926, approximately 0.6 linear feet. Correspondents include Jaime C. de Veyra.

University of Michigan (Ann Arbor, MI). Anti-Imperialist League Papers: 1903–1922, items and 5 volumes. Authors include Jaime C. de Veyra.

University of Michigan, Bentley Historical Library (Ann Arbor, MI). *Microfilm*: 1909–1944, 54 microfilm reels. The papers of Manuel Luis Quezon contain correspondence, speeches, articles, and other papers related to all phases of his career in the Philippines and as Resident Commissioner in the U.S. House of Representatives. Correspondents include Jaime C. de Veyra.

NOTES

1   *Congressional Record*, House, 67th Cong., 4th sess. (15 February 1923): H3696–3698.

2   Gregorio F. Zaide, *Great Filipinos in History: An Epic of Filipino Greatness in War and Peace* (Manila, PI: Verde Book Store, 1970): 616–621; Carlos Quirino, *Who's Who in Philippine History* (Manila, PI: Tahanan Books, 1995): 69; "DeVeyra Buried Today," 8 March 1963, *Manila Times*: 2-A; U.S. Passport Applications, Hawaii, Puerto Rico, and Philippines, 1907–1925, box 4266, vol. 24: Passport Applications-Philippine Islands, National Archives and Records Administration (hereinafter NARA), Washington, DC, http://search.ancestrylibrary.com (accessed 2 March 2015); *Congressional Directory*, 67th Cong., 4th sess. (Washington, DC: Government Printing Office, 1923): 126.

3   Michael Cullinane, *Ilustrado Politics: Filipino Elite Responses to American Rule, 1898–1908* (Quezon City, PI: Ateneo de Manila University Press, 2003): 210–219.

4   Cullinane, *Ilustrado Politics*: 166–167.

5   G. H. Blakeslee, "The First Philippine Assembly," 25 January 1908, *Outlook*: 174–179, quotation on p. 178.

6   Zaide, *Great Filipinos in History*: 618; Peter W. Stanley, *A Nation in the Making: The Philippines and the United States, 1899–1921* (Cambridge, MA: Harvard University Press, 1974): 168.

7   "Five Natives: Philippine Commissioners Are Selected," 16 October 1913, *Boston Daily Globe*: 11; Stanley, *A Nation in the Making*: 205–206; Zaide, *Great Filipinos in History*: 618.

8   *Diario de Sesiones de la Cámara de Representantes*, 11 January 1917 (Manila, PI: Bureau of Printing, 1918): 433; Jaime C. de Veyra Certificate of Election (endorsed 17 March 1917), Committee on Elections (HR65-AJ1), 65th Congress, Records of the U.S. House

of Representatives, Record Group 233, NARA; "Yangco and Veyra Chosen to Be Resident Commissioners to U.S.," 11 January 1917, *Cablenews-American* (Manila, PI): 1.

9   "The New Resident Commissioners," 12 January 1917, *Cablenews-American Daily* (Manila, PI): 6.

10 "New Filipino Agents in United States," 20 April 1917, *Christian Science Monitor*: 7.

11 De Veyra Certificate of Election (endorsed 9 February 1920), Committee on Elections (HR68-AJ2), 68th Congress, Record Group 233, NARA; *Congressional Directory*, 67th Cong., 4th sess.: 126.

12 Zoilo M. Galang, ed., *Leaders of the Philippines* (Manila, PI: National Publishing Company, 1932): 16–18.

13 "Filipino Women Have Made Great Strides, One of Them Says," 2 May 1920, *Boston Globe*: SM15; "Status of Philippine Women High," 26 October 1922, *Christian Science Monitor*: 3; "Mother is 'Boss,'" 5 June 1922, *Los Angeles Times*: sec. 3, p. 11; "Says Suffrage Is in Grasp of Filipino Women," 27 April 1922, *Baltimore Sun*: 11.

14 "Mme De Veyra Shows Filipino Progress," 10 January 1921, *Boston Globe*: 4.

15 *Congressional Record*, House, 65th Cong., 3rd sess. (16 February 1919): 3523–3524.

16 "New Philippine Delegates," 13 January 1917, *Washington Post*: 2; "New Filipino Agents in United States."

17 Public Law 64-240, 39 Stat. 545 (1916); "Philippine Issue to be Discussed," 8 December 1917, *Christian Science Monitor*: 11; Jaime C. de Veyra, "The Philippine Elections," 6 July 1919, *New York Times*: 30.

18 "New Philippine-American Chamber of Commerce," January 1920, *Bankers' Magazine*, vol. 100: 72; "Trusts American Capital," 23 June 1921, *New York Times*: 28; Hearing before the House Committee on Insular Affairs, *Indebtedness of the Philippine Government*, 67th Cong., 1st sess. (1921): 18–19; Hearing before the House Committee on Ways and Means, *Internal-Revenue Revision*, 67th Cong., 1st sess. (1921): 22–24; Hearing before the House Committee on Insular Affairs, *Increase of Salaries of Auditor and Deputy Auditor of the Philippine Government*, 67th Cong., 4th sess. (1922): 3–6.

19 Frank H. Golay, *Face of Empire: United States-Philippines Relations, 1898–1946* (Quezon City, PI: Ateneo de Manila University Press, 1997): 171–172.

20 Bernardita Reyes Churchill, *The Philippine Independence Missions to the United States, 1919–1934* (Manila, PI: National Historical Institute, 1983): 9–17.

21 Churchill, *The Philippine Independence Missions to the United States, 1919–1934*: 13, 15, 17–18, 305.

22 Ibid., 9–17, 27; *Congressional Record*, Appendix, 66th Cong., 1st sess. (11 June 1919): 8848; Churchill, *The Philippine Independence*

Missions to the United States, 1919–1934: 27; "Filipinos Press Claims," 5 June 1920, *Christian Science Monitor*: 10.

23 Gerald E. Wheeler, "Republican Philippine Policy, 1921–1933," *Pacific Historical Review* 28 (1959): 377–390; Eugene Trani and David L. Wilson, *The Presidency of Warren G. Harding* (Lawrence: University Press of Kansas, 1977): 158–159.

24 Woodrow Wilson, Eighth Annual Message, December 7, 1920, in *American Presidency Project*, ed. John T. Woolley and Gerhard Peters, http://www.presidency.ucsb.edu/ws/index.php?pid=29561 (accessed 15 January 2016). See also Jaime C. de Veyra, "The Philippine Problem: The Truth about the Philippines," 5 March 1921, *The Independent* 7, no. 309: 12–14.

25 Churchill, *The Philippine Independence Missions to the United States, 1919–1934*: 27.

26 "Filipino Independence Gets a Boost in House," 17 December 1920, *Los Angeles Times*: 11.

27 "Policy in Philippines Waits on Wood's Report," 15 March 1921, *New York Tribune*: 4; "Seek Philippine Independence," 15 March 1921, *Washington Post*: 6; "Wants Filipinos Given Short Test," 2 June 1921, *Washington Post*: 4.

28 *Condition in the Philippine Islands: Report of the Special Mission to the Philippine Islands to the Secretary of War*, 67th Cong., 2nd sess., H. Doc. 325 (1922): 10–12.

29 *Condition in the Philippine Islands*: 45–46.

30 "Criticize Philippine Report," 2 December 1921, *Washington Post*: 6; *Congressional Record*, Appendix, 67th Cong., 2nd sess. (5 January 1922): 13263–13268.

31 *Congressional Record*, House, 67th Cong., 2nd sess. (21 June 1922): 9110–9112, quotation on p. 9110. Towner also inserted the mission's petition for independence into the *Record*.

32 Churchill, *The Philippine Independence Missions to the United States, 1919–1934*: 29–52; "Insist All Filipinos Want Independence," 25 July 1922, *New York Times*: 9; *Congressional Record*, House, 67th Cong., 2nd sess. (30 June 1922): 9821–9844.

33 *Congressional Record*, House, 67th Cong., 4th sess. (15 February 1923): 3696–3698; "Seeks Constitution for the Philippines," 16 February 1923, *Washington Post*: 4.

34 "Jaime C. de Veyra," *Biographical Directory of the United States Congress, 1774–Present*, http://bioguide.congress.gov/scripts/biodisplay.pl?index=D000276; Zaide, *Great Filipinos in History*: 618–619.

35 "New Filipino Commissioner," 18 February 1923, *Baltimore Sun* 2; "De Veyra Buried Today"; "Jaime C. de Veyra," *Biographical Directory of the United States Congress, 1774–Present*, http://bioguide.congress.gov/scripts/biodisplay.pl?index=D000276.

"WITHOUT FREEDOM
WEALTH IS NOTHING,
CULTURE IS MEANINGLESS,
EXISTENCE ITSELF IS ONLY THE
PROCESSION OF IDLE IMAGES
ON A PURPOSELESS SCREEN."

Jaime C. de Veyra
Congressional Record, February 15, 1923

Teodoro R. Yangco
1861–1939

RESIDENT COMMISSIONER 1917–1920
NACIONALISTA FROM THE PHILIPPINES

Known as the "Rockefeller of the Philippines," Teodoro Yangco, whose business acumen and wealth made him the islands' leading philanthropist, enjoyed a brief, symbolic term as a Resident Commissioner in the U.S. Congress. Yangco followed in the tradition of Benito Legarda and Manuel Earnshaw when he was selected as one of the islands' two concurrent Resident Commissioners on a track reserved for leading industrialists and merchants. These men tended to be gradualists on the independence question as opposed to their colleagues, who came from overtly political backgrounds and tended to espouse the popular will of Filipinos who favored immediate autonomy. But as a staunch ally of Manuel L. Quezon, who sometimes disagreed with his friend on tactics but not objectives, Yangco believed that, in the wake of the Jones Act, full freedom remained the central aspiration for Filipinos. "I am a business man and have [been] much involved in this question of Philippine independence," Yangco noted in 1919. "I am supposed to be a conservative. I believe still the time has come for independence. We are grateful to America for the great things she has done for us, and our desire now to separate from her side is only the natural desire of the child when he comes of age to leave the care and control of a parent."[1]

Teodoro Rafael Yangco was born in San Antonio, Zambales Province, Philippines, on November 9, 1861, the only child of the troubled union of "Capitan" Luis Rafael Yangco, a wealthy entrepreneur and industrialist, and Ramona Arguelles. When Teodoro was four, his father built a grocery store in Manila and moved away to manage it. For six years, Ramona raised Teodoro alone in San Antonio, where private tutors educated the boy. In 1871, at the beckoning of Luis, 10-year-old Teodoro traveled 120 miles to live with his father and attend Ateneo de Manila University, one of the Philippines' most prominent finishing schools. His father eventually remarried to Victorina Obin, and from this union Teodoro gained three step-siblings: Pacita, Luisa, and Luisito.[2] Teodoro graduated from Ateneo de Manila University with a bachelor of arts degree in 1880. He enrolled in the law program at the University of Santo Tomas for one year, but his father encouraged him to pursue a commercial degree instead of law. Yangco studied business in Madrid for a year but left disgusted. "Except for the fact that I was entitled to a vacation," he recalled, "my time was wasted. I learned little or nothing of value." Yangco moved on to Ealing College, a small school in West London, where he lived between 1882 and 1886.[3]

Upon returning to the Philippines in 1887, Yangco worked for his father to learn the business from the ground up. As a self-made entrepreneur, Luis Yangco did not provide his son any special favors and, in fact, verged on being overbearing. "Now Teodoro," he said, "you'll work as a clerk in my office. Don't think that simply because you have studied in Europe you can be a manager right away." A salaried employee, Yangco clerked and slowly worked his way up to manager after a 10-year apprenticeship. His father garnished his wages during that time, using that money to construct a private department store, Bazar Siglo XX (Twentieth Century Bazaar), in Teodoro's name. During the 1896 Philippine Revolution, when Luis was arrested and imprisoned for six months, Teodoro managed the family business. As a reward for his successful work, Yangco received a hefty raise and 13 ships to start his own business. He continued to manage his father's firm while, in his spare time, building his own shipping company.[4]

In 1907 Teodoro broke ties permanently with his father when Luis accused his son of using "insulting language" and abruptly disinherited him. Undeterred,

the younger Yangco formed a transportation firm that managed shipyards and shuttled commercial merchandise. Its reach was extensive, as it operated between eight cities throughout the Philippines. Additionally, Yangco was the proprietor of the Twentieth Century Bazaar store, started a dry dock and slipway operation, and expanded his real estate holdings. As a director of the Philippine National Bank and president of the Philippines Chamber of Commerce, Yangco worked with numerous government and business officials throughout the Philippines.[5]

Philanthropy became a central aspect of Yangco's life—which, by all accounts, was simple and unostentatious, given the magnitude of his wealth. He sponsored projects such as the building of schools and playgrounds around the country. Yangco also sponsored a number of Filipino students who studied in Europe and the United States.[6] The pious, lifelong bachelor was particularly active in charity work for children and even adopted several boys. Two boys, Lucio and Simplicio Godino, were conjoined twins whom he adopted in 1919 after their mother's death, saving them from being relegated to life as a circus act.[7]

Yangco toured the United States during the time of the 1915 World's Fair in San Francisco and visited a number of cities, including Washington, New York, and Chicago. A tall man with wavy dark hair and deep-set eyes beneath large brows, he made favorable impressions on American captains of industry, such as International Harvesters' Cyrus McCormick.[8] In several news interviews, he stressed Filipinos' desire for eventual independence and their satisfaction with Governor General Francis Burton Harrison. Yangco, who believed that Filipinos were not ready to govern themselves immediately, endorsed a protectorate system as the nation moved toward independence.[9]

With the passage of the Jones Act in the waning months of the 64th Congress (1915–1917), the Resident Commissioners' political emphases were in transition. The new law provided a path to independence that, initially, did not seem to require the vocal advocacy that had long been the approach of past Resident Commissioners, most notably Manuel Quezon. By the start of the 65th Congress (1917–1919), American critics pointed to Philippine

politicians' "excessive" focus on achieving Philippine independence at the expense of its economic development.[10] This type of criticism reinforced the need for a Resident Commissioner with sterling business credentials.

These factors weighed on Quezon and Philippine assembly speaker Sergio Osmeña as they considered candidates to succeed Manuel Earnshaw. Newly elected to the Philippine senate, Quezon exercised considerable control over the selection process. In late 1916, he approached Yangco and offered him the Resident Commissioner post. Yangco initially refused Quezon's offer, noting that it was a "fixed principle of his life" to stay out of politics. But Quezon, with whom Yangco had an almost fraternal bond, eventually persuaded his friend; Yangco himself recognized "the vital necessity of sending a recognized business leader to represent the aspirations of the Filipino people." Quezon later described why Yangco was an ideal choice, noting, "We need a man in the United States who is deeply interested in our institutions as well as in the development of our natural resources."[11]

On January 10, 1917, the Philippine assembly elected Yangco by a nearly unanimous 68 votes (two other opposition candidates garnered a single vote each). The legislature simultaneously elected Jaime de Veyra—a newspaperman-turned-politician—to serve alongside Yangco in the other Resident Commissioner slot.[12] News coverage in the United States pointed to the different roles de Veyra and Yangco would play. The former "was named to represent the political aspirations of the Filipino people, while Yangco will represent the business interests—a division of labor that has been followed in the appointment of Philippine resident commissioners since the office was first created."[13] The *Cablenews-American* approvingly noted that Yangco's "broad sympathy with all modern progress, whether social, political or industrial, especially fits him to represent the Philippines in Washington, under this new phase of relations between the Islands and the United States." Before leaving the Philippines, Yangco conducted a fact-finding trip to assess the islands' business needs. Shortly before his departure for Washington in early April 1917, the *Cablenews-American* described him as "the right man for the place," one who would follow in "Earnshaw's shoes."[14]

In a legislative sense, Yangco's service was remarkably threadbare. Part of this lack of production derived from the institutional roadblocks that greeted every Resident Commissioner. House Rules circumscribed their powers—most notably preventing them from holding a committee assignment or voting on the House Floor. During his three-year term, overlapping with parts of the 65th and 66th Congresses (1917–1921), the *Congressional Record* mostly just notes his attendance. After taking his seat on May 1, 1917, Yangco gave just two floor speeches in that span, both of which eulogized the life of William A. Jones of Virginia, chairman of the Insular Affairs Committee and sponsor of the bill that bore his name and set the Philippines on the long path to eventual independence. Yangco was also appointed to Jones's funeral committee. But he authored no bills or resolutions, nor did he follow the example of other Resident Commissioners by offering testimony to the various congressional committees considering legislation that might affect the Philippines. Whereas his colleague Jaime de Veyra served as a vocal advocate for Philippine independence in the mold of Quezon, Yangco had a far less overtly political role. While Resident Commissioners generally straddled a line between being legislators and diplomats, Yangco especially appears to have been more focused on representing Filipino institutions and business interests far outside the hall of the House.[15]

Yangco and Quezon enjoyed warm relations for many years, but a lingering strain seemed to fall upon their friendship, in part because of Quezon's pragmatic political wrangling that ushered the Jones Act into law. Yangco disapproved of Quezon's support for the Clarke Amendment to the Jones Act of 1916, which promised independence for the Philippines rather quickly after the law's enactment. Like many business elites who valued the trade relationship in place with the United States, Yangco at first preferred a slower, more incremental path to independence.[16] Quezon, too, professed to support graduated independence, an ideal embodied in the original language of the Jones Act. But looking to pacify

independence supporters in Washington and Manila who backed the Clarke Amendment, Quezon publicly supported it (Congress later stripped the fast-track provision from the final legislation). Yangco questioned Quezon's political expediency. In 1917, when Yangco first arrived in Washington to assume his duties as Resident Commissioner, Quezon invited him to stay at his home. Yangco reluctantly accepted and, when he arrived, left his baggage at the curb while knocking on Quezon's door. "I did not bring it," Yangco explained, "because before I accept your hospitality I want you to know that I am opposed to your policies." The outgoing Resident Commissioner put his arm around Yangco and gently ribbed him, "You are a saint." Later he would tell Yangco, "If all my friends were as frank and sincere with me as you are, I would be a different man."[17]

Whatever his personal inclinations, Yangco's work in Washington undergirded the push for independence in the waning years of the Woodrow Wilson administration. But Yangco provided implicit proof for Filipinos' fitness for self-rule almost exclusively through his personal example as a cultured philanthropist and business elite rather than through Quezon-like political maneuvering.

Yangco settled in Washington's Cleveland Park neighborhood in a residence he shared with his staff assistant, a chef, two servants, a chauffeur, and three adopted children.[18] His biographer maintains that, while he entertained at many of the city's finest hotels, he also kept his distance from the political intrigue of the wartime capital and "quietly evaded all attempts to make him a party to the artificiality and insincerity that characterized" its social life. Yangco also continued his philanthropic activities by giving generously to the American Red Cross—notably outbidding the financier Bernard Baruch during a wartime DC charity gala—and helping to save one of the capital's African-American churches from lapsing into foreclosure.[19] This charitable aspect of his time in DC won wide press coverage, and that seemed to be the point. In many respects, he served as a cultural ambassador whose refinement, wealth, and generosity countered coarse stereotypes about Filipinos and perceptions that the islands' political elite were calculating opportunists.[20]

Yangco, of course, also helped to promulgate business opportunities for the islands. He and colleague Jaime de Veyra played support roles when the First Independence Mission visited the United States in spring 1919. Led by Quezon and drawing from the islands' leading political class, technocrats, and businessmen, the mission included a special committee focused on commerce, Yangco's area of expertise. In late 1919, Yangco and de Veyra encouraged the formation of the Philippine American Chamber of Commerce, a New York-based group dedicated to promoting trade relations between the United States and the Philippines.[21] After the mission departed, the Resident Commissioners also oversaw the establishment of a Philippine press bureau, which sought to carry on the public relations work initiated by the delegation. With a small staff in Washington and an agent in New York, the bureau's mission was to distribute print materials about the Philippines to U.S. media outlets.[22]

In February 1920, Yangco announced that he would resign as Resident Commissioner, noting that he was eager to return home to attend to his large business empire. He did not, however, give up his role of being an ambassador of Filipino business, representing the Philippine Chamber of Commerce at the Pan-Pacific Commercial Conference in Honolulu, Hawaii. Yangco continued to advocate for Filipino independence as he traveled the world and raised his children.[23] He provided scholarships for students and gave to numerous charities and civic organizations on the islands, including the Young Men's Christian Association, for which he was dubbed the "father of the YMCA in the Philippines." On April 20, 1939, Teodoro Yangco died in Manila at age 77 after a series of complications from pneumonia. His remains were interred in the Manila North Cemetery.[24]

FOR FURTHER READING

Ruiz, Demetrio E., Jr., "Teodoro Rafael Yangco: His Life and Business Career (1861–1939)" (master's thesis, University of Santo Tomas, Philippines, 1975).

Stagg, Samuel Wells. *Teodoro Rafael Yangco, Leading Filipino Philanthropist and Grand Old Man of Commerce* (Manila, PI: University of the Philippines, 1934).

NOTES

1   George T. Shoens, "Free Philippines Now," 11 May 1919, *New York Times*: 36.

2   Samuel W. Stagg, *Teodoro Rafael Yangco: Leading Filipino Philanthropist and Grand Old Man of Commerce* (Manila, PI: University of the Philippines, 1934): 45–51.

3   Stagg, *Teodoro Rafael Yangco*: 59; Demetrio E. Ruiz Jr., "Teodoro Rafael Yangco: His Life and Business Career, 1861–1939," (master's thesis, University of Santo Tomas, Philippines, 1975): 65, 69–72.

4   Ruiz, "Teodoro Rafael Yangco": 89, 93–101.

5   "Teodoro R. Yangco," *Biographical Directory of the United States Congress, 1774–Present*, http://bioguide.congress.gov/scripts/biodisplay.pl?index=Y000004; "Old Yangco Disinherits His Elder Son, Teodoro," 19 October 1907, *Manila Times*: 1; "Teodoro R. Yangco Passes Away at 77," 21 April 1939, *Manila Tribune*: 4; Zoilo M. Galang, ed., *Leaders of the Philippines: Inspiring Biographies of Successful Men and Women of the Philippines* (Manila, PI: National Publishing Company, 1932): 55–56; Luis Yangco quotation from Gregorio F. Zaide, ed., *Great Filipinos in History: An Epic of Filipino Greatness in War and Peace* (Manila, PI: Verde Book Store, 1970): 630–631. For an extensive description of Yangco's business empire, see Ruiz, "Teodoro Rafael Yangco," chapters 6–8.

6   Fernando A. Bernardo, *Silent Storms: Inspiring Lives of 101 Great Filipinos* (Pasig City, PI: Anvil, 2000): 221–223; "Leader of Business in Manila is Here," 12 December 1915, *San Francisco Chronicle*: 24; "Yangco Pensionado Goes," 29 September 1918, *Manila Times*: 2; *Congressional Directory*, 66th Cong., 1st sess. (Washington, DC: Government Printing Office, 1919): 129. Dubbed *pensionados*, many of the students returned to the Philippines as civil servants. Yangco also defrayed the expenses of training the first group of Filipino nurses at a Manila hospital.

7   "Filipinos, Aged 11, Quarrel Seldom and Are Very Active and Healthy," 25 November 1919, *San Francisco Chronicle*: 13; "Twins, Joined Together, Visiting Boys Are Opposed to Operation," 25 November 1919, *San Francisco Chronicle*: 13.

8   Stagg, *Teodoro Rafael Yangco*: 125–131; "Leader in Business of Manila Is Here," 12 December 1915, *San Francisco Chronicle*: 24.

9   "Leader in Business of Manila Is Here"; "Tribal Feeling Block to Rule by Filipinos," 21 February 1916, *Christian Science Monitor*: 8; "Filipinos Not Yet Ready for Freedom," 21 April 1916, *The Republic* (Rockford, IL): 1.

10 Stagg, *Teodoro Rafael Yangco*: 135–136. See also "Practical Politics in Philippines," 9 September 1915, *Indianapolis Star*: 8.

11 Stagg, *Teodoro Rafael Yangco*: 136.

12 *Diario de Sesiones de la Cámara de Representantes* vol. 12 (Manila, PI: Manila Bureau of Printing, 1918): 430–431; Teodoro R. Yangco Certificate of Election (endorsed March 17, 1917), Committee on Elections (HR65-AJ1), 65th Congress, Records of the U.S. House

of Representatives, Record Group 233, National Archives and Records Administration, Washington, DC; "Yangco and Veyra Chosen to be Resident Commissioners to U.S.," 11 January 1917, *Cablenews-American* (Manila, PI): 1; "The New Resident Commissioners," 12 January 1917, *Cablenews-American* (Manila, PI): 6.

13 "Two Filipinos Appointed Resident Commissioners," 11 March 1917, *Indianapolis Star*: 2.

14 "The New Resident Commissioners"; "The Right Man for the Place," 28 March 1917, *Cablenews-American* (Manila, PI): 6; "Yangco Goes to Learn of Trade," 6 March 1917, *Manila Times*: 2.

15 *Congressional Record*, House, 65th Cong., 1st sess. (1 May 1917): 1659; *Congressional Record*, Index, 65th Cong., 2nd sess.: 375; *Congressional Record*, Index, 65th Cong., 3rd sess.: 225; Stagg, *Teodoro Rafael Yangco*: 137. Stagg suggests Yangco and colleague Jaime de Veyra helped to secure tariff legislation that benefited the Philippines, but no record of such a bill is listed in the *Congressional Record*, nor is there committee testimony that alludes to such legislation.

16 "Filipinos Not Yet Ready for Freedom"; "Tribal Feeling Block to Rule by Filipinos."

17 Stagg, *Teodoro Rafael Yangco*: 140–141, 163–167.

18 *Fourteenth Census of the United States, 1920: Population*, Washington, District of Columbia, Roll T625_210, sheet 2B, Library of Congress, Washington, DC, http://search.ancestrylibrary.com (accessed 8 February 2016).

19 "Yangco Donates On Eve of Departure," 5 April 1917, *Cablenews-American* (Manila, PI) 2; Stagg, *Teodoro Rafael Yangco*: 140, 143–146, 151–152.

20 "Filipinos to Help Win War," 1 October 1917, *Washington Post*: 8; "Philippine Issue to be Discussed," 8 December 1917, *Christian Science Monitor*: 11; Stagg, *Teodoro Rafael Yangco*: 159–162. According to Stagg, Yangco's reputation preceded him. President Wilson acquainted himself with Yangco after hearing of his philanthropic efforts and receiving a Filipino hat as a Christmas gift.

21 "$10,000,000 Bank Being Formed in Philippines," 26 April 1916, *Colorado Springs* (CO) *Gazette*: 6; "To Aid Philippine Trade," 12 December 1919, *New York Times*: 28.

22 Bernardita Reyes Churchill, *The Philippines Independence Missions to the United States, 1919–1934* (Manila, PI: National Historical Institute, 1983): 9–26.

23 "Sunday School Work," 11 April 1922, *Washington Evening Star*: 16; Carlos Quirino, ed., *Who's Who in Philippine History* (Manila, PI: Tahanan Books, 1995): 206.

24 Stagg, *Teodoro Rafael Yangco*: 151–152; "Don Teodoro Yangco, Philanthropist and Benefactor, Dies; Burial Sunday," 21 April 1939, *Philippines Herald*: 2; "Teodoro Yangco Passes Away at 77"; "Manila North Cemetery," http://www.manila.ph/manilanorthcem.htm (accessed 13 April 2011).

Isauro Gabaldon
1875–1942

RESIDENT COMMISSIONER 1920–1928
NACIONALISTA FROM THE PHILIPPINES

Wealthy and well connected, Isauro Gabaldon was part of a cohort of rising politicians who helped transform the Philippines and dominated the territorial government in the early 20th century. By the time he became Resident Commissioner, the islands were already along a path toward independence, but a presidential administration change only a short while later completely altered that trajectory. As a result, Gabaldon spent his eight years on the Hill fighting congressional efforts to reassert control over the insular government. As he once told colleagues, "on every occasion which I have addressed the Congress … I have declared that immediate, absolute, and complete independence is the desire of the great majority of the 12,000,000 inhabitants of the islands. Nothing less than this … will be satisfactory to the Filipino people."[1]

Isauro Gabaldon was born in the northern Philippine town of San Isidro, Central Luzon, on December 8, 1875. The landlocked Nueva Ecija Province, where he spent his earliest years, offered limited educational opportunities; Gabaldon's well-to-do family instead sent the four-year-old to Spain for his primary education in the city of Tébar, about 120 miles southeast of Madrid. At the age of 16, he attended the colleges in Quintanar del Rey and Villanueva de la Jara in Cuenca, earning a bachelor's degree from the latter school in 1893. "My dream was to be a military man," Gabaldon recalled years later. "But my father was against it. In school I was strong in philosophy and letters. And when the time came for me to decide, the happy mean was chosen: I took up law."[2]

Gabaldon studied at the Universidad Central in Madrid for five years, but returned to the Philippines after his father's death, earning a law degree from Manila's University of Santo Tomas in 1900. That same year he married Bernarda Tinio, whose family had considerable wealth and land. The couple raised two children, Teresa and Senen.[3] After passing the bar

in 1903, Gabaldon worked in private practice for three years. In addition to his work as a lawyer, Gabaldon was an oil and gold executive, and he owned several large rice-producing estates.[4]

Gabaldon made a rapid transition into politics and, though he at first avoided party labels, he struck an alliance with other up-and-coming nationalist politicos, such as Manuel L. Quezon, Sergio Osmeña, and Jaime de Veyra.[5] In 1906 he won election as governor of his home province, Nueva Ecija. As with other provincial governors, such as Osmeña and de Veyra, he left the governorship before his three-year term expired, running for a seat in the newly formed national assembly. Elected as a member of the Nacionalista Party on July 13, 1907, Gabaldon served two terms (1907–1912) in the national assembly representing Nueva Ecija. In Manila, he chaired the committee on provincial and municipal governments and served on three other panels: police, accounts, and agriculture.[6] While in the legislature, he authored a bill subsequently named after him that provided 1 million pesos to construct modern public schools throughout the islands, but particularly in the *barrios* (neighborhoods). Despite his vast wealth, he earned a reputation for keeping a watchful eye on the *aparcería* (sharecropping) system, protecting the rights of agricultural laborers and small farmers.

From 1912 to 1916, Gabaldon again served as provincial governor in Nueva Ecija, but with the enactment of the Jones Act in 1916 and the creation of a popularly elected senate, Gabaldon sought and won a seat in the newly formed legislative chamber. During his three years in the senate, he chaired the committee on accounts and served on the agriculture, commerce, communications, railroads, and rules committees.[7]

In February 1920, the Philippine assembly nominated Gabaldon as its candidate for the Resident Commissioner post vacated by Teodoro Yangco, who was returning to the

Philippines to focus on the private sector. With Speaker Sergio Osmeña's backing, Gabaldon won the support of Nacionalista leaders, but still faced some opposition from the party. He was challenged for the nomination by Teodoro M. Kalaw, a key Quezon aide, but prevailed by a 53 to 16 margin. The assembly elected Gabaldon over the minority party candidate, Tría Tirona, on February 7, 1920, by a vote of 69 to 3.[8] Gabaldon later comfortably won re-election in February 1923, for the period from March 4, 1923, to March 4, 1926, and again in late 1925, for the period March 4, 1926 to March 4, 1929.[9]

By the time Gabaldon arrived in Washington early in the fall of 1920, Congress had already gone home to finish election-year campaigning. As was customary for Resident Commissioners, Gabaldon submitted his election credentials first to the President, who then informed the legislature. Gabaldon spent nearly two months in the capital settling himself and his family before the House convened for a lame-duck session on December 6, 1920.

Like other Resident Commissioners, House Rules barred him from committee service and voting on the House Floor, but he made it clear that he planned to use the power of publicity to an extent that neither his colleague, Jaime de Veyra, nor his immediate predecessor, Teodoro Yangco, had done. Even before the start of the session, he honed a message that would be the hallmark of his eight-year career as Resident Commissioner. "It is of the utmost importance to continue friendly relations between the Philippines and the United States that Congress should take up the question of independence without further delay," he told the *Christian Science Monitor*. "The officials of the Philippines and the masses of the Filipino people are alike insistent that independence shall be granted. As we have demonstrated our ability to govern ourselves just as often as we have had the opportunity to demonstrate it, there is absolutely no question as to our ability to do so in the future."[10]

At the time, however, the political calculus in Washington greatly complicated Gabaldon's task. Both Congress and the White House were controlled by Republicans, the party which traditionally sought to

maintain U.S. control in the Philippines. Moreover, the new President, Warren G. Harding, had chaired the Senate's Committee on the Philippines in the 66th Congress (1919–1921) and had a poor view of President Woodrow Wilson's efforts to expedite Philippine independence.[11]

On March 3, 1921, the final day of the 66th Congress, Majority Leader Frank Mondell of Wyoming asked unanimous consent to allow Gabaldon to speak on the floor. The Resident Commissioner opened his inaugural speech to the House by reminding Congress that its "promise" of freedom remained "unredeemed." Gabaldon reassured his colleagues that Filipinos appreciated U.S. efforts to improve schools and public health on the islands. He described the Philippines' two-decade apprenticeship in government, highlighting the stability of the insular legislature and local governments, and discounted the threat of Japanese invasion. But Filipinos, he said, expected independence sooner rather than later. "It will be the greatest example of international square dealing in the history of the ages."[12]

Gabaldon and fellow Resident Commissioner Jaime de Veyra met with Harding shortly after his inauguration, but the President refused to commit one way or the other on the matter of independence. His inclinations became clear enough when shortly afterward he dispatched a fact-finding mission to assess the islands' "fitness" for self-rule. Harding assured the Resident Commissioners that he would not make a policy decision until the investigators submitted a formal report.[13] Perhaps sensing the drift of the new administration, Gabaldon tried to preempt the mission by recommending a four- to five-year period of "probational independence."[14]

Led by General Leonard Wood and former Governor General W. Cameron Forbes, both of whom opposed independence, the mission visited the islands from May through August 1921. After interviewing a wide range of people, including resident Americans and Filipino political leaders, the mission advised Harding to strengthen the governor general's office and retain the islands because, in its opinion, the Philippines had not yet mastered self-rule.[15] Harding unsurprisingly endorsed the report.

Gabaldon and de Veyra protested the recommendations, especially the suggestion to embolden the governor general at the expense of the Philippine legislature.[16] In a floor speech refuting the principal findings of the Wood–Forbes report, Gabaldon alleged that it was a thinly veiled attempt to "find excuses for delaying independence." To critics who claimed that Japan would exercise undue influence in the Pacific, he claimed the Philippines were perfectly capable of defending its borders and pointed to provisions in the Washington Naval Conference of 1921, a treaty signed by the United States, Great Britain, Japan, and France, that all but eliminated the threat. In the final analysis, he claimed, "The [Wood–Forbes] report is a clever, but unworthy attempt to change the issue from that of stable government to a multitude of other conditions not required by Congress."[17]

After Harding appointed Wood to the office of governor general in the fall of 1921, the relationship between Filipino leaders and the American administration quickly deteriorated.[18] The situation became so dire that in 1923 the islands sent another delegation to Washington to lobby Congress and the new President, Calvin Coolidge. Members responded by submitting six bills between December 1923 and March 1924, beginning the process toward independence.[19] Coolidge, however, rejected the suggestion outright and instead asked Congress to again strengthen the governor general's office.[20]

Despite Coolidge's opposition, many in Congress sided with the Philippines, and in February 1924, Gabaldon testified on behalf of H.J. Res. 131, which cleared the way for a new constitution and immediate independence. Gabaldon's testimony described the stability of the insular government as well as its loyalty during the First World War. The Philippines, he noted, "not only … maintained peace and order but also performed the international obligations of America" in the Pacific.[21] The House Insular Affairs Committee withheld its report on the bill until its chairman, Louis Fairfield of Indiana, introduced H.R. 8856 two months later, providing for a measure of self-government, but still giving the United States veto power over the proposed commonwealth legislature. Filipinos rejected the bill, and the whole effort stalled heading into the fall elections.[22]

In late 1924, Gabaldon found himself in the middle of an anti-independence backlash. Led in part by the Philippine American Chamber of Commerce, the effort to maintain American control in the Philippines took a nasty turn when, from late November 1924 to January 1925, the *Washington Post* ran a 41-part series titled "Isles of Fear" written by Katherine Mayo.[23] Mayo held a number of nativist and anti-Catholic beliefs, and her articles directly challenged Gabaldon's claims that the Philippines had established a stable government and were ready for independence.[24] She accused Filipino officials of widespread graft and rampant corruption, and her articles used crude stereotypes to depict Filipinos as lazy, irresponsible, and incapable of managing a modern nation-state.[25]

In response, Gabaldon and fellow Resident Commissioner Pedro Guevara, who had earlier succeeded de Veyra in the House, penned a detailed reply in the *Washington Post* dismantling Mayo's assertions.[26] Gabaldon also denounced Mayo's thesis on the House Floor, calling it "unjust" and "wholly unnecessary," a "wholesale indictment of my people." He implied that Mayo invented her data and that she had a singular purpose: to conjure up "material with which she might blacken the character of the Filipino people and belittle their civilization, customs, culture, achievements, and progress."[27]

Over time, congressional intransigence seemed to take its toll on Gabaldon. His rhetoric took a sharper tone as he began to, in his words, "speak plainly" about the Philippines' status. In 1926, for example, Jonathan Wainwright of New York proposed sending a delegation to the Philippines every two years to investigate the political situation.[28] Gabaldon roundly opposed the bill, and the fact that its author was "one of the recognized foremost opponents of independence," he said, "does not add to my enthusiasm for the measure." Gabaldon envisioned the delegations traveling to the islands to "look the Filipinos over, dine and confer with the American opponents" of independence, and then "return and advise Congress" to retain the islands.[29] But even that criticism failed to gain

traction. Wainwright's measure passed the House and was reported out of the Senate Committee on Territories before the Senate decided not to fund the missions.[30] On the last day of the 69th Congress (1925–1927) in March 1927, Gabaldon somberly admitted to the House that there was a "growing belief in the Philippines that America does not intend to ever give us independence."[31]

In his final year in the House, Gabaldon marshalled resources to try and beat back a number of discriminatory measures. In January 1928, Frank Willis, chairman of the Senate Committee on Territories and Insular Possessions, submitted S. 2292, increasing the salaries of 13 presidential appointees, and directed $125,000 from Filipino revenue taxes toward hiring additional assistants and technical advisers. Another Willis bill, S. 2787, circumvented the Philippine senate and proposed empowering the governor general to appoint provincial governors for the Muslim and other non-Christian provinces. In the House, Insular Affairs Committee Chairman Edgar Kiess of Pennsylvania submitted companion bills, H.R. 8567 and H.R. 10074, respectively. When both the Secretary of War Dwight F. Davis and newly appointed Governor General Henry L. Stimson testified in support of the measures, Manuel Quezon asked independence allies in the Senate to fight back. Meanwhile, the Resident Commissioners readied to testify in committee hearings.[32]

On January 31, 1928, both Gabaldon and Guevara testified before the House Insular Affairs Committee against the proposals to increase the salaries and staffs of the islands' presidential appointees. In a prepared statement, Gabaldon blasted the effort as "tyrannical" and scolded Congress for not consulting the Philippine legislature on tax issues. "It would seem," Gabaldon said, "that the representative system of government implanted in the islands imposed upon this Congress the duty of adhering to the fundamental principle of government that 'taxation without representation is tyranny.'"[33] According to the Jones Act, Gabaldon reminded the committee, the avowed purpose of the United States was to set the islands on the path to self-rule and independence "and certainly you would be doing the opposite of that policy if you make

the Philippine participation in governmental affairs a mere fiction instead of a real fact."

The following day the Resident Commissioners were scheduled to testify before the Senate Committee on Territories and Insular Affairs, with Guevara taking the lead. But in between hearings, Guevara suffered a heart attack. Gabaldon, concerned for his colleague's health and hoping for time to prepare new remarks, asked Chairman Willis to postpone the hearing, which Willis promptly denied. Gabaldon learned of this while visiting Guevara in the hospital.

Incensed, Gabaldon appeared before the committee later that day and registered his displeasure in no uncertain terms. Only Chairman Willis and one other Senator had bothered to attend the hearing. Gabaldon complained that the 45 minutes allotted him to speak had been cut to 15 minutes just before the hearing opened and, after describing Guevara's condition, said that it would be an "unnecessary and a useless expenditure of your time as well as mine to proceed as I intended." Gabaldon simply submitted his statement and Guevara's into the record, fully aware that the Senators would ignore them before convening an executive session immediately afterward. "We do not want hearings to be dragging out," Willis told Gabaldon during the testimony. "You see we have other matters: Porto Rico, Hawaii."[34] The Willis and Kiess measures never made it to a vote on the floor, but because of Congress's maneuvering, the Philippine legislature later appropriated $125,000 to expand the staff of the governor general.[35]

Barely a month later, Gabaldon informed the House that he would resign as Resident Commissioner. Frustrated in Washington, he wanted to run for a seat in the Philippine legislature and breathe new life into the independence battle at home.[36] As a parting shot, he inserted an incendiary farewell address into the *Congressional Record*, what political observers described as "the most bellicose formal announcement" ever made by a Philippine Resident Commissioner.[37] The national press corps quickly picked it up, particularly his claim that every U.S. dollar invested in the Philippines was an "additional nail in the coffin of our independence."[38]

Gabaldon ran through a laundry list of what he described as insults and half-truths directed at the insular government that repeatedly seemed to frame the debates about independence. The Wood–Forbes Mission report provided a perfect example. Philippine officials exhausted themselves having "to deny the many counts … against our readiness to govern ourselves," he said. Gabaldon held special contempt for Katherine Mayo and her series of influential articles, saying, "She misrepresented us in the most vile and venomous manner that a human being could stoop to, and we were obliged to answer her." As for the Wainwright fact-finding bill and other such dilatory proposals, Gabaldon predicted that Congress would always have Members who "oppose us."[39]

Gabaldon also inverted the argument that American rule provided protection from Japanese imperialism. Not only was a major U.S. military presence on the islands "a menace," he said, it made the Philippines a more attractive target. Strategically, the islands were a liability for the U.S. military, he added, noting "there is nothing in the world to prevent Japan from taking the Philippines if she desires." Gabaldon predicted that, if such a war took place, the Philippines "would be reduced to a no-man's land by the time the Americans and the Japanese got through fighting for its possession."[40]

But the Resident Commissioner saved perhaps his sharpest remarks for the empty promises of the Philippines' governors general, especially those made by Stimson. Stimson's insistence that economic development be linked to political independence was little more than a smokescreen for a reassertive U.S. imperialism, he said, pointing out, "The very reason that we have not been given our independence is the investment of American capital in the islands."[41] Greater autonomy was no substitute for independence.

Speaking for the "Filipino race and for the Philippines nation to be," Gabaldon encouraged his countrymen, "Stand firm. Insist upon that which has been promised us. Autonomy will perhaps give our leaders more power, but only more power over you. Independence alone will place power exclusively in your own hands."[42]

Philippine leaders roundly denounced Gabaldon's address. In some parts, it read like a stump speech, and, in fact, it became the blueprint for his campaign for a seat in the Philippine legislature. In other parts, it read like a declaration of a new political party, marking a clear break with the Nacionalistas, including both Quezon and Osmeña. Philippine leaders scrambled to reassure Stimson that the Resident Commissioner had gone rogue and did not speak for the insular government, as the New York Times reported.[43] Writing a half-century later, one historian suggested that raw "political ambition" and the belief he could wrest power from Quezon motivated Gabaldon to resign and run for the insular legislature.[44]

But betting against Quezon and the political establishment proved an unwise wager.[45] Gabaldon's scorched-earth campaign won him few friends, and he blasted the Nacionalistas for backing off demands for complete independence in exchange for a circumscribed form of autonomy.[46] The Manila Times advocated against his "non-cooperation" platform and recommended that Gabaldon prepare for "a stinging rebuke at the polls" if he continued on.[47] On Election Day in early June, the Nacionalistas retained control of both houses of the Philippine legislature, and Gabaldon lost to Aurelio Cecilio, 7,263 to 6,442 votes.[48] After his defeat, Gabaldon's resignation as Resident Commissioner became effective on July 16, 1928.[49]

While Gabaldon did not return to a career in electoral politics, he remained involved in the independence movement, returning to Washington as a member of an independence mission in 1933. He died on December 21, 1942, in Manila during the Japanese occupation of the Philippines and was interred at the Cementerio del Norte in Manila.[50]

NOTES

1 Congressional Record, House, 69th Cong., 2nd sess. (4 March 1927): 5955.

2 Zoilo M. Galang, ed., Leaders of the Philippines: Inspiring Biographies of Successful Men and Women of the Philippines (Manila, PI: National Publishing Company, 1932): 277.

★ ISAURO GABALDON ★

3   Anthony R. Tuohy, ed., "Hon. Isauro Gabaldon Gonzalez," *Album Histórico de la Primera Asamblea Filipina* (Manila, PI: I.F., 1908): 41; Galang, *Leaders of the Philippines*: 276–278; "Isauro Gabaldon," National Historical Institute of the Philippines, accessed 14 April 2011, http://www.nhi.gov.ph/downloads/fishgov0053. pdf (site discontinued); U.S. Passport Applications, Puerto Rico and Philippines, 1913–1925, box 4233, vol. 2, National Archives and Records Administration (hereinafter NARA), Washington, DC, http://search.ancestrylibrary.com (accessed 25 March 2015). Reference to Gabaldon's marrying into wealth is made in Michael Cullinane, "*Ilustrado* Politics: The Response of the Filipino Educated Elite to American Colonial Rule, 1898–1907," (PhD diss., University of Michigan, 1989): 523n12.

4   Philippines Senate, "Isauro Gabaldon," Former Senators' Profiles, http://www.senate.gov.ph/senators/former_senators/isauro_gabaldon.htm (accessed 18 February 2016).

5   Cullinane, "*Ilustrado* Politics: The Response of the Filipino Educated Elite to American Colonial Rule, 1898–1907": 247, 384, 403, 435–436.

6   Galang, *Leaders of the Philippines*: 276.

7   "Gabaldon Chosen to Replace Yangco as Commissioner to U.S.," 7 February 1920, *Manila Times*: 1; Galang, *Leaders of the Philippines*: 276; "Isauro Gabaldon," National Historical Institute of the Philippines.

8   *Diario de Sesiones de la Cámara de Representantes*, vol. 15 (Manila, PI: Bureau of Printing, 1924): 545–546; "Gabaldon Chosen to Replace Yangco as Commissioner to U.S."; "Resident Commissioners to Washington Elected," 8 February 1920, *Cablenews-American* (Manila, PI): 1; Isauro Gabaldon certificate of election, (endorsed 9 February 1920), Committee on Elections (HR66-AJ2), 66th Congress, Records of the U.S. House of Representatives, Record Group 233, NARA; *Congressional Directory*, 69th Cong., 2nd sess. (Washington, DC: Government Printing Office: 1927): 131.

9   "New Filipino Commissioner," 18 February 1923, *Baltimore Sun*: 2; *Diario de Sesiones de la Cámara de Representantes*, vol. 18 (Manila, PI: Bureau of Printing, 1931): 1638–1645.

10 "Filipinos Demand Freedom at Once," 18 October 1920, *Christian Science Monitor*: 1.

11 Peter W. Stanley, *A Nation in the Making: The Philippines and the United States, 1899–1921* (Cambridge, MA: Harvard University Press, 1974): 251–258.

12 *Congressional Record*, House, 66th Cong., 3rd sess. (3 March 1921): 4482–4484. Gabaldon had issued a public statement in early January making essentially the same points. See "Filipinos' Stand on Independence Given," 2 January 1921, *Baltimore Sun*: 2.

13 "Policy in Philippines Waits on Wood's Report," 15 March 1921, *New York Tribune*: 4; "Harding Sees Filipinos," 15 March 1921, *New York Times*: 10.

14 "Wants Filipinos Given Short Test," 2 June 1921, *Washington Post*: 4.

15 *Condition in the Philippine Islands: Report of the Special Mission to the Philippine Islands to the Secretary of War*, 67th Cong., 2nd sess., H. Doc. 325 (1922): 10–12, 45–46.

16 "Criticize Philippine Report," 2 December 1921, *Washington Post*: 6.

17 *Congressional Record*, House, 67th Cong., 2nd sess. (20 January 1922): 1483–1487, quotation on p. 1484; "Commissioner Attacks Report on Philippines," 21 January 1922, *Washington Post*: 10.

18 Bernardita Reyes Churchill, *The Philippine Independence Missions to the United States, 1919–1934* (Manila, PI: National Historical Institute, 1983): 53–63.

19 Churchill, *The Philippine Independence Missions to the United States, 1919–1934*: 74–80, 87. The bills were H.R. 2817, H.R. 3924, H.J. Res. 127, H.J. Res. 131, S. 912, S. Res. 35.

20 The mission statement is reprinted in *Congressional Record*, House, 68th Cong., 2nd sess. (6 June 1924): 11094–11095. Coolidge's letter to the mission is reprinted in *Independence of the Philippines*, 69th Cong., 1st sess., S. Doc. 77 (3 March 1926): 2–4. Coolidge commented on the Philippines in his third, fourth, fifth, and sixth annual messages. See *American Presidency Project*, http://www.presidency.ucsb.edu.

21 Hearing before the House Committee on Insular Affairs, *Philippine Independence*, 68th Cong., 1st sess. (17 February 1924): 25–27; Churchill, *The Philippine Independence Missions to the United States, 1919–1934*: 88–89.

22 Churchill, *The Philippine Independence Missions to the United States, 1919–1934*: 99–105. Changes also included the following: Commonwealth officials would support and defend the Philippines' constitution instead of the U.S. Constitution; no one with military experience would serve as U.S. commissioner; the power to muster the armed forces would remain with the President; and only the U.S. Supreme Court would have jurisdiction over the Philippines.

23 Ibid., 122–124. See also *Congressional Record*, House, 70th Cong., 1st sess. (3 March 1928): 4016.

24 Churchill, *The Philippine Independence Missions to the United States, 1919–1934*: 122–124; "'Isles of Fear' to Present Truth About Philippines," 28 November 1924, *Washington Post*: 10. The articles were compiled into a single volume, Katherine Mayo, *The Isles of Fear: The Truth About the Philippines* (New York: Harcourt, Brace, and Company: 1925). For biographical information about Mayo, see "Katherine Mayo, Writer, Is Dead," 10 October 1940, *New York Times*: 25.

25 See, for instance, the second Mayo installment, Katherine Mayo, "Warned that Chaos in Philippines Forbade Full Success," 30 November 1924, *Washington Post*: 1. The editorials are "Conditions in the Philippines," 7 December 1924, *Washington Post*: EF1; "Vetoing Seditious Propaganda," 11 December 1924, *Washington Post*: 6; "The Philippines As They Are," 24 January 1925, *Washington Post*: 6.

26 Isauro Gabaldon and Pedro Guevara, "'Isles of Fear' Articles Answered by Filipinos," 7 December 1924, *Washington Post*: 2. See also Vicente G. Bunuan, "Filipino Progress Called Refutation of Miss Mayo," 25 January 1925, *Washington Post*: E6; Vincente G. Bunuan, "Morality and Stability Urged as Reasons for Filipino Independence," 26 January 1925, *Washington Post*: 13.

27 *Congressional Record*, House, 68th Cong., 2nd sess. (3 January 1925): 1167–1173, quotations on p. 1167.

28 *Congressional Record*, House, 69th Cong., 1st sess. (21 June 1926): 11710.

29 *Congressional Record*, House, 69th Cong., 2nd sess. (4 March 1927): 5957.

30 *Congressional Record*, Index, 69th Cong., 1st sess.: 683; *Congressional Record*, Index, 69th Cong., 2nd sess.: 270.

31 *Congressional Record*, House, 69th Cong., 2nd sess. (4 March 1927): 5957.

32 Churchill, *The Philippine Independence Missions to the United States, 1919–1934*: 185–187.

33 Hearing before the House Committee on Insular Affairs, *Employment of Certain Civilian Assistants in the Office of the Governor General of the Philippine Islands*, 70th Cong., 1st sess. (31 January 1928): 1–6, quotations on p. 1–2.

34 Hearing before the Senate Committee on Territories and Insular Possessions, *Appointment of Governors of the Non-Christian Provinces in the Philippine Islands*, 70th Cong., 1st sess. (1 February 1928): 1–17, quotations on p. 2–3, 14–17; "Gabaldon Accuses Senator Willis of Lack of Courtesy," 7 March 1928, *Baltimore Sun*: 13; *Congressional Record*, House, 70th Cong., 1st sess. (3 March 1928): 4015–4021.

35 Churchill, *The Philippine Independence Missions to the United States, 1919–1934*: 185–189; *Congressional Record*, Index, 70th Cong., 1st sess.: 531, 539, 801.

36 *Congressional Record*, House, 70th Cong., 1st sess. (9 March 1928): 4410; "Gabaldon to Quit His House Seat," 4 March 1928, *Washington Post*: 5.

37 "Territories: Gabaldon's Going," 19 March 1928, *Time*, http://www.time.com/time/magazine/article/0,9171,786723,00.html (accessed 14 April 2011).

38 See for example, "Filipino Quits Congress to Aid Liberty Move," 7 March 1928, *Los Angeles Times*: 6; "Filipino Envoy Demands Liberty," 8 March 1928, *Christian Science Monitor*: 6; "Filipino Quits Congress with Attack on U.S.," 6 March 1928, *Baltimore Sun*: 1.

39 *Congressional Record*, House, 70th Cong., 1st sess. (3 March 1928): 4016–4017.

40 Ibid., 4020–4021.

41 Ibid., 4015.

42 Ibid., 4017.

43 "Regret Gabaldon's Action," 9 March 1928, *New York Times*: 27; "Gabaldon's Views Not Favored Here," 8 March 1928, *Manila Times*: 1.

44 Churchill, *The Philippine Independence Missions to the United States, 1919–1934*: 194.

45 Ibid.; "Filipino Quits Congress With Attack on U.S."

46 "Gabaldon Refuses to Back Aquino," 3 June 1928, *Manila Times*: 1.

47 "New Attack on U.S. Policy Opens in Philippines," 16 April 1928, *Chicago Tribune*: 32; "Cooperation Is Issue Confronting Filipinos," 17 April 1928, *New York Times*: 50. The *Manila Times* editorial was reproduced in "Lack of Cooperation in Philippines Scored," 26 April 1928, *New York Times*: 15.

48 "Belmonte Faction Given Much Credit for Downfall of Resident Commissioner Gabaldon," 7 June 1928, *Manila Times*: 1.

49 "Gabaldon Defeated in Philippines Vote," 7 June 1928, *Washington Post*: 4; "Isauro Gabaldon," *Biographical Directory of the United States Congress*, http://bioguide.congress.gov/scripts/biodisplay.pl?index=G000001; *Congressional Record*, House, 70th Cong., 1st sess. (9 March 1928): 4410.

50 "Isauro Gabaldon," *Biographical Directory of the United States Congress*; Churchill, *The Philippine Independence Missions to the United States, 1919–1934*: 432; Frank H. Golay, *Face of Empire: United States-Philippine Relations, 1898–1946* (Quezon City, PI: Ateneo de Manila University Press, 1997): 322, 325–326; "Manila North Cemetery," http://www.manila.gov.ph/manilanorthcem.htm (accessed 13 April 2011).

Pedro Guevara
1879–1938

RESIDENT COMMISSIONER 1923–1935
NACIONALISTA FROM THE PHILIPPINES

The longest serving Resident Commissioner from the Philippines and a protégé of Manuel L. Quezon, Pedro Guevara waged a difficult battle promoting Philippine independence while fighting congressional measures to curb territorial sovereignty and economic progress. Guevara acted for much of his career as the voice of the Philippine legislature in Congress in a low-key style of delivery that relied on prepared statements rather than fiery, impromptu speeches. Guevara began his career a stalwart proponent of independence, saying, "For 25 years I and my people have lived under the American flag. Yet wherever I go Americans take me for … some other Oriental. Americans know very little about us or our country, and they care even less than they know. To continue American control, under such conditions, is an injustice to the Filipinos."[1] But his perspective shifted in his final years as Resident Commissioner, and disagreements with his patron Quezon over the best path to independence led to his quiet retirement from politics.

Pedro Guevara was born on February 23, 1879, in Santa Cruz, Laguna Province, Luzon, Philippines. The son of Miguel Guevara and Maria G. Valenzuela, he attended local schools some 60 miles to the south of Manila. Guevara's family sent him north to the capital to attend a finishing school, Ateneo Municipal de Manila, and then Colegio de San Juan de Letran. Guevara earned a liberal arts degree at the latter school in 1896, finishing at the head of his class. When the 1896 revolution broke out, Guevara fought the Spanish and earned the rank of lieutenant colonel for his service, including helping to lead Filipino forces in the Battle of Mabitac. In the Philippine-American War, he joined the insurrectionaries who opposed U.S. occupation forces, serving as aide and private secretary to General Juan Cailles, commander of Philippine rebels in Laguna Province. After the war ended, Guevara joined the Philippine constabulary, a paramilitary unit that maintained peace. After five years of service, Guevara returned to civilian life and, in a pattern reminiscent of others who later became Resident Commissioners, worked as a journalist. He became chief editor of *Soberanía Nacional (National Sovereignty)*, a newspaper that championed Philippine independence, and also served as city editor for four other newspapers. During this time, Guevara studied at La Jurisprudencia, a Manila law school, and passed the bar in 1909. He married Isidra Baldomero, and the couple had one son, Pedro Jr.[2]

As with many other contemporary politicos—Isauro Gabaldon, Jaime de Veyra, and Sergio Osmeña among them—Guevara easily transitioned from being an editorialist to an elected public servant. His political career began in 1907, when he was elected as municipal councillor in San Felipe Neri, Rizal Province. Two years later he won election to the Philippine assembly, representing Laguna Province, and he was re-elected in 1912 to a second term. In 1916, under the provisions of the Jones Act, he was elected to the first of two terms in the Philippine senate, representing a district that included Manila and the provinces of Rizal, Laguna, and Bataan. He served in the senate until his election as Resident Commissioner. A well-respected jurist, Guevara chaired the Philippine delegation to the Far Eastern Bar Conference in Beijing, China, in 1921. A year later he joined a group of prominent Filipinos who traveled to Washington, DC, as part of the second Philippine independence mission.[3]

Upon Guevara's return to the Philippines, senate president and Nacionalista Party powerbroker Manuel Quezon tapped his fellow senator to succeed Jaime de Veyra as Resident Commissioner. Domestic political jockeying momentarily complicated his nomination, however, when the insular government set a special election

Image courtesy of the Filipinas Heritage Library

to fill the impending senate vacancy. Democrats put forward a nominee, but the Nacionalistas failed to produce a consensus candidate. Desperate to retain the seat, Quezon stalled by encouraging Guevara to remain in the senate until a suitable candidate could be found. The U.S. House of Representatives threatened not to seat the new Resident Commissioner so long as he held his Manila seat, forcing Guevara to resign and leaving Quezon to bargain with Governor General Leonard Wood on the timing of a special election. Nevertheless, the Filipino legislature elected Guevara as Resident Commissioner on February 17, 1923.[4] He won re-election in 1925, 1929, 1932, and 1934 and served continuously until the position was reorganized under the Commonwealth of the Philippines in 1935.

When Guevara set off on the long voyage to Washington, DC, in August 1923, a "monster parade" accompanied him to his ship, the Associated Press reported. A marching band and military cadets joined the throng, with Guevara at its head wearing a *barong*, a long embroidered shirt that symbolized Filipinos' wish for independence.[5] Guevara arrived in the U.S. capital in mid-September, months before the 68th Congress (1923–1925) was set to convene in early December. Like his predecessors, he played the part of diplomat rather than legislator, in some measure because House Rules prevented him from holding a committee assignment or voting on final legislation on the floor. But he also seemed quite comfortable working the press and serving as a public advocate. In that aspect, he went to work immediately. Even before he claimed his seat, he weighed in on independence and growing tensions with the controversial Governor General Wood.

From the start, Guevara's independence pitch was more nuanced than that of his colleague, Isauro Gabaldon, who demanded nothing short of immediate and unfettered self-rule. Guevara, the *Los Angeles Times* noted, "was the opposite of the agitator type," and while journeying to Washington, he told Filipinos who met him during a brief layover in Honolulu that the key to eventual independence hinged on their ability to demonstrate "self-control" in overseeing their affairs. While he demanded a "final solution" to the Philippines' status, he envisioned it ideally as a kind of protectorate system "with a localized responsibility, capable of bringing about the necessary harmony and co-ordination of the different departments of Government, for its efficient operations."[6] He admitted that Japanese and European encroachments might be a concern with full independence and, to that end, preferred "a protectorate from the United States." But, given a choice between complete independence with no special grant of U.S. military protection or the ambiguous governance reasserted by U.S. officials after President Woodrow Wilson left office, Guevara had a clear choice: "We unquestionably stand for the former."[7]

Guevara's unhappiness with the current structure, like that of so many Filipinos, derived from the ambiguities of the Jones Act. On the one hand, the act granted the islands a greater role in self-rule, including a popularly elected senate. After several years, Manila officials believed that they had fulfilled the spirit and the letter of that legislation by creating a stable government. But, on the other hand, the governor general still was empowered to override the government and Filipino legislative initiatives "may be disregarded any time." While Filipinos were blamed "for any inefficiency or failure" of governance, the governor general seemed to accrue all credit for what went right.[8]

The newest occupant of the governor general's post, Leonard Wood, irritated matters by trying to reassert control over the islands. In July 1923, his actions provoked a mass resignation of Filipino politicos, including Quezon, from the governor general's cabinet. Later that fall, when Secretary of War John Weeks sent a memorandum of endorsement to Governor General Wood, Quezon and Philippine house speaker Manuel Roxas ordered Guevara to visit Secretary Weeks to express their displeasure with Wood's executive encroachments. Impatient for action, the territorial legislature then dispatched a special mission to Washington to request Wood's recall and lobby for immediate independence.[9] "We do not object to General Wood personally," Guevara noted, trying to frame the issue as something larger than a personal spat, "but to the office which he occupies and the method of his appointment."[10] In Boston for a speech at the Harvard Union, Guevara told the *Christian Science Monitor*, "The struggle with General Wood is merely a small incident in the bigger fight for full self-government."[11]

President Calvin Coolidge defended Wood and used subsequent annual messages to request that Congress grant the governor general more resources at the expense of the insular government.[12] Despite the Coolidge administration's clear efforts to reassert control over the islands, independence efforts percolated in Congress in 1924. In February, the special mission, accompanied by Guevara, testified before the Senate Committee on Territories and Insular Possessions to support S. 912, a bill authored by Chairman William King of Utah that authorized Filipinos to convene a constitutional convention. Once ratified and approved, U.S. military forces would withdraw within six months. Predictably, administration officials lined up against the bill. Secretary of War Weeks argued independence would precipitate a political collapse while the Navy's Admiral Hilary P. Jones testified about the need to retain the Philippines to ensure U.S. strategic interests in East Asia. Governor General Wood echoed these sentiments in a telegram to the committee that Guevara and Gabaldon roundly condemned.[13] War Department staff later asked the House Insular Affairs Committee to stall on its review of S. 912, effectively killing it.[14]

Insular Affairs Committee Chairman Louis Fairfield of Indiana submitted H.R. 8856 just as momentum on S. 912 waned. The House bill granted commonwealth status to the islands, allowed for a Filipino to be elected as governor general, continued a bicameral legislature, and also set out a judicial system. Controversially, however, it created a presidentially appointed post of U.S. commissioner empowered to veto legislation, contracts and the governor general's executive actions, and to muster the armed forces of the Philippines. The commonwealth period would last for 30 years, after which Filipinos would vote in a plebiscite to maintain commonwealth status or to declare independence.

Delegates from the independence mission supported the broad outlines of the Fairfield bill but balked at the 30-year commonwealth period and the notion of a commissioner with unchecked power. Though Fairfield was amenable to changing the bill, little support existed in Manila, and the chairman sidelined the entire effort.[15] Later that Congress, Guevara attempted to revive interest in H.R. 8856. "The structure of our political institutions," Guevara said, was built on a "weak base" of limited sovereignty. Emphasizing that Congress "has never been reluctant … in the prompt solution of those problems affecting the life, happiness, and prosperity" of its citizens, he asked the Rules Committee to send the bill to the House Floor, but it never resurfaced.[16] Soon all momentum stalled as Congress adjourned for the presidential nominating conventions and the fall elections.[17]

A wave of negative propaganda designed to curb Philippine autonomy broke across the U.S. press in late 1924. From November 1924 to January 1925, the *Washington Post* published "Isles of Fear," authored by Katherine Mayo, who trafficked in racist stereotypes and belittled the Philippines' push for independence. Retentionists, including the *Post* editorial board, seized on the series and praised it for confirming their views.[18] Guevara was one of a number of Filipino officials who refuted Mayo, publishing a response with Isauro Gabaldon in the *Post*. In a New York City speech, Guevara alleged Mayo's work as one component of a "campaign of misrepresentation waged by the irreconcilable opponents of Philippine independence … for their own benefits or that of the interests they represent." He stressed that Mayo's portrayals failed to convey the true "life, culture, and spirit of a people or race."[19]

Guevara also fought against attempts to separate parts of the Philippines from the insular government. In May 1926, Robert Bacon of New York submitted H.R. 12772 to create a separate province intended to resolve the "fundamental antipathy" between the Christian Filipinos in the Luzon and Visayan Islands and Muslim Filipinos, or Moros, in the Mindanao, Basilan, Palawan, and Sulu Archipelago. According to Bacon, the Moros were "an altogether distinct people from the Christian Filipinos

… not only in language and religion but in physical type and mental outlook."[20] The first Philippine commission established a single province for Moro territory under the control of a military governor.[21] Bacon's bill enabled the governor general to make these appointments without the consent of the Philippine senate. He argued that the Moros were essentially a distinct people and that the insular government had made no real attempt to integrate them. Bacon's underlying goal, however, seemed to be securing key natural resources in Moro lands—namely, rubber.[22]

Guevara responded to Bacon on the House Floor one month later. He dismissed the racial distinctions between Christian and Muslim Filipinos, saying that "differences in religion and civilization are the natural result of the political situation which the Filipino people have been forced to endure for the last 300 years" under foreign rule. Guevara admitted that the Moros had no representatives in the Philippine legislature, but under the Jones Act, only the U.S. Congress could grant that right. To resolve the issue, Guevara suggested an "amendment to the present organic law … which would enfranchise the Moros and permit them to elect their own legislators and governors with … the same freedom of choice as that now enjoyed by Christian Filipinos." Guevara concluded, "Disintegration of … the Philippine Islands can serve no useful purpose." Members of the Committee on Insular Affairs agreed, and Bacon's bill never left committee.[23]

After four years of stalwart opposition to Wood and his policies, Guevara was presented with an opportunity to reset relations when the governor general died unexpectedly in August 1927. Guevara informed Manila that the Coolidge administration wanted suggestions about selecting a new governor general. The primary candidate was Henry L. Stimson, the former Secretary of War in the William H. Taft administration. President Coolidge asked Stimson to visit the Philippines to assess the effectiveness of the insular government. A retentionist himself, Stimson nevertheless proved amenable to all sides. Unlike Wood, Stimson honored Philippine sovereignty where it existed and treated Filipino colleagues with respect. With widespread support in Manila and Washington, President

Coolidge nominated Stimson on December 13, 1927. When the Senate confirmed him four days later, Guevara praised the appointment, calling it "a new era for the islands [sic] government and people."[24]

Despite this attempt to moderate relations with the insular government, President Coolidge continued to request more resources for the governor general's office in his annual messages. In January 1928, Frank Willis, chairman of the Senate Committee on Territories and Insular Possessions, submitted S. 2292. That bill proposed an increase in the salaries of 13 presidential appointees and directed $125,000 from Philippine internal revenue taxes toward hiring additional assistants and technical advisers. A companion bill (H.R. 8567) was submitted by House Insular Affairs Committee Chairman Edgar Kiess of Pennsylvania. These measures placed the appointments of technical advisers solely in the governor general's hands. Another Willis bill, S. 2787, and its companion, H.R. 10074, proposed the appointment of governors for the Muslim and non-Christian provinces of the islands without the Philippine senate's consent. Secretary of War Dwight F. Davis and Governor General Stimson testified in support of each of these bills to the dismay of Quezon, who coordinated with Senate allies to block their passage and asked other members to submit independence bills as substitutes. Guevara prepared for battle in the committee rooms.[25]

Guevara sparred with Chairman Kiess while testifying against H.R. 8567. Among his eight points of disagreement with the legislation, he argued that the Kiess bill would weaken the Jones Act by curtailing the Philippine legislature's power to appropriate funds by eliminating the "functions of the departments and bureaus of the Philippine government." Such an action would reinforce "the colonial nature of the system of government implanted in the Philippine Islands." Frustrated by Guevara's stonewalling, Kiess demanded to know why the Philippine legislature seemingly opposed any congressional action. Guevara answered, "We are opposed to any amendment to the Jones Act which will mean a backward step" in achieving Philippine sovereignty.

After testifying for two hours, Guevara suffered a heart attack and was taken to a local hospital. He was scheduled to testify against S. 2292 before the Senate Committee on Territories and Insular Affairs the next day, but Gabaldon took his place.[26] Although S. 2292 and S. 2787 passed the respective committees of jurisdiction in both chambers, neither came to the House nor Senate Floors for a vote, and the House versions languished in committee.[27]

Guevara balanced expanding Philippine sovereignty with preserving its economy, particularly the sugar industry. In March 1928, beet sugar proponent Charles Timberlake of Colorado submitted H.J. Res. 214, a bill to reduce the duty-free importation of Philippine sugar from an unlimited number to 500,000 tons. Timberlake noted precedent for his legislation and argued that U.S. authorities "never contemplated forcing the American farmer into competition with tropical labor 7,000 miles across the Pacific." Timberlake partially framed his legislation as preventing the Philippines from becoming "dependent on a single competitive export crop" in accordance with "the universally accepted principle of crop diversification." Guevara asked Timberlake if it was fair for the United States "to send any of its products to the Philippine Islands without any limitations … while the Philippine Islands are … limited in the sending of their products" to the United States, but Timberlake dodged the question. Guevara countered with his standard proposal for independence, "May I suggest that the best remedy is to get rid of the Philippine Islands, and we are now ready to be gotten rid of by the United States."[28] The bill died when Governor General Stimson blasted it in the press.[29]

When the House adjourned in May 1928, Guevara remained in the United States. In June he joined Quezon at the Democratic and Republican presidential nominating conventions to promote Philippine independence. At the Republican convention in Kansas City, Missouri, the pair successfully lobbied against the inclusion of a platform that called for limiting Philippine rights. In Houston, Texas, Guevara and Quezon, with an assist from Senator King, convinced Democrats to retain a platform calling for independence that echoed the 1924 platform.[30]

Isauro Gabaldon resigned in July 1928, leaving Guevara the sole Filipino Resident Commissioner for nine months just as the battle over sugar tariffs was heating up. In December 1928, the House Ways and Means Committee convened hearings on tariff readjustments in anticipation of President-elect Herbert Hoover's request to revise the Tariff Act of 1922. A worldwide depression in sugar prices and the rise of an aggressive sugar lobby threatened the free trade privileges enjoyed by the Philippines since the enactment of that legislation.

Testifying before the committee in early 1929, Guevara started with a simple question that echoed his perpetual message: "[W]hile the Philippine Islands are under the American flag, will the United States be justified in imposing limitation on our present free trade?" Guevara reminded members that imposing trade restrictions was tantamount to "economic slavery, because while the United States is free to send to the Philippine Islands all her products and merchandise, we will not be free to export" the same products. When committee members asked Guevara repeatedly what the Philippines did to cultivate trade with neighboring countries, Guevara reiterated that U.S. tariff restrictions compelled nations to restrict trade against the Philippines as a territory of the United States.[31]

On March 7, 1929, President Hoover called an extraordinary session of Congress to consider proposals for agriculture relief and tariff revisions. In light of these initiatives, the Philippine legislature sent a special mission to Washington to negotiate tariff revisions. Arriving in April 1929, the mission was led by Philippine house speaker Manuel Roxas and senator Sergio Osmeña and joined by newly elected Resident Commissioner Camilo Osias.[32]

The next hurdle Guevara and the mission faced came in the form of H.R. 2667, submitted by Ways and Means Committee Chairman Willis Hawley of Oregon. It called for a revision of the tariff schedules. The bill passed the House without many changes that affected the Philippines. But led by beet supporter Chairman Reed Smoot of Utah, the Senate Committee on Finance offered amendments sharply increasing the duty on sugar and other products from the Philippines. In contrast to Osias's fiery testimony,

Guevara submitted a prepared statement to the committee in June 1929, again requesting equal treatment between the United States and Philippines. He once more leveraged the economic conflict to request independence. Retained as a territory, Guevara noted, the matter amounted to interstate commerce. Passing the amendments, however, "would place the United States in the same position of Great Britain in her dealings with the thirteen American Colonies which brought about their separation from the mother country."[33] Smoot's amendments gained little traction before the committee reported the bill in September 1929.

When the bill reached the Senate Floor, fresh amendments spurred a renewed campaign for independence. Louisiana Senator Edwin Broussard again sought to increase the sugar duty, but also offered a path to independence. Some Senators balked when the independence issue crept into the tariff debate. Both amendments failed, but this opened the door for Guevara and Osias to once again campaign for the release of the Philippines. Guevara addressed the House on December 7 and again on December 13, each time stressing the economic argument for an independent Philippines. Despite rising sentiment and support from Democratic Members, Republicans in both chambers stood firm against independence.[34] The final act, popularly known as the Smoot–Hawley Tariff, became law in June 1930. It did not significantly affect Philippine exports, but neither did it feature the independence provisions Guevara and his colleagues had encouraged.[35]

Guevara carried forward his comparison of the islands to the American colonies as he continued his pleas for independence across the United States.[36] In the summer of 1931, Quezon published a report postulating a 10-year trial period of autonomous government ending in a plebiscite. The report muddled the insular government's official stance on independence. Quezon seemed to favor an American protectorate with only limited independence. The legislature instructed Guevara to continue to press for full independence and urged him weeks later to correct a *Washington Post* editorial which had presumed Moro

opposition to independence.[37] Guevara struggled to respond to this misinformation as Congress prepared to convene the 72nd Congress (1931–1933) in December 1931, and government leaders Osmeña and Roxas themselves traveled to Washington to make their case.

Despite the efforts of retentionists to portray the Philippines as deeply riven over the question of independence, supporters in Congress had grown plentiful enough by 1932 to advance a new bill for Philippine independence. Named for the chairman of the House Insular Affairs Committee, Butler Hare of South Carolina, the proposal, once approved by the insular legislature, would provide for an immediate constitutional convention followed by an eight-year schedule for independence. Speaker John Nance Garner of Texas rallied Democratic support and brought the bill to the floor under a suspension of the rules, limiting debate to 40 minutes.

During debate, Guevara proclaimed that this bill would "decide the fate of 13,000,000 people." Describing prior legislative efforts as temporary fixes, Guevara deemed that the Hare measure embodied the "redemption of American pledges ... and the fruition of our hopes for separate nationhood." At the conclusion of Guevara's unusually impassioned rhetoric, many Members rose in applause. With Guevara watching, the House approved the bill by a large majority, 306 to 47.[38] The Hawes–Cutting bill, a competing Senate version of the Hare bill, led a conference committee to increase the window to independence to 10 years, but the final legislation was completed before the year was out.

Congress had passed the legislation over the stern objections of the Hoover administration, however, and President Hoover vetoed the bill on January 13, 1933. Wasting no time, the House overrode the veto that same day 274 to 94. After the vote, Guevara expressed "the gratitude of the Filipino people, which I say to both Republicans and Democrats for their altruistic stand on the ... independence question."[39] The Senate followed suit on January 17 by a vote of 66 to 24, and the combined Hare–Hawes–Cutting Act became law.[40] However, the Philippine legislature still had to approve the measure, and infighting there scuttled the bill. Guevara sided with his mentor Quezon, who feared a loss of influence, had the bill succeeded. After Quezon rallied the votes to reject the independence bill in the Philippine senate, Guevara accompanied him back to Washington to produce another independence bill.[41]

Throughout early 1934, Guevara and Osias occupied opposite sides of the Hare–Hawes–Cutting law debate. Whereas Osias publicly split from Quezon over rejecting the law in December 1933, Guevara lobbied for passage of another bill. In January 1934, Guevara submitted a concurrent resolution from the Philippine legislature rejecting the Hare–Hawes–Cutting Act. He expressed his "profound gratitude" for Congress's actions, but his "patriotic duty" compelled Guevara to take another course. Acknowledging that "many of the Members of this House voted … in the belief that my stand was an expression of the will of the Filipino people whom I represent," Guevara subordinated his preference for the Hare–Hawes–Cutting bill to "the majority of the Philippine Legislature," who rejected it.[42]

Quezon found a favorable climate for a new independence bill in Washington, where the new Franklin D. Roosevelt administration was eager to be done with the issue. Negotiations resulted in the Tydings–McDuffie Act (H.R. 8573, S. 3055), which granted independence and removed military bases from the Philippines while providing authorization to negotiate for a future U.S. naval presence. Guevara endorsed the bill as "the epitome and synthesis of America's aim and purpose in the Philippines" and further ensured that this attempt at independence would meet approval in the Philippine legislature.[43] The bill quickly passed both the House and Senate, and President Roosevelt signed it into law on March 24, 1934.[44]

Guevara involved himself little in negotiations over Tydings–McDuffie, focusing instead on the preservation of the Philippine economy. Days after passage of Tydings–McDuffie, Guevara protested a clause in H.R. 9790 that raised the price of coconut oil to 3 cents per pound. He cautioned that the price increase could "dynamite" approval of the new independence bill because the tax

would exacerbate the "economic sacrifices of the Filipino people, which are already … unbearable" and cripple the nation's prominent coconut industry. Guevara pointed out the "inconsistency" of Congress to pass "a new organic law and, before the President's signature to it is dry, penalize the recipient with additional burdens and oppressive inflictions." Guevara sent letters to President Roosevelt as well as six prominent Senators and submitted a public statement voicing his objections. Representative John McDuffie of Alabama echoed Guevara's concerns and suggested that the tax violated the spirit of the independence measure that bore his name. Under this onslaught, the tax bill wallowed in committee, and the Philippine legislature approved Tydings–McDuffie in May 1934.[45]

Guevara's next economic hurdle was a direct consequence of the national bank emergency and the devaluation of the dollar. Representative McDuffie introduced H.R. 9459 and Senator Millard Tydings of Maryland introduced S. 3530 to settle the resultant devaluation profit in the Philippine currency reserves, enabling the U.S. Treasury to transfer the balance to the Philippine insular government. While advocating for the bill, Guevara noted how the devaluation hurt the Philippines' ability to collect duty rates and obtain full returns on railroad bonds. In two cases, Guevara estimated the Philippines lost about $13 million. Guevara appealed to his colleagues' sense of fair play in restoring the funds. In a practical sense, the restoration of the funds would "forestall economic complications and … prevent financial debilitation" in a nation on the verge of independence. The Tydings bill passed the Senate easily and, after a vigorous debate in the House, passed on a 188 to 147 vote. President Roosevelt signed it into law on June 19, 1934.[46]

As early as June 1934, Guevara showed signs that he had wearied of Filipino politics, feeling that he had been buffeted by insular divisions one time too many. Reports emerged about Guevara advocating for a protectorate for the Philippines, claiming that full independence would lead to disaster. His political patron Quezon dismissed the claims. Guevara had also applied to be a delegate at the 1934 Philippine constitutional convention. In light of the rumored statements, Quezon threatened to pull his support for Guevara's candidacy.[47] However, the threat did not hurt Guevara's prospects, as he was selected to the constitutional convention in July 1934 and was re-elected as Resident Commissioner one month later.[48] The constitutional convention worked from July 1934 to February 1935 on a draft which President Roosevelt approved in March. Following a plebiscite, the Philippines was established as a commonwealth in May 1935.[49]

During his last term in the 74th Congress (1935–1937), Guevara continued to focus on preserving the economy and the security of the Philippines. He lobbied the House to relax tariffs in the Jones–Costigan and Revenue Acts of 1934. Guevara also began openly advocating for a protectorate system rather than complete independence, fearing that Japan was a "real menace to Philippine independence." He relayed open threats made by a Japanese diplomat in Manila before asking the House to consider amending H.R. 3482, a bill pledging the commitment of U.S. military forces to Latin American countries, to include the Philippines. Richard Welch of California reminded the House that Guevara "was in favor of absolute independence" during debate over the Tydings–McDuffie Act. "I have not changed my mind," Guevara replied, but he stated that he wished for "independence for the Filipino people, but not for the benefit of some other nation" to swallow it up. Guevara held no faith in the ability of a neutralization treaty to protect his nation after Japan's decision to ignore the Kellogg–Briand Pact and leave the League of Nations. When Welch continued to needle Guevara, the Resident Commissioner countered, "[I]f reversing my opinion … will mean security for the Philippine Islands I will not hesitate to reverse my stand or my opinion." H.R. 3482 did not pass, but a companion Senate bill (S. 707) added the Philippines to the protection list and it became law.[50]

In August 1935, Guevara returned to Manila to vote in the presidential elections, and he brought his protectorate proposal with him. In accordance with these views, he rescinded his support of the Tydings–McDuffie Act. Nevertheless, he endorsed Manuel Quezon's campaign for president of the Philippine Commonwealth. In a newspaper interview at his home, Guevara stated his preference for a protectorate in the presence of Quezon and two other public figures, General Emilio Aguinaldo and Bishop Gregorio Aglipay, who were running against Quezon. Guevara claimed to have spoken with a number of Members of Congress "and it is my opinion that a … majority would favor the extension of American protection to the islands." The reporter noted that in private Quezon reacted with "tacit approval."[51] Soon afterward, though, he blasted Guevara's proposal in a public statement.[52]

One week after Quezon won the presidency in a landslide, Guevara announced his retirement from politics effective on October 1, 1935, even though his term as Resident Commissioner did not officially expire until February 14, 1936.[53] After leaving office, he started a private law practice in Manila. The *Philippines Free Press* complimented his "long and distinguished career in government, culminating in his many years as Resident Commissioner in Washington."[54] Besides law, Guevara pursued a number of business interests and continued to advocate for a Philippine protectorate as a private citizen.[55]

On January 19, 1938, Guevara suffered a fatal stroke while arguing a case before the Philippine supreme court and died in Manila. Calling him "one of the dearest friends I have ever had," President Quezon credited Guevara as a "devoted and very able public servant" who "stood his ground regardless of whether or not it affected him adversely politically." Guevara was interred in the Cementerio del Norte in Manila.[56]

NOTES

1   Guevara quotation from "Filipinos Hoping For Protectorate," 8 November 1923, *Christian Science Monitor*: 2.

2   *Congressional Directory*, 74th Cong., 1st sess., 2nd ed. (Washington, DC; Government Printing Office, 1935): 129; "Death Strikes Guevara in Act of Pleading Case Before Supreme Court," 20 January 1938, *Manila Tribune*: 1; "Pedro Guevara, Jr.," 22 November 1947, *Washington Post*: B2. Pedro Guevara Jr., was born circa 1903. "Filipinos Elect an 'Independent,'" 7 March 1923, *Christian Science Monitor*: 1.

3   *Congressional Directory*, 74th Cong.: 129; "Death Strikes Guevara In Act of Pleading Case Before Supreme Court"; Bernardita Reyes

Churchill, *The Philippine Independence Missions to the United States, 1919–1934* (Manila, PI: National Historical Institute, 1983): 37–38, 428.

4 Frank H. Golay, *Face of Empire: United States-Philippine Relations, 1898–1946* (Quezon City, PI: Ateneo de Manila University Press, 1997): 242–244; Churchill, *The Philippine Independence Missions to the United States, 1919–1934*: 67; Pedro Guevara certificate of election, (endorsed 24 February), Committee on Elections (HR68-AJ2), 68th Congress, Records of the U.S. House of Representatives, Record Group 233, National Archives and Records Administration, Washington, DC; "Gabaldon, Guevara Re-elected," 10 November 1925, *Manila Times*: 1; "Philippine Legislature Elects Commissioners," 8 February 1929, *Washington Post*: 9; "To Represent Philippines Here," 23 August 1934, *Wall Street Journal*: 5.

5 Associated Press, "Manila Holds Huge Parade in Honor of New Agent to U.S.," 12 August 1923, *Chicago Tribune*: 13.

6 "Independence Haste Decried," 12 September 1923, *Los Angeles Times*: 17; "Philippine Envoy Seeks Settlement," 17 September 1923, *New York Times*: 19.

7 "Filipinos Hoping for Protectorate," 8 November 1923, *Christian Science Monitor*: 2.

8 "Philippine Envoy Seeks Settlement."

9 Churchill, *The Philippine Independence Missions to the United States, 1919–1934*: 70–74.

10 "Hart Defends Leonard Wood," 9 November 1923, *Boston Daily Globe*: 24. See also "First Philippine Plea Is Given to President," 16 December 1923, *Washington Post*: 14; Churchill, *The Philippine Independence Missions to the United States, 1919–1934*: 77.

11 "Philippine Envoy Seeks Settlement."

12 Coolidge commented on the Philippines in his third, fourth, fifth, and sixth annual messages. See Gerhard Peters, "State of the Union Addresses and Messages," in *American Presidency Project*, ed. John T. Woolley and Gerhard Peters, http://www.presidency.ucsb.edu/sou.php.

13 Churchill, *The Philippine Independence Missions to the United States, 1919–1934*: 91–92.

14 Hearing before the Senate Committee on Territories and Insular Possession, *Philippine Independence*, 68th Cong., 1st sess. (11, 16 February and 1, 3 March 1924); Churchill, *The Philippine Independence Missions to the United States, 1919–1934*: 89–90.

15 Churchill, *The Philippine Independence Missions to the United States, 1919–1934*: 101–102. The amended bill removed the independence plebiscite and reduced the probationary period to 20 years. Commonwealth officials would support the Philippine constitution instead of the U.S. Constitution and no one with military experience would serve as U.S. commissioner. Regarding executive and legislative branch powers, the power to muster the armed forces would remain with the U.S. President; the U.S. Supreme Court also would have jurisdiction over the Philippines.

16 *Congressional Record*, House, 68th Cong., 2nd sess. (16 December 1924): 698.

17 Churchill, *The Philippine Independence Missions to the United States, 1919–1934*: 99–105.

18 Ibid., 122–124; "'Isles of Fear' to Present Truth About Philippines," 28 November 1924, *Washington Post*: 10. The articles were compiled into a single volume, Katherine Mayo, *The Isles of Fear: The Truth About the Philippines* (New York: Harcourt, Brace, and Company: 1925). For biographical information about Mayo, see "Katherine Mayo, Writer, Is Dead," 10 October 1940, *New York Times*: 25. For the *Post*'s supportive editorials, see "Conditions in the Philippines," 7 December 1924, *Washington Post*: EF1; "Vetoing Seditious Propaganda," 11 December 1924, *Washington Post*: 6; and "The Philippines As They Are," 24 January 1925, *Washington Post*: 6.

19 *Congressional Record*, House, 68th Cong., 2nd sess. (3 March 1925): 5348–5350, quotation on p. 5349. Gabaldon's remarks about the Mayo articles are in *Congressional Record*, House, 68th Cong., 2nd sess. (3 January 1925): 1167–1173.

20 *Congressional Record*, House, 69th Cong., 1st sess. (6 May 1926): 8831.

21 Bonifacio S. Salamanca, *The Filipino Reaction to American Rule, 1901–1913* (Hamden, CT: Shoe String Press, 1968): 113–117, 256n107.

22 Golay, *Face of Empire*: 266–267.

23 *Congressional Record*, House, 69th Cong., 1st sess. (26 June 1926): 12063–12066; *Congressional Record*, Index, 69th Cong., 1st sess.: 810.

24 Churchill, *The Philippine Independence Missions to the United States, 1919–1934*: 181, 184–185; "Coolidge to Receive Filipino Legislators," 22 September 1927, *Washington Post*: 1; "Stimson Named for Governor of Philippines," 13 December 1927, *Christian Science Monitor*: 1; "Senate Confirms Morrow as Envoy," 18 December 1927, *New York Times*: 23; Larry G. Gerber, "Stimson, Henry Lewis," *American National Biography* 20 (New York: Oxford University Press, 1999): 787–790; *Congressional Record*, House, 70th Cong., 1st sess. (21 December 1927): 916–917.

25 Churchill, *The Philippine Independence Missions to the United States, 1919–1934*: 185–187.

26 Hearing before the House Committee on Insular Affairs, *Employment of Certain Civilian Assistants in the Office of the Governor General of the Philippine Islands*, 70th Cong., 1st sess. (31 January 1928): 7, 19–20. Gabaldon described Guevara's condition in Hearing before the Senate Committee on Territories and Insular Possessions, *Appointment of Governors of the Non-Christian Provinces in the Philippine Islands*, 70th Cong., 1st sess. (1 February 1928): 2; Churchill, *The Philippine Independence Missions to the United States, 1919–1934*: 187.

27 Churchill, *The Philippine Independence Missions to the United States, 1919–1934*: 185–189; *Congressional Record*, Index, 70th Cong., 1st sess.: 531, 539, 706, 731.

28 *Congressional Record*, House, 70th Cong., 1st sess. (22 March 1928): 5212.

29 Churchill, *The Philippine Independence Missions to the United States, 1919–1934*: 188–189; *Congressional Record*, Index, 70th Cong., 1st sess.: 736.

30 Churchill, *The Philippine Independence Missions to the United States, 1919–1934*: 189–190; "To Work For Philippines," 6 April 1928, *New York Times*: 4. The 1924 and 1928 platforms are similar. See George Thomas Kurian, ed., *The Encyclopedia of the Democratic Party*, vol. 3 (Armonk, NY: M.E. Sharpe, Inc., 1997): 520–521, 531.

31 Hearings before the House Committee on Ways and Means, *Tariff Readjustment–1929*: *Vol. V, Schedule 5, Sugar, Molasses, and Manufactures of*, 70th Cong., 2nd sess. (21–22 January 1929): 3288–3292. Guinn Williams of Texas made a similar statement on Guevara's behalf, see *Congressional Record*, House, 70th Cong., 2nd sess. (24 January 1929): 2194–2197.

32 Herbert Hoover, "Proclamation 1870—Requesting an Extra Session of Congress on Agricultural Relief and Tariff Changes," 7 March 1929, in *American Presidency Project*, ed. John T. Woolley and Gerhard Peters, http://www.presidency.ucsb.edu/ws/?pid=22069 (accessed 12 February 2016); Churchill, *The Philippine Independence Missions to the United States, 1919–1934*: 198–201, 204–206.

33 "Urges Wide Powers in Flexible Tariff," 17 July 1929, *New York Times*: 11.

34 "Haitian Policy of U.S. Praised and Condemned," 14 December 1929, *Chicago Daily Tribune*: 10; *Congressional Record*, House, 70th Cong., 1st sess. (7, 13 December 1929): 261–262, 618–630; Golay, *Face of Empire*: 281–282.

35 Hearings before the Senate Committee on Finance, *Tariff Act of 1929*: *Vol. XVII, Special and Administrative Provisions*, 71st Cong., 1st sess. (12–13 June and 15–18 July, 1929): 260–262; Golay, *Face of Empire*: 278–282. Smoot–Hawley became law as Public Law 71-361, 46 Stat. 590 (1930).

36 "Filipino Pleads for Freedom at Politics Parley," 1 July 1930, *Christian Science Monitor*: 5; "Guevara Makes Plea for Filipino Freedom," 28 October 1930, *New York Times*: 52; "Reasserts Filipino Stand," 23 May 1931, *New York Times*: 8.

37 Golay, *Face of Empire*: 296–298; Pedro Guevara, "Moros Declared to Favor Philippine Independence," 20 September 1931, *Washington Post*: M7.

38 "House Votes to Free Philippines in 1940; Stimson Is Opposed," 5 April 1932, *New York Times*: 1; *Congressional Record*, House, 72nd Cong., 1st sess. (4 April 1932): 7401–7412, Guevara quotation on p. 7410.

39 *Congressional Record*, House, 72nd Cong., 2nd sess. (13 January 1933): 1769.

40 Theodore Friend, *Between Two Empires: The Ordeal of the Philippines, 1929–1946* (New Haven, CT: Yale University Press, 1965): 106–108; "Hail Defeat of Veto: Filipino Commissioners Call Independence Grant Unprecedented," 18 January 1933, *New York Times*: 2.

41 Friend, *Between Two Empires*: 129–130.

42 *Congressional Record*, House, 73rd Cong., 2nd sess. (4 January 1934): 128–129.

43 *Congressional Record*, House, 73rd Cong., 2nd sess. (19 March 1934): 4836.

44 President Roosevelt's special message was reprinted in *Congressional Record*, House, 73rd Cong., 2nd sess. (2 March 1934): 3580–3581; *Congressional Record*, House, 73rd Cong., 2nd sess. (19 March 1934): 4225, 4831, 4842; *Congressional Record*, Senate, 73rd Cong., 2nd sess. (20 March 1934): 4921, 5164; Public Law 73-127, 48 Stat. 456 (1934); Golay, *Face of Empire*: 320–327.

45 "Calls Oil Tax Move Blow at Philippines," 3 April 1934, *New York Times*: 2; "Filipino Says Tax on Oil Is Ruinous," 2 May 1934, *New York Times*: 8; *Congressional Record*, House, 73rd Cong., 2nd sess. (29 May 1934): 9864–9868; *Congressional Record*, Index, 73rd Cong., 2nd sess.: 613; Golay, *Face of Empire*: 327–328. Guevara also testified against the passage of H.R. 7835. See Hearings before the Senate Finance Committee, *Revenue Act of 1934*, 73rd Cong., 2nd sess. (12–15 March 1934): 389–394.

46 Guevara's appeal is in *Congressional Record*, House, 73rd Cong., 2nd sess. (11 June 1934): 11079–11080; *Congressional Record*, Senate, 73rd Cong., 2nd sess. (13 June 1934): 11273; *Congressional Record*, House, 73rd Cong., 2nd sess. (14 June 1934): 11351–11546; Golay, *Face of Empire*: 329–330; Philippine Currency Act, Public Law 73-419, 48 Stat. 1115 (1934). Per Golay, the devaluation profit is the dollar value increase of gold equivalent to the currency reserves on deposit in the U.S. when the convertibility of the dollar was suspended.

47 "Guevara Statement Stirs Manila Storm," 19 June 1934, *New York Times*: 8; James G. Wingo, "Guevara Still in the Fight," 7 July 1934, *Philippines Free Press*: 9.

48 "Philippine Elections," 12 July 1934, *Wall Street Journal*: 4; "Solons Select New P.I. Envoys to Washington," 21 August 1934, *Philippines Herald*: 1, 2.

49 H. W. Brands, *Bound to Empire: The United States and the Philippines* (New York: Oxford University Press, 1992): 160–161.

50 *Congressional Record*, House, 74th Cong., 1st sess. (21 January 1935): 716–717; *Congressional Record*, Index, 74th Cong., 1st sess.: 633, 770. The bill became law as Public Law 74-56, 49 Stat. 218 (1935).

51 Vicente Albano Pacis, "A Philippine Protectorate?," 1 October 1935, *Washington Post*: 9.

52 "Quezon is Opposed to U.S. Protectorate," 24 August 1935, *New York Times*: 7.

53 Guevara did not submit a formal letter of resignation. The terms of the Tydings–McDuffie Act limited the Philippines to one Resident Commissioner with the inauguration of the Commonwealth. With Quezon elected and prepared to appoint a new commissioner, and with the House of Representatives on recess until January 1936, Guevara saw no official reason to return to the United States.

54 "Guevara Will Retire From Political Life," 25 September
    1935, *Philippines Herald*: 1; "Guevara is Opening Manila Law
    Office," 26 September 1935, *Philippines Herald*: 1; "Guevara's
    Protectorate Stand," 5 October 1935, *Philippines Free Press*: 28.
    President Quezon appointed Quintin Paredes to serve as Resident
    Commissioner on February 14, 1936. See also "Quintin Paredes,"
    Biographical Directory of the United States Congress, 1774–Present,
    http://bioguide.congress.gov/scripts/biodisplay.pl?index=P000050.

55 Vicente Albano Pacis, "The New Philippines," 14 December 1935,
    Washington Post: 9; "Filipino Urges U.S. Pact," 16 February 1936,
    New York Times: 26; "Guevara Heads Mining Firm," 24 January
    1937, *Tribune* (Manila, PI): 10.

56 "Death Strikes Guevara in Act of Pleading Case Before Supreme Court."

William P. Jarrett

1877–1929

DELEGATE 1923–1927
DEMOCRAT FROM HAWAII

Known alternately as "Big Bill," "Silent Bill," and "Quiet Bill" to his constituents, soft-spoken William (Bill) Paul Jarrett became the first Democratic Delegate from Hawaii in the U.S. Congress. Elected in 1923, he devoted his time in the House to securing more autonomy and infrastructure for the Hawaiian Islands. A low-key, but productive, legislator, Bill Jarrett sponsored several bills during his tenure that sailed to passage. One of a handful of prominent Hawaiian Democrats, Jarrett lost re-election to a third term in 1926 to one of the islands' rising Republican stars.

William P. Jarrett was born on August 22, 1877, in Honolulu, in the Kingdom of Hawaii, to William Haalilio Jarrett and Emma Kaoo Stevens Jarrett. His father worked as a mechanic and foreman for the public works department and served as superintendent of the wharves in Honolulu.[1] The younger Jarrett received his education at the Saint Louis preparatory school in Honolulu before pursuing a career in law enforcement. In 1908 Jarrett married Mary H. K. Clark, with whom he had six children. Jarrett's home life endured its share of tragedy. Their first child, Mary, was barely a year old when she died in 1910. Jarrett's wife died giving birth to the couple's sixth child on December 4, 1919; the baby passed away four days later.[2] He remarried in 1921 to Elizabeth (Bessie) Neal, widow of civil engineer John W. Neal.[3]

Jarrett first ran for deputy sheriff of Honolulu as a Democrat in 1906, seeking office against an established assistant sheriff when Democrats were relatively unpopular across Hawaii. When reviewing candidates across the political spectrum during the lead-up to the race, the *Evening Bulletin* labeled Jarrett "The Fearless Deputy."[4] He was a shoo-in as sheriff of Honolulu in 1908 and was nominated by acclamation. Republicans labeled him as too soft, which his Democratic cohorts reveled in, saying,

"It's an awful charge against a man to say that he is kind hearted, isn't it?"[5] Jarrett admitted he was a poor speaker early in his campaigns but "when it came to action he believed he could say he was there with the goods."[6] Jarrett served as the popular sheriff of Honolulu for three terms.

In 1914, during Jarrett's third term as sheriff, Democrat Lucius E. Pinkham was appointed territorial governor of Hawaii by President Woodrow Wilson. Pinkham, the first Democratic governor, hurried to sweep Democrats into administrative positions across the island. Caught up in that wave was Jarrett, who received an appointment to the position of high sheriff, the head of law enforcement for the territory and warden of Oahu Prison. Jarrett's appointment came as part of Pinkham's effort to recognize and incorporate Native Hawaiians in his administration.[7]

Jarrett immediately set about reforming prison life. He instituted an honor system, created a central committee of inmates organized to make their own laws, and set prisoners to work mostly unguarded. Under his direction, the prisoners built their own new prison to replace the decrepit jailhouse known as the "Reef."[8] Jarrett served two four-year terms as high sheriff, during which his popularity soared across the islands. Inmates reportedly wept when Jarrett resigned his position at the end of his two terms.[9]

Jarrett's popularity outside Oahu helped him secure a position as a Democratic national committeeman from Hawaii over a rival subset of Democrats led by island party co-founders Lincoln McCandless and John H. Wilson. In the 1916 race for committeeman, McCandless's group originally declared victory for their candidate, Wilson, based on his strong support in Oahu. They were shocked to receive a letter from Jarrett demanding they issue his certificate of nomination after results poured in from the other islands handing him landslide victories. Jarrett accused his opponents of fraud in the initial results and

labeled the Oahu and Maui returns "a huge joke."[10] However, when Jarrett joined Wilson on the trip to plead their respective cases before the national committee, the two got along famously and Jarrett readily conceded to Wilson when faced with his connections on the mainland. This congeniality only endeared Jarrett to Democrats in general and Wilson in particular.[11]

This rapport paid dividends for Jarrett in 1922, when incumbent Republican Delegate Henry Baldwin quickly tired of Washington and perennial candidate and Democratic Party leader McCandless suddenly decided he had had enough of politics and dropped out of the race. John Wilson, remembering his 1916 traveling companion, recruited Jarrett. Voters found Jarrett's quiet, responsible nature refreshing in the wake of the wealthy, verbose McCandless. Wilson's biographer noted, "The less Silent Bill said, the more people cheered."[12] He opened his speeches simply, "I'm Bill Jarrett" and inevitably paused for a lengthy standing ovation.[13] The pro-Republican *Maui News* criticized the former high sheriff for his lack of experience compared to Republican candidate and territorial senator John Wise, urging Hawaii not to send a "green horn" to Washington.[14] Republicans, confident right up through Election Day in a very GOP-friendly environment, were shocked when returns showed Jarrett with an approximately 3,000-vote majority. His election marked him as the first Democrat to represent Hawaii nationally since its annexation, and mainland papers repeatedly referred to him as "the most popular man of Hawaiian blood in the Territory," gleefully reporting big *pake* dinners held in his honor.[15] At one of these dinners, Jarrett urged constituents only half-jokingly to write down what his goals should be and "not to expect him to remember thousands of things he is asked to work for."[16]

Upon arrival at the Capitol, Jarrett was assigned to four committees: Agriculture; Public Lands; Post Office and Post Roads; and the Territories. He left the first two in the 69th Congress (1925–1927) and joined the Committee on Military Affairs instead.[17] During his two terms in Congress, Jarrett upheld his tight-lipped reputation, preferring to extend his remarks in the *Congressional*

Record rather than make speeches either on the floor or in committee. Despite his inexperience and minority status in the Republican-controlled House, Jarrett took to legislating quickly, making friends with fellow Representatives of both parties and testifying regularly before committees, though he remained soft-spoken even then.

Jarrett broke from his typical demeanor in one of the very few speeches he gave on the floor on January 21, 1924, a lengthy lecture on Hawaii's history and the islands' interaction with the American mainland. He emphasized Hawaii's self-sufficiency, which had become difficult to maintain under the restrictions of the Organic Act. He insisted, "Hawaii is an integral part of the United States, not acquired by conquest, but annexed by treaty." Jarrett launched into this uncharacteristic speech immediately following the passage of his first piece of legislation in the House (H.R. 4121), which extended several appropriations aid laws applicable to states to the Hawaiian Territory, including the Federal Farm Loan Act and the Sheppard–Towner Maternity and Infancy Act. It also included disbursement of funds for the construction of roads and vocational rehabilitation. The bill passed by voice vote and became law only two months later.[18]

Emboldened by his legislative success, Jarrett soon introduced another bill (H.R. 6070) providing for federal support and approval of a territorial law providing a nonexclusive franchise to develop infrastructure—particularly electrical utilities—in the district of Hamakua. All franchises had to be approved by Congress under the Organic Act. Jarrett testified before the House Committee on the Territories, emphasizing the need for federal approval despite completion of territorial legislation, but he kept his remarks brief and focused on the mechanical aspects of the bill and its process, letting longtime Washington secretary Bertram Rivenburgh hammer out the details.[19] Jarrett secured more funds to bolster Hawaiian infrastructure in the 69th Congress, when he worked closely with Louis Cramton of Michigan and Fiorello La Guardia of New York to approve a territorial act that provided a franchise to establish electrical power on the island.[20]

Jarrett spent much of his tenure struggling with the bureaucracy imposed by the Organic Act. He introduced a bill allowing the governor of Hawaii, a federally appointed official, to issue patents of residence to homesteaders in Hawaii, bypassing individual congressional approval. Jarrett defended the right of the residents to retain their homes and said, "These people went in there in good faith and got those lots and built homes, and thought they were doing right, and now they come to find out they have not got title and this is the only way they can get it."[21] Jarrett then drew up the report for a bill (H.R. 4985) to repeal a proviso that limited expenditures for "maintenance, supervision, and improvement" in an area of the Hawaii Volcanoes National Park that contains active volcanoes. Safe roads around the volcanoes were projected to cost roughly 10 times more than the previously allotted funds. Both bills breezed through the House and Senate and became Private Law 127 and Public Law 68-198, respectively.[22]

His ability to pass legislation waned in the 69th Congress as House Republican opposition to his bills increased. Despite having Republican territorial governor Wallace Farrington's support, joint resolutions (H.J. Res. 240 and H.J. Res. 267) asking the President to call a Pan Pacific Conference on Education, Rehabilitation, Reclamation, and Recreation at Honolulu, Hawaii, went nowhere. Republican Representative James Begg of Ohio called the proposed $20,000 appropriation for travel merely recreational and "a free trip to Honolulu." Jarrett argued the conference held educational benefits similar to the Pan-American Union, but he ultimately received little support.[23] He also attempted an alliance with Delegate Daniel Sutherland of Alaska to introduce a bill (H.R. 10432) that exempted Hawaiian public school teachers and territorial officials from federal income tax. Testifying before a subcommittee of the Committee on Ways and Means, Jarrett argued teachers were being taxed twice. "The teachers believe that they are not being treated right, and that they should be treated the same as the teachers on the mainland," Jarrett opined, pointing out the difficulty of drawing talent from the mainland.[24] The House took no further action, and his successor resubmitted the resolution (H.R. 14465) to no avail.

Jarrett's reputation bore him through the 1924 election. Republicans ran Phillip L. Rice, a member of the influential Rice family and World War I veteran, to contest the Delegate seat in 1924, but Jarrett outpaced his previous victory with a roughly 4,000-vote majority.[25] Two years later, he faced former Navy commander Victor S. (Kaleoaloha) Houston. Jarrett's personal popularity finally faded, as he was unable to spend enough time in Hawaii to maintain his connections. Island Democrats attempted to discredit Houston by arguing his Navy service had disqualified him as a resident of Hawaii, but without effect. Republicans argued the territory needed a Republican in Congress as tariff policy, a hallmark of the party's platform, became ever more important. Hawaiians swept Republicans into office at all levels of the government in November 1926.[26] Houston prevailed over the incumbent, winning 52.5 percent of the vote.

Bill Jarrett fell ill shortly after returning to Hawaii. The illness lingered for more than a year, and Jarrett died on November 10, 1929. His successor, Delegate Houston, announced his death on the House Floor, saying "He was a true Hawaiian—able, courteous, friendly, hospitable, and dignified."[27]

NOTES

1   "William Jarrett Dead," 25 February 1903, *Hawaiian Star*: 4; No Title, 25 February 1903, *The Independent* (Honolulu, HI): 3.

2   "Sheriff's Baby Daughter Dies," 31 May 1910, *Hawaiian Star*: 1; "Sheriff Jarrett's Wife Dies—Baby Son Lives," 5 December 1919, *Maui News* (Wailuku, HI): 8.

3   No Title, 26 August 1921, *Maui News* (Wailuku, HI): 2.

4   "The Beacon Blue Book—Who's Who In Hawaiian Politics," 20 October 1906, *Evening Bulletin*: 5.

5   "Democratic Lineup Made," 24 September 1908, *Hawaiian Star*: 3; "Fern Answers Some Critics," 22 October 1908, *Pacific Commercial Advertiser*: 8.

6   "W. A. Kinney at Aala Park," 27 October 1908, *Hawaiian Gazette*: 1, 10.

7   "Slate is Being Picked for Governor Pinkham," 17 April 1914, *Hawaiian Gazette*: 1; "Henry Resigns; Jarrett Appointed," 28 April 1914, *Hawaiian Gazette*: 7.

8   "Hawaii Boasts Something New in Prison Life," 25 October

1915, *Honolulu Star-Bulletin*: 1; "Bill Jarrett Wins Election," 10 November 1922, *Los Angeles Times*: 13.

9   Bob Krauss, *Johnny Wilson*: *First Hawaiian Democrat* (Honolulu: University of Hawaii Press, 1994): 183; "Bill Jarrett Wins Election."

10 "Jarrett Claims Election; Fraud Shell is Hurled," 26 April 1916, *Honolulu Star-Bulletin*: 1.

11 Krauss, *Johnny Wilson*: *First Hawaiian Democrat*: 139.

12 Ibid., 183.

13 "Bill Jarrett Wins Election."

14 "The Optimistic Pessimist," 24 October 1922, *Maui News*: 4.

15 "Delegate-Elect to Congress Hawaii's Most Popular Man," 10 November 1922, *St. Louis Post-Dispatch*: 21; "Hawaii Democrats Eat 7 Tons of Food At Big 'Luau' Fete," 10 December 1922, *Washington Post*: 1.

16 "Big Pake Dinner for Bill Jarrett," 12 December 1922, *The Garden Island*: 1.

17 David T. Canon, Garrison Nelson, and Charles Stewart III, *Committees in the U.S. Congress, 1789–1945*, vol. 3 (Washington, DC: CQ Press, 2011): 546.

18 *Congressional Record*, House, 68th Cong., 1st sess. (21 January 1924): 1225–1226; Public Law 68-35, 43 Stat. 17 (1924).

19 Hearings before the House Committee on Territories, *Electric Light and Power Within the District of Hamakua*, 68th Cong., 1st sess. (31 March 1924): 1–3. H.R. 6070 went into effect as Public Law 68-391, 43 Stat. 853 (1925).

20 *Congressional Record*, House, 69th Cong., 1st sess. (19 April 1926): 7769–7770.

21 Hearings before the House Committee on The Territories, *Land Patents, Territory of Hawaii*, 68th Cong., 1st sess. (28 January 1924): 2.

22 House Committee on Public Lands, *To Repeal the First Proviso of Section 4 of an Act to Establish a National Park in the Territory of Hawaii*, 68th Cong., 1st sess., H. Rept. 442 (3 April 1924): 1–2.

23 *Congressional Record*, House, 69th Cong. 1st sess. (21 June 1926): 11706–11708.

24 Hearing before a Subcommittee of the House Committee on Ways and Means, *Income Tax on Territorial Employees of Alaska and Hawaii*, 69th Cong., 1st sess. (2 April 1926): 1–2.

25 Office of the Clerk, U.S. House of Representatives, "Election Statistics, 1920 to Present," http://history.house.gov/institution/election-statistics/election-statistics/.

26 "Hawaii Goes Republican," 29 November 1929, *Christian Science Monitor*: 13.

27 "'Bill' Jarrett Passes," 12 November 1929, *Honolulu Star-Bulletin*: 6; *Congressional Record*, House, 71st Cong., 2nd sess. (2 December 1929): 7–8.

"He was a true Hawaiian—
able, courteous, friendly,
hospitable, and dignified."

Victor S. (Kaleoaloha) Houston
Honolulu Star-Bulletin, November 12, 1929

Victor S. (Kaleoaloha) Houston
1876–1959

DELEGATE 1927–1933
REPUBLICAN FROM HAWAII

Victor Houston, a former U.S. Navy officer descended from a prominent Hawaiian family, represented the Territory of Hawaii for six years. His career as Territorial Delegate overlapped with the onset of the Great Depression, an economic crisis that motivated him to steer federal money to Hawaii and weigh in on immigration issues important to the islands' agricultural industry. In a year in which many Republican candidates went down to defeat for overseeing a battered economy, Houston's congressional career ended abruptly, though not primarily for reasons related to the Depression. Rather, to great effect, his Democratic opponent bludgeoned Houston's political position on a sensational murder case that had racial undercurrents.

Victor Stewart (Kaleoaloha) Houston was born on July 22, 1876, in San Francisco, California, to Edwin Samuel Houston, a rear admiral in the U.S. Navy and a Pennsylvania native, and Caroline Poor Kahikiola Brickwood, a native of Honolulu. His mother was from one of Honolulu's old and established families; her father, A. P. Brickwood, was the longtime postmaster of Honolulu.[1] Victor had one sister named Edna.[2] He attended grade school abroad in Dresden, Germany; Lausanne, Switzerland; the Force School in Washington, DC; and Werntz Preparatory School in Annapolis, Maryland.

In 1897 Houston graduated from the U.S. Naval Academy. A year later, he served aboard the USS *Iowa*, as it investigated the sinking of the USS *Maine*, which helped to precipitate the outbreak of the Spanish-American War.[3] The Navy first assigned Houston to Honolulu, Hawaii, in late 1909 to serve as a lighthouse inspector for the district of Hawaii.[4] It was during his one-year stint in that position that Houston married his cousin, the former Pinao G. Brickwood, in 1910. The couple raised an adopted daughter, Gwendolyn. Pinao died in 1936.[5]

Houston served 32 years in the Navy and eventually commanded the cruiser USS *St. Louis*. He retired as a commander in 1926, was recalled to active duty during World War II, and advanced to the grade of captain on the retired list in 1943.

Though Houston had declared Hawaii as his residence for nearly two decades, his naval career kept him away at overseas posts nearly all that time. He had very little practical experience in island politics. Therefore, when he decided to make his first run for elective office by entering the GOP primary in early September 1926, he hoped to secure the party nomination for Hawaii's lone Territorial Delegate seat in the U.S. Congress on the strength of connections in Washington that he had built up during his naval service. He argued that he could make the best case for commercial development on the islands that would match, if not outpace, federal appropriations for military installations. "I believe that the greater service we are destined to render is as a commercial base rather than as a military outpost," he declared in a campaign advertisement. To that end, he advocated securing federal money to dredge and enlarge the harbors at Hilo, Kahului, Kauai, and Honolulu.[6] "Unknown in Hawaiian politics until a bare month ago," the *Honolulu Star-Advertiser* observed the morning after the primary, Houston easily topped his nearest opponent, A. L. Louisson.[7]

In the general election, Houston challenged the popular two-term incumbent, Democrat William P. Jarrett, a former law enforcement officer and warden of the Oahu Prison. Democrats attacked Houston as being little more than a carpetbagger, a claim that he and other surrogates actively refuted during the campaign. "I have been a registered voter here and during the last four and a half years have voted in this Territory," Houston said. "Before that I voted for [Jonah] Kuhio. I have claimed my

residence in Hawaii for the last 18 years, as the books of the Navy Department in Washington prove."[8]

The principal policy issue, however, revolved around commercial development and the tariff. Houston opposed efforts to undermine tariff barriers that protected industries and, ultimately, he argued, wage earners. Of particular concern, he claimed, were Democratic efforts to effect tariff changes that would have lowered or removed supports for Hawaii's sugar industry.[9] On Election Day, November 2, 1926, Houston captured majorities on the islands of Hawaii, Maui, Molokai, Lanai, and Kauai; only Oahu broke for Jarrett. Territory-wide, Houston prevailed with 18,160 votes to Jarrett's 16,372, roughly 52.5 to 47.5 percent.[10] The *Honolulu Star-Advertiser* described Houston's campaign as "clean-cut, clear-cut, straightforward … free from invective, vituperation and mud-slinging." The editors congratulated voters "for their foresight in sending him to Congress. They will not regret it."[11]

After Delegate Houston was sworn into the House on opening day of the 70th Congress (1927–1929), he was placed on eight standing committees. While eight committees was atypical for most Members at the time, House leaders often assigned Delegates to a range of panels to give them jurisdictional oversight of important issues in their territories.[12] Houston served on three of these committees for the entirety of his House career: Agriculture; Post Office and Post Roads; and Territories. Additionally, he served on the following panels: Military Affairs (70th–71st Congresses, 1927–1931); Naval Affairs (70th Congress); Immigration and Naturalization (72nd Congress, 1931–1933); Merchant Marine and Fisheries (72nd Congress); and Public Lands (71st and 72nd Congresses, 1929–1933).[13]

While Houston delivered relatively few floor speeches during his career—usually less than a dozen in any given session—he spent the bulk of his time testifying before House and Senate committees on a range of bills that affected Hawaiian interests. His legislative wheelhouse was what one would expect, mainly relating to the large military presence on the island, particularly the Navy. He spoke on issues related to pay for officers and retirees, the transfer of

military lands to the territory, military construction, military housing at Wheeler Army Airfield, funding for the Hawaiian National Guard, and federal acquisition of private fishery rights in Pearl Harbor. Houston also weighed in on the need for federal money for infrastructure improvements and public works projects, including dredging Honolulu Harbor and building roadways.[14] Another primary area of focus for Houston was agriculture, including monitoring both tariff rate schedules for produce and the immigration status of Filipinos to meet the labor needs of the islands' sugar and pineapple industries.

During Houston's freshman term in the 70th Congress, he tended to local concerns. Testifying before the Ways and Means Committee as it considered a tariff rate adjustment for domestic sugar, he argued that Hawaii should be considered a "domestic" producer and that the rate should be hiked from 2.2 cents per pound to 3 cents. He also argued that coffee growers in Hawaii and Puerto Rico, who tended to be small-scale growers, should be protected by a higher tariff on their product as well (5 cents per pound). Houston noted that Hawaii produced 7 million pounds of coffee per year and Puerto Rico produced more than 25 million. Both territories, he estimated, were capable of producing 200 million pounds per year.[15] In early 1928, Houston testified before the Committee on World War Veterans' Legislation in support of his bill H.R. 9584, which sought to extend the total and permanent disability rating to servicemen who had contracted leprosy in Hawaii.[16]

During his second term in the 71st Congress (1929–1931), Houston's focus turned to the islands' economy as the country slid into the Great Depression. Often economic questions intertwined with immigration issues in Hawaii's multiracial economy. In the second session of the 71st Congress, he testified before the House Committee on Immigration and Naturalization, which was considering legislation to restrict Filipino immigration to the United States. Richard Welch of California, chairman of the Labor Committee, introduced a bill to curb the flow of immigrants, which he described as an "invasion" of the Pacific Coast and a problem that exacerbated the already difficult employment situation in the midst of the economic crisis.[17] Critics disparaged the suggestion as patently unfair to people already living under the U.S. flag. Delegate Houston agreed with that sentiment, but objected primarily on the grounds that cutting off the Filipino immigrants to Hawaii would devastate the agriculture industry on the islands because those immigrants provided the bulk of the unskilled labor. Houston argued that Hawaii ought to receive an exemption to any such ban.

Under examination by committee members who probed into the history of Hawaii's diverse population, Houston noted, "We in Hawaii have heretofore rather prided ourselves that because of lack of racial prejudice in the islands, and a good bit of that lack of racial prejudice has come about by reason of the attitude of the Native Hawaiians themselves, we have always felt that there is a real melting-pot there and it is working and may possibly serve as an example to the rest of the world."[18] Indeed, Hawaii managed to win an exemption for Filipino laborers not on the merits of Houston's defense of Hawaii's multiracial society, but through the agriculture lobby marshaled by the islands' wealthy planters.[19] Houston also believed the National Origins Act of 1924 ought to be amended to allow U.S. citizens to bring Asian wives into the U.S. and put them on the path to citizenship. Conversely, he recommended amending a loophole in the Cable Act of 1922 that denied women of U.S. citizenship their citizenship rights if they married a non-U.S. citizen of Asian descent.[20]

Additionally, Houston secured a payment of federal highway funds to Hawaii of nearly $1 million, money that the Bureau of Public Roads had withheld from the islands from 1917 to 1925 because it had made the administrative decision that the World War I–era law covering such appropriations did not apply to the territory. Houston convinced his colleagues that it had, in fact, been the intent of Congress that Hawaii should be covered.[21]

Houston weighed in on American governance of its other Pacific territories. He testified in the fall of 1930 before the American Samoan Commission, a group created by the President to recommend legislation to Congress on how to organize the ceded territory. Houston believed that the territory could not be placed on the road to statehood, yet should be given autonomy. He suggested that through an organic act Samoa should create a government with the designation of something like dominion status. "In other words, [Samoans] will govern themselves with an American advisor who will not be a governor but simply an advisor to the governing authority." He also believed that, since Samoans were "under the American flag and cannot owe their allegiance to any other country, it would be only fair to give them an American citizenship status."[22]

During the 72nd Congress, Houston introduced a bill (H.R. 5130) "to enable the people of Hawaii to form a constitutional government to be admitted into the Union on equal footing with the states." But it died quietly, being referred to the Committee on Territories, where no action was taken. Nor, apparently, did Houston speak on behalf of the bill on the House Floor.[23] Of even greater consequence was the fact that the influential Hawaiian planter class was unsupportive, given that the act of empowering elected representatives might dilute their lobbying influence in Washington, DC.[24]

In early 1932, Houston testified before the Committee on Insular Affairs in a hearing about independence for the Philippine Islands, noting in his prepared statement "that I am wholeheartedly in favor of independence for the Philippines because many of the questions that are bound up in [Hawaiian] interest will be solved automatically by such definite action."[25] The primary question he was concerned with, however, was an economic one. He favored inserting a provision in the legislation to exempt the Territory of Hawaii from any federal immigration restrictions imposed on an independent Philippines. The free flow of Filipino laborers into Hawaii was critical to the sprawling sugar and pineapple industries on the islands.

Houston had won easy re-election in 1928 against Democrat Bertram Rivenburgh, capturing 72 percent of the vote. Two years later, after the onset of the Great Depression, he claimed a narrower victory over Democratic stalwart Lincoln McCandless with 53 to 47 percent of the vote.[26]

A longtime rancher and farmer and a former member of the Hawaii territorial house and senate, McCandless, one of the islands' wealthiest landowners, was again Houston's Democratic opponent in the general election of 1932. Republicans nationally were on the defensive as the Great Depression deepened and Democratic presidential candidate Franklin D. Roosevelt swept down-ticket Democrats into Washington. But Houston's biggest hurdle was a contentious local campaign stirred by a sensationalized, racially charged murder case in which he had intervened.

McCandless attacked Houston for tinkering in what became known as the Massie case, in which five nonwhite men were charged with raping Thalia Massie, the wife of a naval officer, in the fall of 1931.[27] The alleged perpetrators stood trial, but the jury was deadlocked. Afterwards, the alleged victim's husband, Thomas Massie, her mother, and several other white U.S. Navy personnel kidnapped and shot one of the alleged rapists.

Houston spent time testifying before congressional committees to defend the Hawaiian judicial system in the wake of the hung jury.[28] When another Hawaiian jury found Thomas Massie and his codefendants guilty in April 1932, Houston urged Governor Lawrence Judd to pardon them, which he did, commuting their sentences to an hour shortly after the judge handed down a sentence of 10 years. Houston had advised Judd, "Since justice seems to have been served by the recent findings, may I as an individual urge you to exercise your pardoning powers at the appropriate time? I also recommend that you allow the present defendants to remain in the custody of the Navy until the matter is finally disposed of. I am convinced the Hawaiian interests will be best served by the suggested action."

Houston believed that pardoning the defendants was the surest way to preserve home rule and prevent Congress from imposing harsh restrictions already percolating their way in committee on the territorial government.[29] McCandless, according to the *New York Times*, called that position "an act of treachery to the Hawaiian race."[30] Shortly before the election, on the campaign stump, McCandless pilloried Houston. "How did the delegate show his love for Hawaii?" he asked an audience. "He telegraphed from the other side to let the navy men go.

And back they went to the man of war.... I want you people to remember that. Send him back to the man of war where he comes from."[31]

McCandless also capitalized on the economic crisis to score political points against Houston. He criticized Houston's advocacy on behalf of Filipinos seeking to immigrate to Hawaii to serve as agricultural laborers, insisting that the work they performed on sugar and pineapple plantations ought better be left to citizens of the island. He further suggested that Houston served an "invisible government" dominated by Hawaiian planters.[32]

Houston countered the charge by noting that Hawaii was unable to supply the necessary native labor force and that, once it had a sufficient homegrown pool of labor, he would favor immigration restrictions. He also suggested that Democrats in Congress were leading efforts to rein in home rule on the islands and that McCandless's claims to the contrary were spurious.[33] Houston, the *Star-Bulletin* editors reminded readers, "has always stood while Hawaii was under fire. He was out in front defending Hawaii's name." His experience and knowledge of DC would prove crucial, the editors insisted, in the campaign to retain self-government on the islands. By contrast, McCandless was "completely inexperienced in the work of government ... absolutely untried in Washington and would be without experience and friends when Hawaii's affairs came up for consideration in the legislative halls and executive departments."[34]

But the headwinds against Republicans nationally, combined with the charges that the incumbent had betrayed Native Hawaiian interests in the Massie case, created an electoral wave that McCandless rode to victory. McCandless racked up more than a 4,000-vote lead in Oahu and narrowly won Kauai. When the votes were tallied from across the islands, McCandless prevailed with 29,431 to Houston's 27,017 (52 to 48 percent).[35]

Aside from his World War II naval service, Houston largely retired from public life after leaving Congress. From 1935 through 1941, Houston served in an appointed position on the Hawaiian Equal Rights Commission. From 1945 to 1951, he was a member of the Hawaiian Homes Commission. He also served on the islands' Territorial

Loyalty Board in the early 1950s.[36] He died in Honolulu on July 31, 1959, less than a month before Hawaii formally became the 50th U.S. state.

On the House Floor, Delegate John A. Burns of Hawaii memorialized Houston by recalling his reaction just months earlier to Hawaii's admittance into the union. "It's not a time for whooping it up," Houston said. "It's time for sober happiness, for really enjoying the situation. We have the same rights as the citizens on the mainland."[37] It was that fidelity to Hawaiian culture and his workmanlike attitude, Burns observed, that made Houston such an asset to the island's constituents. "Victor Houston was sincerely dedicated to the advancement of Hawaiians of Polynesian ancestry. Every available opportunity to stimulate their pride in themselves and their traditions and to encourage the Hawaiians to hold and work for the highest possible aspirations was made by him," Burns said. "His contributions to the institutions of Hawaii were substantial and material. Hawaii is a better place for his having lived and worked."[38]

MANUSCRIPT COLLECTION

Hawaii State Archives (Honolulu, HI). *Papers*: 1877–1940, circa 21 feet. The papers focus primarily on Victor Houston's time as Territorial Delegate.

NOTES

1   "Is in the Navy," 1 July 1898, *Hawaiian Gazette* (Honolulu, HI): 2; "Admiral Houston's Wife an Island Girl," 9 March 1905, *Hawaiian Star* (Honolulu, HI): 5.

2   "Victor S. K. Houston, Former Delegate, Dies," 1 August 1959, *Honolulu Star Bulletin*: 2.

3   "Sticks to Hawaii Defense Despite His Navy Heritage," 18 January 1932, *Baltimore Sun*: 1.

4   "Changes in the Light House Rule: Lt.-Cmdr Houston Goes Back to Navy and Civilian Will Succeed Him," 21 October 1910, *Hawaiian Gazette*: n.p.

5   Local newspapers indicate that the couple was married in the summer of 1910, but no news articles cover the marriage announcement or the wedding ceremony. See also *Congressional Record*, House, 86th Cong., 1st sess. (20 August 1959): 16551.

6   Campaign ad, "Hawaii Destined to Become Great Commercial Base Rather than a Military Outpost," 1 October 1926, *Honolulu Advertiser*: 3.

7   "G.O.P. Delegate Foretold By Vote, Republicans Say," 3 October 1926, *Honolulu Advertiser*: 1.

8   "Republicans Hear Ticket Headliners," 19 October 1926, *Honolulu Advertiser*: 2.

9   See Houston's election advertisements: 29 October 1926, *Honolulu Advertiser*: 3; and 30 October 1929, *Honolulu Advertiser*: 2.

10   "Election Statistics" maintained by the House do not carry results for Hawaii from this era—other than what appears to be an incomplete set for the 1926 election. Instead, these figures are taken from Houston's biographical entry in the *Congressional Directory* editions of the 70th through the 72nd Congresses. See also "Republican Landslide Registered," 3 November 1926, *Honolulu Advertiser*: 1.

11   "Victor Houston, Hawaii's Next Delegate to Congress," 3 November 1926, *Honolulu Advertiser*: n.p.

12   A leading source on congressional committees indicates no committee assignments in the 71st Congress for Houston; the *Congressional Directory* for that Congress, however, indicates that Houston did serve on Agriculture; Military Affairs; Post Office and Post Roads; Public Lands; and Territories. See David Cannon et al., *Committees in Congress, 1789–1946*, vol. 3 (Washington, DC: Congressional Quarterly Press, 2002): 518.

13   Cannon et al., *Committees in Congress, 1789–1946*, vol. 3: 518.

14   Hearings before the House Committee on Rivers and Harbors, *Honolulu Harbor, Hawaii*, 72nd Cong., 2nd sess. (23 December 1932): 1–9.

15   Hearings before the House Committee on Ways and Means, *Tariff Readjustment–1929*, 70th Cong., 2nd sess. (20–22 January 1929): 3235–3242, 8413–8423.

16   Hearing before the House Committee on World War Veterans' Legislation, *World War Veterans' Legislation, H.R. 10160*, 70th Cong., 1st sess. (13 March 1928): 223–229.

17   "Urges Filipino Exclusion" 26 March 1930, *New York Times*: 20; "Filipino Exclusion," 11 April 1930, *Wall Street Journal*: 17.

18   Hearings before the House Committee on Immigration and Naturalization, *Exclusion of Immigration from the Philippine Islands*, 71st Cong., 2nd sess. (10–12 April, 7–8 May 1930): 238–248, quotation on p. 245. See also Houston's testimony in Hearings before the Senate Committee on Immigration, *Suspension for Two Years of General Immigration into the United States*, 71st Cong., 3rd sess. (15–16, 18 December 1930): 63–66.

19   Roger Bell, *Last Among Equals: Hawaiian Statehood and American Politics* (Honolulu: University of Hawaii Press, 1984): 56.

20   Hearings before the House Committee on Immigration and Naturalization, *Wives of American Citizens of Oriental Race*, 71st

Cong., 2nd sess. (4 March 1930): 578–585; Hearings before the House Committee on Immigration and Naturalization, *Amendment to the Women's Citizenship Act of 1922, and for Other Purposes*, 71st Cong., 3rd sess. (17 December 1930 and 23 January 1931): 18–21.

21 Hearings before the House Committee on Territories, *Payment to Hawaii of Federal Road Funds*, 71st Cong., 3rd sess. (20, 22 January 1931): 1–20; *Congressional Record*, House, 71st Cong., 3rd sess. (11 February 1931): 4626–4627.

22 Hearings before the Commission Appointed by the President of the United States in Accordance with Public Res. No. 89, *American Samoa*, 70th Cong., 2nd sess. (18–20 September 1930): 30–33, 90–91.

23 *Congressional Record*, House, 72nd Cong., 1st sess. (9 December 1931): 265.

24 Bell, *Last Among Equals*: 56.

25 Hearing before the House Committee on Insular Affairs, *Independence for the Philippine Islands*, 72nd Cong., 1st sess. (12 February 1932): quotation on p. 450, full testimony from p. 450–457.

26 See Houston's entries in the *Congressional Directory* for the 71st and 72nd Congresses. *Congressional Directory*, 71st Cong., 1st sess., 1st ed. (Washington, DC: Government Printing Office, 1929): 129; *Congressional Directory, 1932*, 72nd Cong., 2nd sess., 1st ed. (Washington, DC: Government Printing Office, 1932): 127.

27 Douglas O. Linder, "The Massie Trials: A Commentary," http://law2.umkc.edu/faculty/projects/ftrials/massie/massietrialsaccount.html (accessed 17 March 2015).

28 "Delegate Defends Justice In Hawaii," 12 January 1932, *New York Times*: 3; Hearing before the Senate Committee on Territories and Insular Affairs, *Proposed Investigation of the Government of the Territory of Hawaii*, 72nd Cong., 1st sess. (16 January 1932): 42–46; Hearing before the House Committee on Naval Affairs, *Hawaiian Situation*, 72nd Cong., 1st sess. (11–14 January 1932): 327–330; Hearing before the Senate Committee on Territories and Insular Affairs, *Administration in Hawaii*, 72nd Cong., 2nd sess. (16 January 1933): 14–28.

29 Russell Owen, "Judd Frees All in Massie Case," 5 May 1932, *Boston Globe*: 1. See also "Massie Case Issue in Hawaiian Primary," 3 October 1932, *Baltimore Sun*: 14; "Massie Pardon Demanded by Congressmen," 3 May 1932, *Baltimore Sun*: 1.

30 "Hawaiians Choose House Candidates," 3 October 1932, *Washington Post*: 5; "Democrats Sweep Hawaiian Elections," 10 November 1932, *New York Times*: 13.

31 "Houston Again Attacked By Democrats," 1 November 1932, *Honolulu Star-Bulletin*: 2.

32 "Democrats Sweep Hawaiian Elections"; "Protest Guides Hawaii's Choice," 10 November 1932, *Los Angeles Times*: 5.

33 "Houston Turns on Democrats and Home Rule," 2 November 1932, *Honolulu Star-Bulletin*: 1; "Houston Looks for Citizens to Man Industry," 2 November 1932, *Honolulu Star-Bulletin*: 13.

34 "Hawaii Needs Houston," 5 November 1932, *Honolulu Star-Bulletin*: 6. See also "Send Houston Back," 7 November 1932, *Honolulu Star-Bulletin*: 6.

35 For election results, see *Congressional Directory*, 73rd Cong. (June 1933): 128. See also "Kauai, Oahu, Swing Victory to M'Candless," 9 November 1932, *Honolulu Star-Bulletin*: 1, 3.

36 Hawaii State Archives Digital Collections, http://digitalcollections.hawaii.gov/greenstone3/library/collection/governm1/browse/CL1/8 (accessed 27 September 2017).

37 *Congressional Record*, House, 86th Cong., 1st sess. (20 August 1959): 16551.

38 Ibid.

"HIS CONTRIBUTIONS
TO THE INSTITUTIONS OF
HAWAII WERE SUBSTANTIAL
AND MATERIAL. HAWAII
IS A BETTER PLACE FOR HIS
HAVING LIVED AND WORKED."

John A. Burns
Congressional Record, August 20, 1959

Camilo Osias
1889–1976

RESIDENT COMMISSIONER 1929–1935
NACIONALISTA FROM THE PHILIPPINES

After starting his career as an educational reformer in the Philippines, Camilo Osias moved into politics in the 1920s, first as a Philippine senator and then as a Resident Commissioner in Congress. His colleagues in the U.S. House of Representatives widely admired Osias for his eloquent oratory and his fervent support of immediate independence, quickly dubbing him "Mr. Philippine Freedom."[1] His persistent advocacy paid off in 1932 with the passage of the Hare–Hawes–Cutting Act, which would have put the Philippines on the road to complete independence had not a struggle for power in Manila derailed it. Osias admitted that American rule came with certain benefits, "but … precisely because we are pleased to recognize that America has been so successful in her work in the Philippines, we now come to you and say that the greatest manifestation of gratitude that we can show you is no longer to tie ourselves to the apron strings of a benign guardian but to ask that you set us free."[2]

Camilo Osias was born in Balaoan, a small town in the Philippines' La Union Province a few miles inland from the South China Sea, on March 23, 1889. His father, Manuel Osias, was a farmer and clerk for the local justice of the peace, and his mother, Gregoria Olaviano, was a homemaker. Osias was the second youngest of four surviving siblings, two boys and two girls. Four other siblings had died in infancy. The family led a simple, modest existence, supplementing Manuel's income by harvesting fruit from trees on their lot and repairing fishing nets. "Like most families in our community," Osias wrote years later, "our family in hardships tilled the soil to obtain additional sustenance, worked on watery fields or in the streams for additional food, and performed chores to gain some coins to satisfy our limited wants and needs. The neighborhood was a happy and quiet place in which to lead [a] simple and frugal life."[3]

As a young boy, Osias planned to become a priest, but when the Philippine Revolution erupted in 1896, he studied in San Fernando, where he quickly mastered Spanish. During the American military occupation of the Philippines, Osias became proficient in English while attending high school in Balaoan.[4] In 1905 he was selected as a *pensionado* (a government-funded student) to study in the United States. He moved to Macomb, Illinois, to attend the Western Illinois State Teachers College, earning recognition as a stand-out public speaker and graduating in 1908. Two years later, he earned a bachelor of science degree in education from Columbia College of Columbia University in New York City. He also received a graduate degree from the Columbia University Teachers College with a specialty in school administration and supervision.[5]

After returning to the Philippines, he married Ildefonsa Cuaresma, a former public school teacher from Bacnotan, near his hometown, in 1914. The couple raised seven children, Camilo Jr., Salvador, Victor, Apolinario, Rebecca, Benjamin, and Rosita. Ildefonsa, who had headed the Philippine Young Women's Christian Association (YWCA) and campaigned widely for her husband in his early career, was herself a political power and formidable public speaker. "Tales of her exploits as a stump speaker during the electoral campaign when Mr. Osias was running for senator from the Second Senatorial District are, to this day, tea table bon mots," explained a *Washington Post* profile.[6] After more than 20 years of marriage, Camilo divorced Ildefonsa and married Avelina Lorenzana in Reno, Nevada. That marriage produced no children.[7]

When Osias first returned to the Philippines in 1910, he established himself as one of the islands' leading educators. For several years, he taught in La Union Province before moving to Manila, where he served as the academic supervisor of city schools. From 1915 to 1916,

Image courtesy of the Filipinas Heritage Library

he worked as the first Filipino superintendent of schools in Bataan and Mindoro. He next held several high-ranking jobs in the Philippine bureau of education, including as assistant director, where he endeavored to hire more Filipino teachers and administrators.[8] In December 1921, Osias left government service to become the first president of the private National University in Manila. During his 13-year tenure, Osias imposed curriculum reforms and raised academic standards. He was also a prolific author and traveled widely in Japan and China, speaking about educational reform.[9]

Filipino political leaders took notice of Osias early on. In 1919 Manuel L. Quezon, the islands' former Resident Commissioner who became president of the Philippine senate, invited Osias to join the first independence mission to the United States. While on Capitol Hill, Osias testified with the independence delegation before a joint hearing of the House Committee on Insular Affairs and the Senate Committee on the Philippines about how improved education has "contributed materially and greatly to the economic growth of the Philippines."[10] Afterward, Ohio Senator Warren G. Harding pulled Quezon aside and told him, "If you have half a dozen men like your Osias, you are entitled to your independence."[11]

Working with Quezon elevated Osias's profile and drew him further into politics.[12] In 1922 he returned with another independence delegation that included Quezon and pro-nationalist leaders Emilio Aguinaldo and Sergio Osmeña.[13] While campaigning for Quezon's ticket a year later, Osias recalled, "People many a time privately told me that they would vote for me if I were the candidate."[14]

They had that chance in 1925, when the local Partido Nacionalista (Nationalist Party) faction nominated Osias as its candidate for the Philippine senate. As a Nacionalista, Osias was committed to the principle of "independence, immediate, absolute, and complete." For Osias, the campaign against Alejandro de Guzman for the second senatorial district "was long and arduous." He recalled, "I was on the move night and day, attending conferences, meeting leaders and voters, delivering from five to 10 speeches daily at public rallies." On Election Day, Osias

swept his way to an overwhelming majority, claiming by his own estimate the largest margin of victory ever won by a Filipino political candidate.[15]

Osias served in both the seventh and eighth legislatures, where his interests centered on education initiatives and infrastructure projects.[16] He chaired the senate's committee on education and led a joint panel that reviewed the Philippine school system.[17]

On February 7, 1929, when one of the Philippines' two Resident Commissioners, Isauro Gabaldon, resigned his seat in Washington, the territorial legislature elected Osias to succeed him.[18] His election had wide support, but was not without detractors mostly from the Partido Democrata (Democratic Party) who did not agree with the pro-independence agenda of the Nacionalistas. Others questioned if he was sufficiently versed in business and economics to represent the islands on vital trade questions. After a failed attempt by the opposition to challenge the constitutionality of his appointment, Osias took his seat in the House at the opening of the 71st Congress (1929–1931) during a special session called by President Herbert Hoover in April 1929.[19]

In most aspects, his service deviated little from the pattern established by other Philippine Resident Commissioners over the last few decades. Per House Rules, he had no vote on the House Floor, nor did he serve on any committee. Without votes to trade, he acted more like an ambassador than a legislator, lobbying key committee members and executive department officials on Philippine interests pending before the federal government.

Osias brought his wife and five children as well as a small army of staff to Washington. But unlike some of his predecessors who had amassed independent fortunes, he found the transition—traveling halfway around the world and acquiring new housing—a burden on a government salary. He embarked with just $1,000 to help establish his entourage in the federal capital. But on the long ocean voyage to Seattle, he won $14,000 in a poker game, which helped to ease the burden. After arriving in the capital, the Osias family bought a house once owned by Wisconsin Senator Robert La Follette.[20]

Once ensconced in Washington, Osias wasted no time designing a plan to secure complete independence for the Philippines, "the first and foremost mission expected of me by the Filipino people," he said. It was a "complex and many-sided" issue, he acknowledged, and it "meant intensive and extensive fighting and campaigning in and out of the American Congress."[21]

The same day he took the oath of office, Osias, his colleague Pedro Guevara, and leaders of the Philippine legislature visited Secretary of State Henry L. Stimson, former governor general of the islands, to state their case for independence.[22] Only months later Osias and Guevara visited President Herbert Hoover to apprise him of the warm welcome for the islands' new governor general, Dwight F. Davis.[23]

Osias quickly identified three different attitudes in Congress when it came to Philippine issues. The first group was composed of Members who supported independence for any number of reasons. The second group opposed independence either on the grounds that Filipinos were ill-prepared for it or because they favored imperial rule. The final group was simply "uninformed, uninterested, or apathetic."[24]

Osias spent the bulk of his time trying to win Members over to his side and build support for Philippine issues. This included lobbying each category of Member—for, against, or ambivalent—as well as delivering speeches to clubs, civic groups, churches, universities, and business groups. Osias also recalled that the process involved endless hours of committee testimony: "Guevara and I, through various means befriended members of Committees that had the remotest relations to insular affairs."[25]

Osias often camped out on the House Floor to follow debates, looking for opportunities to talk in support of independence, sometimes on subjects far afield from the Philippines. Once, when the House considered an appropriations bill for indigenous Indians in the territories of Alaska and Hawaii, Osias jumped to his feet and highlighted how Congress often categorized the Philippines differently than it did America's other territories.[26]

Afterward, a Congressman found Osias at his seat. "That speech of yours is going to cost me money," he ribbed the Resident Commissioner. "I just lost a bet for dinner, because I thought you cannot possibly bring in Philippine Independence in the course of your remarks on the Bill that had nothing to do with your country. And I'll be darned if you didn't." "Well, for listening," Osias replied, "I'll foot the bill."[27]

With the onset of the Great Depression, Osias used the opportunity to suggest that immediate Philippine independence would reduce costs for the federal government. As the 71st Congress entered its second session and the economic crisis deepened, he became ever more strident on that issue. When competition for jobs led to violent conflict between Filipino and white workers on the West Coast, there was discussion about banning foreign laborers.

In late January 1930, Osias condemned the proposed immigration ban, pointing out that the Filipinos were still under U.S. rule. American shipping interests had recruited young Filipino men as a cheap source of labor by portraying America as a "land of opportunity and promise," he said, before criticizing Congress for faulting Filipinos who chose to come. "But so long as we are under that flag," he shouted, motioning to the Stars and Stripes hung behind the Speaker's rostrum, "we will continue to enjoy its most priceless heritage—citizenship. But for the sake of our independence we are willing to become a foreign country and take our place among the foreign nations."[28]

Biding his time, Osias listened with "religious attention" as California Congressman Richard Welch explained his bill "to exclude certain citizens of the Philippine Islands from the United States." When Welch finished his statement, Osias obliterated it. The bill was "violative of the spirit of justice," "makeshift," and "unnecessary," he said. "What is necessary is to set us free," Osias thundered to loud applause from the galleries. "If we are to be treated as a foreign people for purposes of immigration, we must first be given the category of a free and independent nation."[29]

Late in the 71st Congress, Osias went before both the House Rules Committee and the Senate Committee on Immigration to vigorously oppose a proposal to ban immigration from the Philippines. "What are we?" he asked the somewhat hostile Senate panel. "I would like to say that the Congress of the United States can not well afford to let another generation of Filipinos go without a definite citizenship."[30]

Much of the debate around citizenship and independence was inextricably linked to the unique economic arrangement between the United States and the Philippines. In mid-June 1929, in some of his earliest committee testimony, Osias argued against restrictive quotas and new taxes on coconut oil and sugar in what would become the Smoot–Hawley Tariff Act. He prodded the United States to live up to the ideal of free trade and argued that, by hampering the Philippine economy, the United States was hurting the robust import business of its own producers. "What America does in the Philippines is the basis of interpretation of America's motives and principles by the peoples in the Pacific borders," he told the Senators. "It is therefore a business and a moral asset for America to see to it that nothing that she does or omits to do … will result in shaking the faith and confidence or lessening the friendship of the peoples in the Orient."[31]

A month later, again before the Senate Finance Committee, Osias urged Congress to limit restrictions on Philippine trade. After lobbyists for U.S. cotton, dairy, and meat interests asked the committee to impose duties on competitive Philippine products, Osias railed against the suggestion, asking the committee for more equitable trade terms.[32] Approved and signed into law in June 1930, the final Smoot–Hawley Tariff bill retained many of the existing trade provisions, as Osias had wished, but it also included a provision restricting the amount of foreign material in Filipino products.[33]

By the time the 72nd Congress (1931–1933) convened in December 1931, the movement for independence had gathered supporters in Congress, and in early 1932, a bill named for Butler Hare of South Carolina, chairman of the House Insular Affairs Committee, began to move through the House. It permitted the Philippine legislature to immediately call a constitutional convention, provided for a plebiscite on the draft constitution, kept import and immigration quotas low, and implemented a full tariff schedule on Philippine products after an eight-year transition period.[34] Osias believed the Hare bill was not perfect—certain provisions for a long-term U.S. military presence rankled him, for instance—but he got the sense that it was passable on Capitol Hill. He, along with senior Philippine legislators, appeared before the House Committee on Insular Affairs in early February 1932 to press for its passage.[35]

Speaker John Nance Garner of Texas maneuvered the bill onto the floor by bringing it up under suspension of the rules, requiring a two-thirds vote after just 40 minutes of debate. This tactic prevented the powerful farm bloc from inserting amendments that would have implemented harsher tariffs and granted immediate independence.[36]

At the end of the House debate on the Hare bill, Osias took to the floor and provided an oratorical flourish that punctuated the debate. Referencing the portraits of the Marquis de Lafayette and George Washington hanging astride opposite ends of the Speaker's rostrum, he beseeched colleagues to approve the measure. Watching from the public galleries was a large contingent of Filipinos, including Philippine house speaker Manuel Roxas and Philippine senate president Sergio Osmeña, both of whom supported the independence bill. "The thought uppermost in my mind and my fervent prayer in this hour of solemn decision is that the Members of this body may incarnate in themselves the spirit of Lafayette and Washington," Osias declared to an ovation, "and, by their wisdom and statesmanship, bring into being another starry banner that shall symbolize sovereignty in the Philippine republic that is to be and enable the Filipino people to consummate their own glorious destiny." With Osias watching, the House approved the Hare bill by a large majority, 306 to 47.[37]

A separate, but similar, measure had been introduced in the Senate in early 1932 by Harry B. Hawes of Missouri and Bronson M. Cutting of New Mexico. But in a presidential election year, with opponents pushing hard to kill the bill, the Senate did not pass its version until mid-December 1932. A conference committee swiftly settled the few differences between the Hare bill and the

Hawes–Cutting measure, changing the transition period before independence to 10 years.[38] On December 22, the Senate approved the conference report, passing the newly named Hare–Hawes–Cutting Act; the House followed six days later without even a quorum of its members present, in a division vote of 171 to 16. "In the light of colonial records this Philippine bill, on the whole, is just, fair, and reasonable," Osias judged.[39]

On January 13, 1933, President Herbert Hoover vetoed the Hare–Hawes–Cutting bill, but the House quickly overrode him, 274 to 94. "A law granting us independence," Osias reminded the chamber, "would be a crowning glory to America's stewardship of the Philippine Islands."[40] The Senate followed the House four days later, overriding the veto 66 to 26.[41]

Importantly, the final version required the Philippine legislature to approve the independence act. Insular politics immediately came into play as Manuel Quezon, concerned that Osmeña, who had helped negotiate the Hare–Hawes–Cutting Act, might challenge him for political supremacy on the islands, set out to thwart the independence bill.[42] For much of 1933, the Partido Nacionalista fractured into pro and anti factions, and on October 7, 1933, Quezon presided over a lopsided Philippine senate vote, rejecting the independence bill 15 to 4.[43]

When Quezon began negotiating a nearly identical second independence bill, what would become the Tydings–McDuffie Act of 1934, Osias blasted him in the press for the maneuvering. In late December 1933, when Quezon led a new mission to Washington and received a chilly reception from the Franklin D. Roosevelt administration, the Resident Commissioner was not surprised. "It was a colossal blunder not to have accepted the bill, and then worked for a better bill later," Osias told the *New York Times*. "Acceptance would not have jeopardized our chances to obtain a modified measure."[44]

As a result of their divergent positions on the first independence bill, Quezon pulled his support from Osias, imperiling his chances for re-election by the Philippine legislature as Resident Commissioner.[45] Osias did not take that act of political revenge quietly. He had thrown himself

unconditionally behind the Hare–Hawes–Cutting bill so fervently that he had damaged his political prospects on the islands. "This Osias is a bridge burner, all right," one observer noted. "No matter how precious and costly a certain bridge may be, if it is his bridge he burns it. That is all a part of the Osias urge. That is in his nature. That is in his blood."[46]

Seeing the writing on the wall, Osias campaigned in the spring of 1934 for his old senatorial district seat. The controversy around the Hare–Hawes–Cutting Act dominated the election, pitting those for the bill against those who opposed it, though Osias maintained that the internecine warfare over the independence act had been "wasteful, divisive, and unnecessary." But he was on the losing end of the fight, noting that his former constituents "sacrificed" him: "My two terms as Commissioner away from the Philippines cooled the affection of the electorate toward their former Senator."[47] Voters rejected him in the June 5 election, with Quezon actively campaigning against him.[48] The antis, under Quezon's leadership, swept to electoral victory.

In an unusual move, Osias's supporters in the U.S. Filipino community circulated a petition, eventually signed by more than 140 Members of Congress, requesting that the newly elected, decidedly "anti-Philippine" legislature re-elect Osias.[49] But in late August 1934, Philippine legislators backed lawyer Francisco Delgado to succeed Osias, who refused to resign his position and stayed on until the conclusion of the official end of the term of the 73rd Congress (1933–1935) in early January 1935 (the House had actually adjourned *sine die* in mid-June 1934 ahead of the fall elections).[50]

After his House career, Osias continued in politics, winning election as one of the more than 200 delegates chosen to serve at the constitutional convention provided for under the terms of the Tydings–McDuffie bill. Shortly after the constitution was ratified, Osias was elected to the first national assembly, at that point a unicameral legislature in which he chaired the committee on public instruction.[51]

During World War II, Osias served under the KALIBAPI, the Japanese-dominated, single-party occupation government.

The Japanese later imprisoned him for his suspected pro-Americanism. He was also briefly held after the war by U.S. occupation forces on suspicion of treason, but a court later cleared him of collaboration with Japanese occupiers. After the war, Osias served two more stints in the Philippine senate, the first from 1947 to 1953 as minority floor leader, majority floor leader, and president. And the second from 1961 to 1967. In 1953 he ran for the presidency of the Philippines, but lost the nomination. Osias died in Manila on May 20, 1976, at the age of 87.[52]

FOR FURTHER READING

Bananal, Eduardo. *Camilo Osias: Educator and Statesman* (Quezon City, PI: Manlapaz Publishing Co., 1974).

Osias, Camilo. *The Story of a Long Career of Varied Tasks* (Quezon City, PI: Manlapaz Publishing Co., 1971).

NOTES

1   Camilo Osias, *The Story of a Long Career of Varied Tasks* (Quezon City, PI: Manlapaz Publishing Co., 1971): 191–192.

2   *Congressional Record*, House, 71st Cong., 2nd sess. (29 January 1930): 2649–2650.

3   Osias, *The Story of a Long Career of Varied Tasks*: 17–18.

4   Eduardo Bananal, *Camilo Osias: Educator and Statesman* (Quezon City, PI: Manlapaz Publishing Co., 1974): 1–5.

5   Bananal, *Camilo Osias*: 5–10; *Congressional Directory*, 73rd Cong., 1st sess. (Washington, DC: Government Printing Office, 1933): 129. See also "Camilo Osias," *Biographical Directory of the United States Congress, 1774–Present*, http://bioguide.congress.gov/scripts/biodisplay.pl?index=O000118.

6   "Political Flair of Mrs. Osias Is Asset Here," 14 October 1929, *Washington Post*: 7; "Dinner for Mrs. Osias," 22 April 1930, *New York Times*: 34.

7   Bananal, *Camilo Osias*: 129; *Congressional Directory*, 73rd Cong., 1st sess.: 129.

8   Fernando A. Bernardo, *Silent Storms: Inspiring Lives of 101 Great Filipinos* (Pasig City, PI: Anvil Publishers, 2000): 63–65.

9   Zoilo M. Galang, ed., *Leaders of the Philippines: Inspiring Biographies of Successful Men and Women of the Philippines* (Manila, PI: National Publishing Company, 1932): 50; Bernardo, *Silent Storms*: 64; "Filipino Returns to United States as High Official," 12 April 1929, *Christian Science Monitor*: 3.

10 Hearings before the Senate Committee on the Philippines and the House Committee on Insular Affairs, *Philippine Independence*, 66th Cong., 1st sess. (2–3 June 1919): 57–72, quotation on p. 57–58; Osias, *The Story of a Long Career of Varied Tasks*: 147–152; "Envoys Speak for the Filipinos," 21 April 1919, *Christian Science Monitor*: 9.

11 Osias, *The Story of a Long Career of Varied Tasks*: 149.

12 Ibid., 147–152; Bananal, *Camilo Osias*: 24–27.

13 Charles Edward Russell, "Delegates Coming to Urge Independence for Filipinos," 20 March 1922, *Christian Science Monitor*: 5.

14 Bananal, *Camilo Osias*: 26–27; Osias, *The Story of a Long Career of Varied Tasks*: 169–171.

15 Osias, *The Story of a Long Career of Varied Tasks*: 170–171.

16 For a listing of the Philippine senate in the 1920s, see the Philippine senate's historical tables at https://www.senate.gov.ph/senators/senlist.asp#sixth_leg (accessed 13 January 2016).

17 Osias, *The Story of a Long Career of Varied Tasks*: 172, 176; "Filipino Returns to United States as High Official."

18 "Philippine Legislature Elects Commissioners," 8 February 1929, *Washington Post*: 9.

19 Bananal, *Camilo Osias*: 28–30; Osias, *The Story of a Long Career of Varied Tasks*: 181–182.

20 Osias, *The Story of a Long Career of Varied Tasks*: 181, 183–184.

21 Ibid., 191.

22 "Filipinos See Stimson," 16 April 1929, *New York Times*: 33.

23 "Filipinos Visit Hoover," 22 August 1929, *New York Times*: 22.

24 Osias, *The Story of a Long Career of Varied Tasks*: 191.

25 Ibid., 191–192.

26 *Congressional Record*, House, 71st Cong., 2nd sess. (13 December 1929): 626–630. See also *Congressional Record*, House, 71st Cong., 2nd sess. (20 December 1929): 1022–1025.

27 Osias, *The Story of a Long Career of Varied Tasks*: 192–193. See also "House Applauds Philippine Appeal: Representatives Cheer Speech of Osias, Urging Immediate Independence," 14 December 1929, *New York Times*: 4.

28 "Free Philippines Put Before Rights," 30 January 1930, *New York Times*: 4. See also *Congressional Record*, House, 71st Cong., 2nd sess. (29 January 1930): 2649–2650.

29 *Congressional Record*, House, 71st Cong., 2nd sess. (25 March 1930): 6110.

30 Hearings before the House Committee on Rules, *Immigration*, 71st Cong., 3rd sess. (5, 10 February 1931): 69–75; Hearings before the Senate Committee on Immigration, *Suspension for Two Years of General Immigration into the United States*, 71st Cong., 3rd sess. (15, 16, 18 December 1930): 50–62, quotation on p. 52.

31 Hearings before a Subcommittee of the Senate Committee on Finance, *Tariff Act of 1929*, 71st Cong., 1st sess. (14–15, 17–18 June 1929): 263–271, quotation on p. 269.

32 Hearings before the Senate Committee on Finance, *Tariff Act of 1929*, 71st Cong., 1st sess. (16 July 1929): 262–263; "Protest by Filipino," 17 July 1929, *Wall Street Journal*: 2; "Three More Tariff Protests Received," 17 July 1929, *Washington Post*: 3.

33 Tariff Act of 1930, Public Law 71-361, 46 Stat. 590 (1930).

34 Theodore Friend, *Between Two Empires: The Ordeal of the Philippines, 1929–1946* (New Haven, CT: Yale University Press, 1965): 90.

35 Hearing before the House Committee on Insular Affairs, *Independence for the Philippine Islands*, 72nd Cong., 1st sess. (9 February 1932): 352–371, quotation on p. 352.

36 "House Votes to Free Philippines in 1940; Stimson Is Opposed," 5 April 1932, *New York Times*: 1; *Congressional Record*, House, 72nd Cong., 1st sess. (4 April 1932): 7401–7412.

37 *Congressional Record*, House, 72nd Cong., 1st sess. (4 April 1932): 7411. Osias also delivered a longer address the day after the vote. See *Congressional Record*, House, 72nd Cong., 1st sess. (5 April 1932): 7480–7484.

38 Friend, *Between Two Empires*: 96.

39 For the House debate, see *Congressional Record*, House, 72nd Cong. 2nd sess. (29 December 1932): 1075–1095, Osias quotation on p. 1095.

40 *Congressional Record*, House, 72nd Cong., 2nd sess. (13 January 1933): 1764.

41 Friend, *Between Two Empires*: 106–108; "Hail Defeat of Veto: Filipino Commissioners Call Independence Grant Unprecedented," 18 January 1933, *New York Times*: 2.

42 Nick Cullather, "Philippines," in *The Encyclopedia of the United States Congress*, ed. Donald C. Bacon, Roger H. Davidson, and Morton Keller (New York: Simon and Schuster, 1995): 1543; Friend, *Between Two Empires*: 131–132. For Hare–Hawes–Cutting, see Public Law 72-311, 47 Stat. 761 (1933).

43 Friend, *Between Two Empires*: 129–130.

44 "Filipinos in Dispute on Independence," 26 December 1933, *New York Times*: 5; "Filipino Leaders to Ignore Osias," 27 December 1933, *New York Times*: 8.

45 "Osias Will Return to D.C. Tomorrow," 22 December 1933, *Washington Post*: 12; "Filipinos Reappoint Guevara, Drop Osias," 21 August 1934, *Christian Science Monitor*: 5.

46 Juan A. Cabildo, "What of Camilo Osias?," 22 August 1943, *Philippines Herald Magazine*: 10, 19, 21, quotation on p. 21.

47 Osias, *The Story of a Long Career of Varied Tasks*: 220–221.

48 "Filipinos Reappoint Guevara, Drop Osias," 21 August 1943, *Christian Science Monitor*: 5.

49 James G. Wingo, "141 Congressmen Want Osias Back," 25 August 1934, *Philippine Free Press*: 38.

50 "Osias Will Not Resign Position," 23 August 1934, *Philippine Herald*: 3.

51 Osias, *The Story of a Long Career of Varied Tasks*: 222–227.

52 "Osias, Statesman, Dies at 87; FM Pays Tribute," 21 May 1976, *Philippines Bulletin Today*: 16; "Osias, 87, Dies," 21 May 1976, *Philippines Daily Express*: 3; Bananal, *Camilo Osias*: 53–86, 108–120.

Francisco A. Delgado
1886–1964

RESIDENT COMMISSIONER 1934–1936
NACIONALISTA FROM THE PHILIPPINES

Francisco Delgado served little more than a year as the Philippine Islands' Resident Commissioner, bridging the brief period between passage of the landmark Tydings–McDuffie Act of 1934 and the establishment of the Philippine Commonwealth in 1936. Delgado spent his time in Washington mostly as a caretaker, protecting Philippine interests by criticizing tariffs and taxes that threatened to restrict economic growth. "There is a fine market in the Philippines for American goods, provided that the buying capacity of the Filipinos is not reduced," Delgado told a House committee. "But every time that you pass legislation which in any way hampers, or is liable to hamper, the economic situation out there, wages are affected, values go down, and, of course, when the laboring man earns less, he has less money, no matter what you do in the way of tariff legislation, he cannot buy anything but what he can afford, whether he likes it or not."[1]

Francisco Afan Delgado was born in Bulacan, Bulacan Province, Philippines, on January 25, 1886, to Nemesio and Manuela Afan Delgado. His mother hoped that he would become a priest, but Delgado was drawn toward a career in law after serving as a stenographer for a judge. He studied at San Juan de Letran and Ateneo de Manila schools for his primary education. He also attended Colegio Filipino, a law school. As a *pensionado* (a student sent by the government to study abroad), he attended Compton High School in Compton, California, for his senior year. He later recalled that his motto as a student was "Industry and Concentration." He was among the first group of Filipino students to study in the United States and "a member of the brain aristocracy of his times," according to a later observer.[2]

Delgado moved to Bloomington, Indiana, and earned a bachelor of laws degree at Indiana University in 1907. He then attended the University of Chicago and Yale, earning a master of laws degree at the latter school in 1908. After graduation, Delgado passed the Indiana state bar and briefly worked in an Indianapolis law firm. According to one source, he was the first Filipino to serve as an active member of the American Bar Association. He eventually led the Philippines Bar Association and directed the International Bar Association. Delgado married Rosario Montenegro in 1915, and the couple had three children, Rosario, Concepcion, and Arturo.[3]

When Delgado returned to the Philippines in 1908, he was employed as a law clerk and later as chief of the legal division of the executive bureau. In 1913 he left government service to start his own law firm, where he worked for the next two decades building a reputation as one of the islands' top lawyers. During World War I, Delgado served in the Philippine national guard and was a member of the islands' national council of defense.[4]

In June 1931, Delgado won popular election to the Philippine house of representatives, where he represented Bulacan, his home province. He was re-elected to a second term in June 1934.[5] Delgado chaired the committee on external relations, a panel specially created by the legislature to help in the transition from colonial rule to independence.[6]

In the legislature, Delgado often won arguments by combining his natural charisma with sheer willpower. He was "handsome … with an aristocratic moustache," the *Philippines Herald Mid-Week Magazine* said in 1934. Colleagues respected him and often bent to his forceful, lawyerly arguments. "When he is discussing important bills and wants them to be approved, he … pounds the table, and issues forth arguments after arguments, and delivers the goods home."[7]

On August 22, 1934, by unanimous resolution, the Philippine house of representatives, with the senate

concurring, elected Delgado as Resident Commissioner to the post being vacated by Camilo Osias.[8] On the same day, the senate, with the backing of President Manuel L. Quezon, chose Pedro Guevara to another term in the other Resident Commissioner post.[9] The *Herald* welcomed the selection of Delgado, calling it an "appointment that inspires the confidence that our case in the United States will be in safe keeping."[10] Delgado's work on the external relations committee made him familiar with the issues and ensured he would follow the legislature's instructions. Moreover, the *Herald* observed, "he knows the peculiar American psychology."[11]

But for a man used to being in the center of things, there was concern that Delgado would "feel homesick in Congress." On Capitol Hill, the *Herald* noted, "he will be expected to discuss only matters that pertain to the Philippines, and only when some congressman implores the speaker that the privilege of the floor be extended to him."[12]

Delgado headed to Washington during a unique, uncertain period in Philippine history. When Congress passed the Tydings–McDuffie Act in April 1934, the very nature of the Philippines' relationship with the United States changed: as a first step toward independence, the islands quickly drafted and approved a constitution creating the commonwealth of the Philippines. As a result, Delgado inherited a responsibility devoid of what had traditionally been the Resident Commissioner's foremost political concern.[13]

With the establishment of the commonwealth, many Filipinos began focusing on other issues. Moreover, Congress had grown less hospitable to Philippine concerns now that the islands were on the path to independence. As a result, Delgado faced strong headwinds delivering his message in Washington. The vocal isolationist camp on Capitol Hill was unreceptive, eager to wash their hands of U.S. entanglements in the Pacific, and commercial interests, especially the powerful southern agriculture sector which had for decades competed with Philippine exports, looked to stifle trade and regain to expand its market share.

Delgado also did not have much time to pursue an agenda in the House: He and Guevara were the last Resident Commissioners elected by the territorial legislature. For the previous 30 years, the Philippines had sent Resident Commissioners to Congress in pairs, one elected by the assembly and the other by the commission. Under Tydings–McDuffie, however, the new Philippine Commonwealth agreed to a change limiting the islands to only one Resident Commissioner appointed by President Quezon. Delgado's term, like Guevara's, was set to expire once a constitutional convention had been held and the new form of government ratified. The compressed legislative schedule for the 74th Congress (1935–1937) also worked against Delgado. The House adjourned *sine die* in late August 1935 and did not come back until early January 1936 for the next session, about a month before Delgado's term in office lapsed.

Delgado's first significant statement as Resident Commissioner, given in an interview with the *New York Times*, revealed that he and Guevara were not on the same page. Both hoped to maintain the strong commercial relationship with the States, but the two disagreed about Japan's goals in the Pacific.[14] Even as Japan bolstered its navy, Delgado downplayed the threat of Japanese expansion, claiming that it had no "immediate intentions" toward the Philippines or its resources, and rejected the idea that the United States should boost its military presence. He went on to suggest that the Philippines could become "the Switzerland of the Far East"—a neutral country without a military, he added. "Our strength will lie in our weakness."[15]

The unevenness of that approach—rejecting the U.S. military while pressing for a preferential economic relationship with Washington—seemed to contradict Quezon and Guevara, who accepted that the price of maintaining special access to U.S. markets would be an ongoing political relationship. Otherwise friendly observers in Manila looked dimly on Delgado's statement. "Such sophistry and naïveté on the part of the new resident commissioner reminds one indeed of Osias in his first days on Capitol Hill," declared the *Philippines Free Press*. "The more Delgado talks the more he sounds like his predecessor."[16]

When the 74th Congress opened in January 1935, Delgado took the oath of office and settled into his office in the House Office Building (now the Cannon building). Since House Rules prevented Delgado from serving on committees or voting on the House Floor, he treated his role in much the same manner as his predecessors, more like a diplomat than a legislator. Delgado made connections with prominent Filipinos living in the States, including Vicente Villamin, an economist and the head of the Philippine American Chamber of Commerce. He testified before congressional committees and lobbied key lawmakers and administration officials in the War and Treasury Departments. For a legislator without any actual legislative power, he worked to build personal relationships and expected to entertain colleagues at his home in Washington. "We have to do this to make up for our lack of a vote in Congress," he explained. "I don't want to be a four-flusher but I don't want to be called stingy either. I will stay within my means and do my best."[17]

The first time Delgado appeared before a congressional committee was on February 5, 1935, when he testified before the Senate Committee on Agriculture and Forestry to address the precipitous decline in Philippine imports of finished U.S. cotton products and the massive inroads made by Japanese exporters in 1934. After the United States raised rates on Philippine exports, he noted, the purchasing power of the average Filipino plummeted. But Japanese goods were cheaper and, by 1935, accounted for more than half the textile imports.[18]

Delgado struck a theme he repeated throughout his tenure, that Filipinos could only be good consumers of U.S. products if they had money in their pockets.[19] If U.S. agricultural interests "look at the commerce between our two countries in its entirety and from a national viewpoint," he told the committee, "they will reach the conclusion that it is as much to their best interests, as it is to ours to maintain and reinforce the purchasing power of the Philippine people by encouraging their material development and refraining from advocating legislation that might blight or blast their economic life."[20] It was not enough for the Philippines to simply hike tariff rates on Japanese goods, he said. America

and the Philippines needed a long-term deal to keep supply up and prices down.[21]

The same day he offered his inaugural testimony, Delgado appeared as a witness before the House Committee on Immigration and Naturalization to testify on a repatriation program for unemployed Filipinos living in the United States. While he understood why the United States would want to send the jobless back to the Philippines, he encouraged the committee to make repatriation voluntary and to allow repatriates to later return to the United States, arguing in both cases that this would encourage Filipinos to return to the islands.[22]

But the overwhelming bulk of Delgado's legislative emphasis concerned tariffs, taxes, and quota reductions that adversely affected the Philippines' primary agricultural exports. In May 1935, for instance, Delgado testified before a special House subcommittee of the Agriculture Committee, protesting the implementation of a special 10-cent-per-pound tax on U.S.-produced oleomargarine that used unprocessed imported fats or oils as ingredients.[23] That excise tax would have doubled the rates set by the Revenue Act of 1934 (H.R. 7835).[24]

According to Delgado, the taxes in both the existing law and the new bill—H.R. 5587, authored by Richard Kleberg of Texas—encouraged American oleomargarine makers to replace Philippine coconut oil with domestic cottonseed oil to save money.[25] Delgado cast the Kleberg bill as an especially egregious "violation of the covenant and trade agreements" established in the Tydings–McDuffie Act. Moreover, he said, the high taxes threatened to ruin America's reputation in the Philippines and "mar the high plane and moral value" that previous policies had helped create.[26]

The Kleberg bill never cleared committee, but the 5-cent coconut oil excise tax that had been inserted into the 1934 revenue bill was included in the annual revenue bill in the summer of 1935. When the Revenue Act of 1935 (H.R. 8947) came to the House Floor for consideration in late August, Delgado again denounced the coconut oil tax as "a flagrant violation of the trade compact contained in the Tydings–McDuffie Act."[27] Several days later, after passing both the House and Senate, the revenue bill, complete with the new tax, was signed into law by President Franklin D. Roosevelt.

During the 74th Congress, Delgado also attacked the Jones–Costigan Act of 1934 as especially injurious to the Philippines' sugar industry, particularly since federal officials had persistently urged Philippine sugar producers to increase their crop for more than a decade. But now that yearly production had been ramped up to about 1.5 million long tons, Jones–Costigan limited duty-free entry of Philippine sugar to the United States to just 850,000 tons, leaving the islands with a huge surplus. "What perplexes us is that you virtually tell us in this law of March 24, 1934, to make preparation to enter the competitive markets of the world, on the one hand, and on the other you set up barriers in that same law that would render such preparations impossible of realization," he said.[28]

Delgado also sought to secure a nearly $24 million line of credit for the Philippines through the U.S. Treasury that Congress had authorized in the 73rd Congress (1933–1935). The act was intended to offset losses incurred by the commonwealth's reserve fund in the United States when Treasury officials failed to convert a nearly $56 million Philippine deposit into gold. When the price of gold increased a short while later, the Philippines missed out on millions in profit. The line of credit at the Treasury Department was meant to cover the difference.[29]

Congress, however, had only authorized the Treasury credit and had yet to appropriate the funds to pay for it, and, by the time Delgado arrived in Congress, the Senate was considering whether to repeal the credit altogether.[30] In early January 1935, Delgado and Guevara appeared before the Senate Appropriations Committee to try and convince it to approve the necessary funds to cover the credit. In oral and written testimony, the Resident Commissioners pointed out that not only did the credit have the backing of the White House and the Treasury and War Departments, it had also been codified into law.[31] Despite their impassioned plea, the issue remained unresolved by the end of Delgado's term. The Senate eventually passed a measure to repeal the credit, and Delgado's successor, Quintin Paredes, took up the cause again in 1936.

In the fall of 1935, Delgado ushered a large congressional delegation trip to the Philippines to attend the inauguration of Manuel Quezon as commonwealth president. It was a lavish, around-the-world junket funded by the commonwealth, which Delgado called a necessary "gesture of goodwill" and demonstrated "the profound gratitude and friendship" between the United States and the Philippines. Nearly 50 Members of Congress joined Vice President John Nance Garner in attending the inauguration.[32] This was, in some aspects, part of a larger lobbying and diplomatic effort by commonwealth officials to convince key members of Congress to revise harmful trade provisions in Tydings–McDuffie and other bills.[33]

On February 14, 1936, when the Philippines inaugurated its commonwealth government, Delgado's term of service in the House came to an end. Earlier the *Philippines Herald Mid-Week Magazine* had predicted the islands would call on Delgado for some other service, "knowing that whatever task is assigned or sacrifice demanded of him, he will always be at the service with the best that there is in him."[34] President Quezon appointed Delgado to serve as an appeals court justice in the Philippines, where he remained for about a year.[35] For much of the next decade, he worked as a private attorney.

In 1945 President Harry Truman appointed Delgado to the Philippine War Damage Commission. Confirmed by the U.S. Senate, Delgado served in that capacity for five years. He also served as a delegate to the United Nations Conference on International Organization in San Francisco in 1945. Delgado was elected to the Philippine senate and served there from 1951 to 1957.[36] From September 1958 to January 1962, he served as the Philippines' ambassador to the United Nations. Delgado died in Manila on October 27, 1964.[37]

NOTES

1   *Congressional Record*, House, 74th Cong., 1st sess. (30 July 1935): 12127. This is part of Delgado's testimony before a House Special Subcommittee of the Committee on Agriculture, which he inserted into the *Record*. The full transcript is on pages 12122–12131. See also Alfonso Ponce Enrile, "An Appraisal of F. A. Delgado," 27 November 1935, *Philippines Herald Mid-Week Magazine*: 5.

2   Francisco Delgado, Box 46, *Biographical Directory of the United States Congress* Research Collection, Office of the Historian, U.S. House of Representatives; Zoilo M. Galang, ed., *Leaders of the Philippines: Inspiring Biographies of Successful Men and Women of the Philippines* (Manila, PI: National Publishing Co., 1932): 197–199; "Our Resident Commissioners," 25 August 1934, *Philippines Herald*: n.p.

3   *Congressional Directory*, 74th Cong., 2nd sess. (Washington, DC: Government Printing Office, 1935): 130; Galang, *Leaders of the Philippines*: 197–199.

4   "Francisco A. Delgado," *Biographical Directory of the United States Congress, 1774–Present*, http://bioguide.congress.gov/scripts/biodisplay.pl?index=D000218.

5   *Congressional Directory*, 74th Cong., 2nd sess.: 130.

6   Eugenio E. Santos, "Within The Committee Rooms," 22 August 1934, *Philippines Herald Mid-Week Magazine*: 7, 23.

7   Santos, "Within The Committee Rooms": 7.

8   Creed F. Cox (War Department) to South Trimble (Clerk of the House), 12 October 1934, House Committee on Elections, 74A-J1, Record Group 233, National Archives and Records Administration (hereinafter NARA), Records of the U.S. House of Representatives, Washington, DC; President Franklin D. Roosevelt to Speaker Joseph Byrns, 3 January 1935, House Committee on Elections, 74A-J1, Record Group 233, NARA.

9   "Solons Select New P.I. Envoys to Washington," 21 August 1934, *Philippines Herald*: 1.

10 "A Happy Choice," 22 August 1934, *Philippines Herald*: 4; "Guevara, Delgado Elected to Congress Posts by Legislature," 22 August 1934, *Philippines Herald*: 1.

11 "Our Resident Commissioners"; "Delgado Promises to Abide by Legislature And Heads," 23 August 1934, *Philippines Herald*: 1.

12 "Our Resident Commissioners."

13 Enrile, "An Appraisal of F. A. Delgado": 5.

14 "Philippine Plots by Japan Scouted," 30 December 1934, *New York Times*: 15; *Congressional Record*, House, 74th Cong., 1st sess. (6 February 1935): 1617.

15 "Philippine Plots by Japan Scouted."

16 James G. Wingo, "Delgado Doings; Immediate Withdrawal Proposal," 16 February 1935, *Philippines Free Press*: 9.

17 Wingo, "Delgado Doings; Immediate Withdrawal Proposal."

18 Hearings before the Senate Committee on Agriculture and Forestry, *Causes of the Loss of Export Trade and the Means of Recovery*, 74th Cong., 1st sess. (5 February 1935): 457–463.

19 "Philippines Seek a Trade Exchange," 25 December 1934, *Washington Post*: 2.

20 *Causes of the Loss of Export Trade and the Means of Recovery*: 461.

21 Ibid., 462.

22 Hearings before the House Committee on Immigration and Naturalization, *Extending the Time for Voluntary Return of Unemployed Filipinos to the Philippines*, 74th Cong., 1st sess. (5–6 February 1935): 26–30.

23 *Congressional Record*, House, 74th Cong., 1st sess. (30 July 1935): 12122–12131; Hearing before a Special Subcommittee of the House Committee on Agriculture, *Oleomargarine*, 74th Cong., 1st sess. (May–July 1935): 92–96.

24 Revenue Act of 1934, Public Law 73-216, 48 Stat. 680 (1934).

25 *Congressional Record*, House, 74th Cong., 1st sess. (30 July 1935): 12125.

26 Hearing before the House Committee on Agriculture, *Trade Relations with the Philippines*, 74th Cong., 1st sess. (28 May 1935): 303–304.

27 *Congressional Record*, House, 74th Cong., 1st sess. (24 August 1935): 14636–14637.

28 Ibid., 14638.

29 "Monetary Issue Tangles Affairs of Philippines," 15 February 1936, *Christian Science Monitor*: 1; Public Law 73-419, 48 Stat. 1115 (1934).

30 "From Across the Sea," 20 March 1936, *Chicago Daily Tribune*: 16; Vicente Albano Pacis, "After the Ball," 16 March 1936, *Washington Post*: 9; "Monetary Issue Tangles Affairs of Philippines."

31 Hearings before the Senate Subcommittee of the Appropriations Committee, *Second Deficiency Appropriations Bill for 1935*, 74th Cong., 1st sess. (June 1935): 90–101.

32 "Philippines to Be Host," 11 September 1935, *New York Times*: 5; "Garner Acclaimed by Seattle Throng," 16 October 1935, *New York Times*: 18.

33 Enrile, "An Appraisal of F. A. Delgado": 5.

34 Ibid.

35 "Francisco A. Delgado," *Biographical Directory of the United States Congress, 1774–Present*, http://bioguide.congress.gov/scripts/biodisplay.pl?index=D000218.

36 Philippines Senate, "Francisco A. Delgado," Former Senators' Profiles, http://www.senate.gov.ph/senators/former_senators/francisco_delgado.htm (accessed 21 December 2015).

37 "Francisco A. Delgado," *Biographical Directory of the United States Congress, 1774–Present*, http://bioguide.congress.gov/scripts/biodisplay.pl?index=D000218; "Delgado, Former UN Envoy, Dies," 28 October 1964, *Manila Chronicle*: 1.

Samuel Wilder King
1886–1959

DELEGATE 1935–1943
REPUBLICAN FROM HAWAII

Samuel Wilder King dedicated his life to Hawaiian statehood, but he died shortly before his dream was realized. King had long advocated for his home to become an equal and vital part of the American nation, consistently characterizing the Hawaiian people as being quintessential American citizens. A veteran of both World Wars and a graduate of the U.S. Naval Academy, he fought both literally and figuratively for Hawaiians' democratic freedoms for more than 40 years. In a 1937 congressional hearing for statehood, King proudly noted that the "agitation for statehood is more my responsibility than that of any other individual."[1]

Samuel Wilder King was born in Honolulu on the island of Oahu, in the Kingdom of Hawaii, on December 17, 1886. He was the son of James A. King, a shipping magnate and minister of the interior for the Republic of Hawaii, and Charlotte Holmes Davis, part-Hawaiian descendant of Oliver Holmes, chief and governor of the island of Oahu. Samuel attended St. Louis School in Honolulu and graduated from Honolulu High School. King's generation came of age during the turbulent period in Hawaiian history that saw the overthrow of the Native Hawaiian monarchy and the establishment of the white-dominated republic that preceded American annexation. King embraced his new nation. In 1905 he was appointed to the U.S. Naval Academy by Jonah Kuhio Kalanianaole, one of the earliest Native Hawaiians to enter the academy after Victor S. (Kaleoaloha) Houston.[2] After graduation in 1910, King entered the Navy and served in World War I. In 1912 he married Pauline Evans, and together they had five children, Charlotte, Samuel P., Davis, Evans, and Pauline.[3] He retired from the Navy in 1924 as a lieutenant commander, remaining in the Navy Reserve until 1928. After his retirement, King settled into the real estate business in Hawaii.

King began speaking out for Native Hawaiians nationally as early as 1924, when he wrote a letter to the editor of the *New York Times* titled "Lo, the Poor Nordic," passionately defending them against mainland stereotypes and lifting up his former patron, the late "Prince Kuhio," for his support of the Hawaiian Homes Act, designed to encourage modern farming on the island.[4] King campaigned actively for the Republican Party, serving as a precinct worker in Oahu for several years. In 1932 he was appointed to fill an unexpired term on the Honolulu board of supervisors, now the city council, and later that year won election to a three-year term. He also served on the three-member Home Rule Commission, which visited Washington, DC, in 1933 to blunt any efforts to revise the Organic Act of the territory to replace government officers with nonresidents.[5]

Following his 1932 re-election loss to Democrat Lincoln McCandless, respected Republican Delegate Victor Houston mulled his political future, leaving the party in limbo heading into the 1934 elections. Houston refused to officially comment on his future plans until the summer of 1934. In the meantime, King returned from Washington, DC, disheartened by Congress's casual response to Hawaiian concerns. In an action that seemingly sidelined Houston, King immediately declared his candidacy for the Republican nomination. "Upon my return from Washington last November, I felt so deeply the false position Hawaii had been put into in Washington," he said, "that I expressed my willingness to be a candidate for delegate from Hawaii."[6]

Running unopposed in the Republican primary freed King to campaign almost exclusively on the cause nearest his heart: achieving statehood for the islands.[7] Meanwhile, McCandless narrowly won the Democratic primary, fending off charges that he had placed personal ambition

before the needs of the electorate.[8] On the campaign stump, King pointed to congressional Republicans' support for the sugar industry and recent opposition to a 1933 bill seeking to supplant the territorial governor with a mainland appointee as proof that the GOP was friendlier to Hawaiian interests.[9] The *Honolulu Star-Advertiser* endorsed the Republican and his argument that islanders owed a debt to the GOP. The *Honolulu Star-Advertiser* also hastened to point out King's naval service and his relative youth compared to the 75-year-old McCandless.[10]

In the November election, King won 51 percent of the vote, defeating McCandless by fewer than 2,000 votes out of the roughly 61,000 cast. McCandless contested the election, but his protest did not prevent King's seating at the opening of the session. Ultimately, the House committee overseeing the election found no evidence of the fraud and voter intimidation that McCandless had alleged. The committee faulted King for failing to file timely reports of his campaign expenditures, violating the spirit, if not the letter, of the Corrupt Practices Act. The Elections Committee, however, decided "that a strict interpretation of the requirements of the law … might result in a wrong and injustice to the contestee and cloud a distinguished and honorable career." McCandless's case was dismissed in May 1936.[11]

King arrived in the capital in late December 1934 to the welcome of many former Navy friends.[12] He prioritized securing important territorial rights for Hawaii, with the ultimate goal of statehood. To that end, King requested to be placed on eight committees, all, he explained, "which have matters of vital interests to the Territory of Hawaii before them."[13] In the 74th Congress (1935–1937), leadership granted his request and he took seats on all eight committees: Agriculture; Immigration and Naturalization; Merchant Marine and Fisheries; Military Affairs; Naval Affairs; Post Office and Post Roads; Public Lands; and Territories. He later joined the Committee on Rivers and Harbors in the 75th Congress (1937–1939) and the Committee on Insular Affairs in the 76th Congress (1939–1941).

One of the first bills King submitted sought to grant Hawaii a constitution, state government, and admission to the Union. The bill quietly died after field hearings in Honolulu in October 1935. Frustrated, King took a different tack. In conjunction with Senator Millard Tydings of Maryland, who submitted S. Con. Res 18, King introduced a concurrent resolution (H. Con. Res. 20) to form a joint committee on Hawaii primarily to investigate the possibility of Hawaiian statehood. In debate over the resolution, King insisted, "There is no argument against Hawaii as to size, as to numbers, as to wealth, as to its capacity to maintain a republican form of government, nor as to the historical obligation of the United States to at some time grant it statehood."[14] The committee, chaired by Utah Senator William H. King, organized in the fall of 1937 aboard the USS *Malolo* headed towards Honolulu. During the month of October, the committee held 17 hearings on the islands on Hawaii's potential for statehood.[15] Despite King's personal popularity and his continued lobbying as a member of the committee, it ultimately recommended in early 1938 that the question of statehood be deferred until the "sentiment of the people" could be decided.[16] King was critical of the process. "A period of 16 days is really not enough time in which to get the whole picture of Hawaii," he lamented on the final day of hearings.[17]

In response to the joint committee's report, King waged a two-front campaign for statehood. The statehood plebiscite that he had urged at home on the islands eventually reached the ballot in 1940. Fearing the sudden ascendant militarism in Japan, Hawaii avoided the question of "immediate" statehood on the ballot. Many politicians viewed the sizable population of Japanese immigrants on the island as a security threat. Intolerance simmered in the months prior to the plebiscite as Japanese-American citizens were terminated from defense jobs and rumors spread of the immigrant community's support for the Japanese military. In the last push before the plebiscite, King returned home to personally campaign for statehood in an attempt to distract from the narrative of barely contained racial conflict. The plebiscite ultimately succeeded with 67 percent of voters confirming a preference for statehood. However, the vague wording scuttled any momentum King had hoped to wrest from its passage.[18]

In Washington, at the beginning of the 76th Congress, he once more reintroduced a bill for Hawaiian statehood. Addressing concerns that Hawaii was populated by a large number of noncitizens, King sponsored measures designed to create pathways to citizenship for these inhabitants. Both of his immigration bills were reported out of the Immigration and Naturalization Committee without amendment, and King's bill (H.R. 159) to naturalize all Hawaiian women born prior to Hawaiian annexation passed both chambers by unanimous consent and became law in July 1940. King continued to offer bills expanding citizenship for inhabitants of Hawaii, viewing each bill as a stepping stone to statehood.

King often pointed to the obstructive nature of the Organic Act in managing Hawaiian affairs when the territorial government found its progress stymied by federal law. He submitted bills to allow for the reapportionment of Hawaii's legislature in 1939 and 1940, insisting that reapportionment had "lagged behind" the population shifts on the islands. He cajoled the House to release the bills from the Committee on Territories, where they languished, in order that Hawaiian citizens of "each economic group" would receive "proportionate membership in the legislature" rather than be controlled by the more densely populated island of Oahu.[19]

King also prioritized the needs of the key Hawaiian agriculture industry. He criticized a provision in the 1937 sugar bill (H.R. 7667) that prohibited Hawaii from refining sugar and placed a quota on the importation of the islands' sugar, the primary crop in the territory. President Franklin D. Roosevelt initially promised to veto the measure unless the provisions limiting Hawaiian imports were stripped from the bill. When challenged on the quota, the bill's proponents cited poor working conditions in Hawaii, which King rejected out of hand. The Members making these claims "have never been to the islands and have never seen the community," he insisted. He leaned on the Texas delegation, many of whom were longtime allies of Hawaiian Delegates in Congress. Backed by Majority Leader Sam Rayburn, Agriculture Committee Chairman John Marvin Jones submitted a cursory amendment to

remove the offending quotas, but they confined their speeches largely to praise of the Roosevelt administration for the expected veto. The amendment predictably failed, and, worse, Roosevelt's promised veto never came. Attempting to make the best of a frustrating law, King admitted that the bill at least offered "recognition of our status as a domestic producer."[20]

King ran unopposed in the 1936 primary and went on to win the general election against Democrat Bertram Rivenburgh with nearly 70 percent of the vote.[21] In 1938 he defeated Democrat David Trask with 59 percent of the vote. King then ran unopposed in 1940, the same year he shepherded a plebiscite on statehood to passage by a margin of 2 to 1. King declared himself "deeply gratified" with Hawaiian voters heading into the 77th Congress (1941–1943), hoping to generate support in Congress off the strength of the vote.[22]

In the wake of the surprise attack on Pearl Harbor in Oahu, King urged full-scale war on Japan to "destroy her as a military power."[23] The Delegate spent much of his time traveling to and from his home territory to report on the situation and aftereffects of martial law. He praised the Hawaiian people who helped fight off the Japanese assault and assisted in the rebuilding. Japanese aggression had inspired "a deep anger and unity of purpose," King remarked, "which might otherwise have been more slowly acquired."[24]

On October 8, 1942, King abandoned his candidacy for a fifth term, despite receiving more votes in the primary than any Hawaiian candidate of either party combined, and instead re-entered the Navy Reserve as a lieutenant commander. "I cannot remain in civil life when the training I received as a naval officer may better serve our country's present needs in active service," King declared in a radio address to the islands, announcing his decision.[25] "Now, with a war on," he remarked in the closing days of his final term, "I feel that Uncle Sam deserves to realize something on the four year investment he made in me many years ago."[26]

King joined a select group of Representatives who left the House for military service.[27] During World War II, he was stationed in the Pacific, where he helped coordinate the attack on Saipan. He retired from the Navy permanently in 1946, having attained the rank of captain. Returning home, he once again took up the banner of statehood, serving as a charter member of the Hawaii Statehood Commission from 1947 to 1953 and as chairman beginning in 1949.[28] In 1950 delegates to the Hawaiian constitutional convention unanimously voted him president of the proceedings.[29]

In 1953 King was nominated by President Dwight D. Eisenhower to serve as territorial governor of Hawaii. In his nomination hearing before the Committee on the Interior and Insular Affairs, he was enthusiastically recommended by his longtime friend and ally, Delegate Joseph Farrington. "The people of Hawaii believe," said Farrington, "that Samuel Wilder King is better equipped than any other man in the Territory to meet the unique responsibilities of that office at the present time."[30] The committee unanimously approved his nomination, making him the first territorial governor of Hawaiian ancestry. His appointment coincided with the Democratic revolution of 1954 that swept Republicans out of elected office in the territory. During his governorship, King made liberal use of his veto, which prompted Democrats in the legislature to propose a more gradual approach to statehood, beginning with the right for Hawaiians to elect their own governor.[31] King served as governor until his abrupt resignation on July 31, 1957, when he was passed over for a second term.[32] Afterwards, King resumed his real estate business. He then won election as a Republican to the territorial house of representatives in 1958.

Though King long stated he hoped to be the first governor of the state of Hawaii as soon as statehood was achieved, he fell ill and died of a heart attack on March 24, 1959, following major surgery. Only a week prior President Eisenhower had signed the Hawaii Admission Act, and Hawaii entered the Union as the 50th state on August 21, 1959.

MANUSCRIPT COLLECTION

Hawaii State Archives (Honolulu, HI). *Papers*: 1905–1959, 40.3 linear feet. The Samuel Wilder King papers primarily document his service as Hawaii's Delegate in the U.S. House of Representatives, but also include material on his business career and his service in the U.S. Navy. The collection includes correspondence, subject files, speeches, campaign and bill files, and covers such topics as Hawaii statehood, agricultural issues, and public works projects.

NOTES

1   *Congressional Record*, House, 75th Cong., 1st sess. (21 August 1937): 9624–9627.

2   Rod Ohira, "King Refused '2nd-class' Citizenship for Hawaii," 27 September 1999, *Hawaiian Star-Bulletin*: n.p.

3   "Islanders Pay Their Last Tribute to King," 31 March 1959, *Honolulu Star-Bulletin*: 1.

4   Samuel Wilder King, "Lo, the Poor Nordic," 13 April 1924, *New York Times*: 19.

5   Roger Bell, *Last Among Equals*: *Hawaiian Statehood and American Politics* (Honolulu: University of Hawaii Press, 1984): 59.

6   "Samuel Wilder King to Seek Delegate Office," 8 July 1934, *Honolulu Advertiser*: 1.

7   Bell, *Last Among Equals*: 62.

8   "Wilson-Wright Combine, Claim Of McCandless," 21 September 1934, *Honolulu Advertiser*: 7.

9   "Bitterness Enters Campaign Finale," 4 October 1934, *Honolulu Advertiser*: 1.

10 Editorial, "Samuel Wilder King for Delegate," 10 October 1934, *Honolulu Advertiser*.

11 House Committee on Elections No. 2, *Contested Election Case of Lincoln Loy McCandless, Contestant, Versus Samuel Wilder King, Contestee, from the Territory of Hawaii*, 74th Cong., 2nd sess., H. Rept. 2736 (1936): 1–3; *Congressional Record*, House, 74th Cong., 2nd sess. (2 June 1936): 8705.

12 "Samuel W. King To Arrive Soon From Hawaii," 1 December 1934, *Washington Post*: 13.

13 Arguments and Hearings before the House Elections Committee No. 2, *Lincoln Loy McCandless v. Samuel Wilder King*, 74th Cong., 2nd sess. (2–3 March 1936): 129.

14 *Congressional Record*, House, 75th Cong., 1st sess. (21 August 1937): 9624–9627.

15 Hearings before the Joint Committee on Hawaii, *Statehood for Hawaii*, 75th Cong., 2nd. sess. (6–22 October 1937): v, 1–3.

16 Edward C. Krauss, "Statehood for Hawaii?," 20 March 1938, *Los Angeles Times*: A4.

17 *Statehood for Hawaii*: 555.

18 Bell, *Last Among Equals*: 67–74.

19 *Congressional Record*, Appendix, 76th Cong., 2nd sess. (2 April 1940): 1816–1821.

20 "Sugar Bill Voted; House Defies Veto," 7 August 1937, *New York Times*: 1; "Approves New Sugar Act," 4 September 1937, *New York Times*: 27.

21 "Voting Heavy in Hawaii," 4 October 1936, *New York Times*: 44; *Congressional Directory*, 75th Cong., 1st sess. (Washington, DC: Government Printing Office, 1937): 129.

22 Radford Mobley, "Hawaii Looks Toward Statehood," 2 November 1940, *Christian Science Monitor*: WM7; "Hawaii Votes For Statehood in Plebiscite," 7 November 1940, *Atlanta Constitution*: n.p.; Robert C. Schmitt, *Historical Statistics of Hawaii* (Honolulu: University Press of Hawaii, 1977): 603.

23 Robert C. Albright, "Joint Session Will Get War Message Today," 8 December 1941, *Washington Post*: 1.

24 "Sees Pearl Harbor Gains: Hawaiian Delegate Says Anger of U.S. Spurs War," 3 January 1942, *New York Times*: 3.

25 *Congressional Record*, Appendix, 77th Cong., 2nd sess. (29 October 1942): A3845; "King, Hawaii Delegate, Won't Seek Reelection," 9 October 1942, *Washington Post*: B17.

26 Hope Ridings Miller, "Finishing Fourth Term in Congress, Delegate King Looks Forward to New Assignment—In the Navy," 20 November 1942, *Washington Post*: B12.

27 "Samuel Wilder King," *Biographical Directory of the United States Congress, 1774–Present*, http://bioguide.congress.gov/scripts/biodisplay.pl?index=K000214.

28 Ohira, "King Refused '2nd-class' Citizenship for Hawaii."

29 "King Led in Political, Military, Civic Fields," 25 March 1959, *Honolulu Star-Bulletin*: 1A.

30 Hearing before the Senate Committee on Interior and Insular Affairs, *Nomination of Samuel Wilder King*, 83rd Cong., 1st sess. (19 February 1953): 2.

31 "Hawaii Studying New Plea to U.S.; Territory May Ask for Right to Elect Own Governor—GOP Against Plan," 13 May 1956, *New York Times*: 46; Bell, *Last Among Equals*: 230.

32 "Hawaii Governor, Denied 2nd Term, Resigns Suddenly," 26 July 1957, *Los Angeles Times*: 6.

Quintin Paredes
1884–1973

RESIDENT COMMISSIONER 1935–1938
NACIONALISTA FROM THE PHILIPPINES

As the first Resident Commissioner to represent the Philippines after it became a commonwealth of the United States, Quintin Paredes worked to revise the economic relationship between his native archipelago and the mainland. Paredes championed Philippine independence, constantly reminding policymakers of his home's history as a valuable and vital trading partner. In testimony before congressional committees and in speeches on the floor of the U.S. House of Representatives, Paredes countered common misconceptions about Filipinos and worked to place the islands on stable economic footing as they moved toward independence.

One of 10 children, Quintin Paredes was born in the northwestern town of Bangued, in the Philippines' Abra Province, on September 9, 1884, to Juan Felix and Regina Babila Paredes. Around the time of Quintin's birth, Juan Felix opened a primary school in Bangued and earned a reputation as a strict and uncompromising educator. Quintin attended his father's school until he was about 11 years old, at which point he began studying at a satellite campus of the University of Santo Tomas and later at the Colegio de la Purissima Concepción in the coastal city of Vigan.[1]

In the late 1890s, the Spanish-American War interrupted Paredes's education, and he returned home from school as the American military advanced up the islands. At one point, his family housed two U.S. troops who had been captured as prisoners of war, and because of the close quarters in the Paredes family home, the GIs taught Quintin how to speak English. When U.S. forces finally captured Bangued, the military made Quintin and his brother, Marin, interpreters even though neither brother was proficient. "The truth is," Quintin later remembered, "I had to learn English from the barrel of a gun!"[2]

After the war, Paredes served as deputy treasurer of Abra, collecting taxes from all corners of the province.[3] He eventually moved to Manila and studied law under the direction of another of his brothers, Isidro. He worked during the day, studied at night, and after passing the bar exam, Paredes briefly took a job with the Filipino government in Manila before moving to the private sector.[4] Paredes married Victoria Peralta, and the couple had 10 children.[5]

In 1908 Paredes joined the solicitor general's office in Manila as a prosecuting attorney and rapidly rose to the solicitor general post in 1917. The very next year, Paredes accepted the job as attorney general, becoming the Philippines' top lawyer. Within two years, he became secretary of justice in the cabinet of Governor General Francis Burton Harrison, a former Member of the U.S. House of Representatives from New York. President Woodrow Wilson nominated Paredes to serve as an associate justice on the Philippine supreme court, but Wilson's administration ended before the confirmation went through. Paredes also served as an officer in the Philippine national guard during the mobilization for World War I.[6]

After 13 years as an attorney for the government, Paredes resigned as secretary of justice ahead of the administration change in Manila and formed his own law firm in 1921. As Paredes's daughter would later write, "The courtroom drama fascinated him more than anything else."[7]

In 1925, after four years of private practice, Paredes fell into political office by something of an accident. While stumping for his nephew's assembly campaign in Abra, local leaders asked Paredes to run for the seat instead. His nephew agreed to the plan, dropped out, and threw his support behind Paredes. Parades won and eventually served four terms in the territorial legislature. His early career in the Philippine house was ambitious. He chaired the rules committee and led a revolt against house leadership, challenging Manuel Roxas, the sitting speaker, in an effort

Image courtesy of the Franklin D. Roosevelt Presidential Library/
National Archives and Records Administration

to empower the rank and file. "If the Chair does not have the full support of the substantial number of the majority," Paredes reportedly said, "trouble is bound to brew and the program of legislation cannot be carried out effectively."[8] The coup attempt failed, but Paredes won the position of speaker pro tempore after Roxas went on a trade mission to the United States and immediately used his new power to quicken the legislative pace.[9]

Elected speaker pro tempore again in 1931, Paredes led the Philippine house's opposition to the Hare–Hawes–Cutting Act, in which the U.S. Congress promised the Philippines its independence after a phase-in period of 10 years. But the new act needed the approval of the Philippine legislature to go into effect.[10] And as Paredes understood the law, the Hare–Hawes–Cutting Act would have crippled the islands' economy and imposed severe immigration quotas for Filipinos going to America.[11] In many respects, the controversial independence bill became a litmus test in the Philippine house. Eventually, opponents of the measure generated enough support to oust Roxas, the speaker, who backed the bill, and install Paredes in his place.[12] During this period, Paredes and senate president Manuel L. Quezon became close allies. Quezon had smoothed Paredes's move up to the speakership, and, by 1934, the *Philippines Herald* described Paredes as Quezon's "mightiest political general."[13] But Paredes's deft handling of the house, combined with his growing national profile, also set him on a collision course with Quezon over control of the islands' future.[14]

Despite his outsized role in the debate surrounding independence, Paredes, according to one description, was "quiet, observant, and thoughtful, the very figure of efficient activity and erudition."[15] He was cool under pressure, calculating, patient, and obsessed with legislative details, further straining his relationship with Quezon.[16] For Paredes, it was not enough to simply achieve independence for the islands; the legislation granting independence needed to give the archipelago every chance to thrive as an autonomous nation. "If you want to do anything," he once said, "always do it well. Then perhaps luck will come."[17]

In 1934 Congress revisited Philippine independence and passed the Tydings–McDuffie Act, which made the Philippines a commonwealth of the United States and addressed some of the criticisms that had doomed the Hare–Hawes–Cutting Act. Per the new agreement, after 10 years and the adoption of a new constitution, the Philippines would officially become an independent country. The change in insular status injected a new dynamic in the islands' politics. With Tydings–McDuffie in place, the main issue dividing the ruling Partido Nacionalista—the terms for an independent Philippines—no longer dominated the debate. In the assembly, Quezon decided the reunited majority party now needed a speaker who could appeal to everyone, not just to those who opposed the earlier independence bill. Quezon was the clear head of the ruling party, but Paredes had been a strong, independent speaker, and his popularity had skyrocketed. Quezon considered Paredes dangerous on two fronts: Paredes, with his loyal following, directly threatened Quezon's personal authority; and, constitutionally, Paredes's authority as speaker might limit the president's power, motivating Quezon to decentralize power in the legislature by empowering the committees.[18]

Quezon quickly convinced a number of assembly members to support his committee overhaul. When the majority party named Paredes to the weakened speaker's office, he rejected the nomination. "Paredes wanted the position of speaker to be strong, so that the system of checks and balances as practiced in the U.S. government could function in the Philippines," wrote an historian of the controversy. For his part, Paredes preferred to serve in the rank and file rather than stand as "a puppet Speaker."[19]

Even with Paredes out of leadership, Quezon still considered him a political threat. Unable to fully dilute the former speaker's influence, Quezon did the next closest thing: he offered Paredes a job more than 8,000 miles away as the Philippines' Resident Commissioner to the U.S. Congress. Paredes knew that if he took the appointment in Washington, he would likely lose power back home. At first, he rejected the post, but after Quezon questioned his commitment to public service, Paredes accepted on December 21, 1935.[20] "I consider it my duty to counteract all reactionary measures in Congress prejudicial to the Philippines," he said after being sworn in by Philippine officials.[21]

Paredes sailed for the United States on January 11, 1936, devoting his short time at home to studying the economic relationship between the commonwealth and the United States. He pledged to revise sections of the Tydings–McDuffie Act that he believed would both hinder trade and impede the Philippines' economic growth.[22] Tariffs on Philippine goods exported to the United States were set to rise gradually in 1940 so that, by the time the commonwealth became independent, Philippine businesses would have to pay the taxes in full. Many observers expected Congress to renegotiate the terms of the deal, but by the time Paredes arrived in Washington, nothing had been finalized.[23]

Shortly after noon on Friday, February 14, 1936, Paredes walked to the well of the House and took the oath of office as a Member of the 74th Congress (1935–1937). The day before, he had met briefly at the White House with President Franklin D. Roosevelt, Secretary of War George Dern, and Creed Cox of the Bureau of Insular Affairs. Paredes also revealed that Quezon had asked him to open an embassy in DC.[24]

As Resident Commissioner, Paredes focused on two main objectives. First, he remained committed to revising the tariff rates in Tydings–McDuffie. For an island nation that traded almost exclusively with the United States, "the [law's] provisions will wreck our economic structure," he said in an interview with the *Christian Science Monitor* in May 1936, and he feared the restrictions in Tydings–McDuffie would "breed discontent and unrest, and perhaps disorder in the islands."[25] Parades hoped certain changes would buy the Philippines' economy enough time to hold its own on a global playing field. Secondly, he sought to convince Congress to protect a nearly $24 million line of credit at the Treasury Department after a reserve fund the Philippines stored with the United States missed out on an easy chance to gain in value with the gold standard.[26]

In the House, Paredes also addressed a handful of other, more immediate issues that affected Filipinos living in the United States. After the Merchant Marine Act of 1936 forced shipowners in the New York area to fire nearly 3,000 Filipinos because they had been classified as "aliens," Paredes threw his support behind a measure introduced by Senator Allen Ellender of Louisiana to allow the sailors who had legally lived in the United States before the passage of Tydings–McDuffie to get their jobs back.[27] Similarly, Paredes lobbied the Senate Appropriations Committee to remove discriminatory language against Filipino government workers in a funding bill for the Treasury Department and U.S. Post Office.[28]

A month before Paredes arrived in Washington, Democratic Senator Alva Adams of Colorado introduced a bill to overturn an earlier law that authorized the Treasury Department to set aside nearly $24 million in credit for the Philippines. The government had opened the line of credit after the commonwealth's reserve fund housed in the United States failed to earn value following an increase in the price of gold. The controversy dated back to 1932, when the Philippine government followed the advice of American officials and stored roughly $56 million in U.S. banks. Almost from the start Philippine leaders had asked to convert that cash deposit into gold, but Treasury officials never followed through. After the price of gold increased, the Philippines lost out on substantial profit, and the $24 million credit was meant to cover the difference of the Philippines' investment.[29]

Unfortunately for the Philippines, Congress had only authorized the Treasury credit and had never appropriated any money for it. Moreover, a number of Members supported Senator Adams's effort to repeal the credit altogether.[30] Seeing as how Paredes had been in Washington for only a few days when he first went before the Senate Banking and Currency Committee to discuss the currency issue, he admitted that he was "not very familiar with the technical questions involved."[31] The committee agreed to reschedule, giving Paredes time to prepare over the next week.

When Paredes testified before the Senate committee again on March 5, 1936, he implored the panel to fund the back payment, arguing that U.S. officials had never

acted on the Philippines' request to convert its deposit into gold.[32] Despite his appeal, the Senate committee went ahead with the repeal measure, claiming that Congress misunderstood the situation when it first authorized the credit line.[33] The Senate passed Adams's repeal bill on May 18, 1936, which Paredes called both "surprising" and "most unfair." When the House received the bill, however, the Committee on Insular Affairs took no action on it during the legislative session.[34]

Although Congress had taken the lead on the Treasury issue, it more or less deferred to the President on the tariff, and the House spent little time revisiting the scheduled rate hikes in Tydings–McDuffie during Paredes's time on the Hill. Nevertheless, Paredes made the Philippines' trade relationship the first thing he spoke about on the floor. He commended Congress for paving the way for the Philippines' full political independence but cautioned the House against ending America's open economic ties to the Pacific. Paredes sympathized with Congress's efforts to combat the Great Depression, but he didn't want to see a similar financial catastrophe hit the islands. He pointed out that, in the short while since Tydings–McDuffie went into effect, Congress had already gone after the Philippines by lowering the sugar quota, capping cordage exports, and levying new taxes on coconut oil. While he did not expect special treatment for the Philippines, Paredes wanted Congress to follow the "spirit" of the independence agreement, urging the House to lift some of the new fees.[35]

A month later, in May 1936, Paredes again spoke on the House Floor about the U.S.–Philippine trade partnership, pointing out that Congress, not the Philippines, dictated the terms of the relationship which had started out "on the basis of free trade." Imposing new taxes to protect American farmers, he argued, would undercut that foundation. "Fair treatment for our Philippine sugar industry will not injure a single beet-sugar or cane-sugar producer in the United States…. All we ask is that, while under the American flag, we be treated fairly and equitably with other Territories and possessions of the United States," he said defiantly.[36]

In March 1937, during testimony on sugar quotas

before a House Agriculture subcommittee, Paredes drove home his point. He knew that domestic sugar producers would call for higher tariffs to protect their product, "but it is a fact that in the case of the Philippines there exists an implied contract derived from the independence law not to impose taxes…. By subjecting our sugar to excise taxes provided in the bill this preference is wiped out and the spirit of the independence law violated." The main problem, Paredes noted, was that the Philippines had little influence in Washington. He reminded the subcommittee that he couldn't vote on tariff bills, "which makes the imposition of excise taxes on Philippine sugar sound like taxation without representation."[37]

During Paredes's House career, isolationist Members who wanted the United States to pull out of the Pacific, regardless of the impact on the commonwealth's economy, appeared to have a controlling interest in Congress. The *Washington Post* noted in a separate article that such thinking also permeated public opinion. As early as the summer of 1936, Paredes reported renewed "prejudices" against the Philippines. Both Democrats and Republicans, the *Post* said, accused the commonwealth of "[forcing] America to grant independence out of ingratitude." The paper also suspected that the public relations campaign by "American labor, sugar, dairy, cordage and other industries" to cast the Philippines as a direct competitor likely helped sour the mood on the Hill.[38]

The Roosevelt administration took a less drastic approach, however, and in 1937, after President Quezon suggested moving Philippine independence up to as early as 1938, he and FDR agreed to create the Joint Preparatory Committee on Philippine Affairs in order to study trade issues affecting the two countries, specifically tariff rates.[39] "If and when independence does finally come," Paredes wrote to the editor of the *Baltimore Sun* in the spring of 1937, just two months after being assigned to the joint committee, "I hope that the American people will find no necessity for ending the mutually beneficial United States-Philippines trade relations." Paredes pointed out that exports from his commonwealth did not so much compete with America's domestic industries as they complemented the United States' existing markets for "sugar, coconut oil, tobacco, [and] cordage." Moreover, he wrote, higher tariffs would discourage the Philippines, already one of the United States' largest customers, from importing American goods.[40]

Paredes was the only Member of the House to sit on the joint committee, which held hearings in Washington, San Francisco, and Manila and included a three-month investigation in the Philippines. After a year of work, the members of the committee agreed to keep the date of Philippine independence set at 1946, but they decided to slow down the rise in tariffs affecting Philippine exports. With an agreement in principle, the committee recommended that the full rates go into effect by 1960, giving the commonwealth's economy an extra 15 years to adjust to independence.[41]

Paredes resigned from the House before Congress took a close look at the Joint Preparatory Committee's recommendations.[42] His initial reluctance to accept the position as Resident Commissioner, combined with some later remarks he made in the summer of 1937, suggest that he had set his sights on returning to the Philippines as quickly as he could. On August 18, 1937, just days before he left for Manila to participate in the Joint Preparatory Committee hearings, Paredes used the "Extensions of Remarks" section of the *Congressional Record* to deliver a speech titled "United States-Philippine Affairs." What started out as a summary of the Joint Preparatory Committee's agenda soon had the feel of a farewell address. After applauding the House for "making the newcomer feel comfortable," he continued, "I have nothing but thanks for all the many courtesies extended to me here. I appreciate the privilege of having served with you in this I consider the greatest legislative body in the world." He even touted his likely successor, Joaquin M. Elizalde.[43]

In case there was any doubt about Paredes's desire to return home, mainland newspapers began reporting in April 1938, months before Paredes formally announced his resignation, that Elizalde, "who, authoritative sources said would succeed Quintin Paredes as resident Philippine commissioner in the United States," had already sailed for

Washington. Three months later, after Congress adjourned for the year, Paredes set off for home in order to leave enough time to campaign for his old seat in the Philippine legislature. He officially resigned from the House on September 29, 1938.[44]

Despite their earlier rivalry, Quezon complimented Paredes. "There is no gainsaying the fact that you are entitled to a great amount of the credit for assisting in the passage of many pieces of legislation favorable to the Philippines and vigorously fighting unjust and adverse bills which embodied threats of harm to us economically as well as politically," Quezon told him.[45]

Once back in the Philippines, Paredes reclaimed his seat as a representative of the Abra Province, serving as floor leader in the assembly. He later won election to the Philippine senate, serving from 1941 to 1945. With the outbreak of World War II, Paredes did not flee the islands, but served in the Japanese occupation government as a commissioner of public works and as secretary of justice, "motivated by a patriotic desire to protect the Filipinos when he took the Cabinet position," his defense lawyers would later argue.[46]

In the spring of 1945, U.S. military forces arrested Paredes, and the commonwealth government later charged him with 21 counts of treason as an active collaborator.[47] Despite these accusations, voters elected Paredes, who was out on bail, to the Philippine house a month later in 1946.[48] After courts acquitted him in 1948, Paredes returned to serve in the Philippine legislature throughout the 1950s.[49] In 1952 the Philippine senate elected him as its president.[50] He also resumed his law practice and was later president of a bank. He died in Manila on January 30, 1973.[51]

"An admiring nation will remember him for his untiring labors on behalf of Philippine independence," said former Resident Commissioner Carlos Peña Romulo. "He may well be the last of this fearless breed, the versatile group of men of wide learning and deep human concerns who passionately devoted their lives to the cause of their people."[52]

FOR FURTHER READING

Paredes-San Diego, Lourdes. *Don Quintin of Abra* (Quezon City, PI: L. Paredes-San Diego, 1985).

NOTES

1 Lourdes Paredes-San Diego, *Don Quintin of Abra* (Quezon City, PI: L. Paredes-San Diego, 1985): 7, 9, 11–12.

2 Paredes-San Diego, *Don Quintin of Abra*: 14–16.

3 Ibid., 17.

4 Ibid., 19–23. Paredes's brother held lessons in his home in Manila and called his informal law school the *"Escuela de Leyes."*

5 *Congressional Directory*, 75th Cong., 1st sess. (Washington, DC: Government Printing Office, 1905): 129–130; Paredes-San Diego, *Don Quintin of Abra*: 8–21; Zoilo M. Galang, ed., *Leaders of the Philippines: Inspiring Biographies of Successful Men and Women of the Philippines* (Manila, PI: National Publishing Company, 1932): 268–270.

6 *Congressional Directory*, 75th Cong., 1st sess.: 129–130; Paredes-San Diego, *Don Quintin of Abra*: 22–36.

7 Paredes-San Diego, *Don Quintin of Abra*: 37.

8 Ibid., 42.

9 Ibid., 45–47.

10 H. W. Brands, *Bound To Empire: The United States and the Philippines* (New York: Oxford University Press, 1992): 149–155.

11 Paredes-San Diego, *Don Quintin of Abra*: 50–51.

12 Robert Aura Smith, "Roxas Fights Back at Manuel Quezon," 27 August 1933, *New York Times*: E2; Estrellita T. Muhi, "The Philippine Legislature, 1916–1935," in *Philippine Legislature: 100 Years*, ed. Cesar P. Pobre (Quezon City, PI: Philippine Historical Association, 2000): 136–137; Paredes-San Diego, *Don Quintin of Abra*: 52–54.

13 Eugenio S. De Garcia, "The Man Quintin Paredes," 5 September 1934, *Philippine Herald Mid-Week Magazine*: 3.

14 Paredes-San Diego, *Don Quintin of Abra*: 69–77.

15 Galang, *Leaders of the Philippines*: 270.

16 De Garcia, "The Man Quintin Paredes": 18, 22.

17 Galang, *Leaders of the Philippines*: 270.

18 Stephen W. Stathis, *Landmark Legislation, 1774–2012*, 2nd. ed. (Los Angeles: CQ Press, 2014): 244; Richard T. Jose, "The National Assembly of the Philippine Commonwealth, the National Assembly of the Second Philippine Republic and the Congress of the Philippine Commonwealth, 1935–1946," in *Philippine Legislature: 100 Years*, ed. Cesar P. Pobre (Quezon City, PI: Philippine Historical Association, 2000): 142–148.

19 Jose, "The National Assembly of the Philippine Commonwealth, the National Assembly of the Second Philippine Republic and the Congress of the Philippine Commonwealth, 1935–1946": 148. See also Paredes-San Diego, *Don Quintin of Abra*: 76–77.

20 Jose, "The National Assembly of the Philippine Commonwealth, the National Assembly of the Second Philippine Republic and the Congress of the Philippine Commonwealth, 1935–1946": 148; Paredes-San Diego, *Don Quintin of Abra*: 77; *Congressional Directory*, 75th Cong., 1st sess.: 130.

21 "Paredes Promises to be Faithful to New Trust," 21 December 1935, *Philippines Herald*: 1.

22 "Free Trade with U.S. Must be Continued, Paredes States," 10 January 1936, *Philippines Herald*: 3.

23 Erwin D. Canham, "New Philippines Delegate Finds Problems Facing Him," 13 February 1936, *Christian Science Monitor*: 1.

24 "President Greets Philippine Official," 14 February 1936, *Chicago Daily Tribune*: 9; "Paredes Calls on President Roosevelt," 14 February 1936, *Philippines Herald*: 1; "Parades Here to Plan Philippines' Legation," 14 February 1936, *Washington Post*: 1; "A Man in the News: Favorable Tariff Rates Sought for Philippines," 6 May 1936, *Christian Science Monitor*: 6.

25 "A Man in the News: Favorable Tariff Rates Sought for Philippines."

26 Canham, "New Philippines Delegate Finds Problems Facing Him"; "Monetary Issue Tangles Affairs of Philippines," 15 February 1936, *Christian Science Monitor*: 1. See also "A Man in the News: Favorable Tariff Rates Sought for Philippines."

27 "Asks Aid for Filipinos," 27 January 1938, *New York Times*: 14.

28 "Filipinos to Lose Jobs With U.S., Paredes Says," 12 February 1938, *Washington Post*: X2.

29 "Monetary Issue Tangles Affairs of Philippines."

30 "From Across the Sea," 20 March 1936, *Chicago Daily Tribune*: 16; Vicente Albano Pacis, "After the Ball," 16 March 1936, *Washington Post*: 9; "Monetary Issue Tangles Affairs of Philippines."

31 Hearing before the Senate Committee on Banking and Currency, *Philippine Currency Reserves*, 74th Cong., 2nd sess. (27 February and 5 March 1936): 16.

32 *Philippine Currency Reserves*: 19–41.

33 Senate Committee on Banking and Currency, *Philippine Currency Reserve on Deposit in the United States*, 74th Cong., 2nd sess., S. Rept. 1702 (1936): 1, 3.

34 "Assails Philippine Bill," 7 August 1937, *New York Times*: 13; *Congressional Record*, Senate, 74th Cong., 2nd sess. (18 May 1936): 7414–7419.

35 *Congressional Record*, House, 74th Cong., 2nd sess. (15 April 1936): 5526–5528. See also "Philippines Seek Modification of Coconut Oil Tax," 15 April 1936, *Christian Science Monitor*: 6.

36   *Congressional Record*, House, 74th Cong., 2nd sess. (28 May 1936): 8215, 8217.

37   Hearings before a Special Subcommittee of the House Committee on Agriculture, *Sugar*, 75th Cong., 1st sess. (19 March 1937): 251.

38   Vicente Albano Pacis, "Forsaken Philippines," 29 July 1936, *Washington Post*: X7.

39   Franklyn Waltman, "U.S.-Philippine Group Named to Study Trade," 19 March 1937, *Washington Post*: 2; "Experts Ponder Economic Liberty for Philippines," 15 April 1937, *Christian Science Monitor*: 1; Erwin D. Canham, "Philippines: Dare U.S. Set Isles Adrift?," 22 November 1937, *Christian Science Monitor*: 1; Pacis, "Forsaken Philippines."

40   Quintin Paredes, "Letters to the Editor: The Philippines, A Source of Needed Products and a Profitable Market," 14 May 1937, *Baltimore Sun*: 14.

41   *Report of the Joint Preparatory Committee on Philippine Affairs* (20 May 1938) part I: 1–4, and part VII: 1–14, https://archive.org/details/JointPreparatoryCommiteeOnPhilippineAffairs (accessed 26 May 2016); "Gradual Duty Rise Asked for Filipinos," 6 April 1938, *New York Times*: 10; "U.S. and Philippines Seek to Extend Transition Period," 7 April 1938, *Christian Science Monitor*: 2; William V. Nessly, "Report Urges Tariff Stay For Filipinos," 29 November 1938, *Washington Post*: X1; "U.S. Keeps Grip on Philippine Trade Till '60," 6 April 1938, *Baltimore Sun*: 1.

42   President Roosevelt sent the report of the Joint Preparatory Committee to Congress in late January 1939, four months after Paredes resigned from the House. See "Proposed Delay in Philippine Independence Up to Congress," 24 January 1939, *Christian Science Monitor*: 4; "Philippine Issue Faces Congress," 25 January 1939, *Atlanta Constitution*: 20; "Philippine Report," 25 January 1939, *Wall Street Journal*: 6.

43   *Congressional Record*, Extension of Remarks, 75th Cong., 1st sess. (18 August 1937): 2152.

44   "Reported Successor to Paredes en Route," 25 April 1938, *Washington Post*: X3; "Philippine Leader Sails for States," 25 April 1938, *Los Angeles Times*: 6; "Paredes to Leave Post Here to Seek Seat in Assembly," 8 September 1938, *Washington Post*: X9.

45   "Elizalde Named P.I. Commissioner," 29 September 1938, *Philippines Herald*: 1.

46   "Filipinos Will Try Paredes for Treason," 16 June 1947, *Atlanta Constitution*: 3.

47   "M'Arthur Frees 7,000 Civilians in Luzon Drive," 18 April 1945, *Chicago Daily Tribune*: 5; "Six Members of Filipino Puppet Cabinet Seized," 23 April 1945, *Chicago Daily Tribune*: 5; "Foreign News Briefs: Filipinos Indicted," 15 March 1946, *Los Angeles Times*: 5.

48   "Poll Nearly Conceded," 26 April 1946, *Christian Science Monitor*: 7.

49   Paredes-San Diego, *Don Quintin of Abra*: 95–101.

50   "Philippine Senators End 35-Day Deadlock," 6 March 1952, *New York Times*: 4.

51   Paredes-San Diego, *Don Quintin of Abra*: 83–93, 95–101.

52   "Paredes, 'Old Guard,' Dies," 31 January 1973, *Bulletin Today* (Manila, PI): 1.

Joaquin M. Elizalde
1896–1965

RESIDENT COMMISSIONER 1938–1944
NO PARTY AFFILIATION, FROM THE PHILIPPINES

Joaquin Miguel (Mike) Elizalde, a wealthy businessman, won appointment as Resident Commissioner from the Philippines in 1938 as war clouds converged in the Pacific.[1] In the U.S. House of Representatives, he threaded the needle between preparing his home islands for independence while assuring the United States of Philippine allegiance in the face of imminent conflict with Japan. He displayed remarkable skill as a diplomat, protecting business interests and Filipino laborers in the United States and serving as an articulate, widely admired spokesman for the commonwealth. He was, said one colleague during the war, "the leading spirit of bracing up the morale of his conquered and ill-treated people."[2] Elizalde transformed the Resident Commissioner's office into the functional equivalent of the Philippine Embassy, an office he later held as the islands' first ambassador to the United States in 1946. Representative Estes Kefauver of Tennessee, who served with Elizalde in the House, attributed Elizalde's success to his personable, even humble, approach that complemented his steadfast devotion to the islands: "He is as plain as an old shoe and is a real friend of his people."[3]

Joaquin Miguel Elizalde was born on August 2, 1896, in the Philippine capital of Manila to José Joaquin Elizalde and Maria del Carmen Diaz Moreu Elizalde. The family was of Castilian Spanish descent; Joaquin Elizalde was a Spanish citizen until the 1930s. Sources vary, but the most reliable suggest that he became a Philippine citizen in 1933.[4] He was schooled in Spain, in Switzerland at Dr. Schmidt's Institute in St. Gallen, and in London, England, at St. Joseph's College and the London School of Economics. According to at least one source, Elizalde also served in the Spanish army for a year.[5]

As the scion of one of the islands' most respected families, Elizalde moved easily among the Filipino elite and, by his early 30s, had positioned himself as one of the Philippines' captains of industry.[6] From 1918 to 1934, he was a managing partner of Ynchausti y Cia, a trading company that his family founded in the mid-19th century. When Elizalde took over as president in 1934, it became Elizalde & Company, Inc. At various points in his career, he also was a leading figure in a web of interconnected companies that ranged from insurance sales to steamships and in other companies producing or trading in rope, gold, iron, cattle, lumber, paint, sugar, and distilled spirits.[7] Elizalde was an avid golfer, director of the Manila Polo Club, and a member of a championship polo team comprising his brothers in the 1930s. He married Elena von Kauffmann in Manila on May 17, 1924. That marriage produced two daughters, Cecilia and Elenita. The couple divorced in 1957. Elizalde remarried to Susan Magalona Ledesma, and the couple had two children, Maria Theresa and Juan Miguel.[8]

Like many Philippine Resident Commissioners before him, Elizalde was propelled by business success into public service. In 1934, as the islands began to ready for independence, he was appointed president of the National Development Company of the Philippines. Three years later, President Manuel L. Quezon tapped him as an economic adviser. He also had a seat on the National Economic Council, which he held until 1941 and then again from 1952 to 1953.

When Quintin Paredes resigned as Philippine Resident Commissioner, President Quezon appointed Elizalde his successor on September 29, 1938, several months after the 75th Congress (1937–1939) had adjourned *sine die*.[9] Elizalde, whose "right hand quivered like a leaf when he was taking the oath," was sworn in as Resident Commissioner by a clerk in the War Department in the presence of Secretary of War Harry Woodring on October

1, 1938.[10] In a prepared statement, Elizalde pledged to devote his office to protecting the rights of Filipinos living in America and noted, "Friendship with the United States stands as the cornerstone for the perpetuation of American ideals and democratic institutions established in the Islands."[11] He retained the office for the next six years.

Due to the outbreak of World War II, controversy accompanied Elizalde's elevation to the post. Filipino laborers working in the United States, as well as other expatriates, doubted that Elizalde would effectively represent the Philippine people and felt that his loyalty would tilt toward big business. They also groused over his Spanish ancestry. Several weeks after his swearing-in, a New York–based businessman, Porfirio U. Sevilla, publisher of the *Philippine-American Advocate* magazine, filed a lawsuit in DC district court, claiming that Elizalde lacked the citizenship qualifications to serve as Resident Commissioner and had not been appointed legally. The suit was dismissed in 1940 when the court refused to hear it.[12]

Over the course of his first year in office, however, Elizalde won over many of his critics. Even as the United States restricted its trade with Japan, he worked to protect the islands' economy in the run-up to independence and became a vocal advocate for Filipinos living and working in America, particularly on the West Coast and in Hawaii.

Elizalde's policy positions and legislative activities tended to reflect his business background. As a firm supporter of independence, he believed the colonial system had depressed the Philippine economy. He believed that only by giving the island territory the freedom to set the terms of its own international commerce would the situation improve.

Elizalde wanted to see the United States and the Philippines gradually unwind in such a way that necessary trade between the islands and the mainland would not be disrupted. In November 1938, in one of his first acts as Resident Commissioner, one that would typify his tenure, he spoke at the National Foreign Trade Council convention in New York City, urging the United States to implement a reciprocal free trade agreement and avoid protectionist legislation.[13]

He carried that message onto the House Floor a year later, calling for an amendment to the Philippine Independence Act to keep tariffs from rising against the islands' major exports, including coconut oil, cigars, pearl buttons, and embroidery. "Mr. Speaker," Elizalde said in one of his rare floor speeches, "I must repeat that what we ask here is, to us, emergency legislation, which will benefit not only the Filipinos but the Americans in the Philippines who, over the past 40 years, have devoted their energies, in partnership with us, to build up a flourishing Philippine–American trade."[14] The bill, H.R. 268, which kept in place many of the favorable trade policies between the United States and the Philippines through independence, scheduled for 1946, passed that day under suspension of the rules.[15] Elizalde also later successfully opposed changes that would have cut the quota on Philippine sugar exports in 1940.[16]

As often as he pushed for big trade interests in the Philippines, he also looked out for the interests of Filipinos working in the United States and its territories. It became a common refrain during Elizalde's career. In 1939, for instance, the Resident Commissioner's office intervened on behalf of 6,000 Filipino asparagus pickers in California who went on strike to protest wage cuts. Elizalde managed to restore their salaries and won plaudits for his efforts.[17]

That same year, Elizalde backed a bill (H.R. 3657) sponsored by Representative Caroline O'Day of New York to extend U.S. citizenship to any Filipino serving on a merchant or fishing ship who had legally been admitted to the United States for permanent residence before 1934. Appearing before a somewhat hostile House Committee on Immigration and Naturalization, Elizalde argued that, based on their years of service and the fact that Filipinos were denied the right to serve on flagged U.S. ships by the Merchant Marine Act of 1936, the thousand or so sailors affected by the bill ought to be granted citizenship in order to get their jobs back or apply for new ones.[18] Despite his forceful protests, the bill appears to have died in committee.

A year later, Elizalde spoke out in favor of New York Representative Vito Marcantonio's bill (H.R. 7239) to extend naturalization to Filipinos who were legal residents of the United States prior to 1934—a much broader category that encompassed agricultural laborers on the West Coast and in Hawaii as well as individuals who worked in shipping—roughly 75,000 individuals in total. While Elizalde's official position was that the Philippine government was doing its utmost to convince these individuals to return to the islands, the reality was that they had established lives in the United States and had children who were legal citizens. "They are practically men without a country," Elizalde told the Committee on Immigration and Naturalization. "They cannot be blamed for their plight; they are innocent victims of circumstances."[19]

Elizalde pointed out that, since the Independence Act, Congress increasingly had treated Filipinos residing in the United States as aliens. He argued that both governments ought to find a solution for the "Filipinos who can no longer return to their country, who have dedicated the best years of their life to the United States only to see themselves considered in the same category as aliens.... Invariably they have assimilated completely the philosophy of the American life."[20] The committee, especially its West Coast members, met this with thinly concealed contempt, and the bill died in committee. A nearly identical bill authored by Marcantonio in 1942, to which Elizalde gave his full-throated support, suffered a similar fate.[21]

In late 1939, when he returned to the Philippines for the first time since he took office, Elizalde was greeted at the airport by an official welcoming party and received an "ovation" like those reserved for Quezon.[22] The *Philippine Free Press* named him its "Man of the Year" for 1940: "Mike Elizalde began a new era of U.S.-Philippine goodwill in Washington. He has cultivated and impressively won the friendship and confidence not only of Federal officials but also Washington correspondents (who broadcast the news from the world's No. 1 news center), the American people (upon whose attitude will depend the extent of help the U.S. will give to his country's aspirations for an independent existence), and U.S. Filipinos (whose interests he has championed more effectively than any of his predecessors because he sees in them not the

Philippines' lost generation but potential assets of the future independent republic)."[23]

Perhaps just as important, the newspaper explained, was that Elizalde's "shrieking success" had transformed the Resident Commissioner "into possibly the most glamorous Philippine office next to the Commonwealth presidency."[24] It was all the more remarkable, since he had very little legislative power in Washington. As per House Rules, Elizalde never served on a committee. He spoke sparingly on the House Floor, but, like his predecessors, he spent far more time testifying before House and Senate committees. In large measure, he combined the roles of publicist and diplomat. "In every possible way, Elizalde drives home the problems of the Philippines," noted one observer. "He takes them to officials in Government departments by direct dealing. He gives an occasional party to which those who manage to get things done in Washington come, not just the possessors of big names on the social surface. He makes an occasional radio speech and his staff gets out a magazine to acquaint Americans in general with island problems."[25]

Elizalde, who insisted on being called "Mike," was often found socializing in neighborhoods dotted with embassies and peopled by diplomats. He had extensive contact with the press and appeared regularly in profiles and in the society page. "He is of medium height, has friendly brown eyes that peer out through his glasses, smiles easily, likes shirts with blue stripes, runs to American slang which sometimes bobs up in the middle of his Spanish," said one description.[26] A piece from early 1942 in the *Boston Globe* noted, "He is a snappy dresser, with a liking for somewhat striking patterns in haberdashery, likes to throw big parties and has been quick on moving into a first-name acquaintance even among Washington's most imposing citizens."[27] Elizalde "seems to like everybody," the *Globe* went on, and everyone seemed to like him: "his big old mansion [on] Massachusetts [Avenue] is the haven of friendly and gregarious citizens."[28]

It was not all just socializing for Elizalde, however, as the war in the Pacific magnified the diplomatic aspects of his job. After the Japanese invaded the Philippines in late 1941, President Quezon and many other officials

fled the islands. They set up a satellite government in the States, and on February 5, 1942, Elizalde was sworn into the Commonwealth government cabinet-in-exile in Washington.[29] For a time, Elizalde was his country's principal spokesman. When Japanese broadcasts claimed that the Philippine government had fled Manila ahead of a Japanese offensive, Elizalde bristled, "The Philippine people are prepared to resist to the last."[30]

On December 17, 1941, Elizalde delivered a shortwave radio broadcast, which he would do periodically during the war, to urge his countrymen to defend the islands, stressing full U.S. support in the effort: "Every heart in the United States beats for our welfare.... Everything possible is being done here to give us strength and support. Our faith in America is justified. Have courage and perseverance." He exhorted Filipinos to fight back against Japanese aggression with "cold revenge," and he supported a revision to the Selective Service Act in late December 1941 that allowed Filipinos residing in the United States to join the Army.[31]

For Elizalde, the occupation was personal, as several immediate family members, his estate home, and his businesses were all held by the Japanese. There was a certain amount of chivalric symbolism to Elizalde's actions in the early months of the war. In 1942 he took a leave of absence from the House to take command of the *Limbis*, a 70-foot yacht that President Quezon offered to President Franklin D. Roosevelt on behalf of the islands for the patrol service of the U.S. Coast Guard. Elizalde and his all-Philippine crew plied the waves on local patrol.[32]

The crisis of war and the arrival of Quezon's government-in-exile in early 1942 funneled much of Elizalde's attention to constructing a diplomatic apparatus in the United States. In anticipation of planned independence in 1946, Elizalde had overseen the purchase of a mansion on Sheridan Circle along Massachusetts Avenue's Embassy Row in November 1941.[33] It became the hub of the Philippine mission in the United States, centralizing previously scattered offices. Elizalde ran it like an embassy, moving his offices into the renovated building in 1943. He had a personal staff of 28 people, many of whom worked in the Elizalde businesses back home. It

was an embassy-in-waiting, one correspondent observed: "When independence comes, the resident commissioner's office can be transformed into a smoothly-functioning embassy or legation without a hitch."[34]

During the early part of the war in the Pacific, prior to U.S. intervention, Elizalde walked a tightrope trying to protect key industries while also supporting America's economic and military policy toward an increasingly hostile Japan. On May 10, 1941, he pledged "unqualified approval" of the U.S. decision to include the Philippines in a system that restricted exports that might hurt the defense of the United States or the islands.[35] Elizalde echoed that statement in a hearing before the House Military Affairs Committee the following day, supporting H.J. Res. 183, which extended controls to the Philippines and other U.S. dependencies. "Control of exports of the Philippines entails future far reaching and profound economic problems to us," Elizalde conceded. "But regardless of the sacrifices we may be called upon to make ... the Philippines will accept its share of the burden.... We feel that the spiritual values involved in the present conflict transcend all material considerations."[36]

Even if Elizalde's efforts did not always succeed or even if they required major concessions, they were not "wasted," one observer noted. Instead, "they served to spotlight the status of the Filipinos, loyal nationals of the U.S.," and demonstrated Elizalde's "watchfulness over Filipinos' political rights."[37] In the years before the war erupted in the Pacific, Elizalde squelched rumblings in Congress that a thoroughgoing investigation be launched into the loyalty of the Philippines. "As far as our cultural inclinations are concerned, our entire national life is founded and maintained on American principles and democratic ideals which are so fundamentally instilled that they will be maintained," Elizalde assured his colleagues. "Any influences alien to democracy and free government do not thrive and are not encouraged in the Philippines."[38]

Even in wartime, with manpower sapped by military conscription, Elizalde found himself having to advocate on behalf of Filipino nationals residing in Hawaii who faced employment discrimination. One week after the United

States declared war on Japan, he supported a wartime measure to allow Filipinos to work on public works projects in Hawaii. While the legislation contemplated directly recruiting workers from the Philippines, it simultaneously included sunset provisions on the contracts for the many Filipinos who already lived and worked in Hawaii. The legislation, Elizalde told the House Committee on Territories, would clearly take advantage of Filipinos who would be working in dangerous conditions without the employment protections given to their American counterparts.[39]

Elizalde also cast an eye toward shaping the post-war peace in Asia and the Pacific, free from Japanese occupation and European colonial systems. In a radio address in March 1942, Elizalde urged U.S. officials to consider making a "Pacific charter" that mirrored the principles set forth in the Atlantic Charter to win the hearts and minds of Asian peoples under the yoke of Japanese oppression. "In Asia there is a great mass of colonial subjects who today merely stand on the sidelines," Elizalde noted. "The world must offer Asia something better than the cold comfort of superior protection and patronage."[40]

Elizalde gave very few floor speeches during the six years he served in the House. In fact, the *Congressional Record* records him speaking on the floor only on three occasions. One of those moments occurred on November 10, 1943, when he voiced his support of Senate Joint Resolution 95 to extend President Quezon's term in office beyond November 15, 1943. The proposal stipulated that Quezon remain the Philippine president until the President of the United States "shall proclaim that constitutional processes and normal functions of government shall have been restored in the Philippine Islands." The alternative was a potentially disruptive wartime transition to Vice President Sergio Osmeña, who would automatically succeed Quezon. Elizalde had worked personally with Secretary of War Stimson and others in the administration to convince FDR to invite Quezon to set up a government-in-exile in Washington, DC. He argued that, because Quezon was elected prior to the onset of the war, the term should be extended "strictly on the basis of war necessity" and

government continuity. The measure passed the House by a vote of 181 to 107, with 143 members not voting.[41]

President Quezon's death in the summer of 1944 precipitated a shakeup in the government-in-exile cabinet. When Osmeña ascended to the presidency, Elizalde resigned abruptly as Resident Commissioner on August 8, 1944, a little more than a week after Quezon's passing. He also was dropped from the war cabinet at that time. Reportedly, tensions had simmered between Elizalde and Osmeña for years when the Resident Commissioner first staffed his office with Spanish elites like himself rather than indigenous Filipinos.[42]

Elizalde's departure from the House evoked an outpouring of praise for him that was highly unusual for a colleague who could not trade votes and who had little direct influence. But his colleagues clearly appreciated his powers of persuasion. "Throughout the membership of the House, he had an entrée which assured the cooperation of his colleagues in any problem in which he was interested," Emmet O'Neal of Kentucky observed. "Many of us have envied him as to his ability to accomplish that which he undertook to do. His fine intelligence, persistence, and sound sense are great assets, but his personality and his understanding of human nature are even rarer."[43]

Elizalde's departure from DC was brief. In July 1946, he returned as the independent Philippines' first ambassador to the United States. On the day he presented his credentials to President Harry Truman, Elizalde asked that the United States swiftly enact legislation to grant loans to help the Philippines rebuild after the war left its infrastructure and its economy in ruins. "The future is dark but by no means hopeless," he said. "The Philippines is capable of developing a self-sustaining economy."[44]

During his tenure, which lasted until 1952, the embassy on Sheridan Circle was celebrated as "one of the liveliest gathering places in the city."[45]

Elizalde's public service also included a term on the board of governors of the International Monetary Fund and the World Bank from 1946 to 1950. He was appointed the Philippine secretary of foreign affairs from 1952 to 1953. Later he represented the Philippines at the United Nations in a variety of capacities, including chairman of the Philippine delegation (1953 and 1955) and economic adviser to the Philippine Mission, with the rank of ambassador, from 1956 until his death.

Elizalde, who for years lived in Adamstown, Maryland, just outside Frederick, died after a long illness on February 9, 1965, at Georgetown University Hospital in Washington, DC. He was interred at St. Joseph's Church Cemetery in Carrollton Manor, Maryland.[46]

NOTES

1   Elizalde was appointed by Quezon, and House Records indicate no discernable party affiliation.

2   Quotation is from Texas Congressman Albert Thomas. See *Congressional Record*, Extension of Remarks, 78th Cong., 2nd sess. (6 September 1944): A3897–3898.

3   *Congressional Record*, Extension of Remarks, 78th Cong., 2nd sess. (19 September 1944): A4123–4124.

4   "Joaquin Elizalde Dead; Manila's 1st U.S. Envoy," 10 February 1965, *Washington Post*: C8. Another source suggested that he changed citizenship for purely pragmatic reasons, "to protect the family business." See "The Philippines: Commissioner Mike," 10 October 1938, *Time*: n.p. The 1933 date of citizenship also seems to be corroborated by James G. Wingo, "Honorable Mike Starts New Era," 22 October 1938, *Philippines Free Press*: 19–21.

5   Zilio M. Galang, ed., *Leaders of the Philippines: Inspiring Biographies of Successful Men and Women of the Philippines* (Manila, PI: National Publishing Company, 1931): 290.

6   Galang, *Leaders of the Philippines*: 289.

7   Biographical survey, Box 53, Joaquin Elizalde, *Biographical Directory of the United States Congress* Research Collection, Office of the Historian, U.S. House of Representatives.

8   *Philippines, Select Marriages, 1723–1957*, Library of Congress, Washington, DC, http://search.ancestrylibrary.com (accessed 24 June 2014); "Joaquin Elizalde Dead; Manila's 1st U.S. Envoy."

9   "Joaquin Miguel Elizalde," *Biographical Directory of the United States Congress, 1774–Present*, http://bioguide.congress.gov/scripts/biodisplay.pl?index=E000108; "Elizalde Named P.I. Commissioner," 29 September 1938, *Philippines Herald*: 1.

10 Wingo, "Honorable Mike Starts New Era."

11 Ibid.

12 "Elizalde Called 'Unqualified' in Court Suit," 18 October 1938, *Washington Post*: X7; "Court Refuses to Consider Elizalde Case," 16 April 1940, *Washington Post*: 23. For some background on Porfirio Sevilla and another Elizalde critic, Teddy de Nolaseo, by a critical observer, see Wingo, "Honorable Mike Starts New Era."

13 "Problem in Little," 7 November 1938, *Baltimore Sun*: 8.

14 *Congressional Record*, House, 76th Cong., 1st sess. (31 July 1939): 10598.

15 For the floor debate and passage, see *Congressional Record*, House, 76th Cong., 1st sess. (31 July 1939): 10594–10601. For Elizalde's testimony for the Senate version of this legislation, see the hearing transcript on S. 1028, Hearings before the Senate Committee on Territories and Insular Affairs, *To Amend the Philippine Independence Act*, 76th Cong., 1st sess. (7 March 1937): 197–208.

16 See a transcript of his testimony before the House Agriculture Committee which he later inserted into the *Record*: *Congressional Record*, Extension of Remarks, 76th Cong., 2nd sess. (20 June 1940): A4057–4059. In October 1941, Elizalde supported a bill to amend the Independence Act of 1934 so that all sugar excise tax funds would be used for a defensive military buildup in the Philippines. The bill died in that Congress. See Hearings before the House Committee on Insular Affairs, *Amend the Philippine Independence Act of 1934*, 77th Cong., 1st sess. (9 October 1941): 17–24.

17 In an article from 12 April 1939 printed in the *Manila Tribune* and inserted into the *Record* by John Z. Anderson of California. See *Congressional Record*, Extension of Remarks, 78th Cong., 2nd sess. (19 September 1944): A4142.

18 Hearings before the House Committee on Immigration and Naturalization, *H.R. 3657—To Confer Citizenship on Certain Aliens Serving in Any Capacity Upon Any Merchant or Fishing Vessels of the United States*, 76th Cong., 1st sess. (5 May 1939): 1–14, quotation on p. 9. Representative O'Day spoke up at one point: "My purpose in introducing this bill is merely to clarify the situation of the Filipinos. They are not American citizens. They are not aliens. For that reason they are not allowed to take on these jobs again; but they are not aliens. Now, what are they?" Quotation on p. 13.

19 Hearing before the House Committee on Immigration and Naturalization, *H.R. 1844—To Authorize the Naturalization of Filipinos Who Are Permanent Residents of the United States*, 77th Cong., 2nd sess. (21 January 1942): 21–27.

20 Hearing before the House Committee on Immigration and Naturalization, *H.R. 7239—A Bill To Authorize the Naturalization of Filipinos Who Are Permanent Residents of the United States*, 76th Cong., 2nd sess. (28 March 1940): 50–53.

21 *H.R. 1844—To Authorize the Naturalization of Filipinos Who Are Permanent Residents of the United States*: 21–27.

22 "Manila Hails Elizalde," 10 December 1939, *New York Times*: 46.

23 James G. Wingo, "Joaquin Elizalde: Free Press Man of the Year for 1940," 4 January 1941, *Philippine Free Press*.

24 Wingo, "Joaquin Elizalde: Free Press Man of the Year for 1940."

25 W. B. Ragsdale, "Island Commissioner Here: Philippine Freedom Is Aim of Elizalde," 28 September 1941, *Washington Post*: 18.

26 Ragsdale, "Island Commissioner Here: Philippine Freedom Is Aim of Elizalde."

27 Lemuel F. Parton, "No More Siestas for Mike," 5 January 1942, *Boston Globe*: 12. See also Hope Ridings Miller, "Implications Team Around Report that Col. Romulo Will Succeed 'Mike' Elizalde," 11 August 1944, *Washington Post*: 10.

28 Parton, "No More Siestas for Mike."

29 "Elizalde Takes Over New Philippine Post," 6 February 1942, *New York Times*: 4. Earlier, on September 29, 1941, President Manuel Quezon had appointed Elizalde a member of the Philippine cabinet (without portfolio). He had, since 1936, been a member of the council of state.

30 "Government Fled? No, Says Official Here," 2 January 1942, *Washington Post*: 6. Here is the reporter's description: "He blasted [the report] with his eyes, his short-clipped words and expressive shrugs of his shoulders calling it 'Japanese propaganda' and an effort to dispirit the Philippine population and soldiers."

31 *Congressional Record*, Extension of Remarks, 77th Cong., 1st. sess. (17 December 1941): A5642; "Filipinos in U.S. May Enlist in Army," 3 January 1942, *New York Times*: 3. The revision was included in Public Law 77-360, 55 Stat. 844 (1941).

32 "Elizalde Soon to Take Leave," 24 July 1942, *Washington Post*: 16.

33 Philippines Embassy, "History of the Embassy of the Philippines in Washington, D.C.," http://philippineembassy-usa.org/philippines-dc/embassy-dc/ (accessed 24 July 2015). The 1617 Massachusetts Ave. NW location remained the embassy until the 1990s, when it moved just a few doors away to number 1600.

34 Wingo, "Joaquin Elizalde: Free Press Man of the Year for 1940."

35 "Philippines Accept Export Controls, Elizalde Says," 11 May 1941, *Washington Post*: 15.

36 Hearings before the House Committee on Military Affairs, *Philippine Export Control*, 77th Cong., 1st sess. (12 May 1941): 5–7, quotation on p. 6.

37 Wingo, "Joaquin Elizalde: Free Press Man of the Year for 1940."

38 *Congressional Record*, Extension of Remarks, 76th Cong., 1st sess. (19 May 1939): A2114. He made similar expressions in radio broadcasts and public speeches in the U.S. For examples, see *Congressional Record*, Extension of Remarks, 77th Cong., 1st sess. (21 August 1941): A4045; and an Elizalde speech to the Women's National Democratic Club which Representative Mike Monroney of Oklahoma inserted into the *Record*. See *Congressional Record*, Extension of Remarks, 77th Cong., 2nd sess. (24 March 1942): A1180–1181.

39 Hearing before the House Committee on Territories, *Employment of Nationals in Hawaii*, 77th Cong., 1st sess. (16 December 1941): 7–13.

40 "Filipino Warns Oppressed Asia May Turn on Us," 10 March 1942, *Chicago Tribune*: 3. For the full text of the speech, see the insertion into the *Record* by Representative James Shanley of Connecticut, *Congressional Record*, Extension of Remarks, 77th Cong., 2nd sess. (10 March 1942): A926–928.

41 *Congressional Record*, House, 78th Cong., 1st sess. (10 November 1943): 9376–9397, see especially 9383. See also the debate and Elizalde's answers to questions on the floor from the *Congressional Record*, House, 78th Cong., 1st sess. (9 November 1943): 9352–9356.

42 Ridings Miller, "Implications Team around Report that Col. Romulo Will Succeed 'Mike' Elizalde," 11 August 1944, *Washington Post*: 10.

43 *Congressional Record*, Extension of Remarks, 78th Cong., 2nd sess. (1 September 1944): A3844–3845.

44 "Elizalde Presents Credentials, Seeks Philippine Loan," 26 July 1946, *Washington Post*: 9.

45 Quotation from "Joaquin Elizalde Dead; Manila's 1st U.S. Envoy."

46 "Joaquin Elizalde Dies; First Philippine Envoy," 10 February 1965, *Washington Evening Star*: n.p.; "Elizalde, 68, Dies; Philippine Envoy," 10 February 1965, *New York Times*: 41.

Carlos Peña Romulo
1899–1985

RESIDENT COMMISSIONER 1944–1946
NO PARTY AFFILIATION, FROM THE PHILIPPINES

As the last Resident Commissioner from the Philippines, Carlos Peña Romulo helped lead the island territory through the brutality of World War II and into an independent future. A former journalist whose "Voice of Freedom" radio broadcast went live during some of the heaviest combat in the Pacific theater, Romulo was a tireless advocate for the commonwealth.[1] A chief aide to General Douglas MacArthur in the Pacific and a brigadier general in the Philippine army, Romulo was appointed to the House in the summer of 1944, where he helped secure Congress's support in rebuilding the Philippines. Known as the "General" among his colleagues on the Hill, Romulo was a champion of global democratic reforms and later served as president of the United Nations General Assembly.[2] In the House, Romulo pushed Congress to invest in the islands. "Mr. Chairman, when we are for a free Philippines as a part of this world government," he told the Ways and Means Committee in 1945, "we are for a Philippines that is a product of the United States, that has the ideals of the United States, and that will be spreading the American gospel in the Far East[,] the spearhead so to speak of American democracy."[3]

Carlos Peña Romulo was born on January 14, 1899, to Gregorio and Maria Peña Romulo.[4] The third of six children, Romulo grew up in a prosperous family in Camiling on the island of Luzon, about 100 miles north of Manila. He described his childhood home as a blend of "Malay and Spanish" influences. His grandparents lived across the street, "and there would be times as I grew," he said, "that our town seemed like one large family group, for everyone seemed related to me in some fashion." Outside his neighborhood, rice fields stretched far and wide. "I learned early that all we had had come to us from the land," he wrote as an adult.[5]

As a boy early in the new century, Romulo grew up amid a regime change in the Philippines. His father was a guerrilla fighter against American occupation forces after the War of 1898, and when U.S. troops reportedly hanged one of his neighbors at a nearby park, Romulo resolved to "hate [the Americans] as long as I lived."[6]

His father eventually surrendered and years later even became mayor, but the younger Romulo's lingering resentment toward the United States did not dissipate until he was in high school.[7] After he completed his studies at the University of the Philippines at Manila in 1918, he moved to New York City to attend Columbia University, graduating in 1921. He later received a degree from the University of Notre Dame in South Bend, Indiana, in 1935.[8] He married Virginia Llamas in 1924, and together they had four boys, Carlos, Bobby, Ricardo, and Gregorio. Virginia died in 1968, and Romulo married his close friend, Beth Day, 11 years later.[9]

At the age of 16, Romulo started as a junior reporter for the *Manila Times*. The newspaper paid him only in streetcar tickets, but it gave him the start to what would become an award-winning career in journalism.[10] When Romulo returned to the islands after college, he went back to work as a writer and an editor in Manila. From the early 1920s to about 1941, he thrived in what the *New York Times* called "the hurly-burly Filipino newspaper world." During that period, he grew close to Philippine President Manuel L. Quezon and became increasingly active in the territory's political future, meeting with U.S. officials six different times (1921, 1924, 1928, 1929, 1933, and 1937) to discuss the possibility of an independent Philippines.[11]

During the early stages of World War II, Romulo kept a close eye on the military movements in the Pacific. In 1941 he wrote a series of articles that ran in Manila and the United States, envisioning the arc of the war in his section of the world. His articles won the Pulitzer Prize and caught

the attention of high-ranking officials in the U.S. military who agreed with his take on the approaching conflict.[12] "War is coming, Carlos," General Douglas MacArthur told Romulo, "and when it breaks out I shall ask President Quezon to commission you in the Philippine army and induct you into the United States Army in charge of Press Relations on the Philippine side." "If war breaks," Romulo replied, "there's no place I'd rather be."[13]

Romulo worked closely with MacArthur, dealing directly with the press and bolstering public morale. "Croaking away into the mouthpiece of my phone and into the mike [sic] of the radio, I was the voice of both the Philippine and American Armies."[14] Despite his distance from combat, his work was exceptionally dangerous. Japanese bombers routinely flew overheard. "At times I felt like a condemned prisoner in a death cell, sitting in my little room while the Japanese executioners roamed overhead."[15]

As the fighting intensified in the Philippines, Romulo, along with thousands of American and Philippine troops and civilians, hunkered down on a small peninsula west of Manila called Bataan. After months of suffering, President Franklin D. Roosevelt ordered General MacArthur to withdraw to Australia. A short while later, the Allied forces surrendered. Thousands died in Japanese custody either during the forced march to the prison camps or in the camps themselves. Romulo, however, had narrowly escaped, defiantly writing "I was the last man out of Bataan."[16]

Romulo remained in exile in the States for two years, completely separated from his family with no way of knowing where they were or if they survived.[17] He used his time away to educate people on the conditions in the Pacific and embarked on a remarkable speaking tour throughout America. By late October 1943, he had traveled an estimated 60,000 miles and given 364 speeches in 289 cities all across the country. He was soon appointed secretary of public instruction for the exiled Philippine war cabinet.[18]

Along with his public speaking duties, Romulo assumed additional responsibility after Philippine President Quezon died on August 1, 1944, followed by the quick resignation of the sitting Resident Commissioner, Joaquin M. Elizalde. The new exiled president, Sergio Osmeña, looking to give the Philippines a stronger presence in Congress, appointed Romulo to the seat.[19] A day later the *Washington Post*'s editorial team touted the appointment, given Romulo's recent history "as an emissary between the Filipino and American people," but did not expect him to stay in Washington very long. "His abilities will undoubtedly be needed in spreading the gospel of democracy in the Philippines once more as soon as the liberation in that part of the world gets under way."[20]

Two months after being appointed Resident Commissioner, Romulo returned home for the first time in two years. On October 20, 1944, American forces landed at Leyte Bay, captured the island, and established an Allied beachhead in the Philippines.[21] Romulo was there to act as a "liaison officer" between his old friend General MacArthur and President Osmeña.[22] As brigadier general, Romulo wanted to fight and avenge what he experienced on Bataan, but, as Resident Commissioner, he hung back and landed with MacArthur, calling the day he returned home "the greatest in my life."[23]

After reuniting with his family, Romulo returned to Washington. For much of his first year in the House, while still serving as the Philippines' secretary of public instruction, Romulo led a public education campaign to inform Congress about the living conditions on the war-ravaged islands.[24] His reports were shocking. By the time the fighting ended, much of the Philippines had been reduced to ruins, and what remained needed to be rebuilt. As bad as the Philippines' physical state was, the war's human toll was even more devastating. A staggering number of people, both civilians and soldiers, had died during the conflict, and those who survived were left destitute. At Leyte, Romulo remembered seeing residents "clothed with the pounded bark of trees."[25] In the territory's capital he had seen the bodies of his friends and neighbors "pushed into heaps on the Manila streets, their heads shaved, their hands tied behind their backs, and bayonet stabs running them through and through."[26]

Beginning in September 1945, Romulo began pushing what would become his signature issue: rebuilding the Philippines using the islands' trade partnership with the

United States. He had studied the situation as a member of the Philippine Rehabilitation Commission, which Congress created in 1944 to investigate "all matters affecting post-war economy, trade, finance, economic stability, and rehabilitation of the Philippine Islands."[27] In many respects, the Philippines had to rebuild both its economy and society from scratch.[28]

To start, Romulo wanted Congress to extend an existing preferential trade deal with the Philippines for at least another 20 years. The current agreement was three decades old but was set to expire in a matter of months, as soon as the commonwealth gained its independence. In October 1945, during hearings on the trade extension (H.R. 5185), Romulo told the House Ways and Means Committee that the archipelago's existing trade arrangement was something of a double-edged sword. Although the Philippine economy had become virtually dependent on trade with the United States, the results, Romulo said, could not be ignored: trade with mainland America generated a huge economic boom, complete with better schools, health care, and public services. Relying on one trading partner, however, was dangerous, and operating in the shadow of America's mammoth economy had its drawbacks. Like other Filipinos before him, Romulo worried that, without time to expand its trade portfolio, the Philippines would struggle once the previous agreement ended and America began levying higher rates.[29] "The plan," he said, "is to diversify so that our economy will not be geared entirely to the American economy."[30]

Romulo's goal explained why he supported quota levels on certain products, like sugar, below what the Philippines might actually be able to export. Although supporting quota levels would have been an unusual position for his predecessors, Romulo kept the long-term interests of the archipelago squarely at heart. "The quota," he said, "must be limited to discourage the production of sugar, so that at the end of 20 years our sugar industry will not have to depend on the American market." Romulo's plan would have the islands spread its financial risk over multiple industries. That way, if one failed, the whole economy would not collapse.[31]

Romulo saw federal stimulus as merely a short-term solution, and he wanted to make sure the archipelago's economy could support the far-reaching goals of an independent nation.[32] He promised that, if his commonwealth could rebuild its infrastructure, Philippine businesses "will be able to stand on their own feet" once the 20-year grace period ends.[33]

The trade issue, however, also highlighted the limitations of Romulo's influence in Washington. When one Member seemed cool to the proposal, Romulo reminded him that Congress would be "deciding the fate of 18,000,000 people who have practically no voice in the determination of their destiny except my very weak voice before this committee."[34]

The bill that followed, H.R. 5856, the Philippine Trade Act of 1946, made it out of the Ways and Means Committee in a unanimous vote and was reported to the House in late March 1946.[35] The legislation also had the support of the Harry S. Truman administration, which called it "vital to the welfare of the Philippines," reminding the committee that they all agreed "at least in principle, with the legislation."[36]

Moreover, it seemed, especially on the surface, as though Romulo's testimony had the desired effect. Writing in its report, the committee admitted, "In the course of hearings … it was made abundantly clear that the Philippines, in order to reestablish a normal economy and to develop resources for sustaining its independence, will require the assurance and stability in its trade with the United States."[37] As described by the committee, the bill seemed to fulfill Romulo's wishes—incentivizing the Philippines to diversify its economy—but there was much he disliked about it.[38]

The measure was a unique piece of legislation: a trade bill without the constitutional requirements of a full treaty. Although the Philippines would gain its independence in a matter of months, at the time it was still technically part of America's geopolitical orbit, and, therefore, the trade talks did not fall under the same requirements as those between the United States and other sovereign nations. Normally, the president would have negotiated the details, and the

Senate would have approval authority. For the Philippine Trade Act, however, both the House and Senate needed majority votes, giving the White House more of a behind-the-scenes role.[39]

The day the bill made it to the floor, Robert Doughton of North Carolina, the chairman of the Ways and Means Committee, said it was the product of "earnest, painstaking, and careful consideration, both as to its objectives and the manner in which it was drafted." The chairman then thanked a number of his colleagues and a host of federal officials for their work on the bill; nowhere, however, did he mention Romulo.[40] In fact, it wasn't until later in the day that the bill's author, Representative Jasper Bell of Missouri, even acknowledged Romulo's "distinguished and far-seeing statesmanship."[41]

When the debate manager finally recognized Romulo on the floor, the Resident Commissioner, suffering from a prolonged bout of malaria, spoke honestly about what he saw as the bill's shortcomings. "If I had written this bill as I would have wished," he told the chamber, "it would provide for perpetual free trade" rather than the "graduated tariffs" that would go up each year after an initial grace period. "If I had written it," he went on, "the rights assured to the United States would not appear in the bill at all. They would be assured by a treaty entered into on a basis of a complete equality between our two sovereign nations." Nevertheless, Romulo knew his political limitations and gave the bill his support, calling it "legislation written for reality.... It represents the spirit of realistic compromise which is democracy at its best."[42]

The next day, as debate wound down, Romulo delivered an elegant appeal to the House in favor of the legislation. He hoped the bill would be passed unanimously in order to "bolster the wavering morale of the Filipino people who live today amid the shambles of postwar devastation."[43] He argued that the trade bill would be seen around the world as proof of America's leadership. "At a time when there is too much suspicion rife among the nations of the earth, you will be demonstrating that the greatest force for true world peace and security is the force of friendship, of harmony, of understanding."[44] A few moments later, the Philippine Trade Act cleared the House.[45]

When the bill went to the Senate, Romulo employed many of the same arguments in his testimony before the Committee on Finance that he had used during the House committee markup.[46] After the Senate approved the bill and the two chambers worked out their differences in conference, the Philippine Trade Act became law on April 30, 1946, two months before the archipelago gained its independence.[47]

As with trade, Romulo acted as the moral compass for the Philippine Rehabilitation Act of 1946 (S. 1610), which, unlike the trade bill, pumped capital directly into the war-torn commonwealth. During the initial Senate hearings in late October 1945, Romulo reminded the Committee on Territories and Insular Affairs that the sooner Congress acted, the sooner the archipelago could start the healing process. As with the trade bill, Romulo worked to ensure that the Philippine government was an active partner in developing the legislation. He offered a series of amendments, including one that raised the cost of one section of the bill tenfold, but the Resident Commissioner did not want Congress to simply "gift" funding to the islands. Instead, Romulo sought to cast the bill as "compensation" for the islands' suffering during the war and cited the Treaty of Paris as precedent.[48] After visiting the islands, the Senate committee estimated the total cost of the damage there at roughly $800 million. "Factories, homes, government and commercial buildings, roads, bridges, docks, harbors, and the like are in need of complete reconstruction or widespread repairs," the committee reported.[49] After being cleared by the committee in late November, the full Senate passed the bill unanimously on December 5, 1945.[50]

The House sat on the rehabilitation bill until late February, when the Committee on Insular Affairs finally took it up. Romulo had twice petitioned the House for action and finally testified before Insular Affairs on March 2, 1946, when he revealed that the bill had the full support of the Philippines.[51] The legislation approved compensation for both public and private property destroyed in the war, cleared the way for transfer of raw materials, and provided technical and job training during the reconstruction. "Taken together with the pending Philippine trade bill—and it would be unrealistic to think of Philippine rehabilitation in terms of one bill without the other—this bill represents an integrated approach to the problem of putting the Filipino nation back on its feet," Romulo said. Filipinos' sacrifices and their wartime loyalty deserved nothing less, he reiterated.[52]

Ultimately, the House committee agreed. The rescue bill, it wrote in its report, "recognizes the obligation of the United States to help rehabilitate the economy and physical properties of a people who will become an independent nation July 4, 1946, and whose land was ravaged by participation in the war of the United States against Japan."[53] As reported, the half-billion-dollar bill was meant to kick-start the rebuilding process rather than cover the full cost of the islands' redevelopment.[54]

When the rehabilitation bill went to the floor, Romulo was the first to speak. In a long and moving address, he described the destruction on the islands and the war's human toll, telling the chamber, "The whole future of the Philippines depends upon the help we get from you."[55] The bill, he said, would represent "a rock of strength for American prestige in the Far East, and therefore it is a force for enduring peace throughout the world."[56]

For Romulo's work on the trade and rehabilitation bills, Majority Leader John McCormack of Massachusetts credited him for his "distinguished service." "The position of General Romulo in the hearts and minds of all of the Members is one of extreme closeness; we all have a very high regard for him, and the people of the Philippines are indeed fortunate in having such an outstanding gentleman representing them in this body."[57] A short while later, the House passed the rehabilitation bill and quickly conferenced with the Senate. A week later, the House agreed to the conference report, and the President signed the measure into law on April 30, 1946.[58]

With the success of the trade and rehabilitation bills, Romulo wanted to address one last issue before the Philippines celebrated its independence. In mid-June 1946, he helped manage a bill providing military assistance to the archipelago over the next five years (H.R. 6572). The

war had devastated the Philippine armed forces and left the islands' national security infrastructure in disarray, threatening the entire rebuilding enterprise. Moreover, as Romulo reminded the chamber on the day of the vote, the U.S. government had armed a huge number of Philippine guerrilla fighters in the war against Japan. The Resident Commissioner estimated that there were "more than 300,000 firearms in the hands of people who have no right to hold them," to say nothing of potential outside threats. "I regret to say, however, that the ravages of the recent conflict have so depleted our resources that we will not be able, until our economic rehabilitation is under way, to discharge our responsibility in preserving, in cooperation with the armed forces of the United States, the peace of the Far Pacific, without the material assistance" provided in the bill. The military assistance measure sailed through Congress. Introduced on May 27, 1946, the House passed it by unanimous consent on June 14, and the Senate cleared it four days later. The President signed it into law on June 26, 1946.[59]

Romulo addressed the House for the final time on June 21, 1946. In a lengthy and emotional address, the last Resident Commissioner from the Philippines delivered a broad accounting of the relationship between the archipelago and the mainland, everything from America's imperial ambitions to the Philippine backlash, to the push toward the Philippines' independence. From an institutional stance, he offered an honest assessment of his limited role in the House. "As an insider who is nevertheless an outsider," he said, "I have seen something which it is possible that you yourselves have overlooked. It is this—in the heat of controversy, in the fervor of partisanship, in the bitterness of debate, you have inevitably demonstrated your faith in the ways of democracy."[60]

House Members responded warmly to that farewell speech with a long standing ovation. "It is with the greatest regret that the Members of the House of Representatives take leave of General Romulo's wise counsel, his brilliant logic, his impassioned eloquence [on] behalf of the people whom he so ably served," Republican Representative Karl Stefan of Nebraska said, capturing the mood of many in the chamber.[61]

Although independence dissolved the Philippines' insular relationship with the United States, Romulo was not gone long, and he remained remarkably active on the international stage. In 1945 Romulo had told a House committee that everything changed with the advent of the atomic bomb. "The only permanent things are the intangible things—friendship, good will, faith, justice, right," he said, stressing the need for a central global authority. "I have always believed that humanity is evolving into that goal—hemispheric solidarity; oceanic solidarity; federation and world government."[62] Fittingly, he twice served as ambassador to the United States (1952–1953 and 1955–1962), but he made his biggest mark in his work with the United Nations, which he helped charter. On July 9, 1946, the Philippine president appointed Romulo as the new republic's permanent delegate to the United Nations. The former Resident Commissioner went on to serve as president of the UN General Assembly in 1949 and 1950.

Late in his life, Romulo was criticized for supporting the dictatorial policies of Philippine President Ferdinand Marcos, but he never lost his fighting spirit. When the Soviet Union's leading voice in the UN General Assembly called Romulo "just a little man from a little country," Romulo admitted the delegate was correct about his physical stature and the size of his homeland. But, he said, "It is the duty of the little Davids here to fling pebbles of truth between the eyes of blustering Goliaths—and make them behave."[63] Romulo died in Manila on December 15, 1985.

FOR FURTHER READING

Romulo, Carlos P., *The Romulo Reader*, edited by Liana Romulo (Makati City, PI: Bookmark, Inc., 1998).

NOTES

1   "Voice of Freedom," 21 October 1941, *New York Times*: 16.

2   Hearings before the House Committee on Ways and Means, *Philippine Trade Act of 1945*, 79th Cong., 1st sess. (17 October 1945): 111.

3   *Philippine Trade Act of 1945* (19 October 1945): 130.

4   Parents' names from Carlos P. Romulo, "I Walked With Heroes," in *The Romulo Reader*, ed. Liana Romulo (Makati City, PI: Bookmark, Inc., 1998): 140–141.

5   Romulo, "I Walked With Heroes": 137–139, 144.

6   Romulo, "I Saw the Fall of the Philippines," in *The Romulo Reader*: 16–17; "Carlos Romulo, Was U.N. Founding Father," 16 December 1985, *Sun Sentinel* (Fort Lauderdale, FL): B10.

7   Romulo, "I Saw the Fall of the Philippines": 19.

8   Ibid., 11, 22–23.

9   Romulo, "I See the Philippines Rise," in *The Romulo Reader*: 111; "Carlos Romulo, Was a U.N. Founding Father"; "Carlos P. Romulo, 86, One of the UN's Founding Fathers," 15 December 1985, *Chicago Tribune*: 18.

10 Romulo, "My Brother Americans," in *The Romulo Reader*: 35.

11 Eric Pace, "Carlos Romulo of Philippines, a Founder of U.N. Dies at 86," 15 December 1985, *New York Times*: 1; "Carlos Peña Romulo," *Biographical Directory of the United States Congress, 1774–Present*, http://bioguide.congress.gov/scripts/biodisplay.pl?index=R000419.

12 For more on his Pulitzer Prize, see http://www.pulitzer.org/awards/1942 (accessed 10 September 2015); Pace, "Carlos Romulo of Philippines, a Founder of U.N. Dies at 86."

13 Romulo, "I Saw the Fall of the Philippines": 12.

14 Ibid., 27.

15 Ibid., 28.

16 Col. Carlos P. Romulo, "Col. C.P. Romulo Tells Story of Bataan's Fall," 28 February 1943, *Chicago Tribune*: 1; David M. Kennedy, *Freedom From Fear: The American People in Depression and War, 1929–1945* (New York: Oxford University Press, 1999): 527–531.

17 Romulo, "I See the Philippines Rise": 93, 108.

18 "Party Given for Colonel Romulo," 30 October 1943, *Washington Post*: B3.

19 "New Philippine President Reorganizes War Aides," 11 August 1944, *Atlanta Constitution*: 11; "Osmena Appoints His War Cabinet," 11 August 1944, *New York Times*: 6; "Filipino Chief Reorganizes War Cabinet," 11 August 1944, *Washington Post*: 5.

20 "Filipinos Get Ready," 12 August 1944, *Washington Post*: 4.

21 Kennedy, *Freedom from Fear*: 822.

22 Romulo, "I See the Philippines Rise": 88.

23 Ibid., 76.

24 *Congressional Record*, House, 79th Cong., 1st sess. (24 September 1945): 8924.

25 *Philippine Trade Act of 1945* (17 October 1945): 113. See also Romulo, "I See the Philippines Rise": 80–81.

26 Romulo, "I See the Philippines Rise": 102.

27 House Committee on Insular Affairs, *Establishing the Filipino Rehabilitation Commission*, 78th Cong., 2nd sess., H. Rept. 1507 (23 May 1944): 2. The Filipino Rehabilitation Commission became law on June 29, 1944, as Public Law 78-381, 58 Stat. 626 (1944).

28 *Philippine Trade Act of 1945* (15 October 1945): 49.

29 Ibid., 51.

30 *Congressional Record*, House, 79th Cong., 1st sess. (24 September 1945): 8925.

31 *Philippine Trade Act of 1945* (17 October 1945): 116–117.

32 *Philippine Trade Act of 1945* (19 October 1945): 124.

33 *Philippine Trade Act of 1945* (15 October 1945): 52.

34 *Philippine Trade Act of 1945* (17 October 1945): 112.

35 *Congressional Record*, House, 79th Cong., 2nd sess. (28 March 1946): 2753.

36 House Ways and Means Committee, *Philippine Trade Act of 1946*, 79th Cong., 2nd sess., H. Rept. 1821 (26 March 1946): 5.

37 *Philippine Trade Act of 1946*: 5.

38 Ibid., 1.

39 *Congressional Record*, House, 79th Cong., 2nd sess. (28 March 1946): 2754.

40 Ibid., 2759.

41 Ibid., 2762.

42 Ibid., 2768–2769.

43 *Congressional Record*, House, 79th Cong., 2nd sess. (29 March 1946): 2854.

44 Ibid.

45 Ibid., 2856.

46 Hearings before the Senate Committee on Finance, *Philippine Trade Act of 1946*, 79th Cong., 2nd sess. (1946): 47–48, 141–142.

47 Conference Committee, *Philippine Trade Act of 1946*, 79th Cong., 2nd sess., H. Rept. 1955 (17 April 1946); Public Law 79-371, 60 Stat. 141 (1946).

48 Hearings before the Senate Committee on Territories and Insular Affairs, *Philippine Rehabilitation Act of 1945* (30 October 1945): 143–144, 151.

49 Senate Committee on Territories and Insular Affairs, *Providing for the Rehabilitation of the Philippine Islands*, 79th Cong., 1st sess., S. Rept. 755 (20 November 1945): quotation on p. 1, total damage estimates on p. 3.

50 *Congressional Record*, Senate, 79th Cong., 1st sess. (5 December 1945): 11470.

51 *Congressional Record*, House, 79th Cong., 1st sess. (18 December 1945): A5619; *Congressional Record*, House, 79th Cong., 2nd sess. (23 January 1946): 261.

52 Hearings before the House Committee on Insular Affairs, *To Provide for the Rehabilitation of the Philippine Islands*, 79th Cong., 2nd sess. (2 March 1946): 121–122.

53 House Committee on Insular Affairs, *Providing for the Rehabilitation of the Philippines*, 79th Cong., 2nd sess., H. Rept. 1921 (9 April 1946): 8.

54 Ibid., 9; *Congressional Record*, House, 79th Cong., 2nd sess. (10 April 1946): 3438.

55 *Congressional Record*, House, 79th Cong., 2nd sess. (10 April 1946): 3436.

56 Ibid., 3437.

57 Ibid., 3439.

58 Conference Committee, *Providing for the Rehabilitation of the Philippines*, 79th Cong., 2nd sess., H. Rept. 1957 (17 April 1946); *Congressional Record*, House, 79th Cong., 2nd sess. (18 April 1946): 3987. The Philippine Rehabilitation Act of 1946 became law as Public Law 79-370, 60 Stat. 128 (1946).

59 *Congressional Record*, House, 79th Cong., 2nd sess. (14 June 1946): 6967; Public Law 79-454, 60 Stat. 315 (1946).

60 *Congressional Record*, House, 79th Cong., 2nd sess. (21 June 1946): 7319.

61 Ibid., 7321.

62 *Philippine Trade Act of 1945* (19 October 1945): 129.

63 Pace, "Carlos Romulo of Philippines, A Founder of U.N., Dies at 86."

From Exclusion to Inclusion

1941–1992

Around 9:00 in the morning on April 21, 1945, Daniel K. Inouye, a 20-year-old army lieutenant from Honolulu, Hawaii, was shot in the stomach on the side of a mountain in northwestern Italy. The German bullet went clean out his back and missed his spine by a fraction of an inch. "It felt like someone punched me," he remembered years later. "But the pain was almost non-existent. A little ache, that's all and since the bleeding was not much I said well, I'll keep on going."[1]

Later that morning, Inouye, a pre-med student who had been getting ready for church when Japan bombed Pearl Harbor on December 7, 1941, was hit again. This time a rifle grenade nearly blew off his entire right arm. After picking up his tommy gun with his left hand, he continued to charge up the hill, firing at German soldiers as he went. Eventually shot in the leg, Inouye waited until his men seized control of the mountain before being evacuated.[2] The war in Europe ended 17 days later.

Inouye lived in military hospitals for the next two years to rebuild his strength and learn to do everyday tasks with one arm. The war forced him to adapt, and over the next two decades, the country he nearly died for began to adapt to the war's consequences as well.

For the most marginalized people—women and minorities, especially—World War II had profound implications for what it meant to be American. The sacrifices they made overseas and on the home front challenged the country to confront its legacy of political exclusion: What role would they have in this new world order?

Japanese-American citizens were rounded up and incarcerated in internment camps during World War II. Photographer Dorothea Lange captured this image of a child, wearing a tag as identification, as he waits for a bus to a relocation center in 1942.

Image courtesy of the National Archives and Records Administration

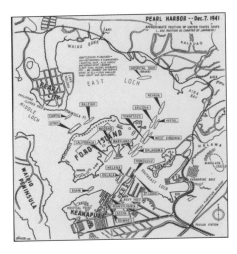

This map details the location of U.S. combat and service ships in Pearl Harbor, Hawaii, on December 7, 1941, the day it was attacked by the Japanese.

Image courtesy of the National Archives and Records Administration

In his painting *Attacked Pearl Harbor* [*sic*] (circa 1947), Henry Sugimoto captures the stunned and anxious reactions of Japanese-American citizens after hearing about the bombing of Pearl Harbor. Sugimoto and his family were removed to internment camps during World War II.

Image courtesy of the Japanese American National Museum, Gift of Madeleine Sugimoto and Naomi Tagawa

For Inouye, the war had something of a twisted logic. "Dec. 7 was the worst date in history for Americans of Japanese ancestry," he told the *Boston Globe* in 1967. "And yet—maybe this is a horrible thing to say—Dec. 7 was one of the greatest breaks we ever had. The hatred erupted and gave us a chance to counteract it."[3]

Of course, not everyone saw the Pearl Harbor attacks as an opportunity for positive change. In their aftermath, the federal government, afraid that immigrants or their family members with Japanese ancestry had helped orchestrate the attacks from U.S. soil, uprooted more than 120,000 Japanese Americans living along the West Coast and placed them in internment camps out of "military necessity." For these people, the war was a period of remarkable emotional and psychological trauma. Beginning in the 19th century, Congress and the courts prevented Japanese immigrants from becoming citizens and from participating in the political process. After 1924 Congress made them ineligible for admission into the United States entirely, and the federal government considered them a direct threat to the nation. The native-born children of Japanese immigrants were U.S. citizens, yet they were imprisoned by their own government, including four who years later would serve in the U.S. House of Representatives. Because their community lacked a voice at almost every level of government, mainland Japanese Americans' political exclusion was quickly compounded by their physical exclusion with internment.

From Hawaii to Capitol Hill, the effects of the war ricocheted across the legislative process over the next 50 years. At first, wartime alliances altered the political math Congress used to determine immigration policy. In 1943 Congress repealed the Chinese Exclusion Act but still kept Asian immigration at a minimum for another two decades. Then the sacrifices and courage of Japanese-American GIs during the war questioned stereotypes at home. Finally, the war against communism encouraged legislators to adopt new visa programs as existing policy became inconsistent with post-war foreign policy needs. In the 1960s, federal lawmakers overturned a century of exclusion and opened citizenship to thousands of Asian immigrants from a host of different countries.

The process did not have a clean narrative arc stretching neatly from exclusion to citizenship. Congress did not swear in its first voting Asian Pacific American (APA) Member, Dalip Singh (Judge) Saund of California, until January 1957, more than a decade after the war. But through fits and starts, exclusion gave way to citizenship, which provided a path to political agency. The decades of discrimination against Asian Americans that culminated in the forced imprisonment of the Japanese-American community during the war left deep and lasting scars. But by the end of the 20th century, APAs in Congress wielded significant political power and forced the country to confront the haunting legacy of internment and prejudice.

This section profiles the 14 APA Members first elected to Congress between 1956 and 1992.[4] Five served as U.S. Representatives, two as Senators, and three held seats in both chambers. Unlike the first section of this book in which every APA Member profiled was a statutory representative, only four of the Members in this section served as Delegates. The first part of this essay provides the general historical context of the war and the experiences of Asian-American communities during this era. The middle section describes the new paths to citizenship and the process of turning that status into political power. Lastly, the discussion turns to the kinds of issues APA Members dealt with during their time in Congress.

This essay groups together the stories of Guam and American Samoa for two reasons. First, both territories became part of America's insular orbit following the Spanish-American War at the turn of the 20th century and both figured prominently in the Pacific theater during World War II. Second, because they were under U.S. jurisdiction at the time, the experiences of the islands' peoples differed significantly from those of immigrants coming from Japan, China, and other independent nations.

WORLD WAR II

Daniel Inouye had just finished brushing his teeth and was dressing in his Sunday best when he looked outside into the bright, early-morning sun on December 7, 1941. He was listening to the radio and buttoning his shirt when a panicked voice cut into the day's programming. "This is no test!" the radio announcer screamed. "Pearl Harbor is being bombed by the Japanese! I repeat: this is not a test or a maneuver! Japanese planes are attacking Oahu!"[5]

Inouye and his father ran outside as dark smoke filled the sky. Japanese warplanes flew overhead. The phone rang. On the other end was the local Red Cross chapter, looking for Inouye. "How soon can you be here, Dan?" the chapter's secretary asked. "I'm on my way," he replied.[6]

Grabbing his bike, the 17-year-old Inouye sprinted for the aid station near Pearl Harbor. As he sped toward the smoke, Inouye noticed his neighbors filling the streets. One of them, an elderly Japanese man, asked him if Germany had attacked, unable to process the reality that his ancestral home had just bombed his adopted one. "In the marrow of my bones," Inouye remembered almost 30 years later, "I knew there was only deep trouble ahead. And then, pedaling along, it came to me at last that I would face that trouble, too, for my eyes were

Seventeen-year-old Daniel K. Inouye was deeply affected by the bombing of Pearl Harbor. He volunteered as a private in the U.S. Army in 1943 and retired as a captain in 1947.

Image courtesy of the Daniel K. Inouye Institute

Smoke billows from the wreckage of the USS *Arizona* on December 7, 1941, in Pearl Harbor.

Image courtesy of the Library of Congress

shaped just like those of that poor old man in the street, and my people were only a generation removed from the land that had spawned those bombers, the land that sent them to rain destruction on America."[7]

Inouye was at the aid station for less than an hour when the next round of bombers swooped into Pearl Harbor. Armed with a stretcher, he and a few others raced to the impact zone and began ferrying out the dead and injured. It was five days before he went home.[8]

During World War II, tens of millions of Americans, nearly 11 percent of the entire population, received some sort of military training. Of those, almost 75 percent wound up overseas, engaged in the European and Pacific theaters. By one estimate, 33,000 *nisei* (the American-born children of Japanese immigrants) served in the armed forces during World War II. For these tens of thousands of Japanese-American troops, however, serving their country was not always a protected right. They fought for a chance to fight for America.[9]

Daniel Inouye was too young to enlist in 1941. But his age was not the only thing that prevented him from signing up. Following the attacks on Pearl Harbor, the federal government reclassified nearly every *nisei* on mainland America and in Hawaii, including almost every *nisei* already in uniform, as an enemy alien unfit to join or serve in the armed forces.[10]

Martial Law

On that fateful day, Hawaii began a complete transformation, one that threatened to upend generations of Japanese Hawaiians' participation in the life of the islands. U.S. officials declared martial law on the afternoon of December 7, and the military assumed all local judicial authority, regulated employment contracts, froze jobs and wages, instituted a curfew, censored the mails, monitored all telephone calls, and had the entire population fingerprinted. Newspapers and magazines, particularly Japanese-language publications, faced new licensing and strict censorship. Authorities implemented food and gasoline rationing and required that all firearms be surrendered. The U.S. Office of Alien Property Custodian seized businesses and properties and froze bank deposits and assets at all Japanese banks.[11]

Still, the treatment of persons of Japanese descent proceeded along two very different paths in Hawaii and on the mainland. In Hawaii, the new military governor, U.S. Army General Delos C. Emmons, ignored orders from Washington to evacuate and intern Japanese Hawaiians.[12] Military intelligence and the Federal Bureau of Investigation (FBI) told Emmons that they had no evidence of any Japanese disloyalty or sabotage. He soon concluded that any effort to intern Japanese Hawaiians, the largest ethnic group on the islands, would be an immense undertaking and would drain the resources needed to bolster the islands' defenses.[13]

In early 1942, General Emmons came under great pressure to relocate and intern Japanese Hawaiians. That pressure intensified following the publication of the Roberts Commission report on Pearl Harbor, directed by Supreme Court Justice Owen Roberts, which falsely suggested that Japanese Hawaiians had provided vital military and naval information to the Japanese consulate that contributed to the Pearl Harbor disaster. Emmons successfully resisted such

Enemy Alien:

A foreign resident in a country with which his or her country is at war.

From left to right: U.S. Army Lieutenant General Delos C. Emmons, Admiral Chester Nimitz, and Rear Admiral Milo Draemel meet at headquarters in Pearl Harbor shortly after the attack on December 7, 1941.

Image courtesy of the Naval History and Heritage Command

During the Battle of Midway, the U.S. Navy decisively turned the tide of the naval war in the Pacific with a devastating attack on the Japanese navy. This photograph shows the *Mikuma*, a Japanese heavy cruiser, after U.S. planes bombed the ship on June 6, 1942.

Image courtesy of the National Archives and Records Administration

drastic actions, however, because powerful white landowners and territorial newspapers backed him. Hawaiian Delegate Samuel Wilder King supported only the arrest of spies.[14]

Crucially, too, Hawaiian businessmen rejected internment. "There are 160,000 of these people who want to live here because they like the country and like the American way of life," wrote the president of the Honolulu chamber of commerce. "The citizens of Japanese blood would fight as loyally for America as any other citizen." But most important of all, the Japanese Hawaiians were the lynchpin of the local economy.[15]

Emmons ended up interning fewer than 1,500 people (about two-thirds of whom were Japanese immigrants and one-third U.S. citizens) whom he considered serious security threats. This came to about 1 percent of the islands' Japanese and Japanese-American population. Pressure for internment eased after the U.S. victory off Midway Island in June 1942 put the Japanese navy on the defensive and tamped down concerns about an invasion of Hawaii.[16] Still, martial law remained in place until President Franklin D. Roosevelt (FDR) lifted it in October 1944 after it became clear that Allied forces had turned the tide against Japan.

"Go for Broke"

While wholesale internment on the islands never came to fruition, life for Japanese Hawaiians remained far different from what it had been before the bombings. In the years leading up to the war, *nisei* served in the military across Hawaii. About 1,500 men had been drafted between September 1940 and December 1941, and on the morning of December 7, for instance, 2,000 Hawaiian *nisei* helped defend the islands when the bombings began, including future U.S. Senator Spark M. Matsunaga of Hawaii, who led a company of troops on nearby Molokai. By nightfall, thousands more *nisei* from the Hawaii territorial guard and the University of Hawaii's reserve officers' training corps helped guard vital points throughout the islands.[17]

Lieutenant General Lucian K. Truscott Jr., right, salutes after fastening the Presidential Unit Citation streamer to the flag of Company L, Third Battalion, of the 442nd Regimental Combat Team, on September 4, 1945. More than 10,000 Japanese-Hawaiian men tried to enlist in the 442nd, an all-*nisei* combat unit that received hard-won commendations.

Image courtesy of the U.S. Army Center of Military History

Daniel K. Inouye, photographed in his U.S. Army uniform on January 1, 1947, fought as a member of the 442nd Regimental Combat Team. On June 21, 2000, Inouye received the Congressional Medal of Honor for heroism in battle during World War II.

Image courtesy of the Daniel K. Inouye Institute

The 100th Infantry Battalion was an all-*nisei* unit of the U.S. Army. Two privates in the 100th, Takeshi Omuro and Kentoku Nakasone, load a machine gun in 1943.

Image courtesy of the U.S. Army Center of Military History

But anti-Japanese hysteria quickly took over, and it was not long before the military stripped *nisei* troops of their weapons and assigned them to menial tasks under armed guard. Less than two months later, on January 21, 1942, the military dismissed all 317 *nisei* from the territorial guard. Six months after that, following the Battle of Midway, the army removed Matsunaga from command and sent him and other *nisei* soldiers to a base in Wisconsin. "Oh, my heavens, that was a sad day," Matsunaga later remembered in an interview with the *Washington Post*. "Just imagine serving there for almost a year and having proven my loyalty.... Boy, I still feel emotional about it when I talk about it."[18]

Pressuring the government for a chance to join the fight, Matsunaga's *nisei* troops petitioned President Roosevelt directly, and with the support of U.S. military officers in Hawaii, the federal government eventually created an all-*nisei* army division, the 100th Infantry Battalion, formed largely out of the young men stationed in Wisconsin.[19]

Not long after, federal officials endorsed the idea of creating an all-*nisei* combat unit, and in January 1943, the War Department put out a call for 1,500 volunteers to form the 442nd Regimental Combat Team. Remarkably, even as the federal government interned Japanese Americans on the mainland, more than 10,000 Japanese Hawaiians, roughly 40 percent of all eligible *nisei* men in Hawaii, tried to enlist. The army ended up taking 2,600 volunteers, including Daniel K. Inouye, who was midway through his freshman year at the University of Hawaii.[20]

The 442nd adopted "Go for Broke" as its motto, borrowing the gambling term for when someone bets it all. "It was no idly chosen phrase," observed the *New York Times* in June 1943. "The Japanese-Americans realize they have perhaps more at stake in this war than the average soldier." At a time when their own government was forcing them to prove their loyalty, the *nisei* troops, the *Times* wrote, "have known from the beginning they would be under close public scrutiny."[21]

The 100th left for North Africa in September 1943 but soon transferred to central Italy, where it faced heavy combat. It eventually became known as the "Purple Heart Battalion" because of its high casualty rate—300 killed, 650 wounded—including Matsunaga, who suffered major injuries to his leg while crossing a mine field.[22]

In the spring of 1944, Inouye and the 442nd shipped out for central Italy and met up with the 100th that June. The two forces went on to see combat in Italy and France, and earned thousands of individual commendations and the nickname the "Army's Most Decorated Unit." Their costliest campaign took place in Bruyères, France, when the 442nd was sent to save a Texas battalion trapped behind German lines. In one week, the unit suffered 800 casualties. The casualty rate was so high over the course of the conflict that more than 15,000 *nisei* troops would serve in the unit.[23]

The harrowing and decorated service of Japanese-American GIs during the war and the fact that they had helped take down the Axis powers helped to transform the old order back home. "Hawaii seemed at a turning point in history, gathering breath as it made ready to push off in directions never before imagined. One could almost feel the ferment of impending change," Inouye later wrote in his memoirs. "The 442nd was very much a part of what was happening." But it was not just because of the accolades and honors they won in combat. "It was more subtle," he said. "We had gone off to war as the sons and grandsons of immigrants, heirs of an alien culture and very much expected—and I suppose, expecting—to resume our unobtrusive minority status if and when we returned. But the army had given us a taste of full citizenship, and an appetite for more of the same. We were the 'can-do' outfit and we were heady with a sense of ourselves."[24]

Internment

Nearly 6,000 miles away from the bloody combat in the French and Italian countryside, Norman Y. Mineta of California, a future 11-term Member of the House, experienced a far different war.

Mineta grew up in San Jose, California, and had just turned 10 when Japan bombed Pearl Harbor in 1941. The same day Inouye and his father ran outside to see black smoke billowing above the naval base in Hawaii, Mineta saw his own immigrant father cry for the first time, unsure of how to process news of the destruction and the uncertain consequences to come.[25]

Despite the attacks having occurred in Hawaii, the bombings had vast and devastating reverberations on the mainland. Inouye, like many Hawaiians of Japanese descent, lived under strict martial law, but he was allowed to stay in Honolulu, help at the Red Cross, finish high school, and enroll in college. For Mineta and the 120,000 Japanese Americans living in California, Oregon, and Washington State, however, the rhythms of everyday life were quickly disrupted by the federal government.

"I don't know what's going to happen to your mother and me," Mineta remembers his dad telling him and his siblings. "But just remember: All of you are U.S. citizens and this is your home. There is nothing anyone can do to take this away from you."[26]

After the Japanese bombing of Pearl Harbor on December 7, 1941, the U.S. government forcibly evacuated Japanese immigrants and their families from their homes. The owner of the Wanto Co. grocery store in Oakland, California, protested the removal by posting this large sign over the closed store that proclaimed "I am an American."

Image courtesy of the Library of Congress

Residents of Japanese ancestry gather on April 6, 1942, at the Wartime Civil Control Administration in San Francisco. Having left their homes, they piled possessions in the street and waited to be sent to internment camps.

Image courtesy of the National Archives and Records Administration

President Franklin D. Roosevelt issued
Executive Order 9066 on February 19,
1942. The order led to the detainment of
persons of Japanese descent, both foreign-
born and American citizens, in internment
camps in six western states and Arkansas.

Image courtesy of the National Archives
and Records Administration

Japanese Americans from California and
Washington State were sent to War Relocation
Authority camps, including Heart Mountain
in northern Wyoming. Here, a man walks
down one of the camp's roads in 1942 as the
mountain rises behind the rows of barracks.

Image courtesy of the National Archives
and Records Administration

On February 19, 1942, however, President Roosevelt issued Executive Order 9066, which authorized military officials in the western states to forcibly remove Japanese immigrants and their families to temporary holding facilities to protect "against espionage and against sabotage."[27] Mineta, dressed in his Cub Scout uniform, and his family were forced to abandon their home, placed on a train, and sent hundreds of miles south to an assembly area at the Santa Anita racetrack outside Los Angeles. The compound was ringed with barbed wire and bright searchlights and staffed with armed military personnel. Mineta and his family stayed in makeshift barracks at the track while the unluckiest evacuees bunked in the horse stables. After four months, the Minetas were placed on another train and sent to an internment camp in Heart Mountain, Wyoming, in a valley just east of Yellowstone National Park. There they found more barbed wire and more machine guns.[28]

The policy of internment became the pivotal event in 20th-century Asian-American history. As thousands of American sailors lay dead or injured, federal officials and many other Americans turned the *issei* (first-generation Japanese immigrants) and *nisei* into enemies of the state. While the U.S. military learned to live with Japanese Hawaiians, whose large numbers helped to ensure the smooth running of the islands' economy, it treated Japanese Americans on the mainland very differently. It suspended Japanese Americans' civil rights wholesale and forced this smaller population from their homes and livelihoods. Internment set back progress in the Japanese-American community for at least a generation.

Within a day or so after the attacks, the FBI arrested 1,500 Japanese immigrants throughout Hawaii and the western states. Armed with lists of "enemy" aliens that had been compiled by the Office of Naval Intelligence and a host of other groups, the FBI swiftly silenced much of the community's leadership. When federal officials turned them over to the Immigration and Naturalization Service (INS), the *issei* were imprisoned in camps scattered across the northern Midwest. By December 8, 1941, the United States had closed its borders to "all persons of Japanese ancestry, whether citizen or alien," and frozen the bank accounts of many Japanese Americans. Within two days, FBI Director J. Edgar Hoover reported that he had "practically all" suspected enemy aliens in custody.[29]

The FBI's efficiency failed to calm the fear rippling across the West Coast and the federal government that Pearl Harbor had been an inside job. "We have thousands of Japanese here," the *Los Angeles Times* reminded its readers. The West Coast was now "a zone of danger" where "alert, keen-eyed civilians" now had to cope with "spies" and "saboteurs." The cartoonist Theodor Geisel, known popularly as Dr. Seuss, stoked that fear when he drew hordes of mainland Japanese armed with explosives. A presidential commission to investigate the Japanese attacks reaffirmed the suspicion that Japanese spies living in America helped plan Pearl Harbor.[30]

In March 1942, FDR issued Executive Order 9102, which created a new agency, the War Relocation Authority (WRA), to carry out the removal.[31] Within weeks, the U.S. Army's Western Defense Command (WDC) had instituted curfews throughout the western states and ordered Japanese Americans to abide by the military's authority.[32]

In the spring of 1942, the government sent all Japanese Americans, regardless of citizenship, living on the West Coast to 17 hastily created assembly centers. Evacuees, whom the WRA called the "incarcerated people," could bring only what they could carry and had little ability to dispose of their other possessions or property. From there they were transported to WRA camps.[33] [**Table 2**]

FDR's first choice to run the WRA was Milton S. Eisenhower, the younger brother of future President Dwight D. Eisenhower. Milton had accepted the job reluctantly, writing in April 1942, "I feel most deeply that when the war is over and we consider calmly this unprecedented migration of 120,000 people, we as Americans are going to regret the unavoidable injustices that may have been done." One western governor cautioned him, "If you bring the Japanese into my state, I promise you they will be hanging from every tree." Milton Eisenhower resigned two and a half months later.[34]

The capacities of the WRA camps varied from 7,500 to 18,000 inmates. Built by the Army Corps of Engineers, the housing blocks were laid out in a grid pattern and surrounded by barbed-wire fences and guard towers. Each block contained 14 barracks made of wood and tar paper, 20 feet by 120 feet, divided into "apartments" of varying sizes. Unmarried adults had the smallest rooms. The largest rooms were reserved for families of six or more individuals. The apartments had no running water, no electricity initially, and no kitchen facilities.[35] One internee recalled finding "a pot-bellied stove, a single electric light hanging from the ceiling, an Army cot for each person and a blanket for the bed."[36] Other buildings housed a central mess hall, communal bathrooms, school, and medical facilities. The bathrooms, one for each gender, had sinks, showers, and toilets, but lacked any measure of privacy.[37]

"We did not know where we were," one internee recalled. "No houses were in sight, no trees or anything green—only scrubby sagebrush and an occasional low cactus, and mostly dry, baked earth."[38]

Most adult internees worked for meager government salaries. They raised crops, cleaned the communal areas, cooked, provided clerical assistance, and transported goods. Unskilled laborers took home $12 per month, skilled

President Franklin D. Roosevelt appointed Milton S. Eisenhower as the first director of the War Relocation Authority in 1942. Eisenhower, however, did not support the policy of removal and internment and resigned less than three months later.

Image courtesy of the Library of Congress

At the Tanforan temporary detention facility in San Bruno, California, a woman looks out through the doorway of a barracks built specifically to house a family. Photographer Dorothea Lange captured this scene at the War Relocation Authority camp in 1942.

Image courtesy of the National Archives and Records Administration

Table 2: The War Relocation Authority Camps, 1942–1946

Name and Location	Opened	Closed
Poston, in Yuma County, AZ	8 May 1942	28 November 1945
Tule Lake, in Modoc County, CA	27 May 1942	20 March 1946
Manzanar, in Inyo County, CA	1 June 1942	21 November 1945
Gila River, in Pinal County, AZ	20 July 1942	10 November 1945
Minidoka, in Jerome County, ID	10 August 1942	28 October 1945
Heart Mountain, in Park County, WY	12 August 1942	10 November 1945
Granada, in Prowers County, CO	27 August 1942	15 October 1945
Topaz, in Millard County, UT	11 September 1942	31 October 1945
Rohwer, in Desha County, AR	18 September 1942	30 November 1945
Jerome, in Drew & Chicot Counties, AR	6 October 1942	30 June 1944

U.S. Army, Western Defense Command, *Final Report: Japanese Evacuation from the West Coast 1942* (Washington, DC: Government Printing Office, 1943): 256; Brian Niiya, ed., *Encyclopedia of Japanese American History* (New York: Checkmark Books, 2001): 174–175, 179, 190, 231–232, 266–267, 276, 337, 350–351, 390, 394–395.

Internees of Tule Lake camp in California plant celery. War Relocation Authority internees raised crops, cleaned, and performed other tasks for small salaries.

Image courtesy of the Library of Congress

Internees wait outside the Japanese American Citizens League in Centerville, California, before boarding buses headed to the Tanforan Assembly Center on May 9, 1942.

Image courtesy of the National Archives and Records Administration

Kibei:

A Japanese term that identifies nisei children who were born in the United States, educated in Japan, and returned to the United States.

workers earned $16, and professionals made $19. The Works Progress Administration also arranged for internees to work outside the camps. In the beginning, inmates helped during local harvests for a day or two. Later, the government authorized longer furloughs in midwestern cities to free up labor for defense work. Other Japanese Americans had indefinite leave to set up permanent resettlements outside the defense area as long as the internee could support him- or herself and reported any changes in address.[39]

On the whole, however, the demand on their time in the camps was light. Handicrafts helped pass the time. Internees built furniture out of spare lumber and set up bonsai gardens outside their apartments. The National Japanese American Student Relocation Council helped college-aged internees enroll in certain midwestern colleges and universities. In other cases, institutions of higher education simply barred the *nisei*.[40]

Parents and elders tried to create as normal an atmosphere as possible for young internees. "In camp we started getting organized because we knew we'd be there for a long time," Mineta later remembered. "There were schools, theaters with candy counters; movies were a dime. So the life was probably typical of what it might have been in any community anywhere, except you had barbed wire, armed guards, the sentries and the search lights."[41]

Such conditions eventually bred generational and cultural transformations. Before the camps, male *issei* heads of family held a significant amount of power. In the camps that status eroded. The Justice Department housed many of the patriarchs in separate facilities, forcing some out of communal activities because of their age or language abilities. Others suffered from depression. As a result, women and children performed much of the labor. They sat on organizations that communicated with the administrators and went out beyond the camps on work-release programs. The WRA banned Japanese-language instruction and outlawed Shinto ceremonies while the camp schools, taught by white teachers, stressed American patriotism. Rather than eating as a family unit, children and teenagers sat with their peer groups in the mess halls. Indeed, most social activities, from movies to sports, separated the young from their elders.[42]

Life in the camps and the stresses of being wrenched away from home also revealed divisions among the internees. Each camp had two extremes. Among the *issei*, who never had the chance to become U.S. citizens, pride in Japan and its culture remained strong. The *kibei*, their U.S.-born children who had been educated in Japan and had come back to the States, shared their parents' resentment that internment destroyed what they had built in America. At the other extreme were the hyperpatriotic *nisei* who belonged to the Japanese American Citizens League (JACL). They had cooperated with federal authorities before the war, identifying people in the Japanese-American community they saw as dangerous. The JACL claimed to speak for all *nisei* and saw relocation as an opportunity to prove their loyalty by cooperating with the program. The League opposed legal efforts to challenge internment and tried to stifle dissent or resistance within the camps.[43]

When the War Department began organizing the 442nd Regimental Combat Team, the WRA tried to identify inmates who would be willing to fight for the same government that imprisoned their families. But in order to qualify for military service, the *nisei* had to prove their loyalty by answering a lengthy questionnaire.[44]

The loyalty survey took questions from the normal draft registration, but, for Japanese immigrants who had been prevented by law from ever becoming U.S. citizens, the survey came as another insult. One question in particular, question 28, asked respondents if they maintained allegiance to the Japanese emperor. For noncitizens, the loyalty questionnaire essentially asked them to become stateless, not Japanese, but not fully American either.[45]

Much of the Japanese-American community had gone to the camps reluctantly, but quietly. For some, it was a way to assist the war effort and prove their loyalty. But over time, opposition within the camps took several forms. Internees criticized the loyalty survey and protested conditions in the camps. Some incidents turned violent. Eventually, the internees challenged the very legality of internment. Perhaps predictably, relatively few of them volunteered for military service. Unlike the high volunteer rates of Japanese Hawaiians who were not subject to imprisonment, by early 1944, only 1,200 mainland *nisei* had signed up.[46]

The WRA, under its wartime head Dillon Myer, struggled with meager resources to make the camps tolerable. The more enlightened administrations, such as the one running the Minidoka camp, worked with the internees to improve living conditions. Other camp officials saw their responsibilities as protecting the country from potential danger. Unsurprisingly, where camps treated inmates with contempt, resistance to internment grew. At Wyoming's Heart Mountain camp, inmates formed the Fair Play Committee and refused to participate in the draft until the government recognized *nisei* citizenship. Most were tried, convicted, and sentenced to prison until President Harry S. Truman issued a mass pardon for *nisei* draft objectors in December 1947. Though Heart Mountain was located far outside the military evacuation zone, camp administrators clamped down on dissent, going so far as to ask the U.S. Office of Alien Property Custodian to shut down the *Rocky Shimpo*, a Japanese-American newspaper published by a small *nisei* community in Denver, Colorado, hundreds of miles away.[47]

Violent outbreaks recurred at a handful of camps. In December 1942, at the Manzanar War Relocation Center, two internees were killed and another 10 were wounded when military police fired tear gas and live ammunition into a crowd of internees who had gathered to protest conditions in the camp. Administrators deported protest leaders to a Justice Department facility and moved 65 internees to another camp as the army tightened security. In April 1943, at the Topaz War Relocation Center, an elderly internee, James Hatsuki Wakasa, was shot to death by a watchtower sentry who claimed that Wakasa had tried to crawl through the fence. Though an initial army inquiry indicated a cover-up (Wakasa had been shot in the chest), a court-martial acquitted the sentry of murder. Later that year, at the Tule Lake Segregation Center, the army declared martial law after internees protested deadly working conditions and the WRA's decision to pay outside farm laborers higher wages than internees. Inmates went on a brief hunger strike as 300 other prisoners were sent to a separate Justice Department facility. The protest slowly dwindled away.[48]

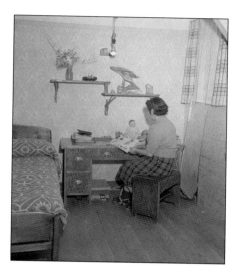

A member of the Nishi family sits in a barrack, furnished with scrap materials and items purchased by mail order, at Minidoka Camp in Idaho in 1942. Minidoka Camp administration officials worked with internees to improve living conditions.

Image courtesy of the National Archives and Records Administration

A *nisei* community in Denver, Colorado, began publishing the *Rocky Shimpo* newspaper during World War II. Hundreds of miles away, administrators of the Heart Mountain relocation camp asked the U.S. Office of Alien Property Custodian to shut down the newspaper in a bid to silence dissent.

Image courtesy of the Library of Congress

Gordon Hirabayashi's draft card lists his name, address, birthplace, and other personal details. "I am a conscientious objector," Hirabayashi wrote neatly in blue ink in the left margin.

Image courtesy of the National Archives and Records Administration

Because many of the internees were American citizens, legal challenges to internment soon appeared before federal judges, and four cases made it to the U.S. Supreme Court.[49] The Supreme Court decided the first two cases, *Hirabayashi v. United States* and *Yasui v. United States*, in June 1943 (Gordon Hirabayashi of Seattle, Washington, and Minoru Yasui of Portland, Oregon, had separately challenged the WDC curfew). But the Justices unanimously sided with the government and stated that the curfew order fell within the "power to wage war successfully," even if that meant singling out a group of people because of their ancestry.[50] One Justice initially dissented and compared the experience of Japanese Americans to Jews in Europe under Nazi Germany, but his opinion was later edited to support the court's consensus that the internment program went "to the very brink" of constitutional authority.[51]

The Supreme Court also ruled on additional cases in late 1944, long after the perceived threat of a Japanese military invasion had passed. In *Korematsu v. United States*, Fred Korematsu of San Francisco challenged the constitutionality of the exclusion and detention orders. Writing the *Korematsu* opinion for the Court (the final tally was a 6 to 3 majority), Justice Hugo Black argued that, because it was impossible to distinguish between loyal and disloyal Japanese Americans, the military had cause to imprison "all citizens of Japanese ancestry." As before, "military urgency" outweighed questions of race and ethnicity in his reasoning. Justices Owen Roberts, Frank Murphy, and Robert Jackson forcefully dissented. Murphy, who questioned the lack of due process, also sneered at the military's professed urgency and noted it took months to implement the full policy. The entire exclusion program, he argued, was a "legalization of racism." For Justice Jackson, *Korematsu* set a risky precedent and validated "the principle of racial discrimination in criminal procedure and of transplanting American citizens."[52]

In *Ex parte Endo*, also decided in December 1944, Mitsuye Endo of Sacramento, California, a *nisei*, applied for a writ of habeas corpus from detention at Tule Lake. In this instance, a unanimous court granted Endo her

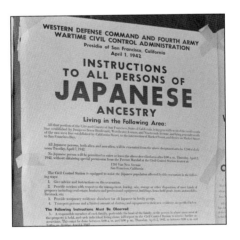

The Western Defense Command posted exclusion orders at First and Front Streets in San Francisco to notify passersby about the evacuation of all persons of Japanese ancestry. "All Japanese persons, both alien and non-alien, will be evacuated … by 12:00 o'clock noon Tuesday, April 7, 1942."

Image courtesy of the National Archives and Records Administration

freedom. Justices Roberts and Murphy found the court's majority opinion too facile, and each filed a concurrence denying the constitutionality of internment. "For the Government to suggest under these circumstances," Murphy concluded, "that the presence of Japanese blood in a loyal American citizen might be enough to warrant her exclusion from a place where she would otherwise have a right to go is a position I cannot sanction."[53]

By the fall of 1944, the Roosevelt administration and the WRA had begun phasing out the camp system and freeing prisoners it deemed "loyal," that is, those who had answered affirmatively to the loyalty questionnaire. When America declared victory over Japan in August 1945, however, the camps still held 44,000 detainees.[54]

The War's Mixed Legacy

Although the war seemed to disproportionately affect Japanese immigrants and their American-born children, it had equally far-reaching effects on other Asian and Pacific Islander Americans. As it did for women and African Americans, the war encouraged Asian immigrants of many nationalities to fill new roles, all the while gaining the moral authority to challenge discrimination on the home front.

But the war's effects were far from uniformly positive. It was a mixed legacy that shaped personal lives and political aspirations for decades. It affected each Asian community in different and unique ways.

Japan's surprise attacks on the United States at Pearl Harbor, for instance, swiftly transformed China and India into U.S. allies, and the domestic atmosphere for immigrants from these countries improved. For Pacific Islanders who initially lived under American protection in the Philippines and Guam, however, the war brought years of brutal Japanese occupation with bloody and devastating consequences. Though no voting APA Representatives served in Congress at the time (nor would they for more than a decade after the war), these upheavals shaped the experiences of the group of APAs who came to Congress in the post-war decades.

IMMIGRANTS AND REFUGEES

For much of the 1930s, Americans had taken on an increasingly positive view of China. Henry Luce's *Time* and *Life* magazines published full-page charts to "educate" Americans on how to distinguish Chinese friends from "Jap" enemies. And in 1942, a Gallup poll listed the Chinese as "hardworking, honest, brave, religious, intelligent, and practical" and the Japanese as "treacherous, sly, cruel, and warlike."[55] The gradual shift away from the 19th century's virulent anti-Chinese policies quickened after Pearl Harbor, as lawmakers redirected their efforts toward Japan. "All at once we discovered the saintly qualities of the Chinese people," said Missouri Representative William Elmer in 1943. "If it had not been for December 7th, I do not know if we would have ever found out how good they were."[56]

The armed forces and defense industries began hiring Chinese Americans, and young Chinese men eagerly volunteered or participated in the military draft. Meanwhile, the number of Chinese Americans in professional and technical jobs

World War II left a mixed legacy for Asian Pacific Americans. As anti-Japanese sentiment rose, this Filipino grocer used his ethnic heritage as an advertisement for his business in San Lorenzo, California, in 1942. The Philippines was a U.S. territory at the time.

Image courtesy of the National Archives and Records Administration

Seventy-eighth Congress of the United States of America;

At the First Session

Begun and held at the City of Washington on Wednesday, the sixth day of January, one thousand nine hundred and forty-three

AN ACT

To repeal the Chinese Exclusion Acts, to establish quotas, and for other purposes.

Be it enacted by the Senate and House of Representatives of the United States of America in Congress assembled, That the following Acts or parts of Acts relating to the exclusion or deportation of persons of the Chinese race are hereby repealed: May 6, 1882 (22 Stat. L. 58); July 5, 1884 (23 Stat. L. 115); September 13, 1888 (25 Stat. L. 476); October 1, 1888 (25 Stat. L. 504); May 5, 1892 (27 Stat. L. 25); November 3, 1893 (28 Stat. L. 7); that portion of section 1 of the Act of July 7, 1898 (30 Stat. L. 750, 751), which reads as follows: "There shall be no further immigration of Chinese into the Hawaiian Islands except upon such conditions as are now or may hereafter be allowed by the laws of the United States; and no Chinese, by reason of anything herein contained, shall be allowed to enter the United States from the Hawaiian Islands."; section 101 of the Act of April 30, 1900 (31 Stat. L. 141, 161); those portions of section 1 of the Act of June 6, 1900 (31 Stat. L. 588, 611), which read as follows: "And nothing in section four of the Act of August fifth, eighteen hundred and eighty-two (Twenty-second Statutes at Large, page two hundred and twenty-five), shall be construed to prevent the Secretary of the

In 1943 Congress repealed the Chinese Exclusion Act to buttress America's wartime alliance with China. But long-standing quotas still kept Asian immigration at a minimum for another two decades.

Image courtesy of the National Archives and Records Administration

increased threefold between 1940 and 1950, with a concentration on engineers and technicians. Chinese-American women, like many women in the United States during the war, also experienced booming rates of employment.[57]

In 1943 nine bills were introduced in Congress to repeal the Chinese Exclusion Act, which was first passed in 1882. FDR urged legislators to overturn the ban to further the war effort. The repeal law erased all six versions of the exclusionary acts and brought Chinese immigration under the quota system in a largely symbolic gesture (China's annual quota was only about 100 people). Importantly, it also opened up the naturalization process to Chinese Americans who were not native-born.[58]

Legislation that granted asylum to war refugees and that also incrementally overturned long-standing immigration policies had a profound impact on APAs. Until the 1990s, only a handful of Asian and Pacific Americans served in Congress, far too few to drive the country's legislative agenda, which more often responded to the exigencies of the Cold War and America's decades-long rivalry with the Soviet Union. But changes culminating in the Immigration and Nationality Act of 1965 had far-reaching consequences for a variety of Asian communities in America as well as the diversity of Asian-American representation in Congress.

Starting in the 1940s, the Cold War began influencing immigration legislation in ways large and small. The Displaced Persons Act of 1948, for instance, started as an effort to assist European war refugees and quickly turned into a way to help Chinese immigrants who became stuck in America after China's communist revolution in 1949. With President Harry S. Truman's State Department taking the lead, federal officials stretched the application of the law and allowed Chinese immigrants to remain in the country rather than face persecution if they were required to return home.[59]

As the anxieties of the Cold War began dictating foreign policy, U.S. politicians saw an opportunity to combat communism abroad by passing more welcoming immigration policies at home. The sterling war record of *nisei* soldiers had helped erase fears about their loyalty and that of their parents. And during the 81st Congress (1949–1951), Minnesota Representative Walter Judd introduced a bill incorporating Asian immigrants into the national origins quota system and opening naturalized citizenship opportunities to all permanent Asian residents in the United States.[60] Judd's measure would also have created something called the Asia-Pacific Triangle, an area of the globe from which immigration to the United States would, with few exceptions, be limited to 100 annual visas per country. It also prohibited Asian immigrants from entering the United States via other Western Hemisphere nations.[61]

A version of Judd's bill eventually passed both the House and Senate, but the conference committee added a clause aimed at likely communist sympathizers and those who belonged to or would later join subversive organizations. Because of that change, President Truman vetoed the bill and called the new section "vague and ill-defined."[62]

Dismayed by the triumph of the communist regime in China, Congress acted in the early 1950s to do more than simply slip Asian refugees into legislative solutions intended for Europeans. In 1953 Congress for the first time passed legislation that included a section explicitly providing for Asian expatriates. The Refugee Relief Act was an umbrella bill that circumvented the national origins quota system and provided entry for more than 200,000 refugees who had been displaced by communist insurgencies around the world. Representative Judd, who had served as a medical missionary in China, took the lead in adding visa provisions for Chinese refugees and for people of Asian descent. Subsequent amendments increased the number of Chinese visas and expanded the program to Africa and the Middle East.[63]

At the height of America's communist paranoia in the 1950s, legislative efforts to thwart suspected communist sleeper cells cast unsettling domestic shadows for Asian Americans, especially as Congress considered the Internal Security Act of 1950. Led by the Senate Judiciary Committee and the House Un-American Activities Committee (HUAC) and sparked in large part by America's war with communists in North Korea, Congress severely circumscribed the movement of suspected communists living in the United States. In a flashback to 1941, Congress built part of the 1950 Internal Security Act on the framework of Japanese-American internment, which empowered the federal government to detain communists in emergency situations.[64]

Later in the decade, Chinese immigrants again were caught up in Cold War concerns. Throughout much of the 1950s, the FBI considered Chinese immigrants a major security threat primarily because it feared they were using forged immigration documents purchased on the black market in Communist China. In an effort to identify communist agents among Chinese immigrants, the INS initiated a confession program in which any Chinese immigrant entering the United States with fraudulent papers could still apply for a visa so long as they were related to a U.S. citizen or permanent resident. In return, the immigrant would have to identify everyone who had helped him or her enter the country illegally. Unsurprisingly, the program produced few confessions.[65]

The procedure, however, showed enough promise that the Immigration Act Amendments of 1957 codified the confession program into law. When he signed the legislation, President Eisenhower, who had urged Congress to show leniency to immigrants who had lied in order to escape the Iron Curtain, admitted ruefully that the bill could have been much better.[66] The confession program largely escaped controversy during its rapid passage, but few Chinese Americans ever participated.[67]

Over the next decade, the refugee crisis continued unabated and, by 1960, had become one of the United Nations' signature issues. Congress, for the most part, kept its attention on the situation in Europe. During debate over the Fair Share refugee bill, for instance, Hawaii Senator Hiram L. Fong introduced an amendment that added visas for 4,500 Chinese refugees, which, he said, would hopefully overturn the common misconception that Asians were "not as good as the people of Europe." Although the Senate added the amendment, the House deleted it from the final version.[68]

Direct legislative solutions were not the only option for Asian asylum seekers. At the time, the U.S. Attorney General's parole power enabled him to temporarily open America's borders in emergency situations. Congress could then pass legislation to allow these refugees to apply for permanent residency

Hiram L. Fong was elected to the U.S. Senate in 1959 following the admission of Hawaii as a state.

Image courtesy of the U.S. Senate Historical Office

status. In 1962, for instance, President John F. Kennedy (JFK) used his parole authority to admit 15,000 Chinese refugees who had settled in temporary camps in Hong Kong.[69]

During World War II, many U.S. soldiers and sailors serving overseas married locals and fathered children, but America's stringent immigration laws prevented most from bringing their new families home after the war. To deal with these wartime complications, Congress passed a series of laws allowing foreign spouses and children of armed services personnel to enter the United States under a nonquota basis. The War Brides Act in 1945, officially known as the Alien Spouses of Members of the Armed Forces Act, applied only to the spouses of white and black soldiers. Less than a year later Congress passed legislation allowing the fiancées of U.S. personnel to bypass the quota system. Chinese war brides, many of whom had married U.S. soldiers of Chinese descent, won this right soon after.[70] The number of Asian war brides, in part, helped to break down some of the general hostility toward Asian immigration.[71]

Overturning Exclusion, Limiting Immigration

The war had far-reaching consequences for other Asian communities that wanted access to America's naturalization process as well. When Dalip Saund first came to the United States from northern India in 1919, he had planned to stay for only a few years, pursue his education, and return home. The immigration official at Ellis Island who stamped his passport shook his hand and told him, "You are now a free man in a free country," but that turned out to be only partly true. Saund moved to California, where anti-Asian policies had created an entire community of second-class citizens. At the University of California, Saund, who later revealed that he had been "cruelly discriminated against many a time because of the place of my birth," socialized only with other Indian immigrants. "Prejudice against Asiatic people in California was very intense in the early twenties and I felt keen discrimination in many ways. Outside of the university atmosphere," he wrote in his memoirs, "it was made quite evident that people from Asia—Japanese, Chinese, and Hindus—were not wanted."[72] Among other policies, the state's alien land laws prevented Saund and other Asian immigrants, including Norman Mineta's parents, from owning land. When Saund moved to Southern California to begin farming, a friend of Saund's in Los Angeles put the leases in his own name to circumvent the land laws.[73]

By midcentury, Saund had carved out what he considered to be a good life in the States. "I was making America my home," he later wrote. He "had married an American girl," and together they had three children. He had a successful farming business and had an active social life. But he could not escape the reality that state and federal laws excluded him from political engagement. "I was dedicated to what is called the American way of life and yet when I looked in front of me I saw that the bars of citizenship were shut tight against me."[74]

In response, Saund helped create the India Association of America in the early 1940s, a group that worked toward winning naturalization rights and, in effect, overturning the alien land laws. The association raised both money and awareness, and it was not long before he received help from national lawmakers.[75] Both Presidents FDR and Truman had recommended extending

Dalip Singh (Judge) Saund came to the United States from India in 1919. Spurred to political engagement by anti-Asian discrimination, he became the first voting Member of Asian descent in the United States Congress in 1957.

Image courtesy of the Library of Congress

Asian Indians the opportunity to become naturalized citizens and including them in the national origins quota system. To that end, Representative Emanuel Celler of New York introduced H.R. 3517 on June 20, 1945. Coming just weeks after V-E Day, it garnered widespread bipartisan support as a way to counter Japan's anti-American propaganda.[76] The Senate later added a clause granting immigration and naturalization rights to people from the Philippines, which was about to gain its independence from the United States. The bill became law on July 2, 1946.[77]

Saund became a U.S. citizen on December 16, 1949. A little more than seven years later, he took the oath of office as the first full-fledged voting Member of Asian descent in the history of the U.S. Congress.

It was around midcentury that public opinion on alien land laws also started to shift, and it was not long before the federal courts began reversing their earlier decisions. On April 17, 1952, in *Sei Fujii v. California*, the California supreme court declared the land laws unconstitutional and added that they violated the United Nations Charter. California voters finally erased the policy in a public referendum in November 1956. Washington State removed the last alien land law on the West Coast 10 years later.[78]

By the early 1950s, attitudes toward the Japanese had also undergone a sweeping transformation. Communist regimes in North Korea and China quickly replaced the conquered Japanese as the main U.S. adversary in the Pacific. Instead, U.S.-occupied Japan became a significant ally in the Cold War and an important forward position for U.S. Armed Forces. Under these circumstances, the last vestige of Asian exclusion in U.S. immigration law finally fell: the inability of the *issei* to become naturalized citizens.

When the 82nd Congress (1951–1953) began in January 1951, the two chairmen of Congress's immigration subcommittees laid out a comprehensive overhaul. Pennsylvania Representative Francis E. Walter and Nevada Senator Patrick (Pat) McCarran, both of whom were fervent anti-communists and isolationists, drafted H.R. 5678, an omnibus immigration bill that built on the Immigration Act of 1924. Hoping to make immigration law a part of the country's Cold War arsenal, they added new features to more easily exclude and deport immigrants they considered to be subversive.[79]

Building on Walter Judd's 1949 immigration bill, Senator McCarran embedded the Asia-Pacific Triangle provision into the new bill. The triangle clause set a limit of 100 visas per country, but enabled all Asian immigrants to apply for naturalization. Judd's triangle provision became something of a sideshow to the larger congressional debate on how best to fight communism. But, crucially, the JACL, the major *nisei* civic association in the country, backed the citizenship provision. Their lobbyists in Washington, Etsu and Mike Masaoka, made their way through the congressional office buildings and argued that McCarran–Walter would honor the parents of those *nisei* soldiers who fought and died for the country in Europe.[80]

Although the bill opened up citizenship to thousands of Japanese immigrants, the final version's limited quotas and anti-communism provisions troubled President Truman, who vetoed it on June 25, 1952. The next day, however, the House overrode the veto, 278 to 112. The Senate followed suit on June 27, 57 to 26, and enacted the McCarran–Walter Immigration and Nationality Act into law.[81]

Senator Patrick McCarran of Nevada was a fervent isolationist, and the namesake of the McCarran–Walter Immigration and Nationality Act of 1952, which excluded and deported immigrants deemed subversive.

Image courtesy of the Library of Congress

Representative Daniel K. Inouye of Hawaii meets with President John F. Kennedy in the Oval Office on April 10, 1962. Inouye lost his right arm during his World War II service with the 442nd Regimental Combat Team.

Photograph by Robert Knudsen; image courtesy of the John F. Kennedy Presidential Library/National Archives and Records Administration

In 1965 Congress passed the Immigration and Nationality Act, making it simpler for immigrants to come to America. The law encouraged Asian immigration and eliminated national quotas. In the years that followed, immigrants from China, India, Japan, and the Philippines reshaped America's demographics.

Image courtesy of the National Archives and Records Administration

Since 1965

McCarran–Walter failed as a comprehensive solution to U.S. immigration policy largely because of its reliance on the controversial national origins quota system developed in the 1920s.[82]

Moreover, international conflicts and changing foreign policies also continued to influence the flow of people from abroad. America's failure to contain communist expansion in Southeast Asia created a tide of political refugees that the United States felt obligated to protect, many of whom had been U.S. allies in the defense of South Vietnam, Laos, and Cambodia. Moreover, the thaw in U.S. relations with the People's Republic of China during the 1970s encouraged more open and welcoming policies.

In 1965 Congress passed the Immigration and Nationality Act, also known as the Hart–Celler Act, making it simpler for immigrants to come to America. It unleashed a host of unintended consequences—chief among them, it opened the doors to large migrations from Asian nations. As such, it serves as a watershed moment in this story.

In the summer of 1963, President Kennedy proposed legislation to phase out the national origins quota system, eliminate the Asia-Pacific Triangle, and institute new entry criteria based on an immigrant's career path and family status. He sent these recommendations to Congress along with requests for the creation of a new advisory immigration board and emergency refugee authority.[83] In the aftermath of JFK's assassination, President Lyndon B. Johnson (LBJ) renewed the campaign for immigration reform.[84]

As Congress took up reform in 1964, both the House and Senate immigration subcommittees heard testimony against the quotas. Secretary of

Eighty-ninth Congress of the United States of America

AT THE FIRST SESSION

Begun and held at the City of Washington on Monday, the fourth day of January, one thousand nine hundred and sixty-five

An Act

To amend the Immigration and Nationality Act, and for other purposes.

Be it enacted by the Senate and House of Representatives of the United States of America in Congress assembled, That section 201 of the Immigration and Nationality Act (66 Stat. 175; 8 U.S.C. 1151) be amended to read as follows:

"SEC. 201. (a) Exclusive of special immigrants defined in section 101(a)(27), and of the immediate relatives of United States citizens specified in subsection (b) of this section, the number of aliens who may be issued immigrant visas or who may otherwise acquire the status of an alien lawfully admitted to the United States for permanent residence, or who may, pursuant to section 203(a)(7) enter conditionally, (i) shall not in any of the first three quarters of any fiscal year exceed a total of 45,000 and (ii) shall not in any fiscal year exceed a total of 170,000.

"(b) The 'immediate relatives' referred to in subsection (a) of this section shall mean the children, spouses, and parents of a citizen of the United States: *Provided,* That in the case of parents, such citizen must be at least twenty-one years of age. The immediate relatives specified in this subsection who are otherwise qualified for admission as immigrants shall be admitted as such, without regard to the numerical limitations in this Act.

"(c) During the period from July 1, 1965, through June 30, 1968,

President Lyndon B. Johnson signs the Immigration and Nationality Act of 1965 on Liberty Island in New York City. The witnesses at the signing include Senator Daniel K. Inouye of Hawaii.

Photograph by Yoichi Okamoto; image courtesy of the Lyndon B. Johnson Presidential Library/National Archives and Records Administration

State Dean Rusk observed that the quota system discriminated against whole groups of people and provided communist countries with a weapon in Cold War propaganda. Attorney General Robert F. Kennedy called the immigration process "a standing affront." "Everywhere else in our national life, we have eliminated discrimination based on national origins," he said. "Yet, this system is still the foundation of our immigration law."[85]

Policy experts did not forecast a huge rise in immigration if national origins quotas were eliminated: 94,000 Asian immigrants could be expected during the first five years (19,000 per year). At that rate, Asian emigration would trend slightly higher than emigration from Europe. The Attorney General expected another 5,000 total would come after removing the Asia-Pacific Triangle.[86]

The bill stalled in the House that year, but LBJ's sweeping victory in the 1964 presidential elections created large Democratic majorities on Capitol Hill and set the stage for another attempt at immigration reform in the 89th Congress (1965–1967). The President urged Congress to scrap the national origins quota system and called it "incompatible with our basic American tradition." Instead, reform proponents sought to replace it with a system that attracted skilled immigrants and those with family already in the States. The same day Johnson submitted his message, companion immigration bills were introduced in the House by Judiciary Chairman Celler and in the Senate by Philip Hart of Michigan.[87]

After the Judiciary Committee cleared Celler's bill, the House spent very little time debating the possible impact on APA immigration. But just before the House voted on the bill, Celler addressed the issue. "With the end of discrimination due to place of birth, there will be shifts in countries other than those of northern and western Europe," the chairman observed. "Immigrants from Asia and Africa will have to compete and qualify in order to get in, quantitatively and qualitatively, which, itself will hold the numbers down." Celler predicted that immigration from Asia would remain low because few people would be able to take advantage of the provision allowing families to reunify in the States.[88] The measure passed, 318 to 25.[89]

The bill's path through the Senate followed a similar course. Despite some lobbying resistance from the JACL, which argued that the decision to prioritize family relations would limit Asian immigration, the Senate passed it in September 1964.[90] Once again the general debate paid little attention to possible consequences other than generalized fears that America was "throwing the doors open and equally inviting people from the Orient, from the islands of the Pacific, from the subcontinent of Asia, from the Near East, from all of Africa, all of Europe, and all of the Western Hemisphere on exactly the same basis," according to Democrat Spessard Holland of Florida.[91]

The Immigration and Nationality Act of 1965 eliminated the national origins quota system, set a ceiling of 290,000 annual visas (120,000 from the Western Hemisphere; 170,000 from the Eastern Hemisphere), and limited yearly emigration from any one country to 20,000. Crucially, it lifted the cap on entries for family reunification. In celebration, Johnson held the signing ceremony outdoors on October 3, 1965, at the foot of the Statue of Liberty.[92]

The Hart–Celler immigration bill quickly became a classic case of unanticipated consequences. Much of the debate had been over allowing more southern and eastern Europeans into the country and over the first entrance caps placed on emigration from the Western Hemisphere. Not even the JACL predicted the large impact the law's changes would have in encouraging Asian immigration.

Total immigration grew to more than 450,000 annual entries, with only one in five coming from Europe. Much of the increase in Asian migration to the United States came through the family reunification clause, leading some Chinese Americans to call Hart–Celler the "Brothers and Sisters Act." Ultimately, immigration officials simply miscalculated how few people it took to create an extensive network of relatives.[93] The bill's provision opening visas for skilled and professional workers also drove a substantial part of the new immigration.[94] Although the new law affected each community in America differently, the rising immigration rates from China, India, Japan, and the Philippines, in particular, helped reshape America's social landscape.

EXPANDING REPRESENTATION: PACIFIC TERRITORIES

Efforts to define the relationship between the United States and its overseas territories that had occupied so much of the story before World War II continued after the conflict, though on a new trajectory. In 1946 the United States followed through on a decades-long promise to give the Philippines complete independence. Hawaii, due in part to its Delegates' strong campaigns for statehood, was little more than a decade away from incorporation into the Union as the 50th state in 1959.

But territorial questions spread beyond these longtime bulwarks of America's presence in the Pacific. In fact, America's Pacific empire at the opening of the 20th century also included the 210-square-mile island of Guam and the multiple islands that make up American Samoa. Placed under American military control, both Guam and American Samoa were vital fueling stations in strategic Pacific locations.

After the United Nations issued a decolonization mandate in 1945, the United States gradually handed over the island governments to the people. In 1947 the Truman administration approved the trusteeship agreement for the Trust Territory of the Pacific Islands that required the United States to "make ample provision for the political, economic, social, and educational development" of certain Pacific territories (Northern Mariana, Caroline, and Marshall Islands) after the war. Nearly a year later, Congress established the Joint Committee on the Trust Territories of the Pacific to oversee the mandate.[95]

Yet, like much of American policy toward the territories, self-determination came piecemeal. The U.S. military maintained a strategic interest in Guam throughout the Cold War, and Guamanians became U.S. citizens in 1950. American Samoa, on the other hand, lost much of its importance as a refueling station as technology improved the range of America's warships. Samoans were also wary of U.S. citizenship and fiercely protected their cultural and political systems.

Regardless of their differences, for Pacific Islanders living under the U.S. flag, gaining access to America's lawmaking process proved to be especially difficult.

American Samoa and Guam to World War II

The United States' relationship with Samoa began out of military necessity. In 1872 the United States cut a deal to build a coaling station at Pago Pago, a vital deepwater harbor, in return for helping Samoa negotiate international disputes. Following the U.S. victory in the Spanish-American War, the Convention of 1900 permanently divided Samoa between Germany and the United States.[96] Guam, which had been captured by the USS *Charleston* during the war, fell within America's jurisdiction.

Congress placed Guam and American Samoa under the control of a rotating cast of U.S. military officers, but the experiences of the two territories differed substantially. In 1900 and again in 1904, American Samoa's political leaders—

UNITED STATES NAVAL STATION, TUTUILA.

THE PROMULGATION OF LAWS REGULATION 1900.

COMMANDER. B. F. TILLEY, U. S. N., COMMANDANT.

No. 1.   PAGOPAGO.   APRIL 24, 1900.

Regulation for the Promulgation of Laws for Tutuila and Manu'a.

1.—The posting of any Law, Regulation, Ordinance, or Notice on the Commandant's Office at Pagopago or at any other public place appointed by the Commandant shall be held a sufficient publication of said Law, Regulation, Ordinance, or Notice.
2.—This Regulation shall take effect upon the date of publication.
3.—This Regulation may be cited as "The promulgation of Laws Regulation, 1900."
Published and Exhibited in the Public Office of the Commandant this 24th day of April, in the year One thousand nine hundred.

B. F. TILLEY, U.S.N.,
COMMANDANT OF THE UNITED STATES NAVAL STATION, TUTUILA.

This Promulgation of Laws Regulation from 1900 details the issuance of laws and ordinances governing the islands of Tutuila and Manu'a in American Samoa. Following the U.S. victory in the Spanish-American War, the Convention of 1900 permanently divided Samoa between Germany and the United States, and the U.S. Navy was responsible for the administration of American Samoa until 1951.

Image courtesy of the National Archives and Records Administration

As governor of Guam, U.S. Navy Captain Roy Smith formed the Guam congress in 1917.

Image courtesy of the Library of Congress

the heads of extended families in Samoan society—agreed to turn over the islands to the United States in the "Instrument of Cession." Their agreement both legitimized American annexation and solidified the *matais* (familial chiefs) as the primary source of local power.[97]

In Guam, on the other hand, island leaders frequently depended on the individual governors to cede local control. In 1917 the governor of Guam, U.S. Navy Captain Roy Smith, formed the Guam congress, an advisory body of Chamorros (Guamanian natives) and statesiders appointed entirely by Smith. Fourteen years later, the then governor, U.S. Navy Captain Willis Bradley, created the second Guam congress, an elected, bicameral legislative body with the same advisory mandate.[98]

On the mainland, however, there was little federal impulse in either the U.S. Navy or the State Department to provide self-determination for either territory.[99]

Post–World War II Guam

In December 1941, Japanese forces invaded Guam, beginning a brutal, three-year occupation. Chamorros were often beaten or executed for small offenses.[100] Delegate Ben Garrido Blaz, who worked in the island's labor camps during the war, recalled having friends simply disappear while he suffered from "the hunger and deprivation of concentration camps."[101] American forces recaptured the island in the summer of 1944, but the effects lingered for the next 50 years. Antonio Borja Won Pat, Guam's first Delegate to Congress, said his experience during World War II largely shaped his congressional career. He said his strong stance as a defense hawk on the House Armed Services Committee came from his "first-hand [experience with] the enslaving hands of a military conqueror."[102]

In large part, the end of the conflict changed U.S. attitudes toward the islands. Guam, for instance, remained under naval rule, but the Navy granted the territorial government "interim" legislative powers in 1947. Won Pat, then the president of the local chamber of commerce, applauded the decision, but told the *Chicago Tribune* in November 1946 that Guam needed "a self-supporting economy before it can be ready for American citizenship."[103]

The war also significantly changed the island. The U.S. military occupied two-thirds of Guam's land, and the island's white population had increased 420 percent during the 1940s. Though still a minority, whites filled nearly half the high-paying jobs, which set up a clash between Guamanians and federal administrators.[104] By 1949, Won Pat had effectively changed his mind about naval control when, as speaker of the territorial assembly, he led a walkout protesting an ongoing power struggle with the then governor, Rear Admiral Charles Pownall.[105]

In September 1949, President Truman transferred control over Guam from the U.S. Navy to the Department of the Interior, and a few months later, on February 19, 1950, Congressman James Peterson of Florida introduced H.R. 7273 that provided for the Guam Organic Act. The bill moved smoothly through Congress and passed with little debate before Truman signed it into law in August. The legislation granted Guamanians citizenship and established a unicameral legislature and an independent judiciary. The governor, appointed by the Interior Department, was given veto power. Guamanians paid federal

U.S. Naval and Marine Corps officers salute as the U.S. flag is raised during the liberation of Guam in 1944.

Image courtesy of the National Archives and Records Administration

income taxes, but the territorial government retained the funds to use at home. In 1968 Guam began directly electing its own governor and lieutenant governor.[106]

Post-war American Samoa and Self-Determination

Unlike Guam, American Samoa stayed under U.S. control for the duration of the Second World War. On June 29, 1951, the Truman administration transferred American Samoa from the U.S. Navy to the Department of the Interior via Executive Order 10264. Though Congress considered conferring citizenship on American Samoans as early as 1933, there was no immediate push for an organic act like that in Guam.[107]

Samoans were protective of their family- and community-based political system and wary of America's involvement. "We're very tribal about our ways," Delegate Eni F. H. Faleomavaega once put it rather succinctly. To date, American Samoans are not U.S. citizens. They are the only people still designated U.S. nationals, a status defined by the Nationality Act of 1940 as those who are not citizens under the U.S. Constitution, but who "owe permanent allegiance to the United States." "I guess our forefathers were very hesitant about getting citizenship, for fear that their lands or their culture will be taken away once they become U.S. citizens," Faleomavaega conjectured.[108]

In 1954, at the behest of the Interior Department, federal officials and island leaders organized a constitutional committee to outline a new civil government in American Samoa. They unveiled a draft constitution six years later, and 68 delegates selected by village and district councils approved the document unanimously.[109]

The Samoan constitution essentially codified the existing political structure: a governor who held full veto power appointed by the Interior Department and a bicameral *fono* (territorial congress). One chamber was made up of the traditional *matais*. Elected representatives from geographical districts comprised the other chamber.[110] Later revisions in 1969 limited the governor's power and expanded the number of *matais* in the *fono*. Samoans began electing their governor and lieutenant governor in 1977.[111]

Congressional Representation

Guam began requesting nonvoting representation in the U.S. Congress as early as 1954, but after 14 years of inaction on the Hill, the territorial legislature created an office to lobby Congress on its behalf. It was an elected position first held by Won Pat, but since it wasn't federally sponsored, it functioned more like a private lobbying firm than a legislative office.[112]

On June 1, 1971, Phillip Burton of California, who served on the House Interior and Insular Affairs Committee, introduced H.R. 8787, which provided for Delegates to Congress representing Guam and the U.S. Virgin Islands. The bill, he said, kept "with the modern trend of democratic governments" in the territories. He believed the needs of the two territories went beyond the jurisdiction of his single committee and with Delegates of their own the territories would have a direct line to Congress. Following a brief debate, the bill granted the new Delegates floor and committee privileges on par with those of the statutory representatives from the District of Columbia and Puerto Rico.[113]

President Harry S. Truman signs the Guam Organic Act of 1950. From left to right: Wyoming Senator Joseph C. O'Mahoney, Carlos Taitano, Harold Seidman, Francis Matthews, New Mexico Senator Clinton P. Anderson, Secretary of the Interior Oscar Chapman, and Nebraska Senator Hugh Butler.

Image courtesy of the Harry S. Truman Library/ National Archives and Records Administration

U.S. Navy scouting pilots discuss plans for patrol flights in the South Pacific during the early 1940s.

Image courtesy of the National Archives and Records Administration

Patsy Takemoto Mink of Hawaii (seated first from right in the second row) and Phillip Burton of California (seated fourth from right in the second row) served on the House Committee on Interior and Insular Affairs. Pictured here with committee staff, Burton introduced legislation to grant Guam and the U.S. Virgin Islands Delegates in the U.S. Congress.

Collection of the U.S. House of Representatives

The Senate passed the bill without amendment by voice vote on March 28. President Richard M. Nixon signed the bill on April 10, 1972, and the following November Guamanians elected Won Pat as their first Delegate.

Like Guam had done two years earlier, American Samoa sent an unofficial "Delegate at Large" to Washington to act as an elected lobbyist for the islands in 1970.[114] On August 2, 1978, Representative Burton introduced H.R. 13702 to provide for a Delegate from American Samoa with the same privileges as other territorial lawmakers. The legislation sailed through Congress and its success surprised even Faleomavaega, who was a congressional staffer at the time.[115] "You wouldn't believe, it was difficult for me even, how do you justify having a congressional delegate from this little, dinky territory, at that time with only about 36 to 40 thousand people," Faleomavaega asked, adding that Burton's belief that every territory "should have representation" was key to its success. President Jimmy Carter signed the bill on October 31, 1978. The first American Samoan Delegate, Fofó I. F. Sunia, was elected in 1980.[116]

The stories of how Guamanians and American Samoans came to be represented in Washington in the 1970s were but two points on a long, arcing dialogue that began in the 1890s about how overseas territories would be administered by or incorporated into the nation. For Guam and American Samoa, especially, the post–World War II period was one of rapid change. Both came out from under military rule and were granted a measure of autonomy as well as representation in Congress. Their new Delegates joined a small cohort of APAs in Congress, pushed for their islands' interests, developed key congressional allies, and participated in the legislative process to a degree earlier statutory representatives had not.

APA MEMBERS ON CAPITOL HILL: LEGISLATIVE INTERESTS AND ACHIEVEMENTS

When considering the legislative agendas and the accomplishments of the Asian and Pacific Islander Americans in Congress during this era, it is important to remember that only 14 APA individuals first won election to the House or Senate in the period from Pearl Harbor to the end of the Cold War in the early

1990s. The most who served in any one Congress in the course of this long span was eight, first in the 97th Congress (1981–1983) and again in the 100th and 101st Congresses (1987–1991). This group proved to be small enough that APA Members did not even form an issues caucus until two decades after women and African Americans had done so in the 1970s.

In many respects, the composition of this group of legislators reflected long-standing immigration patterns. Until the 1970s, Japanese Americans remained the largest APA immigrant community in the United States and half of the 14 APAs who entered Congress were ethnic Japanese. Among them, Hawaii's Patsy Takemoto Mink became the first woman of color to serve in Congress in early 1965. In the first 60 years of Asian Pacific Americans in Congress, all served in the House. When Hawaii entered the Union as a state in 1959, Hiram Fong became not only the first Asian-American Senator, but also the first Chinese American to serve in Congress.

Geographically, these Members hailed from only a handful of areas: six from Hawaii, four from California, and two each from Guam and American Samoa. Still, this represented a change in the power of these individual Members. With the election of Dalip Saund of California in 1956, the era of APAs serving exclusively as statutory representatives, as either Delegates or Resident Commissioners, drew to a close. Of the first 18 APAs who served in Congress through 1945, all were statutory representatives with circumscribed powers. From 1941 to 1991, 10 of the 14 APAs elected to Congress held full voting and membership privileges as Representatives or Senators with no restrictions on their ability to participate in committee, hold leadership posts, or vote on final legislation. The handful who served as Territorial Delegates still were unable to vote on final legislation, though, over time, they enjoyed more privileges in terms of their participation on committees.

It was during this era that, for the first time, APAs served on a broad range of congressional committees that reflected a full spectrum of legislative interests. In 1981 Daniel K. Akaka became the first Asian American to serve on the House Appropriations Committee. California's Robert T. Matsui became the first to serve on several key panels: Interstate and Foreign Commerce (forerunner to Energy and Commerce) in 1979; Judiciary in 1979; and Ways and Means in 1981. Spark Matsunaga broke ground on the House Rules Committee in the 90th Congress (1967–1969). Guamanian Delegate Won Pat became the first to serve on the Armed Services Committee beginning in 1975. In the Senate, Fong became the first to serve on the Judiciary Committee (1961) and the Appropriations Committee (1969), while Inouye joined the Senate Armed Services Committee in 1963.

In more than a century of service in Congress, only a small handful of APAs have ever led committees. It is perhaps unsurprising that Inouye, who served longer than any other APA (a combined 53 years in the House and Senate), led the way in this regard. During his long Senate tenure, Inouye chaired three standing committees (Indian Affairs; Commerce, Science, and Transportation; and Appropriations) as well as two very prominent select committees (the Select Committee on Intelligence and the Select Committee on Secret Military Assistance to Iran and the Nicaraguan Opposition, better known as the Iran-

Hawaiian politicians meet with President Lyndon B. Johnson in 1966. From left, Representative Spark M. Matsunaga, Representative Patsy Takemoto Mink, President Johnson, former Delegate and then Governor John Burns, and Senator Daniel K. Inouye.

Photograph by Yoichi Okamoto; image courtesy of the Lyndon B. Johnson Presidential Library/National Archives and Records Administration

President Lyndon B. Johnson and Hawaii Representative Patsy Takemoto Mink wave before setting off on a flight from Honolulu to Los Angeles after attending the Honolulu Conference on the Vietnam War in 1966.

Photograph by Robert Knudsen; image courtesy of the Lyndon B. Johnson Presidential Library/National Archives and Records Administration

Norman Y. Mineta of California was the first, and to date the only, Asian Pacific American to chair a committee in the U.S. House of Representatives. He oversaw the Committee on Public Works and Transportation in the 103rd Congress (1993–1995).

Image courtesy of the Library of Congress

Spark M. Matsunaga of Hawaii held a leadership role in the Senate, serving as the Democrats' Chief Deputy Whip from the 95th through 100th Congresses (1977–1989).

Collection of the U.S. House of Representatives

Nikkei:

A Japanese term used to identify any person of Japanese descent who emigrated abroad or is the descendant of such individuals.

Diaspora:

The migration of an ethnic group from their home country or region to different parts of the world.

Contra Committee). Akaka led two standing Senate committees (Veterans' Affairs and Indian Affairs). Mineta remains the only APA to ever chair a House committee. He wielded the Public Works and Transportation gavel in the 103rd Congress (1993–1995).

As with committee leadership positions, only a few individuals have moved into party leadership posts. Representative Mink became the first APA to hold a nominal leadership spot when she served for a term as secretary of the House Democratic Caucus in the 94th Congress (1975–1977)—a post traditionally reserved for women Members. In the following Congress, Senator Inouye won election as secretary of the Senate Democratic Conference and remained in that post through the 100th Congress (1987–1989) until his failed run for Majority Leader. He later served as president pro tempore of the Senate, third in line in presidential succession and the member of the majority party with the longest continuous service. In addition to Inouye, Matsunaga also held a position within the Senate Democratic leadership, serving as the appointed Chief Deputy Whip from the 95th through the 100th Congresses (1977–1989).

Remarkably, two of the most powerful APA congressmen—Inouye and Mineta—formed lifelong friendships with other future powerful legislators during the most trying times of their lives, long before any of them served on the Hill. Senator Robert Dole of Kansas had been shot in northern Italy only days before Inouye suffered his own nearly fatal wound. By sheer happenstance, Dole and Inouye both recovered at the Percy Jones Army Hospital in Michigan, where future Senator Philip Hart of Michigan also recuperated from his wartime injuries. While interned at the Heart Mountain camp, a short drive outside of Cody, Wyoming, Mineta, for his part, formed a lasting friendship with future Senator Alan Simpson of Wyoming. Mineta and Simpson first met when their respective Boy Scout troops gathered at the camp for a jamboree, even sharing a tent together. Years later, Inouye, Dole, Mineta, and Simpson would lean on those old friendships during important debates on issues like redress and immigration.[117]

The legislative interests of the APAs of this era largely reflected the unique trajectories of the immigrant or Pacific Islander groups to which they belonged. For the Guamanian and Samoan Delegates, efforts to secure a measure of self-determination and federal appropriations were balanced with a respect for maintaining indigenous culture. Hawaiians aimed to achieve the long-sought goal of statehood. In fighting for redress for World War II internment, Members of Congress who were *nikkei* (those who belonged to the Japanese diaspora, emigrants, or their descendants who reside outside Japan) also raised public awareness of the history of Asian Americans in the 20th century.

Self-Determination

Neither of the Guamanian Delegates in this period, Won Pat nor Blaz, chaired a congressional committee or had a vote on final legislation on the House Floor, but both men worked to give Guam control over its future. Their efforts, however, were frequently thwarted by both mainland opposition and political infighting back home. "Evolution necessary to change a sleepy tropical island into a thriving American community of more than 100,000 persons has been slow and gradual but consistent and steady," Won Pat once told his colleagues.[118]

In 1976 Won Pat and Delegate Ron de Lugo of the U.S. Virgin Islands steered H.R. 9491 to passage, a measure that established constitutional conventions in Guam and the Virgin Islands despite opposition from the Department of the Interior. The proposed constitution for Guam won approval from both President Carter and Congress in 1978 only to stall after the territory's government changed hands. Guam's new Republican administration delayed the ratification vote, during which time support for the constitution crumbled amid claims it continued the status quo under the Organic Act. During a public referendum on August 4, 1979, ratification failed spectacularly.[119]

Won Pat was never able to revive the constitution or any serious discussions on status before his departure from Congress in 1985. His successor, Republican Ben Blaz, introduced the Guam Commonwealth Act in 1988, this time with the full backing of Guam's voters and a local bipartisan Commission on Self-Determination. The bill, however, never made it out of committee.[120]

Commission on Guam War Claims

Even though more than 30 years had passed since the end of World War II, both Won Pat and Blaz confronted issues held over from the conflict. In 1945 Congress passed the Guam Meritorious Claims Act that authorized the Navy Secretary to settle cases of damaged property after the Japanese and American occupations left much of the island in ruins. The Navy dragged its feet, however, and a decade into the claims process the Defense Department ruled that Guamanians had not been U.S. citizens during the war and were therefore ineligible for compensation. The Micronesian Claims Act of 1971 did little to solve the problem and only provoked more criticism. The issue was effectively dropped during the 101st Congress (1989–1991).[121]

In retaking the island of Guam from the Japanese, U.S. forces destroyed the Piti Navy Yard, shown here in 1944.

Image courtesy of the National Archives and Records Administration

The military presence on Guam continued to be a contentious issue well into the 1990s. In an effort to limit military holdings on the islands, Blaz introduced the Guam Excess Lands Act in 1992 which would have transferred 3,000 acres from the Defense Department to Guam in an effort to settle the land claims, but the bill was not acted on.[122]

Cultural Protection and Attention in Washington

In Congress, Pacific Delegates often found themselves having to explain and protect the unique customs of their islands. "Guam is still an unknown quantity," an aide to Won Pat noted in 1978, "so we are engaged in a constant job of education."[123] In some cases, the Delegates had to clarify even basic points. In early 2002, for example, a House colleague mistakenly introduced Delegate Faleomavaega as "the gentleman from Somalia."[124]

For Delegates from the Pacific territories, even the simplest legislative acts could be challenging. All 13 of American Samoa Delegate Fofó Sunia's bills, for instance, never made it past the subcommittee level. "Even if I had only one bill passed that would be a great record," Won Pat reminded his constituents while running for a third term. Personal connections, he said, could help grease the wheels—"You need friends in Congress."[125]

But there were also even larger partisan issues to work around. When Faleomavaega was just a House staffer working for the Committee on Interior and Insular Affairs, Representative Burton taught him an important lesson: Do not make territorial issues "controversial," he said, and ensure they have bipartisan support. "Because the territories are so small, don't get into the arena of the big issues because you will be eaten alive."[126]

Geography also played a role. Unlike the U.S. Virgin Islands or Puerto Rico, whose constituencies lived much closer to the mainland, the Pacific territories were relatively isolated. "Our only disadvantage out here," Won Pat bemoaned to the *Pacific Daily News*, "is that we are just too damn far from the United States."[127] For the Delegates, simply staying in contact with their constituents was difficult. At first, the House would only pay for Won Pat to go home four times a year, but he eventually had his travel and telephone budgets expanded in the 95th Congress (1977–1979). A similar allowance was also approved for the Samoan Delegate. Flights from Hawaii to American Samoa were often limited, however, so when Faleomavaega served as a Delegate a decade later, he tried to go home once a month for at least a week.[128]

Hawaiian Statehood

Along with the decision to grant Guam and American Samoa Delegates in the House, one of the most consequential developments in the history of APAs in Congress during the second half of the 20th century was the successful campaign by Hawaii for statehood. First as a territory and then as a state, Hawaii has sent more APAs to the House and Senate than anywhere else—15 individuals since Delegate Robert W. Wilcox, the first APA to serve on Capitol Hill. Of the six APA Senators in history, five hailed from Hawaii.[129]

Ever since the government annexed the Hawaiian Islands during the late 19th

Robert W. Wilcox was the first Asian Pacific American to represent Hawaii as a Delegate to Congress, from 1900 to 1903.

Collection of the U.S. House of Representatives

century, statehood seemed to loom just out of reach. By fits and starts, however, statehood supporters gradually won concessions and, by the late 1950s, the campaign for Hawaiian statehood faced a familiar hurdle: the confluence of race and politics.[130]

At the time, both Hawaii and Alaska were working toward statehood. Traditionally, Alaska's voters elected Democrats while Hawaiians generally elected Republicans. The assumption in Washington was that these electoral patterns would persist. In the Senate, party divisions were so close that the majority usually held only a one- or two-seat advantage. Admitting either Hawaii or Alaska to the Union separately threatened to tip the scale in either direction. Because of the razor-thin margins, a coalition of conservative Republicans and southern Democrats effectively ruled the Senate, capable of blocking either civil rights legislation or statehood for multiracial Hawaii with equal effectiveness.[131]

By midcentury, the statehood movement in Hawaii seemed well on its way to achieving its goal. It had a majority coalition of white settlers, commonly called *haoles*, and pro-statehood Japanese Hawaiians that outnumbered the anti-statehood block of Native Hawaiians.[132] Congress's earlier fears that statehood would sweep an untold number of communist agents into the national fabric had been neutralized by previous immigration laws.[133] Finally, Hawaii's longtime Delegate in the House, Republican Joseph Farrington, had worked tirelessly to coordinate the statehood campaign in Washington.

When Farrington died in 1954, however, things started to unravel. Although his widow, Republican Elizabeth Farrington, took his seat and resumed the statehood campaign, she struggled against a political realignment back home that was swelling the ranks of the Democratic Party. Complicating the issue, some Democrats in Washington insisted on coupling Alaskan and Hawaiian statehood to maintain party parity in the Senate, but the House Rules Committee Chairman, Howard Smith of Virginia, a dyed-in-the-wool conservative southern Democrat, refused to consider the joint proposal.[134]

During the 85th and 86th Congresses (1957–1961), the fate of Hawaiian statehood largely lay in the hands of two Texans, House Speaker Sam Rayburn and Senate Majority Leader Lyndon B. Johnson, who both thought they saw a parliamentary opening. If they could convince the authorizing committees to make Hawaiian and Alaskan statehood privileged measures, then congressional leaders could still bring the bills to the floor for a vote despite opposition in the House Rules Committee or by southern Democratic opponents.[135]

In April 1956, in a key turning point, Alaskan voters approved a referendum to adopt a proposed state constitution. When Alaskan officials later presented their charter to Congress, the House and Senate were freed from having to pass an enabling act and could immediately start debating the terms of statehood. With Alaska in the pipeline, Johnson informed Hawaii's new Delegate, Democrat John Burns, that his territory would have to wait until the next year for its chance for statehood. Afraid that if Hawaii became a state and elected two GOP Senators he would lose his majority, Johnson instructed Burns to stall attempts to bring up Hawaiian statehood in 1958.[136]

The plan by Rayburn and Johnson to bring Alaska's statehood bill to the

A campaign handbill urges voters to support Elizabeth Farrington in 1955. Farrington succeeded her late husband, Joseph Rider Farrington, as a Delegate from Hawaii in the 83rd and 84th Congresses.

Collection of the U.S. House of Representatives

This 1959 cartoon by Jim Berryman—
"What Did Alaska Have That I Don't
Mister?"—highlights the long-intertwined
push for statehood by Alaska and Hawaii.
Alaska became a state first in January 1959,
and Hawaii followed suit in August 1959.

Image courtesy of the National Archives
and Records Administration

On March 18, 1959, Henry McPhee,
associate special counsel to the President,
looked on as President Dwight D. Eisenhower
signs the bill making Hawaii the 50th state.

Photograph by the National Park Service;
image courtesy of the Dwight D. Eisenhower
Presidential Library & Museum/National Archives
and Records Administration

floor as a privileged measure worked as expected. After overruling objections
and defeating a motion to send it back to committee, the House passed it in
late May and the Senate cleared it in late June. President Eisenhower signed
it into law on July 7, 1958. Keeping his end of the bargain, Delegate Burns
discouraged the chairman of the House Interior and Insular Affairs Committee,
Leo O'Brien, from bringing up Hawaii's accompanying statehood bill.[137]

Throughout July, congressional Democrats contained the political damage
to Burns for putting off the Hawaii bill while House Majority Leader John
McCormack of Massachusetts stated publicly that Hawaiian statehood would
be debated in the next Congress. When the new territorial governor, William
Quinn, and a delegation of Hawaiians lobbied Congress to consider an enabling
bill before adjournment, Johnson promptly shut them down. Later offering
his reassurance, Johnson said, "Due to the wise counsel of Delegate Burns and
others who have put their country ahead of politics, Hawaii has the best chance
for admission at the next session as it has ever had."[138]

When the Hawaiian statehood bill failed to come up in 1958, voices from
across the country, from President Eisenhower to the editorial board of the
New York Times and especially Republicans in Hawaii, lashed out at Congress.
Despite the delay on Capitol Hill, Delegate Burns won re-election that year,
adding to substantial Democratic gains nationwide. The bill to begin the
statehood process for Hawaii was introduced in both houses of Congress in
January 1959. Less than 90 days later Eisenhower signed it into law.[139]

The inhabitants of Hawaii voted for the statehood plebiscite by a 17 to 1 margin on June 27, 1959. Two months later, on August 21, President Eisenhower proclaimed Hawaii the 50th state of the Union.[140] With statehood, the U.S. Senate received its first APA Member, Hiram Fong, and the House its first Japanese American, Daniel Inouye.

LONG ROAD TO REDRESS

Comprehensive legislation apologizing for internment and compensating its victims had to wait for more than a generation after World War II until a phalanx of influential *nikkei* Members of Congress drew attention to the issue. The effort involved pushing back against Cold War–era legislative initiatives that again gave the U.S. government worrisome detention powers while raising awareness about Asian-American experiences and their contributions to U.S. society. This remained a particularly Japanese-American burden, but the community sought to make this a fully American issue—one that required constant education and vigilance. Whether the issue was repealing dangerous laws or providing monetary compensation to detainees, Congress remained a central stage in the redress debates.

When the Roosevelt administration began its internment policy during World War II, thousands of Japanese-American families had little time to arrange their affairs and pack the few things permitted them in the camps. The evacuation was hurried and chaotic. Bank accounts were frozen. Businesses were shuttered. Homes, automobiles, furniture, land, clothes, utensils—all the trappings of everyday life—were abandoned. The cost was staggering. The economic losses to thousands of U.S. citizens and the congressional decision to codify the *nikkei* evacuation and internment into law cast a long and dark shadow over the APA experience for decades afterward.

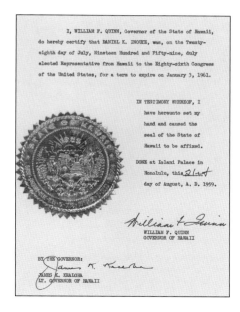

This election certificate formalized Daniel K. Inouye's election to Congress in 1959 as Hawaii's first U.S. Representative. Inouye also was the first Japanese American elected to the House.

Image courtesy of the National Archives and Records Administration

This San Francisco restaurant closed after the federal government mandated the evacuation of Japanese-American citizens during World War II. A sign in the window promises that the restaurant will soon open under new management.

Image courtesy of the National Archives and Records Administration

Japanese Americans line up outside a Civil Control station in San Francisco in 1942 to await processing and evacuation.

Image courtesy of the National Archives and Records Administration

Loyalty

The first stirrings of ameliorative action began even as the war drew to a close, though not in the form of monetary reparations. During internment, some *nisei* men held in the more repressive camps renounced their U.S. citizenship. Some did so out of protest, but others feared the government would deport their immigrant parents (who, by federal law, had been prevented from becoming U.S. citizens) back to Japan after the war and, by giving up their citizenship, the *nisei* could return to Japan to care for them. Uncertain as to the legal precedent in order to renounce one's citizenship, the federal government looked for a way to manage such "disloyal" internees.[141] Working with Congress, the Justice Department crafted a first-of-its-kind policy enabling native-born Americans to renounce their U.S. citizenship. At the time, no such mechanism existed. But the proposed measure allowed the government to retain control over "disloyal" prisoners who voluntarily gave up their citizenship before deporting them to Japan. It became law in July 1944 as an amendment to the Nationality Act of 1940.[142]

Even as Japanese-American detainees were being released from other camps, the WRA turned Tule Lake into a high-security segregation center to hold the roughly 5,500 *nisei* who had either failed the loyalty questionnaire or who sought to go to Japan.[143] More than 1,300 of these "Native American Aliens" were deported. By the end of the war, however, virtually all renunciants and deportees fought to have their citizenship restored despite opposition from the Justice Department. Wayne Collins, a civil liberties lawyer, defended many *nisei*, arguing that they had given up their citizenship under duress or coercion. Some blamed the military and the WRA, but the greatest pressure to renounce came from other militant detainees. By 1959, all renunciants who had applied, both those looking to return from Japan and those in the United States under threat of deportation, had regained their citizenship.[144]

Slowly and incrementally, wartime restrictions also were rolled back. In 1945, four years after the federal government seized the banks, financial records, and assets of Japanese Americans using the Trading with the Enemy Act, Congress voted to unfreeze their money and set aside as much as $10 million in refunds. But because the Office of Alien Property Custodian offered low exchange rates and erected additional hurdles, less than half of the 7,500 Japanese-American depositors redeemed their certificates. More than two decades passed before the U.S. Supreme Court in *Honda v. Clark* forced the custodian to meet all outstanding claims in full.[145]

In 1952 Congress tackled another lingering injustice from the war when it restored seniority benefits to all *nisei* federal employees who had been evacuated. Introduced by Representative George P. Miller of California, the bill expanded a previous law that restored seniority benefits to *nisei* postal workers.[146]

Addressing the far larger injustice of uprooting and incarcerating an entire ethnic group, however, remained an unresolved issue for decades. After the war, former Japanese-American inmates from seven WRA internment camps met in Salt Lake City, Utah, to outline a policy seeking compensation. The delegates settled on reparations: direct payments from the federal government for losses incurred during the forced evacuation.[147]

In 1952 California Representative George P. Miller introduced legislation that restored benefits to *nisei* federal employees who had been evacuated during World War II.

George Paul Miller, Victor Lallier, 1965, Collection of the U.S. House of Representatives

When Republicans took over both chambers in the 80th Congress (1947–1949), the political atmosphere on the Hill warmed to reparations, but hurdles remained. Calculating the cost and verifying property-loss claims proved to be challenging because few records had been kept. Despite some initial help from the WRA, the whole situation was "complicated ... by difficulties in communication with absent owners and local prejudice," the Interior Secretary said in a letter to House Speaker Joe Martin of Massachusetts.[148]

Congressional deliberations also trod carefully around the evacuation's legality. In 1947 the House Judiciary Committee admitted that no one sent to the camps had been guilty of sabotaging America, but the committee nevertheless justified internment as a "military necessity."[149] Even still, the House clearly viewed the evacuees as victims of government overreach. The internees were loyal Americans, the committee wrote and "to redress them would be simple justice." To not do so, the committee believed, would feed into the global communist propaganda criticizing America's civil rights record.[150]

In a message to Congress in February 1948, President Truman reminded the country that more than 100,000 Japanese Americans had been removed from their homes "solely because of their racial origin."[151] Five months later, on July 2, 1948, Truman signed the Japanese-American Evacuation Claims Act into law, but it had limited impact. The legislation covered only "real or personal property" damaged or lost during the evacuation or during internment. Left unaddressed were the unknown costs associated with the stigma of incarceration, the psychological damage, lost earnings, injury or death, and resettlement. The Justice Department struggled to process the 26,000 claims totaling $148 million. In the end, the government awarded just $37 million. In order to keep up with the claims, Congress amended and extended the act, settling the last claim in 1965.[152]

While addressing old injustices, APA advocates in Congress kept a close eye on new legislative efforts that threatened to undermine their constituents' rights. In the late 1960s, the House Un-American Activities Committee lobbied to use the Emergency Detention Act—Title II of the Internal Security Act of 1950—

A Japanese-American child arrives at Lone Pine, California, by train in 1942. He continued on to the Manzanar relocation camp by bus.

Image courtesy of the National Archives and Records Administration

to clamp down on urban riots and student protests. Title II gave the government broad authority to detain suspected communists and other subversives, and the threat of arbitrary arrests, violations of free speech, racism, and internment unsettled many Americans, among them the Japanese-American community that still held painful memories of wartime incarceration.[153]

In response, Hawaii's Senator Inouye submitted a bill to repeal the Emergency Detention Act in the 91st Congress (1969–1971); Representative Matsunaga cosponsored another measure in the House. During debate, Inouye argued that the government's arrest powers terrified those "who are by birth or choice not 'in tune' or 'in line' with the rest of the country."[154] In the following Congress, Matsunaga and Chet Holifield of California sponsored legislation to completely repeal Title II, overriding weaker attempts to simply revise it. Matsunaga used his position on the Rules Committee to prioritize his bill (H.R. 234), casting Title II as a hangover from a darker era, out of place in a changing America. "This is an attempt to erase … the last vestige of any authority to incarcerate people because they are related to people who are at war with us," Speaker Carl Albert said plainly. H.R. 234 overwhelmingly passed the House, 356 to 49.[155] The Senate passed the bill by voice vote. On September 25, 1971, President Richard M. Nixon signed the repeal of the Emergency Detention Act into law.[156]

Remembrance

In the aftermath of internment, a long, stunned silence came over those in the Japanese-American community directly affected by the program. After years of carving out a life in the United States, the trauma of losing a business or a home, of being shipped off to remote camps, of being labeled an enemy, weighed heavily among the *issei* and *nisei*. Historian Roger Daniels, then a professor at the University of California, Los Angeles, once told the story of having *sansei* (the American-born grandchildren of *issei*) students in class who insisted they had been born in Los Angeles in 1943. Given the circumstances, Daniels knew they could have been born only in one of the camps and that their parents never told them about the experience.[157]

Sansei:

A Japanese term that identifies the second generation of Japanese Americans who were born in the United States.

President Gerald R. Ford, surrounded by Asian Pacific American Members of Congress, including Daniel K. Inouye of Hawaii, Patsy Takemoto Mink of Hawaii, Norman Y. Mineta of California, Spark M. Matsunaga of Hawaii, and Hiram L. Fong of Hawaii, signs a proclamation formally terminating Executive Order 9066 and ending the relocation program.

Image courtesy of the Gerald R. Ford Presidential Library/National Archives and Records Administration

By the 1970s, many of the older camp inmates had died or become infirm and leadership had passed to the *nisei*. The younger generation began to process the trauma, drawing inspiration from both the civil rights movement and peace protests. They organized the first visit to Manzanar in late 1969, which sparked annual pilgrimages to other camp sites.[158]

These grassroots efforts helped nudge the nation in its bicentennial year toward reconsidering this troubling aspect of its past. In 1976, on the 34th anniversary of FDR's Executive Order 9066, President Gerald R. Ford signed Proclamation 4417, "An American Promise," which formally ended the relocation program that had remained on the books years after its directives had been abandoned.[159] "We now know what we should have known then—not only was that evacuation wrong but Japanese-Americans were and are loyal Americans," Ford said. "On the battlefield and at home the names of Japanese-Americans have been and continue to be written in America's history for the sacrifices and the contributions they have made to the well-being and to the security of this, our common Nation."[160] The symbolic and often overlooked proclamation served as one of the earliest official statements denouncing the evacuation and internment program.

Ford's statement endorsed remembrance, that by commemorating the event, the sites, and the people, the country could avoid such an unworthy act in the future. This process played out over several decades. By 1980 at least two of the war relocation camps were listed on the National Register of Historic Places: Manzanar in California and Minidoka in Utah. In the 1990s, the effort to raise awareness about the history of internment gained momentum. During the 102nd Congress (1991–1993), the Manzanar War Relocation Center was designated a national historic site. In 1992 the Rohwer Relocation Center Memorial Cemetery gained designation as a national historic landmark while Congress authorized a National Japanese American Memorial to be built with

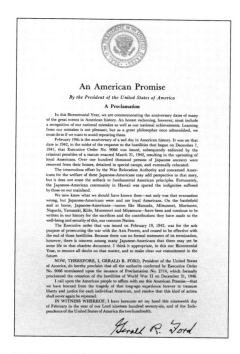

President William J. (Bill) Clinton signs the Asian/Pacific American Heritage Awareness Month Proclamation in 1993, accompanied by, from left to right: Senator Daniel K. Akaka of Hawaii, Representative Norman Y. Mineta of California, Representative Patsy Takemoto Mink of Hawaii, Representative Robert T. Matsui of California, Representative Jay C. Kim of California, Delegate Eni F. H. Faleomavaega of American Samoa, and Delegate Robert A. Underwood of Guam.

Image courtesy of the William J. Clinton Library/National Archives and Records Administration

By the late 1970s, Asian Pacific American Representatives and Senators, including Spark M. Matsunaga of Hawaii, shown serving on the Senate Veterans' Affairs Committee, pushed for recognition of Asian-American heritage.

Image courtesy of the U.S. Senate Historical Office

private funds in Washington, DC. "The lessons learned," Senator Inouye said about the memorial that opened in 2001, "must remain as a grave reminder of what we must not allow to happen again to any group."[161]

Reacting to a National Park Service report about the condition of the internment camps in the West, President William J. (Bill) Clinton directed Interior Secretary Bruce Babbitt to provide recommendations for the preservation of these sites.[162] Just days before he left office, President Clinton issued Proclamation 7395 to establish the Minidoka Internment National Monument in Utah.[163] Meanwhile, Congress passed legislation in the 1990s and early 2000s that added the Granada War Relocation Center to the National Register, appropriated funds for a visitor center at Manzanar, and authorized the study of a memorial on Bainbridge Island, where the first *nikkei* were evacuated in 1942. Toward the end of 2006, President George W. Bush signed into law legislation authorizing $38 million toward the preservation of Japanese-American confinement sites.[164]

These and other efforts helped Americans to contextualize the experiences of the *issei* and the *nisei* during World War II. These efforts also promised to bring the stories of internment to a substantially broader audience.

By the late 1970s, momentum had also started for the commemorative annual recognition of Asian-American heritage. Representative Mineta and New York Representative Frank Horton cosponsored a resolution to set aside one week every year to celebrate the diverse heritage of APAs. Supported by a national coalition of civic groups, including the Organization of Chinese Americans and the JACL, the bill passed the full House in July 1978, 360 to 6, and the Senate passed it two months later.[165] President Carter declared that the first annual Asian Pacific American Heritage Week would take place in May 1979.[166] Congress later expanded the commemoration period and passed H.R. 3802 on May 3, 1990.[167] When he signed the act into law, President George H. W. Bush proclaimed the month of May as the annual Asian Pacific American Heritage Month.[168]

Redress

Efforts at remembrance reinforced the belief that the federal government should act substantively on the legacy of internment before the older generation of Japanese Americans passed from the scene. At the JACL national convention in 1970, a Manzanar pilgrimage organizer, Edison Uno, introduced a resolution calling for reparations to the victims or heirs of "the worst mistakes of World War II." Although the National Council for Japanese American Redress (NCJAR), an offshoot of the JACL, adopted the resolution, it did not follow through.[169] The idea took root, nonetheless. On June 28, 1974, Representative George E. Danielson of California introduced a bill to establish a relocation benefits commission to help victims of the internment camps get financial relief.[170]

Spurred to act as more and more *issei* victims died without seeing government action, the JACL adopted a resolution calling for $25,000 reparation payments to victims of the evacuation or their heirs and established the National Committee for Redress (NCR), headed by John Tateishi. Not everyone agreed, however. The keynote speaker of the 1978 JACL national meeting, Senator Samuel Ichiye (Sam) Hayakawa of California, later dismissed the proposal as "ridiculous." Hayakawa added, "For the JACL to ask for the restitution is merely the rekindling of resentment and racism that no longer exists."[171]

In early February 1979, the JACL president, Clifford Uyeda, along with Tateishi and his NCJAR colleagues arranged to meet with the four Democratic *nikkei* Members of Congress: California Representatives Matsui and Mineta and Hawaiian Senators Inouye and Matsunaga. Inouye and Matsunaga had served in the 442nd Regimental Combat Team and the 100th Infantry Battalion, respectively; Mineta and Matsui had been inmates at Heart Mountain and Tule Lake concentration camps, respectively.[172]

Neither Tateishi nor the JACL leadership had consulted the Congressmen about their redress proposal and simply assumed they would have their support. Inouye provided them with a hard lesson in congressional relations. "I said I think it is premature," Inouye recalled. "I don't think it will fly." The shock was palpable. "They were hoping that all of us would come in flags waving and say let's make the charge up the hill," he added. "I think for a moment they were ready to take away my membership card."[173] From the Congressmen's perspective, the proposal threatened to become a divisive issue. As Mineta's legislative director pointed out, the *nikkei* legislators had "spent their whole lives trying to be seen not as Japanese Americans, but as just plain old Americans." Instead, Inouye asked the NCR to think about a blue-ribbon commission to study the wartime relocation and internment of Japanese Americans.[174]

By and large, the JACL supported Inouye's commission, but the activists remained keenly aware that this decision would delay any action on redress even as the *issei* generation continued to disappear. On August 2, 1979, Senator Inouye introduced S. 1647, the Commission on Wartime Relocation and Internment of Civilians (CWRIC) Act. When Republican Senate Minority Whip Ted Stevens of Alaska approached Inouye about adding Aleutian and Pribilof Islanders, who had also been evacuated, to the commission bill, Inouye, a longtime friend of Stevens, gladly made the addition. This ensured the support of Alaska's delegation and protected the bill from accusations that it benefited

In 1978, when the Japanese American Citizens League proposed reparation payments to Japanese Americans interned during World War II, California Senator Samuel Ichiye (Sam) Hayakawa rejected the idea as "ridiculous."

Image courtesy of the U.S. Senate Historical Office

Members of the National Committee for Redress meet with Senators and Representatives in 1979. Standing (left to right): John Tateishi, Ron Ikejiri, Clifford Uyeda, Ron Mamiya, and Karl Nobuyuki. Seated (left to right): California Representatives Norman Y. Mineta and Robert T. Matsui and Hawaiian Senators Daniel K. Inouye and Spark M. Matsunaga.

Image courtesy of the Japanese American National Museum, Gift of Norman Y. Mineta, 96.370

With the support of Representative Norman Y. Mineta of California, House Majority Leader Jim Wright of Texas introduced a bill in 1979 that created the Commission on Wartime Relocation and Internment of Civilians.

James Claude Wright, Jr., Marshall Bouldin III, 1991, Collection of the U.S. House of Representatives

Formed in 1979, the National Council for Japanese American Redress sought financial compensation for Japanese Americans incarcerated during World War II. This fundraising card proclaims: "We went obediently then. We have remained largely silent since. But no more!"

Image courtesy of Shosuke Sasaki, Densho Digital Repository

special interests. On the whole, the bill's language focused on fact-finding: How was Executive Order 9066 implemented? What was its impact on U.S. citizens and resident aliens? How did the military decide on evacuation and relocation? By emphasizing this approach, Inouye and Matsunaga convinced Hayakawa to cosponsor the bill to maintain a bipartisan and unified *nikkei* front.[175]

In the House, Mineta, who had spent part of his childhood in the Heart Mountain internment camp, could not bring himself to introduce the companion bill, H.R. 5499. It was too personal. But he remembered that Majority Leader Jim Wright of Texas had once told him how outraged he was when the Supreme Court justified the camps and, when asked, the Texan readily introduced the bill with 147 cosponsors on September 28, 1979.[176]

In the Senate, Inouye managed the bill. The Governmental Affairs Committee held hearings on the legislation on March 18, 1980, and featured supportive testimony from the JACL, *nikkei* Congressmen, and from Clarence M. Mitchell of the Leadership Conference on Civil Rights. On the other hand, the NCJAR opposed it for being too timid, instead preferring a bill that would have directly required monetary reparations and an apology. In the end, the committee reported Inouye's commission bill favorably, and on May 22, it passed the full Senate by voice vote.[177]

Two weeks later, the House Judiciary Committee's Subcommittee on Administrative Law and Governmental Relations held hearings on Inouye's bill (S. 1647), on the Wright–Mineta bill (H.R. 5499), and on a third bill that proposed paying out reparations directly (H.R. 5977). Fortunately for the commission's supporters, the subcommittee was chaired by Representative Danielson, who had sponsored the first Japanese-American compensation bill back in 1974. Danielson and the ranking minority member, Robert McClory of Illinois, supported the Wright–Mineta bill and amended it to include the Aleuts and Pribilof Islanders within the scope of the commission's investigation. The full Judiciary Committee approved the bill and reported it to the House, which then passed H.R. 5499, 279 to 109. The Senate then agreed to replace the language of Inouye's bill with the text of the Wright–Mineta bill.[178] On July 31, 1980, in a ceremony in the Cabinet Room, President Jimmy Carter signed the CWRIC Act into law.[179]

The act creating the CWRIC provided for seven commissioners: three to be named by President Carter, two by Senate president pro tempore Warren G. Magnuson of Washington, and two by House Speaker Thomas P. O'Neill of Massachusetts.[180] Four Democrats and three Republicans initially served on the commission that was co-chaired by Joan Z. Bernstein, a former counsel for the Health and Human Services Department, and Representative Dan Lungren of California.[181]

Much of the CWRIC's work involved locating and gathering official documents, memoirs, and personal papers that revealed the federal decision-making processes to implement internment. But the commissioners also wanted to hear and question surviving policymakers and detainees alike. Twenty days of hearings were scheduled around the country in 11 locations between July and December 1981. More than 750 witnesses testified. Both Matsui and Mineta testified about their families' experiences during the evacuation and relocation as well as their time in the camps. The CWRIC also heard from federal officials like John J. McCloy at the War Department, Colonel Karl R. Bendetsen of the WDC, and Abe Fortas of the Interior Department, who had contributed to the decision to go ahead with internment.[182]

Initially, the early testimony held outside Washington, DC, came mostly from *sansei*, who reported how little they had learned about internment from their parents and grandparents. But over time, an increasing number of *issei* and *nisei* witnesses appeared, often telling their stories for the first time. "For over thirty-five years I have been the stereotype Japanese American," Alice Tanabe Nehira told the commission. "I've kept quiet, hoping in due time we will be justly compensated and recognized for our years of patient effort. By my passive attitude, I can reflect on my past years to conclude that it doesn't pay to remain silent."[183] During hearings in Los Angeles, *Time* magazine reported "the audience listened with hushed respect to stories almost too painful to remember, but too important to forget."[184]

As the commission worked on its report throughout 1982, Senator Hayakawa, who taught at an Illinois college during the war, took to the Senate Floor on the 41st anniversary of the Pearl Harbor attacks to adamantly oppose reparations and noted that his "flesh crawls with shame and embarrassment" at the thought. He reminded Japanese Americans of their successful integration into American society, their relative level of wealth and educational achievement, and he warned that, in an era of budget constraints and widespread public concern about Japanese economic gains versus the United States, such a program would invite a "backlash."[185]

The CWRIC issued its report, *Personal Justice Denied*, on February 24, 1983.[186] It presented a narrative about the *nisei* and *issei* that began before the Pearl Harbor attacks and followed their experiences through the end of internment, and it included comparative analyses with the situation in the military and in Hawaii and described the Aleuts' experience. A summary paragraph distilled the commission's basic conclusions:

> The promulgation of Executive Order 9066 was not justified by military necessity, and the decisions which followed from it—detention, ending detention and ending exclusion—were not driven by analysis of military conditions. The broad historical causes which shaped these decisions were race prejudice, war hysteria and a failure of political leadership. Widespread ignorance of Japanese Americans contributed to a policy conceived in haste and executed in an atmosphere of fear and anger at Japan. A grave injustice was done to Americans and resident aliens of Japanese ancestry who, without individual review or any probative evidence against them, were excluded, removed and detained by the United States during World War II.[187]

The public responded favorably to the findings, and there were few objections to the report. The commissioners supported their conclusion unanimously but offered no recommendations and didn't comment on reparations. "It's appropriate that the commission did not deal with the issue of redress," Matsui

President Jimmy Carter signs the Commission on Wartime Relocation and Internment of Civilians Act into law on July 31, 1980. Standing directly behind President Carter, left to right, are Hawaii Senator Daniel K. Inouye, California Representative Norman Y. Mineta, and Hawaii Senator Spark M. Matsunaga.

Image courtesy of the Jimmy Carter Library/National Archives and Records Administration

The Commission on Wartime Relocation and Internment of Civilians holds a hearing in 1981 about the treatment of Japanese Americans during World War II. Initially, young Japanese Americans spoke about how little their grandparents said about internment. Eventually, *issei* and *nisei* witnesses testified before the commission, many telling their stories for the first time.

Image courtesy of the National Archives and Records Administration

The report *Personal Justice Denied* collected the findings of the Commission on Wartime Relocation and Internment of Civilians in 1983.

Image courtesy of the National Archives and Records Administration

said, "because I think the attention of the American public should be on what happened, and the individual tragedies that occurred during [the war]."[188]

Senator Inouye's blue-ribbon panel had accomplished more than anyone dared to imagine. After suffering silently for 50 years, mainland *issei* and *nisei* finally felt free to speak up. Stories they had buried deep inside came spilling out to the surprise of their children and their community. Simply being able to talk about their experiences and having someone confirm that they had undergone a major injustice often meant more than a government check ever could.[189]

Four months after the report came out, the commission published its recommendations on June 16, 1983. The commission unanimously proposed having the federal government apologize "for the acts of exclusion, removal, and detention." It also called for presidential pardons for anyone convicted of curfew and exclusion violations. It asked Congress to direct federal agencies to review "with liberality" all *nikkei* applications for restitution associated with the internment, and it recommended a special foundation created and funded by law for the research and public education of "the causes and circumstances of" internment. All but one of the commissioners further recommended a congressional appropriation of $1.5 billion to pay all surviving evacuees and detainees $20,000 each in reparations.[190]

Most *nikkei* Congressmen cheered the result. Senator Matsunaga announced he would do everything he could to push Congress to fund the recommendations. In the House, Mineta vowed "to develop a plan to implement these long overdue recommendations." Matsui welcomed the recommendations but warned against "false and misleading expectations" about seeing the payments anytime soon. Hayakawa, who had since retired from the Senate, dissented. While he approved of a "national apology for the old injustice," Hayakawa believed "the successes Japanese Americans have enjoyed in business, education, the professions and in politics have amply demonstrated the esteem in which they are held by their fellow Americans." He concluded, "All this is redress enough."[191]

Congress, however, offered a tepid response to the CWRIC recommendations in the 98th Congress (1983–1985). Redress bills were introduced in both the House (H.R. 3387) and Senate (S. 1520) in mid-1983, but neither went anywhere.[192] While Congress generally seemed to support the commission's findings, opponents rejected redress payments as unfair to American taxpayers by making them liable for the transgressions of an earlier generation.[193]

In a fitting bit of commemoration, House Democratic leadership saved the designation H.R. 442 for the redress bill at the opening of the 99th Congress (1985–1987), referencing the wartime heroics of the 442nd Regimental Combat Team.[194] Mineta was the first person to testify on H.R. 442, and he spoke powerfully on how internment affected his family. "I was a U.S. citizen at birth," he reminded a House Judiciary subcommittee. "I had all of the rights promised to all the citizens in the Constitution, and I was 10 ½ years old. There was no reason, absolutely none, to fear me. Was I supposedly a saboteur? A spy? A secret agent? No one has ever explained to me what threat I posed or even could have been seen to pose."[195] But Mineta was not alone in his long-simmering doubt or his lifetime of confusion, and when he spoke in terms of "us," "we," and "our" during his time before the subcommittee, he spoke on behalf of everyone who spent time in the camps. "Mr. Chairman," he said, wrapping up, "there is no statute of limitations on our shame, our damaged honor, or our violated rights, and it has fallen on this subcommittee to set us free." Despite his impassioned testimony, the legislation failed to gain traction.[196]

In the 100th Congress, with Texas Representative Jim Wright now Speaker and with an additional APA Member of the House, Representative Patricia Saiki of Hawaii, redress had its best chance in years.[197] As taken up by the House, the redress bill did three things: It authorized $1.2 billion out of which every surviving member of the camps would be paid $20,000; it advised the Justice Department to clear the convictions of anyone who had resisted imprisonment; and it set aside $50 million to educate the public about the injustices committed by the U.S. government.[198] Representative Don Young of Alaska introduced the Aleut redress bill (H.R. 1631) in March 1987, and Senator Matsunaga introduced a companion redress bill (S. 1009) the next month. When Matsunaga rose to introduce his bill, he declared, "Perhaps the most traumatic experience, the one thing that has haunted Americans of Japanese ancestry for 45 years, was the stigma of being cast as disloyal to their own beloved country, the United States of America."[199]

Throughout the 100th Congress, Matsunaga worked with the American Civil Liberties Union to lobby each Member on the need for reparations. He and Inouye also both testified before the House committees considering the legislation.[200]

Although the Ronald Reagan administration opposed redress, the House quickly moved the bill through the Judiciary Committee, which cleared the measure as Mineta and Matsui looked on. Mineta, working with the Democratic leadership, arranged to have H.R. 442 arrive on the House Floor on September 17, the bicentennial of the signing of the U.S. Constitution.[201] "Great nations demonstrate their greatness by admitting and redressing the wrongs they commit," Mineta told a rapt audience in the House Chamber.[202] In an emotional floor speech, Matsui retold his family's heart-wrenching story of being uprooted from their home. "How could I, as a 6-month-old child born in this country, be declared by my own Government to be an enemy alien?" he asked.[203] One amendment was made to the bill when Representative Lungren asked to have "failure of political leadership" added to the list of causes of the internment.[204]

As before, not everyone believed redress was necessary. Redress supporters, said William Frenzel of Minnesota, were "asking us to purge ourselves of someone else's guilt with another generation's money." But opponents were unable to sway the majority, and after the debate, the House passed the redress bill, 243 to 141. As a former internee, Mineta was technically included in the legislation, but he voted "present" to avoid the appearance of any conflict of interest.[205]

In the Senate, Matsunaga's bill had a slightly more complicated run in which two failed amendments would have stripped funding for or made it virtually impossible to fund redress payments.[206] A third amendment proposed by Senator Jesse Helms of North Carolina demanded the Japanese government compensate the families of those killed in the attacks on Pearl Harbor before

In his testimony about H.R. 442, the redress bill, Representative Norman Y. Mineta of California questioned why he, as a 10 year old, was sent to an internment camp. Like Mineta, this unidentified grandfather and grandson were sent to a camp for the duration of the war.

Image courtesy of the National Archives and Records Administration

Patricia Saiki represented Hawaii in the 100th and 101st Congresses (1987–1991). She added her support to the struggle for redress payments to Japanese Americans.

Collection of the U.S. House of Representatives

The Civil Liberties Act of 1988 became
law on August 10, 1988, and implemented
the recommendations of the Commission
on Wartime Relocation and Internment
of Civilians. The first letters of apology
and redress payments were presented to
the oldest surviving detainees in a public
ceremony on October 1, 1990.

Image courtesy of the National Archives
and Records Administration

President Ronald Reagan signs the Civil
Liberties Act of 1988, providing reparations
to Japanese Americans. Reagan is flanked by
(left to right) Senator Spark M. Matsunaga
of Hawaii, Representative Norman Y.
Mineta of California, Representative Patricia
Saiki of Hawaii, Senator Pete Wilson of
California, Representative Don Young of
Alaska, Representative Robert T. Matsui of
California, Representative William Lowery
of California, and Harry Kajihara, President
of the Japanese American Citizens League.

Image courtesy of the Ronald Reagan Library/National
Archives and Records Administration

any reparations be made to Japanese Americans. Helms's proposal infuriated
Matsunaga, who rushed to highlight its false logic by pointing out that it tied
American citizens to the attacks, an accusation the bill was specifically written
to redress. When Helms refused to relent and demanded a vote, his amendment
failed, 91 to 4.

Following debate in the Senate, Matsunaga brought up H.R. 442, and asked
that the text following the enacting clause be replaced with the substance of his
bill (S. 1009). The bill, which spread reparation payments over five years, passed
on April 20, 1988, by a vote of 69 to 27, a veto-proof majority.[207]

After the House and Senate agreed to the conference report that summer,
President Reagan signed the Civil Liberties Act of 1988 into law on August
10.[208] "Indeed, scores of Japanese Americans volunteered for our Armed
Forces—many stepping forward in the internment camps themselves," the
President said. "The 442nd Regimental Combat Team, made up entirely of
Japanese Americans, served with immense distinction to defend this nation,
their nation. Yet, back at home, the soldiers' families were being denied the
very freedom for which so many of the soldiers themselves were laying down
their lives."[209]

The Civil Liberties Act only authorized the redress payments to the surviving
detainees. The President still had to fit the cost into the federal budget, and
Congress had to approve the necessary appropriations. When both President
Reagan and his successor, George H. W. Bush, asked for less money than expected,
the House Appropriations subcommittee overseeing the legislation responded
by recommending large sums for the redress program. Under the threat of a
presidential veto, however, House leaders removed the funding before bringing
the supplemental budget before the House. "The money was there and ready to
go before it was stripped by a veto threat from the same team that made redress a
campaign issue last year," Representative Matsui said bitterly. "When an election
was on the line, they couldn't say enough about their support for reparations.

Now that 200 survivors are dying each month without the benefit of seeing their dreams completed, they want to block the funding." The only funding that Congress agreed to that year was a small amount for administrative costs.[210]

Having missed the deadline for the 1989 fiscal year, Congress turned its attention to the budget for 1990. When House and Senate budget negotiators reconciled their targets in the spring, $150 million had been slated for redress payments. As before, appropriating money for redress proved to be far more challenging. H.R. 2991 included only $20 million for redress, and during a markup before the full Appropriations Committee, Representative Julian Dixon of California protested the reduction. "This isn't a new program," he complained. "This is a debt." Several efforts to add to the payment appropriations failed until Representative Steny Hoyer of Maryland suggested moving $30 million from the U.S. Census Bureau based in his district toward redress. That broke the impasse in committee, but the final House bill set aside just $50 million for redress, 10 percent of the initial authorization.[211]

When a Senate Appropriations subcommittee approved H.R. 2991, it removed every last cent for redress payments. Senator Ernest Hollings of South Carolina said the committee "couldn't find" the money. One camp survivor attending the Senate markup, Rudy Tokiwa, was appalled. "How long do they expect us to wait?" he asked. "They're just waiting for every one of us to die off." At that point, Inouye stepped in. Taking Hollings aside, the Hawaii Senator suggested turning redress into a federal entitlement program with annual funding of about $500 million. The payments would be done in a timely

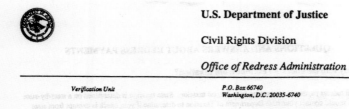

A September 4, 1991, Office of Redress Administration letter informs the recipient of an upcoming redress payment.

Image courtesy of Marjorie Matsushita Sperling, Densho Digital Repository

A woman embraces Representative Norman Y. Mineta of California at a redress check ceremony in 1990.

Image courtesy of the Japanese American National Museum, Gift of Norman Y. Mineta, 96.370

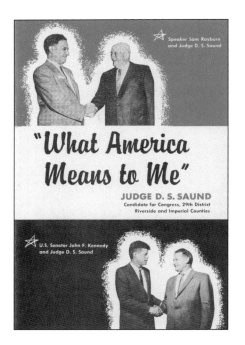

Embodying the transition of Asian Pacific Americans from exclusion to citizenship during the 20th century, Dalip Singh (Judge) Saund published the campaign booklet "What America Means to Me" during his congressional campaign of 1956.

Collection of the U.S. House of Representatives, Gift of Dr. Eric Saund

manner, and the entitlement would be insulated from annual funding fights. The Senate committee agreed to the change, and the full Senate approved H.R. 2991 on September 29, 1989, 74 to 22.[212]

The resulting conference committee agreed to the redress entitlement swap. In the House, Representative Mineta led supporters of the effort. Congress could not prevent elderly internees from dying, he said. "But Congress can make the effort to disburse the redress compensation as quickly as possible." One voice of support came from Representative Newt Gingrich of Georgia, who said that redress was "trying to make sure that those who are now elderly, who once suffered a grievous harm, are given a chance to have their government and the country they love repay that harm before they pass on." The House approved the conference report, 323 to 81, followed by the entitlement waiver, 249 to 166. After the House and Senate cleared the final version that fall, President Bush signed H.R. 2991 into law on November 21, 1989. The first letters of apology and the first redress payments were presented to the oldest surviving detainees in a public ceremony on October 1, 1990. Two years later, Congress amended the Civil Liberties Act in order to provide redress payments to an additional 20,000 camp survivors.[213]

CONCLUSION

Remembrance and redress underscored the profound impact that World War II had on the story of Asian Americans. The echoes of that conflict reverberated for decades afterward. In many ways, the story of seeking and eventually winning redress followed the general contours of the APA experience from the mid- to late-20th century. The decision to evacuate and then imprison 120,000 men, women, and children of Japanese ancestry during World War II capped a century of exclusionary race-based policy that either barred Asian immigrants or denied those already settled in the United States such basic rights as owning property or enjoying opportunities to participate in American society. Only after these exclusionary policies were peeled away one by one did the nation come to terms with the legacies of discrimination and face the historic injustice of internment.

The trajectory of Asian and Pacific Islander Americans during this period moved from exclusion to citizenship. Judge Saund embodied this transition. Though he had been in America since the 1920s, he would not earn his citizenship until the late 1940s. But this opened up possibilities for his political participation that culminated when he won a seat in the U.S. House in 1956. While wartime exigencies caused great hardships for Japanese Americans, they also opened up new possibilities for Asian Indian Americans, such as Saund, and Chinese Americans. Over several decades, immigration prohibitions were relaxed. In its new role as a global power—in part, seeking to appeal to foreign constituencies during the Soviet-American rivalry of the Cold War—the United States created a representational framework for its Pacific territories. On the domestic front, as a small but influential group of APA legislators entered Congress, they were vigilant against dangerous internal security policies that threatened unconstitutional detention, such as Title II of the Internal Security Act that Representative Matsunaga and Senator Inouye helped to repeal.

Secretary of Transportation Norman Y. Mineta, a former Representative from California, and Senator Daniel K. Inouye of Hawaii visit Pearl Harbor in 2004. Mineta, a former internee in the Heart Mountain Camp, and Inouye, a soldier in the 442nd Regimental Combat Team, used their personal experiences as inspiration for political and social change.

Image courtesy of the U.S. Navy

Sometimes change occurs as an unintended consequence of reform, as with the Hart–Celler Immigration Act of 1965 that swung the doors wide open to Asian immigration through family reunification and refugee resettlement policies. More often, efforts at reform percolate through the legislative process slowly, as the case of internment redress illustrates.

But whether gradual or swift, carefully constructed or purposefully undefined, the legislative process turns on representation in Congress and the ability of policy advocates to cultivate key allies. In this sense, the history recounted in this chapter is also the story of the growing political clout of Asian Pacific Americans, especially in Hawaii, California, and America's Pacific territories.

At the beginning of this story, Daniel Inouye, a wounded World War II veteran who fought valiantly with an all-Japanese-American unit, struggled to recuperate from devastating war injuries. Meanwhile, a young boy named Norman Mineta, who, with his family, was uprooted from his home in San Jose and sent to an internment camp in the moonscape terrain of remote Wyoming, tried to find a semblance of normalcy while adjusting to his new surroundings. Remarkably, these very different life experiences and political paths had converged by the early 1990s when Representative Mineta and Senator Inouye served as two of the most senior and influential Members in their respective chambers.

Their stories embodied those of their APA contemporaries on Capitol Hill and portended even greater changes that would come in the following decades.

NOTES

1   Quotation from Senator Daniel K. Inouye, oral history interview by Major Debora R. Cox, 26 April 2000, U.S. Army Medical Department, Office of Medical History: 5. See also Daniel K. Inouye with Lawrence Elliott, *Journey to Washington* (Englewood Cliffs, NJ: Prentice-Hall, Inc., 1969): 149–154; Willard Edwards, "Nisei Hero Inouye Brings Battlefield Courage to Senate," 17 February 1963, *Chicago Tribune*: 11; Caryl Rivers, "A Career of Many Lifetimes," 15 January 1967, *Boston Sunday Globe*: A32; Bill Yenne, *Rising Sons: The Japanese American GIs Who Fought for the United States in World War II* (New York: Thomas Dunne Books, 2007): 215–217.

2   Inouye with Elliott, *Journey to Washington*: 149–154; Yenne, *Rising Sons*: 215–217.

3   Rivers, "A Career of Many Lifetimes."

4   This figure does not include the final Philippine Resident Commissioner, Carlos Peña Romulo, who was appointed to that position by the Philippine government-in-exile in August 1944. Because his career was so brief and fits better within the context of Philippine-U.S. relations, which is broadly covered in Part 1, "Exclusion and Empire, 1898–1946," his profile appears in that section of the book.

5   Inouye with Elliott, *Journey to Washington*: 53.

6   Ibid., 54–55.

7   Ibid., 56.

8   Ibid., 55, 57–61.

9   David M. Kennedy, *Freedom From Fear: The American People in Depression and War, 1929–1945* (New York: Oxford University Press, 1999): 747; Ronald Takaki, *Strangers from a Different Shore: A History of Asian Americans*, rev. ed. (Boston, MA: Back Bay Books, 1998): xiv.

10 Yenne, *Rising Sons*: 34–39.

11 John S. Whitehead, *Completing the Union: Alaska, Hawai'i, and the Battle for Statehood* (Albuquerque: University of New Mexico Press, 2004): 72; Roger Bell, *Last Among Equals: Hawaiian Statehood and American Politics* (Honolulu: University of Hawaii Press, 1984): 77; H. Brett Melendy, *Hawaii: America's Sugar Territory, 1898–1959* (Lewiston, NY: Edwin Mellen Press, 1999): 233, 237.

12 Tom Coffman, *The Island Edge of America: A Political History of Hawai'i* (Honolulu: University of Hawai'i Press, 2003): 79.

13 Gary Y. Okihiro, *Cane Fires: The Anti-Japanese Movement in Hawaii, 1865–1945* (Philadelphia, PA: Temple University Press, 1991): 205; Melendy, *Hawaii*: 237.

14 Sucheng Chan, *Asian Americans: An Interpretive History* (New York: Twayne Publishers, 1991): 124–125; Takaki, *Strangers from a Different Shore*: 383.

15 Takaki, *Strangers from a Different Shore*: 382–383.

16 Ibid., 382; Whitehead, *Completing the Union*: 78; Melendy, *Hawaii*: 234.

17 Whitehead, *Completing the Union*: 84; Takaki, *Strangers from a Different Shore*: 384.

18 Chan, *Asian Americans*: 125; Gavan Daws, *Shoals of Time: A History of the Hawaiian Islands* (Honolulu: University of Hawai'i Press, 1968): 348; quotation in Carla Hall, "The Senator & His Space Refrain," 13 August 1986, *Washington Post*: C1.

19 Hall, "The Senator & His Space Refrain"; Chan, *Asian Americans*: 134; Whitehead, *Completing the Union*: 84–87.

20 Whitehead, *Completing the Union*: 86; Bell, *Last Among Equals*: 82; Takaki, *Strangers from a Different Shore*: 385.

21 "Japanese Excel in U.S. Combat Unit," 6 June 1943, *New York Times*: 33.

22 Chan, *Asian Americans*: 134; Takaki, *Strangers from a Different Shore*: 400.

23 Melendy, *Hawaii*: 238; Chan, *Asian Americans*: 134–135; Yenne, *Rising Sons*: 2.

24 Inouye with Elliott, *Journey to Washington*: 201–202.

25 Johanna Neuman, "Profile: Norm Mineta; What Moves Him?," 25 April 2005, *Los Angeles Times*: B2.

26 Ken Ringle, "The Patriot: Norman Mineta Was Interned by His Country, but Still He Loved It. Then He Changed It," 21 August 2000, *Washington Post*: C1.

27 "Executive Order 9066," National Archives and Records Administration, accessed 6 October 2017, https://catalog.archives.gov/id/5730250.

28 Ringle, "The Patriot"; Berkley Hudson, "'The Hurt is Still There,' Reparations Evoke Painful Recollections," 25 August 1998, *Los Angeles Times*: 10; Michael E. Myers, "As Japanese-Americans, He and His Family Were Interned During War," 22 May 1988, *Los Angeles Times*: 2.

29 Roger Daniels, *Asian America: Chinese and Japanese in the United States since 1850* (Seattle: University of Washington Press, 1988): 202, 205–206; Takaki, *Strangers from a Different Shore*: 386.

30 Daniels, *Asian America*: 199–200; Takaki, *Strangers from a Different Shore*: 380; Chan, *Asian Americans*: 124–125.

31 Roger Daniels, *The Japanese American Cases: The Rule of Law in Time of War* (Lawrence: University Press of Kansas, 2013): 23–24.

32 Roger Daniels, *Prisoners without Trial: Japanese Americans in World War II* (New York: Hill and Wang, 1993).

33 Daniels, *Asian America*: 231, 225.

34 Stephen E. Ambrose and Richard H. Immerman, *Milton S. Eisenhower: Educational Statesman* (Baltimore, MD: Johns Hopkins University Press, 1983); Daniels, *Asian America*: 226–227. In his letter, Eisenhower estimated that 4 in 5 *nisei* were loyal with 50 percent of *issei* "passively loyal."

35 Chan, *Asian Americans*: 127; Takaki, *Strangers from a Different Shore*: 395; Daniels, *Asian America*: 231–232.

36 Takaki, *Strangers from a Different Shore*: 395; Chan, *Asian Americans*: 127.

37 Chan, *Asian Americans*: 128.

38 Takaki, *Strangers from a Different Shore*: 395.

39 Ibid., 396; Chan, *Asian Americans*: 128.

40 Takaki, *Strangers from a Different Shore*: 395; Chan, *Asian Americans*: 128.

41 Betty Cuniberti, "Internment: Personal Voices, Powerful Choices," 4 October 1987, *Los Angeles Times*: 1. See also Irvin Molotsky, "Washington Talk: Friendships, The Heat of War Welds a Bond That Endures Across Aisles and Years," 26 April 1988, *New York Times*: A22; Frank Davies, "Mineta, Ex-Senator Forged Ties at Internment Camp," 2 May 2008, *San Jose Mercury News*: n.p.

42 Chan, *Asian Americans*: 128; Takaki, *Strangers from a Different Shore*: 396.

43 Chan, *Asian Americans*: 129; Daniels, *Asian America*: 221–222.

44 While the initial call to fill the ranks of the segregated battalion would be filled by transfers and volunteers, the draft-registration information eased processing of new recruits. Daniels, *Asian America*: 251n97.

45 The wording of the WRA form for question 27 was "Are you willing to serve in the armed forces of the United States on combat duty, wherever ordered?" And the wording for question 28 was "Will you swear unqualified allegiance to the United States of America and faithfully defend the United States from any or all attacks by foreign or domestic forces, and forswear any form of allegiance or obedience to the Japanese Emperor or any other foreign power or organization?" Daniels, *Asian America*: 261; Chan, *Asian Americans*: 130; Erika Lee, *The Making of Asian America: A History* (New York: Simon and Schuster, 2015): 239.

46 Daniels, *Asian America*: 220; Chan, *Asian Americans*: 133.

47 Takaki, *Strangers from a Different Shore*: 398; Lee, *The Making of Asian America*: 243; Chan, *Asian Americans*: 134.

48 Chan, *Asian Americans*: 129–130, 132–133; Daniels, *Asian America*: 228–230.

49 Peter Irons, *Justice at War: The Story of the Japanese American Internment Cases* (New York: Oxford University Press, 1983); Daniels, *Japanese American Cases*.

50 Paul Finkelman, "*Hirabayashi* v. *United States*," in *The Oxford Companion to the Supreme Court of the United States*, 2nd ed., ed. Kermit L. Hall (New York: Oxford University Press, 2005): 430–431.

51 Finkelman, "*Hirabayashi* v. *United States*."

52 Paul Finkelman, "*Korematsu* v. *United States*," in *The Oxford Companion to the Supreme Court*, 2nd ed., ed. Kermit L. Hall (New York: Oxford University Press, 2005): 561–562. The *Korematsu* decision has never been overturned. See Adam Liptak, "A Discredited Supreme Court Ruling That Still, Technically, Stands," 27 January 2014, *New York Times*, https://www.nytimes.com/2014/01/28/us/time-for-supreme-court-to-overrule-korematsu-verdict.html (accessed 24 August 2016).

53 Irons, *Justice at War*: 343; Daniels, *Japanese American Cases*: 77–78.

54 Takaki, *Strangers from a Different Shore*: 404–505; Chan, *Asian Americans*: 139.

55 Lee, *The Making of Asian America*: 253–254; Chan, *Asian Americans*: 121.

56 Lee, *The Making of Asian America*: 254.

57 Takaki, *Strangers from a Different Shore*: 373–374; Chan, *Asian Americans*: 121–122.

58 Franklin D. Roosevelt, "Message to Congress on Repeal of the Chinese Exclusion Laws," 11 October 1943, in *American Presidency Project*, ed. John T. Woolley and Gerhard Peters, http://www.presidency.ucsb.edu/ws/?pid=16325 (accessed 17 February 2016); Fred W. Riggs, *Pressures on Congress: A Study of the Repeal of Chinese Exclusion* (New York: King's Crown Press, 1950): 210; Stephen W. Stathis, *Landmark Legislation, 1774–2002: Major U.S. Acts and Treaties* (Washington, DC: CQ Press, 2003): 223; Public Law 78-199, 57 Stat. 600 (1943).

59 Displaced Persons Act, Public Law 80-774, 62 Stat. 1009 (1948); Stathis, *Landmark Legislation*: 231; Roger Daniels, *Coming to America: A History of Immigration and Ethnicity in American Life* (New York: Harper Perennial, 1990): 329–330; David M. Reimers, *Still the Golden Door: The Third World Comes to America*, 2nd ed. (New York: Columbia University Press, 1992): 22; Chan, *Asian Americans*: 141; Takaki, *Strangers from a Different Shore*: 417.

60 "Immigration Quotas for Asiatics," *CQ Almanac, 1949*, 5th ed. (Washington, DC: Congressional Quarterly, 1950): 387, http://library.cqpress.com; Reimers, *Still the Golden Door*: 19–20. For more on Judd, see Michael G. Davis, "Impetus for Immigration Reform: Asian Refugees and the Cold War," *Journal of American-East Asian Relations* 7, no. 3/4 (1998): 127–156.

61 Reimers, *Still the Golden Door*: 16–17.

62 "Naturalization of Asians," *CQ Almanac, 1950*, 6th ed. (Washington, DC: Congressional Quarterly, 1951): 240–42, http://library.cqpress.com; U.S. Senate, *Presidential Vetoes, 1789–1976* (Washington, DC: Government Printing Office, 1978): 388.

63 Refuge Relief Act, Public Law 83-203, 67 Stat. 400 (1953); Daniels, *Coming to America*: 336; Stathis, *Landmark Legislation*: 240–241; Reimers, *Still the Golden Door*: 24; Chan, *Asian Americans*: 141.

64 Internal Security Act of 1950, Public Law 81-831, 64 Stat. 987 (1950); Michael J. Ybarra, *Washington Gone Crazy: Senator Pat McCarran and the Great American Communist Hunt* (Hanover, NH: Steerforth Press, 2004): 508, 510; Mitchell T. Maki et al., *Achieving the Impossible Dream: How Japanese Americans Obtained Redress* (Urbana: University of Illinois Press, 1999): 65.

65 Daniels, *Asian America*: 307–308; Lee, *The Making of Asian America*: 276. For more on illegal Chinese immigration during the Cold War, see Mae M. Ngai, "Legacies of Exclusion: Illegal Chinese Immigration during the Cold War Years," *Journal of American Ethnic History* 18, no. 1 (1998): 3–35. And for more general information on the history of illegal immigration, see Mae M. Ngai, *Impossible Subjects: Illegal Aliens and the Making of Modern America* (Princeton, NJ: Princeton University Press, 2004).

66 "Immigration Laws," *CQ Almanac, 1957*, 13th ed. (Washington, DC: Congressional Quarterly, 1958): 670–671, http://library.cqpress.com; Immigration Act Amendments of 1957, Public Law 85-316, 71 Stat. 639 (1957).

67 Bill Ong Hing, *Making and Remaking Asian America through Immigration Policy, 1850–1990* (Stanford, CA: Stanford University Press, 1993): 75.

68 Reimers, *Still the Golden Door*: 24.

69 Daniels, *Coming to America*: 335–336; Reimers, *Still the Golden Door*: 160–161.

70 Daniel J. Tichenor, *Dividing Lines: The Politics of Immigration Control in America* (Princeton, NJ: Princeton University Press, 2002): 188; Daniels, *Asian America*: 306n41; Reimers, *Still the Golden Door*: 21–22; Alien Spouses of Members of the Armed Services Act of 1945, Public Law 79-271, 59 Stat. 659 (1945); Public Law 79-713, 60 Stat. 975 (1946).

71 Philip E. Wolgin and Irene Bloemraad, "'Our Gratitude to Our Soldiers': Military Spouses, Family Re-unification, and Postwar Immigration Reform," *Journal of Interdisciplinary History* 41 (Summer 2010): 27–60.

72 D. S. Saund, *Congressman from India* (1960; repr., Armitsar, India: Satvic Media Pvt. Ltd., 2002): 35–36, 40.

73 Saund, *Congressman from India*: 63.

74 Ibid., 71.

75 Ibid., 72–75.

76 "Naturalization of Natives of India," *CQ Almanac, 1945*, 1st ed. (Washington, DC: Congressional Quarterly, 1946): 710–711, http://library.cqpress.com; Reimers, *Still the Golden Door*: 15.

77 *Congressional Record*, House, 78th Cong., 2nd sess. (14 June 1946): 6933; *Congressional Record*, House, 78th Cong., 2nd sess. (25 June 1946): 7458; *Congressional Record*, House, 78th Cong., 2nd sess. (27 June 1946): 7775; Saund, *Congressman from India*: 75; "Indian Bill Praised," 29 June 1946, *New York Times*: 3; Hing, *Making and Remaking Asian America*: 36–37; Takaki, *Strangers from a Different Shore*: 417; Public Law 79-483, 60 Stat. 416 (1946).

78 Takaki, *Strangers from a Different Shore*: 412–413; Maki et al., *Achieving the Impossible Dream*: 55, 249n11.

79 Daniels, *Asian America*: 305; Tichenor, *Dividing Lines*: 189–190; Stathis, *Landmark Legislation*: 238.

80 Reimers, *Still the Golden Door*: 20; Takaki, *Strangers from a Different Shore*: 413.

81 U.S. Senate, *Presidential Vetoes*: 393.

82 Ibid.; Reimers, *Still the Golden Door*: 61; Immigration and Nationality Act, Public Law 82-414, 66 Stat. 163 (1952).

83 Reimers, *Still the Golden Door*: 63–64; John F. Kennedy, "Letter to the President of the Senate and to the Speaker of the House on Revision of the Immigration Laws," 23 July 1963, in *American Presidency Project*, ed. John T. Woolley and Gerhard Peters, http://www.presidency.ucsb.edu/ws/?pid=9355 (accessed 12 March 2016).

84 Lyndon B. Johnson, "Annual Message to the Congress on the State of the Union," 8 January 1964, in *American Presidency Project*, ed. John T. Woolley and Gerhard Peters, http://www.presidency.ucsb.edu/ws/?pid=26787 (accessed 12 March 2016); Lyndon B. Johnson, "Statement by the President in Response to a Report on Immigration," 17 January 1964, in *American Presidency Project*, ed. John T. Woolley and Gerhard Peters, http://www.presidency.ucsb.edu/ws/?pid=25994 (accessed 12 March 2016).

85 Takaki, *Strangers from a Different Shore*: 518; quotation in Reimers, *Still the Golden Door*: 67.

86 Reimers, *Still the Golden Door*: 74.

87 Ibid., 66; "National Quotas for Immigration to End," *CQ Almanac, 1965*, 21st ed. (Washington, DC: Congressional Quarterly, 1966): 459–482, http://library.cqpress.com. See, for example, James L. Sundquist, *Politics and Policy: The Eisenhower, Kennedy, and Johnson Years* (Washington, DC: Brookings Institution, 1968): 481; Lyndon B. Johnson, "Special Message to the Congress on Immigration," 13 January 1965, in *American Presidency Project*, ed. John T. Woolley and Gerhard Peters, http://www.presidency.ucsb.edu/ws/?pid=26830 (accessed 12 March 2016).

88 Reimers, *Still the Golden Door*: 74.

89 "National Quotas for Immigration to End."

90 Reimers, *Still the Golden Door*: 73; "National Quotas for Immigration to End."

91 Reimers, *Still the Golden Door*: 76.

92 Immigration and Nationality Act of 1965, Public Law 89-213, 79 Stat. 911 (1965); Stathis, *Landmark Legislation*: 267; Lyndon B. Johnson, "Remarks at the Signing of the Immigration Bill, Liberty Island, New York," 3 October 1965, in *American Presidency Project*, ed. John T. Woolley and Gerhard Peters, http://www.presidency.ucsb.edu/ws/?pid=27292 (accessed 12 March 2016).

93 James T. Patterson, *Grand Expectations: The United States, 1945–1974* (New York: Oxford University Press, 1996): 578; Lee, *The Making of Asian America*: 288; Reimers, *Still the Golden Door*: 94.

94 John M. Liu, "The Contours of Asian Professional, Technical and Kindred Work Immigration, 1965–1988," *Sociological Perspectives* 35, no. 4 (1992): 673–704.

95 *Trusteeship Agreement for the Territory of the Pacific Islands*, 80th Cong., 1st sess., H. Doc. 378 (3 July 1947); Public Law 80-204, 61 Stat. 397 (1947); Garrison Nelson, *Committees in the U.S. Congress, 1947 to 1992*, vol. 1 (Washington, DC: Congressional Quarterly Press, 1994): 963. It appears that committee members reported materials through their standing committees. The joint committee disbanded on December 31, 1948.

96 Arnold H. Leibowitz, "American Samoa: Decline of a Culture," *California Western International Law Journal* 10, no. 2 (Spring 1980): 227–229; Sean Morrison, "Foreign in a Domestic Sense: American Samoa and the Last U.S. Nationals," *Hastings Constitutional Law Quarterly* 41, no. 1 (Winter 2013): 75.

97 Arnold H. Leibowitz, *Defining Status*: *A Comprehensive Analysis of United States Territorial Relations* (Dordrecht, Netherlands: Martinus Nijhoff, 1989): 414; Morrison, "Foreign in a Domestic Sense": 76–77.

98 Robert F. Rogers, *Destiny's Landfall*: *A History of Guam*, rev. ed. (Honolulu: University of Hawai'i Press, 2011): 130, 140; Leibowitz, *Defining Status*: 323, 417. Chamorro is the common term used to describe Guam natives before World War II. After the war, Chamorro and Guamanian are considered interchangeable terms. See Gina E. Taitano, "Adoption of 'Guamanian,'" *Guampedia*, accessed 13 October 2015, http://www.guampedia.com/adoption-of-guamanian/.

99 One exception is Senator Millard Tydings of Maryland, who introduced a bill (S. 1450), which died in the 75th Congress (1937–1939), conferring citizenship to Chamorros on Guam. Navy Secretary Claude Swanson was blunt: "These people have not yet reached a state of development commensurate with the personal independence, obligations, and responsibility of United States citizenship," he told a Senate Committee in 1937. The letter from Swanson to Senator Tydings is printed in the Hearings before the Senate Committee on Territories and Insular Affairs, *Citizenship for Residents of Guam*, 75th Cong., 1st sess. (9 April 1937): 2.

100 Leibowitz, *Defining Status*: 323–324.

101 *Congressional Record*, House, 99th Cong., 2nd sess. (26 November 1991): 35435.

102 *Congressional Record*, House, 96th Cong., 2nd sess. (5 March 1980): 4831.

103 Pedro C. Sanchez, *Guam*: *The History of Our Island* (Agana, Guam: Sanchez Publishing House, 1987): 297; Lloyd Norman, "Navy Must Long Rule Guam, Says Island Leader," 10 November 1946, *Chicago Tribune*: 36.

104 Leibowitz, *Defining Status*: 325; James Perez Viernes, "Civil Rights and Citizenship (1898–1950)," *Guampedia*, accessed 13 October 2015, http://www.guampedia.com/chamorro-drive-for-civil-rights/.

105 Doloris Coulter, "Guam Rebels at New Navy 'Rule,'" 3 April 1949, *Washington Post*: B3.

106 Organic Act of Guam, Public Law 81-630, 64 Stat. 384 (1950); Stathis, *Landmark Legislation*: 235; Guam Elective Governor Act, Public Law 90-497, 82 Stat. 842 (1968).

107 There is one instance of a proposed Organic Act for American Samoa. After the *matai* protested a host of U.S. policies and threatened to destabilize the military's authority, Congress authorized the creation of a commission to investigate the governance of American Samoa in 1930. The commission recommended that Samoans be granted American citizenship with a tripartite government but the legislation died in the House in 1933. See Leibowitz, *Defining Status*: 416–417.

108 Eni F. H. Faleomavaega, oral history interview by the U.S. Capitol Historical Society, 11 April 2011, accessed 13 July 2015, http://www.uschs.org/oral-histories/uschs_faleomavaega. htm (site discontinued); Nationality Act of 1940, Public Law 76-853, 54 Stat. 1137 (1940); Morrison, "Foreign in a Domestic Sense": 84, 84n79.

109 Leibowitz, *Defining Status*: 420.

110 Leibowitz, "American Samoa: Decline of a Culture": 251; Morrison, "Foreign in a Domestic Sense": 80.

111 For a full picture of the development of the local legislature, see Fofó I. F. Sunia, *The Story of the Legislature of American Samoa* (New Zealand: GP Printers, 1988); Leibowitz, "American Samoa: Decline of a Culture": 255–256.

112 Leibowitz, *Defining Status*: 339–340.

113 House Committee on Interior and Insular Affairs, *Providing for a Delegate to the House of Representatives for the Unincorporated Territories of Guam and the Virgin Islands*, 92nd Cong., 1st sess., H. Rept. 270 (1971): 2, 4; "Guam, Virgin Islands Delegates," *CQ Almanac, 1972*, 28th ed. (Washington, DC: Congressional Quarterly Inc., 1973): ch. 6, 245; *Congressional Record*, House, 92nd Cong., 2nd sess. (18 January 1972): 26; Public Law 92-271, 86 Stat. 118 (1972).

114 Paramount Chief A. U. Fuimaono first held the position, and Faleomavaega worked on his staff.

115 Hearing before the House Committee on Interior and Insular Affairs, Subcommittee on National Parks and Insular Affairs, *Delegate from American Samoa to the U.S. Congress*, 95th Cong., 2nd sess. (8 August 1978): 1.

116 Faleomavaega, oral history interview; Public Law 95-556, 92 Stat. 2078 (1978).

117 See Richard Ben Cramer, *What It Takes: The Way to the White House* (New York: Vintage Books, 1993): 95–111, 131–136; Ed O'Keefe, "Bob Dole Pays Respects to Daniel Inouye in Capitol Rotunda," 20 December 2012, *Washington Post*, https://www.washingtonpost.com/blogs/2chambers/wp/2012/12/20/bob-dole-pays-respects-to-daniel-inouye-in-capitol-rotunda (accessed 24 August 2016); David M. Shribman, "The Daniel Inouye Generation: Wounded in War, He Just Kept Serving His Country," 19 December 2012, *Pittsburgh Post-Gazette*: B7; Robert D. McFadden, "Daniel Inouye, Hawaii's Quiet Voice of Conscience in Senate, Is Dead at 88," 18 December 2012, *New York Times*: A33; Frank Davies, "Mineta, Ex-Senator Forged Ties at Internment Camp," 2 May 2008, *San Jose Mercury News*: n.p.

118 *Congressional Record*, House, 94th Cong., 1st sess. (9 September 1975): 28034.

119 Leibowitz, *Defining Status*: 336–338. Quotation from Rogers, *Destiny's Landfall*: 242.

120 Blaz introduced H.R. 4100, 100th Cong. (1988).

121 Guam Meritorious Claims Act, Public Law 79-224, 59 Stat. 582 (1945); Bernard Punzalan, "Guam World War II War Claims: A Legislative History," *Guampedia*, accessed 9 March 2016, http://www.guampedia.com/guam-world-war-ii-war-claims-legislative-history/. Under the Treaty of Peace with Japan, the United States excused reparations from Japan and transferred war claims in Guam to its courts. See Stathis, *Landmark Legislation*: 238.

122 *Congressional Record*, House, 102nd Cong., 2nd sess. (5 February 1992): 1692.

123 Lynne Olson, "Territories Still Have Quiet Voices in Congress," 14 May 1978, *Baltimore Sun*: A3.

124 Hearing before the Senate Committee on Energy and Natural Resources, Subcommittee on National Parks, *Miscellaneous National Parks Bills*, 107th Cong., 2nd sess. (12 June 2002): 11.

125 Leanne McLaughlin, "Record is Admirable: Won Pat," 3 September 1976, *Pacific Daily News* (Guam): 24.

126 Faleomavaega, oral history interview.

127 George Blake, "Pat Won! Vows He'll Run Again in '78," 6 September 1976, *Pacific Daily News* (Guam): 2.

128 Faleomavaega, oral history interview.

129 See Appendix B, Asian Pacific Islander Representatives, Senators, Delegates, and Resident Commissioners by State and Territory, 1900–2017.

130 See the general discussions in Bell, *Last Among Equals*, and Whitehead, *Completing the Union*.

131 Bell, *Last Among Equals*: 243, 253–254.

132 Ibid., 257–258.

133 Whitehead, *Completing the Union*: 307; Melendy, *Hawaii*: 277.

134 Office of the Historian, U.S. House of Representatives, "Mary Elizabeth Pruett Farrington," *Women in Congress*, http://history.house.gov/People/Detail/13007?ret=True.

135 Bell, *Last Among Equals*: 237, 273.

136 Ibid., 238, 244, 246; Whitehead, *Completing the Union*: 311.

137 Bell, *Last Among Equals*: 247–249.

138 Whitehead, *Completing the Union*: 312; quotation in Bell, *Last Among Equals*: 250.

139 Whitehead, *Completing the Union*: 314–316; Stathis, *Landmark Legislation*: 252.

140 Daws, *Shoal of Time*: 391; Whitehead, *Completing the Union*: 319, 322–323.

141 Daniels, *Asian America*: 265–266.

142 Chan, *Asian Americans*: 139; Public Law 78-405, 58 Stat. 677 (1944).

143 Lee, *The Making of Asian America*: 239–240.

144 Ibid., 239–241; Daniels, *Japanese American Cases*: 122–124; Maki et al., *Achieving the Impossible Dream*: 54–55.

145 Maki et al., *Achieving the Impossible Dream*: 60–61.

146 Ibid., 55, 250n13.

147 Ibid., 52.

148 Daniels, *Asian America*: 296–297.

149 House Committee on the Judiciary, *Authorizing the Attorney General to Adjudicate Certain Claims Resulting from Evacuation of Certain Persons of Japanese Ancestry Under Military Orders*, 80th Cong., 1st sess., H. Rept. 732 (27 June 1947); Commission on Wartime Relocation and Internment of Civilians (hereinafter CWRIC), *Personal Justice Denied*, Part 1 (December 1982): 50, https://www.archives.gov/research/japanese-americans/justice-denied (accessed 9 January 2017); Maki et al., *Achieving the Impossible Dream*: 54; Daniels, *Asian America*: 296.

150 Daniels, *Asian America*: 297.

151 Japanese-American Evacuation Claims Act, Public Law 80-886, 62 Stat. 1231 (1948); Harry S. Truman, "Special Message to the Congress on Civil Rights," 2 February 1948, in *American Presidency Project*, ed. John T. Woolley and Gerhard Peters, http://www.presidency.ucsb.edu/ws/?pid=13006 (accessed 7 March 2016).

152 Daniels, *Asian America*: 297–298; CWRIC, *Personal Justice Denied*, Part 1: 118; Maki et al., *Achieving the Impossible Dream*: 54.

153 Maki et al., *Achieving the Impossible Dream*: 66; Daniels, *Asian America*: 303n36.

154 Maki et al., *Achieving the Impossible Dream*: 66; Louis Fisher, "Detention of U.S. Citizens," Report RS22130, 28 April 2005, Congressional Research Service.

155 Richard Halloran, *Sparky: Warrior, Peacemaker, Poet, Patriot* (Honolulu, HI: Watermark Publishing, 2002): 140–143.

156 Fisher, "Detention of U.S. Citizens"; Maki et al., *Achieving the Impossible Dream*: 66.

157 Maki et al., *Achieving the Impossible Dream*: 57.

158 Leslie T. Hatamiya, *Righting a Wrong: Japanese Americans and the Passage of the Civil Liberties Act of 1988* (Stanford, CA: Stanford University Press, 1993): 133–134.

159 Gerald R. Ford, "Proclamation 4417—An American Promise," 19 February 1976, in *American Presidency Project*, ed. John T. Woolley and Gerhard Peters, http://www.presidency.ucsb.edu/ws/?pid=787 (accessed 7 March 2016).

160 Gerald R. Ford, "Remarks Upon Signing a Proclamation Concerning Japanese-American Internment During World War II," 19 February 1976, in *American Presidency Project*, ed. John T. Woolley and Gerhard Peters, http://www.presidency.ucsb.edu/ws/?pid=5591 (accessed 7 March 2016).

161 Daniels, *Japanese American Cases*: 193, 195–196; Public Law 102-248, 106 Stat. 40 (1992); Public Law 109-441, 120 Stat. 3288 (2006).

162 Daniels, *Japanese American Cases*: 193–194; William J. Clinton, "Memorandum on Preservation of Japanese-American Internment Sites," 9 November 2000, in *American Presidency Project*, ed. John T. Woolley and Gerhard Peters, http://www.presidency.ucsb.edu/ws/?pid=1011 (accessed 31 March 2016). The NPS Report, *Confinement and Ethnicity: An Overview of World War II Japanese American Relocation Sites*, can be found at https://www.nps.gov/parkhistory/online_books/anthropology74/ (accessed 31 March 2016).

163 William J. Clinton, "Proclamation 7395—Establishment of the Minidoka Internment

National Monument," 17 January 2001, in *American Presidency Project*, ed. John T. Woolley and Gerhard Peters, http://www.presidency.ucsb.edu/ws/?pid=62518 (accessed 31 March 2016).

164 Daniels, *Japanese American Cases*: 195; Public Law 109-441, 120 Stat. 3288 (2006). During 2006, two more World War II *nikkei* sites were added as National Historic Landmarks: the Tule Lake Segregation Center and Granada Relocation Center. See "Tule Lake Segregation Center," National Park Service, accessed 31 March 2016, https://www.nps.gov/nr/feature/asia/2006/tul.htm; "Grenada Relocation Center," National Park Service, accessed 31 March 2016, https://www.nps.gov/nr/feature/asia/2006/gra.htm. President Bush also issued Presidential Proclamation 8327 on December 5, 2008, establishing the World War II Valor in the Pacific National Monument, which included provisions for the Tule Lake Segregation Center to become a National Monument. See George W. Bush, "Proclamation 8327—Establishment of the World War II Valor in the Pacific National Monument," 5 December 2008, in *American Presidency Project*, ed. John T. Woolley and Gerhard Peters, http://www.presidency.ucsb.edu/ws/?pid=85048 (accessed 31 March 2016).

165 "'Asian Heritage Week' Bill Needs Sponsors," 31 May 1978, *International Examiner* (Seattle): 10, http://www.iexaminer.org/iearchives/ (accessed 5 January 2017); *Congressional Record*, House, 95th Cong., 2nd sess. (10 July 1978): 19940–19941.

166 *Congressional Record*, House, 95th Cong., 2nd sess. (19 September 1978): 29969; "Carter Signs Legislation for Asian Heritage Week," 30 November 1978, *International Examiner* (Seattle): 11, http://www.iexaminer.org/iearchives/ (accessed 5 January 2017).

167 *Congressional Record*, Senate, 101st Cong., 2nd sess. (3 May 1990): S5485–S5486.

168 Sharon Shaw Johnson and Marilyn Greene, "Capital Line," 7 May 1990, *USA Today*: 4A.

169 Daniels, *Asian America*: 332; Maki et al., *Achieving the Impossible Dream*: 64; Hatamiya, *Righting a Wrong*: 138.

170 Maki et al., *Achieving the Impossible Dream*: 68; *Congressional Record*, House, 93rd Cong., 2nd sess. (28 June 1974): 21773.

171 Maki et al., *Achieving the Impossible Dream*: 81; Daniels, *Asian America*: 332–333; Hatamiya, *Righting a Wrong*: 139–141.

172 Daniels, *Japanese American Cases*: 148; Maki et al., *Achieving the Impossible Dream*: 86.

173 Daniels, *Japanese American Cases*: 148; quotation in Maki et al., *Achieving the Impossible Dream*: 86.

174 Maki et al., *Achieving the Impossible Dream*: 86; see also Daniels, *Japanese American Cases*: 148.

175 Maki et al., *Achieving the Impossible Dream*: 91–92; Daniels, *Asian America*: 334–335.

176 Maki et al., *Achieving the Impossible Dream*: 92. Backed by JACL members who thought the commission option was too timid, Seattle Congressman Michael E. Lowry introduced a competing redress bill that provided for a formal apology and reparations payments. Because none of the *nikkei* Congressmen supported it, the Judiciary Committee never considered it. See Maki et al., *Achieving the Impossible Dream*: 92–93; Daniels, *Japanese American Cases*: 149.

177 Maki et al., *Achieving the Impossible Dream*: 93–94.

178 Ibid., 95; *Congressional Record*, House, 96th Cong., 2nd sess. (21 July 1980): 18875–18876.

179 Maki et al., *Achieving the Impossible Dream*: 96; Commission on Wartime Relocation and Internment of Civilians Act, Public Law 96-317, 94 Stat. 964 (1980). See also Jimmy Carter, "Commission on Wartime Relocation and Internment of Civilians Act Remarks on Signing S. 1647 Into Law," 31 July 1980, in *American Presidency Project*, ed. John T. Woolley and Gerhard Peters, http://www.presidency.ucsb.edu/ws/?pid=44855 (accessed 9 March 2016).

180 Senator Milton R. Young of South Dakota served as president pro tempore on December 5, 1980. See "President Pro Tempore," U.S. Senate Historical Office, accessed 24 March 2016, http://www.senate.gov/artandhistory/history/common/briefing/President_Pro_Tempore.htm#5.

181 Daniels, *Japanese American Cases*: 150; Daniels, *Asian America*: 335–336. The other members were former Massachusetts Senator Edward W. Brooke; former Justice Arthur J. Goldberg; former Health, Education and Welfare Secretary Arthur S. Fleming; Judge William J. Marutani; and former Washington Senator Hugh B. Mitchell. In early 1981, Reverend Ishmael V. Gromoff, an Aleut, and former Massachusetts Representative Father Robert F. Drinan were added to the commission.

182 Maki et al., *Achieving the Impossible Dream*: 99–100; CWRIC, *Personal Justice Denied*, Part 1: 1; Daniels, *Japanese American Cases*: 153.

183 Lee, *The Making of Asian America*: 312; quotation in Takaki, *Strangers from a Different Shore*: 485.

184 Maki et al., *Achieving the Impossible Dream*: 110.

185 *Congressional Record*, Senate, 97th Cong., 2nd sess. (7 December 1982): 29209–29213, quotation on p. 29213.

186 CWRIC, *Personal Justice Denied*, Part 1: 1.

187 Ibid., 18.

188 Daniels, *Japanese American Cases*: 4; Maki et al., *Achieving the Impossible Dream*: 111.

189 Daniels, *Asian America*: 339.

190 CWRIC, *Personal Justice Denied*, Part 2: *Recommendations*, https://www.archives.gov/research/japanese-americans/justice-denied (accessed 25 March 2016); Maki et al., *Achieving the Impossible Dream*: 112.

191 Maki et al., *Achieving the Impossible Dream*: 113.

192 Ibid., 139, 142. For the testimony of Mineta and Matsui, see Hearings before the House Committee on the Judiciary, Subcommittee on Administrative Law and Governmental Relations, *Japanese-American and Aleutian Wartime Relocation*, 98th Cong., 2nd sess., (20–21, 27 June 1984 and 12 September 1984): 24.

193 Maki et al., *Achieving the Impossible Dream*: 140–145; Daniels, *Asian America*: 340.

194 Both Senators Inouye and Matsunaga served in the 442nd. Maki et al., *Achieving the Impossible Dream*: 153–156.

195 Hearings before the House Committee on the Judiciary, Subcommittee on Administrative Law and Governmental Relations, *Civil Liberties Act of 1985 and the Aleutian and Pribilof Islands Restitution Act*, Part I, 99th Cong., 2nd sess. (28 April 1986): 34.

196 Ibid., 36; Maki et al., *Achieving the Impossible Dream*: 156.

197 Maki et al., *Achieving the Impossible Dream*: 167; *Congressional Record*, House, 101st Cong., 1st sess. (1 August 1989): 2834.

198 "House Votes to Make Amends for Internment," *CQ Almanac, 1987*, 43rd ed. (Washington, DC: Congressional Quarterly, 1988): 278, http://library.cqpress.com; "Internees Gain Reparations," *CQ Almanac, 1988*, 44th ed. (Washington, DC: Congressional Quarterly, 1989): 80–81, http://library.cqpress.com; Bill McAllister, "Amends Sought for 1940s Internment," 12 September 1987, *Washington Post*: A1; Mick Rood, no title, 16 September 1987, States News Service; Jill Lawrence, no title, 17 September 1987, Associated Press; Nathaniel Nash, "House Votes Payments to Japanese Internees," 18 September 1987, *New York Times*: A15; Jill Lawrence, "Mineta Tearfully Recalls 1942 Internment as House Votes Cash Compensation," 18 September 1987, Associated Press.

199 Maki et al., *Achieving the Impossible Dream*: 167, 170. The Aleut redress bill was reported out of the Judiciary Committee in October. "House Votes to Make Amends for Internment"; Halloran, *Sparky*: 210–220.

200 Halloran, *Sparky*: 210–220.

201 Maki et al., *Achieving the Impossible Dream*: 167–169; "House Votes to Make Amends for Internment."

202 "House Votes to Make Amends for Internment."

203 *Congressional Record*, House, 100th Cong., 1st sess. (17 September 1987): 24304.

204 "House Votes to Make Amends for Internment."

205 Ibid.; "Internees Gain Reparations"; McAllister, "Amends Sought for 1940s Internment"; Rood, no title, 16 September 1987; Lawrence, no title, 17 September 1987; Nash, "House Votes Payments to Japanese Internees"; Lawrence, "Mineta Tearfully Recalls 1942 Internment as House Votes Cash Compensation."

206 Maki et al., *Achieving the Impossible Dream*: 171, 181; "Internees Gain Reparations"; Halloran, *Sparky*: 226.

207 *Congressional Record*, Senate, 100th Cong., 2nd sess. (20 April 1988): 7619–7643; "Internees Gain Reparations"; Halloran, *Sparky*: 233–234.

208 "Internees Gain Reparations"; Maki et al., *Achieving the Impossible Dream*: 195–196; Civil Liberties Act of 1988, Public Law 100-383, 102 Stat. 903 (1988).

209 Takaki, *Strangers from a Different Shore*: 485–486; Ronald Reagan, "Remarks on Signing the Bill Providing Restitution for the Wartime Internment of Japanese-American Civilians," 10 August 1988, in *American Presidency Project*, ed. John T. Woolley and Gerhard Peters, http://www.presidency.ucsb.edu/ws/?pid=36240 (accessed 24 March 2016).

210 "House Votes to Make Amends for Internment"; quotation in Maki et al., *Achieving the Impossible Dream*: 201–203.

211 Maki et al., *Achieving the Impossible Dream*: 201, 203–204; "Commerce, Justice, State Cleared for President," in *CQ Almanac, 1989*, 45th ed. (Washington, DC: Congressional Quarterly, 1990): 721–728, http://library.cqpress.com.

212 "Commerce, Justice, State Cleared for President"; Maki et al., *Achieving the Impossible Dream*: 206, 208.

213 "Commerce, Justice, State Cleared for President"; Maki et al., *Achieving the Impossible Dream*: 209–210; Chan, *Asian Americans*: 174; Daniels, *Japanese American Cases*: 163.

Party Divisions in the House of Representatives
85th–102nd Congresses (1957–1993)*

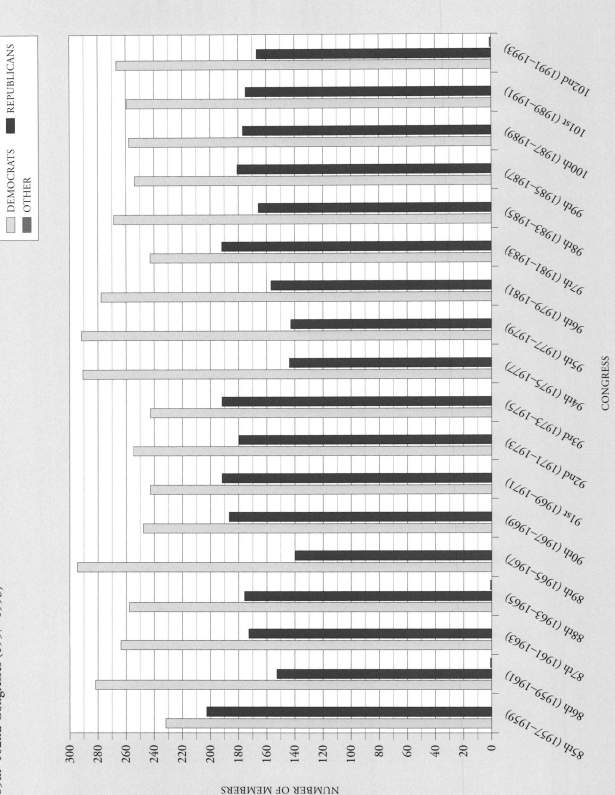

NUMBER OF MEMBERS

CONGRESS

85th (1957–1959)
86th (1959–1961)
87th (1961–1963)
88th (1963–1965)
89th (1965–1967)
90th (1967–1969)
91st (1969–1971)
92nd (1971–1973)
93rd (1973–1975)
94th (1975–1977)
95th (1977–1979)
96th (1979–1981)
97th (1981–1983)
98th (1983–1985)
99th (1985–1987)
100th (1987–1989)
101st (1989–1991)
102nd (1991–1993)

DEMOCRATS   REPUBLICANS
OTHER

Source: Office of the Historian, U.S. House of Representatives, "Party Divisions," http://history.house.gov.

*Party division totals are based on Election Day results.

Party Divisions in the Senate

85th–102nd Congresses (1957–1993)*

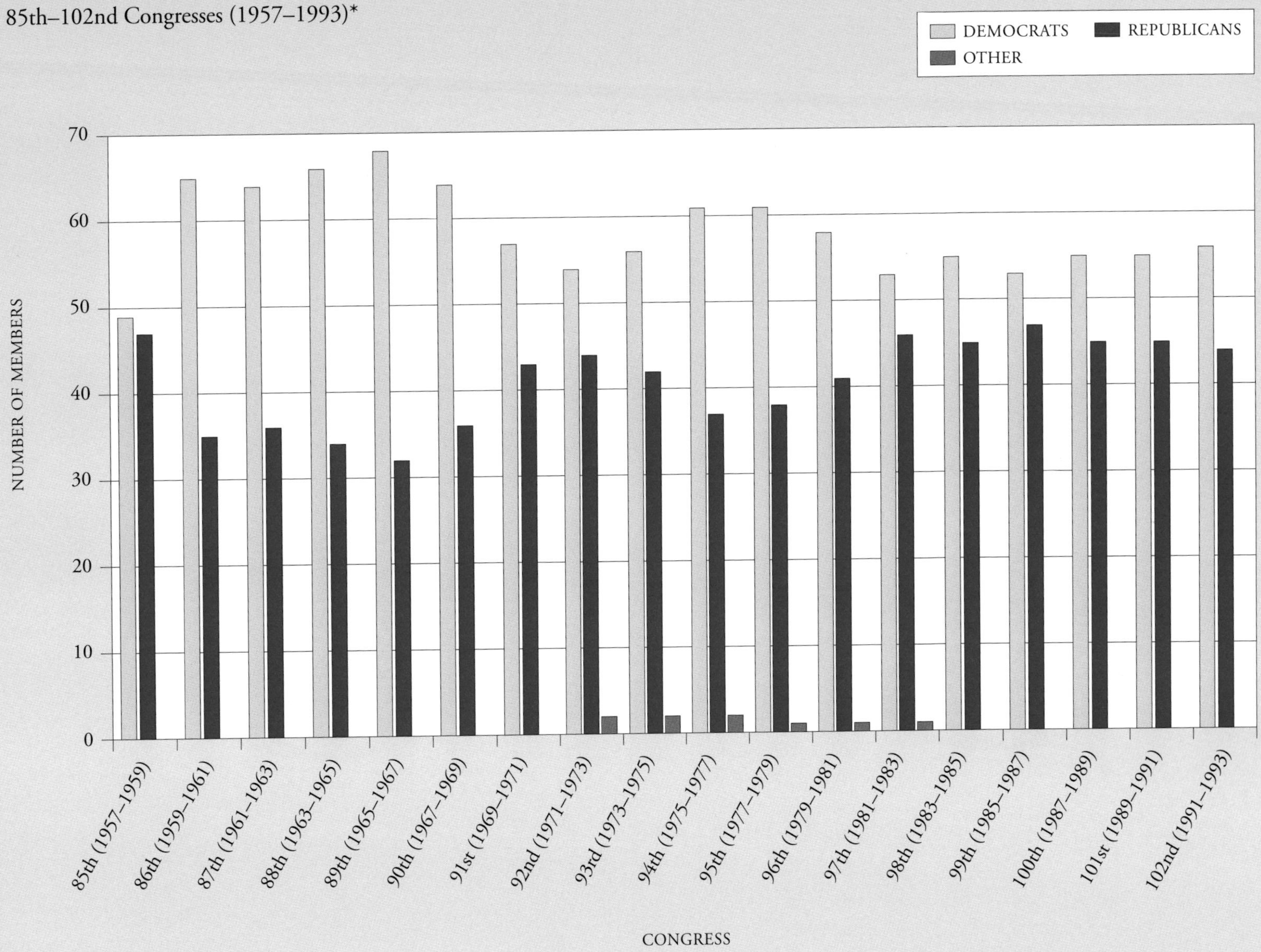
DEMOCRATS
REPUBLICANS
OTHER
NUMBER OF MEMBERS
70
60
50
40
30
20
10
0
85th (1957–1959)
86th (1959–1961)
87th (1961–1963)
88th (1963–1965)
89th (1965–1967)
90th (1967–1969)
91st (1969–1971)
92nd (1971–1973)
93rd (1973–1975)
94th (1975–1977)
95th (1977–1979)
96th (1979–1981)
97th (1981–1983)
98th (1983–1985)
99th (1985–1987)
100th (1987–1989)
101st (1989–1991)
102nd (1991–1993)
CONGRESS

Sources: U.S. Senate Historical Office; *Biographical Directory of the United States Congress, 1774–Present*, http://bioguide.congress.gov.

*Party division totals are based on Election Day results.

Asian and Pacific Islander American Members by Office
First Elected 1956–1991

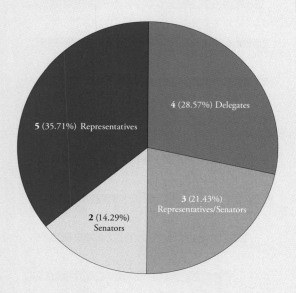

Asian and Pacific Islander American Members by State and Territory
First Elected 1956–1991

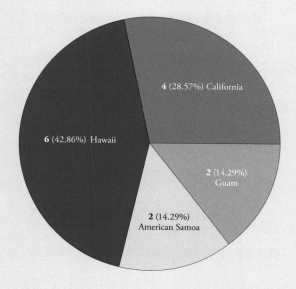

Sources: Appendix A: Asian and Pacific Islander American Representatives, Senators, Delegates, and Resident Commissioners by Congress, 1900–2017; Office of the Historian, U.S. House of Representatives; U.S. Senate Historical Office.

Congressional Service

For Asian and Pacific Islander Americans in Congress First Elected 1956–1991

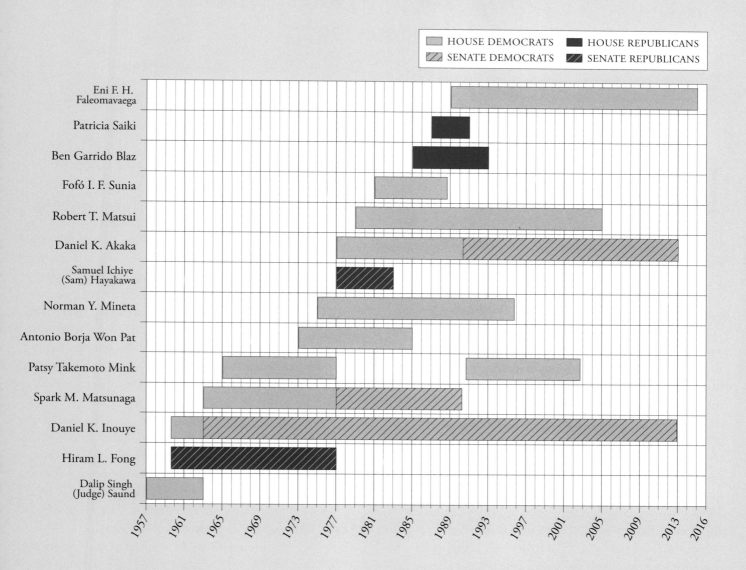

Dalip Singh (Judge) Saund
1899–1973

UNITED STATES REPRESENTATIVE 1957–1963
DEMOCRAT FROM CALIFORNIA

In November 1956, D. S. Saund, who everyone simply called "Judge," became the first person of Asian descent elected to serve as a United States Representative. He was a tireless champion of his southern California district and the farmers who called it home. But his unique backstory—born in India, naturalized U.S. citizen, successful businessman, county judge—also catapulted him to the international stage. During his career in the House of Representatives, at the height of the Cold War, Saund became something of a transcendent politician who had the singular ability to engage audiences abroad. Although he frequently confronted discrimination during his life in the United States, Saund maintained his belief in the promises of American democracy.

Dalip Singh Saund was born on September 20, 1899, and raised in Chhajjalwaddi in the far-northern province of Punjab, India, which at the time was a British colony. Saund's father worked as a construction contractor for the government and died when Saund was only a boy. His parents had lived through the period of British colonialism and neither had attended school, but education was a cornerstone of Saund's life. His father and uncles saved enough money to open a one-room schoolhouse about a half mile from where Saund lived. At the age of eight, his parents sent him to boarding school 16 miles away in the city of Amritsar near the border with modern day Pakistan.[1]

While in college at the University of Punjab, Saund supported the movement for an independent India led by Mohandas Gandhi.[2] Along with his informal lessons in nonviolence and civil disobedience, Saund majored in mathematics, graduated with a BS degree in 1919, and moved to America to further his education. While he waited for his passport, Saund worked to expand his childhood school, planted trees along the roads throughout his village, and helped establish two community banks.[3]

During World War I, Saund read the speeches of President Woodrow Wilson in the news and later discovered the writings of Abraham Lincoln, especially the moving words of the Gettysburg Address.[4] "Lincoln," Saund later wrote, "changed the entire course of my life."[5]

Saund had planned to spend no more than a few years in America learning the fruit-canning business before returning home.[6] His trip west took him from Bombay to England and from England to Ellis Island, New York, where he arrived on September 27, 1920. "You are now a free man in a free country," one of the immigration officers told him.[7] Saund made his way west and enrolled in the University of California's agricultural school and mathematics department as well.[8]

Berkeley, California, was not the most welcoming of places for Indian and Asian students, and "outside of the university atmosphere," he later remembered, "it was made quite evident that people from Asia—Japanese, Chinese, and Hindus—were not wanted."[9] Saund, however, became involved with the local community and then earned MA and PhD degrees in mathematics in 1924.

After he finished his studies, Saund's family informed him that the Indian government had been keeping tabs on his "anti-British utterances in America." Saund decided to stay in California and later authored *My Mother India*, a book about his experiences at home and a critique of British imperialism.[10] He moved south to California's Imperial Valley, where a number of other Indians had settled.[11] His first job, he said, was as "foreman of a cotton-picking gang at a ranch belonging to some Indian friends." Saund saved money and quickly went into the business of growing lettuce. The lettuce market tanked, however, and it was a while before he recouped his losses.[12]

In 1928 Saund married Marian Kosa, the daughter of a close friend and a future teacher in the Los Angeles school

Image courtesy of the Library of Congress

system. Together they had three children: Dalip Jr., who served in the Korean War as a lieutenant in the U.S. Army, and two daughters, Julie and Ellie, who both attended the University of California, Los Angeles.[13]

Initially, Saund's young family settled on a ranch in Westmorland, California, a dry, windy, and hot region of the state just a few miles south of the Salton Sea. The area specialized in sending melons to market before anywhere else, but the Depression hit the local economy hard. Fruit rotted in the field, and harvest work disappeared.[14] Saund came out of the economic collapse relatively unscathed because he grew and baled alfalfa hay and had direct access to Los Angeles.[15] Saund owned his own farming equipment, but because California law prevented people of Asian descent from owning or leasing land at the time, a friend in the valley had to put the contracts in his own name.[16]

As the economy rebounded, Saund stumbled for a spell and plunged into debt. Against advice from friends and business associates, he refused to declare bankruptcy and decided to work his way out of the hole "slowly but surely." "That decision to follow the dictates of my own heart was one of the best decisions I've ever made," he wrote years later.[17] After 20 years of farming, Saund opened his own fertilizer business around 1953, commuting a total of nearly 1,000 miles a week between his home near Los Angeles, where his wife taught and where they raised their children, and his business, headquartered in Westmorland.[18]

Saund closely followed politics during his time in the west, studying the issues of the 1924 and 1928 presidential contests. "By 1932," he wrote in his memoirs, "I had positively and definitely become a Democrat by outlook and conviction."[19] During the 1930s, his home county received a number of benefits from federal New Deal programs created to help struggling farmers and people out of work.[20]

When he was not farming, Saund was a popular speaker in the valley and addressed local groups nearly every week.[21] He learned how to think and speak in the moment, unscripted, during his involvement with the Toastmasters Club.[22]

Saund's political activities could go only so far, however, because, at the time, federal law prevented him

from becoming a U.S. citizen. In the 1940s, he helped organize efforts to open citizenship to people of Indian descent living in the States. He worked long hours to build support, and, eventually, Congress passed a bill allowing Indian immigrants to pursue naturalization.[23] Saund became a U.S. citizen three and a half years later on December 16, 1949.[24]

Saund was elected to the Imperial County Democratic Central Committee in the summer of 1950 and ran for a judgeship in November. He claimed to know every voter in the district and campaigned door-to-door, building momentum. He won, but a higher court vacated his election after it became clear that Saund had not been a U.S. citizen for a full year at the time of his victory.[25]

Two years later, Saund ran again, and in the buildup to the 1952 judicial election, he faced a barrage of discrimination. Voters, and even old friends, told Saund that they liked him well enough but could never bring themselves to "go for a Hindu judge."[26]

As the election heated up, Saund adamantly refused to go negative, his message being, "I am not running against anybody; all I'm asking for is a job, and it's up to you to judge whether I deserve your support or not."[27]

"Doc, tell us, if you're elected, will you furnish the turbans or will we have to buy them ourselves in order to come into your court?" someone later asked him in the middle of a restaurant. "My friend," Saund responded, "you know me as a tolerant man. I don't care what a man has on the top of his head. All I'm interested in is what he's got inside."[28] On Election Day, Saund won by 13 votes.[29]

During his four-year judgeship, Saund worked to institute stiff sentencing that helped clean up blighted areas of Westmorland.[30] He earned the reputation as a first-rate legal mind, going head to head with more practiced attorneys.[31] Saund's judgeship became a huge part of his identity and served as a springboard to national office. When he ran for the House, he ran as "Judge Saund."[32]

In 1954 Saund won election as the head of the Democratic Central Committee for Imperial County. Democrats lost the congressional election that year but made a stronger showing than most political experts expected, encouraging local party officials to go all in for the next race in 1956.[33] Saund had met a number of political kingmakers, and by the next fall, California Democrats began pledging support for Saund—whom they reportedly called "the peacemaker"—if he ever decided to run for Congress. It did not take long. By October 1955, Saund resolved to campaign for a seat in the House from California's 29th District. He knew half of the district well (Imperial County), but anticipated a struggle in neighboring Riverside County. A handful of party leaders from both counties ended up giving him their backing a month later.[34]

When the incumbent Congressman, Republican John Phillips, announced his retirement from the House, six Republicans and two Democrats—Saund included— jumped into the race by early 1956.[35]

Saund's congressional district was created after the 1940 Census, and voters there had elected a Republican to the House ever since. By 1955, however, Democrats had a slight edge in voter registration.[36] Geographically it was huge—larger "than Massachusetts, Rhode Island, and Delaware combined," according to the *New York Times*—and bordered by Nevada to the east, Mexico to the south, and Los Angeles to the west.[37] From a population standpoint, it was one of California's smaller districts, with a total of 233,021 people in 1950; it grew to 378,296 by 1960.[38]

Saund's main opponent in the Democratic primary was a lawyer from nearby Riverside County named Carl Kegley. The race began cordially until Kegley filed legal action to disqualify Saund, arguing the Judge had not been a U.S. citizen long enough to serve in the House.[39] Undismayed, Saund saw it as an opportunity. "When he filed suit against me," Saund remembered a few years later, "it became front-page, headline news in all the Riverside and Imperial County papers. Even if I could have afforded it, I couldn't have bought that kind of publicity."[40]

Saund remained confident in his eligibility throughout the fight, pointing out that, if he won the election, he would take office in January 1957, making him a citizen for just over seven years, as required by the Constitution.[41]

He stayed on message and refused to attack his opponent, eventually winning the primary by more than 9,000 votes.[42]

Going into the general election, Saund played catch-up to his Republican opponent, Jacqueline Cochran Odlum. A decorated Army pilot known for her work as the head of the Women Airforce Service Pilots during World War II, Odlum owned a successful cosmetics company and had long been a supporter of President Dwight D. Eisenhower.[43] Because of the unique backgrounds of the two leading candidates, the race attracted national attention. "A woman's 'smoldering hope' and the success story of an East Indian immigrant are converging into what is likely to be one of the most colorful Congressional contests of 1956," reported the *New York Times*. "Seldom if ever has the American melting pot cooked up a spicier election dish than the contest now simmering in California's 29th Congressional District," read another article in the *Los Angeles Times*.[44]

Throughout the campaign, Odlum reportedly outspent Saund many times over.[45] Saund, however, used a grassroots approach, holding a series of free community barbeques.[46] His phalanx of supporters, including members of his own family, campaigned door-to-door while registering voters.[47] His wife, Marian, and their college-aged daughter, Ellie, spent summer vacation canvassing Riverside, and Saund's son and daughter-in-law came home often to help. "We didn't have time to stop and count how many precincts," Marian said. "We just worked."[48] House Majority Whip Carl Albert of Oklahoma also campaigned for Saund in California, and Harold Cooley of North Carolina wired his support.[49]

Saund's ethnicity and religious beliefs were a constant issue in the race. The Associated Press reminded readers that Saund was "a Sikh Hindu born in India" with "dark-hued" skin before noting that he had been "thoroughly Americanized after 36 years here."[50] Saund bought airtime in Southern California to introduce himself to voters throughout the district.[51] But as the *New York Times* told its readers two weeks before the election, Saund ran up against "considerable racial sensitivity in the area."[52] Years later, Odlum still believed that Saund was, as she said, "a card-toting Communist."[53]

Ultimately, the issues seemed to outweigh everything else. As a farmer who had once struggled to pull himself out of debt, Saund believed in the necessity of farm subsidies, while Odlum, who also ran her own ranch, took a more conditional approach.[54] Odlum touted her connections in Washington, while Saund promised to work hard and used his personal history as proof of his commitment to the district.[55] A few years after the election, Saund criticized the idea of campaigning on political connections writing, "My view was that any congressman who expected to get favors from the big boys in Washington got them only by voting the way the big boys wanted him to vote, not the way the interests of his district would lead him to vote."[56]

During a last-minute debate broadcast a week before the election, Saund pointed out that his political beliefs as a Democrat were often more in line with the popular Republican presidential administration of Dwight Eisenhower than Odlum's own stances as the actual GOP candidate.[57] Saund built on that momentum going into Election Day. When the dust settled, he won, taking 54,989 votes, or roughly 52 percent.[58]

Saund credited his victory to his stance on local issues, especially his commitment to small-scale farmers and small businesses.[59] With his election, Saund became the first Asian American ever to enjoy full voting rights in Congress (he served as a U.S. Representative whose powers were not circumscribed like those of the Delegates and Resident Commissioners who had preceded him.)[60]

"Californians have not always been hospitable to aliens—and especially to aliens of Asian origin," the *Washington Post's* editorial board observed. "In this election they ignored ancestry and considered the individual."[61] "He's growed cotton. He's growed lettuce and beets. He's worked in hay and he's worked for wages. And he won't let any smart aleck lawyers trick him," a district farmer told the culture magazine *Coronet*. "That's why we sent him to Washington."[62]

For the duration of his House career, Saund faced modest competition back home. He won re-election handily in 1958, taking 62 percent of the vote and crushing his Republican opponent, John Babbage, by

almost 26,000 votes.[63] In 1960, although he said he was "running scared," Saund coasted to victory over Republican Charles H. Jameson.[64]

Saund, the *New York Times* wrote shortly after his first election, "is a stocky, dynamic, perpetually grinning man whose walnut skin threatened to handicap him in a race-conscious section where there was some informal school segregation until a couple of years ago. This evidently was more than offset by his manifest dedication to American ideals and by his articulateness—he speaks in a high-pitched, urgent tone, with just a faint alien accent. He looks like an average business man or schoolteacher, and with his serviceable 'border Spanish' has occasionally been mistaken for one of the Mexican-Americans numerous in the district."[65]

Saund's ethnicity may have been an issue in the election, but the Congressman-elect did not want it to influence his service in the House. Saund wanted his committee assignments to reflect his district's interests rather than his personal history and told the press he would like a seat on something other than the Foreign Affairs Committee. "I am not so much concerned with India," he said about a month before the start of the new Congress. "I am concerned with my district right here in California." He wanted to see better farm supports. He wanted the Air Force to build a new base in his district, and he wanted a nuclear power plant built in the "big spaces" outside the valley. "I would prefer to be on the Agriculture and the Armed Services Committee," he had said in late November.[66] On the eve of the new Congress, at least one report had Saund pushing for a seat on the Interior and Insular Affairs Committee.[67]

Saund arrived in Washington on December 17 to look for a home and start organizing his congressional office.[68] He was already something of a national star and, in his first term, Democratic leaders placed him on the Committee on Foreign Affairs despite his earlier reluctance. Saund called the appointment a "high honor," and he remained on the committee for his entire House career. Foreign Affairs was one of the most powerful committees in the House during the Cold War, making it a major coup for a novice lawmaker. In the 86th and 87th Congresses (1959–1963), Saund also served on the Committee on Interior and Insular Affairs.[69]

His national profile aside, Saund tried to stay out of the spotlight as much as he could in order to learn how the House worked—a difficult problem when television cameras from CBS followed him around on Opening Day. He and his wife ate breakfast in the House cafeteria every morning before he went up to his office to answer mail from his constituents.[70] Saund helped veterans and their families access benefits and worked to secure millions in funding for the March Air Force Base and the Naval Auxiliary Air Station and additional money for the Corona Naval Ordinance Laboratory. He collaborated with committee chairmen to fund flood control projects, won funding for irrigation efforts on American Indian land, opened new post offices in his fast-growing district, built new roads, improved airports in the Imperial Valley, and assisted scientists developing new strains of cotton. He worked to protect the Bracero farm labor program, in which immigrants from Mexico took jobs in America's agricultural sector as part of a guest-worker program. And he helped to settle claims Riverside County had against the federal government for repairs to a regional airport.[71]

Saund was a fierce supporter of the 1957 Civil Rights bill. The Judge used his own story to advocate its passage, pointing out that, although being born in India did not prevent him from becoming a Member, being born black in Mississippi would have. "No amount of sophistry or legal argument can deny the fact that in 13 counties in 1 State in the United States of America in the year 1957, not one Negro is a registered voter. Let us remove those difficulties, my friends."[72]

Midway through his first term, Saund fulfilled a campaign promise by flying home to India for the first time in almost 40 years. When he first floated the idea in the days after the 1956 election, Saund billed the trip as a "goodwill" visit sponsored by the State Department to clear up "misunderstanding between the people of the United States and India."[73] India had more or less stayed out of the conflict between the United States and the Soviet

Union during the Cold War, but Saund planned to stress America's "freedom of opportunity."[74] "Look," he wanted to tell the world, "here I am, a living example of American democracy in practice."[75]

It was not until a year later that Saund returned to India as a representative of the Foreign Affairs Committee, "a one-man subcommittee," as the Judge called himself.[76] Saund was quick to acknowledge that racism still existed in the United States, but he hoped to use his personal story to undercut what he called "the Communist lie that racial prejudice against Asians is rampant in America."[77]

Saund, his wife, and their daughter arrived in Calcutta, India, on November 25, 1957, and spent three weeks touring the country. He touted his assignment to the Foreign Affairs Committee as a reflection of America's genuine desire to reach out to the world. More than anything, wrote one reporter, Saund's trip "helped to create a new realization among thinking Indians that they have friends in the United States sincerely devoted to advancing the cause of India."[78] Saund also addressed a joint session of the Parliament of India, speaking honestly about America's failings, but quickly pointing out the steps the United States was taking to correct its wrongs.[79]

During his two-and-a-half-month world tour, Saund visited a host of other locations: "Japan, Hong Kong, South Vietnam, Singapore, Indonesia, the Philippines, Thailand, Burma, India, Pakistan, Israel … Rome, Paris, and London," selling American ideals and encouraging cultural exchange.[80] Eight months after he returned, Saund told the House that the people he met abroad wanted "freedom and the American way of life. Yet we—a Nation of supersalesman [sic], are failing to sell our way of life."[81]

The needs of Saund's constituents remained at the forefront of his legislative agenda during the 86th Congress.[82] His bill to protect the date industry in the valley was perhaps his most hard-fought victory in the House. Date growers from his district had been running up against cheaper imports, and to protect the domestic crop, Saund introduced a bill to subject foreign-grown dates and walnuts to a quality inspection. Although the government already had similar programs for a host of other produce, a number of cabinet departments opposed Saund's bill, as did the large commercial industries that relied on the cheap fruit. The House Agriculture Committee reported Saund's bill favorably, but the Rules Committee sat on it, unwilling to bring it to the floor. In late August 1960, Democratic leadership suspended the rules and allowed for a vote. His bill easily cleared the House but failed to become law.[83]

Using his position on the Interior and Insular Affairs Committee, Saund also helped negotiate a deal between the city of Palm Springs and the residents of the nearby Agua Caliente Reservation. Saund brokered the agreement using two bills (H.R. 8587 and H.R. 6672), whereby existing reservation land would be divided among its residents in a process called "equalization." The holders of tribal lands could then lease their parcels to the city for a period of 99 years in order to meet commercial lending regulations. "This will make possible the development of valuable Indian property, the expansion of business in Palm Springs and the acquisition of the airport by the city," Saund said.[84]

Saund continued to secure funding for flood control in the valley, new infrastructure projects and post offices, and improvements to the military installments in his district. Although he supported the Bracero Program, Saund called for tighter restrictions and criticized the ranchers who exploited the program in order to maximize profit. "American citizens are entitled to jobs on American farms before any imported labor is authorized," he said.[85]

Saund maintained his support for Congress's civil rights legislation and voted in favor of pensions, health insurance for senior citizens, and insurance for the unemployed. On an international scale, Saund wanted to spend less money on military aid and more on cultural exchanges and infrastructure projects in the developing world.[86] For one thing, Saund wanted to see America's huge agricultural surpluses put to use overseas. "A hungry world," he wrote, "would receive the bounty of American farms with much more gratitude than they do the tons of obsolete military hardware under the Mutual Security Program."[87]

Even into the next Congress, Saund remained critical of the federal government's overseas spending. "We must

admit," he said, "that our efforts to promote democracy and build strong free societies in many of the underdeveloped countries of the world through massive expenditures of U.S. funds have been, to say the least, not successful."[88] In defiance of the John F. Kennedy administration, Saund pushed Congress to more closely monitor its foreign investments. In particular, he wanted to ensure that whatever money America gave to the world actually made it to the farmers and rural villagers who needed it the most. "That has been our mistake all along," he said during debate on the Foreign Assistance Act of 1961. "We have been identified with the ruling classes. We have been coddling kings and dictators and protecting the status quo. The status quo for the masses of people in many lands means hunger, pestilence, and ignorance.... And we then wonder why the poor people of the underdeveloped areas of the world do not appreciate the help of Uncle Sam."[89]

Early in the 87th Congress, Saund was named vice chairman of a large congressional delegation participating in the Mexico-United States Interparliamentary Group. With the goal of strengthening ties between legislators of the two countries, four topics dominated the docket: "foreign investments, foreign trade, border affairs, and cultural exchange."[90] Saund, whose district stretched for miles along the U.S.-Mexico border, first submitted the resolution creating the legislative roundtable in 1959, and it became law a year later.[91] He chaired the committee on border affairs at the conference, where the two countries discussed immigration, the Bracero Program, and customs duties.[92] In the end, Saund considered the cross-border sitdown a huge success.[93]

On a flight from Los Angeles to DC on May 1, 1962, the Judge suffered a stroke and was immediately moved to a hospital in Bethesda, Maryland. Saund's family and doctors kept his condition under tight secrecy. His wife reportedly brought work to his hospital room every day while his staff maintained business at his office on the Hill. Saund nevertheless went on to win the party primary a month after his health crisis, and in September his campaign announced he would stand for re-election in the general contest.[94] On Election Day, however, Saund, who had been unable to campaign himself, lost to Republican Patrick M. Martin, taking only 44 percent of the vote.[95]

Saund remained in the Bethesda hospital for the next month until he was well enough to travel. Doctors moved him to a medical facility in San Diego and then, in January 1963, moved him to one closer to home in Los Angeles, where he made "slow but good" improvement.[96] After suffering a second stroke 10 years later, Saund died at his home in Hollywood, California, on April 22, 1973.[97]

The House was in recess when Saund died, but when it gathered again, Members held a memorial service for the Judge in the Capitol and eulogized him on the floor. Colleagues called him "a classic American success story," a "pioneer," and "a gentleman in the best sense of the word."[98] Some said the House was a better place because of his service, which had paved the way for "those generations from and interested in Asian nations."[99] "To chronicle all his legislative achievements and personal successes during his lifetime could not begin to pay Dalip Saund the justice and honor he deserves," Majority Leader Tip O'Neill of Massachusetts said. "Those of us who knew and admired him in the House, remember him as a man of boundless energy, personal integrity, and strong convictions— consistently and tirelessly fighting for the right of 'life, liberty, and the pursuit of happiness' for all Americans."[100]

FOR FURTHER READING

D. S. Saund, *Congressman from India* (1960; repr., Amritsar, India: Satvic Books, 2002).

NOTES

1   D. S. Saund, *Congressman from India* (1960; repr., Amritsar, India: Satvic Books, 2002): 12–15, 20.

2   Saund, *Congressman from India*: 28.

3   Ibid., 30–32.

4   Ibid., 29–30.

5   Ibid., 30.

6   Ibid., 32.

7   Ibid., 33–35, quotation on p. 35; *New York Passenger Lists, 1820–1957, Arrival New York, New York*, microfilm T715 1897–1957, roll no. 2842, p. 31, National Archives and Records Administration,

Washington, DC, http://www.ancestrylibrary.com/ (accessed 30 October 2015).

8   Saund, *Congressman from India*: 42.

9   Ibid., 40.

10 Quotation from Joseph Laitin, "Mr. Saund Goes to Washington," *Coronet* reprinted in the *Congressional Record*, House, 85th Cong., 1st sess. (17 April 1957): 5940; Saund, *Congressman from India*: 44, 47–48.

11 Saund, *Congressman from India*: 45; Gladwin Hill, "Colorful Contest Shaping on Coast," 27 December 1955, *New York Times*: 17.

12 Saund, *Congressman from India*: 46–47.

13 Ibid., 48–50.

14 Ibid., 50–51, 53–55.

15 Ibid., 60–61; Hill, "Colorful Contest Shaping on Coast."

16 Saund, *Congressman from India*: 63–64.

17 Ibid., 64–66.

18 "Mrs. Odlum, Saund Wage Hot Race," 14 October 1956, *Washington Post*: A12; "First India Native Goes to Congress," 11 November 1956, *Atlanta Journal and Constitution*: A9.

19 Saund, *Congressman from India*: 55.

20 Ibid., 56.

21 Ibid., 67–70.

22 Ibid., 69.

23 Ibid., 71–74; "Indian Bill Praised," 29 June 1946, *New York Times*: 3.

24 Saund, *Congressman from India*: 75.

25 Ibid., 76–78.

26 Ibid., 79.

27 Ibid., 80.

28 Ibid., 81.

29 Ibid., 82.

30 Ibid., 81–91; "Hot Race Looms in 29th District," 6 May 1956, *Los Angeles Times*: 45.

31 Laitin, "Mr. Saund Goes to Washington."

32 Bill Becker, "Coast Race Finds Democrat Ahead," 16 October 1960, *New York Times*: 48.

33 Saund, *Congressman from India*: 91–92.

34 Ibid., 93–94; Laitin, "Mr. Saund Goes to Washington."

35 Saund, *Congressman from India*: 94–95.

36 Kenneth C. Martis, *The Historical Atlas of Political Parties in the United States Congress, 1789–1989* (New York: MacMillan Publishing Company, 1989): 197–211; Hill, "Colorful Contest Shaping on Coast."

37 Hill, "Colorful Contest Shaping on Coast." See also Gladwin Hill, "Republicans Lose California Seats," 8 November 1956, *New York Times*: 42.

38 For population figures, see *Congressional Directory*, 85th Cong., 1st sess. (Washington, DC: Government Printing Office, 1957): 18; *Congressional Directory*, 88th Cong., 1st sess. (Washington, DC: Government Printing Office, 1963): 22.

39 Saund, *Congressman from India*: 96–97; "The Southland: Hearing Set on Eligibility of Candidate," 18 April 1956, *Los Angeles Times*: 22; "Appellate Court Refuses to Act in Election Case," 27 April 1956, *Los Angeles Times*: 31.

40 Saund, *Congressman from India*: 97.

41 Ibid.

42 Ibid., 97–98; Seymour Korman, "Adlai Sweeps California," 6 June 1956, *Chicago Daily Tribune*: 1; "Southland: Imperial Provides Major Boost to Odlum Victory," 7 June 1956, *Los Angeles Times*: 41; "Flier, Hindu Judge To Try for Seat From California," 8 June 1956, *Christian Science Monitor*: 19; "Mrs. Odlum, Saund Wage Hot Race."

43 Erik Thomas Robinson, "Jacqueline Cochran," in *American National Biography*, vol. 5 (New York: Oxford University Press, 1999): 117–118.

44 "Congress Only Goal of Jacqueline Odlum," 25 October 1956, *Los Angeles Times*: A14. First quotation from Hill, "Colorful Contest Shaping on Coast." Second quotation from "Hot Race Looms in 29th District."

45 "GOP Primary Expenses Reported at $585,352," 14 July 1956, *Los Angeles Times*: 4; "Mrs. Odlum, Saund Wage Hot Race."

46 Saund, *Congressman from India*: 99.

47 Ibid., 102–103; "Mrs. Odlum, Saund Wage Hot Race."

48 Richard Dyer MacCann, "California Family Shares in Victory of India-Born Contestant for House," 21 November 1956, *Christian Science Monitor*: 10.

49 *Congressional Record*, House, 85th Cong., 1st sess. (14 June 1957): 9197.

50 "The Southland: Hearing Set on Eligibility of Candidate"; "Hot Race Looms in 29th District"; "The Southland: Mrs. Odlum Leads GOP Ticket in Congress Race," 6 June 1956, *Los Angeles Times*: 39; "Mrs. Odlum, Saund Wage Hot Race." See also "Mrs. Odlum, Saund California Rivals," 7 June 1956, *Baltimore Sun*: 2; Edward T. Folliard, "Adlai's Vote Still Soaring in California," 7 June 1956, *Washington Post*: 1; "Party Line Cohesion Is Noted in California's Primary Votes," 7 June 1956, *Washington Post*: 2; Eileen Summers, "Candidate Cochran Sees Agriculture As Top Issue," 7 June 1956, *Washington Post*: 33; "Flier, Hindu Judge To Try for Seat From California."

51 Saund, *Congressman from India*: 105–106; Richard Dyer MacCann, "Democracy Seen in Action," 16 May 1956, *Christian Science Monitor*: 3.

52 Gladwin Hill, "California Leans Strongly to G.O.P.," 21 October 1956, *New York Times*: 1.

53 Jacqueline Cochran, interview by Joe B. Frantz, 7 April 1974, transcript 1, Lyndon Baines Johnson Library, Oral History Collection, Austin, TX, https://www.eisenhower.archives.gov/research/oral_histories/c.html (accessed 11 April 2016).

54 Saund, *Congressman from India*: 103–104; Hill, "Colorful Contest Shaping on Coast"; Eileen Summers, "Candidate Cochran Sees Agriculture As Top Issue," 7 June 1956, *Washington Post*: 33.

55 "A Sikh in Congress: Dalip Singh Saund," 10 November 1956, *New York Times*: 13.

56 Saund, *Congressman from India*: 104–105.

57 Ibid., 105–107; MacCann, "California Family Shares in Victory of India-Born Contestant for House."

58 Office of the Clerk, U.S. House of Representatives, "Election Statistics, 1920 to Present," http://history.house.gov/Institution/Election-Statistics/Election-Statistics/.

59 "Upset Victor," 8 November 1956, *Chicago Daily Tribune*: 11; Richard Dyer MacCann, "California Sends Ex-Asian to House," 8 November 1956, *Christian Science Monitor*: 3; Laitin, "Mr. Saund Goes to Washington." Saund's stance toward agricultural subsidies was something of a region-wide trend, and the strength of farmers in the West "did much to offset the pull of President Eisenhower's coattails" in the congressional races. See John D. Morris, "Farmers Helped House Democrats," 8 November 1956, *New York Times*: 31.

60 Martis, *Historical Atlas of Political Parties in the United States Congress, 1789–1989*: 195–211; "India Immigrant Wins California Seat," 8 November 1956, *Washington Post*: A17.

61 "East Is West," 10 November 1956, *Washington Post*: A8. Not all the press coverage was so welcoming or tolerant. The *Chicago Daily Tribune*, who described Saund as a "detribalized Sikh," recommended that Saund "revert to the costume and customs of his former country…. If he lets his beard grow and oils it until it shines, and puts his hair up under a bright red turban, he can expect to be a marked man in the house [*sic*]." See "Advice to the Sikh Congressman," 14 November 1956, *Chicago Daily Tribune*: 16.

62 Laitin, "Mr. Saund Goes to Washington."

63 "Rep. Saund Faces Fight for Congress," 2 November 1958, *Los Angeles Times*: B2.

64 Bill Becker, "Coast Race Finds Democrat Ahead," 16 October 1960, *New York Times*: 48.

65 "A Sikh in Congress: Dalip Singh Saund."

66 Richard Dyer MacCann, "California Family Shares in Victory of India-Born Contestant for House," 21 November 1956, *Christian Science Monitor*: 10.

67 Don Shannon, "Californians Seek Place on House Rules Group," 3 January 1957, *Los Angeles Times*: 18.

68 "Nehru Meets India-Born Congressman," 19 December 1956, *Los Angeles Times*: 18. For more information on his staff, see Saund, *Congressman from India*: 109–112.

69 Saund, *Congressman from India*: 114–115; Laitin, "Mr. Saund Goes to Washington."

70 "Freshman in Spotlight," 4 January 1957, *New York Times*: 14; Saund, *Congressman from India*: 115–116, 122; *Congressional Record*, House, 85th Cong., 2nd sess. (23 August 1958): 19922.

71 *Congressional Record*, House, 85th Cong., 2nd sess. (23 August 1958): 19922–19923. For additional constituent services, see Saund, *Congressman from India*: 116–122.

72 *Congressional Record*, House, 85th Cong., 1st sess. (14 June 1957): 9197.

73 "Congressman-Elect to Visit Native India," 9 November 1956, *Los Angeles Times*: 22. See also "Rep. Saund to Tell His Story to India," 9 November 1956, *Washington Post*: C4; "Winner on Coast Plans India Trip," 10 November 1956, *New York Times*: 13.

74 "A Sikh in Congress: Dalip Singh Saund."

75 MacCann, "California Family Shares in Victory of India-Born Contestant for House."

76 Saund, *Congressman from India*: 151.

77 "Congressman Born in India to Visit There," 3 May 1957, *Los Angeles Times*: 7. See also "Saund Visits Japan," 31 October 1957, *New York Times*: 8; "Saund Manila Bound," 18 November 1957, *Los Angeles Times*: 5; "The Price of Indonesian Favor," 19 November 1970, *Los Angeles Times*: B4.

78 Quotation from "Rep. Saund Sells U.S. on His Tour," 18 December 1957, *New York Times*: 19. See also "Saund in Indian Homeland," 26 November 1957, *New York Times*: 13; "U.S. Should Sell Itself to Asians, Says Saund," 23 December 1957, *Los Angeles Times*: 6.

79 Josephine Ripley, "A Congressman With a Mission," 8 February 1958, *Christian Science Monitor*: 20.

80 Earl W. Foell, "U.S. Urged to Clarify Motives in Asia," 7 January 1958, *Christian Science Monitor*: 14.

81 *Congressional Record*, House, 85th Cong., 2nd sess. (23 August 1958): 19923. For more on Saund's trip abroad, see Saund, *Congressman from India*: 148–179.

82 Saund, *Congressman from India*: 127.

83 *Congressional Record*, House, 86th Cong., 2nd sess. (1 September 1960): 19359; *Congressional Record*, House, 86th Cong., 2nd sess. (22 August 1960): 17086.

84 *Congressional Record*, House, 86th Cong., 1st sess. (17 August 1959): 16066–16067; *Congressional Record*, House, 86th Cong., 2nd sess. (1 September 1960): 19359; House Committee on Interior and Insular Affairs, *Providing for the Equalization of Allotments on the Agua Caliente (Palm Springs) Reservation in California*, 86th Cong., 1st sess., H. Rept. 903 (14 August 1959); Unpublished hearing before the House Committee on Interior and Insular Affairs, Subcommittee on Indian Affairs, *To Authorize Longer Term Leases on Indian Lands on the Agua Caliente (Palm Springs) Reservation*, 7 August 1959; House Committee on Interior and Insular Affairs, *Authorizing Longer Term Leases of Indian Lands on the Agua Caliente (Palm Springs) Reservation*, 86th Cong., 1st sess., H. Rept. 901 (14 August 1959).

85 *Congressional Record*, House, 86th sess., 2nd sess. (1 September 1960): 19359–19360. On the Bracero program, see also Bill Becker, "Coast Race Finds Democrat Ahead"; *Congressional Record*, House, 86th Cong., 2nd sess. (24 August 1960): 17546–17547.

86 *Congressional Record*, House, 86th Cong., 2nd sess. (1 September 1960): 19361; *Congressional Record*, House, 86th Cong., 1st sess. (9 June 1959): 10341; *Congressional Record*, House, 86th Cong., 1st sess. (17 August 1959): 16080–16083. See also Saund, *Congressman from India*: 181–184.

87 Saund, *Congressman from India*: 187.

88 *Congressional Record*, House, 87th Cong., 1st sess. (16 August 1961): 16060.

89 Ibid., 16061. See also *Congressional Record*, House, 87th Cong., 1st sess. (17 August 1961): 16211–16212; Don Shannon and John H. Averill, "Saund Could be Target of Purge in 1962," 27 August 1961, *Los Angeles Times*: B3.

90 D. S. Saund, *Report of the First Meeting of the Mexico-United States Interparliamentary Group*, 87th Cong., 1st sess., H. Rept. 197 (24 March 1961): iii.

91 Saund, *Report of the First Meeting of the Mexico-United States Interparliamentary Group*: 1.

92 Ibid., 6–8.

93 Ibid., iv.

94 Richard Bergholz, "The Position of Saund is Puzzle to Election," 23 July 1962, *Los Angeles Times*: A4; John H. Averill, "Democrats Worry Over Saund Illness Secrecy," 17 June 1962, *Los Angeles Times*: A4; John H. Averill, "Rep. Saund Will Run Again Despite Illness," 7 September 1962, *Los Angeles Times*: 2; "Rep. Saund of California Campaigns from Hospital," 8 September 1962, *Los Angeles Times*: 16; "Opinions on Health of Rep. Saund Conflict," 17 October 1962, *Los Angeles Times*: 20; "Saund: Mystery Veils His Illness in Capital," 21 October 1962, *Los Angeles Times*: K5; "Rep. Saund Sure He Can Serve, But Leaves Decision to Doctors," 30 October 1962, *New York Times*: 12.

95 "Martin Defeats Saund in Congressional Race," 8 November 1962, *Los Angeles Times*: 2; "Saund Replaced by Native-Son Republican," 9 November 1962, *Washington Post*: A2; Office of the Clerk, U.S. House of Representatives, "Election Statistics, 1920 to Present."

96 "Saund Moved to San Diego Naval Hospital," 30 November 1962, *Los Angeles Times*: 33; "Saund in UCLA Center," 14 January 1963, *Los Angeles Times*: 26; "Ex-Rep. Saund Shows Slow but Good Progress," 10 May 1963, *Los Angeles Times*: 24.

97 "Dalip Saund Dies; Ex-Legislator, 73," 24 April 1973, *New York Times*: 44; "Dalip Saund, 73: Former Congressman," 24 April 1973, *Los Angeles Times*: E18; "Ex-Rep. Dalip S. Saund, First Native of India to Hold U.S. Elective Office," 25 April 1973, *Washington Post*: C11.

98 *Congressional Record*, House, 93rd Cong., 1st sess. (15 May 1973): 15756, 15757, 15759.

99 Ibid., 15758, 15759.

100 Ibid., 15760.

"A HUNGRY WORLD WOULD
RECEIVE THE BOUNTY OF
AMERICAN FARMS WITH MUCH
MORE GRATITUDE THAN THEY DO
THE TONS OF OBSOLETE MILITARY
HARDWARE UNDER THE MUTUAL
SECURITY PROGRAM."

Dalip Singh (Judge) Saund
Congressman from India, 1960

Hiram L. Fong
1906–2004

UNITED STATES SENATOR 1959–1977
REPUBLICAN FROM HAWAII

Known as "the Man of the Pacific," Hiram Fong served nearly two decades as one of Hawaii's first U.S. Senators, acting as a surrogate representative for Asian-American constituents at home and as an ambassador of American policies to Asian people abroad. Several path-breaking aspects distinguished Fong's career. He was the first person of Chinese descent elected to Congress, the first Asian Pacific American elected to the Senate, the first Chinese-American candidate for the presidency, and he remains the only Republican Senator ever elected from Hawaii.[1] While serving in the minority for his entire tenure, Fong supported expanding civil rights programs and liberalizing immigration policies. Simultaneously, he staunchly defended President Richard M. Nixon's Vietnam policies and traveled extensively in Asian nations, calling attention to the growing influence of Asian Americans in the post-war United States. During his time in the Senate, Fong believed himself to be a spokesman for Asian Americans across the country. "I feel sometimes they think I am their senator," he explained. "I try to interpret America to them and to interpret them to America."[2]

Hiram L. Fong was born Yau Leong Fong on October 15, 1906, in Honolulu, Hawaii, to poor Chinese immigrants, Sau Howe Fong and Lum Shee Fong.[3] His father, Sau Howe, worked at the local fertilizer plant while his mother worked as a housekeeper. Hiram was the seventh child and the fifth son of 13 children.[4] He grew up in Kalihi and picked beans, shined shoes, sold newspapers, caught fish, and caddied for golfers to supplement his family's earnings.[5] Fong attended Kalihi-waena Elementary School. He briefly attended St. Louis College and then graduated from McKinley High School in 1924. At his brother's encouragement, Fong took the federal civil service exam while still a high school senior. Unable to afford

college, he worked at the Pearl Harbor naval shipyard as a clerk for three years, staying on a year longer than first planned after he became the family breadwinner following his father's death in 1926. In 1927 he left the position with the understanding he would be hired back should he fail out of the University of Hawaii.[6]

Fong need not have worried, as he breezed through college in three years, taking summer courses to accelerate his studies. He first adopted the name "Hiram" around this time, primarily in his work as editor of the student newspaper *Ka Leo*, though he didn't legally change his name until 1942.[7] During college, Fong developed ties with the Republican Party while serving in 1926 as a paid orator for George Frederick Wright's successful mayoral campaign in Honolulu. After Fong graduated from college with honors in 1930, Mayor Wright appointed him to a clerkship in the city's public works department. Most of his time was spent assisting Wright in his biennial campaigns.[8] After a few years, Fong applied to Harvard Law School and, after being accepted, took out a life insurance policy to ensure his creditors would not go empty-handed should the worst occur. "I figured if I flunked out the first year," he recalled, "I would not owe anyone any money."[9]

Fong returned to Honolulu each summer to work for Wright to afford tuition. After obtaining his law degree in 1935, he returned to Honolulu permanently, passing the bar and accepting the Honolulu attorney general's office position that Mayor Wright had promised. But the work and pay underwhelmed Fong, "I felt, gee whiz, with all my education, is this all I am going to wind up doing?"[10] In 1938 Fong married teacher and longtime sweetheart Ellyn Lo, with whom he eventually had four children, Hiram Jr., Rodney, Merie-Ellen, and Marvin Allan.

A month after the marriage, Fong's mentor George Wright passed away. After three years of struggling to

maintain interest in his work, Fong planned to leave his city job and start his own private practice. Hoping to gain public attention to kick-start his practice, Fong turned to his passion: politics. "So I thought, well I'd better get out … and since I [was] going to get out, I'd better run for office," he recalled.[11] Fong entered the race for one of six territorial house seats in a district encompassing much of the island of Oahu north of Honolulu. He easily won the 1938 Republican primary campaigning on a theme of "local boy makes good" and was swept into office with a surprisingly high vote total for a political newcomer, the second most votes in the district.[12] He resigned from the attorney general's office and opened his own practice.

Drawing on his popularity, Fong asserted his political independence both within the Republican Party and from the "Big Five," the five largest sugar companies with stakes in Hawaiian production. This rankled the establishment and led to a failed attempt to declare his election illegal on the basis that he was employed by the territorial government. Over Republican speaker Roy A. Vitousek's opposition, the legislature seated him by a vote of 27 to 2.[13] The incident only increased his fame and gained him support from organized labor, bolstering both his political position and his law practice. He easily won re-election in 1940.

Just as Fong began to establish himself in the territorial legislature, war erupted in December 1941 when the Japanese attacked Pearl Harbor. He joined the U.S. Army Air Force as a judge advocate in Honolulu in 1942. A first lieutenant in the U.S. Army Reserve, Fong was promoted to captain shortly after being activated as a full-time officer. He initially retained his seat in the territorial legislature, but new War Department regulations prevented active-duty officers from seeking elected office and forced his withdrawal in the 1942 election. The War Department granted Fong permission to run for the legislature in 1944 with the caveat that he could not campaign. His wife Ellyn gamely stumped on his behalf, and Hiram easily won enough votes to regain his seat. He was honorably discharged in February 1945, just days before the new session convened.[14]

Back in the legislature, Fong made a name for himself as a dealmaker willing to upend traditional party dynamics.[15] When his ally Manuel Paschoal stepped aside as speaker in 1948, Fong engineered the "Kauai Inn Agreement," meeting early with 10 Republican colleagues to strike an accord selecting him as the presiding officer. He then demanded an early caucus to ensure his election as speaker before votes could be discussed.[16] Fong served as vice president of the territorial constitutional convention the following year. In 1953 he relied on Democratic votes in a coalition that preserved his speakership. He narrowly lost re-election to the legislature a year later in the Hawaii Democratic revolution of 1954 with the advent of the closed primary in the territory.[17]

"The people have thrown me out. I'm a private citizen now, so I'm taking things easy," Fong said, doing anything but. "I've been retired and I'll stay retired. I don't want people to think I'm a bad loser."[18] To that end, Fong recused himself from politics for five years and turned his attention to his business ventures. He set up the financial services firm Finance Factors Ltd., in 1954 in Wailuku, Maui, to operate alongside his Honolulu legal practice. He diversified his business interests, setting up Finance Realty, Finance Investment, and Finance Home Builders Ltd.[19] In the summer of 1959, however, the prospect of imminent statehood drew him out of self-imposed retirement.

Hawaii had to fill three congressional seats, two Senators and one Representative, simultaneously. Fong entered the race for Senate seat "A," running against Democrat Frank Fasi. Fong's years away from politics had made him a millionaire, and while his entrepreneurial acumen endeared him to the business community, he also had retained support from Chinese Americans and labor organizations such as the International Longshore and Warehouse Union (ILWU). The ILWU's support for a Republican was unusual, but largely attributable to both Fong's personal business practices supporting his unionized employees and the union's distaste for Fasi, who was a virulent anti-communist. Voters embraced Fong's rags-to-riches story, and he won 53 percent of the vote against Fasi in an election that saw significant Republican gains in state elections as well.[20]

Before the election, Fong was neither certain of victory nor how he would be received in Washington, DC. "I was quite fearful—you know, being the first person from Hawaii, and not being a Caucasian," he admitted. "I wondered whether I would be considered too provincial, or too partisan."[21]

Instead, the Republican Party establishment embraced both Fong and his independent streak. Vice President Richard Nixon met Fong and his family at the airport, launching a long friendship that would last through Nixon's presidency. Senate Republicans held a party in Fong's honor after the new Hawaiian delegation was sworn in on August 24, 1959.[22] At that ceremony, Fong won a coin toss for the role of senior Senator over Oren Long. The pair then drew lots to determine the length of each Senator's term; Fong secured the longer term, putting off a re-election campaign until 1964.[23] He earned seats on three committees: Post Office and Civil Service; Public Works; and Interior and Insular Affairs. He joined the Judiciary Committee in the 87th Congress (1961–1963) and the Appropriations Committee in the 91st Congress (1969–1971). He also served on the permanent Select Committee on Aging after the 88th Congress (1963–1965) and retired as that panel's Ranking Member.

Fong requested and was granted placement on the Appropriations Subcommittee on Labor, Health, Education, Welfare and Related Agencies, seeking to check the power of the very unions that had helped launch his Senate career. "I believe labor legislation is essential for our nation as well as for democracy in both unions and business," he said. "Both will have to conform to the laws of the land."[24] His voting record offered a muddier picture. Fong typically took the business side of consumer and labor issues, drawing heavily on his financial background, but liberal Senators counted on Fong's labor connections for his vote on key issues.

While, in the abstract, he frequently condemned communism, he also never turned away known communist leaders from the ILWU, saying of them, "From my

viewpoint, knowing these people, I think what they were doing was that they were just protesting the rule [of] the people in control."[25] He had a long relationship with ILWU leader Jack Hall. "Whenever he wanted legislation, I would see that it would pass," Fong recalled, before clarifying, "as long as it was good legislation."[26]

Hawaii's unions relied on Fong as a go-between with Richard Nixon during his failed 1960 presidential campaign, and they routinely backed the Senator whose advocacy for foreign assistance translated into a steady stream of business through Hawaiian harbors. Scores of shipping containers filled with food supplies and materials set off for ports around the globe, creating work for unionized stevedores and dockhands.[27]

Despite committee appointments oriented toward Hawaiian interests, Fong devoted much of his attention to international affairs, immigration, and defense policy. Between the first and second sessions of the 86th Congress (1959–1961), he undertook a self-funded tour of 13 Asian nations. Fong returned to dispute Democratic presidential candidate John F. Kennedy's assertion that America's prestige had fallen abroad. "I did not find the 'ugly American' on my tour," he insisted, "and I feel we are winning the battle for the minds of people in neutral and free countries of Asia."[28]

Fong urged the use of soft power—exercising economic and cultural influence to improve relations—in Asia whenever possible to combat international communism, an ideology which he described as "the wrong concept of man and the universe."[29] Fong focused on engaging Asian nations with the twin lures of democracy and capitalism. He pressed for continued foreign aid, but disputed China's proposed acceptance into the United Nations, saying the nation still had to prove itself a "good boy."[30] Nevertheless, Fong supported President Nixon's diplomatic talks with China and joined a congressional delegation to the People's Republic of China in 1974. He also prided himself on a friendship with the Republic of China President Chiang Kai-shek, whose funeral he attended the following year.[31] Speaking about strengthening ties with China and other Asian nations,

Fong said late in his career, "America is a two-ocean Nation. We need a friendly Asia-Pacific community, just as much as we need a friendly Atlantic community."[32]

Fong was an early and ardent supporter of the Vietnam War during President Lyndon B. Johnson's administration, and he maintained that support during the Nixon administration in spite of the conflict's increasing unpopularity among his Hawaiian constituents. He routinely opposed efforts to restrict funding for the war and frequently defended the Nixon administration.[33] Fong labeled congressional efforts to diminish the U.S. commitment to Vietnam "hypocrisy" and insisted military action was necessary to combat North Vietnam's aggression against democratic allies.[34]

In line with his interest in Asia, he also urged passage of President Johnson's immigration reform in 1965. Fong's approach reflected his belief in soft power. He pointed to how America inspired nations in Asia and around the world. "Our tenets, regardless of race, creed or color, have inspired freedom-loving people everywhere to look to America as a beacon in their struggle to win freedom and independence," Fong said. "Our opportunity is to live up to their ideals."[35] The Immigration and Nationality Act of 1965 notably discarded an outdated formula that set racial quotas from Asian nations, which scholars have credited with a dramatic rise in immigration by Asian professionals.[36]

Immigration and aid for refugees remained prominent concerns for Fong. In 1971 he introduced 75 private bills, more than any Senator that year, mostly for immigration relief.[37] The Senator endeavored to relieve the plight of refugees from both communist China and the Indochinese conflicts, cosponsoring several bills before securing passage of the Indochina Refugee Children Assistance Act of 1975. Complementing his views on immigration reform, Fong urged both new and established Chinese Americans to integrate more fully into U.S. society.[38]

Senator Fong took seriously his role as a surrogate representative for Chinese Americans and as a link between Asia and the western nations. He followed up on Hawaiian Delegate John Burns's work to establish the East-West

Center in Honolulu and then fought from his seat on the Senate Appropriations Committee for larger expenditures supporting it. Fong pressured colleagues for more funding, saying about the center, "Wherever men can face one another as peers and exchange their considered views on the vital issues of their lives, the constructive potentialities for cooperative peace increase dramatically."[39]

Fong extended that philosophy beyond diplomacy and immigration to civil rights. Though a hawkish supporter of the war in Vietnam, Fong often voted for social legislation that aligned him with Democrats and moderate Republicans. He cast votes for much of President Johnson's Great Society legislation, including the Civil Rights Act of 1964 and the establishment of Medicare in 1965. He supported the Equal Rights Amendment in 1970. Fong also contributed substantially to the Voting Rights Act of 1965, writing an amendment providing for poll watchers to guarantee the safety and fairness of elections.[40]

Hawaiian issues, of course, ranked high on Fong's agenda, and he counted the establishment of the East-West Center and securing funding for federal highways on the islands among his greatest achievements in Congress. One of his first successful bills established the Haleakala National Park on the island of Maui, carving it out from land that had been part of the Hawaii National Park established in 1916, and creating additional jobs in the process. From his seat on the Post Office and Civil Service Committee, Fong tended to the interests of Hawaii's thousands of civil servants. In 1960 and 1962 he drafted legislation raising wages for federal employees. Working from his position on the Public Works Committee, Fong lent his influence to Hawaiian groups seeking federal grants for public works such as dams and harbor improvements. In part for his attention to matters back home, Hawaiian Republicans embraced Fong, even nominating him as a "favorite son" candidate for president at the Republican National Convention in 1964.[41]

Fong's electoral resilience was fully displayed in 1964. Despite a very unfavorable climate for Republicans, Fong, in his re-election bid, comfortably defeated incumbent Democratic Representative Thomas P. Gill, who was supported by Hawaii's other Senator, Daniel K. Inouye, with 53 to 46 percent of the vote. Like the rest of the country, Hawaii elected Lyndon B. Johnson by a landslide over Fong's Senate colleague and GOP nominee, Barry Goldwater. According to some sources, Fong set a senatorial election record nationally by running 32 percent ahead of Goldwater.[42]

Fong had a contentious relationship with Inouye, who had served as a U.S. Representative before becoming the junior Senator from Hawaii. Their enmity originated in territorial politics when Inouye and John Burns headed the increasingly dominant state Democratic Party. Though both Fong and Inouye endeavored to tie Hawaiian industry and jobs to federal spending, their relationship in the normally collegial Senate was often frosty. That tension was exacerbated by Inouye's support in the 1970 Senate election for Fong's opponent, television station owner Cecil Heftel. Fong's continued support for President Nixon's policies, particularly his Vietnam strategy, began to frustrate Hawaiian constituents. He refused to debate Heftel, however, relying on his seniority, experience, and name recognition to make his case against the political newcomer. Fong ultimately prevailed with 52 percent of the vote, his narrowest margin of victory to date.[43]

Barely into his third term, Fong's office faced an unexpected scandal. Robert Carson, a longtime legislative assistant to the Senator, was indicted on charges of bribery, perjury, and conspiracy on January 13, 1971. Allegedly, Carson had attempted to bribe Deputy Attorney General Richard Kleindienst to intercede in a grand jury investigation. While Fong himself remained blameless, rumors flew of an inciting feud between the Senator's office and the attorney general over an appointment to the Ninth Circuit Court of Appeals. Fong prided himself on placing Hawaiians on the federal bench to increase Hawaiian influence. Kleindienst wanted and found someone from his home state of Arizona for the position, and several sources speculated that this competition was at the root of Kleindienst's accusations against Fong's aide Carson. Fong stood by his aide during the trial and appeal process in which Carson was convicted. No accusations or charges

were leveled at Fong, but the scandal rocked an otherwise peaceful and focused office.[44]

Following the bruising 1970 campaign and the Carson scandal, Fong declined to run again in 1976, citing a growing workload and desire to spend more time with his family and friends. At the time of his retirement from the Senate in January 1977, he served as Ranking Member on six committees.[45] Fong returned to his law firm, his plantation on Oahu, and various businesses as chairman of Finance Enterprises Ltd. Fong worked well into his 90s, vowing to "die with my boots on."[46]

Fong died of kidney failure on August 18, 2004, in Kahaluu, Hawaii.[47] His body lay in state in the Hawaiian capitol building in Honolulu before his interment in the city's Nuuanu Memorial Park and Mortuary.[48]

MANUSCRIPT COLLECTION

University of Hawaii at Manoa Library, Archives and Manuscripts Department, Hawaii Congressional Papers Collection (Honolulu, HI). *Papers*: 1910–1990s, circa 559 cubic feet. The Hiram L. Fong papers primarily contain correspondence, legislative files, committee materials, casework, political party materials, administrative papers, public relations files, campaign memorabilia, and audiovisual materials from his years of service in the U.S. Senate. Some personal and family papers are also included. The collection covers Hawaii statehood, Native Hawaiian land claims, the military presence in Hawaii, shipping issues, work of the Judiciary Committee, civil service issues, immigration, and campaigns. A finding aid is available at the repository and online.

Oral History: February 22, 1978–October 12, 1979, 306 pages. Seven interviews conducted by Michaelyn Chou. An index is available.

NOTES

1 "Senator Hiram L. Fong of Hawaii," 17 July 1964, *Christian Science Monitor*: 13.

2 Caspar Nannes, "Senator Fong of Hawaii," December 1973, *The Link*: 21.

3 David Ignatius, "Hiram L. Fong, Republican Senator from Hawaii," in *Ralph Nader Congress Project: Citizens Look at Congress* (Washington, DC: Grossman Publishers, 1972): 1.

4 Michaelyn Pi-Hsia Chou, "The Education of a Senator: Hiram L. Fong from 1906 to 1954" (PhD diss., University of Hawaii, 1980): 59–65.

5 Helen Zia and Susan B. Gall, eds., "Hiram Fong," in *Asian American Biography* (New York: UXL, 2003): 74–76.

6   Chou, "The Education of a Senator": 143–149.

7   Ibid., 48–50, 182–187.

8   Ibid., 242–246; Don T. Nakanishi and Ellen D. Wu, *Distinguished Asian American Political and Governmental Leaders* (Westport, CT: Greenwood Press, 2002): 47–48.

9   Nannes, "Senator Fong of Hawaii."

10   Chou, "The Education of a Senator": 290.

11   Ibid., 314–315.

12   Ibid., 323.

13   Ibid., 340–342.

14   Ibid., 409–417, 429–443.

15   Much of Fong's enmity with party elites could be traced back to his rivalry with Roy Vitousek, who led the Hawaii Republican Club after he left as the speaker of the territorial assembly. Fong undermined Vitousek by elevating Manuel Paschoal—a fellow critic of the old guard—in 1945, using key Democratic votes to do so. When the legislature split evenly in 1947, Democrats offered Fong as a compromise speaker alongside Fong's 1945 Democratic collaborator Charlie Kauhane as vice-speaker. Fong publicly repudiated the resolution, prompting a fistfight in the legislature's lobby as Kauhane accused Fong of manipulating Democrats into a resolution he knew would fail. Fong denied the allegations and used the press gained from the incident to pressure Democrats into electing Paschoal again. For additional detail, see Chou, "The Education of a Senator": 444–445, 474–478.

16   Ibid., 505–507.

17   John S. Whitehead, *Completing the Union: Alaska, Hawai'i, and the Battle for Statehood* (Albuquerque: University of New Mexico Press, 2004): 194; Chou, "The Education of a Senator": 708–711.

18   Gardiner B. Jones, "Fong Thanks Democrats for Fouling Up Sessions," 21 May 1955, *Honolulu Advertiser*: A6.

19   "Senator Hiram Fong 80th Birthday," 1986, pamphlet in files of the U.S. Senate Historical Office, Washington, DC.

20   Whitehead, *Completing the Union*: 317–321; Adam Bernstein, "Hiram Fong Dies; One of First Hawaiian Senators," 19 August 2004, *Washington Post*: B6; "Republican Wins Hawaii Governorship," 30 July 1959, *Chicago Daily Tribune*: 5.

21   Ray Maneki, "Fong Tells Rags to Riches Story," 4 June 1976, *Honolulu Star-Bulletin*, reprinted in *Tributes to The Honorable Hiram L. Fong of Hawaii in the United States Senate*, 94th Cong., 2nd sess., S. Doc. 272 (1977): 21–23.

22   Dillon Graham, "Fong Arrives, Welcomed by Nixon," 24 August 1959, *Washington Post*: A8; Eileen Summers, "Senator's Hello, Hawaiian Style," 25 August 1959, *Washington Post*: B3.

23   *Congressional Record*, Senate, 86th Cong., 1st sess. (24 August, 1959): 16739–16740; "Congress Seats Hawaii Members," 25 August 1959, *Washington Post*: A10.

24   "New Hawaii Senator Favors Union Curbs," 23 August 1959, *Los Angeles Times*: A1.

25   Chou, "The Education of a Senator": 733.

26   Ignatius, "Hiram L. Fong": 6.

27   Hiram Fong, "Mr. Nixon in Hawaii," 12 August 1960, *New York Times*: 18.

28   "Hawaiian Senator Here; Praises Aid for Asians," 5 January 1960, *Los Angeles Times*: 5.

29   Hiram Fong, "Time Is On Our Side," 5 September 1961, *Christian Science Monitor*: 16.

30   "U.S. Prestige High in Orient, Fong Reports," 8 October 1960, *Chicago Daily Tribune*: A7.

31   "Senator Hiram Fong 80th Birthday."

32   *Congressional Record*, Senate, 94th Cong., 2nd sess. (4 March 1976): 5438.

33   Ignatius, "Hiram L. Fong": 19–21.

34   Peter J. Kumpa, "An Angry Debate Is on Party Lines," 20 April 1972, *Baltimore Sun*: A1.

35   "Fong Urges Passage of Immigration Bill," 21 September 1965, *Los Angeles Times*: 5.

36   Mae M. Ngai notably discusses how this influx of Asian immigrants, many of Chinese descent if not immediate origin, led to the rise of a new "model minority" stereotype that shares many similarities with Fong's vision of what the average hardworking Asian immigrant—particularly those converted to Christianity—might have to offer the United States. For more on this, see Mae M. Ngai, *Impossible Subjects: Illegal Aliens and the Making of Modern America* (Princeton, NJ: Princeton University Press, 2004): 266–268.

37   Ignatius, "Hiram L. Fong": 22; Lynda Arakawa, "First Asian in U.S. Senate Broke Barriers," 19 August 2004, *Honolulu Advertiser*: H1.

38   "Immigrant Chinese Told to Integrate," 16 November 1959, *New York Times*: 11.

39   The East-West Center was established in 1960 under the Mutual Security Act of 1960 to "promote better relations and understanding between the United States and the nations of Asia and the Pacific." Mutual Security Act of 1960, Public Law 86-472, 73 Stat. 134 (1960); *Congressional Record*, Senate, 87th Cong., 1st sess. (28 March 1961): 4977.

40   Ignatius, "Hiram L. Fong": 20.

41   "Hiram L. Fong: Legislative Record," campaign literature in the files of the U.S. Senate Historical Office, Washington, DC; "Fong Will Be Nominated as Hawaii's Favorite Son," 14 July 1964, *New York Times*: 21.

42   Ignatius, "Hiram L. Fong": 9; "Senator Hiram L. Fong: Biographical Sketch," accessed 18 May 2016, http://www.senatorfong.com/bio_sketch.html; *Almanac of American Politics*,

1976 (New York: E.P. Dutton & Co., 1975): 206–209; Dale Andrews, "Paradise Found," 23 May 2002, *Roll Call*: 38.

43 *Almanac of American Politics, 1976*: 209; Ignatius, "Hiram L. Fong": 9.

44 Though vocally steadfast in his support, Fong eventually suspended Carson from his duties. Carson faced 18 months in prison following an unsuccessful plea for stay of sentencing. For more on the Carson affair, see Ignatius, "Hiram L. Fong": 15; Ken W. Clawson, "Aide to Fong Is Indicted on Bribe Charge," 14 January 1971, *Washington Post*: A1; John Hall, "Sen. Fong's Indicted Assistant Back at Desk," 10 February 1971, *Los Angeles Times*: B5; "Convicted Aide," 10 November 1972, *Washington Post*: A2.

45 "Sen. Fong to Retire," 15 January 1976, *Washington Post*: A3.

46 Andrews, "Paradise Found."

47 Bernstein, "Hiram Fong Dies."

48 Dan Nakaso, "Hundreds Pay Respects to Fong at Capitol Rites," 27 August 2004, *Honolulu Advertiser*: A1.

Daniel K. Inouye

1924–2012

UNITED STATES REPRESENTATIVE 1959–1963
UNITED STATES SENATOR 1963–2012
DEMOCRAT FROM HAWAII

When Daniel K. Inouye first took his seat in the U.S. House of Representatives in 1959, Speaker Sam Rayburn of Texas took quick stock of the young legislator. "You'll soon be the second most widely recognized member in the Congress," mused the Speaker, who embodied the institution for so many Americans. "We don't have too many one-armed, Japanese Congressmen here."[1] Indeed, Inouye left an indelible mark on Hawaiian politics and on the U.S. Congress, where he served for a combined 53 years in the House and Senate, serving with 412 Senators during his long tenure in that chamber. A proud war veteran and energetic legislator, Inouye battled for party leadership and embraced Members of Congress from across the aisle. On November 20, 2013, President Barack Obama posthumously awarded Inouye the Presidential Medal of Freedom. Senator Inouye "taught all of us that no matter what you look like or where you come from," Obama observed, "this country has a place for everybody who's willing to serve and work hard."[2]

Daniel Ken Inouye was born on September 7, 1924, in Honolulu, Hawaii, to Hyotaro Inouye, a file clerk, and Kame Imanaga, who, as a young orphan, had been taken in by Native Hawaiians.[3] A Methodist minister and his family adopted Inouye's mother, who was homeless. She named Inouye after her adoptive father. "She made it very clear to me from the time I was very young, 'I owe a lot to the Hawaiian [people], and I expect you to repay that debt,'" Inouye said.[4] Inouye graduated from McKinley High School in Honolulu, then known as "Tokyo High" because the city's segregation policies concentrated a high number of ethnic Japanese students at McKinley.[5]

At age 17, Inouye worked for the Red Cross with every intention of becoming a surgeon. "When the war broke out I was a high school senior and preparing myself to go to college and become a doctor," Inouye said. "I had no interest in politics." He rushed to aid the wounded during the devastating attack on Pearl Harbor. Upon turning 18, Inouye applied to enlist in the military but was denied entry because of his race. The U.S. government classified *nisei* (American-born children of Japanese immigrants) unfit for service. "Here I was, though I was a citizen of the United States, I was declared to be an enemy alien and as a result not fit to put on the uniform of the United States," Inouye recalled.[6]

After petitioning the government to reverse its decision, Inouye volunteered again in 1943 and joined the Army as a private, entering the fabled 442nd Regimental Combat Team. Composed primarily of Japanese-American soldiers, the 442nd served with distinction in the French and Italian campaigns during World War II, and the unit famously rescued the "Lost Battalion" of Texans behind enemy lines in France. Inouye later lost his right arm in a return sweep through Italy, crushing his dream of becoming a surgeon.[7] After his injury, Inouye recovered at Percy Jones Hospital in Battle Creek, Michigan, where he met future Senate colleagues Philip Hart of Michigan and Robert Dole of Kansas, with whom he discussed becoming a lawyer and entering national politics.[8]

Inouye spent 20 months in U.S. Army hospitals before being honorably discharged and retiring as a captain on May 27, 1947. He earned a Distinguished Silver Cross, Bronze Star, and a Purple Heart, as well as 12 other medals and citations, for his military service. Though Inouye and the other members of the "Go For Broke" regiment were eventually acknowledged as heroes for their efforts on the Italian front, most received little formal recognition at the time. Only when Hawaiian Senator Daniel Akaka insisted on an Army review of war records nearly a half a century later did their heroism come into focus. Inouye received the Medal of Honor with 21 other Japanese Americans on

June 21, 2000, for his service in World War II. "I take this as the greatest compliment I've ever had," Inouye noted. "I will wear it proudly. And I will not tarnish it."[9]

After the war, with the assistance of the GI Bill, Inouye graduated from the University of Hawaii in 1950. He then pursued a law degree from George Washington University Law School, where he graduated in 1952 before returning to Hawaii. He was admitted to the bar in 1953 and then served as an assistant public prosecutor for Honolulu during 1953 and 1954. Inouye married Margaret Shinobu Awamura, an instructor at the University of Hawaii, on June 12, 1949, and they had one son, Ken, in 1964.[10] Margaret died in 2006, and on May 24, 2008, Inouye married Irene Hirano, president of the U.S.–Japan Council.[11]

Inouye joined a wave of young Japanese-American World War II veterans graduating from college and returning to Hawaii in the early 1950s. This group, respected for their contributions to the war effort and freshly educated, made an immediate impact on Hawaii's political system. "The time had come for us to step forward," Inouye said of this generational shift. "We had fought for that right with all the furious patriotism in our bodies and now we didn't want to go back to the plantation.... We wanted to take our full place in society."[12]

Many of the former members of the 442nd became attached to prominent Democrat John Burns. Burns was the final Hawaiian Delegate to Congress and helped secure statehood for the islands before serving three terms as governor from 1963 to 1974. For much of Inouye's early political career, Burns headed the Hawaiian Democratic Party in spirit, if not always in name.[13] Inouye stood out from this group of Burns protégés and merited special attention from the party. He was elected to the territorial house during the Democratic revolution of 1954, when Democrats swept statewide positions and took control of the legislature long held by Republicans. Inouye served as majority leader in the territorial house until 1958, when he was elected to the territorial senate.

When Hawaii achieved statehood in 1959, Inouye declared his intention to seek a seat in the U.S. Congress. He first planned to run for the Senate, leaving the House seat open for his territorial senate colleague Patsy Takemoto Mink. But he withdrew from the race and ran for the lone U.S. House seat instead when party stalwarts Oren Long and William Heen ran for the Senate.[14] Long noted this deference and pledged to retire after his first term ended, clearing the way for Inouye to run for the vacant Senate seat in 1962.[15] In 1959 this decision put him in direct conflict with Mink for the Democratic nomination to the U.S. House, and he narrowly defeated her in the primary. He faced Dr. Charles H. Silva, director of the territorial department of institutions, in the general election. While his campaign style was described as "sunny" and "outgoing," much of his overwhelming appeal came from his status as a war hero. Inouye won in a landslide, garnering 69 percent of the vote.[16]

His election made him the first Japanese-American Member of Congress, but it was his war injuries that initially made him an object of considerable interest in Washington. When Inouye was sworn in on August 24, 1959, he was asked to raise his right hand for the oath. Upon lifting his left hand, "There was a gasp," Inouye said, noting that many Members did not know he had lost his right arm.[17]

Upon arriving in DC, outgoing Delegate Burns directed Inouye straight to the Texas delegation, with whom Hawaiians had developed a working relationship. Inouye became close with Speaker Rayburn, who steered him to the Agriculture Committee, an influential and helpful assignment for the Hawaiian Islands, notable for their sugar production. In turn, Inouye maintained the friendship between Hawaii and Texas. In 1960 Inouye was an early supporter of Texas Senator Lyndon B. Johnson's presidential campaign before Johnson eventually accepted John F. Kennedy's offer to be the vice presidential nominee.

Inouye toiled quietly for his two terms in the House, trying to foster a larger network of support for future campaigns and to protect the sugar industry in Hawaii. His only substantial piece of legislation passed late in his first term, extending several key provisions to recognize Hawaiian statehood in the Hawaii Omnibus Act (H.R. 11602). The act amended a bevy of existing laws to ensure the new state received the full benefits accorded to the other 49 states.[18] Nevertheless, Inouye's popularity in the islands helped him soar to re-election in 1960; he took 74 percent of the vote against his Republican opponent, Frederick Titcomb.

Senator Oren Long retired, as promised, in 1962 and backed Inouye's candidacy for the open seat. In the general election Inouye faced Ben F. Dillingham, a scion of one of Hawaii's wealthiest families. The *Honolulu Star-Advertiser* embarrassed Dillingham by endorsing Inouye even though Dillingham's father served as the newspaper's vice president. Dillingham also had opposed statehood, which cost him voter support as well.[19] Despite Inouye's early fears about Dillingham's influence, he received more than twice the number of votes, winning 70 percent of the total. His victory made him the first Japanese-American Senator.[20]

Inouye gained a reputation as a prolific legislator, submitting a flurry of bills, resolutions, and amendments. Most of his early legislation tied the Hawaiian economy tighter to federal spending and the federal bureaucracy. He chose his words carefully and rarely made floor speeches in his early terms. He made an early commitment to Senate traditions that held throughout his tenure when his maiden speech in the Senate supported the filibuster because "Hawaii, being a small state, may have to [resort] to the filibuster to get the nation's attention."[21] Much of his influence derived from that respect for the Senate processes, beginning with the role of the committees.

In the 88th Congress (1963–1965), Inouye was initially appointed to two committees, Armed Services and Public Works. He did not remain on either committee long, moving to the Commerce Committee (later named Commerce, Science, and Transportation) in the 91st Congress (1969–1971) and the Appropriations Committee in the 92nd Congress (1971–1973). He remained on both of these committees through the rest of his Senate career, eventually chairing the Commerce Committee in the 110th Congress (2007–2009) and the Appropriations Committee from 2009 until his death. He also served on the Committee on the District of Columbia in the 1970s and joined the Rules and Administration Committee in 1981, in addition to a number of select and joint committees.[22]

Between his workmanlike approach to legislating and his tight ties with the powerful Texas delegation, Inouye's star rose quickly in the national Democratic Party. He published a book, *Journey to Washington*, with author Lawrence Elliott in 1967 detailing his rise to the Senate. In 1968 Inouye served as the keynote speaker at the Democratic National Convention in Chicago, which was rocked by anti-war protests. He spoke passionately about the march of progress and the anger of the country's youth, acknowledging their ideals while questioning their confrontational tactics. He called upon the American people to follow their better instincts. "Fellow Americans, this is our country," Inouye said. "Its future is what we, its citizens, will make it. And as we all know, we have much to do. Putting aside hatred on the one hand and timidity on the other, let us grow fresh faith in our purpose and new vigor in citizenship."[23]

Afterward, President Lyndon Johnson tried to convince Hubert Humphrey to select the Hawaiian as his running mate: "I've never known him to make a mistake. He's got cold, clear courage.... It would be fresh and different. He's young and new. And I think your secretary could call him and say, 'Would you please go to Utah, South Carolina, San Francisco?' And I believe he could go to all of them and never lay an egg." Humphrey declined to nominate Inouye, believing that such a move "just takes it a little too far, too fast."[24] For his part, Inouye claimed he had no interest in the position and was content to remain a Senator.[25]

Inouye gradually shifted his stance on the Vietnam War after Nixon's inauguration. He had steadfastly backed the war during the 1960s, but as opposition built, he stated that he regretted his support and attributed it to his close bond with President Johnson and the Texas delegation.[26] As the war dragged on into Nixon's presidency, Inouye cosponsored the War Powers Act of 1973, which limited the President's ability to engage in conflict overseas by asserting congressional power to place time limits on troop deployments.[27]

Inouye was drawn into direct conflict with the administration in February 1973, when the Senate voted

77 to 0 to launch the Select Committee on Presidential Campaign Activities (known as the Ervin Committee for its chairman, North Carolina Senator Sam Ervin). The Ervin Committee investigated the events surrounding the break-in at the Democratic National Committee's Watergate offices in 1972 and the ensuing cover-up. Inouye was selected to serve, but, wanting to keep his head down, refused the appointment four times. Majority Leader Mike Mansfield of Montana told him that, after eliminating chairmen, party leaders, nonlawyers, and presidential hopefuls, only a select few potential candidates remained. Furthermore, congressional Democrats insisted on his participation due to what was seen as his "Mr. Clean image." With that Inouye agreed to serve.[28]

Within months of joining the investigation, Inouye's name appeared in headlines across the country when John J. Wilson, the attorney representing former Nixon chief of staff, H. R. Haldeman, used a racial slur to describe the Senator from Hawaii. When asked by a United Press International reporter about a line of questioning from Senator Lowell Weicker of Connecticut, Wilson responded, "Oh, I don't mind Senator Weicker.... What I mind is that little Jap," and gestured toward Inouye. Earlier in the investigation, a hot mic had picked up Inouye describing another of Wilson's clients as "a liar." Wilson initially denied having made the comment about Inouye, but later admitted to it. Later, when asked for a response, Inouye simply said, "I think his statement speaks for itself."[29]

In September 1973, Inouye declared the infamous White House recordings featuring President Nixon uttering scandalous expletives and implicating himself in the cover-up "not essential" to the investigation, stating the committee had enough to go on without them.[30] He was lauded in the press for his focus on campaign finance reform and fair, but firm, treatment of witnesses on the committee. Following the committee's revelations and the press they stirred, Inouye called for a constitutional convention to limit the power of the presidency, bringing attention to abuses of power by Republicans and Democrats alike.[31] Now highly visible, thanks to the televised committee proceedings, Inouye's fame expanded nationally.

Given his success on the Ervin Committee, Inouye was appointed to chair the new Select Committee on Intelligence in 1976, established to provide oversight of U.S. intelligence agencies. Persuaded by Mansfield to accept the post after the furor of the Watergate investigation, Inouye struck a careful balance, pledging not to compromise security while ensuring no intelligence agency would "violate the civil rights of any Americans" under his watch.[32] Inouye voiced concerns as early as December 1976 about the stresses and strains that the job had placed on him, and he sought to establish a precedent of brief chairmanships, believing that such turnover was the best means of ensuring that the committee was not unduly influenced by the intelligence organizations reporting to it. "I'm afraid if you stay on too long in this job, you either go a little off," he said, "or you become a part of the institutions.... Either way is wrong."[33] Though he remained on the Intelligence Committee through the 98th Congress (1983–1985), he stepped down as chair after 1977.

Inouye also flexed his muscles on foreign policy from his post as chair of the Foreign Operations Subcommittee of the Appropriations Committee, where he frequently cosponsored foreign aid and investment bills and defended them on the floor. "This country has given much, and, in doing so, we have given truth to the ideals we, as a nation, live by," he said. "We must continue to uphold this humanitarian tradition."[34]

Most of his voluminous floor speeches during the post–Watergate Era centered on aid and investment bills and encouraged a more interconnected planet. Consistent with these beliefs, he also supported opening trade with communist China. In 1984 Inouye developed his foreign policy expertise further, serving as chair of the Senate Democratic Central America Study Group to assess U.S. policy in the region. He also served as senior counselor to the National Bipartisan Commission on Central America, also known as the Kissinger Commission.

In the early 1980s, Senator Inouye again gained national prominence when he spoke out about the Abscam Scandal, an FBI sting operation that targeted Members of Congress.

Inouye criticized the FBI on the Senate Floor in December 1980, sympathizing with observers who worried that the scandal represented a "threat to legislative independence inherent in the Abscam operation."[35] Harrison Williams Jr. of New Jersey was the sole Senator ensnared in the sting. Though uproar persisted on the Senate Floor, the Senate Select Committee on Ethics waited to take up the issue until after the criminal investigation had ended so as not to influence the case.

Following Williams's criminal conviction and sentencing in February 1982, the Select Committee reported the resolution to expel Williams from the Senate. Inouye acted as Williams's advocate on the floor, noting first how extraordinary this resolution was in the history of the Senate. "I believe it is important to note that the Senate of the United States has never expelled a Member except where treason or disloyalty to the Union was involved." He declared the operation was a "manufactured scandal."[36] "I do not believe that a senator should be expelled for being a fool or committing foolish acts," Inouye said.[37] Senators did not agree, and once it became clear that the necessary two-thirds would vote for expulsion, Harrison Williams resigned from the Senate on March 11, 1982.[38] The episode earned Inouye a reputation for loyalty under fire.

Inouye's seniority and success in prior Senate investigatory roles made him a natural choice to lead a new investigation in the wake of another presidential scandal. In late 1986, news organizations brought to light secret operations conducted by National Security Council staff wherein the United States sold arms to Iran and used the profits to fund Nicaraguan Contras, rebel groups opposed to the official Sandinista Junta of National Reconstruction government. Inouye adopted a nonpartisan approach during the so-called Iran-Contra affair, eager to note that the Ronald Reagan administration cooperated in the panel's investigation while also standing behind the committee's conclusion that administration officials subverted the rule of law and misled the American public.[39]

Inouye's nonconfrontational questioning during the nationally televised hearings contrasted sharply with the testimony of charismatic figures like Lieutenant Colonel Oliver North, frustrating his more partisan colleagues. Inouye stood by his methods even as he grew frustrated with witnesses' grandstanding. Inouye stated that the administration's actions derived from "an elitist vision … that trusts no one—not the people, not the Congress, and not the Cabinet. It is a vision of a government operated by persons convinced they have a monopoly on truth."[40] His fairness won plaudits, though his unwillingness to maximize political advantages in the scandal worried some within his party.[41]

Once again thrust into the public eye in a highly publicized investigative panel, Inouye initially thrived under the spotlight, readying his internal campaign to become the next Senate Majority Leader. Inouye had served as secretary of the Democratic Caucus since 1978, placing him in the third-ranking leadership post. Several major newspapers pegged him as the Majority-Leader-in-waiting. In 1986 he reportedly struck a deal with Senator Robert Byrd to help the West Virginian win the post of Senate Majority Leader, with the understanding that Byrd would step aside in 1989 and leave an inside track open for Inouye to run for the post.[42]

However, neither Inouye's experience nor careful positioning secured him the Majority Leader post that eventually went to George Mitchell of Maine. The press blamed a controversial 1987 appropriation that Inouye sponsored and later rescinded to support the construction of religious schools in France, which the Senator himself described as an "error in judgment." Some also recalled Inouye's handling of the Iran-Contra Select Committee that some Democrats described as "lukewarm" for failing to press the case against the Reagan administration. Within the Democratic Caucus, Inouye won the votes of only 14 of the 55 Senators.[43]

When Senator Byrd passed away on June 28, 2010, Inouye became the President pro tempore of the United States Senate, making him the highest-ranking Asian American in the United States and third in the line of presidential succession. While the position did not give him a direct leadership role over policy formation, it nevertheless was valued by Inouye, reflecting his colleagues' acknowledgment that, as the dean of the Senate, he held special knowledge of the chamber's rules, procedures, and practices.

Inouye became famous for supporting earmarks that steered federal dollars to Hawaii. As chairman of the Appropriations Subcommittee on Defense and later as the head of the full committee, he was highly successful in securing money for his constituency. In 1997 alone, federal spending in Hawaii grew $170 million to a total of $8.16 billion, making it the fifth highest per capita recipient of federal funds.

Though his tactics in funneling federal spending to Hawaii made him the target of pork barrel watchdog groups, Inouye refused to apologize for his support of the Hawaiian economy. Inouye often focused on shipping bills.[44] In 1997 he inserted a provision into an annual appropriations bill that provided what he referred to as a "preference" to American Classic Voyages to run the cruise ship industry out of Hawaii. Senator John McCain of Arizona called the provision a government-sponsored monopoly and encouraged President William J. (Bill) Clinton to use his line-item veto against the bill.[45] The provision survived. "Since we're insular and dependent on merchant marine," Inouye had proclaimed, "we find ourselves deeply involved in activities of the sea."

Inouye's history with earmarks included acquiring support for a Hawaiian bank and arranging a $50 million gift to his alma mater, George Washington University.[46] When the push for earmark reform heated up in 2006, Inouye joined his friend, Republican Senator Ted Stevens of Alaska, in dismissing the idea. "I don't see any monumental changes," he declared. "If something is wrong we should clean house, but if they can explain it and justify it, I will look at it."[47] Inouye continued to use earmarks as he had for decades until their eventual ban in 2011.[48]

Inouye took largely liberal social positions on policies such as abortion rights, gun control, and civil liberties. His policies frequently favored the disenfranchised. He was a strong supporter of the Civil Rights Act of 1964 and, as a close friend of Lyndon B. Johnson, stood strongly behind the Great Society programs such as Medicaid, Head Start,

and food stamps. Inouye's stance on civil rights grew out of his own experiences as a Japanese American and living in the patchwork Hawaiian cultural community. During and after the debate over the Civil Rights Act of 1964, Inouye repeatedly evoked Hawaiian values and the wishes of his diverse constituency.

After passage, Inouye shared an advertisement Hawaiians had placed in the *Washington Post* thanking Congress for the bill's passage, "Now we have rules to help us achieve our ideal—an era of universal tolerance, understanding, peace, and aloha."[49] Inouye also supported DC statehood, citing Hawaii's own struggle to join the Union. Inouye served on the Committee on the District of Columbia and was a strong proponent of the Metrorail, specifically the work done to give people living with disabilities access to the system. Inouye cosponsored the District of Columbia Self-Government and Governmental Reorganization Act in 1973 (S. 1435).

This support for the disenfranchised extended to the Asian-American community both inside and outside of Hawaii. Inouye served as a member of the Congressional Asian Pacific American Caucus and, in 1997, joined fellow Hawaiian Senator Daniel Akaka to help Philippine veterans of World War II naturalize as U.S. citizens. Inouye kept his promise to his mother to protect Native Hawaiians when he helped to pass the Native Hawaiian Education Act and the Native Hawaiian Health Care Act in 1988, setting up programs to spur Native Hawaiians' incorporation into American society.

Inouye also stood behind fellow Japanese Americans. In 1981 he proposed the Commission on Wartime Relocation and Internment of Civilians, which led to the 1988 Civil Liberties Act that provided redress to Japanese Americans affected by internment during World War II.[50] Following the attacks of September 11, 2001, Inouye quickly defended American Muslims, comparing the bigotry directed at them to the experience of Japanese Americans following Pearl Harbor.[51]

This interest in preserving the rights of minorities and correcting past wrongs found natural expression through his work on the Select Committee on Indian Affairs.

Inouye wound up on Indian Affairs by chance. As a member of the steering committee, which made committee assignments, he had been directed to fill a vacancy on the select committee. When Inouye could not fill the slot, Senator Byrd suggested Inouye fill the seat himself. Inouye insisted he lacked the expertise, but Byrd responded in jest, "At least you look like one."[52] Though Inouye had initially preferred not to serve on the committee, his interest grew as he learned the extent to which the American government had "shortchanged" American Indians. "By God, did we do all these things?" he recalled thinking. "We should be embarrassed and ashamed of ourselves."[53]

In 1993 Inouye fought to defend the Committee on Indian Affairs (he had introduced successful legislation in early 1993 to remove the term "select" from the committee's name) from the threat of disbandment. Testifying with Senator McCain before the Joint Committee on the Organization of Congress, Inouye argued that the Constitution vested Congress with power over Indian affairs and, thus, the committee could not be removed except by constitutional amendment. "Even if we were not charged with legal obligations and a trust responsibility, we would still have to recognize the moral imperative that we, as a nation, are charged with when it comes to improving the conditions of life in reservation communities," he argued.[54] His commitment to the committee was so strong that, when Senator Wendell Ford of Kentucky retired in 1998, Inouye passed on becoming Ranking Member on the Rules and Administration Committee so he could retain his position on Indian Affairs. He claimed in 1999 that he devoted more time and effort to his work on Indian Affairs than any other committee.[55]

Inouye described his approach to working with Senate colleagues as nonpartisan rather than bipartisan and mused, "I think those of us who get older should make an extra effort to demonstrate what non-partisanship can result in."[56] This independent streak occasionally rankled fellow Democrats. Inouye viewed Senator Stevens as a close friend; the pair often called one another "brother" on the Senate Floor.[57] In 1990 he made a radio ad to

support Republican Senator Mark Hatfield of Oregon, his colleague on the Appropriations Committee.

In 2008, as Senator Stevens faced federal charges and a stiff re-election campaign, Inouye flew out to Alaska to campaign for his old friend.[58] Near the end of his career, Inouye backed Hillary Clinton as his party's nominee for President; Inouye had a long, fruitful relationship with President Bill Clinton's administration. The endorsement created a rift with the eventual nominee, Barack Obama, who spent much of his early life growing up in Hawaii. Until the Obama administration took office in 2009, Inouye's influence within the Democratic Party and particularly within Hawaii had few equals.

Inouye routinely received between three to four times the number of votes his opponents received. Through 1986, Inouye never won less than 73 percent of the vote in his Senate campaigns, thriving on his easygoing, charming demeanor. He was the master "of a sunny, outgoing type of campaigning."[59] His only real electoral challenge came in 1992, facing a broader field of challengers from the Republican, Libertarian, and Green Parties. Republican opponent Richard Reed obtained a secretly recorded tape from Inouye's longtime hairstylist that purported that the Senator had sexually assaulted her in 1975. Reed used the allegation in campaign ads against Inouye. No inquiry was launched, however, since the hairstylist, Lenore Kwock, declined to press charges. Reed took down the ads when Kwock threatened his campaign with a lawsuit. Inouye, who himself welcomed an investigation but otherwise refused to comment on the allegations, won the election with 57 percent of the vote.[60] He returned to his typical overwhelming margins in the following elections, receiving at least 75 percent of the vote in each succeeding election after 1992.

Late in his long career in the public eye, Inouye had ascended to the pinnacle of politics in the Aloha State and had become a revered figure in the U.S. Senate. His efforts to shape the political makeup of Hawaii extended back to his time as a protégé of Delegate John Burns. Early in his career, Inouye often joined Burns and fellow 442nd veteran and Democratic strategist Dan Aoki for breakfast to pick delegates to the Democratic National Conventions.[61] Starting in the mid-1960s and persisting for decades, Inouye had a hand in choosing Democrats for open seats across the state.[62]

Some observers criticized that influence, but Inouye was largely unrepentant. "In certain circles, I'm the godfather," Inouye said. His reach extended deep into state and municipal politics thanks to his broad network of former staffers and assistants. "Like the sun is to our solar system, he is to our state," Honolulu mayor and former legislative assistant Kirk Caldwell said of Inouye.[63] It was a shock, then, when Senator Akaka announced his impending retirement in 2011 and Inouye announced his intention to stay out of the primary process. "I'm a good Democrat, and I want to see a Democrat win that seat," Inouye said in April 2012. By October, however, Inouye had once more tightened his grip on the reins. Representative Mazie Hirono defeated former House Member and longtime Inouye nemesis Ed Case in the primary and won the Senate seat with Inouye's backing.[64]

In early December 2012, Daniel Inouye was hospitalized. He died of respiratory complications at Walter Reed National Military Medical Center on December 17, 2012.[65] When the Senate met on December 18, the presumptive dean of the Senate, Patrick Leahy of Vermont, stood to speak and gestured to Inouye's empty desk, noting, "Today is the first day since Hawaii became a state that it is not represented by Dan Inouye."[66] Inouye's remains were interred at the National Memorial Cemetery of the Pacific in Honolulu, Hawaii.

MANUSCRIPT COLLECTIONS

Library of Congress, Asian Division (Washington, DC). *Oral History*: 2003–2011, 8 linear feet. The collection contains videocassettes, DVDs, photographs, and documents related to an oral history project conducted by the United States Capitol Historical Society to document the service of Asian Americans in Congress. Daniel Inouye is included among the interviewees.

University of Hawaii at Manoa Library, Archives and Manuscripts Department, Hawaii Congressional Papers Collection (Honolulu, HI). *Papers*: 1959–2012, 1,237 linear feet. The collection includes casework, legislation, subject files, and committee-related material. Subjects covered include Watergate, Iran-Contra, and Hawaii-related issues. The papers are currently closed, but researchers may apply to access certain portions.

NOTES

1   Lloyd Shearer, "Sen. Daniel Inouye: Watergate Changed His Life," 11 November 1973, *Parade*: 4.

2   The White House, "Remarks by the President at the Presidential Medal of Freedom Ceremony," press release, 20 November 2013, accessed 27 January 2016, https://www.whitehouse.gov/the-press-office/2013/11/20/remarks-president-presidential-medal-freedom-ceremony.

3   Daniel Inouye and Lawrence Elliott, *Journey to Washington* (Englewood Cliffs, NJ: Prentice Hall, Inc., 1967): 11–17.

4   Tom Coffman, *The Island Edge of America*: *A Political History of Hawai'i* (Honolulu: University of Hawai'i Press, 2003): 299.

5   Shearer, "Sen. Daniel Inouye: Watergate Changed His Life."

6   Mark Preston, "Inouye Reflects on His 40 Years in Congress," 13 September 1999, *Roll Call*: A56–A57.

7   "Daniel Inouye," Academy of Achievement, 12 August 2013, http://www.achievement.org/autodoc/page/ino0bio-1 (accessed 15 March 2016).

8   Preston, "Inouye Reflects on His 40 Years in Congress."

9   Ed Henry, "Inouye Finally Gets His Medal," 26 June 2000, *Roll Call*: 1.

10 Richard Borreca, "Fatal Cancer Could Not Dim Maggie's Grace," 14 March 2006, *Honolulu Star-Bulletin*, http://archives.starbulletin.com/2006/03/14/news/story02.html (accessed 15 March 2016).

11 "About Dan," official website of United States Senator Daniel K. Inouye, accessed 18 December 2012, http://www.inouye.senate.gov/about-dan/biography/ (site discontinued).

12 Sucheng Chan, *Asian Americans*: *An Interpretive History* (New York: Twayne Publishers, 1991): 171.

13 John S. Whitehead, *Completing the Union*: *Alaska, Hawai'i, and the Battle for Statehood* (Albuquerque: University of New Mexico Press, 2004): 178–179.

14 Karen Winkler, "Daniel K. Inouye, Democratic Senator from Hawaii," in *Ralph Nader Congress Project: Citizens Look at Congress* (Washington, DC: Grossman Publishers, 1972): 5.

15 Daniel Inouye, oral history interview by Ronald Sarasin, 3 March 2008, transcript, United States Capitol Historical Society, Washington, DC.

16 Coffman, *The Island Edge of America*: 223; John Ramsey, "All Capitol Eyes Will Be on Long, Fong and Inouye," 21 August 1959, *Washington Post*: B2.

17 Preston, "Inouye Reflects on His 40 Years in Congress."

18 Hawaii Omnibus Act, Public Law 86-624, 74 Stat. 411 (1960). Notable inclusions in the Omnibus Act were amendments to the Internal Revenue Code, the Social Security Act, the National

Defense Education Act, and language in the code of the Interstate Highway System.

19 Winkler, "Daniel K. Inouye, Democratic Senator from Hawaii": 6.

20 "Democrats Record a Sweep in Hawaii," 7 November 1962, *New York Times*: 16.

21 Albert Eisele, "Daniel Inouye's 40-year Climb to Power in the Senate," 4 August 1999, *The Hill*: n.p.

22 For a full listing of Inouye's committee assignments in the Senate, see Garrison Nelson, *Committees in the U.S. Congress, 1947–1992*, vol. 2 (Washington, DC: CQ Press, 1994): 444–446; and Garrison Nelson and Charles Stewart III, *Committees in the U.S. Congress, 1993–2010* (Washington, DC: CQ Press, 2011): 769–771.

23 "Transcript of the Keynote Address by Senator Inouye Decrying Violent Protests," 27 August 1968, *New York Times*: 28.

24 "That Empty Sleeve," March 2009, *Harper's Magazine*: 16.

25 Shearer, "Sen. Daniel Inouye: Watergate Changed His Life."

26 "White House-Backed Keynoter: Daniel Ken Inouye," 27 August 1968, *New York Times*: 28; Shearer, "Sen. Daniel Inouye: Watergate Changed His Life": 6.

27 Helen Zia and Susan B. Gall, eds., *Asian American Biography* (Boston, MA: Cengage Gale, 2003): 97–101.

28 Pete Pichaske, "The Bungled Burglary Made Inouye a 'Star,'" 16 June 1997, *Honolulu Star-Bulletin*, http://archives.starbulletin.com/97/06/16/news/story1.html (accessed 4 August 2015); Shearer, "Sen. Daniel Inouye: Watergate Changed His Life."

29 Douglas Watson, "Haldeman's Lawyer Calls Inouye 'That Little Jap,'" 2 August 1973, *Washington Post*: A23; United Press International, "Haldeman's Lawyer Terms Inouye 'That Little Jap,'" 2 August 1973, *New York Times*: 18; Rudy Abramson, "Offhand Remark in Recess: Wilson, Stung by Questions, Calls Inouye 'That Little Jap,'" 2 August 1973, *Los Angeles Times*: A1.

30 "Inouye Doubts Committee Needs Tapes From Nixon," 10 September 1973, *New York Times*: 21.

31 Roy Reed, "Inouye Is Disturbed by Increase in Criticism of Watergate Panel," 23 January 1974, *New York Times*: 19.

32 John H. Averill, "Inouye Takes Another Sensitive Assignment," 28 May 1976, *Los Angeles Times*: B6.

33 George Lardner Jr., "Inouye Sees Peril in Remaining Too Long on Intelligence Panel, May Quit in 2 Years," 25 December 1976, *Washington Post*: A15.

34 *Congressional Record*, Senate, 94th Cong., 2nd sess. (30 June 1976): 21473.

35 *Congressional Record*, Senate, 96th Cong., 2nd sess. (5 December 1980): 32793.

36 *Congressional Record*, Senate, 97th Cong., 2nd sess. (3 March 1982): 2992.

37 Jonathan Fuerbringer, "The White House Crisis: Man in the News; An Esteemed Colleague: Daniel Ken Inouye," 17 December 1986, *New York Times*: A19.

38 U.S. Senate Historical Office, "The Expulsion Case of Harrison A. Williams, Jr. (1982)," http://www.senate.gov/artandhistory/history/common/expulsion_cases/140HarrisonWilliams_expulsion.htm (accessed 4 August 2015).

39 David E. Rosenbaum, "Iran-Contra Report Says President Bears 'Ultimate Responsibility' for Wrongdoing," 19 November 1987, *New York Times*: A1.

40 "Iran-Contra Hearings: Summing Up a Summer's Work; Final Remarks by Leaders of the Panels: A Litany of Mistakes," 4 August 1987, *New York Times*: A6.

41 Emma Brown, "Daniel K. Inouye, U.S. Senator, Dies at 88," 17 December 2012, *Washington Post*, https://www.washingtonpost.com/local/obituaries/daniel-k-inouye-us-senator-dies-at-88/2012/12/17/61030936-b259-11e0-9a80-c46b9cb1255f_story.html (accessed 18 December 2012).

42 Jack Anderson and Dale Van Atta, "The Byrd-Inouye Leadership Deal," 4 November 1987, *Washington Post*: B11.

43 Preston, "Inouye Reflects on His 40 Years in Congress." For Inouye's quotation, see Irvin Molotsky, "Inouye Concedes 'Error' in Senate," 2 February 1988, *New York Times*: A1.

44 Eisele, "Daniel Inouye's 40-year Climb to Power in the Senate."

45 Adam Bryant, "The Fine Print: Of Arms and Cruise Ships," 11 October 1997, *New York Times*: A1.

46 Paul Kiel and Binyamin Appelbaum, "After Call From Senator's Office, Small Hawaii Bank Got U.S. Aid," 1 July 2009, *Washington Post*, http://www.washingtonpost.com/wp-dyn/content/article/2009/06/30/AR2009063004229.html (accessed 15 March 2016); Kent Jenkins, "Senator Taps U.S. Pockets for Alma Mater Building Fund," 10 October 1993, *Washington Post*: A29; Helen Dewar, "Inouye, Defending 'Five,' Says Senate Is on Trial," 4 December 1990, *Washington Post*: A6.

47 David D. Kirkpatrick, "As Power Shifts in New Congress, Pork May Linger," 24 November 2006, *New York Times*: A1.

48 Inouye chaired the Senate Appropriations Committee at the time and resisted the change for as long as possible. When President Barack Obama joined House Republicans in a refusal to accept the continued use of earmarks, Inouye bowed to pressure. However, he vowed to take up the issue again in the following Congress once "the consequences of this decision are fully understood by the members of this body." He passed away before he was able to revisit the issue. Carl Hulse, "Senate Won't Allow Earmarks in Spending

Bills," 1 February 2011, *New York Times*, http://thecaucus.blogs. nytimes.com/2011/02/01/senate-wont-allow-earmarks-in-spending-bills/ (accessed 2 February 2011).

49 *Congressional Record*, Senate, 88th Cong., 2nd sess. (8 July 1964): 16098.

50 Don T. Nakanishi and Ellen D. Wu, eds., *Distinguished Asian American Political and Governmental Leaders* (Westport, CT: Greenwood Press, 2002): 69–73.

51 Matt Bai, "The Way We Live Now: 10-28-01: Encounter; Hyphenated Americans," 28 October 2001, *New York Times*, http://www.nytimes.com/2001/10/28/magazine/the-way-we-live-now-10-28-01-encounter-hyphenated-americans.html (accessed 15 March 2016).

52 *Congressional Record*, Senate, 102nd Cong., 2nd sess. (8 April 1992): S4997.

53 Preston, "Inouye Reflects on His 40 Years in Congress."

54 Karen Foerstel, "Citing 'Trail of Tears,' Sen. Inouye Entreats Panel to Save His Indian Affairs Committee," 6 May 1993, *Roll Call*: 11.

55 Preston, "Inouye Reflects on His 40 Years in Congress."

56 Daniel Inouye, oral history interview.

57 Kirkpatrick, "As Power Shifts in New Congress, Pork May Linger."

58 David Rogers, "Daniel Inouye 'Lived and Breathed the Senate,'" 17 December 2012, *Politico*, http://www.politico.com/story/2012/12/daniel-inouye-obituary-lived-and-breathed-the-senate-085210 (accessed 12 December 2012).

59 Coffman, *The Island Edge of America*: 223.

60 Derrick DePledge, "Sen. Daniel K. Inouye Dies at Age 88 of Respiratory Illness," 18 December 2012, *Honolulu Star-Advertiser*, http://www.staradvertiser.com/breaking-news/sen-daniel-k-inouye-dies-at-age-88-of-respiratory-illness/ (accessed 27 January 2016); Jane Gross, "Accusations Against Hawaii Senator Meet a Silence in His Seat of Power," 14 December 1992, *New York Times*, http://www.nytimes.com/1992/12/14/us/accusations-against-hawaii-senator-meet-a-silence-in-his-seat-of-power.html (accessed 18 December 2012); "Inouye's Wife Stands By Him Despite Hairdresser's Claims," 19 October 1992, Associated Press; Ken Rudin, "Congressional Sex Scandals in History," 21 January 1998, *Washington Post*, http://www.washingtonpost.com/wp-srv/politics/special/clinton/congress.htm (accessed 28 April 2016); "Report: Inouye Made 'Chubby' Comment to Woman Senator," 22 September 2014, *Honolulu Star-Advertiser*, http://www.staradvertiser.com/breaking-news/report-inouye-made-chubby-comment-to-woman-senator-2/ (accessed 28 April 2016).

61 Coffman, *The Island Edge of America*: 210.

62 Horowitz, "Hawaii's Reigning Son."

63 Ibid.

64 Manu Raju and John Bresnahan, "Inouye Relaxes His Grip on Hawaii," 13 April 2011, *Politico*: 4; Kyle Trygstad, "Daniel Inouye Rooting for Mazie Hirono in Hawaii Primary," 11 October 2011, *Roll Call*, http://www.rollcall.com/issues/57_39/daniel_inouye_rooting_for_mazie_hirono_hawaii_primary-209338-1.html (accessed 27 January 2016).

65 Alexander Bolton and Jonathan Easley, "Hawaii Sen. Inouye Dead at 88," 17 December 2012, *The Hill*: n.p.

66 *Congressional Record*, Senate, 112th Cong., 2nd sess. (18 December 2012): 8103.

"EVEN IF WE WERE NOT
CHARGED WITH LEGAL
OBLIGATIONS AND A TRUST
RESPONSIBILITY, WE WOULD
STILL HAVE TO RECOGNIZE
THE MORAL IMPERATIVE
THAT WE, AS A NATION,
ARE CHARGED WITH WHEN
IT COMES TO IMPROVING
THE CONDITIONS OF LIFE IN
RESERVATION COMMUNITIES."

Daniel K. Inouye
Roll Call, May 6, 1993

Spark M. Matsunaga
1916–1990

UNITED STATES REPRESENTATIVE 1963–1977
UNITED STATES SENATOR 1977–1990
DEMOCRAT FROM HAWAII

A lifetime proponent of peace, Spark M. Matsunaga, the son of an impoverished plantation worker, became a war hero and Member of Congress. Matsunaga believed firmly in gradual reform and the power of one man to change minds, a philosophy he often applied to the legislative process. As a knowledgeable member of the powerful House of Representatives Rules Committee and later as a United States Senator, Matsunaga influenced a broad swath of legislation during his 28 years in Congress. He alternately identified as a lawyer, soldier, peacemaker, poet, technology enthusiast, and a campaigner for equal rights. Fellow Senator Bob Dole of Kansas referred to "Sparky," as he liked to be known, as a "renaissance man."[1]

Spark Matsunaga was born Masayuki Matsunaga on October 8, 1916, in Kukuiula on the island of Kauai in Hawaii. His parents, Kingoro Matsunaga and Chiyono Fukushima, emigrated from Japan and worked on a Kauai sugar plantation. Masayuki grew up in a large family; his mother, Chiyono, was a widow with four children from her previous marriage. Kingoro Matsunaga sustained an injury on the job in the mid-1930s and, after his recovery, dedicated himself to a spiritual life as a Shinto priest. The Matsunaga brothers constructed a Shinto temple in their backyard at their father's instruction. The nickname "Sparky" or "Spark" originated in Matsunaga's youth; childhood friends used it to razz him for his frequent last-place finishes in races. The name stayed with him.[2]

Matsunaga's interest in political office ignited early. While attending Kauai High School, he complained to his *haole* social studies teacher about discrimination against Asians. The teacher replied, "Run for office and fix it." "Ohhh, he put that bug in my head!" Matsunaga recalled. "He planted a seed in my brain. In everything I did I was building steps toward the U.S. Senate."[3] After

graduating high school in 1933, Matsunaga briefly worked as a bookkeeper and then as a sales clerk to save money for college.[4] He participated in Reserve Officers' Training Corps (ROTC) while attending the University of Hawaii in Honolulu. After receiving his bachelor's degree in education in 1941, his ROTC experience led him into the military.

Matsunaga's military career proved to be a defining life experience. He joined the Hawaii National Guard before entering the U.S. Army as a second lieutenant. Matsunaga commanded a company on the island of Molokai when Japanese forces attacked Pearl Harbor on December 7, 1941. Martial law was immediately declared, and Matsunaga took command of the island itself for several months. But after the Battle of Midway in June 1942, the Army removed Matsunaga from command and shipped him and other soldiers of Japanese descent to Camp McCoy in Monroe County, Wisconsin. "Oh, my heavens, that was a sad day," Matsunaga later said.[5]

At the camp, while the soldiers continued training, Matsunaga helped organize a petition to President Franklin D. Roosevelt to allow the troops to prove their loyalty in battle. In early 1943, the government relented and allowed the formation of the 100th Infantry Battalion and later the 442nd Regimental Combat Team, which entered combat in Italy. Matsunaga was wounded twice traversing a minefield, causing severe damage to his right leg. He was awarded the Bronze Star for his service in Italy before being released from active duty in 1945 at the close of the war.

After the war, Matsunaga officially changed his first name to Spark, but kept the name Masayuki.[6] He took a job as a veteran's counselor with the Department of the Interior for two years before joining the War Assets Administration as chief of the Priority Claims Division. He also lobbied Congress on behalf of disabled veterans like

himself. In 1948 he married Helene Hatsumi Tokunaga, with whom he had five children, Karen, Merle, Diane, Keene, and Matthew. Using the GI Bill, Matsunaga pursued a law degree at Harvard University in 1949. He graduated two years later and worked as an assistant prosecutor for the city and county of Honolulu before going into private practice in 1954.

Matsunaga made his entry onto the broader national stage while still in law school when, in 1950, he testified before the Senate Committee on Interior and Insular Affairs in favor of Hawaiian statehood. He cited the patriotism of Japanese-American World War II soldiers and said they deserved "full recognition for the supreme sacrifice which they made for us and our country."[7] He returned to testify in 1954, once more sharing the perspective of a veteran. Later that year, he was elected to the territorial legislature of Hawaii in the Democratic revolution that swept Republicans out of control. He supported the successful abolition of the death penalty in Hawaii in 1957 and went on to serve as the territorial house majority leader in 1958.[8]

In 1959 Hawaii finally attained statehood after Delegate John Burns arranged a compromise admitting Alaska to the Union first. Matsunaga put his name forward for the position of lieutenant governor. However, Burns, the gubernatorial candidate and de facto head of the Democratic Party on the islands, had already handpicked fellow insider Mitsuyuki (Mits) Kido as his running mate. Matsunaga balked; he asked why he had "risked his life in Europe with the 100th to come home and be told not to run for office."[9] He ran anyway and weathered the primary loss. Burns, meanwhile, remained in DC for much of the campaign and lost the governor's race in a Republican landslide. Matsunaga returned to his law practice, but kept an eye on opportunities for national office.

That opportunity arrived in 1962, when Hawaiian Senator Oren Long declined to run for re-election. Representative Daniel Inouye ran for the vacant Senate seat, and redistricting doubled the number of Hawaiian congressional districts from one to two. Both seats were allotted At-Large in 1962 and were vacant, meaning

Matsunaga could come in second overall but still serve in the House. Once again Democratic operatives pleaded with Matsunaga to reconsider, stating he was "upsetting the racial balance that had been so carefully worked out" for the ticket. Furious at the charge, Matsunaga took the issue head-on in the primaries and ended up polling the most votes of any Democrat.[10] In the general election, he ran alongside Democrat Thomas P. Gill against Republicans Albert Evensen and Richard Sutton. Matsunaga received 123,599 votes, only 50 fewer than Gill; neither Republican candidate managed to attain more than 20 percent of the votes.

Upon entering the House in 1963, Matsunaga was appointed to the Agriculture Committee. He also sat on the Post Office and Civil Service Committee in the 89th Congress (1965–1967) before gaining a spot on the powerful Rules Committee in 1967. Matsunaga's seat on the Rules Committee was due to his personal friendship with Speaker John McCormack of Massachusetts. When asked whether he had cleared the appointment with incoming Rules Chairman William Colmer of Mississippi, McCormack scoffed, "Absolutely not. The Rules Committee is an arm of the leadership and the Speaker must have complete freedom to select those members on whose personal loyalty he can reasonably depend."[11]

Despite having no position of defined power on the committee, Matsunaga's command of the House Rules ensured him significant influence over the process of lawmaking. He diluted the power of the chairman by shepherding a rule allowing the majority to call a meeting without the chairman's consent. He frequently cosponsored legislation before it reached the Rules Committee, generating support from moderates on the committee who respected his views. He helped steer several major bills into laws this way, but he did not introduce much legislation himself. His expertise drew acclaim from House leadership. Majority Leader Hale Boggs noted in 1971 that "it's getting to the point where you have to see Sparky Matsunaga to get a bill passed around here."[12] In 1976 he published a book with cowriter Ping Chen titled *Rulemakers of the House*, detailing the evolution of the Rules Committee. At one point during a re-election campaign, Matsunaga defended the importance of his place on the Rules Committee: "The Civil Rights Act of 1968 came out of this committee by an 8-7 vote. So did the Higher Education Act, the Vocational Education Act, the Federal Pay Raise Act, the Gun Control Act and others. You can see the importance of my one vote: Hawai'i's vote."[13]

Matsunaga devoted much of his time and effort to Hawaiian interests, primarily the continuation of sugar subsidies for the island's most important crop. Typically, a seat on the Rules Committee is an exclusive placement; however, Matsunaga negotiated to retain his spot on the Agriculture Committee as well because he "[knew] a lot about sugar." Matsunaga valued the committee membership highly, noting that "sugar is the life-blood of Hawaii."[14] Through his dual positions on Agriculture and Rules, Matsunaga was able to assert his influence in hearings for the Sugar Act Amendments of 1971, speeding its passage. Using his position on the Rules Committee, Matsunaga voted down rules that had the potential to limit sugar benefits on the island, and the bill passed the House under a closed rule on June 10. The Sugar Act Amendments of 1971 maintained favorable prices and quotas for Hawaiian sugar above the world market price, stimulating a key Hawaiian industry.[15]

Throughout his congressional career, Matsunaga tirelessly advocated for peace. In an assigned paper during his first year at the University of Hawaii, Matsunaga wrote, "If we want peace, we must first educate people to want peace. We must replace attitudes favorable to war with attitudes opposed to war."[16] He strongly supported foreign aid as a method of peaceful support to cooperating nations, including India, which he described as "the bulwark of democracy in the East." Matsunaga argued that foreign aid, an unpopular bill in the House, was "a sound investment in our future security."[17]

However, his stance on Vietnam waffled over the years. Shortly after joining the House of Representatives, Matsunaga was recommissioned as a lieutenant colonel in the Judge Advocate General's Corps of the U.S. Army Reserve partially to show support for American troops.[18] For much of the conflict, he viewed the defense of the South Vietnamese government as a moral imperative and supported defense appropriations and the Lyndon B. Johnson administration's decision to escalate U.S. involvement in the conflict. As the war dragged on under the Richard Nixon administration, however, Matsunaga added his voice to those calling for the war's end. In early 1971, he offered one of the earliest resolutions for complete withdrawal of U.S. troops.[19] On February 1, 1971, he spoke in favor of his resolution (H. Con. Res. 101), saying, "The war must end. Congress must move to reassert its constitutional responsibilities to 'raise and support armies' and to 'declare war.'"[20]

Matsunaga had clashed with Nixon's 1968 running mate over civil rights and treatment of Asian Americans. During the presidential election campaign, Republican vice presidential nominee Spiro Agnew casually referred to a *Baltimore Sun* reporter on his campaign jet as a "fat Jap." Matsunaga decried it as a hateful episode, and though Agnew initially shrugged off the concerns as "desperate," he publicly apologized days later.[21]

Matsunaga often spoke in favor of and voted for civil rights legislation, though he resisted its more militant aspects. He waded into the 1964 Civil Rights Bill debate on the House Floor to clearly state, "American society can be true to itself … only as rights are accorded to every person because he is a person."[22] But both before and after passage of the landmark Civil Rights Act of 1964 Matsunaga warned against provoking civil disorder to further the cause of the movement, saying that African Americans should "exercise the patience of Job, and seek to remedy wrongs only through the peaceful means provided by the new law."[23] During the debate on the Voting Rights Act of 1965, Matsunaga more passionately assaulted the hypocrisy that civil rights legislation aimed to correct, noting, "It was not pure chance that under Thomas Jefferson's able draftsmanship the Declaration of Independence should state that 'all men are created equal.' These were not hollow words."[24]

While he occasionally restrained his fervor for the civil rights movement of the 1960s, he never wavered in his effort to restore dignity to Japanese Americans wronged during World War II internment. In 1971 he introduced H.R. 234 to repeal Title II of the Internal Security Act of 1950, an act with similar provisions to the executive order that had enabled the United States to detain 120,000 Japanese Americans during World War II without due process. The Internal Security Act, also known as the McCarran Act after its sponsor, Senator Pat McCarran of Nevada, had been enacted over President Harry Truman's veto. Matsunaga first introduced his repeal bill in 1969 with Representative Chet Holifield of California as a cosponsor. At the time, Matsunaga insisted the provision "violates the constitutional guarantees and judicial traditions that are basic to our American way of life." Despite considerable support, opponents managed to refer the bill to the Committee on Internal Security, the successor of the House Un-American Activities Committee, where it languished.

When the pair reintroduced the bill in the 92nd Congress (1971–1973), Matsunaga used his position on the Rules Committee to have his bill considered before a competing, less effective proposal from Representative Richard Ichord, a conservative Democrat from Missouri who chaired the Internal Security Committee. Ichord's bill would have continued the threat of denying due process to those accused of subversive activities. Matsunaga's compromise forced Ichord's bill to a vote as an amendment to his own. In debate, opponents argued that the provision had never been used and Representative Allen Smith of California declared the bill "much ado about nothing." Representative Joe Evins of Tennessee, floor manager for Matsunaga's bill, came out swinging by denouncing Title II as allowing concentration camps on American soil. Ichord's amendment failed, 272 to 124; H.R. 234 then overwhelmingly passed the House, 356 to 49. The Senate passed the bill by unanimous consent two days later, and President Nixon signed it into law on September 25, 1971.[25]

After his first election, Matsunaga campaigned on his experience and the value of maintaining a strong veteran's voice in Congress for Hawaii. His brochures declared "In the forefront for Hawaii and the Nation," "Keep Hawaii Strong in Congress," and "Spark's rise to national prominence has been phenomenal." The strategy worked, winning Matsunaga overwhelming victories in each election after 1962.[26] In 1964, Representative Thomas Gill unsuccessfully challenged Republican Senator Hiram L. Fong, and state senator Patsy Mink won his spot as Hawaii's junior Representative. Matsunaga and Mink continued to represent Hawaii At-Large until 1970, when the two seats were assigned defined districts. Matsunaga took the district representing urban Honolulu as well as the northwestern Hawaiian islands.

In 1976 Senator Fong announced his retirement. Both Matsunaga and Mink jumped to announce their candidacies to fill the vacant seat. Both candidates attracted fervent support across Hawaii, and experts predicted a close race in the October primary. Ultimately, Matsunaga won with 55 percent of the vote.[27] The brief general election campaign pitted Matsunaga against former Republican Governor William Quinn. Quinn had been out of politics for some time and had lost recognition among an electorate that tilted more Democratic than it had two decades prior. Matsunaga won 54 percent of the vote, amassing a comfortable 40,000-vote margin. Once established in the Senate, he returned to his well-practiced method of touting his experience and clout on Capitol Hill. His victories were much larger in his re-election campaigns in 1982 and 1988, when he won 80 and 77 percent of the vote, respectively.[28]

Reflecting on his arrival in the Senate in 1977, Matsunaga later joked, "I felt very uneasy, very out of place. Everybody else was running for president."[29] Still, he made his mark early. As a freshman, he cast the deciding vote in the Democratic caucus to elect Senator Robert Byrd of West Virginia as Majority Leader. As a reward, Matsunaga was quickly moved from his early provisional appointments on the Commerce and Foreign Relations Committees and granted a seat on the powerful Finance Committee.[30] He was also appointed to the Energy and Natural Resources Committee and the Committee on Veterans' Affairs, although he left Energy and Natural Resources for the Committee on Labor and Human Resources in the 98th Congress (1983–1985).[31]

The Senate marked a change for Matsunaga in more ways than one. Fong had retired in part because he grew tired of the long hours. Matsunaga embraced the workload as he adapted to the culture of the Senate. Despite his ceaseless commitment to the job, he developed a reputation for his good nature among his colleagues and his constituents. He became famous for showing visiting constituents around the Capitol and treating them to lunch in the Senate Dining Room. After his death, the Senate named the center table after him to mark the spot where he so often entertained Hawaiian visitors.[32]

Matsunaga first experienced being in the minority party during his years in the Senate when Republicans regained control of that body in 1981, riding the coattails of President Ronald Reagan's election. During this period, Matsunaga grew more partisan but maintained his amiability. Weeks after reluctantly voting to confirm Alexander Haig as President Reagan's Secretary of State, Matsunaga attended a White House reception for the visiting Japanese prime minister. Despite his best efforts, the Senator found himself lumped in with the Japanese delegation as they were shuffled along the presidential receiving line. Secretary Haig shook Matsunaga's hand and asked if he spoke English. "Yes, Mr. Secretary, I do," Matsunaga replied in a deadpan, "and I had the honor of voting for your confirmation the other day."[33]

Matsunaga spent much of his first term mastering the rhythms of the Senate and forging a cooperative relationship with the senior Senator from Hawaii, Daniel Inouye. They worked closely on legislation important to Hawaii, but each maintained their own legislative focus. Matsunaga added interests in space exploration, alternative energy, and cultural development to his agenda. At the same time, he continued to campaign on behalf of civil rights for Japanese Americans and broader peace initiatives.

Early in his second term, Matsunaga finally achieved a long-sought goal: the establishment of the United States Institute of Peace. He submitted a bill (S. 564) in 1983 to found an Academy of Peace for undergraduates to study the art of diplomacy and peaceful negotiation. More than 140 bills had been introduced during the previous

half-century calling for some sort of agency dedicated to peace.[34] Matsunaga had submitted several similar proposals since entering Congress in 1962. S. 564 garnered 51 cosponsors and seemed bound for passage, but was repeatedly held up in various committees, where it was redesigned to be a grant-making institution.

After suffering a heart attack on January 4, 1984, Matsunaga redoubled his efforts to create his Academy of Peace. He asked Oregon Senator Mark Hatfield, chairman of the Appropriations Committee, to submit the United States Institute of Peace Act as Title XVII of the defense appropriations bill. Hatfield steadfastly backed the amendment, which carried it through committee.[35] Codified in Public Law 98-525, the institute established a nonprofit corporation with federal funding, an appointed board of directors, and the mission to distribute grants, hold conferences, and award the newly minted Medal of Peace.[36] The Institute of Peace was not the academy Matsunaga had originally envisioned, but it carried a mandate to foster peace research in other academic and diplomatic institutions across the nation.

Matsunaga was also taken with emerging technologies, focusing on space exploration and alternative energy sources. While the latter appealed mainly to his love of science, the former tied directly to his tireless efforts for peace. In 1986 he published his second book titled *The Mars Project: Journeys Beyond the Cold War*, advocating cooperation with the Soviet Union to explore the red planet. He was moved to write the book as the Reagan administration pushed the ballistic missile defense system, better known as "Star Wars." Matsunaga addressed the salience of focusing on space exploration at that moment, saying, "They may think I'm out of this world, but one of the objectives I had in mind was to offer something positive in lieu of 'Star Wars' because 'Star Wars' can only lead to our mutual destruction."[37]

Matsunaga was one of the earliest proponents of an international space station, introducing a resolution (S. Res. 488) in favor of its development in 1982. "Space—the last and most expansive frontier—will be what we make it," he wrote in a 1982 editorial.[38] In 1984 Matsunaga sponsored another resolution (S.J. Res. 236) in favor of U.S.-Soviet space cooperation; this one passed the House and Senate and gained Reagan's signature. Studies were launched to address the feasibility of manned spaceflight to Mars. Matsunaga also suggested turning the manned spaceflight program over to the U.S. Air Force, citing the *Challenger* disaster as evidence that NASA had become "overburdened."[39] The International Space Station eventually became a reality in 1998, when the first components were launched for the joint operation.

Another of Matsunaga's longtime goals came to fruition in 1985, when he helped create the U.S. poet laureate position at the Library of Congress. Matsunaga was an amateur poet himself. During Japanese Prime Minister Yasuhiro Nakasone's visit in 1986, Nakasone praised the cherry blossoms at a congressional lunch. Inspired, Matsunaga spontaneously stood and formed a haiku: "Cherry blossoms bloom. Washington is beautified. East and West do meet."[40]

In late 1985, he cosponsored the Arts, Humanities, and Museums Amendments of 1985 along with Republican Senator William Cohen of Maine. This bill (S. 1264) introduced a compromise that combined the position of poet laureate with that of the poetry consultant to the Library of Congress. In floor debate on October 3, 1985, Matsunaga claimed that the United States was behind the times, noting the existence of the position in other developed nations across Europe. He also spoke of poetry's cross-sectional appeal: "It is my hope that the work of the future poet laureate … will also reflect our Nation's great diversity—its multiethnic, multicultural, multiracial heritage, its strength and compassion, and its democratic idealism."[41] The bill passed both chambers by voice vote within a week of each other and became law on December 20, 1985. Robert Penn Warren was chosen as the nation's first poet laureate in early 1986.

The legislation Matsunaga viewed as his crowning achievement came very late in his career. In 1988 working with Representative Robert Matsui of California, among others, Matsunaga obtained redress for Japanese Americans who had been interned during World War II. Like many

of his major accomplishments, this legislation took years to achieve. Matsunaga began lobbying for reparations in earnest shortly after joining the Senate in 1979.[42] He cosponsored Senator Inouye's bill (S. 1647) in August 1979, establishing the Commission on Wartime Relocation and Internment of Civilians, which proceeded to conduct a prolonged study of the effects of internment during World War II. "The proposed study would finally make all the facts known and would allow Congress to decide whether any further action should be taken to compensate victims of the wartime relocation policy," Matsunaga explained just before the bill passed by voice vote.

The commission appointed by Congress published a report in 1983 titled *Personal Justice Denied*, which described internment as a product of "race prejudice, war hysteria and a failure of political leadership" and recommended redress payments to the victims and families.[43] Shortly after the commission started, however, the Senate changed hands and Republicans blocked any legislation based on the commission's report.

By 1987 Democrats had retaken the Senate and once more held both houses of Congress. Throughout the 100th Congress (1987–1989), Matsunaga became a man on a mission, working alongside the American Civil Liberties Union to approach each Member one by one and assert the need for reparations. In January 1987, Majority Leader Tom Foley of Washington introduced H.R. 442 calling for redress. Matsunaga and Inouye both testified before the House committees considering the legislation. Just before the Easter holiday on April 10, Matsunaga rose in the Senate chamber to report the long-awaited findings of the commission, declaring, "Perhaps the most traumatic experience, the one thing that has haunted Americans of Japanese ancestry for 45 years, was the stigma of being cast as disloyal to their own beloved country, the United States of America."[44] On September 17, 1987, the House passed H.R. 442 in a 236 to 137 bipartisan vote.

Despite the success in the House, progress stalled on Matsunaga's Senate version of the bill (S. 1009). The proponents of the legislation began a concerted effort to talk down threats of filibuster from conservative opponents, specifically Senator Jesse Helms of North Carolina, who objected to paying $20,000 to "Japanese." Matsunaga assured him that only Americans who happened to be of Japanese descent were involved, and Helms temporarily relented.[45] After obtaining support from the Reagan administration in early 1988, formal debate finally began on April 19. Senator John Glenn of Ohio introduced the bill and commended Matsunaga on his single-minded pursuit of its passage, saying, "He has been a real bird dog on this one."[46] Matsunaga thanked Glenn and said, "This bill provides a long overdue remedy for one of the worst violations of individuals' civil liberties in our nation's history. Passage of this bill removes a big blot on the Constitution … [by] bringing about personal justice which had been denied by our own government to our own citizens."[47]

Senator Helms tried one final time to upend the bill, introducing an amendment seeking compensation from the Japanese government for the families of those killed at Pearl Harbor before awarding reparations to Japanese Americans. That amendment failed spectacularly, 91 to 4, after Matsunaga pointed out its false logic. Afterward, Matsunaga brought up H.R. 442, which had already passed the House, and asked that the text following the enacting clause be replaced with the substance of his bill. The symbolism of that bill number was lost on no one, as it invoked the all-Japanese-American 442nd Regimental Combat Team in World War II. The bill, which spread $1.3 billion in reparations over five years, passed, 69 to 27, on April 20, 1988.

Reparations began in late 1990, but Spark Matsunaga did not have long to celebrate that achievement.[48] The Senator fell ill in early 1990 with prostate cancer. His condition deteriorated quickly. He cast his final vote on April 3 from a wheelchair, unable to speak.[49] Hawaiian newspapers called for his resignation, intimating that he might be unable to properly represent the interests of the state.[50] Matsunaga waved off the concerns as "trying to make a decision a little too soon."[51]

While seeking treatment in Toronto, Matsunaga died on April 15, 1990. He lay in state in the Hawaiian capitol rotunda before his ashes were interred in Punchbowl National Cemetery in Honolulu. The United States Institute of Peace he had fought so long to create was renamed the Spark M. Matsunaga Institute for Peace and Conflict Resolution shortly after his death on Inouye's suggestion. Speaking at his funeral, Senate Majority Leader George Mitchell of Maine said of him, "Most of all, Spark Matsunaga loved his country enough to make it right when it was wrong."[52]

FOR FURTHER READING

Halloran, Richard. *Sparky: Warrior, Peacemaker, Poet, Patriot.* (Honolulu, HI: Watermark Publishing, 2002).

Matsunaga, Spark M. *The Mars Project: Journeys Beyond the Cold War.* (New York: Hill Wang, 1986).

Matsunaga, Spark M., and Ping Chen. *Rulemakers of the House.* (Urbana: University of Illinois Press, 1976).

MANUSCRIPT COLLECTION

University of Hawaii at Manoa Library, Archives and Manuscripts Department, Hawaii Congressional Papers Collection (Honolulu, HI). *Papers*: 1916–1990, 908 linear feet. The Spark M. Matsunaga papers include correspondence, speeches, schedules, press releases, newsletters, travel files, audiovisual materials, photographs, and memorabilia. The collection covers a wide range of topics, including space exploration, veterans' affairs, health care, natural resources, energy, transportation, taxation, and civil rights, especially redress for Japanese Americans interned during World War II. It includes material from Matsunaga's service in the Hawaii territorial legislature, but primarily documents his career in the U.S. House of Representatives and U.S. Senate.

NOTES

1   *Congressional Record*, Senate, 99th Cong., 2nd sess. (14 August 1986): S11617.

2   Richard Halloran, *Sparky: Warrior, Peacemaker, Poet, Patriot* (Honolulu, HI: Watermark Publishing, 2002): 1–2.

3   Carla Hall, "The Senator & His Space Refrain," 13 August 1986, *Washington Post*: C1.

4   Barbara Bennett Peterson, "Matsunaga, Spark Masayuki," *American National Biography*, vol. 14 (New York: Oxford University Press, 1999): 710.

5   Hall, "The Senator & His Space Refrain."

6   "Senator Spark M. Matsunaga Papers Finding Aid," January 2005, University of Hawaii at Manoa, Honolulu, http://library.

manoa.hawaii.edu/departments/archives/congressional/matsunaga/SMMFindingAid_web.pdf.

7 Hearings before the Senate Committee on Interior and Insular Affairs, *Hawaii Statehood*, 81st Cong., 2nd sess. (1950): 247.

8 "Senator Spark M. Matsunaga Papers Finding Aid."

9 John S. Whitehead, *Completing the Union: Alaska, Hawai'i, and the Battle for Statehood* (Albuquerque: University of New Mexico Press, 2004): 317.

10 Halloran, *Sparky*: 86–87.

11 Ibid., 119.

12 Peterson, "Matsunaga, Spark Masayuki."

13 Halloran, *Sparky*: 125.

14 Sarah Jane Glazer, "Spark M. Matsunaga, Democratic Representative from Hawaii," in *Ralph Nader Congress Project: Citizens Look at Congress* (Washington, DC: Grossman Publishers, 1972): 15; Peterson, "Matsunaga, Spark Masayuki."

15 Glazer, "Spark M. Matsunaga, Democratic Representative from Hawaii": 16–17.

16 Diana Leone, "Peace Institutes Realize Vision," 20 August 2009, *Honolulu Advertiser*, http://the.honoluluadvertiser.com/article/2009/Aug/20/ln/hawaii908200341.html (accessed 29 April 2016).

17 Halloran, *Sparky*: 96–97.

18 "Senator Spark M. Matsunaga Papers Finding Aid."

19 Ralph Nader Congress Project, "Spark M. Matsunaga, Democratic Representative from Hawaii": 17; Halloran, *Sparky*: 134–136.

20 *Congressional Record*, House, 92nd Cong., 1st sess. (1 February 1971): 1281.

21 *Congressional Record*, Senate, 101st Cong., 2nd sess. (19 April 1990): 4460; Halloran, *Sparky*: 126–127.

22 *Congressional Record*, House, 88th Cong., 1st sess. (10 February 1964): 2766.

23 Halloran, *Sparky*: 99.

24 *Congressional Record*, House, 89th Cong., 1st sess. (9 July 1965): 16275.

25 Halloran, *Sparky*: 140–143; Public Law 92-128, 85 Stat. 347 (1971).

26 Ralph Nader Congress Project, "Spark M. Matsunaga, Democratic Representative from Hawaii": 8–9.

27 "Matsunaga Ends Mink's Bid in Hawaii Senatorial Race," 4 October 1976, *Washington Post*: A3.

28 Office of the Clerk, U.S. House of Representatives, "Election Statistics, 1920 to Present," http://history.house.gov/Institution/Election-Statistics/Election-Statistics/.

29 Hall, "The Senator & His Space Refrain."

30 Peterson, "Matsunaga, Spark Masayuki."

31 For a full listing of Matsunaga's committee assignments, see Garrison Nelson, *Committees in the U.S. Congress, 1947–1992*, vol. 2 (Washington, DC: CQ Press, 1994): 570–571.

32 *Congressional Record*, Senate, 101st Cong., 2nd sess. (11 May 1990): S6102; Rudy Maxa, "Hawaii's Senator Who Never Sleeps Says A Millionaire Made Him Do It," 16 March 1980, *Washington Post Magazine*: 4.

33 Halloran, *Sparky*: 159.

34 Spark M. Matsunaga, "An Academy of Peace: Training for a Peaceful Future," February 1985, *The Futurist*: 8.

35 Halloran, *Sparky*: 194–196.

36 Department of Defense Authorization Act, Public Law 98-525, 98 Stat. 2492 (1984).

37 Hall, "The Senator & His Space Refrain."

38 Spark A. Matsunaga, "Find Peace With Russia in Space," 4 July 1982, *Washington Post*: B4.

39 Public Law 98-562, 98 Stat. 2914 (1984); Spark M. Matsunaga, "Put the Air Force Into Space," 13 April 1986, *Washington Post*: B4.

40 Hall, "The Senator & His Space Refrain."

41 Halloran, *Sparky*: 204–205; *Congressional Record*, Senate, 99th Cong., 1st sess. (3 October 1985): 25816.

42 Richard Pearson, "Sen. Spark Matsunaga, Hawaii Democrat, Dies," 16 April 1990, *Washington Post*: D6.

43 Commission on Wartime Relocation and Internment of Civilians, *Personal Justice Denied* (Washington, DC: Civil Liberties Education Fund, 1997): 18.

44 Halloran, *Sparky*: 210–220.

45 Ibid., 224–225.

46 Ibid., 226.

47 "Senate Approves Bill to Settle War Internment," 21 April 1988, *Miami Herald*: A17.

48 *Congressional Record*, Senate, 100th Cong., 2nd sess. (20 April 1988): 7619–7643; Halloran, *Sparky*: 233–234.

49 "Senator Spark M. Matsunaga Papers Finding Aid."

50 Karen Foerstel, "Matsunaga, Stricken With Prostate Cancer, Is Only Coming to Hill for Roll-Call Votes," 19 February 1990, *Roll Call*: n.p.

51 Karen Foerstel, "'I'm Getting Better,' Says Matsunaga: Despite Cancer, He's Far From Resignation," 12 April 1990, *Roll Call*: n.p.

52 *Congressional Record*, Senate, 101st Cong., 2nd sess. (24 April 1990): H1665.

"AMERICAN SOCIETY CAN
BE TRUE TO ITSELF ... ONLY
AS RIGHTS ARE ACCORDED
TO EVERY PERSON BECAUSE
HE IS A PERSON."

Spark M. Matsunaga
Congressional Record, February 10, 1964

Patsy Takemoto Mink
1927–2002

UNITED STATES REPRESENTATIVE 1965–1977; 1990–2002
DEMOCRAT FROM HAWAII

Patsy Takemoto Mink, the first woman of color elected to Congress, participated in the passage of much of the 1960s Great Society legislation during the first phase of her congressional career. After a long hiatus, Mink returned to the House in the 1990s as an ardent defender of the social welfare state at a time when much of the legislation she had helped establish was being rolled back. As a veteran politician who had a significant impact on the nation during both stints in the U.S. House of Representatives, Mink's legislative approach was premised on the belief that representation extended beyond the borders of one's congressional district. "You were not elected to Congress, in my interpretation of things, to represent your district, period," she once noted. "You are national legislators."[1]

Patsy Matsu Takemoto was born in Paia, Hawaii Territory, on December 6, 1927, one of two children raised by Suematsu Takemoto, a civil engineer, and Mitama Tateyama Takemoto. She graduated from Maui High School in 1944 as class president and valedictorian and went on to attend Wilson College in Chambersburg, Pennsylvania, and the University of Nebraska at Lincoln before graduating with a BA in zoology and chemistry from the University of Hawaii in 1948. Mink originally planned to pursue a medical degree, but turned to law school after several medical schools turned down her application. Three years later, she earned a JD from the University of Chicago Law School, the first Hawaiian *nisei* woman to do so. In 1951 she married John Francis Mink, a graduate student in geology at the university. The couple had one child, a daughter named Gwendolyn, and moved to Honolulu. Facing discrimination from bigger firms due to her interracial marriage, Patsy T. Mink went into private law practice and lectured on business law at the University of Hawaii.[2] In 1954 Mink founded the Oahu Young

Democrats and worked as an attorney for the territorial house of representatives in 1955. Mink won election to that body in 1956 and 1958 before winning a seat in the territorial senate, where she served from 1958 to 1959.

In 1959, when Hawaii achieved statehood, Mink set her sights on the new state's lone At-Large seat in the U.S. House of Representatives and began to campaign for the post. Hawaii's Delegate and Democratic "boss," John Burns, remained in Washington, DC, until June, when he suddenly began working behind the scenes to rearrange the Democratic ballot to his liking. He convinced Daniel K. Inouye to abandon his Senate campaign and file for the House seat instead, frustrating Mink's efforts and forcing a primary. Though Mink was also one of Burns's protégés, she frequently broke with party leadership in the territorial legislature. Throughout her career, Mink never had a warm relationship with the state leaders of her party; she attributed their lack of support to her unwillingness to allow the party to influence her political agenda.[3] Additionally, Burns viewed Inouye as his successor, and the two worked together atop the state Democratic Party for many years. The famously liberal International Longshore and Warehouse Union switched their endorsement from Mink to Inouye, who won by a 2 to 1 margin in the primary, leaving Mink to focus on her legal career.[4] Mink returned to politics in 1962, winning a seat in the Hawaii state senate, where she served from 1962 to 1964 and eventually chaired the education committee.

In 1964, after reapportionment created a second seat for Hawaii in the U.S. House, Mink again mounted a grassroots campaign that relied on a staff of unpaid volunteers; her husband, John, served as her campaign manager, "principal sounding board," and "in-house critic."[5] She ran without the blessing of the state Democratic Party leadership, raising campaign funds

largely in small individual contributions. Mink barely edged out two other Democrats in the October primary to secure her spot on the ballot alongside Spark M. Matsunaga, Daniel Inouye's successor in the House. Mink stressed her independence in the general election even as many Democrats arranged deals to support one of the Republican nominees to defeat her.[6] With help from President Lyndon B. Johnson's landslide victory in the presidential race, Mink and Matsunaga were elected as the state's two At-Large Representatives. In a four-way race, she received 27 percent of the total to become the first Asian-American woman and just the second woman from Hawaii to serve in Congress.

In her subsequent five campaigns for re-election, Mink faced a number of difficult primaries in which the local Democratic Party tried to oust her, twice by running women candidates, which Mink interpreted as an effort to deprive her of the gender issue.[7] She proved a durable candidate in the general elections, however, despite being viewed initially as a presidential coattail rider. In 1966 and 1968, in a four-way race for the two House seats, she garnered slightly more than 34 percent of the vote. In the 1966 race, she collected more votes than any of the other three candidates. In 1970 Hawaii was divided into two congressional districts. Representing the outer islands and suburban Oahu, Mink began traveling back to her district every other week to combat the notion that she was a purely national figure with little interest in the local needs of her constituents. The configuration of the new district also forced Mink to shift her campaigning methods, since she could no longer rely on the Honolulu media market to spread her message.[8] Her efforts paid off, however; Mink ran unopposed in 1970 and won 53 percent of the vote in 1972 and 63 percent in 1974.[9]

In the House, Mink successfully sought a seat on the Committee on Education and Labor, on which she served from the 89th Congress (1965–1967) through the 94th Congress (1975–1977). In her second term, she also joined the Committee on Interior and Insular Affairs and, in the 93rd (1973–1975) and 94th Congresses, served on the Budget Committee.

Mink's committee assignments allowed her to concentrate on the same issues that had been the focus of her attention in the Hawaii legislature. Among the education acts Mink introduced or sponsored in the U.S. House were the first childcare bill and legislation establishing bilingual education, student loans, special education, professional sabbaticals for teachers, and Head Start. Starting in 1967, she also put significant effort into passing a bill to institute a national daycare system to support low-income households. The Comprehensive Child Development Act was folded into the Economic Opportunity Act (S. 2007) in 1971. But it failed to become law, in part, because opponents objected that it offered too many incentives for mothers to work outside the home and that it promoted a "communal" approach to rearing children. Though the Economic Opportunity Act passed both houses of Congress, President Richard M. Nixon vetoed it in December 1971.[10] Mink later called the bill's failure "one of the real disappointments" of her political career.[11]

Mink maintained a focus on national issues, especially those affecting Asian Pacific Americans (APA) and the Pacific region. She fought to preserve family reunification provisions in several proposed immigration reform bills and worked alongside Representative Matsunaga to educate Americans about the internment of Japanese Americans during World War II.[12] As a member of the Interior and Insular Affairs Committee, she supported the economic and political development of the Trust Territory of the Pacific Islands. As chair of the Subcommittee on Mines and Mining, she helped author the landmark Surface Mining Control and Reclamation Act of 1975, and in the following year helped to pass a major overhaul of the Mineral Leasing Act of 1920. The House failed to override President Gerald R. Ford's veto of the Surface Mining Control and Reclamation Act, though a similar measure was eventually signed into law in 1977.

During the Johnson presidency, Mink strongly supported the administration's domestic programs that were part of the Great Society legislation, but she was a critic of America's increasing involvement in the Vietnam

War. In September 1967, she refused to support the President's request for an income tax increase because she feared that the new revenues would be used for military action rather than the expansion of social programs. It was, she said, like "administering aspirin to a seriously ill patient who needs major surgery."[13] If inflation threatened the economy, she suggested, the administration should raise taxes on big business and not just the average working taxpayers.[14] In April 1972, she cosponsored Massachusetts Representative Michael Harrington's concurrent resolution (H. Con. Res. 589) calling for an immediate termination of military activity in Vietnam, but the House took no action on it. Her views clashed with those of the three other Members of the Hawaii congressional delegation as well as with those of many of her constituents in a state with a heavy military presence. Years later, however, Mink recalled, "It was such a horrible thought to have this war that it really made no difference to me that I had a military constituency. It was a case of living up to my own views and my own conscience. If I was defeated for it, that's the way it had to be. There was no way in which I could compromise my views on how I felt about it."[15]

Mink also advocated many women's issues in Congress, including equal rights. One of her great legislative triumphs was the Women's Educational Equity Act, passed as part of a comprehensive education bill in 1974. It provided $30 million a year in educational funds for programs to promote gender equity in schools, to increase educational and job opportunities for women, and to excise gender stereotypes from textbooks and school curricula. She realized early in her House career that "because there were only eight women at the time who were Members of Congress, that I had a special burden to bear to speak for [all women], because they didn't have people who could express their concerns for them adequately. So, I always felt that we were serving a dual role in Congress, representing our own districts and, at the same time, having to voice the concerns of the total population of women in the country."[16]

Working with Representative Edith Green of Oregon and Senator Birch Bayh of Indiana, Mink built critical support for Title IX of the Education Amendments of 1972 (S. 659), which barred sexual discrimination in institutions receiving federal funds and opened up opportunities for women in athletics. Though the broad strokes of the legislation were relatively noncontroversial at passage, the House and Senate worked for several months to hammer out more than 250 differences—11 of which dealt specifically with sexual discrimination—between their bills.[17]

As enforcement of Title IX took effect, the full ramifications of the act became clear and many supporters of public school men's sports programs objected to it, believing that their funding was being cut in favor of women's sports under the new statute. In 1975 opponents filed an amendment to the appropriations bill (H.R. 5901) for the Department of Health, Education, and Welfare that would exempt school athletics from Title IX. Despite heavy lobbying by Mink, the amendment survived the House version of the bill. After the Senate struck the amendment in conference, the House faced a tight vote on whether to stand by its position. Just before voting, Mink received an emergency call informing her that her daughter had been in a life-threatening car accident in Upstate New York. Mink rushed to her daughter's side while the voting commenced, ultimately ending in a narrow 212 to 211 victory for Title IX opponents. When newspapers characterized Mink's tearful exit as a result of the vote, her allies leapt to the Congresswoman's defense. Speaker Carl Albert of Oklahoma and Representative Daniel Flood of Pennsylvania explained the circumstances of Mink's absence the following legislative day, and the House voted to "recede and concur" with the Senate, with Mink in attendance. Mink's daughter (and Title IX) survived.[18]

Mink garnered national attention for her fervent support of liberal causes. In 1971 she received an invitation from Oregon Democrats to appear on the Democratic presidential primary ballot in that state in order to draw attention to the anti-war movement. Mink committed to the symbolism of her place in the race with seven weekend visits to Oregon. "My candidacy offers a real and tangible alternative," she said, "based—if any one word can be singled out—on humanism." Ultimately,

Mink received only 2 percent of the vote and withdrew her candidacy afterward. However, she continued to receive votes in Wisconsin and Maryland even after she had ceased campaigning.[19]

In 1976, passing up a bid for what would have been certain re-election to a seventh term in the House, Mink sought the Democratic nomination for a seat in the U.S. Senate. She lost the nomination to fellow House Member Spark Matsunaga.[20] Her supporters criticized Mink for not running a more aggressive campaign, but Mink insisted she had been running for the nomination and not against Matsunaga, a respected colleague.[21] She remained active in politics, serving as Assistant Secretary of State for Oceans and International Environmental and Scientific Affairs from 1977 to 1978. For the next three years, she was president of the Americans for Democratic Action, a liberal political lobbying organization founded in 1947 by an array of scholars, activists, and politicians.[22] Mink returned to Hawaii and was elected to the Honolulu city council, serving there from 1983 to 1987 (from 1983 to 1985 as its chair). She ran unsuccessfully for governor in 1986 and then for mayor of Honolulu in 1988. "Life is not based on being an elected politician," she said during this period. "Politics is a constant involvement in the day-to-day working of society as a whole, one part of which is government."[23]

Despite these electoral setbacks, Mink kept her sights set on returning to public office. An opportunity to return to Congress arose in 1990 when Hawaiian Governor John Waihee III appointed Representative Daniel Akaka to replace the recently deceased Senator Matsunaga. Mink announced her intention to seek both the Democratic nominations for the special election to fill Akaka's vacancy and the November general election for the new term in the 102nd Congress (1991–1993), though she was not the party's choice in either case. Hawaii Democratic Party leaders backed Mufi Hannemann, whose youth and business connections they found appealing. Mink countered by using the campaign slogan "The Experience of a Lifetime," a message that resonated with Hawaiian voters who tended to prioritize seniority and expertise

in their representatives. Both the special election and the primary for the new term were held on September 22, 1990, and Mink edged out her nearest competitor, Hannemann, in both contests by less than 3 percent.[24] She easily won the November general election to the full term in the 102nd Congress and was re-elected comfortably to five subsequent terms with winning percentages ranging from a high of 73 percent in 1992 to a low of 60 percent in 1996.[25]

Mink was once again appointed to the Committee on Education and Labor (later Education and the Workforce) and also was assigned to the Government Operations (later Government Reform) Committee. During the 103rd Congress (1993–1995), she was on the Natural Resources and Budget Committees, serving on the latter through the 105th Congress (1997–1999).

Mink continued to pursue legislative reform in health care and education. Believing that voters cared more about quality health coverage than any other domestic issue, she advocated a universal health care plan that would allow people of all economic backgrounds to receive medical treatment. Mink combined two of her long-standing interests when she cosponsored the Gender Equity Act in 1993. Disturbed that gender discrimination still persisted in the United States 20 years after the passage of Title IX, Mink asserted that targeting gender bias in elementary and secondary education would help reduce inequalities between the sexes. She told the House, "We must assure that schools all across this country implement and integrate into their curriculum, policies, goals, programs, activities, and initiatives to achieve educational equity for women and girls."[26] Mink continued to crusade for women's rights by cochairing the Democratic Women's Caucus in 1995.

In May 1994, Mink joined Representative Norman Mineta of California and other colleagues in forming the Congressional Asian Pacific American Caucus. "We have felt that we have not been consulted on important steps taken by this administration and ones in the past," Mink declared. With so few APA Members of Congress, the caucus welcomed Representatives and Senators as full members, regardless of ethnicity, as long as they represented a district with a large APA constituency.[27] Mink won election as chairwoman of the caucus when Mineta resigned from Congress the following year, and she served in that capacity through 1997.[28]

Throughout her political career, Mink remained true to her liberal ideals. Previously in the majority both in her party affiliation and her political ideology, she often found herself in the minority during her second stretch in the House. During the 1990s, Mink expended considerable effort opposing conservative legislation that challenged the agenda she had promoted in the 1960s and 1970s. An outspoken critic of the welfare overhaul legislation that the Republican-led Congress and the William J. (Bill) Clinton administration agreed upon in 1996, Mink exclaimed, "Throwing people off welfare and forcing them to take the lowest-paying jobs in the community has created a misery index for millions."[29] As Ranking Member of the Education and the Workforce Subcommittee on Oversight and Investigations during the 105th Congress, Mink butted heads with conservative Republicans regarding a proposed $1.4 million investigation of alleged fraud within the Teamsters union. As a loyal supporter of organized labor, Mink accused Republican leadership of sponsoring a "fishing expedition" that wasted "taxpayers' money for sheer partisan political purposes."[30]

After the September 11, 2001, terrorist attacks, Mink also raised concerns about the establishment of the Department of Homeland Security (DHS) in 2002. Created in response to the perceived failures of various U.S. intelligence agencies to uncover plots against the homeland, DHS was charged with preventing further domestic terrorist strikes. Mink feared the sprawling new agency might undermine civil liberties by violating the privacy of American citizens in the name of national security. In favor of full disclosure of government attempts to safeguard the nation from international threats, she proposed that no secrets be kept from the public.[31] "She had already been through that as a Japanese American, seeing people put into detention camps on the basis of what they supposedly were as opposed to what they had actually done," said fellow Hawaii Representative Neil Abercrombie.[32]

On September 28, 2002, after a month-long hospitalization with pneumonia, Patsy T. Mink died in Honolulu, Hawaii. Her name remained on the November ballot, and she was re-elected by a wide margin. Democrat Ed Case defeated Patsy Mink's husband and more than 30 other candidates in the special election to succeed her in the remainder of the 107th Congress (2001–2003) and later won election to the 108th Congress (2003–2005).[33] Shortly after Mink's death, John Boehner of Ohio, chairman of the Education and the Workforce Committee, reflected upon Mink's congressional service: "Patsy Mink was a vibrant, passionate, and effective voice for the principles she believed in. Her passing is a significant loss for our committee, the people of Hawaii and the people of the United States."[34] Norman Y. Mineta, her colleague and a co-founder of the Congressional Asian Pacific American Caucus, called Mink "an American hero, a leader and a trailblazer who made an irreplaceable mark in the fabric of our country."[35]

FOR FURTHER READING

Davidson, Sue. *Jeannette Rankin and Patsy Takemoto Mink: A Heart in Politics* (Seattle, WA: Seal Press, 1994).

Mink, Patsy T., "Energy and Environment: Which is Undermining Which?" *Natural Resources Lawyer* 9 (1976): 19–39.

U.S. Association of Former Members of Congress, Patsy T. Mink, Oral History Interview (1979), Manuscript Room, Library of Congress, Washington, DC.

MANUSCRIPT COLLECTION

Library of Congress Manuscript Division (Washington, DC). *Papers*: 1883–2005 (bulk 1953–2002), 1,530 linear feet. The papers of Patsy T. Mink contain correspondence, memoranda, writings, speeches, notes, interviews, questionnaires, legislative files, testimony, casework, law practice client files, court documents, statements, press releases, appointment books, scheduling files, travel itineraries, campaign files, card files, biographical material, student papers, family papers, scrapbooks, news clippings, printed matter, awards and honors, political ephemera, maps, photographs, and other papers relating chiefly to Mink's service in the U.S. House of Representatives. Subjects include gender equity, Title IX, Women's Educational Equity Act, education, women's rights, welfare, environment, U.S. territories in the Pacific, Asian-American affairs, consumer affairs, civil rights, labor, immigration, health care, Vietnam, and nuclear weapons testing. The collection also documents Mink's private law practice in Honolulu, involvement in Hawaii and national Democratic politics, service in Hawaii's territorial and state legislatures, activities as Assistant Secretary of State for Oceans and International Environmental and Scientific Affairs. Her work as president of Americans for Democratic Action and chairmanship of the Honolulu city council also are represented. A finding aid is available in the repository.

NOTES

1   Patsy T. Mink, oral history interview by U.S. Association of Former Members of Congress, 6 March 1979, 26 March 1979, 7 June 1979, Manuscript Reading Room, Library of Congress, Washington, DC: 74.

2   Don T. Nakanishi and Ellen D. Wu, "Patsy T. Mink," in *Distinguished Asian American Political and Governmental Leaders* (Westport, CT: Greenwood Press, 2002): 129.

3   Mink, oral history interview: 16.

4   John S. Whitehead, *Completing the Union: Alaska, Hawai'i, and the Battle for Statehood* (Albuquerque: University of New Mexico Press, 2004): 315–317; Raymond Moley, "Hawaiian Primaries Show ILWU Power," 11 July 1959, *Los Angeles Times*: B4.

5   Mink, oral history interview: 31.

6   "Fong, Gill Win Hawaii Races; Woman Captures Spot in House Contest," 5 October 1964, *Chicago Tribune*: A6; Mink, oral history interview: 15–16.

7   Mink, oral history interview: 25.

8   Ibid., 22–23.

9   Office of the Clerk, U.S. House of Representatives, "Election Statistics, 1920 to Present," http://history.house.gov/Institution/Election-Statistics/Election-Statistics/.

10 Nancy S. Gates, "Patsy T. Mink, Democratic Representative from Hawaii" in *Ralph Nader Congress Project: Citizens Look at Congress* (Washington, DC: Grossman Publishers, 1972): 9; "Sharpening Day-Care Debate," 11 December 1971, *Christian Science Monitor*: 18.

11 Mink, oral history interview: 46.

12 Diwata Fonte, "For Asian-Americans, Mink's Death Hits 'Deeply,'" 7 October 2002, *Roll Call*: A20.

13 *Current Biography, 1968* (New York: H.W. Wilson Company, 1968): 255.

14 *Current Biography, 1968*: 255.

15 Mink, oral history interview: 98.

16 Ibid., 43.

17 "Title IX: A Sea Change in Gender Equity in Education," 10 July 1997, U.S. Department of Education, https://www2.ed.gov/pubs/TitleIX/part3.html (accessed 1 September 2016).

18 *Congressional Record*, House, 94th Cong., 1st sess. (18 July 1975): 23504–23506; *Congressional Record*, House, 107th Cong., 2nd sess. (17 July 2002): 13370–13371; "Gwendolyn Mink Oral History Interview," Office of the Historian, U.S. House of Representatives, 14 March 2016.

19 Hope Chamberlain, *A Minority of Members: Women in the U.S. Congress* (New York: Praeger Publishers, 1973): 313.

20 *Politics in America, 2002* (Washington, DC: Congressional Quarterly Press, 2001): 290–291.

21 Wallace Turner, "Ex-Gov. Quinn to Face Matsunaga in Hawaii," 4 October 1976, *New York Times*: 10.

22 James T. Patterson, *Grand Expectations: The United States, 1945–1974* (New York: Oxford University Press, 1996): 146.

23 Patsy Sume Saiki, *Japanese Women in Hawaii: The First 100 Years* (Honolulu, HI: Kisaku, Inc., 1985): 132.

24 Tania Cruz and Eric K. Yamamoto, "A Tribute to Patsy Takemoto Mink," *Asian-Pacific Law & Policy Journal* 4, no. 2 (Summer 2003): 594–595.

25 Office of the Clerk, U.S. House of Representatives, "Election Statistics, 1920 to Present," http://history.house.gov/Institution/Election-Statistics/Election-Statistics/.

26 *Congressional Record*, House, 103rd Cong., 1st sess. (21 April 1993): 8021.

27 David S. Broder and Kenneth J. Cooper, "Asian Pacific Caucus," 22 May 1994, *Washington Post*: A10.

28 Alethea Yip, "Mink Leads APA Caucus: Hawaii Representative Warns of Tough Times Ahead," 6 October 1995, *AsianWeek*: 6.

29 *Politics in America, 2002*: 290–291.

30 *Politics in America, 2000* (Washington, DC: Congressional Quarterly Press, 1999): 403–404.

31 *Congressional Record*, House, 107th Cong., 2nd sess. (26 July 2002): 5852.

32 Elissa Gootman, "Patsy Mink, Veteran Hawaii Congresswoman, Dies at 74," 30 September 2002, *New York Times*: B10.

33 James Gonser, "Case Wins; Set Sights on Jan. 4," 2 December 2002, *Honolulu Advertiser*: 1A.

34 Erin P. Billings, "Rep. Mink, First Asian-American Woman Elected to the House Dies," 30 September 2002, *Roll Call*: n.p. See also Gootman, "Patsy Mink, Veteran Hawaii Congresswoman, Dies at 74."

35 Martin Weil, "Rep. Patsy Mink Dies; Hawaiian Pushed Liberal Causes," 29 September 2002, *Washington Post*: A9.

"I ALWAYS FELT THAT WE
WERE SERVING A DUAL ROLE
IN CONGRESS, REPRESENTING
OUR OWN DISTRICTS AND,
AT THE SAME TIME, HAVING
TO VOICE THE CONCERNS
OF THE TOTAL POPULATION
OF WOMEN IN THE COUNTRY."

Patsy Takemoto Mink
oral history interview, 1979

Antonio Borja Won Pat
1908–1987

DELEGATE 1973–1985
DEMOCRAT FROM GUAM

The son of an immigrant from Hong Kong, Antonio Borja Won Pat's long political career culminated in his election as the first Territorial Delegate from Guam—where "America's day begins," a reference to the small, Pacific island's location across the international dateline. Known as "Pat" on Guam and "Tony" among his congressional colleagues, Won Pat's small-in-stature and soft-spoken nature belied his ability to craft alliances with powerful House Democrats and use his committee work to guide federal money towards and protect local interests in Guam.[1] It was these skills and his close relationship with Phillip Burton of California, a powerful figure on the House Interior and Insular Affairs Committee, that helped Won Pat become the first Territorial Delegate to chair a subcommittee. "To speak of Tony Won Pat's life … is to recall the very history of Guam," noted American Samoan Delegate Fofó I. F. Sunia, who memorialized Won Pat on the House Floor after his death. "Every major political accomplishment of the last quarter century in Guam bears Mr. Won Pat's valuable imprint."[2]

Antonio Borja Won Pat was born in Sumay, Guam, on December 10, 1908, to Maria Soriano Borja and Ignacio Won Pat. According to census records, he had at least two brothers, Vicente and Francisco.[3] Ignacio Won Pat was of Chinese heritage, originally from Hong Kong, and had come to Guam with the U.S. Navy to serve as a cook.[4] Later, as a member of the House Armed Services Committee, Won Pat made note of his family history. "And here I am tinkering with parts of the U.S. Navy budget," he observed.[5] Won Pat graduated from the Intermediate School in Agana, Guam, in 1925. He married a native Guamanian (known locally as a Chamorro), Ana Salas Perez, and they had eight children.[6]

Won Pat worked as a teacher at a school (later known as the Dyer School) in Piti, Guam, and then became principal at the Maxwell School in Sumay, where he worked until 1940. He was teaching at George Washington High School when Japan invaded Guam in December 1941. Following the war, Won Pat left teaching and organized the Guam Commercial Corporation, a group of wholesale and retail sellers. In his new career as a businessman, he became president of the Guam Junior Chamber of Commerce.

Won Pat's political career also pre-dated the Second World War. He was elected to the advisory Guam congress in 1936 and served until it was disbanded when war broke out. After the war, Won Pat helped organize the Commercial Party of Guam—the island's first political party. Won Pat served as speaker of the first Guam Assembly in 1948 and was re-elected to the post four times. The Commercial Party evolved into the Popular Party in 1950 and then became the Democratic Party of Guam in 1960. The latter dominated local politics for the next two decades.[7]

Initially, Won Pat supported U.S. naval rule over the island. In 1946 he told the *Chicago Tribune* that Guam needed to achieve greater economic independence before American citizenship. Yet disillusionment over naval leadership led him to change his mind.[8] Won Pat played a key part in the passage of the Organic Act, which granted U.S. citizenship to Guamanians in 1950; he traveled to Washington to testify on behalf of the legislation. In 1964 the Guam legislature authorized an unofficial representative in Washington to lobby for Guam's needs. Won Pat narrowly won election to the new post over the Territorial Party's Felix Lujan Crisostomo and two other independent candidates on March 15, 1965—an election that included personal attacks on Won Pat's Chinese heritage. Still, he won re-election unopposed in 1968.[9] Won Pat later characterized the "unofficial representative" position as having "its genesis in something of a lobbying

concept," and that the position was "a Member of Congress in everything but name" without "the 'power tools' … that other Members had."[10] Won Pat was also a delegate to the Democratic National Convention in 1972.

Won Pat's duties included lobbying for a Territorial Delegate from Guam in the U.S. House of Representatives. He won approval for the office in 1972, despite reservations at the Department of the Interior. The department's Office of the Territories argued that granting Guam a congressional Delegate could be tantamount to bestowing "incorporated" status to the territory, including full constitutional rights and protections.[11]

Having created the Delegate's post, he then ran for it. In what he characterized as a "good, clean race," Won Pat faced Republican territorial senator Pedro (Pete) Diaz Perez.[12] Won Pat emphasized his record during the campaign, especially as Guam's Washington representative, and expressed excitement at having a voice on congressional committees. Whereas Perez wanted to push for a vote in Congress, Won Pat was more hesitant, noting that it was unprecedented for an unincorporated territory to have a vote.[13] Won Pat also took out several full-page ads in the island's largest newspaper, the *Pacific Daily News*, in which he reprinted letters of support and praise from congressional giants such as Majority Leader Hale Boggs of Louisiana and Minority Leader Gerald R. Ford of Michigan.[14] Won Pat defeated Perez with 58 percent of the vote.[15]

Won Pat was able to win most of his elections with similarly comfortable margins. He ran unopposed in 1974, 1976, and 1978. In 1980 he won every precinct, defeating GOP candidate Tony Palomo with 58 percent.[16] Two years later, he narrowly defeated former Marine General Ben Garrido Blaz by less than 1,000 votes (51 percent); turnout for the election was reportedly at 85 percent.[17] Won Pat frequently emphasized his Democratic Party alliances in the House majority during his campaigns. "I know that no one on Guam has the experience in Washington that I have," he noted after he easily won his 1976 primary, despite being hospitalized with an illness right before the election. "The important thing is to have friends…. Our greatest asset [in Washington] is friends.

Because, if we don't have the friends, who the hell is going to support us."[18]

At barely five feet tall, with a tendency to mumble in his Chamorro accent, Won Pat did not command attention. But he maintained a sense of humor. Once, he slipped out of sight behind the rostrum while presiding over a subcommittee hearing and shared a self-deprecating joke with the witness: "You can't see me, much less understand what I am saying."[19] He also proved astute at using both the alliances he campaigned on and his committee work to his advantage. Won Pat became a close ally with the powerful subcommittee chairman on Interior and Insular Affair Committee, Phil Burton. Won Pat was lavish in his praise of Burton's support: "He has consistently shown great sympathy for the people who live in these territories," Won Pat told his colleagues on the House Floor.[20] He later noted that Burton "has shown an enormous capacity for detail and a keen awareness of what was needed by the people of Guam."[21]

Won Pat frequently relied on friends in Congress to aid him when his nonvoting status blocked his ability to look after his constituents' interests. He once bragged to a reporter that when he felt Guam had been left out from a bill, "I'll get some of my friends to amend it right on the floor." He even managed to overcome impediments faced by previous Members who represented a far-flung U.S. territory. Initially, Won Pat's telephone and travel budgets were even less than those of Members who represented suburban districts in the Washington, DC, area. With such a limited budget, the Guamanian Delegate traveled the 19,500-mile round-trip journey home only four times per Congress.[22] However, starting in the 95th Congress (1977–1979), congressional office allowances were pro-rated based on distance from the capital, and Won Pat's $111,115 annual allotment for "official and necessary" expenses was the largest of any House Member.[23]

Without a vote on the House Floor, Won Pat invested himself in committee work. He served on the Committee on Interior and Insular Affairs for his entire career—a key panel on which to keep federal funds flowing to his constituency. Starting in July 1977, federal money was allocated to territories through large Omnibus Territories Acts—sometimes called "Christmas tree" bills for the territories.[24] These allocations were the first checks sent to the Virgin Islands, Guam, and American Samoa as part of a federal anti-recession program and extended to the territories through the work of Puerto Rican Resident Commissioner Baltasar Corrada-del Río, Virgin Islands' Delegate Ron de Lugo, and Won Pat.[25] When the Subcommittee on Pacific Affairs was created in the 96th Congress (1979–1981), it became the bill's originating subcommittee. Won Pat was the subcommittee's first chairman and the first Territorial Delegate to chair a subcommittee. When Pacific Affairs' jurisdiction moved under the Subcommittee on Insular Affairs in the 97th and 98th Congresses (1981–1985), Won Pat chaired that subcommittee.[26]

Won Pat also served on the Armed Services Committee from the 94th to 98th Congresses (1975–1985), a reflection of the U.S. military presence in Guam. In the 97th Congress (1981–1983), he also served on the Veterans Affairs Committee.[27]

Won Pat used his committee work to maximize his advantage. By serving on the Research and Development Subcommittee of the Armed Services Committee, he made himself a target for lobbyists seeking permission to develop new weapons, a position that provided the political capital to seek military spending on Guam. A spot on the Military Installations Subcommittee also allowed him to trade committee votes with others seeking to protect military installations in their districts.[28]

Importantly, too, he helped found the Territorial Caucus and worked closely with Delegate de Lugo, whose post representing the Virgin Islands was created at the same time as Won Pat's. The two met when they were unofficial representatives of their respective territories in the late 1960s.[29]

Won Pat spent his career informing congressional colleagues about the uniqueness of Guam and other U.S. territories. "To a certain extent, Guam is still an unknown quantity," noted one of his press aides in 1978, "so we are engaged in a constant job of education."[30] On February 5, 1973, as

his first act in Congress, Won Pat teamed with Delegate de Lugo to propose an amendment to the Constitution that granted citizens in the Virgin Islands and Guam the right to vote in U.S. presidential elections.[31] He argued that because voters in the territories were American citizens, they should not be penalized as second-class citizens. "In an age when each citizen, no matter whether he lives in California, Maine, or the territories, is vitally affected by Presidential decisions," he told his colleagues, "each American of voting age can make his choice of who will lead his country for the next 4 years." To drive home the point, he emphasized the Guamanians' Vietnam War service. "Guam lost more boys on the field of battle than did any other State or territory on a per capita basis," he reminded his colleagues.[32] The legislation ultimately died in the Judiciary Committee, but Won Pat submitted the same bill in every Congress in which he served.[33]

Won Pat first made mainland headlines in his defense of a local custom: the chewing of betel nuts.[34] The nuts were a part of island culture—especially at weddings and other social gatherings, but the Federal Drug Administration (FDA) claimed they were cancerous and attempted to ban their importation into the mainland United States from Guam. Won Pat publicly took on the FDA by submitting a bill to allow Guamanians to take and chew their betel nuts anywhere in the United States. The Delegate admitted that he had a stash of nuts in his desk, smuggled through U.S. customs by a Guam official. "[B]etel nuts and the people of Guam go together," he told a reporter, comparing the custom to drinking coffee or tea: "a mild stimulant and a source of relaxation at the same time."[35] Though his legislation was unsuccessful, he paved the way for a Guam Delegate Robert A. Underwood's successful override of the embargo in 2001.[36]

The end of the Vietnam War profoundly affected Guam, as the economic infusion that came with using the island to stage troops and supplies suddenly dried up.[37] Following the fall of South Vietnam, refugees flooded into the island. Starting in April 1975, "Operation New Life" sent more than 110,000 refugees by aircraft carrier to Guam. Illness ravaged the refugee populations living in tent cities, and riots broke out. Won Pat supported legislation introduced by Representative Glenn Anderson of California to amend the Migration and Refugee Assistance Act of 1962 to provide for the Southeast Asian refugees. He also submitted his own resolution asking that the President take steps to prevent a disproportionate number of refugees from settling in Guam. "I rise to express my deep pride in the role which our island is playing in the great humanitarian effort to rescue the thousands of South Vietnamese from almost certain death," Won Pat told his colleagues. "Guam, however, is a small island with limited resources. Our ability to do more than lend a temporary helping hand is hindered by an economy which is in precipitous decline.... Under these circumstances, I am deeply concerned that Guam may find itself called upon to provide permanent residence to more individuals than we can reasonably handle."[38] The final camp closed on November 1, 1975. In 1979 Won Pat was part of a group of nine Members of Congress who visited Hanoi to discuss the influx of Indochinese refugees and their destabilizing effect on Southeast Asian nations.[39] But in 1980, he noted that 123,000 refugees remained in Guam and "with the direct assistance of the United States, they have become productive members of the territorial community." He requested that they be granted special status to remain in Guam.[40]

Guam's central role in military strategy remained after the end of hostilities in Southeast Asia because of key Pacific military installations on the island. And despite his nonvoting status, by 1983 Won Pat was recognized as a power broker on military spending.[41] He first attempted the establishment of a national cemetery for military veterans in the 97th Congress, but the bill was held up by the Veterans Administration on the grounds that the agency preferred state or territorial funding. "In my opinion, the least the Federal Government can do is to provide a resting place for former military personnel," he told his colleagues, "and not to leave the burden to the individual States and territories."[42] Won Pat steered a bill to passage that established the Guam National Guard.[43] The island was the only remaining U.S. territory without

a guard unit. "Because of the intense loyalty of the Guamanian people to the American cause, this unit will quickly be filled to its capacity by some of the best trained personnel in the U.S. military," he boasted.[44] In addition, the bill increased the number of appointees allotted to Guam, the Virgin Islands, and Puerto Rico to the United States military service academies. Won Pat also assured continued operation of a naval ship repair facility in Guam, when H.R. 8105 passed both houses in the 96th Congress, with aid from Senator Daniel K. Inouye of Hawaii. "As one who has for some time been warning our colleagues about the danger of the Pentagon's present policy of removing forces from Guam instead of relying upon our bases in foreign areas of the Pacific," Won Pat noted on the House Floor, "I am pleased to see this clear signal from Congress that it recognizes the strategic value of our bases on Guam."[45] One Won Pat aide remembered that, in the late 1970s, naval officers wondered why ships sailed from their base in San Diego to Guam for maintenance and repair. The aide recalled the officers' conclusion: "I don't know, it's the guy Won Pat that did this."[46]

Won Pat's career focus in Congress, however, was Guam's status as a U.S. territory. From his time as an unofficial territorial representative, he favored statehood for Guam, but, as he told the territorial legislature in 1972, "our idealism must be tempered with practicality." As an alternative, Won Pat sought commonwealth status for Guam—a self-governing political unit associated with the United States—at least until the territory could "assume the full responsibilities of a state."[47]

In September 1975, Won Pat submitted H.R. 9491, calling for the creation of a status commission, and H.R. 9492, which provided for establishing a constitution for Guam.[48] He emphasized that his bills offered Guamanians a chance to choose their status—commonwealth, independence, or statehood—but did not guarantee a change in status or a particular relationship. "We on Guam, as American citizens, know from long experience the meaning and importance of self-determination," he said. "Ever since Guam came under the U.S. flag in 1898 our people have pursued with singularity of purpose a single basic goal, full participation in the democratic processes of our country consistent with its high ideals and principles."[49]

The House Committee on Interior and Insular Affairs merged the two bills under H.R. 9491. An amended version passed the House on October 6, 1975, requiring an allowance for the President to veto portions of the constitution and assuring automatic repeal of measures in conflict with the 1950 Organic Act. Senate amendments required that Congress approve Guam's final constitution and merged Won Pat's bill with a similar bill introduced by Delegate de Lugo calling for the establishment of a constitution for the U.S. Virgin Islands. De Lugo's bill, H.R. 9460, passed both chambers and became law on October 21, 1976.[50]

The second Guam Constitutional Convention met from July to December 1977 with Won Pat's daughter, Judith, serving as chairwoman of the committee on women's rights—one of two women among the 34 delegates.[51] The final document defined the structure of the Guamanian government, including residency requirements for elected officials, rules on budgets and appointments, orders of succession, and the future structure of the Guam legislature. Antonio Won Pat was among those who witnessed the constitution's signing on December 15, 1977. Both U.S. President Jimmy Carter and Congress approved it in early 1978.[52]

Yet the Guam constitution's ratification was ultimately derailed by continued confusion over status and a local political fight. Before it could be voted on by Guamanians, the constitution's approval was endangered by a bitter 1978 gubernatorial election. The president of the constitutional convention, Democrat Carl Gutierrez, declared his candidacy for governor as an independent. He chose a Republican running mate—another convention delegate, Dr. Joseph Dizon—and attempted to ride the constitution into the governor's mansion over incumbent Governor Ricardo J. (Ricky) Bordallo. Gutierrez's candidacy effectively split the Democratic vote, opening the door for Republican Paul McDonald Calvo's victory. With an upcoming party change in the governor's mansion, the legislature delayed a plebiscite to approve the constitution.

The necessary Chamorro support for the constitution waned during the delay. Locals—already confused about the contents of the 14-point document—soured on the constitution's lack of clarity about Guam's status. Especially wary of Congress's requirement that the document not alter the existing Organic Act, Chamorros viewed the constitution as a Washington-mandated revision of the Organic Act rather than a declaration of self-determination. Moreover, opposition mounted from a completely different population—special interest groups primarily dominated by "statesiders." The local bar association did not approve of the creation of a separate Guam supreme court with appeals directly to the U.S. Supreme Court instead of the Federal 9th Circuit Court. The teachers union and military personnel stationed on Guam feared the effect of greater local autonomy on their interests. With less than half of Guamanians turning out to vote on August 4, 1979, the constitution received a meager 18-percent approval. Won Pat, who was in DC during the election and referendum, did not provide comment to local newspapers.[53]

Won Pat attempted to jump-start a review of Guam's status in 1983, but the death of his ally, subcommittee chairman Phil Burton, diminished his ability to capture widespread congressional interest.[54] The Guam Delegate introduced a resolution (H. Con. Res. 131) calling on President Ronald Reagan to designate a national official to negotiate status change with Guam in October 1983. "Political status for emerging island entities is more than just theories one reads in freshman college textbooks," he declared. "Political status is a life principle that undergirds all dynamic human society—it is the foundation by which a community of people binds themselves to one another, establishes their identity and develops respect for themselves. More importantly, political status governs the daily relationship between people and their government as equals."[55] The resolution was referred to the Committee on Interior and Insular Affairs where it languished, awaiting comment from the Interior Department.

New Mexico Representative Manuel Luján, Vice Chair of the Interior and Insular Affairs Committee (and later Interior Secretary), then suggested that Guam submit a bill for commonwealth status directly to Congress. At Luján's invitation, Won Pat brought a bipartisan group of Guam legislators to Luján's hometown in Albuquerque, New Mexico, in December 1983 to meet with staffers and members of the Interior Committee. The meeting resulted in another bipartisan Commission on Self-Determination, which drafted a document that granted Guam local self-determination under their own constitution. Under its terms, Department of Interior oversight would cease as would provisions of earlier legislation that limited shipping to Guamanian ports to those under American flags. However, Won Pat never had the self-determination document acted on before he left Congress.[56]

General Blaz returned as Won Pat's opponent in 1984. The incumbent campaigned on a platform similar to what had been effective in the past: "Seniority is the most important role in Congress," he noted in a debate between the two candidates. "[It] gives you power. I am able to accomplish more and more over the years."[57] The local press agreed, telling voters, "Don't risk our rank and influence in Congress … vote for strength and tradition."[58] Shortly before his death in April 1983, Burton had boldly told a reporter that Won Pat was so effective that Guam would lose influence and money if they voted him out. In an analysis entitled "Who Would Serve Guam Best in D.C.?" published on the front page of the *Pacific Daily News*, sources interviewed for the article—including those "knowledgeable about Pacific and territorial affairs"— agreed with Burton's take on the election but they also heralded Blaz's potential as a "new" and "articulate" voice for Guam in Washington. Won Pat's support and strategy ended up backfiring as Guamanians connected his friendliness with the powerful Californian with mainland meddling in the island's affairs.[59]

The close contest between Won Pat and Blaz proved dramatic. In the open primary election, Won Pat lost to Blaz by nearly 2,000 votes.[60] When both moved to the general election, Blaz came out ahead by a narrow margin of 323 votes.[61] The next day, officials found 220 more ballots and computer irregularities that forced election officials to twice count the ballots by hand; recounts put

Blaz in the lead by roughly 350 votes. On November 11, the *Pacific Daily News* reported Blaz had won by 354 votes. "Whatever is decided, I am resigned to accept that decision and to continue to work for my constituents as usual," Won Pat conceded.[62]

Even with his apparent concession, Won Pat had not yet fully resigned himself to the resulting loss. On December 21, 1984, he contested the election before the Committee on House Administration. Won Pat claimed that election officials had improperly dismissed seemingly blank ballots or those marked for both candidates. He also argued that absentee ballots were sent too late to be counted when returned. The Guam Election Commission mailed ballots 21 days before Election Day, even though federal officials had recommended sending them 45 days in advance for timely return by mail. Those ballots received after the polls closed on November 6 were not counted—amounting to 34 percent of all absentee voters, according to Won Pat. Blaz countered with a motion to dismiss Won Pat's claim on January 21, 1985, and later that year, the committee agreed with him, noting the irregular and absentee ballots had been handled legally.[63] The full House defeated Won Pat's challenge on July 24, 1985, in a voice vote.[64]

After his electoral loss, Won Pat lived in Guam but returned to Washington frequently and continued to attend hearings on appropriations for the territories.[65] Won Pat died of a heart attack in a hospital in Silver Spring, Maryland, on May 1, 1987. He was buried in Piti, Guam, at the locally run veterans' cemetery for which he had sought federal funding.[66] Among those offering tributes on the House Floor was Delegate Blaz. "Those who knew Mr. Won Pat know that he was not a giant of a man in stature, but he was a giant of a man in accomplishments," Blaz said in eulogy. "They know that he did not talk very much, but he said a lot. They also know that he was a very, very humble man. He was a common man, but a common man with an uncommon touch."[67] A congressional delegation, mostly made up of other Territorial Delegates, attended his Guam state funeral.[68] In 1988 the Guam International Air Terminal was officially named A. B. Won Pat Guam International Airport Terminal.[69]

MANUSCRIPT COLLECTIONS

University of Guam, Micronesian Area Research Center (Mangilao, GU). *Papers*: 1965–1984, 285 linear feet. The papers of Antonio Borja Won Pat focus mainly on his years in the U.S. House of Representatives. The papers consist of correspondence, briefing material, audiovisual materials, photographs, invitations, cards, and plaques. Topics include the Guam legislature, political campaigns and elections, legislation, committee reports, official trips, district office work, typhoon rehabilitation, refugees, agriculture, schools and education, civil aeronautics, federal appropriations and budgets, and executive branch agency work. A finding aid is available at the repository.

University of Oklahoma, The Julian P. Kanter Political Commercial Archive, Department of Communication (Norman, OK). *Videocassette*: 10 commercials on 1 videocassette. The commercials were used during Antonio Borja Won Pat's Democratic campaign for the 1984 U.S. congressional election in Guam.

NOTES

1 Robert F. Rogers, *Destiny's Landfall: A History of Guam* (Honolulu: University of Hawaii Press, 2011): 226.

2 *Congressional Record*, Extension of Remarks, 100th Cong., 1st sess. (4 May 1987): E1696.

3 *Sixteenth Census of the United States, 1940: Population*, Sumay, Sumay, Guam, Roll T627_4643, page 8A, http://ancestrylibrary.com (accessed 28 January 2016).

4 William L. Wuerch et al., "MARC Working Papers #66: Inventory of the Papers of Antonio Borja Won Pat" (Mangiloa, GU: Micronesian Area Research Center, 1996): 2.

5 Eduardo Lachica, "Despite Obstacles, Won Pat Is Making A Mark in Congress," 22 November 1983, *Wall Street Journal*: 1.

6 There is no reliable source for a list of names for Won Pat's children. A daughter, Judith, later served as speaker of the territorial legislature. Daughter Marilyn Won Pat was also elected to the territorial senate but died in 1990 before she could take her seat. Another daughter, Rosalind Won Pat-Fleet, was commended by Guam Delegate Madeline Bordallo in the *Congressional Record*. The 1940 Census records confirm the names of additional daughters Aveline, Jacqueline, and Ellen. See Wuerch et al., "MARC Working Papers": 2; Rogers, *Destiny's Landfall*: 284; *Congressional Record*, Extension of Remarks, 108th Cong., 2nd sess. (30 June 2005): E1400–E1401; *Sixteenth Census of the United States, 1940*.

7 Wuerch et al., "MARC Working Papers": 2.

8 Ibid., 3. As speaker of the territorial legislature in 1949, Won Pat led a walkout of the general assembly when the military governor refused to support their subpoena of an American witness.

9 Wuerch et al., "MARC Working Papers": 4.

10 Quoted in Arnold H. Leibowitz, *Defining Status: A Comprehensive Analysis of United States Territorial Relations* (Boston, MA: Martinus Nijhoff Publishers, 1989): 340.

11 Wuerch et al., "MARC Working Papers": 5; Leibowitz, *Defining Status*: 342.

12 Wuerch et al., "MARC Working Papers": 5.

13 Pat McElroy, "'Foot in the Door,' Perez Says of Non-Voting Job," 4 November 1972, *Pacific Daily News* (Guam): 6.

14 See, for example, 1 November 1972, *Pacific Daily News*: 11.

15 Office of the Clerk, U.S. House of Representatives, "Election Statistics, 1920 to Present," http://history.house.gov/Institution/Election-Statistics/Election-Statistics/.

16 Wuerch et al., "MARC Working Papers": 5; Office of the Clerk, U.S. House of Representatives, "Election Statistics, 1920 to Present."

17 "Guam Reelects Its Non-Voting Delegate to Seat in Congress," 3 November 1982, *Los Angeles Times*: B12; "Guam Delegate to Congress Is Re-elected by 952 Votes," 3 November 1982, *New York Times*: A23; Office of the Clerk, U.S. House of Representatives, "Election Statistics, 1920 to Present."

18 Wuerch et al., "MARC Working Papers": 5; George Blake, "Pat Won! Vows He'll Run Again in '78," 6 September 1976, *Pacific Daily News* (Guam): 2.

19 Lachica, "Despite Obstacles, Won Pat Is Making A Mark in Congress."

20 *Congressional Record*, House, 95th Cong., 1st sess. (2 May 1977): 1136.

21 *Congressional Record*, House, 95th Cong., 1st sess. (27 September 1977): 31075.

22 William Ringle, "Won Pat Pushy In A Nice Way," 14 February 1973, *Pacific Daily News* (Guam): 10.

23 "Guam Delegate to Have a Dandy Expense Account," 25 November 1976, *Atlanta Constitution*: 8P. Won Pat's allotment was four times that of local District of Columbia Delegate Walter Fauntroy.

24 Leibowitz, *Defining Status*: 34.

25 "First U.S. Countercyclical Funds Are Sent to 4 Island Governments," 10 July 1977, *New York Times*: 16.

26 Lachica, "Despite Obstacles, Won Pat Is Making A Mark in Congress." See *Congressional Directory*, 96th Cong. (Washington, DC: Government Printing Office, 1979): 300; *Congressional Directory*, 97th Cong. (Washington, DC: Government Printing Office, 1981): 295; *Congressional Directory*, 98th Cong. (Washington, DC: Government Printing Office, 1983): 295.

27 Garrison Nelson, *Committees in the U.S. Congress, 1947 to 1992*, vol. 2 (Washington, DC: Congressional Quarterly Press, 1994): 948.

28 Lachica, "Despite Obstacles, Won Pat Is Making A Mark in Congress."

29 *Congressional Record*, House, 100th Cong., 1st sess. (4 May 1987): H3003.

30 Olson, "Territories Still Have Quiet Voices in Congress."

31 *Congressional Record*, House, 93rd Cong., 1st sess. (5 February 1973): 3232.

32 Ibid., 3237–3238.

33 *Congressional Record*, Index, 93rd Cong., 1st sess.: 2227; Donnie Radcliffe, No title, 17 April 1984, *Washington Post*: D1; Lachica, "Despite Obstacles, Won Pat Is Making A Mark in Congress." See, for example, H.J. Res. 442, 94th Cong. (1975).

34 See, for example, his editorial: Antonio Won Pat, "Why Can't Guamanians Chew Betel Nut in the United States?," 22 February 1978, *Baltimore Sun*: A15.

35 Olson, "Territories Still Have Quiet Voices in Congress."

36 "Robert A. Underwood," *Biographical Directory of the U.S. Congress, 1774–Present*, http://bioguide.congress.gov/scripts/biodisplay.pl?index=U000014.

37 Rogers, *Destiny's Landfall*: 228.

38 *Congressional Record*, Extension of Remarks, 94th Cong., 1st sess. (8 May 1975): 13682–13683.

39 Keyes Beech, "9 Congressmen Arrive in Hanoi for Talks on Exodus of Refugees," 9 August 1979, *Los Angeles Times*: B7.

40 *Congressional Record*, Extension of Remarks, 96th Cong., 2nd sess. (23 July 1980): 19342.

41 Lachica, "Despite Obstacles, Won Pat Is Making A Mark in Congress."

42 *Congressional Record*, Extension of Remarks, 96th Cong., 2nd sess. (31 July 1980): 20918.

43 Public Law 96-600, 94 Stat. 3493 (1980).

44 *Congressional Record*, House, 96th Cong., 2nd sess. (13 December 1980): 34060.

45 *Congressional Record*, House, 96th Cong., 2nd sess. (9 December 1980): 32923.

46 Claudine San Nicolas, "Won Pat Contributions: Guam Guard, Ship Facility," 13 May 1987, *Pacific Daily News* (Guam): 4.

47 Leibowitz, *Defining Status*: 335–336; Pat Harrison, "Won Pat: A 'Last' Report," 30 June 1972, *Pacific Daily News* (Guam): 1.

48 Rogers, *Destiny's Landfall*: 234. In 1974 the Republican-led Guam legislature created the Legislative Political Status Commission, the first on the island with the goal of determining the ultimate status of the island. The commission reported that Guam should write a constitution to aid islanders in meeting local economic and social needs. The commission requested that U.S. President Gerald R. Ford send a representative to negotiate terms. Commission members also did not consult Won Pat in their decision, as he was a Democrat and in political opposition with the legislature's majority.

49 *Congressional Record*, House, 94th Cong., 1st sess. (9 September 1975): 28034.

50 Public Law 94-584, 90 Stat. 2899 (1976). For Interior Department objections, see House Committee on Interior and Insular Affairs, *Providing for the Establishment of a Constitution for Guam*, 94th Cong., 1st sess., H. Rept. 508 (1975): 3–4.

51 "Guam Constitution Conventions (ConCon)," Guampedia Foundation, Inc., accessed 21 January 2016, http://www.guampedia.com/guam-constitutional-conventions-concon/. A PDF listing of the delegates for the 1977 Guam Constitutional Convention is available at http://guampedia.media.s3.amazonaws.com/wp-content/uploads/2013/08/2nd-GU_CONCON-delegates.pdf (accessed 21 January 2016).

52 Guampedia Foundation, Inc., "Guam Constitution Conventions (ConCon)."

53 Leibowitz, *Defining Status*: 335–336; Rogers, *Destiny's Landfall*: 242; Wuerch et al., "MARC Working Papers": 6.

54 Rogers, *Destiny's Landfall*: 249.

55 *Congressional Record*, House, 98th Cong., 1st sess. (25 May 1983): 13996.

56 Wuerch et al., "MARC Working Papers": 6.

57 Elaine Santos, "Won Pat, Blaz Face Off," 1 November 1984, *Pacific Daily News* (Guam): 1.

58 No title, 3 November 1984, *Pacific Daily News* (Guam): 33.

59 John M. Simpson, "Who Would Serve Guam Best in D.C.?," 3 November 1984, *Pacific Daily News* (Guam): 1; Richard Person, "Former Delegate From Guam Antonio B. Won Pat, 78, Dies," 3 May 1987, *Washington Post*: D10.

60 "Rival's Tally in Guam Overshadows Incumbent," 3 September 1984, *New York Times*: 9.

61 Office of the Clerk, U.S. House of Representatives, "Election Statistics, 1920 to Present."

62 Stephen Labaton, "Guam's Seat in Congress Still Disputed," 4 June 1985, *Washington Post*: A12; Yvonne Martinez, "It's Blaz By 354 Votes," 11 November 1984, *Pacific Daily News* (Guam): 1.

63 Stephen Labaton, "Former Guam Delegate's Challenge Rejected," 9 July 1985, *Washington Post*: A4; Committee on House Administration, *Dismissing the Election Contest Against Ben Blaz*, 99th Cong., 1st sess., H. Rept. 220 (1985).

64 *Congressional Record*, House, 99th Cong., 1st sess. (24 July 1985): 20180–20181.

65 "Antonio Won Pat, 73, Dies; Guam Delegate to Congress," 3 May 1987, Associated Press; Person, "Former Delegate From Guam Antonio B. Won Pat, 78, Dies."

66 Several sources mark his death date as May 2. These are likely using Guam's Chamorro Standard Time (ChST). According to the *Pacific Daily News*, Won Pat died at 5:00 AM on May 2, 1987, ChST. This converts to May 1, 1987, at 3:00 PM Eastern Standard Time

in Silver Spring, Maryland, the location of his death. See Claudine San Nicolas, "Won Pat: A Chapter Closes," 13 May 1987, *Pacific Daily News* (Guam): 1.

67 *Congressional Record*, House, 100th Cong., 1st sess. (4 May 1987): H3002.

68 "Delegation to Pay Tribute to Won Pat," 11 May 1987, *Pacific Daily News* (Guam): 1.

69 "History and Timeline," A.B. Won Pat International Airport Authority, Guam, accessed 31 March 2015, https://www.guamairport.com/our-business/about/history-and-timeline.

Norman Y. Mineta
1931–

UNITED STATES REPRESENTATIVE 1975–1995
DEMOCRAT FROM CALIFORNIA

Thirty years after being imprisoned by the United States government because of the happenstance of his ancestry, Norman Y. Mineta helped change forever the inner workings of the United States House of Representatives. Over a 20-year career in the House, the San Jose Congressman worked to make the federal lawmaking process more accountable. From the federal budget to the nation's highway system, Mineta and his generation of reform-minded legislators redefined expectations on Capitol Hill. With the moral authority derived from having been unjustly incarcerated as a child, Mineta convinced Congress to address wartime internment and helped the country understand the sins of its past.

Norman Yoshio Mineta was born in San Jose, California, on November 12, 1931, the youngest of five children, to Kunisaku and Kane Mineta. His father, Kunisaku, had arrived from Japan by himself as a teenager 29 years earlier, finding work in a number of jobs before saving up enough money to start his own insurance business in San Jose.[1] Mineta's family settled in the heart of the city's largely Japanese neighborhood. Because California law prevented Asian immigrants from owning property in the state, a local attorney held the house in his name until he signed everything over to Mineta's eldest sister, who was a U.S. citizen by birth, when she turned 21.[2]

Growing up, Mineta attended the San Jose public schools, and every day after class he spent an hour learning Japanese. Over dinner the Minetas would discuss the day's events, and at night their neighbors would often come over to talk about issues facing the community. "My dad was the breadwinner, the community leader, the father who encouraged all of us to participate in community activities," Mineta later remembered. His mother, Kane, was equally active in San Jose's social life, serving on the

Parent-Teacher Association, volunteering with the church, and raising money for the American Red Cross.[3]

But the San Jose community his parents had nurtured was ripped apart on December 7, 1941, when Japan bombed the American military base at Pearl Harbor, Hawaii. Federal officials panicked and ordered the U.S. military to relocate 120,000 Japanese Americans living on the mainland to prison camps often hundreds of miles away from their homes.[4]

Within six months after Pearl Harbor, the government had suspended the Minetas' business license, seized their bank accounts, and moved them out of San Jose. Neighbors disappeared. Mineta's father worried he would never see his family or his home again. Dressed in his Cub Scout uniform, Mineta and his parents were first sent to the Santa Anita racetrack outside Los Angeles, forced to live in small barracks and shower near the horse stables. Even as a boy, Mineta felt the heavy weight of injustice, questioning the presence of armed guards. In the fall of 1942, the government moved the Minetas to a new site in Heart Mountain, Wyoming, their home for the next three years. It was cold and cramped, but they carved out some semblance of a community.[5]

After the war, the Minetas returned to San Jose and began the arduous task of rebuilding their lives. Slowly they and their neighbors reopened businesses and, as the Congressman said years later, "[regained] our standing in the community." They worked to move on from their imprisonment, focusing their energy on the future. Mineta estimated that it took 20 years for his community to recapture what it had lost in 1942.[6] Sixty years later, he was asked if his internment influenced his decision to go into public service. "No question it did," he replied.[7]

Back home, Mineta enrolled at San Jose High School and served as student body president during his senior year.

Norman Yoshio Mineta, George Pollard and Jim Pollard, 1995, Collection of the U.S. House of Representatives

He stayed close to home for college, graduating from the University of California, Berkeley, in 1953 before serving three years as an Army intelligence officer during the Korean War.[8] When he returned to San Jose, Mineta joined his father's insurance firm and began exploring a possible entry into local politics.[9] Mineta had two sons, David and Stuart, with his first wife. When he married his second wife, Danealia, the Congressman welcomed two stepsons, Bob and Mark Brantner.

Early in his life, Mineta had been a staunch Republican. After all, he later said, "It was the damn Democrats that stuck us in those damn camps."[10] But in the 1960s, Mineta grew frustrated with the GOP's approach to the great social issues of the day and left the party.[11] From 1962 to 1964, Mineta served on San Jose's human relations commission, and from 1966 to 1967, he sat on the board of directors of the city's housing authority. That year he jumped to the city council, where he served double duty as vice mayor from 1968 to 1971.[12]

In the spring of 1971, Mineta entered a crowded 15-candidate field to succeed San Jose's outgoing mayor. Mineta's career in local government gave him wide name recognition, and he won the support of a number of San Jose's service organizations. In the two decades since Mineta finished college, San Jose and surrounding Santa Clara County had transformed from farm country into a textbook case of suburban sprawl. Its population had tripled, stressing the public services provided by local government.[13] On Election Day, Mineta took an early lead and never lost it, tallying 62 percent of the vote despite anemic turnout.[14] "It's been full circle," Mineta said of his victory 30 years after being interned.[15]

As mayor, Mineta clamped down on San Jose's runaway development. He worked to funnel growth back toward the city's center, tightening zoning requirements and passing a "pay-as-you-grow" tax to cover the cost of additional public services.[16]

By the early 1970s, Mineta had become part of a new generation of leaders working to redefine political power in America, calling for greater transparency and accountability. He belonged to a number of national organizations, negotiating with the federal government to protect grants to public housing and transportation initiatives. In July 1972, he was one of 16 mayors to meet with President Richard M. Nixon about the costs of rapid development and the possibility that the federal government would kick back billions in revenue to the cities.[17]

Like his jump to the mayor's office, Mineta moved to the House after the incumbent, Republican Charles S. Gubser, decided to retire. And once again Mineta's work in San Jose's local government gave him an early advantage. California's 13th District leaned Republican, but Mineta's success in managing the city's growth, paired with his work on the national circuit, made him widely popular at home. The district stretched south and east away from San Francisco Bay, encompassing Santa Clara County. It also sat astride the southeastern edge of Silicon Valley, the creative tech corridor that became an economic juggernaut by the time Mineta retired. His Republican challenger, George W. Milias, was a well-liked former state assemblyman who had the misfortune of once serving in the Nixon administration. With the Watergate scandal dominating the headlines, Milias could not escape from Nixon's shadow, and Mineta won with almost 53 percent of the vote. Mineta's first election was the closest of his career. He took anywhere from 58 percent (in 1978) to 70 percent (in 1986) of the vote in every subsequent election.[18]

In his first term, Democratic leadership placed Mineta on the Public Works and Transportation Committee, a seat he held for his entire career; he became chairman during the 103rd Congress (1993–1995). During the 94th Congress (1975–1977), Mineta also served on the Post Office and Civil Service Committee before transferring to the Budget Committee, where he spent the next six years (1977–1983). In only his second term, Mineta was appointed by new Speaker Thomas P. (Tip) O'Neill of Massachusetts to the Permanent Select Committee on Intelligence, serving on the highly secretive panel until he stepped down in 1985. Beginning in 1983, Mineta also spent a decade on the Science and Technology Committee (later named the Science, Space, and Technology Committee), a key assignment for a Member representing part of Silicon Valley. In 1993 Mineta stepped down from Science, Space, and Technology to take over the gavel of the Public Works Committee.[19]

As part of the largest Democratic wave in years, Mineta was one of the most promising prospects in a crowd of bright lawmakers. On average, the Watergate Babies, as his highly motivated class of 1975 was called, were 15 years younger than the existing membership. They saw themselves as a political vanguard, and collectively they embodied the deep distrust voters had toward their government.[20] Mineta's generation of lawmakers valued accountability and accessibility, but perhaps none more so than him. "It goes back to my own experience in terms of the evacuation and the internment of those of Japanese ancestry," he said years later. "We didn't have access to our political leaders at the time."[21]

In the 1970s, however, it was the criminal activities of the Nixon White House, the ongoing war in Vietnam, and the old, impenetrable seniority system on Capitol Hill. The new Members promised to reform all of it and to restore confidence in the government.[22] "We came to Congress on a tide of change," Mineta told the *Los Angeles Times* in the summer of 1975, "and there was a sense of euphoria about the Age of Aquarius having hit Capitol Hill."[23]

For the first 30 days of the new Congress, the reform-minded freshmen seemed on course to redefine the art of the possible. They ousted three long-standing committee chairs, brought other chairmen to heel, and weakened the influence of the Ways and Means Committee.[24] In June, after House Democrats failed to override a series of presidential vetoes, Mineta's cohort elected him president of the Democratic freshman class for a six-month term, hoping the former military intelligence analyst and "self-described activist" could organize the freshmen into a potent voting bloc.[25] "Procedural changes have nothing to do with whether the lot of the unemployed gets better or if education gets better," he said. "In terms of what we have been able to get through, it bothers me that we haven't had the programs that benefit people out in the streets."[26]

In one of his first acts as leader of the freshman class, Mineta drew up a "six-point plan" he hoped would harness the restless energy of the young legislators. Nearly every recommendation sought to empower the rank and file. Mineta called for fact-finding roundtables with policy experts and "opinion leaders," regular meetings between freshman officers and the Democratic leadership, stricter oversight of committee activities, a commitment to developing policy in the Democratic Caucus, the creation of national "truth squads" to promote Democratic legislation, and the publication of a freshman newsletter.[27] It was "a pledge," he said, "not to allow things to go on as usual, to reassert Congress as a coequal branch of government."[28]

Mineta helped manage expectations and built rapport between the older and younger generations. While some freshmen talked about removing Carl Albert of Oklahoma from the speakership, Mineta was one of a handful of new California Democrats to reaffirm his commitment to the existing leadership.[29] Mineta was known around the Hill as "energetic, competent, and levelheaded" without being overbearing. He and Speaker Albert had a personal history that dated back to the 1950s. Mineta's brother-in-law knew the Speaker "real well," and Mineta's sister babysat for the Albert family.[30] Midway through his first term as he was running for re-election in June of 1976, Mineta had Majority Leader O'Neill come out to California to help campaign. During a lull in the trip, while O'Neill and a group of legislators relaxed around a hotel pool in San Jose, Mineta broke some surprising news: "Tip," he said, "I just heard on the radio that Carl Albert is retiring. Let me be the first one to support you for Speaker."[31]

Still, he kept leadership on its toes. The way Mineta saw it, years of Democratic control in the House had nurtured a class of party leaders who lost touch with the rank and file. "When was the last time Carl Albert or Tip O'Neill had opposition?" Mineta was quoted as saying in a front-page article in the *New York Times*.[32]

Television, which pulled back the curtain on the political system, became a sticking point between the two generations. "Albert and O'Neill did not grow up in television land," Mineta pointed out. "They can go in and tell a few jokes and buy a few rounds of drinks and people love them and they get re-elected. But we're the products of a different era and a different system." It was a system that rewarded new ways of thinking.[33] "More and more demands are being made by the public," Mineta said. "Watergate heightened the accountability syndrome."[34]

Mineta's early congressional career illustrated just how successful his class was at reforming internal House procedure, especially the committee system. With O'Neill serving as Speaker and the seniority system under attack, Mineta's leadership prospects improved rapidly. In only his second term during the 95th Congress (1977–1979), Mineta was appointed chairman of the Public Works and Transportation Committee's Subcommittee on Public Buildings and Grounds, marking the start of a long reign as a subcommittee chairman. In fact, from 1977 until he became chairman of the full Public Works and Transportation Committee in 1993, Mineta served as chairman of four Public Works subcommittees over the course of eight consecutive Congresses: the Subcommittee on Public Buildings and Grounds (95th Congress), the Subcommittee on Oversight and Review (96th Congress [1979–1981]), the Subcommittee on Aviation (97th–100th Congresses [1981–1989]), and the Subcommittee on Surface Transportation (101st–102nd Congresses [1991–1995]).

Mineta's leadership extended to the Budget Committee as well. Traditionally, the White House managed the federal budget, but after entitlement spending exploded and the Vietnam War dragged on, Congress began formally monitoring legislation that affected the ebb and flow of the country's finances.[35] Almost from the start, Mineta was at the forefront of the House's new oversight responsibility. In the 96th and 97th Congresses, he held the gavel of Budget's Task Force on the Budget Process (the committee called its subcommittees Task Forces), giving him a powerful bird's-eye view of how the federal government managed its money.[36]

Even with his growing profile, Mineta did not hesitate to keep the pressure on his own party. "I see a vacuum right now," he told the *Washington Post* just a few days after the 96th Congress convened. "Just a lot of tinkering and holding patterns."[37]

It was around that time that Mineta saw his stock rise considerably. In early 1979, he was part of a "damage assessment squad" that squeezed House leadership for answers as to why California Democrats missed out on preferred committee assignments.[38] Later that year the *Washington Post* named Mineta as a likely candidate for Transportation Secretary.[39] By 1980, he was short-listed for either chairman of the House Budget Committee or the Democratic Whip's office.[40] Writing a year later, David Broder, one of the country's leading political journalists, noted that, "At 49, Norman Mineta of California is perhaps the most widely admired Democrat to enter the House of Representatives in the 1970s.... Many of his contemporaries regard him as a future prospect for Speaker of the House."[41]

Mineta was soon ensconced in party leadership. He was a utility player on the Democratic Whip team, having been named Deputy Whip-at-Large in the 97th Congress (1981–1983); he quickly moved up a rank and spent the rest of his House career as Deputy Whip.[42] Moreover, in late 1980, Speaker O'Neill appointed Mineta to the powerful Democratic Steering and Policy Committee, where he helped shape the House's legislative agenda.[43] The California Democrat later had roles in the Democratic Congressional Campaign Committee and flirted with a run for party Whip.[44]

If Mineta's early entry into leadership signaled a new era in party mechanics, his work in committees reinforced his generation's influence on policy. The Budget Committee, created a few years earlier in 1974, was somewhat uncharted territory for the House, but that sort of independence seemed to fit Mineta's legislative style. "The new members are very selective," he said in May 1977. "A number of us feel that we don't have to go along with the New Deal approach of throwing money at a problem, hoping it will go away. We want to target our resources."[45]

The federal budget process was an arcane, but immensely powerful, mechanism, and over the course of his four years as chairman of the Budget Process Task Force, Mineta became an ardent supporter of Congress's oversight responsibilities. On Capitol Hill, he became a counterweight to the budget philosophy in the Ronald Reagan administration, warning that if Congress didn't assert itself and make a few changes to the budget process it risked being replaced by White House economists or what he called "a toothless balanced budget constitutional amendment." Mineta's solutions included a mix of reforms to binding resolutions, the reconciliation and appropriations processes, and the act of impounding unspent funds.[46]

As Task Force chairman, Mineta loathed the idea of a balanced budget amendment. "The Constitution is a marvelously simple document, defining only the most basic human rights and the most fundamental structures of government," he observed in testimony submitted to the House Judiciary Committee. A balanced budget amendment was neither of those things, he said, and would "only … cheapen the highest law of our Nation." In fact, Mineta argued that a balanced budget amendment would strip Congress of the very control it wanted (the ability to run deficits was key).[47] Instead, Mineta advocated for sunset laws giving legislators the ability to phase out spending and tax programs deemed unnecessary.[48] "It's more the badness, not the bigness, of government that is bothering people," Mineta said as far back as 1976.[49]

Mineta was front and center during budget negotiations with the Reagan administration. In 1979 he helped shepherd the Democrats' budget through the House. A year later, he was a member of the "Gang of Five" and, in 1982, part of the "Gang of Four," leading the House effort to protect domestic spending. As Speaker O'Neill readily admitted in 1980, a no vote from Mineta could sway any number of other Democrats.[50]

When Mineta's term on Budget expired, he moved to the Science and Technology Committee. Smartphones and laptops were still decades away, but many of the products coming out of his district were going increasingly mainstream. Mineta was at the forefront of changes to intellectual property law as it applied to the tech industry. As early as 1983, back when Silicon Valley was known as "California's so-called Silicon Valley," he introduced legislation to protect the revolutionary designs of computer

chips being made in his district.[51] "Technology is moving so fast the government has no ability to keep track of it," Mineta said a few years later.[52] By the early 1990s, Mineta and his Republican colleague from nearby Stanford, Thomas Campbell, had won "reputations as torch-bearers for Silicon Valley companies."[53] Mineta, Vice President Al Gore once said, "was Silicon Valley before Silicon Valley was cool."[54]

Mineta, however, made his most lasting contributions on the Public Works and Transportation Committee, first at the head of its Aviation and Surface and Transportation Subcommittees and then as full committee chairman. Mineta had pioneered smart-growth policies back in San Jose, making Public Works something of a natural home for the former mayor. The committee was also deceptively powerful. With control over the nation's infrastructure, it could authorize any number of new projects—roads, federal buildings, airports—which meant a fresh source of jobs for each district.[55]

Mineta first led the Subcommittee on Public Buildings and Grounds, but jumped to the Subcommittee on Oversight and Review after one term, bringing with him the drive for openness and accountability. "Oversight requires patient and detailed and continuing effort," he said during the subcommittee's organizational meeting in early 1979, "but I am absolutely convinced that it need not be dull or unimaginative."[56] His jurisdiction spread far and wide across every policy area of every one of the subcommittees: water pollution, public mass transit, aviation safety, flood control, America's highways, disaster relief, and public buildings and grounds. The subcommittee held 12 open hearings and heard from nearly 240 witnesses over a combined 34 days.[57]

Mineta jumped to the Subcommittee on Aviation in the next Congress, starting what would become an eight-year reign as chairman. His subcommittee work reads like a deeply researched market summary of the airline industry, one that prioritized safety and its long-term viability. More than anything, Mineta wanted to make sure the Federal Aviation Administration and other regulatory agencies had the resources they needed to ensure the safety of airline passengers.

Mineta tallied a number of early legislative victories on Aviation, often using his expertise in the budget process to his advantage. As part of the budget reconciliation in 1981, Congress agreed to the Airport Development Authorization Act, which included $450 million for new and improved airports. A year later, Mineta helped attach the Airport and Airway Improvement Act to the Tax Equity and Fiscal Responsibility Act of 1982, providing nearly $20 billion from an industry trust to help limit "wide-spread congestion and delays" at America's airports.[58] Over the next six years, two dozen bills that went before Mineta's Aviation Subcommittee became law.

When Mineta took over the gavel of the Subcommittee on Surface Transportation during the 101st Congress (1989–1991), the future of America's roads in "the post-Interstate period" became his most immediate concern. Mineta also considered "high speed transportation corridors," pipeline safety, sanitary food, and hazardous waste transportation. After two days of hearings, Mineta also worked to include transportation protections in the landmark Americans with Disabilities Act of 1990.[59] "The Americans With Disabilities Act gives us a unique opportunity to complete the work that we first started when we passed the Civil Rights Act some twenty-five years ago," he said in his opening statement during the bill's first hearing.[60]

Along with a number of smaller bills that became law during the next Congress, Mineta's major legislative victory in 1991 was the Intermodal Surface Transportation Efficiency Act, which addressed an issue he had wrestled with since his time as mayor.[61] It was a huge, "revolutionary" law that gave state and local governments more control over the roadways in their districts and authorized vast amounts of money—$151 billion over six years—for a number of different projects. It set the foundation for the National Highway System (NHS) by combining the interstate highway system with a web of other federally funded roads.[62]

After years of success at the subcommittee level, Mineta sought the chairmanship of the full committee before the start of the 102nd Congress (1991–1993), challenging the sitting chairman, 77-year-old Glenn M. Anderson of California, who had represented the Long Beach area since

1969. Mineta's bid was partly successful: The Democratic Caucus voted Anderson out, but handed the committee to Robert Roe of New Jersey instead. Roe, however, was not keen on fighting Mineta and retired after just one term as committee chairman.[63]

Mineta pooled his two decades of experience on Public Works and Transportation and took over the gavel as chairman of the committee for the 103rd Congress. Having led four different subcommittees during his tenure on Public Works, he was fluent in the policy and deeply connected to the issues.

As chairman, Mineta ruled a vast and influential empire. Public Works and Transportation was the largest committee in the House during the 103rd Congress, bigger than either the spending or tax-writing committees. Seven other Californians served with him (three Democrats and four Republicans), and 30 of the 50 states as well as the U.S. Virgin Islands and the District of Columbia were represented on the committee.[64] His jurisdiction included flood control, roads, bridges, dams, public buildings—everything from airports to post offices to the Smithsonian Institution.

Mineta's focus as committee chairman was to prepare the government to meet the sure-to-be weighty demands of the upcoming 21st century. More than anything, he felt the need to make up for lost time. The Cold War had dominated America's discretionary spending for decades, and money that might have gone to improve the country's infrastructure went elsewhere. "Maintenance, new technologies, and leadership suffered often because, in real terms, we had to try to do more with less," Mineta remembered.

Looking forward, he identified two lingering hurdles. "The first challenge," he reiterated, "is to make up for a quarter century of trending downward in infrastructure investments, a trend which has seen the Federal commitment as a share of Gross Domestic Product decline by half. The second challenge is to look ahead to plan for the future with flexibility, with less interference from Washington into local decision-making, and with justification and public scrutiny at the national level for the policies we recommend and enact."[65]

Given the size and scope of the committee's jurisdiction, Mineta saw a tsunami of legislation during the 103rd Congress. House Parliamentarians referred almost 400 bills to Public Works and Transportation, which resulted in 165 hearings and markups; 53 of the 62 bills the committee reported to the full House became law. The panel also approved 168 committee resolutions covering everything from erosion control studies to improvements to federal buildings.[66]

While some of the legislation was as simple as naming post offices or courthouses, Mineta's committee could generate large amounts of goodwill simply by approving a new road or bridge for a Member's district. Mineta guarded this jurisdiction closely, and in 1993, during the annual appropriations process, he got into a very public turf war with Representative Bob Carr of Michigan, who chaired the Appropriations' Subcommittee on Transportation. Congressional authorizers like Mineta determine which agencies and which programs receive federal funding, while appropriators like Carr dole out money for the upcoming fiscal year.

In the House, it is considered bad form for appropriators to clear funding for projects that have not been vetted by an authorizing committee. But in late June, Mineta accused Carr of including hundreds of millions of dollars for the upcoming fiscal year that the Public Works and Transportation Committee had never approved. Mineta quickly convinced the Rules Committee to remove all unauthorized earmarks from the funding bill. Within the month, House leaders were forced to pull it from the floor completely after Mineta doubled down on what he called "backroom political deal-making."[67] House leaders eventually sent the bill back to the Appropriations Committee for changes.[68]

By September tensions were still high, and the House had yet to vote on the transportation bill. Mineta cast the fight as one about "process and rules"; Carr said it was all about "ego."[69] Unable to forge a compromise between the two lawmakers, Speaker Tom Foley of Washington and House leadership ultimately sided with Mineta.[70] "The episode," wrote the Congress-watchers at *CQ Almanac*, "appeared to give the Public Works Committee veto power

over new highway projects, allowing it to block funding for any specific project not included in one of the committee's authorization bills." It was, *CQ* said, "a sweeping victory." Mineta agreed to reform part of how his committee approved projects, but for the most part the chairman from San Jose had substantially increased his influence.[71]

The very next year Mineta ran headlong into an obstinate Senate over a popular highway bill. Back when he chaired the Surface Transportation Subcommittee during the 102nd Congress, Mineta had cleared a bill that created the National Highway System, which targeted federal funding for the most heavily used and most commercially important roads in America. Congress had until 1995 to determine which highways would fall under the NHS, and while most routes had already been selected, Mineta's committee wanted to add a host of new routes to the system. After sifting through Member requests for nearly 300 new road and transit programs, Mineta unveiled a $2 billion bill in mid-May 1994. Demonstrating just how popular Mineta's committee was, the full House approved the highway bill two weeks later by a huge 400-vote majority. The Senate, however, balked at the bill, and talks between the two chambers failed.[72]

Outside his immediate committee jurisdiction, Mineta worked to correct what he considered one of America's worst injustices: the forced internment of Japanese Americans during World War II. For Mineta, this was about as personal an issue as he dealt with in Congress. In the late 1970s, Mineta passed a bill crediting the time internees spent in the camps toward their civil service retirement benefits. Around the same time, a grassroots movement started to pressure the government to formally apologize for its policy of internment and ask for redress. Working alongside Hawaiian Senators Daniel K. Inouye and Spark M. Matsunaga, and California Representative Robert T. Matsui, Mineta helped pass a bill to study the wartime relocation and internment to generate awareness and develop policy.[73]

Out of that study came the Civil Liberties Act of 1988, authorizing the government to pay $20,000 to every surviving internee ($1.2 billion total). It also

required a formal apology for the policy of internment, had the Justice Department clear criminal records from internment, and set aside millions to fund public education initiatives.[74] Mineta was the first person to testify before the House Judiciary Committee about the effect of internment, underscoring the "shame" and "damaged honor" felt by two generations of Japanese Americans for being wrongfully imprisoned.[75] It was an intensely personal bill, but Mineta voted present during its final passage to avoid a conflict of interest.[76]

After Republicans swept the 1994 elections and took the majority in the House for the first time in decades, Mineta retired from Congress on October 10, 1995. He worked in the policy shop of a major defense contractor after leaving the House, and in 2000 President Bill Clinton named him Commerce Secretary. After two years in the Clinton administration, Mineta joined the George W. Bush administration as Transportation Secretary—the only Democrat in Bush's Cabinet—serving from 2001 until 2006. "There are no Democratic or Republican highways," Mineta liked to say, "no such thing as Republican or Democratic traffic congestion."[77] Shortly after Mineta stepped down, President Bush awarded him the Presidential Medal of Freedom for his years of public service. Mineta has since retired from public life.

MANUSCRIPT COLLECTIONS

Japanese American National Museum (Los Angeles, CA). *Papers*: 1975–1996, circa 45 linear feet. The collection consists of correspondence, memoranda, government publications, speeches, newspaper clippings, books, briefings, photographs, audiovisual materials, and meeting notes documenting Norman Mineta's involvement in seeking redress for Japanese Americans interned during World War II. Materials not related to the redress movement include civil rights issues of Asian Americans and Americans from the Pacific Islands, as well as materials that document Mineta's campaign activities. A finding aid is available at the museum and online.

Library of Congress, Asian Division (Washington, DC). *Oral History*: 2003–2011, 8 linear feet. The collection contains videocassettes, DVDs, photographs, and documents related to an oral history project conducted by the United States Capitol Historical Society to document the service of Asian Americans in Congress. Norman Mineta is included among the interviewees.

San Jose State University, Special Collections and Archives (San Jose, CA). *Papers*: 1961–2001, 435.3 linear feet. The Norman Mineta papers document his long-term political service in Congress and the executive branch. The collection consists of legislative files, administrative files, awards and memorabilia, public relations and press files, subject files, U.S. Department of Commerce files, and files from the U.S. Department of Transportation.

NOTES

1　Hearings before the House Committee on the Judiciary, Subcommittee on Administrative Law and Governmental Relations, *Civil Liberties Act of 1985 and the Aleutian And Pribilof Islands Restitution Act*, Part I, 99th Cong., 2nd sess. (28 April 1986): 35; E. Michael Myers, "Congressman Mineta Recalls the Days When the Constitution Failed," 22 May 1988, *Los Angeles Times*: 2; Ken Ringle, "The Patriot: Norm Mineta Was Interned by His Country, but Still He Loved It. Then He Changed It," 21 August 2000, *Washington Post*: C1.

2　Sam Chu Lin, "Working For the People: Norm Mineta Wraps Up More Than Two Decades of Public Service," 6 October 1995, *AsianWeek*: 10; Johanna Neuman, "Profile: Norm Mineta; What Moves Him?," 25 April 2005, *Los Angeles Times*: B2.

3　Chu Lin, "Working For the People: Norm Mineta Wraps Up More Than Two Decades of Public Service."

4　David M. Kennedy, *Freedom from Fear: The American People in Depression and War, 1929–1945* (New York: Oxford University Press, 1999): 748–760.

5　Neuman, "Profile: Norm Mineta; What Moves Him?"; Betty Cuniberti, "Internment: Personal Voices, Powerful Choices," 4 October 1987, *Los Angeles Times*: 1. See also Irvin Molotsky, "Washington Talk: Friendships, The Heat of War Welds a Bond That Endures Across Aisles and Years," 26 April 1988, *New York Times*: A22; Frank Davies, "Mineta, Ex-Senator Forged Ties at Internment Camp," 2 May 2008, *San Jose Mercury News*: n.p.

6　Hearings before the House Committee on the Judiciary, Subcommittee on Administrative Law and Government Relations, *Japanese American and Aleutian Wartime Relocation*, 98th Cong., 2nd sess. (20 June 1984): 74.

7　Norman Mineta, oral history interview by Ronald Sarasin, 11 September 2006, accessed 8 April 2016, transcript, U.S. Capitol Historical Society, Washington, DC: 4, http://www.uschs.org/oral-histories/uschs_mineta.htm (site discontinued).

8　Chu Lin, "Working For the People: Norm Mineta Wraps Up More Than Two Decades of Public Service."

9　"3,000 (Over 18, Under 21) Cast First Ballot Today in Maryland," 13 April 1971, *New York Times*: 26; "Little Sway by Young in Md. Vote," 15 April 1971, *Boston Globe*: 31.

10 David S. Broder, *Changing of the Guard: Power and Leadership in America* (New York: Penguin, 1981): 54.

11 Norman Mineta, "San Jose Mayor Finds Role of Parties Waning," 16 December 1971, *Washington Post*: A14; Broder, *Changing of the Guard*: 54.

12 "Norman Yoshio Mineta," *Biographical Directory of the United States Congress, 1774–Present*, http://bioguide.congress.gov/scripts/biodisplay.pl?index=M000794.

13 *Almanac of American Politics, 1976* (New York: E.P. Dutton & Co., Inc., 1975): 75; "Around the Nation," 15 April 1971, *Washington Post*: A5; Wallace Turner, "Idyllic Valley Now Urban Anthill, Planner Charges," 7 September 1970, *New York Times*: 12; "San Jose Mayor Is a Japanese-American," 15 April 1971, *New York Times*: 21; "3,000 (Over 18, Under 21) Cast First Ballot Today in Maryland."

14 "3,000 (Over 18, Under 21) Cast First Ballot Today in Maryland"; "Nisei Is in Lead," 14 April 1971, *New York Times*: 25; "Mineta is First," 15 April 1971, *Atlanta Constitution*: A20; "San Jose Mayor Is a Japanese-American." For vote totals, see "Little Sway By Young in Md. Vote."

15 "Men and Events," 18 April 1971, *Los Angeles Times*: C5.

16 *Almanac of American Politics, 1976*: 75; Art McGinn, "Can Towns Bar Their Gates?," 10 February 1974, *Atlanta Constitution*: C6; Gary Blonston, "Houses Achangin', Not for Better," 16 February 1975, *Baltimore Sun*: F1; David Homstrom, "Mayors Strike Gold—Citizen Involvement," 1 December 1971, *Christian Science Monitor*: 1.

17 John Herbers, "Despite Problems, Cities Produce Vigorous Mayors," 14 June 1971, *New York Times*: 18; "Revenue Share Consideration Set in Congress, Mayors Told," 18 January 1972, *Atlanta Constitution*: A9; "Mills Quoted as Predicting Action on Revenue Sharing," 9 March 1972, *New York Times*: 33; Peter Negronida, "Daley Leader: Mayors Back Nixon Policy," 22 June 1972, *Chicago Tribune*: 2; John Herbers, "Mayors, In Shift, Back War Policy," 22 June 1972, *New York Times*: 1; "16 Mayors Meet With Nixon," 25 July 1972, *Los Angeles Times*: 2; Martin F. Nolan, "Mayors Fear Bankruptcies Spreading in Public Housing," 7 September 1972, *Boston Globe*: 8; Maurice Carroll, "Mayors Tour City and Assail Nixon For Cuts in Funds," 5 February 1973, *New York Times*: 1; Richard L. Strout, "Mayors Call Nixon Budget Cuts 'Double Cross of City Poor,'" 24 February 1973, *Christian Science Monitor*: 2. For a general account of this generational change, see Broder, *Changing of the Guard*.

18 *Almanac of American Politics, 1976*: 76; *Almanac of American Politics, 1984* (Washington, DC: National Journal, 1983): 109–110; Kenneth C. Martis, *The Historical Atlas of Political Parties in the United States Congress, 1789–1989* (New York: Macmillian Publishing Company, 1989): 237; Office of the Clerk, U.S. House of Representatives, "Election Statistics, 1920 to Present," http://history.house.gov/Institution/Election-Statistics/Election-Statistics/.

19 Garrison Nelson, *Committees in the U.S. Congress, 1947–1992*, vol. 2 (Washington, DC: Congressional Quarterly Inc., 1994): 620–621; Garrison Nelson and Charles Stewart III, *Committees in the U.S. Congress, 1993–2010* (Washington, DC: CQ Press, 2011): 854.

20 Richard L. Lyons, "The New House: Members Mostly Lawyers, More Liberal, Younger," 1 December 1974, *Atlanta Constitution*: 2K; "New Members Bring Slice of Life to House," 11 November 1974, *Chicago Tribune*: 7.

21 Mineta, oral history interview: 8.

22 John A. Farrell, *Tip O'Neill and the Democratic Century* (Boston: Little, Brown and Company, 2001): 384–386; John A. Lawrence, "The Democrats' High-Water Mark," *Politico Magazine*, http://www.politico.com/magazine/story/2014/11/the-democrats-high-water-mark-came-40-years-ago-112492_Page2.html (accessed 13 January 2017).

23 Paul Houston, "Hopes Dimmed: Set Backs Give Freshman New View of House," 22 June 1975, *Los Angeles Times*: A1.

24 Robert Reinhold, "12 Go to Harvard to Study for Jobs in New Congress," 14 December 1974, *New York Times*: 31; Farrell, *Tip O'Neill and the Democratic Century*: 400–402.

25 Richard Lyons, "Caucus Chief Mineta Adopts Activist Role," 5 July 1975, *Washington Post*: A3.

26 Houston, "Hopes Dimmed."

27 Paul Houston, "Mineta Offers Six-Point Plan to Democrats," 26 June 1975, *Los Angeles Times*: B4; Lyons, "Caucus Chief Mineta Adopts Activist Role."

28 Houston, "Mineta Offers Six-Point Plan to Democrats."

29 Paul Houston, "5 Newcomers Give Vote of Confidence to Albert," 17 June 1975, *Los Angeles Times*: A19.

30 Lyons, "Caucus Chief Mineta Adopts Activist Role"; Mineta, oral history interview: 3–4.

31 Tip O'Neill with William Novak, *Man of the House: The Life and Political Memoirs of Speaker Tip O'Neill* (New York: Random House, 1987): 272; Martin Nolan, "O'Neill Views Speaker's Role," 14 June 1976, *Boston Globe*: 1.

32 Majorie Hunter and David E. Rosenbaum, "Defeats Split Bitter House Democrats," 2 July 1975, *New York Times*: A1.

33 Hunter and Rosenbaum, "Defeats Split Bitter House Democrats"; Mary Russell, "Freshmen Feel Frustration," 27 October 1975, *Washington Post*: A1.

34 Jerry Cohen, "Public Is Watching Politics Closer Now," 1 January 1976, *Los Angeles Times*: OC1.

35 Donald C. Bacon, Roger H. Davidson, and Morton Keller, eds., *The Encyclopedia of the United States Congress*, vol. 1 (New York: Simon and Schuster, 1995): 209; Eric Patashnik, "Congress and the Budget since 1974," in *The American Congress: The Building of*

Democracy, ed. Julian E. Zelizer (Boston: Houghton Mifflin, 2004): 671–672.

36 Hearings before the House Committee on Rules, Task Force on the Budget Process, *Congressional Budget Process*, 97th Cong., 2nd sess. (15 September 1982): 2.

37 David S. Broder, "Democratic Party in Transition, but the Question Is, to What?," 14 January 1979, *Washington Post*: A1.

38 Richard L. Lyons, "On Capitol Hill," 25 January 1979, *Washington Post*: A2.

39 Edward Walsh, "Administration Continues Its Search for Appointees to Fill Top Positions," 25 July 1979, *Washington Post*: A7.

40 David Rogers, "The Scent of Change is Strong," 16 November 1980, *Boston Globe*: 49; Mary Russell, "Democrats' Chairs," 11 November 1978, *Washington Post*: A1; Ellen Hume, "California Lawmakers Jockey for Position," 27 November 1980, *Los Angeles Times*: C1.

41 Broder, *Changing of the Guard*: 54.

42 *Congressional Directory*, 95th Cong. (Washington, DC: Government Printing Office, 1977): 17; *Congressional Directory*, 97th Cong. (Washington, DC: Government Printing Office, 1981): 17; "House Committees, 97th Congress, First Session," *CQ Almanac*, *1981*, 37th ed., (Washington, DC: Congressional Quarterly, Inc., 1982): 82, http://library.cqpress.com; "House Party Committees, 99th Congress," *CQ Almanac*, *1985*, 41st ed. (Washington, DC: Congressional Quarterly, Inc., 1986): 73-G–76-G, http://library.cqpress.com.

43 Margot Hornblower and Richard L. Lyons, "House GOP Picks Michel As Leader," 9 December 1980, *Washington Post*: A1; John Jacobs, *A Rage for Justice: The Passion and Politics of Phillip Burton* (Berkeley, CA: University of California Press, 1995): 478.

44 "Democrats in Full Control for 100th Congress," *CQ Almanac*, *1986*, 42nd ed. (Washington, DC: Congressional Quarterly, Inc., 1987): 3–7, http://library.cqpress.com; *Congressional Directory*, 103rd Cong. (Washington, DC: Government Printing Office): 478.

45 Lou Cannon, "The Independent Democrats," 23 May 1977, *Washington Post*: A1.

46 Hearings before the House Committee on Rules, Task Force on the Budget Process, *Congressional Budget Process*, 97th Cong., 2nd sess. (15 September 1982): 2–14; *Almanac of American Politics*, *1982* (Washington, DC: Barone & Company, 1981): 101. See also Zelizer, *The American Congress*: 678.

47 Hearings before the House Committee on the Judiciary, Subcommittee on Monopolies and Commercial Law, *Constitutional Amendments to Balance the Federal Budget*, 96th Cong., 1st sess. (13 June 1979): 423–426.

48 Bacon, Davidson, and Keller, eds., *The Encyclopedia of the United States Congress*, vol. 4: 1899.

49 Albert R. Hunt, "The Watergate Class," 26 March 1976, *Wall Street Journal*: 30.

50 *Almanac of American Politics*, *1984*: 110; "Fiscal 1980 Budget Targets," *CQ Almanac*, *1979*, 35th ed. (Washington, DC: Congressional Quarterly, Inc., 1980): 163–175, http://library.cqpress.com. For Gang of Five, see "First 1981 Budget Resolution: Slim Surplus," *CQ Almanac*, *1980*, 36th ed. (Washington, DC: Congressional Quarterly, Inc., 1981): 108–119, http://library.cqpress.com; Thomas B. Edsall, "Conflict Between Balancing Budget, Old-line Support Wracks Democrats," 13 March 1980, *Baltimore Sun*: A1; William J. Eaton, "House Scuttles Budget Plan," 30 May 1980, *Los Angeles Times*: 1; Martin Tolchin, "House Rejects Budget Compromise As Foes of Military Outlay Prevail," 30 May 1980, *New York Times*: A1; Steven Rattner, "Conferees Approve Budget Plan for '81 and '80 Deficit Rise," 12 June 1980, *New York Times*: A1; Andrew J. Glass, "Key House Democrats Prepare Own 1983 Budget," 9 March 1982, *Atlanta Constitution*: A11; Helen Dewar, "House Approves Stopgap Spending Till End of Fiscal Year, 299 to 103," 25 March 1982, *Washington Post*: A5.

51 Dan Morgan, "Battling to Innovate and Emulate: Intel vs. Nippon Electric," 2 May 1983, *Washington Post*: A1; "Bills Offer Protection for Chips," 11 June 1984, *New York Times*: D1.

52 James A. Martin, "Vendors Decry Stiff U.S. Trade Export Controls: Say Laws Protecting Sensitive Technology Cripple Access to Foreign Markets," 27 April 1987, *Computerworld*: 85.

53 John Hendren, no title, 16 July 1991, States News Service.

54 Ringle, "The Patriot: Norm Mineta Was Interned by his Country, but Still He Loved It. Then He Changed It."

55 John M. Barry, *The Ambition and the Power: A True Story of Washington* (New York: Penguin Books, 1990): 11.

56 House Committee on Public Works and Transportation, Subcommittee on Oversight and Review, *Organizational Meeting*, 96th Cong., 1st sess. (27 February 1979): 2–3.

57 House Committee on Public Works and Transportation, *Summary of Activities*, 96th Cong., 2nd sess., H. Rept. 1565 (2 January 1981): 43–46.

58 House Committee on Public Works and Transportation, *Summary of Activities*, 97th Cong., 2nd sess., H. Rept. 1013 (3 January 1983): 7, 16–18.

59 House Committee on Public Works and Transportation, *Summary of Legislative Activities*, 101st Cong., 2nd sess., H. Rept. 1007 (2 January 1991): 3–5, 77–80.

60 Hearings before the House Committee on Public Works and Transportation, Subcommittee on Surface Transportation, *Americans With Disabilities Act*, 101st Cong., 1st sess. (20 September 1989): 2.

61 Bill Anderson, "Cities and U.S. Tussle over Powers," 7 December 1973, *Chicago Tribune*: 16.

62 House Committee on Public Works and Transportation, *Summary of Legislative Activities*, 102nd Cong., 2nd sess., H. Rept. 1071 (16 December 1992): 81–89.

63 *Politics in America, 1992* (Washington, DC: Congressional Quarterly Inc., 1991): 193, 948; *Politics in America, 1994* (Washington, DC: Congressional Quarterly Inc., 1993): 147.

64 *Congressional Directory*, 103rd Cong. (Washington, DC: Government Printing Office, 1993): 460.

65 House Committee on Public Works and Transportation, *Summary of Legislative Activities*, 103rd Cong., 2nd sess., H. Rept. 877 (22 December 1994): 3.

66 Ibid., 4.

67 Al Kamen, "Chairmen Battle Over Transportation Bill," 28 June 1993, *Washington Post*: A17; William DiBenedetto, "House Action on Transport Bill Delayed By Dispute Over Projects," 7 July 1993, *Journal of Commerce*: B3; Mark Simon, "Mineta—The Roads Warrior," 19 July 1993, *San Francisco Chronicle*: A17. Quotation from Al Kamen, "Stalled in a Transportation Tug of War," 26 July 1993, *Washington Post*: A15.

68 Mark Simon, "Light Rail, BART Funds Imperiled," 28 July 1993, *San Francisco Chronicle*: A17.

69 Eric Pianin, "Turf Battle Stalls Transportation Spending in House," 17 September 1993, *Washington Post*: A17; Martin Tolchin, "2 Powerful Democrats Battle Over Transportation Projects," 22 September 1993, *New York Times*: B9.

70 Eric Pianin, "House Frees Transportation Bill After Carr-Mineta Turf Fight," 23 September 1993, *Washington Post*: A14.

71 "Transportation Programs Score Big Gains," *CQ Almanac, 1993*, 49th ed. (Washington, DC: Congressional Quarterly, 1994): 663–670, http://library.cqpress.com.

72 "Highway Funds Meet Roadblocks," *CQ Almanac, 1994*, 50th ed. (Washington, DC: Congressional Quarterly, 1995): 165–168, http://library.cqpress.com; *Politics in America, 1996* (Washington, DC: Congressional Quarterly Inc., 1995): 118.

73 Mineta, oral history interview: 11.

74 "House Votes to Make Amends for Internment," *CQ Almanac, 1987*, 43rd ed. (Washington, DC: Congressional Quarterly, 1988): 278, http://library.cqpress.com; "Internees Gain Reparations," *CQ Almanac, 1988*, 44th ed. (Washington, DC: Congressional Quarterly, 1989): 80–81, http://library.cqpress.com; Bill McAllister, "Amends Sought for 1940s Internment," 12 September 1987, *Washington Post*: A1; Mick Rood, no title, 16 September 1987, States News Service; Jill Lawrence, no title, 17 September 1987, Associated Press; Nathaniel Nash, "House Votes Payments to Japanese Internees," 18 September 1987, *New York Times*: A15; Jill Lawrence, "Mineta Tearfully Recalls 1942 Internment as House Votes Cash Compensation," 18 September 1987, Associated Press.

75 *Civil Liberties Act of 1985 and the Aleutian And Pribilof Islands Restitution Act*, Part I: 34–36.

76 "House Votes to Make Amends for Internment"; "Internees Gain Reparations"; McAllister, "Amends Sought for 1940s Internment"; Rood, no title, 16 September 1987, States News Service; Jill Lawrence, no title, 17 September 1987, Associated Press; Nash, "House Votes Payments to Japanese Internees"; Lawrence, "Mineta Tearfully Recalls 1942 Internment as House Votes Cash Compensation."

77 Johanna Neuman and Ricardo Alonso-Zaldivar, "The Nation: Mineta, Cabinet's Sole Democrat, Quits," 24 June 2006, *Los Angeles Times*: A6.

Samuel Ichiye (Sam) Hayakawa
1906–1992

UNITED STATES SENATOR 1977–1983
REPUBLICAN FROM CALIFORNIA

Samuel Ichiye (Sam) Hayakawa's journey from academia to Capitol Hill abounded in contradictions, reversals, and some mirthful moments. He began his long career as a successful author of semantics, later transitioning into academic administration, which, in turn, thrust him to national acclaim as the improbable, tam-o'-shanter-topped hero of the law-and-order crowd. Drawing on that popularity, Hayakawa won election to a single Senate term, where his iconoclasm contrasted with an institution rooted in tradition. Along the way, his ideological trajectory arced from New Deal liberalism to a conservatism borne of the perceived excesses of Vietnam Era protests.

Samuel Ichiye Hayakawa was born on July 18, 1906, in Vancouver, British Columbia, Canada, the eldest of four children of Ichiro and Tora Isono Hayakawa. Ichiro had left Japan and joined the U.S. Navy as a mess attendant at age 18. Two years later, he returned to Japan, married Isono, and the couple relocated to Canada.[1] Sam Hayakawa was educated in the public schools of Winnipeg before earning a bachelor's degree from the University of Manitoba in Winnipeg in 1927. A year later, he graduated with a master's degree in English literature from McGill University in Montreal.

In 1929, the year his parents returned to their native Japan, Hayakawa immigrated to the United States, but because of naturalization restrictions that applied to Asians, he would not become a U.S. citizen until 1954. He attended the University of Wisconsin at Madison, earning a PhD in English in 1935. After finishing his studies, Hayakawa stayed and taught at his alma mater. In 1937 he married Margedant Peters, one of his former students. Many states prohibited such interracial marriages, including California, where the young couple wanted to live. So the Japanese-American husband and Caucasian wife ended up residing in Chicago for nearly two decades, where he taught at the Illinois Institute of Technology (1939–1947) and the University of Chicago (1950–1955). The couple raised three children, sons Alan and Mark and daughter Wynne.[2]

After witnessing the ruthless efficiency of the Nazi propaganda machine that aided Adolph Hitler's rise to power, Hayakawa was inspired to write *Language in Action* (1941), a book that cemented his reputation as a semanticist. Selected by the Book of the Month Club, it was eventually revised as *Language in Thought and Action* (1949) and remained a popular text for many decades. Working from the intellectual foundations laid by the Polish semanticist Alfred Korzybski, Hayakawa's principal thrust was that words are not the same as reality; while language can be used to approximate reality, it may also be used to obscure it. The success of the book helped establish Hayakawa in the field and earned him an academic appointment. In the mid-1950s, after discriminatory state laws were abolished, Hayakawa and his family moved to California, where he joined the faculty at San Francisco State College (now University) as a professor of English.

Hayakawa rose to national prominence during an era of collegiate unrest in which thousands of young Americans protested the Vietnam War and fought for civil rights reforms. The Bay Area had become something of a social justice incubator, and in 1968 San Francisco State students, as part of a larger call to improve diversity on campus, initiated a strike to support an African-American teacher who had been suspended. After the school suspended classes and the college president stepped down that November, Hayakawa sat on the faculty committee to find a successor. He became a vocal critic of the protestors. "What my colleagues seem to be forgetting is [that] we also have an obligation to the 17,500 or more students—white,

Image courtesy of the Library of Congress

black, yellow and brown—who are not on strike and have every right to expect continuation of their education." The college trustees, with the support of then Governor of California Ronald Reagan, named Hayakawa as acting president of San Francisco State on November 28, 1968.

When classes resumed a few days later, the protests intensified. Hayakawa called in the police, who arrested dozens of student demonstrators. With television cameras rolling, Hayakawa scrambled onto a sound truck the protestors had commandeered and ripped the cords out of the loudspeaker. The image of a diminutive college administrator wearing a tam-o'-shanter, uncowed by student radicals resonated with Americans who had wearied of college protests and the anti-Vietnam War movement. The strikes and class stoppages continued for months, but Hayakawa was resolute throughout, gaining wide name recognition (the public knew him thereafter as "Samurai Sam") and plaudits from state and national politicians. To defuse tensions, he made some concessions, such as creating a black studies department. In July 1969, college trustees named him the permanent university president, and he held the position until he retired in 1973.[3]

As a young man, Hayakawa aligned with Democrats squarely in the New Deal coalition, which tackled the economic crisis of the 1930s and gave America its social safety net. But over time he became more conservative, partly in reaction to the counterculture of the 1960s and partly to protest the expansion of federal government social programs as part of President Lyndon B. Johnson's Great Society. He became a lightning rod for liberal faculty, who he said "deserted" him during the campus-wide protests. It all made him rethink his longtime political affiliation. "When I kept the university open for the benefit of our students and faculty, I thought I was doing a liberal thing," Hayakawa wrote years later. "I don't know anything more liberal than to maintain education for all who want it."[4] He formally registered as Republican in June 1973, the day after he retired as college president. The government, he had come to believe, was risking the health of the nation by "redistributing income" and "rewarding the unsuccessful."[5] "You should govern a great nation as you fry a small fish,"

Hayakawa said, echoing the Chinese philosopher Lao Tzu, "with only a little amount of stirring."[6]

Three years after retiring, Hayakawa decided to try to unseat California's junior Senator, Democrat John V. Tunney, and announced his candidacy for the GOP nomination on January 20, 1976. It was his first campaign for any elected office, and he introduced himself as a "Republican unpredictable."[7] Observers described it as a "low-key" effort by a political neophyte against a field of seasoned political veterans, but Hayakawa drew on a strong conservative backlash against the social unrest of the era. "I think the triumph of the New Left in the 1960s was really a blow against certain basic American values," he explained to a reporter. "One individual can do damn little about it, I suppose. This is some sort of moral gesture on my part. For after all, it seems to me the Senate is a platform from which you can preach."[8]

He campaigned in what were traditionally heavily Republican parts of the state, mainly in Orange and San Diego Counties, on a platform that opposed big government and deficit spending.[9] His principal primary opponents were eight-term U.S. Representative Alphonzo Bell Jr., and Robert Finch, a former lieutenant governor and cabinet member in the Richard Nixon administration. Finch and Bell did not take Hayakawa's under-the-radar candidacy seriously. Late in the campaign they scrambled to make up ground by hammering at the front-runner's age—Hayakawa would turn 70 before the general election.[10] The strategy failed. Hayakawa's rivals split enough of the vote to allow the former academician to prevail. On June 8, 1976, Hayakawa captured 38 percent of the vote to 26 and 23 percent, respectively, for Finch and Bell.[11]

Hayakawa's general election opponent, Senator Tunney, had served three terms in the U.S. House of Representatives, representing a Riverside district, before winning election to the Senate in 1970. Tunney, however, struggled in his first term. Liberals criticized him for supporting big agribusiness, a logical position for him, given his House district based in the Imperial Valley. Conservatives did not like his generally liberal voting record, and the press often depicted the divorced Tunney as a playboy.[12] During the 1976 Democratic primary, the former student activist Tom Hayden managed to poll 41 percent of the vote against him.[13]

Hayakawa's 1976 Senate campaign cemented his reputation as an iconoclast. At times, the candidate cast himself as a "political innocent," which had an appeal in the aftermath of Watergate. He embraced the role of being the people's candidate. "I admit it," he noted late in the campaign, "I'm a folk hero."[14] He donned the colorful knit tam-o'-shanter that had been his trademark at San Francisco State and even named a campaign train that whisked him from stop to stop along the California coast as the "Tam-O'-Shanter Express."[15] His enthusiastic departure from the niceties of politics and his free-swinging responses broadened his appeal across party lines, particularly in a state where voters often split the ticket in presidential election years. When told that McDonald's restaurant chain operated 100 franchise restaurants in Japan, he replied, "What a terrible revenge for Pearl Harbor." On the hot-button issue of returning control of the Panama Canal to the Panamanians, Hayakawa chirped, "We should keep it. We stole it fair and square." When student radicals heckled him at a campaign appearance, he asked the crowd, "Do the rest of you want to hear my speech?" When the crowd replied resoundingly that they did, Hayakawa shot back, "Well, would you tell those bastards to shut up?"[16]

Though he started out as a decided underdog against Tunney, Hayakawa had the momentum. "There is no way for Hayakawa to win this election but he's going to," observed Franklyn (Lyn) Nofziger, an aide to Ronald Reagan, in the weeks leading up to Election Day.[17] Hayakawa prevailed by a narrow 3 percent margin of victory, 50 to 47.[18] Still, some believed that a man who had spent his life parsing the English language and who had little practical experience would have a hard time transitioning to the U.S. Senate. Colman McCarthy observed shortly afterward, "Hayakawa, the politician, may prove to be much less effective than Hayakawa, the semanticist. His campaign was anything but the age of

enlightenment revisited, and he defeated a man whose work in the Senate had at least some substance."[19]

Tunney resigned from the Senate two days before the start of the 95th Congress (1977–1979) so that the governor could appoint Hayakawa in the waning hours of the 94th Congress (1975–1977) and give him seniority over the incoming class of Senate freshmen.[20] His initial assignments were on the Interior and Insular Affairs Committee and Agriculture and Forestry Committee (later renamed Agriculture, Nutrition, and Forestry). He kept the Agriculture assignment for his entire term, but within a month left Insular Affairs for seats on both the Budget Committee and the Human Resources Committee. At the opening of the 96th Congress (1979–1981), he traded in both those assignments for a seat on the Foreign Relations Committee, where he served the duration of his term in office. In the 97th Congress (1981–1983), Hayakawa also was assigned to the Select Committee on Small Business, which became a standing committee two months after the start of the session.

In his first year, Hayakawa addressed economic issues affecting California. His first legislative effort was a bill friendly to the Pacific tuna fleet that frequently killed porpoises in its nets and led to protests by environmental groups. His bill provided a "technological solution" to the problem and called for a gradual plan that sought to loosen restrictions of the Marine Mammal Protection Act. Hayakawa sought to provide money for further study of the problem and, rather than bar porpoise kills outright, suggested that the tuna catch be reduced only if the porpoise population continued to decline.[21] He also supported building the B-1 bomber, a Cold War Era supersonic aircraft that carried nuclear weapons, since many of the plane's components were manufactured in California.

The same plainspokenness and quirkiness that won him votes back home undercut his effectiveness in the U.S. Senate. Hayakawa had an aloof and generally uncooperative working relationship with Alan Cranston, California's senior Senator and the Democratic Whip. Initially, Cranston described Hayakawa's potential in the Senate this way: "He's unpredictable and will cast a lot of good votes and a lot of bad votes. I don't know how it will add up, but it's great to have a senator who's individualistic and different." But the partnership was not helped by public gaffes. At a committee hearing that both men attended on a California wilderness bill, for instance, Cranston and Hayakawa openly disagreed on it. Hayakawa compounded the awkward encounter when giving remarks against the proposal and nodding at Cranston and saying, "I'm delighted to be here with my colleague from Wisconsin."[22]

Observers complained that Hayakawa had hired an eclectic staff ill-prepared to handle the rigors of representing a huge state like California. Nearing the end of his first year in office, Senate insiders suggested that his name "still conjures up more curiosity than clout" and that the professor had been a poor student in learning the institution's folkways.[23] The press made hay with his habit of napping on the job, first in orientation classes for freshman Senators and, in the years that followed, in committee hearings.[24] "I have a low threshold of boredom," Hayakawa quipped.[25]

A year into his term, Hayakawa wrote an essay for *Harper's Weekly* in which he gainsaid the wisdom of his own appointment to the Senate Budget Committee. "This was ironic because I have the greatest difficulty balancing my own checkbook, and my wife handles our investments," Hayakawa noted. "Putting me on the Budget Committee when I don't understand money at all seemed to me to be appallingly irresponsible on the part of the United States Senate." He added, though, that after being on the committee for several months, he discovered that work on a committee that he described as being comprised of free spenders only involved simple math. "It's all simple addition," Hayakawa deadpanned. "You don't even have to know subtraction."[26]

By the late summer of 1977, Hayakawa already had backed away from the campaign trail rhetoric opposing the transfer of control of the Panama Canal. He claimed that, while his laugh line on stealing it got all the press, his more serious remarks about finding a pragmatic solution to the impasse were ignored. Moreover, Hayakawa insisted he always believed that "our policies toward Panama had

to be examined in the general framework of our relations with the other countries of Latin America."[27] As such, he believed President Jimmy Carter's proposal to relinquish control of the canal was sound and could improve U.S. relations with Panama and the rest of Central America.[28] On March 16, 1978, Hayakawa voted with the majority to return control of the canal to Panama.[29]

But Hayakawa's political positions on several hot-button ethnic and cultural issues began to erode his support among California voters. In 1979 he opposed the Japanese American Citizens League (JACL), which called for the U.S. government to redress civil rights violations committed against Japanese Americans relocated from the West Coast during World War II. Hayakawa described Franklin D. Roosevelt's executive order as being borne not principally of racism, but of "wartime necessity" and "the essence of prudence." He added that the relocation camps sped up a process whereby Japanese Americans were "integrated into [U.S.] society faster than any other non-English-speaking ethnic group in our history. The camps, unjust though they were, forced the Japanese Americans to break out of the West Coast and into the American mainstream."[30] Critics howled in protest not the least because the Canadian-born Hayakawa neither suffered that uprooting nor fought in the U.S. military in the Second World War.

Late in Hayakawa's Senate career, as the congressionally mandated Commission on Wartime Relocation and Internment of Civilians (CWRIC) prepared to release its report, the JACL continued to call for reparations of $25,000 per individual interned, a nearly $3 billion outlay. On the 41st anniversary of the surprise attack on Pearl Harbor, Hayakawa took to the Senate Floor to note that "my flesh crawls with shame and embarrassment" at proposed reparations. He reminded Japanese Americans of their successful integration into American society vis-à-vis other ethnic groups and their relative level of wealth and educational achievement and warned that, in an era of budget constraints and widespread public concern about Japanese economic gains versus the United States, such a program would invite a "backlash."[31] Ultimately, CWRIC recommended reparations along with an acknowledgement of the federal government's violation of Japanese-American civil rights that were eventually embodied in the Civil Liberties Act signed into law by President Ronald Reagan in August 1988.

Hayakawa's views on economic issues, infused with the perspectives of an educator who had spent decades working with young people, reflected mainstream Republican thinking about the value of the free market and the problems with welfare. In 1977 he opposed raising the national minimum wage, arguing that it would have an adverse impact on teenage boys because, when facing elevated wages, employers would cut their workforces. This would hurt particularly minority youth for whom jobs represented economic gain, social advancement, and an opportunity for personal growth. "If an affluent society does not provide boys with challenges," Hayakawa told colleagues on the Senate Floor, "they are compelled by inner necessity to improvise their own."[32]

In 1978 he authored a bill to provide incentives to small-business owners to hire teenagers in urban areas. By the early 1980s, Hayakawa advocated reducing the entry-level minimum wage for teenagers, a time at which it was $3.35 per hour. Amid cries that his plan would create a pool of cheap labor, Hayakawa countered that early employment opportunities presented a crucial step to integrating teenagers into society and steering them away from trouble.[33]

In 1982, amidst a steep economic recession, Hayakawa argued that the "voluntarily unemployed"—those people not looking for jobs or those passing up positions that paid too little—ought to be removed from the food stamp program. The proposal, he admitted, "may seem to lack compassion. However, it is the other way around. The Government is lacking compassion by encouraging people to remain idle.... Lost are the opportunities to gain a foothold on the economic ladder and to obtain the basic dignity and self-respect derived from being a productive member of society."[34]

Given his experience as a school administrator, Hayakawa was an unsurprisingly assertive opponent of federal mandates at all levels of the U.S. education system. He opposed school busing as a means to desegregate schools and wanted to prohibit federal payments to colleges with affirmative action policies, a position which he voiced consistently throughout his Senate career. In April 1979, he took to the Senate Floor to deride the "foolishness" of "forcing preferential quotas" on U.S. universities. His experience as a university president led him to resent such policies, and as a Senator he sought to defund programs implemented by the Department of Health, Education, and Welfare that supported affirmative action. He argued, in part, that such policies undercut the intent of the Civil Rights Act of 1964 and had eroded higher education. "In recent years Washington has pushed its foot in the schoolhouse door and created new and sophisticated priorities," Hayakawa told his colleagues. "Every priority they throw in interferes with the educational process."[35]

Hayakawa repeatedly derided bilingualism efforts in schools and, in April 1981, proposed a constitutional amendment to make English the official language of the United States. He argued, in part, that English proficiency was the great equalizer that helped immigrants assimilate and succeed in the United States: "Participation in the common language has rapidly made available to each new group the political and economic benefit of American society."[36] While Hayakawa supported learning other languages, he opposed the tendency of new immigrants in school to be taught primarily in their native language. He also opposed bilingual ballot provisions, which, he argued, conflicted with naturalization requirements that mandated basic English proficiency. In early 1981, he submitted a bill to repeal the bilingual requirements of the Voting Rights Act extension of 1975.[37] At the heart of his proposals, he once explained, was an attempt to "prevent a growing split among ethnic groups based on their native languages. With each trying to become more powerful than the other, the function of language could change from a means of communication to a tool of cultural assertion."[38]

In early 1982, Hayakawa announced that he would not seek re-election to a second term. "I make this choice without urging or pressure from anyone except my own internal imperative to turn in a record of solid legislative achievement as my small contribution to the history of the state," Hayakawa said. At the time, polls indicated that he was badly trailing the field of candidates for the nomination, including San Diego Mayor Pete Wilson, who would go on to succeed him in the Senate.[39]

After Congress, Hayakawa founded the group U.S. English, a political lobbying organization devoted to "preserving the unifying role of English" in the United States.[40] Hayakawa resided in Mill Valley, California, and passed away February 27, 1992, in Greenbrae. Senator Mark Hatfield of Oregon eulogized him as "a man who had the strength of character to fight unabashedly for what he believed in and for what he felt in his heart was in the best interest of the Nation."[41]

FOR FURTHER READING

Haslam, Gerald W., with Janice E. Haslam. *In Thought and Action: The Enigmatic Life of S. I. Hayakawa* (Lincoln: University of Nebraska Press, 2011).

Hayakawa, S. I. *Language in Thought and Action*, 4th ed. (New York: Harcourt Brace Jovanovich, 1978).

MANUSCRIPT COLLECTIONS

Hoover Institution, Library and Archives (Stanford, CA). *Papers*: 1926–1994, 264.1 linear feet. The collection includes correspondence, memoranda, reports, speeches, clippings, photographs, audiovisual materials, and memorabilia relating to many aspects of U.S. foreign relations and domestic policies, U.S. politics, and the Republican Party. A finding aid is available online and at the repository.

San Diego State University, Special Collections and University Archives (San Diego, CA). *Papers*: 1959–1982, 10.2 linear feet. The papers include correspondence, office memos, invitations, biographical data, press releases, subject files, and reports from Hayakawa's San Diego district office.

NOTES

1   "Ex-Sen. Hayakawa Dies; Unpredictable Iconoclast; Professor: Semanticist First Caught Public's Attention with His Opposition to Students Radicals at S.F. State," 28 February 1992, *Los Angeles Times*: A1; J. Y. Smith, "Outspoken U.S. Senator S. I. Hayakawa Dies at 85," 28 February 1992, *Washington Post*: D4; Katherine Bishop, "S. I. Hayakawa Dies at 85; Scholar and Former Senator,"

28 February 1992, *New York Times*: B6; Samuel W. Crompton, "Hayakawa, S. I.," *American National Biography*, vol. 10 (New York: Oxford University Press, 1999): 372–373.

2   Bishop, "S. I. Hayakawa Dies at 85; Scholar and Former Senator."

3   "Hayakawa, S(amuel) I(chiye)," *Current Biography* 38, no. 1 (January 1977): 20–21; Crompton, "Hayakawa, S. I."; Smith, "Outspoken U.S. Senator S. I. Hayakawa Dies at 85."

4   S. I. Hayakawa, "Toward a Governing Coalition—II. Republicans," in *Emerging Coalitions in American Politics*, ed. Seymour Martin Lipset (San Francisco, CA: Institute for Contemporary Studies, 1978): 425.

5   Tom Goff, "Hayakawa: the Making of a Senator," 4 November 1976, *Los Angeles Times*: B15; S. I. Hayakawa, "Mr. Hayakawa Goes to Washington," *Harper's Magazine* 256 (January 1978): 39–43, quotation on p. 43.

6   Lou Cannon, "Hayakawa Breakfast: Lao-tse or Lausche?," 27 April 1977, *Washington Post*: A1.

7   William Endicott, "Hayakawa Makes It Clear: He'll Seek Tunney's Seat," 21 January 1976, *Los Angeles Times*: C1.

8   Bill Stall, "Hayakawa Puts the Accent on Action in GOP Senate Campaign," 2 April 1976, *Los Angeles Times*: OC-B5.

9   Tom Goff, "Hayakawa: Soft Sell Pays Off," 5 May 1976, *Los Angeles Times*: A3.

10 William Endicott, "Hayakawa's Age Becomes Campaign Issue," 15 May 1976, *Los Angeles Times*: C1.

11 *Almanac of American Politics, 1980* (Washington, DC: National Journal, Inc., 1979): 56.

12 *Almanac of American Politics, 1980*: 52.

13 Tom Goff, "Tunney Defeats Hayden, 59%–41%; Hayakawa Wins," 9 June 1976, *Los Angeles Times*: 3.

14 Larry Stammer, "Hayakawa Cultivates His 'Political Innocent' Image," 4 October 1976, *Los Angeles Times*: B1; Lou Cannon, "Hayakawa's Style: He Shuns Court Jester Role," 27 February 1977, *Washington Post*: A1.

15 Larry Stammer, "Hayakawa Rides Rails to San Diego," 31 October 1976, *Los Angeles Times*: A3.

16 Lou Cannon, "Hayakawa vs. Tunney: Californians' Senate Race is Unusual," 17 October 1976, *Washington Post*: L1.

17 Cannon, "Hayakawa's Style: He Shuns Court Jester Role."

18 Office of the Clerk, U.S. House of Representatives, "Election Statistics, 1920 to Present," http://history.house.gov/Institution/Election-Statistics/Election-Statistics/; Goff, "Hayakawa: the Making of a Senator."

19 Colman McCarthy, "A Semanticist Loose in the Political Stacks," 30 November 1976, *Los Angeles Times*: C7.

20 "Head Start For Hayakawa," 10 December 1976, *Washington Post*: A30.

21 *Congressional Record*, Senate, 95th Cong., 1st sess. (10 February 1977): 4151–4152; Richard Bergholz, "Hayakawa Acts to Aid Tuna Fleet," 22 January 1977, *Los Angeles Times*: A30.

22 Cannon, "Hayakawa's Style: He Shuns Court Jester Role"; Ellen Hume, "Gaffe Puts Hayakawa in Badger State," 27 September 1977, *Los Angeles Times*: B14.

23 Ellen Hume, "Prof. Hayakawa Still a Student in the Senate," 18 September 1977, *Los Angeles Times*: A1; Linda Charlton, "Hayakawa Finds Senate Friends More Interesting Than Ph.D.'s," 27 April 1977, *New York Times*: 18.

24 "Former Prof. Hayakawa Naps in Congress Classes," 16 December 1976, *Chicago Tribune*: 7.

25 Don Shannon, "Sen. Hayakawa Dots the Eyes and Crosses the Press," 5 January 1977, *Los Angeles Times*: 1.

26 "Former Prof. Hayakawa Naps in Congress Classes"; Shannon, "Sen. Hayakawa Dots the Eyes and Crosses the Press"; Hayakawa, "Mr. Hayakawa Goes to Washington"; Hume, "Prof. Hayakawa Still a Student in the Senate."

27 *Congressional Record*, Senate, 95th Cong., 2nd sess. (23 February 1978): 4281.

28 William Endicott, "Hayakawa Ready to Back Panama Canal Treaties," 19 August 1977, *Los Angeles Times*: B12.

29 S. I. Hayakawa, "'Aye' … I Knew that I Had Done the Right Thing," 30 March 1978, *Los Angeles Times*: D7.

30 S. I. Hayakawa, "Reparations for Japanese-Americans? No!," 11 May 1979, *Los Angeles Times*: E7.

31 *Congressional Record*, Senate, 97th Cong., 2nd sess. (7 December 1982): 29209–29213, quotation on p. 29213.

32 *Congressional Record*, Senate, 95th Cong., 1st sess. (7 October 1977): 32867–32870, quotation on p. 32870.

33 S. I. Hayakawa, "Minimum Wage: Helping Hand or Empty Promise?," 4 January 1981, *Los Angeles Times*: F5. For a similar argument, see *Congressional Record*, Senate, 96th Cong., 1st sess. (29 March 1979): 6706–6707; *Congressional Record*, Senate, 96th Cong., 1st sess. (11 July 1979): 18012–18013.

34 S. I. Hayakawa, "Paid by the Government to Do Nothing," 8 September 1982, *New York Times*: A26.

35 *Congressional Record*, Senate, 96th Cong., 1st sess. (30 April 1979): 8935; see also *Congressional Record*, Senate, 97th Cong., 1st sess. (21 May 1981): 10798–10799.

36 *Congressional Record*, Senate, 97th Cong., 1st sess. (27 April 1981): 7444–7445. See also *Congressional Record*, Senate, 97th Cong., 1st sess. (14 October 1981): 23980–23982; *Congressional Record*, Senate, 97th Cong., 1st sess. (24 March 1981): 5088–5089.

37 *Congressional Record*, Senate, 97th Cong., 1st sess. (6 January 1981): 167–168.

38 S. I. Hayakawa, "English By Law," 1 October 1981, *New York Times*: A35. See also *Congressional Record*, Senate, 96th Cong., 1st sess. (1 May 1979): 214–215.

39 Jay Mathews, "Sen. Hayakawa Drops Bid for Reelection," 30 January 1982, *Washington Post*: A5.

40 "About U.S. English: History," accessed 30 October 2014, http://www.usenglish.org/history.

41 *Congressional Record*, Senate, 102nd Cong., 2nd sess. (4 March 1992): 4333.

Daniel K. Akaka

1924–

UNITED STATES REPRESENTATIVE 1977–1990
UNITED STATES SENATOR 1990–2013
DEMOCRAT FROM HAWAII

As the first Native Hawaiian in the U.S. Senate, Daniel K. Akaka used his genial nature and influence in committee to effect change on the national stage. During his 36 years of service in the House and Senate, Akaka built up significant loyalty in Hawaii and within the Democratic Party. However, success eluded him on his signature piece of legislation, a law elevating Native Hawaiians to tribal status with all the privileges commensurate with that designation. "I am not a born politician," Akaka said of his congressional experience. "People tell me I have to be feisty to get my way in Congress. But that's not my style. I use my Hawaiian abilities and the spirit of Aloha that brings people together."[1]

Daniel Kahikina Akaka was born on September 11, 1924, in Honolulu, Hawaii, the son of Kahikina Akaka and Annie Kahoa. His ethnic Chinese father processed sugar and worked as a molder for the Honolulu Ironworks. His Native Hawaiian mother was a homemaker who raised Daniel and his seven brothers and sisters. The family lived in a two-bedroom home with a separate building for the kitchen, cooking on a wood stove.[2] Akaka's family was devoutly religious, a quality that stayed with Akaka throughout his life. He briefly considered following his older brother, Abraham, into the ministry before committing himself to education. He remained close with Abraham, whom he invited to act as a guest chaplain in the House in 1977 and the Senate in 1991.[3]

Akaka attended public schools in Honolulu and graduated from the Kamehameha School for Boys in 1942. After high school, he followed in his father's footsteps and began working as a civilian welder and mechanic for the Hawaiian Electric Company. He joined the U.S. Army Corps of Engineers upon being drafted in 1945 and received an honorable discharge from the Army in 1947. He then served as the first mate on the schooner *Morning Star* out of Hawaii for a year. In 1948 Akaka married Mary Mildred Chong, with whom he had five children, Alan, Millannie, Daniel Jr., Nicholas, and Gerard.

After his year at sea, Akaka attended the University of Hawaii, where he received a bachelor's degree in education in 1952, using benefits from the GI Bill to pay his way. Akaka earned his professional certificate in secondary education and began teaching in 1953 at Kahuku High School. He then moved on to Pearl Harbor Intermediate School and ended his teaching career in elementary schools in suburban Oahu in 1960. After acquiring his professional school administrator's certificate, Akaka transitioned into school administration. He had also worked for the Hawaii department of education as an education program specialist beginning in 1953, a position he held for 18 years.[4] While working as a principal in the Oahu school system, Akaka completed a master's degree in education from the University of Hawaii in 1966. Three years later Akaka became chief program planner for compensatory education for the Hawaii department of education. From 1971 to 1974, he served as director of the Hawaii office of economic opportunity.

Akaka's ascension through the ranks of the Hawaii education department caught the attention of longtime Democratic godfather Governor John Burns.[5] Constantly on the lookout for fresh talent, Burns regularly invited Akaka to the governor's mansion to eat breakfast and discuss the need for a Native-Hawaiian presence in politics. "I had never thought about it before then," Akaka admitted.[6] Incapacitated by cancer late in his third term, Burns urged Akaka to transition from administration to politics. In 1974 Akaka ran in the Democratic primary to be George R. Ariyoshi's running mate for governor. Ariyoshi specifically wanted Akaka on the ticket for lieutenant governor as a Native Hawaiian.

Maintaining a careful ethnic balance in Hawaiian politics had long been a common practice carefully managed by party elites. However, Akaka entered the campaign late and was defeated by Nelson Doi, who went on to win the election for lieutenant governor alongside Ariyoshi. Ariyoshi then hired Akaka as a special assistant in the governor's office, where he served from 1975 to 1976.[7] Akaka's political interest in helping Native Hawaiians began as Governor Ariyoshi's aide when he was directed to organize a program under the Native American Act in Hawaii. During this time, he helped forge the beginnings of ALU LIKE, a nonprofit organization formed to help increase opportunities and standards of living for Native Hawaiians while preserving their unique culture.[8]

A chain of events created a giant vacuum on the national level for Hawaii when Senator Hiram L. Fong retired in 1976. Both of Hawaii's U.S. Representatives, Spark M. Matsunaga and Patsy Takemoto Mink, announced their candidacies to replace the Senator, setting off an intraparty fight among Democrats and opening up both of Hawaii's congressional seats. Akaka declared his candidacy for Mink's seat, which included most of the land outside the population center of Honolulu except for the smaller northwestern islands. He faced Republican Hank Inouye (no relation to Senator Daniel K. Inouye) among other third-party candidates. Akaka ran away with the election, securing 80 percent of the vote.[9]

A liberal Democrat, Akaka tended to vote the party line on the majority of legislation, which helped him advance within the House. Though he often differentiated himself from his party by supporting defense programs largely due to the military bases on Hawaiian soil, Akaka voted with party leadership on issues they deemed essential. As one example, Akaka was crucial to a successful attempt by Democratic leadership to block President Ronald Reagan's funding for the MX missile. Akaka initially voted for the bill, but changed his mind when Illinois Democrat Marty Russo carried him from a phone booth to the chamber to change his vote.[10]

Akaka developed a "Hawaiian style" rapport with his House colleagues. He rejected a more showy or flashy style on the Hill, instead becoming more well known among Members of Congress for his soft-spoken, but affable, manner. Akaka devoted his time in the House to acquiring funding for his home state and focusing on Hawaiian issues, appearing "quietly competent" without gaining visibility either nationally or broadly across Hawaii.[11]

As a freshman House Member, Akaka was tapped to serve on four separate committees, including the Agriculture Committee and the Merchant Marine and Fisheries Committee, both key assignments to oversee legislation affecting Hawaiian industries. Akaka's longest service was on the Select Committee on Narcotics Abuse and Control, where he spent much of his time attempting to draw attention to the drug abuse problems on the islands and writing harsher sentences for dealers.[12] His broader agenda included protection of the sugar and merchant marine industries in Hawaii and fostering a stronger relationship between Hawaii and the federal government. Akaka specifically developed a reputation for being a friend of federal workers, who comprised a large part of his constituency. From 1978 through his final House election in 1988, Akaka never received fewer than 75 percent of the vote. Akaka never went uncontested and usually faced a Libertarian opponent, but for many of these elections, Republicans failed to put forward an opponent.[13]

Akaka entered Congress with the hope of securing a seat on the Appropriations Committee, but was told not to expect much, coming from a small state. He recognized the difficulty of his position. "You cannot get into the committee unless somebody dies, or somebody resigns or leaves the House." When a seat did open up during his second term, Akaka aggressively pursued it and reminded Speaker Tip O'Neill of Massachusetts of his unwavering loyalty. "I think that made a difference," Akaka recalled, "because the next day, Charlie Rangel [of New York] called me and said, 'Danny, you're in.'"[14] From the Appropriations Committee and its Agriculture Subcommittee, Akaka supported the causes of the sugar and pineapple industry, tourism, and environmental protection, issues that loomed large for his constituency. He also continued his advocacy for Native Hawaiians.

Akaka focused on that behind-the-scenes approach to legislating particularly through his seat on the House Appropriations Committee, where he coordinated with fellow Hawaiian Daniel Inouye on the Senate Appropriations Committee.

When Senator Spark Matsunaga died in 1990, Governor John Waihee III appointed Representative Akaka to finish out Matsunaga's unexpired term. Akaka delayed taking the Senate oath of office in order to ensure House passage of funding for various projects relevant to Hawaii, using his seat on the powerful Appropriations Committee. It was unlikely he would be in the same position to influence legislation upon entering the Senate.[15]

Akaka's appointment officially began on May 16, 1990, but he still had to weather a special election in November to fill the remaining four years of Matsunaga's term. His fellow Representative from Hawaii, moderate Republican Patricia Saiki, declared her candidacy to challenge Akaka, and polls placed them in a dead heat. Saiki entered the race with the full backing of the George H. W. Bush presidential administration. With the potential to retake the Senate in 1990, Republicans made the contest a top priority. Akaka waved off the President's endorsement of his opponent, "I know what I'm up against: the White House. I don't think they know what they're up against."[16]

Saiki, with support from the national party, led Akaka in the polls as late as October. While the campaign between the two former teachers remained largely polite and, therefore, true to Hawaiian "Aloha" values, Akaka hit hard on his early Senate service, particularly his work for the sugar industry as well as his party bona fides, in an overwhelmingly Democratic state. "If it were not for the Democrats and the Democratic majority in Congress, Hawaii would suffer," Akaka claimed.[17] In his tightest race since 1976, Akaka won with 54 percent of the vote, surpassing media expectations.[18] Surprisingly, he drew large Japanese-American support despite Representative Saiki's prominent position within that influential Hawaiian community.

Akaka made an immediate impression in the Senate by passing an amendment in the Energy and Natural Resources Committee to rename a scientific research bill in honor of the late Senator Matsunaga, who had authored it. In July Akaka led the effort to defeat New Jersey Senator Bill Bradley's proposal to lower sugar price supports. Bradley's amendment to the annual farm bill would lower price supports for sugar by 2 cents a pound. Bradley denounced the support as "the S&L of the farm program," a reference to the bankrupt savings and loan industry.[19] Akaka built a bipartisan coalition to defeat the measure, and his motion to table Bradley's amendment passed 54 to 44 on July 24, 1990. After his success, Akaka proudly said of his maneuver against Bradley, a former basketball star, "I'm only 5-feet-7, but I slam-dunked him." He touted his triumph as proof of his legislative effectiveness in the 1990 special election.[20]

Akaka was initially appointed to three committees in the 101st Congress (1989–1991): Energy and Natural Resources; Veterans' Affairs; and Governmental Affairs.[21] He served on the latter two committees throughout his tenure in the Senate. His reputation as an ally of federal employees grew out of his position on the Governmental Affairs Committee, renamed the Committee on Homeland Security and Governmental Affairs in 2005 in response to the executive reorganization in the wake of the September 11, 2001, attacks. He chaired the Federal Workforce Subcommittee and regularly reached across the aisle on behalf of federal employees alongside Senators George Voinovich of Ohio and Susan Collins of Maine, both Republicans. Akaka often referred to Voinovich as a "brother," and he engineered whistleblower protection legislation with Senator Collins.

Akaka was the primary sponsor on the Whistleblower Protection Enhancement Act of 2012, which passed the Senate by unanimous consent. Federal worker groups credit him for streamlining the federal hiring process, encouraging telework options, and shepherding to passage the Non-Foreign Area Retirement Equity Assurance Act of 2009, which shifted federal employees in Hawaii, Alaska, and U.S. territories from broad nonforeign cost-of-living adjustments to fairer locality pay levels. The president of the Partnership for Public Service lauded Akaka, "He's not flashy, but he is immensely substantive."[22]

Akaka served on the Banking, Housing, and Urban Affairs Committee during the 107th Congress (2001–2003) and again during his final term from 2007 through 2013. Akaka helped to develop the Dodd–Frank Wall Street Reform and Consumer Protection Act in 2010, authoring the section of the bill establishing the Office of Financial Education in the Consumer Financial Protection Bureau and creating grant programs for consumer education.

Akaka attempted to offer alternatives to predatory financial products like high-interest payday loans. Long an advocate of financial literacy and education, Akaka also sponsored the Excellence in Economic Education Act (S. 1487) in the 106th Congress (1999–2001), which provided federal funding for teacher training and school activities for economic education. Much of his bill passed as part of the No Child Left Behind Act in 2002.

Akaka also sponsored the Credit Card Minimum Payment Warning Act, much of which found its way into the Credit Card Accountability Responsibility and Disclosure Act of 2009. The relevant portions necessitated a box, referred to by his colleagues as the "Akaka Box," on credit card statements that simply displayed the minimum payments required to pay an outstanding balance within 36 months.[23]

As a member of the Senate Veterans' Affairs Committee (1990–2013), Akaka helped to expand federal support for veterans and honor their service with education benefits and medal awards. In 1996 he launched a review of World War II records which led to more than 30 medals being distributed in 2000 to retroactively honor the service of Asian-American soldiers, including Senator Inouye. As chairman of the committee (2007–2011), Akaka pushed the panel to authorize the largest increase ever in funding for the Veterans Administration in 2007. Akaka collaborated with Virginia Senator Jim Webb to rework the GI Bill for veterans of the wars in Iraq and Afghanistan. Akaka and Inouye also provided compensation for Filipino veterans who fought under the U.S. flag in World War II. After many different iterations of the Filipino veterans' bill, the pair finally secured funding in the 2009 stimulus bill through a combined effort, using their positions on the Veterans' Affairs and Appropriations Committees.[24]

Despite having a hand in major pieces of legislation, much of Akaka's work happened behind the scenes to support his state and fellow Asian Americans. "You don't see him introducing legislation or much important legislation," a political observer once noted. "He rarely speaks on the floor. He might be effectively talking one on one with other senators, but no one would see that."[25] Akaka arranged for a Federal Emergency Management Agency office to be located in Hawaii in 1993 following Hurricane Iniki.[26] He maintained an interest in the protection of the natural Hawaiian environment, and he lobbied for the creation of new national parks. Akaka also supported prohibiting the use of U.S. territories in the Pacific as nuclear waste disposal sites, safeguards against introduction of alien species to Hawaii, and the foundation of the Spark M. Matsunaga Renewable Energy and Ocean Technology Center at Keahole Point.[27]

With his Senate appointment in 1990, Akaka became the first Native Hawaiian to serve in that body. Throughout his Senate career, Akaka devoted considerable effort to representing Asian Americans broadly and Native Hawaiians specifically. Akaka helped found the Asian Pacific American Caucus in 1994 and briefly served as its secretary. In 1997 Akaka delivered a stirring condemnation of anti-Asian prejudice on the Senate Floor, specifically denouncing the belittling of Asian-American contributions to the political process in the wake of fundraising scandals featuring Asian-American businessmen and politicians.[28]

In 1993 Akaka secured congressional and presidential apologies for the U.S.-backed 1893 overthrow of the Hawaiian monarchy. Senators Akaka and Inouye both lamented the nature of the kingdom's toppling as a cultural loss. After little debate, the resolution (S.J. Res. 19) passed 65 to 34.[29] Akaka introduced the Senate version (S. 1763) of the Stand Against Violence and Empower Native Women Act in 2011, which was folded into the Violence Against Women Act in 2013, extending protections to Native-American and Native-Hawaiian women.[30]

His signature legislation grew out of his support for Native Hawaiians. Serving on the Permanent Select Committee on Indian Affairs, Akaka threw his weight behind indigenous Hawaiians following a 2000 Supreme Court ruling that struck down a Hawaiian practice in which state officials responsible for dispensing aid to Native Hawaiians were elected by Native Hawaiians. The Court deemed unconstitutional the racial basis for determining these voters. Less than six months later, Senator Akaka and Hawaii Representative Neil Abercrombie first introduced the Native Hawaiian Government Reorganization Act, which became known over time as the "Akaka Bill." The bill reconstituted the Kingdom of Hawaii as a Native-Hawaiian tribal unit similar to other Native-American tribes in the United States, allowing for "government-to-government" interactions and other privileges extended to Native-American tribes.[31]

Proponents of the original legislation argued that Native Hawaiians faced discrimination and loss of opportunity because they lacked the long history of treaties that tribes on the mainland had made with the federal government.[32] Hawaiian Representative Mazie K. Hirono pointed out in 2007 that indigenous Hawaiians, while having no treaties with the federal government, did have a long history of federal statutes providing unique protections for them as a group. In essence, she argued, the bill would be an extension of current federal policy since the United States already treated Native Hawaiians as an indigenous group.[33] Opponents claimed the bill could lead to "an impermissible racial preference in the establishment and operation of a government entity" and likened it to "the ethnic Balkanization of the country."[34]

A specific grievance levied against the Akaka bill noted that, unlike other native tribes, Native Hawaiians tended not to live together in one community continuously, but would be accounted for essentially by race, according to this legislation.[35] Akaka himself said in the 2009 hearing on the bill that the legislation was merely intended to provide parity, to grant only the same privileges to Native Hawaiians already provided to other native tribes.[36]

Senator John Ensign of Nevada feared that the bill would lead to legal gambling on Native-Hawaiian land and repeatedly placed holds on it. In response, Akaka led the Hawaiian delegation in inserting a provision into the bill that prevented any new Native-Hawaiian government from authorizing gambling.[37] Akaka gathered support from an overwhelming majority of Democrats and several Republicans, including allies in Alaska and Republican Governor Linda Lingle of Hawaii. However, President George W. Bush promised to veto the bill. As a result, it languished in Senate committees.

The original bill passed the House in 2000 and 2007, but never made it to a vote on the Senate Floor. Akaka reintroduced the bill each Congress following the 107th Congress. It briefly gained some traction during the 2008 presidential campaign. Then Senator Barack Obama, who was born in Hawaii, spent much of his youth there, and attended high school in Honolulu, vowed to sign the Akaka bill, if elected. Akaka grew more optimistic about the measure's prospects after the 2008 elections increased the Democratic majority in the Senate and ushered Obama into the presidency.[38]

After the bill stagnated under anonymous holds in the Senate for much of the 111th Congress (2009–2011), the Department of Justice requested revisions in 2010. Governor Lingle rejected those revisions and withdrew her support from the bill, which shrank Republican support in the Senate.[39] Unable to overcome Republican opposition, Akaka's efforts sputtered at the close of the 111th Congress. He reintroduced the bill in the 112th Congress (2011–2013), but had no real expectations of passage.

During the struggles to reconcile the bill in 2010, Akaka said of the legislation, "Over the last 10 years we have held hearings, considered various versions of the bill, and marked it up in both chambers. We believe we have a bill that is constitutionally viable, and a bill that can be supported by all."[40] Akaka continued to support the effort through his waning days in the Senate. After his colleague Daniel Inouye died on December 17, 2012, Akaka again pushed in vain for passage of the bill in honor of his late friend, who had been a major proponent of the legislation.[41]

Akaka's quiet, but constant, service in the Senate guaranteed him wide margins in his first two re-election campaigns; he carried more than 70 percent of the vote in both 1994 and 2000.[42] In 2006, however, he faced his only

real electoral test since his 1990 special election. Voicing concerns about the age of Hawaii's two Senators, who were both more than 80 years old at the time, Representative Ed Case challenged Senator Akaka in the Democratic primary. "We have to think how we will move on, we want to have control how we move forward," Case said in his announcement, setting himself up as the vanguard of Hawaii's next generation of leaders. He also claimed a more moderate voting record than Akaka.

The rest of Hawaii's Democrats were unprepared for the announcement, and Inouye immediately requested that Case withdraw.[43] Both the Hawaii and national Democratic establishment shut Case out, but he attracted the support of national business leaders. Despite raising roughly three times more in campaign donations than Case, Akaka felt threatened, as polls showed a surprisingly tight race. He spent the entire month leading up to the primary campaigning in Hawaii and focusing on Case's assertion that he would have voted for the 2002 authorization of force against Iraq, which Akaka had voted against.[44] Akaka survived the primary, garnering 55 percent of the vote. Republicans expected Akaka to be weakened heading into the general election, but Akaka handily defeated opponent Cynthia Thielen in November with 61 percent of the vote.

After the intense primary in 2006, Akaka decided not to run for re-election in 2012. He retired from Congress at the age of 88 and now resides in Pauoa Valley in Honolulu, Hawaii.

MANUSCRIPT COLLECTIONS

Library of Congress, Asian Division (Washington, DC). *Oral History*: 2003–2011, 8 linear feet. The collection contains videocassettes, DVDs, photographs, and documents related to an oral history project conducted by the United States Capitol Historical Society to document the service of Asian Americans in Congress. Daniel Akaka is included among the interviewees.

University of Hawaii at Manoa Library, **Archives and Manuscripts Department, Hawaii Congressional Papers Collection** (Honolulu, HI). *Papers*: 1997–2012, 560 linear feet. The collection reflects Daniel Akaka's service in Congress and includes bill files, subject files, committee materials, staff files, memorabilia, administrative files, and audiovisual materials. The collection is closed.

NOTES

1　Helen Zia and Susan B. Gall, eds., *Asian American Biography*, vol. 1 (New York: UXL, 2003): 1; *Politics in America, 1992* (Washington, DC: Congressional Quarterly Press, 1991): 391.

2　Rosemarie Bernardo, "Lawmaker Courts Supporters With a Gentle, Personal Touch," 18 September 2006, *Honolulu Star-Bulletin*, http://archives.starbulletin.com/2006/09/18/news/story01.html (accessed 26 August 2015).

3　*Congressional Record*, Senate, 105th Cong., 1st sess. (21 October 1997): S10867–S10869.

4　Don T. Nakanishi and Ellen D. Wu, eds., "Daniel K. Akaka," in *Distinguished Asian American Political and Governmental Leaders*, (Westport, CT: Greenwood Press, 2002): 5–8.

5　Bernardo, "Lawmaker Courts Supporters With a Gentle, Personal Touch."

6　Pete Pichaske, "Akaka Eager to Serve 5th Term," 11 October 1999, *Honolulu Star-Bulletin*, http://archives.starbulletin. com/1999/10/11/news/story4.html (accessed 4 March 2016).

7　Lynda Arakawa, "Ethnicity a Factor in Election," 7 April 2002, *Honolulu Advertiser*, http://the.honoluluadvertiser.com/article/2002/Apr/07/ln/ln11a.html (accessed 14 September 2015).

8　Tom Coffman, *The Island Edge of America: A Political History of Hawai'i* (Honolulu: University of Hawai'i Press, 2003): 296–298.

9　Office of the Clerk, U.S. House of Representatives, "Election Statistics, 1920 to Present," http://history.house.gov/Institution/Election-Statistics/Election-Statistics/.

10　*Politics in America, 1992*: 391.

11　As quoted in Maralee Schwartz, "Rep. Akaka Named to Fill Senate Seat From Hawaii," 29 April 1990, *Washington Post*: A4.

12　For a full listing of Akaka's committee assignments in the House of Representatives, see Garrison Nelson, *Committees in the U.S. Congress, 1947–1992*, vol. 2 (Washington, DC: CQ Press, 1994): 10–11.

13　Office of the Clerk, U.S. House of Representatives, "Election Statistics, 1920 to Present."

14　Daniel Akaka, oral history interview by Ronald Sarasin, 16 March 2007, transcript, United States Capitol Historical Society, Washington, DC: 3–4, http://uschs.org/educate/documents-images-and-recordings/ (accessed 28 September 2017).

15　*Politics in America, 1992*: 391.

16　Karen Foerstel, "Sen. Akaka Sworn In To Serve Six Months," 17 May 1990, *Roll Call*: 14.

17　Michel McQueen, "Akaka and Saiki Fight for Hawaii Senate Seat with Some Hula Hoopla but Little Mudslinging," 1 October 1990, *Wall Street Journal*: A16.

18 Office of the Clerk, U.S. House of Representatives, "Election Statistics, 1920 to Present."

19 "House, Senate Vote Against Cut in Sugar Support Price," 25 July 1990, *San Antonio Express-News*: E2.

20 Zia and Gall, eds., *Asian American Biography*: 2–3; *Politics in America, 1992*: 391.

21 For a full listing of Akaka's committee assignments in the Senate, see Garrison Nelson, *Committees in the U.S. Congress, 1947–1992*, vol. 2: 10–11; Garrison Nelson and Charles Stewart III, *Committees in the U.S. Congress, 1993–2010* (Washington, DC: CQ Press, 2011): 560–561.

22 Joe Davidson, "Feds Lose a Friend as Akaka Leaves Senate," 29 November 2012, *Washington Post*, https://www.washingtonpost.com/local/feds-lose-a-friend-as-akaka-leaves-senate/2012/11/29/e85e5ada-3a5b-11e2-8a97-363b0f9a0ab3_story.html (accessed 5 December 2012).

23 *Politics in America, 2010* (Washington, DC: CQ-Roll Call, 2009): 305–306; *Congressional Record*, Senate, 112th Cong., 2nd sess. (28 December 2012): S8498–8499; Joint Committee on Printing, *Daniel Akaka: U.S. Senator from Hawaii Tributes in the Congress of the United States*, 113th Cong., 2nd sess., S. Doc. 3 (2014): vii.

24 *Politics in America, 2010*: 305–306; "Akaka to Renew Fight for Filvets," 17 October 2008, *Filipino Reporter*: 1, 12, 28.

25 Bernardo, "Lawmaker Courts Supporters With a Gentle, Personal Touch."

26 "FEMA to Keep Honolulu Office," 15 June 2005, *Pacific Business News*, http://www.bizjournals.com/pacific/stories/2005/06/13/daily23.html (accessed 18 January 2016).

27 *Politics in America, 2010*: 305–306; Joint Committee on Printing, *Daniel Akaka: U.S. Senator from Hawaii Tributes in the Congress of the United States*.

28 Albert Eisele, "Sen. Akaka's Defense of Asian-Americans," 26 March 1997, *The Hill*: n.p.

29 *Congressional Record*, Senate, 103rd Cong., 1st sess. (27 October 1993): 26423–26429.

30 *Politics in America, 2010*: 305–306; Senate Committee on Indian Affairs, "Senator Daniel K. Akaka Introduces Bill To Protect Native Women Against Domestic Violence And Sexual Assault," press release, 31 October 2011, http://indianlaw.org/safewomen/save-native-women-act-introduced (accessed 29 September 2015).

31 "The Hawaii Decision," 25 February 2000, *Washington Post*: A22.

32 Scott Charton, "Native Hawaiians Push for Status as Indigenous People," 25 August 2000, *Northwest Asian Weekly*: 1.

33 *Congressional Record*, House, 110th Cong., 1st sess. (17 January 2007): E135.

34 "The Akaka State?," 2 June 2006, *Wall Street Journal*: A18.

35 "Aloha, Segregation," 17 December 2009, *Wall Street Journal*: A26.

36 Hearings before the Senate Committee on Indian Affairs, *Native Hawaiian Government Reorganization Act*, 111th Cong., 1st sess. (2009): 3–4.

37 Derrick DePledge, "GOP Senators Quietly Muscle in Against Akaka Bill," 21 July 2005, *Honolulu Advertiser*, http://the.honoluluadvertiser.com/article/2005/Jul/21/ln/507210342.html (accessed 20 January 2016); John Yaukey, "2007 Akaka Bill Gets Reintroduced," 8 May 2009, *Honolulu Advertiser*: B2.

38 B. J. Reyes, "Obama Would Sign Akaka Bill as President," 22 January 2008, *Honolulu Star-Bulletin*, http://archives.starbulletin.com/2008/01/22/news/story05.html (accessed 23 September 2015); Dennis Camire, "Odds for Akaka Bill's Passage Better Than Ever," 8 December 2008, *Honolulu Advertiser*: A1.

39 Richard Borreca, "There's Still Some Life Left in Akaka Bill," 21 November 2010, *Honolulu Star-Advertiser*: n.p.

40 Daniel Akaka, "Hawaii Delegation Agrees on Final Text of Native Hawaiian Government Reorganization Act," press release, 22 February 2010, https://votesmart.org/public-statement/485944/hawaii-delegation-agrees-on-final-text-of-native-hawaiian-government-reorganization-act#.WHj4lVMrKUk (accessed 23 September 2015).

41 Daniel Akaka, "Akaka Calls for Passage of Native Hawaiian Government Reorganization Act in Honor of Senator Inouye," press release, Senate Committee on Indian Affairs, 21 December 2012, http://www.indian.senate.gov/news/press-release/akaka-calls-passage-native-hawaiian-government-reorganization-act-honor-senator (accessed 25 August 2015).

42 Office of the Clerk, U.S. House of Representatives, "Election Statistics, 1920 to Present."

43 Richard Borreca, "Case to Oppose Akaka," 20 January 2006, *Honolulu Star-Bulletin*, http://archives.starbulletin.com/2006/01/20/news/story01.html (accessed 20 January 2016).

44 Nicole Duran, "Where Would You Rather Be?," 13 September 2006, *Roll Call*: 11.

Robert T. Matsui

1941–2005

U.S. REPRESENTATIVE 1979–2005
DEMOCRAT FROM CALIFORNIA

Robert T. Matsui served in the House from 1979 to 2005, but his earliest memories were of an internment camp where his family was separated and where they lived like prisoners, denied their most basic constitutional rights. That experience was formative for Matsui. "Adversity made [Matsui] stronger, and along the way he helped countless others to find strength as well," noted an observer who reflected on Matsui's long political career.[1] A social liberal with a pro-market approach to trade, Matsui's workhorse style of legislating earned the respect of his colleagues on both sides of the aisle during his 26 years in the House.

Robert Takeo (Bob) Matsui was born on September 17, 1941, in Sacramento, California, to Yasuji and Alice Matsui, less than three months before Japan's surprise attack on Pearl Harbor.[2] Both his parents were born in Sacramento. Following the U.S. declaration of war against Japan, six-month-old Robert Matsui and his family were evacuated from their hometown to an internment camp in April 1942 as part of the relocation of Japanese Americans from the Pacific Coast.[3] Becoming family number 25261, the Matsui family initially was sent to the Tule Lake camp in Newell, California—a remote location in the extreme northeast corner of the state. Alice and Robert Matsui were moved to a camp in Caldwell, Idaho, while Yasuji was separated from his family and sent to a Weiser, Idaho, work camp. Alice Matsui gave birth to Robert's sister, Barbara, at the Caldwell facility.[4] Eventually, the Matsui family reunited and returned to Sacramento following their release three years later. Like most internees whose livelihoods were shattered, the Matsui's lost their family produce business in Sacramento during internment. After the war, they had to rebuild their lives.

Robert attended William Land Elementary School, California Junior High, and later graduated from

C. K. McClatchy High School in Sacramento, California, in 1959. In 1963 he graduated from the University of California, Berkeley, with a degree in political science. At Berkeley, he met Doris Okada, another wartime internee who was born at an internment camp in Poston, Arizona.[5] In 1966 Matsui received his JD from the University of California, Hastings College of the Law, in San Francisco and practiced as a lawyer in Sacramento. Robert and Doris married in 1968 and had one son, Brian.

As a young man studying at Berkeley in 1961, Matsui was motivated by the words of President John F. Kennedy's inaugural address to enter into public service. Matsui felt inspired to "look beyond ourselves, and look to our community, our state, and our nation to see how we can improve the lot of every American."[6] At the age of 29, Matsui, a lawyer in a private practice, was encouraged to run for the Sacramento city council in 1971.[7] Reflecting on this first election, Matsui said, "For historical purposes, I think it's good to say people were coming to me, asking me to run, but the reality is that that's not the way these things happen. You have to want it."[8] This election marked the first time the city council was divided into districts. Matsui ran a grassroots campaign and won, earning the distinction as the first Japanese American to hold this position.[9] He served until 1978, and his time on the council included a year as vice mayor of Sacramento in 1977.

Matsui also worked as the campaign manager for U.S. Representative John Moss's 1972, 1974, and 1976 re-election contests.[10] After 13 terms in the House, Moss announced his retirement at the end of the 95th Congress (1977–1979) and suggested that Matsui run for the open seat.[11] He seemed a natural fit. Like Moss, he was a liberal with a pro-business approach.[12] Matsui won a tight, five-way Democratic primary for the urban district, which encompassed the California state capital. In the general

election for the 96th Congress (1979–1981), Republican Sandy Smoley ran a competitive race against Matsui in the largely Democratic district. Speaker of the House Thomas P. (Tip) O'Neill of Massachusetts and President Jimmy Carter both stumped for Matsui, who struggled with name recognition in the campaign.[13] Ultimately, Matsui prevailed by a margin of 13,000 votes, winning 53 percent of the total.[14] "I think there [are] only a few times in a person's life that they have an opportunity to do something very important and this is my opportunity," he told a reporter after the election. "It might be frustrating, at the same time I can do it."[15] He won each of the next 12 general election campaigns by wide margins, and despite weighing a U.S. Senate run in 1990, remained in the House for the duration of his political career.

As a House freshman, Matsui initially was assigned to the Government Operations and Judiciary Committees. One year later, he left Judiciary and won a seat on the influential Interstate and Commerce Committee (later named Energy and Commerce), an assignment previously held by his predecessor John Moss.[16] As a sophomore in the 97th Congress (1981–1983), Matsui left his other committee assignments for a post on the exclusive Ways and Means Committee and a spot on the Select Committee on Narcotics. In the 100th Congress (1987–1989), Matsui left Narcotics, and in the 102nd Congress (1991–1993), he joined the Budget Committee.

It was with the assistance of the California delegation and House leadership that Matsui received the coveted Ways and Means seat.[17] When he became the first Asian-American Member to serve on that panel, Dan Rostenkowski of Illinois, the committee's autocratic chairman, commented that Matsui was philosophically "a pretty good package."[18] In 1993 Matsui became interim chair of the Ways and Means Subcommittee on Human Resources, succeeding Harold Ford Sr. of Tennessee.[19] A year later, Matsui was tapped again to serve as an interim chair, this time on the Ways and Means Subcommittee on Trade when Sam Gibbons of Florida moved up to chair the full committee. "The trade subcommittee has a number of important issues to address this year, and it will take a

concerted effort by our members to meet the challenges ahead of us," Matsui said. "I have the utmost confidence in our committee's ability to meet those challenges."[20] Matsui later left the Subcommittee on Trade and moved to the Subcommittee on Social Security.

On the Ways and Means Committee for most of his congressional career, Matsui used his knowledge of the tax code and the memory of his family's experience with internment to help further social change and to look out for the needs of the most vulnerable Americans. In 1985 Ways and Means took center stage as the Ronald Reagan administration pushed a plan to overhaul the tax code. With Matsui's assistance, Chairman Rostenkowski managed to push through the politically difficult bill (H.R. 3838). The legislation—eventually signed into law as the Tax Reform Act of 1986—reduced the number of tax brackets, altered corporate tax rates, streamlined deductions, and increased personal tax exemptions.[21] In an op-ed, Matsui argued that the bill, "is fairer and better than the current tax code." He added, "It may not be perfect," but "a whole lot more low- and middle-income Americans will be enjoying more of the fruits of their own labor."[22]

Matsui also used his seat on the Ways and Means Committee to push for social equality. "If you think about welfare reform, if you think about the immigrant-bashing, if you think about Medicare/Medicaid cuts, essentially they're going after the powerless groups that have no constituency that is vocal, that votes, that are involved in the political process," he once observed.[23] Matsui challenged the William J. (Bill) Clinton administration to ensure that its welfare reform proposals did not place unrealistic burdens on the recipients of federal aid. During Ways and Means subcommittee testimony in the 103rd Congress, Matsui confronted officials from the Department of Health and Human Services, "Can you discuss this with me in a way that I will feel satisfied and comfortable that we can move forward and that these people will not be screwed?"[24] He railed against President George W. Bush's proposal to privatize Social Security, challenging the administration to produce a solid plan. "If the president and leaders of his party are serious about

Social Security reform, I urge them to come forward with a concrete legislative proposal," he said.[25]

In the House, Robert Matsui championed the cause of Japanese-American redress. Joined by fellow California Representative Norman Y. Mineta, who also spent part of his childhood in internment camps, Matsui fought for reparations. From the beginning, Matsui declared he would not accept any monetary compensation to keep detractors from accusing him of self-interest.[26] During testimony before the House Judiciary Subcommittee on Administrative Law and Governmental Affairs in 1983, Matsui mourned Japanese Americans' loss of constitutional rights.[27]

In the 99th Congress (1985–1987), Matsui and Mineta first introduced the Japanese American reparations bill, the Civil Liberties Act. It was assigned the symbolic number H.R. 442 to honor the Japanese-American 442nd Combat Team, one of the most decorated units of World War II (Senators Spark M. Matsunaga and Daniel K. Inouye of Hawaii served in the 442nd). Referred to the Judiciary Committee, the bill did not make it to the floor. But in the 100th Congress, Mineta and Matsui steered the Civil Liberties Act to House passage on September 17, 1987.[28] In an emotional House Floor speech, Matsui retold his family's heart-wrenching story of being uprooted from their home.[29] In the Senate, Spark Matsunaga introduced the legislation and led the effort to get the bill to the Senate Floor, where it passed with bipartisan support.[30] In August 1988, it won final passage and was signed into law by President Reagan. The Civil Liberties Act recognized the injustice of internment, issued a formal apology to internees, and provided each surviving internee a sum of $20,000 from the United States government.[31]

In the final year of the George H. W. Bush administration, the North American Free Trade Agreement (NAFTA) became a top issue before Congress. The controversial implementation legislation had become a focal point of the 1992 presidential election cycle and a divisive issue for Democrats.[32] Democrats in the House worried about their working-class base and the potential loss of jobs if companies moved to Mexico for cheaper labor. By the time NAFTA came up for consideration in

the House, a pro-NAFTA Democrat, Bill Clinton, was President. But the measure, H.R. 3450, was opposed by Democratic leadership, including Leader Richard Gephardt of Missouri and Whip David Bonior of Michigan. Unable to rely on his party's Whip operation, which was actively rallying support against the legislation, President Clinton turned to Matsui, a free trade proponent and an influential member on the Ways and Means Committee.[33] Without the formal Whip's office, Matsui led the Democratic House NAFTA Liaison Group.[34] He managed most of the floor debate in lieu of the bill's sponsor, Ways and Means Chairman Rostenkowski. Matsui also persuaded Republican colleagues to gather the necessary House votes, noting that "many of us as we began this process of NAFTA, just as you felt about us, had trepidations about whether each of us could trust each other.... Democrats and Republicans, feel that we have reached a new beginning with each other."[35] Led by Republican Whip Newt Gingrich of Georgia, most Republicans stood behind the trade agreement. With only 102 House Democrats supporting the bill, it passed, 234 to 200.[36] President Clinton signed the North American Free Trade Agreement into law on December 8, 1993.[37]

On the whole, Matsui supported free trade policies and stayed true to that interest throughout his congressional career. In 2000 he was called upon again by the Clinton administration to help gather the necessary votes to grant permanent normal trade relations with China (H.R. 4444).[38]

Initially hesitant to accept the job of rounding up the votes, Matsui was convinced by Commerce Secretary William Daley.[39] The China trade bill had two main hurdles to overcome to win support: its economic impact in America and China's human rights record. During debate, Matsui addressed the economic benefits and turned his attention to human rights. "Now, let me also talk about the issue of human rights. China's human rights record is terrible. We understand that. We, obviously, should put the focus on them, and we believe that the Levin–Bereuter bill, will, in fact, do that. But what is really interesting is that many of the Chinese dissidents that have the luxury of living in the United States are opposed to this. But those

that live in China, the Chinese Democracy Movement, they want us to pass this, because they want to engage the United States. They think if they gain economic power, they will be able to oppose the central government of China. So we need to vote yes on this legislation for the future of our country and certainly, for prosperity and peace throughout the world."[40]

Matsui's pragmatic approach to the idea that open trade would promote human rights allowed him to focus on the benefits while rounding up the necessary votes. The effort underscored his reputation as a legislative workhorse. "I enjoy trying to work through a strategy on how you get 218 votes," he said.[41] Matsui saw the open market with China as imperative. "I've always believed that technology and trade were the two engines that really drive economic growth," he observed. "If we want to continue to be the number one nation in the world when it comes to job creation, when it comes to leading the cutting edge, we have to understand that these things are important."[42] The trade relations bill passed the House 237 to 197 and was signed into law on October 10, 2000.

In December 2002, fellow Californian and Democratic Leader Nancy Pelosi tapped Matsui to chair the Democratic Congressional Campaign Committee (DCCC), which supports Democratic House candidates. Matsui was accustomed to fundraising for the party, having co-chaired the party's fundraising commission and serving as the party treasurer during the Clinton administration.[43] As the chair of the DCCC, Matsui assumed the position as the chief fundraiser. In making the announcement, Pelosi noted that Matsui's "legislative and political acumen," made him a natural choice.[44] Upon his selection, Matsui commented, "I think this gives me an opportunity to play a significant role in our efforts to take the House back." He added, "It's an added responsibility, there's no question, but it's one where I'll be able to play a leadership role in terms of the 2004 elections."[45]

But, following the 2004 election cycle, Matsui's health deteriorated. After a brief battle with pneumonia, complicated by a rare blood disease, the 63-year-old Congressman died on January 1, 2005, in Bethesda, Maryland, surrounded by his family. A private person, Matsui had not publicly disclosed his illness, so his sudden passing came as a shock to the congressional community, which held a special memorial service in the U.S. Capitol's Statuary Hall.

Attending the ceremony, former President Bill Clinton eulogized Matsui as embodying "everything that was right with America. And whether he was right on every issue or not, and whether every battle we fought together was the right position or not, he was the right sort of person."[46] Matsui's friend, political commentator Norm Ornstein, recalled the Californian's depth of knowledge on the issues and his equally deep commitment to his constituents. "Bob became a world-class expert on welfare and Social Security," Ornstein said "He was a policy wonk who loved politics, a gentle man who had a fierce attachment to his values and policy views, a partisan who wanted to work with those across the aisle, and a man who could use ferocious rhetoric to defend the downtrodden but who seemed to have no enemies, even among those he excoriated."[47] In his home state of California, Robert Matsui's body lay in state at the capitol in Sacramento. In March 2005, Doris Matsui succeeded her husband in a special election, winning the election with 68 percent to continue, as she put it, "Bob's work" in the House.[48]

MANUSCRIPT COLLECTION

University of California, Berkeley, Bancroft Library (Berkeley, CA). *Papers*: circa 1940–2006, 306.25 linear feet. The Robert T. Matsui papers primarily document his work in the U.S. House of Representatives. The collection includes correspondence, legislative addresses, campaign literature, press releases, schedules, and ephemera. It covers legislation and issues related to health care, Social Security, taxes, and welfare reform; the North American Free Trade Agreement and approval of the Uruguay Round Agreements; civil rights and Japanese-American internment redress; Sacramento regional water and flood control; and district military base closures. Matsui's office and press files, personal correspondence, campaign and political files, compose a significant part of the collection; some Sacramento city council materials also are included. The collection is restricted, but researchers may apply for access. A finding aid is available online.

NOTES

1 Deb Kollars and Will Evans, "Hundreds Say Last Goodbye to Congressman; Touching Tributes Flow As Colleagues, Family, Friends and Others Praise the Sacramento Native," 9 January 2005, *Sacramento Bee*: n.p.

2 Betty Cuniberti, "Internment: Personal Voices, Powerful Choices," 4 October 1987, *Los Angeles Times*: n.p.

3 William Eaton, "Internee Payment Bill Gets Final OK," 5 August 1988, *Los Angeles Times*: 1.

4 Cuniberti, "Internment: Personal Voices, Powerful Choices."

5 Ibid.

6 Robert T. Matsui, interview by Brian Lamb, *American Profile Series*, C-SPAN, 4 October 1988, http://www.c-span.org/video/?4551-1/ life-career-robert-matsui&start=1145 (accessed 13 January 2017).

7 "Matsui, Robert T.," *Current Biography Yearbook 1994* (New York: H.W. Wilson Company, 1994): 368.

8 Ibid.

9 Sam Stanton and Steve Gibson, "Council Win Was First of Many," 3 January 2005, *Sacramento Bee*: A10.

10 *Politics in America, 1990* (Washington, DC: Congressional Quarterly Inc., 1989): 102–103.

11 Stanton and Gibson, "Council Win Was First of Many."

12 *Almanac of American Politics, 1976* (Washington, DC: National Journal Inc., 1975): 56–58.

13 Martin Nolan, "O'Neill Lends Celebrity Status to Congressional Candidates," 21 October 1978, *Boston Globe*: 24; W. Dale Nelson, no title, 5 November 1978, Associated Press.

14 W. B. Rood, "3rd District Campaigners Spending Big," 21 October 1978, *Los Angeles Times*: A23; Office of the Clerk, U.S. House of Representatives, "Election Statistics, 1920 to Present," http:// history.house.gov/Institution/Election-Statistics/Election-Statistics/.

15 "Mr. Matsui Goes to Washington," archived video, 4:14, from NBC Nightly News on 4 February 1978, accessed 4 April 2016, http:// digital.lib.csus.edu/cdm/ref/collection/mats/id/195.

16 Garrison Nelson, *Committees in the U.S. Congress, 1947–1992*, vol. 2 (Washington, DC: Congressional Quarterly Press, 1994): 642–643.

17 Richard Lyons, "On Capitol Hill," 25 January 1979, *Washington Post*: A2; Martin Tolchin, "Congress Plays Party Games by Committee," 25 January 1981, *New York Times*: E5.

18 Tolchin, "Congress Plays Party Games by Committee."

19 Hearing before the House Committee on Ways and Means, Subcommittee on Human Resources, *Selected Aspects of Welfare Reform*, 103rd Cong., 1st sess., (30 March 1993); "Harold E. Ford, Sr.," *Biographical Directory of the U.S. Congress, 1774–Present*, http://bioguide.congress.gov/scripts/biodisplay.pl?index=F000261.

20 Gerard Lim, "Matsui Named Chair of Trade Subcommittee," 17 June 1994, *AsianWeek*: 3.

21 Tax Reform Act of 1986, H.R. 3838, 99th Cong. (1986); "House Approves Major Rewrite of Tax Code," *CQ Almanac, 1985*, 41st ed. (Washington, DC: Congressional Quarterly Inc., 1986): 480–498; Steven W. Stathis, *Landmark Legislation, 1774–2002: Major U.S. Acts and Treaties* (Washington, DC: Congressional Quarterly Press, 2003): 325.

22 *Congressional Record*, Extension of Remarks, 99th Cong., 1st sess. (16 December 1985): E5638.

23 Julie Ha, "Congressman Matsui Criticizes Proposed Medicare Cuts: GOP Plan an Assault on the Elderly," 31 October 1995, *Examiner*: 9.

24 Hearings before the House Committee on Ways and Means, Subcommittee on Human Resources, *Welfare Reform Proposals, Including H.R. 4605, the Work and Responsibility Act of 1994*, Part 1, 103rd Cong., 2nd sess. (26–28 July 1994): 342.

25 Robert Matsui, "What Can Congress Do To Stabilize the Future of Social Security?" 6 December 2004, *Roll Call*: n.p.

26 Hearings before the House Committee on the Judiciary, Subcommittee on Administrative Law and Governmental Relations, *Japanese-American and Aleutian Wartime Relocation*, 98th Cong., 2nd sess., (20–21, 27 June 1984 and 12 September 1984): 24.

27 *Japanese-American and Aleutian Wartime Relocation*: 24.

28 Civil Liberties Act of 1987, H.R. 442, 100th Cong. (1987).

29 *Congressional Record*, House, 100th Cong., 1st sess. (17 September 1987): 24304.

30 S.1009, 100th Cong. (1987).

31 Public Law 100-383, 102 Stat. 903 (1988).

32 "Congress OKs North American Trade Pact," *CQ Almanac, 1993*, 49th ed. (Washington, DC: Congressional Quarterly Inc., 1994): 172–176.

33 Kevin Merida, "The Whip Lashes Out," 10 November 1993, *Washington Post*: C1.

34 *Politics in America, 1998* (Washington, DC: Congressional Quarterly Inc., 1997): 100. House Republicans worked separately with their own NAFTA whip group. See "Congress OKs North American Trade Pact": 178.

35 *Congressional Record*, House, 103rd Cong., 1st sess. (17 November 1993): H29945.

36 "Congress OKs North American Trade Pact": 178.

37 North American Free Trade Agreement (NAFTA) Implementation Act, H.R. 3450, 103rd Cong. (1993).

38 *Politics in America, 2004* (Washington, DC: Congressional Quarterly Inc., 2003): 77; H.R. 4444, 106th Cong. (2000).

39 Ann Scott Tyson, "The Fine Art of Twisting Arms for China Trade," 19 May 2000, *Christian Science Monitor*: 1.

40 *Congressional Record*, House, 106th Congress, 2nd sess. (24 May 2000): H3671.

41 Matthew Vitta, "On Hill, Clinton Turns to Calif. Free-Trader; Matsui Has Key Role on China Legislation," 5 April 2000, *Washington Post*: A17.

42 Vitta, "On Hill, Clinton Turns to Calif. Free-Trader."

43 Paul Houston, "Matsui Named to Top Fund-Raising Post Politics: He and Rockefeller Will Head Democrats' Contribution Drive For 1992 Elections," 5 September 1991, *Los Angeles Times*: 20; Michael Doyle, "Matsui Takes Top Fund-Raising Role," 24 December 2002, *Sacramento Bee*: A1.

44 Doyle, "Matsui Takes Top Fund-Raising Role."

45 Ibid.

46 *Memorial Address and Other Tributes Held in the House of Representatives and the Senate of the United States Together With the Memorial Services in Honor of Robert T. Matsui*, 109th Cong., 1st sess. (Washington, DC: Government Printing Office, 2006): 14.

47 Norman Ornstein, "Bob Matsui: Wonk, Fighter, and All-Around Great Guy," 26 January 2005, *Roll Call*: n.p.

48 Kevin Yamamura and David Whitney, "Matsui's Widow Launches Campaign for Congress," 13 January 2005, *Sacramento Bee*: A3.

"KENNEDY ... REALLY ASKED US
TO LOOK BEYOND OURSELVES, AND
TO LOOK TO OUR COMMUNITY,
OUR STATE, AND OUR NATION TO
SEE HOW WE CAN IMPROVE THE
LOT OF EVERY AMERICAN."

Robert T. Matsui
C-SPAN, October 4, 1988

Fofó I. F. Sunia
1937–

DELEGATE 1981–1988
DEMOCRAT FROM AMERICAN SAMOA

As the first Delegate from American Samoa, Fofó I. F. Sunia spent most of his four terms in Congress trying to give voice to and to carve out a new role for his small, faraway constituency in the South Pacific. He quickly found it to be a constant process of having to educate his colleagues. "To be sitting amongst people who really didn't understand who you are or even why you're here—that struck me as a point of some frustration," Sunia observed. "I guess I was expecting a little bit too much. I thought that everybody was going to know that there was a representative from American Samoa come January and (would say), 'We've got to make way for him' and 'We know all about his territory.' That wasn't so."[1] While he advocated bringing American Samoans further into the political, economic, and military embrace of the mainland, he also was wary of protecting Samoan traditions and culture. Sunia's career collapsed, however, when he was implicated in a fraud scheme to enrich himself by paying ghost employees on his official payroll.

Fofó Iosefa Fiti Sunia was born on March 13, 1937, in Fagasa, Pago Pago, American Samoa. He was the eldest of eleven children of Fiti and Savali Sunia. His father, Fiti, was a minister and Sunia himself later served as a deacon and lay minister in the Christian Congregational Church of Samoa.[2] His brothers, Tauese and Ipulasi, later served as governor and lieutenant governor of American Samoa, respectively. Sunia graduated from Samoana High School in Pago Pago in 1955 before leaving Samoa for Honolulu, Hawaii, to earn his bachelor's degree in economics from the University of Hawaii. After graduating in 1960, he returned to Samoa, working as a translator and interpreter for the territorial governor. In the early 1960s, Sunia founded and edited the *Samoa News*.

Sunia's work for the territorial governor and as a journalist provided a segue into local politics. For much of the 1960s, he served as the territorial election commissioner (1962–1970). He also held a post as the first director of tourism for American Samoa from 1966 to 1972 and was president and chairman of the American Samoan Development Corporation from 1965 to 1971. In 1969 Sunia ran for and won a senate seat in the American Samoa legislature and served from 1970 to 1978. Sunia married Aioletuna V. (Ta'amū) Sunia in 1960, and together they raised eight children: Fiti, Melina, Iosefa, Vaaomala, Alexander, Cynthia, Lupe, and Fiafia.[3] In addition to serving in his church, Sunia also was a *matai*, or chief, of a Samoan clan. Fofó means "talking chief" in Samoan, and Sunia preferred that title to simply being called "chief."

In 1978 Congress extended territorial representation to American Samoa, providing for a Delegate to serve as the islands' representative on Capitol Hill. The territory, located in the Pacific, roughly between Hawaii and Australia, is made up of five islands and two atolls. Its total land area is comparable to the size of Washington, DC, but is more than 7,000 nautical miles away from the nation's capital. In 1980, in the first election for Delegate, Sunia ran as an independent and entered a three-way race for the seat. Although he led the field on election day, he did not secure a majority, carrying nearly 44 percent of the vote against 38 percent for another independent candidate, Eni Fa'aua'a Hunkin Jr., and 18 percent for Democratic candidate I. S. Mulitauaopele. Sunia faced Hunkin in the runoff on November 18, winning with 59 to 41 percent.[4] In the House, Sunia caucused with the Democrats, which controlled the majority. He coasted to re-election in his subsequent three general elections in which he ran as a Democratic candidate. He was unopposed in 1982 and won 65 and 56 percent of the vote against Aumeoualogo Salanoa Soli in 1984 and 1986, respectfully.[5]

When Sunia entered the House at the opening of the 97th Congress (1981–1983), he was assigned to the Merchant Marine and Fisheries Committee (where he served through the 98th Congress [1983–1985]) and the Public Works and Transportation Committee. He held the latter assignment for his entire House career, eventually rising to chair the Subcommittee on Public Buildings and grounds for the 100th Congress (1987–1989) in 1987. Sunia also picked up two additional committee assignments during his career: Interior and Insular Affairs (99th–100th Congresses [1985–1989]) and the Foreign Affairs Committee, during his final term. Like other Territorial Delegates, Sunia could vote in committee, introduce legislation, and hold committee leadership positions, but could not vote on the House Floor.

The *Washington Post* profiled Sunia in a 1982 article with the subtitle, "The Village Chief Brings a Touch of the South Seas." Described by a reporter as a relaxed, jovial, large man—some 300 pounds when he was sworn into office— Sunia emphasized that the easy-going Samoan life could have advantages in frenetic Washington. On Capitol Hill, "everybody's banging their heads against a wall and rushing around," Sunia said. "I figure the guy who walks slowly will stand out. If everybody's yelling, they're going to take notice of the guy that speaks softly."[6] But that low-key approach didn't necessarily translate into visibility right away. *The Almanac of American Politics* called Sunia "something of an unknown quantity" during his first term in Washington.[7]

Without the ability to vote on legislation on the House Floor, Sunia focused on the time-honored tradition of constituent service. He employed an intimate approach with his modest constituency of roughly 34,000 people— right down to writing personal replies to letters that arrived at his DC office. "Many of these people are friends," Sunia explained. "I'd feel guilty if I don't answer personally."[8]

Although his office was a daylong flight away from his home, Sunia decorated it in a fashion resembling "a microcosm of a Samoan village," an aide noted. "A woven mat of pandana leaves hangs on the wall, strewn with pink feathers and pearly shells. There are bowls of teak, conch shells, and bright patterns stenciled on pressed bark."[9]

That décor reflected Sunia's pride in his culture, but it also highlighted a tension between modern notions of progress and the Samoan emphasis on tradition and family. He was quick to point out, for instance, that American Samoa did not fund island-wide welfare programs, it had declined to participate in federal aid initiatives, and it had refused to accept food stamps. "We felt they were really not in line with the ways of our customs and culture," Sunia explained. "While it's always nice to have money, it really would not be helpful in a much larger sense. The very fiber of the place is family units, and families tend to help their own and to help each other. When you start having this almost total dependence on someone else you're going to lose that."[10] Nevertheless, he didn't hesitate to embrace some measure of federal assistance for his largely poor constituency when he supported the Hunger Relief Act of 1984, which covered the states and U.S. territories. "America and its territories promote freedom, equality, and opportunity, and I believe that no American should experience hunger in this land of plenty," Sunia said.[11]

In the long tradition of Delegates for the territories, Sunia spent much of his legislative activity testifying before House and Senate committees, including the House Committee on Interior and Insular Affairs and the Senate Committee on Energy and Natural Resources. One of his principal concerns was that Congress retain sole discretion over amending the American Samoa constitution, rather than delegating the power to the Secretary of the Interior. Sunia believed that as the only unorganized and unincorporated territory in the United States, American Samoa needed its status to be directly addressed by Congress: "A people's constitution, its basic governing document, cannot be placed at the mercy of one man. By giving itself the authority to act on any and all changes, Congress made certain that the Secretary of the Interior did not have unilateral authority to change the American Samoa Constitution and that the territorial government was allowed to develop in an orderly, democratic fashion."[12] At stake in that debate were issues pertaining to traditional Samoan land rights and titles that the Interior Department sought to open to federal court review.[13]

In four Congresses, Sunia introduced just 13 bills, all of which dealt with American Samoa. All died in committee, with just one bill (H.R. 3555, which amended a "joint resolution to provide for accepting, ratifying, and confirming the cession of certain islands of the Samoan group to the United States") receiving even a subcommittee hearing. His floor speeches addressed issues touching on education, unemployment and job creation, protecting American Samoa's tuna fishing and canning industry, infrastructure improvements, and regional security issues in the Pacific islands during the late stages of the Cold War. Among the bills that Sunia authored were measures to amend the National Housing Act to extend loan mortgage insurance programs to American Samoa, to give the Samoan Delegate the right to make appointments to the U.S. service academies, to establish a National Guard in American Samoa, to amend the Social Security Act to create a Medicaid program in Samoa, to exempt Samoan U.S. nationals from having to meet the language requirements for citizenship, and to authorize the American Samoa legislature to draft a constitution for the local self-government of the people of American Samoa.[14] Sunia managed only a handful of cosponsors for these bills; some received none at all.

Without the power to vote, Sunia's legislative accomplishments were often minor. He claimed credit for convincing Congress to permit the duty-free transportation of fish products in the Pacific territories and worked to maintain import fees on tuna shipped to the United States from the Caribbean. Sunia felt that American Samoa's tuna fishing and packing industry, its only major job sector, would risk an "economic disaster" if it faced additional competition. Sunia also pushed for a provision allowing American Samoans to enter into the U.S. Merchant Marine.[15]

Sunia's career imploded during his fourth term in Congress because of a scandal arising from the improper use of his official allowance. He was charged with using tens of thousands of dollars of federal funds to hire employees who did not exist and then distributing the money to the personal account of his principal aide,

Matthew Iuli, and to his own election campaign account.[16] Sunia insisted that he had been unaware of the scheme when Iuli hatched it in 1983.[17] In October 1987, the House Ethics Committee began an inquiry into the allegations.[18] After pleading guilty to a charge of conspiracy to defraud the government, Sunia resigned his seat on September 6, 1988.[19] A month later, Sunia was sentenced to five to 15 months in prison, "for conspiring … to defraud the government of $130,920 through false payroll claims."[20] At his sentencing, Sunia admitted, "I have come to understand the meaning of shame, fear. I have made apologies to my people and I hope they will forgive me."[21] Sunia eventually returned to Pago Pago, where he still resides.

NOTES:

1 Ted Gup, "Samoan Adjusts to Washington," 20 August 1982, *Los Angeles Times*: D5.

2 Ted Gup, "American Samoa's Man in Congress: The Village Chief Brings a Touch of the South Seas," 26 April 1982, *Washington Post*: C1. The 1940 Census records do not provide information on the Sunias. However, several sources list parent and sibling names. See, for example, http://politicalgraveyard.com/families/18853.html (accessed 6 April 2016).

3 *Congressional Directory*, 100th Cong. (Washington, DC: Government Printing Office, 1987): 229.

4 Office of the Clerk, U.S. House of Representatives, "Election Statistics, 1920 to Present," http://history.house.gov/Institution/Election-Statistics/Election-Statistics/.

5 Ibid.

6 Gup, "American Samoa's Man in Congress."

7 *Almanac of American Politics, 1982* (Washington, DC: National Journal Inc., 1981): 1213.

8 Philip Shenon, "In the House, But Without Votes," 12 April 1985, *New York Times*: A14.

9 Gup, "Samoan Adjusts to Washington."

10 Gup, "American Samoa's Man in Congress."

11 *Congressional Record*, House, 98th Cong., 2nd sess. (27 July 1984): 21450–21451.

12 Hearing before the Senate Committee on Energy and Natural Resources, Subcommittee on Energy Conservation and Supply, *Revised Constitution of American Samoa*, 98th Cong., 2nd sess. (8 May 1984): 2–7. See also *Congressional Record*, House, 97th Cong., 2nd sess. (20 May 1982): 10824.

13 Hearings before the House Committee on Interior and Insular Affairs, *Office of Territorial and International Affairs, Department of Interior*, 97th Cong., 1st sess. (15 December 1981): especially 19–22, for an exchange between Sunia and Won Pat.

14 *Congressional Record*, House, 97th Cong., 1st sess. (18 November 1981): 27983; *Congressional Record*, House, 97th Cong., 2nd sess. (10 February 1982): 1401; *Congressional Record*, House, 97th Cong., 2nd sess. (23 February 1982): 2011; *Congressional Record*, House, 97th Cong., 2nd sess. (25 February 1982): 2435.

15 *Almanac of American Politics, 1986* (Washington, DC: National Journal Inc., 1985): 1491; *Congressional Record*, House, 97th Cong., 2nd sess. (13 December 1982): 30245. Sunia had just assumed the chairmanship of the Public Works and Transportation Subcommittee on Public Buildings and Grounds when he ran into ethics problems. Much of the committee's work was conducted after he resigned his seat. A resume of the subcommittee activities is available in House Committee on Public Works and Transportation, *Summary of Legislative Activities, 100th Congress*, 100th Cong., 2nd sess., H. Rept. 1121 (30 December 1988): 59–61.

16 "Samoan Delegate Accused of Fraud," 1 August 1988, *New York Times*: B5. See also "Samoa's House Delegate Accused of Payroll Fraud; $70,000 Allegedly Paid to Ghost Employees," 15 August 1987, *Washington Post*: A3.

17 "Samoan Delegate Enters Plea," 5 August 1988, *New York Times*: A10.

18 Jim Drinkard, "Panel Votes to Begin Preliminary Inquiry Involving Delegate from American Samoa," 28 October 1987, Associated Press.

19 "House Delegate from Samoa Resigns After Guilty Plea," 7 September 1988, *Chicago Tribune*: 4; "House Schedules Disciplinary Hearings Against Sunia in Fraud Case," 10 August 1988, Associated Press.

20 "Samoan Ex-Delegate Sunia Sentenced," 5 October 1988, *Washington Post*: 2.

21 "Ex-Delegate for Samoa Faces Prison Term," 5 October 1988, *New York Times*: A17.

"I FIGURE THE GUY WHO WALKS
SLOWLY WILL STAND OUT. IF
EVERYBODY'S YELLING, THEY'RE
GOING TO TAKE NOTICE OF THE
GUY THAT SPEAKS SOFTLY."

Fofó I. F. Sunia
Washington Post, April 26, 1982

Ben Garrido Blaz
1928–2014

DELEGATE 1985–1993
REPUBLICAN FROM GUAM

In 1985 Ben Garrido Blaz became just the second Delegate to represent the western Pacific island of Guam in Congress. A decorated military veteran who became a politician later in life, Blaz focused on issues of local importance to the island territory. Acutely affected by the Japanese invasion of Guam during World War II, Blaz used his national position to bring attention to the sacrifices and hardships of the era, including his own imprisonment. During his four terms in the House, Blaz led the charge for commonwealth status for his native land. "We in Guam have embarked on a voyage of political self-determination—a desire on our part for greater local autonomy and an equal place in the American political family."[1]

Vicente Tomas (Ben) Garrido Blaz was born February 14, 1928, in Agana, the capital of Guam.[2] Thirteen years old when the Japanese invaded Guam during World War II, Blaz worked in labor camps, building aviation fields, planting rice, and digging trenches until American forces retook the island in 1944.[3] After the war ended in 1945, Blaz returned to school. In 1947 he left Guam after earning an academic scholarship to the University of Notre Dame, where he majored in physics and chemistry and earned a BS in 1951.[4] While in school, he joined the U.S. Marine Corps Reserve at the onset of the Korean War. After graduating from Notre Dame, he was commissioned a second lieutenant. Blaz served two overseas tours in Japan and one in Vietnam. In 1963 he earned an MA in management from The George Washington University, and in 1971 he graduated from the Naval War College in Newport, Rhode Island. Blaz rose to the rank of brigadier general in 1977, becoming the highest-ranking Guamanian to serve in the U.S. military.[5] That same year, he headed the Marine information division that was tasked with improving public relations in the post–Vietnam War era.[6] Blaz's military honors included the Legion of Merit, the Bronze Medal with Combat "V," the Navy Commendation Medal, and the Vietnam Cross of Gallantry.[7] Blaz married Ann Evers, a teacher, and the couple had two sons, Mike and Tom. After retiring from the military in 1981, Blaz returned to his native island, where he taught at the University of Guam. He received an honorary LLD from the University of Guam in 1974.

On August 1, 1950, President Harry S. Truman signed the Organic Act of Guam, granting U.S. citizenship and limited self-government to the inhabitants of Guam. In 1972 the House of Representatives granted congressional representation to Guam and the Virgin Islands. Territorial Delegates were permitted to serve on and vote in committee, but they could not vote on the House Floor. In the 93rd Congress (1973–1975), Democrat Antonio Borja Won Pat became the first Delegate to represent Guam in the U.S. House of Representatives. Despite Won Pat's popularity and his impressive political résumé, which included service as speaker of the Guam assembly, Blaz challenged the longtime Delegate in 1982. "One reason I decided to run," Blaz revealed, "is that I did not get the sense that bureaucrats understand and appreciate Guam's uniqueness.... We're 100,000 American citizens who deserve a rightful spot in the American family."[8] Blaz attempted to offset his opponent's experience by emphasizing the need for a new, more aggressive strategy to represent Guam—especially with regard to the island's political status.[9] Although his first run for Congress was not successful, Blaz earned an impressive 48 percent of the vote against Won Pat.[10]

Encouraged by his strong showing at the polls, Blaz challenged Won Pat again in 1984. Both candidates ran unopposed in the primary, but voters had the option of crossing party lines. Tellingly, Blaz polled nearly 2,000 more votes than the incumbent.[11] During the general

election campaign, 75-year-old Won Pat stressed his seniority in Congress. The challenger countered by reminding voters that his Republican Party affiliation would be an asset for Guam under the Ronald Reagan administration.[12] "Although I'll be a junior [Member] I'm not exactly without friends," Blaz added. "There are many ways to explain clout—seniority is just one of them."[13]

During the tightly contested campaign, Blaz criticized his opponent's attendance record in Congress and accused Won Pat of missing opportunities to improve Guam's economy while serving as its Delegate.[14] He also promised to ensure that Guamanians enjoyed the same privileges as U.S. citizens on the mainland. After the ballots were tallied on Election Day, Blaz had a razor-thin lead of about 300 votes, causing the Guam Election Commission to authorize a recount. On November 11, 1984, the commission certified the election, declaring Blaz the winner by 354 votes.[15] "I'm ready," Blaz remarked. "I've been ready for 40 years. I'm on a mission."[16]

Though eager to start his new career, Blaz still had to contend with the remnants of a competitive and heated campaign. Initially conciliatory, Won Pat contested the election. Citing "substantial irregularities," Won Pat asked the House to overturn the election results, claiming Blaz had not received a majority of the votes. (Unlike most congressional races in the United States, in which Representatives need only capture a plurality, Delegates in Guam must win a majority of votes to avoid a runoff election.) The House denied Won Pat's challenge on July 24, 1985, by a voice vote, citing insufficient evidence. "Deep down inside I didn't have doubts, but the House of Representatives is hard to predict," Blaz commented afterward.[17]

At the beginning of the 99th Congress (1985–1987), the freshman class elected Blaz as its president, marking the first time a Territorial Delegate held this informal leadership position.[18] Blaz received two committee assignments: Armed Services and Interior and Insular Affairs. Both fit his legislative interests and allowed him to oversee and influence legislation affecting Guam. Blaz retained these two assignments during his eight years in the House. In the 100th Congress (1987–1989), he also had

a spot on the Foreign Affairs Committee, which he kept until he left Congress in 1993. From 1985 until 1993, he served on the Select Committee on Aging.

Guam's strategic location in the western Pacific Ocean significantly affected Blaz's legislative focus in Congress. After the Americans regained control of Guam during World War II, the island became a military bastion for the United States and a vital Cold War defense point. Guam's economy prospered with the influx of federal spending for the island's conversion to a military outpost. It continued to flourish after the Vietnam War, with a construction boom sparked by a budding tourism industry—fueled mainly by Japan. Blaz, however, questioned the need for the U.S. military's vast land holdings on Guam throughout the latter half of the 20th century. In 1992 he introduced the Guam Excess Lands Act, which called for the United States to return to Guam specified areas that had been appropriated by the military during World War II. According to the Guam Delegate, U.S. forces increased their presence after they regained control of Guam, instead of downsizing at the war's end. "These lands have remained unjustly inaccessible to my constituents ever since, even though much of it has not been used since the war for any military purpose," Blaz stated. He went on to say that returning the land to the people of Guam would help the nation's economy and "close the books on the issue of excess lands since the military has repeatedly indicated that it has no further use for them."[19]

Throughout his tenure in the House, Blaz sought to publicize Guam's role during World War II. He offered a firsthand account of the hardships the people endured during Japan's nearly three-year occupation. "There are many horrible and appalling stories I could tell about the atrocities inflicted upon our people," he said.[20] Blaz also recalled serving as commanding officer of the same Marine regiment that rescued him and eventually liberated Guam in 1944. "Taking command of the Ninth Marines was and remains the proudest moment of my life," he observed.[21] Building upon legislation drafted by Won Pat in 1983, Blaz introduced a bill to establish a Commission on War Claims to examine assertions of damages that were

suffered by the people of Guam at the hands of Japanese occupation forces. Although he did not attain this goal while he was serving in Congress, Blaz continued to fight for federal reparations for Guam. In 2005 he testified before the House Committee on Resources in favor of the Guam World War II Loyalty Recognition Act. "Loyalty and appreciation for their liberation made many of them hesitant to seek compensation for death, injuries, and damages in the years immediately following liberation," Blaz explained.[22]

While in the House, Blaz worked on a range of issues to fortify Guam's economy. The island relied heavily on the fishing industry. During the 99th Congress, Blaz introduced a bill to amend the Immigration and Nationality Act to allow alien crewmen working on U.S. fishing boats to go ashore while working in Guam. As Guam was the home port for America's western Pacific tuna fleet, which supplied much of the tuna for the United States, the fleet's presence had a major impact on Guam's economy. Blaz's measure called for the continued presence of U.S. fishing fleets and the same shore leave privileges for all crew members, regardless of their national origin. "Since Guam is America's bridge to the Pacific and its finest symbol it is essential that the free enterprise system flourish there," Blaz observed.[23] Blaz's bill became law on October 21, 1986. The Guam Delegate also sought to extend supplemental security income (SSI)—federal benefits for low-income, disabled, or elderly American citizens—to his constituents. Blaz introduced legislation to "reverse the meaningless discrimination" of SSI funding, which included residents of the District of Columbia and the Commonwealth of the Northern Mariana Islands but not the residents of other U.S. territories like Guam. "Affording these benefits to residents of one island and not to another is tantamount to extending benefits to residents of Chicago's North Side but not to fellow Americans in the South Side," Blaz concluded.[24] Blaz also supported federal assistance for educational programs in Guam, including funding for vocational education and improvements to elementary and secondary education. To help the many veterans residing in Guam, Blaz introduced the Veterans'

Educational Assistance Act during his first term in the House. The measure called for expanded eligibility for basic assistance under the GI Bill.

Throughout his tenure, Blaz's most consistent and fervent cause remained improving Guam's political status. He routinely introduced legislation to establish Guam as an American commonwealth rather than an unincorporated U.S. territory. "Commonwealth is the principal issue for Guam," Blaz asserted. "It's not a Democratic issue and it's not a Republican issue. It's a distinctly Guam issue with political, civil and human rights issues in it."[25] On March 7, 1988, the same week as Discovery Day—a holiday commemorating the day Portuguese explorer Ferdinand Magellan landed in Guam—Blaz introduced the Guam Commonwealth Act. Resulting from the work of the bipartisan Commission on Self-Determination, and ratified by Guam's voters, the measure called for complete self-government for the people of Guam, the preservation of the indigenous Chamorro culture, and consultation with the United States about matters that would affect the island. Advocating a partnership with the United States, Blaz reminded his House colleagues of Guam's sacrifices throughout the 20th century. "We on Guam paid our dues—as heavily in war as in peace—to prove our loyalty and pride as members of the American family. Still, we have never enjoyed equal status with other Americans—either politically or economically."[26] Although the Guam Commonwealth Act never made it out of committee, Blaz reintroduced it twice.[27]

Blaz did not limit his quest for equal rights to Guam. In 1991 he came out in support of statehood for the District of Columbia and compared the plight of his constituents with that of the residents of DC. "Yet the people of Guam—Americans all—remain second-class citizens. Like the people of the District of Columbia, they are denied the fundamental rights afforded their counterparts elsewhere," he said.[28] He also backed legislation sponsored by Virgin Islands Delegate Ron de Lugo that called for increased sovereignty of the U.S. territories of the Virgin Islands, Guam, American Samoa, and the Northern Mariana Islands. "The measure before us is the result of careful

consideration and comes to the floor with bipartisan support," Blaz observed. "It contains several items of importance to each of the territorial representatives and the American citizens from the territories and I urge approval of its passage."[29] The final version of the bill, which became law on August 27, 1986, provided additional funding for and greater autonomy over Guam's education system. During the 99th Congress, Blaz demonstrated further solidarity with his nonvoting colleagues and their constituents by introducing legislation to authorize the inclusion in the Capitol's National Statuary Hall Collection of statues from Washington, DC, Puerto Rico, Guam, the Virgin Islands, and American Samoa.[30]

Until his last election in 1992, Blaz encountered only modest competition in his campaigns to serve as Guam's Delegate. In 1986 he trounced Frank Torres, a former adjutant general of the National Guard, with 65 percent of the vote; in his subsequent two elections he easily defeated Vicente Pangelinan, a political veteran who worked for Delegate Won Pat, and Guam governor Ricardo Bordallo, capturing 55 percent of the ballots cast in both contests.[31] In his bid for a fifth term in the House, Blaz faced a strong challenge from Robert A. Underwood, a longtime educator with strong community ties in Guam. Underwood ran an effective grassroots campaign, criticizing Blaz for not spending enough time in Guam. Blaz countered by emphasizing his military and congressional record.[32] During Blaz's re-election, a typhoon hit the island and postponed voting in Guam for nearly a week. By the time voters cast their ballots for Delegate, they already knew that William J. (Bill) Clinton had been elected President. The outcome was significant because Blaz had underscored the value of Guam's Delegate being from the same party as the President.[33] On Election Day, Blaz garnered only 45 percent of the vote. He later offered to help his successor during the transition, remarking that his political career "started and ended on the high road."[34]

After leaving the House, Blaz taught at the University of Guam. He died on January 8, 2014, in Fairfax, Virginia.[35]

FOR FURTHER READING

Blaz, Ben Garrido. *Bisita Guam: A Special Place in the Sun* (Fairfax Station, VA: Evers Press, 1998).

MANUSCRIPT COLLECTION

University of Guam, Micronesian Area Research Center (Mangilao, GU). *Papers*: 1984–1992, 8 linear feet. The Ben Blaz papers document his service as a Delegate in the U.S. House of Representatives. The collection contains bill files, correspondence, news clippings, and reports. An inventory is available online.

NOTES

1   *Congressional Record*, House, 101st Cong., 1st sess. (9 March 1989): 4007.

2   Formerly called Agana, Guam's capital was renamed Hagatna, which is Chamorro. The names of Blaz's parents did not appear in any secondary sources, campaign materials, or newspaper articles. The 1930 Census listed a Vicente G. Blas born in Guam in 1928, to Vicente and Rita Blas. *Fifteenth Census of the United States, 1930: Population*, Piti, Piti, Guam, Roll 2629, sheet 1A, p. 293, Library of Congress, Washington, DC, http://search.ancestrylibrary.com (accessed 25 May 2012).

3   "Vicente Tomas (Ben) Blaz," Bisita Guam with Ben Blaz, accessed 9 January 2012, http://bisitaguam.com/bio/index.html.

4   Neither the name of the high school Blaz attended nor the date of his high school graduation is available on his website, "Vicente Tomas (Ben) Blaz," accessed 11 April 2011, http://bisitaguam.com/bio/index.html. Newspaper accounts provide contradictory information about the high school Blaz attended. See, for example, "Election 1992, a Special Project of the *Pacific Daily News*," 2 November 1992, *Pacific Daily News* (Guam): 2; Jeremiah O'Leary, "Guam Delegate's Rise Parallels Struggle for Civil Rights," 17 July 1989, *Washington Times*: B1.

5   Elaine Santos, "The Delegate," 4 November 1984, *Pacific Daily News* (Guam): 3.

6   Harold J. Logan, "Information Head Says Marines Must Be Open to Scrutiny," 2 July 1977, *Washington Post*: A6.

7   "Vicente Tomas (Ben) Blaz," accessed 11 April 2011, http://bisitaguam.com/bio/index.html; O'Leary, "Guam Delegate's Rise Parallels Struggle for Civil Rights."

8   Susan Kreifels, "'We Deserve a Rightful Spot,'" 29 October 1982, *Pacific Daily News* (Guam): 3.

9   Paul J. Borja, "'No Substitute for Experience,'" 29 October 1982, *Pacific Daily News* (Guam): 3; Kreifels, "'We Deserve a Rightful Spot.'"

10 Office of the Clerk, U.S. House of Representatives, "Election Statistics, 1920 to Present," http://history.house.gov/institution/election-statistics/election-statistics/.

11 "Rival's Tally in Guam Overshadows Incumbent," 3 September 1984, *New York Times*: 9.

12 Elaine Santos, "Won Pat, Blaz Face Off," 1 November 1984, *Pacific Daily News* (Guam): 1.

13 Santos, "The Delegate."

14 "Ben Blaz on Issues," Ben Blaz campaign advertisement, 2 November 1984, *Pacific Daily News* (Guam): 9; "Issues Facing Guam Now," Ben Blaz campaign advertisement, 3 November 1984, *Pacific Daily News* (Guam): 41.

15 Kate Pound, "Recount Set for Delegate Race," 8 November 1984, *Pacific Daily News* (Guam): 1; Yvonne Martinez, "It's Blaz by 354 Votes," 11 November 1984, *Pacific Daily News* (Guam): 1; Office of the Clerk, U.S. House of Representatives, "Election Statistics, 1920 to Present."

16 Paul J. Borja, "Blaz: On a New Mission," 12 November 1984, *Pacific Daily News* (Guam): 1.

17 *Congressional Record*, House, 99th Cong., 1st sess. (24 July 1985): 20180–20181; "House Rejects Bid to Overturn Election of Guam Delegate," 25 July 1985, *Los Angeles Times*: 23; "House Denies Won Pat Challenge," 26 July 1985, *Pacific Daily News* (Guam): 1; Stephen Labaton, "Guam Delegate Resists Demand for Runoff Vote," 6 June 1985, *Washington Post*: A7; Stephen Labaton, "Guam's Seat in Congress Still Disputed," 4 June 1985, *Washington Post*: A12.

18 "Minority Reports," 16 December 1984, *New York Times*: E20.

19 *Congressional Record*, House, 102nd Cong., 2nd sess. (5 February 1992): 1691.

20 *Congressional Record*, House, 99th Cong., 2nd sess. (26 November 1991): 35435.

21 Blaz took command of the Ninth Regiment of the Marines 27 years after the liberation of Guam. Blaz recalled escaping with several companions from a Japanese concentration camp shortly after U.S. troops invaded Guam in 1944. The Marines mistook Blaz for a Japanese soldier and briefly held him as a prisoner of war. According to Blaz, the Japanese captured and killed two Guamanians in his group who ran in a different direction. See Bernard E. Trainor, "Lack of Vote Doesn't Deter Delegate from Guam," 3 February 1988, *New York Times*: B6.

22 Hearings before the House Committee on Resources, *Guam War Claims*, 109th Cong., 1st sess. (20 April 2005); James Brooke, "Decades after Abuses by the Japanese, Guam Hopes the Military Will Make Amends," 14 August 2005, *New York Times*: 16.

23 *Congressional Record*, House, 99th Cong., 2nd sess. (12 May 1986): 10276.

24 *Congressional Record*, House, 102nd Cong., 2nd sess. (18 February 1992): 2452.

25 Tambra A. Bryant, "Guam Dems: Clinton Win Would Help Underwood," 4 November 1992, *Pacific Daily News* (Guam): 3.

26 *Congressional Record*, House, 100th Cong., 2nd sess. (7 March 1988): 3500.

27 For detailed information on the commonwealth movement in Guam, see Robert F. Rogers, "Guam's Quest for Political Identity," *Pacific Studies* 12 (November 1988): 49–70; Robert F. Rogers, *Destiny's Landfall: A History of Guam* (Honolulu: University of Hawai'i Press, 1995): 271–290.

28 Ben Blaz, "Guam: Equal in War, But Not in Peace," 19 October 1991, *New York Times*: 22.

29 *Congressional Record*, House, 99th Cong., 2nd sess. (1 August 1986): 18622.

30 *Congressional Record*, House, 99th Cong., 1st sess. (19 November 1985): 32463.

31 Office of the Clerk, U.S. House of Representatives, "Election Statistics, 1920 to Present"; "About Senator ben" on Senator Vicente (ben) Cabrera Pangelinan's official website, accessed 4 January 2012, http://senbenp.com/?page_id=6; "Guamanians Cast Ballots in U.S. Territory's Primary Election," 6 September 1986, Associated Press.

32 Donovan Brooks, "New Turn on the 'High Road,'" 10 November 1992, *Pacific Daily News* (Guam): 1; Donovan Brooks, "Grassroots, Media Use Called Key to Success," 11 November 1992, *Pacific Daily News* (Guam): 7. For an example of Blaz's campaign advertisements, see "Ben Blaz for U.S. Congress," 1 November 1992, *Pacific Daily News* (Guam): 14.

33 Bryant, "Guam Dems: Clinton Win Would Help Underwood"; Frale Oyen, "Election Postponed," 3 November 1992, *Pacific Daily News* (Guam): 1.

34 Brooks, "New Turn on the 'High Road.'"

35 "Vicente Tomas (Ben) Blaz," accessed 9 January 2012, http://bisitaguam.com/bio/index.html; Matt Schudel, "Vincente T. 'Ben' Blaz, Marine General and Guam Delegate, Dies at 85," 24 January 2014, *Washington Post*, http://www.washingtonpost.com/national/vicente-t-ben-blaz-marine-general-and-guam-delegate-dies-at-85/2014/01/23/a41a445c-8397-11e3-9dd4-e7278db80d86_story.html (accessed 26 February 2014).

Patricia Saiki
1930–

UNITED STATES REPRESENTATIVE 1987–1991
REPUBLICAN FROM HAWAII

Patricia Saiki's revitalization of the Hawaiian Republican Party propelled her to election as the state's first GOP Representative since 1959, when it entered the Union. As a Member of Congress, Saiki focused on economic and environmental legislation important to her Honolulu constituency as well as the international Asian community. In 1990 Saiki left the House to campaign for a Senate seat in a race that many political observers believed might signal a shift in the balance of political power in Hawaii. "Before Pat Saiki was elected to Congress, it was hard for us to relate to young people and tell them, 'It's great to be a Republican,'" noted a Hawaiian GOP member. "Now we can begin to spin the tale that will make people interested in supporting the Republican Party in Hawaii."[1]

Patricia Fukuda was born to Kazuo and Shizue Fukuda on May 28, 1930, in Hilo, on the big island of Hawaii. She graduated from Hilo High School in 1948 and received a bachelor of science degree from the University of Hawaii at Manoa in 1952. In 1954 she married Stanley Saiki, an obstetrician, and they had five children: Stanley, Stuart, Sandra, Margaret, and Laura. Patricia Saiki taught history in Hawaii's public and private schools for 12 years.

Her path to politics began with her work as a union organizer and research assistant to Hawaii senate Republicans. In the mid-1960s, Saiki served as the secretary and then the vice chair of the state Republican Party. She attended the state constitutional convention in 1968, and that year won election to the Hawaii house of representatives, where she served for six years. In 1974 Saiki won election to the state senate, where she served until 1982. In 1982 Saiki left the legislature and made an unsuccessful bid for lieutenant governor. She subsequently oversaw a three-fold expansion in party membership and helped the party raise $800,000 during her two-and-a-half-year tenure

as party chair. Her hand in reviving the Republican Party in the strongly Democratic state aided President Ronald Reagan's victory there in the 1984 presidential election (the only previous Republican presidential candidate to carry the state was Richard Nixon in 1972) and the election of Democrat-turned-Republican Frank Fasi as Honolulu mayor.

After spending nearly two decades in state politics, Saiki decided to run for the U.S. House seat vacated in July 1986 by five-term Democrat Cecil Heftel, who left to run for governor. As the state's population center, the district encompassed Honolulu, its suburbs, and the Pearl Harbor naval base (Hawaii's only other congressional district included the rest of Oahu and the other islands). Tourism and commercial shipping were the lifeblood for the cosmopolitan population of Caucasians, Asian Americans, and Native Hawaiians, most of whom were registered Democrats. The potential for influence in Washington as well as the war on drugs were the major issues leading up to the September special election to fill the remaining four months of Heftel's term in the 99th Congress (1985–1987). Liberal Democratic state senator Neil Abercrombie was the early favorite; however, a third candidate, Democrat Mufi Hannemann, a 32-year-old corporate lobbyist and former White House fellow, entered the race, siphoning off a portion of the liberal vote. Saiki certainly benefited from the Democratic intraparty warfare but she was unable to best Abercrombie in the September 20 special election. He prevailed over Saiki by fewer than 1,000 votes, 30 to 29 percent; Hannemann trailed by about 2,200 votes (28 percent). On the same day, Saiki won the Republican primary to run for a full term in the 100th Congress (1987–1989), while Abercrombie and Hannemann battled for the Democratic nomination for the full term. As the two Democrats faced off in the closed primary, several thousand Saiki supporters temporarily

registered as Democrats to give Hannemann a narrow win and instantly reduce Abercrombie to lame-duck status in the 99th Congress.[2]

In the general election for the 100th Congress, Hannemann had history on his side: ever since the state entered the Union in 1959, Hawaii had sent only Democrats to the U.S. House of Representatives. But Hannemann also faced several obstacles. First, the acrimony from the primary carried over as Abercrombie withheld his endorsement. More importantly, Saiki's ancestral roots as a Japanese American—one-third of the voters shared her ethnic background—helped her popularity. Saiki won the general election with 59 percent of the vote, a 33,000-vote advantage; no previous Hawaiian Republican candidate for the U.S. House had ever polled more than 45 percent of the vote.[3] She became the first Republican to represent Hawaii in the House since Elizabeth Farrington won election as a Territorial Delegate in 1954 (Republican Hiram Fong served in the U.S. Senate from 1959 to 1977). Two years later, Saiki ran unopposed in the 1988 Republican primary. In the three-way Democratic primary, Mary Bitterman, a former director of the Voice of America, emerged as the convincing winner; however, she spent the bulk of her campaign funds securing the nomination, leaving her little money for the general election. She was not able to dent Saiki's record, and the incumbent won comfortably with a 55 percent majority.

Throughout her career, Saiki established a fiscally conservative voting record on economic issues, in line with most of her GOP colleagues. She also supported much of the Reagan and George H. W. Bush administrations' foreign policy programs—voting for aid to the Nicaraguan Contras, funding for the Strategic Defense Initiative, and the death penalty for drug-related murders. Where she parted company with many Republicans was on her moderate stance on touchstone social issues, chief among them reproductive rights. Saiki supported women's reproductive freedom. "I don't want to be sexist about this, but anything that involves a woman's life or career, it's very personal, very close to us," Saiki told the *New York Times*.

"We're the ones who experience it. We're the ones who have to pay for it."[4]

Saiki received seats on the Committee on Banking, Finance and Urban Affairs, the Committee on Merchant Marine and Fisheries, and the Select Committee on Aging. Her seat on Merchant Marine and Fisheries, with assignments on its Oceanography and Fisheries Subcommittee, was particularly important to her oceanside constituency. Saiki worked to preserve the islands' natural beauty and unique resources. She attempted to persuade the Bush administration to suspend military test bombing on the island of Kahoolawe, situated just offshore from Maui. Claimed by U.S. officials in the early 1950s, the island nevertheless retained significant cultural relevance for Native Hawaiians.[5] In 1990 she supported an amendment to revise the annual accrual method of accounting for pineapple and banana growers, whose longer growth and production cycles distorted their income statements and exposed them to excess taxation.[6] Saiki also advocated a ban on environmentally unsound driftnet fishing in the Pacific, urging the U.S. Secretary of State to call an international convention to discuss the topic.[7]

In 1987 Representative Saiki signed on to support H.R. 442, a measure with broad bipartisan support that called for monetary reparations and an official apology to the Japanese Americans who were interned during World War II. Saiki and 62 other Republicans joined 180 Democrats to approve the legislation later that year. After the measure passed the Senate, Saiki was present when President Reagan signed it into law in 1988. She subsequently pressed Congress to expedite payouts.[8]

As an Asian American representing a district in the middle of the Pacific, Saiki also was involved with Pacific Rim issues. She served on congressional delegations that visited Tonga for the birthday of the South Pacific island's monarch and attended the funeral for the Emperor of Japan. In May 1989, several weeks before the Chinese military's massacre of student protestors in Beijing's Tiananmen Square, Saiki introduced a resolution in the House declaring congressional support for democratic rights in the People's Republic of China. "I have been deeply moved by the determination and idealism of the Chinese students," she said. "Fighting in a nonviolent way for what one believes to be true has been a cornerstone of many civil rights movements."[9]

In April 1990, popular, long-serving Hawaii Senator Spark M. Matsunaga died of cancer. Urged by her friend President Bush, Saiki entered the election to fill the islands' vacant seat. "Hawaii needs a Senator who can make the people on Pennsylvania Avenue and Constitution Avenue understand the people on Kamehameha Avenue," Saiki said while announcing her candidacy.[10] Democratic Governor John Waihee III appointed Hawaii Congressman Daniel K. Akaka to serve as interim Senator until the November special election. Akaka's new position made him the favorite to hold onto the seat in the fall.

Yet Saiki proved a formidable opponent. She won the primary against four other Republican candidates with a strong 92 percent of the vote. In the general election, both candidates supported the key economic issues that many Hawaiians favored: maintaining price supports for cane sugar, promoting increased tourism, and halting target practice on Kahoolawe. Saiki proved a more dynamic candidate than the sedate Akaka. She also had repeatedly proved her ability to draw votes from the Japanese-American community. Moreover, the growing suburban, conservative white population allowed her, in the words of one political strategist, to "cut into the Democratic establishment."[11] Political observers believed Saiki might be among a handful of candidates to help Republicans regain control of the Senate. However, Akaka had the support of the well-entrenched Hawaiian Democratic establishment, and his warm, pleasing personality appealed to voters. Saiki lost to Akaka by a healthy margin of about 33,000 votes, 54 percent to 45 percent.

After Saiki left Congress, President Bush appointed her director of the Small Business Administration, where she served from 1991 to 1993. In 1993 she taught at Harvard University's Institute of Politics at the John F. Kennedy School of Government. The following year, she became the first woman candidate on a major party ticket for Hawaii governor. Saiki lost a three-way race to Democratic Lieutenant Governor Ben Cayetano.[12] Patricia Saiki returned to teaching and lives in Honolulu.

MANUSCRIPT COLLECTION

University of Hawaii at Manoa Library, Archives and Manuscripts Department, Hawaii Congressional Papers Collection (Honolulu, HI). *Papers*: circa 1970–2006, 18.5 linear feet. The papers primarily document Patricia Saiki's tenure as a Member of the U.S. House of Representatives. A small portion of the collection concerns her service in the Hawaii state house and the Hawaii state senate. Topics covered include agriculture, environmental issues, and foreign affairs. The papers also contain documents regarding Saiki's appointment and tenure as administrator of the U.S. Small Business Administration. A finding aid is available at the repository and online.

NOTES

1   "Liu: Up & Coming in Republican Politics," 13 February 1987, *AsianWeek*: 5.

2   *Politics in America, 1986* (Washington, DC: Congressional Quarterly Inc., 1985): 389.

3   *Politics in America, 1986*: 389.

4   Robin Turner, "G.O.P. Women Raise Voices For the Right to an Abortion," 31 October 1989, *New York Times*: A1.

5   *Congressional Record*, House, 101st Cong., 2nd sess. (22 October 1990): 32430.

6   *Congressional Record*, House, 101st Cong., 2nd sess. (16 May 1990): 10832.

7   *Congressional Record*, House, 101st Cong., 1st sess. (17 November 1989): 29997.

8   "House Roll-Call Votes," *CQ Almanac, 1987*, 43rd ed. (Washington, DC: Congressional Quarterly, Inc., 1988): 98-H; *Congressional Record*, House, 101st Cong., 1st sess. (4 August 1989): 17145; *Congressional Record*, House, 101st Cong., 1st sess. (26 October 1989): 26241.

9   *Congressional Record*, House, 101st Cong., 1st sess. (23 May 1989): 10013.

10 Maralee Schwartz, "Hawaii GOP Rep. Saiki to Run Against Akaka in Senate Race," 1 June 1990, *Washington Post*: A12.

11 "Republicans Select Woman in Hawaii," 20 September 1994, *New York Times*: A19; Robert Reinhold, "Hawaii Race Tests Democratic Hold," 1 November 1990, *New York Times*: D22; Robert Reinhold, "Republicans Sense Chance in Hawaii," 9 May 1990, *New York Times*: A26.

12 "West: Despite Voter Discontent, Governors Win Re-Election in California and Colorado," 9 November 1994, *New York Times*: B8.

Eni F. H. Faleomavaega
1943–2017

DELEGATE 1989–2015
DEMOCRAT FROM AMERICAN SAMOA

In 1989 Eni F. H. Faleomavaega became only the second Delegate from American Samoa to serve in the House. Upon his departure from Congress 26 years later, Faleomavaega owned the distinction, albeit briefly, as the longest-serving Delegate in House history. As a House committee staffer in the 1970s, Faleomavaega had helped American Samoa gain a House seat and during his time in Congress was "dogged in his determination to improve the economic lot of his island territory," according to one political almanac.[1] Being a Delegate from American Samoa was not always the easiest job, but his strong relationship with Democratic leaders and his work in committee often helped him overcome the circumscribed powers of his office, and earned him the moniker the "champion of the Pacific Islanders."[2]

Eni Faʻauaʻa Hunkin Faleomavaega Jr., was born on August 15, 1943, to Eni Faʻauaʻa Sr., and Taualaitufanuaimeaatamaliʻi. His last name, in Samoan, "means house where important things or decisions are made." Faleomavaega grew up in Vailoatai Village, a fishing and boat-building community along the island's southwest coast. "Our culture is very much closely associated with families," the Congressman said in 2011. "Of course you have your immediate family, and then we also have what is known as the extended family, or you might say clans in that respect. So I might be related to 15 or 20 different clans—both on my mother's side and my father's side."[3]

Faleomavaega's father served in the U.S. Navy, and when the Delegate was just a boy, the military transferred the family to Hawaii, making room deep below deck of an outdated ship for Samoan families by placing makeshift beds in the cargo hold. "It was the most inhumane way of transporting human passengers," Faleomavaega recalled. "It was like a dungeon in there."[4] Faleomavaega spent "about half" his life in Hawaii, graduating from Kahuku High

School in northern Oahu. He spent his first two years of college at nearby Church College, before transferring to Brigham Young University (BYU) in Provo, Utah.[5] In 1966 Faleomavaega graduated from BYU and enlisted in the United States Army. In 1972, after a tour in Vietnam, where he was exposed to the dangerous chemical Agent Orange during his time in Nha Trang, Faleomavaega earned a JD from the University of Houston in Texas. He then accepted a fellowship at the University of California, Berkeley, earning an LLM in 1973.[6] Faleomavaega married Antonina Hinanui; together they raised five children.

Also in 1973, Faleomavaega moved across the country and took a job with Paramount Chief A. U. Fuimaono, American Samoa's "Delegate at Large" and its first elected official in Washington. Since American Samoa did not have an official Delegate in the U.S. House until 1981, Fuimaono worked more like an elected lobbyist for the islands. On issues pertaining to American Samoa and the South Pacific, Fuimaono would often testify before Congress, including the Interior and Insular Affairs Committee's Subcommittee on Territorial and Insular Affairs, chaired by Phillip Burton of California.[7]

In 1975 Faleomavaega made the jump to the House and took a job with Burton's subcommittee. He worked with Burton until 1981, helping to secure representation in the House for his home islands. "I kept asking Congressman Burton … how do we justify having a small little territory being represented in the U.S. House of Representatives as a delegate[?]" Burton told him that size did not matter; American Samoa was a U.S. territory like Guam and the Virgin Islands and was therefore entitled to a voice in the House.[8] Faleomavaega later estimated that the eight years he spent working on Capitol Hill were "probably equivalent to me working in American Samoa for thirty years in trying to understand how the system functions, how it operates."[9]

Faleomavaega returned to American Samoa in 1981 when he became the deputy attorney general, "so I could feel the people's pains and sufferings and so that I might be able to serve them with more meaningful purpose," he would later say.[10] In 1985 voters on the island elected him lieutenant governor.

In early September 1988, American Samoa's first Territorial Delegate, Fofó I. F. Sunia, resigned from the House after pleading guilty to payroll fraud. Faleomavaega, leveraging his wide name recognition as lieutenant governor of the small island chain, ran against American Samoa's former lieutenant governor, Tufele Li'a, to fill the vacancy. At the time, elections in American Samoa differed from many of those on the mainland in that there were no primary campaigns on the islands. Moreover, if no candidate in the general election captured 50 percent of the vote, the race automatically headed to a runoff two weeks later. On Election Day, Faleomavaega captured 3,739 votes—only 358 votes more than his challenger—and failed to reach the 50 percent threshold that would have given him the victory. But a short while later, on November 22, 1988, Faleomavaega won the runoff and became the second Delegate to represent the islands in the House.[11]

Like his first race, a handful of his re-election races were nail biters. During Faleomavaega's career running for Delegate, the total number of votes cast in American Samoa, an island chain with only 56,000 people, exceeded 13,000 only once.[12]

Geographically, American Samoa has slightly more square mileage than the District of Columbia, but the islands have less than one tenth the population of the average congressional district on the mainland.[13] With access to the South Pacific fishery, American Samoa, during Faleomavaega's tenure, was home to large tuna canneries, but for the most part, the federal government helped maintain the territory's standard of living, pumping millions of dollars into the economy every year.[14] In the search for new jobs and better opportunities, many on American Samoa join the U.S. military, giving the islands one of the highest enlistment rates in the country.[15] A number of Samoans also lived full time on the mainland which, for Faleomavaega, translated to unique re-election campaigns. Whereas the vast majority of Members campaigned in their home district, Faleomavaega often campaigned in regions of the country home to high concentrations of his fellow islanders. "I'm probably the only member that has to go to San Francisco, Los Angeles, San Diego, or Hawaii where we have communities … where I would attend their community activities." Often, he said, Samoans living on the mainland would rather talk to him than their actual elected Representative. "We are very tribal in our ways."[16]

When Faleomavaega began his House career, he maneuvered to secure a seat on the Foreign Affairs Committee as quickly as possible. As the new Delegate saw it, the committee's membership did not fully reflect the breadth of America's interests abroad. "The entire mentality of Washington, twenty-two years ago, was Europe and the Middle East," he said in a 2011 oral history. "Asia Pacific was not even on the map. It was not even on the radar screen." But as Faleomavaega understood it, Foreign Affairs was reserved for Members who had already served "at least one or two terms" in the House—meaning that as a freshman, Faleomavaega would likely have been passed over. "So I pleaded my case with the leadership," he later remembered. "I felt there needs to be some diversity here, infusion of the Asia Pacific, if you will. So they allowed me to be member of the Foreign Affairs Committee."[17]

Faleomavaega suspected the House's indifference toward Asia stemmed in part from the makeup of Foreign Affairs' subcommittees. "What was interesting is that when I got onto the Committee, nobody wanted to be on the Asia Pacific subcommittee," he remembered. "Well, I shouldn't say nobody[,] but the fact was that the two subcommittees that members really didn't want to be members of [were] Asia Pacific and Africa."[18] While Faleomavaega believed that the allure of the already well-developed markets in Europe and the Middle East accounted for such neglect, he also believed there was a deeper, more troubling cause of the global disparity on the committee. "I suspect one reason, if you look at the history; America has never had a positive relationship really with the Asia Pacific region."

World War II, the Korean War, the Vietnam War: each conflict likely deepened the prejudice against that section of the world, he said. "In my perspective, I think when we talk about the Asia Pacific … there's unbalance, there's a lot of racial feelings about people coming from the Asia Pacific region, unfortunately, but that's the reality that we're faced with."[19]

That first conversation with party leadership was all Faleomavaega needed; he served on the Foreign Affairs Committee for his entire career. During his quarter-century in the House, the Delegate served on a number of subcommittees: Asia and the Pacific; International Economic Policy and Trade; International Operations; Arms Control, International Security and Science; International Operations and Human Rights; East Asia and the Pacific; the Western Hemisphere; and Asia, the Pacific, and the Global Environment. His longevity on the committee translated into leadership positions by 2001. Beginning with the 107th Congress (2001–2003), Faleomavaega was named the Ranking Democrat on the East Asia and the Pacific Subcommittee, and when his party took back the House in the 110th and 111th Congresses (2007–2011), Faleomavaega served as chairman of the Subcommittee on Asia, the Pacific, and the Global Environment. After the Democrats returned to the minority, Faleomavaega resumed his seat as Ranking Member of the subcommittee.[20]

Faleomavaega's chairmanship of the Subcommittee on Asia, the Pacific, and the Global Environment became an increasingly important assignment as America's economy expanded to markets in China and its surrounding trade partners.[21] As chairman, Faleomavaega held hearings on a host of different issues: human rights, the fishing industry, nuclear and renewable power, climate change, and diplomatic relations with a broad range of Pacific countries—South Korea, the Marshall Islands, Australia, New Zealand, China, and Cambodia. From a general foreign policy perspective, Faleomavaega took a hard line against America's unilateral military interventions, and called for diplomatic solutions that included the international community.[22]

In his second Congress as chairman of the subcommittee, Faleomavaega slowed the pace of hearings and built on the legislative groundwork he set in the 110th Congress, revisiting a number of issues the subcommittee considered earlier: U.S. policy toward North Korea, the South Pacific tuna industry, the continual legacy of Agent Orange, North Korea's nuclear capabilities, Japan's changing role in the regional and global economy, the ramifications of global warming, and America's general policy in the Pacific.[23] As chairman, Faleomavaega also used his influence to look out for the interests of his home islands. Among other measures, the House passed his bill, the Pacific Island Economic and Educational Development Act of 2007 (H.R. 3062), on September 5, 2007. The legislation appropriated $1 million a year for two years to fund cultural and educational exchange programs in the region.[24]

That party leaders selected Faleomavaega to lead a subcommittee was a huge legislative boost for the Delegate. House Rules forbid statutory representatives from voting on the floor, but his ability to craft legislation in the early stages gave Faleomavaega outsized influence. "I think we've come a long way in improving the situation," he said toward the end of his career, "delegates now can vote in committee, can hold chairmanships, can introduce bills, can debate on the floor, do all other things as other members do with that one exception … voting for legislation on the floor.… I do ninety percent of the work, but that ten percent of voting on the floor, even though that isn't the most critical aspect of it, being a full member of Congress is that you vote on final passage of legislation. And we're not allowed to do that simply because of the Constitution."[25]

Faleomavaega also served brief stints on a handful of other committees. He spent two terms (101st and 102nd Congresses [1989–1993]) on the Select Committee on Hunger; one term (102nd Congress [1991–1993]) on the Merchant Marine and Fisheries Committee; one term (103rd Congress [1993–1995]) on the Education and Labor Committee; and two terms (108th and 109th Congresses [2003–2007]) on the Small Business Committee.

Along with Foreign Affairs, Faleomavaega served on the Interior and Insular Affairs Committee for his entire House

career as well, although for the vast majority of his time in Congress the committee was called Natural Resources or just Resources. The committee was and remains a natural home for statutory representatives. "All the issues affecting the territories come under that [committee]," he once pointed out. Traditionally, each Delegate and the Resident Commissioner serves on the panel. As Faleomavaega said, "We are the counterparts to the Secretary of the Interior, who oversees all the U.S. territories."[26]

Faleomavaega sat on a number of different Resources subcommittees during his House career: General Oversight and Investigations; Insular and International Affairs; General Oversight and California Desert Lands; Native American Affairs; National Parks, Forests, and Lands; Native American and Insular Affairs; National Parks and Public Lands; Energy and Mineral Resources; Fisheries Conservation, Wildlife and Oceans; National Parks, Recreations, and Public Lands; Insular Affairs, Oceans and Wildlife; Insular Affairs; Fisheries, Wildlife, and Oceans; Fisheries, Wildlife, Oceans and Insular Affairs; and Indian and Alaska Native Affairs.[27]

Faleomavaega used his seat on the committee to address the immediate concerns of his constituents and campaign for the interests of America's native peoples everywhere. "I've always expressed an interest [in] the rights of the indigenous people throughout the world that I don't think has been given fair treatment, I suppose you might put it in those terms," Faleomavaega said towards the end of his career.[28] Faleomavaega designed his work on behalf of America's indigenous population in large part to raise awareness on issues affecting communities all over the country. One of his first legislative successes in 1990 (H.J. Res. 577) proclaimed November "Native American Indian Heritage Month," which he replicated in 1991 and 1992. In the 102nd Congress, his bill to name 1992 the "Year of the American Indian" garnered 226 cosponsors, and he pushed to improve educational programs for American Indians everywhere.[29] Democratic leaders took notice of his work, and for the 104th Congress (1995–1997) they named him the Ranking Member of the Subcommittee on Native American and Insular Affairs. In the subcommittee,

he submitted a number of bills dealing with the federal recognition of American Indian nations and encouraging the tribes' self-determination. For the 106th Congress (1999–2001), he was also named Ranking Democrat of the Subcommittee on Fisheries Conservation, Wildlife and Oceans.

By the 106th Congress, Faleomavaega's work on the Resources Committee included a strong environmental component with direct bearing on American Samoa's economy. Since his first term, when the House passed Faleomavaega's H. Con. Res. 214 condemning driftnet fishing in the South Pacific, he worked to end the practice of targeting wild tuna stocks while ensuring his territory's financial health.[30]

By 2009 the tuna industry accounted for nearly 60 percent of the economy in American Samoa.[31] In addition to protecting the resource, Faleomavaega also had to protect jobs in his district. To compete with nearby markets in the South Pacific and the robust fishing industry in South America, officials in American Samoa and Washington had kept wages well below the national average. In 2007, after Democrats won back the House partly on promises to increase the minimum wage, Faleomavaega lobbied his party's leadership to exclude American Samoa from the raise. Faleomavaega worried that the major canners in his district would move their operations to markets where labor cost a fraction of what it did on American Samoa. The final legislation, however, mandated an increase in the minimum wage by 2014. Though other issues factored in, too, the bill convinced one of the major tuna processors to move abroad, costing the islands thousands of jobs. On the day the tuna packing plant was scheduled to close, a major tsunami hit the territory, caused vast destruction, and killed two dozen people. Once the islands started rebuilding, Faleomavaega submitted legislation—which Congress passed— delaying the minimum wage increase there.[32] Along with maintaining the cost of labor, Faleomavaega also worked to protect generous tax breaks for the Samoan fishing industry.[33] Given the territory's reliance on a handful of employers, he pushed to diversify American Samoa's revenue sources and encourage investments in aquaculture and seafloor mineral extraction.[34]

In 1988 Congress approved the National Park of American Samoa (the United States' 50th national park), which spread across a number of the territory's islands.[35] Later a group of village chiefs back home approached the Delegate about expanding the park's boundaries to the include parts of nearby islands, Ofu and Olosega. After four years of planning, Faleomavaega earned a major victory in May 2001 when he sponsored H.R. 1712, which added nearly 3,000 acres to the existing tract. The House Resources Committee reported it favorably on March 12, 2002: "Expanding park boundaries to include land and water on the island of Ofu and Olosega would help protect vast coral communities which harbor a great diversity of species and offer excellent scuba diving opportunities," the committee wrote. The new park would also protect a host of reef ecosystems and a variety of birds, turtles, and rare giant clams. Moreover, the committee observed, "The addition of rainforest and coral reef on Ofu and Olosega would provide greater hiking opportunities and help to diversify visitor use and lessen the impact on the reef. In addition," the committee continued, "a high concentration of medicinal plants in the area would be protected. Many of these plants are disappearing and are in need of preservation."[36] When the bill went before the Senate, the Committee on Energy and Natural Resources warmly received Faleomavaega's testimony and favorably reported the legislation.[37] His bill became law on December 16, 2002.[38]

Faleomavaega's concern for the environment extended beyond the needs of his district's economy. In the mid-1990s, he worked to end France's nuclear testing in the Pacific (getting arrested during one protest) and a few years later submitted bills calling for the study of the shark population and the protection of coral reefs.[39] He also worked to amend the National Fish and Wildlife Foundation Establishment Act to make it easier for the organization to accept private donations.[40] In the 107th Congress, Faleomavaega pushed for a stronger tsunami relief program at the National Oceanic and Atmospheric Administration (NOAA) and submitted the Shark Protect

Act of 2001, which outlawed the sale of shark fins.[41] Three years later, he convinced Congress to give the Utrok Atoll a decommissioned NOAA ship that could be used to monitor radiology levels near U.S. nuclear testing sites. The bill also included a number of fisheries regulations.[42]

Throughout his time in the House, Faleomavaega kept American Samoa at the heart of his legislative agenda: everything from trade to the environment, to its relationship with the federal government. The Delegate worked to include American Samoa in a number of federal initiatives during the 1990s, including the Supplemental Security Income Program, programs serving Americans with disabilities, and even a program that issued emergency livestock feed.[43] In the 106th Congress, Faleomavaega amended the Interior Department's appropriations bill for Fiscal Year 2000 to establish a payment plan for American Samoa's existing debt and helped clarify the eligibility of U.S. nationals to donate to political campaigns.[44] He worked to lift the cap on Medicaid spending in the territory and steered to passage a law that required the Internal Revenue Service to treat bonds issued by American Samoa in the same way it treated tax-free bonds issued by the other territories. He also worked on an overhaul of American Samoa's election law which would eliminate the automatic runoff if the islands did not institute a primary season.[45]

Faleomavaega lost re-election in 2014 in a nine-candidate race, taking roughly 31 percent, or 3,157 votes, and finishing second to Aumua Amata Coleman Radewagen, who garnered a 42 percent plurality.[46] The Delegate's health was a major factor in his loss. Late in the race, Faleomavaega had to be flown to Hawaii to receive emergency medical treatment for the lingering effects of his exposure to Agent Orange during his tour in Vietnam more than 40 years earlier. It nearly cost him his life. "There were … a lot of rumors floating around that I'm way too sick," he said a few days after the election. "It's understandable."[47] As Faleomavaega weighed his future, he revealed that he still felt compelled to serve his island territory, working with the next generation back home, "sharing the sense of my experience with our young people," he said.[48] "I go forward, Mr. Speaker," he said in his farewell address on the House Floor a few weeks later, "knowing that the best is yet to come and hoping that I will be remembered for trying my best."[49]

Faleomavaega died at his home in Provo, Utah, on February 22, 2017. "Eni was a restless champion for the rights and advancement of his constituents," House Democratic Leader Nancy Pelosi said in a statement after learning of his death. "His life and leadership powerfully spotlighted the immense contributions of Americans from U.S. territories."[50]

NOTES

1 *Politics in America, 2012* (Washington, DC: CQ-Roll Call, Inc., 2011): 1087.

2 See Hearing before the House Committee on Foreign Affairs, Subcommittee on Asian and Pacific Affairs, *U.S. Policy Toward the South Pacific: Implementation of the Honolulu Summit*, 102nd Cong., 1st sess. (20 November 1991): 80.

3 Eni F. H. Faleomavaega, oral history interview by the U.S. Capitol Historical Society, 11 April 2011, accessed 13 July 2015, http://www.uschs.org/oral-histories/uschs_faleomavaega.htm (site discontinued).

4 Anthony Millican, "Samoans Speak Out," 13 October 1991, *Los Angeles Times*: B3.

5 *Congressional Record*, House, 113th Cong., 2nd sess. (8 December 2014): H8821; Faleomavaega, oral history interview.

6 "Eni F. H. Faleomavaega," *Biographical Directory of the United States Congress, 1774–Present*, http://bioguide.congress.gov/scripts/biodisplay.pl?index=F000010; Faleomavaega, oral history interview; Fili Sagapolutele, "Faleomavaega Speaks for First Time About his Illness," 24 September 2014, http://samoanews.com (accessed 2 September 2015).

7 Hearing before the House Committee on Interior and Insular Affairs, Subcommittee on Territorial and Insular Affairs, *Current Problems in American Samoa*, 93rd Cong., 2nd sess. (2 April 1974): 1–6.

8 Faleomavaega, oral history interview.

9 Ibid.

10 *Congressional Record*, House, 113th Cong., 2nd sess. (8 December 2014): H8822.

11 "Republican is Elected Governor of Samoa," 12 November 1988, *New York Times*: A8; *Almanac of American Politics, 1990* (Washington, DC: National Journal Inc., 1989): 1351. In 2004 Faleomavaega managed to change the election system on the island by introducing a bill that created a primary system, getting rid of

the runoff. See *Almanac of American Politics, 2006* (Washington, DC: National Journal Group Inc., 2005): 1860.

12 Office of the Clerk, U.S. House of Representatives, "Election Statistics, 1920 to Present," http://history.house.gov/Institution/Election-Statistics/Election-Statistics/; "American Samoa–2010 Census Results: Total Population by County," U.S. Census Bureau, accessed 15 July 2015, https://www.census.gov/2010census/news/releases/operations/cb11-cn177.html.

13 According to the U.S. Census Bureau, the average congressional district population following the 2010 Census was 710,767. *Congressional Apportionment: 2010 Census Briefs*, C2010BR-08, prepared by Kristin D. Burnett, U.S. Census Bureau (Washington, DC, issued November 2011): 1.

14 *Almanac of American Politics, 2000* (Washington, DC: National Journal Inc., 1999): 1782; *Almanac of American Politics, 2002* (Washington, DC: National Journal Group Inc., 2001): 1699.

15 Gregg Zoroya, "From Tiny Pacific Islands Comes Outsized Sacrifice," 27 May 2005, *USA Today*: A16.

16 Faleomavaega, oral history interview. See also Jerry Spangler, "Mormon Democrats Link Up in Congress," 31 January 2005, *Deseret Morning News*: n.p.

17 Faleomavaega, oral history interview.

18 Ibid.

19 Ibid.

20 Various issues of the *Congressional Directory*, from the 101st through the 113th Congresses (1989–2013).

21 *Politics in America, 2014* (Washington, DC: CQ-Roll Call, Inc., 2013): 1104; John Pomfret, "As China Rises, So Does its Influence on the Hill," 9 January 2010, *Washington Post*: A1.

22 *Politics in America, 2014*: 1105.

23 House Committee on Foreign Affairs, *Legislative Review Activities of the Committee on Foreign Affairs*, 111th Cong., 2nd sess., H. Rept. 713 (3 January 2011): 75–76.

24 South Pacific Economic and Educational Development Act, H.R. 3062, 110th Cong. (2007).

25 Faleomavaega, oral history interview.

26 Ibid.

27 Various issues of the *Congressional Directory*, from the 101st through the 113th Congresses (1989–2013).

28 Faleomavaega, oral history interview.

29 H.J. Res. 577, 101st Cong. (1990); H.J. Res. 182, 102nd Cong. (1991); H.J. Res. 342, 102nd Cong. (1991).

30 H. Con. Res. 214, 101st Cong. (1989). See also Les Blumenthal, "Lawmakers Call for Consumer Boycott of Drift Net Caught Tuna," 25 October 1989, Associated Press.

31 "Star-Kist Laying Off Hundreds in American Samoa," 25 July 2009, *Daily-Journal Messenger* (Seneca, SC): D1.

32 *Almanac of American Politics, 2006*: 1860; *Almanac of American Politics, 2008* (Washington, DC: National Journal Group Inc., 2007): 1814; David Cohen, "Ravaged Samoa," 1 October 2009, *Forbes*, https://www.forbes.com/2009/10/01/samoa-tsunami-earthquake-opinions-contributors-david-cohen.html#6128ab4c48a2 (accessed 15 July 2015); *Almanac of American Politics, 2012* (Washington, DC: The University of Chicago Press, 2011): 1804; Jonathan Weisman, "Minimum-Wage Hike May Reach to Samoa," 13 January 2007, *Washington Post*: A2; "Wage Bill to Include Territories," 14 January 2007, *Deseret Morning News* (Salt Lake City, UT): n.p.; "American Samoa Cannery to Fire 200 Workers," 6 June 2007, *Honolulu Star-Bulletin*: n.p.; "Tsunami Swamps Samoan Isles," 30 September 2009, *Seattle Times*: A1; "Tsunami Toll Expected to Rise in Samoan Islands," 30 September 2009, *Los Angeles Times*: A23.

33 *Almanac of American Politics, 2008*: 1816.

34 *Politics in America, 2014*: 1104.

35 *Almanac of American Politics, 1998* (Washington, DC: National Journal Inc., 1997): 1566.

36 House Committee on Resources, *Authorizing the Secretary of the Interior to Make Adjustments to the Boundary of the National Park of American Samoa to Include Certain Portions of the Islands of Ofu and Olosega within the Park, and for Other Purposes*, 107th Cong., 2nd sess., H. Rept. 372 (12 March 2002): 2.

37 Hearing before the Senate Committee on Energy and Natural Resources, Subcommittee on National Parks, *Miscellaneous National Parks Bills*, 107th Cong., 2nd sess. (12 June 2002): 9–12, 15–16; Senate Committee on Energy and Natural Resources, *Natural Park of American Samoa*, 107th Cong., 2nd sess., S. Rept. 270 (11 September 2002).

38 For more on the bill, see *Almanac of American Politics, 2002*: 1701.

39 Eni F. H. Faleomavaega, "Perspective on Nuclear Testing: Stop the Rape of the South Pacific," 25 June 1995, *Los Angeles Times*: M5; Ian Christopher McCaleb, "Panel Slams Proposed French Nuke Tests," 13 July 1995, United Press International; Philip Shenon, "French Tow Ships off Site of Atom Test," 3 September 1995, *New York Times*: A9; Scott Kraft, "France Detonates Nuclear Device at Pacific Test Site," 6 September 1995, *Los Angeles Times*: A1; H.R. 3062, 110th Cong. (2007); H.R. 3133, 106th Cong. (1999).

40 H.R. 4010, 106th Cong. (2000).

41 H.R. 3720, 107th Cong. (2002); H.R. 2673, 107th Cong. (2001).

42 H.R. 2584, 108th Cong. (2003).

43 H.R. 189, 103rd Cong. (1993); H.R. 1060, 104th Cong. (1995); H.R. 188, 103rd Cong. (1993); H.R. 185, 103rd Cong. (1993).

44 H. Amdt. 268, 106th Cong. (1999); H. Amdt. 454, 106th Cong. (1999).

45 *Politics in America, 2006* (Washington, DC: Congressional Quarterly Inc., 2005): 1138; H.R. 1448, 107th Cong. (2001); H.R. 982, 108th Cong. (2003); H.R. 2010, 108th Cong. (2003).

46 Office of the Clerk, U.S. House of Representatives, "Election Statistics, 1920 to Present"; Fili Sagapolutele, "1st Woman Elected as American Samoa Delegate," 5 November 2014, Associated Press.

47 Fili Sagapolutele, "Faleomavaega Discusses Future Plans, Which Include Returning Home," 11 November 2014, http://samoanews. com (accessed 2 September 2015).

48 Sagapolutele, "Faleomavaega Discusses Future Plans, Which Include Returning Home."

49 *Congressional Record*, House, 113th Cong., 2nd sess. (8 December 2014): H8822.

50 Max Greenwood, "Eni Faleomavaega, American Samoa's Longest-Serving Delegate, Dies," 23 February 2017, *The Hill*, http://thehill. com/blogs/blog-briefing-room/news/320931-eni-faleomavaega-american-samoas-longest-serving-house-delegate (accessed 30 May 2017); Associated Press, "Eni Faleomavaega, 73, American Samoa's Delegate to Congress," 24 February 2017, *New York Times*: B15; Democratic Leader Nancy Pelosi, "Pelosi Statement on Passing of Former Congressman Eni F. H. Faleomavaega," press release, accessed 30 May 2017, http://www.democraticleader.gov/newsroom/2232017/.

A Growing Diversity

1993–2017

In late April 1975, eight-year-old Anh (Joseph) Cao's long and improbable odyssey to the halls of Congress began as North Vietnamese communists seized the southern capital city of Saigon.[1]

The trajectory of the soft-spoken, bookish Cao toward Capitol Hill stands out as one of the most remarkable in the modern era, even as it neatly encapsulated post-1965 Asian immigration patterns to the United States.

Still, the origins of Cao's story were commonplace. For three decades, conflict and civil war enveloped his country. After the Vietnamese threw off the yoke of French colonialism following World War II, a doomed peace accord in 1954 removed the French military and partitioned Vietnam. The new government in South Vietnam aligned with Western world powers, while North Vietnam allied with communist states. Amid the Cold War, the U.S. backed successive Saigon regimes against communist insurgents before directly intervening in 1965. A massive ground and air war dragged on inconclusively for nearly a decade. More than 58,000 American troops were killed, and more than three million South and North Vietnamese perished.[2] Public opposition in the United States eventually forced an end to the intervention.

America's decision to withdraw from Vietnam shattered Joseph Cao's family just as it did many thousands of others as communist forces soon swamped the ineffectual government and military in the South.

In 2011 Japanese-American veterans received the Congressional Gold Medal for their valor during World War II. The medal included the motto of the 442nd Regimental Combat Team, "Go for Broke."

Nisei Soldiers of World War II Congressional Gold Medal Obverse © 2011 United States Mint

Vietnamese refugees, including this family aboard the USS *Hancock* in 1975, fled their country in four waves from 1975 to the mid-1990s.

Image courtesy of the National Archives and Records Administration

Just days before Saigon fell, Cao's mother, Khang Thi Tran, spirited one of her daughters and two sons, including Anh, to a U.S. airfield. Along with their aunt, the three children were airlifted out and then transported to Guam. As three of more than 130,000 people who evacuated from Saigon and South Vietnam, Cao and his siblings joined the first of four waves of Vietnamese immigration to the United States that stretched into the mid-1990s.[3]

From Guam, the siblings' paths diverged. The aunt kept one of the boys; the daughter traveled to Florida to live with an American foster family; and Anh went to live with a bachelor uncle in Goshen, Indiana. He entered the first grade and learned English from his classmates, delivered newspapers to earn money, and eventually relocated to Houston, Texas. Cao's mother and several siblings remained behind in Vietnam, and for seven years, the communists imprisoned and tortured his father, My Quang Cao, a former officer in the South Vietnamese Army. Eventually, in the early 1990s, the family reunited in America.[4]

Joseph Cao's story, however, was just beginning. After spending years preparing for the priesthood, he left the seminary and went to law school, believing that he could better serve the poor and disadvantaged as a public servant. He settled in New Orleans in a growing Vietnamese community, practiced law, and was drawn into politics as the city fought to recover from the devastation wreaked by Hurricane Katrina in 2005. In 2008, running as a Republican for a seat in the U.S. House of Representatives from a city that Democrats dominated, Cao upended a nine-term incumbent, becoming the first Vietnamese American to win a seat in Congress. "It's like the American Dream," a neighbor and supporter observed.[5]

Cao's story was inextricably linked with late 20th-century immigration. By 2010 Vietnamese Americans numbered 1.7 million and comprised the fourth largest group of Asians in the United States, behind only Chinese, Filipinos, and Indians. Nearly 84 percent of the group was foreign-born, well above the average of Asian Americans generally, and most were refugees who, like Cao, sought safety from political persecution and the ravages of war. They had settled largely in the West and the South in or near urban areas. While Vietnamese Americans had the lowest voter registration rates of the major Asian-American groups, Cao's election marked a moment of ethnic pride and suggested the rising influence of Asian Americans.[6]

The story of the Vietnamese-American community, which grew from several hundred thousand in 1980, was but one piece of a larger mosaic of Asian immigration to the United States. Driven by Cold War conflicts in faraway places like Laos and Cambodia and made possible by the legacy of mid-1960s immigration reform, these trends profoundly affected the story of Asian Pacific Americans (APAs) in Congress.

HART–CELLER LEGACIES

The 1965 Hart–Celler Act overhauled immigration policy in the United States by increasing access for new immigrant groups and producing a demographic revolution in the U.S. population. The long-lasting effects of this legislation have, in large measure, shaped the composition of the modern Congress. Over

President Lyndon B. Johnson delivers remarks at the ceremonial signing of the Immigration and Nationality Act of 1965 on Liberty Island. The law, also known as the Hart–Celler Act, transformed immigration policy in the United States.

Photograph by Yoichi Okamoto; image courtesy of the Lyndon B. Johnson Presidential Library/National Archives and Records Administration

the last 50 years, APA communities in the United States have grown in both number and diversity. As of 2011, APAs (both foreign- and native-born) made up nearly 6 percent of the entire U.S. populace and their total population stood at 18.2 million. More than half of the entire foreign-born population of the United States has entered the country since 1990, and at the time of this writing, APAs represent the fastest-growing group.[7] In fact, in the 30 years between 1980 and 2010, the APA population jumped nearly fourfold.[8]

This population boom has helped to redefine America's electoral makeup and changed the face of the national legislature. Including current Members and first-termers, 28 of the 60 Congressmen and Congresswomen profiled in this book have been elected after 1993 (47 percent). Unlike in the previous 100-plus years when statutory representatives accounted for the bulk of Asian Pacific Americans in Congress, only three of the 28 Members in this section serve or have served as Delegates. The remaining 25 Members represent nearly 70 percent of all APA Representatives and Senators ever elected with full voting rights.

A consequential development in Asian immigration over the last 40 years has been the marked diversity of the people coming to America. No longer a story dominated by Chinese and Japanese immigration, Asian immigration in the modern era involves a greater proportion of immigrants from the Philippines, India, Vietnam, and Korea. Whereas Japanese Americans once accounted for nearly half of the entire Asian-American population, as of 2010, they had dropped to around 7 percent. Chinese Americans make up the largest segment of America's Asian population at around 23 percent. They are followed by Filipinos (roughly 20 percent), Indians (18 percent), Vietnamese (10 percent), and Koreans (also around 10 percent). Many have settled in the States to fill jobs and reunite with family, and many have gone on to become naturalized citizens.[9]

The Members in this section—both former and current—reflect this new diversity. In addition to Joseph Cao, who fled Saigon, Jay C. Kim was born in

Seoul, before Korea's partition, and immigrated to the United States in 1961; Senator Mazie K. Hirono was born in Japan and grew up in Fukushima before moving to Hawaii around the age of eight; David Wu was born in Taiwan and moved to the United States in 1961 to rejoin his father, who was studying in America; Congressman S. Raja Krishnamoorthi and Congresswoman Pramila Jayapal were both born in India; and Senator Tammy Duckworth, whose father was a U.S. military veteran and whose mother was from Thailand and later became a U.S. citizen, was born in Bangkok.[10]

Seven other Members who were born in the United States had at least one parent immigrate from overseas: Charles Djou's father was from Shanghai, China, and his mother was from Bangkok, Thailand; Bobby Jindal's parents came over from India, as did Congressman Ami Bera's and Congressman Ro Khanna's. Congresswoman Judy Chu's mother was from China; Congresswoman Grace Meng's parents emigrated from Taiwan; Steve Austria's father was from the Philippines; and Hansen Clarke's father was from Bangladesh.

America's Pacific territories continue to play a prominent part in the makeup of the modern Congress as well, and they account for the birthplace of four Members in this section: Robert A. Underwood was born in Guam and later served as its Delegate; Gregorio Kilili Camacho Sablan was born in Saipan in the Northern Mariana Islands; Colleen Hanabusa was born in Honolulu when Hawaii was still a U.S. territory; and Congresswoman Tulsi Gabbard was born in American Samoa.

Although the 1965 Hart–Celler Act laid the groundwork for a substantial portion of Asian immigration to America, much of the recent movement between countries has also been driven by job markets both here and abroad.[11]

But even that change can, in large measure, be tied to the 1965 law. Along with family reunification, the Hart–Celler Act created a number of opportunities for professional and highly skilled Asian immigrants. As Erika Lee, a noted historian of the Asian-American experience, has observed, that policy remained firmly in place as the country entered the 21st century. Lee points to U.S. companies in high-tech fields that recruit overseas. In fact, Asian immigrants, she notes, receive nearly 75 percent of all H-1B visas set aside for "highly skilled" immigrant workers.[12] "The majority of new arrivals," Lee wrote in *The Making of Asian America*, "come to join family already here and bring a different set of educational and professional skills than earlier immigrants."[13]

REFUGEE CRISIS

Much of the emigration from South and Southeast Asia can also be traced to a series of laws passed in response to the Vietnam War and the fallout from the West's fight against communism.

Like global conflicts before it, the Vietnam War forced America to confront a serious refugee crisis. The United States had been slow to develop a refugee policy during World War II, and afterward Congress designed the Displaced Persons Act of 1948 to help Europeans who met restrictive credentials—namely, non-Jews and non-Catholics. As the immigration historian Mae M. Ngai has pointed out, over the next two decades America's refugee policy worked on something of "an ad hoc basis" and was often in conflict with international law.[14]

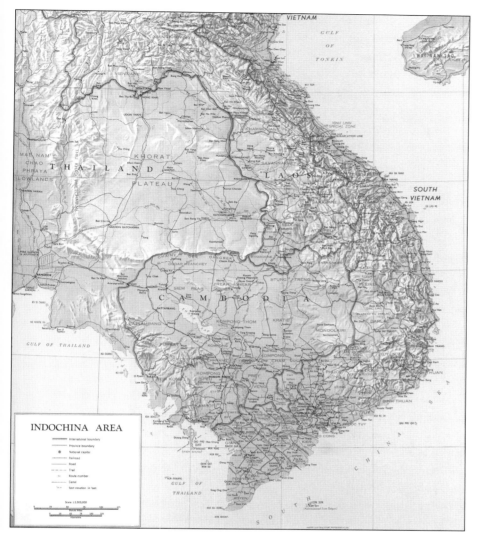

INDOCHINA AREA

International boundary
Province boundary
National capital
Railroad
Road
Trail
Route number
Canal
Spot elevation (in feet)

Scale 1:1,500,000

By the mid-1970s, as governments in South Vietnam, Cambodia, and Laos fell and displaced thousands of people, many Americans, including Members of Congress, opposed proposals to allow them to settle in the United States. When U.S. immigration agencies finally began admitting Southeast Asian refugees, they were quickly confronted by a wave of people in need of help.[15]

In 1975, responding to the refugee crisis, Congress passed the Indochina Migration and Refugee Assistance Act, setting aside $405 million for a two-year evacuation and resettlement program to assist refugees from South Vietnam and Cambodia.[16] Congress quickly amended the law to clear the way for thousands of refugees from Laos.[17]

For the rest of the 1970s, the crisis in Southeast Asia only worsened as a second wave of refugees began fleeing the region. Chinese families escaped Vietnam; Cambodians fled the autocratic and murderous Khmer Rouge regime; Laotians streamed into Thailand. In total, more than 100,000 people in the region fled for their lives. The U.S. government, still struggling with the scope of the crisis, responded by admitting more than 20,000 additional refugees and opening up residency opportunities and access to social services.[18]

Judiciary Committee Chairman Peter Rodino of New Jersey supported the Refugee Act of 1980, calling it "one of the most important pieces of humanitarian legislation ever enacted by a U.S. Congress."

Collection of the U.S. House of Representatives

Amerasian:

Term used to describe the children of U.S. military personnel and Asian partners born outside the United States.

The Refugee Act of 1980 overhauled many of America's humanitarian policies. It broadened the federal designation of "refugee" and opened the door to more people looking to settle in the United States. The legislation also included funding for new relief programs.

Image courtesy of the National Archives and Records Administration

When the 96th Congress (1979–1981) convened, the Indochina refugee crisis remained at full boil. The United States agreed to accept another 15,000 Indochinese refugees over the next year, but the flow of refugees into camps in Thailand, Hong Kong, and other parts of Southeast Asia far surpassed the trickle of asylum-seekers being resettled elsewhere.[19]

To address the refugee crisis, the 96th Congress formed the Select Commission on Immigration and Refugee Policy and tasked it with developing a blueprint for comprehensive reform. Congress eventually created a new office—the Coordinator for Refugee Affairs—and moved many of the refugee programs to the Department of Health and Human Services. It capped the total number of refugees at 50,000, limited the administration's parole power, and required the President to confer with Congress when raising the annual quota.[20]

The Refugee Act of 1980 was the country's most comprehensive refugee legislation and overhauled many of America's humanitarian policies. With new accountability systems in place and federal funding to match, Judiciary Committee Chairman Peter Rodino of New Jersey proclaimed it was "one of the most important pieces of humanitarian legislation ever enacted by a U.S. Congress."[21]

As in previous conflicts abroad, U.S. soldiers serving overseas occasionally fathered children during the Vietnam War. When reports surfaced in the early 1970s that these children, known as "Amerasians" because they were born to an American parent, were being shunned in South Vietnam as *bui doi* (dust or trash), certain Members of Congress took up their cause. On May 21, 1971, Hawaii Representative Patsy Takemoto Mink introduced H.R. 8462, providing special entry visas for Amerasians in South Vietnam, but the bill never made it out of the Judiciary Committee.[22]

Increasing media coverage and lobbying pressure led to improved awareness, but it was not until 1982 that Congress passed the Amerasian Immigration Act, allowing Amerasians to immigrate to the United States under a nonquota visa using the family reunification provision.[23]

PUBLIC LAW 96-212

Ninety-sixth Congress of the United States of America

AT THE SECOND SESSION

Begun and held at the City of Washington on Thursday, the third day of January, one thousand nine hundred and eighty

An Act

To amend the Immigration and Nationality Act to revise the procedures for the admission of refugees, to amend the Migration and Refugee Assistance Act of 1962 to establish a more uniform basis for the provision of assistance to refugees, and for other purposes.

Be it enacted by the Senate and House of Representatives of the United States of America in Congress assembled, That this Act may be cited as the "Refugee Act of 1980".

TITLE I—PURPOSE

Sec. 101. (a) The Congress declares that it is the historic policy of the United States to respond to the urgent needs of persons subject to persecution in their homelands, including, where appropriate,

The program, however, required eligible children to enter the States from a country with which the United States had diplomatic relations. This precluded Vietnam, but it included countries with substantial Vietnamese populations, including the Philippines, South Korea, and Thailand. The bill also prevented the parent or any half-siblings from immigrating to the United States under the same conditions. President Ronald Reagan signed the bill in the fall of 1982, noting it acknowledged "the rightful claim of Amerasian children to American citizenship."[24]

The bill struggled to make much of an impact. Few people took advantage of the program, since most of the qualified participants were still children and were unable to locate sponsorship in America. Critics of the measure called it nothing more than an empty gesture.[25]

Congress revisited the issue of Amerasian immigration in 1987 with new legislation that assumed no documentation would exist to prove American parentage and cleared the way for the child's immediate family to enter the United States as well. The children would be counted against Vietnam's immigration quota, but a provision introduced by Robert Mrazek of New York ensured that they would receive refugee benefits, such as cultural and language training.[26] While the House Judiciary Committee blocked Mrazek's bill, he managed to have it embedded in the omnibus continuing appropriations act.[27]

By 2009, according to the Amerasian Independent Voice of America and the Amerasian Fellowship Association, 75,000 Amerasians and their immediate relations had come to the United States in the decades following the war, while a few hundred stayed in Vietnam. But only around 2 percent ever reunited with their biological American parent.[28]

GEOGRAPHIC DISTRIBUTION

As they have grown in number and diversity, so too have Asian-Pacific American communities spread out across the United States. If the story of the previous era (1941–1992) occurred mostly in the American West and Hawaii, the story of our modern era also takes place along the Eastern Seaboard, the Gulf Coast, and in the Midwest. In an increasingly globalized world, Asian immigrants have begun practicing "transnational immigration" as well, living or commuting between one's home country and the United States.[29]

Although the West Coast remains the home of nearly half the adult APA population (47 percent), communities have sprung up all over the United States. As of the 2010 Census, 20 percent live in the Northeast, 21 percent in the South, and 11 percent in the Midwest.[30] Despite the growing national population, in the 10 years between 2000 and 2010, the proportion of Asian Americans living in the West has actually decreased while rising in the South, the region with the fastest growth rate in the country.[31]

Despite the general tendency to put down roots in the western states, the settlement patterns of the six largest Asian-American communities—Chinese, Filipinos, Indians, Vietnamese, Koreans, and Japanese—seem to share few, if any, commonalities. Of the largest group, 49 percent of adult Chinese Americans live in the West, but a sizable population (27 percent) lives in the Northeast. The vast majority of adult Filipinos living in the United States have settled in the West (66 percent), while the South represents the next largest

Representative Robert Mrazek of New York championed refugee benefits for cultural and language training to children with Vietnamese and American parents.

Collection of the U.S. House of Representatives

Located in a primarily Vietnamese neighborhood of Port Arthur, Texas, the Queen of Peace Shrine and Gardens features a statue of the Virgin Mary in a pagoda. No longer concentrated on the West Coast, Asian-Pacific American communities today exist throughout the United States.

Image courtesy of the Library of Congress

population at 16 percent. Nearly half the adult Vietnamese population lives in the West (49 percent), but a substantial 32 percent also lives in the South, especially along the Gulf Coast. Among adult Koreans, 45 percent live in the West, but nearly equal numbers live in the South and Northeast (23 and 21 percent, respectively.)[32]

At one end of the spectrum, adult Indian Americans are the most geographically dispersed Asian-American community in the United States: 31 percent live in the Northeast, 29 percent in the South, 24 percent in the West, and 17 percent in the Midwest. At the other end are adult Japanese Americans. An overwhelming majority (71 percent) live in the West, followed well behind by the South at 12 percent, the Northeast at 9 percent, and the Midwest at 8 percent.[33]

On a state-by-state level, California led the nation in 2010 with the largest Asian-American population (5,556,592). It was followed by New York (1,579,494), Texas (1,110,666), New Jersey (795,163), Hawaii (780,968), Illinois (668,694), Washington (604,251), Florida (573,083), Virginia (522,199), and Pennsylvania (402,587).[34]

Pacific Diaspora

A movement of people both within the Pacific and from the Pacific to the mainland (and occasionally back to the Pacific) has also begun changing the face of the American electorate. As the historian Paul Spickard has pointed out, "This is not an entirely new phenomenon. Islanders have been moving around the Pacific for as long as memory recalls, for many hundreds of years." "Nor is migration to North America wholly new," he observed, pointing out that Pacific Islanders worked in a host of 19th-century industries on the West Coast. What is different, however, is the "velocity and impact of such movements" in the late 20th and early 21st centuries.[35]

The 2010 Census revealed that 1.2 million people (or 0.4 percent of the entire U.S. population) identified as either Native Hawaiian or Other Pacific Islander, which it defined as "a person having origins in any of the original peoples of Hawaii, Guam, Samoa, or other Pacific Islands."[36] Although statistically small, their numbers increased "more than three times faster than the total U.S. population" between 2000 and 2010, making their growth rate second only to that of the Asian-American community, which the Census counts separately. It is important to note that many Pacific Islanders are American nationals and, therefore, legally able to move to the mainland United States. More than 70 percent of Native Hawaiians and Other Pacific Islanders call the West home, and over half live in Hawaii and California. Another 16 percent live in the South (which also experienced a population surge during the 2000s), 7 percent in the Northeast, and 6 percent in the Midwest. Native Hawaiians represent the largest group, followed by Samoans, and Guamanians or Chamorro.[37]

Many young people from American Samoa, Guam, and the Northern Mariana Islands enlist in the U.S. military, seeking better benefits and higher salaries. Others have settled in Hawaii and on the mainland—particularly California and Utah—to pursue an education, often with the sponsorship of religious organizations.[38]

For Delegate Eni F. H. Faleomavaega, who represented American Samoa in the House from 1989 to 2015, this diaspora often influenced his constituent outreach. "I'm probably the only member that has to go to San Francisco, Los Angeles, San Diego, or Hawaii where we have communities … where I would attend their community activities," he said in a 2011 oral history. In his experience, Samoans living on the mainland often preferred speaking to him instead of their own Representative. "They call me all over the country," he said. "Of course, our men and women in the military, I take care of them. We also have a number from Western Samoa who live in the United States and I try to help them as well."[39]

LEGACY OF EXCLUSION

Yet, despite their often successful political mobilization, Asian Pacific Americans continue to live with a legacy of exclusion that stretches back more than 160 years. "To be Asian American in the twenty-first century," observed the historian Erika Lee, "is an exercise in coming to terms with a contradiction: benefiting from new positions of power and privilege while still being victims of hate crimes and microaggressions that dismiss Asian American issues and treat Asian Americans as outsiders in their own country."[40]

Their growing population, combined with that unique duality—"with histories of both exclusion and inclusion," Lee has written—enables Asian and Pacific Americans to ask what it means to be American even as they shape and reshape the country in the 21st century.[41]

The modern Congress reflects this in ways large and small. But perhaps the most immediate example is its direct link to the legacy of World War II: Three Members first elected to Congress in this era had either personal or familial experience with the forced evacuation and policy of internment that followed the bombing of Pearl Harbor. Congresswoman Doris Matsui was born in the Poston Camp in Arizona; Congressman Mike Honda lived in the Amache Camp as an infant; and Congressman Mark Takano's parents had been interned as well.

PACIFIC ISLANDERS: TERRITORIAL STATUS AND REPRESENTATION

As the number of Asian-American immigrants arriving in the United States steadily rose, Pacific Islanders continued to search for ways to clarify their relationship with the United States government. In the fall of 2008, the Commonwealth of the Northern Mariana Islands (CNMI) was the last of the unincorporated U.S. territories to receive representation in Congress when it elected its first nonvoting Delegate to the House. Since the end of World War II, Guam, the Northern Mariana Islands, and other American possessions in the Pacific grappled with persistent questions concerning political sovereignty and congressional representation. This political upheaval frequently reached the chambers of Congress, involving APA Members and Delegates in a debate that lasted more than three decades.

Administrators process evacuees about to leave the Poston Camp in Yuma County, Arizona, in 1945. California Representative Doris Matsui was born in the camp.

Image courtesy of the National Archives and Records Administration

Trust Territory of the Pacific Islands, or Micronesia

The Northern Mariana Islands consist of 17 islands in the western Pacific Basin just north of the equator. Since 1898, when Guam, the southernmost island of the Marianas, was seized by the U.S. Navy during the Spanish-American War, possession of these islands frequently changed hands. Guam eventually became a U.S. possession, and what was left of the Spanish Empire in the Pacific, including the Northern Mariana Islands, was sold to Germany in 1899. During World War I, however, Germany lost its Pacific colonies to Japan, and during World War II the U.S. military captured two Japanese-held islands (Saipan and Tinian) in the Marianas.[42]

At the end of hostilities in the Pacific, the U.S. Navy retained control of the Japanese South Seas Islands. On July 18, 1947, Congress agreed by joint resolution to authorize President Harry S. Truman's approval of the Trusteeship Agreement for the Territory of the Pacific Islands. The agreement with the United Nations Security Council required the United States to "make ample provision for the political, economic, social, and educational development" of South Pacific territories, creating the Trust Territory of the Pacific Islands (TTPI), commonly referred to as Micronesia.[43]

As in Guam and American Samoa, President Truman had already decided in November 1946 that the U.S. Navy would administer the TTPI on an interim basis, but traditional forms of authority based upon kinship, and which were often specific to each island, remained the basis for local governance. In 1951 President Truman ordered the transfer of administrative responsibilities over Micronesia from the U.S. Navy to the Interior Department, and throughout the 1960s the department granted Micronesians small concessions toward their own self-determination, including the creation of the Micronesian Congress in 1965.[44]

Under obligations to the United Nations, Congress slowly began addressing the status of the Trust Territory in the second half of the 1960s. Senator Hiram L. Fong of Hawaii introduced S. Con. Res. 50 in August 1965, proposing

Palau was one of the islands included in the Trust Territory of the Pacific Islands. Congress created the territory, commonly referred to as Micronesia, in 1947.

Image courtesy of the National Archives and Records Administration

that Micronesia merge with the state of Hawaii, an effort, he claimed, to push Congress to reach a consensus over the fate of the territories.[45] Senator Fong was also among three Members who introduced measures to establish a commission on the TTPI in 1967.[46]

During the 91st Congress (1969–1971), Representative Mink introduced bills to clarify Micronesia's status by either providing for a Trust Territory Organic Act or by authorizing a Micronesian constitutional convention. "Mr. Speaker, all the people of the Pacific who live under the American flag make up my larger unofficial constituency. To these people who have no voice in the governance of their lives I believe all of us owe a special responsibility," Mink said. "Regrettably in our busy lives we do not have the time to devote to these voiceless, powerless, subjugated peoples living on the remote coral atolls of the Pacific."[47] But it soon became clear that no House action would take place unless various agencies of jurisdiction within the federal government agreed to give the TTPI a greater level of autonomy.

Micronesia Flies Apart

In September 1969, officials from three key executive departments—State, Defense, and Interior—began meeting with delegates from the Micronesian Congress's joint committee on future status. The discussions were slow initially. The United States was hesitant to relinquish military control over the region and, while many in the TTPI expressed a desire for independence, the Northern Mariana district representatives went the other way in the hopes of creating a permanent relationship with the United States.[48]

This had been a goal of the Northern Marianas since the 1960s, when the district legislature sponsored a series of plebiscites on the chain's future political status that reaffirmed the electorate's desire to reunite with nearby Guam, citing the neighboring island's economic progress. The passage of the Guam Organic Act of 1950 had only strengthened the reunification movement. Guamanians, however, rejected a referendum proposing to join the Northern Marianas in 1969.[49] The Saipanese—those living in the Northern Mariana Islands' largest and most populous island, Saipan—were most comfortable with English and felt economically burdened by the rest of Micronesia. After Guam's rejection, they more aggressively pursued their own agreement.[50]

By the early 1970s, the situation in Micronesia grew tense and, on February 19, 1971, Northern Mariana officials threatened to leave the Trust Territory. The very next day a fire set by an unknown arsonist destroyed the legislative chambers of the Micronesian Congress in Saipan. The entire Northern Mariana delegation then boycotted a special session scheduled for later in the year.[51]

Northern Mariana officials began negotiating directly with the United States over the chain's political status, retaining a law firm to represent their interests in the capital and establishing the Political Status Commission in 1972. The Northern Marianas also sent representatives to the United Nations Trusteeship Council to report the islands' desire to negotiate for a closer association with the United States, separate from the rest of Micronesia.[52]

Senator Hiram L. Fong of Hawaii, shown here in his office decorated with flowers, proposed that Micronesia merge with the state of Hawaii in 1965.

Image courtesy of the U.S. Senate Historical Office

Representative Phillip Burton of California introduced legislation to create the Commonwealth of the Northern Mariana Islands in 1975.

Image courtesy of the Library of Congress

President Gerald R. Ford signs H.J. Res. 549 into law on February 24, 1976, to form the Commonwealth of the Northern Mariana Islands.

Image courtesy of the Gerald R. Ford Presidential Library/National Archives and Records Administration

Commonwealth of the Northern Mariana Islands and the Associated States

Negotiations on the future status of the Northern Mariana Islands opened on December 13, 1972, and continued for two years. The final agreement allowed for local governance of the islands, but gave the United States the right to control defense and foreign affairs. All federal tax revenue would return to the islands' coffers in addition to an annual federal grant. Finally, it provided for a constitutional convention to outline the new government.[53]

On February 15, 1975, representatives of the Northern Marianas and the U.S. government signed the Covenant to Establish a Commonwealth of the Northern Mariana Islands in Political Union with the United States of America, and the Mariana district legislature approved it five days later. On June 17, 1975, 95 percent of registered voters in the Marianas participated in a plebiscite monitored by the United States; 78.8 percent voted approval of the covenant.[54]

President Gerald R. Ford officially informed the U.S. Congress of the covenant and sent a proposed joint resolution on July 1, 1975. Legislation introduced by California Representative Phillip Burton, who chaired the Interior Subcommittee on Territorial and Insular Affairs, creating the Commonwealth of the Northern Mariana Islands (CNMI) moved swiftly through the House. It unanimously passed the Interior and Insular Affairs Committee and cleared the House by voice vote before the end of the month. Guam Delegate Antonio Borja Won Pat conveyed his constituents' support for the measure as well as his desire "that this union will usher in a new era of good will, mutual cooperation and eventual union of all Chamorros in the Marianas." With minor changes, the Senate concurred on February 24, 1976. In an East Room ceremony on March 24, 1976, President Ford signed the joint resolution into law.[55]

The CNMI was the only part of the Trust Territory to remain directly tied to the United States as a commonwealth. After a long period of negotiations with the U.S. government and several popular referenda, three independent states emerged from the remnants of the TTPI: the Federated States of Micronesia, the

Marshall Islands, and the Republic of Palau. By the end of the 1980s, Congress had passed legislation that formalized a Compact of Free Association between these three island states and the U.S. government. The United States agreed to provide military defense and financial aid while retaining the right to military bases and other strategic considerations.[56]

Guam's Pursuit of Commonwealth Status

For Guamanians, CNMI's commonwealth agreement had bolstered a desire to negotiate one of their own.[57] The struggle for greater political autonomy continued with a new Territorial Delegate, Democrat Robert A. Underwood, who had defeated the Republican incumbent Ben Garrido Blaz in 1992. Underwood introduced the Guam Commonwealth Act (H.R. 1521) in late March 1993.[58] The measure called for the creation of a commonwealth with full self-government, the preservation of Chamorro culture, and the "mutual consent" of Guam and the United States when considering federal policies affecting the territory. The bill also sent an important signal, that Guam remained interested in achieving commonwealth status. But progress remained fitful during the first part of President William J. (Bill) Clinton's administration, in part because of staff turnover in the Interior Department office handling the negotiations.[59]

In 1997 Underwood took to the House Floor to ask his colleagues to consider commonwealth status for Guam. "The 100th anniversary of the Spanish-American War marks an important time period for the United States to, in a sense, come face to face with its imperial past," Underwood declared, "and come face to face with what hopefully will be in the next century a more perfect union not only for the 50 States and the District of Columbia, but all the people who live under the American flag."[60] A House Resources Committee hearing in October 1997, however, marked the end of commonwealth negotiations. The Interior Department pointed to four major demands by Guam that it could not support: insisting that the commonwealth government would have veto power over legislation or regulations applying to Guam; limiting decisions on Guam's political status to Chamorros at the exclusion of other U.S. citizen residents; transferring control over immigration and labor policy to the commonwealth; and creating a joint commission with authority to determine the transfer of military lands in Guam.[61] With the two sides unable to agree on the details, the negotiations ended. On the centennial of the United States capturing Guam in 1998, Delegate Underwood, disappointed, spoke of "a relationship that has not been fully consummated. It is not like a wedding anniversary, but more the recognition of the date when two people first met and began a relationship."[62]

CNMI Congressional Representation

Largely because of the territory's small population, the CNMI commonwealth legislation failed to include language about its representation in the U.S. Congress. During the covenant negotiations, Mariana representatives had proposed the creation of a nonvoting Delegate once the territory's population reached 50,000 people. The 1970 Census had recorded 9,640 inhabitants in the Mariana district, far smaller than the other territories that gained a Delegate in the 1970s: Guam, 84,996; the U.S. Virgin Islands, 62,468; and American

A campaign button touts Antonio Borja Won Pat's experience. Won Pat served as the Delegate from Guam in the U.S. House of Representatives from 1973 to 1984.

Collection of the U.S. House of Representatives

President William J. (Bill) Clinton speaks with Guam Delegate Robert A. Underwood during a Congressional Asian Pacific American Caucus meeting in 1998.

Image courtesy of the William J. Clinton Library/ National Archives and Records Administration

Samoa, 27,159.[63] But U.S. negotiators argued that only Congress could approve a nonvoting Delegate and did not include it in the covenant draft.[64]

As the only U.S. territory without an elected representative in Washington, CNMI followed the strategy other territories had used by sending an unofficial representative—one they called a "resident agent"—to lobby Congress and the executive branch starting in 1979.[65] "I cannot speak for the CNMI on the floor of the House of Representatives," Pedro A. Tenorio, the CNMI's fourth unofficial representative, noted in his testimony before a House subcommittee in 2007, "nor can I defend my people except as an invited witness at hearings such as this one."[66]

In the House, Guam's Delegates often looked after the interests of the CNMI. In January 1997, Delegate Underwood introduced a bill to grant the CNMI a nonvoting Delegate, but nothing came of it in either the 105th or 106th Congresses (1997–2001). But by 2000 Census data put the CNMI population at 69,221, well above the threshold for the territories receiving congressional representation in the 1970s.[67] Underwood introduced his CNMI Delegate bill again in May 2001 during the 107th Congress (2001–2003). "Right now, every American is represented, either full, by their representatives and senators, or partially, like the people of Guam, by the delegate," noted an Underwood spokeswoman. "The only people who are not are the residents of the CNMI."[68] The bill made it out of committee, but the House did not take it up. By the next Congress, Underwood had left Capitol Hill to run for governor of Guam.

Delegate Donna Christensen of the U.S. Virgin Islands eventually took up the mantle, introducing H.R. 3079 in the 110th Congress (2007–2009) on July 18, 2007. The bill to amend the commonwealth covenant extended U.S. immigration laws to the CNMI and provided for a nonvoting Delegate. According to Christensen, closing immigration loopholes to the CMNI provided leverage for the creation of the Delegate position, and she emphasized the strategic, national-security value of both Guam and the CNMI. The bill easily passed the House by voice vote. Bundled with nearly 60 other noncontroversial House-passed bills as S. 2739, it cleared the Senate and became law on May 8, 2008. The following November CNMI elected its first Territorial Delegate, Gregorio Kilili Camacho Sablan.[69]

APA MEMBERS ON CAPITOL HILL: GROWTH, ORGANIZATION, AND REPRESENTATION

In the relatively brief modern era that began in 1993, 28 Asian Pacific Americans have served in Congress. All but one of them have served in the House, and three total have served in the U.S. Senate. Together, they constitute nearly 47 percent of all the Asian Pacific Americans ever to serve in Congress. More APAs serve in the 115th Congress (2017–2019)—18 at the time of this writing—than have ever served before simultaneously.[70]

The reach of the Hart–Celler Immigration Act of 1965 is evident in the story of APAs in the modern Congresses. Whereas Japanese Americans stood out as the largest Asian immigrant community in the previous era and, accordingly, sent more Members to Congress than any other APA ethnic group, the diversity of the modern cohort is perhaps its most striking feature. Fueled by immigration

Donna Christensen, Delegate of the Virgin Islands, worked to establish a nonvoting Delegate for the Commonwealth of the Northern Mariana Islands. The first Delegate from the Northern Mariana Islands, Gregorio Kilili Camacho Sablan, was seated in the U.S. House of Representatives in 2009.

Collection of the U.S. House of Representatives

policies that opened the door to new Asian groups, this group includes Joseph Cao, the first Vietnamese American to serve in Congress, and Jay C. Kim, the first Korean American elected to Capitol Hill. In 1993 Robert C. (Bobby) Scott of Virginia, an African American with Filipino ancestry, won election to the House as the first individual of Filipino heritage to serve in Congress since the last of the archipelago's Resident Commissioners left with the grant of independence in 1946. In 2004 Louisiana's Bobby Jindal became just the second Asian-Indian American elected to Congress, more than 40 years after Dalip Singh (Judge) Saund of California left the House.

Before 1993 only two APA women, both representing Hawaii and both of Japanese ancestry, had ever served in Congress: Patsy Mink and Patricia Saiki. But beginning in 2005, with the election of California's Doris Matsui, who succeeded her late husband Robert T. Matsui in a special election, an additional 10 APA women have been elected to Congress through the 2016 elections. This reflects the general upward trend of women entering political office in recent decades. It also underscores the tendency of minority women to account for a larger percentage of their overall ethnic group in Congress compared to white women.[71] Mazie K. Hirono of Hawaii registered a notable accomplishment in this era when, after three terms as a U.S. Representative, she became the first APA woman ever to serve in the U.S. Senate, succeeding Senator Daniel K. Akaka in 2012.

A majority of these Members came from states that had large APA constituencies and a history of electing Asian Americans to Congress, seven from California and five from Hawaii. But for the first time APA Representatives were elected from more diverse geographic locales, with Virginia's Bobby Scott becoming the first APA Member of Congress to serve from a U.S. state outside of Hawaii or California. Others won election from districts in Ohio, Michigan, New York, Louisiana, and Washington State. Additionally, three new APA Territorial Delegates were elected to Congress in this period.

As with the generation of APAs that served between World War II and the end of the Cold War, this cohort served on a wide range of congressional committees reflecting the complete spectrum of legislative interests.[72] In 2007 Mike Honda became just the second Asian American to serve on the House Appropriations Committee. Steve Austria of Ohio followed him in 2011. California's Doris Matsui became the first to serve on the Energy and Commerce Committee; her husband, Robert T. Matsui, had sat for one term when it was named the Interstate and Foreign Commerce Committee. Tammy Duckworth of Illinois and Tulsi Gabbard of Hawaii, both Iraq War veterans, served on the Armed Services Committee.

While long-serving Hawaiian Senators Akaka and Daniel K. Inouye chaired two Senate committees apiece in this era and a number of subcommittees, only Norman Y. Mineta of California, who led the Public Works and Transportation Committee in the 103rd Congress (1993–1995), chaired a House committee. Several others, however, were tapped as chairmen of subcommittees. In the 105th Congress (1997–1999), Representative Kim led Transportation and Infrastructure's Subcommittee on Public Buildings and Economic Development. In the 110th and 111th Congresses (2007–2011), three APAs chaired House subcommittees: Virginia's Bobby Scott (Crime, Terrorism, and Homeland Security Subcommittee of the Judiciary Committee); American Samoa's Eni F. H. Faleomavaega (Asia, the Pacific, and the Global Environment Subcommittee of the Foreign Affairs Committee); and Washington's David Wu (Technology and Innovation Subcommittee of the Science Committee). In the 114th Congress (2015–2017), Aumua Amata Coleman Radewagen of American Samoa became just the second APA woman (after Patsy Mink) to wield a gavel when she led the Small Business Committee's Health and Technology Subcommittee.

Whereas in prior periods the legislative interests of APAs in Congress reflected the unique trajectories of the immigrant or Pacific Islander groups to which they belonged, organization and coordination have marked APA efforts in the last two decades. With the creation of the Congressional Asian Pacific American Caucus (CAPAC) in 1994 and efforts to collaborate with other minorities in Congress in the early 2000s, an agenda emerged that sought to leverage the power of a growing voting bloc in Congress to address shared areas of interest, from immigration to civil rights.

Congressional Asian Pacific American Caucus

In recent years, APA Members of Congress have taken steps to increase their effectiveness as a group. With American Samoa and the Northern Mariana Islands gaining Territorial Delegates in 1981 and 2009, respectively, the number of Pacific Islanders serving in Congress has increased. With that increase, APA Members began to pool resources and information.

In the mid-1990s, APA Members followed congressional precedent by establishing an informal caucus that provided forums for networking and building influence in Congress. In a manner reminiscent of the creation of

Eni F. H. Faleomavaega, Delegate from American Samoa, addresses a meeting of the Congressional Asian Pacific American Caucus in 2013. Faleomavaega served in Congress from 1998 to 2015.

Image courtesy of the U.S. House of Representatives Photography Office

the Congressional Black Caucus (CBC) and the Congressional Hispanic Caucus (CHC) in the 1970s, the establishment of the Congressional Asian Pacific American Caucus (CAPAC) in 1994 flowed from frustrations that APA concerns were poorly understood and often ignored in Washington, DC.[73]

On May 16, 1994, nearly a dozen charter members joined forces to form CAPAC, drawing its membership from both the House and Senate to raise awareness for APA issues and find legislative strength in numbers.[74] As cofounder Patsy Mink of Hawaii explained at the time, "We have felt that we have not been consulted on important steps taken by this administration and the ones in the past." Mink and others pointed specifically to health care, welfare, and immigration issues. Representative Mineta, whom colleagues elected as the first chairman of the group, recalled that APA Members had worked together on an informal basis for years, but "found that we didn't have the leverage or the clout to get the attention to us on certain issues." When the Clinton administration began to court other minority groups in Congress about proposed health care reforms, but failed to consult with APA Members, Mineta demanded and won a White House meeting with the President for Asian-American legislators.[75]

From the outset, Mineta and others believed that one of the group's organizing principles was to publicize issues affecting APAs within Congress. "We think that this caucus can be used as an education forum," he noted shortly after CAPAC's creation. "We have to educate our colleagues that we're the fastest growing population. We're still evidently a mystery to a lot of our own fellow members in Congress."[76] One of the group's first efforts was to counter anti-immigrant measures that cropped up in debate about an $8.6 billion supplemental bill to address the devastation in Northridge, California, following the 1994 earthquake there. Mineta recalled, "There were amendments being offered that would say for instance that 'none of the programs could be paid to undocumented residents.' My point was: 'How could you exclude emergency food, emergency housing to people just because they happened to be in the eyes of these people illegal aliens[?]'"[77]

CAPAC was distinct from another Asian-focused caucus created in 1994, the Congressional Caucus on India and Indian-Americans (CCIIA), which began as a foreign policy–centered group with Members interested in United States–India relations. Organized by New Jersey Representative Frank Pallone and seven other legislators, CCIIA boomed to more than 100 members within five years. It later expanded its activities toward Asian-Indian immigrant issues within the United States.[78]

CAPAC's rules permitted non-APAs who represented large Asian-American constituencies to serve as full-fledged members with the right to vote on policy and even serve in leadership positions.[79] In fact, three of the caucus's charter members were not of Asian-American descent: Nancy Pelosi and Don Edwards of California and Neil Abercrombie of Hawaii. "It's all about building bridges to a larger group, most of whom are not [of] Asian descent," CAPAC chairman David Wu of Oregon observed in 2002.[80]

Since its founding, CAPAC has had six chairs: Mineta, Mink, Underwood, Wu, Honda, and the current chair, Judy Chu of California. Chu was elected to the post in February 2011.[81]

Hawaii Representative Patsy Takemoto Mink advocates for the needs of the Congressional Asian Pacific American Caucus with President William J. (Bill) Clinton in 1998.

Image courtesy of the William J. Clinton Library/ National Archives and Records Administration

The educational aspect of CAPAC's work remains a strong interest among its members and extends beyond the confines of Capitol Hill. As recently as the 114th Congress, the group has supported the creation of a national Asian-American museum within the Smithsonian Institution. Caucus member Grace Meng of New York has introduced bills to establish the National Museum of Asian Pacific American History and Culture, the most recent version being H.R. 868 in the 115th Congress.[82]

In April 2002, CAPAC, CBC, and CHC formally agreed to work in concert as the so-called Tri-Caucus "with the purpose of addressing issues of mutual concern: civil rights, education, immigration, job training, housing, and economic development."[83] This marked an effort to create a potent congressional voting bloc and signaled the growing influence of minority representatives particularly within the House Democratic Caucus. It reflected shifting nationwide demographics, as urban communities that for decades had been majority African American now included large and growing numbers of Hispanic and APA populations and that the APA population was increasing faster than any other group in the country. The Tri-Caucus agreement also reflected the fact that leaders of the various caucuses chose to coordinate their efforts in key areas so as not to compete for limited federal resources.[84]

LEGISLATIVE INTERESTS

During its more than two decades of existence, CAPAC has acted as something of an informational clearinghouse on a wide array of issues ranging from immigration, to political participation, to racial profiling. The breadth of policy issues that the group has addressed reflects the heterogeneous nature of the APA community. During a 2006 series of floor speeches commemorating Asian Pacific American Heritage Month, then CAPAC Chairman Mike Honda noted,

The diverse Congressional Asian Pacific American Caucus has addressed issues such as immigration, political participation, and racial profiling. This 2014 photograph shows (from left to right) Northern Mariana Islands Delegate Gregorio Kilili Camacho Sablan, California Representative Scott Peters, California Representative Jerry McNerney, Texas Representative Al Green, California Representative Judy Chu, Guam Delegate Madeleine Bordallo, California Representative Xavier Becerra, New York Representative Charles Rangel, Virginia Representative Robert C. (Bobby) Scott, and California Representative Mike Honda.

Image courtesy of the U.S. House of Representatives Photography Office

Petition for a Nonimmigrant Worker

Department of Homeland Security
U.S. Citizenship and Immigration Services

USCIS
Form I-129
OMB No. 1615-0009
Expires 12/31/2018

For USCIS Use Only	Receipt	Partial Approval (explain)	Action Block

Class: _____
No. of Workers: _____
Job Code: _____
Validity Dates: _____
From: _____
To: _____

☐ Classification Approved
☐ Consulate/POE/PFI Notified
  At: _____
☐ Extension Granted
☐ COS/Extension Granted

► **START HERE - Type or print in black ink.**

Part 1. Petitioner Information

If you are an individual filing this petition, complete Item Number 1. If you are a company or an organization filing this petition, complete Item Number 2.

1. **Legal Name of Individual Petitioner**

Family Name (Last Name)	Given Name (First Name)	Middle Name

2. **Company or Organization Name**

The Immigration Act of 1990 created the H-1B visa for specialty workers and allowed employers to hire skilled individuals for three years and to apply for an additional three years of residency. The H-1B visas created a new wave of immigration, as more than half of all H-1B visas since 1990 have been awarded to skilled workers from Asian nations.

Image courtesy of the Department of Homeland Security, U.S. Citizenship and Immigration Services

"As our community expands, we must also continue to educate our fellow citizens about the uniqueness of our experiences. The Asian Pacific Islander American community is often misperceived as monolithic. Our community is extremely diverse in our languages, ethnicities and culture. Aggregating such a large and diverse group makes it difficult to understand the unique problems faced by the individual and subgroups."[85]

Immigration

Immigration has become a perennial issue for APA Members of Congress, particularly regarding preference categories for special professional skills and family reunification. A major piece of legislation with far-reaching implications for Asian immigrants was the Immigration Act of 1990, which modified the H visa for "guest workers," a program that extended back to the Immigration Act of 1952. For many years the H-1 visa existed for professionals in "specialty" occupations that required advanced training. The 1990 measure created the H-1B for specialty workers, allowing employers to hire skilled individuals for three years and to apply for an additional three years of residency. By the mid-1990s, the H-1B requests from information technology companies boomed as the high-tech industry blossomed. The 1990 act increased the number of such H visas from 54,000 to 140,000. By the time Congress passed the American Competitiveness in the Twenty-first Century Act in 2000, the number of H-1B visas alone had been increased to 195,000.[86]

The H-1B visas created a new wave of immigration, as more than half of all H-1B visas since 1990 have been awarded to skilled workers from Asian nations: India, China, Taiwan, South Korea, and the Philippines. In some years, Asians accounted for 80 percent of all such recipients, and, by the late 1990s, the number of Asian migrants on such temporary visas exceeded the number of individuals admitted as permanent residents on employment-based visas.[87] This created a complex immigration picture, since many of these individuals brought families to the United States or started families while in the country. Often these families had mixed statuses as immigrants with parents who were worker nonimmigrants and children who were American citizens.[88]

In 2006, during the 109th Congress (2005–2007), a proposed immigration bill addressing border security and a path to legalized status for the more than 11 million estimated undocumented immigrants stalled in Congress. During congressional debate about various proposals, CAPAC called attention to aspects of immigration reform that directly affected Asian Pacific Americans, but which had received little attention by Congress or the media—issues like family reunification and the long backlog in the family immigration system, especially for applicants from Asian nations.[89]

To highlight these and other immigration-related issues, CAPAC created its Immigration Task Force. In the 114th Congress, the task force listed among its top priorities preserving "our longstanding tradition of family-based immigration," reducing wait times for family reunification and related visa applications, providing "legal status and a path to permanent residence for undocumented immigrants" who pay taxes and abide by the law, and easing restrictions on workers with H-1B visas.[90]

Increasing Political Participation

Any analysis of Asian Pacific Americans' political participation presents challenges because of their diversity and relatively small numbers. Yet, in recent decades, the accelerating population growth of APAs has increased their influence within the general electorate, especially in the western states where, as of 2010, they made up 11 percent of the region's combined population. In California, 15 percent of the population is of APA descent, and in Hawaii it is 57 percent.[91]

Recent surveys analyzing the six largest APA ethnic groups suggest that their voting-registration patterns are comparable to the general population.[92] [**Table 3.1**] Voter turnout among these groups has been generally high. For instance, in the 2004 election, 65 percent of Asian Americans went to the polls, about 15 percent higher than the general electorate.[93] [**Table 3.2**]

Table 3.1: Voter Registration and Voting Percentages, 2008

U.S. Asian Groups	Percent Registered	Percent Voted
Japanese	81	76
Filipino	78	70
Asian Indian	76	63
Korean	70	65
Chinese	68	64
Vietnamese	64	63
U.S. Asians	72	66
General U.S. Population	75	70

Source: Pew Research Center, "The Rise of Asian Americans," (4 April 2013): 163, http://www.pewsocialtrends.org/2012/06/19/the-rise-of-asian-americans.

Table 3.2: Voter Turnout, 2000 to 2012 (in thousands)

Group	2000	2004	2008	2012
U.S. Asians	2,045	2,768	3,357	3,904
General U.S. Population	110,826	125,736	131,144	132,948

Source: *The Diversifying Electorate—Voting Rates by Race and Hispanic Origin in 2012 (and Other Recent Elections)*, P20-568, prepared by Thom File, U.S. Census Bureau (Washington, DC, issued May 2013).

Table 3.3: Political Ideology Percentages, 2012

U.S. Asian Groups	Conservative	Moderate	Liberal
Filipino	33	42	20
Korean	33	30	30
Japanese	28	36	29
Chinese	21	39	31
Vietnamese	19	34	34
Asian Indian	18	39	37
U.S. Asians	24	37	31
General U.S. Population	34	37	24

Source: Pew Research Center, "The Rise of Asian Americans": 158.

A recent Pew Research Center study attempted to plot the political spectrum in the United States by asking respondents to identify their political ideologies. In 2010 the U.S. population as a whole identified as more than a third "moderate," a third "conservative," and a quarter "liberal." Asian Americans, however, identified themselves as more than a third "moderate," but almost a third "liberal," and just under a quarter "conservative." In short, the six largest Asian Americans groups are left of center as a whole in a right-of-center country. These summary figures, though, hide wide variations that exist among the different ethnicities. [**Table 3.3**]

A 2008 study conducted by the Russell Sage Foundation discovered that, when it came to party identification, a large number of Asian Pacific Americans did not identify with any party. In fact, nonidentifiers turned out to be a plurality of responses (35 percent), followed by Democrats (31 percent), Independents (20 percent), and Republicans (14 percent).[94]

Given the relatively recent trends toward a better understanding of the characteristics of the Asian Pacific American electorate, voter organization and registration became a particular area of emphasis for CAPAC.[95] In the aftermath of Hurricane Katrina, CAPAC Chairman Honda traveled to southern Louisiana to advise the Vietnamese community that was still struggling to recover from the devastation on how to be more politically active. That visit served to inspire Joseph Cao's political career and his historic election to the House just two years later, when he became the first Vietnamese American elected to Congress.[96]

Civil Liberties

The policy of internment during World War II burned a deep mental scar in the Japanese-American community that redress has not been able to fully heal. Accordingly, APA Members of Congress and activists have often taken it upon themselves to ensure that such a traumatic event is never repeated, particularly in instances where internment by group characteristics has been raised as a

Hurricane Katrina ravaged the Gulf Coast in 2005. California Representative Mike Honda, chair of the Congressional Asian Pacific American Caucus, traveled to southern Louisiana to assist the local Vietnamese community. His visit inspired Anh (Joseph) Cao to enter politics; Cao later became a Member from Louisiana and the first Vietnamese American in Congress.

Image courtesy of the Library of Congress

legitimate policy. For instance, during the summer of 1990, California state assemblyman Gil Ferguson authored a resolution hailing Japanese-American internment as justified. It sparked a 70-minute debate in the California state assembly that was mostly spent denouncing Ferguson's resolution. Many legislators simply abandoned the floor to register their disgust with Ferguson's measure. In the end, the resolution was soundly defeated, 60 to 4.[97]

Civil liberties gained renewed national attention for Asian Pacific American Members of Congress, particularly in the months after the terrorist attacks of September 11, 2001, as the nation prepared for the "War on Terror." Overnight, Americans of South-Asian heritage were identified by some as possible terrorists and businesses, residences, and individuals seen as Muslim (including the non-Muslim Sikhs) were attacked. On September 15, 2001, Balbir Singh Sodhi, owner of a gas station in Mesa, Arizona, was killed in an act of retaliation for the terrorist attacks.[98] Senator Inouye of Hawaii defended American Muslims in the aftermath of 9/11, comparing the bigotry directed at them to the experience of Japanese Americans following Pearl Harbor. "The lessons learned must remain as a grave reminder of what we must not allow to happen again to any group," Inouye warned.[99]

Roughly 18 months later, during an interview on a phone-in radio talk show, North Carolina Congressman Howard Coble, the chairman of the House Judiciary's Subcommittee on Crime, Terrorism, and Homeland Security favorably cited President Franklin D. Roosevelt's internment of Japanese Americans when responding "to a caller's suggestion that Arabs in the United States be imprisoned as an anti-terrorist measure." Several APA Members quickly responded, including Representatives Honda, Wu, and Robert T. Matsui of California. "If we do not accurately portray the past," Wu told the press, "we risk repeating it."[100]

More recently, CAPAC has expressed concerns over various public Justice Department investigations of Chinese-American scientists that have been dropped with no charges, reminiscent of the long and drawn-out case of the physicist Wen Ho Lee over possible espionage. "We cannot tolerate another case of Asian-Americans being wrongfully suspected of espionage," said CAPAC Chairwoman Judy Chu. "The profiling must end."[101]

Guam War Claims

For decades, Guamanian Delegates in Congress sought restitution for damages incurred and wrongs committed during World War II. Over the course of the nearly three-year Japanese occupation of Guam, Chamorros of all ages were raped, beaten, or executed for small offenses. Many were subjected to forced marches and confinement in concentration camps. Others endured Japanese language and cultural assimilation schools.[102] Into the 21st century—more than 70 years after the war ended—Guam's Delegates still pursued claims for compensation for island residents suffering the aftereffects of the destruction of life and property.

Following up on the efforts of both Delegates Won Pat and Ben Blaz, Robert Underwood introduced a war claims measure in each of the 104th, 105th, and 106th Congresses (1995–2001).[103] His bills, which requested $20,000 for the descendants of those killed, $7,000 for the injured, and $5,000 to those subjected to forced marches or imprisonment, were all bogged down because Congress balked at the eventual cost and did not have access to what it considered to be an authoritative list of claimants. Underwood estimated the cost of the bill at up to $50 million, but the Congressional Budget Office scored the legislation at three times that amount in 2000.[104]

A change of strategy in the 106th Congress (1999–2001) finally overcame concerns about cost. Underwood began working with Hawaii Senator Inouye to create a fact-finding commission to identify claimants and estimate a more accurate cost.[105] He quickly recrafted the most recent version of his bill, H.R. 755, the War Restitution Act. The House Committee on Resources reported the bill as the Guam War Claims Review Commission Act, which established a five-member Guam War Claims Commission within the Department of Interior to determine through oral testimony and documentary evidence who was eligible for compensation and how much it would cost.[106] The House passed the amended bill on September 12, 2000, but the Senate was unable to take action on the measure before the end of the Congress.

Undeterred, Underwood introduced an identical bill (H.R. 308) in January 2001 at the start of the 107th Congress. Moments before the bill was approved by voice vote in March, Underwood hoped that with its passage "the World War II generation of the people of Guam … will be finally made whole." American Samoan Delegate Eni Faleomavaega further testified that every Guam Delegate from Underwood back to Won Pat had sought this "long, long overdue" legislation. Indeed, Underwood credited his predecessor, Delegate Ben Blaz—a Republican, who had been imprisoned by Japanese forces during World War II—for lobbying on his behalf, despite the fact that Underwood had once criticized Blaz on his lack of progress on the war claims issue.[107]

It was November 2002 before Underwood's bill cleared the Senate. President George W. Bush signed the Guam War Claims Review Commission Act into law on December 16, 2002. It marked Underwood's last act in Congress: "Suffice to say that I had to evade legislative minefields, be mindful of the legislative clock and listen to the sage advice of experienced legislators like Daniel Inouye, Daniel Akaka, and Norman Mineta," he recalled.[108]

After receiving more than 5,300 responses to questionnaires in addition to the 18 boxes of claims, Delegate Won Pat had saved, the commission opened in September 2003.[109] The panel took the testimony of a "'parade of survivors' and their pitiful, agonizing, horrifying testimonies," according to one local observer, before issuing its report on June 9, 2004. It recommended formal recognition by Congress for Guam's suffering and loyalty.[110] The proposed monetary compensation was greater than what Underwood had suggested in his bills: $25,000 to the immediate survivors of Guamanians who died because of the Japanese occupation; $12,000 for those who suffered at the hands of the Japanese and still were living in 1990; and the establishment of a foundation to fund World War II Loyalty Scholarships.[111]

Underwood's successor, Delegate Madeleine Bordallo, worked to implement the commission's recommendations. In an effort to enact the report's findings, former Delegate Blaz testified before the House Resources Committee in

Over several decades, Guam Delegates Ben Garrido Blaz, pictured here, Antonio Borja Won Pat, Robert A. Underwood, and Madeleine Bordallo each attempted to secure restitution for damages incurred during World War II.

Collection of the U.S. House of Representatives

2004. In a voice described as "booming at times and choked with emotion," he appealed to his former colleagues: "If we are fellow Americans, the time is now. If we are yours, you should take us as your own. The time has come."[112]

Beginning with the 109th Congress, Delegate Bordallo repeatedly proposed a bill to provide restitution for Guamanian war claims. Titled the Guam World War II Loyalty Recognition Act, the legislation passed the House during the 110th and 111th Congresses, but failed to become law.[113] At a 2009 hearing held by the House Armed Services Committee, testimony by Guamanian Delegates and Guam's residents highlighted the harrowing stories of survivors.[114] After years of consideration, Congress included the Guam World War II Loyalty Recognition Act in the National Defense Authorization Act for Fiscal Year 2017. President Barack Obama signed it into law in late December 2016.[115]

Congress Recognizes APA History

Until relatively recently, so little was known about the history of Asian Pacific Americans within the institution of Congress that, at the press conference announcing the creation of CAPAC, reporters stumped the newly installed chairman, Norman Mineta, when they asked him who the first Asian-American Member was or how many total had served on Capitol Hill. "We have to write our own history," Mineta remarked.[116]

The 1990s and early 2000s marked a period of remembrance and reflection as long-standing historical narratives about the United States' century-long role as a Pacific power were supplanted by more complex and nuanced interpretations. In concert with federal efforts to memorialize internment and the legacies of World War II discussed in the previous section of this book, these new perspectives often illuminated the experiences and pivotal contributions of Asian and Pacific Americans to the national storyline.

Hawaii Senator Daniel K. Akaka introduced legislation in 1992 to acknowledge U.S. complicity in the overthrow of the Hawaiian monarchy at the end of the 19th century and to provide an apology to Native Hawaiians.

Image courtesy of the Library of Congress

Veterans of the 442nd Regimental Combat Team, the 100th Infantry Battalion, and the Military Intelligence Service, which included Japanese-American soldiers, receive the Congressional Gold Medal on November 2, 2011.

Image courtesy of the U.S. House of Representatives Photography Office

As the centennial of the downfall of the Hawaiian monarchy approached, people began paying greater attention to the violent transfer of power in 1893 and the key role of U.S. sugar planters, financiers, and missionaries in the overthrow. In 1992, during the 102nd Congress (1991–1993), Senator Daniel Akaka first introduced a measure that acknowledged U.S. complicity in the rebellion and issued an apology to Native Hawaiians. The bill eventually worked its way through both chambers in the following Congress. On October 27, 1993, after little debate, the resolution (S.J. Res. 19) passed the Senate, 65 to 34. Less than a month later, the House passed the joint resolution, and President Bill Clinton signed it into law in late November.[117]

Senators Akaka and Inouye both lamented the nature of the kingdom's toppling and the damage the overthrow caused to the indigenous population; yet, the resolution also highlighted the native peoples' "determination to preserve, develop and transmit to future generations their ancestral territory, and their cultural identity." While carefully refraining from establishing precedent or labeling Native Hawaiians definitively as Native Americans, it noted that the centennial marked a timely moment for the United States to "acknowledge the historic significance of the illegal overthrow of the Kingdom of Hawaii, [and] to express its deep regret to the Native Hawaiian people."[118]

Remembrance found expression in other venues, too. As the World War II generation slowly passed from the scene in the 1990s and early 2000s, momentum built to commemorate the contributions of groups whose service had never formally been recognized, including the Tuskegee Airmen, Native-American Code Talkers, and the Women Airforce Service Pilots (WASPs). During the 111th Congress (2009–2011), California Senator Barbara Boxer introduced a resolution (S. 1055) to award the Congressional Gold Medal to the Japanese-American army units of the European theater, the 100th Infantry Battalion, and the 442nd Regimental Combat Team, as well as the Military Intelligence Service

The 442nd Regimental Combat Team, composed almost entirely of Japanese Americans, trains at Camp Shelby, Mississippi, in 1943.

Image courtesy of the Library of Congress

Senator Daniel K. Inouye speaks to fellow veterans of the 442nd Regimental Combat Team as they receive the Congressional Gold Medal on November 2, 2011.

Image courtesy of the U.S. House of Representatives Photography Office

The Congressional Asian Pacific American Caucus meets with President Barack Obama in the Cabinet Room of the White House in 2011. Left to right on the far side of the table: Northern Mariana Islands Delegate Gregorio Kilili Camacho Sablan, California Representative Judy Chu, President Obama, Guam Delegate Madeleine Bordallo, California Representative Doris Matsui, and Texas Representative Al Green.

Image courtesy of the Barack Obama Presidential Library/National Archives and Records Administration

that had Japanese-American soldiers serving in the Pacific theater. Since the earliest Congresses, the Congressional Gold Medal has been the highest national expression of appreciation for a recipient's distinguished achievements and contributions. After both houses of Congress swiftly passed Boxer's resolution, President Obama signed it into law on September 23, 2010.[119]

Congressional leaders presented the Congressional Gold Medal to veterans from the three units at a ceremony in the Capitol on November 2, 2011. Representatives from each group accepted the award, including Senator Inouye, a veteran of the 442nd and himself a Medal of Honor recipient. Wearing a dark navy blazer with a 442nd patch sewn on the breast pocket, Inouye recalled that, while officials first believed Japanese Americans "were unfit to put on a uniform," they were determined "to show their patriotism." He added, "This has been a long journey" to achieving recognition.[120] The Congressional Gold Medal toured the United States in 2013 and 2014 and was displayed in seven cities. It remains on permanent display at the Smithsonian Institution's National Museum of American History in Washington, DC, as part of "The Price of Freedom" exhibit.[121]

CONCLUSION

In June 2016, the Associated Press reported new Census numbers underscoring perhaps the most underappreciated characteristic of America's ever-changing demographics: Asian Americans remained "the fastest growing racial group in the United States." Between 2010 and 2016, the Asian-American population had jumped from 17.3 million to 21 million. That growth, according to the Associated Press, had been driven, in large part, by migration.[122]

If these current population figures are any indication, the story of this period—larger numbers, greater diversity, and a more pronounced legislative agenda in Congress—has the potential to continue well into the 21st century.

But whatever changes occur over the next few decades, they will happen on the shoulders of the APA Members who have come before, and those Members came from all over. The congressional narrative is no longer dominated by Japanese-American legislators from California and Hawaii and, instead, features the life stories and family histories of immigrants from China, Vietnam, Korea, the Philippines, and India, to name a few.

On Capitol Hill, greater legislative influence has accompanied that new diversity. Although few APA Members have chaired committees or subcommittees in the modern era, the creation of CAPAC has given an added lift to the most pressing issues in recent Congresses: immigration, civil liberties, territorial interests, and public education campaigns to ensure America never again approves a policy as destructive as internment. Asian Pacific Americans have also served as cabinet members (Mineta) and as president pro tempore in the Senate (Inouye).

With a history that is, at turns, both heart-wrenching and awe-inspiring, Asian Pacific Americans in Congress have fought to overcome a century of exclusion to take their rightful place in both Congress and the American narrative.

NOTES

1   Neely Tucker, "The Possible Dream: Louisiana's Historic New Congressman Seems to Surprise Everyone but Himself," 30 December 2008, *Washington Post*: C1.

2   Fredrik Logevall, *Embers of War: The Fall of an Empire and the Making of America's Vietnam* (New York: Random House, 2012): xv.

3   Pew Research Center, "The Rise of Asian Americans" (4 April 2013): 7, 47–48, http://www.pewsocialtrends.org/2012/06/19/the-rise-of-asian-americans/ (accessed 1 August 2016).

4   Tucker, "The Possible Dream"; "My Quang Cao, Father of U.S. Rep. Anh 'Joseph' Cao, Dies," 21 October 2010, *New Orleans Times-Picayune*: n.p.

5   Tucker, "The Possible Dream."

6   Pew Research Center, "The Rise of Asian Americans": 47, 163.

7   Erika Lee, *The Making of Asian America: A History* (New York: Simon and Schuster, 2015): 284, 286, 373.

8   Pew Research Center, "The Rise of Asian Americans": 19.

9   Ibid.; Lee, *The Making of Asian America*: 287.

10   Katherine Skiba, "Duckworth Keeps Her Eyes on Prize," 3 March 2016, *Chicago Tribune*: C6.

11   Pew Research Center, "The Rise of Asian Americans": 9; Lee, *The Making of Asian America*: 284.

12   Lee, *The Making of Asian America*: 286. See also Phung Su, "Immigration Act of 1990," in *Asian Americans: An Encyclopedia of Social, Cultural, Economic, and Political History*, vol. 2, ed. Xiaojian Zhao and Edward J. W. Park (Santa Barbara, CA: Greenwood, 2014): 538–540; John S. W. Park, "H-1B Visa," in *Asian Americans: An Encyclopedia of Social, Cultural, Economic, and Political History*, vol. 2: 475–478.

13   Lee, *The Making of Asian America*: 287.

14   Mae M. Ngai, *Impossible Subjects: Illegal Aliens and the Making of Modern America* (Princeton, NJ: Princeton University Press, 2004): 234–236.

15   Sucheng Chan, *Asian Americans: An Interpretive History* (New York: Twayne Publishers, 1991): 154–156; Lee, *The Making of Asian America*: 325, 340.

16   Indochina Migration and Refugee Assistance Act of 1975, Public Law 94-23, 89 Stat. 87 (1975); Stephen W. Stathis, *Landmark Legislation, 1774–2002: Major U.S. Acts and Treaties* (Washington, DC: Congressional Quarterly Press, 2003): 294–295; Chan, *Asian Americans*: 156; David M. Reimers, *Still the Golden Door: The Third World Comes to America* (New York: Columbia University Press, 1992): 179.

17   Public Law 94-24, 89 Stat. 89 (1975); Ronald Takaki, *Strangers from a Different Shore: A History of Asian Americans*, rev. ed. (Boston: Little, Brown, 1998): 461–462; Lee, *The Making of Asian America*: 329, 340; Stathis, *Landmark Legislation*: 296; Chan, *Asian Americans*: 156; Public Law 94-313, 90 Stat. 691 (1976).

18   Lee, *The Making of Asian America*: 340; Chan, *Asian Americans*: 161; Takaki, *Strangers from a Different Shore*: 452, 454; Reimers, *Still the Golden Door*: 179–180.

19   Reimers, *Still the Golden Door*: 181; Chan, *Asian Americans*: 157.

20   Roger Daniels, *Coming to America: A History of Immigration and Ethnicity in American Life* (New York: Harper Perennial, 1990): 345; Reimers, *Still the Golden Door*: 195–196.

21   Adam Clymer, *Edward M. Kennedy: A Biography* (New York: William Morrow, 1999): 314; Stathis, *Landmark Legislation*: 307; Chan, *Asian Americans*: 161; Reimers, *Still the Golden Door*: 196; Lee, *The Making of Asian America*: 341–342.

22   Sabrina Thomas, "The Value of Dust: Policy, Citizenship and Vietnam's Amerasian Children," (PhD diss., Arizona State University, 2015): vi, 43–44, 47, 51; *Congressional Record*, House, 92nd Cong., 1st. sess. (17 May 1971): 15248.

23   Thomas, "The Value of Dust": 44–45, 68; Amerasian Immigration Act, Public Law 97-359, 96 Stat. 1716 (1982).

24   Chan, *Asian Americans*: 163; Ronald Reagan, "Remarks on Signing a Bill Providing for the Immigration of Certain Amerasian Children," 22 October 1982, in *American Presidency Project*, ed. John T. Woolley and Gerhard Peters, http://www.presidency.ucsb.edu/ws/?pid=41904 (accessed 19 April 2016).

25   Thomas, "The Value of Dust": 112–113.

26   Ibid., 185–186; Chan, *Asian Americans*: 163.

27   Thomas, "The Value of Dust": 188–189; Public Law 100-202, 101 Stat. 1329 (1987).

28   David Lamb, "Children of the Vietnam War," June 2009, *Smithsonian Magazine*, http://www.smithsonianmag.com/travel/children-of-the-vietnam-war-131207347/ (accessed 1 June 2016); Thomas, "The Value of Dust": 176.

29   Lee, *The Making of Asian America*: 358–359.

30   Pew Research Center, "The Rise of Asian Americans": 33.

31   *The Asian Population: 2010*, C2010BR-11, prepared by Elizabeth M. Hoeffel, Sonya Rastog; Myoung Ouk Kim, and Hasan Shahid, U.S. Census Bureau (Washington, DC, issued March 2012): 6.

32   Pew Research Center, "The Rise of Asian Americans": 33; Hoeffel et al., *The Asian Population: 2010*: 17–19.

33   Pew Research Center, "The Rise of Asian Americans": 33.

34   *The Asian Population: 2010*: 7–8.

35   Paul Spickard, "Introduction: Pacific Diaspora?," in *Pacific Diaspora: Island Peoples in the United States and Across the Pacific*, ed. Paul Spickard, Joanne L. Rondilla, and Debbie Hippolite Wright (Honolulu: University of Hawaii Press, 2002): 2, 16–17.

36   *The Native Hawaiian and Other Pacific Islander Population: 2010*, C201BR-12, prepared by Lindsay Hixson, Bradford B. Hepler, and Myoung Ouk Kim, U.S. Census Bureau (Washington, DC, issued May 2012): 1–2.

37   *The Native Hawaiian and Other Pacific Islander Population*: 4–5, 7, 15, 19. It was not until the 1990 U.S. Census that federal officials began enumerating Pacific Islanders separately

from Asian Americans. See Karen Nero, "The End of Insularity," in *The Cambridge History of the Pacific Islanders*, ed. Donald Denoon et al. (Cambridge, UK: Cambridge University Press, 1997): 448.

38 James Ciment, "Samoan Americans," in *Asian American History and Culture: An Encyclopedia*, vol. 2, ed. Huping Ling and Allan Austin (New York: Sharpe Reference, 2010): 530–531; James Brooke, "On Farthest U.S. Shores, Iraq Is A Way to A Dream," 31 July 2005, *New York Times*: A18; Lee Davidson, "One of Every Four Tongans in U.S. Calls Utah Home," 12 September 2011, *Salt Lake Tribune*, http://archive.sltrib.com/story.php?ref=/sltrib/politics/52551592-90/california-family-hawaii-population.html.csp (accessed 22 June 2016). For slightly earlier migration trends, see Craig R. James, "From Village to City: Samoan Migration to California," in *Pacific Diaspora: Island Peoples in the United States and Across the Pacific*, ed. Paul Spickard, Joanne L. Rondilla, and Debbie Hippolite Wright (Honolulu: University of Hawaii Press, 2002): 121–122.

39 Eni F. H. Faleomavaega, oral history interview by U.S. Capitol Historical Society, 11 April 2011, accessed 13 July 2015, Washington, DC, http://www.uschs.org/oral-histories/uschs_faleomavaega.htm (site discontinued). See also Davidson, "One of Every Four Tongans in U.S. Calls Utah Home"; Jerry Spangler, "Mormon Democrats Link Up in Congress," 31 January 2005, *Deseret Morning News*: n.p.

40 Lee, *The Making of Asian America*: 391, 393–394, quotation on p. 391.

41 Ibid., 396, 402.

42 Arnold H. Leibowitz, *Defining Status: A Comprehensive Analysis of United States Territorial Relations* (Dordrecht, Netherlands: Martinus Nijhoff, 1989): 484–487.

43 *Trusteeship Agreement for the Territory of the Pacific Islands*, 80th Cong., 1st sess., H. Doc. 378 (1947); Public Law 80-204, 61 Stat. 397 (1947).

44 Leibowitz, *Defining Status*: 493, 499–500; Howard P. Willens and Deanne C. Seimer, *An Honorable Accord: The Covenant between the Mariana Islands and the United States* (Honolulu: University of Hawaii Press, 2002): 3–5. Shortly thereafter the islands of Saipan and Tinian were returned to naval command. The two Marianas Islands came under the Interior Department again in 1962 after a plebiscite in early 1961 that indicated little support for continued naval administration of the islands. See Leibowitz, *Defining Status*: 527n19.

45 "Study of Annexation of Pacific Islands Urged," 5 August 1965, *Los Angeles Times*: 19.

46 In the 90th Congress (1967–1969), Fong introduced S. Con. Res. 24; Representative Jonathan Bingham of New York introduced H.J. Res. 594; and Senate Majority Leader Mike Mansfield of Montana introduced S.J. Res. 96. The Johnson administration then put forward its own proposal (S.J. Res. 106) introduced by Washington Senator Henry Jackson. Hearings were held on the administration's joint resolution by the Interior and Insular Affairs Committee leading to its Senate passage in late May 1968. The House, though, took no action before the end of the Congress. See Senate Committee on Interior and Insular Affairs, *The Covenant to Establish A Commonwealth of the Northern Mariana Islands*, 94th Cong., 1st sess., S. Rept. 433 (22 October 1975): 38–39.

47 *Congressional Record*, House, 91st Cong., 1st sess. (4 August 1969): 22138.

48 Leibowitz, *Defining Status*: 501.

49 Observers thought the vote was poorly organized and badly publicized, hiding a greater desire for reunification. Others suspected lingering bad feelings from the Japanese occupation of Guam when people from the Northern Marianas assisted in the occupation. Leibowitz, *Defining Status*: 527–528.

50 Ibid., 528; Willens and Siemer, *An Honorable Accord*: 7, 22–23.

51 Leibowitz, *Defining Status*: 528–529; Willens and Siemer, *An Honorable Accord*: 24.

52 *The Covenant to Establish A Commonwealth of the Northern Mariana Islands*: 56, 62; Leibowitz, *Defining Status*: 528–529.

53 "Mariana Islands," *CQ Almanac, 1976*, 32nd ed. (Washington, DC: Congressional Quarterly Inc., 1977): 264–266, http://library.cqpress.com.

54 Leibowitz, *Defining Status*: 520, 532.

55 Gerald R. Ford, "Letter to the Speaker of the House and the President of the Senate Transmitting Proposed Legislation To Provide Commonwealth Status for the Northern Mariana Islands," 1 July 1975, in *American Presidency Project*, ed. John T. Woolley and Gerhard Peters, http://www.presidency.ucsb.edu/ws/?pid=5036 (accessed 26 April 2016); *Congressional Record*, House, 94th Cong., 1st sess. (21 July 1975): 23670; Gerald R. Ford, "Remarks Upon Signing Legislation Approving the Covenant Establishing Commonwealth Status for the Northern Mariana Islands," 24 March 1976, in *American Presidency Project*, ed. John T. Woolley and Gerhard Peters, http://www.presidency.ucsb.edu/ws/?pid=5750 (accessed 20 April 2016); Public Law 94-241, 90 Stat. 263 (1976).

56 Leibowitz, *Defining Status*: 508, 639–653. The Compact of Free Association was established between the United States and the Federated States of Micronesia and the Marshall Islands on January 14, 1986, while the Compact with the Republic of Palau was approved "in principle" on November 14, 1986. Compact of Free Association Act, Public Law 99-239, 99 Stat. 1770 (1986); Public Law 99-658, 100 Stat. 3672 (1986). After seven failed referenda, Palau finally ratified the agreement in 1994, when 75 percent of the population approved of the Compact, as required by the Palau Constitution. See Robert G. Sutter, "Palau: Briefing Paper," Report 95-40 S, 23 December 1994, Congressional Research Service.

57 For opinions on reunification in the late 1970s, see "A Unified Guam and Marianas? It's Marianas' Turn to Say 'No,'" 24 October 1976, *Pacific Daily News* (Guam): 3.

58 Its numerical designation had been chosen with care. Ferdinand Magellan had "allegedly discovered Guam" in 1521. See Vivian Loyola Dames, "Rethinking the Circle of Belonging: American Citizenship and the Chamorros of Guam" (PhD diss., University of Michigan, 2000): 527.

59 Dames, "Rethinking the Circle of Belonging": 498n121.

60 *Congressional Record*, House, 105th Cong., 1st sess. (10 February 1997): H401.

61 Hearing before the House Committee on Resources, *H.R. 100, H.R. 2370, and S. 210*, 105th Cong., 1st sess. (29 October 1997): 24.

62 Quoted in Dames, "Rethinking the Circle of Belonging": 55.

63 *Census of Population and Housing*, vol. 1: *Characteristics of the Population*, parts 54–58 (Washington, DC, issued July 1973), https://www.census.gov/prod/www/decennial.html (accessed 15 June 2016).

64 Willens and Siemer, *An Honorable Accord*: 184–185.

65 Dames, "Rethinking the Circle of Belonging": 501n130; Willens and Siemer, *An Honorable Accord*: 185.

66 Hearing before the House Committee on Natural Resources, Subcommittee on Insular Affairs, *Current Economic, Social, and Security Conditions of the Commonwealth of the Northern Mariana Islands*, 110th Cong., 1st sess. (19 April 2007): 13.

67 Gebe Martinez, "Derogatory Rohrabacher Remarks Anger Guam," 18 January 1997, *Los Angeles Times*: 14; Steve Limtiaco, "Underwood Wants Delegate Seat for CNMI," 25 May 2001, *Pacific Daily News* (Guam): n.p.; *Recent Population Trends for the U.S. Island Areas: 2000 to 2010*, Report P23-213, prepared by Justyna Goworowska and Steven Wilson, U.S. Census Bureau (Washington, DC, issued April 2015).

68 Limtiaco, "Underwood Wants Delegate Seat for CNMI."

69 *Congressional Record*, House, 110th Cong., 1st sess. (11 December 2007): H15224; Consolidated Natural Resources Act, Public Law 110-229, 122 Stat. 754 (2008).

70 As of July 1, 2017, the closing date of this publication.

71 See Appendix B: Asian and Pacific Islander American Representatives, Senators, Delegates, and Resident Commissioners by State and Territory, 1900–2017.

72 See Appendix C: Asian and Pacific Islander American Members' Committee Assignments (Standing, Joint, Select) in the U.S. House and Senate, 1900–2017.

73   For the story of the formation of the Congressional Black Caucus, see Office of the Historian, *Black Americans in Congress, 1870–2007* (Washington, DC: Government Printing Office, 2008): 373–376, also available online at http://history.house.gov/Exhibitions-and-Publications/BAIC/Historical-Essays/Permanent-Interest/Congressional-Black-Caucus/. For information on the origins and development of the Congressional Hispanic Caucus and the Congressional Hispanic Conference, see Office of the Historian, *Hispanic Americans in Congress, 1822–2012* (Washington, DC: Government Printing Office, 2013): 482–486, also available online at http://history.house.gov/Exhibitions-and-Publications/HAIC/Historical-Essays/Strength-Numbers/Caucus-Conference/.

74   Congressional Asian Pacific American Caucus, "Purpose, Mission, & Goals," http://capac-chu.house.gov/about-me/purpose-mission-goals (accessed 12 June 2015); David S. Broder and Kenneth J. Cooper, "Politics: Asian Pacific Caucus," 22 May 1994, *Washington Post*: A10. For more on issues caucuses in Congress, their role in the legislative process, and why they are formed, see Susan Webb Hammond, *Congressional Caucuses in National Policy Making* (Baltimore, MD: Johns Hopkins University Press, 1998): 36–53.

75   Sam Chu Lin, "New Asian Pacific American Congressional Caucus Forms In the Capital," 27 May 1994, *AsianWeek* (San Francisco, CA): 1.

76   Lin, "New Asian Pacific American Congressional Caucus Forms In the Capital."

77   Ibid.

78   Sanjeev Khagram, Manish Desai, and Jason Varughese, "Seen, Rich, but Unheard? The Politics of Asian Indians in the United States," in *Asian Americans and Politics*: *Perspectives, Experiences, Prospects*, ed. Gordon H. Chang (Stanford, CA: Stanford University Press, 2001): 258–284. See also *Congressional Record*, Extensions of Remarks, 103rd Cong., 1st sess. (26 January 1993): 1305–1306.

79   Diwata Fonte, "Caucus Courts Diversity; Asian Group Finds Strength in Numbers," 4 November 2002, *Roll Call*: n.p.

80   Fonte, "Caucus Courts Diversity"; Broder and Cooper, "Politics: Asian Pacific Caucus."

81   See Appendix H: Congressional Asian Pacific American Caucus Chairmen and Chairwomen, 1994–2017.

82   "National Asian Pacific American Museum Gets Congressional Push," 12 April 2016, NBC News, http://www.nbcnews.com/news/asian-america/national-asian-pacific-american-museum-gets-congressional-push-n554316 (accessed 10 May 2016); H.R. 4307, 114th Cong. (2015); H.R. 868, 115th Cong. (2017).

83   "Minorities in Congress Join Forces," 30 May 2002, *Sun Reporter* (San Francisco, CA): 2; *Congressional Record*, House, 108th Cong., 1st sess. (19 May 2003): 12138; Karen Branch-Brioso, "Minority Caucuses Join Forces to Increase Influence in House," 24 April 2002, *St. Louis Post-Dispatch*: A9.

84   "Minorities in Congress Join Forces"; Peter Brand, "Minority Caucuses Form Alliance," 1 June 2002, *Atlanta Inquirer*: 3.

85   *Congressional Record*, House, 109th Cong., 2nd sess. (9 May 2006): 2317.

86   Immigration Act of 1990, Public Law 101-649, 104 Stat. 4978 (1990); Park, "H1-B Visa": 475–478; see also Lee, *The Making of Asian America*: 286.

87   Park, "H1-B Visa": 477.

88   Ibid.

89   "Congressional Asian Pacific American Caucus Calls for Comprehensive Immigration Reform," 19 September 2006, *The Asian Reporter* (Portland, OR): 1. Immigration remained high on the CAPAC agenda during the Obama administration, too. See Daniel Newhauser, "Obama Will Meet Asian Caucus," 4 August 2011, *Roll Call*: n.p.

90   "Support Comprehensive Immigration Reform," CAPAC Immigration Task Force, accessed 23 June 2016, http://capac-chu.house.gov/issue/immigration.

91   *Asian Population*: *2010*: 6, 7.

92 Two national surveys have been conducted within the past decade explicitly to study Asian American political participation. The National Asian American Survey (NAAS), conducted in 2008, was published by the Russell Sage Foundation in 2011. The Pew Research Center conducted their Asian-American Survey in 2012, published it in June 2012, and updated it online in April 2013. These two studies represent some of the latest and most detailed work on Asian American political participation and political attitudes.

93 The NAAS was published as Janelle Wong, S. Karthick Ramakrishnan, Taeku Lee, and Jane Junn, eds., *Asian American Political Participation*: *Emerging Constituents and Their Political Identities* (New York: Russell Sage Foundation, 2011): 55.

94 Wong et al., *Asian American Political Participation*: 132, table 4.1.

95 Alison McSherry, "Asian-Americans See Gains in Political Clout," 17 March 2009, *Roll Call*: n.p.

96 Tucker, "The Possible Dream."

97 Ralph Frammolino, "Colleagues Leave Ferguson Adrift: Internment," 30 August 1990, *Los Angeles Times*: 1.

98 Lee, *The Making of Asian America*: 386.

99 Matt Bai, "The Way We Live Now: 10-28-01: Encounter; Hyphenated Americans," 28 October 2001, *New York Times*, http://www.nytimes.com/2001/10/28/magazine/the-way-we-live-now-10-28-01-encounter-hyphenated-americans.html (accessed 2 August 2016).

100 Associated Press, "Key Lawmaker Defends WWII Internment of Japanese," 6 February 2003, *Chicago Tribune*: 14; Janet Hook, "The Nation; Internment Remarks by Lawmaker Anger Peers," 7 February 2003, *Los Angeles Times*: A17.

101 Matt Apuzzo, "After Missteps, U.S. Tightens Rules for Espionage Cases," 26 April 2016, *New York Times*, http://www.nytimes.com/2016/04/27/us/after-missteps-us-tightens-rules-for-national-security-cases.html (accessed 1 August 2016). On Wen Ho Lee, see Dan Stober and Ian Hoffman, *A Convenient Spy*: *Wen Ho Lee and the Politics of Nuclear Espionage* (New York: Simon & Schuster, 2001).

102 Leibowitz, *Defining Status*: 323–324.

103 See, for example, Guam Restitution Act, H.R. 2041, 104th Cong. (1995); Guam War Restitution Act, H.R. 2200, 105th Cong. (1997). Senator Daniel K. Inouye of Hawaii also introduced similar bills in the Senate in the 104th and 105th Congresses (1995–1999).

104 Steve Limtiaco, "Guam War Reparation Bill Stalls," 12 July 1999, *Pacific Daily News* (Guam): A2; Steve Limtiaco, "Congress Yet to Hear Guam Bills," 27 October 2000, *Pacific Daily News* (Guam): A1.

105 Limtiaco, "Guam War Reparation Bill Stalls."

106 The commission consisted of two members selected by the Secretary of Interior and one each by the U.S. President, Guam's governor, and Guam's Delegate. Limtiaco, "Congress Yet to Hear Guam Bills."

107 *Congressional Record*, House, 107th Cong., 1st sess. (13 March 2001): H849–H850; Robert Underwood, "Legislature Must Step Up for War Reparations," 1 August 2004, *Pacific Daily News* (Guam): A14; Robert Underwood, "Ben Blaz Deserved to be a Commission Member," 26 October 2003, *Pacific Daily News* (Guam): A16.

108 Underwood, "Legislature Must Step Up for War Reparations"; Guam War Claims Review Commission Act, Public Law 107-333, 116 Stat. 2873 (2002).

109 Mark-Alexander Pope, "Panel: Thousands Submitted Questionnaires," 2 December 2003, *Pacific Daily News* (Guam): A3; Dionesis Tamondong, "Commission Traces History," 8 December 2003, *Pacific Daily News* (Guam): A1.

110 Victor Toves, "Is Alternate Path Needed to Settle War Claims?," 29 September 2004, *Pacific Daily News* (Guam): A19; Guam War Claims Review Commission, "Report on the Implementation of the Guam Meritorious Claims Act of 1945" (June 2004): 79, https://www.chamorroroots.com/warclaimdocs/GuamWarClaimsReviewCommission/GWCRC_Final_Report_060904.pdf (accessed 21 June 2016).

111 Bernard Punzalan, "Guam World War II War Claims: A Legislative History," *Guampedia*, accessed 16 June 2016, http://www.guampedia.com/guam-world-war-ii-war-claims-legislative-history/.

112 Frank Oliveri, "Bush Official Says Little On Guam War Claims Report," 22 July 2004, *Honolulu Advertiser*: A7.

113 Delegate Bordallo's bills passed the House as H.R. 1595 in the 110th Congress (2007–2009) and H.R. 44 in the 111th Congress (2009–2011). H.R. 1595 was proposed during the 109th Congress (2005–2007) but was not voted on.

114 Hearing before the House Committee on Armed Services, *Assessing the Guam War Claims Process*, 111th Cong., 1st sess. (2 December 2009).

115 Gaynor Dumat-ol Daleno, "House Passes War Reparations for Guam," 20 May 2016, *Pacific Daily News* (Guam): A3; National Defense Authorization Act for Fiscal Year 2017, Public Law 114-328, 130 Stat. 2000 (2016).

116 Broder and Cooper, "Politics: Asian Pacific Caucus."

117 *Congressional Record*, Senate, 103rd Cong., 1st sess. (27 October 1993): 26423–26429.

118 S.J. Res. 19, 103rd Cong. (1993); Public Law 103-150, 107 Stat. 1510 (1993).

119 For more on the history of Congressional Gold Medals, see Office of the Historian, U.S. House of Representatives, "Congressional Gold Medal Recipients," http://history.house.gov/Institution/Gold-Medal/Gold-Medal-Recipients/.

120 Martin Snapp, "Battlefield Exploits Earn Japanese-American Veterans the Congressional Gold Medal," 10 November 2011, *Oakland Tribune*, http://www.eastbaytimes.com/columns/ci_19307182 (accessed 1 August 2016); Gregg K. Kakesako, "Congress Honors Japanese-American Veterans," 2 November 2011, *Honolulu Star-Advertiser*: n.p.

121 "Congressional Gold Medal Tour around Seven Cities," 20 September 2012, *North American Post* (Seattle, WA): 2. A digital exhibition focusing on the medal and featuring stories about Japanese-American soldiers was also created. See "Congressional Gold Medal Digital Exhibition to Highlight Nisei Soldier Stories," 11 December 2014, *North American Post* (Seattle, WA): 3.

122 Jesse J. Holland, "Census: Asians Remain Fastest Growing Racial Group in US," 23 June 2016, Associated Press, http://bigstory.ap.org/article/544b8c3d65394c17b960518d39eb96e9/census-asians-remain-fastest-growing-racial-group-us (accessed 1 July 2016). The article, citing U.S. Census officials, includes the statement: "The nation's Asian population grew at 3.4 percent between July 2014 and 2015, with migration responsible for the majority of the growth."

Party Divisions in the House of Representatives
103rd–115th Congresses (1993–2019)*

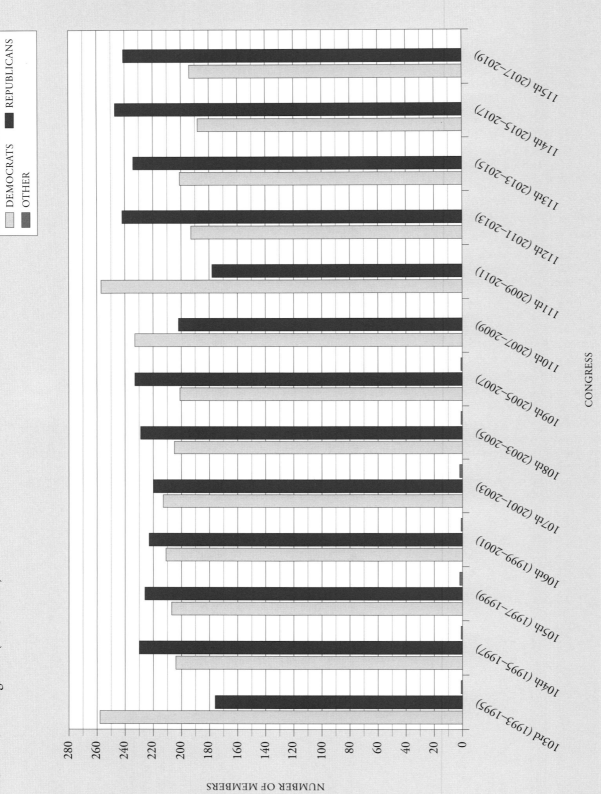

CONGRESS

NUMBER OF MEMBERS

DEMOCRATS ☐   REPUBLICANS ■
OTHER ▨

103rd (1993–1995)
104th (1995–1997)
105th (1997–1999)
106th (1999–2001)
107th (2001–2003)
108th (2003–2005)
109th (2005–2007)
110th (2007–2009)
111th (2009–2011)
112th (2011–2013)
113th (2013–2015)
114th (2015–2017)
115th (2017–2019)

Sources: Office of the Historian, U.S. House of Representatives, "Party Divisions," http://history.house.gov.

*Party division totals are based on Election Day results.

Party Divisions in the Senate

103rd–115th Congresses (1993–2019)*

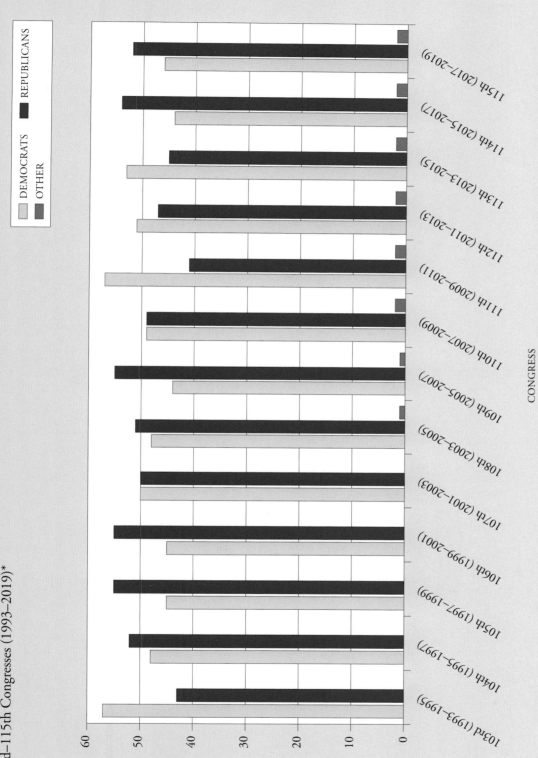

NUMBER OF MEMBERS

CONGRESS

DEMOCRATS
REPUBLICANS
OTHER

103rd (1993–1995)
104th (1995–1997)
105th (1997–1999)
106th (1999–2001)
107th (2001–2003)
108th (2003–2005)
109th (2005–2007)
110th (2007–2009)
111th (2009–2011)
112th (2011–2013)
113th (2013–2015)
114th (2015–2017)
115th (2017–2019)

Sources: U.S. Senate Historical Office; Biographical Directory of the United States Congress, 1774–Present, http://bioguide.congress.gov.

*Party division totals are based on Election Day results.

Asian and Pacific Islander American Members by Office
First Elected 1992–2017*

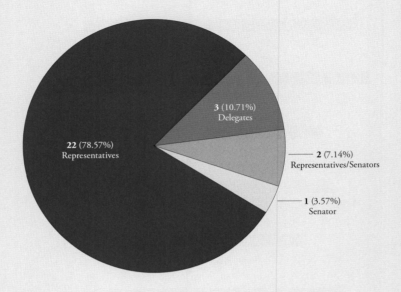

Asian and Pacific Islander American Members by State and Territory
First Elected 1992–2017*

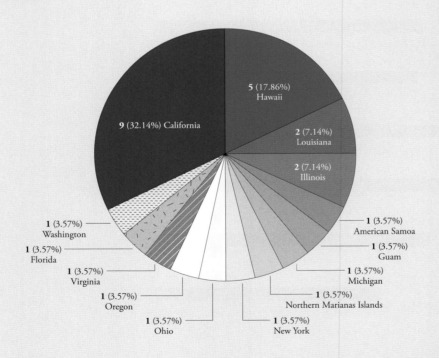

Sources: Appendix A: Asian and Pacific Islander Representatives, Senators, Delegates, and Resident Commissioners by Congress, 1900–2017; Office of the Historian, U.S. House of Representatives; U.S. Senate Historical Office.

*115th Congress (2017–2019) as of July 1, 2017.

Congressional Service

For Asian and Pacific Islander Americans in Congress First Elected 1992–2017*

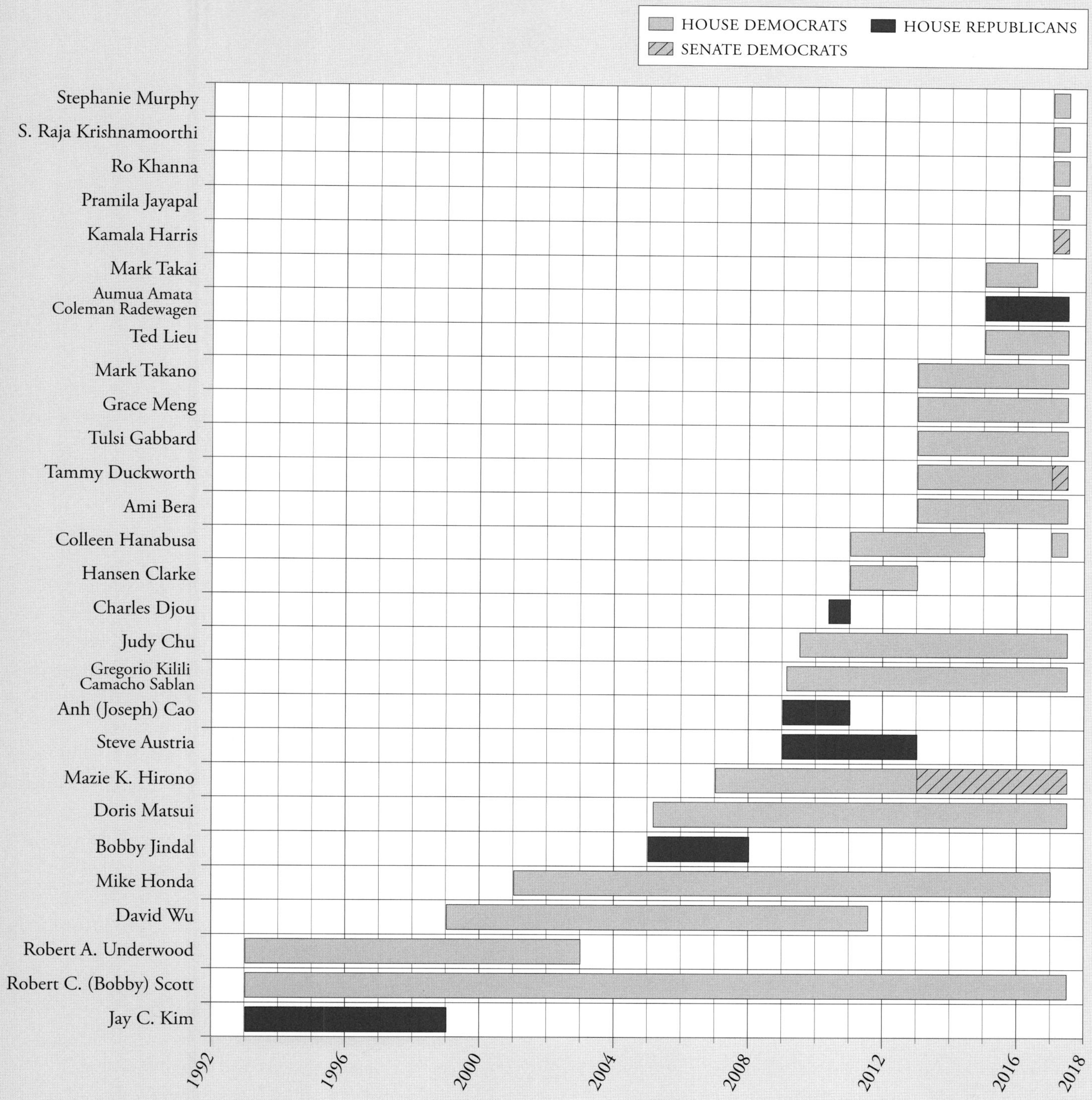
HOUSE DEMOCRATS
HOUSE REPUBLICANS
SENATE DEMOCRATS
Stephanie Murphy
S. Raja Krishnamoorthi
Ro Khanna
Pramila Jayapal
Kamala Harris
Mark Takai
Aumua Amata Coleman Radewagen
Ted Lieu
Mark Takano
Grace Meng
Tulsi Gabbard
Tammy Duckworth
Ami Bera
Colleen Hanabusa
Hansen Clarke
Charles Djou
Judy Chu
Gregorio Kilili Camacho Sablan
Anh (Joseph) Cao
Steve Austria
Mazie K. Hirono
Doris Matsui
Bobby Jindal
Mike Honda
David Wu
Robert A. Underwood
Robert C. (Bobby) Scott
Jay C. Kim
1992
1996
2000
2004
2008
2012
2016
2018

*As of July 1, 2017.

Jay C. Kim
1939–

UNITED STATES REPRESENTATIVE 1993–1999
REPUBLICAN FROM CALIFORNIA

A war survivor and refugee, Jay C. Kim became the first Korean American elected to Congress. "In a free enterprise system, hard work pays off," the often outspoken Congressman noted, summing up his political philosophy. "I've always believed that. If you don't work hard, you're going to fall behind."[1] After building his own engineering business, Kim won a U.S. House seat just two years after his initial entrée into politics. As a new Congressman, he voiced skepticism over House Rules and practices that solidified power among a small group of senior Members. However, Kim's own difficulties with campaign finance violations effectively ended his career in elected office.

Chang Joon Kim was born in Seoul, Korea, on March 27, 1939.[2] His birth name meant "Golden Splendid Law," but he later legally changed his name to Jay.[3] Kim's father was a restaurant manager before the Korean War, but, as Jay Kim recalled, his well-educated family members were marked as enemies by North Korean forces. The family's home was destroyed, and they walked 90 miles to safety. Kim's adopted brother was later executed by North Korean communist officials.[4]

Jay Kim graduated from Po Sung High School, Seoul, South Korea, in 1956 before finishing his education in the United States. In 1961, fresh out of one year of service in the South Korean Army, Jay Kim immigrated to the United States at the age of 22.[5] He married Jung Ok (June) in 1962; the couple had met in Seoul. He earned a BS in engineering from the University of Southern California in 1967. Two years later, he earned an MS in environmental engineering from the same institution. Kim later earned a PhD from Hanyang University, Seoul, South Korea, in 1993.

Kim worked in restaurants and grocery stores when he first arrived in the United States. Later, with a Small Business Administration loan, he founded JAYKIM

Engineers, a firm that designed highways and water reclamation plants. Primarily procuring government contracts, JAYKIM Engineers was one of five minority-owned firms hired to demolish buildings damaged during the 1992 riots in Los Angeles and its suburbs.[6]

Kim entered electoral politics to "make government run more like a business," placing first in a nine-candidate race for the Diamond Bar, California, city council in 1990. One year later, he was elected mayor.[7]

In 1992 local Republican officials courted Kim to run for the U.S. House in a newly created congressional district. The new district sat at a crossroads between Los Angeles, San Bernardino, and Orange counties. It encompassed most of the city of Ontario, an airport, an industrial base, and several high-income neighborhoods. The Los Angeles County Fairgrounds, a low-security prison in Chino, and President Richard Nixon's Presidential Library were also located within its boundaries.

With only two years of political experience, Kim faced veteran political opponents in the GOP primary: Pomona assemblyman Charles Bader and lawyer James Lacy. Kim campaigned on lower taxes and privatizing government services. He opposed amnesty for undocumented immigrants, but supported abortion rights, arguing the government had no business getting involved in women's reproductive decisions. Kim won the primary with a 30-percent plurality—with 889 more votes than his closest opponent.[8] In his conservative district, Kim handily won the general election with 60 percent against Democrat Bob Baker, an intelligence analyst and Vietnam veteran.[9]

Alleged campaign ethics issues surfaced shortly after Kim took office, ensuring that he would face primary challenges throughout his House career. His campaigns, including his run for city council, were plagued by careless bookkeeping and disclosure irregularities.[10]

Less than a year after his election, the *Los Angeles Times* reported that JAYKIM Engineering had spent $400,000 on his campaign, which constituted an illegal corporate contribution. Federal officials investigated, and Kim admitted that he should have paid the company from the campaign coffers to rent office space. Still, no formal legal or ethics charges were brought against him.[11]

Given this rocky start, Kim faced challengers in the 1994 Republican primary but captured a 41 percent plurality in the four-person field. In the general election, Kim easily won with 62 percent of the vote against Pomona-based urban developer Ed Tessier.[12] In the 1996 primary, Yorba Linda-based businessman Bob Kerns had little financing but attacked Kim's ongoing ethics challenges. Kim won with 58 percent of the vote and, in the general election, defeated Democrat Richard L. Waldron with 59 percent of the vote.[13]

Throughout his career, Kim served on the Public Works and Transportation (later Transportation and Infrastructure) Committee. He sought a seat on this panel with the goal of streamlining and trimming government spending.[14] Kim also served on the Small Business Committee in the 103rd Congress (1993–1995).

As the first Korean American elected to Congress, Kim traveled to South Korea following his election and the Korean-American community in southern California quickly embraced him as a surrogate representative.[15] At first, Kim didn't embrace that role. When he arrived in Washington, Republicans tried to place him on the Foreign Affairs Committee—specifically the Asia subcommittee—an assignment he initially declined. Kim claimed he did not have a special agenda nor did he wish to be labeled a spokesperson on South Korea and for Korean Americans. Yet, after his re-election and as part of the new GOP majority in 1995, he accepted the assignment on the renamed International Relations Committee. He served on the panel for two terms.[16]

Representative Kim had an outsized presence for a freshman lawmaker.[17] He amassed one of the House's most conservative records and earned a reputation for being outspoken. As a political newcomer, Kim recalled being "shocked" to see Members gather in various caucus groups on the House Floor; a colleague had to tell him about party bloc seating tradition in the chamber wherein Republicans sat to the left of the House rostrum.[18]

With an outsider's perspective on Congress, Kim embraced the role of being among the institution's loudest critics. One of his first speeches highlighted his cynicism over the political process on Capitol Hill. "In the few short months that I have been here I have learned that this beltway is the land of the easy promise," Kim said. "It's the place where special interests prevail, where truth is tempered by political expediency, where honesty and values take a back seat to business-as-usual politics."[19]

Kim's disillusionment solidified during his freshman orientation, during which a senior Member steered him toward more powerful committee assignments in order to draw larger campaign contributions.[20] Kim was among several freshmen who sought to abolish select committees, launching a salvo against the seniority system which gave long-serving Members greater power. Kim also proposed cutting committee sizes and budgets by 25 percent, claiming that such cost-saving measures would improve Congress's reputation. "The war cry is, eliminate gridlock," he observed, starting "by eliminating the overwhelming power of the seniority system."[21]

One of Kim's primary legislative interests was helping private entrepreneurs with government contracts, the same kind of work he did as an engineer.[22] One of his earliest legislative proposals was the Highway Construction Private Investment Act that helped entrepreneurs get contracts to repair and build roadways. "The private sector is always looking for sound investments. The public sector is always looking for more projects," he noted. "This private-public partnership I am proposing beneficially addresses both needs. It's a win-win concept."[23]

Kim also sought federal reimbursement for road maintenance to keep up with increased traffic from Mexico after the North American Free Trade Agreement (NAFTA) took effect in 1994, and to allow repair shops and vehicle dealerships to access and operate onboard vehicle diagnostics under the Clean Air Act. He successfully

funneled aid for several local projects: $151 million for sewer recycling in Orange County, $91 million for road improvements and carpool connector lanes on major highways passing through his district.[24]

Kim was a vocal opponent of President William J. (Bill) Clinton's health care plan, specifically opposing any mandated contribution from employers for coverage, a centerpiece of the plan. "Employer mandates are nothing more than a tax on jobs," he said. "They are nothing more than a job-killing payroll tax, a tax that American workers will pay in the form of reduced wages and lost jobs. In other words, there is no such thing as a free lunch."[25]

Kim offered an amendment to prohibit taxpayer money on employer mandates. When he submitted his amendment, Kim was dismayed to learn of the Rules Committee's lopsided roster that strongly favored the majority party. When the leadership pulled the bill from the floor before Kim was able to get a vote on it, he concluded they were "scared to vote on my amendment," describing the episode as the "truth held hostage."[26]

Immigration and foreign policy rose to the top of Kim's congressional agenda. "If you're an immigrant in this country, you can lose everything except an accent," Kim noted.[27] Drawing from his experience, he supported aid to legal immigrants, including a successful effort in 1996 to differentiate benefits given to legal and undocumented immigrants. "It is an insult to legal immigrants to lump them together with illegal aliens, who are lawbreakers," Kim argued.[28] In the 103rd Congress, he sought to amend a housing bill limiting undocumented immigrants to seven days of assistance under emergency food and shelter programs for the homeless, citing a desire to "put Americans' needs first."[29] His amendment was approved 220 to 176, and the bill passed the House.[30]

Kim was one of North Korea's strongest critics. He supported cutting off food aid to that nation until the Pyongyang government entered talks with South Korea. Kim was horrified when the Clinton administration threatened to veto a Foreign Relations Committee bill because it did not provide enough aid to North Korea in 1996—this shortly after a North Korean submarine

foundered in South Korean waters and was discovered with "armed commandos" aboard.[31] Kim offered a resolution to condemn North Korean action. "The Clinton administration American taxpayer-funded aid to North Korea has grown faster than to any other country in Asia," Kim explained on the House Floor. "Is this what Americans are subsidizing? Commando raids and military attacks on our own troops and our allies?"[32]

Revelations of further campaign finance violations dogged Kim during his final term in the House. In 1995 and 1996, the *Los Angeles Times* and *Orange County Register* broke the initial story that five Korean companies made illegal contributions to his campaign. The companies pled guilty (and paid fines amounting to $1.6 million) after compensating their employees special bonuses with the expectation that these employees would donate the amount to Kim's campaign.[33] Kim claimed no knowledge of the scheme.[34]

Kim's claims of innocence came under fire, however, when revelations were published that the plan was allegedly hatched at a club meeting for Korean businessmen in July 1992 during which he was a featured speaker. Moreover, two former campaign treasurers testified that Kim's wife, June, had kept track of off-the-book, illegal donations. Seokuk Ma, his campaign treasurer in 1994, was convicted of concealing illegal contributions in April 1997. Ma told authorities that, due to Korean cultural norms, he could not question his superiors, and he did not challenge June Kim when she asked him to sign blank election report forms. "My culture is very different," he testified, "I respect Congressman Kim very much. If they ask me to do something like that, I cannot refuse."[35]

On August 11, 1997, both Jay and June Kim pleaded guilty to misdemeanor violations of federal election law, including three counts of accepting illegal campaign contributions totaling more than $230,000.[36] Kim was sentenced to one-year probation (during two months of which he was required to wear an electronic ankle monitor), 200 hours of community service, and a $5,000 fine. He kept his congressional seat but was only permitted to travel between his Washington-area home in Fairfax

County and the Capitol, attending sessions wearing his ankle monitor and holding meetings with constituents via satellite communication.[37] Though he had initially pledged to observe a three-term limit, Kim ran for re-election in 1998. He finished third in an eight-way open primary, losing to the eventual winner, Republican Gary Miller, and his closest Democratic opponent, Eileen Ansari. Kim was the only House incumbent to lose in a primary election that year.[38]

Afterward, Kim and his wife divorced, and he taught political science courses at a South Korean university for the next year.[39] In 1999 he returned to his home in Washington's Virginia suburbs and also took up residence in San Bernardino County so as to be eligible to run in the 2000 election for a U.S. House seat in a district neighboring his old one.[40] The new district—centered on the city of San Bernardino, or the heart of the "Inland Empire," and the fast-growing, eastern Los Angeles suburbs—was one-third Hispanic, with a majority of registered Democrats.[41] The long-shot campaign drew detractors from Kim's own party.[42] Kim garnered just 8 percent of the vote, losing the open primary to Rancho Cucamonga businessman Elia Pirozzi and the eventual winner, Joe Baca.[43] He went on to chair the Washington Korean-American Forum, a think tank focused on improving U.S. relations with South Korea. Kim remarried a colleague, Jennifer Ahn.

NOTES

1 Quoted in *Almanac of American Politics, 1996* (Washington, DC: National Journal Inc., 1995): 199.

2 *Politics in America, 1994* (Washington, DC: Congressional Quarterly Inc., 1993): 220.

3 Claire Spiegel and K. Connie Kang, "The Fast, Rocky Rise of Jay Kim," 27 October 1993, *Los Angeles Times*: 1.

4 *Congressional Record*, House, 104th Cong., 1st sess. (28 July 1995): H7979.

5 Spiegel and Kang, "The Fast, Rocky Rise of Jay Kim."

6 *Politics in America, 1994*: 220.

7 Spiegel and Kang, "The Fast, Rocky Rise of Jay Kim."

8 *Almanac of American Politics, 1994* (Washington, DC: National Journal Inc., 1993): 186; *Politics in America, 1994*: 220.

9 Office of the Clerk, U.S. House of Representatives, "Election Statistics, 1920 to Present," http://history.house.gov/Institution/Election-Statistics/Election-Statistics/.

10 *Politics in America, 1996* (Washington, DC: Congressional Quarterly Inc., 1995): 183; Spiegel and Kang, "The Fast, Rocky Rise of Jay Kim."

11 Kim sold the company shortly after his election to his son-in-law. See *Almanac of American Politics, 1996*: 199; Spiegel and Kang, "The Fast, Rocky Rise of Jay Kim"; *Politics in America, 1996*: 183; "FBI Searches Former Offices of Rep. Kim," 3 October 1993, *Washington Post*: A11. JAYKIM Engineers collapsed in mid-1993 shortly after he sold it, defaulting on a $1 million loan guaranteed by Kim and his wife.

12 James V. Grimaldi, "Kim Sweeps 4 Aside in Heading for Easy Win," 8 June 1994, *Orange County Register* (CA): A3.

13 Office of the Clerk, U.S. House of Representatives, "Election Statistics, 1920 to Present."

14 *Politics in America, 1994*: 220.

15 Jake Doherty, "Korean-Americans Hail Kim's Victory," 8 November 1992, *Los Angeles Times*: 11.

16 Garrison Nelson and Charles Stewart, III, *Committees in the U.S. Congress, 1993–2010* (Washington, DC: Congressional Quarterly Press, 2011): 790.

17 *Almanac of American Politics, 1994*: 186.

18 Spiegel and Kang, "The Fast, Rocky Rise of Jay Kim."

19 *Congressional Record*, House, 103rd Cong, 1st sess. (22 April 1993): H2011.

20 Robert W. Stewart, "After Winning Office Comes the Actual Office," 17 December 1992, *Los Angeles Times*: B1.

21 *Congressional Record*, House, 103rd Cong., 1st sess. (11 March 1993): H1217.

22 *Almanac of American Politics, 1996*: 199.

23 *Congressional Record*, House, 103rd Cong, 1st sess. (20 May 1993): H2605; H.R. 2225, 103rd Cong. (1993).

24 *Almanac of American Politics, 1998* (Washington, DC: National Journal Inc., 1997): 246.

25 *Congressional Record*, House, 103rd Cong, 2nd sess. (10 August 1994): H7305.

26 *Congressional Record*, House, 103rd Cong, 2nd sess. (3 August 1994): H6743.

27 *Politics in America, 1994*: 220; Spiegel and Kang, "The Fast, Rocky Rise of Jay Kim."

28 Quoted in *Politics in America, 1998* (Washington, DC: Congressional Quarterly Inc., 1997): 206.

29 *Politics in America, 1996*: 183.

30 See H.R. 3838, 103rd Cong. (1993); H. Amdt. 778, 103rd Cong. (1994).

31 See Kevin Sullivan, "N. Korean Submarine Found Beached Off S. Korea," 19 September 1996, *Washington Post*: A22; Nicholas D. Kristoff, "One Commando Still at Large In Korea Submarine Manhunt," 6 November 1996, *New York Times*: A14.

32 *Congressional Record*, House, 104th Cong., 2nd sess. (27 September 1996): H11399.

33 Mark Grossman, *Political Corruption in America*, vol. 1 (Amenia, NY: Grey House Publishing, 2008): 273.

34 *Politics in America, 1998*: 205.

35 Ibid., 204.

36 Chae Reed, "Jay Kim," in *Distinguished Asian Americans*, ed. Hyan-chan Kim (Westport, CT: Greenwood Press, 1999): 158; "CA41: Kim Pleads Guilty to Illegal Contributions," 11 August 1997, Reuters; Dena Bunis, "Ex Rep. Jay Kim May Seek House Seat Again," 4 December 1999, *Orange County Register* (CA): B4; Senate Committee on Governmental Affairs, *Investigation of Illegal or Improper Activities in Connection With 1996 Federal Election Campaigns*, vol. 4, 105th Cong., 2nd sess., S. Rept. 167 (1998): 5683, 5690. The Senate committee investigating foreign contributions to federal elections quoted the *Washington Post*'s claim that Kim's case constituted "the largest amount of criminal campaign violations ever committed by a member of Congress."

37 John Mercurio, "Kim Struggles in Comeback," 6 March 2000, *Roll Call*: n.p.; Reed, "Jay Kim": 158. The Committee on Standards of Official Conduct did not immediately pursue an investigation against Kim because a moratorium on filing ethics complaints against Members was in place while the committee's rules and structure were being overhauled. See "Gingrich Case Prompts Ethics Overhaul," *CQ Almanac, 1997*, 53rd ed. (Washington, DC: Congressional Quarterly Inc., 1998): ch. 1, 32–35.

38 *Politics in America, 2000* (Washington, DC: Congressional Quarterly Inc., 1999): 195.

39 Mercurio, "Kim Struggles in Comeback."

40 Tom Gorman, "Former Rep. Kim, Convicted in 1997, May Run Again," 4 December 1999, *Los Angeles Times*: B1.

41 *Politics in America, 2002* (Washington, DC: Congressional Quarterly Inc., 2001): 145; *Almanac of American Politics, 2002* (Washington, DC: National Journal, Inc., 2001): 267.

42 Gorman, "Former Rep. Kim, Convicted in 1997, May Run Again"; Mercurio, "Kim Struggles in Comeback."

43 *Almanac of American Politics, 2002*: 269.

Robert A. Underwood
1948–

DELEGATE 1993–2003
DEMOCRAT FROM GUAM

Robert A. Underwood served five terms as Guam's Delegate in the U.S. House of Representatives before running unsuccessfully for governor of the territory. As Guam's third Delegate, Underwood continued his two predecessors' push for commonwealth status for the tiny island in the western Pacific. His experience as an educator, along with his respect for Guam's Chamorro culture, shaped much of his legislative agenda during his time in the House. Using his position to draw attention to the pressing needs of the territory, Underwood fought for increased recognition for Guam and for its inclusion in federally funded programs. "When you're a small territory, the nexus of your relationship to the federal government is the basis for your representation in Washington," Underwood noted. "It's always trying to understand that and take advantage of it and try to fix the problems with that. That's the nature of the representation that comes from a small territory."[1]

Robert A. Underwood was born July 13, 1948, in Tamuning, a town on the west coast of Guam. Both his father, John, and his mother, Esther Flores Taitano, were teachers.[2] After graduating from Tamuning's John F. Kennedy High School in 1965, Underwood attended California State University in Los Angeles, earning a BA in history in 1969 and an MA in history in 1971. Influenced by his parents' vocation, Underwood embarked on a 20-year career in education.[3] From 1972 to 1976, he was a high school teacher, a school administrator, and a curriculum writer for Guam's public schools. He then worked at the University of Guam from 1977 to 1992 as an instructor for and a director of the Bilingual Bicultural Training Program and a director of Project BEAM (Bilingual Education Assistance from Micronesia). He was also a professor of education, the dean of the College of Education, and the academic vice president of the university. During this period, Underwood also earned an EdD from the University of Southern California in 1987 and graduated from Harvard's Management Development Program in 1988.[4] Underwood married Lorraine Aguilar, also a teacher, and the couple had five children: Sophia, Roberto, Ricardo, Ramon, and Raphael.[5]

In 1992 Underwood left the University of Guam to challenge four-term incumbent Ben Garrido Blaz in the election for Guam's congressional Delegate seat. Long active in the debate on Guam's political status, Underwood was familiar with the issues affecting the island and pledged to use his experience in public policy to help Guam at the national level.[6] He relied on strong ties to the community that he built during his career as an educator and his familial connections, which included his grandfather James H. Underwood, a former U.S. Marine and the postmaster of Guam.[7] He directed a successful grassroots campaign, walking to small villages and meeting with voters.[8] Underwood's electoral prospects received an unanticipated boost when an impending typhoon postponed voting in Guam for nearly a week. Thus, Guamanians knew before going to the polls that William J. (Bill) Clinton had succeeded in his bid to unseat President George H. W. Bush. This was an important development since both Underwood and Blaz had emphasized the significance of Guam's having a Delegate from the same party as the President.[9] Ultimately, Underwood benefited from a desire for political change and bested Blaz with 55 percent of the vote.[10] "I feel gratified, but that has to end real quick," Underwood remarked. "There's a lot of work ahead."[11] In subsequent elections, Underwood cruised to victory. In 1994 and 1996, he ran unopposed. He faced minimal opposition in his final two elections, defeating Manuel Cruz, a labor union president, with 76 and 78 percent of the vote, respectively.[12]

During his first term in the House, Underwood was assigned to the Armed Services, Natural Resources, and Education and Labor Committees. He remained on Armed Services and Natural Resources throughout his five terms in the House but left Education and Labor after the 103rd Congress (1993–1995).[13] Lacking the ability to vote on the final passage of legislation, Underwood used his committee work as a vital tool to represent his constituents. His spot on Natural Resources—an essential seat for Territorial Delegates—allowed him to weigh in on and influence legislation affecting Guam and the other U.S. territories. Located west of the International Date Line, Guam is a strategic U.S. military stronghold because of its proximity to East Asia. As the U.S. military presence on the island grew after World War II and the Cold War, Guam's economy became closely linked to the armed forces. Underwood's seat on the Armed Services Committee allowed him to cultivate military connections and monitor any changes that might affect the island. In addition to his committee work, Underwood also chaired the Congressional Asian Pacific American Caucus during the 106th Congress (1999–2001).

Underwood wasted no time taking up the issue of Guam's political status. Since the passage of the Organic Act in 1950, which granted Guamanians U.S. citizenship and limited self-government, the island's political future remained a significant topic of debate. Underwood, a longtime advocate of Chamorro rights and increased independence for Guam, backed the commonwealth movement. On March 30, 1993, he introduced his first piece of legislation, the Guam Commonwealth Act (H.R. 1521). The measure called for the creation of a commonwealth with full self-government, the preservation of Chamorro culture, and the "mutual consent" of Guam and the United States for federal policies affecting the territory. Although the measure did not make it to the House Floor for a vote, Underwood introduced the legislation multiple times during his House tenure. In 1997 he took to the floor asking his colleagues to consider commonwealth status for Guam. "The 100th anniversary of the Spanish-American War marks an important time

period for the United States to, in a sense, come face to face with its imperial past and come face to face with what hopefully will be in the next century a more perfect union not only for the 50 States and the District of Columbia, but all the people who live under the American flag," Underwood declared.[14]

As a nonvoting Delegate, Underwood faced unique challenges. "So essentially we are Members, but not entirely," Underwood said, explaining the role of Territorial Delegates. "The island or jurisdiction each respective delegate represents is not often afforded the attention that their jurisdictions deserve, and by our unique status we must introduce very unique legislation tailor-made for our respective jurisdictions."[15] Underwood drafted legislation that focused primarily on issues that pertained solely to Guam and particularly on protecting the interests of its native inhabitants. One such matter concerned lands that had been taken from the Chamorros by the U.S. military after World War II. "Returning Federal excess lands to the people of Guam is not just a good thing to do," Underwood told his House colleagues. "It is the right thing to do, the just thing to do." The freshman Delegate achieved a major legislative victory when his bill, the Guam Excess Lands Act, became law in 1994. The new law transferred more than 3,000 acres of federal land to Guam for parks, new schools, and affordable housing.[16]

Bolstered by this success, Underwood sought to tackle a related long-standing dispute between Guam and the United States. The federal government owned a substantial portion of the island, whose land mass was barely more than 200 square miles. In the wake of security demands after World War II, the U.S. military took control of large tracts of land in Guam. With the end of the Cold War, the local government called for the return of the unused land. Criticism of the American government intensified after the U.S. military relinquished a substantial stretch of land in 1994 to the U.S. Fish and Wildlife Service for use as a refuge.[17] In response to frustration over U.S. land practices, Underwood introduced the first Guam omnibus legislation in congressional history. He considered the Guam Land Returns Act, a provision giving Guam the right of "first refusal of declared excess lands" by the federal government, the most important segment of the bill. The Guam Delegate hoped to develop a process for acquiring excess land that would differ from the standard practice, which gave federal agencies interested in obtaining the unused property priority over the local government.[18] Labeling the topic "one of the most contentious issues in Guam history since the end of World War II," Underwood guided his bill through the House. It became law in 2000.[19]

Following the lead of his predecessors Antonio Borja Won Pat and Ben Garrido Blaz, Underwood drew attention to the hardships Guamanians endured during World War II. During Japan's three-year occupation, the people of Guam suffered forced labor and internment. Although he was born a few years after the war ended, Underwood had a personal connection to the period; his two older siblings died as infants during the occupation. Reflecting on his parents' reaction to their loss, Underwood said, "They taught me that in the midst of difficult circumstances, we should learn lessons about dignity and courage and not bitterness or resentment."[20] Inspired by the Chamorros' strength, Underwood focused his legislative energy on reparations for the victims of the occupation. During the 107th Congress (2001–2003), he oversaw the passage of the Guam War Claims Review Commission Act. The bill, which became law in 2002, established a commission to oversee and settle claims made by Guamanians after World War II. Although the law did not authorize any payments, it was viewed as an important step in the eventual monetary compensation of the victims of the war.[21] In the interest of his constituents' safety, Underwood also asked American military personnel to search for unexploded mustard gas bombs left in Guam during World War II.[22]

Underwood's goal of ensuring fair treatment for all Americans often extended to other U.S. territories. In 1996 he inserted language into a telecommunications bill that would extend domestic rates and access to new technology to Guam and other Pacific territories.[23] He also introduced legislation to extend federal benefits for low-income and older U.S. citizens and those with disabilities

to qualifying residents of Guam and the Virgin Islands. As a lifelong educator, Underwood wanted U.S. territories included in national education policy, and he expressed frustration when Guam, the Virgin Islands, Puerto Rico, and the Commonwealth of the Northern Mariana Islands were omitted from President George W. Bush's No Child Left Behind proposal.[24] "We will not be ignored and we will be included so that every child, whether they are from California, Texas or more familiar locations like Guam will not be left behind," Underwood said.[25] Although he was able to secure more federal money to build schools and train teachers, Underwood was not satisfied with federal funding for public education in Guam.[26]

Underwood also fought to preserve Guam's unique cultural identity. He had chaired the Chamorro Language Commission before coming to Congress and had led a movement to incorporate the Chamorro language and culture into the curriculum at the University of Guam.[27] His commitment to protect Guam's indigenous customs and traditions continued during his House tenure. In 2001 Underwood achieved an important victory when he convinced the Food and Drug Administration to allow the importation of betel nuts into the U.S. mainland. Chewed by many Pacific Islanders, the betel nut, a product of the areca palm tree, is a significant part of the Chamorro culture.[28] In the 106th Congress (1999–2001), Underwood introduced a bill to establish a standard time zone for Guam and the Northern Mariana Islands. Signed into law in 2000, the new legislation "will prove to be a source of pride when people refer to our time zone as Chamorro Standard Time," Underwood remarked.[29] Rather than criticizing legislation that would declare English the official language of the U.S. government, Underwood sent House Members a "Dear Colleague" letter poking fun at the bill by offering a mock "ketchup-only" measure. "I was surprised to learn salsa has replaced ketchup in sales as our nation's leading condiment," Underwood wrote. "I hope you share my concern that a country built on ketchup should take steps to ensure the predominance of this vegetable as our national condiment."[30] Speaking at the Democratic National Convention in 2000, Underwood highlighted the unique nature of Guam and the other Pacific Islands, concluding his speech in Chamorro as a tribute to his native land.[31]

In 2002 Underwood announced his decision to not seek a sixth term in the House. "Ten years in Washington is a long time, and I had hoped to have a good career in Congress, and I felt that I've done well, but it's also time to come back home," Underwood remarked.[32] Still interested in public service, he entered the race for governor of Guam in 2002. In the campaign against Guam senator Felix Camacho, Underwood, heavily outspent by his Republican opponent, employed a grassroots strategy like the one he used when he ran for Delegate.[33] Underwood lost the election, garnering 45 percent of the vote to Camacho's 55 percent.[34] "This is not the end. It is just another chapter," he told his supporters after the loss.[35] But four years later he again lost to Camacho. Named professor emeritus by the University of Guam in 2000, Underwood was selected as the university's president in 2008.

NOTES

1   Jennifer Yachnin, "Guam Delegate Hopes to Exchange Long Flights for Governorship," 26 September 2002, *Roll Call*: 14.

2   "Underwood & Ada for Governor and Lt. Governor," accessed 7 November 2002, http://www.underwoodada.com/?ua=profiles (site discontinued).

3   Yachnin, "Guam Delegate Hopes to Exchange Long Flights for Governorship."

4   Underwood's *curriculum vitae* was posted on the University of Guam's website, accessed 11 January 2012, http://www.uog.edu/dynamicdata/PresidentsOffice.aspx (site discontinued).

5   "Robert Underwood," 2 November 1992, *Pacific Daily News* (Guam): 3.

6   Underwood's campaign materials underscored his familiarity with important issues in Guam and his desire to bring change to the island. See "The Time Is Right for a Change," 4 November 1992, *Pacific Daily News* (Guam): 27.

7   Robert F. Rogers, *Destiny's Landfall: A History of Guam* (Honolulu: University of Hawai'i Press, 2011): 267.

8   Marshall Santos, "Democrats Win 2–1 Advantage," 9 November 1992, *Pacific Daily News* (Guam): 3.

9   Tambra A. Bryant, "Guam Dems: Clinton Win Would Help Underwood," 4 November 1992, *Pacific Daily News* (Guam): 3; Frale Oyen, "Election Postponed," 3 November 1992, *Pacific Daily News* (Guam): 1.

10   Office of the Clerk, U.S. House of Representatives, "Election Statistics, 1920 to Present," http://history.house.gov/Institution/Election-Statistics/Election-Statistics/.

11   Donovan Brooks, "Grassroots, Media Use Called Key to Success," 11 November 1992, *Pacific Daily News* (Guam): 7.

12   Office of the Clerk, U.S. House of Representatives, "Election Statistics, 1920 to Present"; Jacob Leon Guerrero, "Underwood to House: Halt A–76," 12 April 2000, *Pacific Daily News* (Guam): 5A.

13   When the Republican Party took control of the House in 1995, many committee names were changed, including Armed Services, which was renamed National Security during the 104th and 105th Congresses, and Natural Resources, which was renamed Resources for the rest of Underwood's tenure. Before the 104th Congress, Natural Resources was known as the Interior and Insular Affairs Committee—a name dating back to 1951. For information on committee histories and name changes, see Garrison Nelson, *Committees in the U.S. Congress, 1947–1992*, vol. 2 (Washington, DC: CQ Press, 1994).

14   *Congressional Record*, House, 105th Cong., 1st sess. (10 February 1997): H401.

15   *Congressional Record*, House, 106th Cong., 1st sess. (29 June 1999): 4999.

16   *Congressional Record*, House, 103rd Cong., 1st sess. (18 May 1993): 2500.

17   During World War II, the U.S. military seized a large tract of land in northern Guam that made up nearly one-third of the island. In 1994 the military relinquished the land it no longer needed to the U.S. Fish and Wildlife Service, which added the area to an existing national wildlife refuge. Many Guamanians thought the land should have been returned to them. There was also concern that the new wildlife reserve would lead to more destruction by the brown tree snake, which was introduced to the island during World War II and which devastated many indigenous bird species. William Branigin, "Guam Sees Predator in Wildlife Effort: Expansion of Refuge Acreage Smacks of Colonialism," 15 April 1994, *Washington Post*: A21.

18   *Congressional Record*, House, 106th Cong., 2nd sess. (30 October 2000): 11574.

19   Yachnin, "Guam Delegate Hopes to Exchange Long Flights for Governorship"; *Congressional Record*, House, 106th Cong., 2nd sess. (30 October 2000): 11574; Public Law 106-504, 114 Stat. 2309 (2000).

20   Robert Underwood, "Recognize Chamorro Character," 13 July 2011, *Pacific Daily News* (Guam): n.p.

21 *Congressional Record*, Extension of Remarks, 107th Cong., 1st sess. (30 January 2001): E49–E50; *Almanac of American Politics, 1998* (Washington, DC: National Journal Inc., 1997): 1565; Dionesis Tamondong, "Delegate Returns to Hall," 6 July 2000, *Pacific Daily News* (Guam): 2A; Public Law 107-333, 116 Stat. 2873 (2002).

22 Steve Limtiaco, "Delegate Urges Federal Action on Buried Weapons," 4 October 2000, *Pacific Daily News* (Guam): 5A; *Almanac of American Politics, 2002* (Washington, DC: National Journal Inc., 2001): 1698.

23 *Congressional Record*, House, 104th Cong., 2nd sess. (1 February 1996): 2237.

24 Tanya M. C. Mendiola, "Underwood Wants Guam Included in Education Plan," 2 February 2001, *Pacific Daily News* (Guam): 7A.

25 Scott Radway, "Delegate Wants Unity," 9 August 2001, *Pacific Daily News* (Guam): 1A; Mendiola, "Underwood Wants Guam Included in Education Plan."

26 Radway, "Delegate Wants Unity."

27 "Robert Underwood," *Guampedia*, accessed 7 January 2011, http://guampedia.com/robert-underwood/.

28 Theresa Merto, "Delegate's Address Encourages Listeners," 9 August 2001, *Pacific Daily News* (Guam): 3A; *Congressional Record*, House, 106th Cong., 2nd sess. (30 October 2000): H11574.

29 Theresa Merto, "Chamorro Time Measure Awaits Clinton's OK," 17 December 2000, *Pacific Daily News* (Guam): 5A.

30 Emily Hancock, "Guam Delegate Pours It on English-Only Measure," 20 October 1995, *Houston Chronicle*: 14.

31 Steve Limtiaco and Dionesis Tamondong, "Underwood Steps Up," 19 August 2000, *Pacific Daily News* (Guam): 1A.

32 Limtiaco and Tamondung, "Underwood Steps Up."

33 Theresa Merto, "The Count Continues," 6 November 2002, *Pacific Daily News* (Guam): 1.

34 "Results," 6 November 2002, *Pacific Daily News* (Guam): 3.

35 Scott Radway, "Underwood Keeps Spirits High upon Defeat," 6 November 2002, *Pacific Daily News* (Guam): 2.

David Wu

1955–

UNITED STATES REPRESENTATIVE 1999–2011
DEMOCRAT FROM OREGON

David Wu, who immigrated to America in the 1960s, had never held political office before he won a seat representing the suburbs of Portland, Oregon, in the U.S. House of Representatives in 1998. Described by one journalist as "an energetic fusion of gabby extrovert and musing intellectual," Wu pursued an ambitious agenda during his House career and was not afraid to break with Democrats or businesses in his district on hot-button issues.[1] "We have a certain bandwidth," Wu said of Congress's capacity to juggle multiple issues. "Education has always been a top priority. Human rights is a particular passion of mine. There hasn't been a lot of legislation in Congress on that," he said in 2008. "I've been outspoken. Health care and energy are things that are very, very important to Oregon and the district."[2]

David Wu was born on April 8, 1955, on the island of Taiwan off the coast of mainland China. When he was only an infant, his father, Keh Chang (K. C.) Wu left to study in New York, leaving Wu, his mother Helen, and his sisters back home. In 1961 Wu and the rest of his family immigrated to America, reunited with his father, and settled in southern California after K. C. took a job with a defense contractor.[3] Wu learned to speak English in the first grade and was quickly drawn to classes in science, math, and technology.[4] In 1977 he graduated from Stanford University in Palo Alto, California, with a degree in biology before beginning medical school at Harvard University in Cambridge, Massachusetts. While training to become a doctor, however, Wu realized that he found policy more interesting than medicine.[5] He left Harvard for Yale Law School, earning a JD in 1982.

Wu settled in Portland in his late 20s and, after clerking for a federal judge on the Ninth Circuit, began a successful career as a lawyer for the region's technology companies.[6] He was active in his community, serving on Portland's planning commission for three years in the late 1980s, occasionally writing op-eds for his local paper and leading the drive to make Suzhou, China, Portland's sister city. Wu had worked on Jimmy Carter's and then Gary Hart's presidential campaigns, but in Portland his political activities generally took place behind the scenes.[7] Wu's first marriage ended in divorce in 1992. He married his second wife, Michelle Maxine Wu, about four years later. They separated in late 2009 and later filed for divorce. Together they have a son and a daughter.[8]

During the 105th Congress (1997–1999), three-term Democratic Representative Elizabeth Furse decided not to run for re-election, opening a seat from Oregon's 1st District, which encompassed downtown Portland and stretched northwesterly toward the coast and included all of Clatsop, Columbia, Washington, and Yamhill Counties as well as parts of Multnomah and Clackamas Counties.[9] The area was home to a number of major technology companies, earning northwestern Oregon the nickname of "Silicon Forest," a riff on California's famed Silicon Valley.[10]

Despite having little political experience, Wu declared his candidacy for the House in the summer of 1997.[11] Although he knew the tech sector inside and out, Wu's main campaign theme became access to universal education.[12] He wanted to pump federal money into the nation's Head Start preschools, hire 100,000 new public school teachers, invest in research and job training, and make college more affordable with federal grants.[13] He supported gun control, wanted to see Congress reinforce Social Security, and lauded efforts in Oregon to protect migratory salmon populations.[14]

His main opponent in the party's primary was Linda Peters, chairwoman of the Washington County board of commissioners, who drew early funds from national groups, forcing Wu to lend his campaign money from

his personal savings.[15] Peters then missed the deadline to appear in the statewide Oregon voters' guide, and on May 3, 1998, Wu picked up a major endorsement from the *Oregonian* newspaper. "Peters has the resume," the editors wrote, "but Wu has the chops. He displays the sharp intellect and grasp of detail that the job demands, and he exudes the passion and energy that the voters deserve. He's simply a better fit for the future of this diverse, evolving district."[16] Wu defeated Peters with about 53 percent of the vote.[17]

With the open seat, the 1st District's general election quickly garnered national attention.[18] Wu's main opponent was Molly Bordonaro, a young Republican from Portland's wealthy western suburbs who also had never held public office.[19] Just as he did during the primary election, Wu touted his educational reforms as the lynchpin of his campaign.[20] By August, the local Portland paper called the contest in the 1st District "the hottest congressional race in the state."[21]

Wu received campaign help from House Democrats and, by mid-September, he had taken the lead in the polls.[22] On the eve of the election, the press asked Wu what he envisioned for Portland's future. "I'd like to see a 21st century where all children start life well taken care of," he said, emphasizing the importance of early education. "I would like to see, in my lifetime, the final triumph of democracy around the world, everywhere, people being able to … enjoy the human rights that we sometimes take for granted in this country."[23]

On Election Day, Wu won in a nail-biter, taking 50 percent of the vote. His 1998 victory was the closest in his career. Over the next decade, Wu never won with less than 55 percent of the electorate. In 2008, riding the wave of Democratic excitement at Barack Obama's presidential candidacy, Wu captured nearly 72 percent, his largest margin of victory.[24]

In his first term, Democrats assigned Wu to committees where he would spend his entire House career, the Committee on Education and the Workforce (later renamed the Committee on Education and Labor), and the Committee on Science (later renamed the Committee on Science and Technology, then renamed again as the Committee on Science, Space, and Technology). Combined, the two committees perfectly fit his legislative agenda. "I see myself in a sweet spot, in a really, really sweet spot," he told the *Oregonian* a decade after receiving his initial assignments. "It's a sweet spot because it's economic growth. It's jobs."[25] During the 110th Congress (2007–2009), Wu also served a brief stint on the Foreign Affairs Committee.

Outside of his immediate committee jurisdiction, Wu joined the New Democrat Coalition, and in the 107th Congress (2001–2003), he served as chairman of the Congressional Asian Pacific American Caucus.[26]

In the House, it did not take Wu long before he made headlines for a controversial decision to oppose a trade deal with China that companies in his district, including juggernauts Nike and Intel, supported.[27] For years, Congress had refused to grant China permanent most favored nation (MFN) status (later called permanent normal trade relations) because the federal government claimed China had committed human rights violations against its citizens. MFN status carried with it generous trade terms, making it a huge economic boost.[28] Because of certain loopholes, however, China had enjoyed MFN benefits for years and, by the 1990s, had become one of America's main trading partners.[29]

For Wu, who had spent his earliest years in the shadow of Beijing, the human rights situation in China struck a chord.[30] He had opposed MFN status for China for almost a decade and, in 1991, said it would be "an act of political cowardice" if the United States relaxed trade restrictions before China improved its human rights record.[31]

As a corporate lawyer, Wu had once called himself "a foot soldier of capitalism," but he also believed "that the marketplace must be leavened by" a general sense of decency, that the United States had a moral obligation to use its purchasing power to spur democratic reform.[32] "I believe in engagement. I believe in trade. We're not going to shut it down, but we have to do everything we can to help create some breathing space for progressive forces within China."[33]

"He's a key vote in a lot of ways," one of Nike's lobbyists said in the spring of 2000. "There's a lot of attention on Mr. Wu right now." Such a spotlight was rare for a freshman legislator, but Wu worked closely with the Democratic Whip's office to generate opposition to the measure.[34] Nevertheless, the China trade bill passed in a bipartisan vote.[35] It was not the last time Wu bucked powerful interests back home either. In 2005 Wu emerged as the only member of the Oregon delegation to oppose the construction of a casino in the Columbia River Gorge, protesting the possible environmental impact on the area.[36]

Nor was Wu afraid to cross party leaders on controversial votes. In 2003, for instance, Wu voted for a Republican bill to expand the country's Medicare program. Democrats decried the proposal for threatening the stability of the program, and throughout the vote Wu sat stoically as Members buzzed around him. According to the *Washington Post*, a rotating cast of Democrats lobbied him, but Wu stayed silent until the final seconds when he voted yes after enough Republicans had switched their votes to pass the measure.[37] Wu was one of just 16 Democrats to vote for the bill, and he shocked some constituents back home. "In my view," Wu told the *Oregonian* after the vote, "I delivered to my constituents and my conscience the right thing to do."[38]

Wu also pursued a number of local projects for his district. In 2002, for instance, he introduced the Fort Clatsop National Memorial Expansion Act, authorizing the Interior Department to buy land adjacent to the existing national memorial—the location where Meriwether Lewis and William Clark had wintered during their western expedition—in order to create a trail system linking the memorial to the Pacific Ocean.[39] President George W. Bush signed it into law on August 21, 2002. Two years later Wu helped direct tens of millions in federal funding to companies in Oregon that were developing safety equipment for the U.S. military, and he also helped procure $15 million to dredge the shipping canal in the Columbia River.[40]

For Wu, serving on the Education Committee was deeply personal, and he credited the educational opportunities he had as a child for the success he experienced as an adult. "Education was my way up in the world," he said during his first campaign in 1998. "To me this is not the issue du jour. This is my life."[41] Wu served on multiple subcommittees: Employer-Employee Relations (106th Congress [1999–2001] and 108th through 109th Congresses [2003–2007]); Early Childhood, Youth and Families (106th Congress); 21st Century Competitiveness (107th through 109th Congresses); Higher Education, Lifelong Learning, and Competitiveness (110th and 111th Congresses [2007–2011]); and Health, Employment, Labor, and Pensions (110th and 111th Congresses).

In his first few terms, Wu introduced a number of educational initiatives, but he found limited success. His bills included proposals to reduce class size, to improve classroom technology, to create new work-study programs, and to open funding for colleges and universities "serving Asian Americans and Pacific Islanders." He also worked to simplify the process of transferring from two-year to four-year universities. His efforts to reform certain types of student loans and their tax requirements attracted a good deal of support, and he recruited 85 cosponsors for his Student Loan Fairness Act of 2005. "Making it harder for students to go to college not only undercuts our promise to individuals, it undermines America's economy and world leadership," he said in 2006.[42]

When Democrats retook the House in the 110th and 111th Congresses, Wu continued pushing the issues. He worked to expand visa quotas for immigrant employees with advanced degrees who worked for companies that funded college scholarships, and after a flood ravaged the town of Vernonia, Oregon, in 2007, Wu petitioned the Appropriations Committee in 2008 to help the school district buy new technology.[43] He also sought to improve the education and training opportunities available to military veterans living in rural areas.

Along with the Education Committee, the Science Committee was something of a natural home for Wu. Although he had hoped for a seat on the Judiciary Committee to work on intellectual property law, Wu settled into a number of Science subcommittees: Space

and Aeronautics (106th through 111th Congresses [1999–2011]); Technology (106th Congress); Energy (107th and 108th Congresses [2001–2005]); and Environment, Technology, and Standards (109th Congress [2005–2007]). When the Democrats regained the majority following the 2006 elections, Wu was named chairman of the Science Committee's Subcommittee on Technology and Innovation for both the 110th and 111th Congresses, where he worked to both strengthen federal initiatives helping startup technology firms and to improve math and science education.[44]

Wu notched an early legislative victory in the 110th Congress when he introduced the Technology Innovation and Manufacturing Stimulation Act of 2007 (H.R. 1868) on February 15, 2007. The bill funded the National Institute of Standards and Technology for two years and created a number of new research and development programs at the 106-year-old organization. Wu's subcommittee considered the bill two months later and, after amending it twice, passed it by voice vote. Once the measure cleared the full committee on April 30, the House approved it four days later, 385 to 23. Although the Senate never considered it, H.R. 1868 became law after the House attached it to the America COMPETES Act, which President Bush signed into law in early August 2007.[45]

That summer Wu won another legislative battle when the Science and Technology Committee approved his amendment to the Solar Energy and Advancement Act, clarifying language in the bill that made community colleges eligible to receive federal grants for training programs in solar power. Although the House never took up the bill, sections of it, including Wu's amendment, were wrapped up in the Energy Independence and Security Act of 2007.[46]

As subcommittee chairman in the 111th Congress (2009–2011), Wu wanted to leverage government resources to ignite innovation. "It meshes every priority I can think of. It meshes with everything I've been doing," Wu said, noting the support from Democratic leaders. "The speaker [Nancy Pelosi] is really hip to innovation," he pointed out. And the Obama administration, he said, also "really gets it in terms of innovation."[47]

As chairman of the Technology and Innovation Subcommittee in the 111th Congress, Wu used his seat to help better prepare the country to deal with natural disasters, holding hearings on earthquakes, hurricanes, and wildfires. In an effort to coordinate the federal agencies that helped predict and respond to natural disasters, his bill, the Natural Hazards Risk Reduction Act of 2010, passed the House in a landslide vote, 335 to 50, on March 2, 2010.[48] Unfortunately for Wu, the Senate never considered it.

In addition to natural disasters, Wu's subcommittee conducted hearings on a multitude of different subjects from 2007 to 2011, including the effect of globalization on domestic innovation, federal initiatives for small design and tech firms, the commercial ramifications of federal research, federal cybersecurity policy, the development and regulation of new medicine, airline security technology, environmentally sensitive construction technologies, and improvements to America's energy grid.[49]

Following an accusation that the press described as "an unwanted sexual encounter … with a young California woman," Wu resigned from the House on August 3, 2011. He had initially decided not to stand for re-election in 2012, but after pressure from Democratic leadership and in the face of a looming ethics investigation, Wu stepped down.[50]

MANUSCRIPT COLLECTION

Library of Congress, Asian Division (Washington, DC). *Oral History*: 2003–2011, 8 linear feet. The collection contains videocassettes, DVDs, photographs, and documents related to an oral history project conducted by the United States Capitol Historical Society to document the service of Asian Americans in Congress. David Wu is included among the interviewees.

NOTES

1 Steve Suo, "Wu vs. Bordonaro: An Ambitious Race for First in the 1st: Wu," 4 October 1998, *Sunday Oregonian*: A1. His hometown newspaper, the *Oregonian*, once described Wu as "a wild card." See Jeff Kosseff, "Wu Proves to be a Wild Card in Congress," 1 September 2006, *Oregonian*: A1.

2 Jeff Kosseff, "District 1–Wu Pushes Energy, Health, Education," 21 October 2008, *Oregonian*: A4.

3 Suo, "Wu vs. Bordonaro, An Ambitious Race in the 1st: Wu"; "2000 Democratic National Convention Day 2, Afternoon," C-SPAN video, 3:49:03, 15 August 2000, http://www.c-span.org/video/?158806-1/2000-democratic-convention-day-2-afternoon (accessed 24 August 2015); *Politics in America, 2004* (Washington, DC: Congressional Quarterly, Inc., 2003): 840; *Almanac of American Politics, 2000* (Washington, DC: National Journal Group, Inc., 1999): 1334–1335. His father's name, and much of his family's naming history, is found in David Wu, "Newly Born on the 4th of July," 13 July 1997, *Sunday Oregonian*: C5. Wu's mother's name comes from a photo caption from "David Wu," 4 November 1998, *Oregonian*: A1.

4 Steve Suo, "Wu Wants to be the Talk of the Town in the 1st District: Voter Guide," 26 April 1998, *Sunday Oregonian*: D1; Jeff Kosseff, "Northwest Legislators Strut Their Science Stuff," 30 April 2007, *Oregonian*: B1.

5 "David Wu, Democrat Voter Guide," 26 April 1998, *Sunday Oregonian*: D9; Suo, "Wu Wants to be the Talk of the Town in the 1st District: Voter Guide."

6 Suo, "Wu Wants to be the Talk of the Town in the 1st District: Voter Guide"; Suo, "Wu vs. Bordonaro, An Ambitious Race in the 1st: Wu."

7 Ibid.

8 Kevin Freking, "In Wake of Sex Allegation, Congressman Will Resign," 26 July 2011, Associated Press; Bill Graves, "Congressman Wu, Wife Separating," 29 December 2009, *Oregonian*: n.p.; Janie Har and Charles Pope, "Sealed Divorce Filing Said to Address Wu's Pill Use," 8 April 2011, *Oregonian*: n.p.

9 Office of the Historian, U.S. House of Representatives, "Elizabeth Furse," *Women in Congress*, http://history.house.gov/People/Detail/13522?ret=True.

10 *Congressional Directory*, 106th Cong. (Washington, DC: Government Printing Office, 1999): 220–221; *Almanac of American Politics, 2000*: 1334.

11 Jeff Maples and Harry Bodine, "Beaverton Mayor Apparently Won't Seek 1st District Seat," 24 August 1997, *Sunday Oregonian*: C2.

12 Don Hamilton, "Democrats Kick Off 1st District Race," 19 November 1997, *Oregonian*: E2.

13 Steve Suo, "1st District Race Shows Varying Styles," 15 February 1998, *Sunday Oregonian*: B7; Steve Suo, "1st District Candidates Throw Spotlight on Education," 1 March 1998, *Sunday Oregonian*: C1.

14 "1998 Voters' Guide: 1st Congressional District," 14 May 1998, *Oregonian* (West Zoner): 13.

15 Steve Suo, "Powerful PAC Puts Peters on Wish List," 14 December 1997, *Sunday Oregonian*: B2; Steve Suo, "1st District Money Race on in Big Way," 2 February 1998, *Oregonian*: A1.

16 "Steve Suo, "Peters Misses Deadline, Won't Appear in Voters' Guide," 22 March 1998, *Sunday Oregonian*: B2; Steve Suo, "Peters and Wu Run an Even-Money Race," 16 April 1998, *Oregonian*: D9. Quotation from "Wu for 1st District Demos," 3 May 1998, *Sunday Oregonian*: F4.

17 Steve Suo, "Wu Finally Wins in 1st District," 22 May 1998, *Oregonian*: D1.

18 Jeff Maples, "Northwest Key to Locking Up House," 18 January 1998, *Sunday Oregonian*: B2; "1st District Differences," 23 May 1998, *Oregonian*: D14; James Mayer, "Wu, Bordonaro Low-Key at Start of High-Stakes Race," 14 August 1998, *Oregonian*: C7.

19 Steve Suo, "Wu, Bordonaro Draw Images for Microscope," 23 September 1998, *Oregonian*: A1.

20 Don Hamilton, "Gephardt Makes Early Plug for Wu," 28 August 1998, *Oregonian*: C1.

21 Hamilton, "Gephardt Makes Early Plug for Wu."

22 "Poll Gives Wu Edge over Bordonaro," 11 September 1998, *Oregonian*: D12.

23 "David Wu: What He Says," 4 October 1998, *Sunday Oregonian*: A14.

24 Office of the Clerk, U.S. House of Representatives, "Election Statistics, 1920 to Present," http://history.house.gov/Institution/Election-Statistics/Election-Statistics/.

25 Charles Pope, "Wu Sees Himself at Nexus of Innovation," 12 April 2010, *Oregonian*: n.p.

26 *Almanac of American Politics, 2002* (Washington, DC: National Journal Group, Inc., 2001): 1276; *Politics in America, 2004*: 840.

27 Dave Hogan, "Wu At the Center of U.S.-China Trade Debate," 13 March 2000, *Oregonian*: A1; Don Hamilton, "Trade with China Becomes Issue in 1st District Race," 13 May 2000, *Oregonian*: D1.

28 For more on America's trade history with China, see James Mann, *About Face: A History of America's Curious Relationship with China, from Nixon to Clinton* (New York: Vintage Books, 2000); Hogan, "Wu at the Center of U.S.-China Trade Debate."

29 "U.S. Acts to Ease Trade with East Bloc," *CQ Almanac, 1990*, 46th ed. (Washington, DC: Congressional Quarterly, 1991): 204–206, http://library.cqpress.com; "Jackson-Vanik Waiver," *CQ Almanac, 1989*, 45th ed. (Washington, DC: Congressional Quarterly, 1990): 145–146, http://library.cqpress.com.

30 Associated Press, "Lawmaker's Opposition to China Trade Bill May Make his Re-Election Tougher," 23 April 2000, *St. Louis Post-Dispatch*: A5.

31 David Wu, "U.S. Stance on China Mistaken," 17 July 1991, *Oregonian*: D7.

32 David Wu, "Trade with China: Americans Should Stand Firm in Support of Human Rights," 10 November 1995, *Oregonian*: B9.

33 Hogan, "Wu at the Center of U.S.-China Trade Debate."

34 Ibid.; Associated Press, "Lawmaker's Opposition to China Trade Bill May Make His Re-Election Tougher"; Dave Hogan, "Wu, Others Take Stand Against Trade," 30 March 2000, *Oregonian*: D7; Hamilton, "Trade with China Becomes Issue in 1st District Race."

35 Hogan, "Wu, Others Take Stand Against Trade." For more on the politics of trade with China and the events surrounding the vote, see "Lawmakers Hand Clinton Big Victory in Granting China Permanent Trade Status," *CQ Almanac, 2000*, 56th ed. (Washington, DC: Congressional Quarterly, 2001): ch. 20, 3–24, http://library.cqpress.com.

36 *Politics in America, 2008* (Washington, DC: Congressional Quarterly, Inc., 2007): 835.

37 David S. Broder, "Time Was GOP's Ally on the Vote," 23 November 2003, *Washington Post*: A1.

38 Quotation from Jim Barnett, "Background Check," 25 November 2003, *Oregonian*: A6; Jeff Mapes, "Wyden, Wu Test Waters Among Constituents on Medicare Bill Vote," 5 December 2003, *Oregonian*: A1; Jim Barnett and Tom Detzel, "Congress: Looking Ahead Issues for Northwest Lawmakers Range from the Economy to Forests to ID Theft," 20 January 2004, *Oregonian*: A6; *Politics in America, 2006* (Washington, DC: CQ Press, 2005): 853.

39 House Committee on Resources, *Fort Clatsop National Memorial Expansion Act of 2002*, 107th Cong., 2nd sess., H. Rept. 456 (14 May 2002).

40 Jim Barnett, "Election 2004 1st Congressional District," 15 October 2004, *Oregonian*: A1.

41 Suo, "Wu vs. Bordonaro: An Ambitious Race for First in the 1st: Wu."

42 Jim Barnett and Michelle Cole, "Federal Cuts Sting Social Services," 3 February 2006, *Oregonian*: B1; Robert Landauer, "State Student Aid Increasingly Anemic," 16 March 2003, *Oregonian*: F4.

43 Michelle Trappen, "Funding for Vernonia Schools Gets Initial OK," 25 June 2008, *Oregonian*: E2.

44 "Wu for 1st District Demos"; Jeff Kosseff, "Northwest Legislators Strut Their Science Stuff," 30 April 2007, *Oregonian*: B1.

45 House Committee on Science and Technology, *Summary of Activities of the Committee on Science and Technology*, 110th Cong., 2nd sess., H. Rept. 935 (2009): 54–55; Public Law 110-69, 121 Stat. 572 (2007).

46 House Committee on Science and Technology, *Solar Energy Research and Advancement Act of 2007*, 110th Cong., 1st sess., H. Rept. 303 (3 August 2007): 52; *Summary of Activities of the Committee on Science and Technology*, H. Rept. 935: 66–67; Public Law 110-140, 121 Stat. 1492 (2007).

47 Pope, "Wu Sees Himself At Nexus of Innovation."

48 House Committee on Science and Technology, *Natural Hazards Risk Reduction Act of 2009*, Part 1, 111th Cong., 2nd sess., H. Rept. 424 (26 February 2010): 13–18, 58–64. Wu's quotation appears on page 61.

49 *Summary of Activities of the Committee on Science and Technology*, H. Rept. 935: 303–331; House Committee on Science and Technology, *Summary of Activities of the Committee on Science and Technology*, 111th Cong., 2nd sess., H. Rept. 698 (2010): 237–278.

50 Charles Pope, Beth Slovic, and Harry Esteve, "Pressure Increases for Wu to Resign," 24 July 2011, *Oregonian*: n.p.; Aaron Blake, "Oregon Rep. Wu Faces Sex Allegation," 24 July 2011, *Washington Post*: A3; Charles Pope, "Embattled Wu Won't Seek Re-Election," 25 July 2011, *Oregonian*: n.p.; Chris Cillizza, "Democratic Leaders Call for Ethics Investigation of Wu," 25 July 2011, *Washington Post*: A3; Freking, "In Wake of Sex Allegation, Congressman Will Resign."

"I WOULD LIKE TO SEE,
IN MY LIFETIME, THE FINAL
TRIUMPH OF DEMOCRACY
AROUND THE WORLD,
EVERYWHERE, PEOPLE BEING
ABLE TO ... ENJOY THE HUMAN
RIGHTS THAT WE SOMETIMES
TAKE FOR GRANTED
IN THIS COUNTRY."

David Wu
Sunday Oregonian, October 4, 1998

Mike Honda
1941–

UNITED STATES REPRESENTATIVE 2001–2017
DEMOCRAT FROM CALIFORNIA

Over the course of his 16-year career in Congress, the affable Mike Honda quietly attained positions of authority in the House Democratic Caucus, serving on the party's Steering and Policy Committee and rising to a seat on the House Appropriations Committee. An advocate of tolerant and inclusive policies, Honda led the Congressional Progressive Caucus and the Congressional Asian Pacific American Caucus and helped found the LGBT Equality Caucus. According to a political scientist based in Honda's hometown of San Jose, Honda "really puts the K in 'Kumbaya.'"[1]

Mike Honda was born on June 27, 1941, in Walnut Grove, California. His parents, Giichi (Byron) and Fusako Honda, worked on farms in the Bay Area. When Honda was six months old, the Franklin D. Roosevelt administration incarcerated thousands of Japanese Americans following the attack on Pearl Harbor. Honda's family was among 7,000 individuals sent to the Granada War Relocation Center in Colorado.[2] Honda remained imprisoned even after his father joined the U.S. Military Intelligence Service (MIS) in 1943 to teach Japanese to American servicemen. Nearly 70 years later, the elder Honda and the MIS received a Congressional Gold Medal for their service during the war.[3]

After the war, the family returned to the Bay Area and settled in San Jose. Mike Honda graduated from San Jose High School in 1959 and served with the Peace Corps in El Salvador from 1965 to 1967. He graduated in 1968 from San Jose State University with a bachelor's degree.[4] Honda married Jeanne Yoshida in 1967, and they had two children, Mark and Michelle. A longtime educator, Jeanne died in 2004 after battling cancer.[5]

Honda worked as a teacher and principal in San Jose throughout the 1970s and 1980s, while earning a master's degree from his alma mater in 1974. In 1971 Honda joined the San Jose planning commission and served for a decade.[6] Honda then served on the San Jose school board for the next nine years (1981–1990) before winning election to the Santa Clara county board of supervisors. In 1996 Honda was elected to the California state assembly, representing San Jose.[7]

In December 1999, after his local Congressman Thomas Campbell opted to run for the Senate, Honda declared his candidacy for the open House seat. Both the national Democratic Party and President William J. (Bill) Clinton offered support.[8] After winning the party nomination, Honda—whose campaign platforms included more funding for America's school systems, improved civil rights protections, and open trade with China—faced off against Republican Jim Cunneen in the general election. Honda won with 54 percent of the vote. For much of his career, Honda won re-election by overwhelming majorities, often taking upwards of 70 percent of the vote.[9]

Centered in Santa Clara County, California's 15th District encompassed parts of Silicon Valley, Santa Clara, and San Jose. Although redistricting shifted its boundaries and renumbered it the 17th District, high-tech manufacturing and computer science continued to dominate the local economy. The district had the highest concentration of Asian residents anywhere in mainland America.[10]

In the House, Honda served on several different committees: Budget (107th Congress [2001–2003] and 112th Congress [2011–2013]); Science (107th through 109th Congresses [2001–2007]); and Transportation and Infrastructure (107th through 109th Congresses [2001–2007]). Starting with the 110th Congress (2007–2009), when Democrats regained the majority, Honda served on the powerful Appropriations Committee for the balance of his career.[11] In the 112th Congress, Democrats named him Ranking Member of the Legislative Branch Subcommittee.

In the 114th Congress (2015–2017), he served as Ranking Member of the Subcommittee on Commerce, Justice, Science, and Related Agencies.

Honda used his committee assignments to pursue the interests of his tech-savvy district and fought for improved support for nanotechnology.[12] But with new technology came new security gaps, so Honda pressed for more funding to protect individual identities and guard America's computer grid, including the Cyber Security Research and Development Act.[13]

The former teacher also focused on educational opportunities. Honda led the creation of the National Commission on Educational Equity and Excellence to make recommendations for improving education access to the U.S. Department of Education.

Following the terrorist attacks on September 11, 2001, Honda recalled Japanese-American internment and warned against renewed racial profiling.[14] In 2002 he voted against the authorization for the use of military force against Iraq and later worked to improve security at the U.S. Capitol.[15]

As a leader in the Congressional Progressive Caucus, Honda disagreed with President Barack Obama's administration on its combat policy in Afghanistan and later chaired the Progressive Caucus's Budget Task Force.[16]

Honda overcame an early fear of public speaking by singing karaoke, and he continued to sing in Washington. "It is a great leveler," he said. "Everyone makes themselves vulnerable."[17] On the Hill he developed a reputation as a coalition builder, serving as the chairman of the Congressional Asian Pacific American Caucus, where he worked on immigration policy. Honda championed lesbian, gay, bisexual, and transgender rights while in Congress. He created the Anti-Bullying Caucus and the Transgender Equality Task Force in his fight to protect those who faced discrimination, such as his transgender grandchild. He also helped found the LGBT Equality Caucus.[18]

But changes back home to both California's primary system and to the makeup of Honda's constituency combined to make him electorally vulnerable. Numerous young Democrats in the Bay Area had become restive over the lack of turnover among an aging group of leaders. In 2011 the state of California replaced its closed primary system with a nonpartisan open primary that pitted the top two contenders against each other in the fall, regardless of party affiliation. In 2012 a young Democrat, Eric Swalwell, defeated longtime Democratic Representative Pete Stark under these new rules.[19]

During this time, Honda's district had become increasingly diverse. The Asian-Indian and Filipino-American population in the district had quadrupled, and the Chinese- and Vietnamese-American population had tripled. "Asian-American politics is a lot different than other ethno-American politics," Professor Melissa Michelson of Menlo College said. "It's a much weaker pan-ethnicity because there are so many different languages, different religions." Honda, in his early 70s, now faced a challenge from a younger Asian-Indian Democrat, Ro Khanna.[20] Khanna had worked in President Obama's Commerce Department from 2009 to 2011 and was the highest-ranking Asian Indian American in the U.S. government.[21]

Honda won the June 3, 2014, primary with 49 percent of the vote (Khanna took 27 percent), but because neither candidate captured a majority, the two faced off again in the general election that November. Election forecasters expected Khanna to pick up both Republican votes and support from the other Democratic candidates.[22] In late September, the Khanna campaign filed a complaint with the House Ethics Committee against Honda for using his official staff for campaign purposes.[23] Nevertheless, Honda won re-election in a close race that was not decided until the Friday morning after Election Day.[24]

When Honda announced his candidacy for re-election in June 2015, Khanna had already made it clear that he intended to challenge Honda again.[25] In late July, however, the House Committee on Standards of Official Conduct announced that it would look into the 2014 complaint made by Khanna because of findings made by the Office of Congressional Ethics, its independent investigatory arm.[26] After edging out Honda in the June 2016 primary, Khanna beat Honda in the fall general election with 61 percent of the vote.[27]

NOTES

1   *Almanac of American Politics, 2016* (Bethesda, MD: Columbia Books & Information Services, 2015): 215.

2   *Politics in America, 2006* (Washington, DC: CQ Press, 2005): 100; "My Story," Representative Mike Honda's official website, accessed 20 November 2015, https://honda.house.gov/mike/my-story (site discontinued); Rep. Mike Honda, "Honda Marks 70th Anniversary of Closing of Amache Internment Camp," press release, 15 October 2015, https://honda.house.gov/news/press-releases/honda-marks-70th-anniversary-of-closing-of-amache-internment-camp (site discontinued); Zachary Coile, "Tears of Joy and Hard Memories: Japanese American Memorial Opens," 30 June 2001, *San Francisco Chronicle*: A3; Mary Anne Ostrom, Edwin Garcia, and Hallye Jordan, "Honda Lauds Diversity, Attention to Education," 17 August 2000, *San Jose Mercury News*: A16.

3   Rep. Mike Honda, "Honoring the Unsung Heroes of World War II," 10 November 2011, *San Jose Mercury News*: n.p.; Peter Delevett, "In San Jose's Japantown, Vigil Commemorates 70th Anniversary of FDR's Internment Order," 19 February 2012, *San Jose Mercury News*: n.p.

4   "My Story"; *Politics in America, 2006*: 101.

5   Ryan Kim, "Jeanne Yoshida Honda—Wife of Congressman," 18 February 2004, *San Francisco Chronicle*: A15; Barbara Feder Ostrov, "Jeanne Honda, Legislator's Wife, Dies," 17 February 2004, *San Jose Mercury News*: B1.

6   *Almanac of American Politics, 2002* (Washington, DC: National Journal, Inc., 2001): 198.

7   Melody Petersen, "Health High on Honda's Agenda," 11 January 1995, *San Jose Mercury News*: B1; De Tran, "District 23 Success Depends on Who Can Turn Out Voters," 11 February 1996, *San Jose Mercury News*: B1.

8   Mary Anne Ostrom, "Honda Touted for House Seat," 7 December 1999, *San Jose Mercury News*: B1; Mark Simon, "Assembly Democrat to Seek Campbell's Seat," 8 December 1999, *San Francisco Chronicle*: A3; Mary Anne Ostrom and Moan Levey, "Honda Enters Race for House," 8 December 1999, *San Jose Mercury News*: B1; Lori Aratani, "Demo Leaders Spur Honda's Campaign," 24 February 2000, *San Jose Mercury News*: B1.

9   Carolyne Zinko and Mark Simon, "Party Favorites Cunneen, Honda Lead in 15th District Primary," 8 March 2000, *San Francisco Chronicle*: A8; Mark Simon, "Muscle Flex Pays Off for Honda," 9 March 2000, *San Francisco Chronicle*: A15; Lori Aratani, "Honda, Cunneen Gear Up for House Contest," 9 March 2000, *San Jose Mercury News*: B1; Lori Aratani, "Debate Opens in 15th District," 7 September 2000, *San Jose Mercury News*: B1; Lori Aratani, "Cunneen, Honda Debate," 14 September 2000, *San Jose Mercury News*: B4; Editorial, "Vote For Cunneen In 15th

District As A Moderate Republican," 15 October 2000, *San Jose Mercury News*: C6; Hallye Jordan and Lori Aratani, "Mike Honda: Regular Guy with Warmth, Experience," 24 October 2000, *San Jose Mercury News*: A12; *Almanac of American Politics, 2002*: 198–199; Office of the Clerk, U.S. House of Representatives, "Election Statistics, 1920 to Present," http://history.house.gov/Institution/Election-Statistics/Election-Statistics/.

10 *Politics in America, 2002* (Washington, DC: Congressional Quarterly, Inc., 2001): 95; *Almanac of American Politics, 2004* (Washington, DC: National Journal Group, 2003): 205; *Politics in America, 2014* (Washington, DC: CQ-Roll Call, Inc., 2013): 102.

11 Josh Richman, "Bay Area Representatives to Join Powerful Panel," 14 December 2006, *Contra Costa Times*: F4; "Mike Honda Named to Powerful Appropriations," 22–26 December 2006, *AsianWeek*: 9.

12 *Politics in America, 2002*: 95; *Politics in America, 2004* (Washington, DC: Congressional Quarterly, Inc., 2003): 96; *Politics in America, 2006*: 100.

13 *Almanac of American Politics, 2006*: 207; Public Law 107-305, 116 Stat. 2367 (2002).

14 *Politics in America, 2004*: 96.

15 *Politics in America, 2008* (Washington, DC: Congressional Quarterly, Inc., 2007): 100; *Politics in America, 2010* (Washington, DC: Congressional Quarterly, Inc., 2009): 99–100.

16 *Politics in America, 2012*: 93.

17 Mark Leibovich, "The Karaoke Congressman Has the Floor," 12 June 2002, *Washington Post*: C01.

18 *Almanac of American Politics, 2010*: 183; *Politics in America, 2006*: 100.

19 *Almanac of American Politics, 2014* (Chicago: University of Chicago Press, 2013): 185.

20 Josh Richman, "With Demographic Shifting, Congressman Mike Honda Faces Political Challenge of His Life," 17 May 2014, *Oakland Tribune*: n.p.

21 Sunita Sohrabji, "The Biennial Question: Is Ro Running for Congress?," 1 February 2013, *India-West* (San Leandro, CA): A21; Josh Richman, "Rep. Mike Honda Digs In against Potential Challenger Ro Khanna," 3 February 2013, *Oakland Tribune*: n.p.

22 Josh Richman, "Congressional District 17: Honda Easily Finishes First, Will Face Khanna in November Showdown," 3 June 2014, *Oakland Tribune*: n.p.; Ritu Jha, "Honda Triumphs, Khanna Lives to Fight Another Day," 13 June 2014, *India Abroad* (New York): A6.

23 Josh Richman, "Ro Khanna Supporters File Ethics Complaint against Mike Honda," 26 September 2014, *Oakland Tribune*: n.p.; Josh Richman, "Rep. Mike Honda Email Leaker Revealed as Former Aide Arrested for Death Threats," 3 October 2014, *Oakland Tribune*: n.p.

24 Josh Richman, "Ro Khanna Concedes Hours after Mike Honda Declares Victory," 7 November 2014, *Oakland Tribune*: n.p.; Sunita Sohrabji, "Honda Wins Fierce CA17 Race," 14 November 2014, *India-West* (San Leandro, CA): A1.

25 Heather Somerville and Josh Richman, "Khanna Launches New Campaign to Oust Congressman Mike Honda," 30 May 2015, *Oakland Tribune*: n.p.

26 Aaron Kinney, "Ethics Inquiry of Honda Extended," 21 July 2015, *San Jose Mercury News*: B3; Ritu Jha, "Office of Congressional Ethics Reviews Mike Honda's Office," 24 July 2015, *India Abroad* (New York): A7; "Rep. Honda under Investigation by House Ethics Committee," 24 July 2015, *India-West*: A27.

27 Khanna won 51,919 votes (39 percent) to Honda's 49,720 (37 percent). Eric Kurhi, "Mike Honda vs. Ro Khanna: Rematch Set in District 17 Congressional Race," 8 June 2016, *Oakland Tribune*: n.p.; Eric Kurhi, "Dead Heat in Primary to Call," 9 June 2016, *San Jose Mercury News*: B1; Giovanni Albanese Jr., "Ro Khanna Edges Out Honda to Win CA Primary," 17 June 2016, *India-West* (San Leandro, CA): A1; Eric Kurhi, "Khanna Claims Win; Results Not Final," 24 June 2016, *East Bay Times*: B6; Eric Kurhi, "Ro Khanna Defeats Mike Honda," 9 November 2016, *San Jose Mercury News*: S3; Eric Kurhi, "Khanna Ousts Honda," 10 November 2016, *San Jose Mercury News*: B1; Giovanni Albanese Jr., "Ro Khanna Victorious in CA 17th Congressional Election," *India-West* (San Leandro, CA): A1; "General Election—Statement of Vote, November 8, 2016," Alex Padilla, California secretary of state, accessed 10 January 2017, http://www.sos.ca.gov/elections/prior-elections/statewide-election-results/general-election-november-8-2016/statement-vote/.

Over the course of his
16-year career in
Congress, the affable
Mike Honda
quietly attained positions
of authority in the House
Democratic Caucus....
An advocate of
tolerant and inclusive
policies, Honda led
the Congressional
Progressive Caucus and
the Congressional Asian
Pacific American Caucus
and helped found the
LGBT Equality Caucus.

Bobby Jindal
1971–

UNITED STATES REPRESENTATIVE 2005–2008
REPUBLICAN FROM LOUISIANA

Bobby Jindal was a fast-rising, intelligent "wunderkind technocrat" in the Republican Party when he won election to a U.S. House seat representing a district outside New Orleans in 2004, becoming the second Indian American elected to the House.[1] The gulf region's response to and recovery from a crippling 2005 hurricane season defined Jindal's House career and eventually catapulted him to the Louisiana governor's mansion. The son of Indian immigrants seeking higher educational opportunities, Jindal became a rallying point for the Indian-American community. "What makes the American system so successful is the fact that immigrants and their children born here can get ahead," he declared upon his first election to the House. "[They] can do very well, just do hard work."[2]

Born in Baton Rouge, Louisiana, on June 10, 1971, Piyush Jindal was the son of Indian immigrants from the Punjab region of northern India. Jindal later insisted on being called "Bobby" after the youngest son in the television show *The Brady Bunch*. His parents had come to the United States so his mother, Raj Gupta Jindal, could pursue graduate work in nuclear physics at Louisiana State University.[3] His father, Amar, was an engineer—the only one of nine siblings to finish high school. Bobby Jindal has a younger brother, Nikesh.[4]

Jindal graduated from Baton Rouge High School in 1988 before earning degrees in biology and public policy from Brown University in Providence, Rhode Island, in 1991. Jindal was named a Rhodes scholar and studied at Oxford University, earning a master of letters in 1994. Jindal worked briefly for a consulting firm after graduation before taking on the position of president of the University of Louisiana school system in 1999. Bobby Jindal married chemical engineer Supriya Jolly, and they have three children: Selia, Shaan, and Slade.[5]

Jindal's interest in politics came early. During college, he interned in Louisiana Representative Jim McCrery's office. The eager Jindal personally asked McCrery what he could do to contribute to the Congressman's policy initiatives and McCrery shuttled him off to do research on Medicare. Two weeks later, Jindal delivered a thick report that impressed his boss.[6]

Jindal was preparing to attend Harvard Medical School when he was offered a secretary position in the Louisiana cabinet, heading the Department of Health and Hospitals. Jindal served for two years, never pursuing medical training. Thereafter, public service became his calling. "After my daughter was born, I really started thinking about the fact that I wanted her to grow up here in Louisiana like I did," Jindal recalled. "I realized so many of my friends were leaving home, and I wanted to be a part of turning that around."[7] Jindal served as executive director of the National Bipartisan Commission on the Future of Medicare in 1998. In 2001 President George W. Bush appointed him Assistant Secretary for Planning and Evaluation in the Department of Health and Human Services.

Jindal's first attempt at elected office came when he ran for Louisiana governor in 2003, losing narrowly to Democrat Kathleen Babineaux Blanco, 52 percent to 48 percent. A year later, when Louisiana Representative David Vitter vacated his House seat to run for the U.S. Senate, Jindal launched a campaign for the congressional seat. The district stretched from east of New Orleans, north across Lake Pontchartrain to the Mississippi border. Made up of primarily white-collar conservatives in the fast-growing New Orleans commuter suburbs, the constituency was 80 percent white.[8] Jindal capitalized on the notoriety he gained in his close gubernatorial loss. "When God closes one door, he opens another," he said to a crowd of GOP

Image courtesy of the U.S. House of Representatives Photography Office

supporters when he announced his candidacy in January 2004. "I understand there's a job opening here."[9] Jindal did not live in the district before running, but his popularity catapulted him to front-runner status.[10] In August, his nearest competitor, then state representative (and future U.S. House Majority Whip) Steve Scalise, withdrew from the race ostensibly because Jindal's popularity and funding made him a clear favorite. Some observers were already calling Jindal "Congressman."[11] Jindal raised more money than needed, contributing the excess to other GOP campaigns.[12] He won the general election with a comfortable 78 percent.[13]

Jindal was the first Indian American to win election since the first Asian-American Representative, Dalip Singh (Judge) Saund of California, left office in 1963. But Jindal tended to play down his heritage. "We'll be eating a lot of turkey over the holidays—with some crawfish on the side," Jindal told reporters after his election. "(Louisiana) is the life we know. This is our culture. This is our home."[14] Nevertheless, Jindal recognized the significance of being the son of immigrants in Congress. "I am very, very honored by the well wishes and support from the Indian American community. I guess the reason I ran for office in the first place is that I saw my parents [sic] experience in this country," he told an Indian-American newspaper. "I want to make sure that the opportunities that brought our parents here in the first place continue to exist for the second, third and fourth generations as well."[15]

An effective and prolific fundraiser, Jindal amassed a campaign re-election war chest as a freshman Member that matched those of congressional veterans.[16] He won re-election easily in 2006 with 88 percent of the vote.[17] Jindal initially requested seats on the Energy and Commerce or Ways and Means Committees when he arrived in Congress. He did not receive a seat on either panel, as freshmen rarely get such plum assignments. He instead served on the Education and the Workforce, Homeland Security, and Resources Committees in the 109th Congress (2005–2007). In the 110th Congress (2007–2009), he left Education and the Workforce and remained on the other two panels until he left the House mid-Congress in 2008.

Natural disaster defined Jindal's House career after Hurricane Katrina struck southern Louisiana on August 29, 2005, just nine months after he came to Congress. The powerful storm surge overwhelmed New Orleans's levee system resulting in 15- to 20-foot floods which left 80 percent of the city under water.[18] At the time, Katrina was the costliest hurricane in U.S. history and one of the five deadliest, and it was followed less than a month later by Hurricane Rita, prompting large-scale evacuations of already storm-damaged areas. According to *Congressional Quarterly*, nearly two-thirds of the bills Jindal submitted over the next 18 months were related to the storms, their aftermath, and other natural disasters.[19]

Jindal's first act fell in line with his conservative beliefs. He initially teamed with Senator Vitter to author a law banning local municipalities from confiscating guns from citizens during natural disasters. This followed New Orleans's confiscation of 700 weapons in the storm's chaotic aftermath. The city returned the weapons in April 2006 after the National Rifle Association (NRA) threatened a lawsuit.

Jindal introduced the Hurricane Regulatory Relief Act on October 6, 2005; he immediately gained the support of Education and Workforce Committee Chairman (and soon-to-be Republican Leader) John Boehner of Ohio. The bill was aimed at streamlining aid to students, teachers, and displaced workers. It adjusted financial aid awards to students whose circumstances changed because of the storms, allowed teachers credentialed in Louisiana to find employment in the state in which they resided, and allowed affected states to allocate funding to emergency loans and early retirement distributions to displaced workers.[20]

Jindal was frustrated with the pace of government assistance, citing rules and regulations as the source of the delays. "People are starting to come home and businesses are beginning to reopen, critical infrastructure is slowly being rebuilt and we need to facilitate this recovery by ensuring that the state, local and federal governments are made completely user friendly," Jindal told his colleagues. He emphasized that his bill did not create greater

bureaucracy: "Too often government proves its existence by adding rules and regulations, which can turn the rebuilding process into a vast quicksand, holding back growth. This is a perfect time to clean our regulatory house and make sure Louisiana is a welcoming, supportive state in which to live and work."[21] Jindal also introduced legislation that created the Louisiana Hurricane and Flood Protection Council, a group charged with overseeing the Army Corps of Engineers in their efforts over the next 20 years to bolster infrastructure against damaging natural disasters.[22]

Post-storm difficulty in Jindal's district shifted his traditionally pro-business stance when he fought against insurance companies dropping policies and raising premiums in Katrina's wake. Jindal supported Democratic legislation that compelled insurance companies to share their data on losses, and he requested that the federal flood insurance program be able to borrow additional funds to cover homeowners' losses.[23] Jindal worked with then Florida Governor Charlie Crist—whose state had faced a damaging 2004 hurricane season—to brainstorm ideas on how to reform the insurance industry in areas at high risk for hurricanes. Jindal showcased the Homeowners' Defense Act of 2007, sponsored by Florida Representatives that had recently passed the House, as an example of good federal involvement with the insurance industry. The legislation allowed state-sponsored insurance funds to pool catastrophic risk and created a fund for low-interest loans to homeowners affected by natural disasters.[24]

Jindal criticized the Federal Emergency Management Agency (FEMA), charged with aiding the immediate aftermath and long-term recovery from the storm. In March 2006, he announced the allocation of more than $79 million in FEMA grants to parishes in his district.[25] In April 2006, Jindal hosted the Senate Homeland Security & Governmental Affairs Committee for a field hearing at the Louisiana supreme court building in New Orleans. The hearing focused on FEMA waste, fraud, and abuse.[26] Jindal was particularly critical of the high levels of formaldehyde found in FEMA trailers serving as temporary shelters for hurricane victims. (Tests revealed the presence of the poison exceeded Environmental

Protection Agency standards by 83 percent.)[27] He also faulted FEMA for hiring out-of-state contractors to clear debris, distribute supplies, and oversee reconstruction rather than award contracts to local Louisiana businesses.[28] Jindal's work in disaster relief earned praise from across the political spectrum. A local Democratic sheriff noted that Louisianans were frequently disappointed with the government response "from top to bottom," but that there were "some people who distinguished themselves, and Bobby Jindal was one of them."[29]

Jindal also sought increased oil drilling in the Gulf of Mexico, a potential boon to the southern Louisiana economy that had been crippled by the 2005 hurricanes. In his first term, Jindal helped to pass a law opening 8.3 million acres to drilling in the Gulf of Mexico—according to Jindal, this was the culmination of a long-term fight among Louisiana politicians spanning 50 years.[30] The House-passed bill, enacted as part of a larger tax and trade bill, split drilling revenues evenly between federal and gulf state governments.[31]

Jindal attempted to balance his drilling bill with certain environmental protections, including those benefiting gulf state fishing operations. He offered an amendment to a Department of the Interior and Environment Appropriations Act allocating $2.5 million to combat "dead zones" in the Gulf of Mexico. In these areas, pollutants were causing algal blooms, which sucked oxygen out of water, making it unsustainable for sea life.[32] With one eye on Louisiana's fishing industry, Jindal opposed a request to put oysters on the endangered species list in November 2005—"This is a victory for common sense," he said, when the requester withdrew his petition.[33] Citing its importance for protecting against hurricane storm surge, Jindal introduced legislation adding 3,000 acres to Jean Lafitte National Historical Park and Preserve—a series of six sites throughout the southern Louisiana peninsula.[34]

On January 23, 2007, Jindal announced his intention to fulfill a past political ambition to run for Louisiana governor. He resigned from the House nearly a year later, on January 14, 2008, to focus on his gubernatorial campaign.[35] His victory in the governor's race was embraced

by both the Indian-American community and Republican Party.[36] In 2009 the GOP selected Jindal for the high-profile role of delivering the response to Democratic President Barack Obama's first State of the Union Address. In 2015, after running in a crowded Republican primary field, he suspended his campaign for the GOP nomination for President.[37]

FOR FURTHER READING

Jindal, Bobby. *Leadership and Crisis* (Washington, DC: Regnery Publishing, 2010).

NOTES

1 Mike Sager, "Bobby Jindal, All American," October 2008, *Esquire*, http://www.esquire.com/features/bobby-jindal-all-american-1008 (accessed 24 February 2011).

2 Subhash Vohra, "Newly Elected Indian-American Congressman Talks About His Hopes and Plans," 19 November 2004, *Voice of America News*: n.p.

3 *Almanac of American Politics, 2006* (Washington, DC: National Journal Inc., 2005): 737.

4 Adam Nossiter, "A Son of Immigrants Rises in Deeply Southern State," 22 October 2007, *New York Times*: 1.

5 Stephanie Boswell, "Supriya Jindal Says Life as the Wife of a Politician is Hectic," 1 January 2007, *New Orleans CityBusiness* (North Shore Report): n.p.

6 *Politics in America, 2008* (Washington, DC: Congressional Quarterly Inc., 2007): 433. McCrery would later serve as Jindal's 2008 gubernatorial campaign chairman.

7 Emily Peters, "Bobby Jindal," 4 January 2004, *Daily Town Talk* (Alexandria, LA): 12F.

8 *Politics in America, 2006* (Washington, DC: Congressional Quarterly Inc., 2005): 443; *Almanac of American Politics, 2006*: 737.

9 Doug Simpson, "Bobby Jindal to Seek Vitter's South Louisiana Congressional Seat," 29 January 2004, Associated Press.

10 *Politics in America, 2008*: 432.

11 "Two Months to Go, but Jindal has Won,'" 27 August 2004, *India Abroad* (New York): A8.

12 *Politics in America, 2006*: 443.

13 Office of the Clerk, U.S. House of Representatives, "Election Statistics, 1920 to Present," http://history.house.gov/Institution/Election-Statistics/Election-Statistics/.

14 Peters, "Bobby Jindal."

15 Lavina Melwani, "Mr Jindal Goes to Washington," 5 December 2004, *Little India* (Torrington, CT), http://www.littleindia.com/nri/1490-mr-jindal-goes-to-washington.html (accessed 6 January 2016).

16 Bill Walsh, "Bobby Jindal's Fund-raising Effort Is Termed 'Amazing,'" 9 April 2005, *New Orleans Times-Picayune*: 9.

17 Office of the Clerk, U.S. House of Representatives, "Election Statistics, 1920 to Present."

18 Anne Waple, "Hurricane Katrina," December 2005, National Oceanic and Atmospheric Administration (NOAA), National Climatic Data Center, accessed 9 December 2015, http://www.ncdc.noaa.gov/extremeevents/specialreports/Hurricane-Katrina.pdf; David L. Johnson, "Hurricane Katrina, August 23–31, 2005," NOAA, National Weather Service, accessed 9 December 2015, http://www.nws.noaa.gov/om/assessments/pdfs/Katrina.pdf.

19 *Politics in America, 2008*: 432.

20 "U.S. Congressman Bobby Jindal's Hurricane Relief Bill Aids Teachers, Students, and Displaced Workers," 7 October 2005, *New Orleans CityBusiness*: n.p.

21 "Congressman Bobby Jindal Calls for Legislation to Ease Recovery Efforts," 12 October 2005, *New Orleans CityBusiness*: n.p.

22 H.R. 5448, 109th Cong. (2006). It died in the Transportation and Infrastructure Committee.

23 "Rep. Bobby Jindal Pushes for More Insurance Pay Outs for Residents of Louisiana," 31 January 2006, *New Orleans CityBusiness*: n.p. Specific legislation includes: the Flood Insurance and Modernization Act of 2007 (H.R. 3121, 110th Cong. [2007]), which died in conference; Hurricanes Katrina and Rita Flood Insurance Buy-In Act of 2005 (H.R. 3922, 109th Cong. [2005]), which died in the Financial Services Committee; and the National Flood Insurance Program Further Enhanced Borrowing Authority Act of 2005, which became Public Law 109-106, 119 Stat. 2288 (2005).

24 Sarah Chacko, "Jindal Looks to Fla. for Insurance Ideas," 13 December 2007, *The Advocate* (Baton Rouge, LA): 26. H.R. 3355, 110th Cong. (2007). The bill passed the House, but died in committee in the Senate.

25 "Rep. Bobby Jindal Praises $80M FEMA Infusion," 14 March 2006, *New Orleans CityBusiness*: n.p.

26 "Rep. Bobby Jindal to hold FEMA Fraud Hearing Monday in N.O.," 8 April 2006, *New Orleans CityBusiness*: n.p.

27 "Rep. Bobby Jindal Slames FEMA for Trailer Negligence," 19 July 2007, *New Orleans CityBusiness*: n.p.

28 "Rep. Bobby Jindal Tells FEMA That There is No Excuse for Not Hiring LA Firms," 12 October 2005, *New Orleans CityBusiness*: n.p.

29 Quotation in *Politics in America, 2008*: 432.

30 Littice Bacon-Blood, "Jindal Upbeat on Oil Royalties," 4 October 2006, *New Orleans Times-Picayune*: 1.

1   Patrick Courreges, "Jindal Warns Nation's Eyes on State," 29 December 2006, *The Advocate* (Baton Rouge, LA): 1.

2   "Rep. Jindal's 'Dead Zone' Bill Faces Debate," 26 June 2007, *New Orleans CityBusiness*: n.p.

3   Janet McConnaughey, "Petition to List Oysters as Endangered is Pulled," 8 November 2005, Associated Press.

4   "Bobby Jindal, R-Kenner, Expects Backing for Jean Lafitte Expansion," 25 September 2006, *New Orleans CityBusiness*: n.p. H.R. 162 expired in the House. H.R. 162, 110th Cong. (2007).

5   Jan Moller, "Jindal Quietly Begins His Run," 23 January 2007, *New Orleans Times-Picayune*: 2.

6   See Robert Travis Scott, "India Relishes Jindal's Success; But Some Say He Plays Down His Heritage," 28 October 2007, *New Orleans Times-Picayune*: 1.

7   Philip Rucker et al., "Jindal Suspends Presidential Campaign: 'This is not My Time,'" 17 November 2015, *Washington Post*, https://www.washingtonpost.com/news/post-politics/wp/2015/11/17/jindal-suspends-presidential-campaign/ (accessed 9 December 2015).

Steve Austria
1958–

UNITED STATES REPRESENTATIVE 2009–2013
REPUBLICAN FROM OHIO

Becoming just the second person of Filipino heritage to serve as a voting Representative in Congress, Steve Austria won election to the U.S. House of Representatives amid the worst financial crisis since the Great Depression.[1] As a proponent of shrinking government services and spurring small business growth, Austria quickly worked his way onto the influential Appropriations Committee, where he could tend to the economy of his southwestern Ohio district. But when Ohio's congressional delegation shrank by two seats during reapportionment after the 2010 Census, Austria's House career ended abruptly.

Steve Austria was born in Cincinnati, Ohio, on October 12, 1958, to Clement and Jean Brockman Austria. His father, a medical doctor, was born in the Philippines and fought alongside Filipino rebels and General Douglas MacArthur against Japanese forces during World War II. Clement later immigrated to the United States from Tiaong, Quezon, to the Cincinnati area, where he attended medical school; Jean Austria worked as a nurse.[2] By observing his father's work on the Greene County Central Committee of the Republican Party, Steve Austria became interested in politics and "realized that through public service I could have a positive impact on people's lives."[3] The oldest of nine children, Austria grew up in Xenia, Ohio, a community about an hour's drive northeast of Cincinnati. In 1977 he graduated from Carroll High School in Riverside, Ohio, and in 1982 earned a bachelor of arts degree in political science from Marquette University in Milwaukee, Wisconsin. Austria worked for more than 15 years as a financial advisor. He married Eileen Crotty, whom he met in the 1980s while putting up campaign signs during an Ohio state senate election.[4] The couple raised three sons: Brian, Kevin, and Eric.

When Austria embarked on his political career by succeeding his father on the GOP's Greene County

Central Committee, Clement Austria counseled him to campaign door-to-door to get to know voters. "My father was absolutely right. I never lost an election, and I credit that to my father's advice and all the time I spent in the district, listening to constituents," Steve Austria recalled years later.[5] In 1998 he challenged incumbent Republican state representative Marilyn Reid in the GOP primary. Austria upended Reid, who was in the midst of an ethics scandal, and went on to win the general election. He served briefly in the Ohio state house of representatives from 1999 to 2000 before winning election to the state senate. Austria served in that chamber from 2001 to 2008, rising to the position of majority whip during his last three years there. He also chaired the judiciary and highways and transportation committees.[6] His focus in both chambers was to crack down on crime. Austria authored bills to increase penalties for child rapists and for offenders who solicit sex with minors online; he also helped pass a bill that allowed Ohioans to carry concealed weapons.[7]

When nine-term incumbent U.S. Representative David L. Hobson announced his retirement from Congress, Austria joined the race for the vacant seat. The district, which was adjacent to Republican Leader John Boehner's Cincinnati-centered district, encompassed six counties (and parts of two others) in the southcentral portion of the state, from the Miami Valley region near Dayton to just south and east of Columbus. The district was a mixture of rural and residential areas, with industrial and agriculture businesses; it was also home to several military facilities, including Wright–Patterson Air Force Base and the Springfield Air National Guard Base.

The Austrias had a long connection to Hobson, and one political almanac described Hobson as a political mentor to Steve. Eileen Austria was also a longtime staffer for Hobson going back to his time in the Ohio legislature

and later served as his congressional district director.[8] As the favorite in the GOP primary, Austria defeated three opponents with 55 percent of the vote; his next closest competitor, Ron Hood, a former state representative, garnered 34 percent.[9]

In the 2008 general election, Austria faced attorney Sharen Swartz Neuhardt. Austria benefitted from the fact that the district was conservative-leaning; he also enjoyed a fundraising advantage of $1.2 million to Neuhardt's $900,000. However, the campaign was not without its challenges. A political blogger claimed that Austria plagiarized portions of columns he wrote for a local newspaper. Another paper, the *Dayton Daily News*, rendered an editorial judgment that "What he's most likely to do is to settle into a long, long career of keeping people back home happy, while remaining on the congressional back benches."[10] But these bumps in the road were soon overshadowed by the revelation that for six years Neuhardt housed a Rwandan refugee who was not legally in the country.[11] Austria eventually pulled away with a comfortable, 58-percent majority of the vote on Election Day.[12] Afterward, as the economic crisis in the fall of 2008 deepened, he told the press, "The No. 1 issue we've got to get to work on is the economy. We've got to create new jobs and bring new businesses into the area. We've got to keep government spending under control, and I'm going to have a challenge in D.C. to do that."[13] Austria became just the second person of Filipino heritage—behind Robert C. (Bobby) Scott of Virginia—to serve as a full voting Member of the House.[14]

In 2010 Austria won easy re-election to the House—cruising through his primary and winning the general election against Democrat William R. Conner 62 to 32 percent, with two other minor party candidates capturing the remainder of the vote.[15] In that election, control of the majority swung to Republicans on a wave of discontent with President Barack Obama and the Affordable Care Act. "The American people have spoken loud and clear," Austria said after the election. "They are tired of Washington not listening to them and pushing through policies for the expansion of government and creating more spending. We

as Republicans are going to stop that and turn this country around. That all starts with helping the job creators."[16]

At the opening of his first term in 2009, Austria won assignments to the House Budget and Homeland Security Committees. Given that he was a member of the House minority, these were solid committee assignments. Moreover, fellow GOP freshmen named him president of their class.[17]

At the opening of the 112th Congress (2011–2013), after Republicans captured the House majority, Austria moved to the exclusive Appropriations Committee and gave up his prior assignments. On Appropriations, Austria held seats on three subcommittees: Commerce, Justice, Science and Related Agencies; Military Construction, Veterans Affairs and Related Agencies; and State, Foreign Operations and Related Programs.

Recovering from the economic crisis and battling the federal deficit consumed Austria's legislative agenda. South Central Ohioans had elected him on a platform that called for shrinking the size of the federal government. *Politics in America* said he was not so much of a "conservative firebrand" as he was "a reliable Republican vote and a consistent critic of what he calls unsustainable budget deficits."[18] Austria spoke on the floor on a number of occasions but usually in sharply messaged one-minute speeches or in colloquies. Invariably, these revolved around his fiscally conservative views. In a March 2009 colloquy on the economy, the economic stimulus, and carbon use cap-and-trade proposals, Austria said, "When you start combining, increasing taxes, when you start combining the debt that we are just continuing to increase, to try and tax and spend your way out of an economic crisis I don't believe is the right way to go. We can do better than that."[19] In another colloquy a few weeks later, Austria advocated relief for families and small businesses through tax cuts, noting, the "Federal Government right now thinks that they can just spend all they want for as long as they want, just continue to borrow, and now they're going to start taxing families and all so that they can keep this feel-good spending going on. And I think the Americans, as they begin to realize what's going on here in D.C., are

becoming more and more outraged, and businesses are already very concerned on how they're going to be able to continue to survive."[20]

In early 2009, in the first major vote of his career, he joined with his Republican colleagues who unanimously opposed a nearly $800 billion economic stimulus bill (which the Democratic majority passed). His comments to the *Columbus Dispatch* at the time compared the stimulus bill to the Keynesian economics of the New Deal. He drew criticism for his claim that President Franklin D. Roosevelt "tried to borrow and spend, he tried to use the Keynesian approach, and our country ended up in a Great Depression. That's just history." He later withdrew the statement, insisting that he meant to convey the idea that Roosevelt, who was elected three years after the crisis began, implemented policies that did not help end the economic crisis.[21] While Austria voted with his party on most major issues, he was one of several dozen Republicans to vote for an expansion of the State Children's Health Insurance Program (S-CHIP).

Like most freshman Members, Austria was attentive to his district. With his district's heavy military presence, he promoted it as a region that could help lead U.S. cybersecurity policy and the use of advanced security and military applications (such as Unmanned Aerial Vehicles—UAVs) through partnerships among local universities and private businesses. He supported federal loan guarantees to help build a uranium enrichment plant in a neighboring district. In the 111th Congress, he introduced a bill that barred the use of funds to transfer enemy combatants from Guantanamo Bay to any facility in Ohio and advocated keeping the Guantanamo detention facility open. In the 112th Congress, as he had in the prior one, he authored the Health Savings and Affordability Act, which would have expanded health insurance deductions and health savings accounts. Referred to the Ways and Means Committee, the proposal received no major action. Austria also introduced the Colonel Charles Young Home Study Act to direct the Interior Department to conduct a study of the National Historic Landmark site in Xenia, Ohio, for possible inclusion in the National Park System. Young,

an African-American U.S. Army intelligence officer and commander in the Spanish-American War, helped lead the 1916 hunt for Pancho Villa in Mexico.[22]

After the 2010 Census and resulting reapportionment, Ohio lost two of its 18 House seats. When the Ohio legislature drew up the new map, it dismantled Austria's district, throwing most of his constituency into a new district where Republican Mike Turner had the upper hand as a five-term House veteran. Austria faced the unpalatable options of taking on Turner or moving out of the new district into a neighboring one where he would challenge Republican Steve Stivers, a first-term incumbent but also a close ally of Speaker Boehner.[23] On December 29, 2011, Austria announced that he would retire from Congress rather than wage an uphill fight in a GOP primary that "pitted friends against friends."[24]

His announcement spared the party a bruising primary. Nevertheless, Austria was unhappy with what he perceived to be an unfair process. "I have thoroughly enjoyed working on behalf of every one of my communities, both large and small, and regret that I will not be able to continue the work I have truly been committed to, due to the redrawing of the maps," Austria said. He also noted, "Since the redistricting process began, it has been done in secrecy and with closed door deals. I join my constituents, who are frustrated and disappointed about the new maps forced upon them and the fact that they didn't have a vote in the process."[25]

During his farewell speech on the House Floor, Austria thanked his colleagues, staff, and family, noted his pride in his Asian-American heritage, and reflected on his House career and his future. "Often, as I walk through the Halls of the Capitol or am traveling throughout the district, folks will come up to me and remind me that, when one door closes, another opens and that God has a plan for us all."[26] After he left the House in 2013, Austria returned to Beavercreek, Ohio, where he founded a consulting firm. He also is a member of the Republican National Committee's Asian American Advisory Council.[27]

NOTES

1 Lorraine Tong, "Asian Pacific Americans in the United States Congress," Report 97-398, 7 May 2013, Congressional Research Service: 2.

2 *Almanac of American Politics, 2010* (Washington, DC: National Journal Inc., 2009): 1180. His mother's name is referenced in "Austria to Adjust to Quick Pace," 9 January 2009, *Filipino Reporter*: 6. See also "A Win by Austria Will Make History," 8 August 2008, *Filipino Reporter*: 1.

3 *Politics in America, 2012* (Washington, DC: CQ-Roll Call, Inc., 2011): 771.

4 Mary McCarty, "Steve Austria Looks Back on Career in Congress," 31 December 2012, *Dayton Daily News*: n.p.; *Almanac of American Politics, 2010*: 1179–1181.

5 McCarty, "Steve Austria Looks Back on Career in Congress."

6 "A Win by Austria Will Make History."

7 *Almanac of American Politics, 2010*: 1180.

8 McCarty, "Steve Austria Looks Back on Career in Congress"; *Almanac of American Politics, 2010*: 1179–1181.

9 *Politics in America, 2010* (Washington, DC: Congressional Quarterly Inc., 2009): 793.

10 *Almanac of American Politics, 2010*: 1181.

11 *Almanac of American Politics, 2012* (Washington, DC: National Journal Inc., 2011): 1280.

12 Office of the Clerk, U.S. House of Representatives, "Election Statistics, 1920 to Present," http://history.house.gov/Institution/Election-Statistics/Election-Statistics/.

13 Sean Golden, "Austria to Fill Seat Vacated by Retiring Rep. Hobson," 5 November 2008, *Lancaster Eagle Gazette* (OH): 1A.

14 Tong, "Asian Pacific Americans in the United States Congress."

15 Office of the Clerk, U.S. House of Representatives, "Election Statistics, 1920 to Present."

16 Joe Giessler, "Steve Austria Coasts Past Conner to Second Term," 3 November 2010, *Lancaster Eagle Gazette* (OH): n.p.

17 *Politics in America, 2010*: 793.

18 *Politics in America, 2012*: 770.

19 *Congressional Record*, House, 110th Cong., 1st sess. (11 March 2009): H3328.

20 *Congressional Record*, House, 110th Cong., 1st sess. (31 March 2009): H4245; see also *Congressional Record*, House, 111th Cong., 1st sess. (19 July 2011): H5169.

21 *Politics in America, 2010*: 793; *Politics in America, 2012*: 770–771.

22 See, for example, William Hershey, "Keep Guantanamo Open, U.S. Rep. Austria Says; Legislator Had Just Returned From Fact-finding Mission," 12 January 2010, *Dayton Daily News*: A4.

23 "Ohio Republican Rep. Steve Austria Retiring," 30 December 2011, *Washington Post*, https://www.washingtonpost.com/blogs/the-fix/post/ohio-republican-rep-steve-austria-retiring/2011/12/30/gIQAECkwQP_blog.html (accessed 20 March 2015); Jonathan Strong, "How Rep. Steve Austria Became a Sacrificial Republican," 17 January 2012, *Roll Call*: n.p.

24 "Ohio Republican Rep. Steve Austria Retiring."

25 Josh Lederman, "Ohio Rep. Steve Austria to Retire, Sparing GOP Primary Showdown," 30 December 2011, *The Hill*: n.p.; Alex Isenstadt, "Departing Ohio Rep. Steve Austria Knocks Boehner," 4 January 2012, *Politico*: n.p.

26 *Congressional Record*, House, 112th Cong., 2nd sess. (11 December 2012): H6691.

27 Republican National Committee, "RNC Launches National Advisory Councils," press release, 3 March 2014, https://www.gop.com/rnc-launches-national-advisory-councils/ (accessed 27 August 2015).

"THE AMERICAN PEOPLE
HAVE SPOKEN LOUD AND
CLEAR. THEY ARE TIRED
OF WASHINGTON NOT
LISTENING TO THEM AND
PUSHING THROUGH POLICIES
FOR THE EXPANSION
OF GOVERNMENT AND
CREATING MORE SPENDING."

Steve Austria
Lancaster Eagle Gazette, November 3, 2010

Anh (Joseph) Cao
1967–

UNITED STATES REPRESENTATIVE 2009–2011
REPUBLICAN FROM LOUISIANA

Anh (Joseph) Cao, a refugee of the Vietnam War and one-time Jesuit seminarian, pulled off an improbable election victory to serve in the House of Representatives in the 111th Congress (2009–2011). Running as a Republican in a historically Democratic-leaning district, Cao (pronounced "gow") dispatched a nine-term incumbent to represent much of the city of New Orleans. As the first Vietnamese American to serve in Congress, his win highlighted the new political activism of the Vietnamese community in post-Katrina New Orleans. Cao's idealism, notion of service to the indigent, and willingness to cross party lines to support measures he felt best met the needs of his largely poor, minority constituency often put him at odds with his party's leaders on health care and economic stimulus during the Great Recession. "I don't want to conform to any ideology, to be put into a little corner," Cao said shortly after his election.[1] A longtime political associate observed, "It's hard to categorize him as a Republican or Democrat. In his heart, Anh is a Jesuit."[2]

Anh (Joseph) Cao was born on March 13, 1967, in Saigon (now Ho Chi Minh City), Vietnam. Cao was the fifth of eight children. His father served as an officer in the South Vietnamese Army and was later imprisoned by North Vietnamese officials during the Vietnam War. At age eight, Cao immigrated to the United States with two siblings, older sister Thanh and younger brother Khanh. During the Fall of Saigon in 1975, as North Vietnamese troops overran South Vietnam's capital, Cao's mother took the three children to a nearby airfield and, while she remained behind, spirited them onto a military transport with their aunt. The younger brother lived in Guam with the aunt; the sister went to Florida to live with a foster family; and Anh lived for the first several years in the United States with an uncle in Goshen, Indiana, before

they relocated to Texas. Cao learned English from his elementary school classmates in Goshen.[3] He graduated from Jersey Village High School in Jersey Village, Texas, in the northwestern suburbs of Houston. He earned a bachelor of science degree in physics from Baylor University in Waco, Texas, in 1990.

Cao's Catholic faith had a profound influence on him as he came of age and later shaped his views on social policy. After college, he entered the seminary with the Society of Jesus, better known as the Jesuit order. His first assignment was at Grand Coteau, Louisiana, to begin training for the priesthood. For the next two years, the Jesuits sent Cao to Brownsville, Texas; Montgomery, Alabama; Tijuana, Mexico; and Hong Kong, China, to help the poor. To further his religious studies, he earned a master's degree in philosophy from the Jesuit-run Fordham University in New York City in 1995. He was then sent to the Jesuit-founded Loyola University in New Orleans to study law.[4]

During his outreach to the poor, Cao had an experience that altered his path to the priesthood. "In life's journey, you sometimes reach a level of uncertainty that you have to make such a leap," he once explained. "I was working in extremely poor conditions, and I wanted to promote social change. I came to believe, over the course of two or three years, that the best way to do that would be to enter public office. It would also allow me to have a family— the celibate life can be quite lonely. So I drafted a course of action for myself to enter politics. But it was a quite painful discernment. It implied I would have to leave the seminary. I would have to start life over again. I would have to make that leap of faith."[5] In 1996 he left the Jesuits and, while reestablishing himself, lived with his sister Thanh in Northern Virginia. A year later, Cao returned to Loyola and earned his law degree in 2000. He worked as an immigration lawyer and personal injury lawyer. While

studying law, he met a pharmacy student, Hieu (Kate) Hoang, who had once been one of his catechism students at the local Catholic church. They married in 2001 and later had two daughters, Sophia and Betsy.

Cao's initial experience with politics came at the local level as a community advocate for the approximately 15,000 Vietnamese who lived in suburbs east of New Orleans. In 2005 Hurricane Katrina devastated the city and large swaths of southern Louisiana, flooded Cao's home, and left his neighborhood in tatters. Afterwards, many of the city's 460,000 residents fled. By some estimates, only 190,000 remained. But the Vietnamese community stayed virtually intact and rebuilt. The storm and its aftermath also forced that small community of fishermen and business owners to become, according to one observer, more vocal in asserting its interests.[6]

Cao's first run for political office was inspired when, in early 2006, the city announced plans to place a waste landfill in their community. Cao led the opposition and provided legal advice to fight the move. At one meeting between city residents and federal officials, Congressman Mike Honda of California, head of the Congressional Asian Pacific American Caucus, urged the Vietnamese community in New Orleans to become more politically active.[7] In 2007 Cao heeded that call. The city scrapped its plan for the landfill because of the protests. That success propelled Cao to run for a seat in the Louisiana state house of representatives. With no organized support, he ran as an independent and finished fifth in a six-candidate field. The *Times-Picayune* later described it as an "inauspicious" political start.[8] But Cao's effort won the notice of Bryan Wagner, a Republican and former city councilman in the 1980s—reportedly, the first to be elected to the council since Reconstruction. He persuaded Cao, a lifelong independent, to join the Republican Party.

In 2008 Cao challenged nine-term, Democrat incumbent William Jefferson. Jefferson, an Ivy League-trained lawyer, had been a force in local politics for two decades and was immensely popular with the city's majority black population in no small measure because he was the first African American ever to represent the city

and the first since Reconstruction to represent Louisiana in Congress.[9] His district took in almost all of the city of New Orleans, including the French Quarter, sweeping out far to the east to encompass the less populous portions of Orleans Parish. It also swung across the Mississippi River to take in several West Bank towns and then west through Jefferson Parish and into portions of the towns of Metairie and Kenner, the largely white suburbs west of the city. The total population of the heavily Democratic district was 60 percent African American.

Recent scandals hobbled Jefferson's re-election bid. In 2006 the Federal Bureau of Investigation raided his House office and his home, where agents found more than $90,000 in cash stuffed into his freezer, part of a larger amount of $400,000 that the government claimed was bribe money from contractors seeking his help to secure federal government work in Africa. The Democratic Caucus stripped him of his seat on the Ways and Means Committee in May 2006, and a little more than a year later, the Justice Department indicted Jefferson on bribery charges.[10] Nevertheless, he did not resign from the House and while his case worked its way through the courts, Jefferson eventually prevailed in a competitive 2008 Democratic primary.[11]

Meanwhile, Cao ran a quiet campaign and won the Republican primary unopposed. His under-the-radar approach was strategic, he later recalled, meant to lull Democrats into a false sense of security. "We sat there and waited, we didn't do any hoopla," Cao noted. "We stayed low profile."[12] His areas of local focus were coastal restoration, levee protection, and redevelopment of New Orleans after Katrina. Education and health care policy were two other areas of interest for Cao.

After Jefferson won his primary, Cao's campaign went into high gear. "We started sprinting," Cao recalled, buying advertising time to highlight Cao's character and honesty and stressing the need for open government. Cao won the backing of several high-profile politicians and received a helping hand from Mother Nature. When Hurricane Gustav forced the postponement of the Louisiana primary elections in early September, it set the entire process back

a month. This separated the 2nd District election from the presidential election in early November, where the African-American Democratic candidate, Barack Obama, won by large margins on his way to his historic election as President, a trend which likely would have helped Jefferson in the House race.

As it was, Jefferson's campaign ran out of resources, and the postponement complicated his task by dampening voter turnout. Additionally, white Democrats largely repulsed by Jefferson's ethics problems either did not vote or defected to Cao. Turnout in the postponed general election on December 6, 2008, was light, with little more than 65,000 voters casting ballots. Cao carried the more conservative Jefferson Parish outside the city with 60 percent of the vote. Jefferson won Orleans Parish, but only with 51 percent. Just a month earlier in the presidential election, Obama won Orleans Parish with nearly 80 percent of the vote.[13] Cao won the overall with 49.5 percent to Jefferson's 46.8 percent. Green Party and Progressive Party candidates split the remainder.[14] Observers hailed it as the biggest upset of the 2008 election cycle and dubbed Cao the "dragon slayer."[15]

Cao's election also garnered headlines because it made him the first Vietnamese American ever to serve in Congress. At a post-election celebration, Cao told a crowd, "Never in my life did I think I could be a future congressman. The American dream is well and alive."[16] A point of pride for Vietnamese Americans nationally, his victory also was touted by congressional Republicans as the future of their party. "As House Republicans look ahead to the next two years, the Cao victory is a symbol of what can be achieved when we think big, present a positive alternative, and work aggressively to earn the trust of the American people," House GOP Leader John Boehner of Ohio told his colleagues shortly after the election.[17] He titled that memo to House Republicans "The Future is Cao."[18]

Others saw that future as being quite delimited, judging Cao's victory to be a one-off event: a Republican elected in an overwhelmingly Democratic district against a damaged, weakened opponent. Just the day after his election Cao was pegged as a "short-timer," an "aberration," a "one-term

wonder," and Democrats instantly targeted him for the next election cycle.[19]

Shortly after the opening of the 111th Congress (2009–2011), Cao won assignments to three committees that had direct bearing on his port city district: Homeland Security; Transportation and Infrastructure; and Oversight and Government Reform. Yet, despite the GOP's promotion of his historic election and his strong set of committee assignments, Cao was an uncertain ally for party leaders from the start. They may have claimed him as their future, but he soon proved to be a difficult vote, sometimes flirting with and at other times joining Democrats on some of the 111th Congress's landmark legislation.

In the wake of the 2008 recession, the first major bill considered by the Democratic-controlled Congress and backed vigorously by the White House was an economic stimulus bill widely seen as the public-focused companion to the large lifeline (Troubled Asset Relief Program) that Congress threw to the big financial institutions in the fall of 2008. Believing they had been cut out of the drafting process, House Republicans, led by GOP Whip Eric Cantor of Virginia, declared that no Republican would vote for the bill.

By the eve of the vote, Cao, ever watchful for federal money to help his district continue its Katrina recovery, was the lone Republican still offering his support. The White House, eager to say that the measure had bipartisan support, lobbied Cao intensely. He later recalled that White House chief of staff Rahm Emanuel "insinuated" that Cao's vote might translate into re-election support. But on the day of the vote, when Cao realized that New Orleans would get only 20 percent of the average amount that other congressional districts would receive from the bill ($330 million as opposed to $1.7 billion), he joined every other Republican in voting no.[20]

Philosophically, Cao also seemed to diverge from his party on one of the defining political issues of the decade. Whereas Republicans uniformly rejected a major health care reform law backed by Democrats, Cao believed such legislation was necessary and would benefit his constituents. "I listened to the countless stories of Orleans and Jefferson parish citizens whose health care costs are exploding—if they are able to obtain health care at all," Cao explained. "Louisianans need real options for primary care, for mental health care, and for expanded health care for seniors and children."[21] Years of tending to the poor and participating in the post-Katrina recovery in New Orleans informed that viewpoint, but Cao's vigorous anti-abortion position also shaped his vision of health care reform. The caveat was that he would never support a bill which allowed federal money to be used to conduct abortions.

Political calculations weighed heavily on Cao, too. In August 2009, he candidly stated, "I know that voting against the health care bill will probably be the death of my political career, but I have to live with myself." He later had to walk back that statement because supporters and donors perceived that he was throwing in the towel on his re-election chances.[22] Moreover, Republican leaders placed intense pressure on him to maintain uniform GOP solidarity against the measure. With Whip Cantor at his side on the House Floor seeking to convince him to vote no, Cao nevertheless cast a yes vote and was the only Republican who voted for the bill that passed the House in the fall of 2009. Afterward he explained that he voted in the best interests of his constituents: "Today, I obtained a commitment from President Obama that he and I will work together to address the critical health care issues of Louisiana including the FMAP [Federal Medical Assistance Percentage] crisis and community disaster loan forgiveness, as well as issues related to Charity and Methodist Hospitals. And, I call on my constituents to support me as I work with him on these issues.… I have always said that I would put aside partisan wrangling to do the business of the people. My vote tonight was based on my priority of doing what is best for my constituents."[23]

Senate revisions to the health care bill eventually forced Cao to reconsider his support. While he applauded President Obama "for his strength and determination in pushing for health care reform in the face of great adversity," he balked at the latest version of the bill that had removed Hyde Amendment language banning the use of federal dollars for abortions and also stripped

protections for medical providers who refused to assist in abortion procedures because of personal conscience. He called the changes "devastating in their effects" and pulled his support.[24]

On the day before the vote, Cao expressed empathy with those priced out of the health care market, but stressed the moral imperatives that drove his opposition. "I understand the crushing costs of health care. I understand that we have to fight the insurance companies. But I also understand that abortion is wrong," he said on the floor. Ultimately, Cao voted no.[25]

Nevertheless, the House passed the Affordable Care Act and President Obama signed it into law in March 2010. The net effect of Cao's waffling was to enrage at one point or another both conservatives and progressives in his district.

On other hot-button social issues, Cao was far out of step with social conservatives. He cosponsored and voted for the Hate Crimes Prevention Act of 2009 (Matthew Shepard and James Byrd Law) that provided federal and local law enforcement with more resources to investigate and prevent hate crimes and stiffened federal criminal penalties for individuals convicted of carrying out hate crimes. He also supported legislation to repeal the U.S. military's "don't ask, don't tell" policy that prevented gay men and women from serving openly.

Cao was an ardent advocate for his constituents—never more so than in the wake of the single most salient event to affect them during the 111th Congress: the massive, slow-motion disaster that unfolded when the British Petroleum (BP) Deepwater Horizon wellhead spewed millions of gallons of crude oil into the Gulf of Mexico over the course of a month in the late spring of 2010. In June, when Members of Congress grilled BP America President Lamar McKay over his company's handling of the massive spill disaster, Cao noted that, while some Members of Congress were calling for McKay to resign, "in the Asian culture we do things differently. During the Samurai days, we just give you a knife and ask you to commit hara-kiri."[26]

Cao sought to protect the watermen in his district, many of them Vietnamese who were virtually put out of business. He called for swift disbursements from the $20 billion fund that BP had agreed to set aside for victim compensation and environmental remediation efforts. Along with Mike Honda of California, the chairman of the Congressional Asian Pacific American Caucus, he called for better communication from BP and the federal government, including bilingual information where appropriate—important for many in the Vietnamese community—immediate financial assistance and job training, and the direct intervention of federal agencies such as the Environmental Protection Agency and the Department of Health and Human Services to address public health concerns and long-term environmental damages. "This nation knows now how devastating the oil spill has become for the Gulf's environmental ecosystem," Cao and Honda wrote in an editorial. "What it has yet to realize, however, is the potential impending devastation to the other equally vital onshore ecosystems—social, economic, and cultural—the most vulnerable of which is the Southeast Asian and African-American fishing and seafood industry communities."[27]

Cao spoke on the floor on dozens of occasions during his single term in the House, but with few exceptions, his remarks were usually relegated to one-minute speeches. No significant piece of legislation bore his name or primary sponsorship. While he introduced 22 measures, from protesting Vietnamese human rights abuses to improving the Federal Emergency Management Agency and disaster response, to allowing states and local governments to revise disaster recovery and mitigation plans, none became law. A handful of his amendments to major bills were passed on the House Floor, including an amendment to the Small Business Jobs Act of 2010 that provided federal funding to organizations and institutions serving small businesses along the Gulf Coast that had suffered from the oil spill.[28]

From his election night in 2008, Democrats marked Cao for the 2010 election cycle. Cedric Richmond, a longtime state representative, announced in September 2009 that he would seek the Democratic nomination to challenge Cao. Richmond had opposed Jefferson in the crowded 2008 Democratic primary, but had fallen short due to lack of name recognition. Even before Cao's

turnabout on the health care legislation, Richmond argued that Cao's vote against the 2009 stimulus, which included money for coastal restoration and flood prevention, threatened the well-being of New Orleans's residents.[29]

The electoral math for Cao to win re-election was complicated enough, but his position on hot-button issues also led social conservatives within his own party to target him. Conservative Christian interest groups ran ads during the campaign attacking his record of support for gay rights. One demanded, "Who is Rep. Joseph Cao representing in Washington?" before claiming that he sought "to advance the radical social agendas of homosexual activists" by placing voters' "personal liberties at jeopardy."[30]

In an historic election that yielded Republicans a gain of 65 seats, sweeping them back into the House majority, Cao was one of the few GOP losses on the national map. Richmond prevailed handily, winning 65 percent of the vote to Cao's 33 percent.[31] Cao gave no farewell address in the House Chamber, nor were any made by colleagues on his behalf. After he left the House in January 2011, Cao returned to New Orleans, where he currently practices law. In 2016 he ran as an unsuccessful Republican candidate for a U.S. Senate seat from Louisiana.

NOTES

1 Adam Nossiter, "History and Amazement in House Race Outcome," 8 December 2008, *New York Times*: A18.

2 Amanda Ruggeri, "Republican Cao's Unlikely Journey from Seminary to Congress," 4 March 2009, *U.S. News and World Report*, https://www.usnews.com/news/articles/2009/03/04/republican-joseph-caos-unlikely-journey-from-seminary-to-congress (accessed 6 April 2011).

3 Neely Tucker, "The Possible Dream: Louisiana's Historic New Congressman Seems to Surprise Everybody but Himself," 30 December 2008, *Washington Post*: C1; Nossiter, "History and Amazement in House Race Outcome." See also Gerard Shields, "Difficult Early Life Forged Cao's Character," 18 January 2009, *Advocate* (Baton Rouge, LA): A12.

4 "History," on Anh (Joseph) Cao's campaign website, accessed 5 November 2008, http://www.voteforanhcao.com/mission.html (site discontinued).

5 Tucker, "The Possible Dream."

6   Ruggeri, "Republican Cao's Unlikely Journey from Seminary to Congress." See also Ylan Q. Mui, "After the Storm, Mr. Cao Goes to Washington," 14 December 2008, *Washington Post*: B2.

7   Tucker, "The Possible Dream."

8   Michelle Krupa, "Anh 'Joseph' Cao Beats Rep. William Jefferson in 2nd Congressional District," 6 December 2008, *New Orleans Times-Picayune*: n.p.

9   See Office of the Historian, U.S. House of Representatives, "Black-American Representatives and Senators by State and Territory, 1870–Present," http://history.house.gov/Exhibitions-and-Publications/BAIC/Historical-Data/Black-American-Representatives-and-Senators-by-State-and-Territory/. For more on Louisiana's only other black representative until Jefferson's election in 1990, see Office of the Historian, U.S. House of Representatives, "Charles Edmund Nash," *Black Americans in Congress*, http://history.house.gov/People/Detail/18846.

10 *Almanac of American Politics, 2010* (Washington, DC: CQ Press, Inc., 2009): 660.

11 *Almanac of American Politics, 2010*: 660.

12 Shields, "Difficult Early Life Forged Cao's Character."

13 *Almanac of American Politics, 2010*: 660.

14 Office of the Clerk, U.S. House of Representatives, "Election Statistics, 1920 to Present," http://history.house.gov/Institution/Election-Statistics/Election-Statistics/.

15 Tucker, "The Possible Dream"; Nossiter, "History and Amazement in House Race Outcome."

16 Rick Jervis, "Vietnamese Hail Cao's Win over Jefferson in La.," 8 December 2008, *USA Today*: n.p.

17 John McCardle, "Cao Pegged as Short-Timer Following Historic Win," 9 December 2008, *Roll Call*: n.p.

18 Paul Kane, "GOP Finds an Unlikely New Hero in Louisiana," 9 December 2008, *Washington Post*: A1; Josh Kraushaar and Andy Barr, "Boehner: The Future of GOP Is Cao," 9 December 2008, *Politico*, http://www.politico.com/story/2008/12/boehner-future-of-gop-is-cao-016336 (accessed 9 December 2008).

19 McCardle, "Cao Pegged as Short-Timer Following Historic Win"; Kraushaar and Barr, "Boehner: The Future of GOP Is Cao."

20 Bob Woodward, *The Price of Politics* (New York: Simon and Schuster, 2012): 16–18, 21.

21 "Health Care's LONE Republican Supporter Is Rep. Anh 'Joseph' Cao," 8 November 2009, *Huffington Post*, http://www.huffingtonpost.com/2009/11/08/joseph-cao-health-cares-l_n_349779.html (accessed 24 February 2011).

22 John McCardle, "Frankly Speaking, Cao's Candor Not Always Good," 6 August 2009, *Roll Call*: n.p.

23 "Health Care's LONE Republican Supporter is Rep. Anh 'Joseph' Cao."

24 *Congressional Record*, House, 111th Cong., 2nd sess. (16 March 2010): H1471.

25 *Congressional Record*, House, 111th Cong., 2nd sess. (20 March 2010): H1749.

26 "Joseph Cao Tells BP Exec: In Samurai Days, You'd Kill Yourself," 15 June 2010, *CBS News*, http://www.cbsnews.com/news/joseph-cao-tells-bp-exec-in-samurai-days-youd-kill-yourself/ (accessed 24 February 2011).

27 Mike Honda and Anh "Joseph" Cao, "BP Oil Spill's Impacts on Vulnerable Minority Communities," 9 August 2010, *The Hill*: n.p. See also Mireya Navarro, "Spill Takes a Heavy Toll on Gulf Workers' Psyches," 17 June 2010, *New York Times*: A19; and Cao's interview, "Oil Spill Impacts Vietnamese-American Workers," 17 May 2010, National Public Radio, http://www.npr.org/templates/transcript/transcript.php?storyId=126883721 (accessed 8 July 2015).

28 See H. Amdt. 702 to H.R. 5297, 111th Cong. (2010).

29 John McCardle, "Richmond Makes Bid Against Cao Official," 9 September 2009, *Roll Call*: n.p.

30 David Gibson, "Louisiana's Anh 'Joseph' Cao, First Vietnamese-American in Congress, a Rare GOP Loss," 3 November 2010, *Politics Daily*: n.p.

31 Office of the Clerk, U.S. House of Representatives, "Election Statistics, 1920 to Present."

"NEVER IN MY LIFE DID I
THINK I COULD BE A FUTURE
CONGRESSMAN. THE AMERICAN
DREAM IS WELL AND ALIVE."

Anh (Joseph) Cao
USA Today, December 8, 2008

Charles Djou
1970–

UNITED STATES REPRESENTATIVE 2010–2011
REPUBLICAN FROM HAWAII

In May 2010, Charles Djou won a surprise special election victory to become only the second Republican since statehood to represent Hawaii in the U.S. House of Representatives. Although his career on Capitol Hill lasted only a few months, Djou worked to control spending and lower taxes, and he was not afraid to break ties with his party on issues he felt strongly about.

Charles J. Djou was born in Los Angeles, California, on August 9, 1970. Both of his parents had immigrated to the United States from across the Pacific. His father was born in Shanghai, China, and fled to Hong Kong during the Chinese Communist Revolution in the late 1940s. Djou's mother grew up in Bangkok, Thailand.[1] When he was a boy, Djou's family moved to Hawaii and settled on the southeastern side of Oahu.[2] He graduated in 1988 from the famed Punahou School in Honolulu and traveled east for college, earning both a bachelor of arts degree in political science and a bachelor of science degree in finance from the Wharton School of the University of Pennsylvania in 1992.[3] Four years later he earned a law degree from the University of Southern California in Los Angeles.

In 2001 Djou joined the United States Army Reserve and served in Afghanistan's Kandahar Province with the 3rd Brigade Combat Team, 10th Mountain Division, a light infantry division, from 2011 to 2012.[4] Afterward, in his private career, Djou worked as an attorney for a small number of firms in Hawaii. He married Stacey Kawasaki, whom he had met shortly after law school when they worked for the same law practice. They have three children, Nick, Tori, and Alli.[5]

In 1998 Djou waged an unsuccessful campaign for a seat in Hawaii's state house of representatives. But two years later, he ran again and won, serving the Kahaluu and Kaneohe areas on Oahu's east coast. In the state house, he served on the finance committee, the labor and public employment committee, the public safety and military affairs committee, and the transportation committee.[6] He had a reliably conservative voting record, opposing legislative pay raises and working to shrink Hawaii's spending.[7] As a member of the finance committee, Djou led the push to open its budget deliberations to public view.[8] In mid-January 2002, in just his first term, Djou was elected party floor leader, becoming the youngest Republican officer in the Hawaiian legislature's history.[9]

After one term, redistricting erased his seat in the state house and drew him into a neighboring district represented by a fellow incumbent.[10] In response, Hawaii Republicans began drafting Djou to run for lieutenant governor. Djou declined, however, and began exploring a run for the Honolulu city council.[11]

To prepare for the city council run, Djou moved to East Honolulu, not far from where his wife's family lived. By the summer of 2002, he began to earn solid reviews in the Honolulu newspapers.[12] To combat what he saw as runaway spending, Djou wanted to refocus the city's finances on "core city services, like road paving and law enforcement salaries."[13] Honolulu's public service sector "should be something that hums neatly and efficiently in the background," he said.[14] Djou won the general election that November, beginning what became nearly a decade-long stint on the city council.[15]

Djou became perhaps the most prominent conservative on the city council during the 2000s. He fought tax increases, looked to cap spending, and repeatedly voted against the city's budget, which grew year after year. He worked to pass ethics reform, improve Honolulu's recycling program and increase its use of "alternative energy."[16] Djou cycled on and off as chairman of the powerful zoning committee, using his influence to put a proposal to build a $5 billion rail project up for a public vote.[17]

Early in 2010, the incumbent Representative from Hawaii's 1st District, Neil Abercrombie, resigned from the House to focus on his gubernatorial campaign, opening a seat that encompassed Djou's hometown.[18] Abercrombie had served in the House since 1991, creating a 20-year backlog of Honolulu politicians looking to serve in national office. Djou, according to one Capitol Hill newspaper, had been planning for an eventual House campaign as early as November 2007.[19] Following Abercrombie's resignation, Djou decided to run for both the special election to serve out the remainder of the 111th Congress (2009–2011) as well as the general election for the 112th Congress (2011–2013) in November 2010.[20]

Republicans on the mainland quickly took interest in Djou's candidacy. In the first half of 2009, the National Republican Congressional Committee, the party's House campaign arm, included Djou in its "Young Guns" program and ran ads criticizing Abercrombie for his support of the recent stimulus package. Taking a more moderate stance, Djou argued that Republicans and Democrats needed to "work together" to spend the funds "wisely."[21] "For me," Djou said a few weeks later, "my campaign has been about bringing a sense of accountability and responsibility back to the federal government."[22]

Based on the returns from the 2008 election, when Democrats won by a landslide in the 1st District, Djou's candidacy looked like a longshot.[23] But he remained optimistic heading into 2010, saying, "I think the Republican Party does have a good message about diversifying our economy, about trying to keep more money in the pocketbooks of consumers."[24]

Djou's platform included a number of traditional Republican initiatives, such as job creation, trade, lowering taxes, balancing the budget, limiting earmarks, and reducing spending.[25] In theory, Djou also supported reforming parts of America's health care system but wanted to see Congress include changes to malpractice insurance and to allow insurance companies to sell plans across state lines.[26] "Djou is everything the GOP could hope for in a viable Hawaii candidate," said one editorial in the *Honolulu Star-Bulletin* later that month, "local,

moderate, against all tax increases and is even an officer in the Army Reserve."[27]

Despite some conservative tendencies in the district, Hawaii was historically Democratic and was President Barack Obama's home state. Djou maintained a much more moderate tone compared to the election politics on the mainland, and his long service on the Honolulu city council also made him well versed in the district's issues. Political handicappers predicted a close race.[28] "Nothing can make a powerful statement for the Republicans about the 2010 midterm elections than to send a Republican from Barack Obama's hometown to the Congress in the special election," Djou told *Roll Call* in March 2010.[29]

Hawaii conducted the special election almost entirely by mail-in ballot, and on May 22, Djou defied the early odds and won, taking 39.4 percent of a surprisingly large turnout and beating the two leading Democrats, state senator Colleen Hanabusa and former U.S. Representative Ed Case, who split the Democratic vote.[30] Djou became only the second Republican Representative from Hawaii to serve in the House (before statehood, Hawaii had sent a number of Republican Delegates to the House). "The congressional seat is not owned by one political party," Djou said after his victory. "This congressional seat is owned by the people."[31]

Two days after his victory Djou and his family flew to Washington.[32] Just after 5:00 p.m. on May 25, 2010, Charles Djou took the oath of office and was sworn in by Speaker Nancy Pelosi. After introductory remarks by Congresswoman Mazie K. Hirono of Hawaii and House Minority Leader John Boehner of Ohio, Djou addressed the chamber. "I want all the voters to know that every single day I have the privilege of serving them I will never, ever forget the trust and confidence they have vested in me," he said. "It is a testimony to the greatness of the United States of America that I, a son of immigrants from China and Thailand, have the privilege of calling myself a Member of the United States Congress."[33]

House Republicans assigned Djou to two popular and powerful committees, the Armed Services Committee and the Budget Committee.[34] On the Armed Services Committee, a natural home for the Army reservist with a large military constituency, he served on two subcommittees,

the Subcommittee on Readiness and the Subcommittee on Terrorism, Unconventional Threats and Capabilities.

His first appearance with the Budget Committee occurred on June 9, 2010, when the House heard testimony from Federal Reserve Chairman Ben Bernanke. From his seat on the dais, Djou questioned Bernanke about the viability of additional economic stimulus and whether new free trade agreements would help the U.S. economy.[35] A month later, during another Budget Committee hearing on the effects of the 2009 stimulus, Djou seemed to reach across the aisle, telling the Secretary of Agriculture that he was "far more concerned about fixing things and looking forward in the future than continuing to lay partisan blame."[36]

Entering the House in late May during an election year, however, left Djou with little time to legislate. He introduced his first bill (H.R. 5720) on July 13, 2010, and offered his final bill of the 111th Congress only a month later, just before Congress recessed for the summer. In total, Djou introduced 12 resolutions during the 111th Congress, including two bills to rename post offices in Honolulu; the FACT Act (H.R. 5857), which would have lowered corporate income tax; the Family Reunification Act of 2010 (H.R. 5880), which would have amended certain immigration requirements; and the Citizenship and Service Act of 2010 (H.R. 6327), which would have enabled undocumented young people to become "conditional permanent" U.S. residents if they met certain educational qualifications. Djou also broke from his party on a handful of hot-button issues. He was one of only five Republicans to vote for the repeal of the military's "don't ask, don't tell" policy and later was one of only eight Republicans to vote for an immigration overhaul.[37]

On the House Floor, Djou often used his congressional megaphone to recognize and praise the accomplishments of his constituents.[38] He also spoke in favor of America's trade deal with South Korea and supported the House GOP's crowd-sourced budget-reducing tool called YouCut.[39]

During debate on H.R. 5822, the Military Construction and Veterans Affairs and Related Agencies Appropriations Act of 2011, Djou sided with the Obama administration and lamented the decision by House Republicans not to include his amendment that would have restored funding to help America's Armed Forces begin moving from Okinawa, Japan, to Guam. Later, toward the end of the 111th Congress, Djou strongly supported H. Res. 1735, which condemned North Korea for attacking South Korea on November 23, 2010. "We must strengthen our bonds between the United States and South Korea to stand as a bulwark against the aggressive and repressive North Korean Government," he said.[40]

Djou's career in the House lasted only a few months. Whereas Democrats had split the ticket during the special election, he faced only Colleen Hanabusa heading into the general election. Djou was in a dead heat with Hanabusa by mid-October and raised more than a half million dollars as voting neared.[41] In an effort to help his candidacy, House Minority Leader Boehner promised to assign him to the powerful Appropriations Committee if the GOP took the House.[42] Two weeks before Election Day, however, Djou experienced a large setback when Hanabusa won the endorsement of the *Honolulu Star-Advertiser*.[43] In the end, Djou took 46 percent of the vote and lost the general election by 11,417 votes.[44]

After his loss, Djou returned to Capitol Hill for the remainder of the Congress. In his last address, Djou thanked the voters of the 1st District for the opportunity to serve them in the House. "I believe that a vibrant two-party democracy is better at preserving liberty than one-party monolithic rule," he said. "But I also believe one of the beauties of our Nation is that the voters always have the final say.... Yielding to the final word of the voters is something that I always will respect."[45]

After leaving the House, Djou returned to Hawaii. In 2012 he won the Republican nomination for his old seat, but lost in the general election. He ran again in 2014, but lost in the GOP primary. In June 2016, Djou entered a three-way race for mayor of Honolulu against the incumbent Kirk Caldwell and the city's previous mayor Peter Carlisle. In a close campaign, Djou came in second to Caldwell, but since neither candidate received a majority of the votes, the election headed to a runoff. Djou ended up losing the runoff later that November.[46]

NOTES

1 "Charles," on Charles Djou's official campaign website, accessed 10 August 2015, http://djou.com/about.

2 Suzanne Roig, "5 Vie for East Oahu Council Seat," 10 September 2002, *Honolulu Advertiser*: B3.

3 "Charles Djou," *Biographical Directory of the United States Congress, 1774–Present*, http://bioguide.congress.gov/scripts/ biodisplay.pl?index=D000611; Charles Djou's LinkedIn page, accessed 10 August 2015, https://www.linkedin.com/in/charles-djou-31305a29.

4 "Charles," on Charles Djou's official campaign website, accessed 10 August 2015, http://djou.com/about.

5 "Stacey," on Charles Djou's official campaign website, accessed 10 August 2015, http://djou.com/stacey.

6 "Statewide Summary Report," Office of Elections, State of Hawaii, 3 November 1998, http://elections.hawaii.gov/election-results/ (accessed 27 April 2016); "The 2002 Hawaii State Legislature," 16 January 2002, *Honolulu Advertiser*: A12.

7 Pat Omandam, "House Hammers Out Bill-Recall Agreement," 21 February 2001, *Honolulu Star-Bulletin*: n.p.; Pat Omandam, "Republicans Stop 4 House Bills," 7 March 2001, *Honolulu Star-Bulletin*: n.p.; "Djou Announces Council Run," 25 February 2002, *Honolulu Star-Bulletin*: n.p.

8 Pat Omandam, "Let the Sun Shine In, Say Republicans," 17 March 2001, *Honolulu Star-Bulletin*: n.p. See also Richard Borreca, "Open State Budget Details to Public, Legislator Urges," 2 April 2001, *Honolulu Star-Bulletin*: n.p.; Richard Borreca, "Budget Papers Now Open to Public," 7 April 2001, *Honolulu Star-Bulletin*: n.p.

9 Lynda Arakawa, "House in Squabble Over Republican's Double Duty," 20 January 2002, *Honolulu Advertiser*: A29. See also Pat Omandam, "Djou's Dual House Roles Spark Bitter Political Debate," 19 January 2002, *Honolulu Star-Bulletin*: n.p.; Pat Omandam, "Bill Would Move Up Primary Election," 26 January 2002, *Honolulu Star-Bulletin*: n.p.; Walter Wright, "Legislator to Run for Council," 25 February 2002, *Honolulu Advertiser*: B3.

10 "Djou Announces Council Run," 25 February 2002, *Honolulu Star-Bulletin*: n.p.

11 Richard Borreca, "Republican Party Convention Starts Amid Calls for Energetic Diligence," 20 May 2001, *Honolulu Star-Bulletin*: n.p.; Walter Wright, "Legislator to Run for Council"; "Djou Announces Council Run."

12 "Ernie Martin, Rep. Djou Run for City Council," 19 July 2002, *Honolulu Advertiser*: B2; "Djou Announces Council Run"; Roig, "5 Vie for East Oahu Council Seat."

13 Roig, "5 Vie for East Oahu Council Seat."

14 Treena Shapiro, "Election 2002," 20 October 2002, *Honolulu Advertiser*: A27.

15 Treena Shapiro, "Election 2002," 6 November 2002, *Honolulu Advertiser*: A5.

16 Robbie Dingeman, "Council Weighing Property Tax Hike," 25 January 2003, *Honolulu Advertiser*: B1; "The Hot Seat," 27 September 2009, *Honolulu Advertiser*: B1; "Djou Seeks Backing for Spending Caps," 23 December 2003, *Honolulu Advertiser*: B6; Robbie Dingeman, "Djou Seeks Earlier Start for Curbside Recycling," 12 March 2006, *Honolulu Advertiser*: A34; Johnny Brannon, "Recycling Takes New Turn," 6 September 2007, *Honolulu Advertiser*: B1; B. J. Reyes, "Councilmen Find Allies to Fight Recycling Cut," 20 May 2009, *Honolulu Star-Bulletin*: n.p.

17 Sean Hao, "Council Votes 9-0 to Put Rail on Ballot," 24 July 2008, *Honolulu Advertiser*: A1.

18 Shira Toeplitz, "GOP Says Aloha to 2010 Special Election," 15 December 2009, *Roll Call*: n.p.

19 Shira Toeplitz, "The Farm Team: Hawaii," 5 February 2008, *Roll Call*: n.p.; "Hawaii: City Councilman Eyes Abercrombie Seat in '10," 16 October 2008, *Roll Call*: n.p.; Shira Toeplitz, "Winds of Change Could Be Blowin'," 20 January 2009, *Roll Call*: n.p.; Chad Blair, "Charles Djou Running for Congress," 19 March 2008, *Pacific Business News*: n.p. Djou also appeared to be keeping his options open. The *Honolulu Star-Bulletin* reported in November 2008 that Djou had also filed papers to seek the office of lieutenant governor during the 2010 election cycle. See Richard Borreca, "More Change to Occur in Next Election," 9 November 2008, *Honolulu Star-Bulletin*: n.p.

20 Richard Borreca, "Candidates Tossing Hat in Early, Too," 12 December 2009, *Honolulu Star-Bulletin*: n.p.

21 Aaron Blake, "NRCC Picks 13 Challengers with 'Young Guns' Potential," 30 July 2009, *The Hill*: 4. Quotations from Richard Borreca, "Republican Attack Ads Target Abercrombie," 21 February 2009, *Honolulu Star-Bulletin*: n.p. See also "Hawaii EMILY's List Backs Hanabusa in 1st District," 8 October 2009, *Roll Call*: n.p.

22 Derrick DePledge, "Case Sets His Sights on Returning to Congress," 29 March 2009, *Honolulu Advertiser*: A1.

23 Office of the Clerk, U.S. House of Representatives, "Election Statistics, 1920 to Present," http://history.house.gov/Institution/ Election-Statistics/Election-Statistics/.

24 Derrick DePledge, "Republicans Urged to Unite," 17 May 2009, *Honolulu Advertiser*: A21.

25 Jeremy B. White, "GOP Has Big Mauka to Climb in Hawaii," 7 July 2009, *Roll Call*: n.p.; B. J. Reyes, "2 TV Debates Might be the Key to Victory," 2 May 2010, *Honolulu Star-Bulletin*: n.p.

26 Derrick DePledge, "Local Democrats, Republicans Join Debate on Health Care Reform," 21 August 2009, *Honolulu Advertiser*: n.p.; Derrick DePledge "Health Care Fires Up Crowd," 26 August 2009, *Honolulu Advertiser*: n.p.

7   Richard Borreca, "Special Election Offers 3 Distinct Candidates," 24 March 2010, *Honolulu Star-Bulletin*: n.p.

8   David Shapiro, "Congressional Race Intriguing Contest," 14 October 2009, *Honolulu Advertiser*: n.p.; Shira Toeplitz, "GOP Says Aloha to 2010 Special Election," 15 December 2009, *Roll Call*: n.p.

29 Shira Toeplitz, "NRCC Weighs Playing in Pair of Specials," 3 March 2010, *Roll Call*: n.p.

30 Philip Rucker, "Republican Captures House Seat in Hawaii," 24 May 2010, *Washington Post*: A2; "Djou Win Reflects Unrest of Voters," 24 May 2010, *Honolulu Star-Bulletin*: n.p.

31 Mark Sappenfield, "Charles Djou: How Did a Republican Win in Obama's Hawaii Hometown?," 23 May 2010, *Christian Science Monitor*: n.p.

32 Craig Gima, "East Honolulu Went to Djou," 24 May 2010, *Honolulu Star-Bulletin*: n.p.

33 *Congressional Record*, House, 111th Cong., 2nd sess. (25 May 2010): 9269–9270.

34 The House approved his assignments by way of H. Res. 1415, 111th Cong. (2010).

35 Hearing before the House Committee on the Budget, *State of the Economy: View from the Federal Reserve*, 111th Cong., 2nd sess. (9 June 2010): 30–32.

36 Hearing before the House Committee on the Budget, *The American Recovery and Reinvestment Act of 2009, an Update*, 111th Cong., 2nd sess. (14 July 2010): 31.

37 Jan Austin, ed., "Key Votes: In the House," *CQ Almanac, 2010*, 66th ed. (Washington, DC: CQ-Roll Call Group, 2011): Appendix C, 18–24; Mark Niesse, "Outside Image Coveted by Hawaii Congress Nominees," 10 October 2010, Associated Press.

38 *Congressional Record*, House, 111th Cong., 2nd sess. (17 June 2010): 11130; *Congressional Record*, House, 111th Cong., 2nd sess. (17 June 2010): E1141; *Congressional Record*, House, 111th Cong., 2nd sess. (10 August 2010): 1548; *Congressional Record*, House, 111th Cong., 2nd sess. (23 September 2010): 16487; *Congressional Record*, House, 111th Cong., 2nd sess. (29 September 2010): 17373.

39 *Congressional Record*, House, 111th Cong., 2nd sess. (27 July 2010): 14097–14098; *Congressional Record*, House, 111th Cong., 2nd sess. (30 June 2010): 12411.

40 *Congressional Record*, House, 111th Cong., 2nd sess. (30 November 2010): 18376.

41 B. J. Reyes, "Candidates Talk Cash, Little Trash," 14 October 2010, *Honolulu Star-Advertiser*: n.p.; B. J. Reyes, "Djou, Hanabusa in Dead Heat," 24 October 2010, *Honolulu Star-Bulletin*: n.p.; B. J. Reyes, "Djou Holds Slim Lead in Congressional Race," 25 October 2010, *Honolulu Star-Advertiser*: n.p.

42 "Djou, Hanabusa Raise Similar Amounts in September," 18 October 2010, Associated Press; "Djou Doubles Foe's Contributions in October," 23 October 2010, Associated Press; B. J. Reyes, "Djou Promised Seat on House Appropriations Committee," 12 October 2010, *Honolulu Star-Advertiser*: n.p.; B. J. Reyes, "GOP Leader Promises Djou Key Money Post," 13 October 2010, *Honolulu Star-Advertiser*: n.p.

43 "Send Hanabusa to Serve in D.C.," 21 October 2010, *Honolulu Star-Advertiser*: n.p.

44 B. J. Reyes, "Djou, Hanabusa Invest Shoe Leather," 30 October 2010, *Honolulu Star-Advertiser*: n.p.; B. J. Reyes, "Hanabusa Tops Djou for House Seat," 2 November 2010, *Honolulu Star-Advertiser*: n.p.

45 *Congressional Record*, House, 111th Cong., 2nd sess. (21 December 2010): 23238.

46 "Djou, Carlisle to Face Caldwell in Honolulu Mayoral Race," 8 June 2016, Associated Press; "Rail Takes Center Stage in Honolulu Mayoral Race," 27 July 2016, Associated Press; "Honolulu Mayor Race Heads to Runoff Election," 14 August 2016, Associated Press; Gordon Y. K. Pang, "Caldwell Beats Djou to Win Reelection as Honolulu's Mayor," 8 November 2016, *Honolulu Star-Advertiser*, http://www.staradvertiser.com/2016/11/08/breaking-news/caldwell-leads-challenger-djou-in-early-results/ (accessed 1 June 2017).

Hansen Clarke
1957–

UNITED STATES REPRESENTATIVE 2011–2013
DEMOCRAT FROM MICHIGAN

In 2010 Hansen Clarke unseated a seven-term incumbent in the Democratic primary before going on to represent the city of Detroit in the U.S. House of Representatives for one term. His path to the House was as unique as it was unconventional. Clarke had a casual, approachable way about him, and he asked people to refer to him simply as "Hansen."[1] In 2005 the *Detroit Free Press* called his life an "underdog story … a classic," an "up-from-the-east-side hard-luck tale."[2] Indeed, the struggle of his childhood shaped his political philosophy and oriented him toward policies that he hoped would help both Michigan's disadvantaged citizens and its businesses.

Hansen Clarke was born Molik Hashim in Detroit, Michigan, on March 2, 1957, the son of an African-American mother and a Bangladeshi father.[3] His father, Mozaffar Ali Hashim, worked at a Detroit automobile factory, but he died when Clarke was only eight years old, leaving his mother, Thelma Clarke, to raise him on a school crossing guard's salary.[4] His neighbors stepped in to help, and when he was 14 years old Clarke moved east to New Hampshire to attend Phillips Exeter Academy, one of the country's elite high schools. Surrounded by wealth and prestige, Clarke felt out of place and, after two years, returned home to Detroit. "All I knew was this block," he said years later, standing outside his childhood house in what one national magazine called "one of the toughest neighborhoods on the east side."[5] Phillips Exeter might as well have been a world away. "I couldn't handle it," he recalled.[6]

Clarke eventually accepted a scholarship to Cornell University and moved back east to study art.[7] Tragedy struck when his mother died in 1976. As he grieved, Clarke returned to Detroit and scraped by, eventually going on government assistance. In 1978 he changed his name to Hansen Clarke to honor his mother. Ultimately, he made it back to Cornell with the help of his godmother

and graduated with a bachelor's degree in fine arts in 1984. Three years later Clarke earned a law degree from Georgetown University in Washington, DC.[8]

After law school, Clarke began practicing as an attorney. He cemented his local public service credentials while running the Detroit district office of U.S. Representative John Conyers of Michigan and working for Wayne County Executive Edward H. McNamara.[9] Clarke made the jump to elective office in the early 1990s, serving in the Michigan state house of representatives from 1991 to 1992 and again from 1999 to 2002. In 2003 he began an eight-year stint in the state senate.

In 2005 Clarke ran a very personal race for mayor of Detroit, filling his campaign with vignettes from his childhood and reflecting on the example set by his mother. As a candidate, Clarke promised to clean up Detroit and hoped to convince people to stay in the city rather than move to the suburbs. He ran as a reform candidate, pledging to dismantle the patronage system in city hall and "change the political culture of the city."[10] Despite his populist message, Clarke finished fourth in the city primary.[11]

After the election, Clarke returned to the state senate and his seat on the appropriations committee, where he protected funding for his beleaguered city.[12] In 2008, as Michigan reeled from the housing crisis, he introduced a popular bill to protect homeowners in foreclosure from being evicted.[13] Later that year, he pushed the governor to overhaul the Detroit public schools as the city system struggled financially.[14]

By 2010, as term limits were about to force Clarke out of the state senate, he flirted with a run for governor before deciding to challenge Congresswoman Carolyn Cheeks Kilpatrick, who had represented Detroit in the U.S. House since 1997.[15] In the race for the 13th District, Clarke had an early advantage over Kilpatrick, whose son

had previously been mayor of Detroit and faced a slew of federal corruption charges.[16]

Clarke's campaign for the House harkened back to his earlier run for mayor, focusing on the emotion and power of his life story. At the heart of the 13th District was his old neighborhood, which had been plagued by violence and loss over the years.[17] It was a struggle Clarke knew intimately.[18] "All my life I've been afraid that I'm going to wind up on the streets," he said in 2010.[19] Despite having a law degree from one of the country's leading schools, Clarke held on to his taxi license for two decades just in case things went south again.[20] "I still hate that I had to leave," Clarke confessed during his earlier mayoral campaign. "I wanted to make it here, to show what could be done in Detroit."[21]

Clarke ran perhaps the most unique race of the 2010 election cycle. "I'm from the neighborhood," he reminded his local paper. "So I don't think we're going to need a lot of money for commercials."[22] Instead, as reported by the *Detroit Free Press*, he "used an unconventional campaign strategy, enlisting homeless people and panhandlers to spread his message, going to soup kitchens and shelters to tell people they could, in small and large ways, control their own fate."[23] Clarke's empowerment narrative allowed him to reach voters everywhere and seemed to blur conventional party divisions, never more directly during the election than when he described his brand of politics as equal parts "Newt Gingrich and Malcolm X."[24]

Clarke's House campaign received a boost shortly before the primary when Detroit's major newspaper, the *Detroit Free Press*, endorsed him. Clarke cast himself as the city's best shot to replace Kilpatrick in the House and a few days later won with 47 percent of the vote, which, in the heavily Democratic 13th District, was tantamount to winning the general election. "This was bigger than an opponent and not about the incumbent or a family," Clarke said the night he won. "You must be mindful that elected officials come and go, but people, not politicians, always have the power."[25] In the general election, Clarke buried his Republican opponent, John Hauler, with 79 percent of the vote.[26]

Clarke's message to Detroit had always been resilience. Even after his victory he continued to appeal directly to people who struggled to get by but who time and again rebounded from setback. Clarke promised to represent every part of his constituency, from rich to poor, but he was not afraid to cast his story in stark relief to the wealthier Detroit suburbs which had been devastated by the housing market collapse. "The people out there were making six figures a year and now a lot of them are in foreclosure," he said to a homeless audience shortly after the November elections. "They think this is the end of the world for them, but you and I know better. People like us are strong, not despite what we have been through, but because of it."[27]

Although Democrats had lost their House majority in the 2010 elections, Clarke had a full legislative agenda when he arrived in Washington: job creation, foreclosure relief, and insurance premium reform.[28] For Clarke, the act of legislating was about people and "knowing what they're going through." But Clarke also pointed out that he was not in Washington merely to represent the interests of the underserved. "I've got to work for the employers as well," he observed, "because that's the only way my folks are going to get employed."[29]

In the House, Democratic leaders appointed Clarke to two committees, the Committee on Homeland Security and the Committee on Science, Space, and Technology.[30] On the Homeland Security Committee, Clarke served on the Border and Maritime Security Subcommittee and the Emergency Preparedness, Response, and Communications Subcommittee. On the Science, Space, and Technology Committee, Clarke served only on the Subcommittee on Research and Science Education.

That Clarke was not appointed to one of the powerful money committees did not stop him from trying to pump federal tax dollars directly to Detroit. Shortly before he took office, Clarke told *Newsweek* magazine, "I'm a Democrat because I believe tax dollars can be used for the common good, but between Milton Friedman and John Maynard Keynes I come right down the middle. As a progressive I want to pay down the debt. I think it can be done by cutting some taxes, and by putting people back to work."[31]

By the fall of his first term, Clarke had sketched out a revolutionary plan using a similar principle to rescue his hometown: the federal government would return to the city every single tax dollar it collected from Detroit for five years. Clarke estimated his program would be worth $2 billion a year and believed it would balance the city's budget, cover many of Detroit's pension plans, and help pay down its debt. Detroit would also continue to receive the same Medicare and Social Security grants it had always received. To encourage people to move back into the city, Clarke wanted Detroit to slash its property taxes and abolish its personal income tax. Clarke figured Detroit could be the country's pilot program which, if it succeeded, Congress could apply to other cities.[32]

Clarke's rescue plan never made it beyond the idea stage, but he was active on a number of legislative fronts. During the 112th Congress (2011–2013), he introduced 26 bills, four House Resolutions, and 12 floor amendments. Some were broad, ambitious pieces of legislation, like his Detroit Growth and Sustainability Act, which authorized $500 million in loans to his hometown. Others were more itemized efforts, like his push to suspend the import fees on products used by the auto industry. Clarke spoke passionately on the floor about reducing America's debt burden, improving America's educational system, and protecting America's labor unions.[33] He also offered floor amendments to appropriations bills to boost funding for certain programs, including $5 million for the Women, Infants, and Children Farmers Market Nutrition Program, which the House approved as part of the consolidated funding bill in late 2011. In the summer of 2011, he teamed up with Republican Representative Dan Benishek of northern Michigan to tour each other's district and encourage job creation across the state.[34]

Clarke's time on Capitol Hill was cut short, however, after Michigan lost a seat in the House following the 2010 Census. When the state redrew its district boundaries, the mapmakers moved much of Clarke's core support to the newly redrawn 14th District. In August 2011, Clarke announced he would seek the seat in the new 14th District. By fall he faced a tough primary contest against multiple candidates, including another Democratic House incumbent, Gary Peters, who had formerly represented the 9th District.[35] During the campaign, Clarke refused to participate in any of the primary debates after reports surfaced claiming that his mother's death certificate recorded her race as white. Clarke's campaign released a statement in late June 2012 criticizing "the use of racist rhetoric and race-baiting" during the campaign, and a few days later came out with even stronger language accusing his opponents of going "after my dead parents" because "they can't attack my record."[36] By early August, however, polls showed Clarke trailing by a wide margin, and he was never able to make up the difference. Clarke did well among voters in the city, but he could not match Peters's support in the adjacent suburbs.[37]

After losing in the Democratic primary, Clarke finished out the 112th Congress. Two years later, when Peters announced he would run for the Senate, Clarke announced his candidacy for Michigan's 14th District.[38] Over the summer of 2014, polls showed him with a comfortable lead and wide name recognition.[39] Clarke ran on a plan to help lower America's student-loan debt, but after national women's organizations threw their support behind his main opponent in the primary, Southfield mayor Brenda Lawrence, Clarke saw his numbers slip.[40] On August 5, he lost in the Democratic primary.[41]

NOTES

1 Bob Campbell, "Yes, Politicos Really Do Have a Heart," 8 August 2010, *Detroit Free Press*: A24.

2 Nichole M. Christian, "Clarke Has Done His Neighborhood Proud," 1 July 2005, *Detroit Free Press*: 12.

3 Dawson Bell, "Clarke Runs His Campaign Like He Lives, from the Heart," 20 July 2005, *Detroit Free Press*: 1.

4 "Rep. Kilpatrick Vanquisher, Hansen Clarke, Has Some Story," 4 August 2010, National Public Radio, http://www.npr.org/sections/thetwo-way/2010/08/04/128978167/rep-kilpatrick-vanquisher-hansen-clarke-has-some-story (accessed 20 March 2015); Aziz Haniffa, "Hansen Hashim Clarke," 25 February 2011, *India Abroad* (New York): A17-A18.

5 Zev Chafets, "Rep. Hansen Clarke and Detroit's New Renaissance," 29 December 2010, *Newsweek*, http://www.newsweek.com/rep-

hansen-clarke-and-detroits-new-renaissance-69073 (accessed 17 June 2015).

6 Quotations from Christian, "Clarke Has Done His Neighborhood Proud." See also Bell, "Clarke Runs His Campaign Like He Lives, from the Heart."

7 Bell, "Clarke Runs His Campaign Like He Lives, from the Heart." See also "Media Center: Biography," on Hansen Clarke's official campaign website, accessed 21 August 2015, http://www.hansenclarkeforcongress.com/media-center/.

8 Bell, "Clarke Runs His Campaign Like He Lives, from the Heart"; Christian, "Clarke Has Done His Neighborhood Proud"; "Questions & Answers: State Sen. Hansen Clarke, Find the Waste, Serve the Citizens," 20 July 2005, *Detroit Free Press*: 9; *Congressional Record*, House, 112th Cong., 2nd sess. (10 July 2012): H4690; Kathleen Gray, "Clarke Out of Debates, Alleges 'Racist Rhetoric,'" 30 June 2012, *Detroit Free Press*: A1.

9 Ann L. Brownson, ed., *Congressional Staff Directory, 1990/1* (Mount Vernon, VA: Staff Directories, Ltd., 1990): 375; "Biography," official website of Hansen Clarke, accessed 18 June 2015, archived at http://webarchive.loc.gov/all/20120105224404/https://hansenclarke.house.gov/about-me/full-biography.

10 "Questions & Answers: State Sen. Hansen Clarke, Find the Waste, Serve the Citizens."

11 Marisol Bello, "Running for Mayor, Who Spent What?," 23 July 2005, *Detroit Free Press*: 3; Kathleen Gray and Hugh McDiarmid Jr., "In a Minute: Michigan News Briefs," 18 August 2005, *Detroit Free Press*: 3.

12 "*Free Press* Endorsements," 6 August 2006, *Detroit Free Press*: 2; "Questions & Answers: State Sen. Hansen Clarke, Find the Waste, Serve the Citizens."

13 Gina Damron, "Detroit: Meeting Looks at Eviction Reprieve," 15 June 2008, *Detroit Free Press*: 3.

14 Chastity Pratt Dawsey, "Detroit Lawmaker Pushes for State to Force DPS Change," 6 November 2008, *Detroit Free Press*: 4.

15 Chris Christoff, "The Fallout of Cherry's Dropout," 6 January 2010, *Detroit Free Press*: A2.

16 Chris Christoff, "Clarke Quits 1 Race, Weighs Another," 16 January 2010, *Detroit Free Press*: A3; Kathleen Gray, "Clarke Is Challenging Rep. Kilpatrick For Seat," 9 March 2010, *Detroit Free Press*: A3; Todd Spangler, "Rep. Kilpatrick Has Smaller War Chest Than '08," 16 July 2010, *Detroit Free Press*: A6.

17 Bell, "Clarke Runs His Campaign Like He Lives, from the Heart"; Campbell, "Yes, Politicos Really Do Have a Heart."

18 Kathleen Gray, "Tough Past Fueled Clarke's Victory," 5 August 2010, *Detroit Free Press*: A10.

19 Chafets, "Rep. Hansen Clarke and Detroit's New Renaissance."

20 Bell, "Clarke Runs His Campaign Like He Lives, from the Heart."

21 Christian, "Clarke Has Done His Neighborhood Proud."

22 Gray, "Clarke Is Challenging Rep. Kilpatrick."

23 Kathleen Gray, "Tough Past Fueled Clarke's Victory," 5 August 2010, *Detroit Free Press*: A10.

24 Gray, "Tough Past Fueled Clarke's Victory."

25 "*Free Press* Endorsements," 1 August 2010, *Detroit Free Press*: A26; Kathleen Gray, "Clarke: 'I Have the Chance To Make Real Changes,'" 5 August 2010, *Detroit Free Press*: A1; Kathleen Gray, "Clarke Upsets Kilpatrick as Family Dynasty Ends," 4 August 2010, *Detroit Free Press*: A4.

26 Office of the Clerk, U.S. House of Representatives, "Election Statistics, 1920 to Present," http://history.house.gov/Institution/Election-Statistics/Election-Statistics/. Clarke won 100,885 out of 127,076 votes. Four other candidates took a combined two percent of the overall vote.

27 Chafets, "Rep. Hansen Clarke and Detroit's New Renaissance."

28 Todd Spangler, "Clarke Is Ready to Start Helping State," 6 January 2011, *Detroit Free Press*: A11.

29 Todd Spangler, "Mr. Clarke Goes to Washington," 21 November 2010, *Detroit Free Press*: A25.

30 Todd Spangler, "Michigan Has Power Drain in Congress," 8 August 2010, *Detroit Free Press*: A20.

31 Chafets, "Rep. Hansen Clarke and Detroit's New Renaissance."

32 Todd Spangler, "U.S. Rep.'s Long-Shot Plan To Fix Detroit," 28 September 2011, *Detroit Free Press*: A1.

33 *Congressional Record*, House, 112th Cong., 2nd sess. (29 March 2012): H1796; *Congressional Record*, House, 112th Cong., 1st sess. (19 July 2011): H5162; *Congressional Record*, House, 112th Cong., 2nd sess. (11 December 2012): H6686–6687.

34 "Michigan US Reps. Benishek, Clarke Going on the Road," 25 July 2011, Associated Press.

35 Kathleen Gray, "Redrawn Maps Create Uncertainty For State Dems," 21 August 2011, *Detroit Free Press*: A10; Kathleen Gray, "Clarke to Run in New 14th; Conyers Weighing Options," 23 August 2011, *Detroit Free Press*: A3; Kathleen Gray, "Peters Ahead of Clarke in Cash As Costly Race Looms," 18 October 2011, *Detroit Free Press*: A3; Kathleen Gray, "Competitive Races Form In New Districts," 17 April 2012, *Detroit Free Press*: A5.

36 First quotation from Kathleen Gray, "Clarke Out of Debates, Alleges 'Racist Rhetoric.'" Second quotation from Kathleen Gray, "Clarke Gains An Endorsement, Criticizes Attacks," 4 July 2012, *Detroit Free Press*: A3. See also Kathleen Gray, "5 Candidates Find Common Ground," 2 July 2012, *Detroit Free Press*: A3.

37 Kathleen Gray, "Conyers, Peters on Way to Big Victories, Latest Poll Shows," 3 August 2012, *Detroit Free Press*: n.p.; Kathleen Gray, "Campaigns Down to Wire—And Getting Downright Nasty," 6

August 2012, *Detroit Free Press*: n.p.; Kathleen Gray, "Conyers And Peters on Track Back to U.S. House," 8 August 2012, *Detroit Free Press*: n.p.

38 Kathleen Gray, "Michigan Has No Shortage of Candidates For Upcoming Tough Congressional Races," 23 April 2014, *Detroit Free Press*: A4; Kathleen Gray, "Familiar Faces Fill Race For Zigzagging 14th District," 26 June 2014, *Detroit Free Press*: A4.

39 Kathleen Gray, "Clarke Surges Ahead in 14th District House Race," 16 July 2014, *Detroit Free Press*: A6.

40 Kathleen Gray, "Money, Endorsements, Voter Outreach Key as Race Reaches Final Days," 31 July 2014, *Detroit Free Press*: A9; Kathleen Gray, "Hobbs, Lawrence In Tough U.S. House Battle," 6 August 2014, *Detroit Free Press*: A10.

41 Kathleen Gray and Todd Spangler, "Primary Victors Facing Big Tests," 7 August 2014, *Detroit Free Press*: A1.

Mark Takai
1967–2016

UNITED STATES REPRESENTATIVE 2015–2016

DEMOCRAT FROM HAWAII

I mmediately after finishing graduate school, Mark Takai dedicated himself to public service. He served the state of Hawaii for the rest of his life, first in the state house of representatives and then in Congress. During his legislative career, Takai drew on his experiences as a college athlete, small-business owner, and Iraq War veteran. He consistently stressed "putting Hawaii and its people first." His political career ended abruptly when he was diagnosed with cancer, and he announced that he would not seek re-election barely a year into his first term in the U.S. House of Representatives. After his death, Hawaii's governor, David Ige, eulogized his longtime friend: "Mark humbly and effectively served the people of his state House and Congressional districts. In the often tumultuous world of politics, he has been a shining example of what it means to be a public servant."[1]

Kyle Mark Takai was born on July 1, 1967, in Honolulu, Hawaii, to Erik, an electrical engineer, and Naomi Takai, a public servant in the city and county of Honolulu. Mark, his brother, and two sisters grew up in suburban Honolulu. In 1985 Takai graduated from Pearl City High School in Pearl City, Hawaii, and then attended the University of Hawaii in Manoa, Hawaii, where he was editor-in-chief of the school newspaper, student body president, and a champion swimmer.[2] He graduated with a bachelor's degree in political science in 1990 and earned a master's in public health in 1993. Takai met his future wife, Sami Aya, while attending college, and they married soon after graduation and had two children, Matthew and Kaila. Mark and Sami ran a small insurance brokerage and consulting firm from their home in Hawaii.[3]

Takai began a lengthy career in politics in 1994, winning election to the Hawaii house of representatives from the Aiea region in western Honolulu County. He vigorously defended funding for state schools and his

alma mater, the University of Hawaii, proposing a fund to match public donations with state money to maintain the school's sports programs. He also procured funding for the university's library and labs.[4] Takai's decision in 1999 to join the Hawaii Army National Guard reinforced his support for veterans' issues. He introduced legislation creating the Hawaii Medal of Honor—the first of its kind in the nation—to salute the state's fallen soldiers and their families. He also supported the creation of the Veterans Treatment Court, which pooled the resources of the state courts and federal veterans' affairs services to offer better access to treatment and counseling for veterans seeking employment and health care.[5]

As a member of the National Guard, Takai was twice called to active duty for six-month periods. He remained in Hawaii in an administrative capacity as the deputy state surgeon in 2005 and then deployed to Iraq as a preventive medical officer in 2009. He retained his seat in the state legislature during both activations and relied primarily on David Ige, then a state senator, to help cover his legislative duties.[6] He returned from deployment to serve as vice speaker from 2005 to 2006. From 2012 to 2013, Takai served as president of the Hawaii National Guard Association and was instrumental in bringing the national conference to Hawaii in 2013.[7] By 2015 he had attained the rank of a lieutenant colonel.

The opportunity for Takai's congressional candidacy arose when Colleen Hanabusa vacated her House seat representing urban Oahu to run for the U.S. Senate. Takai entered a Democratic primary field that included six other candidates, among them state senate president Donna Mercado Kim. Takai won a 43 percent plurality in the October primary.[8] He faced former Representative Charles Djou in the general election. Both candidates touted their military service, but the campaign largely boiled down to

fundamental differences in political philosophy about the size of the government. Takai also stressed the importance of a united Hawaiian delegation.[9] Takai received the endorsement of the *Honolulu Star-Advertiser*, which provided him with a boost in an unusually close campaign for the Democratic stronghold. Takai prevailed, winning 52 percent of the vote.[10]

Coming out of that tight race, Takai displayed optimism for bipartisanship in the weeks before the Opening Day of the 114th Congress (2015–2017). "I do believe we have a window of opportunity to bring everybody together to deliver for this nation," he said, "and I want to be part of that."[11] He focused much of his attention on his committee assignments, Armed Services and Small Business. He prioritized small businesses, protecting the environment, reforming student loan debt, and improving veterans' care. His first proposed legislation would have made it easier for Filipino veterans of World War II to reunite with their families living in the United States.[12]

In November 2015, Takai announced he had been diagnosed with pancreatic cancer. The following May, Takai shared that the cancer had spread despite treatment and that he had decided not to seek re-election. "In life, we often make plans for ourselves," he observed. "I had envisioned a long career in the U.S. House of Representatives, building up the seniority and influence that were key to Sen. (Daniel) Inouye's ability to deliver for Hawaii. But as often happens, we find ourselves on a different journey than what we had planned."[13] Mark Takai died on July 20, 2016, at his home in Honolulu.

NOTES

1 Kevin Dayton, "U.S. Rep. Mark Takai Dies after Battle with Pancreatic Cancer," 20 July 2016, *Honolulu Star-Advertiser*, http://www.staradvertiser.com/breaking-news/u-s-rep-mark-takai-dies-after-battle-with-pancreatic-cancer/ (accessed 22 July 2016).

2 Emily Langer, "Hawaii Democrat Was in His First Term in House," 21 July 2016, *Washington Post*: B6; "Mark Takai, Congressman from Hawaii, Dies at 49," 23 July 2016, *New York Times*: D6; Kevin Dayton and Sophie Cocke, "Takai Leaves 'Legacy of Courage, of Service, and of Hope,'" 21 July 2016, *Honolulu Star-Advertiser*,

http://www.staradvertiser.com/hawaii-news/takai-leaves-legacy-of-courage-of-service-and-of-hope/ (accessed 22 July 2016).

3 Langer, "Hawaii Democrat Was in His First Term in House."

4 Fred Lewis, "K. Mark Takai: Forever a Rainbow," 21 July 2016, *Honolulu Star-Advertiser*, http://www.staradvertiser.com/sports/k-mark-takai-forever-a-rainbow/ (accessed 22 July 2016).

5 Langer, "Hawaii Democrat Was in His First Term in House"; Mark Niesse, "Isle Veterans Court Sought," 25 April 2010, *Honolulu Advertiser*, http://the.honoluluadvertiser.com/article/2010/Apr/25/ln/hawaii4250370.html (accessed 2 August 2016); *Almanac of American Politics, 2016* (Columbia Books & Information Services, 2015): 564.

6 "Hawaii Rep. Takai to be Deployed to Kuwait," 19 January 2009, *Honolulu Advertiser*, http://the.honoluluadvertiser.com/article/2009/Jan/19/br/hawaii90119062.html (accessed 2 August 2016).

7 "Takai Ends Re-election Bid To Focus on Cancer Fight," June 2016, *National Guard*: 8.

8 *Almanac of American Politics, 2016*: 565.

9 B. J. Reyes, "In Televised Debate, Takai Aims to Link Djou to Tea Party," 12 October 2014, *Honolulu Star-Advertiser*, http://www.staradvertiser.com/hawaii-news/in-televised-debate-takai-aims-to-link-djou-to-tea-party/ (accessed 28 July 2014).

10 Office of the Clerk, U.S. House of Representatives, "Election Statistics, 1920 to Present," http://history.house.gov/Institution/Election-Statistics/Election-Statistics/.

11 B. J. Reyes, "Takai Heads to Washington with Hope for Bipartisan Unity," 17 November 2014, *Honolulu Star-Advertiser*, http://www.staradvertiser.com/hawaii-news/takai-heads-to-washington-with-hope-for-bipartisan-unity/ (accessed 28 July 2014).

12 Dayton and Cocke, "Takai Leaves 'Legacy of Courage, of Service, and of Hope'"; *Almanac of American Politics, 2016*: 565.

13 Dayton, "U.S. Rep. Mark Takai Dies after Battle with Pancreatic Cancer."

"I DO BELIEVE WE HAVE A
WINDOW OF OPPORTUNITY
TO BRING EVERYBODY
TOGETHER TO DELIVER
FOR THIS NATION, AND I
WANT TO BE PART OF THAT."

Mark Takai
Honolulu Star-Advertiser, January 19, 2009

★ PART TWO ★

Current Asian and Pacific Islander
American Members

★ INTRODUCTION ★
Profiles of Current Members

More than a century ago, Delegate Robert W. Wilcox of Hawaii became the first of 60 Asian Pacific Americans (APAs) to serve in the U.S. Congress.[1] The history of APAs in Congress contains many of the same themes that resonate in the larger chronicle of American democracy: a pioneering spirit, times of struggle and perseverance, the gradual attainment of power, advancement through unity, and remarkable legislative achievements.

The 18 APAs (13 Representatives, two Delegates, and three Senators) who serve in the 115th Congress (2017–2019) have inherited that long historical legacy that extends back to the first Hawaiian Delegates and Philippine Resident Commissioners. As the largest group of Asian and Pacific Islander legislators to serve simultaneously in the history of the institution, this cohort accounts for nearly one-third of all APAs who have ever held seats in Congress. The majority of these legislators first took office after 2013.

The biographical profiles of these current Members, like those of their predecessors, contain information on precongressional careers, first House or Senate campaigns, committee and leadership positions, and legislative achievements. Because these Members are incumbent, comprehensive accounts of their congressional careers must await a later date. Their profiles are arranged in two distinct groups. First, the 13 Asian Pacific Americans who have served two terms or more in Congress are arranged in alphabetical order and profiled in 750-word entries. Second, the five freshman APA Members of the 115th Congress appear at the end of this section and are profiled in résumé format entries. All current Members were given the opportunity to review their profiles before the book was published.

Among the individuals profiled in this section is Representative Robert C. (Bobby) Scott of Virginia, whose 24 years of congressional service make him the longest-serving APA among the group of current Members. Also included in this section is Mazie K. Hirono of Hawaii, who served three terms in the U.S. House of Representatives (2007–2013) and then won election to the U.S. Senate seat once held by Daniel K. Akaka. Hirono is the first Asian-American woman to serve in the Senate and one of only a handful of APAs who have served in both chambers. Since Hirono won election to the Senate, two other APA women have joined her: Tammy Duckworth of Illinois and Kamala Harris of California.

As these members leave Congress, their profiles will be updated in the online version of *Asian and Pacific Islander Americans in Congress*—available at http://history.house.gov—to reflect a more complete account of their congressional careers and their contributions to the rich history of Asian Pacific Americans in Congress.

NOTES
1   The closing date for this volume was July 1, 2017.

Image courtesy of the Member

Ami Bera
1965–

UNITED STATES REPRESENTATIVE 2013–
DEMOCRAT FROM CALIFORNIA

In 2012 Ami Bera became the third Indian American elected to Congress when he defeated a longtime incumbent. Trained as a physician, he focuses on health care legislation. "My parents emigrated here from India in the 1950s with very little but the dream of a better life," Bera said. "I grew up believing America was a land of opportunity, where if you worked hard and played by the rules, you could reach your full potential."[1]

Ami Bera was born on March 2, 1965, in Los Angeles, California. His mother was a public school teacher, and his father was an engineer and small-business owner.[2] Bera earned a bachelor of science degree in biological sciences from the University of California, Irvine, in 1987 and earned an MD degree from the same university in 1991.

Bera has been a physician for more than 25 years and practices internal medicine. He also served as the part-time medical director of care management for a seven-hospital system in the Sacramento area in the late 1990s. Bera was the chief medical officer for Sacramento County from 1999 to 2004. He also taught at the University of California, Davis, School of Medicine and served as associate dean from 2004 to 2008. Bera is married to Dr. Janine Bera, and the couple has one daughter, Sydra.

Bera made an unsuccessful attempt in 2010 to unseat Republican Congressman Dan Lungren in a close race that drew national attention.[3] In 2012 Bera challenged Lungren again in a new district that encompassed the eastern Sacramento suburbs, home to tech and health care businesses.[4] In California's new open primary, in which all candidates run in the primary and the top two vote-getters, regardless of party, compete in the general election, Bera trailed Lungren by 13 percentage points.[5] Endorsed by former President William J. (Bill) Clinton and the *Sacramento Bee*, Bera touted his long experience in health care and efforts to defend women's health and reproductive rights.[6] The race was too close to call on Election Day and remained undecided for more than a week. On November 16, 2012, Lungren conceded.[7] The final tally put Bera up with 52 percent of the vote. Bera won re-election in 2014 with a 50.4 percent majority and in 2016 with 51 percent.[8] Bera has served on the Foreign Affairs and the Science, Space, and Technology Committees in the 113th, 114th, and 115th Congresses (2013–2019).

Bera's primary legislative focus is general access to medical care. He has opposed cuts to Medicare and advocated increasing the number of doctors in the Veterans Affairs (VA) health care system, noting that veterans have waited up to two months for appointments. "Now, these are men and women who stepped up to answer the call to duty, to protect our freedoms … and we need to give them that same duty when they return," he said on the House Floor. "You have to have the necessary health care professionals that can address these needs in a timely manner."[9]

Bera introduced legislation easing immigration restrictions for doctors and medical students, expanding health savings account benefits for children under age 27, and implementing best practices and standards in VA facilities.[10] His first bill in Congress recognized National Minority Cancer Awareness Week. "Despite medical advances that save many lives in our country," he noted, "there's been limited progress in ending the racial and ethnic disparities in health."[11] He also sponsored the Dispose Responsibly of Your Pills (DROP) Act to make more disposal sites available for unwanted prescription medication.[12]

Bera has been an outspoken proponent of women's health, including protecting a woman's right to make reproductive choices. He submitted the Women's Preventive Health Awareness Campaign Act in direct response to the Pain-Capable Unborn Child Protection Act, which prohibited late-term abortion.[13] Bera's bill directed the Secretary of Health and Human Services to implement a public outreach campaign for women's preventive health.[14] He invoked his experience as a medical doctor on this issue, noting his bill was "not only smart medicine; it will get to the core of empowering patients, of empowering women and of empowering families to make the decisions that best fit within the context of their lives."[15]

Bera also sought aid to alleviate California's drought in 2014, noting that Folsom Lake, a water supply for many of his constituents, had nearly emptied.[16] He opposed a bill seeking to divert water to southern California by repealing environmental regulations protecting fish runs. He noted that the drought could not pit sections of the state against each other and supported later legislation that balanced long- and short-term drought solutions.[17]

NOTES

1 "Ami Bera Sworn into 113th Congress," 3 January 2013, States News Service.

2 *Congressional Record*, House, 113th Cong., 1st sess. (20 March 2013): H1711.

3 *Almanac of American Politics, 2014* (Washington, DC: National Journal Inc., 2013): 157.

4 *Politics in America, 2014* (Washington, DC: Congressional Quarterly Inc., 2013): 84; *Almanac of American Politics, 2014*: 156.

5 Torey Van Oot, "Lungren-Bera Rematch Part of Democratic Effort to Retake House," 9 June 2012, *Sacramento Bee*: A3.

6 *Almanac of American Politics, 2014*: 157; Laurel Rosenhall, "Capitol Alert: Bill Clinton Stumps for California Dems in Tight Congressional Races," 9 October 2012, *Sacramento Bee*: n.p.; Torey Van Oot, "Capitol Alert: Ami Bera Puts Focus on Women's Health Issues in Final Stretch," 30 October 2012, *Sacramento Bee*: n.p.

7 "Rep. Lungren Concedes Defeat in Calif.," 17 November 2012, United Press International.

8 Office of the Clerk, U.S. House of Representatives, "Election Statistics, 1920 to Present," http://history.house.gov/Institution/Election-Statistics/Election-Statistics/.

9 *Congressional Record*, House, 113th Cong., 2nd sess. (25 July 2015): H6849.

10 H.R. 2484, 113th Cong. (2013); H.R. 4951, 113th Cong. (2014); H.R. 1272, 114th Cong. (2015); H.R. 5465, 113th Cong. (2014); H.R. 3951, 114th Cong. (2015).

11 Remarks made in recognition of National Minority Health Month, see *Congressional Record*, House, 113th Cong., 1st sess. (25 April 2013): H2313; for the designation of National Minority Cancer Awareness Week, see H. Res. 154, 113th Cong. (2013).

12 H.R. 2463, 114th Cong. (2015).

13 H.R. 2457, 113th Cong. (2013). The Pain-Capable Unborn Child Act was submitted as H.R. 1797, 113th Cong. (2013) and H.R. 36, 114th Cong. (2015).

14 H.R. 2457, 113th Cong. (2013); H.R. 2355, 114th Cong. (2015).

15 *Congressional Record*, House, 113th Cong., 1st sess. (18 June 2013): H3691.

16 *Congressional Record*, House, 113th Cong., 2nd sess. (5 February 2014): H1621.

17 *Congressional Record*, House, 113th Cong., 2nd sess. (4 February 2014): H1552.

Judy Chu
1953–

UNITED STATES REPRESENTATIVE 2009–
DEMOCRAT FROM CALIFORNIA

Image courtesy of the Member

The first Chinese-American woman elected to Congress in history, Judy Chu has been a cross-ethnic coalition builder throughout her career.

Judy Chu was born in Los Angeles, California, on July 7, 1953, to Judson and May Chu. Her father, a second-generation Chinese American, was a radio technician, and her mother, a war bride from China, worked in a cannery and as a stay-at-home mom.[1] Chu grew up in a predominantly African-American neighborhood in south Los Angeles.[2] She graduated from Buchser High School in Santa Clara, California, in 1970.

Chu earned a BA in mathematics from the University of California, Los Angeles (UCLA), in 1974, an MA degree in 1977, and a PhD degree in 1979 from the California School of Professional Psychology, Los Angeles. She was a faculty member of UCLA's Asian American Studies Center before becoming a professor of psychology at East Los Angeles College in 1988. Chu is married to Michael Eng, a lawyer and elected official.

Chu entered politics to oppose an "English-only" anti-immigrant movement in Monterey Park in the 1980s.[3] She was elected to the Garvey School Board of Education in 1985. In 1988 she won election to the Monterey Park City Council and served as mayor three times during her 13-year tenure. Chu won a California state assembly seat in 2001, earning a reputation for bridging ethnic lines.[4] In 2006 Chu won a seat on the California Board of Equalization, the state's elected tax authority.

In February 2009, Congresswoman Hilda Solis resigned from the House of Representatives to serve as President Barack Obama's Secretary of Labor. Her district encompassed the eastern edge of Los Angeles with a majority-Hispanic, working-class electorate that was nearly two-fifths foreign born.[5]

After announcing her candidacy, Chu faced 11 opponents in the open primary. With key endorsements from the local Democratic Party and Los Angeles Mayor Antonio Villaraigosa, Chu won a 32 percent plurality. She won the general election in July 2009 with 62 percent.[6] In 2010 she was re-elected with a 71 percent majority. After reapportionment reshaped her district, Chu was re-elected in the next three general elections with 64, 59, and 67 percent of the vote.[7]

Chu was sworn in to the 111th Congress (2009–2011) on July 16, 2009. She served on the Education and Labor, Judiciary, and Oversight and Government Reform Committees. In the 112th Congress (2011–2013), she remained on the Judiciary Committee and picked up a seat on the Small Business Committee. Chu was also elected to chair the Congressional Asian Pacific American Caucus starting in the 112th Congress.[8] In the 115th Congress (2017–2019), Chu earned a seat on the prestigious Ways and Means Committee.

One of Chu's first priorities was a congressional resolution of regret for the Chinese Exclusion Act of 1882. In 2012 Chu succeeded: both the House and Senate unanimously passed a resolution to "acknowledge the injustice of the Chinese Exclusion Act, express regret for the lives it destroyed, and make sure that the prejudice that stained our Nation is never repeated again."[9]

Chu has championed greater protections for the San Gabriel Mountains. In June 2014, she introduced the San Gabriel National Recreation Area Act (H.R. 4858) to declare large portions of the mountains a national recreation area. She followed that bill with a request for President Obama to take executive action. In October 2014, President Obama responded by declaring much of the area a national monument. She introduced subsequent bills to further expand the national monument designation.

As Ranking Member of the Subcommittee on Access to Capital, Chu worked to help entrepreneurs. Chu's bill, the Commercial Real Estate and Economic Development Act (H.R. 2266), passed in 2015. The legislation reintroduced the Small Business Administration's Section 504 refinancing to help small businesses refinance old, expensive real estate debt at current low interest rates.

In 2011 Chu's nephew committed suicide after being hazed while serving with the Marines in Afghanistan.[10] In 2016 she successfully included language into the 2017 National Defense Authorization Act that requires improved anti-hazing reporting and policies.

As the representative of a large immigrant and minority constituency, Chu brought national attention to the need for comprehensive immigration reform. In the 113th Congress (2013–2015), Chu was one of the five original House cosponsors of H.R. 15, a comprehensive immigration reform bill. Despite the bill's bipartisan support in the House and Senate, the Speaker would not bring it to the floor for a vote. However, Chu has continued her efforts to bring about immigration reform.

NOTES

1 "Judy Chu," in Don T. Nakanishi and Ellen D. Wu eds., *Distinguished Asian American Political and Governmental Leaders* (Westport, CT: Greenwood Press, 2002): 39; *Politics in America, 2012* (Washington, DC: Congressional Quarterly Inc., 2011): 127.

2 "Judy Chu," in Nakanishi and Wu eds., *Distinguished Asian American Political and Governmental Leaders*: 39; Jean Merl, "Judy Chu's Victory Makes History," 16 July 2009, *Los Angeles Times*: A3.

3 *Politics in America, 2012*: 126.

4 Richard Winton, "Chu is Known as a Bridge Builder," 18 May 2001, *Los Angeles Times*: 4; Stephanie Chavez, "Assemblywoman Praised for Reaching Across Ethnic Divide," 1 July 2001, *Los Angeles Times*: 3.

5 *Politics in America, 2012*: 126.

6 Evelyn Larrubia, "Big Names in Race to Replace Solis," 23 December 2008, *Los Angeles Times*: 3; Jean Merl, "Party Endorses Chu," 19 April 2009, *Los Angeles Times*: A36; Jean Merl, "Endorsements May Sway Key Latino Base," 17 May 2009, *Los Angeles Times*: A38; Josh Kurtz, "Chu Tops Field in Special Election to Replace Solis," 20 May 2009, *Roll Call*: n.p.; Carla Hall, "32nd Congressional District; Two Chus Are Among Choices," 21 May 2009, *Los Angeles Times*: 12; Rebecca Kimitch, "Judy Chu Wins 32nd Congressional District Race," 15 July 2009, *San Gabriel Valley Tribune* (CA): n.p.

7 *Almanac of American Politics, 2014* (Washington, DC: National Journal Inc., 2013): 216. Office of the Clerk, U.S. House of Representatives, "Election Statistics, 1920 to Present," http://history.house.gov/Institution/Election-Statistics/Election-Statistics/.

8 Rebecca Kimitch, "Judy Chu Off to Washington after Election Win," 15 July 2009, *Pasadena Star-News*: n.p.; Garrison Nelson and Charles Stewart III, *Committees in the U.S. Congress, 1993–2010* (Washington, DC: Congressional Quarterly Press, 2011): 636; *Congressional Directory*, various editions.

9 H. Res. 683, 112th Cong. (2012); *Congressional Record*, House, 112th Cong., 1st sess. (1 June 2011): H3810.

10 Sarah D. Wire, "Rep. Judy Chu's Nephew Took His Own Life After Military Hazing; Now She's Seeking Justice for Him and Other Families," 10 May 2016, *Los Angeles Times*, http://www.latimes.com/politics/la-pol-ca-chu-military-hazing-20160510-snap-story.html (accessed 21 June 2017).

Image courtesy of the Member

Tammy Duckworth
1968–

UNITED STATES REPRESENTATIVE 2013–2017
UNITED STATES SENATOR 2017–
DEMOCRAT FROM ILLINOIS

Senator Tammy Duckworth is an Iraq War veteran, Purple Heart recipient, and former Assistant Secretary of the Department of Veterans Affairs (VA). She was among the first Army women to fly combat missions during Operation Iraqi Freedom. Duckworth served in the Reserve Forces for 23 years before retiring from military service in 2014 at the rank of lieutenant colonel. She was elected to the U.S. Senate in 2016 after representing Illinois's Eighth Congressional District in the U.S. House of Representatives for two terms.[1]

Duckworth earned a bachelor's degree in political science from the University of Hawaii and a Master of Arts in international affairs from George Washington University. Following graduation, Duckworth moved to Illinois to pursue a PhD in political science at Northern Illinois University. She worked at NIU's School of Nursing, researching public health and environmental causes of cancer and later worked for Rotary International.

In 2004 Duckworth was deployed to Iraq as a Black Hawk helicopter pilot for the Illinois Army National Guard. On November 12, 2004, her helicopter was hit by a rocket-propelled grenade, and Duckworth lost her legs and partial use of her right arm.

Duckworth spent the next year recovering at Walter Reed Army Medical Center, where she quickly became an advocate for her fellow soldiers and testified before Congress about caring for veterans and wounded warriors. Following her recovery, she became director of the Illinois Department of Veterans Affairs. She worked to create a tax credit for employers who hired veterans, establish a first-in-the-nation 24/7 veterans' crisis hotline, and develop innovative programs to improve veterans' access to housing and health care.

In 2009 President Barack Obama named Duckworth as Assistant Secretary of Veterans Affairs. In that role, Duckworth coordinated a joint initiative with the U.S. Department of Housing and Urban Development to end veteran homelessness. She also created the Office of Online Communications to improve the VA's accessibility and worked to address the unique challenges that Native American and female veterans face.

Since her recovery, Duckworth has resumed flying as a civilian pilot and fulfilled a promise she made at Walter Reed by completing several marathons. In her spare time, she volunteers at local food pantries and enjoys couponing and flea markets. In 2015 Duckworth completed her PhD in human services at Capella University.

In the House, Duckworth advocated for working families and job creation, introducing bills such as the Friendly Airports for Mothers Act to ensure new mothers have access to safe and clean lactation rooms in airports, which passed the Senate with bipartisan support. She introduced the In the Red Act to reduce student debt, the Get the Lead Out Act to keep America's drinking water safe, and bipartisan legislation to help close the skills gap and help people find good-paying jobs. Duckworth also co-sponsored the No Budget, No Pay Act, which would ensure members of Congress get paid only if they pass a budget.

She served on the House Armed Services Committee and the House Oversight and Government Reform Committee, where she was Ranking Member of the Transportation and Public Assets Subcommittee. She introduced and helped pass several important policies on these committees, including the Clay Hunt Suicide Prevention for American Veterans Act to help reduce suicide among veterans and improve VA mental health services and the Troop Talent Act, which helps returning veterans find jobs in the private sector. She also cut waste and fraud at the Pentagon and throughout government, including passing a common-sense provision to reduce redundancy in armed forces uniforms that the nonpartisan U.S. Government Accountability Office found will save taxpayers more than $4 billion over five years.

In the Senate, Duckworth serves on several committees that give her an important platform to advocate for Illinois's working families and entrepreneurs: Environment and Public Works; Energy and Natural Resources; Commerce, Science, and Transportation; and Small Business and Entrepreneurship. As Senator, she advocates for practical, common-sense solutions needed to move the country forward such as rebuilding crumbling infrastructure, keeping water systems safe and lead-free, growing manufacturing jobs while supporting minority-owned small businesses, investing in communities that have been ignored, and making college more affordable. Duckworth continues her lifelong mission to support and protect veterans while ensuring America stands fully behind the troops its sends into danger overseas.

Duckworth lives in Hoffman Estates with her husband, Bryan, an Army cyber warrant officer, and their daughter Abigail.

NOTES

1   "About Tammy," on Senator Tammy Duckworth's official website, accessed June 1, 2017, https://www.duckworth.senate.gov/content/about-tammy.

Image courtesy of the Member

Tulsi Gabbard
1981–

UNITED STATES REPRESENTATIVE 2013–
DEMOCRAT FROM HAWAII

As one of the first female combat veterans elected to Congress, Tulsi Gabbard entered the U.S. House of Representatives with a high profile that quickly earned her prominent committee and party positions. Gabbard developed a reputation for reaching across the aisle and advocating for military servicemembers and veterans. "People at home don't care whether you've got a D or R in front of your name," she said. "They want you to get things done."[1]

Tulsi Gabbard was born in American Samoa on April 12, 1981, the daughter of teachers and entrepreneurs, Mike and Carol Gabbard. As a teenager, she cofounded with her father the Healthy Hawai'i Coalition, a nonprofit organization focused on educating children about clean water and protecting Hawaii's environment.[2] In 2002, at age 21, Gabbard became the youngest woman elected to the Hawaii house of representatives.[3]

Gabbard enlisted in the Hawaii Army National Guard in April 2003.[4] Although she was not on the mandatory deployment roster, Gabbard left her re-election campaign and volunteered to deploy to Iraq with her unit, the 29th Infantry Brigade Combat Team, so she could stand alongside her fellow soldiers. She served a 12-month tour at Logistical Support Area Anaconda in Iraq, working in a field medical unit.

After returning from her deployment, Gabbard rejoined her nonprofit and led an investigation into beach pollution.[5] In 2006 U.S. Senator Daniel K. Akaka's office hired her as a legislative aide. She completed Officer Candidate School at the Lyman Ward Military Academy in Alabama in 2007, becoming the first woman to earn the distinguished honor graduate title in the academy's 50-year history. In 2009 Gabbard again voluntarily deployed with her unit to Kuwait, where she served as a military police platoon leader and trainer for the Kuwait National Guard's counterterrorism unit.

In that same year, Gabbard completed a bachelor's degree in international business through Hawaii Pacific University. In 2010 she was elected to the Honolulu city council, where she served as chair of safety and government affairs and vice chairman of budget.[6]

In May 2011, Gabbard announced her candidacy for Hawaii's 2nd Congressional District that encompassed suburban and rural Oahu and all the neighboring islands. She entered a six-person Democratic primary race led by former Honolulu Mayor Mufi F. Hannemann. Gabbard attracted support from progressive and environmental organizations.[7] She won the primary by more than

20 percent.[8] She highlighted President Barack Obama's support for veterans during a prominent slot at the 2012 Democratic National Convention.[9] Gabbard cruised to victory against Republican opponent Kawika Crowley, garnering 79 percent of the vote.[10]

The 113th Congress (2013–2015) featured a record number of Congresswomen. Gabbard stood out as one of the first female combat veterans elected to Congress and as the first practicing Hindu elected to Congress. She chose to take her oath of office on the *Bhagavad-Gita As It Is*.[11] Democratic leadership chose Gabbard as vice chair of the Democratic National Committee. She also obtained assignments to three committees: Armed Services, Homeland Security, and Foreign Affairs. In the 113th Congress, she left Homeland Security to serve on the Armed Services Committee, reflecting her own military service and the large military presence in her district.

In her first term, Gabbard introduced the Helping Heroes Fly Act (H.R. 1344) to improve the treatment of severely injured and disabled veterans going through airport security. She noted the everyday hardship this caused and stressed "the difference between a smooth and dignified screening experience or one that is filled with frustration, shame, and pain" was important, especially for injured veterans. President Obama signed the bill into law in 2013.[12]

She joined the bipartisan outcry against "deep and systemic issues" in the Department of Veterans Affairs, requesting an executive order allowing veterans to use their veteran IDs to get private medical care.[13] She also called for reforms to how the military handles sexual assault cases, claiming legislation would "stem the growing cancer of sexual assault on men and women in the military."[14]

Gabbard ran unopposed in the August 2014 primary. She again defeated the GOP challenger, Crowley, with roughly 79 percent of the vote. In the 2016 general election, Gabbard won with 76 percent of the vote. In April 2015, Gabbard married cinematographer Abraham Williams.[15]

Echoing her opposition to the Iraq War and the overthrow of Libya's Muammar Gaddafi in 2011, Gabbard has strongly opposed U.S. military action to overthrow Syrian President Bashar al-Assad in the Syrian civil war. In her second term, she introduced H.R. 4108 to prohibit the use of U.S. funds for the provision of assistance to Syrian opposition groups and individuals with that aim.[16]

NOTES

1   John Powers, "Making a Splash: Is Tulsi Gabbard the Next Democratic Party Star?" 25 June 2013, *Vogue*, http://www.vogue.com/865223/making-a-splash-is-tulsi-gabbard-the-next-democratic-party-star/ (accessed 29 February 2016).

2   Lynda Arakawa, "State's Political Balance Shifting in Legislature," 6 November 2002, *Honolulu Advertiser*: 1A.

3   Kevin Dayton, "Lingle Spent $5.4M to Win Governor's Race," 6 December 2002, *Honolulu Advertiser*: 1B.

4   Espanol Zenaida Serrano, "State Legislator 'Honored' to Serve," 20 April 2003, *Honolulu Advertiser*: 25A.

5   Eloise Aguiar, "Sand Clean at 4 Sites, Test Finds," 22 April 2006, *Honolulu Advertiser*: 1B.

6   Rob Shikina, "Medical Waste Continues to Wash Up at West Oahu Beaches," 16 January 2011, *Honolulu Star-Advertiser*: n.p.

7   B. J. Reyes, "Governor's Wife, Other Women Back Gabbard," 15 April 2012, *Honolulu Star-Advertiser*: n.p.; B. J. Reyes, "Democratic Primary Will Likely Determine House Race," 25 June 2012, *Honolulu Star-Advertiser*: n.p.

8   Gordon Pang, "Gabbard Upsets Hannemann," 11 August 2012, *Honolulu Star-Advertiser*: n.p.

9   "Gabbard at Dem Convention: Obama Best for Vets," 5 September 2012, *Associated Press*.

10 Office of the Clerk, U.S. House of Representatives, "Election Statistics, 1920 to Present," http://history.house.gov/Institution/Election-Statistics/Election-Statistics/.

11 Matthew Brown, "Tulsi Gabbard, First Hindu in Congress, to Take Oath over the Bhagavad Gita," 12 November 2012, *Deseret Morning News*: n.p.

12 *Congressional Record*, House, 113th Cong., 1st sess. (21 May 2013): H2819–2825; Helping Heroes Fly Act, Public Law 113-27, 127 Stat. 503 (2013).

13 Chris D'Angelo, "Vets 'We Have to Do Better'; Congresswoman Gabbard Says Veterans Deserve Immediate Care," 3 June 2014, *The Garden Island*: n.p.; Janis L. Magin, "Hawaii Veterans Have Longest Waits for Appointments as New Patients," 9 June 2014, *Pacific Business News*: n.p.

14 Stewart Powell, "Military Sexual-Assault Bills Compete; Senators' Vote on 2 Measures Approaching," 6 March 2014, *San Antonio Express-News*: A7.

15 Emmarie Huetteman, "Tulsi Gabbard, Rising Democratic Star From Hawaii, Makes Mark on Party by Defying It," 28 November 2015, *New York Times*, http://www.nytimes.com/2015/11/29/us/politics/tulsi-gabbard-rising-democratic-star-from-hawaii-makes-mark-on-party-by-defying-it.html (accessed 29 February 2016); Helena Andrews-Dyer, "Tulsi Gabbard's Getting Married Today," 9 April 2015, *Washington Post*: n.p.; Office of the Clerk, U.S. House of Representatives, "Election Statistics, 1920 to Present."

16 See Congresswoman Tulsi Gabbard, "Reps. Tulsi Gabbard, Austria, Scott Introduce Legislation to End Illegal War to Overthrow Syrian Government of Assad," press release, 19 November 2015, http://gabbard.house.gov/index.php/press-releases/520-reps-tulsi-gabbard-austin-scott-introduce-legislation-to-end-illegal-u-s-war-to-overthrow-syrian-government-of-assad.

Image courtesy of the Member

Colleen Hanabusa
1951–

UNITED STATES REPRESENTATIVE 2011–2015; 2016–
DEMOCRAT FROM HAWAII

A prominent Hawaiian Democrat and labor lawyer, Colleen Hanabusa worked her way to the forefront of Democratic politics in the state through 12 years in the Hawaii senate. Hanabusa first won election to the U.S. House of Representatives in 2010 and returned in a 2016 special election following the death of Representative Mark Takai.

Colleen Hanabusa was born on May 4, 1951, in Honolulu, Hawaii, to June and Isao Hanabusa, gas station proprietors in Waianae.[1] She graduated from Honolulu's St. Andrew's Priory School in 1969, before attending the University of Hawaii in Manoa. There she earned bachelor's degrees in economics and sociology in 1973, a master's degree in sociology in 1975, and a law degree in 1977. Hanabusa spent 20 years in private practice. Her rising profile as a labor lawyer led to a successful campaign for a state senate seat in 1998. She served as president of the senate from 2007 until 2010 and was the first woman to lead either chamber of the Hawaiian legislature.[2]

Hanabusa first ran for national office in a 2003 House of Representatives special election, when she lost the Democratic nomination for an open seat in the 2nd District, centered on downtown Honolulu. She then competed for the same House seat in 2006 but again lost in the Democratic primary.[3] In May 2010, Hanabusa ran in the 1st District race to fill the vacancy caused by the resignation of Representative Neil Abercrombie. In a winner-take-all special election, conducted solely by mail-in ballots, with no primary and no runoff, Hanabusa faced Republican candidate Charles Djou and former Democratic Representative Ed Case. Hanabusa and Case split the Democratic vote, while Honolulu city councilman Djou garnered a winning plurality of 39 percent.[4]

In the 2010 general election rematch months later, the competition between the Djou and Hanabusa campaigns intensified. Hanabusa capitalized on a late endorsement from Case and strong get-out-the-vote efforts to win 53 percent of the vote. The election marked the first ousting of an incumbent Representative in Hawaiian history.[5] Hanabusa's success stood out among the tide of Republican midterm victories.

Hanabusa took office in the 112th Congress (2011–2013) and joined the Armed Services and Natural Resources Committees. Operating in the minority, Hanabusa focused on supporting Hawaiian labor and infrastructure. She worked alongside Senator Daniel K. Inouye in the 112th Congress to direct grants to Hawaiian veterans and testified before the Budget Committee in favor of federal funding for the East-West Center and the Pacific Tsunami Warning Center.[6] Hanabusa advocated for passage of the Native American Housing Assistance and Self-Determination Reauthorization Act (NAHASDA) of 2014. Though the bill (H.R. 4277) passed by voice vote in the House, it did not clear the Senate. She also made regular floor speeches in defense of President Barack Obama and his signature Patient Protection and Affordable Care Act of 2010.

Hanabusa bested Djou again in 2012, winning 54 percent of the vote.[7] A month later, Senator Inouye succumbed to respiratory complications. Senator Inouye's staff insisted he had handpicked Hanabusa as his successor, sending a letter to Governor Abercrombie making this wish known. But Abercrombie appointed Lieutenant Governor Brian Schatz to fill Inouye's remaining term. Hanabusa stated that she respected "the process and the governor's right to choose a successor" but hinted she would run against Schatz in the next election.[8]

At the beginning of the 113th Congress (2013–2015), Hanabusa positioned herself as a successor to the legislative interests of Inouye and fellow Senator Daniel K. Akaka. She re-introduced Senator Akaka's bill for Native-Hawaiian self-government.[9] While Hanabusa increased her congressional profile, she narrowly lost the August primary by 1,769 votes, but a dangerous tropical storm delayed the vote in two precincts and led to a protracted count process.[10] Though Hanabusa originally requested a further delay to recover from the storm, she decided not to challenge the election results a week later.[11]

At the end of her term in the House, Hanabusa returned to Honolulu to resume practicing law.[12] In 2016, when Congressman Mark Takai announced he would not seek re-election (and subsequently lost his battle with cancer), Hanabusa announced her candidacy for the open seat.[13] On Election Day, Hanabusa won both the general election to the 115th Congress (2017–2019) with 68 percent of the vote, as well as the special election to the remainder of the 114th Congress (2015–2017) receiving 61 percent of the vote.[14] Hanabusa took her seat on November 14, 2016. She returned to the Armed Services and Natural Resources Committees, and joined the Committee on Science, Space, and Technology. She is also a member of the House Democratic Leadership and the Democratic Steering and Policy Committee.

NOTES

1   "Biographies—Colleen Hanabusa," 15 January 2011, *National Journal*: 18–19.

2   "Hawaii's Race for Congress," 16 April 2010, *Honolulu Advertiser*: A20.

3   "Hanabusa Takes Office as a Freshman in a Minority," 5 January 2011, *Honolulu Star Advertiser*: n.p.

4   Derrick DePledge, "Hawaii May Hold a Special Congressional Election in May," 5 January 2010, *Honolulu Advertiser*: n.p.; Stu Woo, "U.S. News: Republican Wins Hawaii Seat—Democrats Gird for Fall Rematch, Saying Special-Election Rules Aided Victory," 24 May 2010, *Wall Street Journal*: n.p.

5   B. J. Reyes, "Hanabusa Sweeps Districts," 4 November 2010, *Honolulu Star-Advertiser*: n.p.; Office of the Clerk, U.S. House of Representatives, "Election Statistics, 1920 to Present," http://history.house.gov/Institution/Election-Statistics/Election-Statistics/; Mark Niesse, "Democrat Colleen Hanabusa Wins Hawaii Race for Congress," 15 November 2010, *Asian Reporter*: n.p.

6   Hearings before the House Committee on the Budget, *Member's Day*, 112th Cong., 1st sess. (30 March 2011): 75–79.

7   Office of the Clerk, U.S. House of Representatives, "Election Statistics, 1920 to Present"; Derrick DePledge, "Hanabusa Weighs U.S. Senate Run; Rents Apartment in District," 10 June 2011, *Honolulu Star-Advertiser*: n.p.; Sean Sullivan, "The Case for Colleen Hanabusa," 18 December 2012, *Washington Post*: n.p.

8   Kyle Trygstad, "Hawaii: Abercrombie Appoints Lt. Gov. Brian Schatz to Senate," 26 December 2012, *Roll Call*: n.p.

9   U.S. Rep. Colleen Hanabusa, "Hanabusa to Work on Armed Services, Positioning for Asia-Pacific Pivot," 6 January 2013, *Honolulu Star-Advertiser*: n.p.; Richard Borreca, "In Inouye's Absence, State Loses Big Federal Projects," 7 April 2013, *Honolulu Star-Advertiser*: n.p.

10 Richard Borreca, "For Hanabusa, Last Days with Inouye Instructive," 20 April 2014, *Honolulu Star Advertiser*: n.p.

11 Maya Rhodan, "Hawaii Democratic Senate Primary Finally Ends As Rep. Colleen Hanabusa Concedes," 20 August 2014, *Time*, http://time.com/3148542/hawaii-democratic-primary-finally-ends-as-rep-colleen-hanabusa-concedes/ (accessed 27 May 2015).

12 Duane Shimogawa, "Former Hawaii Congresswoman Colleen Hanabusa Forms New Law Company," 26 May 2015, *Pacific Business News*, http://www.bizjournal.com/pacific/news2015/05/26/former-hawaii-colleen-hanabusa-forms.html (accessed 27 May 2015).

13 Cathy Bussewitz, "Former US Rep. Colleen Hanabusa Announces Congressional Run," 2 June 2016, *Washington Times*, http://www.washingtontimes.com/news/2016/jun/2/former-us-rep-colleen-hanabusa-announces-congressi/ (accessed 13 January 2017).

14 Office of the Clerk, U.S. House of Representatives, "Election Statistics, 1920 to Present."

Image courtesy of the Member

Mazie K. Hirono
1947–

UNITED STATES REPRESENTATIVE 2007–2013
UNITED STATES SENATOR 2013–
DEMOCRAT FROM HAWAII

An immigrant from Japan who came to Hawaii as a child, Mazie Hirono credits her mother's bravery for inspiring her decades-long political career. "My mother decided that she needed to get us all away so that we could have a chance at a better life; [she showed] tremendous courage and risk taking. She showed me that one person can make a difference. So my path to the U.S. Senate was a highly unlikely one, but it also points out not only how one person can make a difference, but also what a great country the United States is."[1]

Mazie Hirono was born in Fukushima, Japan, on November 3, 1947, the daughter of Laura Chie Hirono. Laura Hirono left an abusive marriage by escaping with her elder son Roy and daughter Mazie aboard a ship bound for Hawaii. The family lived in a single room in a boarding house, and, at age 10, Mazie Hirono started working to support the family.[2] Hirono became a naturalized American citizen in 1959, when Hawaii became a state. She later married Leighton Kim Oshima and has one stepchild.

After graduating from Kaimuki High School in Honolulu, she earned a psychology degree at the University of Hawaii in Manoa in 1970.[3] She became active in politics by managing several state legislative campaigns.[4] Hirono earned a juris doctorate degree from Georgetown University in Washington, DC, in 1978. She later served as deputy attorney general of Hawaii in the anti-trust division and worked in a private legal practice. In 1980 she won a seat in the Hawaii state house of representatives, serving until 1994, when she was elected lieutenant governor. Hirono lost a close race for governor in 2002.[5]

In 2006 Hirono entered the Democratic primary to succeed Representative Ed Case of Hawaii, who had announced his bid for a seat in the U.S. Senate. The district—one of two in Hawaii—included parts of Oahu outside Honolulu and the rest of the Hawaiian Islands; the constituency had a large Asian population (28 percent) and had only ever elected Democrats.[6] With wide name recognition and the backing of national women's rights organizations, Hirono campaigned on her work in education, land reform, and workers' compensation, winning the primary with 22 percent of the vote against nine other contenders.[7] In the general election, she won 61 percent of the vote. She garnered majorities of 70 percent or more in the next two elections.[8]

Joining a new Democratic majority in the 110th Congress (2007–2009), Hirono served on the Education and Labor Committee and the Transportation and Infrastructure Committee, staying with both throughout her House career.

She also served briefly on the Small Business and the Ethics Committees and the Democratic Steering and Policy Committee.[9]

In the House, Hirono introduced the Native Hawaiian Government Reorganization Act, which sought recognition for a Native-Hawaiian government, similar to those of Native Americans on the mainland.[10] The bill passed the House, but died in the Senate.[11] Hirono also pursued legislation to help low-income Native Hawaiians purchase homes.[12] She advocated for early childhood instruction, introducing the Providing Resources Early for Kids (PRE-K) Act to provide grants to states to hire more qualified educators, to buy supplies, and for nutrition funding for preschools.[13] She championed growing American tourism by introducing the bipartisan VISIT USA Act.[14]

In 2011, when Senator Daniel Akaka announced his retirement, Hirono entered the primary to succeed him, winning with 57 percent of the vote against former Representative Case.[15] Running on her efforts to protect Social Security and investments in early childhood education and alternative energy, Hirono won 62 percent of the vote in the general election against Republican Linda Lingle.[16]

Hirono received seats on the Senate Armed Services, Judiciary, and Veterans' Affairs Committees in the 113th Congress (2013–2015). As the only immigrant serving in the Senate, Hirono threw herself into drafting the Senate's 2013 comprehensive immigration reform legislation, successfully including 11 amendments and prioritizing family unity.[17]

During the 114th Congress (2015–2017), Hirono became Ranking Member on the Armed Services Committee's Seapower Subcommittee. She left the Judiciary Committee and took seats on the Intelligence, Small Business and Entrepreneurship, and Energy and Natural Resources Committee—where she served as Ranking Member on the Water and Power Subcommittee. In the 115th Congress (2017–2019), she served as Ranking Member on the National Park Subcommittee. Hirono also moved from the Select Committee on Intelligence back to the Judiciary Committee.[18]

NOTES

1 Women's Media Center, "A Personal Interview with Mazie Hirono, Hawaii's First Woman Senator," accessed 2 June 2016, http://www.womensmediacenter.com/feature/entry/a-personal-interview-with-mazie-hirono-hawaiis-first-woman-senator.

2 "Mazie K. Hirono Bio," Mazie K. Hirono's official campaign website, accessed 8 November 2006, http://mazieforcongress.com/index.cfm/preset/bio (site discontinued); *Almanac of American Politics, 2008* (Washington, DC: National Journal Inc., 2007): 511; "About Mazie," on Senator Mazie Hirono's official website, accessed 16 February 2016, https://www.hirono.senate.gov/about; *Politics in America, 2010* (Washington, DC: Congressional Quarterly Inc., 2009): 309.

3 *Politics in America, 2012* (Washington, DC: CQ-Roll Call, Inc., 2011): 297.

4 *Politics in America, 2010*: 310.

5 *Almanac of American Politics, 2008*: 511.

6 Ibid., 510–511; "It's Official: Hirono Enters Race for U.S. House," 28 April 2006, *Honolulu Advertiser*: 3B.

7 *Almanac of American Politics, 2008*: 511; Nicole Duran "Primaries in Paradise: Hirono Leads Democratic Field But No Sure Thing," 21 September 2006, *Roll Call*: n.p.

8 Office of the Clerk, U.S. House of Representatives, "Election Statistics, 1920 to Present," http://history.house.gov/Institution/Election-Statistics/Election-Statistics/.

9 *Congressional Directory*, various editions; Garrison Nelson and Charles Stewart III, *Committees in the U.S. Congress, 1993–2010* (Washington, DC: Congressional Quarterly Press, 2011): 757–758; *Congressional Record*, House, 112th Cong., 1st sess. (14 July 2011): H5050.

10 See H.R. 505, 110th Cong. (2007); *Congressional Record*, House, 111th Cong., 2nd sess. (23 February 2010): H722; *Congressional Record*, House, 110th Cong., 1st sess. (7 May 2007): H4535.

11 See H.R. 862, 111th Cong. (2009) and H.R. 1250, 112th Cong. (2011).

12 H.R. 835, 110th Cong. (2007); H.R. 2786, 110th Cong. (2007); *Congressional Record*, House, 110th Cong., 1st sess. (27 March 2007): H3166; *Congressional Record*, House, 110th Cong., 1st sess. (24 July 2007): H8310. The legislation sought to bolster previous laws setting aside land for indigenous Hawaiians—dating back to the Hawaiian Homes Commission Act of 1921.

13 *Congressional Record*, House, 110th Cong., 1st sess. (18 June 2007): H6589; H.R. 3289, 110th Cong. (2007); H.R. 2655, 110th Cong. (2007); *Politics in America, 2010*: 309.

14 H.R. 3341, 112th Cong. (2011).

15 "Hirono Announces She Will Run For Akaka's Senate Seat," 19 May 2011, *Honolulu Star-Advertiser*: n.p.; Derrick DePledge, "Case, Hirono Duke It Out" 27 July 2012, *Honolulu Star-Advertiser*: n.p.; DePledge, "Hirono Beats Case" 12 August 2012, *Honolulu Star-Advertiser*: n.p.

16 Office of the Clerk, U.S. House of Representatives, "Election Statistics, 1920 to Present."

17 "Immigration," on Senator Mazie K. Hirono's official website, accessed 16 February 2016, https://www.hirono.senate.gov/issues/immigration.

18 "About Mazie."

Image courtesy of the Member

Ted Lieu
1969–

UNITED STATES REPRESENTATIVE 2015–
DEMOCRAT FROM CALIFORNIA

Ted Lieu was already an experienced legislator when he won election to the western Los Angeles seat in the U.S. House of Representatives vacated by veteran Representative Henry Waxman. A lawyer with technical expertise who shares the immigrant experience, Lieu has made the most of his social media platforms. Upon his election to Congress, he addressed his active communications strategy, "I just give people more and more information, and try to make them look at a situation from a different view."[1]

Ted W. Lieu was born on March 29, 1969, in Taipei, Taiwan, to George and Kerry Lieu.[2] His family immigrated to suburban Cleveland, Ohio, in 1972, where they sold gifts at flea markets and saved to open a gift store. The business eventually expanded to several locations, with Ted and his siblings often helping out. Lieu graduated from St. Ignatius High School in Cleveland in 1987. He then earned bachelor's degrees in computer science and political science from Stanford University in Stanford, California, in 1991. Three years later, Lieu completed his law degree at Georgetown University in Washington, DC. From there, he went on to serve as a judge advocate general in the U.S. Air Force from 1995 to 1999. He continues to serve as a colonel in the Air Force Reserve. After leaving the service full time, Lieu moved to Torrance, California, where he practiced law and served as the city's environmental quality commissioner.[3] He and his wife, Betty, a water commissioner, have two children, Brennan and Austin.

Lieu first won elected office in 2002, serving on the city council in Torrance, California. In 2005 he won a special election to the California state assembly, where he served until he won election to the California state senate in 2010. Lieu also ran in the Democratic primary for California state attorney general but fell short against eventual winner Kamala Harris.[4] As a state senator, he led California's opposition to the Supreme Court's *Citizens United* ruling and successfully guided legislation allowing undocumented immigrants to take the state bar exam.[5]

In 2013 longtime Representative Henry Waxman announced his retirement, setting up a scramble for the reliably Democratic coastal Los Angeles district. Eighteen candidates, mostly Democrats, leaped into California's open primary. Lieu announced his candidacy in January 2014 and obtained the endorsement of both the Democratic Party and Los Angeles Mayor Eric Garcetti. As the establishment favorite, Lieu received 19 percent of the vote, second only to the leading Republican on the ballot, Los Angeles County Deputy District Attorney

Elan Carr.[6] Advancing to face Carr in the general election, Lieu received the endorsement of the *Los Angeles Times*, which cited his legislative experience as a factor in their decision.[7] Lieu cruised to victory in November, winning 59 percent of the vote.[8]

Lieu was elected president of his freshman class of Democrats for the 114th Congress (2015–2017).[9] He received assignments on the Budget Committee and Oversight and Government Reform Committee. In the 115th Congress (2017–2019), he left both committees and joined the Foreign Affairs and Judiciary Committees. He was named a Democratic Assistant Whip in 2017.[10]

In keeping with his district, which has many high-tech companies, Lieu prioritizes protection of consumer privacy, advances in cybersecurity, and solutions for climate change. Lieu pushed for better care for homeless veterans and improvements to the Veterans Affairs health care system while opposing privatization, representing pressing concerns in his district. Operating in the minority, Lieu introduced the Quarterly Financial Report Reauthorization Act (H.R. 3116) in July 2015, renewing a study conducted by the U.S. Census Bureau, which provides a crucial indicator of the economic health of various industries. The bill passed the House by voice vote and the Senate by unanimous consent, before being signed into law in October 2015.[11] Seven different legislative provisions sponsored by Lieu were signed into law during his freshman term in office.

Lieu's family and colleagues describe him as quiet and thoughtful, though he maintains an aggressive social media presence, particularly following the 2016 election. "I will not cede public discourse to anyone," he insisted, stating an obligation to speak out against anyone he viewed as peddling falsehoods on social media.[12]

Lieu won re-election to the House in 2016, winning 66 percent of the vote.[13]

NOTES

1 David Mendez, "From Council to Congress: Torrance's Ted Lieu Says He's Ready to Take On National Political Stage," 27 November 2014, *Orange County Register* (CA): n.p.

2 Sarah D. Wire, "These Californians All Have Tickets to the State of the Union Address," 12 January 2016, *Los Angeles Times*, http://www.latimes.com/politics/la-pol-ca-state-of-the-union-san-bernardino-20160112-htmlstory.html (accessed 18 May 2017).

3 "Biography," on Congressman Ted Lieu's official website, accessed 10 May 2017, https://lieu.house.gov/about/full-biography/.

4 Mendez, "From Council to Congress: Torrance's Ted Lieu Says He's Ready to Take On National Political Stage."

5 *Almanac of American Politics, 2016* (United States: Columbia Books and Information Services, 2015): 263.

6 Asher Klein, "Crowded Race to Replace Waxman in 33rd House District: Elan Carr and Ted Lieu Will Face Off," 26 June 2014, *Orange County Register* (CA): n.p.

7 Editorial, "Elections 2014; Ted Lieu for Congress," 26 September 2014, *Los Angeles Times*: A16.

8 Office of the Clerk, U.S. House of Representatives, "Election Statistics, 1920 to Present," http://history.house.gov/Institution/Election-Statistics/Election-Statistics/.

9 Mendez, "From Council to Congress: Torrance's Ted Lieu Says He's Ready to Take On National Political Stage."

10 Congressman Ted Lieu, "Rep. Lieu on Appointment as Assistant Whip," press release, 10 January 2017, accessed 18 May 2017, https://lieu.house.gov/media-center/press-releases/rep-lieu-statement-appointment-assistant-whip.

11 *Congressional Record*, House, 114th Cong., 1st sess (24 September 2015): H6198; Ted Lieu, "Congressman Lieu Statement on Passage of Quarterly Financial Report Reauthorization Act," press release, 22 July 2015, accessed 18 May 2017, https://lieu.house.gov/media-center/press-releases/congressman-lieu-statement-passage-quarterly-financial-report.

12 Karen Heller, "Ted Lieu Is Out-Tweeting Trump, and It's Making Him a Political Star," 30 March 2017, *Washington Post*, http://www.washingtonpost.com/lifestyle/style/ted-lieu-is-out-tweeting-trump-and-its-making-him-a-political-star/2017/03/30/a087d670-fec2-11e6-8ebe-6e0dbe4f2bca_story.html (accessed 10 May 2017); Steve Lopez, "Trolling the Tweeter in Chief: California Congressman Stands Up to Trump, Using the President's Favorite Weapon," 15 March 2017, *Los Angeles Times*, http://www.latimes.com/local/california/la-me-lopez-lieu-twitter-resistance-20170315-story.html (accessed 18 May 2017).

13 Office of the Clerk, U.S. House of Representatives, "Election Statistics, 1920 to Present."

Image courtesy of the Member

Doris Matsui
1944–

UNITED STATES REPRESENTATIVE 2005–
DEMOCRAT FROM CALIFORNIA

Congresswoman Doris Matsui has represented a diverse, urban, and growing district in Sacramento, California, since 2005. In more than a decade in the U.S. House of Representatives, she has gained a reputation as a savvy, pragmatic legislator invested in working with colleagues on a bipartisan basis. Now a senior member of the Energy and Commerce Committee, she has won legislative achievements in health care reform and mental health care, expansion of Internet access to low-income consumers, support for clean technology, and protection of net neutrality. She has been an early leader in practical responses to climate change by working constantly to ensure adequate flood control for Sacramento, which sits at the confluence of two great rivers.

She was born Doris Okada in a Japanese-American internment camp in Poston, Arizona, on September 25, 1944. Her parents, Ichiro and Matsuye Miyamoto Okada met at the Poston War Relocation Center.[1] The family later settled on a farm in Dinuba in California's Central Valley. In 1966 Doris Okada earned a bachelor of arts degree in psychology from the University of California, Berkeley, where she met Robert T. Matsui. The couple married that year and had one son, Brian. In 1978 Robert was elected to the U.S. House of Representatives to represent Sacramento.

In 1992 President-elect William J. (Bill) Clinton appointed Doris Matsui to his eight-member transition board and asked her to serve in the White House as deputy assistant to the President and deputy director of public liaison, a position she held for six years. In 1998 Matsui joined a Washington government relations firm, where she specialized in medical technology, telecommunications, and financial services.[2]

Robert T. Matsui died on January 1, 2005, from a rare bone marrow disorder, and Doris Matsui won the special election to succeed him a little more than two months later. She received 68 percent of the vote and was sworn into Congress on March 10, 2005. "Despite tragedy and heartbreak, life indeed goes on," Matsui said at her swearing-in, "and I know that somewhere Bob is looking down and smiling."[3] She won her next six general re-election bids with 70 percent or more.[4]

Matsui was assigned to the Energy and Commerce Committee in 2008 and currently serves on the Health, Communications and Technology, Environment, and Digital Commerce and Consumer Protection Subcommittees. Matsui's first committee assignment was to the powerful Rules Committee, where she later supported Speaker Nancy Pelosi of California in moving key legislation, including the Affordable Care Act and Dodd–Frank financial reform. She served on the Rules Committee through the 111th Congress (2009–2011) and was vice chair of the Rules and Organization of the House Subcommittee in the 110th and 111th Congresses (2007–2011). She sat on the Science Committee in the 109th Congress (2005–2007) and the Transportation and Infrastructure Committee in the 110th Congress (2007–2009).[5]

Matsui has promoted the arts, humanities, and cultural institutions throughout her career, serving as a member of the Board of Regents for the Smithsonian Institution and as a board member of the National Symphony Orchestra.

Matsui has been a vocal supporter of comprehensive mental health care reform, passing into law the Excellence in Mental Health Act in 2014, landmark legislation that provided for community behavioral health clinics.

Matsui has emerged as a leader in promoting technology jobs in Sacramento and expanding Internet access to low-income consumers. During the 114th Congress (2015–2017), she introduced a bill to support companies developing clean technology to combat climate change.[6]

Matsui is also an advocate for net neutrality. Working alongside Senator Patrick Leahy of Vermont, Matsui sought authority for the Federal Communications Commission to prevent Internet service providers from opening "fast lanes" for some content at the expense of other data.[7]

As one of the youngest members of the generation of Japanese Americans interned by their own government during World War II, Matsui has supported efforts to preserve internment sites "as the physical reminder of past inequality."[8] While securing anti-terror funding for her district, she also cited America's history of internment as a warning against potential civil liberties abuses in efforts to combat terrorism. "The government at all levels was blinded by war," Matsui observed, "and it is imperative that we learn the lesson this moment in history has taught us."[9]

NOTES

1   *Congressional Record*, House, 109th Cong., 2nd sess. (1 March 2006): H479.

2   *Politics in America, 2006* (Washington, DC: Congressional Quarterly, Inc., 2005): 81.

3   Erica Werner, "Doris Matsui Takes Over for Late Husband," 11 March 2005, *Ventura County Star* (Camarillo, CA): 3.

4   Kevin Yamamura, "Matsui Headed to Congress," 9 March 2005, *Sacramento Bee*: A1; Office of the Clerk, U.S. House of Representatives, "Election Statistics, 1920 to Present," http://history.house.gov/Institution/Election-Statistics/Election-Statistics/.

5   H. Res. 1256, 110th Cong. (2008); *Congressional Record*, House, 110th Cong., 2nd sess. (10 June 2008): H5126.

6   Melanie Turner, "House Passes Matsui Bill that Would Boost U.S. Clean-Tech Industry," 28 July 2010, *Sacramento Business Journal*: n.p.

7   Brian Fung, "Democrats Propose Law putting Brakes on Internet Fast Lanes," 18 June 2014, *Washington Post*: A13.

8   *Congressional Record*, Extension of Remarks, 110th Cong., 2nd sess. (14 February 2008): E196.

9   *Congressional Record*, House, 109th Cong., 2nd sess. (1 March 2006): H479. See, for example, David Whitney, "Matsui Backs Boost in Anti-Terror Grants," 14 June 2007, *Sacramento Bee*: B2.

Image courtesy of the Member

Grace Meng
1975–

UNITED STATES REPRESENTATIVE 2013–
DEMOCRAT FROM NEW YORK

As a lifelong resident of Queens, Grace Meng has staked her career on protecting the interests of her New York City constituents. In the state assembly, she became known for focusing on results and putting aside party and personal politics. "That's the one thing I probably don't like about politics," she said during her first congressional campaign, "the focus on the individual. To me, it's more important to get it done, whether I get the credit for it or not."[1]

Grace Meng was born in Queens, New York, on October 1, 1975, the daughter of immigrants Shiao-Mei and Jimmy Meng, who owned and operated a lumber company.[2] She graduated from Stuyvesant High School in New York City in 1993 and then attended the University of Michigan in Ann Arbor, where she studied Chinese and history. After receiving her BA in 1997, Meng considered teaching but shifted her focus to law. She returned to New York and received her JD from Yeshiva University in New York City in 2002.[3] She briefly worked as a public interest lawyer and at a public relations firm before volunteering at her father's Flushing-area district office after his election as the first Asian-American member of the New York state assembly. Meng led her father's district office after his election. In 2005 she married Korean-American dentist and professor Wayne Kye, with whom she has two sons, Tyler and Brandon.[4]

In 2008 Meng defeated her opponent, Ellen Young, by 18 percent to win a seat in the New York state assembly.[5] Meng dedicated her time to constituent services, a priority she continues to pride herself on, given the unique and diverse needs of her congressional district.[6] She also built a reputation for bipartisanship, stating, "Being the only Asian American in the State Legislature, I've had no choice but to reach across the aisle." Among her key legislative achievements were eliminating the term "Oriental" from most state documents as well as authoring the Reverse Mortgage Act of 2009.[7] Seven of her bills in the assembly were ultimately signed into law. She easily won re-election in 2010 and was later selected as a delegate to the 2012 Democratic National Convention.[8]

When U.S. Representative Gary Ackerman retired from his district in northern Queens, Meng entered the race for the vacant seat. New York's 6th Congressional District, home to sizable Chinese and Korean immigrant communities, included a portion of Meng's assembly district in Flushing. Endorsed by Ackerman and Representative Joe Crowley, she ran on a platform of improving transportation, increasing school funding, and bringing more jobs to the area through tax incentives.[9] Meng won the primary with 52 percent of the vote, defeating three other candidates for the nomination.[10] She defeated Republican councilman Daniel J. Halloran III in the general election with 60 percent of the vote, becoming the first Asian-American Member of Congress from New York.[11]

In the 113th Congress (2013–2015), Meng was appointed to the Foreign Affairs and Small Business Committees. On the latter, she served as Ranking Member on the Contracting and Workforce Subcommittee. Meng won appointment to the prestigious Appropriations Committee at the start of the 115th Congress (2017–2019).

Representative Meng has remained district-focused while serving in Congress. She established the Quiet Skies Caucus to prioritize eliminating noise pollution due to the frequency of flights near her Queens district as well as the Congressional Kids' Safety Caucus.[12] She also sought a National Park Service study to mark historic sites in Queens (H.R. 3222) and was successful in securing its inclusion in the 2015 National Defense Authorization Act.[13]

Meng proved to be an unusually active freshman legislator. She successfully passed legislation through the House amending the International Religious Freedom Act of 1998 to classify the desecration of cemeteries as a violation of religious freedom, and President Barack Obama signed it into law on August 8, 2014.[14] From her position on the Foreign Affairs Committee, she fought for funding and protection for the State of Israel, reflecting the large Jewish population within her district.[15]

Meng won re-election unopposed in 2014, after which Democratic Party leadership selected her as an Assistant Whip.[16] In the 114th Congress (2015–2017), Meng continued to support her district by focusing on small businesses and defending the rights of women and minorities. She has maintained her reputation as an active legislator. She reintroduced her Anti-Spoofing Act that passed the full House during the 113th Congress and successfully shepherded legislation to strike all uses of the term "Oriental" from federal law. President Obama signed it into law in May 2016.[17]

Meng won re-election to the 115th Congress with 72 percent of the vote.

NOTES

1 David W. Chen, "A Breakthrough Candidate and Potential Star," 27 June 2012, *New York Times*, http://www.nytimes.com/2012/06/28/nyregion/grace-meng-is-rising-star-for-asian-new-yorkers.html (accessed 9 March 2016).

2 *Politics in America, 2014* (Washington, DC: Congressional Quarterly, Inc., 2013): 677.

3 Chen, "A Breakthrough Candidate and Potential Star"; Charles Lam, "Rep. Grace Meng on Civic Engagement, Public Service, and Being Chinese American," 28 February 2013, *Northwest Asian Weekly*, http://www.nwasianweekly.com/2013/02/rep-grace-meng-on-civic-engagement-public-service-and-being-chinese-american-the-first-asian-american-congressperson-from-the-east-coast-speaks-with-the-asian-weekly/ (accessed 14 March 2016).

4 "Grace Meng, Wayne Kye," 12 June 2005, *New York Times*: 14.

5 Sally Goldenberg and Maggie Haberman, "Silver's Golden in Primary Win," 10 September 2008, *New York Post*: 15; Jonathan P. Hicks, "In Assembly Seat's Past, a Hint of Musical Chairs," 11 September 2008, *New York Times*, http://www.nytimes.com/2008/09/12/nyregion/12flushing.html (accessed 10 March 2016).

6 Daniel Edward Rosen, "Lost in Translation Pol: Non-English Signs an Emergency Risk," 14 April 2010, *Daily News* (New York): 44; Leigh Remizowski, "At a Glance," 21 April 2010, *Daily News* (New York): 28.

7 Chen, "A Breakthrough Candidate and Potential Star."

8 Joe Anuta, "Meng, Stavisky Win Dem Delegate Spots," 30 January 2012, *TimesLedger* (New York): n.p.

9 Joe Anuta, "Meng Explains Bid for House," 25 May 2012, *TimesLedger* (New York): n.p.

10 Joe Anuta, "Meng Clinches Dem Primary," 27 June 2012, *TimesLedger* (New York): n.p.

11 Office of the Clerk, U.S. House of Representatives, "Election Statistics, 1920 to Present," http://history.house.gov/institution/election-statistics/election-statistics.

12 Grace Meng, "Airplane Noise in Queens," 30 August 2013, *New York Times*: 18.

13 *Congressional Record*, House, 113th Cong., 2nd sess. (15 September 2014): H7494–7495.

14 *Congressional Record*, House, 113th Cong., 2nd sess. (28 May 2014): H4850–4851.

15 Dmitriy Shapiro, "N.Y. legislator Grace Meng an Emerging Pro-Jewish Voice in Congress," 3 June 2014, *Washington Jewish Week*, http://www.jns.org/latest-articles/2014/6/3/ny-legislator-grace-meng-an-emerging-pro-jewish-voice-in-congress#.U49byiiGdot (accessed 11 March 2016).

16 Congresswoman Grace Meng, "Meng Named Assistant Whip," press release, 15 April 2015, accessed 14 March 2016, https://meng.house.gov/media-center/press-releases/meng-named-assistant-whip.

17 Madina Toure, "Meng Bill Seeking Removal of 'Oriental' Term Now Law," 30 May 2016, *TimesLedger* (New York): n.p.

Aumua Amata Coleman Radewagen
1947–

DELEGATE 2015–
REPUBLICAN FROM AMERICAN SAMOA

Image courtesy of the Member

Amata Coleman Radewagen became the first woman elected to represent the territory of American Samoa in 2014. She holds the title of "Aumua" (orator/talking chief) from the village of Pago Pago in American Samoa's capital. Radewagen has dedicated her career to bridging the gap between Washington, DC, and the Pacific Islands. Notably, Radewagen campaigned unsuccessfully for 10 straight congressional elections before winning. When asked about her perseverance, she responded, "My Dad's motto, '*Sulu o le tautua*,' remains what I stand for, 'Torch of service.'"[1]

Amata Coleman was born on December 29, 1947, to Nora Stewart Coleman and Peter Tali Coleman, the first popularly elected governor of American Samoa.[2] One of 13 children, she counts Pago Pago, American Samoa, as her hometown. She attended Sacred Hearts Academy, a Roman Catholic preparatory school for girls in Honolulu, before earning a bachelor's degree in psychology from the University of Guam in 1975. She completed additional studies at George Mason University in Fairfax, Virginia, and Loyola Marymount University in Los Angeles, California. She married Fred Radewagen, with whom she has three children: Erika, Mark, and Kirsten.

Radewagen built up a résumé of pro-democracy international work on advance teams for presidential trips during the George H. W. Bush administration. Beginning in 1992, she taught democratic governance to professionals and politicians in countries such as Kazakhstan, Cambodia, Kyrgyzstan, and Morocco. During this time, Radewagen was diagnosed with breast cancer; she began advocating on behalf of cancer awareness in 1993. She also served as chief diplomatic correspondent for the *Washington Pacific Report* from 1984 to 1997.[3] Beginning in 1997, Radewagen became a mainstay in the U.S. House of Representatives, working for Philip Crane of Illinois before moving to the office of J. C. Watts of Oklahoma in 1999. She then joined the staff of the House Republican Conference, where she worked until 2005, at which point she returned to Pago Pago to work as a community activist.[4]

Radewagen first ran for the office of Delegate from American Samoa in 1994 against incumbent Democrat Eni F. H. Faleomavaega. Though she only received 21 percent of the vote, Radewagen continued to campaign for the position in every following election. She failed to secure the Republican nomination in 1996 and 2000 and ran with no declared party affiliation in 1998.[5] In 2014 Faleomavaega's declining health and long absences from the public eye became a concern for constituents.[6] A known quantity after years of campaigning, Radewagen stumped on improving infrastructure and education for the territory's youth. The Pacific island was still recovering from the effects of the 2008 global recession and a 2009 tsunami; reliant on federal aid, constituents were eager for a more active voice in Washington. She went on to win 42 percent to Faleomavaega's 31 percent.[7]

Upon entering the 114th Congress (2015–2017), Radewagen was appointed to three committees: Natural Resources, Veterans' Affairs, and Small Business. She was vice chairman of the Natural Resources Subcommittee on Indian, Insular and Alaska Native Affairs and chairman of the Small Business Subcommittee on Health and Technology. In the 115th Congress (2017–2019), she continued serving on the same three committees and as the chairman of the Small Business Committee's Health and Technology Subcommittee. Her years as a Hill staffer helped her form working relationships with other Republicans and provided her more support for legislation favoring the territory.

Radewagen's primary agenda has been to preserve the political will of the people of American Samoa. In June 2015, she supported an appellate court judge's decision not to grant birthright citizenship to people of the territory, insisting that American Samoans "should have the final say in matters concerning their political status."[8] Later that year, she pushed to delay a planned minimum wage increase in the territory, explaining that the island's economy had yet to recover from the 2008 recession. The bill (H.R. 2617) passed the House by voice vote and became law in October 2015.[9] In late 2016, she submitted a bill (H.R. 6452) to ensure access to Pacific fisheries for the territories following the regulations of international convention. This bill, supporting a crucial industry in American Samoa, passed the House by unanimous consent and was signed into law by President Barack Obama on December 16, 2016.[10] Radewagen has been a consistent voice for veterans' affairs, a key constituency in American Samoa, which maintains the highest rate of enlistment in the U.S. armed forces.[11]

Radewagen handily won re-election in 2016 with 74.5 percent of the vote against four independent competitors, none of whom garnered more than 15 percent of the vote.[12]

NOTES

1   "Aumua Amata Launches Her Campaign for Delegate Seat," 9 June 2014, *Samoa News*, https://samoanews.com/aumua-amata-launches-her-campaign-delegate-seat (accessed 14 November 2014).

2   Eric Pace, "Peter Coleman, 77, Governor of American Samoa," 1 May 1997, *New York Times*: 16.

3   "Aumua Amata Radewagen's Biography," Project Vote Smart, accessed 8 May 2017, https://votesmart.org/candidate/biography/128380/aumua-amata-radewagen#.WRCgGlXyuUl.

4   "Aumua Amata Launches Her Campaign for Delegate Seat."

5   Office of the Clerk, U.S. House of Representatives, "Election Statistics, 1920 to Present," http://history.house.gov/Institution/Election-Statistics/Election-Statistics/.

6   Timothy Cama, "American Samoa Delegate Loses Seat," 5 November 2014, *The Hill*, http://thehill.com/blogs/ballot-box/house-races/223113-american-samoa-delegate-loses-seat (accessed 1 May 2017); "Am. Samoa: Candidates Line Up for Run at Faleomavaega's Seat; Memorial Day: Faleomavaega Again a No Show," 26 May 2014, *Hawai'i Free Press*, http://www.hawaiifreepress.com/ArticlesMain/tabid/56/ID/12720/Am-Samoa-Candidates-Line-up-for-Run-at-Faleomavaegas-Seat.aspx (accessed 1 May 2017).

7   Office of the Clerk, U.S. House of Representatives, "Election Statistics, 1920 to Present"; "Aumua Amata Launches Her Campaign for Delegate Seat."

8   *Almanac of American Politics, 2016* (United States: Columbia Books and Information Services, 2015): 2041.

9   *Congressional Record*, House, 114th Cong., 1st sess. (28 September 2015): H6281–H6284; Public Law 114-61, 129 Stat. 545 (2015).

10 *Congressional Record*, House, 114th Cong., 2nd sess. (8 December 2016): H7540; Ensuring Access to Pacific Fisheries Act, Public Law 114-327, 130 Stat. 1974 (2016).

11 *Congressional Record*, Extension of Remarks, 114th Cong., 1st sess. (16 November 2015): E1623.

12 Office of the Clerk, U.S. House of Representatives, "Election Statistics, 1920 to Present."

Image courtesy of the Member

Gregorio Kilili Camacho Sablan
1955–

DELEGATE 2009–
DEMOCRAT FROM NORTHERN MARIANA ISLANDS

Representing an archipelago of 14 volcanic islands, some active, 15 time zones from Washington, DC, Gregorio Kilili Camacho Sablan is the first Delegate to represent the Northern Mariana Islands in the U.S. House of Representatives. Early in his first term, Sablan, who prefers to go by Kilili, noted, "We've been a commonwealth for 33 years, and we became citizens in 1986. We've got a lot of catching up to do."[1]

Gregorio Kilili Camacho Sablan, born on the island of Saipan on January 19, 1955, is the third of seven children born to Jesus Diaz Sablan and Victorina Camacho Sablan.[2] Sablan graduated from Marianas High School before attending the University of Guam, Armstrong University at Berkeley, and the University of Hawaii at Manoa. He served in the United States Army from 1981 to 1986. Sablan and his wife, Andrea, have six children, six grandchildren, and two great-grandchildren.

In 1976, when Sablan was 21 years old, President Gerald R. Ford approved Public Law 94-241, formalizing a covenant between the Northern Mariana Islands and the United States. The new commonwealth government was established on January 9, 1978, and three years later Sablan began working for the first governor, Carlos S. Camacho. Sablan hailed from a political family—his uncle, Vicente D. Sablan, and his grandfather, SN. Sablan, both served as mayors of Saipan—and, like his older relatives, he gravitated to public service. In 1982 Sablan, running as a Democrat, was elected to the commonwealth legislature, where he served until 1986. After his stint in the legislature, Sablan worked as an aide to Senator Daniel K. Inouye of Hawaii and later to the commonwealth governor. Sablan was appointed executive director of the Commonwealth Election Commission in 1999.[3]

In May 2008, more than 30 years after the original covenant, President George W. Bush signed Public Law 110-229, granting the islands a Delegate in the U.S. House of Representatives. Sablan left his position with the election commission and entered a nine-way race for the new seat.[4] In the early 1980s, he was chairman of the Northern Marianas Democratic Party, but Sablan had grown frustrated with what he considered a highly unorganized local Democratic Party and opted to run as an independent instead. His biggest competition came from Republican Pedro A. Tenorio, the incumbent Washington representative.[5] Sablan edged out Tenorio by 357 votes, winning 24 percent of the total vote. In 2010 he won re-election in a four-way contest with

43 percent of the vote, and he has not dipped below 65 percent of the vote in subsequent elections.[6]

Once in Congress, Sablan caucused with House Democrats and was assigned to the Committee on Natural Resources and the Committee on Education and Labor for the 111th Congress (2009–2011). He has served on Natural Resources for his entire House career. In the 112th Congress (2011–2013), Sablan left Education and Labor and, for one term, had a seat on the Agriculture Committee. He returned to the renamed Education and the Workforce Committee for the 113th, 114th, and 115th Congresses (2013–2019). In the 115th Congress (2017–2019), Sablan was also assigned to the Veterans' Affairs Committee.

Focusing on the basic needs of his constituents and seeking parity for the Northern Marianas in federal law, Sablan has introduced more than 40 bills during his career. His first bill conveyed submerged land rights to the Northern Mariana Islands.[7] "The Northern Mariana Islands is the only U.S. jurisdiction that does not have ownership of the submerged lands three miles off its shores," he noted. Sablan's bill passed the House in the 111th and 113th Congresses, and a companion measure (S. 256) was enacted into law in 2013.

In the 112th Congress, as a member of the Agriculture Committee, he added a provision to the 2014 Agricultural Act to create a pilot program to bring the Marianas into the Supplemental Nutrition Assistance Program. He also authored legislation to increase federal support for education in the Northern Marianas and other U.S. insular areas.[8] The necessary change in funding formulas for low-income island students was successfully included in the 2015 Every Student Succeeds Act.[9]

Sablan makes it a point to educate Congress on living conditions in the Northern Marianas. About half of his constituents are below the federal poverty line and lack basic necessities, such as reliable access to fresh drinking water. "[Y]ou're lucky enough to get two to three hours of water a day," he said on the House Floor in 2009. "And not just that, but, you can't drink that water anyway."[10] Since then, with Sablan's support, federal funding for water infrastructure in the Marianas has increased sevenfold.

NOTES

1 Kris Kitto, "This Man Is No Island," April 20, 2009, *The Hill*: n.p.; quotation in *Congressional Record*, House, 111th Cong., 1st sess., (14 May 2009): H5657.

2 "Full Biography," on Congressman Gregorio Kilili Camacho Sablan's official website, accessed May 21, 2012, http://sablan. house.gov/about-me/full-biography; "About," Kilili for Congress Facebook Page, http://www.facebook.com/pages/Kilili-for-Congress/112096108825189?sk=info (accessed 9 May 2012).

3 "Progress in the Pacific," 15 November 1986, *Christian Science Monitor*: 19; "Full Biography"; *Politics in America, 2012* (Washington, DC: CQ-Roll Call, Inc., 2011): 1090.

4 *Congressional Record*, House, 111th Cong., 1st sess. (24 March 2009): H3785; "Full Biography."

5 From 1978 to 2008, the Northern Mariana Islands elected a "resident representative to the United States." This representative was not a Member of the House of Representatives but served as an advocate for the Northern Mariana Islands. Frank S. Rosario, "Sablan Leads CNMI's U.S. Congress Delegate Race," *Pacific Magazine*, www.pacificmagazine.net (accessed November 5, 2008).

6 *Politics in America, 2010* (Washington, DC: Congressional Quarterly, Inc., 2009): 1130; *Politics in America, 2012*: 1090; Office of the Clerk, U.S. House of Representatives, "Election Statistics, 1920 to Present," http://history.house.gov/Institution/Election-Statistics/Election-Statistics/.

7 H.R. 934, 111th Cong. (2009); H.R. 670, 112th Cong. (2011); and H.R. 573, 113th Cong. (2013).

8 H.R. 428, 113th Cong. (2013); H.R. 851, 114th Cong. (2015). The legislation to increase federal support for the insular territories is listed in the Agricultural Act of 2014, Public Law 113-79, 128 Stat. 816 (2014).

9 See Section 1014 of the Every Student Succeeds Act, Public Law 114-95, 129 Stat. 1802 (2015).

10 *Congressional Record*, House, 111th Cong. 1st sess. (14 May 2009): H5656–H5657.

Robert C. (Bobby) Scott
1947–

UNITED STATES REPRESENTATIVE 1993–
DEMOCRAT FROM VIRGINIA

Image courtesy of the Member

Robert C. (Bobby) Scott was born in Washington, DC, on April 30, 1947, the son of Charles Waldo Scott, a doctor, and Mae Hamlin Scott, a teacher. He was raised in Newport News, Virginia. When Virginia officials resisted court-ordered public school integration in the late 1950s, Scott's parents sent him to Groton School, a college preparatory school in Massachusetts.[1] He graduated with a bachelor of arts in liberal arts from Harvard University in 1969, and he earned a juris doctor degree at Boston College four years later.[2] While in law school, Scott served in the Massachusetts National Guard and later in the U.S. Army Reserve.

After law school, Scott returned to Newport News and opened a private law practice. From 1975 to 1980, he served as president of the local chapter of the National Association for the Advancement of Colored People. In 1977 he won election to the Virginia house of delegates. He served for five years until his election to the Virginia senate, where he served for another decade. Scott is divorced and has no children. He is a member of St. Augustine's Episcopal Church in Newport News.

Scott first attempted to win national office in 1986 when he challenged two-term Republican incumbent Herbert H. Bateman for a seat in the U.S. House of Representatives. The campaign garnered wide name recognition for Scott, although he lost the general election by a margin of 56 to 44 percent.[3]

Following the 1990 Census, Virginia underwent reapportionment that increased its congressional delegation from 10 to 11. In order to comply with the Voting Rights Act, the Virginia assembly created a majority-black district spanning from southeast Richmond into portions of Newport News and Norfolk at the mouth of the Chesapeake Bay in southeastern Virginia. Scott, who had represented portions of the new district in the state legislature, ran for the seat. In the Democratic primary, he received two-thirds of the vote, defeating two African-American women, one a member of the house of delegates and the other chair of the state retirement system. In the general election, he prevailed handily over Republican candidate Daniel Jenkins, winning 79 percent of the vote.[4]

Scott was the first black elected official since John Mercer Langston (1890–1891) to represent Virginia and, because of Scott's Filipino ancestry on his mother's side of the family, the first American of Filipino ancestry to serve as a U.S. Representative.[5] Despite court-ordered redistrictings, Scott has never been seriously challenged in his 12 re-election bids. He has never received less than 66 percent of the vote and has run unopposed in multiple elections.[6]

When Scott was sworn in to the 103rd Congress (1993–1995), he was appointed to three committees: Judiciary, Education and Labor, and Science, Space, and Technology. He served on the Science, Space, and Technology Committee for two years (1993–1995) and continued to serve on the Judiciary Committee until the conclusion of the 113th Congress (2013–2015). Scott continues to serve on the Education Committee, though he took a leave of absence during the 108th Congress (2003–2005) to serve on the prestigious Budget Committee. During the 114th and 115th Congresses (2015–2019), he has served as Ranking Member on the Education and the Workforce Committee.

Congressman Scott has earned a reputation as a forthright progressive, opposing efforts to amend the Constitution to outlaw flag desecration and promote prayer in public schools.[7] He is also a strong advocate of reforming the juvenile justice system and reducing crime by using prevention and intervention strategies. Scott has consistently fought against employment discrimination in organizations that use federal funds. In 1997 Scott was a leading proponent of expanding the Individuals with Disabilities Education Act, which requires every state to provide a free, appropriate public education for children with disabilities. He opposed the war in Iraq and was a strong supporter of the Affordable Care Act.

Scott also cosponsored the Death in Custody Reporting Act, signed into law in 2000, which requires states to report the deaths of individuals in the custody of law enforcement or in the process of arrest.[8] Scott reintroduced the bill each Congress following its 2006 expiration and secured passage in 2013.[9] He also played a crucial role in the passage of the Fair Sentencing Act of 2010, which reduced mandatory minimum sentences in many drug cases.[10]

In 2015 Scott was one of the four primary negotiators of the Every Student Succeeds Act, which reauthorized the Elementary and Secondary Education Act for the first time in 13 years, replacing the No Child Left Behind Act.[11]

NOTES

1   *Politics in America, 2006* (Washington, DC: Congressional Quarterly, Inc., 2005): 1058; "About Bobby," on Representative Bobby Scott's official website, accessed 4 April 2016, http://bobbyscott.house.gov/about/biography.

2   "Robert C. Scott," *Contemporary Black Biography*, vol. 23 (Detroit, MI: Gale Group, 1999).

3   Office of the Clerk, U.S. House of Representatives, "Election Statistics, 1920 to Present," http://history.house.gov/Institution/Election-Statistics/Election-Statistics/; *Politics in America, 2006*: 1058.

4   Office of the Clerk, U.S. House of Representatives, "Election Statistics, 1920 to Present"; "Robert C. Scott," *Contemporary Black Biography*.

5   "About Bobby." Thirteen Filipinos served as Resident Commissioners for the nearly 50 years of Philippine annexation by the United States after the Spanish-American War in 1898. None of the Resident Commissioners were American citizens.

6   Office of the Clerk, U.S. House of Representatives, "Election Statistics, 1920 to Present"; *Politics in America, 2008* (Washington, DC: Congressional Quarterly, Inc., 2007): 1044.

7   *Politics in America, 2006*: 1057.

8   "About Bobby"; *Congressional Record*, House, 106th Cong., 2nd sess. (24 July 2000): H6737; H.R. 1800, 106th Cong. (1999); Death in Custody Reporting Act, Public Law 106-297, 114 Stat. 1045 (2000).

9   H.R. 2908, 110th Cong. (2007); H.R. 3971, 110th Cong. (2008); H.R. 7227, 110th Cong. (2008); H.R. 738, 111th Cong. (2009); H.R. 2189, 112th Cong. (2011); H.R. 1447, 113th Cong. (2013). Death in Custody Reporting Act of 2013, Public Law 113-242, 128 Stat. 2860 (2014).

10   "The Fair Sentencing Act Corrects a Long-time Wrong in Cocaine Cases," 3 August 2010, *Washington Post*: A14; Fair Sentencing Act, Public Law 111-220, 124 Stat. 2372 (2010).

11   "Scott Statement on Senate Passage of Bipartisan Bill to Fix No Child Left Behind," press release, accessed 1 May 2016, http://democrats-edworkforce.house.gov/media/press-releases/scott-statement-on-senate-passage-of-bipartisan-bill-to-fix-no-child-left-behind.

Image courtesy of the Member

Mark Takano
1960–

UNITED STATES REPRESENTATIVE 2013–
DEMOCRAT FROM CALIFORNIA

Mark Takano won election in 2012 as the first openly gay person of color in Congress. A high school teacher with three decades of experience, Takano focuses on education benefits for veterans from his position on the Veterans' Affairs Committee.

Mark Takano was born December 10, 1960, in Riverside, California. The son of Japanese Americans, his parents and grandparents were uprooted from their California and Washington state homes and sent to internment camps during World War II. After the war, they resettled in Riverside County.[1] Takano attended La Sierra High School in Riverside, graduating as class valedictorian in 1979. He received an AB degree in government from Harvard University in 1983. Takano planned to attend law school but decided to try teaching in the Boston suburbs. He earned his teaching certificate from the School of Education at the University of California, Riverside, upon returning to California to teach English and social studies at Riverside's Rialto High School. Takano also served on the board of trustees at Riverside Community College. Eventually becoming the board's longest-serving member, he twice served as its president.[2]

Takano first ran for a Riverside County-based U.S. House of Representatives seat in 1992, losing to Republican Representative Ken Calvert by 519 votes. He lost a rematch against Calvert in 1994.[3] In 2012 redistricting created a new U.S. House district encompassing the western parts of Riverside County, including a cache of traditionally Democratic voters.[4] Takano announced his candidacy in July 2011.[5] In California's new open primary, wherein the top two candidates advance to the general election regardless of party affiliation, he emerged in second place behind Republican Riverside County supervisor John Tavaglione in a five-candidate race.[6] Takano stressed job creation and training as well as education reform in the general election and defeated Tavaglione with 59 percent of the vote.[7]

Takano's initial committee assignments included Science, Space, and Technology and Veterans' Affairs. Midway through the 113th Congress (2013–2015), he picked up a seat on the Education and the Workforce Committee. Takano now serves as the Vice Ranking Member of the Veterans' Affairs Committee and was its Ranking Member in the 114th Congress (2015–2017). Much of his legislation originated from this committee work. His first bill in Congress was the VetSuccess Enhancement Act, which extended the period during which veterans with service-connected disabilities could enroll in the Veterans Administration training and rehabilitation programs.[8]

Student veterans are a particular focus for Takano. His Work-Study for Student Veterans Act allowed veteran students to get paid jobs on campuses or in Department of Veterans Affairs facilities.[9] The Veterans Education Outcomes Act, introduced in March 2014, attempted to help the federal government better track data on veterans through school and subsequent employment.[10] "In order to know if we are properly serving our student veterans and how we can improve this service, we need to see the numbers," Takano said.[11] He also introduced the Warriors' Peer-Outreach Pilot Program Act, which granted paid work-study jobs for veterans using the GI Bill for peer outreach and mentoring programs.[12] Takano was a cofounder of the bipartisan Work for Warriors Caucus to promote awareness for a California-based program to reduce unemployment among National Guard members.[13] His GI Bill Fairness Act ensures that wounded Guard members receive full GI Bill benefits.[14]

Takano often weighs in on broader education policy. He seeks legislation increasing transparency of charter schools and protecting students who attend for-profit colleges from fraudulent practices. His Job Skills for America's Students Act encouraged partnerships between businesses and schools, awarding tax credits for offering technical and skill training.[15] Takano's Helping Schools Protect Our Children Act provided training for teachers to spot signs of sexual abuse.[16]

Takano is also an advocate for lesbian, gay, bisexual, and transsexual (LGBT) rights. His support for immigration reform is often couched in a call to defend binational LGBT families. Takano cosponsored legislation ensuring that veteran benefits be awarded to LGBT families even in states where gay marriage was not recognized. "Our veterans have sacrificed so much for our country, and all our returning heroes deserve to enjoy the same benefits and freedoms, no matter who they love or where they live," he declared.[17] Takano also introduced the Social Security and Medicare Parity Act, which would close loopholes in the Social Security Act to guarantee survivor benefits to same-sex couples.[18]

Mark Takano won re-election in 2014 and 2016 with 57 and 65 percent of the vote, respectively.[19]

NOTES

1 "Biography," on Congressman Mark Takano's official website, accessed 4 March 2016, http://takano.house.gov/about/biography.

2 *Almanac of American Politics, 2014* (Washington, DC: National Journal Inc., 2013): 254.

3 Office of the Clerk, U.S. House of Representatives, "Election Statistics, 1920 to present," http://history.house.gov/Institution/Election-Statistics/Election-Statistics/.

4 *Almanac of American Politics, 2014*: 254; Phil Willon, "Democrats See New Chances in Inland Empire," 16 March 2012, *Los Angeles Times*: A1.

5 "CA: Takano Plans Run in New District," 5 July 2011, *The Frontrunner*: n.p.

6 "Tavaglione, Takano Discuss Issues in Debate for Election to New 41st District," 11 October 2012, *Riverside County Record* (CA): 3.

7 *Almanac of American Politics, 2014*: 254; Office of the Clerk, U.S. House of Representatives, "Election Statistics, 1920 to Present."

8 H.R. 844, 113th Cong. (2013).

9 H.R. 1453, 113th Cong. (2013).

10 H.R. 4248, 113th Cong. (2014).

11 "Veterans Education Outcomes Act Introduced by Democrat/Republican," 20 March 2014, *Riverside County Record* (CA): 13.

12 H.R. 3056, 113th Cong. (2013).

13 Congressman Mark Takano, "Rep. Mark Takano and Rep. Paul Cook Form Bipartisan Work for Warriors Caucus," press release, 8 November 2013, https://takano.house.gov/newsroom/press-releases/.

14 H.R. 1141, 114th Cong. (2015).

15 H.R. 1271, 113th Cong. (2013).

16 H.R. 5127, 113th Cong. (2014).

17 "Takano Helps Introduce Bipartisan Bill To Protect LGBT Veterans and Families," 28 November 2013, *Riverside County Record* (CA): 3.

18 H.R. 5182, 113th Cong. (2014); H.R. 2025, 114th Cong. (2015).

19 Office of the Clerk, U.S. House of Representatives, "Election Statistics, 1920 to Present."

First Term Asian and Pacific Islander American Members of the 115th Congress

Image courtesy of the Member

Kamala Harris

UNITED STATES SENATOR

DEMOCRAT FROM CALIFORNIA

Congressional Committees: Budget, Environment and Public Works, Homeland Security and Governmental Affairs, Select Committee on Intelligence

Born: October 20, 1964, Oakland, California

Family: Doug Emhoff (spouse)

Education: BA, Howard University, Washington, DC, 1986; JD, University of California, Hastings College of the Law, San Francisco, California, 1989

Military: N/A

Political Career: District attorney of San Francisco, California, 2004–2011; attorney general of California 2011–2017

Professional Career: Lawyer

Publications: *Smart on Crime: A Career Prosecutor's Plan to Make Us Safer* (San Francisco, CA: Chronicle Books, 2009).

SOURCES

Online *Biographical Directory of the United States Congress, 1774–Present*: http://bioguide.congress.gov; individual Member offices.

The closing date for this volume was July 1, 2017.

Image courtesy of the Member

Pramila Jayapal

UNITED STATES REPRESENTATIVE
DEMOCRAT FROM WASHINGTON

Congressional Committees: Budget, Judiciary

Born: September 21, 1965, Chennai, Tamil Nadu, India

Family: Steve (spouse); Janak, Michael (children)

Education: BA, Georgetown University, Washington, DC, 1986; MBA, Northwestern University, Evanston, Illinois, 1990

Military: N/A

Political Career: Washington state senate, 2015–2016

Professional Career: Community organizer, immigration nonprofit founder, public health advocate

Publications: *Pilgrimage to India: A Woman Revisits Her Homeland* (Seattle, WA: Seal Press, 2001).

Image courtesy of the Member

Ro Khanna

UNITED STATES REPRESENTATIVE
DEMOCRAT FROM CALIFORNIA

Congressional Committees: Armed Services, Budget

Born: September 13, 1976, Philadelphia, Pennsylvania

Family: Ritu (spouse)

Education: AB, University of Chicago, Chicago, Illinois, 1998; JD, Yale University, New Haven, Connecticut, 2001

Military: N/A

Political Career: Deputy Assistant Secretary, U.S. Department of Commerce, 2009–2011; member, California Workforce Development Board, 2012–2016

Professional Career: Lawyer, professor

Publications: *Entrepreneurial Nation: Why Manufacturing is Still Key to America's Future* (New York: McGraw-Hill Education, 2012).

Image courtesy of the Member

S. Raja Krishnamoorthi

UNITED STATES REPRESENTATIVE

DEMOCRAT FROM ILLINOIS

Congressional Committees: Education and the Workforce, Oversight and Government Reform

Born: July 19, 1973, New Delhi, India

Family: Priya (spouse); Vijay, Vikram, and Sonia (children)

Education: BA, Princeton University, Princeton, New Jersey, 1995; JD, Harvard Law School, Cambridge, Massachusetts, 2000

Military: N/A

Political Career: Board of Illinois Housing Development Authority, 2005–2007; Illinois special assistant attorney general, 2006–2007; deputy state treasurer of Illinois, 2007–2009; vice-chair of the Illinois Innovation Council, 2014–2015

Professional Career: Small business executive, attorney

Publications: N/A

Image courtesy of the Member

Stephanie Murphy

UNITED STATES REPRESENTATIVE

DEMOCRAT FROM FLORIDA

Congressional Committees: Armed Services, Small Business

Born: September 16, 1978, Ho Chi Minh City, Vietnam

Family: Sean (spouse); Liem and Maya (children)

Education: BA, College of William and Mary, Williamsburg, Virginia, 2000; MSFS, Georgetown University, Washington, DC, 2004

Military: N/A

Political Career: N/A

Professional Career: Consultant, businesswoman, foreign affairs specialist (U.S. Department of Defense), college faculty member

Publications: N/A

"THE HISTORY OF APAs
IN CONGRESS CONTAINS
MANY OF THE SAME THEMES
THAT RESONATE IN THE
LARGER CHRONICLE OF
AMERICAN DEMOCRACY."

Introduction to Current Asian
and Pacific Islander American Members

★ PART THREE ★

Appendices

Asian and Pacific Islander American Representatives, Senators, Delegates, and Resident Commissioners by Congress, 1900–2017

The membership listed in this appendix applies to the total number of Members, House and Senate, in a particular Congress. For details about each Congress, please consult the footnotes.

CONGRESS	TOTAL MEMBERSHIP	HOUSE	SENATE
56th (1899–1901)	1	Robert W. Wilcox (HI)[1]	N/A
57th (1901–1903)	1	Robert W. Wilcox (HI)	N/A
58th (1903–1905)	1	Jonah Kuhio Kalanianaole (HI)	N/A
59th (1905–1907)	1	Jonah Kuhio Kalanianaole (HI)	N/A
60th (1907–1909)	3	Jonah Kuhio Kalanianaole (HI) Benito Legarda (PI) Pablo Ocampo (PI)	N/A
61st (1909–1911)	4	Jonah Kuhio Kalanianaole (HI) Benito Legarda (PI) Pablo Ocampo (PI)[2] Manuel L. Quezon (PI)	N/A
62nd (1911–1913)	3	Jonah Kuhio Kalanianaole (HI) Benito Legarda (PI) Manuel L. Quezon (PI)	N/A
63rd (1913–1915)	3	Manuel Earnshaw (PI) Jonah Kuhio Kalanianaole (HI) Manuel L. Quezon (PI)	N/A
64th (1915–1917)	3	Manuel Earnshaw (PI) Jonah Kuhio Kalanianaole (HI) Manuel L. Quezon (PI)[3]	N/A
65th (1917–1919)	3	Jaime C. de Veyra (PI) Jonah Kuhio Kalanianaole (HI) Teodoro R. Yangco (PI)	N/A
66th (1919–1921)	4	Jaime C. de Veyra (PI) Isauro Gabaldon (PI)[4] Jonah Kuhio Kalanianaole (HI) Teodoro R. Yangco (PI)	N/A
67th (1921–1923)	3	Jaime C. de Veyra (PI) Isauro Gabaldon (PI) Jonah Kuhio Kalanianaole (HI)[5]	N/A

CONGRESS	TOTAL MEMBERSHIP	HOUSE	SENATE
68th (1923–1925)	3	Isauro Gabaldon (PI) Pedro Guevara (PI) William P. Jarrett (HI)	N/A
69th (1925–1927)	3	Isauro Gabaldon (PI) Pedro Guevara (PI) William P. Jarrett (HI)	N/A
70th (1927–1929)	3	Isauro Gabaldon (PI)[6] Pedro Guevara (PI) Victor S. (Kaleoaloha) Houston (HI)	N/A
71st (1929–1931)	3	Pedro Guevara (PI) Victor S. (Kaleoaloha) Houston (HI) Camilo Osias (PI)	N/A
72nd (1931–1933)	3	Pedro Guevara (PI) Victor S. (Kaleoaloha) Houston (HI) Camilo Osias (PI)	N/A
73rd (1933–1935)	2	Pedro Guevara (PI) Camilo Osias (PI)	N/A
74th (1935–1937)	4	Francisco A. Delgado (PI)[7] Pedro Guevara (PI)[8] Samuel Wilder King (HI) Quintin Paredes (PI)[9]	N/A
75th (1937–1939)	3	Joaquin M. Elizalde (PI)[10] Samuel Wilder King (HI) Quintin Paredes (PI)[11]	N/A
76th (1939–1941)	2	Joaquin M. Elizalde (PI) Samuel Wilder King (HI)	N/A
77th (1941–1943)	2	Joaquin M. Elizalde (PI) Samuel Wilder King (HI)	N/A
78th (1943–1945)	2	Joaquin M. Elizalde (PI)[12] Carlos Peña Romulo (PI)[13]	N/A
79th (1945–1947)	1	Carlos Peña Romulo (PI)[14]	N/A
80th–84th (1947–1957)	0	N/A	N/A
85th (1957–1959)	1	Dalip Singh (Judge) Saund (CA)	N/A
86th (1959–1961)	3	Daniel K. Inouye (HI)[15] Dalip Singh (Judge) Saund (CA)	Hiram L. Fong (HI)

CONGRESS	TOTAL MEMBERSHIP	HOUSE	SENATE
87th (1961–1963)	3	Daniel K. Inouye (HI) Dalip Singh (Judge) Saund (CA)	Hiram L. Fong (HI)
88th (1963–1965)	3	Spark M. Matsunaga (HI)	Hiram L. Fong (HI) Daniel K. Inouye (HI)
89th (1965–1967)	4	Spark M. Matsunaga (HI) Patsy Takemoto Mink (HI)	Hiram L. Fong (HI) Daniel K. Inouye (HI)
90th (1967–1969)	4	Spark M. Matsunaga (HI) Patsy Takemoto Mink (HI)	Hiram L. Fong (HI) Daniel K. Inouye (HI)
91st (1969–1971)	4	Spark M. Matsunaga (HI) Patsy Takemoto Mink (HI)	Hiram L. Fong (HI) Daniel K. Inouye (HI)
92nd (1971–1973)	4	Spark M. Matsunaga (HI) Patsy Takemoto Mink (HI)	Hiram L. Fong (HI) Daniel K. Inouye (HI)
93rd (1973–1975)	5	Spark M. Matsunaga (HI) Patsy Takemoto Mink (HI) Antonio Borja Won Pat (GU)	Hiram L. Fong (HI) Daniel K. Inouye (HI)
94th (1975–1977)	7	Spark M. Matsunaga (HI) Norman Y. Mineta (CA) Patsy Takemoto Mink (HI) Antonio Borja Won Pat (GU)	Samuel Ichiye (Sam) Hayakawa (CA)[16] Hiram L. Fong (HI) Daniel K. Inouye (HI)
95th (1977–1979)	6	Daniel K. Akaka (HI) Norman Y. Mineta (CA) Antonio Borja Won Pat (GU)	Samuel Ichiye (Sam) Hayakawa (CA) Daniel K. Inouye (HI) Spark M. Matsunaga (HI)
96th (1979–1981)	7	Daniel K. Akaka (HI) Robert T. Matsui (CA) Norman Y. Mineta (CA) Antonio Borja Won Pat (GU)	Samuel Ichiye (Sam) Hayakawa (CA) Daniel K. Inouye (HI) Spark M. Matsunaga (HI)
97th (1981–1983)	8	Daniel K. Akaka (HI) Robert T. Matsui (CA) Norman Y. Mineta (CA) Fofó I. F. Sunia (AS) Antonio Borja Won Pat (GU)	Samuel Ichiye (Sam) Hayakawa (CA) Daniel K. Inouye (HI) Spark M. Matsunaga (HI)
98th (1983–1985)	7	Daniel K. Akaka (HI) Robert T. Matsui (CA) Norman Y. Mineta (CA) Fofó I. F. Sunia (AS) Antonio Borja Won Pat (GU)	Daniel K. Inouye (HI) Spark M. Matsunaga (HI)

CONGRESS	TOTAL MEMBERSHIP	HOUSE	SENATE
99th (1985–1987)	7	Daniel K. Akaka (HI)	Daniel K. Inouye (HI)
		Ben Garrido Blaz (GU)	Spark M. Matsunaga (HI)
		Robert T. Matsui (CA)	
		Norman Y. Mineta (CA)	
		Fofó I. F. Sunia (AS)	
100th (1987–1989)	8	Daniel K. Akaka (HI)	Daniel K. Inouye (HI)
		Ben Garrido Blaz (GU)	Spark M. Matsunaga (HI)
		Robert T. Matsui (CA)	
		Norman Y. Mineta (CA)	
		Patricia Saiki (HI)	
		Fofó I. F. Sunia (AS)[17]	
101st (1989–1991)	9	Ben Garrido Blaz (GU)	Daniel K. Akaka (HI)[19]
		Eni F. H. Faleomavaega (AS)	Daniel K. Inouye (HI)
		Robert T. Matsui (CA)	Spark M. Matsunaga (HI)[20]
		Norman Y. Mineta (CA)	
		Patsy Takemoto Mink (HI)[18]	
		Patricia Saiki (HI)	
102nd (1991–1993)	7	Ben Garrido Blaz (GU)	Daniel K. Akaka (HI)
		Eni F. H. Faleomavaega (AS)	Daniel K. Inouye (HI)
		Robert T. Matsui (CA)	
		Norman Y. Mineta (CA)	
		Patsy Takemoto Mink (HI)	
103rd (1993–1995)	9	Eni F. H. Faleomavaega (AS)	Daniel K. Akaka (HI)
		Jay C. Kim (CA)	Daniel K. Inouye (HI)
		Robert T. Matsui (CA)	
		Norman Y. Mineta (CA)	
		Patsy Takemoto Mink (HI)	
		Robert C. (Bobby) Scott (VA)	
		Robert A. Underwood (GU)	
104th (1995–1997)	9	Eni F. H. Faleomavaega (AS)	Daniel K. Akaka (HI)
		Jay C. Kim (CA)	Daniel K. Inouye (HI)
		Robert T. Matsui (CA)	
		Norman Y. Mineta (CA)[21]	
		Patsy Takemoto Mink (HI)	
		Robert C. (Bobby) Scott (VA)	
		Robert A. Underwood (GU)	

CONGRESS	TOTAL MEMBERSHIP	HOUSE	SENATE
105th (1997–1999)	8	Eni F. H. Faleomavaega (AS) Jay C. Kim (CA) Robert T. Matsui (CA) Patsy Takemoto Mink (HI) Robert C. (Bobby) Scott (VA) Robert A. Underwood (GU)	Daniel K. Akaka (HI) Daniel K. Inouye (HI)
106th (1999–2001)	8	Eni F. H. Faleomavaega (AS) Robert T. Matsui (CA) Patsy Takemoto Mink (HI) Robert C. (Bobby) Scott (VA) Robert A. Underwood (GU) David Wu (OR)	Daniel K. Akaka (HI) Daniel K. Inouye (HI)
107th (2001–2003)	9	Eni F. H. Faleomavaega (AS) Mike Honda (CA) Robert T. Matsui (CA) Patsy Takemoto Mink (HI)[22] Robert C. (Bobby) Scott (VA) Robert A. Underwood (GU) David Wu (OR)	Daniel K. Akaka (HI) Daniel K. Inouye (HI)
108th (2003–2005)	7	Eni F. H. Faleomavaega (AS) Mike Honda (CA) Robert T. Matsui (CA)[23] Robert C. (Bobby) Scott (VA) David Wu (OR)	Daniel K. Akaka (HI) Daniel K. Inouye (HI)
109th (2005–2007)	8	Eni F. H. Faleomavaega (AS) Mike Honda (CA) Bobby Jindal (LA) Doris Matsui (CA)[24] Robert C. (Bobby) Scott (VA) David Wu (OR)	Daniel K. Akaka (HI) Daniel K. Inouye (HI)
110th (2007–2009)	9	Eni F. H. Faleomavaega (AS) Mazie K. Hirono (HI) Mike Honda (CA) Bobby Jindal (LA)[25] Doris Matsui (CA) Robert C. (Bobby) Scott (VA) David Wu (OR)	Daniel K. Akaka (HI) Daniel K. Inouye (HI)

CONGRESS	TOTAL MEMBERSHIP	HOUSE	SENATE
111th (2009–2011)	13	Steve Austria (OH) Anh (Joseph) Cao (LA) Judy Chu (CA)[26] Charles Djou (HI)[27] Eni F. H. Faleomavaega (AS) Mazie K. Hirono (HI) Mike Honda (CA) Doris Matsui (CA) Gregorio Kilili Camacho Sablan (MP) Robert C. (Bobby) Scott (VA) David Wu (OR)	Daniel K. Akaka (HI) Daniel K. Inouye (HI)
112th (2011–2013)	13	Steve Austria (OH) Judy Chu (CA) Hansen Clarke (MI) Eni F. H. Faleomavaega (AS) Colleen Hanabusa (HI) Mazie K. Hirono (HI) Mike Honda (CA) Doris Matsui (CA) Gregorio Kilili Camacho Sablan (MP) Robert C. (Bobby) Scott (VA) David Wu (OR)[28]	Daniel K. Akaka (HI) Daniel K. Inouye (HI)
113th (2013–2015)	13	Ami Bera (CA) Judy Chu (CA) Tammy Duckworth (IL) Eni F. H. Faleomavaega (AS) Tulsi Gabbard (HI) Colleen Hanabusa (HI) Mike Honda (CA) Doris Matsui (CA) Grace Meng (NY) Gregorio Kilili Camacho Sablan (MP) Robert C. (Bobby) Scott (VA) Mark Takano (CA)	Mazie K. Hirono (HI)

CONGRESS	TOTAL MEMBERSHIP	HOUSE	SENATE
114th (2015–2017)	15	Ami Bera (CA) Judy Chu (CA) Tammy Duckworth (IL) Tulsi Gabbard (HI) Colleen Hanabusa (HI)[29] Mike Honda (CA) Ted Lieu (CA) Doris Matsui (CA) Grace Meng (NY) Aumua Amata Coleman Radewagen (AS) Gregorio Kilili Camacho Sablan (MP) Robert C. (Bobby) Scott (VA) Mark Takai (HI)[30] Mark Takano (CA)	Mazie K. Hirono (HI)
115th (2017–2019)*	18	Ami Bera (CA) Judy Chu (CA) Tulsi Gabbard (HI) Colleen Hanabusa (HI) Pramila Jayapal (WA) Ro Khanna (CA) S. Raja Krishnamoorthi (IL) Ted Lieu (CA) Doris Matsui (CA) Grace Meng (NY) Stephanie Murphy (FL) Aumua Amata Coleman Radewagen (AS) Gregorio Kilili Camacho Sablan (MP) Robert C. (Bobby) Scott (VA) Mark Takano (CA)	Kamala Harris (CA) Mazie K. Hirono (HI) Tammy Duckworth (IL)

1   Robert W. Wilcox was elected on November 6, 1900, upon the formation of the Territory of Hawaii.

2   Pablo Ocampo lost re-election midway through the 61st Congress.

3   Manuel L. Quezon resigned on October 15, 1916.

4   Isauro Gabaldon was elected on February 7, 1920.

5   Jonah Kuhio Kalanianaole died in office on January 7, 1922.

6   Isauro Gabaldon resigned on March 6, 1928, effective July 16, 1928, having been nominated for election to the Philippine house of representatives.

7   Francisco A. Delgado served until February 14, 1936, in accordance with the newly formed Commonwealth of the Philippine Islands.

8   Pedro Guevara served until October 1, 1935.

9   Quintin Paredes was appointed on December 21, 1935.

10 Joaquin M. Elizalde was appointed on September 29, 1938, to fill the vacancy caused by the resignation of Quintin Paredes.

11 Quintin Paredes resigned on September 29, 1938.

12 Joaquin M. Elizalde resigned on August 9, 1944.

13 Carlos Peña Romulo was appointed on August 10, 1944, to fill the vacancy caused by the resignation of Joaquin M. Elizalde.

14 Carlos Peña Romulo served until July 4, 1946, when the office of Resident Commissioner from the Philippines terminated.

15 Daniel K. Inouye was elected on August 21, 1959, upon the admission of Hawaii into the Union.

16 Samuel Ichiye (Sam) Hayakawa was elected to the 95th Congress (1977–1979), and subsequently appointed to the 94th Congress (1975–1977) on January 2, 1977, to fill the vacancy caused by the resignation of John V. Tunney.

17 Fofó I. F. Sunia resigned on September 6, 1988.

18 Patsy Takemoto Mink was elected on September 22, 1990, by special election, to fill the vacancy caused by the resignation of Daniel K. Akaka.

19 Daniel K. Akaka was appointed on April 28, 1990, effective May 16, 1990, to fill the vacancy caused by the death of Spark M. Matsunaga. Akaka was elected on November 6, 1990, by special election, to complete the term ending January 3, 1995.

20 Spark M. Matsunaga died in office on April 15, 1990.

21 Norman Y. Mineta resigned on October 10, 1995.

22 Patsy Takemoto Mink died in office on September 28, 2002.

23 Robert T. Matsui died in office on January 1, 2005.

24 Doris Matsui was elected on March 8, 2005, by special election, to fill the vacancy caused by the death of her husband, Robert T. Matsui.

25 Bobby Jindal resigned on January 14, 2008, to serve as Governor of Louisiana.

26 Judy Chu was elected on July 14, 2009, by special election, to fill the vacancy caused by the resignation of Hilda Solis.

27 Charles Djou was elected on May 22, 2010, by special election, to fill the vacancy caused by the resignation of Neil Abercrombie.

28 David Wu resigned on August 3, 2011.

29 Colleen Hanabusa was elected to the 114th Congress, on November 8, 2016, by special election, to fill the vacancy caused by the death of Mark Takai. She was simultaneously elected to the 115th Congress.

30 Mark Takai died in office on July 20, 2016.

*The closing date for this volume was July 1, 2017.

Asian and Pacific Islander American Representatives, Senators, Delegates, and Resident Commissioners by State and Territory, 1900–2017*

States and Territories are listed in descending order according to the number of Asian and Pacific Islander Americans that each has sent to Congress. Unless noted, Members are Representatives.

STATE/TERRITORY	MEMBER	YEAR MEMBER TOOK OFFICE
California (13)	Dalip Singh (Judge) Saund	1957
	Norman Y. Mineta	1975
	Samuel Ichiye (Sam) Hayakawa[d]	1977
	Robert T. Matsui	1979
	Jay C. Kim	1993
	Mike Honda	2001
	Doris Matsui	2005
	Judy Chu	2009
	Ami Bera	2013
	Mark Takano	2013
	Ted Lieu	2015
	Kamala Harris[d]	2017
	Ro Khanna	2017
Philippine Islands (13)**	Benito Legarda[a]	1907
	Pablo Ocampo[a]	1907
	Manuel L. Quezon[a]	1909
	Manuel Earnshaw[a]	1912
	Jaime C. de Veyra[a]	1917
	Teodoro R. Yangco[a]	1917
	Isauro Gabaldon[a]	1920
	Pedro Guevara[a]	1923
	Camilo Osias[a]	1929
	Francisco A. Delgado[a]	1934
	Quintin Paredes[a]	1935
	Joaquin M. Elizalde[a]	1938
	Carlos Peña Romulo[a]	1944
Hawaii (11)	Hiram L. Fong[d]	1959
	Daniel K. Inouye[c]	1959
	Spark M. Matsunaga[c]	1963
	Patsy Takemoto Mink	1965
	Daniel K. Akaka[c]	1977

STATE/TERRITORY	MEMBER	YEAR MEMBER TOOK OFFICE
	Patricia Saiki	1987
	Mazie K. Hirono[c]	2007
	Charles Djou	2010
	Colleen Hanabusa	2011
	Tulsi Gabbard	2013
	Mark Takai	2015
Hawaii Territory (5)	Robert W. Wilcox[b]	1900
	Jonah Kuhio Kalanianaole[b]	1903
	William P. Jarrett[b]	1923
	Victor S. (Kaleoaloha) Houston[b]	1927
	Samuel Wilder King[b]	1935
American Samoa (3)	Fofó I. F. Sunia[b]	1981
	Eni F. H. Faleomavaega[b]	1989
	Aumua Amata Coleman Radewagen[b]	2015
Guam (3)	Antonio Borja Won Pat[b]	1973
	Ben Garrido Blaz[b]	1985
	Robert A. Underwood[b]	1993
Illinois (2)	Tammy Duckworth[c]	2013
	S. Raja Krishnamoorthi	2017
Louisiana (2)	Bobby Jindal	2005
	Anh (Joseph) Cao	2009
Florida (1)	Stephanie Murphy	2017
Michigan (1)	Hansen Clarke	2011
New York (1)	Grace Meng	2013
Northern Mariana Islands (1)	Gregorio Kilili Camacho Sablan[b]	2009
Ohio (1)	Steve Austria	2009
Oregon (1)	David Wu	1999
Virginia (1)	Robert C. (Bobby) Scott	1993
Washington (1)	Pramila Jayapal	2017

a Resident Commissioner   b Delegate   c Senator and Representative   d Senator

Note: The following states and territories have never elected an Asian Pacific Islander to Congress: Alabama, Alaska, Arizona, Arkansas, Colorado, Connecticut, Delaware, District of Columbia, Georgia, Idaho, Indiana, Iowa, Kansas, Kentucky, Maine, Maryland, Massachusetts, Minnesota, Mississippi, Missouri, Montana, Nebraska, Nevada, New Hampshire, New Jersey, New Mexico, North Carolina, North Dakota, Oklahoma, Pennsylvania, Puerto Rico, Rhode Island, South Carolina, South Dakota, Tennessee, Texas, Utah, Vermont, Virgin Islands, West Virginia, Wisconsin, Wyoming.

*The closing date for this volume was July 1, 2017.

**The United States and the Republic of the Philippines signed the Treaty of General Relations and Protocol on July 4, 1946, to provide recognition of independence of the Philippines from American sovereignty.

Asian and Pacific Islander American Members' Committee Assignments (Standing, Joint, Select) in the U.S. House and Senate, 1900–2017

This appendix lists alphabetically all the congressional committees on which Asian and Pacific Islander American Members served. Several features will help readers track Asian and Pacific Islander membership on committees over time:

- In instances where a committee's name (rather than its primary jurisdictional duties) has changed, a "See also" note refers researchers to prior or latter committee name iterations. These name iterations are listed in chronological order.

- In instances where a committee on which an Asian and Pacific Islander Member served was disbanded and its jurisdiction subsumed by another committee, a "Jurisdiction reassigned" note is provided. Not all reassigned jurisdictions are listed. Researchers are referred only to the committees with expanded jurisdictions on which Asian and Pacific Islander Members later served.

- In instances where a committee was disbanded and no jurisdictional transfer occurred, only the Congress and date ranges of the committee are provided.

- Members' terms of service on committees reflect the years they served on the committees; the Congress range is provided in a separate column. Please be aware that, because this appendix accounts for Members joining or leaving committees because of deaths, resignations, and special elections, in some instances service dates are not coterminous with Congress dates.

- Resident Commissioners from the Philippine Islands did not receive committee assignments.

- The closing date for this volume was July 1, 2017.

HOUSE STANDING COMMITTEE	TERM	CONGRESS	HOUSE STANDING COMMITTEE	TERM	CONGRESS
Agriculture [1820–Present]			**Armed Services [1947–1995; 1999–Present]**		
16th Congress–Present			*80th through 103rd Congresses; 106th Congress–Present*		
Jonah Kuhio Kalanianaole	1913–1922	63rd–67th	*(See also the following standing committees: Military Affairs; Naval Affairs; National Security)*		
William P. Jarrett	1923–1925	68th	Antonio Borja Won Pat	1975–1985	94th–98th
Victor S. (Kaleoaloha) Houston	1927–1933	70th–72nd	Ben Garrido Blaz	1985–1993	99th–102nd
Samuel Wilder King	1935–1943	74th–77th	Robert A. Underwood	1993–1995	103rd
Daniel K. Inouye	1961–1963	87th		1999–2003	106th–107th
Spark M. Matsunaga	1963–1967	88th–89th	Charles Djou	2010–2011	111th
	1971–1975	92nd–93rd	Colleen Hanabusa	2011–2015	112th–113th
Daniel K. Akaka	1977–1981	95th–96th		2017–	115th
Gregorio Kilili Camacho Sablan	2011–2013	112th	Tammy Duckworth	2013–2017	113th–114th
			Tulsi Gabbard	2015–	114th–115th
Appropriations [1865–Present]			Mark Takai	2015–2016	114th
39th Congress–Present			Ro Khanna	2017–	115th
Daniel K. Akaka	1981–1990	97th–101st	Stephanie Murphy	2017–	115th
Mike Honda	2007–2017	110th–114th			
Steve Austria	2011–2013	112th			
Grace Meng	2017–	115th			

Banking and Currency [1865–1975]

39th through 93rd Congresses
(See also the following standing committees: Coinage, Weights, and Measures; Interstate and Foreign Commerce; Banking, Finance, and Urban Affairs; Energy and Commerce)

Daniel K. Inouye	1959–1961	86th

Banking, Finance, and Urban Affairs [1977–1995]

95th through 103rd Congresses
(See also the following standing committees: Coinage, Weights, and Measures; Banking and Currency; Interstate and Foreign Commerce; Energy and Commerce)

Patricia Saiki	1987–1991	100th–101st

Budget [1974–Present]

93rd Congress–Present

Patsy Takemoto Mink	1975–1977	94th
	1993–1999	103rd–105th
Norman Y. Mineta	1977–1983	95th–97th
Robert T. Matsui	1991–1993	102nd
Mike Honda	2001–2003	107th
	2011–2013	112th
Robert C. (Bobby) Scott	2003–2005	108th
	2007–2009	110th–111th
Steve Austria	2009–2011	111th
Charles Djou	2010–2011	111th
Ted Lieu	2015–2017	114th
Pramila Jayapal	2017–	115th
Ro Khanna	2017–	115th

Coinage, Weights, and Measures [1867–1947]

40th through 79th Congresses
(Jurisdiction reassigned to the following standing committees: Banking and Currency; Interstate and Foreign Commerce. See also the following standing committees: Banking, Finance, and Urban Affairs; Energy and Commerce)

Robert W. Wilcox	1901–1903	57th
Jonah Kuhio Kalanianaole	1905–1922	59th–67th

Economic and Educational Opportunities [1995–1997]

104th Congress
(See also the following standing committees: Education and Labor; Education and the Workforce)

Patsy Takemoto Mink	1995–1997	104th
Robert C. (Bobby) Scott	1995–1997	104th

Education and Labor [1867–1883; 1947–1995; 2007–2011]

40th through 48th Congresses; 80th through 103rd Congresses; 110th and 111th Congresses
(See also the following standing committees: Economic and Educational Opportunities; Education and the Workforce)

Patsy Takemoto Mink	1965–1977	89th–94th
	1990–1995	101st–103rd
Eni F. H. Faleomavaega	1993–1995	103rd
Robert C. (Bobby) Scott	1993–1995	103rd
	2007–2011	110th–111th
Robert A. Underwood	1993–1995	103rd
Mazie K. Hirono	2007–2011	110th–111th
David Wu	2007–2011	110th–111th
Judy Chu	2009–2011	111th
Gregorio Kilili Camacho Sablan	2009–2011	111th

Education and the Workforce [1997–2007; 2011–Present]

105th through 109th Congresses; 112th Congress–Present
(See also the following standing committees: Education and Labor; Economic and Educational Opportunities)

Patsy Takemoto Mink	1997–2002	105th–107th
David Wu	1999–2007	106th–109th
	2011	112th
Bobby Jindal	2005–2007	109th
Gregorio Kilili Camacho Sablan	2013–	113th–115th
Robert C. (Bobby) Scott	1997–2003	105th–107th
	2005–2007	109th
	2011–	112th–115th
Mark Takano	2014–	113th–115th
S. Raja Krishnamoorthi	2017–	115th
Mazie K. Hirono	2011–2013	112th

Energy and Commerce [1981–1995; 2001–Present]

97th through 103rd Congresses; 107th Congress–Present
(Jurisdiction reassigned to the following committee: Science. See also the following standing committees: Coinage, Weights, and Measures; Banking and Currency; Interstate and Foreign Commerce; Banking, Finance, and Urban Affairs)

Doris Matsui	2008–	110th–115th

Ethics [2011–Present]

112th Congress–Present
(See also the following standing committee: Standards of Official Conduct)

Mazie K. Hirono	2011	112th

Foreign Affairs [1822–1975; 1979–1995; 2007–Present]

17th through 93rd Congresses; 96th through 103rd Congresses;
110th Congress–Present
(See also the following standing committee: International Relations)

Dalip Singh (Judge) Saund	1957–1963	85th–87th
Ben Garrido Blaz	1987–1993	100th–102nd
Fofó I. F. Sunia	1987–1988	100th
Eni F. H. Faleomavaega	1989–1995	101st–103rd
	2007–2015	110th–113th
David Wu	2007–2009	110th
Ami Bera	2013–	113th–115th
Tulsi Gabbard	2013–	113th–115th
Grace Meng	2013–2017	113th–114th
Ted Lieu	2017–	115th

Government Operations [1953–1995]

83rd through 103rd Congresses
(See also the following standing committees: Post Office and Post Roads;
Post Office and Civil Service; Government Reform; Oversight
and Government Reform)

Robert T. Matsui	1979–1981	96th
Patsy Takemoto Mink	1990–1993	101st–102nd

Government Reform [1999–2007]

106th through 109th Congresses
(See also the following standing committees: Post Office and Post Roads;
Post Office and Civil Service; Government Operations; Oversight
and Government Reform)

Patsy Takemoto Mink	1999–2002	106th–107th

Homeland Security [2005–Present]

109th Congress–Present

Bobby Jindal	2005–2008	109th–110th
Steve Austria	2009–2011	111th
Anh (Joseph) Cao	2009–2011	111th
Hansen Clarke	2011–2013	112th
Tulsi Gabbard	2013–2015	113th

Immigration and Naturalization [1893–1947]

53rd through 79th Congresses
(Jurisdiction reassigned to the following standing committee: Judiciary)

Victor S. (Kaleoaloha) Houston	1931–1933	72nd
Samuel Wilder King	1935–1943	74th–77th

Insular Affairs [1899–1947]

56th through 79th Congresses
(Jurisdiction reassigned to the following standing committee: Public Lands.
See also the following standing committees: Interior and Insular Affairs;
Natural Resources; Resources)

Samuel Wilder King	1939–1943	76th–77th

Interior and Insular Affairs [1951–1993]

82nd through 102nd Congresses
(See also the following standing committees: Public Lands; Territories;
Insular Affairs; Natural Resources; Resources)

Dalip Singh (Judge) Saund	1959–1963	86th–87th
Patsy Takemoto Mink	1967–1977	90th–94th
Antonio Borja Won Pat	1973–1985	93rd–98th
Ben Garrido Blaz	1985–1993	99th–102nd
Fofó I. F. Sunia	1985–1988	99th–100th
Eni F. H. Faleomavaega	1989–1993	101st–102nd

International Relations [1975–1979; 1995–2007]

94th and 95th Congresses; 104th through 109th Congresses
(See also the following standing committee: Foreign Affairs)

Eni F. H. Faleomavaega	1995–2007	104th–109th
Jay C. Kim	1995–1999	104th–105th

Interstate and Foreign Commerce [1892–1981]

53rd through 96th Congresses
(See also the following standing committees: Coinage, Weights, and Measures;
Banking and Currency; Merchant Marine, Radio, and Fisheries; Banking,
Finance, and Urban Affairs; Energy and Commerce)

Robert T. Matsui	1979–1981	96th

Judiciary [1813–Present]

13th Congress–Present
(See also the following standing committee: Immigration and Naturalization)

Robert T. Matsui	1979	96th
Robert C. (Bobby) Scott	1993–2015	103rd–113th
Judy Chu	2009–2017	111th–114th
Ted Lieu	2017–	115th
Pramila Jayapal	2017–	115th

Merchant Marine, Radio, and Fisheries [1932–1935]

72nd and 73rd Congresses
(Jurisdiction reassigned to the following standing committee:
Interstate and Foreign Commerce. See also the following standing
committee: Merchant Marine and Fisheries)

Victor S. (Kaleoaloha) Houston	1931–1933	72nd

Merchant Marine and Fisheries [1887–1932; 1935–1995]

50th through 72nd Congresses; 74th through 103rd Congresses
(Jurisdiction reassigned to the following standing committees: National Security; Resources; Science; Transportation and Infrastructure. See also the following standing committee: Merchant Marine, Radio, and Fisheries)

Samuel Wilder King	1935–1937	74th
	1939–1943	76th–77th
Daniel K. Akaka	1977–1981	95th–96th
Fofó I. F. Sunia	1981–1985	97th–98th
Patricia Saiki	1987–1991	100th–101st
Eni F. H. Faleomavaega	1991–1993	102nd

Military Affairs [1822–1947]

17th through 79th Congresses
(Jurisdiction reassigned to the following standing committee: Armed Services. See also the following standing committee: National Security)

Jonah Kuhio Kalanianaole	1917–1922	65th–67th
William P. Jarrett	1925–1927	69th
Victor S. (Kaleoaloha) Houston	1927–1933	70th–72nd
Samuel Wilder King	1935–1943	74th–77th

National Security [1995–1999]

104th and 105th Congresses
(See also the following standing committees: Military Affairs; Naval Affairs; Armed Services; Merchant Marine and Fisheries)

Robert A. Underwood	1995–1999	104th–105th

Natural Resources [1993–1995; 2007–Present]

103rd Congress; 110th Congress–Present
(See also the following standing committees: Public Lands; Territories; Insular Affairs; Interior and Insular Affairs; Resources)

Eni F. H. Faleomavaega	1993–1995	103rd
	2007–2015	110th–113th
Patsy Takemoto Mink	1993–1995	103rd
Robert A. Underwood	1993–1995	103rd
Gregorio Kilili Camacho Sablan	2009–	111th–115th
Colleen Hanabusa	2011–2015	112th–113th
	2017–	115th
Aumua Amata Coleman Radewagen	2015–	114th–115th
Bobby Jindal	2007–2008	110th

Naval Affairs [1822–1947]

17th through 79th Congresses
(Jurisdiction reassigned to the following standing committee: Armed Services. See also the following standing committee: National Security)

Victor S. (Kaleoaloha) Houston	1927–1929	70th
	1931–1933	72nd
Samuel Wilder King	1935–1943	74th–77th

Oversight and Government Reform [2007–Present]

110th Congress–Present
(See also the following standing committees: Post Office and Post Roads; Post Office and Civil Service; Government Operations; Government Reform)

Anh (Joseph) Cao	2009–2011	111th
Judy Chu	2009–2011	111th
Tammy Duckworth	2013–2017	113th–114th
Ted Lieu	2015–2017	114th
S. Raja Krishnamoorthi	2017–	115th

Post Office and Civil Service [1947–1995]

80th through 103rd Congresses
(Jurisdiction reassigned to the following standing committee: Government Reform and Oversight. See also the following standing committees: Post Office and Post Roads; Government Operations; Government Reform; Oversight and Government Reform)

Spark M. Matsunaga	1965–1967	89th
Norman Y. Mineta	1975–1977	94th

Post Office and Post Roads [1808–1947]

10th through 79th Congresses
(See also the following standing committees: Post Office and Civil Service; Government Operations; Government Reform; Oversight and Government Reform)

Jonah Kuhio Kalanianaole	1903–1905	58th
	1913–1917	63rd–64th
William P. Jarrett	1923–1927	68th–69th
Victor S. (Kaleoaloha) Houston	1927–1933	70th–72nd
Samuel Wilder King	1935–1937	74th

Private Land Claims [1816–1911]

14th through 61st Congresses

Robert W. Wilcox	1901–1903	57th
Jonah Kuhio Kalanianaole	1905–1911	59th–61st

Public Lands [1805–1951]

9th through 81st Congresses
(See also the following standing committees: Post Office and Post Roads; Territories; Insular Affairs; Interior and Insular Affairs; Natural Resources; Resources)

William P. Jarrett	1923–1927	68th–69th
Victor S. (Kaleoaloha) Houston	1927–1933	70th–72nd
Samuel Wilder King	1935–1937	74th

Public Works and Transportation [1975–1995]

94th through 103rd Congresses
(See also the following standing committees: Rivers and Harbors; Transportation and Infrastructure)

Norman Y. Mineta	1975–1995	94th–103rd
Fofó I. F. Sunia	1981–1988	97th–100th
Jay C. Kim	1993–1995	103rd

Resources [1995–2007]

104th through 109th Congresses
(See also the following standing committees: Public Lands; Territories; Insular Affairs; Merchant Marine and Fisheries; Interior and Insular Affairs; Natural Resources)

Eni F. H. Faleomavaega	1995–2007	104th–109th
Robert A. Underwood	1995–2003	104th–107th
Bobby Jindal	2005–2007	109th

Rivers and Harbors [1883–1947]

48th through 79th Congresses
(Jurisdiction reassigned to the following standing committee: Public Works. See also the following standing committees: Public Works and Transportation; Transportation and Infrastructure)

Samuel Wilder King	1937–1943	75th–77th

Rules [1849–1853; 1880–Present]

31st and 32nd Congresses; 46th Congress–Present

Spark M. Matsunaga	1967–1977	90th–94th
Doris Matsui	2005–2011	109th–111th

Science [1995–2007]

104th through 109th Congresses
(See also the following standing committees: Merchant Marine and Fisheries; Science and Technology; Energy and Commerce; Science, Space, and Technology)

David Wu	1999–2007	106th–109th
Mike Honda	2001–2007	107th–109th
Doris Matsui	2006–2007	109th

Science and Technology [1975–1987; 2007–2011]

94th through 99th Congresses; 110th and 111th Congresses
(See also the following standing committees: Science, Space, and Technology; Science)

Norman Y. Mineta	1983–1987	98th–99th
Mike Honda	2007	110th
David Wu	2007–2011	110th–111th

Science, Space, and Technology [1987–1995; 2011–Present]

100th through 103rd Congresses; 112th Congress–Present
(See also the following standing committees: Science and Technology; Science)

Norman Y. Mineta	1987–1993	100th–102nd
Robert C. (Bobby) Scott	1993–1995	103rd
Hansen Clarke	2011–2013	112th
David Wu	2011	112th
Mark Takano	2013–	113th–115th
Ami Bera	2013–	113th–115th
Colleen Hanabusa	2017–	115th

Small Business [1975–Present]

94th Congress–Present

Jay C. Kim	1993–1995	103rd
Eni F. H. Faleomavaega	2003–2007	108th–109th
Mazie K. Hirono	2007–2009	110th
Judy Chu	2011–	112th–115th
Grace Meng	2013–2017	113th–114th
Mark Takai	2015–2016	114th
Aumua Amata Coleman Radewagen	2015–	114th–115th
Stephanie Murphy	2017–	115th

Standards of Official Conduct [1967–2011]

90th through 111th Congresses

Robert C. (Bobby) Scott	2008–2009	110th

Territories [1825–1847]

19th through 79th Congresses
(Jurisdiction reassigned to the following standing committee: Public Lands. See also the following standing committees: Interior and Insular Affairs; Natural Resources; Resources)

Jonah Kuhio Kalanianaole	1903–1922	58th–67th
William P. Jarrett	1923–1927	68th–69th
Victor S. (Kaleoaloha) Houston	1927–1933	70th–72nd
Samuel Wilder King	1935–1939	74th–75th
	1941–1943	77th

Transportation and Infrastructure [1995–Present]

104th Congress–Present
(Jurisdiction reassigned to the following standing committee: Interior and Insular Affairs. See also the following standing committees: Rivers and Harbors; Merchant Marine and Fisheries; Public Works and Transportation)

Mike Honda	2001–2007	107th–109th
Mazie K. Hirono	2007–2013	110th–112th
Doris Matsui	2007–2008	110th
Anh (Joseph) Cao	2009–2011	111th
Jay C. Kim	1995–1999	104th–105th
Norman Y. Mineta	1995–1997	104th

Veterans' Affairs [1947–Present]

80th Congress–Present

Antonio Borja Won Pat	1981–1983	97th
Mark Takano	2013–	113th–115th
Aumua Amata Coleman Radewagen	2015–	114th–115th
Gregorio Kilili Camacho Sablan	2017–	115th

HOUSE STANDING COMMITTEE	TERM	CONGRESS	HOUSE STANDING COMMITTEE	TERM	CONGRESS
Ways and Means [1795–Present] *4th Congress–Present*			Judy Chu	2017–	115th
Robert T. Matsui	1981–2005	97th–108th			

HOUSE SELECT COMMITTEE	TERM	CONGRESS	HOUSE SELECT COMMITTEE	TERM	CONGRESS
Select Committee on Aging [1975–1993] *94th through 102nd Congresses*			**Select Committee on Narcotics Abuse and Control [1976–1993]** *94th through 102nd Congresses*		
Spark M. Matsunaga	1975–1977	94th	Daniel K. Akaka	1978–1979	95th
Ben Garrido Blaz	1985–1993	99th–102nd		1981–1990	97th–101st
Patricia Saiki	1987–1991	100th–101st	Robert T. Matsui	1981–1987	97th–100th
Select Committee on the Events Surrounding the 2012 Terrorist Attack in Benghazi [2014–2017] *113th through 114th Congresses*			**Select Committee on U.S. National Security and Military/Commercial Concerns with the People's Republic of China [1998–1999]** *105th and 106th Congresses*		
Tammy Duckworth	2014–2017	113th–114th	Robert C. (Bobby) Scott	1998–1999	105th–106th
Select Committee on Hunger [1984–1993] *98th through 102nd Congresses*			**Select Committee on the Outer Continental Shelf (Ad Hoc) [1975–1980]** *94th through 96th Congresses*		
Eni F. H. Faleomavaega	1989–1993	101st–102nd	Patsy Takemoto Mink	1975–1977	94th
Permanent Select Committee on Intelligence [1977–Present] *95th Congress–Present*			**Select Committee on Population [1977–1979]** *95th Congress*		
Norman Y. Mineta	1977–1985	95th–98th	Daniel K. Akaka	1977–1979	95th

JOINT COMMITTEE	TERM	CONGRESS	JOINT COMMITTEE	TERM	CONGRESS
Joint Committee on Disposition of Executive Papers [1945–1970] *79th through 91st Congresses*			**Joint Committee on the Library of Congress [1806–Present]** *9th Congress–Present*		
Hiram L. Fong	1969–1970	91st	Daniel K. Inouye	1982–1987	97th–99th
Joint Committee on Hawaii [1937–1939] *75th Congress*			**Joint Committee on Printing [1947–Present]** *80th Congress–Present*		
Samuel Wilder King	1937–1939	75th	Daniel K. Inouye	1995–2009	104th–110th
Joint Committee on Immigration and Nationality Policy [1953–1970] *82nd through 91st Congresses*			**Joint Committee on Taxation [1926–Present]** *69th Congress–Present*		
Hiram L. Fong	1970	91st	Spark M. Matsunaga	1987–1990	100th–101st

Agriculture and Forestry [1884–1977]
48th through 94th Congresses
(See also the following standing committee: Agriculture, Nutrition, and Forestry)

Samuel Ichiye (Sam) Hayakawa	1977	95th

Agriculture, Nutrition, and Forestry [1977–Present]
95th Congress–Present
(See also the following standing committee: Agriculture and Forestry)

Samuel Ichiye (Sam) Hayakawa	1977–1983	95th–97th

Appropriations [1867–Present]
40th Congress–Present

Hiram L. Fong	1969–1977	91st–94th
Daniel K. Inouye	1971–2013	92nd–112th

Armed Services [1947–Present]
80th Congress–Present

Daniel K. Inouye	1963–1971	88th–91st
Daniel K. Akaka	2001–2013	107th–112th
Mazie K. Hirono	2013–	113th–115th

Banking, Housing, and Urban Affairs [1971–Present]
92nd Congress–Present

Daniel K. Akaka	2001–2003	107th
	2007–2013	110th–112th

Budget [1974–Present]
93rd Congress–Present

Samuel Ichiye (Sam) Hayakawa	1977–1979	95th
Kamala Harris	2017–	115th

Commerce [1825–1946; 1961–1977]
19th through 79th Congresses; 87th through 94th Congresses
(Jurisdiction reassigned to the following standing committee: Environment and Public Works. See also the following standing committee: Commerce, Science, and Transportation)

Daniel K. Inouye	1969–1977	91st–94th

Commerce, Science, and Transportation [1977–Present]
95th Congress–Present
(See also the following standing committee: Commerce)

Daniel K. Inouye	1977–2013	95th–112th
Spark M. Matsunaga	1977–1991	95th–101st
Tammy Duckworth	2017–	115th

District of Columbia [1816–1977]
14th through 94th Congresses
(Jurisdiction reassigned to the following standing committee: Governmental Affairs. See also the following standing committee: Homeland Security and Governmental Affairs)

Daniel K. Inouye	1971–1977	92nd–94th

Energy and Natural Resources [1977–Present]
95th Congress–Present
(See also the following standing committee: Interior and Insular Affairs)

Spark M. Matsunaga	1977–1985	95th–98th
Daniel K. Akaka	1990–2009	101st–110th
Mazie K. Hirono	2015–	114th–115th
Tammy Duckworth	2017–	115th
Samuel Ichiye (Sam) Hayakawa	1977	95th

Environment and Public Works [1977–Present]
95th Congress–Present
(See also the following standing committee: Public Works)

Mazie K. Hirono	2013–2015	113th
Tammy Duckworth	2017–	115th
Kamala Harris	2017–	115th

Finance [1816–Present]
14th Congress–Present

Spark M. Matsunaga	1977–1990	95th–101st

Foreign Relations [1816–Present]
14th Congress–Present

Spark M. Matsunaga	1977	95th
Samuel Ichiye (Sam) Hayakawa	1979–1983	96th–97th

Governmental Affairs [1977–2004]
95th through 108th Congresses
(See also the following standing committees: District of Columbia; Homeland Security and Governmental Affairs; Post Office and Civil Service)

Daniel K. Akaka	1990–2005	101st–108th

Homeland Security and Governmental Affairs [2005–Present]
109th Congress–Present
(See also the following standing committees: District of Columbia; Governmental Affairs; Post Office and Civil Service)

Kamala Harris	2017–	115th
Daniel K. Akaka	2005–2012	109th–112th

Human Resources [1977–1979]
95th Congress
(See also the following standing committee: Labor and Human Resources)

Samuel Ichiye (Sam) Hayakawa	1977–1979	95th

Indian Affairs [1993–Present]
103rd Congress–Present
(See also the following select committee: Indian Affairs)

Daniel K. Inouye	1993–2013	103rd–112th
Daniel K. Akaka	1993–2013	103rd–112th

Interior and Insular Affairs [1948–1977]
80th through 94th Congresses
(See also the following standing committee: Energy and Natural Resources)

Hiram L. Fong	1959–1961	86th–87th

Judiciary [1816–Present]
14th Congress–Present

Hiram L. Fong	1961–1977	87th–94th
Mazie K. Hirono	2013–2015	113th
	2017–	115th

Labor and Human Resources [1979–2001]
96th through 106th Congresses
(See also the following standing committee: Human Resources)

Spark M. Matsunaga	1982–1990	97th–101st

Post Office and Civil Service [1947–1977]
80th through 94th Congresses
(Jurisdiction reassigned to the following standing committee: Governmental Affairs. See also the following standing committee: Homeland Security and Governmental Affairs)

Hiram L. Fong	1959–1977	86th–94th

Public Works [1947–1977]
80th through 95th Congresses
(See also the following standing committees: Commerce; Environment and Public Works)

Hiram L. Fong	1959–1969	86th–90th
Daniel K. Inouye	1963–1969	88th–90th

Rules and Administration [1947–Present]
80th Congress–Present

Daniel K. Inouye	1982–2013	97th–112th

Small Business [1981–2001]
97th through 106th Congresses
(See also the following select committee: Small Business; and the following standing committee: Small Business and Entrepreneurship)

Samuel Ichiye (Sam) Hayakawa	1981–1983	97th

Small Business and Entrepreneurship [2001–Present]
107th Congress–Present
(See also following standing committee: Small Business)

Mazie K. Hirono	2015–	114th–115th
Tammy Duckworth	2017–	115th

Veterans' Affairs [1971–Present]
92nd Congress–Present

Spark M. Matsunaga	1977–1990	95th–101st
Daniel K. Akaka	1990–2013	101st–112th
Mazie K. Hirono	2013–	113th–115th

Special Committee on Aging [1961–Present]
87th Congress–Present

Hiram L. Fong	1963–1977	88th–94th

Temporary Select Committee: Study the Senate Committee System II [1984]
98th Congress

Spark M. Matsunaga	1984	98th

Permanent Select Committee on Ethics [1977–Present]
95th Congress–Present

Daniel K. Akaka	2001–2006	107th–109th

Select Committee on Equal Education Opportunity [1970–1972]
91st and 92nd Congresses

Daniel K. Inouye	1970–1972	91st–92nd

Select Committee on Indian Affairs [1977–1993]
95th through 102nd Congresses
(See also the following standing committee: Indian Affairs)

Daniel K. Inouye	1979–1993	96th–102nd
Daniel K. Akaka	1991–1993	102nd

Permanent Select Committee on Intelligence [1976–Present]
94th Congress–Present

Daniel K. Inouye	1976–1985	94th–98th
Mazie K. Hirono	2015–2017	114th
Kamala Harris	2017–	115th

Special Committee: Official Conduct [1977]
95th Congress

Daniel K. Inouye	1977	95th

Select Committee on Presidential Campaign Activities [1973–1974]
93rd Congress

Daniel K. Inouye	1973–1974	93rd

Select Committee: Secret Military Assistance to Iran and the Nicaraguan Opposition [1987]
100th Congress

Daniel K. Inouye	1987	100th

Select Committee on Small Business [1950–1981]
81st through 96th Congresses
(Jurisdiction reassigned to the following standing committee: Small Business. See also the following standing committee: Small Business and Entrepreneurship)

Samuel Ichiye (Sam) Hayakawa	1979–1981	96th

Select Committee: To Study Law Enforcement Undercover Activities of Components of the Department of Justice [1982–1983]
97th Congress

Daniel K. Inouye	1982	97th

MEMBER	TERM	CONGRESS	MEMBER	TERM	CONGRESS

Delegates, Representatives, and Resident Commissioners Who Served Full or Partial Terms Without Committee Assignments

Benito Legarda	1907–1912	60th–62nd
Pablo Ocampo	1907–1909	60th
Manuel L. Quezon	1909–1916	61st–64th
Manuel Earnshaw	1912–1917	63rd–64th
Jaime C. de Veyra	1917–1923	65th–67th
Teodoro R. Yangco	1917–1920	65th–66th
Isauro Gabaldon	1920–1928	66th–70th
Pedro Guevara	1923–1936	68th–74th
Camilo Osias	1929–1935	71st–73rd

Francisco A. Delgado	1934–1936	74th
Quintin Paredes	1935–1938	74th–75th
Joaquin M. Elizalde	1938–1944	75th–78th
Carlos Peña Romulo	1944–1946	78th–79th
Robert W. Wilcox	1900–1901	56th, 2nd sess.
Colleen Hanabusa	2016	114th

Senators Who Served Full or Partial Terms Without Committee Assignments

Samuel Ichiye (Sam) Hayakawa	1976	94th, 2nd sess.

Sources: David T. Canon, Garrison Nelson, and Charles Stewart III, *Committees in the U.S. Congress, 1789–1946*, 4 vols. (Washington, DC: CQ Press, 2002); various editions of the *Congressional Directory* (Washington, DC: Government Printing Office); various editions of the *Congressional Quarterly Almanac* (Washington, DC: Congressional Quarterly, Inc.); various editions of the *Congressional Record*; Garrison Nelson, *Committees in the U.S. Congress, 1947–1992*, 2 vols. (Washington, DC: Congressional Quarterly Press, 1994); Garrison Nelson and Charles Stewart III, *Committees in the U.S. Congress, 1993–2010* (Washington, DC: CQ Press, 2011); various editions of Congressional Committee Prints (Washington, DC: Government Printing Office).

Asian and Pacific Islander Americans Who Have Chaired Congressional Committees, 1975–2017*

Prior to 1975, no Asian Pacific American had served as chairman of a full congressional committee.

CONGRESS	MEMBER (PARTY-STATE)	HOUSE COMMITTEE
103rd (1993–1995)	Norman Y. Mineta (D-CA)	Public Works and Transportation
104th–115th (1995–2019)	N/A	N/A

CONGRESS	MEMBER (PARTY-STATE)	SENATE COMMITTEE
94th (1975–1977)	Daniel K. Inouye (D-HI)	Select Intelligence
95th (1977–1979)	Daniel K. Inouye (D-HI)**	Select Intelligence
96th–99th (1979–1987)	N/A	N/A
100th (1987–1989)	Daniel K. Inouye (D-HI)	Indian Affairs Select Secret Military Assistance to Iran and the Nicaraguan Opposition
101st (1989–1991)	Daniel K. Inouye (D-HI)	Indian Affairs
102nd (1991–1993)	Daniel K. Inouye (D-HI)	Indian Affairs
103rd (1993–1995)	Daniel K. Inouye (D-HI)	Indian Affairs
104th–106th (1995–2001)	N/A	N/A
107th (2001–2003)	Daniel K. Inouye (D-HI)***	Indian Affairs
108th–109th (2003–2007)	N/A	N/A
110th (2007–2009)	Daniel K. Akaka (D-HI) Daniel K. Inouye (D-HI)	Veterans' Affairs Commerce, Science, and Transportation
111th (2009–2011)	Daniel K. Akaka (D-HI) Daniel K. Inouye (D-HI)	Veterans' Affairs Appropriations
112th (2011–2013)	Daniel K. Akaka (D-HI) Daniel K. Inouye (D-HI)	Indian Affairs Appropriations
113th–115th (2013–2019)	N/A	N/A

*The closing date for this volume was July 1, 2017.

**Daniel K. Inouye stepped down as Chairman on January 27, 1978, but remained on the committee.

***Daniel K. Inouye became Chairman on June 6, 2001.

Asian and Pacific Islander American Chairs of Subcommittees of Standing and Select Committees in the U.S. House and Senate, 1965–2017*

This table is based on information drawn from the *Congressional Directory*, various historical directories, and the *United States Code Congressional and Administrative News*.

Prior to the 89th Congress, there were no Asian Pacific American subcommittee chairs.

CONGRESS	MEMBER (PARTY-STATE)	HOUSE COMMITTEE	SUBCOMMITTEE
89th (1965–1967)	Spark M. Matsunaga (D-HI)	Agriculture	Domestic Marketing and Consumer Relations
90th–92nd (1967–1973)	N/A	N/A	N/A
93rd (1973–1975)	Patsy Takemoto Mink (D-HI)	Interior and Insular Affairs	Mines and Mining
94th (1975–1977)	Patsy Takemoto Mink (D-HI)	Interior and Insular Affairs	Mines and Mining
95th (1977–1979)	Norman Y. Mineta (D-CA)	Public Works and Transportation	Public Buildings and Grounds
96th (1979–1981)	Norman Y. Mineta (D-CA)	Budget	Budget Process
	Norman Y. Mineta (D-CA)	Public Works and Transportation	Oversight and Review
	Antonio Borja Won Pat (D-GU)	Interior and Insular Affairs	Pacific Affairs
97th (1981–1983)	Norman Y. Mineta (D-CA)	Public Works and Transportation	Aviation
	Antonio Borja Won Pat (D-GU)	Interior and Insular Affairs	Insular Affairs
98th (1983–1985)	Norman Y. Mineta (D-CA)	Public Works and Transportation	Aviation
	Antonio Borja Won Pat (D-GU)	Interior and Insular Affairs	Insular Affairs
99th (1985–1987)	Norman Y. Mineta (D-CA)	Public Works and Transportation	Aviation
100th (1987–1989)	Norman Y. Mineta (D-CA)	Public Works and Transportation	Aviation
	Fofó I. F. Sunia (D-AS)	Public Works and Transportation	Public Buildings and Grounds
101st (1989–1991)	Norman Y. Mineta (D-CA)	Public Works and Transportation	Surface Transportation
102nd (1991–1993)	Norman Y. Mineta (D-CA)	Public Works and Transportation	Surface Transportation
103rd–104th (1993–1997)	N/A	N/A	N/A
105th (1997–1999)	Jay C. Kim (R-CA)	Transportation and Infrastructure	Public Buildings and Economic Development
106th–109th (1999–2007)	N/A	N/A	N/A
110th (2007–2009)	Eni F. H. Faleomavaega (D-AS)	Foreign Affairs	Asia, the Pacific, and the Global Environment
	Robert C. (Bobby) Scott (D-VA)	Judiciary	Crime, Terrorism, and Homeland Security
	David Wu (D-OR)	Science and Technology	Technology and Innovation
111th (2009–2011)	Eni F. H. Faleomavaega (D-AS)	Foreign Affairs	Asia, the Pacific, and the Global Environment
	Robert C. (Bobby) Scott (D-VA)	Judiciary	Crime, Terrorism, and Homeland Security
	David Wu (D-OR)	Science and Technology	Technology and Innovation

CONGRESS	MEMBER (PARTY-STATE)	HOUSE COMMITTEE	SUBCOMMITTEE
112th–113th (2011–2015	N/A	N/A	N/A
114th (2015–2017)	Aumua Amata Coleman Radewagen (R-AS)	Small Business	Health and Technology
115th (2017–2019)	N/A	N/A	N/A

CONGRESS	MEMBER (PARTY-STATE)	SENATE COMMITTEE	SUBCOMMITTEE
90th (1967–1969)	Daniel K. Inouye (D-HI)	Armed Services	Treatment of Deserters From Military Service
91st (1969–1971)	Daniel K. Inouye (D-HI)	Armed Services	H.R. 3832, Grade of General for Assistant Commandant of the Marine Corps
92nd (1971–1973)	Daniel K. Inouye (D-HI)	Appropriations	District of Columbia
	Daniel K. Inouye (D-HI)	Commerce	Foreign Commerce and Tourism
93rd (1973–1975)	Daniel K. Inouye (D-HI)	Appropriations	Foreign Operations
	Daniel K. Inouye (D-HI)	Commerce	Foreign Commerce and Tourism
94th (1975–1977)	Daniel K. Inouye (D-HI)	Appropriations	Foreign Operations
	Daniel K. Inouye (D-HI)	Commerce	Foreign Commerce and Tourism
95th (1977–1979)	Daniel K. Inouye (D-HI)	Appropriations	Foreign Operations
	Daniel K. Inouye (D-HI)	Commerce, Science, and Transportation	Merchant Marine and Tourism
	Spark M. Matsunaga (D-HI)	Finance	Tourism and Sugar
96th (1979–1981)	Daniel K. Inouye (D-HI)	Appropriations	Foreign Operations
	Daniel K. Inouye (D-HI)	Commerce, Science, and Transportation	Merchant Marine and Tourism
	Daniel K. Inouye (D-HI)	Select Intelligence	Budget Authorization
	Spark M. Matsunaga (D-HI)	Finance	Tourism and Sugar
97th (1981–1983)	Samuel Ichiye (Sam) Hayakawa (R-CA)	Agriculture, Nutrition, and Forestry	Forestry, Water Resources, and Environment
	Samuel Ichiye (Sam) Hayakawa (R-CA)	Foreign Relations	East Asian and Pacific Affairs
	Samuel Ichiye (Sam) Hayakawa (R-CA)	Small Business	Advocacy and the Future of Small Business
98th–99th (1983–1987)	N/A	N/A	N/A
100th (1987–1989)	Daniel K. Inouye (D-HI)	Appropriations	Foreign Operations
	Daniel K. Inouye (D-HI)	Commerce, Science, and Transportation	Communications
	Spark M. Matsunaga (D-HI)	Finance	International Trade
	Spark M. Matsunaga (D-HI)	Labor and Human Resources	Aging

CONGRESS	MEMBER (PARTY-STATE)	SENATE COMMITTEE	SUBCOMMITTEE
101st (1989–1991)	Daniel K. Inouye (D-HI)	Appropriations	Defense
	Daniel K. Inouye (D-HI)	Commerce, Science, and Transportation	Communications
	Spark M. Matsunaga (D-HI)	Finance	Taxation and Debt Management
	Spark M. Matsunaga (D-HI)	Labor and Human Resources	Aging
102nd (1991–1993)	Daniel K. Inouye (D-HI)	Appropriations	Defense
	Daniel K. Inouye (D-HI)	Commerce, Science, and Transportation	Communications
103rd (1993–1995)	Daniel K. Akaka (D-HI)	Energy and Natural Resources	Mineral Resources Development and Production
	Daniel K. Inouye (D-HI)	Appropriations	Defense
	Daniel K. Inouye (D-HI)	Commerce, Science, and Transportation	Communications
104th–106th (1995–2001)	N/A	N/A	N/A
107th (2001–2003)	Daniel K. Akaka (D-HI)	Armed Services	Readiness and Management Support
	Daniel K. Akaka (D-HI)	Energy and Natural Resources	National Parks
	Daniel K. Akaka (D-HI)	Governmental Affairs	International Security, Proliferation, and Federal Services
	Daniel K. Inouye (D-HI)	Appropriations	Defense
	Daniel K. Inouye (D-HI)	Commerce, Science, and Transportation	Communications
108th–109th (2003–2007)	N/A	N/A	N/A
110th (2007–2009)	Daniel K. Akaka (D-HI)	Armed Services	Readiness and Management Support
	Daniel K. Akaka (D-HI)	Energy and Natural Resources	National Parks
	Daniel K. Akaka (D-HI)	Homeland Security and Governmental Affairs	Oversight of Government Management, the Federal Workforce, and the District of Columbia (OGM)
	Daniel K. Inouye (D-HI)	Appropriations	Defense
111th (2009–2011)	Daniel K. Akaka (D-HI)	Homeland Security and Governmental Affairs	Oversight of Government Management, the Federal Workforce, and the District of Columbia (OGM)
	Daniel K. Inouye (D-HI)	Appropriations	Defense
112th (2011–2013)	Daniel K. Akaka (D-HI)	Homeland Security and Governmental Affairs	Oversight of Government Management, the Federal Workforce, and the District of Columbia (OGM)
	Daniel K. Inouye (D-HI)	Appropriations	Department of Defense
113th–115th (2013–2019)	N/A	N/A	N/A

*The closing date for this volume was July 1, 2017.

Asian and Pacific Islander Americans in Party Leadership Positions, 1975–2017*

CONGRESS	MEMBER (PARTY-STATE)	CAUCUS/CONFERENCE	POSITION
HOUSE OF REPRESENTATIVES			
94th (1975–1977)	Patsy Takemoto Mink (D-HI)	Democratic Caucus	Secretary
95th–115th (1977–2019)	N/A	N/A	N/A

CONGRESS	MEMBER (PARTY-STATE)	CAUCUS/CONFERENCE	POSITION
SENATE			
95th (1977–1979)	Daniel K. Inouye (D-HI)	Democratic Conference	Secretary
	Spark M. Matsunaga (D-HI)	Democratic Conference	Chief Deputy Whip
96th (1979–1981)	Daniel K. Inouye (D-HI)	Democratic Conference	Secretary
	Spark M. Matsunaga (D-HI)	Democratic Conference	Chief Deputy Whip
97th (1981–1983)	Daniel K. Inouye (D-HI)	Democratic Conference	Secretary
	Spark M. Matsunaga (D-HI)	Democratic Conference	Chief Deputy Whip
98th (1983–1985)	Daniel K. Inouye (D-HI)	Democratic Conference	Secretary
	Spark M. Matsunaga (D-HI)	Democratic Conference	Chief Deputy Whip
99th (1985–1987)	Daniel K. Inouye (D-HI)	Democratic Conference	Secretary
	Spark M. Matsunaga (D-HI)	Democratic Conference	Chief Deputy Whip
100th (1987–1989)	Daniel K. Inouye (D-HI)	Democratic Conference	Secretary
	Spark M. Matsunaga (D-HI)	Democratic Conference	Chief Deputy Whip
101st–110th (1989–2009)	N/A	N/A	N/A
111th (2009–2011)	Daniel K. Inouye (D-HI)	N/A	President Pro Tempore
112th (2011–2013)	Daniel K. Inouye (D-HI)**	N/A	President Pro Tempore
113th–115th (2013–2019)	N/A	N/A	N/A

*The closing date for this volume was July 1, 2017.

**Daniel K. Inouye served as president pro tempore from June 28, 2010, until his death on December 17, 2012.

Asian and Pacific Islander American Familial Connections in Congress

WIDOWS WHO HAVE SUCCEEDED THEIR LATE HUSBANDS

Doris Matsui of California (2005–Present), wife of Robert T. Matsui of California (1979–2005)

Congressional Asian Pacific American Caucus Chairmen and Chairwomen, 1994–2017*

In 1994 Members of Asian and Pacific Islander descent created the Congressional Asian Pacific American Caucus (CAPAC). Inspired by the Congressional Black and Hispanic Caucuses, CAPAC was created for Members to formally coordinate efforts to advance legislation pertaining to the interests of the Asian Pacific American community. Since its formation, the bipartisan and bicameral caucus has educated congressional colleagues on the history of the growing Asian Pacific American community in the United States and continues to build recognition in Congress.

CONGRESS	MEMBER'S NAME
103rd (1993–1995)	Norman Y. Mineta (D-CA)
104th (1995–1997)[1]	Norman Y. Mineta (D-CA)
	Patsy Takemoto Mink (D-HI)
105th (1997–1999)	Patsy Takemoto Mink (D-HI)
106th (1999–2001)	Robert A. Underwood (D-GU)
107th (2001–2003)	David Wu (D-OR)
108th (2003–2005)[2]	David Wu (D-OR)
	Mike Honda (D-CA)
109th (2005–2007)	Mike Honda (D-CA)
110th (2007–2009)	Mike Honda (D-CA)
111th (2009–2011)	Mike Honda (D-CA)
112th (2011–2013)	Judy Chu (D-CA)
113th (2013–2015)	Judy Chu (D-CA)
114th (2015–2017)	Judy Chu (D-CA)
115th (2017–2019)	Judy Chu (D-CA)

1   In the 104th Congress, Norman Y. Mineta served as Chairman from May 1994 to October 1995, and Patsy Takemoto Mink served as Chairwoman from October 1995 to January 1997.

2   In the 108th Congress, David Wu served as Chairman from January to December 2003, and Mike Honda served as Chairman from January 2004 to December 2004.

*The closing date for this volume was July 1, 2017.

Constitutional Amendments, Treaties, Executive Orders, and Major Acts of Congress Referenced in the Text

TITLE	CITATION: PUBLIC LAW (P.L.) AND STATUTE (STAT.)	MAIN PROVISIONS
DOMESTIC POLICY *(excluding Acts related to Revenues/Tariffs)*		
CIVIL RIGHTS LEGISLATION		
FOURTEENTH AMENDMENT (1868)	14 Stat. 358	Declared that all persons born or naturalized in the United States were citizens and that any state that denied or abridged the voting rights of males over the age of 21 would be subject to proportional reductions in its representation in the U.S. House of Representatives. Approved by the 39th Congress (1865–1867) as H.J. Res. 127. Ratified by the states on July 9, 1868.
IMMIGRATION AND NATURALIZATION POLICIES		
CHINESE EXCLUSION ACT (1882)	22 Stat. 58	Banned Chinese laborers from immigrating to the United States for 10 years and denied citizenship to all foreign-born Chinese. Also listed penalties for employers who violated the act. Exempted some Chinese laborers and merchants who entered the United States from other destinations. Passed by the 47th Congress (1881–1883) as H.R. 5804. Amended by the Geary Act (27 Stat. 25) amendments in 1892.
GEARY ACT (1892)	27 Stat. 25	Extended Chinese Exclusion Act (22 Stat. 58) for 10 years and enabled the removal of Chinese immigrants who lived illegally in the United States. Immigrants arrested under this act had to provide residency certificates to maintain legal residency. Passed by the 52nd Congress (1891–1893) as H.R. 6185.
EXECUTIVE ORDER 589	N/A	Enabled the Secretary of Commerce and Labor to restrict Japanese and/or Korean laborers from entering the continental United States and U.S. territories through Canada, Hawaii, and Mexico via passports issued by the Japanese government. Issued on March 14, 1907, by President Theodore Roosevelt.
IMMIGRATION ACT OF 1917	P.L. 64-301; 39 Stat. 874	Increased entry restrictions for foreigners who immigrated to the United States. Prohibited immigration from specific regions of Asia. Required a literacy test. Streamlined deportation procedures. Passed by the 64th Congress (1915–1917) over a presidential veto as H.R. 10384.
EMERGENCY QUOTA ACT (IMMIGRATION RESTRICTION ACT OF 1921)	P.L. 67-5; 42 Stat. 5	Limited the number of immigrants entering the United States to 3 percent of the foreign-born population listed in the 1910 Census. Set the total limit to approximately 357,000 immigrants per year. Passed by the 67th Congress (1921–1923) as H.R. 4075.

TITLE	CITATION: PUBLIC LAW (P.L.) AND STATUTE (STAT.)	MAIN PROVISIONS
IMMIGRATION ACT OF 1924 (JOHNSON–REED ACT)	P.L. 68-139; 43 Stat. 153	Lowered annual immigration quotas of all foreign nationalities living in the United States by 2 percent based on population determined by the 1890 Census. Established a strict apportionment system based on country of origin. Authorized strict quota of a minimum of 100 immigrants from Asian and African countries to the United States and reduced total immigration limit to 150,000 per year. Passed by the 68th Congress (1923–1925) as H.R. 7995.
NATIONALITY ACT OF 1940	P.L. 76-853; 54 Stat. 1137	Defined nationality at birth in the mainland United States and in U.S. territories. Limited nationality cases to certain courts and revised eligibility requirements for naturalization. Also enabled Filipinos who had served in the U.S. Armed Forces to become naturalized citizens. Outlined how a naturalized citizen could forfeit that status. Passed by the 76th Congress (1939–1941) as H.R. 9980.
WAR BRIDES ACT (1945)	P.L. 79-271; 59 Stat. 659	Enabled honorably discharged U.S. military personnel to bring foreign spouses and children to the United States if they applied for admission within three years of the act's passage and met necessary requirements. Passed by the 79th Congress (1945–1947) as H.R. 4857.
DISPLACED PERSONS ACT OF 1948	P.L. 80-774; 62 Stat. 1009	Authorized the admission of European refugees displaced by World War II to the United States for two years after its enactment based on the quotas stated in the Immigration Act of 1924 (P.L. 68-139). Also enabled resident aliens to adjust their immigration status. Passed by the 80th Congress (1947–1949) as S. 2242.
IMMIGRATION AND NATIONALITY ACT OF 1952 (McCARRAN–WALTER ACT)	P.L. 82-414; 66 Stat. 163	Revised parts of Immigration Act of 1924 (P.L. 68-139) and retained the national origins quota system, but repealed the exclusion of Asian immigrants. Passed by the 82nd Congress (1951–1953) over a presidential veto as H.R. 5678.
REFUGEE RELIEF ACT (1953)	P.L. 83-203; 67 Stat. 400	Authorized the annual admission of more than 200,000 refugees from anywhere in the world to the United States beyond the established quota numbers per the Immigration and Nationality Act of 1952 (P.L. 82-414). Passed by the 83rd Congress (1953–1955) as H.R. 6481.
IMMIGRATION AND NATIONALITY ACT OF 1965 (HART–CELLER ACT)	P.L. 89-236; 79 Stat. 911	Superseded the Immigration Act of 1924 (P.L. 68-139) by eliminating the national origins quota system. Initiated a new preference system with annual numerical ceilings for immigrants. Applied a quota on immigrants from the Western Hemisphere. Passed by the 89th Congress (1965–1967) as H.R. 2580.
INDOCHINA MIGRATION AND REFUGEE ASSISTANCE ACT OF 1975	P.L. 94-23; 89 Stat. 87	Provided relocation and resettlement aid for immigrants who left Southeast Asia and were unable to return to their home countries. Passed by the 94th Congress (1975–1977) as H.R. 6755.
REFUGEE ACT OF 1980	P.L. 96-212; 94 Stat. 102	Amended the Immigration and Nationality Act of 1965 (P.L. 89-236) and the Migration and Refugee Assistance Act of 1962 (P.L. 87-510). Established a federal office to process refugees for U.S. settlement and expanded the term "refugee" to include anyone in the world who fled his or her original country to avoid persecution based on race, religion, or political alignment. Created special category for asylum seekers. Increased the numerical ceiling for immigrants entering the United States. Passed by the 96th Congress (1979–1981) as S. 643.

TITLE	CITATION: PUBLIC LAW (P.L.) AND STATUTE (STAT.)	MAIN PROVISIONS
AMERASIAN IMMIGRATION ACT (1982)	P.L. 97-359; 96 Stat. 1716	Amended the Immigration and Nationality Act of 1965 (P.L. 89-236) to permit Amerasian children—children with American fathers—born in Southeast Asia between 1950 and 1982 to immigrate to the United States upon a guarantee by an American sponsor. Passed by the 97th Congress (1981–1983) as S. 1698.
APPROPRIATIONS ACT FOR THE FISCAL YEAR 1988, AND FOR OTHER PURPOSES (AMERASIAN IMMIGRATION) (1987)	P.L. 100-202; 101 Stat. 1329	Authorized executive branch agencies to maintain admission and protection programs for Indochinese refugees in the border regions of Cambodia, Laos, and Thailand. Instructed the President to consider larger admission allocations for Amerasian children and their immediate families. Passed by the 100th Congress (1987–1989) as H.J. Res. 395.

INTERNMENT POLICIES AND REDRESS LEGISLATION

EXECUTIVE ORDER 9066	N/A	Enabled the Secretary of War and military commanders to designate military areas and control access of U.S. citizens or residents to those areas. Those living within the areas were subject to any and all rules imposed by military authorities. Issued on February 19, 1942, by President Franklin D. Roosevelt.
EXECUTIVE ORDER 9102	N/A	Authorized the formation of a War Relocation Authority in the Executive Office of the President. Designated a director to create and carry out removal and relocation of Japanese Americans and Japanese immigrants from military areas as defined by Executive Order 9066 (Authorizing Secretary of War to Prescribe Military Areas). Issued on March 18, 1942, by President Franklin D. Roosevelt.
JAPANESE-AMERICAN EVACUATION CLAIMS ACT (1948)	P.L. 80-886; 62 Stat. 1231	Enabled the U.S. Attorney General to examine claims of Japanese Americans who were removed and relocated. Limited submission claims to specific types and capped monetary compensations to a maximum of $2,500 per individual. Passed by the 80th Congress (1947–1949) as H.R. 3999.
INTERNAL SECURITY ACT (McCARRAN ACT) (1950)	P.L. 81-831; 64 Stat. 987	Established a five-member Subversive Activities Control Board selected by the President to determine communist affiliations of organizations. Provided for registration and possible internment of communist sympathizers or anyone suspected of subversive activities and exclusion as inadmissible aliens. Passed by the 81st Congress (1949–1951) over a presidential veto as H.R. 9490.
PRESIDENTIAL PROCLAMATION 4417	N/A	A proclamation declaring the end of Executive Order 9066. Issued on February 19, 1976, by President Gerald R. Ford.
COMMISSION ON WARTIME RELOCATION AND INTERNMENT OF CIVILIANS ACT (1980)	P.L. 96-317; 94 Stat. 964	Established a seven-member commission to review the implementation of Executive Order 9066 and its impact on U.S. citizens and permanent resident aliens. The commission reviewed U.S. military directives that required the relocation and/or detention of Japanese Americans, Japanese resident aliens, and permanent resident aliens of the Aleutian and Pribilof Islands. Passed by the 96th Congress (1979–1981) as S. 1647.
CIVIL LIBERTIES ACT (1988)	P.L. 100-383; 102 Stat. 903	Issued a formal apology for the internment of Japanese Americans and the confiscation of Aleutian property during World War II. Provided financial compensation to internment survivors and Aleutian property owners. Passed by the 100th Congress (1987–1989) as H.R. 442.

**ACTS RELATED
TO TERRITORIES**

TITLE	CITATION: PUBLIC LAW (P.L.) AND STATUTE (STAT.)	MAIN PROVISIONS
ANNEXATION OF THE HAWAIIAN ISLANDS (NEWLANDS RESOLUTION) (1898)	30 Stat. 750	Authorized the annexation of the Republic of Hawaii to the United States and outlined a civilian government. Prohibited Chinese immigration to the Hawaiian Islands and the mainland United States per the Chinese Exclusion Act (22 Stat. 58) and subsequent amendments. Passed by the 55th Congress (1897–1899) as H.J. Res. 259.
HAWAIIAN ORGANIC ACT (1900)	31 Stat. 141	Designated Hawaii as an incorporated territory and granted U.S. citizenship to citizens of Hawaii. Established a territorial government that included executive, judiciary, and legislative branches. Designated a Territorial Delegate to Congress. Made Chinese immigrants subject to the Geary Act (27 Stat. 25) and prevented Chinese laborers from entering the United States via Hawaii. Passed by the 56th Congress (1899–1901) as S. 222.
PHILIPPINE ORGANIC ACT (1902)	P.L. 57-235; 32 Stat. 691	Established a territorial government for the Philippine Islands. Authorized the creation of a presidentially appointed Philippine commission and a popularly elected Philippine assembly. Created two Resident Commissioner positions in the U.S. House of Representatives for the Philippines. Passed by the 57th Congress (1901–1903) as S. 2295.
AN ACT PROVIDING FOR THE QUADRENNIAL ELECTION OF MEMBERS OF THE PHILIPPINE ASSEMBLY AND RESIDENT COMMISSIONERS TO THE UNITED STATES (1911)	P.L. 61-376; 36 Stat. 910	Extended terms of service for Philippine assembly members and Resident Commissioners from two to four years. Fixed start of the Philippine legislature to mid-October, but enabled members to set start dates. Enabled Resident Commissioners Benito Legarda and Manuel L. Quezon to serve through the Philippine legislature's current term. Passed by the 61st Congress (1909–1911) as H.R. 32004.
JONES ACT OF 1916 (PHILIPPINE AUTONOMY ACT)	P.L. 64-240; 39 Stat. 545	Established a more autonomous Philippine government by providing for a popularly elected bicameral legislature. Reduced Resident Commissioners' terms from four years to three. Passed by the 64th Congress (1915–1917) as S. 381.
HARE–HAWES–CUTTING ACT OF 1932	P.L. 72-311; 47 Stat. 761	Provided for complete independence of the Philippines following a 10-year transitional period if approved by the Philippine government. Reduced the number of Resident Commissioners from two to one, appointed by the Philippine government. Passed by the 72nd Congress (1931–1933) over a presidential veto as H.R. 7233. Not approved by the Philippine government.
TYDINGS–MCDUFFIE ACT (PHILIPPINES INDEPENDENCE ACT) (1934)	P.L. 73-127; 48 Stat. 456	Provided for complete independence of the Philippines following a 10-year transitional period if approved by the Philippine government and contingent upon the adoption of a Philippine constitution within two years of the legislation enactment. Also capped Philippine immigration to the United States at 50 persons per year. Passed by the 73rd Congress (1933–1935) as H.R. 8573. Approved by the Philippine government.
THE TRUSTEESHIP AGREEMENT FOR THE TRUST TERRITORY OF THE PACIFIC ISLANDS (1947)	P.L. 80-204; 61 Stat. 397	Authorized President Harry S. Truman's trusteeship agreement with the United Nations. Supported educational, political, and economic development of the South Pacific Territories (Mariana, Caroline, and Marshall Islands) obtained from the Japanese after World War II. Deemed administration of Guam and American Samoa interrelated. Passed by the 80th Congress (1947–1949) as H.J. Res. 233.

TITLE	CITATION: PUBLIC LAW (P.L.) AND STATUTE (STAT.)	MAIN PROVISIONS
GUAM ORGANIC ACT (1950)	P.L. 81-630; 64 Stat. 384	Transferred Guam federal jurisdiction from U.S. Navy to Department of Interior. Granted U.S. citizenship to Guam's residents and established a three-branch structure of government. Passed by the 81st Congress (1949–1951) as H.R. 7273.
HAWAII STATEHOOD ADMISSION ACT (1959)	P.L. 86-3; 73 Stat. 4	Provided official statehood in the United States and for the formal ratification of the state constitution adopted by Hawaiians on November 7, 1950. Passed by the 86th Congress (1959–1961) as S. 50.
DELEGATE TO THE HOUSE OF REPRESENTATIVES FROM GUAM AND U.S. VIRGIN ISLANDS (1972)	P.L. 92-271; 86 Stat. 118	Created nonvoting Delegate positions in the U.S. House of Representatives for Guam and the U.S. Virgin Islands beginning in the 93rd Congress (1973–1975). Passed by the 92nd Congress (1971–1973) as H.R. 8787.
DELEGATE TO THE HOUSE OF REPRESENTATIVES FROM AMERICAN SAMOA (1978)	P.L. 95-556; 92 Stat. 2078	Created a nonvoting Delegate position in the U.S. House of Representatives for American Samoa. Passed by the 95th Congress (1977–1979) as H.R. 13702.
CONSOLIDATED NATURAL RESOURCES ACT OF 2008	P.L. 110-229; 122 Stat. 754	Created a nonvoting Delegate in the U.S. House of Representatives for the Commonwealth of the Northern Mariana Islands. Passed by 110th Congress (2007–2009) as S. 2739.

FOREIGN POLICY
(excluding acts related to revenues and tariffs)

TITLE	CITATION	MAIN PROVISIONS
TREATY OF TRADE, CONSULS, AND EMIGRATION (BURLINGAME TREATY) (1868)	16 Stat. 739	Amended previous agreements between the United States and China. Outlined property rights, trade privileges, and emigration procedures. Approved by the Senate during the 40th Congress (1867–1869) on July 28, 1868.
RECIPROCITY TREATY OF 1875	19 Stat. 625	Permitted the duty-free importation of sugar and other products from the Hawaiian Islands to the United States. Enabled Americans to export duty-free products to Hawaii. Approved by the Senate during the 44th Congress (1875–1877) on March 18, 1875.
TREATY OF PARIS (1899)	30 Stat. 1754	Formally concluded the Spanish-American War. Spain ceded Cuba, Guam, Puerto Rico, and portions of the West Indies to the United States. Spain also surrendered the Philippines to the United States for $20 million. Approved by the Senate during the 55th Congress (1897–1899) on February 6, 1899.
CONVENTION TO ADJUST THE QUESTION BETWEEN THE UNITED STATES, GERMANY, AND GREAT BRITAIN IN RESPECT TO THE SAMOAN ISLANDS (1900)	31 Stat. 1878	Partitioned the jurisdiction of certain Samoan Islands between the United States, Great Britain, and Germany. Approved by the Senate during the 56th Congress (1899–1901) on January 16, 1900.
PHILIPPINE REHABILITATION ACT (1946)	P.L. 79-370; 60 Stat. 128	Established a presidentially appointed war commission to review damage claims and award compensation for damages that occurred during the Japanese occupation of the Philippines. Allocated $120 million for infrastructure. Passed by the 79th Congress (1945–1947) as S. 1610.

TITLE	CITATION: PUBLIC LAW (P.L.) AND STATUTE (STAT.)	MAIN PROVISIONS
PAYNE–ALDRICH TARIFF ACT (1909)	P.L. 61-5; 36 Stat. 11	Lowered duties to a general level of 38 percent while making sizable cuts on certain duties. Established a tariff board to advise the President and U.S. Court of Customs Appeals. Passed by the 61st Congress (1909–1911) as H.R. 1438.
PHILIPPINE TARIFF ACT (1909)	P.L. 61-7; 36 Stat. 130	Established duties on products imported to the Philippines. Passed by the 61st Congress (1909–1911) as H.R. 9135.
UNDERWOOD–SIMMONS ACT (REVENUE ACT OF 1913)	P.L. 63-16; 38 Stat. 114	Reduced the average duty rate from 38 percent to less than 30 percent. Reduced duties on many items and expanded free list. Enabled the President to negotiate reciprocal agreements. Established a comprehensive federal income tax. Passed by the 63rd Congress (1913–1915) as H.R. 3321.
JONES–COSTIGAN ACT (SUGAR ACT OF 1934)	P.L. 73-213; 48 Stat. 670	Amended quotas and taxes on different kinds of sugar. Prohibited the importation and processing of sugars from insular territories. Passed by the 73rd Congress (1933–1935) as H.R. 8861.
PHILIPPINE TRADE ACT (1946)	P.L. 79-371; 60 Stat. 141	Established trade relations between the United States and the Republic of the Philippines by providing for a graduated introduction of customs duties. Prescribed duty-free quotas on certain items. Passed by the 79th Congress (1945–1947) as H.R. 5856.

Glossary

A

"Aliens ineligible for citizenship" Legal term describing those immigrants prohibited from attaining U.S. citizenship through naturalization, e.g., Asians (U.S. legislation limited naturalization to white individuals or African descendants). The prohibition on Asians becoming naturalized citizens was eliminated in stages between 1943 and 1952.

Amerasian The children of U.S. military personnel and Asian partners born outside the United States.

Annexation The action or process of joining or uniting with, especially in the case of a nation acquiring a territory.

Archipelago A chain or cluster of islands located in the same body of water.

Assembly Center Temporary detention centers established by the Wartime Civil Control Administration in March 1942 to facilitate the forced evacuation of 120,000 Japanese Americans primarily from California, Washington, and Oregon. The evacuation of citizens and residents to the assembly centers was completed by mid-September 1942.

Asylum A secure place of refuge, shelter, or retreat.

At-Large Representative In modern practice, a Representative elected in a state that has only one seat apportioned to it in the U.S. House. For many years states that were apportioned more than one Representative could elect an At-Large Representative in statewide voting even when a majority of the state delegation was elected by single-member, geographically defined districts. Until the mid-20th century, At-Large Representatives were often elected immediately following decennial apportionment. At-Large elections in states with more than one seat in the U.S. House were abolished by federal law in 1968.

B

Bicameral A legislative body having two legislative chambers or houses.

C

Caucus A meeting of party members in each chamber (House Republicans and Senate Republicans refer to their gatherings as a "conference"). A caucus is used primarily to select candidates for office and to consider other important business for furthering party interests. The term also describes an organization of House and Senate Members that is devoted to a special interest or legislative area.

Census An official count of a population that includes various related statistics. The U.S. Constitution mandates that a nationwide census be taken every 10 years.

Chamorro Indigenous inhabitants of the Mariana Islands and Guam who migrated from Southeast Asia almost 3,000 years ago. The term also denotes a distinct Austronesian language.

Cold War The state of ideological, economic, political, military, and cultural warfare pitting a capitalist United States against a communist Soviet Union (USSR) from 1947 until 1991. Developing from divergent American and Soviet foreign policies concerning the restoration of Europe after World War II, the conflict spread from Europe to the rest of the world. Although there were no direct military conflicts, the Soviet and American superpowers tried to alter the international balance of power in their favor by competing globally for allies, strategic locations, natural resources, and influence in Asia, Africa, and Latin America. The Cold War ended with the collapse and disintegration of the USSR in 1991.

Colonialism The practice of a group of people who form a community in a new country or territory while remaining subject to their parent state. It also describes a policy of exploitation of a less-powerful country or territory by a dominant nation.

Committee (Standing, Joint, Select, or Special) A standing committee is permanently established by House and Senate Rules and has the ability to receive and report bills and resolutions to the full chamber. A Joint Committee is also established by House and Senate Rules with membership comprised of an equal number of Representatives and Senators and a chairperson that traditionally rotates between a House and a Senate Member each Congress. A Select or Special Committee is established by resolution for a defined period of time, is usually created to investigate a specific legislative issue, and may or may not have legislative authority.

Commonwealth A state in which the supreme power is vested in the people; a republic or democratic state.

Concentration Camps See "Relocation Centers."

Constituents People living within the geographic area that a Member of Congress represents.

D

Delegate A nonvoting official in the U.S. House currently representing the following territories: the District of Columbia, Guam, American Samoa, the U.S. Virgin Islands, and the Northern Mariana Islands. Delegates serve two-year terms. Delegates cannot vote in the full House but are permitted to vote in committees and can introduce and cosponsor legislation. Under a House Rule in place from 1993 to 1994 and again from 2007 to 2011, Delegates were temporarily permitted to vote in the Committee of the Whole, during consideration of appropriations, authorization, and tax bills for amendment. If the votes of the Delegates were decisive on any vote in the Committee of the Whole, the amendment was automatically voted on again in the full House, where the Delegates could not vote.

Detention Centers See "Relocation Centers."

Diaspora The migration of an ethnic group from their home country or region to different parts of the world.

District A geographical area represented by a U.S. Representative.

E

Empire Political dominion by a sovereign state over one or more subject territories.

Enemy Alien A foreign resident in a country with which his or her country is at war.

Evacuation Camps See "Relocation Centers."

Exclusion The act of barring or keeping out of a physical place or society.

H

Haole A Hawaiian term that means "foreigner" but is mainly used to identify Caucasians.

House Rules The rules and precedents that govern the conduct of business in the House. These rules address duties of officers, the order of business, admission to the floor, parliamentary procedures on handling amendments and voting, and jurisdictions of committees. Whereas the House re-adopts its rules, usually with some changes, at the beginning of each Congress, Senate rules carry over from one Congress to the next.

I

Ilustrados Wealthy, educated Filipinos who mostly lived in the territory's major cities during the era of Spanish rule (1600–1896). Many *ilustrados* fought against the Spanish during the 1896 revolution and against the United States during the Philippine-American War (1899–1902). Others cooperated with U.S. forces and helped develop a new territorial government. After both wars, *ilustrados* sought professional careers in business, education, and politics, including service as Resident Commissioners to the U.S. Congress.

Imperialism The policy of extending the authority of an empire or nation over foreign countries or territories; acquiring and maintaining political control over colonies and dependencies.

Incarceration See "Internment."

Incumbency The holding of an office or the term of an office (usually political).

Insular Territory A commonwealth, freely associated state, possession, or territory that falls under the jurisdiction of the U.S. government but is not a state or federal district.

Internment An umbrella term used by the federal government and generally accepted by the American public to describe the systematic removal, relocation, and detainment of nearly 120,000 Japanese Americans and Japanese immigrants primarily from the West Coast during World War II. The majority of internees were American citizens who—in addition to being denied due process and other constitutional rights—lost their possessions, homes, property, and businesses when they were forcibly moved to relocation centers in remote locations in the interior West. In recent decades, some leading scholars have contested the use of the term, arguing that "incarceration" is a more accurate description of the policy.

Internment Camps See "Relocation Centers."

Issei A Japanese term that identifies the generation of emigrants who left Japan to settle in the United States.

J

Japanese American Citizens League (JACL) A national civic organization formed in San Francisco, California, in 1929 from the merger of local West Coast *nisei* groups. The JACL lobbied against legal discrimination and confronted misperceptions about Japanese Americans' loyalty to the United States.

K

Kibei A Japanese term that identifies *nisei* children who were born in the United States, educated in Japan, and returned to the United States.

M

Model Minority A journalistic description of Asian Americans that stresses their economic success and compliance towards general societal norms. The term has been used to denigrate other ethnic and racial groups while penalizing more recent Asian immigrants.

N

Naturalization The action of admitting an alien to the position and privileges of a native-born citizen or subject.

Nikkei A Japanese term used to identify any person of Japanese descent who emigrated abroad or is the descendant of such individuals.

Nisei A Japanese term that identifies the generation of Japanese Americans who were born in the United States from their *issei* immigrant parents.

P

Plantation An estate or farm, especially in a tropical or subtropical country, on which crops such as coffee, tobacco, or sugarcane were cultivated often by enslaved or contract laborers; also used to denote a company of settlers or colonists.

Plebiscite A vote by which the people of an entire country or district express an opinion for or against a proposal especially on a choice of government or ruler following the call for a referendum.

Possession See "Insular Territory."

Primary A preliminary election usually between aspirants from the same political party held to determine who will serve as the party's candidate in the general election.

R

Redistricting The redrawing of U.S. House districts within states following the constitutionally mandated decennial census and the apportionment of seats. State legislatures draw new districts based on population declines or increases that result in the subtraction or addition of House seats apportioned to the state.

Redress Satisfaction or compensation for a wrong sustained or the loss resulting from such a wrong. It was also the name given to a grassroots movement organized by Japanese-American groups to seek restitution for being interned by the federal government in violation of their civil rights during World War II, which resulted in loss of their possessions, homes, property, and businesses.

Refugee A person who seeks refuge in a foreign country as a result of warfare, religious persecution, or political persecution in their home country.

Relocation Centers The official term for the 10 War Relocation Center facilities where 120,000 Japanese Americans, both immigrants and native-born citizens, were incarcerated for much of World War II. During and since World War II, these facilities have also been called "relocation centers," "detention centers," "evacuation camps," "internment camps," and "concentration camps." Federal officials frequently referred to them as "concentration camps" during the war at a time when the label was associated with the Boer War and the Cuban rebellions of the 1890s. Many of the post-war histories and studies of this event have used "relocation," "evacuation," and "internment." More recent studies have begun to use "incarceration" as a more accurate term.

Renunciant A person who makes a formal resignation of some right or trust, including citizenship.

Reparations The act of making amends for a wrong done; offering compensation.

Resident Commissioner of the Philippine Islands
A Member of Congress who served in the U.S. House of Representatives as an advocate for the Philippines. Per the Philippine Organic Act of 1902 and the Jones Act of 1916, Resident Commissioners were elected by the Philippine legislature from 1907 to 1936 and served in pairs. Philippine presidents appointed subsequent Resident Commissioners from 1936 to 1946 per the Tydings–McDuffie Act of 1934. They served in fixed terms that ranged from two to four years. Many sought greater autonomy for the Philippines but were unable to vote on final legislation or serve on committees per House Rules. A total of 13 Resident Commissioners from the Philippines served in the House from 1907 to 1946.

Retention An action to hold or keep something or someone fixed in a place or position.

S

Sansei A Japanese term that identifies the second generation of Japanese Americans who were born in the United States.

Social Darwinism A 19th-century sociological theory, now discredited, that argued that societies advance because of intense competition and conflict between social groups. According to the theory, social elites acquired their status as a result of their biological superiority over weaker social groups.

Special Election An election held by a state to fill a vacancy created when a Member of Congress dies, resigns, or is expelled. All House vacancies must be filled by election; Senate vacancies usually are filled by temporary appointments until a special election can be organized.

Statutory Representation A position defined by congressional mandate rather than by the U.S. Constitution. Territorial Delegates and Resident Commissioners are statutory representatives. Senators and Representatives are constitutional representatives.

Surrogate Representation The act of serving as a representative of or spokesperson for a group of persons united by gender or race and not confined to the boundaries of a congressional district or state. This representational style was prevalent among some minorities in Congress—particularly after the 1960s—to advance a legislative agenda important to minorities nationwide. To a degree, each minority group in Congress has adopted some form of "surrogate representation."

T

Treaty A contract between two or more nation states relating to peace, commerce, or other international relations.

U

Unincorporated Territory An insular area that the United States controls but that has not been fully incorporated into the Union and where Congress has determined that only select parts of the U.S. Constitution apply. Citizens of an unincorporated territory receive some constitutional protections but not all the rights enjoyed by the citizens of U.S. states.

U.S. National A person who lives in an unincorporated territory. Their citizenship is defined by the Fourteenth Amendment of the U.S. Constitution or from specific statutes. U.S. Nationals receive some constitutional protections but are exempt from all the rights reserved to citizens of U.S. States.

W

Whip An assistant House or Senate Floor leader who helps round up party Members for quorum calls and important votes. Coined in the British Parliament, this term is derived from "whipper-in," a person who keeps the dogs from straying during a fox hunt.

Index

Member names appear in **bold** (surnames in **ALL CAPS**)
Bold page numbers denote Member profiles
Italicized page numbers denote references to images and image captions

A

Abelarde, Pedro E., 17, 55–56
Abercrombie, Neil, 363, 401, 424, 426, *451*, 453, 522, 548–49
Abscam scandal, 340–41
Ackerman, Gary, 556
Adams, Alva, 235–36
Adams, Ansel, *291*
Aglipay, Gregorio, 194
Agnew, Spiro, 351
Aguinaldo, Emilio, 48, 51, *51*, 66, 105, 124, 136, 140, 146, 194, 214
Air Force, United States, 320–21, 330, 354, 506, 552
AKAKA, Daniel K., 14, 71, *292*, 336, 342, 344, 362, **396–403**, *397*, 451–52, 459–61, *460*, 539, 546, 549, 551, 580, 591, 594
  chairmanships and, 282, 400, 452, 591, 594
  committee assignments of, 281–82, 398–400, 582, 585, 587–90
  early political career of, 396, 398
  House career of, 398–99
  military service of, 396
  Native Hawaiian advocacy and, 398, 400–1, *460*, 461, 549
  Senate career of, 362, 399–403, 427
  sugar industry and, 399
al-Assad, Bashar, 547
Alaska, 215, 285–86, 343, 399, 401
  Aleutian Islands, 293–94, 297, 309n–310n, 600
  constitution of, 285
  Pribilof Islands, 293–94, 600
  statehood and, 285–86, *286*, 350
Alaska–Yukon–Pacific Exposition, 116
Albert, Carl, 290, 319, 361, 379–80
Alexander & Baldwin, 67. *See also* sugar industry
Alien land laws, 10, 34, 39–40, 272–73, 318
Alien Property Custodian, U.S. Office of, 260, 267, *267*, 288
Alien Spouses of Members of the Armed Forces Act, 272
Alunan, Rafael, *7*
Amache Camp. *See* Granada War Relocation Center
Amerasian Immigration Act of 1982, 442–43, 600
Amerasian Independent Voice of America, 443
Amerasians, 442–43, 600
American Civil Liberties Union, 297, 354
American Indians, 34, 215, 321, 343, 398, 400–1, 432, 461, 544, 551
American Red Cross, 175, 259, 263, 336, 376
American Samoa, 277–80
  Asian Pacific American representation and, 3, 12–13, 279–80, 412–16, 428–35,

452, *452*, 558–59, 581
  citizenship and, 277, 279–80, 306n, 559
  constitution of, 279, 414
  creation of Territorial Delegate position and, 280, 412, 428, 449–50, 602
  diaspora and, 4–5, 430, 440, 444–45, 546
  economy of, 415, 428, 432–33, 559
  fono, 279
  Instrument of Cession, 278
  statehood and, 207
  territorial status of, 2, *2*, 17, 43, 207, 259, 276–79, *277*, 369, 421–22, 446
  World War II and, 277–79
American Samoan Commission, 207
American Sugar Refining Corporation, 149
Americans with Disabilities Act, 382
Anderson, Clinton P., *279*
Anderson, Glenn M., 370, 382
Ansari, Eileen, 478
Anti-Bullying Caucus, 496
Anti-Saloon League, 117
Aoki, Dan, 343
apportionment and redistricting, 20, 76, 229, 358, 506, 509, 529, 542, 562
Ariyoshi, George R., 396, 398
Army, United States, *11*, 40, 61–62, *62*, 73, 84, 206, 244, 250, 256, *259*, *261*, 262–65, *262*, 267, 282, 318–19, 330, 336, 348, 351, 378, 396, 428, 461, 503, 509, 520, 522–23, 544–546, 560, 562
  U.S. Army Forces in the Far East (USAFFE), 62
Arthur, Chester A., 37, *37*
Asia-Pacific Triangle, 270–71, 273–75
Asian Pacific American Heritage Month, 292, *292*, 454
Asian Pacific American Heritage Week, 293
Asian Pacific American Members of Congress, characteristics
  background and pre-congressional experience of, 50–51, 75, 261–69
  committee assignments, 582–90
  committee chairmanships of, 12, 340–42, 380, 452, 490, 559, 591–94
  discrimination and, 105, 115, 318–19, 340, 351, 353, 400
  diversity of, 3–4, 13, 270, 281, 292, 439–40, 443–44, 450–52, *454*, 455–56, 463
  experience in Washington, DC, 52–53
  family and ethnic roots of, 3–5, 281, 319–20, 328, 338, 366, 396, 400, 426, 438–40, 450–52, 462, 474, 476, 500, 502, 506, 508, 512, 515, 540, 542, 562, 596
  language barrier and, 50, 73, 75, 105–6, 136, 140–41, 149, 212, 232, 320, 391
  leadership positions and, 282, 341–42, 379–80, 420, 431, 463, 549, 595
  legislative interests of, *21*, 54–62, 64–66,

77, 81–84, 280–300, 454–61
  military service of. *See* military service, Asian Pacific American Members of Congress
  statutory representation and, 3, 6, 11, 24n, 52–53, 85–86, 90n, 102–255, 258, 279–80, 366–75, 412–23, 428–35, 439, 480–85, 558–61, 580–81
  surrogate representation and, 2, 23n, 328, 332, 358, 361–62, 400–10, 430, 445, 447, 476, 607
  women Members of Congress and, 12, 14, 281, *281*, 358–65, 424–27, 451, 539, 542–51, 554–59, 566–68
Asiatic Barred Zone, 10, 40–42
AUSTRIA, Steve, 440, 452, **506–10**, *507*

B

Babbage, John, 320
Babbitt, Bruce, 292
Baca, Joe, 478
Bacon, Robert, 189–90
Bader, Charles, 474
Bailey, Thomas A., 5
Baker, Bob, 474
Baker, Newton, 167
Baldwin, Henry Alexander, 25n, 200
Bandholtz, Harry H., 146, 148
Bankhead, William, *83*
Baruch, Bernard, 175
Bateman, Herbert H., 562
Bayh, Birch, 361
Becerra, Xavier, *12*, *454*
Begg, James, 201
Bell, Alphonzo, Jr., 390
Bell, Jasper, 64, 252
Bendetsen, Karl R., 295
Benishek, Dan, 529
BERA, Ami, 440, **540–41**, *540*
Bernanke, Ben, 523
Bernstein, Joan Z., 294
Berry, Francis J., 148
Berryman, Clifford K., *33*
Berryman, Jim, *286*
Beveridge, Albert, *43*, 43–45
Bingham, Jonathan, 465n
Bitterman, Mary, 426
Black, Hugo, 268
Blaine, James G., 69
Blakeslee, George H., 136, 139, 143n
Blanco, Kathleen Babineaux, 500
BLAZ, Ben Garrido, *21*, 278, 282–84, 307n, 368, 372, **418–23**, *419*, 449, 458–62, *459*, 480, 483
Blount, James, 70
Boehner, John, 363, 502, 506, 509, 515, 522–23
Boggs, Hale, 350, 368
Bonior, David, 407
Bordallo, Madeleine, 373n, *454*, 459–60,

459, *462*, 469n
Bordallo, Ricardo J. (Ricky), 371, 422
Bordonaro, Molly, 488
Box, John C., 120
Boxer, Barbara, 461–62
Boykin, Frank W., *12*
Bracero Program, 321–22
Bradley, Bill, 399
Bradley, Willis, 278
Brands, H. W., 17, 54, 57
Brinkley, Alan, 5
Broder, David, 380
Brooke, Edward W., 309n
Broussard, Edwin, 192
Bureau of Insular Affairs, United States, *2*, 52, 55, 57, *57*, 124, 128, 130–31, 139–40, 142, 150–51, 235
Bureau of Public Roads, United States, 76, 207
Burlingame Treaty. *See* Treaty of Trade, Consuls, and Emigration
Burns, John A., 209, 211, *281*, 285–86, 332–33, 338, 343, 350, 358, 396
Burton, Phillip, 279–80, *280*, 284, 366, 368, 371–72, 428, 448, *448*
Bush, George H. W., 292, 298–300, 399, 407, 426–27, 480, 558
Bush, George W., 292, 309n, 384, 401, 406, 459, 483, 489–90, 500, 560
Bush, John E., 104
Butler, Hugh, *279*
Byrd, Robert, 341–43, 352
Byrnes, John W., *12*

C

C. Brewer & Company, 67. *See also* sugar industry
Cailles, Juan, 186
Caldwell, Kirk, 344, 523
California
  anti-Asian discrimination in, 316, 319–20
  anti-Asian policies of, 9–10, 37–39, 272–73, 318, 376
  anti-Asian violence in, 37–38
  Asian Pacific American representation and, 301, 316–27, 376–95, 404–11, 474–79, 494–98, 540–43, 552–55, 564–67, 580
California Gold Rush, 9, 34, 36
Calvert, Ken, 564
Calvo, Paul McDonald, 371
Camacho, Carlos S., 560
Camacho, Felix, 484
Cambodia, 4–5, 274, 431, 438, 441, 558, 600
  immigration and, 13
Camp McCoy, 348
Campbell, Thomas, 381, 494
Cannon, Joe, 76, 116, 140
Cantor, Eric, 515–16

Emmons, Delos, 260–61, *260*
Endo, Mitsuye, 268–69
Ensign, John, 401
Environmental Protection Agency, United
  States, 503, 517
Equal Rights Amendment, 332
Ervin Committee. *See* Select Committee on
  Presidential Campaign Activities
Ervin, Sam, 340
Escamilla, Antonio G., 140–42
Espinas, J. E., *60*
Evensen, Albert, 350
Evins, Joe, 352
Executive Order 10264, 279. *See also*
  American Samoa
Executive Order 589, 598
Executive Order 9066, 264, *264*, *290*, 291,
  291, 294–95, 600. *See also* internment
Executive Order 9102, 264, 600. *See also*
  internment

F

Fairfield, Louis, 181, 189
FALEOMAVAEGA, Eni F. H., 279–80, 284,
  292, 307n, 412, **428–35**, *429*, 445, 452,
  452, 459, 558–59, 592
familial connections, 596
Farrington, Elizabeth, 285, *285*, 426
Farrington, Joseph, 230, 285, *285*
Farrington, Wallace R., 120, 201
Fasi, Frank, 330, 424
Fauntroy, Walter, 373n
Federal Bureau of Investigation (FBI), United
  States, 260, 264, 271, 340–41, 514
Federal Drug Administration (FDA), United
  States, 369
Federal Emergency Management Agency
  (FEMA), United States, 400, 503, 517
Federated States of Micronesia, 448, 466n
Ferguson, Gil, 458
Finch, Robert, 390
Fish and Wildlife Service, United States, 482,
  484n
Fisher, Walter, 118
Fleming, Arthur S., 309n
Flood, Daniel, 361
Florida
  Asian Pacific American representation and,
    568, 581
Foley, Tom, 354, 383
Fong Yue Ting v. United States. See Supreme
  Court, United States
FONG, Hiram L., 10, *17*, 19, 71, 84,
  271, *271*, 281, 287, *290*, **328–35**, *329*,
  352–53, 398, 426, 446–47, *447*, 465n
Forbes, W. Cameron, 58, *59*, 160, 168, 180
Ford, Gerald R., *13*, *290*, 291, *291*, 360, 368,
  374n, 448, *448*, 560, 600
Ford, Harold, Sr., 406
Ford, Wendell, 343
Fortas, Abe, 295
442nd Regimental Combat Team, 11, *11*, *22*,
  261, 262–63, *262*, 266, *274*, 293, 296,
  298, *301*, 310n, 336, 338, 343, 348,
  407, *436*, 461–62, *461*, *462*
Fourteenth Amendment, 34, 87n, 598
Frear, Walter Francis, *8*, 73, 118, 120
Frenzel, William, 297

Frick v. Webb. See Supreme Court, United
  States
Friedman, Milton, 528
Frye, William P., *46*
Fuimaono, A. U., 307n, 428
Furse, Elizabeth, 486

G

GABALDON, Isauro, *35*, 58–59, 93n,
  167–68, **178–85**, *179*, 186, 188–89, 191,
  195n, 214
GABBARD, Tulsi, 440, 452, **546–47**, *546*
Gandhi, Mohandas, 316
Garcetti, Eric, 552
Garner, John Nance, 192, 216, 224
Garrison, Lindley Miller, 92n
Gear, George D., 105
Geary Act of 1892, 598, 601
Geisel, Theodor, 264
Gephardt, Richard, 407
GI Bill, 84, 338, 350, 396, 400, 421, 565
Gibbons, Sam, 406
Gila River War Relocation Center, 265. *See
  also* internment
Gill, Thomas P., 332, 350, 352
Gillett, Frederick, 168
Gingrich, Newt, 300, 407, 528
Glenn, John, 355
Goldberg, Arthur J., 309n
Goldwater, Barry, 333
Good, James W., *7*
Goodness, P. J., *17*
Gore, Al, 381
Government Accountability Office, United
  States, 545
Granada War Relocation Center, 265, 292,
  309n, 494. *See also* internment
Great Depression, 60, 81, 204, 206, 208, 215,
  236, 318, 390, 506, 509
Great Society legislation, 13, 332, 342, 358,
  360, 390
Green, Al, *454*, *462*
Green, Edith, 361
Gromoff, Ishmael V., 309n
Guam, 277–80, 449
  Asian Pacific American representation and,
    12, 14, 279–84, 366–75, 418–23, 428,
    480–85, 581
  citizenship and, 277–79, 283, 306n, 366,
    418, 482
  Cold War and, 12, 277, 482
  Commission on Self-Determination, 283,
    372, 421
  commonwealth status of, 372, 418, 421,
    449, 480, 482
  constitution of, 283, 370–72, 374n
  creation of Territorial Delegate position,
    279–80, 368, 450, 602
  economy of, 278, 366, 369–70, 420–21,
    482
  immigration and, 449
  Legislative Political Status Commission,
    374n
  statehood and, 370
  territorial status of, 2, 17, 277–78, 370–72,
    421–22, 446–47, 465n
  war claims and, 420, 458–60, 468n
  World War II and, 259, 269, 277–79,

283–84, 418, 420–21, 423n, 468n,
  482–83, 484n
Guam Commonwealth Act, 283, 421, 449,
  482
Guam Excess Lands Act, 284, 420, 482
Guam Land Returns Act, 482
Guam Meritorious Claims Act, 283
Guam Organic Act, 278, *279*, 283, 366, 371,
  418, 447, 482, 602
Guam War Claims Commission, 459, 468n
Guam War Claims Review Commission Act,
  459, 483
Guam World War II Loyalty Recognition Act,
  421, 460
Guantanamo Bay, 509
Gubser, Charles S., 378
GUEVARA, Pedro, *7*, 8, *35*, 60, *60*, 93n,
  169, 181–82, **186–97**, *187*, 215, 222, 224
Gutierrez, Carl, 371

H

H. Hackfeld & Company, 67. *See also* sugar
  industry
Haig, Alexander, 353
Haldeman, H. R., 340
Haley, James A., *12*
Hall, Jack, 331
Halloran, Daniel J., III, 557
HANABUSA, Colleen, 440, 522–23, 532,
  548–49, *548*
Hannemann, Mufi, 362, 424, 426, 546
Harding, Warren G., 41, 58–59, 119,
  167–68, 180–81, 214
Hare, Butler, 60, 192, 216
Hare–Hawes–Cutting Act, 60–61, 192–93,
  212, 217, 234, 601
Harrington, Michael, 361
HARRIS, Kamala, 539, 552, **566**, *566*
Harrison, Francis Burton, *8*, 151, 174, 232
Hart, Gary, 486
Hart, Philip, 275, 282, 336
Hart–Celler Act of 1965. *See* Immigration
  and Nationality Act of 1965
Hatfield, Mark, 343, 353, 394
Hauler, John, 528
Hausserman, John W., *62*
Havana, Cuba, 42–43, *43*
Hawaii
  Asian Pacific American representation and,
    12–13, 328–64, 396–403, 424–27,
    520–25, 532–34, 546–51, 580–81
  economy of, 339, 342
  statehood and, 3, 8–11, 35, 44, 69, 75,
    77, 80–86, *83*, 118, 122n, 209, 226,
    228–30, 276, 281–82, 284–87, *286*,
    330, 338–39, 350, 358, 520, 522, 550,
    602
  sugar in, 338, 351, 399
  See also Hawaii Territory
Hawaii Admission Act, 230
Hawaii Omnibus Act, 338, 344n
Hawaii Territory, 8–9, 66–84, 601
  annexation of, 2, 6, 9, 32, 37, 43–44, *44*,
    68–75, *69*, *70*, *72*, *73*, 77–79, *81*, 85,
    104, 106, 108, 114, 118, 200, 226, 229,
    284, 601
  anti-Asian discrimination in, 70–74,
    78–84, 119–20, 228, 348

Asian Pacific American representation and,
  1, 3, 9, 19, 35, 75, 102–22, 198–210,
  226–31, 581
Bayonet Constitution, 67–69, 102, 112,
  114
citizenship and, 74, 78, 83, 229
congressional delegations to, 9, 69, 72, 76,
  76, 116
constitution of, 70–71, 73, *73*, 81, 84,
  102, 114, 207, 228, 230, 424
Democratic revolution of 1954, 84, 230,
  330, 338, 350
economy of, 8–9, 66–68, 76–78, 82, 106,
  112, 116–19, 127–28, 200, 204, 206–8,
  229, 261, 264
Equal Rights Commission, 82–83, 208
Equal Rights League, 69, 104
haoles and, 9, 66–69, 71, 73–75, 77–79,
  102, 104–6, 108, 112, 114–15, 119–20,
  285, 348
Home Rule Commission, 80, 226
homesteading in, 76–77, 79, 106, 118–19,
  201
immigration and, 71–72, 74, 78–79,
  206–8
Japanese-American internment in, 260–63
leprosy and, 77, 106–8, 115, 206
Liberal Patriotic Association, 102
maps of, *67*, *81*
migration to mainland United States, 37,
  44, 74
monarchy in, 6–7, *6*, 9, 67–72, *68*, *69*,
  71, *72*, 76–77, 102, 104, 106, 112,
  114–16, 118, 226, 400, *460*, 461
revolution in, 67–71, 102, 104
suffrage in, 67, 69–71, 104–5, 108, 120
sugar industry in, 9, 66–67, *67*, 71, 76–78,
  78, 81, 85, 118–19, 206–7, 229
tariffs and, 9, 67, 77–78, 206
Territorial Loyalty Board, 209
World War II and, 42, 84, 260–63, 264,
  338
See also statehood
Hawaii Volcanoes National Park, 201
Hawaiian Homes Commission Act, 9, 76–77,
  79, 112, 119, 208, 226, 551n
Hawaiian Independent Party (HIP), 74, 104
Hawaiian Organic Act, 9, 73–74, 76–77,
  81, 85, 104, 108, 109n, 114, 119, 121n,
  200–1, 226, 229, 601
Hawaiian Rehabilitation Bill, 77, 119–20
Hawaiian Sugar Planters' Association (HSPA),
  81–83
Hawes, Harry, 60, 216
Hawley, Willis, 191
Hay, John, 34
HAYAKAWA, Samuel Ichiye (Sam), 293–96,
  293, **388–95**, *389*, 593
Hayden, Tom, 391
Heart Mountain Relocation Center, *6*,
  264–65, *264*, 267, *267*, 282, 293–94, *301*,
  376. *See also* internment
Heen, William, 338
Heftel, Cecil, 333, 424
Helms, Jesse, 297–98, 355
Hemenway, James, 115
Hernández, Joseph Marion, 24n